VISIONS: THE CANADIAN HISTORY MODULES PROJECT

Post-Confederation

Editorial Board:

NELSON / EDUCATION

NELSON / EDUCATION

Visions: The Canadian History Modules Project
Post-Confederation

by P.E. Bryden, Colin Coates, Maureen Lux,
Lynne Marks, Marcel Martel, Daniel Samson

**Vice President,
Editorial Director:**
Evelyn Veitch

**Editor-in-Chief,
Higher Education:**
Anne Williams

Executive Editor:
Laura Macleod

Marketing Manager:
Amanda Henry

Senior Developmental Editor:
Linda Sparks

**Photo Researcher/
Permissions Coordinator:**
Nicola Winstanley

Content Production Manager:
Christine Gilbert

Production Service:
MPS Content Services

Copy Editors:
Kelli Howey, Rodney Rawlings,
Karen Rolfe, Wendy Yano

Proofreader:
MPS Content Services

Production Coordinator:
Ferial Suleman

Design Director:
Ken Phipps

Managing Designer:
Franca Amore

Interior Design:
Greg Devitt

Cover Design:
Martyn Schmoll

Cover Image:
Canadian Artillery in Action:
Detail of: Kenneth Forbes
Canadian Artillery in Action CWM
19710261-0142, Beaverbrook
Collection of War Art. ©
Canadian War Museum; Rally in
support of doctors image: Morris
Predinchuck fonds, Saskatchewan
Archives Board; Mistahimusqua
(Big Bear) Cree Leader: Library and
Archives Canada, C1873.

Compositor:
MPS Content Services

Printer:
RR Donnelley

**Library and Archives Canada
Cataloguing in Publication**

Visions : the Canadian history
modules project, editor's choice :
post-Confederation / P.E. Bryden ...
[et al.].—1st ed.

Includes bibliographical
references.
ISBN 978-0-17-650281-2

1. Canada—History—1867—
Textbooks.   I. Bryden, Penny

FC500.V57 2010 971.05
C2010-900596-1

ISBN-13: 978-0-17-650281-2
ISBN-10: 0-17650281-5

● TABLE OF CONTENTS

INTRODUCTION

The past is a foreign country; they do things differently there.
—*The Go-Between*, L.P. Hartley (1953)

As editors and authors of the first set of modules in *Visions: The Canadian History Modules Project*, we tried to achieve a number of objectives. We wanted to provide introductory Canadian history students with a solid foundation for learning how to think like a historian in the context of their introductory Canadian history course. We also wanted instructors to be able to choose among a variety of teaching topics set within a common pedagogical framework that would support their students in their aim to become more sophisticated historical thinkers.

Each of the modules is designed to introduce a topic or key question that is commonly taught in introductory Canadian history classes. The short introductions set the basic context for the topic and draw attention to major historiographical themes and issues that have emerged as historians have studied it. They also attempt to show the interplay between the primary and secondary sources and illustrate how historians have used a wide variety of evidence to create their picture of the past. It is important for the students to note, however, that these introductions are merely starting points. Their job is to connect the material in the modules to the course lectures and core textbooks. A set of questions at the end of the introduction presents the framework for thinking critically about the material that follows. Each module contains a selection of primary sources from a broad range of materials, including government documents, diary entries and private letters, contemporary newspapers, and oral history interviews, as well as visual evidence in the form of maps, paintings, illustrations, and cartoons. Finally, a selection of secondary sources, the work of professional historians, foregrounds both the ways in which historians construct a narrative about the past and gives students insights into the differing ways in which evidence can be used.

The use of primary sources in conjunction with secondary sources is an essential component in the postsecondary study of history. To use an analogy, if the textbook for the course tells the overarching story of the history of Canada, the readings presented in these modules provide the rich detail that flesh out particular aspects of that story. They add the details that sensitize students to other viewpoints, other experiences, and other worldviews. If the past is indeed a foreign country, as Hartley said, then these modules are meant to give us an introduction to the tools to understand the assumptions, priorities, culture, and experience of people who lived 20 years ago or 200 years ago.

Learning to approach source material in a careful and nuanced way not only enhances students' ability to think critically, but also helps lower the barriers between the past and the present. It is important to apply these same critical approaches not only to the primary sources, but also to the secondary material. Historical actors are not the only ones influenced by the times in which they live. By showcasing different interpretations of evidence, we hope to help students realize that the past is not a set narrative, but rather that history is an argument created by historians based on how they choose and interpret the available evidence. Just as there are arguments today about issues such as climate change and how to interpret the scientific evidence for human impacts on climate, there are arguments among historians regarding a wide array of issues, from what Confederation meant to whether or not Canadians in the late nineteenth century experienced the secularization of their society.

iv

We have carefully selected material that meets rigorous criteria of readability, significance, and variety. We include modules that cover a variety of approaches—social, political, environmental, religious, and so on—and a wide geographical range. One of the most difficult aspects of creating a reader is the need to exclude topics because of space limitations. In the case of *Visions*, however, the project has been conceived from the start as a living, growing database. We have therefore had the luxury of knowing that topics we were unable to cover in the first release will not be neglected but can be added as the project unfolds. To the instructors using this text we say, if you don't see what you need for your students, please join us!

> Laura Macleod (Executive Editor, History)
> P.E. Bryden (University of Victoria)
> Colin Coates (Glendon College, York University)
> Maureen Lux (Brock University)
> Lynne Marks (University of Victoria)
> Marcel Martel (York University)
> Daniel Samson (Brock University)

AS LONG AS THE SUN SHINES AND THE WATERS FLOW

Treaties and Treaty-Making in the 1870s

Maureen Lux
Brock University

AS LONG AS THE SUN SHINES AND THE WATERS FLOW: TREATIES AND TREATY-MAKING IN THE 1870s

● **Introduction by Maureen Lux**

3

● INTRODUCTION

Maureen Lux

Treaties and treaty-making probably marked the very first relations between Aboriginal people and newcomers to northern North America. Fairly equal power relations characterized those early pacts for military or commercial alliance. But the most important document in the history of treaty-making, the Royal Proclamation of 1763, set out the means by which agreements regarding territory could be concluded. Although enacted by the British to create institutions for governing its newly acquired territories after the Seven Years' War, the Proclamation also attempted to keep peace with the Aboriginal nations of the interior by holding back agricultural settlers from the Thirteen Colonies. Thus the Proclamation acknowledged Aboriginal rights to the lands, while also asserting Crown title. The Crown alone could negotiate with Aboriginal people for access to their lands, while the negotiations were required to be conducted in a public forum.

In 1850, in a departure from previous treaties for military alliance or for small parcels of land, the Robinson Treaties with the Aboriginal people of Lakes Huron and Superior regions covered huge districts in preparation for commercial development, and created the precedent for the western Numbered Treaties beginning in the 1870s. Unlike earlier pacts, the Robinson Treaties in what would become Ontario provided for reserve lands, annual cash payments (annuities), and promises of continued fishing and hunting rights. Moreover, it was Aboriginal resistance to incursions into their lands, not royal edict, that forced treaty negotiations.[1]

The Numbered Treaties began with Treaty One in 1871 in southern Manitoba and eventually extended to Treaty Eleven in 1921, which covered a vast segment of the Northwest Territories (see Document 1: Historical Indian Treaties). But this implies an orderly and coherent approach that was far from the case. The Hudson's Bay Company sale of Rupert's Land to the newly created Canadian government in 1869 prompted armed resistance by residents at Red River, who demanded a voice in the new order. The Red River resistance likewise highlighted the need to make some accommodation with Aboriginal peoples of the West who demanded an agreement before they would allow access to their lands.

The first seven treaties to 1877 covered the southern plains from Ontario to the Rockies, serving the government's nation-building project of railway construction and settlement. As the selection from Sarah Carter's *Aboriginal People and Colonizers of Western Canada to 1900* shows, Aboriginal leaders saw the treaties as a way to protect their interests in the land, but especially to ensure the peoples' survival and future livelihood in vastly changed circumstances. The image "Conference with the Chiefs (Treaty One) September 9, 1871" clearly shows that treaty negotiations were conducted in the oral traditions of the Aboriginal nations. The written text of the treaties, however, purported to represent the substance of the agreements. Fundamental misunderstandings emerged about what the parties thought or assumed they were doing when they made the treaties. The concerns varied from one treaty to another, but in general the Aboriginal negotiators, based on their cultural and oral traditions, understood they were sharing the land with the newcomers, not "surrendering" it. As Derek Whitehouse argues in "The Numbered Treaties: Similar Means to Dichotomous Ends" both government and First Nations negotiators understood that treaties were a viable way to meet their respective goals, however much those goals were at odds.

In Treaty Seven, as the selections from *The True Spirit and Original Intent of Treaty 7* makes clear, the surrender of land was not discussed during negotiations; elders understood

4

that the agreement was in fact a treaty of peace. It is clear that the "spirit and intent" of the treaty agreements was not necessarily represented in the written version of the treaties, creating hardship in the immediate post-treaty period and controversy ever since.

Elders have kept their histories alive, but only recently have notions of what constitutes a historical source evolved to include Aboriginal peoples' oral tradition. As we come to understand the treaties as binding agreements made in the presence of the Creator that created a relationship between newcomers (the Crown) and Aboriginal people to share the land and its benefits, and not simply a contract that surrendered the land in return for specific obligations, we can come to realize that indeed all Canadians are treaty people.

NOTES

1. J.R. Miller, *Lethal Legacy: Current Native Controversies in Canada* (Toronto: McClelland and Stewart, 2004), 119, 124; Gerald Friesen, *The Canadian Prairies: A History* (Toronto: University of Toronto Press, 1987), 136.

QUESTIONS

1. Why would Aboriginal elders understand that the treaties were agreements to share, not cede or surrender, the land?
2. Only recently have historians begun to listen to Aboriginal accounts of treaty negotiations. Why?
3. Why were there such fundamental misunderstandings between government and Aboriginal negotiators over what was agreed upon in treaty discussions?
4. The written text of Treaty 7 (Document 8) refers to the Queen and "her Indians." What does this indicate about the Crown's view of the treaty relationship?
5. Why was it important for the government to photograph Mistahimusqua (Big Bear) in chains?
6. On the signature page of the written text of Treaty 7 (Document 8) note the prominence of North-West Mounted Police (NWMP) officers. What does this say about how Canada exerted control over the West?

FURTHER READINGS

Erasmus, Peter. *Buffalo Days and Nights*, ed. Irene Spry, 1976, reprint (Calgary: Glenbow Alberta Institute, 1999).

Miller, J.R., *Compact, Contract, Covenant; Aboriginal Treaty-Making in Canada* (Toronto: University of Toronto Press, 2009).

Morris, Alexander, *The Treaties of Canada with the Indians of Manitoba and the North-West Territories*, 1880, reprint (Toronto: Coles Publishing, 1971).

Ray, Arthur J., Jim Miller, and Frank Tough, *Bounty and Benevolence: A History of Saskatchewan Treaties* (Montreal and Kingston: McGill-Queen's University Press, 2000).

Tobias, John, "Protection, Civilization, Assimilation: An Outline History of Canada's Indian Policy," in *As Long as the Sun Shines and Water Flows*, Ian A.L. Getty and Antoine S. Lussier, eds. (Vancouver: UBC Press, 1983), 13–30.

Treaty Elders of Saskatchewan, with Harold Cardinal and Walter Hildebrant, *Our Dream Is That Our Peoples Will One Day Be Clearly Recognized as Nations* (Calgary: University of Calgary Press, 2000).

5

▲ Document 1: Historical Indian Treaties

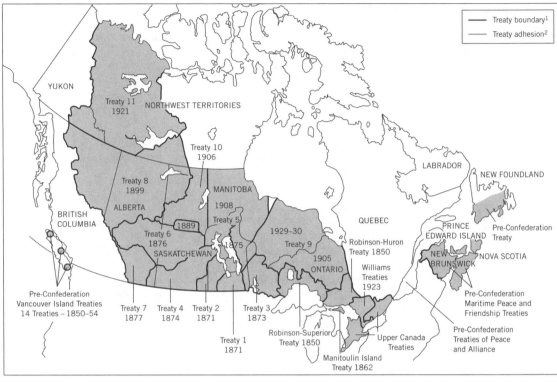

● **Historical Indian Treaties**

Source: Adapted from Canada, Indian Treaties, MCR 4162. "The Atlas of Canada, 1991, Natural Resources Canada, 4 March 2009, http://atlas.nrcan.gc.ca/site/english/maps/archives/5theditions/historical/mcr4162; and from *Ways of Knowing: An Introduction to Native Studies in Canada* 1E. Belanger, Yale D. © 2010 Nelson Education Ltd. Reproduced by permission. www.cengage.com/permissions.

▲ Document 2: Treaty Talks

"Conference with the Chiefs (Treaty One) September 9, 1871". This illustration, while likely romanticized, clearly shows the oral nature of treaty talks conducted in at least two, sometimes many, different languages. Hand gestures and displays of emotion, crucial to the context of negotiations, become lost in the treaties' written version.

Source: *Canadian Illustrated News*, 09 September 1871, Vol. IV, No. 11, 161. Library and Archives Canada, C056472.

7

▲ Document 3: Treaty Six

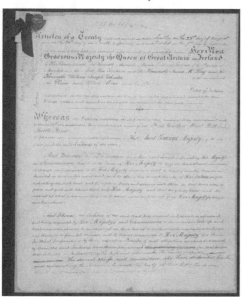

Page 1 of Treaty Six signed at Fort Carlton and Fort Pitt, 23 August and 28 August, 1876. The images in Documents 2 and 3 refer to different treaties, but all treaties were negotiated using translators, and all treaties were eventually written in English. Imagine how many ways misunderstandings might make their way into the legalistic (and privileged) treaty texts.

Source: Manuscript original of western Treaty 6 (IT296) signed at Fort Pitt on September 9, 1876 by Alexander Morris, Lieutenant-Governor of the Northwest Territories, and representatives of the "Plain and Wood Cree". © Indian and Northern Affairs Canada. Reproduced with the permission of the Minister of Public Works and Government Services Canada (2009). Source: Library and Archives Canada/RG10, Indian Affairs, D-10-a, IT296, Microfilm Reel T-9940/e004156541.

▲ Document 4: Treaty Six Chiefs

● Ahtahkakoop (left front) and Mistawasis (right front) influential Treaty Six Chiefs at Fort Carlton in 1876 (front centre, Chief Flying in a Circle; left rear, Chief Osoup; right rear, Peter Hourie, interpreter). Note the Chiefs wearing their Treaty medal.

Source: Library and Archives Canada, C19258.

▲ Document 5: Mistahimusqua (Big Bear) Cree Leader

● Mistahimusqua (Big Bear) Cree leader who participated in Treaty Six talks at Fort Pitt in September 1876, but refused to sign until 1882. Here he is photographed in chains for his supposed role in the Riel Rebellion 1885.

Source: Library and Archives Canada, C1873.

8

▲ Document 6: Herd of Buffalo in Foothills of Rocky Mountains

● **What does this image and the next tell you about the pace of change on the prairies?**

Source: Glenbow Archives NA-1041-15.

9

▲ Document 7: Pile of Buffalo Skulls, Saskatoon, Saskatchewan, August 9, 1890

Source: Glenbow Archives NA-354-30.

▲ Document 8: Text of Treaty 7

Treaty Seven Elders and Tribal Council et al.

The text following contains the articles of the treaty as presented by the treaty commissioners. As is clear from the evidence of the elders, this document does not represent the true spirit and original intent of the treaty that was made at Blackfoot Crossing. The elders say that the treaty as presented to them a year after the negotiations does not contain all of the agreements concluded between the commissioners and chiefs. Many contentious issues concerning the written treaty remain unresolved, especially issues relating to the translation. Many elders have stated that the written treaty they were given was written prior to the arrival of the commissioners, and that agreements made during the negotiations were never incorporated into the final treaty text. The elders feel that much discussion, analysis, and amendment are still required before the written treaty contains the true spirit and original intent of the agreement. In addition to the fundamental issue of whether the treaty represents a land surrender, the elders point to the careless drafting and translation of the treaty.

Elder Louise Crop Eared Wolf* cites examples of gross misrepresentations of names on the treaties as evidence of the incompetence of the translators and those who wrote the treaty. Improper translations and spellings of the Blackfoot names appended to the treaty abound. She identified over eighty errors made by the translators. Some of the worst examples include the recoding of Crowfoot's name as Chapo-Mexico instead of Issapo-maksika; Chapo-Mexico has no meaning and sounds more like an English word. The name of another leading Siksika elder, Old Sun, was recorded as Matose-Apiw, which is simply incomprehensible in Blackfoot. Stamis-cotocar, for Stami-kso-tokan (Bull Head) of the Tsuu T'ina, again has no meaning in Blackfoot, as there are no "r's" in the Blackfoot language. Natose-onistors is a misrepresentation of Natoso-nista, which was wrongly translated as Medicine Calf instead of Powerful Calf. Takoye-stamix is an incorrect representation for Sakoi-yi-stamik (Last Bull, which was also mistranslated as Fiend Bull.) Issokoi-ya-wotanni or Cougar Shield was translated as Sakoye-aowotan, which means Heavy Shield. Crop Eared Wolf points out that this latter translation is an example of a very poor understanding of the language, since even though the words are close in sound—*issokoioyi* for "cougar" and *issokoi* for "heavy"—a real Blackfoot speaker would know the difference. Also Pitah-siksinum, meaning White Eagle, is the wrong spelling and translation of Pitai-siki-namm, which means Black Eagle. Pitah-otsikin, which means "disgusting," was used to represent Pitai-tsi-kinn, which means Eagle Moccasin.

*Louise Crop Eared Wolf: "My comments regarding all the mispronounced Blackfoot names of chiefs of the Bloods, Blackfoot, and Piegan give enough evidence to show that the interpreter (James Bird) at the Treaty 7 peace-making agreement was not a fluent speaker of the Blackfoot language at the time. How could he have accurately explained the articles of the treaty if he was unable to master the Blackfoot terms of the names in Blackfoot. My belief is that our ancestors were not made aware of all the English terms of the treaty."

Source: From *The True Spirit and Original Intent of Treaty 7*, Treaty 7 Elders and Tribal Council with Walter Hildebrandt, Sarah Carter and Dorothy First Rider. Chapter 6, pp. 230–31. Montreal and Kingston: McGill-Queen's University Press, 1996. Reprinted with permission from McGill-Queen's University Press.

When recording the names of the Stoney chiefs on the treaty documents, the officials used the Cree language and the not Stoney-Siouan language. Chief Jacob Bearspaw is written as Mas-gwa-ah-sid, Cree for Bear's Paw, and Chief Jacob Goodstoney is written as Ki-chi-pwat, the Cree word for Big Stoney. The use of Cree to record Stoney names underlines the claim of the Stoney elders that their chief adviser, Reverend John McDougall, officially representing their position during the negotiations, was not a competent translator. McDougall knew Cree but not the Nakota-Siouan language.

The written treaty text below must therefore be read with the understanding that the Treaty 7 elders see it as something that does not fully represent what was agreed to at Blackfoot Crossing.

"THE TREATY WITH THE BLACKFEET; NUMBER SEVEN"

Articles of a Treaty made and concluded this twenty-second day of September, in the year of our Lord one thousand eight hundred and seventy-seven, between Her Most Gracious Majesty the Queen of Great Britain and Ireland, by her Commissioners, the Honorable David Laird, Lieutenant-Governor and Indian Superintendent of the North-West Territories, and James Farquharson McLeod, C.M.G., Commissioner of the North-West Mounted Police, of the one part, and the Blackfeet, Blood, Peigan, Sarcee, Stony, and other Indians, inhabitants of the territory north of the United States boundary line, east of the central range of the Rocky Mountains, and south and west of Treaties Numbers Six and Four, by their head Chiefs and minor Chiefs or Councillors, chosen as hereinafter mentioned, of the other part:

Whereas the Indians inhabiting the said territory, have pursuant to an appointment made by the said Commissioners, been convened at meeting at the "Blackfoot crossing" of the Bow River, to deliberate upon certain matters of interests to her Most Gracious Majesty, of the one part, and the said Indians of the other;

And whereas the said Indians have been informed by Her Majesty's Commissioners that it is the desire of Her Majesty to open up for settlement, and such other purposes as to Her Majesty may seem meet, a tract of country, bounded and described as hereinafter mentioned, and to obtain the consent thereto of her Indian subjects inhabiting the said tract, and to make a treaty, and arrange with them, so that there may be peace and good will between them and Her Majesty, and between them and Her Majesty's other subjects; and that her Indian people may know and feel assured of what allowance they are to count upon and receive from Her Majesty's bounty and benevolence;

And whereas the Indians of the said tract, duly convened in council, and being requested by her Majesty's Commissioners to present their head Chiefs and minor Chiefs, or Councillors, who shall be authorized, on their behalf, to conduct such negotiations and sign any treaty to be founded thereon, and to become responsible to Her Majesty for the faithful performance by their respective bands of such obligations as should be assumed by them, the said Blackfeet, Blood, Piegan and Sarcee Indians have therefore acknowledged for that purpose, the several head and minor Chiefs, and the said Stony Indians, the Chiefs and Councillors who have subscribed hereto, that thereupon in open council the said Commissioners received and acknowledged the head and minor Chiefs and the Chiefs and Councillors presented for the purpose aforesaid:

And whereas the said Commissioners have proceeded to negotiate a treaty with the said Indians; and the same has been finally agreed upon and concluded as follows, that is to say: the Blackfeet, Blood, Piegan, Sarcee, Stony and other Indians inhabiting the district hereinafter more fully described and defined, do hereby cede, release, surrender, and yield up to the Government of Canada for Her Majesty the Queen and her successors forever,

11

all their rights, titles and privileges whatsoever to the lands included within the following limits, that is to say:

Commencing at a point on the international boundary due south of the western extremity of the Cypress Hills; thence west along the said boundary to the central range of the Rocky Mountains, or to the boundary of the Province of British Columbia; thence north-westerly along the said boundary to a point due west of the source of the main branch of the Red Deer River; thence south-westerly and southerly following on the boundaries of the tracts ceded by the Treaties Numbered Six and Four to the place of commencement; and also all their rights, titles and privileges whatsoever, to all other lands wherever situated in the North-West Territories, or in any other portion of the Dominion of Canada:

To have and to hold the same to Her Majesty the Queen and her successors forever:

And Her Majesty the Queen hereby agrees with her said Indians, that they shall have right to pursue their vocations of hunting throughout the tract surrendered as heretofore described, subject to such regulations as may, from time to time, be made by the Government of the country, acting under the authority of Her Majesty; and saving and excepting such tracts as may be required or taken up from time to time for settlement, mining, trading or other purposes by her Government of Canada, or by any of her Majesty's subjects duly authorized therefor by the said Government.

It is also agreed between Her Majesty and her said Indians that reserves shall be assigned them of sufficient area to allow one square mile for each family of five persons, or in that proportion for larger and smaller families, and that said reserves shall be located as follows, that is to say:

First—The reserves of the Blackfeet, Blood and Sarcee bands of Indians, shall consist of a belt of land on the north side of the Bow and South Saskatchewan Rivers, of an average width of four miles along said rivers, down stream, commencing at a point on the Bow River twenty miles north-westerly of the "Blackfoot crossing" thereof, and extending to the Red Deer River at its junction with the South Saskatchewan; also for the term of ten years, and no longer, from the date of the concluding of this treaty, when it shall cease to be a portion of said Indian reserves, as fully to all intents and purposes as if it had not at any time been included therein, and without any compensation to individual Indians for improvements, of a similar belt of land on the south side of the Bow and Saskatchewan Rivers of an average width of one mile along said rivers, down stream; commencing at the aforesaid point on the Bow River, and extending to a point one mile west of the coal seam on said river, about five miles below the said "Blackfoot crossing"; beginning again one mile east of the said coal seam and extending to the mouth of Maple Creek at its junction with the South Saskatchewan; and beginning again at the junction of the Bow River with the latter river, and extending on both sides of the South Saskatchewan in an average width on each side thereof of one mile, along said river against the stream, to the junction of the Little Bow River with the latter river, reserving to Her Majesty, as may now or hereafter be required by her for the use of her Indian and other subjects, from all the reserves hereinbefore described, the right to navigate the above mentioned rivers, to land and receive fuel and cargoes on the shores and banks thereof, to build bridges and establish ferries thereon, to use the fords thereof and all the trails leading thereto, and to open such other roads through the said reserves as may appear to Her Majesty's Government of Canada, necessary for the ordinary travel of her Indian and other subjects, due compensation being paid to individual Indians for improvements, when the same may be in any manner encroached upon by such roads.

Secondly—That the reserve of the Piegan band of Indians shall be on the Old Man's River, near the foot of the Porcupine Hills, at a place called "Crow's Creek."

12

And Thirdly—The reserve of the Stony band of Indians shall be in the vicinity of Morleyville.

In view of the satisfaction of Her Majesty with the recent general good conduct of her said Indians, and in extinguishment of all their past claims, she hereby, through her Commissioners, agrees to make them a present payment of twelve dollars each in cash to each man, woman, and child of the families here represented.

Her Majesty also agrees that next year, and annually afterwards forever, she will cause to be paid to the said Indians, in cash, at suitable places and dates, of which the said Indians shall be duly notified, to each Chief, twenty-five dollars, each minor Chief or Councillor (not exceeding fifteen minor Chiefs to the Blackfeet and Blood Indians, and four to the Piegan and Sarcee bands, and five Councillors to the Stony Indian Bands) fifteen dollars, and to every other Indian of whatever age, five dollars; the same, unless there be some exceptional reason, to be paid to the heads of families for those belonging thereto.

Further, Her Majesty agrees that the sum of two thousand dollars shall hereafter every year be expended in the purchase of ammunition for distribution among the said Indians; provided that if at any future time ammunition became comparatively unnecessary for said Indians, her Government, with the consent of said Indians, or any of the bands thereof, may expend the proportion due to such band otherwise for their benefit.

Further, Her Majesty agrees that each head Chief and minor Chief, and each Chief and Councillor duly recognized as such, shall, once in every three years, during the term of their office, receive a suitable suit of clothing, and each head Chief and Stony Chief, in recognition of the closing of the treaty, a suitable medal and flag, and next year, or as soon as convenient, each head Chief, and minor Chief, and Stony Chief shall receive a Winchester rifle.

Further, Her Majesty agrees to pay the salary of such teachers to instruct the children of said Indians as to her Government of Canada may seem advisable, when said Indians are settled on their reserves and shall desire teachers.

Further, Her Majesty agrees to supply each head and minor Chief, and each Stony Chief, for the use of their bands, ten axes, five handsaws, five augers, one grindstone, and the necessary files and whetstones.

And further, Her Majesty agrees that the said Indians shall be supplied as soon as convenient, after any band shall make due application therefor with the following cattle for raising stock, that is to say: for every family of five persons, and under, two cows; for every family of more than five persons, and less than ten persons, three cows; for every family of over ten persons, four cows; and every head and minor Chief, and every Stony Chief, for the use of their bands, one bull; but if any band desire to cultivate the soil as well as raise stock, each family of such band shall receive one cow less than the above mentioned number, and in lieu thereof, when settled on their reserves and prepared to break up the soil, two hoes, one spade, one scythe, and two hay forks, and for every three families, one plough and one harrow, and for each band, enough potatoes, barley, oats, and wheat (if such seeds be suited for the locality of their reserves) to plant the land actually broken up. All the aforesaid articles to be given, once for all, for the encouragement of the practice of agriculture among the Indians.

And the undersigned Blackfeet, Blood, Piegan and Sarcee head Chiefs and minor Chiefs, and Stony Chiefs and Councillors, on their own behalf and on behalf of all other Indians inhabiting the tract within ceded do hereby solemnly promise and engage to strictly observe this treaty, and also to conduct and behave themselves as good and loyal subjects of Her Majesty the Queen. They promise and engage that they will , in all respects, obey and abide by the law, that they will maintain peace and good order between each other and between themselves and other tribes of Indians, and between themselves and

13

others of Her Majesty's subjects, whether Indians, Half breeds or whites, now inhabiting, or hereafter to inhabit, any part of the said ceded tract; and that they will not molest the person or property of any inhabitant of such ceded tract, or the property of Her Majesty the Queen, or interfere with or trouble any person, passing or travelling through the said tract or any part thereof, and that they will assist the officers of Her Majesty in bringing to justice and punishment any Indian offending against the stipulations of this treaty, or infringing the laws in force in the country ceded.

In witness whereof Her Majesty's said Commissioner, and the said Indian head and minor Chiefs, and Stony Chiefs and Councillors, have hereunto subscribed and set their hands, at the "Blackfoot crossing" of the Bow River, the day and year herein first above written.

(Signed) DAVID LAIRD,
Gov. of N.W.T. and Special Indian Commissioner.
JAMES F. MCLEOD,
Lieut.-Colonel, Com. N.-W.M.P.
and Special Indian Commissioner

CHAPO-MEXICO(or Crowfoot),	His x mark
Head Chief of the South Blackfeet.	
MATOSE-APIW (or Old Sun),	" x "
Head Chief of the North Blackfeet.	
STAMISCOTOCAR (or Bull Head),	" x "
Head Chief of the Sarcees.	
MEKASTO (or Red Crow),	" x "
Head Chief of the South Bloods.	
NATOSE-ONISTORS (or Medicine Calf.).	" x "
POKAPIW-OTOIAN (or Bad Head).	" x "
SOTENAH (or Rainy Chief),	" x "
Head Chief of the North Bloods.	
TAKOYE-STAMIX (or Fiend Bull).	" x "
AKKA-KITCIPIMIW-OTAS (or Many Spotted Horses).	" x "
ATTISTAH-MACAN (or Running Rabbit).	" x "
PITAH-PEKIS (or Eagle Rib).	" x "
SAKOYE-AOTAN (or Heavy Shield),	" x "
Head Chief of the Middle Blackfeet.	
ZOATZE-TAPITAPIW (or Setting on an Eagle Tail).	His x mark
Head Chief of the North Piegans.	
AKKA-MAKKOYE (or Many Swans).	" x "
APENAKO-SAPOP (or Morning Plume).	" x "
*MAS-GWA-AH-SID (or Bear's Paw).	" x "
*CHE-NE-KA (or John).	" x "
*KI-CHI-PWOT (or Jacob).	" x "
STAMIX-OSOK (or Bull Backfat).	" x "
EMITAH-APISKINNE (or White Striped Dog).	" x "
MATAPI-KOMOTZIW (or the Captive or Stolen Person).	" x "
APAWAWAKOSOW (or White Antelope).	" x "
MAKOYE-KIN (or Wolf Collar).	" x "
AYE-STIPIS-SIMAT (or Heavily Whipped).	" x "
KISSOUM (or Day Light).	" x "
PITAH-OTOCAN (or Eagle Head).	" x "
APAW-STAMIX (or Weasel Bull).	" x "

14

ONISTAH-POKAH (or White Calf).	His x mark
NETAH-KITEI-PI-MEW (or Only Spot).	" x "
AKAK-OTOS (or Many Horses).	" x "
STOKIMATIS (or The Drum).	" x "
PITAH-ANNES (or Eagle Robe).	" x "
PITAH-OTSIKIN (or Eagle Shoe).	" x "
STAMIX-OTA-KA-PIW (or Bull Turn Round).	" x "
MASTE-PITAH (or Crow Eagle).	" x "
†JAMES DIXON.	" x "
†ABRAHAM KECHEPWOT.	" x "
†PATRICK KECHEPWOT.	" x "
†GEORGE MOY-ANY-MEN.	" x "
†GEORGE CRAWLOR.	" x "
EKAS-KLINE (or Low Horn).	" x "
KAYO-OKOSIS (or Bear Shield).	" x "
PONOKAH-STAMIX (or Bull Elk).	" x "
OMAKSI SAPOP (or Big Plume).	" x "
ONISTAH (or Calf Robe).	" x "
PITAH-SIKSINUM (or White Eagle).	" x "
APAW-ONISTAW (or Weasel Calf).	" x "
ATTISTA-HAES (or Rabbit Carrier).	" x "
PITAH (or Eagle).	" x "
PITAH-ONISTAH (or Eagle White Calf.).	" x "
KAYE-TAPO (or Going to Bear).	" x "

Signed by the Chiefs and Councillors within named in presence of the following witnesses, the same having been first explained by James Bird, Interpreter.

(Signed) A.G. IRVINE, *Ass't Com.*, N.-W.M.P.

> J. MCDOUGALL *Missionary.*
> JEAN L'HEUREUX.
> W. WINDER.
> T.N.F. CROZIER, *Inspectors.*
> E. DALRYMPLE CLARK, *Lieut. and Adjutant.* N.-W.M.P.
> A. SHURTLIFF,
> C.E. DENING,
> W.D. ANTROBUS, *Sub-Inspectors.*
> FRANK NORMAN, *Staff Constable.*
> MARY J. MACLEOD.
> JULIA WINDER.
> JULIA SHURTLIFF.
> E. HARDISTY.
> A. MCDOUGALL.
> E.A. BARRETT.
> CONSTANTINE SCOLLEN, *Priest,* witness to signatures of Stonixosak and those following.
> CHARLES E. CONRAD.
> THOS. J. BOGG.

---

* Stony Chiefs.
† Stony Councillors

Article 1: The Numbered Treaties: Similar Means to Dichotomous Ends

Derek Whitehouse

On 2 August 1871, the Canadian government and the Indians of the North-West Territories signed the first of the Numbered Treaties. By the end of 1877 an additional six Treaties had been negotiated, effectively opening the North-West for settlement. Events leading up to the negotiations, and the negotiations themselves, provide clear evidence that dichotomy existed between the goals that the Indians hoped to achieve through the Treaty process and those the government hoped to attain. The Indians,[1] realizing that their environment was changing, sought to protect their culture from threatening forces such as non-native agricultural settlement and diminishing buffalo herds. The government, meanwhile, strove to encourage the absorption of the Indian cultures into broader Euro-Canadian society, not only because it wanted to open the North-West for settlement, but also because it believed that assimilation was in the best interest of the Indian peoples. Despite the disparity in the objectives that each party sought, both considered the Treaties to be tools that were essential to achieving their goals. Thus, in the first seven Numbered Treaties, the government and the Indians employed similar means toward very dissimilar ends.

Until recent decades, the historical analysis of Canada's past down-played or overlooked the contributions of aboriginal peoples. As James W. St.G. Walker noted of historical works such as Donald Creighton's *Canada: The Heroic Beginnings,* Indians were often presented as "not even minor actors in the Canadian drama, simply stage-props against which others work[ed] out their roles."[2]

A case in point is the work of Allan Harper. In 1947, Harper wrote that, during the Numbered Treaty process, discussion was controlled by the government and "confined to a careful explanation of the terms, answering questions, firmly rejecting exorbitant demands, and dispelling false notions about the government's assumption ofobligations."[3] Similarly, in 1932, G.F.G. Stanley argued that the negotiation of the Treaties "was confined to an explanation of the

Source: *Past Imperfect,* Vol. 3 (1994): 25–45. Reprinted with permission from Derek Whitehouse-Strong.

terms" by the government and that "the Indians never understood what was happening."[4] Until the 1970s, historians portrayed Canada's aboriginal peoples as passive victims of dominant outside forces.

By the 1970s, however, historians were beginning to revise the image of the Indian peoples as victims. Fur trade historians like A.J. Ray spearheaded the revisionists' efforts. Writing in 1978, Ray argued that historical analyses which assumed "that the Indians were ruthlessly exploited and cheated in all areas and periods by white[s] [...] gives us only half the story."[5] A reinterpretation of Canada's past which recognized the contributions made by the Indian peoples would result in new perceptions of Indians as active and creative agents in the historical process. Ray realized that treating the largely ignored aboriginal peoples as active participants in Canada's past was essential to the appropriate placement of the Indian in the historical record.[6]

While the process of reinterpreting Canada's past began with fur trade historians such as A.J. Ray and Donald B. Freeman,[7] historians working in other fields also reassessed the Indian perspective. Sylvia Van Kirk, for example, argued that the fur trade "was not simply an economic activity, but a social and cultural complex."[8] Consequently, when examining the role that Indian, Métis, and white women had in the fur trade, Van Kirk asserted that the "examination of the role played by women as actors upon the fur trade stage is essential to a full understanding of the complexities" of early Western Canadian society.[9] Thus, in viewing Canada's aboriginal peoples as active agents of history, historians developed new interpretations of economic, social, religious, and political interactions between white and Indian.[10]

J.R. Miller noted, however, that most efforts of historians to restore the Canadian aboriginal to the position of an active historical agent have focused upon the period preceding the 1860s. Indeed, as late as 1990, Miller argued that "studies of Indian-white relations after Confederation [...] have thus far largely proved resistant to reinterpretation."[11]

Articles by Jean Friesen, D.J. Hall, and John Leonard Taylor, however, are notable exceptions in that they demonstrate that the revisionists are no longer emphasizing the pre-Confederation period. Taylor, for example, maintained that the Numbered Treaties were the product of Indian and government interactions, and not, as Harper had argued, the result of the government dictating terms that the Indians had either to "accept or reject."[12] Taylor understood the Treaty process as having been an open negotiation in which the Indians introduced innovations that the government was subsequently forced to accept. If the government had not accepted the innovations, it "would have had even more difficulty getting the treaties, if [it] had been able to get them at all."[13]

Duncan Campbell Scott, Canada's Deputy Superintendent General of Indian Affairs from 1913 to 1932, attested to the underlying continuity of the government's Indian policy some thirty years after the completion of the first seven Numbered Treaties. In 1909, Scott stated that "the true and uniform policy [of the government] [...] has made the Canadian Indian believe the British sovereign is his great parent and [he] himself is a child under beneficent protection."[14] He went on to say that "the happiest future for the Indian race is [...] absorption into the general population, and this is the object of the policy of our government."[15] Toward this goal, the government believed that

> agriculture, education, and religion would, in time, provide the Indian with far more than he had lost. Eventually the settlement of the West would uplift the native from his state [of savagery or barbarism].[16]

The Canadian government genuinely believed that its goal of assimilation was in the best interest of the Indian peoples. The Numbered Treaties were intended to provide the tools which government officials thought were necessary to facilitate this assimilation: reserve agriculture, schools, and missionaries.[17]

Much of the Canadian population shared the government's desire to absorb the Indian peoples into broader Euro-Canadian society. For decades, official documents and reports, and "the works of scientists, social scientists, travellers, humanitarians, and missionaries"[18] had served to shape the perception that assimilation was not only in the best interest of the Canadian population, but also of the aboriginal peoples themselves. As a result of these varied influences, a paternalistic approach to the assimilation of the Indians was seen as both "desirable [...] and necessary. With the Indian as the ward of the state, steps could be taken to protect him from the harmful effects of white culture while teaching him its benefits."[19]

Imperialistic influences also strengthened and confirmed the idea that the assimilation of the Indian was the true and correct policy to follow. Colonies within the British Empire, historian Walter Houghton argued, had been founded

> it was said—and believed—by the generous and altruistic desire of spreading throughout the habitable globe all the characteristics of Englishmen—their energy, their civilization, their religion and their freedom.[20]

Consequently, those directing the government's Indian policy saw themselves as fulfilling this aspect of Britain's destiny. What could be better for an improvident, intemperate, and latently indolent people who were prone to privation[21] than to become active members of a nation destined to assume the role of dominance in the British Empire? The government expected that agriculture would help the Indians overcome the inherent weaknesses that it believed they shared as peoples, and thus it would aid their eventual assimilation into Canadian society. The aboriginal peoples would then become part of that which "represent[ed] man's highest achievement in the development of governmental and social institutions."[22] In order for the Indians to be assimilated, however, the government knew that the cultural identity of the Canadian aboriginals would have to be eliminated. On a cultural level, the Indian would have to adopt the traditions and practices of the white man.[23]

In 1877, the prominent American anthropologist Lewis Henry Morgan put to print a theory, the essence of which many of his era were already familiar with. Morgan asserted that all societies passed through the stages of savagery and barbarism on their way to becoming civilized.[24] Consequently, because passage from one level of development to the next was thought to be unilinear, "each step [...] was regarded as essential to the next and [thus] could not be transcended."[25] According to the unilinear evolutionists argument, it followed that because many of the Indian bands in the North-West engaged in hunting and gathering subsistence, they were in the initial, savage phase of the evolutionary path. Subscribing to Morgan's theory, the government believed that the Indians would have to pass through barbarism, a stage which was characterized by domestication

17

and cultivation, before they could become civilized. Reserve agriculture was, therefore, to be the Indian peoples' "place of probation, a training ground in the lessons of civilization and citizenship."[26]

Besides viewing the Treaties as a means to encourage the assimilation of the Indian, government officials also intended to use the Treaties to open the North-West for settlement in accordance with its national policy.[27] The Royal Proclamation of 1763 made it illegal for anyone, save the Crown, to purchase land in "Indian Country."[28] Although this provision "did not apply to the Hudson's Bay Company lands, [it did] set out the basis" by which these lands would be settled after their transfer to Canada in 1870.[29] It was necessary, therefore, for the government to extinguish Indian title to land in the North-West before settlement could begin. Alexander Morris, the lieutenant governor of the North-West Territories from 1872 to 1876, summarized this objective during the discussions concerning Treaty One and Treaty Two. According to Morris,

> it was desirable to secure the extinction of the Indian title not only to the lands within Manitoba, but also to so much of the timber grounds east and north of the Province as were required for immediate entry and use, also of a large tract of cultivate ground west of the Portage, where there were very few Indian inhabitants.[30]

Regarding the completion of Treaty Three, he continued:

> and so was closed, a treaty, whereby a territory was enabled to be opened up, of great importance to Canada, embracing as it does the Pacific Railway route to the North West Territories—a wide extent of fertile lands, and, as is believed, great mineral resources.[31]

Extinguishing Indian title to land in the North-West so that settlement could commence thus constituted the second goal of the government's Treaty policy.

Morris' words demonstrate that pressures on land, resulting from the government's settlement policy, were the primary motivators behind the government's decision to treat. That settlement pressures were of such great import to the Canadian government can be largely attributed to the fact that, with an annual federal budget of only $19 million and with the construction of a transcontinental railway a national preoccupation, the government was seeking to devote only as many resources as were necessary to negotiating treaties with the Indians.[32] Indeed, Joseph Howe, Secretary of State for the Provinces cautioned Treaty Commissioner Wemyss Simpson to

> endeavour to secure the session [*sic*] of the lands upon terms as favourable as possible to the Government, not going as far as the maximum sum hereafter named unless it be found impossible to obtain the object for a less amount.[33]

In addition, Prime Minister Alexander Mackenzie pointed out that, when compared to "other countries," Canada's Treaty policy was not only "a humane, just, and Christian policy," it was also "the cheapest."[34] Only when it was so required by settlement pressures, therefore, would the government be induced to negotiate.

The requests of the Indian peoples themselves had little impact on the timing of negotiations when settlement pressures were not at issue. Indeed, some of the bands who would eventually be included under Treaty Six had requested negotiations toward an agreement a full five years before actual proceedings began. The government, however, did little to address the "[general] feeling of discontent and uneasiness," arising from the fact that they had not been treated with, "[that] prevailed [...] amongst the Assiniboines and Crees."[35] Only when the Indians threatened to disrupt survey and telegraph crews was the government finally compelled to negotiate.[36]

Settlement pressure of a different type was the key factor in the government's movement to negotiate Treaty Seven. On this occasion, it was white settlers who pressured the government for an agreement in order to allay growing concerns regarding their own safety. Father Constantine Scollen noted that

> The Blackfeet are extremely jealous of what they consider their country and have never allowed any white men, Half-breeds, or Crees to remain in it for any length of time

[...] [As such, the settlers] are anxious that a treaty be made as soon as possible, so that they may know what portions of land they can hold without fear of being molested.[37]

Consequently, it was again in the government's interest to obtain a treaty, despite the fact that, unofficially at least, the Blackfoot were not seeking such an agreement.

Humanistic, expansionistic, imperialistic, and nationalistic beliefs, values, and ideas thus shaped the Canadian government's Indian policy. Furthermore, it is clear that the government engaged in the treaty-making process for two main reasons. First, negotiations were initiated to facilitate the Euro-Canadian agricultural settlement of the North-West. Second, the Treaty concessions provided the means by which the distinctiveness, uniqueness, and heritage of the Indian could be eliminated, and what was left could be absorbed into the Euro-Canadian culture.

For the Indians, however, the Treaties served an entirely different function. Aware that the Treaties would open the North-West up for rapid settlement, the aboriginal peoples also understood that settlement was inevitable, with or without the Treaties. Consequently, the Indians sought to use the concessions that they gained under the Treaty system to ensure that their culture would survive, an end antithetical to that being sought by the government. To achieve their goal, the Indians, much like the government, expressed an interest in schools and in missionaries and "were desirous of according to the wish of their great Mother" that they "discard their former precarious mode of living and adopt the agricultural pursuits of the white man."[38] Aware that social and economic pressures were making it inevitable that their way of life was coming to an end, the aboriginal peoples sought to adopt a new way of life, one which would allow them to retain their independent cultures.

The Ojibwa and the Swampy Cree, who were among the first Indian peoples to be involved in the Numbered Treaty process, had outwardly expressed concern regarding the "influx of population" onto their lands. Indeed, Alexander Morris noted that "the Indians in Manitoba [...] had in some instances obstructed settlers and surveyors"[39] until their calls for a Treaty were met. Thus, while governmental policy dictated that Treaties were to be negotiated only when so required by settlement pressures, the Indian peoples were still able to "[rush] the government's timetable somewhat."[40]

Concerns about the influx of white settlers also affected the tribes involved in later negotiations. The Plains Cree were aware that great numbers of white settlers would soon be entering their lands. During Treaty Six negotiations, Star Blanket, the Chief of the Wood Indians, cautioned those of his people who opposed the Treaty:

[When the buffalo are gone] what then will be left us with which to bargain? With the buffalo gone we will have only the vacant prairie which none of us have learned to use. Can we stop the power of the white man from spreading over the land like the grasshoppers that cloud the sky and then fall to consume every blade of grass and every leaf on the trees in their path? I think not. Before this happens, let us ponder carefully our choice of roads.[41]

Indeed, in 1875, the Reverend George McDougall had been informed by certain Cree that "they were unanimous in their determination to oppose the running of lines, or the making of roads through their country, until an agreement between the Government and them had been effected."[42] This concern was echoed by the Plains Assiniboine who, on hearing that they would be treated with, informed Alexander Morris that "foolish men have told us that the Great Chief would send his young men to our country until they outnumbered us, and that then he would laugh at us."[43]

The Blackfoot, who in 1877 were signatories to Treaty Seven, also saw the early signs of white settlement. Unlike many of the tribes further east, however, they themselves were not seeking a Treaty. It is likely, nevertheless, that factors such as the diminishing buffalo herds and the steady increase of white settlers into their region would have eventually "disposed the Blackfoot towards making a treaty."[44] Indeed, the likes of the Reverends George and John McDougall and Fathers Scollen and Fourmond had penetrated as far south as the Bow River by 1877. This fact "not only indicates the hold the missionaries were gaining on the prairie Indians but also how much the Blackfoot hold on their native land was slipping."[45]

19

The Blackfoot's concern over the diminishing buffalo herds had also been voiced by the other Plains tribes who had realized, at least as early as the 1850s, that the herds were becoming more scarce.[46] From that time on, the Cree, for example, had attempted to protect the herds by calling on the government to limit the hunting of these creatures to Indians alone.[47] Yet, it was not until 1876 that "the North-West Council [considered] the framing of a law to protect the buffaloes."[48] Nothing ever came of the Council's consideration, however, and less than three years later the buffalo had disappeared from Canada. Despite attempts to protect the buffalo, the Cree had largely accepted the fact that their way of life was coming to an end. Star Blanket addressed this concern when he said:

> We have always lived and received our needs in clothing, shelter, and food from the countless multitudes of buffalo that have been with us since the earliest memory of our people. No one with open eyes and open minds can doubt that the buffalo will soon be a thing of the past. Will pass? No! They will die and become just a memory unless we find another way.... The mother earth has always given us plenty with the grass that fed the buffalo. Surely we can learn the ways that made the whiteman strong.[49]

Thus, Canada's aboriginal peoples realized that an adaptation to a new way of life was required, and, like the government, most saw agriculture as the answer.

Many Canadians were likely surprised to learn that the Indians were willing to take up cultivating the soil. Most Euro-Canadians believed that Indians resisted change and had lived in their current state for untold centuries. The Methodist missionary John MacLean described Canadian efforts to "civilize" and "uplift" the Indian peoples:

> We wish to make them white men, and they desire to become better Indians. They believe the native culture is best suited for themselves, and having developed under it, and enjoyed it so long, they care not to give it up for an untried system.[50]

The missionary John McDougall, who in 1876 was a commissioner for the government's treaty negotiations, concurred. He wrote that the

> aboriginal man with his traditions unchanged through the centuries met face to face representatives of another old but ever-changing race to negotiate in peace and friendship their future negotiations in this new land.[51]

Much of the Euro-Canadian populace thus believed that the cultures of the Indian peoples were static.

The perception that the Indian way of life was unchanging proved to be unfounded, however. In the two centuries prior to the signing of the Numbered Treaties, many aboriginal peoples had adapted to the new economies that had been created by the fur trade. That the Indians understood the concepts of dynamic economies is evident when one examines the adaptability of the Plains Cree. Prior to European contact, the Cree were primarily woodland hunters and gatherers.[52] After 1670, however, they had assumed a middleman role in the fur trade. When the fur traders themselves began to move into the interior, thus effectively bypassing them, the Cree had adapted again by moving on to the Plains and becoming buffalo hunters.[53] Although they were perhaps caught off guard by the rapidity with which they were required to adapt,[54] the Indian peoples accepted the fact that their lifestyle would have to change again. What the aboriginals were concerned with, however, was the impact that this change would have on their culture.

The desire of Beardy, the Chief of the Willow Crees, to negotiate in a place that "had been revealed to him in a vision"[55] provides clear evidence that the Indians believed the Treaties to be an important means of preserving Native culture. In Cree culture, as in almost all Plains cultures, the dream or vision was of great significance. The Plains Indian perceived dreams to be sources of powerful knowledge and insight. As scholar Joseph Epes Brown argued, the "nature of the received vision often obligate[d] the recipient to externalize the experience and thus ... share the power with the larger community."[56] To ensure that the Treaty would be negotiated successfully and that his people would achieve what they

20

desired from these proceedings, Beardy sought to re-enact his vision. The government negotiators, however, misunderstood his intentions and assumed that Beardy was merely being difficult. Consequently, the government negotiators would only treat with the Willow Crees at the location they themselves had designated.[57]

The Indians of Treaty Six[58] realized that, in order to protect their culture from being destroyed by the inevitable incursion of white settlers onto their lands, they had to reach an agreement with the government. As a result, they took an active role in the Treaty negotiations. Entering the talks, the government was prepared to offer essentially the same concessions that had been granted under the first five Treaties. Regarding Treaty One, the government had intended only to establish reserves and grant annuities in exchange for the surrender of Indian title to their lands. The Indians, however, eventually extracted additional concessions such as the provision of agricultural and educational assistance.[59] Similarly, the Indian signatories to Treaty Three were able to obtain further allowances from the government including an increase in the allotment of land from 100 acres for each family of five to 640 acres and an increase in annuities from $3 to $5.[60]

The government had acceded to the Indians' demands as they were consistent with their goals of assimilation. For the Indian peoples to be able to cultivate those reserve lands that were to be set aside for them, they had to be provided with the implements and the knowledge necessary to undertake such a task. As Henry Prince, Chief of the St. Peter's band, asked when he was informed that the government wanted the Indians to take up agriculture but would provide them with only land and annuities, "[How could] the Queen expect the Indian to cultivate the land? They cannot scratch it—work it with their fingers. What assistance will they get if they settle down?"[61] Wemyss Simpson apparently concurred when he wrote that the aforementioned concessions were given "with a view to inducing the Indians to adopt the habits and labours of civilization."[62]

Those concessions which were granted under Treaties One through Five, however, did not fully address the apprehensions that the Plains Cree had concerning the protection of their culture. Consequently, much like the Saulteaux of Treaty One, the Cree were able to demand and receive additions

to the Treaty which the government had not originally intended to grant.[63] These new concessions, namely the granting of $1000 a year for three years, the medicine chest clause, and the pestilence/famine clause, addressed the concerns of the Plains Cree regarding their adaptation to, and survival in, their new environment.[64]

The government agreed to pay a sum of $1000 to those bands who were "settled on the reserves and [who were] engaged in cultivating the soil."[65] Consequently, only those Indians who were already considered to be in the process of becoming civilized were to receive benefits from the clause. The government therefore regarded the $1000 as further contributing to the eventual assimilation of the Indian and achieving the ultimate goal of its Indian policy.

The monetary concession itself had been made in response to Cree demands for "food in the spring" when they began to farm[66] In the spring, and especially during the initial years of cultivation, great expenditures of time and energy would have to be made in ploughing, seeding, and cultivating the land. Consequently, the Indians would have to abandon non-agricultural means of acquiring sustenance, such as hunting, gathering, and trapping, to ensure that their agricultural efforts were as successful as possible. The Indians believed that a secure source of food would assist them in their adaption to reserve agriculture and thus help them to preserve a unique and separate identity in Euro-Canadian society.

With regard to the pestilence/famine clause and the medicine chest clause, both were applicable only to those Indians who had signed Treaty Six.[67] Again, the government considered these concessions as aiding the inevitable assimilation of the Plains Cree as they addressed specific concerns that the Cree had expressed. Alexander Morris was aware that "small-pox had destroyed [the Plains Cree] by hundreds a few years before"[68] and that epidemics of scarlet fever and measles had also recently affected the region. In addition, the fact that the buffalo herds were rapidly disappearing had raised concerns about starvation at a time when adaption to a new method of subsistence, namely agriculture, was required.[69] In the words of Morris, the Indians "dreaded pestilence and famine."[70] The government regarded sustenance requirements as being specific to the Plains Cree alone, however. Indeed, with the exception of "spring provisions for several years" as provided in

Treaty Eight, these "pestilence/famine concessions," or any that were similar, were not repeated in subsequent agreements.[71]

The Indians viewed the pestilence/famine clause as a means of insuring themselves against any hardships that they might have encountered during their initial attempts to cultivate their reserve lands including both crop failure and destruction.[72] Big Child, Chief of the Carlton Indians, noted:

> It is well known that if we have plenty in our gardens and crops we would not insist on getting more provisions, but it is only in the case of extremity and from the ignorance of Indians in commencing to work the land that we speak. We are in the dark. This is no trivial matter with us.[73]

Knowing that the buffalo would soon be gone and that agriculture was to become their main means of support, the Indians were acutely aware of the dangers that could arise if they proved slow to learn proper agricultural techniques or if some disaster befell them. If either situation were to occur without the protection and assistance of the government, the Indians knew that they would starve.

The medicine chest clause addressed specific concerns held by the Cree regarding the aforementioned epidemics that had recently swept through the Plains. As a result of smallpox alone, hundreds of Plains Cree had died and many more had become seriously ill by the early 1870s. In one band alone, over fifty individuals had perished.[74] To make matters worse, during times of affliction many hunters and trappers were either killed or incapacitated to the point where they were unable to perform everyday duties. As a result, starvation and economic difficulties (the latter exacerbated by the need to destroy the property of those who had been infected) often accompanied and outlasted the epidemics. The Indians were aware that a vaccine to combat the disease did exist, but it was not readily available to them.[75] Thus, the aboriginal peoples believed that having a medicine chest on each reserve would help to ensure that both unnecessary deaths and economic hardships resulting from illnesses were minimized.

A consideration of the roles of both the Indian peoples and the Canadian government in the Numbered Treaty process, reveals that both parties sought similar terms to achieve dichotomous ends. While both the Indians and the Canadian government supported the concept of reserve agriculture as outlined in the Treaties, each saw cultivation as a way to help achieve different goals. The Indians recognized that their environment was changing and considered reserve agriculture to be the best method of adapting to a new way of life. In making this transition, however, the Indians attempted to protect their people from being assimilated into white society, thus preserving their separate identities. The government, on the other hand, saw both the Treaties and reserve agriculture as the most practical way to achieve the goals of its Indian policy. By utilizing the Treaties to open up the North-West for settlement, the government hoped to bring about that which it considered to be in the best interest of the Indian peoples: their assimilation into white society.

NOTES

1. It should be noted that many different groups of Indians were involved in the Numbered Treaty process, including various bands of Ojibwa, Cree, Assiniboine, and Blackfoot. For a brief introduction to the first seven of the Numbered Treaties, refer to Gerald Friesen, *The Canadian Prairies: A History* (Toronto. 1987). 138–146.

2. James W. St.G. Walker, "The Indian in Canadian Historical Writing, 1972–1982" in Ian A.L. Getty and Antoine S. Lussier, eds., *As Long as the Sun Shines and the Water Flows: A Reader in Canadian Native Studies,* (Vancouver, 1983), 346. Reprinted from Canadian Historical Association *Historical Papers* (1971), 21–47.

3. Allan G. Harper, "Canada's Indian Administration: The Treaty System," *America Indigena* 7, 2 (April, 1947), 145

4. G.F.G. Stanley, "The Indian Background of Canadian History" in Canadian Historical Association Report (1932), 20. Quoted in Jean Friesen, "Magnificent Gifts: The Treaties of Canada with the Indians of the Northwest 1869–76," *Transactions of the Royal Society of Canada,* Fifth Series, 1. (1962), 42.

5. Arthur J. Ray, "Fur Trade History as an Aspect of Native History" in R. Douglas Francis and Donald B. Smith, eds., *Readings in Canadian History* (Pre-Confederation) (Toronto, 1982), 151

6. Ibid., 149–151

7. See A. J. Ray, *Indians in the Fur Trade 1660–1870* (Toronto, 1974) and A. J. Ray and Donald B. Freeman *Give us Good Measure: An Economic Analysis of Relations Between the Indians and the Hudson's Bay Company Before 1763* (Toronto, 1978).

8. Sylvia Van Kirk, Many Tender Ties: *Women in Fur-Trade Society, 1670–1870* (Winnipeg, 1980), 2

9. Ibid., 8

10. D.J. Hall, "'A Serene Atmosphere'? Treaty 1 Revisited," *Canadian Journal of Native Studies* 4, 2 (1984), 322. Also note works such as J.R. Miller, *Skyscrapers Hide the Heavens: A History of Indian-White Relations in Canada,* rev. ed. (Toronto, 1991) and John Webster Grant, Moon of Wintertime: *Missionaries and the Indians of Canada in Encounter since 1534* (Toronto, 1984).

11. J.R. Miller, "Owen Glendower, Hotspur, and Canadian Indian Policy," *Ethnohistory* 37, (Fall, 1990), 388

12. Harper, "Canada's Indian Administration," 145

13. John Leonard Taylor, "Canada's Northwest Indian Policy in the 1870s: Traditional Premises and Necessary Innovations" in Richard Price, ed., *The Spirit of the Alberta Indian Treaties,* (Montreal, 1980), 6. Also see Friesen, "Magnificent Gifts" and Hall, "Serene Atmosphere."

14. Brian E. Titley, *A Narrow Vision: Duncan Campbell Scott and the Administration of Indian Affairs in Canada* (Vancouver, 1986), 27. For an analysis of the government's Indian strategy prior to the Indian Act and how their post-Confederation goals could be considered to be an extension of a somewhat continuous policy, refer to John E. Leslie and Ron Maguire, *The Historical Development of the Indian Act* (Ottawa, 1978).

15. Ibid., 34

16. Doug Owram, *Promise of Eden: The Canadian Expansionist Movement and the Idea of the West 1856–1900* (Toronto, 1981), 132

17. It should be noted that although missions were outside the purview of the government, both the government and the Indians wished to see them established on reserves. As such, although not prescribed by the Treaties themselves, the establishment of missions was integral to the objectives of both the Indians and the government.

18. L.F.S. Upton, "The Origins of Canadian Indian Policy," *Journal of Canadian Studies* 8, 4 (1973), 5. Alsosee Grant, Moon of Wintertime, 85.

19. Owram, *Promise of Eden,* 132

20. Walter E. Houghton, *The Victorian Frame of Mind: 1830–1870* (New Haven, 1957), 47

21. Marcel Giraud, *The Métis in the Canadian West* Vol. I trans. George Woodcock, (Lincoln, 1986), 349–351

22. Owram, *Promise of Eden,* 126

23. John MacLean, *Indians of Canada: Manners and Customs* (Toronto, 1889), 263

24. Abraham Rosman and Paula G. Rubel, *Tapestry of Culture,* 2nd ed. (New York, 1985), 14. See also Ixwis Henry Morgan, "Ancient Society" in Paul Bohannan and Mark Glazer, eds., *High Points in Anthropology* (New York, 1973), 30-60. Morgan's theory concerning the evolutionary development of societies was an embodiment of Social Darwinism, a theory that held that societal evolution represented progress. Historian, Laurence S. Fallis Jr., noted of intellectual thought in mid-to-late nineteenth-century Canada that the "idea of progress by making change appear to be natural, if not inevitable, made change acceptable." Laurence S. Fallis Jr., "The Idea of Progress in the Province of Canada: A Study in the History of Ideas" in W.L. Morton, ed., *The Shield of Achilles: Aspects of Canada in the Victorian Age* (Toronto, 1968), 173. The "cultural advancement" of the Indian peoples was thus held by much of the Euro-Canadian population as being in the best interest of all concerned, particularly with regard to the Indians.

25. [missing from original document]

26. Ibid., 19. See also Carter, *Lost Harvests,* 36–45 where it is noted that some Indian peoples possessed agricultural experience that pre-dated the Treaty era. Indeed, Carter notes that in "nineteenth-century Manitoba before the treaties of the 1870s, Indian participation in gardening and farming was not uncommon." Ibid., 40

27. Friesen, *The Canadian Prairies,* 184–186

28. Leslie, *The Historical Development,* 3–5

29. Richard C. Daniel, *A History of Native Claims in Canada: 1867–1979* (Ottawa, 1979), 2. As Daniel noted, the terms of the purchase agreement effectively extended the terms of the Royal Proclamation to the newly acquired North-West. Article 14 of the Imperial Order in Council that gave effect to the transfer stated that "[a]ny claims of the Indians to

23

compensation for lands shall be disposed of by the Canadian government in communication with the Imperial Government; and that the Company shall be relieved of all responsibility in respect to them." Ibid., 1–2

30. Alexander Morris, *The Treaties of Canada with the Indians of Manitoba and the North-West Territories, 1880* (Toronto, reprint, 1971), 26. Morris was the chief negotiator for the crown during the negotiations of Treaties Three, Four, Five, and Six. He also revised Treaties One and Two. Jean Friesen, "Alexander Morris" in Francess G. Halpenny, ed., *Dictionary of Canadian Biography* 11, (Toronto, 1982), 612.

31. Ibid., 46

32. Miller, *Skyscrapers Hide the Heavens,* 162. See also Gerald Friesen, *The Canadian Prairies,* 177–8 regarding the funding that the government supplied for the construction of the C.P.R. including "direct grants of $25 million." Also note Carter, *Lost Harvests,* 22.

33. As quoted in Daniel, *A History of Native Claims,* 6.

34. As quoted in Miller, *Skyscrapers Hide the Heavens,* 162.

35. Morris, *The Treaties of Canada,* 171

36. Ibid., 172

37. Ibid., 249

38. Ibid., 40

39. Ibid., 25–26

40. "Hall, "A Serene Atmosphere," 323. Also see John Tobias, "Canada's Subjugation of the Plains Cree," *Canadian Historical Review* 44, 4 (1983), 519–548. Tobias provides an alternate view to that of Hall. While Hall qualifies his remark with the term "somewhat," Tobias down-plays the government's role, at least with regards to Treaty One. I would argue that until settlement became a governmental priority, the Indians were able to do little to make their demands carry much weight. This is evident in the five-year interval between when the Plains Cree expressed a desire to treat and the beginning of negotiations. Again, in the above case, the government acted only when it perceived that its plans regarding settlement might be threatened.

41. Peter Erasmus, *Buffalo Day sand Nights* (Calgary, 1976), 249. Historian Olive Patricia Dickason makes note of the English spelling of Star Blanket's true Indian name, Ahchacoosacootacoopits, in *Canada's First Nations: A History of Founding Peoples from Earliest Times* (Toronto, 1992), 300. Similarly, Alexander Morris noted the spelling of Star Blanket's name as Ah-tak-ah-coop in *The Treaties of Canada,* 213.

42. Morris, *The Treaties of Canada,* 173

43. Ibid., 174

44. John Leonard Taylor, "Two Views on the Meaning of Treaties Six and Seven," in Richard Price, ed., *The Spirit of the Alberta Indian Treaties* (Montreal, 1980), 26

45. James MacGregor, *Father Lacombe* (Edmonton, 1978), 233

46. Carter, *Lost Harvests,* 35–36

47. Tobias, "Canada's Subjugation of the Plains Cree," 106

48. Morris, *The Treaties of Canada,* 241

49. "Erasmus, *Buffalo Days and Nights,* 250

50. John MacLean, *Canadian Savage Folk: The Native Tribes of Canada* (Toronto, 1896), 543

51. John McDougall, *Opening the Great West: Experiences oaf Missionary in 1875–76* (Calgary, 1970), 58

52. It should be noted that there is a historical debate concerning the western extent of the Cree borders. John S. Milloy argued for the traditionally accepted interpretation that the Cree "adopted a plains way of life in the 1790s" in *The Plains Cree: Trade, Diplomacy and War, 1790 to 1870* (Winnipeg, 1988), xiv. According to Milloy, the Plains Cree became "clearly identifiable" when they "own[ed] horses" and had "a different relationship to the buffalo herds and to the Europeans" than their Woodland Cree ancestors. Ibid., 23–26. Milloy, argued that the Plains Cree's "transition from beaver to buffalo, from forest to plain, was completed" during the 1790s. Ibid., 27. Dale Russell, however, reinterpreted the archival and secondary resources and contended that the Cree of the mid-1700s did not shift "from the forests to the grasslands. Rather, they were then, and continued to be, a parkland group." Dale Russell, *Eighteenth-Century Western Cree and their Neighbours* (Hull, 1991), 218. Russell believed that the western limits of the Cree had been placed 800 kilometres too far east by previous scholars (Ibid., 212) and that the change in the role of middleman Cree to Plains Cree was gradual and somewhat minimal as they already possessed experience at living in a Parkland environment.

53. Tobias, "Canada's Subjugation of the Plains Cree," 105

54. MacGregor, *Father Lacombe*, 231

55. Morris, *The Treaties of Canada*, 176

56. Joseph Epes Brown, *The Spiritual Legacy of the American Indian* (New York, 1992), 15

57. Morris, *The Treaties of Canada*, 176. See also Ibid., 225.

58. Tobias, "Canada's Subjugation of the Plains Cree," 106–107. It is important to note that not all members of the Plains Cree considered the final text of Treaty Six to be adequate for ensuring the protection of their culture. Big Bear and Little Pine did not sign the Treaty as they believed it would result in a "loss of autonomy" for their people and result in their being "enslave[d]."

59. Hall, "A Serene Atmosphere," 327–331. These concessions took the form of outside promises which were not adhered to by the government until 1875. That the government was willing to agree to these concessions is evident in that Treaty 3, signed in 1873, contained distinctly similar provisos.

60. Gerald Friesen, *The Canadian Prairies*, 141. See also Morris, *The Treaties of Canada*, 320–327.

61. Ibid., 327

62. *Morris*, The Treaties of Canada, 40

63. The additional concessions that were granted to the Indian signatories of Treaty Six were agreed to by the government as they were not considered to run contrary to the government's goal of assimilating Indian culture. As will be seen, these concessions were in fact considered to help facilitate that goal.

64. That these terms were introduced by the Indians is evident in the transcripts of the negotiations. For example, Morris implies as much when he states of the Treaty that "it is more than has been done anywhere else; I must do it on my own responsibility, and trust to the other Queen's councillors to ratify it." Morris, *The Treaties of Canada*, 215.

65. Ibid., 354–355

66. Ibid., 252

67. Ibid., 354–355

68. Ibid., 178

69. George Brown and Ron Maguire, Indian Treaties in Historical Perspective, (Ottawa, 1979). 36

70. Morris, *The Treaties of Canada*, 178

71. Brown and Maguire, *Indian Treaties*, 38

72. Sarah Carter has noted that there were many problems attached to farming in the North-West. "Crops were often damaged by frost and scourged by squirrels, gophers, and dogs. Grasshopper plagues occurred almost annually." Carter, *Lost Harvests*, 42.

73. Erasmus, *Buffalo Days and Nights*, 252. Dickason makes note of the English spelling of Big Child's true Indian name, Mistawasis, in *Canada's First Nations*, 300. Similarly, Alexander Morris noted the spelling of Big Child's name as Mis-tah-wah-sis in Morris, *The Treaties of Canada*, 213.

74. Ibid., 212

75. Ibid., 204–212

25

■ Article 2: Canada's Colony and the Colonized

Sarah Carter

'A Unique and Unenviable Place': Canadian Federal Indian Policy

When Manitoba and the North-West Territories joined Confederation in 1870, the vast majority of

Source: Sarah Carter, *Aboriginal People and Colonizers of Western Canada to 1900* (Toronto: University of Toronto Press, 1999), selections from Chapter 6 (pp. 111–130). © University of Toronto Press Inc., 1999. Reprinted with permission of the publisher.

the residents were Aboriginal people, and largely unknown to them, their lives from then on were to be greatly influenced by policies and legislation developed for nearly 100 years in Eastern Canada, and inherited from British imperial practices. The British North America Act of 1867 had given the Canadian federal government jurisdiction over Indians and Indian reserves. In Western Canada, by 1870 there had been over two centuries of European contact, but no formal challenges to Aboriginal land ownership, except within the territory covered by the Selkirk Treaty. The 1870s represents an important watershed for many reasons. The era of efforts to impose the values and institutions of the immigrants or colonists began (although not in earnest until after 1885), and this coincided with the destruction and disappearance of the buffalo economy, just after a devastating epidemic of smallpox and famine. Yet while economic security, independence, and opportunities were to a great extent diminished beginning in the 1870s, Aboriginal people, of course, continued to take action, and make decisions and adopt strategies that influenced the course of events. However, their ability and freedom to control their own lives was increasingly constrained in the last decades of the nineteenth century.

Recent approaches to many of the fundamental documents of Aboriginal and Canadian legal history stress that First Nations were 'not passive objects, but active participants, in [their] formulation and ratification.' To appreciate the meaning of many of these documents then, and the often radically different interpretations of them, it is not enough to have an understanding of the European, written perspective alone. The central policy pursued by the British following the military defeat of the French at Quebec was given expression in the Royal Proclamation of 1763, and this was to form the foundation of the principles governing relations between First Nations and the Crown. The proclamation recognized the 'nations or tribes' of Indians to the west of the British colonies as continuing to own their lands, despite the extension of the new British sovereignty and protection, and directed that the Indians be left undisturbed on these lands. These nations could not sell their lands, however, until they were brought within a colony, and then they could sell only to the Crown, and only through collective and voluntary public action. The proclamation is generally described as a unilateral declaration of the British Crown, but Aboriginal nations played an active role in its genesis, bringing their own considerations, their own power, range of choices, and perspectives, to the agreement. First Nations did not see themselves as dependent, conquered victims of a foreign power, and they proposed peaceful government-to-government relationships of equality, retaining their lands and sovereignty. Different objectives and visions are embedded within the text of the proclamation, and this is why the document is open to differing interpretations.

Beginning in the 1790s, with the arrival of the United Empire Loyalists, the British negotiated treaties with First Nations to permit the expansion of non-Native settlement, generally adhering to the principles established in the Royal Proclamation. At first these were for relatively small parcels of land in exchange for a once-for-all payment. Responsibility for Indian affairs was originally in the hands of a branch of the British military. After the War of 1812, and the decline of the strategic importance of Aboriginal people as military allies, pressure mounted to change the basis of British Indian policy. Missionaries in British North America, as well as a humanitarian lobby in Britain, urged that the Indian Department should take the lead in encouraging Aboriginal people to change their way of life. There was also the example of the United States, where, in the last decade of the eighteenth century, the federal government declared a policy designed to make farmers out of Native Americans, responding to the widely held belief that Native Americans had no choice but to give up their vast tracts of land, with the advantage that they could be taught to farm. From 1828, the British Indian Department sought to foster the creation of self-supporting, as well as self-governing Aboriginal agricultural communities in British North America. In that year the Indian Superintendent of Upper Canada proposed a new function for the department: it would take the lead in 'civilizing' the Indians by encouraging them to settle on reserves, and take up agriculture as a livelihood. Reserves, land set aside for the exclusive use of Indian bands, were now included in the treaties, and the concept of annual payments, or annuities, was introduced. To facilitate the new program, in 1830 in the colonies of Upper and Lower Canada, jurisdiction over the management of Indian affairs shifted from military to civil authorities.

These policies have been assigned 'good marks' by many historians who see in this era the genesis of a humanitarian, benevolent approach to Canada's Aboriginal people. In the British territories, in contrast to the United States (this line of argument goes), there was no hostility, no disposition to eliminate or to coerce; rather, the government played an active role in eliminating reasons for conflict, well in advance of sustained settlement. It is certainly the case that at the same time as the Americans were pursuing the policy of 'removal,' a sizeable portion of the Aboriginal population of the older provinces of Canada remained resident on reserves. Yet there are more cynical views of Britain's 'humanitarian' policy. There was concern about the spread of American 'republican' ideas, and there were good reasons to encourage Aboriginal people to look to Britain as

26

their chief benefactor to gain their loyalty. The concept of reserves and agriculture, which should have ideally allowed Aboriginal people to subsist on a radically reduced land base, permitted a humanitarian veneer to be attached to a policy that was simply aimed at removing an obstacle to non-Aboriginal economic development and settlement.

The direction of the new policy was not entirely unwelcome in the Aboriginal communities. Conscious of the rapid changes unfolding around them, Aboriginal people were not averse to new economic accommodation. With an eye towards preparing themselves to cope with dwindling game and other resources, a number of bands of Upper Canada, even before the adoption of the 'civilizing' program, had used some of the proceeds from land surrenders to fund the establishment of farms and schools with the assistance of missionaries. Aboriginal governments were in favour of agriculture, and the maintenance of the integrity of their society and culture within an agricultural context. For a time beginning in the 1830s there was a progressive partnership in development with Aboriginal governments deciding the degree, nature, and direction of change. They rejected initiatives such as an 1846 effort to introduce the concept of reserve subdivision and individualized property-holding. These councils remained self-governing, with control over their population, land, and finances, until 1860, when responsibility for Indian affairs was transferred from the British government to the government of the United Canadas.

This self-governing status, however, and the progressive partnership, did not last. Colonial legislation of the late 1850s, the transfer of authority over Indian affairs from Britain to the colony, and Confederation radically altered the standing of Aboriginal people. The other parties, groups, or regions that became part of Confederation were consulted and negotiated with, often resulting in contentious and protracted debates. In Canada East, or Quebec, for example, there were concerns about the preservation of their language, religion, culture, and institutions. Aboriginal nations were not consulted, and they were to occupy what historian John Milloy has described as 'a unique and unenviable' place in the new nation. Through the British North America Act, and the legislation aimed at Aboriginal people combined in the comprehensive Indian Act of 1876, the federal government took extensive control of the Aboriginal nations, their land, and their finances. Traditional forms of government were replaced by government/Indian agent–controlled models of government. There was no Aboriginal participation in the formulation and ratification of this legislation; there were protests and objections raised, but these were ignored.

The Indian Act of 1876 incorporated and consolidated earlier legislation of the Assembly of the United Canadas, including the Gradual Civilization Act of 1857 and the Enfranchisement Act of 1869. These acts were based upon the assumption that it was only through individualized property that Aboriginal people could become industrious and self-reliant. With the act of 1857 the Indian Department became an aggressive and disruptive agent of assimilation. It stipulated that any Indian, if he was male, free of debt, literate, and of good moral character, could be awarded full ownership of 50 acres (20 hectares) of reserve land, and would thereby be enfranchised. He would then cut his tribal ties and cease to be an Indian. The goal of full civilization through the enfranchisement of individuals was to be accompanied by the disappearance of Aboriginal communities. In the 1860s there was even more overt encroachment on Aboriginal independence and further destruction of self-government. Enfranchisement had attracted very few qualified candidates, and the tribal governments and their leaders were seen as the obstacles. Self-government had to be abolished. This argument was accepted by the new Canadian government, and the 1869 Enfranchisement Act greatly increased the degree of government control of on-reserve systems. There was to be very little meaningful Aboriginal participation in their own governance. Although chiefs and councillors were to be elected by all male band members over the age of twenty-one, the superintendent general of Indian Affairs decided the time, manner, and place of election, and these officials were to serve at Her Majesty's pleasure, and could be removed by this same official. Band councils were also limited in their areas of jurisdiction, and faced an all-encompassing federal power of disallowance. As historian John Milloy concluded, 'For the original people there was to be no partnership, no degree of home rule to protect and encourage the development of a valued and variant culture, as was the case with French Canada.'

27

A significant feature of the colonial legislation, later incorporated in the 1876 Indian Act, was the effort to impose Euro-Canadian social organization and cultural values, and English common law, in which the wife was virtually the property of her husband. The act assumed that women were subordinate to males, and derived rights from their husbands or fathers. Women were excluded from voting in band elections and from partaking in band business. They had to prove to government officials that they were of good 'moral' character before they were entitled to receive an inheritance. Beginning with the 1869 act, an Indian woman who married a non-Indian man lost her status as a registered Indian, as did her children. So upon marriage to a non-Indian, the woman would no longer be eligible for residency on reserve land. Even if her non-Indian husband died, her status would not be affected—only remarriage to a status Indian man could reinstate her. On the other hand, white women who married Indian men, and their children, obtained legal status as Indians, and all could reside on reserve land. Another section of the act stipulated that, if an Indian woman married an Indian from another band, she was automatically transferred to the band of her husband, regardless of her personal wishes. This legislation entirely ignored Aboriginal marriage and residency customs, and it was to be keenly resented by women as well as men.

The Indian Act of 1876, which has been described as a 'formidable dossier of repression' and which established race-based laws and limitations in Canada, was originally passed with 100 sections, and this nearly doubled in the next thirty years, to 195. It consigned Aboriginal people to the status of minors; they were British subjects but not citizens, sharing the status of children, felons, and the insane, and it established the federal government as their guardians. Those who came under the act were not allowed to vote in federal or provincial elections, and as they were not voters they were legally prohibited from the professions of law and politics, unless they gave up their Indian status. Through the administration of this act, government agents were able to control minute details of everyday life. There were restrictions on Aboriginal peoples' ability to sell their produce and resources, on their religious freedom and amusements. Many of the clauses of the act were based upon nineteenth-century negative stereotypes of Indians as drunkards, as immoral, as incapable of handling money. The act criminalized for Indians the consumption of alcohol. It also specifically denied Indians rights available even to complete newcomers to the country. It stipulated, for example, that 'no Indian [...] shall be held capable of having acquired or of acquiring a homestead [...]'

The Numbered Treaties

The First Nations of Western Canada were not informed about this formidable dossier of repression when they entered into treaties in the 1870s. The Indian Act was simply unilaterally imposed, and by not communicating anything about this legislation, government and Crown representatives at treaty negotiations seriously misrepresented the nature of the relationship Aboriginal people were entering into. Aboriginal people were, however, active participants in the treaty negotiations, and the agreements reached reflect the concerns and goals of both sides, although it is now increasingly recognized that these were not fully represented in the written texts of the treaties. There were eight 'numbered treaties' covering the territory of Western Canada (excluding most of British Columbia) made between 1871 and 1899. The written texts of the treaties, prepared well in advance of the sessions, but subject to some change as a result of negotiations, have generally been understood until recently to represent the meaning of these treaties, although that meaning has been open to many interpretations. They have been depicted as just and benevolent instruments through which non-Aboriginal Canada systematically extended its jurisdiction, while offering kindly and generous aid to a population greatly in need of such assistance. The treaties have also been described as tragic misunderstandings, disreputable documents, that were imposed upon a people who had no idea of what was happening. Research that has drawn upon oral history has demonstrated that a focus upon the written text alone projects narrow perceptions of the treaties. The meaning cannot be derived and interpreted from the written words alone as the written texts do not include the Aboriginal understandings. There has also been a Eurocentric tendency to look only at government/and Crown policy and diplomacy with regard to treaty-making, yet Aboriginal societies also had their policy, protocol, ceremonies, and laws. Aboriginal groups had a lengthy history of treaty-making with other First Nations for military, trade, and other purposes. There has been a focus upon the power and authority of the Crown commissioners, but what about the power and authority of the Aboriginal negotiators?

There was significant Aboriginal input with regard to the timing of the treaties, and they were responsible for the introduction of some of the clauses and terms of the agreements. Through treaties Aboriginal people sought to secure not only physical, but cultural survival; to gain assistance in the transition to new economies based on agriculture and husbandry; and to establish peaceful, equitable relations. Canada sought through treaties to acquire legal title to the land in order to complete the transcontinental railway (promised and held out as an enticement to British Columbia in 1871), which would in turn encourage immigration, establish a prosperous economy, and strengthen industry in Eastern Canada. Aboriginal title was to be removed with as little expense as possible, avoiding costly military campaigns. Canadian authorities were also concerned to stop American intrusion north of the forty-ninth parallel, as causes of potential serious international disputes escalated in the 1870s. There were also officials, such as Alexander Morris, who seriously believed that Canadians were honour- and duty-bound to 'elevate' the Aboriginal residents of Western Canada. There was a moral imperative here to export what was perceived as a superior way of life to people assumed to be inferior. It is important to keep in mind that members of a colonizing society can hold powerful convictions that they are behaving altruistically towards the colonized.

Until recently, in written histories the numbered treaties were generally presented as one of the deliberate, orderly, and wise policies pursued by the federal government to ensure the peaceful settlement and prosperous development of the Canadian West. Yet it now seems that there was no particular plan or direction; the pattern and timing of treaty-making, as well as some important clauses, were to a great extent the result of pressure brought to bear by Aboriginal people. In the 1870s Aboriginal people were interested in entering into agreements that could assist them to acquire economic security in the face of a very uncertain future. There was also a great deal of unease and anxiety about the intentions of the government, and concerns were voiced that their land might be taken without consultation. It was learned with alarm that the HBC had 'sold' their land; there had never been any recognition that this company with whom they had traded had any jurisdiction over their land. As legal scholar Sharon Venne recently wrote, 'In present circumstances, it would be tantamount to Pepsi Cola or another such company gaining title to the lands of another country merely by engaging in trading.' Great indignation over the HBC claiming to have sold their land, and then surveying and claiming tracts of land around posts in advance of treaties, was expressed at Treaty Four proceedings: 'A year ago these people [the HBC] drew lines, and measured and marked the lands as their own. Why was this? We own the land; the Manitou [or Great Spirit] gave it to us. There was no bargain; they stole from us [...]' Word of troops stationed at Red River in 1870 heightened fears of hostile intentions. The appearance of railway and telegraph surveyors in advance of treaties caused concern. In central Saskatchewan and in Alberta, the NWMP arrived suddenly in advance of treaties and, without permission or consultation, built posts. Pressure for agreements that would provide economic security was brought to bear through messages, deputations to Crown representatives, and interference with survey work.

The numbered treaties appear to be remarkably similar documents. In each of the written treaties, the First Nations agreed to 'cede, release, surrender, and yield up to the Government of Canada for Her Majesty the Queen,' large tracts of land. They were promised, however, that they could continue their vocations of hunting throughout the surrendered tract, except those tracts taken up 'from time to time for settlement.' Reserves of land were to be set aside. (The precise amount of land varied considerably from treaty to treaty. For example, in Treaties Three, Four, and Five, each family of five was allowed one section, or 640 acres [260 hectares], whereas in Treaties One and Two each family was allotted 160 acres [65 hectares].) These reserves were to be administered and dealt with for the residents by the government. Annual payments (varying from five to twelve dollars) were promised to each man, woman, and child, with bigger payments for chiefs and councillors, who were also to receive suitable suits of clothing. They were promised implements, cattle, and seed for the encouragement of agriculture. In Treaties One to Six, the government agreed to

29

maintain schools on reserves, and, in Treaty Seven, to pay the salary of teachers. The signatories solemnly promised to strictly observe the treaty, to conduct and behave themselves as good and loyal subjects of the Queen, to obey and abide by the law, to maintain peace and good order. Closer inspection of the individual treaties, however, reveals significant differences in the circumstances and negotiating tactics of both sides, and in the written and oral accounts of proceedings. There were unique features to each of the agreements, and different understandings of these agreements emerged.

The earliest of the treaties illustrate the concern about future livelihood that was foremost in the minds of Aboriginal spokesmen, and the effective negotiating skills of Aboriginal leaders. They also indicate that verbal promises and statements were regarded by Aboriginal people as every bit as binding as those which appeared on the written text. The signatories to the 1871 Treaties One and Two were Saulteaux and the Cree of Manitoba. Their concern about future livelihood was shared by Crown negotiators, who clearly indicated that they wished to encourage an agricultural economy. Alexander Morris, who was the Queen's representative in the treaties made between 1873 and 1876 (Treaties Three to Six), felt that it was Canada's duty to make the new wards self-supporting through agriculture. Initially, however, the Crown negotiators did not intend to provide direct assistance in the transition to an agricultural economy in the way of implements, draught animals, and other necessities of a settled and agricultural lifestyle. In Eastern Canada, agriculture as well as education had received official support and encouragement from government, but specific clauses were not included in treaty terms as obligations upon the Crown. This situation changed in the numbered treaties as a result of the bargaining of Aboriginal negotiators. In Treaty One, specific requests were made for implements, cattle, wagons, and housing. The Crown commissioners orally agreed to this assistance, but the clauses did not appear in the printed versions of Treaties One and Two. Controversy soon surrounded the so-called outside promises, the clauses that related to agricultural assistance, and there was discontent over the non-fulfilment of these terms. These were 'outside' only to the non-Aboriginal negotiators to the treaties; to Aboriginal negotiators, who remembered precisely what had been promised orally, they were an intrinsic part of the treaties. Before the Treaty One negotiations, government surveyor S.J. Dawson had warned his superiors that this would be the case, as 'though they have no means of writing, there are always those present who are charged to keep every word in mind.' Dawson cited the example of an Ojibway principal chief who began an oration by repeating almost word for word what Dawson had said two years earlier. Crown officials agreed to make these a formal part of the treaties in 1875 as a result of the pressure brought to bear by Aboriginal people. The numbered treaties that followed included the terms that provided for agricultural transition in the formal, written treaties.

Treaty Six was made at Fort Carlton and Fort Pitt in 1876 with Plains Cree and Assiniboine. This treaty exemplifies the themes mentioned above; in particular, there was concern about future livelihood. Aboriginal negotiators demanded further clauses that provided for agricultural assistance, and help in making a transition to a new life. As a result of their bargaining, novel terms were added to Treaty Six, including assistance in the event of famine or pestilence, and an additional clause providing for a medicine chest. Reflecting a concern for the future health of their people, the Aboriginal negotiators succeeded in exacting the promise that a medicine chest would be kept at the home of the Indian agent for the use and benefit of the Indians. A troubling aspect of this agreement is that, like Treaty Four, concluded in 1874 at Fort Qu'Appelle with the Cree, Saulteaux, and Assiniboine, a vast number of people, including most of the Cree and prominent leaders, were not informed of the proceedings and were not present. Chief Big Bear, a prominent Plains Cree leader, was not invited by the representatives of the Crown to the original negotiations for Treaty Six.

Studies of Treaty Six that focus upon Aboriginal perspectives reveal fundamentally different understandings of what was agreed to at these proceedings. At the heart of the difference is the certainty that the land was not surrendered, or sold; rather, Aboriginal negotiators agreed to share and to coexist as equals with non-Aboriginals. Given the nature of leadership in Plains societies, and the limits on the powers of the chiefs who entered into treaty, they would not have had the authority to sell or surrender the land. Elders maintain that the land was never sold in the treaty process, and that the wording 'cede, surrender […]' was not included in the original treaty. They accepted the idea that the Queen wanted to make a treaty to share the land with her people, who were in poverty, and the concept of sharing was acceptable. As Harold Cardinal said in an address to Queen Elizabeth II in 1973, 'Our Treaties were agreements between two peoples from different civilizations to share their resources so that each could grow and successfully meet changes brought on by the passage of time.'

Oral histories with the people of Treaty Seven, made in 1877 with the Siksika, Blood, Peigan, Tsuu T'ina, and Nakoda (Stoney) peoples, indicate that a peace treaty was concluded, not a land surrender. They were asked and agreed to put away their weapons, live in peace and harmony, and share the land. But the emphasis on peacemaking was left unrecorded, and instead land surrender was made the most significant part of the written treaty. In the oral record there is no memory of the issue of land surrender being raised and discussed at the proceedings, and no realization that the land was ceded for ever. There is also little trace of the issue being raised in the documentary record of the treaty proceedings. Government officials were anxious to hastily conclude a treaty with the southern Alberta peoples in 1877, and did not want to raise issues such as land surrender as it could well mean that the treaty would be rejected. The Blackfoot were perceived as war-like, volatile, and dangerous as they were well armed. There was concern about potential Blackfoot alliances with the Lakota, who had defeated Colonel George Custer in 1876 and taken up residence in Canadian territory. To the south, in the spring and summer of 1877, there were numerous small battles between the U.S. military and the non-treaty Nez Percé, whose destination was Canada. The making of Treaty Seven coincided with the Nez Percé moving closer and closer to the camp of Sitting Bull, and there was great alarm about the formation of an alliance.

Research into First Nations' perspectives on Treaty Seven has revealed other factors that would have impeded understanding of the concepts embedded in the written document. In Blackfoot there is no equivalent word for 'cede,' and terms such as 'square mile' could not have been translated properly. In Blackfoot there is now a term for mile (*ni'taa'si*), but it entered the language in the early 1900s with the establishment of mission schools, as

did the term now used for square (*iksisttoyisi*). There was no word for 'Canada,' only a word for the territory of their own nation. The translators at the proceedings were not competent in all of the Aboriginal languages present, nor could they have understood the Victorian jargon of the commissioners. In the written text of the treaty, there are more than eighty examples of gross misrepresentations of the names of chiefs and headmen signatories, clearly indicating that the translators were not real Blackfoot speakers. The names of Nakoda chiefs, who spoke a Siouan language, were recorded in Cree, indicating that the translator for them, Reverend John McDougall, was not competent in their language.

Conflicting perceptions and interpretations of the treaties are at the root of many contemporary issues. Until recently the treaties have been narrowly interpreted by government and in the courts to mean the words on the written documents. Those who prepared these written documents likely did not fully understand or appreciate what the Aboriginal participants believed they had agreed to. From the government's perspective, treaties were straightforward agreements to secure title to land and resources for settlement and development. First Nations draw attention to the verbal promises and the negotiations, and ask that treaties be understood, not according to the technical meaning of the words, but in the sense that they were understood by Aboriginal people. There must be recognition of the 'spirit' of the treaties, and there should be a flexible and generous interpretation of the terms. The Supreme Court of Canada has found that courts cannot begin with the assumption that the written text of the treaties manifests a shared communication between the treaty parties. Instead, the courts must take into account the historical context and perception each party might have as to the nature of the undertaking.

An understanding of the spirit of the treaties also requires an appreciation of Aboriginal concepts, philosophies, and ceremonies. It is consistently explained by Elders of the First Nations that the Creator bestowed sacred responsibilities upon them to act as custodians of the land, and that it could therefore not have been possible for them to even consider breaking this inviolable sacred relationship and to cede, surrender, release, and yield up the land. This would be tantamount to giving up their life. According to Harold Cardinal, to the Cree

31

the treaty relationship is rooted in the principles embodied in the term *meyo witchi towin*, meaning 'good, healthy, happy, respectful relationships among equal parties.' The parties agree to act according to the divinely inspired principles of *wak koo too win*, meaning a perpetual relationship patterned after familial concepts. The relationship with the Crown was understood to consist of mutual ongoing sharing arrangements that would guarantee each other's survival and stability. The concept of *wi taski win*, or sharing the blessing of the land in mutual harmony, provided that the sharing arrangements would be fair to each of the parties, enabling both to enjoy the prosperity of the land and *pim atchi hoowin*, or make a living. Through the pipe ceremonies conducted by First Nations when making treaties for the goals of peace and harmony, the most powerful spirits were called upon to assist in maintaining the peace agreement and accompanying commitments of promises. If the agreement was broken, the powerful spirits of the sun, water, thunder, and wind might unleash their wrath upon the attending parties. The serious consequences to breaking vows made to the spirits was a way of ensuring that peace and harmony would be preserved at all costs. The sweet-grass used in the ceremony represented an undertaking between the parties both that their relationship would be non-coercive and that it would be governed according to precepts of honesty, integrity, good faith, gentleness, and generosity. That these ceremonies took place affirms the sacred nature of the agreements and mutual commitments. As Cardinal wrote in his 1969 *The Unjust Society*, 'To the Indians of Canada, the treaties represent an Indian Magna Carta.'

The North-West Mounted Police

The fact that the non-Aboriginal settlement of Western Canada proceeded relatively peacefully, and that 'law and order' was to a great extent observed, has almost entirely to do with the strategies and actions of First Nations. These strategies, outlined above, featured the negotiation of treaties in order to ensure that resources would be shared, that independence and integrity would be retained, and that a useful partner in the creation of an enriched way of life would be obtained. Aboriginal negotiators solemnly promised that they would in all respects obey and abide by the law. Even leaders such as Big Bear, who rejected 'taking treaty'

for almost a decade, advised and adopted non-confrontational strategies. Despite persistent rumours of Indian 'uprisings' in Western Canada, there were no such events with the exception of Frog Lake (1885; discussed in chapter 7). Promises to maintain peace and good order were observed. Yet credit for the peaceful and orderly settlement of the West is generally attributed in written histories to the NWMP, as well as to the treaties, although these are traditionally perceived as entirely a British-Canadian strategy. Both are often presented as essential components of the vision of one man, Prime Minister Sir John A. Macdonald, who had a grand dream and design for a strong and stable Dominion from sea to sea. While the treaties established the foundation, it was this small force of intrepid few that introduced, and then maintained, law and order, according to many histories of the Canadian West. The force was launched in 1873, and 300 of them, dressed in scarlet to distinguish them from the American cavalry, dressed in blue, made the much-celebrated 'march west' the following year.

A great deal has been written about the Mounties. There are first-hand accounts, academic as well as popular works of history, fiction, and a 'Heritage Minute.' As historian Keith Walden has written, this vast body of literature has made mythic heroic figures of the Mounties. Most of the accounts contain a heavy cultural bias, as they describe these few men as members of a superior and more powerful yet humane culture, bringing stability and peace, law and order, to a wild and savage people in a fretful, uninhabitable land. The force is invariably depicted as having forged outstanding relations with Aboriginal people, who welcomed, appreciated, and respected them. They stopped the whisky trade; pacified warlike Indians; and explained the law to them, administering it in equal doses to white and Indian alike. They stood as sterling examples of manly attributes such as integrity, sobriety, and courage.

As Walden observed, none of this is very plausible as few of the residents of Western Canada could possibly have so willingly accepted the intrusion of outsiders into their affairs. There is an element of plausibility, however. The police were welcomed by some leaders and groups. Red Crow, Crowfoot, and other Blackfoot leaders were grateful that the American whisky trade was curtailed. Major James Walsh *did* forge outstanding relations with Sitting Bull and his people when they sought refuge across the border from 1876 to 1881. Yet the Mounties were outsiders intruding into the lives of Aboriginal people, and their actions were not always appreciated. There were indignant reactions to police posts being placed in the path of the buffalo, without the government first conferring with them about these establishments. A post such as Fort Calgary was placed at a popular camping and fording site without permission or consultation. As Walter Hildebrandt has argued, the police were sent in the vanguard of a 'new order for the white settlers' to pacify the people in what Prime Minister Macdonald called 'that fretful realm' and make the West a safe place to settle. They were more a military, occupying force than a police force. Their function was to assist in expanding British-Canadian influence, without the costs incurred in costly wars of conquest. They served in a military rather than a police capacity at occasions such as treaty negotiations. At Treaty Seven, the police brought and fired cannons, which the Blackfoot found menacing. As agents of the government they assisted in enforcing the Indian Act and related policies of the Department of the Interior and of Indian Affairs, and soon after their arrival they became vital enforcers of extremely unpopular coercive measures and laws that monitored, controlled, and restrained people. They had powers that were unprecedented in the history of police forces; not only did they introduce and enforce Canadian law, they were also given powers as magistrates and so administered the same laws. Many of the predominantly young men who made up the force were also a far cry from the exemplary models of behaviour that most of the police literature would have us believe, and this caused consternation among Aboriginal leaders. The police indulged in considerable drinking, and brawling among themselves and with the 'citizens.'

Missionary John McDougall was critical of the conduct of the police, whom he found to be fond of whisky, drinking all they could lay their hands on, while supposedly putting down the whisky trade. He also felt that some of the laws and policies the police enforced were foolish and unnecessary. Yet despite his criticisms, McDougall contributed to the 'myth of the Mountie.' In his *Opening the Great West*, McDougall wrote that 'here in the mid-summer of 1875 the fact remained that the major sense of all men in this big West was to respect the Police and obey the law. Thus without any bloodshed an immense lawless region was being justly and peaceably administered

[...]' Despite cherished non-Aboriginal origin narratives about Western Canada, the new realm was not, in the last three decades of the nineteenth century, as peaceable as McDougall described, nor was it as lawless as he described in the preceding years. As in other colonial settings, there was considerable resistance to aspects of the foreign presence that caused colonial authorities grave concern, although there was also accommodation to other aspects. Yet it remains the case that in Western Canada there simply was not the record of continuous violence and conquest that characterized not only the western United States, but many of Britain's imperial enterprises. This had as much to do with the strategies and actions of the Aboriginal residents as with the policies of government and the actions of a handful of police.

Bibilography

Borrows, John. 'Wampum at Niagara: The Royal Proclamation, Canadian Legal History, and Self-Government.' In *Aboriginal and Treaty Rights in Canada: Essays on Law, Equality, and Respect for Difference,* ed. Michael Asch, 155–72. Vancouver: University of British Columbia Press, 1997.

Cardinal, Harold. 'Treaty Eight: The Right to Livelihood.' Unpublished LLM thesis, Harvard University Law School, 1996.

Chartrand, Paul L.A.H. *Manitoba's Métis Settlement Scheme of 1870.* Saskatoon: Native Law Centre, 1991.

Flanagan, Thomas, and Gerhard J. Ens. 'Métis Land Grants in Manitoba: A Statistical Study.' *Histoire sociale/Social History* 27/23 (1994): 65–88.

Francis, R. Douglas. *Images of the West.* Saskatoon: Western Producer Prairie Books, 1989.

Friesen, Jean. 'Magnificent Gifts; The Treaties of Canada with the Indians of the Northwest, 1869–76.' *Transactions of the Royal Society of Canada,* series 5, vol. 1 (1986): 41–51.

Hildebrandt, Walter. *Views from Fort Battleford: Constructed Visions of an Anglo-Canadian West.* Regina: Canadian Plains Research Center, 1994.

Milloy, John S. 'The Early Indian Acts: Developmental Strategy and Constitutional Change.' In *As Long as the Sun Shines and Water Flows,* ed. Ian A.L. Getty and Antoine S. Lussier, 56–64. Vancouver: UBC Press, 1983.

Morris, Alexander. *The Treaties of Canada with the Indians of Manitoba and the North-West Territories.* 1880. Reprint. Toronto: Coles Publishing, 1971.

33

Owram, Douglas. *Promise of Eden: The Canadian Expansionist Movement and the Idea of the West, 1856–1900*. Toronto: University of Toronto Press, 1980.

Sprague, D.N. *Canada and the Métis, 1869–1885*. Waterloo: Wilfrid Laurier University Press, 1988.

Stanley, G.F.G. *The Birth of Western Canada: A History of the Riel Rebellions* 1936. Reprint. Toronto: University of Toronto Press, 1975.

Tobias, John. 'Protection, Civilization, Assimilation: An Outline History of Canada's Indian Policy.' In *As Long as the Sun Shines and Water Flows*, ed. Ian A.L. Getty and Antoine S. Lussier, 13–30. Vancouver: UBC Press, 1983.

Treaty Seven Tribal Council, Walter Hildebrandt, Dorothy First Rider, and Sarah Carter. *The True Spirit and Original Intent of Treaty 7*. Montreal: McGill-Queen's University Press, 1996.

Venne, Sharon. 'Understanding Treaty 6: An Indigenous Perspective.' In *Aboriginal and Treaty Rights in Canada: Essays on Law, Equality and Respect for Difference*, ed. Michael Asch, 173–207. Vancouver: University of British Columbia Press, 1997.

Walden, Keith. 'The Great March of the Mounted Police in Popular Literature, 1873–1973.' *Canadian Historical Association Historical Papers* (1980): 33–56.

■ Article 3: The True Spirit and Original Intent of Treaty 7

Treaty Seven Elders and Tribal Council et al.

INTRODUCTION

Otsistsi Pakssaisstoyiih Pi
(the year when the winter was open and cold)

WILTON GOODSTRIKER

Among all First Nations people, there is and has always been a recording of significant events in our history. Our ancestors were just as anxious to leave a record of their story as we are today. I wish that somehow we could let them know that we have remembered, but then again, they probably knew all along that we would.

The stories have been recorded in many forms, through our winter-counts, on the land, but most importantly in the minds and spirit of our people. In these ways, the stories have been passed down from one generation to another throughout the ages.

Throughout this document, we will share the various methods that the First Nations people of Treaty 7 used to record our history.

In the winter-counts of the First Nations of the Treaty 7 area, the year 1877 is referred to as *otsistsi pakssaisstoyiih pi** (Blackfoot—the year when the winter was open and cold). Among the other nations, it is known as "the year when there was great hunger," "the year when the long rains did not come," "the year of starvation and hunger," or "the year when the first snow was late." In any event, to our people it was to be a year which was not going to be normal. To the elders, something was going to be wrong.

It was also the year that a treaty (Treaty 7) was entered into between the First Nations people of this area and the representatives of the Queen of Britain. Interesting is the fact that the treaty did not make its way onto any of the winter-counts of the First Nations people. However, the memory of that occasion is vivid among our people, and the story has been told many times among Niitsitapi (the real people) throughout the years since that time. This story is about *istsist aohkotspi* (the first time that we received gifts and money) at Soyooh

---

*Blackfoot is an oral language, and over the years several Blackfoot dictionaries have been produced. For consistency in this book, we will use Don Frantz's *Blackfoot Dictionary of Stems, Roots and Affixes* (Toronto: University of Toronto Press, 1995), second edition, unless otherwise noted. This choice is not intended to raise Frantz's dictionary as a final authority for usage, since each Blackfoot tribe has its own legitimate dialect and usage.

Source: Treaty 7 Elders and Tribal Council with Walter Hildebrandt, Dorothy First Rider, and Sarah Carter, *The True Spirit and Original Intent of Treaty 7* (Montreal and Kingston: McGill-Queen's University Press, 1996), pp. 3–5, 11–15, 111–119, 191–201. Reprinted with permission.

34

pawahko (ridge under water) or Blackfoot Crossing. In our languages there is no word for treaty; the event is simply referred to as *istsist aohkotspi* or *iitsinnaihtsiiyo'pi* (the time when we made a sacred alliance). Among our people, there are several ways to make an alliance and we will examine these closely in the hope that the reader will come to understand the complex ways of our people. The alliance process of the First Nations played a major role at Blackfoot Crossing.

The memory of a people is made accurate with the help of ceremony. This memory is a precious gift among our people.

The Story

"Sit here my child, and watch me close as I prepare the sacred smudge. I will then tell you a story. The reason I will use the smudge is so you will never forget that which I will share with you. And in time, when it is your turn to share, you will share with your children exactly as I will share with you. In this way, things will never change."—Sa'ksisakiaaksin (Laurie Big Plume)

Laurie Big Plume went on to tell me many stories. I remember one time when he told me that "The Christian story always begins with 'In the beginning.' Our story, if we were to write it down, would start with 'Before the beginning.'" I asked him at one point, "How old are our ways?" and he replied, "The ways of the White people are a child compared to our ways."

History has been documented in many ways, and in large part what we know of the past is dependent on information gained through archaeology and to some extent anthropology. Among our people, oral history is perhaps the most accurate. Our people's memory goes back to the beginning of time and in some respects beyond. Our story has come through seven ages, the last one being referred to as *i'kookaiksi* (the age when the people used tipi designs). We are still in this age and will be for as long as the people use the tipi design. This era dates back some five hundred years, and it will be the one that we will concentrate on for the purposes of this document. It is an era that saw the coming of the horse, of the immigrant nations to our land, and of new ways to a people.

One must keep in mind the history of a people when attempting to understand their perspective, their spirit and intent, in their dealings with the newcomers. This story will take you into the world of the First Nations. We will share our history, our alliance process, and our ceremony as they pertain to the treaty. Constant through the ages have been the use of ceremony and the need to document our history accurately. The latter has been done by way of marking in some way on the land, in our winter-counts, and, in all cases, in the oral history, which has been the most accurate method.[...]

Alliances have always been common to our people. There were alliances for trade, for cohabitation of territory. *Innaihtsiini* are sacred alliances of peace between individuals, families, and nations. These alliances find their beginning in the sacred ways of the Plains people, and they go back for thousands of years. Each year one would still witness these in our sacred ceremonies.[...]

STORYTELLING

Storytelling is a great gift among our people. A requirement among our people is for young children to spend much time with grandparents. It is the responsibility of grandparents to teach legends and stories and the ways of our people. In this way a closeness develops between the very young and the old. Our people do not believe in old-age homes.

I was a small child when I witnessed my first storytelling session among the old ones. Those present were my grandfather Many Fingers, Old Man Rabbit, Shot Both Sides, Low Horn, and Old Black Plume. For several days they shared stories, legends, and history. There was always great care in correcting each other when there was error found in one of the accounts. In this way, when everybody left for home, they all left with the same story to be retold at another time. For many years I have heard these stories, and they remained unchanged. It is in this way that our history and heritage have been accurately handed down through the ages. Because our languages are not written, we rely heavily on the oral traditions and on the winter-counts. Among our elders, it is only when individuals could recount stories without error that they were allowed to teach history. When young people were present at these storytelling sessions, they weren't allowed to make noise or be up walking around. From an early age, the young were taught to be careful listeners. A great deal of tenderness and gentleness was required when talking to young people. The elders would talk to the young ones in a low voice, sometimes so low and gentle that the children would think that they were dreaming. In this way a child would never forget.

The teaching of history among our people was given to everyone. Only a select few, however, were privy to sacred teaching, and throughout our recent documented history, this is the information which has been absent. The elders were very careful in the sharing of this kind of information. For the first time, and under the close authority of the elders, this document will attempt to shed some light on those areas which pertain to the events at Soyooh pawahko (ridge under water or Blackfoot Crossing).

SWEETGRASS

The sweetgrass with its three strands represents a harmony which is necessary between the Giver of Life, all that lives, and Mother Earth. It is a harmony which cannot be deliberately imbalanced or separated by man. This is common knowledge among the buffalo people, the Plains tribes. It was this understanding that our leaders and elders took with them to the talks at Blackfoot Crossing in 1877. This was the harmony which for some reason to this point has not been mentioned in the official accounts of Treaty 7. From an early age each young person is taught about this gift of the Giver of Life, and throughout one's lifetime, many times one will experience the ceremonies where it is used. It is a ceremony that played a major part in the talks at Blackfoot Crossing.

THE SACRED SMUDGE

The sacred smudge is a ceremony given to Niitsitapa (the real people) by the Giver of Life. Along with this precious gift there are spiritual laws which govern the use of the smudge: it is used only when there are very important issues to be discussed, the issues cannot be of a negative nature, and spiritual guidance is asked for so that all that will be discussed will be treated with the highest regard for honesty. The sacred smudge is often used in the teaching of sacred information so that the one being taught will never forget. The person teaching or sharing the information will also ask for

spiritual guidance, so that he or she will share in exactly the same way as they were taught themselves. When using the smudge, the people present are conducting themselves with the knowledge that the Giver of Life is witness to the proceedings. The smudge is used for cleansing first of all the participants and then the area or environment where the ceremony is being conducted so that everything will be done in a clean and pure way. The ceremony is as old as time and can never change in process because it is a sacred gift to all First Nations. The ceremony itself is a prerequisite to the use of the sacred pipe.

THE STORY OF BLACKFOOT CROSSING

Many stories have been told surrounding the events which took place at Blackfoot Crossing in the fall of 1877, but seldom from the perspective of the First Nations people themselves. In many cases, vivid accounts have been solicited from our people as to the happenings during those few days in September, but noticeable is their reluctance to mention the ceremony attached to the participation of the First Nations. In some instances, the reluctance comes from their not wanting to share that which is sacred; in others, they were not privy to the information. On the part of historians and academics, the reason is oftentimes an ignorance of the complex ways of a people they simply do not know. Thus, in various published accounts, the occasions that involved ceremony are often recorded inaccurately or it is indicated that no record exists of what took place. A good example of this kind of reference is found in documents of the officials at Blackfoot Crossing. The officials simply reported that on the evening of the twentieth there appeared to be much joy and singing well into the night. In actuality, there were prayers and ceremonies in each of the camps of the various nations. This had been going on for several days, and the purpose was to seek guidance as the nations prepared to discuss important issues pertaining to their survival. By that time, all of the various nations were well informed about the deceit that their neighbours to the east and south had experienced at the hands of government and military officials. Many treaties had been entered into, and in most cases, the promises made had been broken over and over. It was common knowledge that the newcomers were not honest people. Before we go into the actual events and talks at Blackfoot Crossing, there is one more ceremony that needs mention, as it was probably the most important ceremony of this occasion. This ceremony took place in the few days prior to the actual discussions of the treaty.

There is a ceremony known to our people as *kano'tsississin* (where everybody smokes ceremony). At times it has been referred to as the "big smoke." It was one of the few ceremonies that brought together all those affiliated in some way with the sacred smudge—elders, medicine pipe holders, members of sacred societies, leaders, and war leaders. One requirement was that those in attendance would bring with them their pipes and knowledge of sacred songs and prayers. The elders conducted the ceremony. They played a key role even in the everyday lives of the people. Important decisions affecting the people were never made in the absence of or without consultation with the elders. The ceremony was, and is, held during the winter moons of our people or, if we use the new calendar moons, from September to March. It began at sundown and ended at sunrise and lasted throughout the night. One could hear the songs and prayers, which are as old as time, with each of the participants asking for guidance in whatever was going to happen. Many of the people in attendance would have their faces painted with sacred ochres to protect them from anything that would be negative in nature. Throughout our recorded history, this painting of the faces has been erroneously termed "war paint." Among our people, there is no such thing as war paint. As with all ceremonies, the sacred smudge was at the centre of all activity. Prior to any pipe being used, the first requirement was to place the sweetgrass on some coals, and in doing this, you would ask the Giver of Life to guide you in what you will say and that you will only hear good things. The pipe would then be taken and again you would ask the Giver of Life to give you courage and strength as the stone of the pipe is strong and that you will talk straight (honestly) as the stem of the pipe is straight. You would then ask the same of those who would join you in smoke.

At Blackfoot Crossing, the ceremony was initiated on the advice of Father of Many Children, who had been present at the signing of the Lame Bull Treaty of 1855. On his urging, the ceremony would give protection against the authorities' apparent disregard of the provisions in the American treaty and the subsequent starvation and hardships of the people. By this time, Father of Many Children was a respected elder and teacher among his people. Many of the participating leaders at Blackfoot Crossing were medicine pipe holders. Each of the five nations had beaver bundles as well as medicine pipes at the time.

Not surprising is the fact that in 1991 the chiefs of Treaty 7, on the advice of their elders, initiated this whole treaty review project by participating in the same ceremony. Their teaching had remained constant in the ways of their people. The songs which were heard were the same songs as those heard in September 1877. This ceremony has remained unchanged throughout the ages, and it is still very much in use today. The chiefs, in authorizing this review, felt that it was important to document the stories of their elders so that, for generations to come, those who would read the story would somehow get a much better understanding of the spirit and intent of the First Nations people with respect to their participation in Treaty 7.

These, then, were some of the ceremonies held in those few days in September of 1877. The sad note is the fact that no descriptions of them found their way into the official accounts of the time. Perhaps those who were responsible for the recording had viewed ceremony as a small detail, insignificant and not worth mention in official documents. To the First Nations people, this was the spirit of the whole process. Only ceremony could seal an accord that would last "as long as the sun would shine, and as long as the river would flow." I once asked Dan Weasel Moccasin where this expression came from. His response was, "The term 'as long as the sun shines and the rivers flow' comes directly out of the way of the pipe. The way of our people is the way of the pipe. Since then there is much sadness each time there is effort to renege on promises they feel were made to them upon a sacred oath."[...]

CHAPTER THREE

The First Nations' Perspective on Treaty 7

WHAT DID TREATY 7 MEAN TO THE FIRST NATIONS?

The leaders who accepted Treaty 7 believed that it was first and foremost a peace treaty. All the Treaty

7 First Nations were unanimous on this point: that through the agreement with the British Crown and the Canadian representatives, the First Nations would cease to war among themselves and that peace would be preserved between the First Nations and the Canadian authorities. Peace and order were essential for the protection of the settler populations that were to be ushered onto the prairies under various schemes initiated within the framework of John A. Macdonald's National Policy. The resulting stability in the newcomer settlements would help to realize the agricultural potential of the West that so many central Canadian explorers and politicians had desired. To some degree the peace process had already been set in motion with the arrival of the North-West Mounted Police in southern Alberta in 1874-75. Their presence and the stability they were able to establish by stopping the whiskey trade were much appreciated by the First Nations people of southern Alberta. Indeed, some historians say that Colonel Macleod became somewhat of a hero among the Blackfoot Confederacy for the authority he was able to establish in the aftermath of clearing Whoop-Up Country of the outlaw traders who had generated so much of the violence that had plagued the territory for the previous decade.

In fact, from the point of view of the elders, it was above all a peace treaty that the Canadian government had desired for this territory. Peace had not been of central importance in the other prairie treaties. The First Nations genuinely appreciated the peace and stability that was brought to the southern territory of the Canadian plains. In return, the First Nations agreed to end hostilities among themselves, promising not to interfere with the peaceful settlement of the newcomer agriculturalists who had been arriving to share the land. There was nothing said among the elders about this peace being in any way linked to giving up land; rather they viewed the peace as being of benefit to all the groups agreeing to the treaty.

In the view of the government, the most significant part of the written treaty involved the surrender of land—not peace. However, peace must have been prominent in the minds of the commissioners who set out to sign Treaty 7, since the tribes of southern Alberta, having had the least contact of any Aboriginal peoples with settler society up to this point, were thought to be a serious threat to settlement.

This fact was most trenchantly underlined by Father Scollen's letter warning the treaty commissioners that these southern Alberta nations were the most "warlike" on the plains. Scollen and others were also concerned about the potential alliance between Sitting Bull's Lakota at Wood Mountain and the tribes of the Blackfoot Confederacy. Thus, it was the Canadian officials, perhaps more so than the First Nations' attending the talks, who wanted to be assured of peace and who raised the issue specifically during the treaty discussions. Certainly they wanted to avoid other international incidents like the one precipitated by the arrival of Sitting Bull or the crisis produced by the Cypress Hills Massacre of 1873.

The First Nations at Blackfoot Crossing were very familiar with the treaty process. Indeed, a number of Blackfoot chiefs had signed the Lame Bull Treaty of 1855, which allowed road development into the West in return for peace with the tribes across the American plains and promised payments to those who signed. This treaty was not understood to be a land surrender but rather a peace treaty, and the tribes at the time were left to move freely over rather large territories. However, the nature of the peace agreed to under Treaty 7 was understood in different ways by the First Nations. Each nation's interpretation of the treaty—just what the peace was to achieve, and who was to benefit—depended on the historical situation that each found itself in at the treaty signing.

The Stoneys, traditional enemies of the other four nations that accepted the treaty, believed that peace meant that they would no longer be fighting with nations of the Blackfoot Confederacy and the other First Nations to whom they had been hostile at various times in the past. As understood by members of the Blackfoot-speaking nations, peace meant not only the kind of peace they enjoyed in the American territories into which their hunting territory still extended, but also the cessation of hostilities with the Stoneys and Cree, and the prohibition of the whiskey trade. But aside from these slight differences in perception, what is clear is that all the First Nations understood the agreement reached at Blackfoot Crossing to be first and foremost a peace treaty. Secondarily, it represented their agreement to share the land and its resources with the newcomers in return for a variety of compensation benefits understood to be their "treaty rights" or "treaty promises."

Blood Tribe

According to Pete Standing Alone, the Blood word for treaty, *innaihtsiini*, means that two sides must "achieve a common purpose." A treaty had to be approached with care and caution. One tried not to be aggressive when negotiating a treaty, as it was a serious undertaking and the consequence of failure might be too great. It was therefore with much gravity that Treaty 7 was pursued. Various interpretive language was used by the Blood elders to describe what the treaty meant to them and their ancestors. Fred Gladstone said that a treaty meant having peace between peoples or tribes; it was a "negotiation between two peoples." Rosie Red Crow indicated that the treaty meant that "we all agreed to be on friendly terms." Wallace Mountain Horse described the treaty process as it had affected the Bloods when they made treaty with both the Cree and the Crow peoples at various times in his memory. He reiterated that the treaty meant an agreement "not to fight anymore." Mountain Horse also discussed the significance of the role of the North-West Mounted Police in pacifying the territory of southern Alberta; this was seen as an important achievement by the Bloods. However, he lamented the fact that the recording of what was said about peace was one-sided, leaving it to look as though the land surrender was the most important issue discussed when in fact for the Bloods peace was most important. Louise Crop Eared Wolf said that the fundamental beliefs of the Bloods would not have allowed them to give away the land: "We believed and understood [that we would] share this territory amongst each other and we also believed that the land could not be given away because of its sacredness; therefore, it did not belong to us or anybody else. The earth is just put there by our creator for only our benefit and use."

Adam Delaney stressed that surrendering land is a concept foreign to the Bloods. Treaties can be made in three situations. Payments are made between in-laws when couples marry; payments can be made between spiritual persons to break a taboo; and finally, treaties are made between nations or tribes to signify peace and friendship or to end wars.

To illustrate the Blood understanding of what happened at Blackfoot Crossing, Louise Crop Eared Wolf related the story of Red Crow: "At the signing of the treaty at Blackfoot Crossing, Red Crow pulled out the grass and gave it to the White officials and informed them that they will share the grass of the earth with them. Then he took some dirt from the earth and informed them that they could not share this part of the earth and what was underneath it, because it was put there by the Creator for the Indians' benefit and use."

Peigan Nation

According to John Yellowhorn, it was the government that wanted the peace treaty, and it was at the government's initiative that the negotiations commenced. People were told that "they would have a much better life if they made the treaty." The reoccurring theme of peace was stated rather differently by Sally Provost: "It's a sign of peace to say we accept the treaty [...] they were just promising and promising, and we were going to get help for the rest of time." That was how important peace appeared to be for the government. Sally Provost also mentioned that the government wanted peace in order to "civilize the Indians." Nick Smith remembered that the main purpose of the treaty was that "we will make peace here with everyone." The "Queen's representatives will make laws for us." Unfortunately, these laws were used "to control us," and the peace that was sued for under the guise of the government "caring for" the First Nations was instead used to restrict and control them. The peace meant that the First Nations' way of life would be changed, for the officials told them, "These are the laws you will abide by." Hugh Crow Eagle remembered his grandfather saying that the treaty was for peace and friendship, "not only with the White man but also with all other tribes that we may have been fighting."

The North-West Mounted Police were considered significant not only for their past service in driving out the whiskey traders but also for enforcing the new laws that were established. Peace would be more complicated than simply not fighting: "You will no longer live the way you were used to. You will be taken care of by the Queen and her representatives. She sent them here. The Red Coat was sent here to watch and take care of you. We will make peace with everyone and we will live in harmony with one another."

For Cecile Many Guns, to make peace meant "no more fighting between anyone, everybody will be friends, everybody will be in peace." Tom Yellowhorn noted with disappointment that the Peigan's initial enthusiasm for the peace treaty grew into bitterness when the seriousness with which they took the agreement was later not reciprocated by the government. In subsequent years the Peigan were "sorry that they made this treaty." For the Peigan the ceremony of peace making was solemn, undertaken with much gravity, especially when they smoked the peace pipe: "They prayed that they would be friends." Yellowhorn thought that the government officials who signed Treaty 7 were serious as well; Macleod in particular was respected. When Macleod said that the First Nations would be thought of by the Queen as "my children," the Peigan thought a great obligation would be attached to so solemn and important a commitment. But disappointment soon followed: "They thought they were going to get money, that they'll own the land and still be free in the country. But this [disappointment] was after, when they found out that they had to stay on the reserves." Macleod had convinced the Peigan that the Queen "was going to treat them good." As Tom Yellowhorn bitterly concluded, in the wake of the treaty "they put up the Indian Act to punish Indian people and protect the White man." In fact, the Indian Act of 1876 had already been enacted.

Elder Ida Yellowhorn remembered: " Long Pipe Woman said that the Peigan leaders understood the making of the treaty as a peace treaty. She said that the leaders said that we should take the White man as our children and share our land with them."

Siksika Nation

The Siksika interpreted Treaty 7 as a commitment to peace in return for government assistance. Philip Many Bears remarked that "the police were to take care of us." For Arthur Yellow Fly, the terms of the peace treaty included "no more killing, no more whiskey trafficking, no more fighting with White men and other Native tribes." The end of warfare and violence was also foremost in the mind of Josephine Weasel Head, who remembered stories about her people deciding that they "wanted to save children from bloodshed and smallpox, also to stop the fighting between tribes." Stemming the violence that accompanied the economic exploitation in the free-wheeling days of Whoop-Up Country was foremost in the memory of Frankie Turning Robe, who stated that "whiskey trading was killing people. Crowfoot was thinking of his people when

he signed." In return for the Siksika's agreement to stop fighting, the Mounties were "assigned to watch over the Native people." There was to be "no more bloodshed between White and Indian."

For Augustine Yellow Sun, peace was agreed to in return for money, freedom to hunt, and rations: "The way I heard it is that treaty money was used to keep us from fighting." The government gave people $12 each for the peace agreement: "The treaty money was used as a token of peace to us at the treaty. Many material things were promised." The Siksika believed the agreement was honestly sought by the government: "We were a treaty people and really thought that we would be taken care of." But Jim Black noted that the Siksika were soon to be disappointed: "Fifty thousand dollars was given out—that was cheap compared to the land we were cheated out of."

To illustrate the point that the Blackfoot tribes had no intention of selling land, Reverend Arthur Ayoungman told a story about Crowfoot that had been related to him by Joe Crowfoot, the grandson of Crowfoot and a former chief of the Siksika himself. A few years after the making of Treaty 7, Crowfoot met with government officials in an evening meeting at his lodge, where a fire was going. Crowfoot took some earth in one hand and, throwing it into the fire, said that the earth would not burn. He then said that if he took money and threw it in the fire, it would burn and disappear. Finally he said that he would rather keep the earth because it will not burn. Ayoungman related the story to underline the contention of the Blackfoot tribes that the earth could not be sold.

Stoney Nakoda Nation

The understanding that Treaty 7 was a peace treaty is very strong among the Stoney. Lou Crawler Sr. recalled that it was "a peace agreement between First Nations and Europe." The nature of the agreement, according to Carl Simeon, was explained by Chief Bearspaw: "He said he [the Stoneys] will camp and live wherever he likes and he will not kill any White man." Della Soldier believed that peace was agreed to in return for land for the Stoney "and to choose more land in the future."

Morley Twoyoungmen remembered leaders of the Stoneys asking why the NWMP cannons were pointed in a threatening manner. The chiefs said, "You talk of peace while there are guns pointing at me. This is not peace … lay down your guns." Similar sentiments were echoed by John and Gordon Labelle. George Ear described the agreement as "a peace treaty between two races." Ear too recalled the request to turn away the cannons "if he [Commissioner Laird] really wants peace."

The Stoneys remembered discussions between their leader Bearspaw and Crowfoot: "Bearspaw told Crowfoot that there were only two options: one was to make war and fight back. But this would make things worse. Women and children will be killed. On the other hand, if we signed the treaty we would be without any worries and would be happy with each other. Crowfoot answered: 'Yes, that is why I want to make peace.'"

"Peace every day" would be valued by the Stoneys according to Joe Brown. "Before there was killing and stealing—because of the killing the treaty was made." The prospect of no more violence was a relief to all sides.

Lily Wesley contended that the peace that was agreed to was not a land surrender; it was meant to "stop the fighting." The stories Wesley remembered suggest that Whites feared an Indian war greatly, that many things were offered to secure peace and that "the White people were very persuasive using slick words." It was clearly the Whites who wanted the treaty most desperately. But according to Wesley, the Stoneys were deceived by the many promises given to get peace. The government ploy was to pacify the tribes initially with false promises so that they would not resist and talk back.

Lazarus Wesley stated that Queen Victoria was highly regarded by the Stoneys and that they solemnly agreed to stop the antagonistic practices that had existed up to that time. The treaty would stop horse stealing, and the parties agree "not to kill each other anymore—to have peace in the land."

In summary, the Stoney attitude was "let's shake hands; as long as we live, we will not oppose each other in any way." This was the meaning that the Stoneys believed both sides understood.

For Lazarus Wesley, the treaty was a comprehensive negotiation between nations: "Countries sign treaties so as not to have war and prevent devastation." The main point of a treaty was "to make peace, to shake hands, to make promises and agreements." In return "we will no longer fight over the land because the NWMP will protect us." Wesley remembered that

John McDougall, as he talked about the treaty prior to the meetings at Blackfoot Crossing, emphasized the peace that was to be gained by accepting the treaty. McDougall vowed: "We will be going to other tribes and tell the others about the [treaty] money to be given out, and that you will lay down your weapons and make peace and there will be no more animosity between the Indian people and the government's people. The government will look after you." The Methodist mission started at Morleyville in 1873 was originally set back in the forest so that it could be defended against attack. Only in 1875, when the NWMP arrived, was the mission church moved to its present location on the valley bench of the Bow River at the junction of Jacob's Creek.

The treaty meant money for Gwen Rider: "It was signed so they would receive money and to have peace." She, like a number of others, stressed that it was the government that wanted the treaty most and this was because "hostility existed between White and Native people."

Bill Mclean had perhaps the most detailed recollection of Treaty 7 as a peace treaty. Mclean remembered the significant role that John McDougall played in talking about the treaty prior to its signing. The missionaries talked about how a treaty would soon be made and the Stoneys would be part of it; they told the Stoneys about a "peace making." There had always been tribal wars but McDougall presented an ominous picture to the Stoneys; he talked about the government's intentions and "how White people would flood the land." Mclean felt that the missionaries had a strategic place among the tribes and acted as government agents, passing along messages the government wanted to get to the First Nations people: "The missionaries told the people when and where the treaty would be made." After reflecting on the nature of this peace making, he concluded that the treaty had been pre-written, even though it ought to have been a matter of "two parties coming together discussing an issue and coming to an agreement." Mclean, like John Snow, thought that the Stoneys had said much more in the treaty making than was recorded; the Stoneys had been able to say what they wanted "but no one wrote it down."

Elva Lefthand recalled that ancestors had talked of Bearspaw having said, " If I sign this treaty, everything I say now will have to be honoured. And there will be no more fighting. The fighting will have to stop." For the Stoneys, peace was the most important reason for accepting the treaty.

Tsuu T'ina Nation

Like the other five nations, Tsuu T'ina emphasized that the treaty was a peace treaty. Hilda Big Crow, Dick Big Plume, Louise Big Plume, Lucy Big Plume, Helen Meguinis, Clarabelle Pipestem, and Rosie Runner all echoed the words of Maurice Big Plume, who said that the treaty meant that Native people and Whites alike would "live as brothers and sisters in peace." The peace, according to Tom Heavenfire, meant that the Tsuu T'ina would be protected: "We were going to live our lives by the laws that White people brought," laws intended to "keep peace" and to "protect families."

CHAPTER FIVE

Treaty 7 in Its Historical and Political Context

INTRODUCTION

Past and present perspectives vie for prominence in the continual debate about what constitutes the history of any event. While the facts of an event remain unaltered, interpretations change and new stories come to light. Such is the case with Treaty 7. The history of Treaty 7, as Treaty 7 people understand it, has always been there, but it has not been part of the mainstream story of Canada. In most historical accounts, Treaty 7 is simply recounted as an event that paved the way to nationhood, making the West safe for settlement by Ontarians and Europeans. But the treaty has a different significance for the Treaty 7 First Nations because in their histories they emphasize issues that have little to do with nation-building. They even disagree with how the Canadian government continues to define its lawful obligations under Treaty 7.

It is only recently that non-Aboriginal Canadians have been willing to listen to what First Nations have to say about their history, and to acknowledge that official histories may have to be changed to accommodate the Aboriginal point of view.

One of the fundamental problems associated with coming to an understanding of Aboriginal-White relations has to do with the fact that Canadian intellectuals generally eschew a colonial framework and scarcely mention imperialism as a factor in the settlement of the West. Told from the point of view of the "victors," or the newcomer settlers, Canadian history emphasizes the perspective of the dominant society. Token recognition is extended to tragedies related to the history of the Aboriginal peoples—the unfortunate disappearance of the buffalo, disease, alcohol—but it is assumed that everything worked out for the best in the long run. Established historians such as Arthur Lower, Donald Creighton, and George Stanley consistently maintain that Canada's Indian policy was honourable, if at times misguided. Intentions were always good. In the long view of Aboriginal-White relations, the "partnership" forged between newcomers and Aboriginal peoples has served both sides well—it was inevitable that Canada's history in the Northwest turned out as it did. The effects of empire-building, according to the establishment historians, has on balance been to the benefit of all concerned in this spread of "civilization." In the words of George Stanley:

The gravest problem presented to the Dominion of Canada by the acquisition and settlement of Rupert's Land and the North-West was the impact of a superior civilization upon the Native Indian Tribes. Again and again, in different places and in different ways, the problem has unfolded itself at the contact of European and savage. Too often the advent of the white man has led to the moral and physical decline of the Native. In Africa, Melanesia and America, the clash of peoples in different stages of development has spelled disaster to the weaker. The European, conscious of his material superiority, is only too contemptuous of the savage, intolerant of his helplessness, ignorant of his mental processes and impatient at his slow assimilation of civilization. The savage, centuries behind in mental and economic development, cannot readily adapt himself to meet the new conditions. He is incapable of bridging the gap of centuries alone and unassisted. Although white penetration into Native territories may be inspired by motives of self-interest, such as trade and settlement, once there, the responsibility of "the white man's burden" is inevitable.[1]

However euphemistically writers like Stanley portray the process, we can no longer ignore colonialism and its imperial context as we write the history of the Canadian West. As cultural critic Edward Said notes:

The global reach of classical nineteenth and early twentieth century European imperialism still casts a considerable shadow over our own times. Hardly any North American, African, European, Latin American, Indian, Caribbean, Australian individual—the list is very long—who is alive today has not been touched by the empires of the past. Britain and France between them controlled immense territories: Canada, Australia, New Zealand, the colonies of North and South America and the Caribbean, large swatches of Africa, the Middle East, the Far East (Britain will hold Hong Kong as a colony until 1997), and the Indian subcontinent in its entirety all these fell under the sway of and in time were liberated from British and French rule.[2]

Imperial powers played a major role not only in physically neutralizing indigenous populations but in creating and sustaining negative images of Aboriginal peoples. The dissemination of these negative images helped those in power justify, to themselves, the removal of Aboriginal peoples from their traditional lands. Said has called this the "struggle over geography": "That struggle is complex and interesting because it is not only about soldiers and cannons but about ideas, about forms, about images and imaginings."[3]

After justifying their right to move into and control new territory, the European powers went wherever they could: "Scarcely a corner of life was left untouched by the facts of empire; the economies were hungry for overseas markets, raw materials, cheap labour, and hugely profitable land, and defense and foreign-policy establishments, were more and more committed to maintaining vast tracts of distant territories and large numbers of subjugated people. When the Western powers were not in close, sometimes ruthless competition with one another for more colonies ... they were hard at work settling, surveying, studying, and of course ruling the territories under their jurisdictions."[4]

The Aboriginal people of southern Alberta were not a pool of cheap labour, nor a new market to be exploited, but they did occupy valuable land and stood in the way of those who wanted to exploit coal, oil, and other minerals in and along the Rocky Mountains. The invasions and intrusions of traders, surveyors, and settlers were experienced by the indigenous people as the National Policy became the driving force behind the Canadian expansion into the Northwest. The same forces at work in other parts of the world were at work in the Canadian West. These forces were defined by Said as follows: "'Imperialism' means the practice, the theory and attitudes of a dominating metropolitan centre ruling a distant territory; 'colonialism,' which is almost always a consequence of imperialism, is the implanting of settlements on distant territories."[5] Imperialism can be exercised in a variety of ways, including force, political collaboration, economic pressure, and social or cultural co-option; it is the process of establishing and maintaining an empire. The accumulation of wealth that invariably takes place is accompanied by productions and portrayals—books, newspapers, visual images—that justify and document the need of the colonizers to dominate the land and make it bountiful in ways that those who originally occupied it have been unable to do. Thus, terms such as "inferior," "subject race," "subordinate people," "dependency," "expansion," and "authority" come into common use by the colonizer.

Those agents of colonialism who exercised power used concepts and languages that gradually became familiar to the colonized and over time became part of the culture of domination. As the agents of empire sought to exploit spices, sugar, slaves, coal, rubber, cotton, opium, tin, gold, oil, and silver, they found it difficult to maintain these huge empires. They needed "immense will and self-confidence even arrogance"[6] in order to rule the indigenous people and convincingly portray them as subordinate, less advanced, and inferior. Thus, a process of "education" began whereby the colonizers tried to persuade the colonized that what the colonizers were doing was right, that they should accept the colonizers' notions of what was best for the lands they were living on. It was, as Stanley put it, the "white man's burden" to persuade the indigenous people that the newcomers' way was the best way. The newcomers promoted the idea of a partnership, but in this partnership the colonizers would try to convince the colonized that what was being done was in their own best interests.

Thus, to understand properly what happened in the Treaty 7 area, one must acknowledge the concepts of imperialism and colonialism, for these concepts shaped the relations between Aboriginal and newcomer, and were behind the forces that permanently changed the landscape and lifestyle of

43

the Aboriginal peoples of the western prairies. The history of Treaty 7 must be broadened to allow the voices of the colonized to be heard.

UNDERSTANDING TREATY 7

The numbered treaties, from 1 to 7, were substantially similar, but each one dealt with particular circumstances and contained distinct clauses. While there can be unanimity on the meaning of certain clauses, in general the texts of the treaties can be interpreted in a variety of ways. It is questionable whether a "mutually understood agreement" was ever arrived at between a people representing a written culture on the one hand and a people representing an essentially oral culture on the other. Indeed, many indigenous cultures throughout the world were at a distinct disadvantage as the nation-states that had been growing since the mid-eighteenth century expanded their interests. In the period from the late eighteenth century to the twentieth century, the world witnessed "the construction of the state in the image and interests of the new middle classes."[7] The expansion of these nation-states saw the subordination of classes, ethnic groups, and races to a dominant class or racial group. The interests of one particular class or group were privileged at the expense of the interests of the others. What emerged in each instance was a so-called national culture that in fact was little more than the culture favoured by those who made up the dominant group or class. By the twentieth century it was clear that the dominant class was the middle class, and its cultural forms and economic interests were favoured. In most nation-states this meant that the culture of the subordinated class, ethnic group, or race was either suppressed or expropriated as nominally part of the "national" culture. National identity and culture were "disseminated throughout the whole of society in several ways, such as the spread of literacy, the 'invention of tradition,' the standardization of 'national' language the establishment of public education, religious evangelism, promotion of economic individualism."[8] What went hand in hand with the valorizing of a national culture was the diminution of other cultures: "Local, 'unprogressive,' and particularist attitudes and practices, such as minority religion, dialect and minority languages, folk customs and traditions rooted in agrarian economy and so on, were either taken over (or tidied up) as folklore of

the 'nation' or discouraged and even prescribed as 'superstitious,' 'barbaric' or 'unprogressive.'"[9]

At times the subordinated groups were described in national narratives as "noble savages," especially when any threat from them had dissipated. What they learned from their experiences was that it was best to become assimilated within the dominant culture if they hoped to survive. Their real culture was somewhere far in the distant past: "Nostalgia could be indulged, and the 'primitive people' could be safely used as a moral, because they could not or soon would not pose any political, social or cultural problem in their own right and on their own behalf. Meanwhile the middleclass reformers of the early nineteenth century rapidly developed strategies for 'modernizing' these primitive people, along with the lower classes."[10] While the "noble savage" was idealized, the cultural practices of subordinated groups were belittled. This condemnation included "merely oral culture, communalism (if not communism) and sociability, apparently improvident and opportunistic work patterns and domestic economy, 'immoral' sexual practices, a tendency to nomadism if not outright vagabondage, 'superstitions' or false religion and an ad hoc and adaptive attitude to 'improvement' and new technology, an ad hoc practical approach to leadership, work organization and the 'moral economy' and 'irrational' or merely 'traditional' ideas of social land economic justice."[11]

The dominant middle-class society was either unwilling or unable to see Aboriginal culture as a successful and long-term accommodation to its environment. Thus, the dominant culture that emerged was a literate society directed by Christian principles. In the Canadian West, the dominant culture had a specific agenda: " Just as important were ideas of economic self-sufficiency and individualism and settled, disciplined and investment oriented work habits and domestic economy. These would be supported by a middle-class sexual morality and model of domesticity and reinforced by a more routine, 'orderly' and hierarchical pattern of leadership in work and social life; and a market-oriented, competitive attitude to labour and its rewards. Finally there should be acceptance of regular institutions of surveillance, control and policing."[12] The agents of this European culture, which was making its way across North America in a search for wealth, were not always primarily interested in controlling the indigenous populations—at least not at first. Early in the contact period, they needed the expertise and knowledge of indigenous people in order to establish their own position of strength. The need to denigrate and then to convert and civilize the Aboriginal only came once the economic advantaged had been secured. Those who at first had been important "partners" were soon to become major impediments to "civilization."

By the time the treaties were being negotiated on the prairies, the Euro-Canadian leadership were confident that they were powerful enough to secure agreements that would allow White settlements to be established and to thrive. Unknown to the Aboriginal leadership, the treaties were to privilege the written culture of the dominant society while denigrating the oral culture of the Aboriginal treaty makers. For this newly emerging middle-class power, the land had to be made "bountiful," and in its estimation the Aboriginal peoples had not succeeded in this. There were no cultivated fields or estates by which Euro-Canadians measure success. In fact, when the treaties were being negotiated, the Aboriginal peoples were viewed as an obstacle to the colonization schemes envisaged for the West by Euro-Canadian elites. The treaties were seen by people like Father Scollen, Reverend McDougall, Colonel Macleod, and Commissioner Laird as expedient means of beginning the process of assimilation through which (they believed) the Aboriginal populations would eventually disappear. It is clear that Canadian officials and religious leaders were preparing the Aboriginal population for the White settlers who they knew would be arriving in large numbers to take over the land. These agents of Euro-Canadian society showed scarcely any ability to appreciate the "communal economy and social practices"[13] of the populations with whom they came into contact. They did not approach the treaty process as equals negotiating with equals but rather as superiors with inferiors. This was a major disadvantage for the Aboriginal leadership, who came to negotiate Treaty 7 in good faith. The attitude of the Canadian treaty makers was paternalistic and condescending—they would do what they thought was best for the Aboriginal peoples, even to the extent of ignoring what the Aboriginal leaders clearly wanted to include in the treaty.

Thus, a major problem with the treaties was that ideologically and culturally the treaty makers for the Crown did not respect the Aboriginal leadership and

what it represented: "the white policy-makers' idea of the nature and powers of native chiefs was in part a relic of the earlier political culture of monarchy and court government and the idea that a European monarch was treating a weaker or lesser peer, the chief, in The New World, Africa or Australia."[14] They did not respect the authority or legitimacy of the chiefs with whom they were negotiating, and perhaps they never had any intention of honouring what they were negotiating: "The treaties, circumstances and perceptions of the Canadian Government and its officers profoundly altered the political and social organization of the Native people, according to white assumptions and practices that had been formed in North America but they were also informed by models of social structure and relationships developed in Britain. To some extent, at least, the chiefs were made something like a cross between a Highland laird…[and] an idealized version of the professionalised landed gentleman and the Victorian public school ideal of the gentlemanly public official."[15]

The Aboriginal leaders were allowed to feel that they were negotiating as equals, but the Euro-Canadians did not respect their culture and they saw their nations as inferior. The Aboriginal leaders could hardly be expected to know that these men they were bargaining with in good faith had little resolution to take seriously the discussions that the Aboriginal leadership solemnized by smoking the pipe.

The power relationship between the Aboriginal government and the Canadian government was not equal, and leaders such as Crowfoot and Red Crow were aware that military force was being used to slaughter indigenous people in the United States. By accommodating the newcomers, the Aboriginal people hoped to work out an arrangement to share the land so that both sides could benefit from living side by side. They could not have known that the newcomers expected more than a commitment to share the land, that in fact they wanted to take what they could, even if it meant disregarding the treaties. The Aboriginal leadership did not know about the cultural attitudes that had long been evolving in Europe, which privileged the culture of one class above that of all others. Anything not European was subordinated, and values that were not middle class were dismissed or ignored. What happened in western Canada in the 1870s was only one incident in the global process of subjugation that was played

45

out wherever colonial fragments of the British Empire took hold. There never was a reconciliation between what was actually discussed at Blackfoot Crossing in September 1877 and what was included in the written legal text of the Treaty 7 document. The territorial imperative of the Crown is still imposed today upon the First Nations of Treaty 7.

CONTEXT OF TREATY 7: SOME CONSIDERATIONS

A problem with understanding Treaty 7 arises out of the way in which it has been described and represented to date. Until very recently the treaty has been explained in the context of nation-building, usually in an academic discourse by male writers who are defending a linear approach. Their chosen form is the essay, which usually presumes a monological or single perspective, with a narrator arbitrarily organizing evidence to produce the Truth—a single unassailable verity. Much of the writing done about Treaty 7 assumes this tone of truth, of finality: that we (Euro-Canadians) are right and their (the Aboriginal peoples') opinions are of no consequence. This position has been allowed to go unchallenged—until only very recently—because few of these authors have considered what Aboriginal people themselves thought or think of the treaty; they either never asked, or when they have, they have selectively asked only certain people. The result has been that areas of the treaty that are clearly problematic have been glossed over and the discourse of those who hold power has allowed authors to ignore difficult issues. The consequence has been to discredit the voices of those who disagree with the "official" government line on what the treaty means.

What is clear is that there is no agreed-upon interpretation of Treaty 7; nor is there agreement on what motivated both sides to agree to the treaty. Studies based on a single perspective have failed to stop the nagging questions about the treaty. Over the years academics have come to the recognition that a dialogic (dual or multiple) perspective is needed to understand historical events such as Treaty 7. What becomes evident when a dialogical approach is used is that on some points there is agreement while on others there is divergence of opinion. One of the crucial differences between the perspectives of the Canadian government and the First Nations is that the government side has privileged the written form of representation, while the First Nations side has relied (and still does) on an oral discourse. Thus, while the Crown thought that what was written down was the final word, the Aboriginal people believed that what was said in the discussions at Blackfoot Crossing was as valid as what was written down.

Problems relating to language are at the very core of the Euro-Canadian's difficulty in understanding the Aboriginal world view. The spoken languages of Aboriginal peoples have been ignored by dominant imperial cultures, and the failure to recognize or acknowledge Aboriginal culture constitutes a form of cultural subjugation. As Sakej Youngblood-Henderson has written: "Everywhere we are born into language, everywhere it binds our consciousness. Its mystery and development reflect our particular habits, those of our linguistic heritage. Our language [or languages] contain the essential ways in which we experience and interact with our culture. Thus, our linguistic understanding [the world view in English] is our map that a particular language creates in order to navigate the larger worldview. These understandings become, then, in some sense, most of the worldview."[16]

Youngblood-Henderson argues that the noun-centred objectifying languages of the Eurocentric world view help users of these languages to reify and classify the world environment. By contrast, Aboriginal languages are verb-centred and reflect an apprehension of the world that is in a constant state of flux or change. Thus, there are very few fixed or rigid objects in the Aboriginal world view: "With the fluidity of semantic-phonemes comprising the verb sounds, every speaker can create new vocabulary 'on the fly,' custom tailored to meet the experience of movement to express the very finest nuances of meanings."[17] Youngblood-Henderson maintains that such different ways of seeing the world mean that these languages cannot be easily translated—that simply translating a word by itself does not relay with it the world view that the language as a whole contains.

The fundamental assumptions underlying European and Aboriginal languages are so radically different that simple translation is impossible. For the Aboriginal, "to see things as permanent is to be confused about everything: an alternative to that understanding is the need to create temporary harmonies through alliances and relationships among all forms and forces—this process is a never-ending source of wonder to the indigenous mind and to other forces who contribute to the harmony."[18]

To ignore Aboriginal languages and to insist on assimilation or "cognitive imperialism" is to deny and destroy the Aboriginal sacred understandings. Young-blood-Henderson concludes that "cultural and cognitive racism must be exposed and resolved. Under modern thought, at least in theory, every language describes the world completely, though each in its own way. The Aboriginal languages and worldviews must be strengthened and developed with their own contexts. Any interference is domination, both cognitively and culturally. Thus every Aboriginal language has the right to exist without conforming to Eurocentric languages or worldviews … The failure to admit differences in worldview is also domination."[19]

Thus, a fundamental problem continues to exist in the discourse between those who have held power and those who have not or those who have represented a new way of life and the indigenous populations.[...]

Notes
Chapter Five

1. Stanley, *The Birth of Western Canada*, 194.
2. Said, *Culture and Imperialism*, 5–6.
3. Ibid., 7.
4. Ibid., 8.
5. Ibid., 9.
6. Ibid., 11.
7. Kelly, "Class, Race and Cultural Revolution," 19.
8. Ibid., 20.
9. Ibid., 21.
10. Ibid.
11. Ibid.
12. Ibid., 22.
13. Ibid., 24.
14. Ibid., 35.
15. Ibid., 36.
16. Youngblood-Henderson, "Governing the Implicate Order," 3.
17. Ibid., 8.
18. Ibid., 9.
19. Ibid., 19.

INDUSTRIALIZATION AND WOMEN'S WORK, 1870s-1920s

Lynne Marks
University of Victoria

INDUSTRIALIZATION AND WOMEN'S WORK, 1870s-1920s

Introduction by Lynne Marks

51

● INTRODUCTION

Lynne Marks

What historians term the "Industrial Revolution" occurred first in England in the late eighteenth and early nineteenth centuries, and began in Canada in the 1850s, accelerating in the 1870s and 1880s. Revolution is perhaps not the best term for what was in fact a very ragged and uneven process which included some or all elements of the following:

1. A shift from making products in the home or in small workshops to making them in factories.
2. A move from making things by hand to the use of machines to assist in the production of goods.
3. The subdivision of formerly skilled labour, in which a product (such as a shoe or a coat) which had once been made by one worker with all the skills necessary to make the entire product, was now made by many workers, each with very limited skills, doing only one piece of the job—such as sewing on buttons, or ironing the finished garment.

In Canada, as elsewhere, some economic sectors industrialized much earlier than others, as did some regions, particularly areas of Ontario, Quebec and the Maritimes. Both men and women were dramatically affected by industrialization, particularly those who were employed within newly industrialized sectors of the economy, or who had family members so employed. Until fairly recently, most Canadian historians have focused primarily on the ways in which industrialization affected male workers. This has meant that they have looked almost exclusively at the industrial workplaces where most men worked. They have focused on important questions such as the ways in which the introduction of machines, or other new ways of organizing work, dramatically reduced or eliminated the need for male skilled labour in many industries, as well as undermining the control many men had formerly had over the pace and nature of their work. They also documented the ways in which working men used unionization and strikes to challenge some of the more negative effects of industrialization, despite a legal framework that provided no rights to workers attempting to unionize.

As we will see in this module, historians of women's work have also looked at issues of women's paid work following the coming of industrialization. However, given the impact which industrialization had on all facets of women's work, both paid and unpaid, some of these historians have focused on the home as well as the workplace. Women's historians have tended to see industrialization as leading to a dramatic separation of home and workplace. They have argued that prior to industrialization both men and women worked in and around the home, either working on complementary tasks on the farm, or with the husband working as an artisan (for example as a shoemaker or a tailor) at a home workshop, often assisted by family members. With the coming of factory production, those earning wages in the factory would have to leave home, often for twelve or more hours a day, leading to a major separation between home and workplace. As the readings suggest, in working-class families married women and younger children would generally stay at home, while husbands and older children would be most likely to go out to work in factories and at other waged work. Bettina Bradbury, one of the historians used in this section, agrees that in general, industrialization did lead to an increased separation of home

52

and workplace. However, like other historians who have recently critiqued the model that sees industrialization as leading to a sharp distinction between home and work, she argues that working-class married women, in particular, often integrated paid work into the home, pointing to the need to complicate the dichotomy between home and work.

The lack of household technology in this period and the many tasks required of married women made it very difficult for them to take on waged work outside of the home. An example of the kind of backbreaking work required in completing basic household tasks can be seen in one woman's recollections of doing laundry in Northern Ontario in the 1930s. The task took a full day ("Blue Monday"), and all of her physical strength and energy—and this woman had access to water in her home, which many nineteenth century women did not.

The articles illustrate as well that most women who went out of the home to work for wages were single, younger women. Legislation to protect child workers was limited, enforcement was lax, and thus many of these young women were very young indeed. The document by Videre demonstrates that even in the early twentieth century girls younger than fourteen were working 10 or more hours at factory labour. While Videre, a middle-class journalist posing as a factory worker, was concerned about the moral dangers facing the factory girls, she did note that the young women seemed to enjoy the camaraderie of the factory, even though the actual jobs were very repetitive and boring. Testimony from female factory workers before the Royal Commission on Labour and Capital provide more evidence of the harsh working conditions facing women and children in the factories, including the fact that children who failed to work steadily during ten to twelve hour workdays could face physical punishment from foremen. MacKenzie King, who prior to becoming Prime Minister of Canada was active in labour relations research, points to some of the most dismal working conditions in this period, those facing the women, children and men working in the sweated industries of garment making.

More generally, women in the paid workforce earned less, generally considerably less than men, even when they were doing the same work. Frager and Patrias demonstrate clearly that the arguments used to justify lower wages for women had little basis in reality, but made life very difficult for women trying to survive on their own, and made the situation almost impossible for widows and deserted wives with young children. As Bradbury has noted in other work, these women, facing destitution, often were forced to leave their children in orphanages for several years, because they could not afford to support them and were often only able to reclaim them when they were of an age to contribute financially to the household.

In the late nineteenth and early twentieth centuries new jobs began to emerge for young single Caucasian women with adequate education. These women were increasingly hired as teachers, particularly in the many rural one-room schools of the time, or as junior teachers in the graded urban schools. Female teachers were considered appropriate for these positions, both because they could be paid less than men, and because women's apparently "natural" nurturing qualities made them seem particularly suitable for teaching younger children. Over the nineteenth century most clerical and sales work had been done by young men, who could expect to move up to better positions. However, by the end of the century opportunities in these fields emerged for women, as the development of larger bureaucracies led to the need for an increasing number of clerical workers who could be expected to be satisfied with dead end, low paid work, and as the rise of department stores led to the need for an increased sales staff, again, with no expectations of promotion. Young women generally preferred these jobs to factory work, but such positions were not available to all. Female applicants were expected to be "respectable", often needing references from their clergyman. Religious and racial discrimination meant that many clerical jobs were closed to Jewish women, while women of colour faced barriers that not only kept them out of clerical work, but most factory work as well. While Japanese and Aboriginal women on the west coast were employed at back-breaking labour in the salmon canneries, across most of Canada women of colour were generally restricted to domestic service, at least until the Second World War, which dramatically expanded the demand for female factory workers.

As Frager and Patrias and the Videre piece make clear, domestic work was the least favoured option for young women seeking paid employment. These positions were lonely and low status, provided minimal free time, and also left young women vulnerable to sexual harassment from male household members. Most young women facing harassment did not resort to the methods of Carrie Davies, a young domestic servant who in 1915 in Toronto shot and killed her employer, Charles Massey, who had tried to "take liberties" with her. Davies was fortunate, in that the fact that she had managed to maintain her "purity" [virginity] helped lead to her acquittal on a murder charge. Many other servants were not so lucky—if left pregnant by male household members they lost their jobs and character references, and often had no choice but to take up sex trade work. Other women chose sex trade work over domestic work and the very limited alternative forms of paid work available to young women—particularly to women of colour.

While few women took the direct approach of Carrie Davies, some working-class women did take an active role in trying to improve their lives through unionization or other forms of activism. Women workers faced a number of barriers to active involvement in unions, as many unions of skilled workers were not supportive of women workers. A more inclusive union, the Knights of Labour of the late nineteenth century, tried to bring male and female workers together, and made major efforts to encourage women's unionization. The Knights' efforts allowed women to achieve at least limited economic successes in some workplaces in the 1880s. Some historians have argued that women workers tended to be less interested in unionization themselves, as they saw themselves as only temporary workers who would leave the paid workplace upon marriage. Many married working-class women who, as Bradbury argued, worked very hard within the home to keep their families adequately fed and clothed, could be very militant in defending their families' standard of living when their husbands were on strike. In one of many examples, during a coal miners' strike in Ladysmith, British Columbia in 1912–3, when the provincial government called in the army against the strikers, who were striking for safer working conditions and reasonable wages, the women of the community were active in organizing against the employer and the state, and played a significant role in the violence against strike breakers. These "amazons," as the judges called them, demonstrated that working-class women were not necessarily silent and powerless in the face of challenges to their families' livelihoods.

QUESTIONS

1. According to the readings, what impact did industrialization have on working-class women?
2. In late-nineteenth century working-class households, what family members were most likely to go out of the home to work for pay, and why? Why do you think married women are more likely to work outside the home today than they were in this period?
3. What explanations do Frager and Patrias put forward to explain women's secondary status within the labour force, and what explanations do they reject, and why? Are you convinced by their arguments?

4. In this period what impact did technology have on women's work both inside and outside of the home?
5. Did you find anything particularly surprising in the article by Videre? Do you think her article is a useful source for understanding the experience of nineteenth-century female factory workers? Would the testimony of female factory workers to the Royal Commission be more or less valuable? Please explain.

FURTHER READINGS

Acton, Janice; Goldsmith, Penny; Shepard, Bonnie, eds., *Women at Work: Ontario 1850–1930* (Toronto: Women's Press, 1974).

Bradbury, Bettina, *Working Families: Age, Gender and Daily Survival in Industrializing Montreal*, (Toronto: McClelland and Stewart, 1993).

Frager, Ruth, *Sweatshop Strife: Class, Ethnicity and Gender in the Jewish Labour Movement of Toronto, 1900–1939* (Toronto: University of Toronto Press, 1992).

Hinde, John, "Stout Ladies and Amazons": Women in the British Columbia Coal-Mining Community of Ladysmith, 1912–14," *BC Studies*, (Summer 1997).

McIntosh, Robert, "Sweated Labour: Female Needleworkers in Industrializing Canada," *Labour/Le Travail* 32 (Fall 1993): 105–138.

Myers, Sharon, "'Not to be Ranked as Women': Female Industrial Workers in Turn-of-the Century Halifax," in *Separate Spheres: Women's Worlds in the 19th-Century Maritimes*, Janet Guildford and Suzanne Morton eds. (Fredericton, NB: Acadiensis Press, 1994), 161–183.

55

▲ Document 1: "A Little Independence: Factory Girls, 1912"

June 1: How I got my first job in a Toronto biscuit factory

"If only one of us would go and work as a factory girl, we should understand better the real conditions …"All winter, the committee of our University Women's Club delegated to study industrial conditions had been at work. We had gathered statistics, read books, held meetings … been addressed by speakers … gone through factories by the kindly permission of their owners … But we still felt there were some things in the life of a factory girl that we had not yet gripped. …

I have called myself 'Videre' because I went "to see" the land. I have been practically a wage-earning woman as much as I have been a journalist drawing a regular salary, and have also been to some extent an employer of others' labour, in that I have had from time to time stenographers doing special work for me. … In fact, I feel that I could no longer afford the cheaper line of labour. I have also been connected for some years with the work of a downtown church, and have in that way become acquainted with many whom I am glad to call personal friends, in all ranks of labour. I have, too, had something to do with the investing of money, and realize that a man has a right to expect a certain income from the wealth he has amassed … If I may put my creed in such form, I believe in the right of the individual to acquire an honest fortune if he has the skill. I believe also in the brotherhood of man, though I do not interpret it to mean that God made men free and equal, as has been stated on the American dollar. If He made men free, He never could make them equal. …

I arrayed myself in a $1.25 shirtwaist, a ten-cent collar, a hat once good but a little tawdry from the dew and dust of last summer, and confronted the foreman of one of our biscuit factories.

I had to wait standing for half an hour at a desk in the hallway for him, when I stated my object, but I remembered that of course a working woman's time did not count for very much, and that I would probably have to stand all day when I succeeded in getting a job.

"What have you worked at before?" the foreman asked. … "Worked on papers," I answered meekly. …" Well, you'll find the work here very different from that you've been used to. …" "Yes," I replied, "they say it's healthier to work on biscuits than on paper." "Yes, that's right." I think I finished plaintively. "If you gave me a chance I think I could soon get onto the trade."

"Well, all right. Be here at 7.30 Monday morning," he said, and abruptly left. …

It was scarcely 5 o'clock when I awakened that Monday morning, but I dared not to go to sleep again for fear of losing my job. … I tied up my necessities for the week in a brown manila wrapping paper and with my bundle under my arm and $5.00 in my pocket I stole away from my little world.

A mite of a girl was standing at the foreman's office where I waited myself that morning for directions. "Are you waiting for a job?" I asked. … "I was told to come," said the mite. "So was I," I replied confidently. "How old are you?" "Fourteen." That was an irrelevant question, I have since learned. All children applying for work at factories know enough to be fourteen. [By law children under 14 were not allowed to work in factories. Child labour legislation was first passed in Ontario in the 1880s.]

Source: Videre articles in the *Toronto Star,* 1912, "A Little Independence: Factory Girls," in *The Canadian Worker in the Twentieth Century,* Irving Abella and David Millar, eds. (Toronto: Oxford University Press, 1978) [abridged].

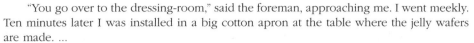

"You go over to the dressing-room," said the foreman, approaching me. I went meekly. Ten minutes later I was installed in a big cotton apron at the table where the jelly wafers are made. ...

The foreman passed a few minutes afterwards, and I dropped my little jelly-scraper and seized an opportunity. "You didn't tell me," I said, "whether I was to be on time work or piece work." "Oh, I'll put you on time work," he said in a kindly voice. ... I was too unsophisticated yet to comprehend the advantage he was affording me. "How much will I get?" I asked. "Oh, I'll give you $5.00 a week. ..." I went back attentively to my jelly-box and scraper. My thoughts, if fully concentrated on my work, would read something like this: "Dab-a-jelly, turn-a-biscuit, dab-a-jelly, turn-a-biscuit, dab-a-jelly, turn-a-biscuit."

But you soon begin to work mechanically. Most of the workers seem inclined to sing while working, though singing is against the rules. I found myself contracting a habit of ceaseless humming. Fortunately my weird melodies were drowned by the whir of the machinery.

... These are selections I heard sung on my first day as a factory hand: "I love to tell the story," "Count your many blessings." "Blest be the tie that binds." And a snatch of a love song that I did not recognize. I have listened to the singing of many hymns, but I seldom had them go to my heart more deeply than did these under the circumstances. To offer this, I was given to understand that several little misses of 15 and 16 could tell quite shady stories.

Being an inexperienced worker ... before an hour I had my hands and the handle of my scraper all daubed with jelly. ... I was directed to a sink at the other end of the room. A woman joined me there, with a marshmallow pail to wash. "Been here long?" I asked. "Over a year," she answered. She was a patient, earnest-looking woman of about 30. "How much do you get?" I asked. She turned her eyes full upon my face. "Five dollars a week." I shall never forget, I think, the look in those eyes. It could not have been a look of appeal, for I was but a fellow-worker. It was just a long, long look.

June 4

I joined a group for lunch at noon. There was a moment of silence as they waited for the forelady to ask the blessing. We don't have blessings in boarding houses, so naturally I felt it was not a bad crowd I had fallen among. ... There seems to be a continued shifting in these occupations. The workers grow tired of the monotony of their labour, and change from chocolates to lace, and from lace to gum, and from gum to feathers, and so on [from a factory that makes chocolates, to one that manufactures lace, etc.] ... Quite a percentage of my fellow workers in this factory were new employés of a month or so. One would think it would be to an employer's advantage to pay higher prices to those already trained in his service, and prevent thus this system of eternal change. ...

It was decided finally that a girl I shall call Alma had better take me in hand in a search for a room that night. Alma was one of the most relied-upon employés, had been six years with the firm. She drew a salary of $6.00 per week. She paid $1.25 rent for a nice, but tiny box of a room at the end of a hall. Her meals cost $2.25 per week. She had thus $2.50 per week for clothing, laundry, and other expenses. She was one of the best provided-for of the employés. ... The average wage paid these women was from $4.60 to $5.25 per week. ... I found a number of girls who had left other factories because they were paid lower wages than they were paid here, for instance $3.50 in the chocolate industry, $4.00 in the cigar trade. The few getting $6.00 per week were mostly boarders. Among the most interesting of my new friends was one I shall call blue-eyed Alice, a girl of 14, getting a wage of $4.50 per week. I met her also at the sink at the close of the day. She

57

was elated and sparkling. "I got a hustle on to-day," he said. "I packed seven trays. They are 15¢ a tray piece work. Perhaps they will make it up to me on pay day. But the others tell me I mustn't go so fast, or they will cut the price on the trays when they find out how many we can do." And next day, acting on the hint, she did but five.

I found this sentiment very common among the workers, that an unusually quick worker was likely to cut the price of piece work. ... Next day I learned from Alice that though she was only 14 last November, she had left school two years ago, and has been employed in four different industries: chocolates, gum, feather, and biscuits. ... I noticed that she could not read the typewritten directions hanging about three feet above her head in the dressing room. Her face was pale and anaemic. Is it possible that the grim red walls of our factories are red sometimes with the life-blood from the cheeks of our children, as well as with bricks from the Don Valley?

"How would Alice manage to get away from school at 12 without the teacher noticing her disappearance?" I asked a couple of other little girls.

"Oh, it would be like this. She would move and be transferred to another school and then never turn up after transferring."

There was a slightly festive air about the factory on pay day. "I never care for pay day," said Alice, "I give all my money to my mother. She lets me have a quarter, generally."

Her father was living. There were but three children in the family. The eldest was employed in paper-box making. The night of that same pay day, I took Alma to a five-cent show. At 9.20 my Alice came marching in with a younger child. ...

I cannot leave my companions in the factory without speaking of the many little kindnesses they showed me as a stranger, the sacrifices even, that they were willing to make. I was late, for example, the second morning. Alma waited for me rather than let me go in alone. I noted the flush on her face when the foreman asked her what was the matter. This being late means docking 10¢. During my last afternoon I had a misfortune. I upset from the top of the pile a wooden box containing about twenty pounds of biscuits. ... My Alice left her work and scraped up biscuits with all the strength of which she was capable, that I might not get into trouble with the foreman when he came upstairs.

June 6

I went at the close of my first factory day with Alma to the house where I could get my meals for $2.25 per week. The meals were really better than I expected at this rate. We had spare ribs, potatoes, tapioca pudding and tea. This was, I later learned, a meal a little below par. The next night we had fish, potatoes, and raw tomatoes (the second week in May). Breakfast consisted of porridge, steak or bacon, and fruit (sliced oranges, jelly, etc.) ... the linen was coarse but clean. As descriptive of the social surroundings. I will give just a sentence I heard the other day from the lips of a stenographer. "In those cheap boarding places the girls are usually a great deal nicer than the men, for you find so many real nice girls in the city on very poor pay." [Many cannot afford these meals and just "take something."]

We went out on our search for a room. ... I could not, at the outside price, pay more than $1.50 a week. We found a very nice clean little room a few doors from my boarding place at this very rate. It was over the kitchen and heated by a stove-pipe, but a fair size and with a good closet. The landlady impressed upon me that I must buy my own soap and matches. ... My landlady told me in a very kindly way that she could not afford to let the girls have hot water for washing and gas for ironing in the summer. She did not mind all in the winter time, when the fire was on. She even gave them the privilege of cooking some things then.

I believe she told the truth. She could not afford it. She was paying $35.00 a month for a nine-roomed house. ... It had taken often two tons of coal a month to heat the house during the past winter. ... Her rooms would sometimes be vacant. You can readily see ... the difficulty she would have been in had she not herself had children at work. Her daughter was a book binder, getting $7.00 a week. She paid $4.00 a week at home for her board, she told me. She aroused my envy with her pretty velvet waist and lace collar. That "paper business" I had left was not so bad.

I should consider myself as well and safely lodged in this house as in most houses. We did not have the use of the parlour at all, and took our gentleman friends to our rooms. But that is so in almost all rooming houses.

"Do you shut your door when you have a gentleman in?" I asked of the girl in the next room. "Oooh, yes," she said expressively. "Shut it and lock it."

My oft-reiterated complaint in this house was that the bathroom was in such a dangerously unsanitary condition. I presume it was the landlady's fault. ...

I sat down at my window that evening and went over the things I had to be thankful for as a factory girl. There was a glorious view of the sunset between the chimneys. ... I was thankful for a nice clean room in a nice house and on a rather nice street.

But I began to see myself confronting certain financial difficulties. I had just $1.25 weekly left for clothing and other expenses. ... I must have soap, coarse soap. ... So many of my companions lived at home, helped the family by contributing $2.50 or $3.00 of their earnings, but they had their laundry done, and had all the rest for clothes and pin money. ... At night they changed their working skirts and put on nice quiet suits and hats to go out into the streets. I would not have recognized them as the same girls passing in a crowd. I like new clothes as well as any girl, and I wished very much I could afford things like theirs. I wanted also to take Alma to the five-cent show. ...

I used to think that any girl who worked all the time should have something laid up in case of sickness, and not be dependent upon charity, if she were ill a few weeks. It looked to me as if she were not very provident ... but it is hard to save when the necessities of life are demanding every cent. Then too, ... I wanted church collection. I had paid at least 25¢ too much for my room to begin with. I could not afford $2.25 for my meals. I find I can't afford three meals every day. ... By going without breakfast one morning a week, I could afford Sunday dinner. ... I had begun to know what it was to be "just a little hungry." ... Nibbling at occasional biscuits while at work no doubt allayed my appetite too. ... I discovered that eggs, even at two for five, were rather expensive. It would be cheaper to get three bananas for 5¢ and make them last three days for lunches, and thus save difficulties about cooking. I remembered then the words of a barrister in the flat across the hall from my old room. I had told them I was cooking an egg for lunch that night before I left for my job. "Eggs!" called the barrister, "you can't afford eggs! Eggs are dear. It's bread and tea *you* want."

[...]

"Here," says one girl, "is how I spend my evenings." Monday night, an "occasional." That means a man who just calls upon one sometimes. Tuesday, my "steady". Wednesday, another "occasional." Thursday, "steady." Friday, another "occasional." Saturday and Sunday, "steady." The "steady" worked three nights a week, so she filled up her programme as above, according to her own words. She was a very attractive girl, around whom the attention of our boarding house seemed to gravitate. And again, if I may put myself in another girl's place, "Monday night Will comes; Tuesday I sew; Wednesday night Will comes again; Thursday night I sew; in short, I sew every other night, for Will and I are engaged." You see, there is the light of love and romance in the life of the girl worker just as in the mansions of Rosedale. [...]

What girls need is not so much a place to go into as a place to go out to. We need open-air skating at a lower rate. Regular rink charges are so high that we can't go unless John or Jimmy takes us ... Outdoor ball games are good for us, if they do not necessitate too much expense, as tennis often does. We like gymnastic apparatus, and after a hard day's work you'll pardon us for saying that we like something more exciting than a sermon or some lectures We are fond of music, and often wish that there was a popular music hall in Toronto, like we hear of in Germany.

But do not think that we want to take all these things and give nothing back. In a certain young people's society of a certain downtown church in this city, ... [$760] was given by less than a hundred of Toronto's young workers, mostly girls (it is safe to say, generally, on small salaries). They were contributing also to the pastor's salary and other funds ...

June 20

I had worked in the average and the almost-ideal factory. I decided for my third experience I would look up a place, well, say not too near the celestial regions. I applied for a job in a little office on one of the upper floors ... It is no exaggeration whatever to say that one needed a shovel as well as a broom to get the dirt and dust off these stairs ... There was a manager and a forewoman in the office, though I learned later that the forewoman was usually in the work room. "Had I any experience in edging or lining boxes?" she asked. "No, but I think I could learn," I said.

Again no references were required. "Come on tomorrow at eight o'clock," I was told. This sounded quite luxurious. The hours were 8 to 6. I was to get $4.00 a week, time work ... Beginners were taken on, it is true, at $4.00 a week, but as soon as they could earn over $4.00 a week they were put on piece work. ...

It was by no means a light or pleasant room, however, and the lowness of the ceilings, and the machinery whirring overhead, added to its depressing effect ... There was a good deal here of the same spirit of kindness among the employés that I had found in the other factories. They seemed anxious, all of them, to see me pick up the work quickly and do well at it, ready to tell me how slow they had been at first and how discouraged. [...]

They seemed to me to be in need of more workers. I found out later that they had to work evenings sometimes. I shuddered at the thought of these little kiddies of 14, 15 and 16 coming back to work at night at nine or after in a section [of the city] like this. ...

There was no lunch room. I did not expect it after the stairs. I ate my lunch on a window sill looking down into the back yards across the lane ... old barrels, and boxes, and rusty scraps of tin, and old hat-brims, and worn-out shoes ... Wouldn't the air be cleaner, I wonder, for us all to breathe, if the back yards of the city were looked after once in a while? ... I turned my back directly towards the window in order to gulp down and keep down the rest of the lunch.

[...]

July 2

I was sitting in a group of my 14-year-old factory friends at noon hour when I propounded the question rather tentatively, "Wouldn't you rather do housework for somebody, girls, than to work in a factory? You get bigger pay."

The young faces around me drooped a little. Instantly I perceived that I had offended. I had made what is called "a break."

"Mother says," said one, "that I cannot do housework unless I do it in my own house." This "mother says no" reason is a very common one for girls not going into housework. Mother does not like the social standing for her daughter. Besides, the little girlie helps

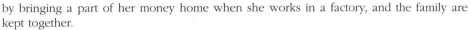

by bringing a part of her money home when she works in a factory, and the family are kept together.

"You are not thought as much of," says another. "You have to work harder at it," says a third. ... "It is every night in the week but one, and Sundays too."

I put the same question to Alma, the more mature girl, in her little $1.25 room. "I don't like being bossed so much," she answered. "At the factory, when your work's done, your time's your own. You can go where you like."

Aside from the reasons given, there is a lure about the factory. ... The girls like to be where there is "something doing," where things happen, where the joke is being bandied and the bit of gossip, good- or ill-natured, whichever it may be, passed along. The kitchen looks a lonely place down behind the board fences and between the brick walls. ...

Our pretty sentiment about the servant girl's good home is more or less flimsy farce. The home where she is employed is not in any sense her home. ... Home is where love is, where they have a community of interests. The servant girl occupies no such place in your dwelling. Which one of your home circle would feel he "belonged," if he or she had to eat alone in the kitchen and live apart from the rest? ...

One must allow too for the mating instinct. ... The girl in the factory has "bows" in her hair and "beaux" in her train. The girl in the kitchen is shut away from these lords of creation. ... She is only out one night a week and altogether she feels that the back gate is a sort of limit to her prospects. ... Besides, when John calls on your servant girl, he has to go in by the back gate. If he is a somewhat proud young man, he does not like it. A month later, when she has taken a place at the factory, he can call at the front door of the boarding house and ask for "Miss Samson Johnson," or whatever it is. They both feel that she now has a different standing in the world.

Above all, it is this loss of caste, this social slur that women themselves have put upon housework, that accounts for the unwillingness of our girls to do it.

61

▲ Document 2: "The Sweating System in Canada", 1898

Speaking generally, the sweating system denotes a condition of labor in which the remuneration is quite disproportionate to the amount of work done: or, to borrow mathematical phraseology, in which a maximum amount of work, in a given time, is performed for a minimum wage. It is also usually understood that the hours of labor are long, and that the place in which the work is done, and the environments to which the workers are subjected, are unhealthy, and such as to prove injurious to their physical and moral well-being. Excessive work, low wages, long hours and unhealthy surroundings are the distinguishing characteristics of the so-called sweating system.

[...] In the home-shops [in Montreal] women are almost exclusively employed. The work done is that on the cheaper grades of clothing and consists largely in the making up of pants and vests. Many of them are employed at $2 and $2.50 a week, and $3 is regarded as a good wage [...]

Where the workshop is in a separate establishment the hours are regulated by the Provincial factory and workshops acts; but, where the shop is in the home it is frequently unknown to the inspectors, and the period of labor often extends beyond fifteen and sixteen hours a day. To those who work in their homes there is, in many cases, no limit save that of physical endurance; for where the individuals or families are dependent solely on the amount earned by sewing, nothing but excessively long hours can enable them to gain a subsistence with so small a remuneration. There are many who work in homes for fifteen or sixteen hours daily, and who realize only from $3 to $5 a week. The task system, which is common in New York tenements, has also found its way into some of the shops in Canada. It is a scheme whereby one employee, or a group of employees, are allotted what is nominally supposed to be one day's work, and receive only one day's pay for the whole of it, though to complete it satisfactorily may require two or even three days. The baneful effects of excessive work of this sort upon the workers require no comment [...]

Not infrequently men and women, boys and girls, are crowded together in a room hardly large enough for a half or a third of the number. The atmosphere of the place, already noxious by reason of the presence of too many persons in so confined a space, is still more vitiated by the fetid odors arising from the gas, irons and dampened cloths. The running of machines and the pressing of garments create an incessant noise of the most distracting kind. Where the work is done in homes it is sometimes made up in the living apartments of the family, or the sleeping rooms [...]

Source: Excerpt from Letter to the Editor, The Toronto MacKenzie King, "The Sweating System in Canada," unsigned article in the *Globe*, November 19, 1898.

▲ Document 3: Domestic Servants, Early 20th Century

● These domestic servants would almost certainly be washing this stack of dishes without the benefit of hot and cold running water. If they were lucky, they might have a tap with cold water in the kitchen, and would have to heat water on the stove. In many homes they would also have to carry water into the kitchen from an outside tap or well.

63

Source: Canada's Visual History, Vol. 30.12. Vancouver Public Library, Special Collections 2266.

▲ Document 4: Oral History Excerpt "Laundry"

Laundry

For centuries the techniques by which North American housewives did their laundry remained static. It was an arduous, physically demanding task which required the greater part of a whole day and had to be done on a regular basis, usually once a week and normally on Monday. Since the early nineteenth century domestic scientists and home economists were concerned with analyzing and simplifying "blue Monday." The various descriptions ranging over more than one hundred years show a marked similarity that corresponds closely to the following description from Flin Flon in the 1930s [an oral history interview from Manitoba].

Imagine, if you can, one of those blistery hot summer days, the kind when all you want to do is go sit in the lake. But it's Monday; so I can't. For Monday is washday. So I get up at 4:30 a.m. to start the fire in the stove—a fire and when it's already hot enough to fry eggs on the rocks! When the fire's going I fill the copper boiler with water and carry it from the tank to the stove and then lift it onto the stove—heavy work that and already the sweat is pouring down my back. It makes me hot just to think of it. Then I go get the washing. Baskets of dirty things—clothes, bed sheets, towels and his dirty work clothes and I carry them into the kitchen and sort them into piles and then by 6:30 I'm ready to start scrubbing. Each thing to wash you wet in the warm water and then throw it in the boiler to boil awhile. The steam rises everywhere till the whole house is like one of them Finnish saunas. Then you take a wooden spoon and start fishin'. One at a time you pull the steamy things out of the boiler and you hold them there heavy and steaming that they are—my, them wet things get heavy till your arm aches. Then when they cool enough to touch you start scrubbing, rubbing the thing against the scrub board and rubbing with soap and a scrub brush. Oh and I forgot the soap, which you couldn't forget because you had to get it ready the day before by taking a bar of soap and grating it into flakes so it would dissolve easier. So then you scrub each thing and there were hundreds and the steam is boiling and the clothes are hot and heavy and when you've scrubbed it you throws it into a pail of warm water for rinsing then you squeeze it out, and you have to squeeze so hard and your arms are already tired and it is so hot. Then you rinse again and wring and then pile all the stuff into the basket and carry it outside and one by one hand each piece on the line to dry and you have to hang them just right or you'll never iron the wrinkles out and that takes till 6:30 or 7:00 of an evening when he wants his supper and you to go sleep like the dead, hot and weary and worn to the bone. (That were some hard work let me tell you and we never had no help from no one and that's what it used to be like to do my washing.) Oh, but I forgot. All the while you had to keep stoking up the stove to keep it hot enough to keep the water boiling so's it got as I hated it, it was so hot and all the water splashed on the floor so when I finished I had to scrub the kitchen floor too. And we didn't have no plastic clothes line, only linen so it had to be strung up before the clothes could be hung. And of course you were forever slipping in the water and losing your balance and hitting that fiery stove and of course the kids wanted looking after all day at the same time. Well that was Blue Monday all right.
(Generation I, b. 1896)

▲ Document 5: Excerpts from the Royal Commission on the Relations of Labor and Capital, 1889

[The Royal Commission was instituted by Sir John A. Macdonald in 1887, in part to try to demonstrate that his Conservative party was a "friend of labour." The commission was intended to investigate all aspects of the relationship between labour and capital in Canada, and the commissioners travelled across the country taking testimony from employers and employees. Women workers were very much underrepresented among those giving testimony, at about 5 per cent of all witnesses, even more underrepresented than the percentage of women in factories more generally (approximately 15 to 20 percent overall).]

Quebec Evidence

Miss _____, of Quebec, employee in a woolen factory, sworn.

By Mr. HELBRONNER:

Q. You received no subpoena, you came of your own free will?

A. Yes, sir.

Q. Will you state what you wish to say to this Commission?

A. It is because of the work. The work is too hard for the pay. We are not paid proper prices for the work we do.

Q. What wages do you get now?

A. 45 cents a day.

Q. What kind of work do you do? Are you obliged to stand?

A. We are always standing.

Q. Are you permitted to sit?

A. No, sir; they will not permit us to sit.

Q. Are you fined when you sit?

A. No, sir; but they say our work does not allow of our sitting down.

Q. Do any workwomen earn less than you?

A. There are some; the highest is 50 cents.

Q. And the lowest?

A. The lowest is 15 cents.

Q. Are those that earn 15 cents children?

A. Children of about 12 years of age.

Q. Do you spin or do you weave?

A. We spin. [...]

By MR. BOIVIN:

Q. Do you think the work given to little girls of twelve years of age, is too hard for them?

A. Some have too hard work; it is a work that requires them to keep their arms up all the time.

Source: Excerpts from the Royal Commission on the Relations of Labor and Capital, 1889.

By MR. HELBRONNER:

Q. Could your work not be done sitting as well as standing?

A. When things go well, we might have sit down; but they will not let us sit. There is a bobbin to be put in, high up, and we have our arms over our head all the time.

Q. Have you anything else to complain of in the factory?

A. We are hard driven by the foreman at times. Sometimes for the least little thing the foreman tells us to go. Then, if we are sick, they say it is not because we are sick we stay away because we want to amuse ourselves; and all the time we may be as sick as well as others.

Q. Do the foreman ill-treat the children, are they brutal to them?

A. Yes, sir.

Q. Do they strike them?

A. No; they do not strike them, but they treat them roughly.

Q. Little girls or little boys?

A. Little girls.

Q. As to little girls who earn 15 cents, are their wages raised often, or do they work a long time at 15 cents?

A. It is always the same.

Q. Their wages are raised when they grow big enough to take the places of grown girls?

A. Yes; to take the places of grown girls. Some of the foremen are cruel. There is one, the foreman in our room, who, a short time ago, pushed a girl to make the others laugh; sometimes they want to joke the girls, and in passing he gave a kick to one who was at her work. She made a face at him, and he kicked her in passing …

Q. Have you ever seen little girls cry, and heard them complain of having been roughly treated?

A. Yes, sir. It has been said that we do not work on feast days; we work on every feast day. We may not work all the whole day, but we work part. It has been said that we do not work on feast days, but even when we say we will not work, they tell us to leave; some were sent away because they would not work on holy days.

Q. You worked on Epiphany, and the next day you had no work?

A. The next day we had no work.

Nova Scotia Evidence

MISS _____, employé, cotton factory, sworn.

By MR. ARMSTRONG:

Q. What department do you work in?

A. I work in the spinning room.

Q. What do you earn per week?

A. The most I have earned is $6 a fortnight.

Q. Are there any young girls in that room?

A. Yes

Q. Do you know their ages?

A. Twelve would be the youngest.

Q. How many are there in the room aged 12?

A. I could not say.

Q. How much do they earn?

A. They earn $2 a week.

Q. Are there any fines imposed on the young girls in your room?

A. Yes; when they are late. [...]

Q. Are all subject to fines, the big girls and the little ones alike?

A. Yes.

Q. What time have they to be there in the morning?

A. They have to be there at a quarter past six.

Q. If they are not there exactly on time are they fined?

A. Yes.

Q. They do not get any grace?

A. No.

Q. What time have they for dinner?

A. They have an hour. [...]

Q. Is there much dust in the spinning room?

A. Yes; there is a good deal.

Q. Is there so much that you have to open the windows?

A. No; the windows are never opened.

Q. Don't you find it too warm in summer?

A. Yes. [...]

Q. Do they work after six o'clock?

A. No; we would not do it. The manager wanted us to do it and he said before he would let the Halifax people have their own way he would send for English spinners, but as long as the steam had gone down he concluded to let us go. [...]

Q. Is any abusive language used towards those employed in that room?

A. Yes; when they are not doing the work quick enough.

Q. Who does this?

A. There is an under boss that does it.

Q. Does he swear at them?

A. Yes.

Q. Does he cuff any of them?

A. He kicks the boys when they are not doing the work.

Q. Have any of them cried on account of being kicked?

A. Yes.

Q. Does he ever cuff the little girls?

A. No; I never saw him beat the girls.

Q. But you have seen him kick the boys until they have cried?

A. Yes.

[...]

▲ Document 6: Toronto Textile Factory, 1908

● These workers are required to stand for their entire workday. Do you see any guards on the machines to protect the workers from fast moving belts and other dangers? Many workers lost fingers and hands, or suffered other injuries through factory work. Do you see the foreman watching to ensure that workers keep up to the pace of the machines?

Source: James Collection, City of Toronto Archives (137) , Fonds 1244, Item 137.

▲ Document 7: Mothers and Children at Home, 1913, Toronto

● What can you determine about the living conditions of these mothers and children from this picture? Might they be sharing a kitchen to try and make ends meet, as Bradbury suggested was one survival strategy for poor families? Why would this picture have been taken? Government nurses and charity workers felt that they had the right to enter the homes of the poor at this time.

Source: Canada's Visual History, Vol. 51.17. Courtesy: Department of Health Collection, City of Toronto Archives, Series 372, Sub-Series 32, Item 243

▲ Document 8: Children Gathering Coal Cinders from a Toronto Rail Yard

70

● Why are these children gathering coal cinders? This picture would have most likely been taken by middle class reformers to demonstrate the shiftless ways of the poor, and the improper ways in which poor parents raised their children, without any recognition of the integral role that the scavenging of children could play in the survival of poor families.

Source: Library and Archives Canada, C-85579

■ Article 1: Industrial Capitalism and Women's Work

Ruth A. Frager and Carmela Patrias

"Z" left school at the age of fourteen to help her family. Her father made a living hauling goods, and her mother supplemented the family's income by taking in boarders. For the first few months after leaving school, Z helped her mother with domestic chores. But although she needed the help, the mother wanted Z to find a better way to earn a living than 'slaveying' for boarders. Z found a job in a candy factory, wrapping chocolate bars, but left after several months because of poor health.

After a short rest, Z found a job in a millinery factory, trimming women's hats. She quickly became skilled at this, and, within the first six weeks her wages rose from six to nine dollars a week. But she had to leave because the employer 'yelled and swore at the workers so shockingly that Z's nerves gave out.' After resting a week, she found another millinery job but soon left the new job because she was earning only six dollars and had no prospect of advancement. She next found a job in a store, selling women's hats for ten dollars a week, but her health declined again, partly because she found it hard to stand all day long. After recuperating, she decided not to go back to making women's hats because even though she had a talent for this, the trade was characterized by substantial seasonal unemployment.

Z found the prospect of clerical work more attractive, so one of the family's boarders started helping her learn to type and improve her spelling. The Toronto researcher who investigated Z's case around 1920 concluded that 'as she is the type of girl who can obey orders and carry out routine work well, and as she is likewise faithful and industrious, she has a fair prospect of success up to the point where her limited general education closes the door to further progress on those lines.'

As Z's case reveals, industrialization created new types of paid employment for females. To both Z

Source: Abridged from Ruth A. Frager and Carmela Patrias, "Industrial Capitalism and Women's Work," *Discounted Labour*, pp. 17-53. © University of Toronto Press Inc., 1995. Reprinted with permission of the publisher.

and her mother, factory work seemed preferable to domestic work, and clerical work seemed better yet. Z's frequent changing of jobs indicates that she was ambitious to find the best possible employment and that the prospects available to her were limited, characterized by low wages, long and irregular hours, and health hazards. Z's eleven-year-old brother would also discover that his job prospects were limited once he left school. But although working-class males and females faced certain common constraints in the world of paid labour, females also encountered gender-based obstacles.

The First and Second Industrial Revolution

Industrial capitalism fundamentally transformed Canadian society, dramatically altering the very nature of work. In the process, Canada changed from a predominantly rural society based on small-scale, independent commodity production to a predominantly urban one based on the factory system.

By the 1850s, the first industrial revolution was underway. Transportation networks improved dramatically as canals and railways were built, making it more feasible to sell products to larger markets. Steam power was central to this transformation, for steam engines propelled ships and locomotives. Produced by burning coal, steam also powered the new machines that were being developed for the emerging factories. Resource industries such as lumbering and mining expanded, and large saw mills, flour mills, and textile mills developed. A fairly wide range of factories arose, including those manufacturing boots and shoes, clothing, furniture, stoves, and agricultural implements such as reapers and mowers. Yet, in this phase of industrialization, mechanization was still limited. Of greater impact on the organization of production was the gathering together of workers into larger workplaces.

As the early twentieth century dawned, industrial capitalism accelerated, ushering in the second industrial revolution, which extended up to the Second World War. Electricity (often generated from rivers and waterfalls) emerged as the key power source. Mechanization increased dramatically, fundamentally changing almost all industrial sectors. New industries, including steel, automobiles, pulp and paper, and electrical appliances, became prominent. As more

71

efficient methods of administration became increasingly important, large centralized office bureaucracies developed, and offices expanded further to deal with a flood of paperwork.

Urban centres expanded rapidly as industrial growth pulled more people in from rural areas and from abroad to work in factories and other expanding workplaces. From 1891 to 1921, the populations of the two most important industrial cities, Montreal and Toronto, almost tripled, surpassing 615,000 in Montreal and 520,000 in Toronto. Several cities experienced even more dramatic growth rates, and by 1921 the populations of Winnipeg, Vancouver, Hamilton, and Ottawa exceeded 100,000. By then, half the nation's population was classified as urban.

Yet industrial development was highly uneven, not only because of dramatic regional variations, but also because the pace of change varied from sector to sector and even within particular sectors. In the late nineteenth century, significant industrial development occurred in the Maritimes as well as central Canada. But by the early twentieth century, the nation's industrial heartland centred in Ontario and, to a lesser degree, Quebec, notably in a string of industrial cities extending from Windsor along the Great Lakes to Montreal. Some sectors of the economy industrialized more rapidly than others so that, in the late nineteenth century, new factories coexisted with older forms of production even in the most industrialized parts of the country. During the first industrial revolution, in particular, mechanization had been uneven. But even during the second industrial revolution, characterized by the rise of large corporations, small firms continued to compete with one another in such sectors as clothing and food processing. Frequent economic downturns in the late nineteenth and early twentieth centuries, moreover, reinforced the unevenness of industrial development.

The Reorganization of Work

The rise of industrial capitalism entailed major changes in the organization of work, as employers sought to break up the artisans' traditional control over their trades. This was not simply a question of gathering more workers under one roof so as to manufacture more items to sell to a larger market. Employers strove to make their businesses more competitive and more profitable by cheapening the cost of labour. To do so, they transformed the labour process in two main, interrelated ways, both of which involved the process of deskilling. Employers often increased the division of labour: instead of one or two people making an entire product from start to finish, the steps involved in making that product would be broken down and divided among a group of less skilled—hence less expensive—workers, each of whom would specialize in a particular task. Employers also resorted to mechanization to cut labour costs.

As managers coordinated the actions of growing numbers of workers and machines, new rhythms of work formed. Instead of the more natural variations in the pace of work in artisanal workshops, factory labour became highly regimented. Long hours became commonplace, and the pace was often gruelling, as employers sought to maximize the utility of expensive machines. Although the assembly line did not become widespread in this period, those women and men who worked on the line had to keep up with the rapid pace set by the line itself. More commonly, the system of piecework was used to speed up workers. Under this system, instead of paying the worker a set wage per hour, the worker was paid according to the number of items (or parts of items) she or he had produced. Instead of timing average workers, employers frequently set piece rates according to the time required by the fastest workers. When they believed that workers were able to earn too much money under the established rates, employers often reduced piece rates. As factory inspectors emphasized, piecework seriously strained workers' nerves.

Some employers used time and motion studies to speed up workers and to ensure that tasks would be performed in set ways so as to ensure maximum efficiency. For the worker, the result was not only monotonous work but also the risk of what would now be called repetitive strain injuries. A middle-class reformer who disguised herself as a 'factory girl' in order to investigate working conditions, in 1912, captured the monotony of making jelly wafers at a biscuit factory: 'Dab-a-jelly, turn-a-biscuit, dab-a-jelly, turn-a-biscuit, dab-a-jelly, turn-a-biscuit.' [See Videre article in this module.] Lunch or supper breaks were short, and there were often very few other breaks in the day, even for using the washroom.

In the nineteenth century, a rigid system of fines sometimes formed part of the regimentation of factory work. Workers who arrived five or ten minutes late might find their pay docked for the whole morning. In some workplaces, employers docked people's pay for work that they judged to be imperfect, even though such judgments could be subjective and the imperfections might have resulted from problems that were beyond the individual worker's control. In a Halifax textile factory, for example, a weaver received a fine because oil had dripped from the loom onto the cloth, even though oiling the machine was not her responsibility. Talking, singing, and laughing were forbidden in some workplaces, and management used fines to enforce these prohibitions. Employers appear to have fined women and children much more than adult male workers, presumably because the employers viewed women and children as more docile and therefore more likely to put up with the penalties. Some employers also used corporal punishment to discipline child workers, sometimes quite brutally.

Mechanization, together with employers' desire to cut costs, introduced new hazards into the workplace. Improperly maintained steam-driven equipment could explode. Various kinds of machinery could ensnare fingers and sometimes limbs. The threats to health increased as employers proved reluctant to spend money on proper ventilation and on safety guards for machinery. While tuberculosis was known as the 'tailors' disease' because of its link to the harmful lint and fumes in clothing factories, lung problems related to poor ventilation plagued workers in other trades as well. Lives were shortened and even lost due to job-related diseases and workplace accidents.

Children served as an important pool of cheap labour, particularly during the first industrial revolution. Some, especially those working in textile mills, were only nine or ten years old. While some urban boys plied street trades such as selling newspapers or shining shoes, the intense subdivision of labour in certain sectors in the late nineteenth century enabled a significant number of boys and girls to find factory jobs, often working with light machinery. Over all, fewer girls than boys took up wage earning, for girls often had to help their mothers at home. Parental decisions about whom to send out to work were influenced by the fact that a girl's earning power was commonly less than her brother's. Although the scarcity of historical studies of child labour makes it difficult to generalize, existing studies suggest that, at least in Ontario, employers came to rely less on

child labour as factories became more mechanized in the early 1900s.

Employers were sometimes frank about why they employed women. As a cigar manufacturer from London, Ontario, explained in the late nineteenth century, the employment of women 'is more profitable to us or we would not employ them.' He also valued female employees because he believed they were more tractable. 'Women do not go on strike and do not get drunk,' he maintained. A late-nineteenth-century printer advanced similar arguments: 'The proprietor says he likes to have girls because they never ask for a raise of wages, and he can get rid of them some day when he does not need them. They get married.'

Women at Work

Although employers commonly viewed them as cheap labour, most females who went out to work did so because of pressing economic need. For many working-class families in particular, the wages of the male head of the family were simply not enough. At a time when many workers believed that men should bring home a family wage, this ideal did not correspond to reality for most working-class households. In Toronto in 1921, for example, the average annual wage of adult male blue-collar workers constituted only two-thirds of what was necessary to keep a family of five above the poverty line. Hence, secondary wage-earners were necessary, if these families were to cover basic items such as food and rent. In addition, in a period before social welfare measures such as unemployment insurance and socialized medicine, families often needed additional wage earners to help them cope with emergencies resulting from layoffs, sickness, and deaths.

Although some working-class wives and mothers took regular jobs outside the home, most did not, for it was difficult to combine homemaking with going out to work.

The Women Who Went Out to Work

Since working-class families requiring secondary wage earners were reluctant to send wives out to work, the vast majority of females who went out to work were young and unmarried. Most females engaged in paid labour as an interval between leaving school and marrying. Hence the proportion

73

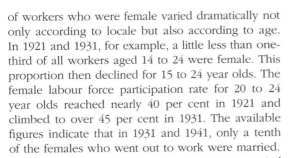

of workers who were female varied dramatically not only according to locale but also according to age. In 1921 and 1931, for example, a little less than one-third of all workers aged 14 to 24 were female. This proportion then declined for 15 to 24 year olds. The female labour force participation rate for 20 to 24 year olds reached nearly 40 per cent in 1921 and climbed to over 45 per cent in 1931. The available figures indicate that in 1931 and 1941, only a tenth of the females who went out to work were married.

It would be incorrect to view young, unmarried female income earners as independent women who controlled their own earnings and lived on their own while enjoying freedom from parental control. Most female income earners were embedded in the family economy. Many of these young women lived with their families and contributed all or most of their earnings to their families. Indeed a significant number of them handed their unopened pay envelopes over to their mothers. Many other young women probably retained only a small portion of their pay for their own purposes and routinely handed over the rest. Young women who had left rural families to come to the city to take up paid labour, sometimes lived with surrogate families, often consisting of members of extended families or relatives of former neighbours. Those who lived in 'respectable' boarding houses faced constraints imposed by boarding-house keepers who sought to maintain their reputation for respectability by restricting opportunities for socializing with the opposite sex. Given how difficult it was for female income-earners to earn a living wage, notions of their independence are misleading. These young women may have challenged parental authority to a certain extent by going out to unchaperoned dance halls or taking up the latest fashions (such as bobbing one's hair), but they did not necessarily abandon family loyalties or neglect family obligations. In fact, many took pride in their economic contributions to their families' well-being.

While many women faced limited job opportunities, difficult working conditions, and low wages, they were not simply victims. Like Z, they were active agents in the paid labour force, manoeuvring within sharp constraints to make the most of their limited options. Some obtained a sense of satisfaction from doing their jobs well, even though the jobs could be tedious. Women who went out to work because they and their families needed the money sometimes found other benefits as well. Many appear to have especially enjoyed the camaraderie with female co-workers, and those who were looking for male friends, perhaps seeking marriage partners, may have enjoyed mingling with male co-workers as well. Those who did manage to support themselves usually took pride in their ability to do so, and, as we shall see, those who performed white-collar work took pride in the higher status that this type of work often afforded.

In the rare situations where women possessed scarce skills and could bring in somewhat better wages, there could be other important benefits. A study of skilled female textile workers recruited in the early twentieth century from England for the mills of Paris, Ontario, for example, indicates the advantages that such women enjoyed. Their greater earning power, combined with the possibility of life-long work in the textile mill, enabled some to escape troubled marriages and meant that the single women among them did not necessarily have to marry for economic reasons. In a town where so many mothers continued to go out to work, moreover, accommodations, such as flexible employment hours and commercial laundries providing door-to-door delivery, developed to facilitate the combination of outside work with household responsibilities.

Far more often, however, working-class women who had to support children without the aid of husbands were in a very vulnerable position, especially because women's jobs usually paid so little. Aging widows found it difficult to compete for jobs with young women in their late teens or early twenties. And, of course, it was hard to combine income earning with household responsibilities, particularly if the children were young. Widows and deserted wives constituted a small but significant group of female income earners who confronted particular hardships.

Factory Work

The manufacturing sector was an important source of jobs, especially for women who lacked the language skills or the formal education required for white-collar work. [...] Within manufacturing, females represented a significant proportion of workers—roughly one-quarter from 1891 to 1911 and around one-fifth from 1921 to 1941. Women in factories tended to concentrate in a few areas: the textile, clothing, boot and shoe, food-processing, and tobacco industries. The highest proportion of female workers was in the clothing industry. [...]

These women typically earned little. In the late nineteenth and early twentieth centuries, many factory women did not make enough to be economically self-sufficient, let alone support elderly parents, young children, or an ailing husband (or other partner). Those who managed to eke out a living wage for themselves usually remained poor and seldom had savings for unemployment, illness, or old age. [...] Throughout the period under consideration, factory women earned roughly half as much as men. With so many jobs off limits to females, women workers' intense competition for the available 'women's work' helped to keep their pay low. Yet they still earned less when they had the same jobs as men.

The Gender Division of Labour

Even though women workers constituted an important pool of cheap (and reputedly docile) labour, women were not pulled into the paid labour force indiscriminately. Many jobs were off limits to women because of the ways in which the prevalent gender ideology intertwined with men's material self-interest, as employers, as workers, and as heads of families.

The gender division of labour was commonly seen as natural, fixed, and immutable. Some industries were deemed totally unsuitable for women. Even where they found work, they usually encountered a distinct differentiation between 'women's' and 'men's' work and thus seldom competed directly with men for jobs. To contemporaries, these distinctions seemed to reflect common sense. Women seemed incapable of heavy work, such as making steel, cutting down trees, or mining coal. Women's jobs were generally regarded as an extension of work that women had traditionally done in the home. They were seen as naturally good at delicate work by virtue of their nimble fingers, their patience, and attentiveness to detail. Beyond this, they were believed to be good at putting up with tedious, repetitive tasks and were often believed to be unsuitable for tasks requiring considerable exercise of individual judgment. They were not seen as skilled workers, nor were they seen as having mechanical ability.

Such 'logic' was, in fact, heavily shaped by customs, indeed stereotypes, rooted in deep beliefs about what constituted 'womanhood' and 'manhood.' At the most basic level, it did not occur to anyone that women could fill men's jobs. Employers would not hire them, and women themselves would not apply because they shared the conventional assumptions that they were by nature unsuited for such work. As a woman who spent years on an assembly line making watches explained succinctly: 'Girls just didn't do men's jobs.' For her, as for so many others, this fact was strongly related to the man's role as family breadwinner: 'Yes, the men were better paid too. We just took that for granted, I supposed because they had families.' A woman who packed cereal for years explained: 'I was still a woman, and I don't believe in taking a man's job.' Thus, in many cases, there was no need to patrol the boundaries of the gender division of labour.

This division of labour was so entrenched that it resulted in certain rigidities. A shortage of women workers in an early-twentieth-century New Brunswick candy factory, for example, did not lead management to hire men to fill women's jobs, even though the shortage limited production and some of the women's jobs paid relatively well.

None of this was inevitable, however. In theory at least, many new factory jobs could have emerged without necessarily being coded as female or male and, in practice, the gender designation of some jobs could change over time and from place to place. Consider the assumption that heavy work was for men. Not only did women perform heavy work on struggling family farms and in working-class households, but the definition of certain jobs as physically demanding—and hence men's jobs—could be arbitrary. In the late-nineteenth-century shoe industry, for men and women held different jobs, partly on the grounds that women needed to sit while working whereas men, being physically stronger, could stand. Yet many women in the textile industry, as well as a number of other sectors, worked at tasks that required them to stand for hours on end. Moreover, while some of the machines involved in shoe-making required that the operator stand in order to exert more leverage, a number of shoe-making machines were built in such a way that the operator had to stand—apparently not for any functional reason but rather to define the task as men's work, worth higher pay. Gendered assumptions can clearly be embedded in new technology

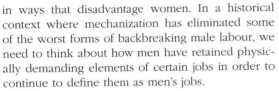

in ways that disadvantage women. In a historical context where mechanization has eliminated some of the worst forms of backbreaking male labour, we need to think about how men have retained physically demanding elements of certain jobs in order to continue to define them as men's jobs.

[...]

The common conception of female workers as less skilled than males is itself problematic. It is difficult to assess the levels of skill in any job objectively and precisely. Some jobs were clearly less skilled than others, and this reality is crucial to the notion of deskilling. A person needs more skill to make a complete coat from start to finish than to sew in coat linings all day long. But assessments have often been shaped by subjective perceptions of what is skilled and what is not, and these perceptions have been shaped by ideological factors. In other words, skill is socially constructed. To analyse the social construction of skill in particular historical circumstances, one needs to examine how common particular skills have been, the types of people who have possessed such skills, the nature of access to various forms of training and experience, and the extent to which groups of workers have been able to defend their claims to particular skills. In the garment industry, for example, women's sewing abilities were demeaned. Sewing skills they had learned from their mothers and performed in their own homes were seen as simply natural to them and evaluated in a context where women's household skills and household labour were generally undervalued.

William Lyon Mackenzie King was right when he observed at the turn of the century that, in the clothing industry, 'the reward for female labour is still greatly at a discount as compared with that of the opposite sex.' In fact, one late-nineteenth-century clothing manufacturer was uncommonly frank when asked what he paid for his help. 'I don't treat the men bad, but I even up by taking advantage of the women,' he replied. 'I have a girl who can do as much work, and as good work as a man; she gets $5 a week. The man who is standing next to her gets $11.' He explained that the other 'girls' averaged $3.50 per week and some of them made a mere two dollars. As this example suggests, low wages for women—both when they were doing the same jobs as men and also more broadly—need to be viewed partly in terms of manufacturers' strategies, for some manufacturers deliberately tried to buy off male workers at the women's expense.

The notion that a woman's 'proper place' was in the home ('a man's castle') meant that women who did go out to work were often not viewed as legitimate participants in the paid labour force, even though a significant number of them had no men to support them. Since women were not expected to be self-supporting or supporting dependants, the common presumption was that they were working merely for 'pin money,' for small luxuries. They were also assumed to be temporary workers, employed for a short time before marriage or, if married, working only while their husbands were ill or unemployed. Practices such as paying women less than men for the same work, or laying women off first, were thus based on the assumption that women could not do the work as well as the man who stayed in the trade for years.

In fact, women workers often did leave their jobs. Many did get married. Others withdrew briefly if their mothers or male relatives needed help at home. The relatively few married women who worked outside their homes frequently moved in and out of the paid labour force in a pattern of their own, often regulated by pregnancies. After a baby was weaned, a woman might return to her paid job, only to leave it when the next child was born. As the children grew older and were able to contribute to the family income, a woman might concentrate on her domestic responsibilities, perhaps to return to paid labour only when her children had left home.

Many women changed jobs frequently, particularly if they lacked scarce skills. They might move from one type of factory work to another and from factory work to waitressing or fruit picking and then back to the factories again. Females like Z were responding to the boredom of repetitive work and the difficult working conditions in many workplaces. While employers used high rates of turnover to justify confining women to relatively unskilled, low-wage jobs, this rationale became a self-fulfilling prophecy. The poor jobs encouraged even more transiency and also caused women to hope all the more to be able to leave paid employment upon marriage, thus reinforcing heterosexuality. At the same time, those who faced racist discrimination had less flexibility in moving from one job to another, as did those who tended towards a particular sector for ethnocultural

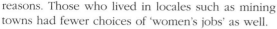

reasons. Those who lived in locales such as mining towns had fewer choices of 'women's jobs' as well.

In any case, it is misleading to think of females as temporary income earners and males as workers who stayed at a job permanently. For women, the interval between leaving school and marrying might last nearly a decade, particularly for working-class females who quit school at age fourteen or fifteen. Female textile workers in Quebec who began work in the early 1900s sometimes continued these jobs for fifteen years. Nor did the male income earner necessarily devote a lifetime to his job. White-collar males in more prestigious occupations were more likely to fit the image, but many working-class males were relatively transient, particularly if they lacked scarce skills.

Hence we need to question the common perception that women's short-term stint in the paid labour force legitimated confining them to relatively unskilled, low-waged work. Ultimately, there were other powerful forces keeping women's earnings low.

Examples from the unionized shops in Toronto's men's fine clothing industry in 1920 highlight the weakness of conventional rationales. In these cases, the women who did the same work as the men invariable earned considerably less. Sometimes the women did have less experience than the men. Male buttonhole makers, for example, had an average of nineteen years of experience and received an average wage of $36 per week, while female buttonhole makers had an average of only seven years of experience and received an average wage of only $22 per week. Given that one could learn to be a fairly fast and efficient buttonhole maker in far less than seven years, it is doubtful that the discrepancy between men's and women's skills was sufficiently great to warrant such wide pay differentials. Moreover, in a few cases in 1920, women and men performed the same jobs in these shops, and the women had experience equal to or greater than the men, yet the women still earned dramatically less.

[...]

In a sense, women have been the opposite of the legendary King Midas, whose touch turned objects into gold. Because women themselves have been devalued, a woman's touch has had a negative effect. Women did not simply fill jobs deemed unskilled: certain kinds of jobs were seen as less skilled and less remunerative *because* women did them. And, in circular fashion, the presence of women in devalued jobs reconfirmed notions of women as lacking skill.

[...]

Although male unionists sometimes allied themselves with women workers to resist harsh employers, there were instances where male unionists did their utmost to try to ensure that certain jobs would be reserved for men. For craft workers, opposition to female labour stemmed partly from the exclusivist aspects of pre-industrial artisanal traditions. In addition, the defensive actions of these male workers need to be seen in a context where they were often struggling against powerful employers in an era that was profoundly anti-union.

Indeed, employed males, especially working-class males, feared that the employment of women would intensify job competition, thereby allowing employers to undercut wages and hence undermining the men's ability to provide for their families.

[...]

The printing trade reveals how men could use their unions to exclude women from the better jobs. Traditionally, typesetting had been done by hand, demanded considerable skill, and was mainly a male job. The International Typographical Union largely succeeded in excluding women from typesetting. But the invention of the linotype machine towards the end of the nineteenth century threatened these male craft workers. Newspaper publishers argued that operating a linotype machine should be women's work since its keyboard resembled the typewriter, which was already identified with female labour. In Toronto, through a series of strikes, the male unionists succeeded in ensuring that men would be the ones who operated the new linotypes, at wage rate regulated by the union.

[...]

Restricting women's access to paid employment was part and parcel of women's subordination in the family and in society more broadly. The logic of the family wage was faulty. While many people believed that women should not take 'men's jobs' because the men were their families' breadwinners, men who were not supporting families did not necessarily earn less than men who were. Nor did a man with five children to support earn more than a man with just one child. Moreover, the whole emphasis on the family wage was built on the presumption that the male head of the household would devote all his

77

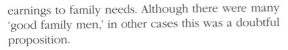

earnings to family needs. Although there were many 'good family men,' in other cases this was a doubtful proposition.

Ethnicity and Race

The gender division of labour intersected with ethnic and racist prejudices to exclude minority women from a wide range of 'women's jobs.' While employers had a great deal of power to determine whom to exclude from these jobs, the prejudices of other workers also often constrained minority women. Those affected included women from southern and eastern Europe, and especially those from China, Japan, and India. African-Canadian women—whose presence and disadvantaged position predated industrialization—and indigenous women also faced similar problems. [...]

Those Chinese women who did come to this country could seldom obtain factory work, particularly in central Canada. Discrimination limited them to work for Chinese-Canadian employers in small restaurants, laundries, or fruit and vegetable businesses. Some Chinese-Canadian and Japanese-Canadian women found work in the fish canneries of British Columbia in the early twentieth century, sometimes working with babies strapped to their backs. But the main workforce in these plants consisted of Aboriginal women and immigrant Chinese men. Although Aboriginal females in northern canneries sometimes did jobs that were performed by immigrant Chinese males in less remote locations, Aboriginal women and Chinese-Canadian men did not do the same jobs in the same canneries. In this sector, the Aboriginal women received lower pay and even shorter stints of seasonal work than the immigrant Chinese males. Members of these groups obtained cannery jobs because the working season was too short and the pay was too low to attract males or females of European heritage.

Racist exclusion from other work and a perceived shortage of Euro-Canadian female workers led many Chinese males in western Canada to take conventionally female work. As Euro-Canadian miners struggled to push them out of the mines, Chinese immigrant men found jobs in British Columbia in domestic service, restaurants, laundries, and canneries. Some worked in shoe, cigar, and clothing factories at jobs typically filled by women in central Canada. These Chinese men were often stereotyped

as effeminate. Racism was thus reinforced by linking Chinese males in the inferior status of women.

As they battled poverty, women and men of African descent also found that the intensity of racism barred them from many types of employment. Because men from this group earned such low wages, women's contributions to the family income were especially crucial. But African-Canadian women could generally only work as domestic servants. As one Toronto woman recalled, 'We weren't allowed to go into factory work until Hitler started the war.'

Among immigrants from southern and eastern Europe, women tended to marry relatively young, partly because of skewed sex ratios, and they tended not to go out to work. A significant number helped to build family farms out west or to run small family businesses in cities. Many who did work for wages were in domestic service or held related jobs as hotel maids or dishwashers and waitresses in restaurants. Some did typical 'women's jobs' in factories. Immigrant Ukrainian women, for example, worked in garment factories, cigar factories, paper-box factories, and meat-packing plants in cities such as Winnipeg, Montreal, and Edmonton. The clothing industry employed women from a number of backgrounds, including Italian, Polish, and Macedonian immigrants. Some women immigrants also found their way into southern Ontario's textile mills and canneries.

Immigrants frequently sought out workplaces where they could share the companionship and the familiar language of people from their own backgrounds. Jewish immigrants from eastern Europe exhibited one of the highest rates of occupational concentration. They gravitated towards the clothing industry not only because many other sectors would not hire Jews but also because of their cultural background and their experiences in eastern Europe. Many Jewish immigrants had worked in this sector before emigrating, partly because of severe anti-Semitic occupational restrictions and partly because of the religious injunction against wearing clothing that mixed wool and linen, which led religious Jews to depend on Jewish-made clothing to avoid violating sacred law. In Canada, the Jews already entrenched in the garment industry attracted many more, forming a concentration that helped maintain Jewish cultural practices and the Yiddish language. Yet, on the whole, economic factors and discriminatory employment practices probably played stronger roles than culture in determining the occupational distribution of particular racial and ethnic groups.

Service Jobs

Many females seeking work because of pressing economic need took jobs as domestic servants, especially if other jobs were not available to them. For a long period, this was the most common job for females, accounting for approximately one-third of all females who went out to work at the beginning of the twentieth century. Because industrialization and urbanization led more women to try for jobs in factories, offices, and shops, the relative importance of domestic service declined somewhat, to about one-fifth of the female workforce in the interwar years. Yet it remained an important occupation for females as middle-class housewives sought to employ a live-in domestic servant to lighten their own domestic work and to symbolize their family's status.

Most working-class women who went out to work preferred factory work to domestic service. Many of them felt that it was degrading to serve others in this way. Indeed, employers usually expected servants to be highly deferential. Although some employers were kinder than others, the 'mistress' commonly 'consider[ed] the servant a piece of machinery to perform her work,' according to a disheartened 'servant girl' who wrote a letter to the editor of the Toronto *Globe* in 1886. The live-in servant also suffered from lack of privacy and from isolation from family and friends. Her isolation was especially intense in situations where she was the only servant, as was commonly the case. Women who toiled in other people's homes frequently lost the possibility of having families of their own. The pay was low, the work was heavy: hauling water, scrubbing and polishing floors on their hands and knees, scouring pots and pans, and so on. The hours were unusually long. Many were on call twenty-four hours a day, perhaps with only a half day off per week. One woman explained her avoidance of such work: 'I don't like being bossed so much ... At the factory, when your work's done, your time's your own. You can go where you like.' In addition, the servant was sometimes subjected to sexual harassment by males in the household. If she fell out of favour and lost her job, she lost her bed and board as well. Hence many women who needed to earn a living avoided domestic service if they possibly could. The result was a great deal of transiency in this occupation and an overall shortage of servants.

A poignant letter from an early-twentieth-century servant to a Toronto newspaper portrayed some of the occupational difficulties. "All day long I serve and scrub and bake and then wash dishes, polish silver, press clothes until well into the night,' the writer explained. 'I wear a frilly head band that seems like a lead weight on my throbbing temples ... I say "Yes sir," and "Yes madame" with a pleasant smile, when I feel like screaming and telling the whole shooting match to go to hades ... I am tender with [the employer's] little children and I humor their childish whims; my own are in a foster home and indifferently cared for. But I do it all gladly, and I am well satisfied that my meagre wage is enough to pay for the bite that keeps my children alive.'

[...]

Related jobs in the service sector included not only hotel maids but also laundry workers and restaurant staff. These were low-status jobs commonly requiring little training but much endurance. [...]

Prostitution

When women's job choices were so limited and the available jobs commonly entailed such harsh circumstances and low pay, some women turned to prostitution. While many commentators viewed prostitutes as depraved and sinful women and argued that it was their depravity that turned them into prostitutes, some working-class voices held that women turned to prostitution because otherwise they could not earn enough to eat. Although some, like Toronto's Mayor William Howland, believed that 'a good woman will die first,' others differed sharply. 'Is it any wonder that girls go wrong?' asked an 'Unemployed Working Girl' in a letter to one of the garment unions in 1914. Explaining that one Toronto clothing firm offered an experienced female worker a mere four dollars per week, she declared that such meagre wages could not be stretched to cover room and board and other absolute necessities. Some of those who turned to prostitution in desperation did so on a temporary basis, depending on the availability of other jobs, while others resorted to prostitution on the side to supplement their earnings from 'respectable' jobs that did not pay a living wage.

The circumstances of some live-in domestic servants drove them to prostitution. Some had been

79

seduced or raped by male employers and then lost their jobs. Having been 'dishonoured' and kicked out on the streets, such women may have had little recourse other than prostitution, partly because they usually needed a letter of reference from the former employer (or other evidence of 'good character') in order to obtain a new position in domestic service. Besides, as 'fallen women,' they could not realistically expect that marriage would rescue them from the need to be self-supporting.

But while some desperate women resorted to prostitution as a survival strategy, others were tricked or trapped into this line of work. Horrified moral reformers publicized sensationalist stories of 'pure,' unsuspecting, young women caught in the grips of the 'white slave trade' and forced into a life of prostitution. According to these accounts, procurers lured women through false promises of marriage or even fake marriage ceremonies and sometimes drugged and kidnapped them. While such stories were exaggerated, some women were undoubtedly coerced into prostitution.

This was not the whole story, however, for some women workers apparently became prostitutes because they believed that work in the sex trade was easier and more lucrative than toiling away at a 'legitimate' job such as domestic service or garment work. They may have believed that prostitution would enable them to escape to a life that provided for more than bare necessities. Domestic servants who saw first-hand how the middle class lived, and department store employees who toiled in the midst of a multitude of appealing goods they could not afford on their meagre salaries, may have been especially susceptible to such dreams.

There was a hierarchy among prostitutes. Those who serviced wealthy customers might earn a great deal and work in luxurious surroundings, at least for a time, and a few might achieve upward mobility, becoming wealthy 'madams' who ran their own 'high-class' brothels. Raw frontier towns like Dawson City, in the Yukon, provided special possibilities because of their raucous atmosphere and high numbers of single men. Yet many prostitutes faced police harassment, imprisonment, fines, violence at the hands of pimps and customers, and intense social ostracism (including from their own families). They also risked sexually transmitted diseases such as syphilis and gonorrhea (especially before the development of penicillin in the 1940s), as well as unwanted pregnancies, sometimes leading to death from botched illegal abortions. The stress arising from the hazards of the job, together with the stigma of being social outcasts, led to high rates of alcoholism and drug addiction, especially to morphine and heroin, which resulted in further health problems.

Women from especially disadvantaged backgrounds may have felt driven to prostitution because discrimination sharply limited their prospects for employment and earnings in 'legitimate' sectors. The immigrants among them may have been especially vulnerable to procurers' machinations because they felt lost in a strange, new country. Among the worst off were Vancouver's immigrant Chinese 'crib prostitutes' at the turn of the century. Having been forced into prostitution under miserable working conditions in tiny cells, their impoverished 'careers' typically lasted only six to eight years before death. Moreover, prostitutes from 'non-preferred' immigrant groups, together with African Canadian and First Nations prostitutes, faced especially harsh treatment from the legal system.

Conclusion

While prostitution constituted one of the most difficult options for women needing to earn money, most female job seekers encountered serious limitations in many other areas as well. Industrial capitalism had changed Canadian society fundamentally, transforming much of the world of work. Within the factories, women were commonly channeled into jobs perceived as resembling the kinds of unpaid work performed by housewives. The gender division of labour seemed natural, relegating women to jobs that required nimble fingers, patience and attentiveness to detail—but not mechanical ability or the exercise of individual judgment. Yet many women preferred factory work to domestic service even though factory work commonly entailed harsh circumstances and low pay. Women from non-Anglo-Celtic backgrounds faced further obstacles that limited their employment options. In broad terms, some of the worst outrages of industrial capitalism pertained to women's work. [...]

80

■ Article 2: The Home as Workplace

Bettina Bradbury

This chapter is an attempt to look into the households of the families that became largely dependent on wages in Upper Canada and Ontario between the 1850s and the end of the century.[1] Such working-class families were a minority of the province's population throughout the nineteenth century. By the end of the century, however, as artisanal production diminished and as wage-earning opportunities increased in factories, in workshops, and on construction sites, a majority of the households in the growing cities and in many smaller towns and villages had become dependent on wages. While many of the tasks performed by wives and children in working-class homes were similar to those done in agricultural, artisanal, or even professional and bourgeois households, dependence on wages shaped their work in specific ways.

It is not easy to look inside the homes where women of the emerging working class worked to feed, clothe, and nurture their husbands, relatives and children.[2] The key lies in finding both an adequate theoretical approach and the sources that will allow us to see and understand what they were doing, how they did it, and the relationship between their daily tasks and the transformations occurring in the wider economy. Canadian historians have written more about the work performed in the homes of farm and pioneer women than about their counterparts in the newly emerging manufacturing towns and cities of Canada.[3] [...] To see into the daily lives of working-class women, men, and children, to describe the tasks they performed at home and to hear their voices is a challenge. We have to learn about their work in different ways, piecing together fragments from censuses, contemporary investigations, newspapers, civic documents, and records kept by charities or the legal system. We have to listen carefully to what husbands and fathers said about their families, their wives, and their work. The evidence for this chapter is drawn largely from such sources. I also

draw on secondary studies of particular towns and communities by historians whose main interest was not work done in the home, but whose findings tell us something about wage labour and some family strategies for survival. Only occasionally do these sources allow us to see things from the women's point of view. They do underline the importance of such labour.

[...]

Wage-Earning and Working-Class Households

MALE FAMILY HEADS

Over the second half of the nineteenth century, women in cities, towns, and villages across Ontario were increasingly likely to need the wages of other household members to perform much of their daily labour. In two-parent families the principal earner was usually the husband. As the children grew up, boys were more likely to be secondary earners than girls, but both contributed wage and domestic labour to the family economy. Most wives and mothers worked for wages only in emergencies. Their money managing and stretching was a full-time occupation. The amounts the family head could earn, the frequency he could find work, and how often he was paid, along with his willingness to hand it over to his wife for 'the necessaries of life' dictated the family's standard of living and determined what other kinds of work were done by his wife and children.

The spread of wage labour that accompanied the growth of construction and industry in Ontario's economy did not guarantee wages that would enable most men to feed, clothe and house their families as well as pay for medical care, fuel, basic furniture, schooling, and modest entertainment.

A Kingston labourer, James Rushford, was adamant when he gave evidence to the Royal Commission on the Relations between Labour and Capital in 1888: 'A labourer who gets only $1.00 a day and has two or three small children cannot half support his children and clothe them the way he should, and he cannot pay school taxes and give them an education. There are hundreds of them that way.'[4] His claim is supported by evidence taken by reporters for the Bureau of Industries across Ontario in 1889. That year,

Source: Abridged from Bettina Bradbury, *Labouring Lives: Work and Workers in Nineteenth-Century Ontario*, Paul Craven, ed. (Toronto: University of Toronto Press, 1995). Reprinted with permission.

the labourers who were surveyed averaged $302.60 in annual wages. Their expenses totalled an average of $343.07. Even with the additional $37.26 raised by other family members such budgets did not balance.

A difficulty in balancing budgets was not limited to labourers and their wives. Most blacksmiths and carpenters living in Toronto in 1888 and 1889 did not earn enough to allow their wives to balance their budgets.[5] 'Do you think a man who has $1.75 a day can support his family comfortably if he is sober, and industrious, and intelligent?' Mr. Carson asked R. Clements, a carpenter who was a witness at the same hearings in Ottawa in May 1888. 'It would depend upon the size of his family. If he had a small family, of course he could do it by being economical,' Clements replied. Only when asked by the chairman, 'Does it not depend a great deal upon the wife?' did he reply 'Exactly.'[6]

A wife's ability to perform her main task—transforming the wages of others into food, meals, clothing, and comfortable shelter and raising the children depended on her husband's earning, the number of children she had, the size and age of the family, and how often her husband could find work. The irregularity of work was a constant difficulty. Employment possibilities varied greatly between trades, with the seasons, and with economic ups and downs. Toronto workers surveyed by the Bureau of Industries in 1888 averaged about 268 days of employment—forty-four weeks if they worked six full days a week.[7] The workers giving evidence at the Royal Commission hearings of the same year suggested that much shorter work periods were more common. Few men in construction worked more than eight months a year.[8] A Windsor carpenter, George Jenkins, said there was 'not a man in Windsor with whom I am acquainted who makes full time.' Some averaged eight or nine months, some seven. The likelihood of steady work depended on the nature of the work available and hence varied across the province.[9]

Seasonal unemployment was often predictable. Some men were used to finding alternative winter work in the shanties. Men and women could negotiate credit if they knew work would resume at some particular time. Cyclical unemployment was more devastating, especially in the Great Depression which started in the United States in 1873 and then spread out across Quebec and Ontario.[10] At first some women could stretch what money they had, borrow

from friends, or negotiate credit. As men found fewer and fewer days work, family members sought other ways to get by, some eventually selling their furniture to pay the rent and then turning to charity. At Toronto's main institution offering relief to people living in their own homes, the House of Industry, the numbers shot up. In 1874 about 560 families living at home received help. By 1877 over 1,000 were being given some fuel or bread. Between 1874 and 1877 the number of four-pound loaves of bread distributed doubled from around 12,000 to over 28,000 and the amount of coal from 250 to 500 tons. The soup kitchen increased its output from 90 gallons a day in 1873 to 170 in 1876. The numbers receiving aid only began to fall after 1881.[11]

Lack of work and illness quickly ate into all wages, placing different burdens on the wage earner and those responsible for making ends meet at home. Illness was widespread. The poorest were usually the most vulnerable as the effects of inadequate diets were compounded by the unsanitary state of the parts of town where they so often lived, especially in the larger cities. When a *Globe* reporter interviewed an unemployed Toronto labourer, Mr. Gloynes, in February 1883, he was coughing 'in an ugly fashion.' He explained that his two greatest fears were sickness and lack of work.[12] Some men belonged to benevolent societies and some unions provided for periods of sickness or for the death of the wage-earner. In 1888, the International Moulders' Union, for instance, paid four dollars a week when a member was sick. Unionized cigarmakers in Stratford reported receiving five dollars a week. While this might cover a family's rent it was not enough for food as well, even in the smallest family.[13]

WAGE-EARNING OFFSPRING

Working-class families were most vulnerable to poverty before their children reached working age. Once the children were old enough to earn, many of them were sent out to seek some form of paid labour. From the 1860s on, more children were able to find some kind of work, although the possibilities varied from town to town and year to year. The proportion of sixteen-year-old boys reporting a job in Hamilton, for example, rose from 51 per cent in 1851 to 66 per cent twenty years later. Girls' participation in the formal market was more erratic, falling in Hamilton for all age groups—among sixteen-year-olds from 34 per cent in 1851 to 26 per cent in 1871.[14] Some off-spring undertook full-time work. Others found odd jobs or seasonal work. The particular local economies of parts of cities, or of small towns offered specific possibilities. In Chatham the pickling and canning works employed some fifty to seventy men, women, and children, black and white, between July and the end of October. In 1887 the men could earn $1.25 a day, and boys and girls about 60 cents. They worked for sixty hours a week. The local reporter felt it necessary to explain that this employment of children was 'not in any way due to the dissipation of parents here.' Rather the factory was a resort for people when regular work was slack during the summer. In Cornwall, in contrast, where wages were lower than in most other parts of the province, many children under fourteen, as well as those aged four-teen to eighteen were reported to work in the mills 'mainly because the wages paid to heads of families are insufficient to maintain all without the aid of the children.'[15]

In some trades boys in their late teens and early twenties could rival the earning power of their fathers. But daughters, wives, and young sons could not. The wages of older sons in particular offered the possibility of major improvements in a family's standard of living, often after years of scrimping on what the husband could earn alone. The need for older children's wages reshaped the relationships within working-class families, and the nature of childhood changed, as growing numbers of children remained with their parents longer than in the days of pre-industrial or even early industrial capitalism. Where earlier a craftsman might have apprenticed a son out to learn a trade, increasingly the sons stayed home, contributing some or all of their wages to the family economy. Girls were as likely to help their mothers with domestic work in the home as to seek wage labour.[16]

In many families, income was so low that even the small wages a youngster under fourteen or so could earn made an important difference to the family budget. Contemporary reformers expressed horror at finding such children in factories, too often ascribing it to the greed or dissipation of parents. But the parents themselves could be acutely aware that they were sacrificing their children's education for the money they so badly needed. The moulder Thomas Picket expressed some of the anguish many

men must have felt when they were obliged to make this choice:

> I have four boys. I mean to give them a fair education, but the little one of my boys has been able to clothe himself. I merely mention these facts to show that there must be thousands of working men worse off than I am [...] I do not believe five percent of our trade or of any mechanical trade can save a dollar in Toronto.[17]

[...] The small amounts such youngsters could earn underlines the need for extra cash. Boys under sixteen working as moulders making agricultural implements, for example, earned an average of only $3.18 a week during the last week of April in 1884, compared to the $11.00 male moulders earned. Boy woodworkers earned $3.63 compared to the $8.73 of adults, while girl bookbinders brought in only $2.47, and adult women a dollar more.[18] Nevertheless, family income increased more rapidly with a steadily earning teenage son than with a pay increase or extra day's work for the father.

When a woman's husband died, the earnings of her children were one of her principal ways of getting by. A working-class widow could seldom manage alone even if her husband had worked in one of the rare workplaces that gave some kind of pension to widows or had made provision for her through life insurance or a will.[19] [...] The children of widows were among the youngsters reported to be working in various kinds of factories across the province, like the glove works in Brockville. In Aylmer many of the women working in the canning factory were reported to be 'widows and the daughters of widows who must work at something for a living.'[20]

Female wages were generally so low that deserted wives and all widows but the wealthy lived in precarious states of dependence on others. Those unable to live by their own earnings or by those of their children and who found no other ways of making money turned to relief agencies and charities, often making up the majority of those helped.[21] Widows predominated among the clients of the Toronto House of Industry, and their ways of getting by starkly reveal the difficulties faced by women heading a family when few jobs were available to women, when wages could be as little as half those of men, and when support systems or day care were few or non-existent. Most widows with young children found work they could do from their homes, partly because the skills they possessed were ones that were done in the home—cooking, sewing, washing, and caring for children or the sick—and partly so they could earn and care for their children at the same time. Seldom did such earning prove sufficient. We will return shortly to such home-based tasks.

[...]

Working at Home

The diverse domestic tasks that women performed for their own families and at times for others were increasingly the major kind of work performed in Ontario homes. As live-in apprenticeships declined, as growing numbers of men and sons and daughters left their homes daily to work for wages or attend school, the home became feminized—a place where women worked with some help from their children. Clearly that work was not independent from the wage-earning of other family members. The tasks and rhythms were more varied than those of factory workers, but this did not make the home some kind of separate, pre-industrial enclave.

As long as there were some wage-earners in a family, some of the timing of that work was determined by the hours that wage earners were away. Furthermore, in the early years of industrial development, employers were able to keep wages relatively low precisely because women's domestic labour provided such a large proportion of family subsistence. Its benefits clearly accrued both to wage-earners and to the owners of mills and factories able to pay accordingly.[22]

Women's work in the home was crucial. Whether a family could muster one or several wage-earners, most wives had to work hard at making the money earned go as far as possible. They were the ones who had to 'study how long she must make the bag or barrel of flour last.' Among the 'more prosperous working-class families,' Jeanne Boydston has argued, 'household manufacturing, and gardening ... functioned as means of avoiding cash outlays,' while shopping carefully or in bulk might save money. In poorer families 'wives (as well as children) were responsible for finding ways to increase the household provisions without spending cash'—including scavenging and even at times stealing.[23]

At the core of the work in homes across the province were the production or purchase of food and the preparation of meals, sewing, and mending, and cleaning—what Marvin McInnis refers to as 'conventional household tasks'—that went into caring for families of all classes in cities, as on farms.[24] Most of this was women's work, whether it was performed by the mistress of the house, her children, or a servant. What distinguished working-class homes was the need to rely on a wage to pay for many of these goods and services, as well as for shelter, education, and other expenses.

The tasks and aptitudes that went into this work were ones that married women could use to raise the standard of living of their husbands, children, and themselves. Most entered married life having helped their mothers on farms or in cities, or spent time as a domestic in the homes of others. They drew on skills learned, often applying them in new and changing circumstances. Daughters, widows, and wives in need of extra cash could also trade their skills for fees or wages if necessary. They might use them separately—cooking and selling meals, taking in washing, sewing dresses, or knitting. Or they might wield them in combination by taking in boarders or working as a general servant. But work in the home included more than cooking, cleaning, sewing, and the production of goods. Women's domestic labour involved services too—feeding babies, looking after children, caring for sick and elderly relatives, providing sexual satisfaction for husbands, and dealing with the disagreements and worries of old and young alike.[25] Most of these services could also become the basis of raising cash if necessary.

What was produced, rather than purchased, scrounged, bartered or, in some cases, stolen, depended on the amount of cash or credit available, on the abilities and values of housewives, and on the possibilities of making and saving money in particular neighbourhoods and towns. In the majority of working-class homes survival depended on some blend of production, exchange, purchase, and sometimes scrounging or theft. The relative weight and significance of these is virtually impossible to measure. The ways of getting by ranged from the purchase of all household needs—the assumption behind most analyses of the cost of living—to relative self-sufficiency in food and clothing.[26]

Working-class women's main source of help in their own daily work was their children. They taught their sons and daughters to perform domestic labour largely by demanding that they help with every kind of chore. Boys were expected to chop wood, carry coal, fetch water, and run errands. Girls learned cooking, sewing, cleaning, and nursing by doing them at their mothers' side. Children made work for mothers, and children worked for them. historian John Bullen wrote, 'At any hour of the day, youngsters could be found sweeping steps, washing windows, and scrubbing floors.'[27] Truant officers investigating children's absences from school found girls cleaning, babysitting, sewing, and caring for sick members of the family. Children of either sex might carry laundry 'to and from their homes while older siblings assisted with washing and ironing" or they might help change sheets, clean rooms, serve meals, and wash dishes, especially in homes with boarders. Mothers sent them out to find discarded coal, wood, fallen foodstuffs, and anything else that might be used in the home.[28]

Youngsters were particularly good at scrounging, that art of turning someone else's rubbish into useable items, although this particular skill was by no means limited to the young. The greater the discrimination that faced old and young alike for their sex, class or race, the greater likelihood they would have to turn to such means of getting by. Blacks living in St John's Ward in Toronto were referred to disparagingly by a local policeman as 'finders.' From his description, their methods sound particularly systematic. 'They sally out just at daybreak' and, dividing 'into squads slowly patrol Yonge, King and Queen streets on both sides.'[29]

Such activities shifted rather too easily into theft. The thin line was not necessarily clear to children, nor did it always matter to desperate parents. Respectability was not a luxury that everyone could afford to uphold. The theft of just a few sticks of firewood earned a young Toronto girl fourteen days in prison in 1859 because the magistrate considered 'pilfering wood' to be so common that punishment was necessary despite the 'pinching distress in the city.'[30] When Thomas and Mary Pool convinced a local magistrate in Barrie that their children had stolen clothes off a neighbour's clothes line only as a prank because they had quarrelled with the plaintiff's children, who knows what the truth was?[31] Street trades, prostitution, and theft offered children sources of economic independence that could strain their relations with their parents. But the money they helped earn or save could also enable a family to get by. As more and more were able to find jobs, the possibility of a better standard of living based partially on children's earnings increased for families with offspring of earning age.

Throughout the century the numerous attempts to get more and more children into school were intended in large part to prevent children from contributing to the family economy, especially in towns. Whereas rural children's contribution to farm work was generally accepted, 'working-class parents of absent children were periodically assailed by charges of criminal neglect and indifference […] The exigencies of working-class family life ran counter to nineteenth-century educators' instincts for punctuality, regularity, and permanence.'[32]

The compulsory education laws pitted the educators' desires against family needs. 'The compulsory education law is intended for the benefit of young children whose parents desire to obtain money for their services when they should be in school: who are willing to sacrifice the future advancement of their offspring for their own immediate gain,' wrote the Toronto inspector of schools in 1874.[33] Such laws could not eliminate such contributions to the family economy, as the truant officer quoted above discovered. Home responsibilities did not prevent children from enrolling in school; rather they 'precluded regular attendance at school.' setting up urban patterns of absenteeism different from the seasonal ones of agricultural areas. Children continued to stay home to cut wood, mind ill family members, and perform household tasks.[34] But from mid-century on, they also spent more time in school. Regulations regarding attendance were tightened, and growing numbers of parents sought better chances for their own children.

As keeping children home to help with the 'trivial' pursuits related to women's work at home came under growing public attack, women were more and more likely to perform their domestic tasks at home unaided by youngsters. At the same time their older sons in particular were more likely to find work. Yet the laws passed during the 1880s acknowledged the economic need of some families by allowing children 'employed in any manufactory' to attend school only half time.[35] Paid, formal labour

85

was thus legitimated, while helping a mother with household tasks was less acceptable.[36] As schooling and wage labour drew their sons and daughters out of the home, mothers spent more time working in the home alone with their babies and pre-school children.

[...]

Home-based Tasks: From Stretching Wages to Making Money

Food and Meals

The largest part of most nineteenth-century working-class family budgets was food. In the budgets collected by Young in 1873, food purchases took up about half of family incomes. Here was an area where a wife's abilities could have a real influence on her family's standard of living. Saving money on food might involve careful shopping, learning how to use the cheapest cuts of meat, seeking out bargains at market or at specific shops, raising food, or scrounging for it. Wives could also minimize expenditures by eating the cheapest foodstuffs themselves, saving the better food for the wage-earning members of the family.[37] While few working-class families could achieve self-sufficiency in food, many could avoid being totally dependent on the market by keeping a garden or a few animals. Families of all classes had a better chance of ensuring that their milk was pure, their meat healthy, and their vegetables fresh in the summer if they kept animals or a garden. [...]

Small towns usually offered more space for gardens and animal keeping than a city like Toronto. The 1871 census reports that residents of Thornhill to the north of Toronto harvested apples in great quantities. About half the urban households there produced butter; a few kept pigs.[38] In Hespeler, whose wage-earning residents, male and female, were mostly employed in the local woollen mill, some 30 per cent of the 151 families had pigs, and about 40 per cent had killed swine or sold them for slaughter or export. A third of the families also had milk cows. Just over one in ten local families were making their own butter, half grew potatoes and about a quarter grew apples.[39] [...]

Lorna McLean has uncovered relatively high rates of animal holding in Ottawa, where 'a wide variety of animals' were kept in 1871. Pigs were kept in back yards across the city, and in houses near to

unoccupied 'grazing' space by the river or railway yards. There too, working-class families of Irish or French-Canadian background were especially likely to keep pigs. She estimates that a '150 pound pig sold with a dressed weight of approximately 100 pounds could pay the rent for two to three months, or provide enough cash to purchase part of the winter's fuel.' Or it could provide 'bacon, ham, pork, and lard for the family'. [...]

As cities became more densely populated, pigs, goats, and other animals were increasingly viewed as undesirable. By the 1860s large towns like Toronto and even Brantford had regulations prohibiting 'horses, cows, cattle, goats, sheep, swine or geese' from running at large, as well as a complex system of fines and maintenance costs for the owners of errant animals.[40] Similar by-laws were passed during the 1870s in Ottawa.

Yet pigs, cows and the occasional goat continued to 'run the streets' of Ontario towns. In Ottawa they were reported to 'disturb neighbours' gardens,' and 'run wild' well into the 1870s, resulting in fines of one dollar for a pig owner and two dollars for a goat owner. [...]

Poultry was cheaper to keep and needed less room than either pigs or cows. As laws and lack of space curtailed the possibility of keeping larger animals, chickens remained a possibility. They had the added advantage of not wandering, and were often kept in basements. In Ottawa the local paper warned residents that this practice not only caused smells, but could spread disease. When poultry were first counted in the census in 1891, there were over 18,000 in Toronto, a significant member in a city with about 27,000 families.[41] Keeping hens could save the housekeeper the cost of eggs—some 12 to 20 cents a dozen in the early 1870s, 15 to 25 cents in the early eighties.[42]

Whether women bought or raised animals, vegetables or fruit, nineteenth-century cooking entailed considerably more preparation than it does today. Animals raised at home had to be butchered, skinned, and hung. Fowl had to be plucked and their innards removed. Home-grown and purchased vegetables alike had to be washed, and sugar, flour, barley, and other grains picked over carefully to remove impurities.[43] Only then could cooking begin. In poorer homes cooking was very simple, limited by the income of the family, the number of pots, and the space on the stove. An 'ordinary meal' consisted of meat and potatoes, bread, tea, sugar, and perhaps coffee. Bread was the basis of most working-class diets. Some wives made it; more bought it.[44] Increasingly bread was the one food most likely to be bought ready made. [...]

The technology of cooking and all other domestic labour remained rudimentary in working-class homes. While capitalism had introduced major changes to the machinery of production, the only significant changes in nineteenth-century homes were the replacement of fireplaces for cooking with cook stoves, the connection of growing numbers of households to the city water supply, and, for the middle-class families, the growing use of gas and electricity. The American historian Susan Strasser has shown what a full-time, labour-intensive, physically demanding job housework was for most married women during the nineteenth century. She argues that the advent of new fuels—first lighting oils, then, at the end of the century, electricity—together with the spread of running water, lightened women's tasks, changed the rhythms of work in the home, and created new kinds of dependency.[45] Ruth Schwartz Cowan has examined similar changes but argues, in contrast, that most nineteenth-century changes lightened men's and children's rather than women's labour and that women's work intensified as higher expectations about cleanliness and cooking prevailed.[46]

No Canadian research has examined what expectations were in working-class homes, or what technology existed. Neither electricity nor gas appears to have been installed in most working-class homes till after the turn of the century. Men in cities might chop firewood after work or on their days off and carry it in to the stove, but the long hours of their work made it likely, as Cowan suggests, that wives and children would have had to do so at times.

Fuel for heating and light used up about 10 per cent of the working people's budgets recorded by Young in 1873. Some economies could be made if families could afford to buy their wood and coal in bulk at cheaper times of year. Many, however, could not. When money was short, children were sent to scrounge for wood on construction sites or wharves, for wood shavings in mills, or for discarded lumps of coal and scraps of wood in back alleys and in rail and factory yards.[47] When every cent counted, such small economies made a difference. In the most

desperate cases, people burned anything they could to keep warm. When Bridget Clark, a thirty-year-old Toronto widow, applied for charity in the winter of 1867, she had burned an old bedstead for want of fuel.[48] [...]

Some poor families bought stoves second-hand, and in dwellings where several families lived together they might share the stove. A widow, Bridget Murphy, and a deserted wife, Johanna Canrahan, were using the same stove in their shared house at the rear of King Street when they applied for help from the House of Industry in 1867. That same year the wife of a policeman who had lost his job, probably for drinking, captured the pity of the visitor from the House of Industry by reporting how she had gone to her former mistress as she had no fuel to roast the piece of meat she had for their Christmas dinner.[49] [...]

Carrying water was as physically demanding as carrying wood or coal. "A 2-gallon (9-L) bucket of water weights about 16 lb (7.3kg),' quite a weight for a sick or pregnant woman obliged to lug it upstairs or across a muddy backyard.[50] The water that working-class wives used for cooking, washing, laundry, and cleaning came from a variety of sources. Evidence taken at the Royal Commission on the relations of Labour and Capital gives us glimpses of the provision of water in different Ontario towns. In Windsor, most households were connected to the municipal water system, which pumped water from the Detroit River, but a few wells were still in use. The local health officer was busily persuading the locals to switch to river water, although a few stuck to the 'idea that water from the river is scarcely good because it has not the old well flavour attached to it.' Given that the community upstream was sending its sewage into the river, their resistance was perhaps more rational than he implied! In Cornwall some houses still had not water laid on in the late 1880s. Paul Dane, a weaver at the Stormont cotton mill, reported that his family got their drinking water from a well and their washing water out of the canal. By hauling their own water they could save paying a man to bring it from the waterworks every month.[51]

In St Thomas there was no waterworks, 'except from the creek." Household water all came from wells, many of which were believed to be contaminated.[52] In 1888 the collector of information for the Bureau of Industries reported that the sanitary condition of St. Thomas was anything but satisfactory.

Diphtheria and typhoid fever have been prevalent, the former in most cases being attributable to poor ventilation in old dwelling houses with low ceilings, and kitchen garbage thrown out upon the ground undergoing decomposition for want of drains. Fully three-fourths of the well water is condemned by the public and the board of health.[53]

Little wonder the citizens greeted the installation of water-supply systems with 'civic celebrations and rhapsodic editorials.'[54]

As the century advanced, women in the larger cities were more and more likely to live in houses connected to the civic water system. [...] Doucet and Weaver suggest that the families of labourers were the least likely to be served and acknowledge how difficult it could be for them to persuade their landlords to connect their dwellings to the main.[55]

Poor families were consistently those least likely to benefit from city water supplies.[56] The wives of poorly paid workers, of sick or unemployed men, and widows continued to rely on water from wells and cisterns, collecting it themselves or badgering their husbands and offspring to do so. Even when the house was connected to the water mains, most wives had only one tap, not always conveniently located. They still had to carry water to the stove to heat and to wherever the washing was done.

Nor was the carrying of tubs, pails, and basins of water finished once the washing or cleaning was done. Not only did many houses not have a water connection, but sewers were often rudimentary. Women continued to heave water out windows and dispose of their slops in the easiest ways possible, to the great and justified concern of health reformers and passers-by alike. [...] The rudimentary state of sewers, often little more than open gutters or ditches, compounded the sanitary problems, especially in the densely populated parts of the cities.

Washing, Cleaning, and Charring

The need to carry water, the weight of wet clothes, and the physical labour required to wring them out and hang them to dry made washing the most hated of nineteenth-century household tasks. In summer firing up the stove to boil water overheated the houses, while in winter fingers froze in the icy rinsing water. Susan Strasser describes the work involved:

Without running water, gas, or electricity, even the most simplified hand laundry process consumed staggering amounts of time and labor. One wash, one boiling, and one rinse used about fifty gallons of water—or four hundred pounds—which had to be moved from pump or well or faucet to stove and tub, in buckets and wash boilers that might weight as much as forty or fifty pounds. Rubbing, wringing, and lifting water-laden clothes and linens ... wearied women's arms and wrists and exposed them to caustic substances.[57]

[...]

Hauling large containers of boiling water was heavy, and dangerous, as in the case of an Ottawa woman who scalded herself with boiling water while doing her housework.[58] [...] In small urban homes with little outside space, it was also a challenge to get the clothes dry. On wet winter days the washing was hung in front of fireplaces or around stoves, creating a fire hazard. Outside clothes-lines criss-crossed the backyards and alleys, draping parts of the city in washing that stands out clearly in nineteenth-century photographs.

For most working-class women the technology of washing was simple—a washing tub and a washboard powered by their own exertion. [...]

Washing took so much time, water, and energy that women tried to avoid it if they could. [...][59] Those able to pay for their laundry to be done were only too happy not to have this messy, wet, and lengthy task performed in their own homes. For those working-class wives whose family income had reached this level, hiring a washerwoman must have been a major time and energy saver.[60]

Many washerwomen were widows, wives of sick men, or deserted women often with several children too young to earn even a child's pittance. [...] The rewards were small and unpredictable, never furnishing even the most basic living unless combined with other income or ways of economizing. [...] Hard-pressed widows who scraped 'together a paltry existence by scrubbing floors and taking in washing' were among those most likely to have to turn to charities like the Toronto House of Industry for food and fuel. Some washed in their own homes; more, perhaps lacking even the basics for washing, went 'out to wash and scrub.'[61] They tended to cluster together, sharing housing, child care, and poverty in poorer parts of the cities, which, like lower St. John's Ward, were not too far from wealthier homes where they might find work. [...]

Sewing and Knitting for Family and Pay

Like cleaning and washing, the skills involved in fabric making and transformation—knitting, sewing, mending, and in some cases spinning or weaving, were among the ones that women drew on for their own families and to raise money when necessary. Most women could sew at least well enough to mend clothes and make dresses, one of the last kinds of clothing to be available ready-made. Since clothing was a flexible expense, a wife's abilities could make major savings. In the budgets of 1873 outlined in Table 1, shoes and clothing absorbed somewhere between 12 and 16 per cent of expenditures. Ready-made men's clothing dropped in price in the later decades of the century as more and more was produced in factories, but new clothes were a luxury, bought infrequently and in good times only. Most women's clothes were home-made well into the twentieth century, so the cost of much women's and children's clothing was in the cloth. Women mended and remade their own clothes and those of their children.

Among working-class families it appears to have been increasingly rare for women to spin or weave at home.[62] Cloth could be bought at reasonable prices, daughters working in textile mills might bring small amounts home, and neighbours could exchange scraps. Knitting, in contrast, for those who could get wool, provided cheap socks, sweaters, gloves, and other winter clothing, or could be done to raise money.[63] [...]

Sewing was the skill most likely to enable a woman to add to the family's revenues.

Across the province, in villages, small towns, and big cities women found numerous different ways to use their sewing to complement the wages of others, to tide them over in bad times, or to support themselves and their children. Some women whose husbands were unemployed or sick or had deserted them or died set up independently in their own homes as dressmakers, sewing for neighbours in exchange for other goods or services, or for customers for cash. Others no doubt found work at small local enterprises, relying on word of mouth, personal contacts, or advertisements in the papers. Until after the turn of the century, women's clothing continued to be custom-made by skilled seamstresses working from their homes or small shops. This practice provided employment possibilities for many women.[64] As the century advanced, more women sewed at home for factory owners who put out men's clothing and paid by the piece.

Sewing for cash thus took place in many different ways, some organized by the women themselves, others by industrial capitalists. Some women were skilled workers who made complete garments; others only completed work begun elsewhere. In the 1860s in Glencairn, a small lumber-milling village in the midst of Simcoe County farming country, the local shoemaker's wife, for example, earned 30 cents for 'facing mitts' and a further $1.40 for making 'pants and a vest.'[65] [...] An Ottawa woman, possibly short of money after Christmas or, more likely having trouble balancing the budget when costs were highest and income invariably low, advertised in the local paper for 'employment in sewing. Would either sew at residence of employer or take sewing home to do.'[66]

Sewing, like washing or knitting, could be done at home. That made it desirable for women who were sick or weak or had children to supervise. Thus Elizabeth Waters of Pine Street in Toronto started 'taking in sewing for a living' after her 'health became bad' and she could no longer go out to service. Mrs Clark's history was similar. This widow, who was looking after her two children and her seventy-six-year-old mother, 'used to go out to scrub and wash,' but she had hurt her leg and could 'only sew.' [...]

Growing numbers of women, helped often by their children, found employment sewing at home on work put out by clothiers. In 1868 the *Globe* described whole families in Toronto that worked at home making some of the coarser descriptions of men's garments for the ready-made clothing market:

> Often, in such instances, the child of eight or nine summers is made a source of material help … In the same way the female head of the house, a group of daughters, and perhaps, the male members of the family if no better occupation is available, turn in to assist the father in adding to their means of support.[67]

Nearly thirty years later A.W. Wright still found that the women he visited in their homes were helped by children 'of very tender years.' The women and children worked irregularly, but for many more hours than allowed by the factory acts, which did not cover such workplaces.[68]

Homework was widespread. In Hamilton at William Sanford's enterprise, only about 10 per cent of the workers were employed within the factory in 1874. Some two thousand women worked outside.[69] Alexander Whyte Wright's 1896 'Report upon the Sweating System in Canada' gives some idea of the conditions of this kind of home work at the close of the century. He set out to determine the extent to which manufacturers were giving 'out work directly to people who make them up in their own homes,' giving it out to subcontractors, or having work done within their factories.[70] He found a mixture of all three, with the proportions varying in different towns:

> In Hamilton … the greater part of the work is done by contractors and the balance by people who work at home. In Toronto the same system prevails, though in that city the proportion of work done in private houses is greater. In Ottawa, Montreal and Quebec the contract system scarcely exists … the greater part of the work is done by families in their homes.[71]

When Mackenzie King investigated how uniforms for the military and postal workers were being made two years later, he found a similar situation.[72] In 1901 when a question about the number of homeworkers was first included in the census, some 7,500 women across Ontario were working in their homes manufacturing for the garment industry.[73]

It was cheaper for capitalists to pay women to work outside the factory stitching together parts of garments that had been cut out by the more highly paid male workers under the factory roof.[74] There were no rents to pay, and the huge pool of females seeking work in their homes guaranteed that wages could be kept down and that they were unlikely to organize. [...]

Women working at home for clothing manufacturers used whatever space was available for their sewing machines and bundles of clothing, frequently setting up in their bedrooms or living rooms. [...] They never made a whole garment. They sewed together the parts and returned them to the contractor or factory. From the 1860s on they were expected to do their sewing on a sewing machine, and these were vigorously promoted by manufacturing companies, which arranged credit financing as well as repossession in cases of non-payment.[75]

The money women received varied, but it was always very little. The clothing-trades employers had no compunction about exploiting them both as female workers and as women working at home. Their pay was by the piece, and only by sustained labour, by working 'their nails bare' could they make even minimal earnings. Production was seasonal, characterized by dull seasons when little work was available.[76] Women sewing for an Ottawa dry goods firm that put out all its work in the late 1880s received 65 cents for a coat and $1.50 for a dozen shirts without collars, $1.80 with. The employer, Mr. Charles Bryson, like so many other employers in the garment industry, had no idea how long it took a woman to make a coat. And, like other clothing contractors, he rationalized their exploitation by maintaining that the women sewed in their spare time, sitting down to the work 'any time they … got to themselves.'[77] They did not. In 1868 the *Globe* reporter estimated that the mothers and daughters he visited were working '16 to 18 hours steadily for six days a week.'[78] Mackenzie King found women working similar hours in 1898.[79] [...]

The great advantage of homework for these women was, of course, that they could combine it with child care and housework. Mothers called on children of all ages to help while also keeping an eye on younger ones. For, as Jean Thompson Scott remarked in her study *The Conditions of Female Labour in Ontario*, published in 1892,

> Women whose husbands are dead or are not able to support them, will not go out as long as they have children at home to care for, but prefer if they can, to engage in some work which will keep them at home … In many cases they take in sewing or dressmaking, and do tailoring for the wholesale trade at their homes.[80]

Youngsters helped with sewing. They also went to the factory to collect the bundles of clothing and to return the completed garments. Without this 'cheap or free labour of children,' argues John

Bullen, 'families would have gained virtually nothing for their efforts.'[81]

Clothing was the main but not the only industry where homework occurred. In almost any trade that entailed sewing, some work seems to have been put out during the 1850s and sixties. The *Globe* reported in 1868 that women who had built up their skill in the millinery and fur trades before their marriage occupied 'an idle hour at the fireside in the winter time stitching [to] augment their husbands' salary [...] to the extent of six or seven dollars a week.' Women working at home in this trade were reported to be mostly sewing buffalo robes.[82] In Ottawa and Hull during the early 1860s some '20 or 30 families' were employed at home making paper boxes for the Eddy Company. [...]

Women who combined sewing at home, washing for others, or charring by the day with the cooking, washing, cleaning, and child care they performed for their own families did not work what we would recognize today as a double day. The labour for their own families and that performed for others were sometimes combined, sometimes separate. Some took place in their own homes, some in the houses of others. Their work for others seldom took up a specific part of the day and their own labour another. Rarely did their money-generating efforts fill up such a chunk of their day that it was reported to census takers or enumerators for city directories Usually it was not wage-earning, but payment or services rendered—with no fixed rate and no guarantee that it would continue. It was so like their own housework that it has faded from most historical records.

Taking In Boarders

For many women attempting to add to their family income, it could be more profitable to draw on their skills in combination by taking in a boarder or two than attempt to sell them separately by sewing, cooking, cleaning or washing. Recently arrived male and female immigrants, unmarried labourers seeking work in single-enterprise towns, young people new to the city and seeking work often had neither a mother nor a wife to feed, clothe, and care for them. This need for room and board opened up possibilities to many women seeking extra cash.
[...]

Boarding arrangements varied. Some families took one or two extra people into their homes. Other women, sometimes widows or deserted wives, set up more formal boarding or lodging houses, ranging from cheap and often dirty lodging houses to clean, well-furnished rooms with baths and toilet facilities. Such institutions were distinguished by the clientele they aimed at and the comfort they could offer. According to C.S. Clark, lodgers were lucky to have a sheet on their bed in some. 'Double, triple and even quadruple beds' were stuffed into 'single rooms and closets.' Flimsy partitions between rooms hid neither snores nor conversations.[83]

Boarders were a mixed blessing. Taking them in usually involved cooking their meals as well as providing sleeping space and bedding. Lodgers who simply rented a room, eating their meals elsewhere, seem to have become common only at the end of the century.[84] Providing bed and board meant extra cooking, cleaning, washing, and even sewing for the housewife and the children. 'Family run boarding houses daily called on children to change sheets, clean rooms, serve meals and wash dishes. Some homes took in extra customers, or 'mealers,' at the dinner hour, often resulting in several sittings a day.'[85] Many working-class houses simply didn't have the extra labour power, the space, or the money to pay for bed linen.

Furthermore, boarders could be demanding about what they were fed, occasionally creating such a disturbance that they ended up in court.[86] Two male boarders in Ottawa in 1866 experienced the full force of their landlady's wrath when they complained about the quality of the 'grub' she provided. They tried to take her to court, but the case was dismissed.[87] Nor could boarders always be relied on to pay their board, behave respectably, or leave without some of their landlord's possessions. [...]

Providing, exchanging, and selling services

Work in the home involved much more than the production or purchase of food, its transformation into meals, and sewing, washing, and cleaning. Most women who married had children who required care as infants, socialization, and some supervision. Husbands expected attention and sexual satisfaction. All family members were liable to fall sick frequently, especially in the crowded, poor dwellings of the lower levels of the urban working class. Elderly parents, even lodgers, might have to be cared for because they were either sick or simply old and frail. These services were fitted into a woman's daily routine, sometimes upsetting it completely, at others involving little mental or physical energy.

Like sewing, washing, or taking in boarders, these services could also be a source of extra money if necessary. Daughters or mothers might sell their bodies—regularly to make ends meet or occasionally in desperation or to pay for special treats. Women sometimes combined prostitution with selling alcohol illegally from their homes—another way of raising money at home, but prostitutes were most often single girls. Younger girls worked and lived together, often under the control and shelter of a madam, in a brothel that was both workplace and home. They appear to have moved frequently, sometimes to other established brothels, sometimes setting up more cooperative arrangements with other prostitutes. Older women were more likely to work the streets.[88]

Prostitution was not the only way women could use their bodies to earn needed cash. Women with an adequate supply of milk might make money feeding other people's children or deserted babies. Formal advertisements for wet-nurses seem pretty rare, but there are enough in newspapers of the 1850s and 1860s to make it clear that this was a fairly widespread practice.[89] [...] Wet-nursing was likely to be a temporary occupation, governed by the capacity of women's bodies.

Married women, widows, and young girls alike, in contrast, could look after other people's offspring. Young girls seeking to help the family finances were in demand to look after children. Advertisements specified the qualities desired—'clean and careful girl' wanted 'to take charge of baby,' 'nurse to take charge of children,' or '13-14 year old girl as nanny.'[90] Older sisters cared for younger siblings. Mothers kept an eye on the children of others going out to work. [...]

Conclusion

The growth of industry in nineteenth-century Ontario transformed, but did not eliminate, the importance of the home as a workplace. The household remained the principal workplace, although there were changes in who worked there and the work they did. In the first half of the century farmers, artisans, professionals, and early industrial capitalists worked essentially out of their homes. Apprentices, domestics, and some farm labourers worked and lived in the homes of others. Homes were the major base for the domestic production of foodstuffs and clothing—largely the work of women. They were also the base for the production of a wide variety of other commodities, ranging from coffins and candles to sausages and cheese, that might be in the work of either men or women. Housework continued to be the main occupation of the majority of the adult female population as well as of a large number of girls working in their own homes as well as in those of others.

Between 1850 and 1900 the varied employment undertaken in the home remained crucial to working-class survival, to the functioning of the labour market, and to the wider economy. Dependence on wages was seldom total. Women, helped by their children, and sometimes by the wage-earners too, found ways to produce and exchange goods and services that mitigated the dangers of relying entirely on wages.

The particular balance between purchase and production varied with the amount of wages earned, the life-cycle stage of the family, the local cost of food and rent, and the nature of the community in which working-class families lived. Overall, however, there were at least four changes in the second half of the century. Work in the home became increasingly female as more men, older sons, and some daughters were drawn into wage labour. Wage dependency increased as the possibilities of keeping animals and even gardens diminished and as people grew accustomed to goods like store-bought bread and manufactured men's clothing and aspired to a higher standard of living measured in part by store-bought furniture and kitchen utensils. As a corollary, the home production of food, clothing, and other goods diminished and the relative importance of good shopping and money management in the arsenal of a housewife's skills increased. Finally, by the last two decades of the century, male workers, especially those in organized skilled trades increasingly pushed for a wage that would support a whole family and began to talk in a way that at once celebrated women's role in the home but rendered their domestic labour less visible.

Despite these changes, the work done in homes across the province continued to be crucial to the survival and reproduction of the working class. Cash was not good to eat; wages had to be transformed into food, clothing, and shelter.[91] And they had to be stretched when money was low, work was irregular, or wage-earners were sick. As a result of lengthy strikes and long periods of unemployment or illness, some of the time working-class men and women had to continue to survive without wages. This could be done by wives' and daughters' drawing on housekeeping skills like washing, sewing, and cooking to earn cash. Mothers and sons and daughters could seek paid wage labour themselves. Or families could try to survive as much outside the cash economy as possible by scrounging, begging, or stealing food and clothing or by turning to charity. Thus, while working-class households as a whole were increasingly likely to buy rather than produce some of their basic foodstuffs, clothing, and household linen, there were fluctuating proportions of the working class that relied on home production, exchange, and various other non-wage means of survival. [...]

When wives could save money or make money by producing foodstuffs or other household needs themselves, they raised their family's standard of living. They also gave themselves some autonomy, a measure of independence from their reliance on the wages of others. For much of the century, that autonomy was limited by law. Even after the law was changed to give married women the right to keep their own property and wages separate from their husband's, the economy and wider society offered working-class wives little chance to accumulate much of either. The importance of their work sustaining and perpetuating their families and the working class kept most women close to home. They were increasingly dependent on the wages of others to perform their daily tasks, which society was less and less likely to view as work.

Notes

1. My ways of looking at what was going on in nineteenth-century Ontario homes are influenced by my study of Montreal during the same period. See Bettina Bradbury, *Working Families: Age, Gender and Daily Survival in Industrializing Montreal* (Toronto: McClelland and Stewart 1993). For a careful analysis of some of the concepts used in that study see Cynthia Coimacchio, 'Beneath the "Sentimental Veil": Families and Family History in Canada,' *Labour/Le Travail* 33 (Spring 1994), 279–302.

2. The writing to date has over-dichotomized the study of the family wage economy, ascribing wages largely to men and offspring, and domestic labour to wives. While work on women's labour has revealed the variety of means by which they stretched their husbands' wages, little attention in Canada, or elsewhere, has been paid to non-wage strategies that were more likely to be undertaken by men— hunting, fishing, producing a variety of goods for sale, etc. Even the question of men holding several occupations has received little attention.

3. On rural women see especially Marjorie Cohen, *Women's Work, Markets, and Economic Development in Nineteenth-Century Ontario* (Toronto: University of Toronto Press 1988); Eliane Leslau Silverman, *The Last Best West: Women on the Alberta Frontier, 1880–1930* (Montreal: Eden Press 1984); Rosemary Ball, '"A Perfect Farmer's Wife": Women in 19th Century Rural Ontario,' *Canada: An Historical Magazine* 3, no. 2 (December 1975).

4. RCRLC, 2045.

5. Bureau of Industries, 1888, 1889.

6. RCRLC, 1121.

7. Bureau of Industries, 1889, 28; Gagan and Gagan, 'Working Class Standards of Living'; Bureau of Industries, 1888, 42.

8. RCRLC, 1078, 1108, 679, 687, 866, 424.

9. See Bureau of Industries, 1887, 23, for an example which lists the number of workers employed by town in each range of days.

10. More research on how people managed during this great depression would be useful. See Debi Wells, '"The Hardest Lines of the Sternest School": Working-Class Ottawa and the Depression of the 1870's' (MA thesis, Canadian Studies, Carleton University 1982).

11. Toronto House of Industry, Annual Reports, 1873–82.

12. *Globe*, 3 February 1883, cited in David M. Sobel, 'Household Economies and Material Life: Family Survival in Southern Saint John's Ward, 1879–1885' (Major research paper, History, York University 1982), 48.

13. RCRLC, 147; Bureau of Industries, 1888, 132.

14. Katz, Doucet, and Stern, *The Social Organization*, 254. I look more explicitly at girls and domestic labour in

Bettina Bradbury, 'Gender at Work at Home,' in Bettina Bradbury, ed., *Canadian Family History: Selected Readings* (Toronto: Copp Clark Pitman 1992).

15. Bureau of Industries, 1887 Report, 38.

16. Katz, *The People of Hamilton*, 273–6; Katz et al., *the Social Organization*, 254–6, 312–19; see also my *Working Families*, 144–50.

17. RCRLC, 154–6.

18. Bureau of Industries, 2884, 33–41; See also Craig Heron in this volume.

19. Lorna McLean, 'Single Again: Widow's Work in the Urban Family Economy, Ottawa, 1871.' *Ontario History* 83, no. 2 (June 1991). We need to know more about how working-class families used life insurance during the nineteenth century and about the prevalence of work-based pension and insurance schemes.

20. Bureau of Industries, 1889, 10.

21. RCRLC, 159, 286, 592, 803, 618, 924, 969–70.

22. Jeanne Boydston, 'To Earn Her Daily Bread: Housework and Antebellum Working Class Substance,' *Radical History Review* 35 (1986), 9.

23. *Ontario Workman*, 14 August 1873, 3; my thanks to Chris Burr for this reference Boydston, 'To Earn Her Daily Bread,' 13-15. Her ideas are developed more subtly and at greater length in her *Home and Work: Housework, Wages and the Ideology of Labour in the Early Republic* (New York: Oxford University Press 1990).

24. R. Marvin McInnis, 'Women, Work and Childbearing: Ontario in the Second Half of the Nineteenth Century,' *Histoire sociale/Social History* 24, no. 48, 249.

25. My discussion here draws on Luxton, *More than a Labour of Love*, 18. See also Veronica Strong-Boag, 'Keeping House in God's Country: Canadian Women at Work in the Home,' in Craig Heron and Robert Storey, eds., *On the Job*, 125; Susan Strasser, *Never Done: A History of American Housework* (New York: Pantheon Books 1982), 6, 36–8 Ruth Schwartz Cowan, *More Work for Mother: The Ironies of Household Technology from the Open Hearth to the Microwave* (New York: Basic Books 1983).

26. The budgets produced by the Ontario Bureau of Industries, like Marx's theorization of the 'means of subsistence,' assume all household needs are purchased. Boydston, in 'To Earn Her Daily Bread,' 9, and *Home and Work*, xiii–xix, ably shows how the distinctive value of housewives' labour is largely unrecognized in traditional Marxist analyses.

27. John Bullen, 'Hidden Workers: Child Labour and the Family Economy in Late Nineteenth-Century Urban Ontario,' *Labour/Le Travail* 18 (1986), 166, reprinted in Bradbury, Canadian Family History.

28. Bullen, 'Hidden Workers," 174.

29. Quoted in David M. Sobel, 'Household Economies and Material Life: Family Survival in Southern Saint John's Ward, 1879–1885' (Major Research Paper, History, York University 1982), 13.

30. *Globe*, 7 March 1859.

31. Christine Stansell, *City of Women: Sex and Class in New York, 1789–1860* (Chicago and Urbana: University of Illness Press 1987), 203–7; *Barrie Northern Advance*, 22 June 1864.

32. 46. Susan E. Houston and Alison Prentice, *Schooling and Scholars in Nineteenth-Century Ontario* (Toronto: University of Toronto Press 1988), 98, 217–8.

33. Ontario, *Annual Report of the Normal, Model, High and Public Schools for the Year 1874*, quoted in Bullen, 'Children of the Industrial Age: Children, Work and Welfare in Late Nineteenth Century Ontario' (PhD dissertation History, University of Ottawa 1989), 340.

34. Houston and Prentice, *Schooling and Scholars*, 217–18; Bullen, 'Children of the Industrial Age,' 340, 326.

35. Ontario, *Statutes*, 1881, Chap. 30, quoted in Bullen, 'Children of the Industrial Age,' 342.

36. This discrepancy was partly remedied in 1891 when a new law allowed a child to be absent from school with permission from a justice of the peace or the principal if 'the services of such child are required in husbandry or urgent and necessary household duties, or for the necessary maintenance of such child or of some person dependent upon him.' Ontario, *Report of the Minister of Education for the year 1891* (Toronto 1891), 155, quoted in John Bullen, 'Children of the Industrial Age,' 345.

37. Laura Oren, 'The Welfare of Women in Labouring Families: England, 1860–1950,' in Mary S. Hartman and Lois Banner, eds, *Clio's Consciousness Raised: New Perspectives on the History of Women* (New York: Harper Colophon Books 1974).

38. MS Census, Thornhill, 1871.

39. MS Census, Hespeler, 1871.

40. By-laws regarding pound keepers and roving animals were passed in 1968 and amended in 1869, 1874, and 1876. These early amendments are found

in by-law 474, *Consolidated By-Laws of the City of Toronto* (Toronto 1876), 196–205.

41. Cohen, *Women's Work*, 166.

42. The families whose expenditures were surveyed in 1873 (Young, *Labour in Europe*) paid between 15 and 42 cents a week for eggs, with the exception of two reporting no expenditure. They may well have had their own chickens. For prices see Ontario, Department of Immigration Report, 1881, *Sessional Papers* (6), 1882, 41.

43. On cooking in the nineteenth century see Strasser, *Never Done*, 11–31; Cowan, *More Work for Mother*, 40–67; and Una Abrahamson, *God Bless Our Home: Domestic Life in Nineteenth Century Canada* (Canada: Burns and MacEachern 1966), 162–73. Purchased food was especially likely to be adulterated and contain impurities. Some discussion of this can be found in RCRLC, 96.

44. A Chatham labourer, William Partridge, pieced together a living digging out cellars, mixing mortar, carrying hods, or doing anything that came in handy. He reported that they sometimes bought bread and other times made it. He told the commissioners in 1888, 'We buy both [bread and flour]; sometimes we get two two-pound loaves for nine cents.' RCRLC, 461.

45. Strasser, *Never Done*.

46. Cowan, *More Work for Mother*, 66–8.

47. Bullen, 'Children of the Industrial Age,' 124.

48. Toronto House of Industry, 1867, case no. 5.

49. Toronto House of Industry, cases no. 687, 1881 and 418, 1880 quoted in Sobel, 63; cases no. 23 and 96–7, 1867.

50. Letty Anderson, 'Water Supply,' in Norman R. Ball, ed., *Building Canada: A History of Public Works* (Toronto: University of Toronto Press 1991), 196.

51. RCRLC, 385, Evidence of Dr. John Coventry, Medical Health Officer, Windsor; 1094–5, Evidence of Paul Dane, Cornwall, weaver.

52. RCRLC evidence of Dr. Hohn B. Tweedale, Physician to the Board of Health at St. Thomas, 501.

53. Bureau of Industries, 11.

54. Anderson, 'Water Supply,' 196.

55. Doucet and Weaver, *Housing*, 442.

56. G.P. deT. Glazebrook, *The Story of Toronto* (Toronto: University of Toronto Press 1971), 129; Sobel, 'Household Economies,' 25–6.

57. Strasser, *Never Done*, 105.

58. *Ottawa Citizen*, 24 July 1877.

59. Diary of W.A. Stephens, Wednesday, 16 March 1856, privately held. She paid 7s 6d board weekly.

60. See Stanislas Lortie, 'Compositeur typographe,' in Pierre Savard, *Paysons et ouvriers québécois d' autrefois*, 90, 106, 111.

61. James Pitsula, 'The Relief of Poverty in Toronto, 1880–1930' (PhD dissertation, History, York University 1970), 112; Toronto House of Industry, 1867, nos 28, 63, 102. When such women applying for help described what they did, going out 'washing and scrubbing' were invariably linked. Few of these really poor women appear to have taken in washing—perhaps because they lacked the facilities in their own houses to do large amounts of washing.

62. On the earlier nineteenth century around Montreal see David-Thiery Ruddel, 'Consumer Trends, Clothing, Textiles and Equipment,' and on rural families in eastern Ontario see Janine Roelens and Kris Inwood, '"Labouring at the Loom": A Case Study of Rural Manufacturing in Leeds County, Ontario, 1870,' *Canadian Papers in Rural History*, 7 (Gananoque, Ontario: Langdale Press 1990).

63. Traill underlined the importance of this skill for settlers in 1855: "There is no country where there is so much knitting-work done as in Canada.' She gave the example of a settler's young daughter who had provided for her clothing before her marriage with the fruits of her knitting. *The Canadian Settler's Guide*, 184.

64. See, for example, the reminiscences of M. Alberta Auger, reproduced in Beth Light and Joy Parr, eds, *Canadian Women on the Move, 1867–1920* (Toronto: New Hogtown Press and OISE 1983), who apprenticed in a woman's home in Salem, Ontario, early in the twentieth century.

65. M.N. Stephens, 'Journal no. 1,' 1869–70, Archives of Ontario, MU 6009. In such small local economies where formal exchange was largely organized through the account books of the general store, little cash actually changed hands. It is hard to know whether the women would ever have benefited individually from their efforts, for the money made was credited to their husband's accounts, as was to be expected at a time when economically and legally a wife's identity disappeared into that of her husband.

66. *Ottawa Citizen*, 28 December 1878.

67. *The Globe*, 28 October 1868.

68. 'Report upon the Sweating System in Canada,' Canada, *Sessional Papers* 61, 1896, 7–8, 11.

69. Canada, House of Commons, *Journals*, 1874, App. 3, 'Report of the Select Committee on the Manufacturing Interests of the Dominion', 22–4.

70. 'Report upon the Sweating System,' 1896, 3.

71. 'Report upon the Sweating System,' 1896, 5–6.

72. William Lyon Mackenzie King, *Report to the Honourable the Postmaster General on the Methods Adopted in Canada in the Carrying Out of Government Clothing Contracts* (Ottawa: 1900).

73. *Census of Canada*, 1901.

74. On the sweating system and the clothing trades in general in Canada see Michelle Payette-Daoust, 'The Montreal Garment Industry, 1871–1901' (MA thesis, History, McGill University 1986); Mercedes Steedman, 'Female Participation in the Canadian Clothing Industry, 1890–1940' (PhD dissertation, University of London 1990). [...]

75. Bradbury, *Working Families*, 139.

76. *The Globe*, 28 October 1868.

77. RCRLC, evidence of Charles Bryson, dry goods merchant, Ottawa, 1164. Similar quotations can be found in other evidence at the Royal Commission of 1888 as well as in all the investigations of industry undertaken during the nineteenth century.

78. *The Globe*, 28 October 1868.

79. William Lyon Mackenzie King, 'Report,' 12–14; *Globe*, 19 November 1898, 1.

80. Bullen, 'Children of the Industrial Age,' 25.

81. Bullen, 'Children of the Industrial Age,' 133.

82. *The Globe*, 28 October 1868, 1.

83. Boarding houses and brothels mixed at times—at least in the rhetoric of reformers. See Lori Rotenberg, 'The Wayward Worker: Toronto's Prostitute at the Turn of the Century,' in Action et al., *Women at Work: Ontario 1850–1930* (Toronto: Women's Educational Press 1974), 42–3. C.S. Clark describes the disgusting people one could meet and places one might find in Toronto at the end of the century in *Of Toronto the Good* (Montreal: The Toronto Publishing Company 1898; repr. Coles 1970).

84. Richard Harris suggests that in 1900 three-quarters of Toronto lodgers in private homes were boarders rather than roomers, though by the First World War roomers predominated. 'The End Justified the Means: Boarding and Rooming in a City of Homes, 1890–1951,' *Journal of Social History* 26, 2 (Winter 1992), 335–9.

85. Bullen, 'Children of the Industrial Age,' 134.

86. *Ottawa Citizen*, 15 January 1877.

87. *Ottawa Citizen*, 6 January 1866, 2. Lorna McLean found that four of the forty-six widows living in Bytown in 1871 and listing a job reported keeping a boarding house; 'Home, Yard and Neighbourhood,' 86.

88. Mariana Valverde, *The Age of Light, Soap, and Water: Moral Reform in English Canada, 1885–1925* (Toronto: McClelland and Stewart 1991), 82–3; Lori Rotenberg, 'The Wayward Worker,' 33–70; Constance Backhouse, 'Nineteenth Century Canadian Prostitution Law: Reflection of a Discriminatory Society,' *Histoire sociale/Social History*, 18 no. 36 (November 1985); Lorna McLean, 'Behind Bars: Women and the Criminal Justice System in Four Communities in Ontario, 1840–1881,' paper presented to the Canadian Historical Association, 1993; Clark, *Of Toronto the Good*, 86–136; Debra Clipperton, 'In Bad Company: Prostitution and Brothel Life in Toronto, 1871' (graduate paper, History, York University 1994).

89. *Ottawa Citizen*, 7 January 1854, 5 September 1873; *London Free Press*, 8 October, 19 December 1861; 28 June, 29 July 1862.

90. *Ottawa Citizen*, 26 May 1875; 12 January 1878, 4; 8 February 1878, 4.

91. Michael Merrill, 'Cash Is Good to Eat: Self-Sufficiency and Exchange in the Rural Economy of the United States,' *Radical History Review* 4 (Winter 1977).

IMMIGRATION IN THE LATE NINETEENTH AND EARLY TWENTIETH CENTURY CANADA

Lynne Marks
University of Victoria

IMMIGRATION IN THE LATE NINETEENTH AND EARLY TWENTIETH CENTURY CANADA

Introduction by Lynne Marks

99

● INTRODUCTION

Lynne Marks

When late–nineteenth century Canadian political leaders dreamed of greatness for Canada, they knew that there was one absolute precondition for such greatness—large-scale immigration. In the 1870s and 1880s Canada's population remained relatively small, at just over 4.3 million in 1881, and still under 5 million in 1891. Major population growth was necessary to increase Canada's visibility as a player in the British empire and beyond, but it was also an integral part of any plan of national economic growth, and it was most definitely a centrepiece of Sir John A. Macdonald's national policy, a policy intended to make Canada a great nation "from sea to sea." The newly acquired Northwest Territories could not live up to their destiny as part of an expanded Canadian nation if they were not settled, and settled soon, by a massive influx of new farmers. The original inhabitants of the land, the First Nations, had been forced to settle on reserves in the 1870s and 1880s, freeing the land for "true" settlement, by Euro-Canadian farmers, but such settlement was slow to develop. In order to ensure the success of new industries designed to be nurtured by the National Policy tariff, Canada's growing factories needed workers, and they also needed consumers for their goods, both in the cities and on the farms. If the Canadian Pacific Railway, another key piece of the national policy, was to be built to tie the country together both politically and economically, many railway construction workers were needed, workers who were willing to work for low wages, under dangerous conditions.

While immigration rates were low in the first three decades after Confederation, immigrants began to pour into Canada at a much faster rate in the post-1896 period. With the closing of the American frontier of free land, the Canadian prairies began to look more appealing to prospective immigrants, who were also encouraged by a major advertising campaign conducted in European countries by the federal government. Many immigrants also came to Canada's growing cities, or to work on the resource frontiers. Between 1896 and 1914 over 3 million immigrants arrived in Canada, with over 400,000 arriving in 1913 alone. Between the end of the First World War and 1930, almost 1.5 million more immigrants arrived.

Canadian political leaders were pleased to welcome more immigrants, but they did not want just anyone. In late–nineteenth century Canada, a very clear racial hierarchy existed, with white British Protestants at the top. More British immigrants were needed if Canada was to maintain its destiny as a British, Protestant nation. But not enough British immigrants were coming to Canada, and some of the working-class urban British immigrants who did come were in fact seen as less than desirable, particularly as Prairie farmers, despite the value placed on Britishness to Canadian identity. Another group of British immigrants were the over 80,000 poor children, either orphans or children with parents considered too poor to care for them, who were brought from Britain between 1880 and 1930. The idea was that by integrating them into Canadian families they would have a chance at a better life than in Britain, but the reality for most was that they served as unpaid drudges in Canadian homes and on farms and though British, were commonly looked down upon as "off-scourings of the slums."

So although British "stock" was the ideal, poor British immigrants often failed to live up to this ideal, causing Canadian leaders to look beyond Britain to find many of its new settlers. The next most "desirable" immigrants were those from other countries in northern and western Europe, who were seen to have similar qualities of morality, self-control, rationality, and a strong work ethic as those that English Canadians associated with the British ideal. Further down the racial hierarchy were the southern and eastern Europeans, such as the Russians, Ukrainians, and Italians. These peoples were seen as less "white" in the racial categories of the time than the British and other northern European peoples, and thus less desirable as immigrants. Nonetheless, eastern European peasants, in particular, were seen as potentially valuable prairie farmers, and Russians and Italians alike were seen as being at least potentially assimilable to English Canadian values and ways of life.

Other groups were less acceptable. The Jews, particularly the poorer eastern European Jews who began immigrating in large numbers in the 1880s, were even less desirable than their eastern European compatriots, both as non-Christians, and as primarily urban dwellers. Below the Jews on the racial hierarchy were those who could never aspire to being white. The largest groups of non-white immigrants of the late nineteenth and early twentieth centuries were the Chinese and Japanese, most of whom emigrated to British Columbia. While most white Canadians shared a common racism against Asians in this period, as you can see in the House of Commons debate on the *Chinese Exclusion Act* of 1923 (officially known as "An Act Respecting Chinese Immigration"); the oral history interviews with Margaret Chan, George Nitta, and Fred Soon; and Timothy Stanley's article, anti-Asian racism was particularly virulent in British Columbia. The Chinese were viewed as unfair competition, particularly by white workers, because they generally received lower wages than these workers. They were also viewed as "immoral" and as unassimilable.

At the same time, as historian Donald Avery noted a number of years ago, large Canadian employers, such as the CPR and the mining and lumbering companies, were much more concerned about acquiring large numbers of employees willing to work for low wages than they were about these employees race or religion. Such employers had enough clout with the federal government to ensure that their employment needs were met through government immigration policy. As a result, Chinese immigrants were brought to Canada during the building of the CPR, where their willingness to work for low wages, and to take on many of the dangerous tasks involved in building a railroad through the mountains, made them very appealing to employers. With the completion of the railway in 1885, the government became much more ready to heed white demands for limiting Chinese immigration. Thus in 1885 the federal government imposed the first head tax of $50, to be paid by each Chinese immigrant coming to Canada. Public pressure, particularly from British Columbia, led to the raising of this head tax to $100 in 1900 and $500 in 1903, and ultimately to the *Chinese Exclusion Act* of 1923, which legislated the exclusion of all Chinese immigrants other than those deemed to be merchants, diplomats, or foreign students. During the period that the act was in force, from 1923 to 1947, fewer than 50 Chinese people were allowed to enter Canada. Chinese Canadians also lost the right to vote in 1874, and did not regain it until 1947.

While the first historians to study Canada's history of racism toward Chinese immigrants focused on the exclusionary legislation of Canadian governments, and the racist actions of white employers, school boards, unions, and individuals, more recent scholarship has begun to see the Chinese not simply as passive victims, but also as active agents who spoke up strongly against the discriminatory treatment they faced. The article by Timothy Stanley is an example of this more recent work, which demonstrates how Chinese students in Victoria, and their community, protested strongly against the racist segregation imposed by the local school board.

Other immigrant groups from Asia, particularly the Japanese and the Sikhs, also faced significant racism and exclusionary legislation, although such legislation took different forms, because of the nature of the relationships between the Canadian government and India and Japan.

While Asian immigrants faced the most virulent racism, other groups, such as the Italians, eastern Europeans, and Jews, also faced racist attitudes. Italians and eastern Europeans were relegated to the dirtiest and most dangerous jobs in many of their workplaces, while Jews were informally barred from many clerical and professional positions. Canada also allowed only tiny numbers of Jews into Canada in the 1930s and early 1940s, at a time when Jews were desperate to escape Europe.

While many historians have studied the racism of Canadian society toward various immigrant groups, other historians have focused on the motives of the immigrants themselves. Why did so many immigrants come to Canada, given the racism of Canadian society at this time? Economic motives were a primary factor for many immigrants. Economic conditions in their home countries could be extremely dire, with hunger or imminent starvation driving people to immigrate to try to improve their situations and those of their families. In many other cases, the subdivision of arable land in one's home country over the generations had led to landlessness, or to peasants farming tiny pieces of land that were too small to sustain families. Many of those facing such prospects in their home countries were eager to take up the Canadian government's offer of free land for homesteading on the Canadian prairies. Like Veronia Kokotailo's family described here, they did not find an instant paradise on the prairies. The government provided no assistance to most new settlers, and life could be very hard indeed, with food often scarce and shelter rudimentary in the early years, and with men having to leave for several months a year to earn much-needed cash. While Veronia's family ultimately survived and even prospered, many would-be homesteaders found the prospect of carving a farm out of the prairies to be an impossible task, and gave up their homesteads.

Many others who left their home countries to improve their economic prospects in Canada did not see themselves as permanent immigrants. These "sojourners," as immigration historians have termed them, were primarily male workers who planned to travel to Canada for a summer, or for a year or two, to make enough money to assist their families back in the home country, and ideally to be able to buy more land at home. As historians have recently noted, such sojourners had a very transnational perspective, not simply in travelling between Canada and their home country, but often travelling between a number of countries, including the United States and Australia, in search of well-paying work. Robert Harney's article shows clearly some of the difficulties facing Italian sojourners, both in the harsh conditions they faced in Canadian work camps and cities, and in the tensions their absence could create for wives and other members of their families in Italy. Other immigrant groups also tended to be more likely to be sojourners than permanent settlers, including many Chinese and Japanese. As the John Madokoro oral history interview demonstrates, some who planned to return home changed their minds, particularly if they were able to bring their wives over, and remained as permanent settlers. Immigration restrictions made it very difficult for Chinese workers to bring over their wives and other family members, so most Chinese communities were made up primarily of single men, or men whose wives remained in China. The Stanley article demonstrates that some wealthier Chinese did have their families in Canada, where their children faced significant racism in B.C. schools.

While economic reasons played a major role in the decisions of many to immigrate, others came to avoid persecution in their home countries. This was certainly true of most Jewish immigrants from the 1880s on, who left Eastern Europe to avoid the increasingly powerful discriminatory laws they faced within the Russian empire, as well as the rising tide of pogroms, or massacres of Jews, by members of the local population. Those immigrating to avoid persecution saw themselves as permanent settlers, although in many cases husbands and fathers would emigrate first, and send for the rest of their families as soon as they had earned enough money to pay for the tickets.

Once in Canada, most immigrants sought to learn English and Canadian ways. At the same time, most communities continued to value their own culture and religion and developed various institutions to maintain them. Many communities developed after-school programs that taught their children the languages and sometimes the religion of their home cultures. Stanley's article and the oral history interviews with Tommy Kimoto and Myer Freedman demonstrate that this was common in the Chinese, Japanese, and Jewish communities, but many other ethnic communities also developed such schools. In this way, long before the development of official multicultural policy, children, many of whom faced racism in the Canadian context, could learn pride in their ethnic, religious, and racial heritages.

QUESTIONS

1. What were some of the different motives of immigrants in coming to Canada? Can you identify these motives in various oral history interviews and in the three articles?
2. What arguments were put forward for and against Chinese immigration in the 1923 House of Commons debates? In what ways do J.S. Woodsworth's ideas reflect those we hold today? In what ways do they seem to fit more with the values of 1923?
3. Robert Harney suggests that the experience of sojourning was a negative one for Italian men. Why? Do you agree with his analysis? Why or why not?
4. George Nitta, one of the oral history interviewees, suggested that racism became less acceptable in Canadian society following the Second World War. Why do you think this may have been true?
5. In what ways are our attitudes toward immigration today similar to or different from those of the late-nineteenth and early-twentieth centuries?
6. Can we talk about immigration as a gendered experience (i.e., being different for men and women)? How might the documents and articles be used to demonstrate this?

FURTHER READINGS

Irving Abella and Harold Troper, *None is Too Many: Canada and the Jews of Europe, 1933–1948* (Toronto, Lester. 1991).

Kay Anderson, *Vancouver's Chinatown: Racial Discourse in Canada, 1875–1980* (Montreal and Kingston: McGill-Queen's University Press, 1995).

Donald Avery, *"Dangerous Foreigners": European Immigrant Workers and Labour Radicalism in Canada, 1896–1932* (Toronto: McClelland and Stewart, 1979).

Marlene Epp, Franca Iacovetta, and Frances Swyripa, eds., *Sisters or Strangers?: Immigrant, Ethnic, and Racialized Women in Canadian History* (Toronto: University of Toronto Press, 2004).

Franca Iacovetta, ed., with Paula Draper and Robert Ventresca, *A Nation of Immigrants: Women, Workers, and Communities in Canadian History, 1840s–1960s* (Toronto: University of Toronto Press, 1998).

Joy Parr, *Labouring Children: British Immigrant Apprentices to Canada, 1869–1924* (London: Croom Helm, 1980).

Patricia Roy, *A White Man's Province: British Columbia Politicians and Chinese and Japanese Immigrants, 1858–1914* (Vancouver: UBC Press, 1989).

103

▲ Document 1: Immigrant Boy Ploughing Farm, c. 1900

● Immigrant boy ploughing at Dr. Barnardo's Industrial Farm, c. 1900. This boy would be one of over 80,000 poor British children sent to Canada between 1880 and 1930. Canadians at that time might 'read' the photo as showing how the children were prepared for their work on Canadian farms. How would we read it today?

Source: Library and Archives Canada, PA 117285

▲ Document 2: Interview with Margaret Chan

Margaret was born in southern China around 1902. She was in her mid-eighties and living in Vancouver at the time of her interview for this book.

Her story is historically significant because she immigrated in 1910—a time when very few Chinese women came to Canada because of the racist Canadian Head Tax and the traditional Confucian views of the role of women. The "relatives" who sponsored her were probably very wealthy, since they had to pay $500 for her to come to Canada.

Margaret was one of the first Chinese girls to go through public school in Victoria. She spoke about having to go abroad to teach because of racist policies that prevented her from teaching in Canada. [...]

My father was a gambler and he smoked opium too. He was not able to support his two daughters. So he gave me away. I became the adopted daughter of my relatives. My relatives brought me over to Canada when I was eight years old. They didn't treat me good, so I ran away. Treat me like a slave girl! I had to work and got no food. My aunty was not good to me—always beat me, made me do all the work. My uncle was good. My aunty's so cruel. She didn't have time to teach me anything—my aunty was sick with asthma. Finally, they were going back to China, and they going to sell me to some people with a lot of children—so I run away to the Oriental Home. I was thirteen and a half, maybe fourteen.

The Oriental Home was run by the Women's Missionary Society in Victoria. They saw the plight of the women in those days—under great suffering. That place could house forty-five people. Some of them were Japanese women deserted by their terrible husbands. So we all run to this home. It's called the Oriental Home—got Japanese and Chinese. It's like an orphanage I, Margaret, was one of their occupants, and they helped me out immensely. We went to church three times a day then.

I went to school. I like learning things. I had to write the English exam three times to get my grade eleven.[...] My schoolteacher, Miss Martin, was my best friend. I got a few friends—they're nice to me. You got to have friends to survive.[...]

After I finished grade eleven, I went to Vancouver to work in a fruit store, as a clerk, for about a year. Well, we worked hard—cold! Then we were half-starved.[...] But we worked *very* hard. Never got-money, and cold—worked overtime too.

Then I went back to Victoria to go to normal school (formerly a school for high school graduates preparing to be teachers). I worked very hard to reach my ambitions. I was the only Chinese girl among many girls and boys. I worked very hard with the help of the teacher in the Oriental Home, Miss Martin. She helped me with my preparation for my teaching course.[...]

After I finished normal school, I went back to work in a fruit store again. They paid $12 a week. No, that was not good! I borrowed $50 from Miss Martin, and went back to Hong Kong to try and get a teaching job. In those days in Canada, they discriminate against us Chinese. They don't give us a chance to teach here. I got my teacher's diploma, but they wouldn't give me a licence in Victoria, British Columbia.

I taught in Hong Kong, but then they didn't pay me enough. So when opportunity came along, I took a chance and went to Dutch East Indies (Indonesia). I taught in a

Source: *Jin Guo: Voices of Chinese Canadian Women*, The Women's Book Committee, Chinese Canadian National Council (Women's Press, 1992), 27–29.

105

multimillionaire's home, as a governess. I taught seven grandchildren and the millionaire's daughter. I was very lonely. They didn't pay me too much, so I went back to Hong Kong and taught in a village.[…]

I returned to Canada on the boat, *Empress of Hong Kong,* in 1934. Depression time was really bad. I worked in a fruit store again. I lived in a place where the landlady was my matchmaker. She asked, "How come you didn't get married?" She introduced me to my husband who wanted a wife without having to pay.[…] He tried to kid me. But I was foolish enough to marry him, thinking he never was married. He was older than me by five, six years. He was a cheater, fooled me because I was by myself—had no family here. When I married him, I was a working girl. I got some money. I sent $300 Canadian back to the village to his mother because I married her son.

I got married in 1935 in North Bay. We moved from place to place. When his cousin went to China, my husband took his job in Timmins. He worked as a housecook. I worked as a housemaid. So have to go wherever he goes.[…]

▲ Document 3: Interview with Japanese Canadians Who Settled in the Clayoquot Sound Area, B.C.

JOHN MADOKORO: Most of the first generation didn't come here to live, they came here to make money. There was no work in Japan. The fishing was poor and the farming was poor, so they would come to Canada to make a bundle and go back. At that time Canadian money was worth a lot. If you had a hundred Canadian dollars, boy oh boy. My father went back to Japan to marry, but then he bought an acre of property here and built a nice house in Tofino and then he never talked about going back.

HAROLD KIMOTO: Between Tofino and Clayoquot there were about 30 families. We all settled here in the spring or fall of 1923. We were like the pioneers, the first Japanese group. Maybe some Japanese were just here to work and then go back to Japan, but Dad and Mum couldn't afford to go back. We had ten children, at least until one drowned.

TOMMY KIMOTO: I was born in 1915, pretty near pension age now. I was six or seven when we moved up to Clayoquot. We went up in dad's fishboat. I was seasick most of the way up.[…]

I guess you could say the place on Clayoquot was more or less a shack, but it was nice there. We used to grow Japanese vegetables and things.[…]

The wife of the secretary of our fishing co-op used to teach Japanese. We used to study out of a Japanese textbook, just enough so we could keep talking to our parents. It was tough on kids you know, five or six hours of school and then three hours of Japanese school.[…]

JOHN MADOKORO: I was the first Jap boy to go to school. We all went, myself, my sister, my brother. We didn't have a hard time. We got along good with the boys. I would fight, you see, and they were scared of me.

Source: *Settling Clayoquot,* BC Sound Heritage Series, BC Archives, No. 33, p. 51. Reprinted with permission from Bob Bossin.

▲ Document 4: Interview with Mrs. Wappel

The transcription captures a fragment of the reminiscences of a woman who came to Canada from Central Europe as a child in 1931. The reader should understand that despite the cheerful tone of Mrs. Wappel's account, she and her family, like most immigrants, experienced many difficulties both before emigrating and upon arriving in Canada. They lived as Hungarians in a territory ceded to Roumania after World War I. The decision to emigrate led to a lengthy separation from her father—first when he went ahead to Canada looking for work, and later when he had to leave Montreal to find work in Toronto. Finally, her account of the warmth and happiness of a household of nineteen Hungarians living as "one big family" should give pause to those who measure immigrant well-being in terms of achieving single family dwellings without boarders or multi-generational families.

Mrs. Wappel is talking about Toronto in the 1930s.

[Sharing houses, as described below, with each family having a separate room and cooking facilities, was one common way for immigrants to manage on small incomes. Another way was to open a boarding house, as mentioned in the Harney piece, Article 2, in which the wife and daughters of the house provided food and laundry services for the boarders, usually from their own ethnic group, who rented rooms in their home.]

MRS. WAPPEL: With your permission, I would like to tell you about this house that we moved into. It was at 102 Darcy St. The reason I think it's fascinating is because I think back how on earth 19 people could live in a two-storey house, in harmony, relative harmony. One bathroom, literally one bathroom, one tub. And today people are complaining if they only have two bathrooms in a family. So it shows that when you must make do, you can.

So, this particular house [...] I must describe it room by room I think. Downstairs, the so-called living-room was occupied by the owner of the house, a Mr. G. Gruber, who worked at Canada Goodyear [...] right. He was a mechanic, and a very good one, and he had a steady job. And he was sort of [...] every one-held him in awe, because he bought this house. Now this house was *the* house. Now, everyone said "Oh! if he ever is unable to make the payments he'll loose [sic] everything." So for this reason he rented every nook and cranny that he could. And as I said, downstairs, in the so-called living-room, he and his wife and their 13-year old son [...] there was a double bed and a single bed for the boy, and I don't know, not much else, because it wasn't used as a living-room. It was the bedroom.

And the very next room—I don't know what that would have been, I guess maybe just an extra bedroom—lived two old maids, whom I adored. They were, I would say, in their late fifties, or early sixties. But when you are fourteen, anybody over thirty-five is an old maid. But the Misses Faluba fascinated me. They worked in a factory on fur coats. They used to do the finishing for fur coats. These two ladies were very tiny, petite ladies, and some of these coats were huge, and it must have been very, very hard work. I remember they used to be very tired when they would come home. Their great passion was playing cards. They loved playing cards. And I think even bigger than that, their passion was for

Source: From the Oral History Sources Collection, *Polyphony: The Bulletin of the Multicultural History Society of Ontario,* Fall/Winter 1977, 26–29. Reprinted with permission from the Multicultural History Society of Ontario.

107

the past. And they used to regale me with stories of when they were debutantes back in the old country, and the handsome hussars who danced with them. [...] The next room was the dining room, which was a large room. I remember we had a piano, a grand piano. I don't know why we had a grand piano, but we brought it from Montreal. We lived upstairs in this house, and there was no room in our room, so our grand piano was put into the dining room downstairs. Now in the dining room, there was a bed, in which the grand-mother slept—Mr. Gruber's mother, who was in her middle fifties—and an adult son, who slept on a couch in that same dining room.

Beyond that was the kitchen, with one sink and gas stove. And beyond that was a so-called summer kitchen, in which there were 2 beds, where the youngest boys, the younger brothers of Mr. Gruber slept. Now Johnny was 17 and Steve was 19. Johnny was going to school, yet Steve was working. He used to go by bicycle, I remember, on Carlaw somewhere, in a doll factory. And he was working with paints, and he was allergic to these paints, and often his hands were just a mass of eruptions, because of the allergy I suppose. But that certainly would not have been a serious enough reason to leave your job, simply because your hand was raw. And I suppose he wore gloves when he worked.

So these were the people downstairs; three in the front room, two in the next, that's five, the grandmother and the adult son, that's seven, the two younger sons—nine. These were the people downstairs.

Now upstairs in the small front room lived a Mr. Kovacs who fascinated me because he was a vegetarian.[...]

Now the next room was occupied by the Suto family. These were our *komas*—our [...], my mother and father were the godparents of one of their children, who originally found the job for my father. Now they had the front room, which was their bedroom. They had a double bed and two beds, two small beds, for the two smaller children, and they had a little kitchen in the back, so that was [...] they had a kitchen and a room.

The next room was ours. Ah, there was one bed in it, which was mine, and my mother sewed there. There was a large dining sort of table and mother's sewing machine, and this was where I slept, and this is where she sewed and this is where the ladies came to try on the dresses. And we had a kitchen too. Now in the kitchen they had a double bed, where my father and mother slept.

And finally there was the last room where Mr. Eckhart was. He was a fascinating man, because he was a junk man. (Now these are all Hungarians.) He used to get up at two o'clock in the morning, and [...] with a push cart, and he would go to [...] one of the wealthy districts. [...] And he would pick up things in the garages that were left out for the garbage people, or simply go through some of the garbage. And by morning he would have this two-wheeled hand cart piled up to as high as it would go, and he would pull it home.[...] And he would sell these things.

[He] was an intelligent man, but he had no trade. He was an intellect and there was absolutely no work he could get. And this was the only thing he could do, honestly. [...]

So there were nine people, downstairs, upstairs there was Mr. Kovacs, the four Sutos, that's five, three of us, that's eight, and Mr. Eckhart, that's nine. So how many. is that? That's eighteen people. But for some reason there was an extra one, and I can't think of who [...] nineteen. And we had one bathroom.

Now you would think in a crowded house like that, we would be, there would be dirt, cockroaches, dirty bathroom. [...] Not at all! It was considered bad manners to leave a speck, literally a speck on the sink in the bathroom. [...]

The windows were cleaned at least once a week. The curtains were crisp. No one ever felt dirty. Nothing was dirty.

▲ Document 5: Group of Immigrant Workers in C.N.R. Construction Camp, 1913

A group of workers: Canadian, American, Swedish, Italian, and Scots in a C.N.R. construction camp 1913, Agabob, B.C. Many of these workers, particularly but probably not exclusively the Italians, would have been "sojourners," workers who came for a summer to earn money before returning home. Note the all-male nature of such work camps.

Source: Library and Archives Canada, C-0476150.

109

▲ Document 6: Arrival of Immigrants at Union Station, 1910

● Arrival of immigrants at Union Station, 1910 Toronto. These immigrants are arriving in family groups, often meeting other family members who arrived in Canada before them.

Source: Library and Archives Canada, C-047042.

▲ Document 7: Interviews with Immigrants to Vancouver in the Late-Nineteenth and Early-Twentieth Centuries

George Nitta

George Nitta is a third-generation Canadian citizen, even though he was born in Japan in 1903. His father and grandfather before him were fishermen on the coast of British Columbia.

My mother was visiting in Japan and she went over for a little longer than what she expected, so I was born in Japan in 1903. That meant I was supposed to be Japanese, so when I got to be 18 or 19 I was naturalized in order to get my rights as a Canadian. My grandfather had come over here about 100 years ago, and then he called over his son, my father. My grandpa was a naturalized Canadian and so was my father, so my children are fourth generation Canadian.

Those were the "dog days" then. Discrimination was floating in the air. For example, they wouldn't allow anyone of Oriental descent into the White Lunch Restaurant. And it was the same thing in the public swimming pool. In the movie theatres, upstairs was for coloured people, including us. I was kind of fed up after I found out that I didn't have equal rights, and I thought I'd better go to some other country. But after the war, everybody realized discrimination is real bad for all of us, and now it doesn't matter what colour your skin is, a Canadian is a Canadian. But it wasn't like that before the war.

So, I was helping my father and I didn't even get the chance to go to school. Because those days we worked all year round, we sweated, and no 8- or 10-hour day either. We worked 12 and 15 hours a day, and maybe we managed to save $300 or $400 a year. The only reason we survived was because everything was cheap then. Once the fishing season was over, then it was another job, eh? And you couldn't choose, you know. You went to work at sawmills, logging, railway, anything you could get. Well, so I had to help my father support the family, and the only time-off he gave me, when I could go to school, was after January 1st to maybe the beginning of May, when we'd go back to fishing. So I'd study only a few months a year, and I'd have to keep starting and starting—night school, eh? Even for white Canadians, it wasn't easy then, so I had quite a few white schoolmates at night school. [...]

Myer Freedman

Myer Freedman was born in Poland in 1910. He came to Canada in 1914.

My father and my family came here because of the terrible pogroms [massacres of Jews] that took place in Europe, and they just felt there was no future there, and thank God they did or I wouldn't be alive. In our village where I was born, on the border between Poland and Russia, there are no Jews left, period. They've all been killed off because the succeeding wars just travelled all over that area.

Dad came here in 1910, and brought my mother and me here in 1914. He never did really learn to speak English well, 'cause he immediately had to make a living and try and get enough money to bring his family over. And the only means that he could was by being a peddler. So my two uncles who preceded him here, two uncles and an aunt,

Source: *Opening Doors*, BC Sound Heritage Series, pp. 20, 37–38, 63–64, 111. Reprinted with permission from Daphne Marlatt and Carole Itter.

111

pooled their resources and bought him a horse and a wagon for something like $40 and he went out peddling and meagerly put together enough money so that he could bring us out here four years later. Then he opened a second-hand store, after I had been here about three years—I remember distinctly the time 'cause I went out on his horse and wagon with him.

[...] We used to hold services, to my earliest recollection, in a rented store on Union Street. Then a movement was made to buy a building of our own, and it still exists, on Heatley and Pender, and that served as a synagogue for quite a while.

We had our Hebrew School, an after-hours type of a school for extra-curricular learning of language. I went to Strathcona School in the daytime, then always put in 2 hours in the late afternoon, 5 days a week and Sunday, in that particular building. [...] That was the original synagogue which later became our school. When we were using the [store as a] synagogue on Union Street, we had a Hebrew school in an old store at the corner of Jackson Avenue and Georgia, and the kosher butcher shop was just about three or four doors away from that particular spot. [...]

Fred Soon

Fred Soon was born in Canton, China in 1908. He immigrated to Canada with his uncle and cousins in 1921.

When we landed in Vancouver, we were put in the Immigration Building—you might call it like a jailhouse—and we were there for 3 weeks. My father had to go through a lot of red tape and that was done with paying a head tax of $500 and then I was able to stay in Canada. In the Immigration Building, we each had a bed. No furniture, naturally, not even a night table. There were probably a dozen people in a big open room. No privacy, everything was public, you couldn't even write a letter. Those are the days we don't like to remember. The past is the past and I really don't want to dwell on it.

When I first arrived in Vancouver, I regarded it as a hostile land. I mean, I had to tread very carefully—that was my impression when I landed. But my elders always taught me not to make trouble when you don't have to.

In those days, you were called a "landed immigrant," but there was no such thing as a full citizen, because you were not allowed to vote. You didn't have the franchise and you were not naturalized. We weren't naturalized until 1947, after the Second World War. Before then, you were treated just like a political football, like an object and it didn't matter how badly you were treated. There was no way to vent your sorrow and be able to do anything about it, because what the political parties were doing was for the privilege of their own citizens.

The CCF was one of the groups that protested, but not just one group or one party, a lot of people protested—conscientious people protested. There was discrimination against the Oriental in general. And jobs were very limited. The Chinese mostly confined themselves to lumbering, restaurants, farming, sawmills, and logging camps. In other words, they did manual or menial labour work. [...]

We lived in a community house along Keefer and Pender. There was about 10 or 12 people there, all single. They all came from China, and they left their wives in China. There was a public kitchen and everybody had their own room and the house was rented. Very seldom people bought a house.

I didn't have the opportunity of higher education. My father was a worker, he didn't have too much money. I wanted to finish high school and he said, "Forget it, you won't get very much ahead." Then I wanted to go to a technical school, I wanted to be a mechanic or an engineer and start out in the technological field. I tried to do that, and before the season was half over my father took me out of that school. "Are you crazy? You'll never get a job, you'll never get anything like that. Even in a garage they won't hire you." I took a commercial course, because he said when you take a commercial course, you don't have to rely on people to hire you, you can own a business, you can hold on to your job.

▲ Document 8: Excerpts from House of Commons Debate Regarding the *Chinese Exclusion Act* of 1923

MR. MACKENZIE KING: [Liberal Prime Minister] I might take advantage of this moment to say just a word as to the point of view from which the government has introduced this legislation. In dealing with the subject of immigration from the Orient there are two aspects which it seems to me, the committee will do well to keep more or less continuously in mind. First there is the aspect of our international relations with the great countries that lie on the other side of the Pacific. There is the other aspect, which perhaps appeals more immediately to us, of our own economic conditions and the problems in this country that arise therefrom, particularly where certain classes of our labour are brought into competition with labour from countries which have standards different from our own. As long as we keep these two points of view clearly in mind and distinguish between them [...] I think there should be little difficulty in solving the problem as between the Orient and ourselves. If, however, we lose sight of the international aspect and use expressions— either unguardedly or for other reasons—which are certain to be repugnant to peoples of another part of the world, I am afraid that instead of helping to relieve a very serious situation we shall only be creating—perhaps not for ourselves but for others—a situation which will be infinitely worse. [...]

MR. TOLMIE: [Simon Fraser Tolmie, Conservative MP for B.C. and later to become Premier of B.C.] British Columbians as a whole are anxious to maintain international relations and also to maintain our high standard as a Christian community; but we do not want to do that at the expense of giving up our country to the Asiatics.

We might glance just for a moment at the result of past legislation. In 1885, we had a head tax passed of $50 a head on Chinese. In 1901, this was increased to $100; in 1904, to $500, and in 1919, an order in council was passed keeping out skilled and unskilled labour. Then certain privileges were extended to students, and as has already been pointed out by one of the representatives from British Columbia, the Chinese abused that privilege. After a "student" came in he would attend a school for a short time, and then he would be found peeling potatoes in some hotel kitchen. He was not a student at all, but simply a labourer. We extended certain privileges to merchants, and in one year, 1921, no less than 1,145 "merchants" came in under that heading. In 1904, the Chinese population of Canada was only 14,000. It is now 58,000 and 38,000 of those are located in British Columbia. This indicates that our past legislation has been totally inadequate to meet the situation. I feel, like some hon. gentlemen who have spoken already, that if we do not have total exclusion, we must have something as close to that as possible, if we are going to get along and attain the ends we desire. [...]

113

Source: Excerpts from Hansard, House of Commons Debate, 1923, regarding the *Chinese Exclusion Act of 1923*, officially known as "An Act Respecting Chinese Immigration."

I have lived in British Columbia all my life, and I can remember when in Victoria there was only one Chinese merchant; now we have thousands of them located there, and there are thousands of them in Vancouver. We have them controlling several lines of agricultural work; we have them controlling practically, or very nearly, the whole of the fishing business and gaining on us every year, and they are becoming more powerful now that they have money as they did not have before. If the white people of British Columbia are going to be able to compete with these Chinese, they must lower their standard of living, live under cheaper conditions and in cheaper houses, wear cheaper clothes and eat less food. The Chinese do not and never will assimilate with our people, as has been proved to be the case in every country in which they have settled. [...]

I might refer for a moment to conditions existing across the Pacific, the tremendous populations there. In China alone there is a population of 400,000,000, many of whom have been kept on the edge of starvation owing to the heavily populated condition of the country, with the result that it has been found in all countries where they have settled, they are able to put up a class of work more cheaply and under rougher conditions than any other labour that is to be found in the world.

I quite agree that we should like to have oriental trade, but if we are going to permit any laxity in connection with Chinese immigration or make too many concessions in order to get this trade, we shall find in all probability that we shall secure this trade at the expense of many of the industries of the country. One of our principal troubles in the past has been I think the inability of the people east of the Rocky mountains to grasp the Asiatic situation in its full significance. Many persons in the professions have contended that we should allow more Chinese to come into the country. I can quite understand that, because there are no Chinamen in this country engaged in these professions; and the professional people have taken good care to preclude Chinese competition against themselves, having fenced their professions around with various regulations to render such competition impossible. But the farmers, the labourers, the laundry people, the restaurant people, the tailors, and now even the merchants of the country are feeling this competition. In British Columbia we have passed year after year certain legislation asking the federal government to put into effect a proper exclusion of Asiatics. This matter has been urged principally by the business organizations who have passed resolutions and forwarded them to Ottawa. The business people have fallen into line behind these resolutions but with no definite results, for we find to-day that the Chinese are still coming in across the Pacific and locating in our country in large numbers, in spite of such regulations as have been enforced; which proves that our laws have been inadequate in the past to meet this situation. The Chinese question has now assumed very serious proportions, so that we have to-day a difficult oriental problem to solve. I think that the people of Canada must wake up to the danger from this Asiatic invasion from across the Pacific. If we hope to preserve this country to the white man, our legislators and the members of this House should realize the great responsibility that rests on their shoulders not only for the protection of those people who are now in this country, but in the interests of the generations to come. I must oppose the bill in its present form and hope the minister will have a suitable amendment to offer.

After Recess

[...] MR. MCBRIDE: [Thomas McBride, MP from B.C. for the Progressive Party] Mr. Chairman, [...] Expression has been given here to the opinion that it is quite satisfactory to the people of British Columbia to allow the entry of Chinese students. Well, I cannot see the matter in that light. Why should British Columbia educate the people of the Orient? Why cannot the orientals build schools in their own countries and get European teachers to come out and

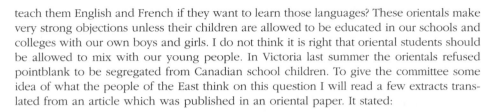
teach them English and French if they want to learn those languages? These orientals make very strong objections unless their children are allowed to be educated in our schools and colleges with our own boys and girls. I do not think it is right that oriental students should be allowed to mix with our young people. In Victoria last summer the orientals refused pointblank to be segregated from Canadian school children. To give the committee some idea of what the people of the East think on this question I will read a few extracts translated from an article which was published in an oriental paper. It stated:

> There is danger ahead. Discrimination has been shown in the school question and in the fishing question. This question is a life and death struggle to us Japanese, and we should determine our objective.

This is rather strong language from people who come into our country although they know we do not want them here. The orientals must know that they are not wanted in British Columbia. And what is their object in coming into this country if they are putting up a "life and death struggle" as they call it? In my opinion their object is to get control of the Pacific coast, including all British Columbia. [...]

In South Africa the people are talking of segregating the Chinese; that may have to be done yet in British Columbia, for the two races should not be brought together. It seems to me that if the good Lord had intended orientals and white people to live in the same country he would not have put the Pacific ocean between them. I think the people of the East should remain in their own countries. I do not see why we should admit them here and educate them in our own schools and colleges. I could cite a number of cases where the mingling of oriental children with our children in British Columbia has been a great detriment to the latter. The eastern ideals of morality and citizenship are entirely different to ours, and I do not see why our children's ideals should be lowered by their contact with the children of orientals.

MR. MACKENZIE KING: Mr. Chairman, I should like to remove a misapprehension under which my hon. friend is apparently labouring. He seems to think that it is the intention to have such students educated in British Columbia. As a matter of fact the clause in the bill relating to students has reference to universities conferring degrees. Undoubtedly if any university hesitates to take Chinese students they will not be admitted there. For instance, if the University of British Columbia thinks well not to admit Chinese students, why certainly these students will not go to that university. But Toronto, Kingston and Montreal universities are willing and anxious to take Chinese students. It seems to me it would be a mistake on the part of our people if we prevented educated young men and women from China getting the benefits of higher education here and then returning home to do what they can to acquaint the Orient with what my hon. friend has spoken of as the higher standards of living on this continent. I think we ought to be prepared, if we have it, to spread the light of our civilization in the Orient, and so far as I can see it our universities afford one of the best means to that end.

MR. WOODSWORTH: [J.S. Woodsworth was a major leader in the social gospel movement and in the 1930s would become the first leader of the CCF party (precursor to the NDP) Dealing with these two points it seems to me we are nothing less than hypocritical if we talk about the immoralities of the Chinese and yet permit them to come under conditions that would breed immorality. We object to their coming because they make poor citizens, and then take from them the very things that are necessary to make them good citizens—that is the presence of their wives and children with them. I am not pleading that several wives should be admitted. That is not in accordance with our law in this country, but it

115

would seem to me that if a man is to live in this country the least that can be done is to see that his wife, if she so desires, is permitted to come. I am not urging that she should be asked to come if the immigrant does not want to bring her. The minister suggests that a good many do not wish to establish homes in this country. We have heard it said again and again on the floor of this House that one of the dangers is that too many will come and establish residence in this country, and will bring their families, and that thus we shall have an oriental population. Those of us who have lived on the coast recognize that there is already a very considerable number of Chinese in this country who have their wives. There is a very considerable number of children who are growing up in the schools. We have to deal with them, and I cannot think that we are travelling along the right lines when we make arbitrary restrictions of this kind. A good deal has been said on the side of the exclusion of the Chinese from this country. I should like to make a few general observations, because I think we must recognize that this is by no means a small problem. No one who has lived where there is the conflict of two civilizations, of two different types of people, can be oblivious to the seriousness of the problems which arise. I am not making light of them. I confess that I am not at all sure that we are prepared at the present time to receive more orientals than we have. I know that at the present time at the coast conditions are far from satisfactory, and it may be necessary to have total exclusion for some time, until we are prepared to deal properly with the matter. At the same time I fancy any one who has listened dispassionately to the discussions on the floor of this House from time to time will recognize that there is an immense amount of prejudice towards the orientals. For example, not only on the floor of the House but in the West we have complaints about the low sanitary standards of the Chinese, and yet a year or two ago the oriental nurses or girls who wished to train as nurses were excluded from the Vancouver general hospital.

An HON. MEMBER: Hear, hear.

MR. WOODSWORTH: An hon. member says "hear, hear". It may be well from one standpoint, that the white nurses shall not be contaminated by the presence of yellow nurses—Chinese or Japanese—but I submit, since we have large numbers of orientals already in the country, that in some way or another we ought to permit them to live up to our standards. We fail to do so with danger to ourselves and to our civilization. [...] If in order to maintain our standards—and I think we should do that—it is thought desirable to exclude certain classes, I would feel that at least we should give very generous treatment to the student classes to which reference is made in this act. It seems to me that we must very definitely and consciously attempt to overcome the prejudices which we have against men of other races and other colours than our own. All students of ethnology will recognize that after all there are a great many more things in common between the different races than things which separate us, and the apparent divergences are not so great as sometimes we imagine. The stranger has always been regarded as more or less of an enemy, and we are naturally content to look down upon those who are not of our own kind.

In view of the fact that the world has become so unified industrially and commercially, and in its political relationships, it would seem as if we had arrived at that juncture where we should very definitely attempt to establish a better understanding among the great peoples of the earth. I was very much interested in a resolution, to which reference was made on the floor of the House some few weeks ago, which was forwarded by the Federation of Canadian Students, urging that scholarships be established by the government of Canada which would bring considerable numbers of the representatives of various nations to this country, and on the other hand would send out Canadian students to those countries for the purpose of studying conditions there. If this suggestion could be carried out it would be a very definite contribution on our part towards establishing better world relationships. [...]

▲ Document 9: Chinese Railway Workers, 1881

● Chinese workers on the CPR line, 1881. The Chinese played a major role in building the CPR, particularly in the mountains, where they faced significant danger as well as backbreaking labour.

Source: Boorne and May/Library and Archives Canada/C-006686B.

■ Article 1: White Supremacy, Chinese Schooling, and School Segregation in Victoria: The Case of the Chinese Students' Strike, 1922–1923

Timothy J. Stanley

In September 1922, the Victoria School Board moved to segregate the Chinese students enrolled in the district. On September 5, the first day of classes, the principals of the Boys' Central and the George Jay Schools called the Chinese students out of their classes, lined them up, and marched them down to the schools which had been set aside for the Chinese only.[1] Much to the surprise of the Victoria School board and its officials, the Chinese community did not passively acquiesce to this discriminatory move. When Principal J.A. Cunningham of Boys' Central School and his charges reached the segregated King's Road School,

> a Chinese boy holding the reputation of being the quietest and most studious in the class shouted something in the Oriental lingo, and like a flash the parade disbanded, leaving Principal Cunningham in the middle of the roadway and wondering how he could overcome the difficulties of the situation.[2]

Similar events took place with the students from the George Jay School.[3] The Chinese community had organized a student strike against the public school system of Victoria in an effort to pressure the school board into allowing their children to return to their former schools. Despite various attempts at resolution in the coming months, the deadlock between the Chinese community and the Victoria School Board lasted for the rest of the school year. To maintain the strike, the Chinese community even established its own school for the children involved. Consequently during the 1922–23 school year, 'less than

Source: *Histories of Canadian Children and Youth*, Nancy Janovicek and Joy Parr, eds., (Toronto: Oxford University Press, 2003), pp. 126–43. Reprinted with permission from Historical Studies in Education.

six' Chinese students attended the public schools in Victoria, compared to 216 the previous year.[4]

School segregation can be seen as a particular instance of white supremacy: the political and social system predicated on the supposed existence and natural dominance of a white 'race'.[5] In British Columbia, white supremacy was often expressed in the notion that BC was, and should be, a white man's country. Non-whites, including the Chinese, were by definition alien to this country. White supremacist opinion consequently represented the Chinese to be morally, culturally, and biologically different from whites. For example, shortly before World War One, a commentary in *British Columbia Magazine* presented its readers with the following characterization of the 'Oriental'.

> Racially he is as opposite to the Anglo-Saxon in life, thought, religion, temperament, taste, morals, and modes, as ice is to fire. AND HE CAN NEVER BE OTHERWISE. There is the test; this is the touchstone that irrevocably fixes the difference. He cannot be changed, even by centuries of contact, any more than the leopard can change his spots. He may adopt certain of the white man's vices, because to him these seem virtues; but he will not take up any of the white race's virtues, because these seem, either as vices to him or negligible trifles. So that, to begin with, in this review you may set it down as unalterable that, racially, the yellow man can never become a white man.[6]

Opinions of this sort made socially constructed divisions of the human species into groups such as 'Anglo-Saxons' and 'Orientals' appear natural, at the same time that they rationalized the dominance of one over the other. Such opinions were often used to exclude the Chinese and members of other groups from participation in white society and to justify discriminatory measures directed against them. For example, in 1885, in order to defend extending British Columbia's disenfranchisement of the Chinese to the federal level, Sir John A. Macdonald told the House of Commons that the Chinese immigrant 'has no British instincts or British feelings or aspirations', and that the Chinese in Canada constituted 'an Asiatic population, alien in spirit, alien in feeling, alien in everything'.[7] Discriminatory measures, like disenfranchisement, in turn codified and reinforced representations of the Chinese as Other.[8]

The result was that, by the turn of the century, a patchwork of discriminatory legislation, petty regulations, and racist social practices effectively circumscribed the daily lives of the Chinese residents of British Columbia. Amongst other things, these measures limited their sectors of economic activity, sanctioned their places of residence, and deprived most of them of family life.[9] The Chinese lived in 'A World of Their Own',[10] more often than not, effectively isolated from meaningful interaction with white society. Thus, for some whites, like the *Victoria Daily Colonist*'s 1902 labour columnist, T.H. Twigg, school segregation seemed to involve little more than 'carrying into the schools what already exists in every other institution of society—the branding of Chinese as Ishmaelites'.[11]

Even though it was not the only instance in which Chinese children attending public schools in British Columbia were segregated,[12] the 1922–23 dispute between the Chinese community and the Victoria School Board poses some of the most important questions for our understanding of how white supremacy functioned. The sustained and organized response of the Chinese community evident in this dispute suggests that white supremacy should not be seen as a static, one-way system. Rather it points to the fact that discriminatory legislation, government regulations, and racist social practices were continually being challenged by affected groups. For example, racist legislation was at various times in full effect, suspended pending court challenges, unenforceable, or being systematically ignored.[13] Far from being static, white supremacy, therefore, needs to be understood as a dynamic system continually in flux. The advantages of such an understanding become apparent through an examination of the factors shaping the response of the Chinese community during the 1922–23 Victoria school segregation controversy as well as those shaping the actions of the school board.

The ever-changing nature of white supremacy would have been readily apparent to Chinese children attending Victoria public schools before 1922. Few of these children could have escaped school segregation, or threats of school segregation, at some point in their careers. School segregation was first proposed in 1901, and put into effect for all the Chinese students in the district between 1902 and 1905.[14] Partial school segregation in the lower grades, either for all Chinese students, or for those who were older than the average for their grade levels, was in effect during much of the period between 1908 and 1922.[15]

Chinese resistance to school segregation in large measure accounts for this shifting pattern. As early as 1902, Chinese merchants whose children attended public schools in Victoria directly intervened with the school board to respond to calls for school segregation.[16] Segregated classes had to be closed, due to lack of enrolment, in 1904 and again in 1916.[17] In 1907 and 1908, legal challenges were made to segregation and exclusion of Chinese students from the district.[18] In 1921–22, older Chinese students in segregated schools may have deliberately subverted school discipline to protest segregation.[19]

Pressure for school segregation also varied in its intensity and in its nature. Most often calls for school segregation were motivated by the supposed moral and physical threat that the Chinese posed to white children. For years Chinatown had been vilified as the moral opposite of white society, as a breeding ground for depravity and disease.[20] Chinese children, it was often feared, would spread the contagions of Chinatown to white children.

The moral and physical threat to their white classmates that Chinese students could supposedly transport from Chinatown was well summarized by Vancouver City Council in 1914 when it called for school segregation. This call was in response to an incident in which a Chinese servant, who was also a public school student, was accused of murdering the white woman who employed him. Council stated that

> by being indiscriminately thrown into association with Orientals many years their senior, our children are wantonly exposed to Oriental vices at an age when revolting incidents may be indelibly stamped upon their minds. Furthermore the health of our children is endangered by such close association with Oriental children, many of whom hail from habitations where reasonable sanitation and cleanliness are not only despised but utterly disregarded. In

some cases, these Orientals come into our public school classrooms with their apparel polluted with the fumes of noxious drugs and germs of loathsome diseases on their persons.[21]

School segregation, it was argued, was essential for the protection of white children.

The physical threat of disease probably motiv-ated residents in the area of Victoria's Rock Bay School to call for school segregation in 1901,[22] while the threat posed by alleged improper sanitation was certainly an issue when the Victoria Trades and Labour Council resurrected the matter the following year.[23] This theme was returned to in 1922 by Muni-cipal School Inspector, George H. Deane, when he reintroduced the subject to the Victoria School Board. 'There is a danger in these Chinese boys, many of whom cannot even speak English, coming from the unsanitary living quarters downtown and mixing with other children with no attempt at segregation', he told the board. 'We know that it is not only a ten-dency with the Chinese to live in unsanitary quarters, but a practice.'[24]

What most captured the imaginations of white parents was the moral threat posed by older Chinese students in the lower grades.[25] Thus, school segrega-tion again became an issue in Victoria in 1908 when white residents threatened to pull their children out of the Rock Bay school[26] after one of the older Chinese students was expelled for 'employing his spare-time in drawing obscene pictures in the exer-cise books of little white children'.[27] White girls were believed to be particularly vulnerable to the threat of older Chinese boys. There was a brief scare in 1909 over the risks facing white girls teaching English in Chinatown,[28] and similar concerns motivated the Vancouver City Council's call for school segregation in 1914. But the fears that underlay these concerns were made the most explicit in popular fiction. One novel, published in serial form in the *Vancouver Sun* in 1921, described the unusually 'hopeless despair' felt by two parents who woke up one morning to discover that their daughter had eloped during the night:

Pretty Eileen Hart, the pride of her mother, the apple of her father's eye, and only eighteen years old, had run away and

married—a Chinaman. The horror of it turned them sick. She had been better dead. Eileen, with her beauty, her daintiness, her originality—they had always been specially proud of this and her daring—was now Mrs Wong Fu![29] Since Eileen had met Wong Fu, an older student, at school, where she was seduced by his more worldly ways, the distraught father placed the blame squarely on 'this *damned system of co-education*' and 'co-education with the spawn of these yellow dogs'.[30]

However, not all white British Columbians accepted that the Chinese constituted a real physical and moral threat. School personnel in particular ques-tioned this notion. For example, in 1902 in response to the Trades and Labour Council's pressure to effect school segregation, Victoria's Superintendent F.H. Eaton noted that far from causing problems, the Chi-nese children were 'getting on very well' and that 'they were obedient, attentive, and studious, and often set a good example in these things to the other children of the various rooms'.[31] According to the *Victoria Daily Colonist*, he was using even stronger language a few months later when he referred to reports that the Chinese were causing problems as 'pure fabrications'.[32] In 1914, Principal Cunningham of the Boys' Central School questioned the school board's policy of segregating primary students. He noted that the Chinese students 'make good use of the educational chances available in the higher grades, and are docile and easy to teach', but pointed out that they entered the higher grades with little flu-ency in English. 'Hence', he informed the board, 'it is no remedy to establish a separate graded school for the Chinese, who would thus never thoroughly learn English or western ways.'[33]

In fact, white attitudes towards the Chinese were to a large extent class-based. Before the First World War, it was mainly working-class organizations, and politicians pandering to the working-class vote, who called for school segregation.[34] The drive towards school segregation in 1902 was spearheaded by the Victoria Trades and Labour Council. In 1907–8, it was the Asiatic Exclusion League, an organization actively supported by white trade unions, that pressured for action against Chinese students who were suppos-edly using schools to evade the immigration head tax. These concerns were motivated by fears that the Chinese were cheap labourers who were undercutting the wages of white workers. Indeed, working-class opinion was so inimicable to the Chinese that it is likely that otherwise class-conscious white workers did not see their fellow Chinese workers as workers at all.[35] During the summer of 1907, fears that Chinese labourers were using the school system to circumvent the immigration head tax led the Victoria School Board to refuse admission to Chinese students unless they spoke sufficient English as 'to be amenable to the ordinary regulations of school discipline',[36] thus effectively barring recent Chinese immigrants from the district. In January 1908, it ruled that it would admit only native-born Chinese students who met the English test.[37] Fear of competition from cheap Chinese labour even led the provincial government to pass an order-in-council complaining that Chinese students were only using the educational system 'to increase their efficiency and to render them better able to compete with white labour'.[38] By contrast, upper-class whites living in Victoria, themselves often the employers of Chinese servants and industrial workers, probably saw the Chinese as no threat at all, but merely a rather exotic aspect of life in British Columbia.[39] They may well have been somewhat bemused by calls for school segregation.[40]

However, even those whites who opposed the excesses of white supremacist opinion shared the view that the Chinese were alien. They, too, took for granted that BC was a white society. For example, when he criticized the board's policies in 1914, Principal Cunningham commented that the problem of how best to provide for the Chinese students was one 'which is inevitable with so many children of Chinese nationality residing and growing up in a white country'.[41]

Class-based attitudes began to shift during the First World War. Increasingly, it was the white middle classes, rather than the working class, which saw the Chinese as a threat.[42] The problem for white opinion was that the Chinese were no longer just cheap labour, but were entering other fields of endeavour. The contradiction was summarized by *The Daily Colonist* in 1922: 'So long as Orientals, or the members of any foreign race, are property owners in British Columbia our municipalities cannot refuse to provide for the education of their children.'[43] In a political and social system predicated on the rights of property-owners, the Chinese, although a 'foreign

race', were now property-owners. This posed more of a problem for white property-owners than white workers. In this respect it should be noted that it was the Board of Trade and the Chamber of Commerce whose calls for school segregation, and laws barring the Chinese from owning land, led to the actions of the school board in 1922.[44] As the *Daily Colonist* editorial pointed out, it was the children of Chinese property-owners who were being segregated. Most of the Chinese children in the public schools of British Columbia during this era were likely the sons and daughters of merchants or professionals. This was for the simple reason that most of the Chinese children in Canada by this time came from this class.

Discriminatory immigration measures maintained male Chinese workers as cheap labour by transferring the costs of reproducing their labour to China. This was primarily achieved through the head tax on Chinese immigration (raised to $500 by 1904) which, however much it inhibited male labourers from entering Canada, effectively barred their wives and dependent children from immigrating.[45] Merchants and their families, by contrast, were specifically excluded from the head tax provisions. The net effect of these measures was that most of the Chinese families in Canada, and much of the second generation, would have been from the merchant class.[46]

That school segregation was primarily directed against the children of Chinese merchants becomes apparent from the response of the Chinese community in Victoria to the school board's decision to impose segregation. From the very beginning of the 1922–23 school segregation controversy, the Chinese Consolidated Benevolent Association (CCBA) played a key role in organizing this response. The CCBA, whose membership theoretically included all the Chinese living in Victoria, had always been controlled by the merchant-elite of the community. It was formed in 1884 by a group of Victoria merchants who received a charter from the Chinese Consulate in San Francisco, and a year later it incorporated under the BC statutes.[47] It functioned as 'a *de facto* Chinese government in Canada',[48] not only operating welfare institutions such as a Chinese hospital, but also resolving disputes internal to the community and providing support for those Chinese caught in disputes outside the community.[49] It was in this latter role that it first became involved in the 1922–23 school segregation issue. At a school board meeting early in 1922, the CCBA directly challenged Inspector Deane's charges of improper sanitation on the part of Chinese students.[50] During the summer, after the board announced its plans to proceed with segregation, the CCBA, this time in conjunction with other Chinese organizations, again protested.[51] It was the CCBA that organized the students' strike and established the Victoria Overseas Chinese Resist School Segregation Association (*Weiduoli Huaqiao Kangzheng Fenxiao Tuantihui*), an *ad hoc* organization which was to coordinate the fight against the school board in the coming months.[52]

The students' strike and ensuing deadlock must have come as a surprise to the trustees of the Victoria School Board. While they were well aware that the Chinese were opposed to segregation,[53] from their point of view they were merely extending to the middle grades an existing system of partial segregation already in effect in the lower grades. The response of the Chinese must have seemed extreme to say the least. Indeed, throughout the segregation dispute, the Victoria Chinese community demonstrated a high degree of solidarity. When segregation was first proposed, the school inspector granted special permits which allowed twenty Chinese students to attend integrated classes on the grounds that their English was good enough.[54] Despite this, the twenty children granted permits also boycotted classes.[55] For a time in October, five Chinese students showed up for class at the King's Road School, but they too withdrew after a while.[56]

What the school board had not taken into account was the depth of Chinese resentment of school segregation. In particular, second-generation Chinese Canadians, who may have made up to 85 per cent of the students attending Victoria schools,[57] had a great deal to lose. The stakes involved for them were made clear by Low Kwong Joe, the President of the Chinese Canadian Club, an organization of second-generation people. In a letter to the *Victoria Daily Times*, he admitted that for several years Chinese in Victoria had accepted the principle of separate classes for the Chinese students in the lowest grades on the grounds that 'segregation would enable the children better to acquire a knowledge of English'. Quite the contrary had proved to be the case, however. Now the Chinese were being asked to accept segregation up to the level of the high school entrance class. According to Joe,

If we accept this we have no reason to expect any better result, so the next step will be on the grounds of imperfect knowledge of English we will be prevented from the entrance classes or the High School. You can therefore see, Mr. Editor, how serious the question is for us. It is not the 200 children now affected that we have to think of, but the whole of our future is involved in this question. We cannot afford to take any other attitude than the one we have taken.

We ask ourselves this question: What can be the purpose behind this movement? Can it be the intention to prevent us securing an English education so that our children can be permanently ignorant, so that they must remain labourers to be exploited? Being ignorant of the language we will be unable to take our part by the side of other Canadians, and we will then be pointed out as those who refuse to learn the customs or social life of the country—in fact, refuse to assimilate. It will have been forgotten by then that it was not because we did not want to learn, but because certain narrow-minded autocrats have taken upon themselves the responsibility of preventing our learning.[58]

In other words, second-generation Chinese Canadians saw school segregation as an attempt to prevent them from learning English. This not only threatened to maintain their separation from white society; it also threatened to make the second-generation children of merchants into cheap labour like most of the first generation. In addition, by maintaining the pariah status of the Chinese, it also laid the basis for their potential expulsion from Canada.[59]

Throughout the 1922–23 school segregation crisis, the Chinese Canadian Club played an important role in exposing the school board's agenda. The racist nature of the school board's actions had been evident to the Chinese in Victoria from the beginning of the dispute. This was apparent in several letters to the editor published in the English-language papers. For example, one Chinese letter-writer saw the school board's actions as 'purely and simply a matter of discrimination', while another asked what the reasons for the board's actions were: 'Surely they are not moved to act simply out of racial prejudice', he commented ironically.[60] However as the deadlock continued, it was the Chinese Canadian Club that took on the role of responding to the school board's allegations in the white newspapers. For example, when the school board claimed that segregation was necessary because Chinese students were retarding the progress of white students, the Chinese Canadian Club published a list of the names, ages, and class rankings of ninety-four Chinese students, formerly attending non-segregated schools, who were above their class averages. In addition it published the names of another seventeen students who were below their class averages but were two years younger than their classmates. It pointed out that in these classes 'all questions and answers are given in English, and that the Chinese children could not stand so high up in their classes unless they understand the questions asked them, and could answer intelligently.'[61]

Collecting the kind of information that the Chinese Canadian Cub used to respond to the school board indicates that there was a high degree of organization and solidarity within the Chinese community. This organization and solidarity is also apparent in the other element of the Chinese community's response to segregation: the creation of a Chinese-language school for the children involved in the strike. Plans for the creation of the *Weiduoli Bu Zhonghua Yixue* (Victoria Chinese Free School) were first discussed on October 5, 1922, when some of Victoria's most 'prominent Chinese residents' met to discuss the formation of a Chinese-language school since 'the school board persists in upholding school segregation'.[62] By the end of October, quite detailed plans for the Chinese Free School were announced. The school, which would not charge tuition, had been 'specially established to support the students on strike against school segregation'. It would hold classes in the CCBA building and be divided into two grades—a 'national grade' for students ages seven to twelve, and a higher grade for students thirteen to eighteen. Its staff of seven teachers and one principal would teach a curriculum which would 'normally' include Chinese language, calligraphy, arithmetic and English.[63]

Chinese nationalism was an integral element in the school. This was evident in its 'Guiding Principles' which stated, 'Established in order to support

understanding of Chinese [language] amongst the students of the western schools on strike to resist school segregation, the school will nourish knowledge amongst the overseas people of the homeland's common written characters and stimulate the overseas people to have the idea that patriotism wipes out shame.'[64] In other words, the school was primarily intended to instill Chinese nationalist feeling and knowledge of written Chinese amongst the striking students in order to strengthen their resolve while the strike lasted.

It may be that the nationalist character of this school was the result of expediency. A white sympathizer of the Chinese, Harry Hastings, claimed that the Chinese had 'no intention of establishing their own English schools at an additional cost to themselves when they are already paying more than their share through the school tax.'[65] In addition, the Chinese would have drawn upon readily available resources to create such a school. At this time the Chinese community of Victoria had its own network of day and evening Chinese-language schools.[66] The existence of this network of Chinese schools was even apparent in the announcement of the creation of the Chinese Free School which made careful provision to insure that the school would not take away students from any existing schools.[67] Because of this network, a Chinese-language school would have been easier to establish. But the nature of the school also points to the fact that, during this era, the Chinese community used Chinese nationalism instrumentally to challenge white hegemony. Indeed the Chinese community had invented a common identity as Chinese largely in response to the threat of white-supremacist exclusion.

Although white opinion portrayed the Chinese in Canada as monolithic, they did not see themselves as such. Most of the Chinese immigrants to Canada came from Guangdong province in South China. However, they spoke several, often mutually unintelligible, dialects of Cantonese and Hakka. Their loyalties tended to be based on their county of origin, rather than any broader identification.[68] Settlement patterns in Canada further compounded these centrifugal tendencies as people from the same districts, speaking the same dialects, grouped together in certain localities, or else established monopolies in certain industries or trades, in order to survive in the new world. It was only very slowly that institutions such as the CCBA, or pan-local organizations such as the clan associations, 'invented' a common identity as Chinese.[69]

The promotion of literacy in written Chinese was an important element in overcoming the barriers of dialect and home origin. For over two thousand years written Chinese had made possible the political unification of China. Through written texts, officials, who would need interpreters to speak face to face, could communicate effectively. Written Chinese fulfilled the same function amongst the Chinese communities of Canada. As written Chinese could be understood without reference to spoken languages, it provided a common language accessible to all the Chinese in Canada.

Life in a country like Canada placed a premium on literacy. The ever-changing nature of white supremacy meant that previously barred areas of endeavour might suddenly open up, thus providing work or new opportunities for investment. By the same token, a district, or economic sector, that had earlier welcomed the Chinese might suddenly become hostile. In the former case one's economic well-being could depend upon accurate information and in the latter case, one's very survival might depend upon it. Chinese-language newspapers, like *The Chinese Times*, provided this kind of information.[70] The fact that literacy in Chinese allowed for confidential communications with family or business partners in China would have provided an added incentive to learn how to read and write.

At the same time, the periodic efforts of white supremacy to further restrict the Chinese provided an incentive to organize beyond the local level. Such organization in turn presupposed a common identity and a common language. The utility of organizing beyond the local level was apparent in the 1922–23 school segregation dispute. One of the first acts of Victoria's Resist School Segregation Association was to write to other communities, and even China, to request support.[71] In response, the Vancouver Chinese Benevolent Association established the Vancouver Resist School Segregation Rear Support Association to raise money and provide moral support to the Chinese in Victoria. It also held several public meetings which claimed that unless school segregation was stopped in Victoria, it would not only spread to Vancouver school, but all sectors of Chinese endeavour in Canada.[72]

Knowledge of written Chinese thus became a resource for survival in the new world at the same time that it provided a common language and common identity. Chinese-language schools, therefore, were inseparably nationalist and anti-racist institutions. This is apparent in the case of the Chinese Public School, the most important and oldest of the Chinese language schools in Victoria. The Victoria Chinese Public School had originally been established under the auspices of the CCBA as the *Lequn Yishe* (Happy Masses Free School) in 1899.[73] The school itself was formed as the result of a burgeoning consciousness of being Chinese amongst the merchant class. Quoting an anonymous Chinese, the *Victoria Daily Colonist* claimed that the school was created because 'we are Chinamen wherever we go [...] and find that, in view of the international commercial relations now opening up, it is necessary to have an education in Chinese as well as English.'[74] In 1907–8, this school was called upon to provide for the schooling in Chinese and English of those students who were refused entry into the Victoria public school system. Consequently it became overcrowded and a new building was established, this time with the help of the Imperial Qing government. For a short time it was called the Imperial Chinese School, although the name subsequently was changed to the Chinese Public School.[75]

The school's importance is indicated by its enrolment. From 1908 to 1923, between 43 and 127 students a year attended the school.[76] For example, in 1914–15, it enrolled ninety students in six classes. The four upper classes were held during the evening as they were made up of students who attended the white public schools during the day. The two lower classes were held during the daytime.[77]

For the Chinese, this school was a 'public' school in the true sense. This was not only reflected in its name but also in its practices. It charged no tuition, was open to all Chinese children, and its activities were regularly followed in the Chinese-language press.[78] It was financed through the revenues of, and answerable to, the local Chinese government: the Chinese Consolidated Benevolent Association. In addition, it sought to instill in its students a collective consciousness through public speaking and observance of Chinese holidays such as Confucius' birthday. Its teachers were brought over from China and its language of instruction was Cantonese, even though most of its students spoke local dialects.[79] Its curriculum also appears to have been closely modeled on that of schools in China, as the school was inspected by official educational delegations from China on a number of occasions and pronounced up to standard each time.[80]

White supremacy provided an additional incentive for Chinese-language schools in Canada to be similar to their counterparts in China. The conditional nature of the Chinese presence in Canada meant that Chinese entrepreneurs or professionals might easily find their ambitions blocked in Canada, in which case, China could provide the best area of endeavour. It is likely that both white society and first-generation Chinese pressured second-generation children to seek fame and fortune in China.[81]

White supremacy is also important in explaining an additional feature of the Chinese Public School. In comparison to the Chinese attending the white public schools, the Chinese Public School appears to have enrolled a higher proportion of girls. In 1915, for example, of the school's ninety students, sixty-two were boys and twenty-eight girls. In 1914–15, the segregated school board school on Fisguard Street enrolled eighty-one boys and only seventeen girls. The next year at Rock Bay, there were forty boys and five girls.[82] Although it is no doubt true that some Chinese girls did not attend schools of any kind during this era,[83] and that the schooling of girls was devalued by Chinese patriarchy, it appears that the Chinese schools may well have been less hostile to Chinese girls than white schools. This points to the fact that white supremacy had a different effect on Chinese males compared to Chinese females. This differential effect can be seen in the gender imbalance created by immigration patterns.[84] It can also be seen in the discussions of school segregation which, as should be apparent, were gendered. Thus school segregationists often spoke of 'Chinese boys' in contrast to 'white boys and girls' and since white girls were perceived to be particularly at risk from Chinese boys, for example, the City of Vancouver had called for segregation in 1914.

Much of the gender imbalance amongst Chinese students in the white school system can only be accounted for by the racist violence which was a constant reality facing the Chinese in British Columbia. Women and children, the Chinese believed, were especially vulnerable to this violence. As the market gardener Sing Cheung Yung explained to the 1902 Royal Commission on Chinese and Japanese Immigration when asked why he left his family in China, 'the people in this country talk so much against the Chinese that I don't care to bring them here.'[85]

Racist violence was certainly a constant reality confronting Chinese students in the white public schools. A number of incidents of such violence are reported in the English and Chinese-language newspapers throughout this era. At the turn of the century assault on Chinese occasioned negative newspaper comments in both Vancouver and Victoria.[86] These assaults could have tragic results as was evident in 1904 when a Victoria Chinese youth had to have his leg amputated after being run over by a streetcar following an assault by a group of white boys.[87] In 1908, white boys were reported to be making 'an organized attempt to prevent Chinese pupils from attending the Rock Bay and Central Schools'.[88] Again in 1915, a Chinese schoolgirl was so seriously injured when she was stoned by a group of white boys that she required major surgery to save her life.[89] In 1922, tensions were sufficiently high in Vancouver that a snowball fight at Lord Strathcona School, on the edge of Chinatown, ended in the stabbing of a white boy.[90] Several years later, going to and from school was still an ordeal for Chinese students. One student who attended school in Vancouver recorded in his autobiography: 'We had trouble with the white kids on our way to and from school. We walked in groups for protection, the small kids following closely behind the bigger, stronger boys.'[91] Given this kind of violence, the Chinese community inevitably kept its youngest children and girls out of the white public schools, but allowed them to attend Chinese institutions in the relative safety of Chinatown. Therefore it is not surprising that the Chinese Public School's classes for its youngest students were day classes, nor that more Chinese girls attended it proportionally than attended the white public schools.

From the foregoing it is apparent that white supremacy needs to be understood as a complex system, one whose many dimensions were continually being challenged by the Chinese and other groups. School segregation was an on-again, off-again phenomenon as it swung back and forth between Chinese resistance and white opinion. White opinion about the Chinese itself was in constant flux as it

125

varied considerably in intensity and content with time and class origins.

To acknowledge that white supremacy was in constant flux is not to render it any more palatable as a system. Rather it is to try to come to terms with its true horror: to recognize that for Chinese Canadians, their presence in British Columbian society was always contingent, and subject to potential renegotiation and exclusion. For the Chinese in Canada, coming to terms with white supremacy at least in part involved the creation, through the devices of literacy and Chinese-language schooling, of a domain separate and distinct from that of white society. This domain existed largely beyond the ken of white society and proved to be the greatest resource available to the Chinese in resisting white oppression. Its existence made possible their invention as a community, and enabled organized, community-wide, politically conscious challenges to white domination such as the 1922–23 students' strike. The fact that this Chinese domain, and its institutions such as *The Chinese Times* and the Victoria Chinese Public School, are still present in British Columbia is a testament to the persistence of the Chinese community in challenging supremacy. It is also a testament to the fact that the creation of a realm open to the full participation of all the peoples of Canada remains unfinished.

Notes

1. 'Chinese Pupils Start "Rebellion"', *Victoria Daily Times*, Sept. 6, 1922, 2.
2. Ibid.
3. Ibid.
4. British Columbia, Department of Education, *Annual Report of the Public Schools of the Province of British Columbia, 1922–1923* (Victoria: King's Printer, 1923) [henceforth *Annual Report*], F45, and 'Orientals Health Menace in Schools, Inspector Asserts', *Victoria Daily Times*, Jan. 12, 1922, 18.
5. White supremacy is in this respect a particular form of racism. In this paper, the usage of the term 'racism' is intended to follow that of Robert Miles, who has argued that 'racism "works" by attributing meanings to certain phenotypical and/or genetic characteristics of human beings in such a way as to create a system of categorization, and by attributing additional (negatively evaluated) characteristics to the people sorted into these categories.' See Robert Miles, *Racism* (London: Routledge, 1989), 3. 'Races' should be understood as 'socially imagined rather than biological realities' (Ibid., 71). See also Ashley Montagu, ed., *The Concepts of Race* (New York: Free Press), 1964.
6. Ernest McGaffey, 'British Columbia and the Yellow Man', *British Columbia Magazine* 8, (Mar. 1912): 198.
7. Canada, House of Commons, *Debates, Vol. XVIII* (Ottawa: King's Printer, 1885), 1582 1589.
8. For a discussion of how European representations of the people of the Near East have made them Other, see Edward W. Said, *Orientalism* (New York: Vintage, 1979).
9. These measures and many of their consequences are documented in several histories of the Chinese in Canada and histories of racist discourse in BC. See David T.H. Lee (Li Donghai) *Jianada Huaqino shi [A history of the Chinese in Canada]* (Taibei: Zhonghua Da Dian Bianyin Hui, 1967); W. Peter Ward, *White Canada Forever: Popular Attitudes and Public Policy Toward Orientals in British Columbia* (Montreal: McGill-Queen's University Press, 1978); Harry Con et al., *From China to Canada: A History of the Chinese Communities in Canada*, ed. Edgar Wickberg, Generations: *A History of the Canada's Peoples* (Toronto: McClelland and Stewart Ltd., 1982); Anthony B. Chan, *Gold Mountain: The Chinese in the New World* (Vancouver: New Star Books, 1983); Peter S. Li, *The Chinese in Canada* (Toronto: Oxford University Press, 1988); Patricia E. Roy, *A White Man's Province: British Columbia Politicians and Chinese and Japanese Immigrants, 1858–1914* (Vancouver: University of British Columbia Press, 1989). Two important doctoral dissertations are: Gillian Creese, 'Working Class Politics, Racism and Sexism: The Making of a Politically Divided Working Class in Vancouver, 1900–1939' (Ph.D. diss., Carleton University, 1986), and Kay Anderson, '"East" as "West": Place, State and the Institutionalization of Myth in Vancouver's Chinatown, 1880–1980' (Ph.D. diss., University of British Columbia, 1987). Paul Yee's *Saltwater City: An Illustrated History of the Chinese in Vancouver* (Vancouver: Douglas & McIntyre; Seattle: University of Washington Press, 1988), while intended for a non-academic audience, provides superb insights into the historical experiences of the Chinese in Canada.
10. Roy, *A White Man's Province*, 13.

11. Cited by Mary Ashworth, *The Forces Which Shaped Them: A History of the Education of Minority Group Children in British Columbia* (Vancouver: New Star Books, 1979), 58.

12. School segregation was also in effect at various times in Vancouver, New Westminster, and Nanaimo. Two excellent studies are Ashworth, 'Chapter Two, The Chinese', in *The Forces Which Shaped Them*, 54–90 and David Chuenyan Lai, 'The Issue of Discrimination in Education in Victoria, 1901–1923', *Canadian Ethnic Studies/Études Ethniques au, Canada* XIX, 3 (1987): 47–67. Lai provides a particularly detailed account of segregation in Victoria. See also Lee, *Jianada Huaqiao shi*, 357–8; Ward, *White Canada Forever*, 62–4, 127–8; Wickberg, *From China to Canada*, 128–30; and Roy, *A White Man's Province*, 24–7, 276n31. On segregation in Victoria, see also Liu Guangzu, 'Weibu Huaqiao sanshi nian fendou shiji', [The record of accomplishments of thirty years of struggle by the Victoria Overseas Chinese] in *Jianada Weiduoli Zhonghua Huiguan/Zhonghua Xuexiao chengh qishiwu/liushi zhounian tenan* [Special publication commemorating the seventy-fifth anniversary of the founding of the Victoria Chinese Consolidated Benevolent Association and the sixtieth anniversary of the founding of the Chinese School] (Victoria: Chinese Consolidated Benevolent Association, 1960), Part IV, and on Nanaimo, see '*Jishi Dong Ya xuetong*', [Angry glares at East Asian students' *Chinese Times (Da Han gongbao)*, Nov. 8, 1921, 3. Since 1907, the *Chinese Times* has been published in Vancouver by the Zhigongdang, a.k.a. the Chinese Free Masons. During the era under consideration here it was continually publishing news about the Chinese communities across Canada. It paid particular attention to racist violence, anti-Asian discrimination, and calls for exlusion [sic]. This makes it one of the most important sources on white supremacy during this era. Fortunately, an English-language index of the paper's news columns on the Chinese communities of Canada, including some translations of variable quality, are available through the Chinese Canadian Research Collection (CCBC) located at UBC Special Collections. The CCRC contains much of the background research for *From China to Canada*.

13. Such was the case with the Coal Mines Regulations Act, which supposedly kept the Chinese out of the coal mines. See Roy, *A White Man's Province*, 77–81, 134–42, and 167–72.

14. 'Chinese Pupils Will Sit Alone', *Victoria Daily Colonist*, Nov. 13, 1902, 3, and Ward, *White Canada Forever*, 63.

15. See 'Chinese Question to Again be Considered', *Victoria Daily Colonist*, ct. 14, 1908, 7; 'Secures Quarters for Chinese Pupils', *Victoria Daily Colonist*, Oct. 15, 1908, 2; 'Chinese Problem Solved', *Victoria Daily Times*, Oct. 15, 1908, 3; and 'Education of the Chinese Arranged', *Victoria Daily Colonist*, Oct. 24, 1908, 3. On its first day of opening, only sixteen out of an expected forty students showed up at segregated facilities rented in Chinatown. 'Chinese School is Opened Today', *Victoria Daily Times*, Nov. 2, 1908, 2. At this time there were fifty-four Chinese and two Japanese enrolled in the district. See 'Chinese Question to Again Be Considered', *Victoria Daily Colonist*, Oct. 14, 1908, 7. This 'Fisguard Street School' remained in operation from 1908 through to 1915. See British Columbia, Department of Education, *Annual Report, 1908–1909*, A XX; *Annual Report, 1909–1910*, A XXI; *Annual Report, 1910–1911*, A XXV; *Annual Report, 1911–1912*, A XXIX; *Annual Report 1912–1913*, A XXIV; *Annual Report, 1913–1914*, A XXVI; *Annual Report, 1914–1915*, A XXVII. In 1915–16, this school was closed and the Chinese students moved to Rock Bay School which was closed quite quickly due to 'a lack of enrolment'; see *Annual Report, 1915–1916*, A 43 and A XII. The Rock Bay School re-opened in 1919, with 44 Chinese students (43 boys, 1 girl) and by 1921 had 171 (167 boys, 4 girls) students in 3 divisions. See *Annual Report, 1919–1920*, C12; *Annual Report 1920–1921*. C12; and *Annual Report, 1921–1923*, C15. The annual reports do not make clear whether these segregated classes applied to immigrant Chinese or the native-born. In fact there are some indications that the Rock Bay School may have contained both while earlier schools had not. See, for example, 'Chinese Segregation', *Victoria Daily Colonist*, Oct. 11 1922, 4.

16. 'The Chinese Enter a Protest', *Victoria Daily Colonist*, June 11, 1902, 3.

17. See Ward, *White Canada Forever*, 63 and *Annual Report, 1915–1916*, A 43.

18. See, for example, 'Victoria West School Plans', *Victoria Daily Times*, Sept. 24, 1907, 6 and 'Government to Defend Action', *Victoria Daily Colonist*, Sept. 24, 1907, 7.

19. See 'Says Chinese Are Menace in Schools', *Victoria Daily Colonist*, Jan. 12, 1922, 9 and 'No More Chinese Teachers Her', ibid., Aug. 30, 1922, 5. This report of disciplinary problem is in such contrast to other assessments of the Chinese that it suggests an unusual problem. Chinese schoolchildren were under tremendous pressure from their own community to act properly in school. On a number of occasions the Chinese Benevolent Association in Vancouver held meetings with Chinese students attending white public schools at which no less a person than the Chinese Consul lectured them on the need to behave. See 'Zhonghua Huiguan zhixun xuesheng jishi' [Chinese Benevolent Association instructs students in important matters], *Chinese Times*, Sept. 7, 1920, 3. See also 'Lim Lingshi Bugao' [An Announcement from Consul Lim], ibid., Nov. 8, 1922, 2–3.

20. Anderson, '"East" as "West"', thoroughly documents how Vancouver's Chinatown was constructed in white opinion as the antithesis of white society.

21. City of Vancouver, *Council Minutes,* City of Vancouver Archives, Vol. 10, Apr. 8, 1914, 122 cited by Anderson, '"East" as "West"', 152.

22. 'To Exclude the Chinese', *Victoria Daily Colonist*, Feb. 14, 1901, 8. On the issue of motivation, see Roy, *A White Man's Province*, 24.

23. 'Chinese in Schools', *Victoria Daily Colonist*, Mar. 13, 1902, 2. See also, 'The World of Labour', ibid., Apr. 20, 1902, 9.

24. 'Says Chinese are Menace in Schools', ibid., Jan. 12, 1922, 9 and 'Orientals Health Menace in Schools, Inspector Asserts', in *Victoria Daily Times*, Jan. 12, 1922, 18.

25. Older Chinese boys in the public school were a recurring issue. These were English as Second Language students who were placed in primary classes. Most often, they were only one or two years older than the average white student in the class. In some instances, however, they were as much as ten years older, being sixteen- to eighteen-year-olds.

26. 'Will have Separate School for Chinese', *Victoria Daily Colonist*, Apr. 4, 1908, 2.

27. 'Orientals in the Schools', ibid., Mar. 28, 1908, 3. See also ibid., Mar. 28, 1908, 1 and 3.

28. "Says Danger Has Been Magnified', ibid., July 30, 1909, 7. See also Lai, 'Discrimination', 54.

29. Hilda Glynn-Ward, *The Writing on the Wall*, with an introduction by Patricia E. Roy (Toronto: University of Toronto Press, 1974), 85. This novel has been called the worst piece of literature in Canadian history. See Terrance Craig, *Racial Attitudes in English Canadian Fiction* (Waterloo, Ontario: Wilfrid Laurier University Press, 1987).

30. Glynn-Ward, *The Writing on the Wall*, 84–5. Emphasis in the original.

31. 'Chinese in The Schools', *Victoria Daily Colonist*, Mar. 13, 1902. 2.

32. 'Chinese in the Schools', ibid., Nov. 12, 1902, 6. The teachers in the district also felt the Chinese caused no problems. See also Eaton's comments at the Nov. 12. 1902 meeting of the school board to the effect that the case for segregation had not been proven. See 'Chinese Pupils Will Sit Alone', *Victoria Daily Colonist,* Nov. 13, 1902, 3. Similar opinions were expressed by officials of the Vancouver School District in 1907 in response to calls for segregation. The *Vancouver Daily Province* reported 'the opinion of the school authorities' that 'the Oriental children are model pupils and exceedingly apt. It is stated that they are well dressed and cleanly, and give practically no trouble to the teaching staff. See 'Orientals in City Schools Do Not Exceed 150', *Vancouver Daily Province*, Sept. 13, 1907, 1.

33. 'Chinese Children in Public Schools,' *Victoria Daily Times*, Feb. 2, 1914, 12.

34. This was apparent in the platforms of the Labour candidates in the 1902 local elections in Victoria. See 'With the Labor Candidates', *Victoria Daily Colonist*, Dec. 21, 1902, 3.

35. Gillian Creese, 'Exclusion or solidarity? Vancouver Workers Confront the "Oriental Problem"', *BC Studies*, 80 (Winter 1988-89): 24–51.

36. 'Chinese and City Schools', *Victoria Daily Times*, Aug. 31, 1907, 1.

37. 'Again Urges Claims of Chinese Scholars', *Victoria Daily Colonist*, Aug. 13, 1908, 2, and 'Chinese Question Is Knotty Proposition', ibid., Sept. 11, 1908, 2.

38. 'Takes Action in Chinese Question', ibid., Nov. 15, 1907, 7. The same issue was also raised in Vancouver during this era largely under the inspiration of the Asiatic Exclusion League. Ironically, the anti-Chinese and anti-Japanese riot of Sept. 7, 1907 may have moderated demands for segregation. It is also apparent most Asian students were concentrated in schools bordering Chinatown and the Japanese quarter. See 'Orientals in City Schools Do Not Exceed 150', *Vancouver Daily Province*,

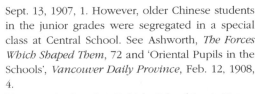

Sept. 13, 1907, 1. However, older Chinese students in the junior grades were segregated in a special class at Central School. See Ashworth, *The Forces Which Shaped Them*, 72 and 'Oriental Pupils in the Schools', *Vancouver Daily Province*, Feb. 12, 1908, 4.

39. Margaret A. Ormsby, *British Columbia: A History* (Vancouver: MacMillan of Canada, 1958), 303.

40. For example, when segregation was first proposed in Victoria, one trustee reportedly commented that 'if our Anglo-Saxon civilization could not withstand the effects of educating a hundred or so of Chinese, it was time that the school board should be abolished.' See 'To Exclude the Chinese', *Victoria Daily Colonist*, Feb. 10, 1901, 8.

41. 'Chinese Children in Public Schools', *Victoria Daily Times*, Feb. 2, 1914, 12.

42. For example, in the late 1910s and early 1920s, white merchants led a campaign to keep Vancouver's Chinese community from expanding into the Grandview-Woodlands area of East Vancouver. See Anderson, '"East" as "West"', 206–9.

43. 'Segregation in Schools', *Victoria Daily Colonist*, Oct. 14, 1922, 4.

44. See 'Aim Resolutions Against Orientals', *Victoria Daily Colonist*, Nov. 29, 1921, 3; Wickberg, *From China to Canada*, 137.

45. The role of immigration regulations in maintaining a split labour market is explained by Li, *Chinese in Canada,* 33–52. An important discussion of the differential effect of immigration laws and the nature of work for Chinese women and men is provided by Tamara Adilman, 'A Preliminary Sketch of Chinese Women and Work in British Columbia 1858–1950', in *Not Just Pin Money: Selected Essays on the History of Women's Work in British Columbia*, ed. Barbara K. Latham and Roberta J. Pazdro (Victoria: Camosun College, 1984), 52–78.

46. Intermarriage with white women would have been virtually impossible for bachelor Chinese males. Often there were legal hurdles. See, for example, 'Sheng Zhengfu quid huang bai tonghun' [Provincial Government outlaws yellow white intermarriage], *Chinese Times*, Apr. 10, 1917, 2–3.

47. Lee, *Jianada huaqiao shi*, 176–8.

48. See Chan, *Gold Mountain*, 89.

49. Ibid., 86–89.

50. 'Weibu Zhonghua Huiguan shang xuewubu shu' [Victoria Chinese Consolidated Benevolent Association sends letter to school board], *Chinese Times*, Feb. 22, 1922, 3. See also Lai, 'Discrimination', 55. One of the strengths of Lai's study is that he had access to the CCBA archives.

51. 'Oppose Plan of Segregation', *Victoria Daily Colonist*, Sept. 9, 1922, 1. The fact that the CCBA joined with the Chinese Chamber of Commerce and the Chinese Canadian Club in making this protest suggests that merchants and second-generation Chinese were particularly concerned about school segregation. See also, 'Showdown in School Crisis', *Victoria Daily Colonist*, Oct. 8, 1922, 3.

52. Lai, 'Discrimination', 57. Formation of such *ad hoc* organizations was quite common during this era. For example, in 1923 many such groups were formed across Canada to protest the federal government's proposed Chinese Immigration Act. See Chinese Canadian Research Collection, Box 4, folder for 1923.

53. See 'Board Does Not Yield to Plea', *Victoria Daily Colonist*, Aug. 30, 1922, 5.

54. Strike supporters firmly denounced the permit system as 'one of favoritism, permits being granted to the wealthier ones with the intention of preventing cohesion amongst the Chinese'. See 'Chinese Segregation', *Victoria Daily Colonist*, Oct. 15, 1922, 4. Apparently one permit had been granted to the Inspector's insurance agent.

55. 'Chinese Picketing Schools; Five Boys Start Work To-Day', *Victoria Daily Times*, Oct. 9, 1922, 1.

56. Ibid., Oct, 1922.

57. Letter from P. Lee, 'Chinese Segregation', *Victoria Daily Colonist*, Oct. 15, 1922, 4.

58. 'Chinese Segregation', *Victoria Daily Times*, Oct. 11, 1922, 4.

59. Lack of English had often been used to justify differential treatment. This was not only evident in school segregation but in other areas. For example, it was claimed that since the Chinese did not speak English, they were a safety threat in the mines. During World War I, by studying English the miners of Cumberland circumvented an attempt by the provincial government to get the Chinese out of the mines. See, for example, 'Yaoyinm: kuanggong zhizhao zhi shencha' [Examination of Cumberland miner's certificates], *The Chinese Times*, Sept. 5, 1916, 3.

60. See 'School Problem', 'Chinese in Schools', and 'Chinese in Schools', three letters to the editor in

129

the *Victoria Daily Colonist*, Sept. 10, 1922, 4. See also 'Segregation', *Victoria Daily Times*, Sept. 14, 1922, 4.

61. 'Chinese Segregation', *Victoria Daily Colonist*, Nov. 26, 1922, 14. For other interventions, see the letters, 'Chinese Segregation', *Victoria Daily Colonist*, Oct. 15, 1922, 4 and 'Chinese Segregation', *Victoria Daily Times*, Nov. 2, 1922, 4.

62. 'Huaren kangzheng fenxiao zhi judong' [Activities of Chinese resisting school segregation], *Chinese Times*, Oct. 7, 1922, 3.

63. 'Weiduoli bu Zhonghua Yizue zhaosheng jian zhang' [Brief rules of the call for students of the Victoria Chinese Free School], reproduced by Lai, 'Discrimination', 61.

64. Ibid.

65. 'Chinese Segregation', *Victoria Daily Colonist*, Oct. 13, 1922, 4.

66. See Lee, *Jianada Huaqiao shi*, 312–47, for a discussion of Chinese-language schooling amongst the Chinese communities of Canada.

67. 'Zbonghua Yixu zhaosheng' [Call for students of the Chinese Public School].

68. This, for example, accounts for the stormy reception of Sun Yat-sen in 1910 when he spoke in Vancouver's Chinatown. He spoke a different dialect from the Sye-Yip people who were the majority there. See Chang Yung Ho's account of this meeting in Yee, *Saltwater City*, 40–1, 44–5.

69. Chuen-Yan David Lai, 'Home County and Clan Origins of Overseas Chinese in Canada in the Early 1880s', *BC Studies* 27 (Autumn 1975): 3–29. On the use of the term 'invent' here, see Roy Wagner, *The Invention of Culture* (Chicago: University of Chicago Press, 1981).

70. See Chinese Canadian Research Collection, Box 4.

71. See 'Zhonghua Huiguan suo jie zhongyao wenjian' [Chinese Benevolent Association office receives important letter], *Chinese Times*, Oct. 3, 1922, 3. Such activities led to fears amongst the whites of Victoria that a boycott of Canadian goods would be effected in China; see, for example, 'Chinese Here May Retaliate', *Victoria Daily Colonist*, Oct. 16, 1922, 1.

72. For example, 'Bokuan ju Weibu Kangzheng Fenxiao Tuan' [Funds assist Victoria Resist School Segregation Association], *Chinese Times,* Dec. 20, 1922, 2.

73. Previously, Chinese schools in Canada were really little more than spaces in the backs of shops where merchants taught basic literacy. Lee, *Jianada Huaqiao shi*, 323.

74. 'A Chinese School', *Victoria Daily Colonist,* Jan. 18, 1899, 6.

75. Lim Bang, 'Weibu Zhonghua Huiguan zhi yuange ji qiaxiao chuangli zhi yuanqi' [The origins of the Victoria Chinese Consolidated Benevolent Association and the reasons for the creation of overseas schools], *Zhonghua Huiguan/Huaqiao Xuexiao jinian gikan,* Part IV, 1–5; Guan Qiyui, 'Jianada Huaqiao jiaoyu shilue' [A short History of Overseas Chinese Education in Canada], ibid., Part IV, 17–18. See also 'Benxiao xiaoshi [A history of our school], ibid., Part III, 54–8.

76. Ibid., Part V, 26.

77. 'Weibu Huaqiao Gongxue baogao ce' [Text of the report of the Victoria Chinese Public School], *Chinese Times*, July 13, 1915, 1.

78. Even though it was based in Vancouver, the *Chinese Times* regularly reported on the activities of the school, its graduation ceremonies, and social events. See, for example, 'Weibu Huaqiao Gopngxiao dierci gingyou jicheng' [Victoria Chinese Public School holds second annual picnic], *Chinese Times*, July 20, 1920, 3.

79. The *Chinese Times* reported that 'every girl and boy who graduates from the first class can leave behind their local dialects and are fluent in Cantonese when reading and speaking.' 'Weibu qikao zhuzhong Shenghua Guoyu ying sheng zhi tese' [Special characteristics of the pronunciation of Cantonese and Mandarin at the Victoria end of term examinations], *Chinese Times*, July 17, 1915, 3. The writer complained that Victoria's Cantonese was not standard as it 'suffered from the influence of the students'.

80. For example, Cai Yuanpei, the principal of Beijing University, led such a delegation which inspected schools in Victoria and Vancouver in 1918.

81. See, for example, '"All For China"', *Victoria Daily Colonist*, Aug. 13, 1909, 4.

82. *Annual Report, 1914–15*, A XXXVIII and *Annual Report, 1915–1916,* A XLI.

83. See Yee, *Saltwater City*, 44–6.

84. During this era the male/female ratio amongst Chinese in Victoria was six to one; in other centres in BC it was as high as twenty to one. See *Census of Canada*, 1921, Vol. 1, 542.

85. Cited by Chan, *Gold Mountain*, 129.

86. 'Youthful Viciousness', *Victoria Daily Colonist*, Nov. 16, 1899, 5 and Ill Mannered Boys', *Vancouver Daily Province,* Jan. 15, 1901, 4.

87. 'The Injured Chinaman', *Victoria Daily Colonist*, Apr. 6, 1904, 4.

88. *Victoria Daily Times*, Nov. 4, 1908, 5. This report was untitled.

89. 'Huanu beiwu' [Chinese girl assaulted], *Chinese Times*, Feb. 26, 1915, 3.

90. 'Huatong cishang xitong' [Chinese youth stabs western youth], *Chinese Times*, Feb. 4, 1922, 3.

91. Sing Lim, *West Coast Chinese Boy* (Montreal: Tundra Books, 1979), 23.

Article 2: Men Without Women: Italian Migrants in Canada, 1885–1930

Robert Harney

In July of 1908, the lead article of the *Rivista di Emigrazione* described emigration as the 'greatest social phenomenon of our epoch whether one is speaking of the demographic impact on the country, its economy, its moral condition, levels of criminality, state of public health, in fact, of any aspect of the people's life.'[1] Since that time, both in countries of emigration and in immigrant-receiving countries, historians have created a rich literature about migration's demographic and economic impact. From Robert Foerster's *Italian Emigration of Our Times* (1919) to recent studies of remittances and *ritornati*, we have shown the way in which emigration affected class structure in the Italian South.[2] Much less has been said of emigration's impact on the people's morale [...]

This essay concentrates on the Italian emigrant as a man of his family and of his *paese* (agrotown or village). It suggests that his intentions when he began his sojourn in North America defined whether or not the length of his stay caused extraordinary stress on him and also on those he had left behind. For, just as the hometown remained at the centre of his concern, so the migrant retained his place in the social organization of the village or in the inheritance structure and plans for the family. The debate over

Source: From *A Nation of Immigrants: Women, Workers and Communities in Canadian History, 1840s–1960s*, Franca Iacovetta, ed., with Paula Draper and Robert Ventresca (Toronto: University of Toronto Press, 1998, 206–230). (Originally from *The Italian Immigrant Woman in North America*, Betty Boyd Caroli, Robert F. Harney and Lydiio F. Tomasi [Toronto: Multicultural History Society of Ontario, 1978, 79–101]). Permission granted by the American Italian Historical Association.

the role of nuclear and extended families in South Italian life is tedious, but all would agree that family members were expected to suppress their individualism and to work for what Constance Cronin had labeled a synthetic person, the family.[3] Such a view of the family is not, of course, uniquely Italian. The family as a functioning economic unit occurs in most rural and pre-industrial settings. [...]

The decision to migrate, then, was not usually made by the individual, particularly not if he was a young man: 'The actual decision itself is thrashed out in the nuclear family.'[4] (The corollary would be that the decision to end a sojourn abroad will also not be the result of individual decision). In fact, the migrant, like the cash remittances and the *ritornati*, was a constantly accounted for unit of the family and town which he left behind.[5]

The mayor of a small town in Basilicata informed a parliamentary committee in 1907 that 'the population [of his town] was 2400 souls of whom about 600 were in America.' At first glance that is an extraordinary view to take of the fact that one quarter of the population, and probably at least half of the productive men and boys, were residing in foreign lands.[6] But the mayor did not see those men as future Canadians, Americans, or Argentinians. They remained in his mind the husbands, sons, fiancés, and fathers of the women in his town. In this essay, we try to share the mayor's perspective. The role of the migrants as cheap foreign labour and potential Canadian or American citizens has been studied; their roles as wage earners and sources of 'cash money' for the Italian South is receiving more attention now. Here we look at the impact of emigration on family life, on morals, health, and the state of mind of the migrant and his people. [...]

The so-called 'target migrant'—the man who goes abroad or to the city in search of cash money for a specific family objective—expects certain things of his sojourn away from the village and plans to be away for a certain amount of time. In turn, his family and dependents expect certain things of him and have at least a rough estimate, based on local folk wisdom, of how long it should take him to achieve these objectives.[7] Obviously, a sojourn which goes beyond the customary time causes anxiety for all involved. The daughter awaiting a dowry, the empty conjugal bed, the aging parent, or just a Mediterranean spring missed—all put pressure upon the migrant. In this essay we will be dealing with migrants betrayed, thwarted in their schedule by the Canadian economy, by dishonest men, and by harsh winters. The betrayal turned seasonal migration into long-term sojourning and turned momentary success in achieving the financial goal of migration into new depths of indebtedness. Unexpectedly long separation brought disruption and perhaps some of the social pathology which the critics of emigration feared.

How long could commitment to family obligations survive the great distance and increasing time that lay between the sojourner and his origins? One Lithuanian who came as a migrant to Canada in the 1920s told me that when he returned to Vilnius after fifty years in Canada, he went immediately to his sister in order to apologize for failing to send her dowry money to her a half-century earlier.[8] Did young migrants from Calabria have a less filial or familial sense of duty than that?

A tradition of happy endings has grown up to obscure the disruption and pain caused by long sojourning abroad. The *ritornato*, the rich *cafone,* the *Americano* with the diamond stickpin who returns to buy the land that he once sharecropped and to marry the girl of his dreams or take up with the wife whom he has not seen for many years—both the latter as virginal as when he left for America—is migration study's version of the Western melodrama.[9] In the same genre, of course, are the happy vineyard owners who send to Italy for brides who have been fluttering expectantly for many years: 'In his absence, members of the extended family or clan will provide protection and supervision for his immediate family. He can return at any time, assured of a physical home, a social niche and at least some income.'[10] How does that sanguine view of the modern migrant correspond to De Nobili's survey of Calabria in 1907? 'Adulteries, infanticides, and vendettas are the order of the day—manifestations of that abnormal social

state brought on by emigration and the consequent disequilibrium of the sexes.' One critic clearly understood the difference between inheriting the earth and losing one's soul. 'The country is covered with houses, the houses of the new landowners, but from their houses and those of the former owners is banished an ancient heritage and an ancient nobility—the moral integrity of the *foco-bio*.'[11] The same cash money which confused and brought mobility to the social and cadastral structure also deeply affected family structure.[12] However, the physical absence of the migrant himself, especially if it was unexpectedly prolonged, ravaged any dream of a well-ordered future for South Italian families. It changed the distribution of inheritances, the meaning of marriage alliances, and the feelings of people toward one another.

Canada had a higher percentage of 'target migrants' in its Italian immigration after 1900 than the United States did. There were sound economic reasons for that, but there was also terribly fraudulent advertising of work and exploitation of migrants, so Canada also had a very high percentage of seasonal and 'target migrants' trapped into longer sojourns. The gap between the intention of the sojourner and his fate seems particularly great when one looks back at Canada in the 1900s. In that sense, it becomes an especially fruitful setting for the study of the impact of long-term sojourning.

One reason that Canada had more migrants and fewer immigrants than the United States was that neither the Dominion nor the Italian government encouraged settlers from Italy. The Italian Commissariat of Emigration issued several *bollettini* on conditions in Canada which pointed out that the country was not suitable for colonizing except by wealthy peasants. In 1901, the Italian consul in Montreal went so far as to fault 'the lightheartedness with which the Canadian government seeks to people the desert plain of the Dominion.' He concluded that Canada was no place for 'experiments with our peasantry.'[13] Nor did Sifton, the Dominion's powerful Minister of the Interior, view Italians as useful immigrants.[14] So the climate of opinion was as frigid as the climate itself. Nonetheless, a well organized system of seasonal migration to Canada developed at the beginning of the century.[15] Before World War I, thousands of Italian labourers, particularly from Calabria, the Abruzzi, Basilicata, and Friuli were induced to migrate to Canada. There is little doubt that most of those who came through the network fit the definition of 'target migrants.' They came intending brief sojourns, usually hoping for a summer's work in the railway, timbering, and mining camps of the Canadian North.[16]

False newspaper reports were printed in Montreal and distributed throughout Calabria. Workers were led out of Italy overland through Chiasso and Switzerland and then on to the Channel ports and England where they made the crossing on Cunard, CP, and Beaver Lines ships. They were escorted by a variety of sinister labour and travel agents, and so they reached Canada much in the manner of migrants travelling with a foreman to seasonal work on the European continent. Solimbergo, the Italian consul in Montreal, 'found out that of all Italian emigrants who were already in Canada not one thought it of any use to become a colonial [...] the emigrants are going to Canada in order to find work.'[17] At first the seasonal work offered by the great Canadian labour-intensive employers such as the railroad, mining, and lumber companies served the interests of the target migrants well.[18] Struggle for control of the labour pool, though, led to dislocation in the system. Every year a certain number of seasonal migrants became a winter residue in the country. In some years, for example, 1901 and 1904, simply too many migrants were brought over.

Men who had come for single 'campaigns' found that crooked bankers, foremen, boardinghouse keepers, and late thaws made it impossible to hold to their family and community schedule for migration.[19] The same commerce of migration which made the system efficient and drew the target migrants, also led to cutthroat competition between *padroni* and dishonest labour bureaux. That in turn led to imbalances in the labour supply and lost time for the migrants. In 1901, a correspondent for the *Corriere della Sera* accompanied a group—'almost entirely young men, representing the best portion of our country population of the South.' He soon learned how the system could fail the target migrant and his family plans. His group was met in Montreal, where they had been promised work, by agents of the Donnor Emigration Company, which had sponsored their crossing. The migrants were told that they could only have work in British Columbia. Most had no idea where that was. Those who refused the terms

were abandoned. Those that remain here,' he went on, 'seek to house themselves as best they can. Many found their way into different houses, and when it came to paying were driven into the streets as they had no money, their belongings having previously been retained.'[20]

Canadian immigration statistics are virtually useless for the study of return flows to Italy, so it is difficult to estimate the number of migrants caught in the country each year as winter approached.[21] If a man did not get home at season's end, it was quite likely that he would not do so for another year, and perhaps many more. The boardinghouses were run by *padroni*, the camp commissaries were exorbitant and dishonest, and there was little or no work for foreigners in the winter except city snow removal. Some were lucky and found factory work or steady work in street railway construction; many others never escaped the seasonal cycle of work and consequently found their sojourn becoming a form of exile.[22]

It is a truism of migration studies that people who regard themselves as sojourners, regardless of how long they dwell in a host country, continue to think of the problems and needs of their home town as paramount.[23] If it is true that the sojourner was preoccupied with what he had left behind, then we should study him not just as an urban problem or a potentially assimilable immigrant, but also in his own existential frame of reference. Italian migrants were, first and foremost, men away from loved ones and familiar places. They were men entrusted with responsibilities who sensed the proximity of failure, usually failure to bring family levels of existence into harmony with rising expectations. They were men with the increase[d] and natural suspicion that things would not be, indeed could not possibly be, as they should be when and if they managed to get back home.[24] The abnormality of their own existence had to have, they thought, its mirror image in the *paese* [home community].

This essay speculates on the impact of separation and uncertainty on the sojourner. It does not matter whether each migrant eventually became a rich and respected *ritornato* with many children and a Fascist party card, or sent for a wife and became part of the Italian-Canadian bourgeoisie. Any seasonal or 'target migrant' who did not return after the first season slipped into an abnormal existence; so did the people left behind.

One reason historians have shied away from studying the turn of the century in terms of migration disruption is distrust of the sources. We do not have much chance to employ the survey and interviewing techniques used by the anthropologists and sociologists who study contemporary migration.[25] Only bits of oral history material survive, along with risky inferences from migration statistics, to suggest the migrant's real frame of mind. What we are left with is the very suspect literature of those opposed to emigration in Italy and of the missionaries, social workers, and restrictionists in North America. Obviously, with such sources it is too easy to paint a picture of emigration and the migrant's life as pathological. What follows is not a vindication of such literature, but the modest suggestion that it makes sense to think of the man separated from his people as being in an abnormal situation and to use the questions raised by the anti-immigrant literature to propose avenues of research.

We know the economic consequence of the migrant's commitment to his hometown—that willingness to be crowded in cheap boarding houses, to depend on *padroni*, to show little interest in the host country, and to risk no 'cash money' on North American situations. Now we must look at the migrant's frame of mind itself. Let us begin with his hometown world which concerns him so much. His failure to return after a season's work may have been eased by remittances (although more often than not, it was lack of funds which made him stay in Canada). Then, too, there are things money can't buy. If he was a young man, the girl of his choice may not have waited. If he was a father and a husband, he worried about the virtue of his womenfolk.

Anti-emigration literature concentrated on the impact of sojourning on sexual morality. As migration increased, there apparently was an increase in cuckolding and bastardy in the Italian countryside, as there was of prostitution in the cities.[26]

What is one to make of such evidence? It also reflected an old Mediterranean assumption that healthy people left alone copulate, and that women particularly are helpless in the face of temptation. 'Modesty is not natural in women but imposed on them. [...] The emigration of men, fathers, brothers, husbands, lovers, eliminates the coercion and lets natural and unbridled instincts emerge.'[27] The author's view of women and their instincts was primitive, but one can wonder whether it was more so than that of the young, under-educated, rural men and jealous husbands who were the migrants themselves. Moreover, one can also assume that, among men thrown together in work gangs, camps, and boardinghouses, such a view of women became accentuated. The coarse jokes, thwarted young appetites, the dreams of women left behind and inaccessible women seen in the host country, the banter about *comuti*, the fragmentary news from home, all colluded to paint a picture of the hometown which would increase the migrant's tension.[28] The reality of the impact of migration on the countryside hardly mattered as much as the imaginations of those abroad in causing tension and misunderstanding.

It is unlikely that simply the absence of men would destroy the inbred, umbertine, and Catholic values of most peasant women. Moreover, few towns or families were so completely decimated by migration that some older guardian of the family's good name was not about to cluck over impropriety. [...]

[Nevertheless] the possibilities of family disintegration, cuckolding, and dishonour haunted men whose sojourn grew uncontrollably and the phantom that lived with them was, at least in part, created by fear and guilt about how well they were fulfilling family obligations.

Of course, not all the migrants had the same social and familial stress upon them. Many young men had only limited responsibility and had in some sense been ejected from the family inheritance structure with a cash settlement which paid their fare in the New World. (If, however, they were beyond puberty, they might already have had the pressure from a potential bride and the need to meet the property conditions of forming a new nuclear family.) [...] Many married men had become such multiple migrants that they managed to return once a year, beget children, settle family affairs, and thus mitigate the burden of uncertainty that came with long-term sojourning.[29] [...]

The Italian critics of emigration, just like racist restrictionists in North America, saw the male sojourner as a dangerous and amoral beast preying upon North American women. The fear and jealousy of the sexual prowess of strangers along with an almost colour racism against Italian bachelors makes it impossible to study this aspect of the migrant's life through the layers of prejudice in North American sources. For example, Toronto's local muckracking newspaper, *Jack Canuck*, carried lurid accounts of Italian labourers having carnal knowledge of young girls and infecting them.[30]

Years ago, Robert Forester remarked that 'plenty of testimony exists to show that loose living on the part of male Italians abroad is common. Our witnesses, who are generally also critics, affirm that there is often a ready frequenting of prostitutes, a class of persons all but absent from the Italian countryside and village.'[31] Perhaps the Italian literature deserves more attention since it has no racist edge. The critics of emigration, as umbertine Italian gentlemen, held the rather simple physical and ecological view of sex which we spoke of when dealing with the family without its menfolk. Illicit sex would take place if physical and social barriers were not erected against it. To the critics, the migrants abroad were men with the barriers removed. They would be unfaithful to wives and fiancées. They would spend in bordellos money earned for a sister's dowry or saved for a few *tomoli* of land. [...]

No doubt travelling only with other males produced an earthy camaraderie typical of a peasant work force. Whatever the culture or education of the sojourners, life in isolated work camps brutalized them in the truest sense of the word. Men became *bestie* (brutish) under the impact of conditions, and work camp life in Canada was usually worse than in the United States.[32]

The decline into brutishness which took place was not one into unbridled sexuality. The workers were too isolated, tired, frugal, and the host society too prejudiced against them for moral decline to take that form. Rather, the failure came in terms of personal dignity, outward appearance, language, and manner. The process enabled North American racists to remark that such conditions could only be imposed on victims who were 'the sons of backward civilization and know not what twentieth-century living is.'[33]

Interviews with men who were young migrants in those isolated camps refer over and over to becoming *bestie*, to feeling inadequate and inferior not just to the Anglo-Celtic Canadians but to city folk generally. Men came to feel like the *foresee*, 'the man who lives *fuori*,' those too poor and brutish to live in a nucleated agrotown, the unclean, impoverished shepherds and others who held their head downcast

when they entered town, 'and in the face of *stranieri*, nearly always more educated and civil than they, felt themselves humiliated by their ignorance, as men and as Italians.'[34]

They were men who had not eaten anything but stew on mouldy bread and sardines for months on end, and had only eaten in the company of other men. They were men who were 'deprived of the refining influences of women and the soothing touch of childhood.' And their decline was not just in concern for their physical appearance:

> Camp life is an unnatural life, and in it the coarse, vulgar elements of human nature come to the surface; the indecent story, the vulgar joke and the immoral picture are introduced and passed around. If intoxicants are within reach, the men will drink and gamble.[35]

The quote may have the speech rhythm of a born-again preacher or Salvation Army sergeant, but there is no reason to doubt its essential truth.

In general, the brutalization of foreign migrant workers was worst in the most isolated settings. Even in those settings, though, controls existed to keep them from the immorality and sexuality which the critics in Italy assumed. First of all, the very system which drew 'target migrants' to Canada kept them in groups based upon their *paese*. [...]

This meant that often the eyes of the village followed the migrant into the remotest setting. If a man became a drunkard, consorted with the rare prostitutes to be found in the North, dabbled in perversion [sic], or just seemed to go a little crazy, word might get back to the family and town. [...] The other powerful force which kept most of the 'sins against chastity' of the migrants at the level of fantasy was the deep prejudice toward them among their hosts. Literature about 'dirty foreign navvies' abounds and would seem to imply that the migrants were unlikely to find female companionship among the natives easily or without a price.[36] [...]

The abnormality of life for the migrants came not from promiscuity but from total physical and cultural frustration. The same was probably true for the vast majority of women left behind in the *paese*. Perhaps the substitutions were just as debilitating for the family structure. Commissionaires in most camps sold alcohol. The U.S. Industrial Commission of 1901 claimed that unemployed Italians spent 'almost all the idle time […] in the saloons and in other resorts of their countrymen,' a strange new image for an abstentious wine-drinking people. [...]

In the long run, the same combination of external and internalized social coercion which guarded the *villagio pettegolo*, 'the gossipy village,' existed in the migrant camps. The backbiting *paisano* or solicitous relative, the hostile women of the host society, combined with levels of filial piety, parental duty, and morality in the migrant to serve as a brake on his decline into brutishness. He might drink more, he might find a prostitute, he certainly became coarser and more vulgar than he had been when he left Italy, but he probably had not broken faith with the commitments which had sent him forth. He still worked to send money home for specific purposes; he still intended to marry someone from his *paese* (most often someone whom he or his family had chosen before he left), or to return to his wife.

Each migrant seems to have measured time differently according either to his nature, or to the original purpose of his sojourn, and to the situation in his town or origin. To the extent, though, that migration was a form of suspended animation, the sojourn had no time dimension. If a young man were a bachelor, he was held between youth and manhood in regard to marriage, inheritance, and indeed to carrying weight with family and *paesani*. Oral history interviews with immigrants from half-a-dozen countries show that what Arensberg said of the Irish countrymen held true in most rural communities. 'The "boy" reaches adult status when he marries and inherits the farm. The family and the land are both involved in the crucial reorganization.'[37] Young men who had married but had no children before they migrated were often just like bachelors. Their counsel was worth little, and until they had saved money to start a household, would not increase in value. Their absence was a temporary solution to problems of space and fecundity even if the larger problem of owning arable land could only be solved by a long and successful sojourn. Fathers of families worried more; they had more that could go awry or dishonour them at home. For all these men seasonal migration, repeated trips across the oceans, and even accepting immigration were options; the degree to which they entertained each option was entangled

with their fortunes in America and the nature of news from home. Out of that cluster of concern emerged the real measurement of each man's sojourn time.[38]

If a man escaped the confined world of labour camps in summer and large *padrone*-owned boardinghouses[39] in winter and still had not found means to return to Italy or continued to have a 'target' need for cash, he might begin to look for a change to become *bordante*[40] in one of the larger cities with a family from his *paese*. This meant that some of his job transience had declined and usually coincided with the transition to city street work or factory work.[41] The value of the system to husband and wife was obvious. It provided sheltered work at home which enabled her to continue her economic role in the family. The increase in the atmosphere of *civile e gentile* for the migrant *bordante* was also obvious, but what did the system of *conviveza* mean for the moral life of the migrant and for the maintainance of his commitments to his village of origin?

In the first place, if each good-sized Little Italy was a combination of many little *paese*, the little *paese* broke down further into houses where families took in *paesani* and relatives. Historians have long known this, but have not thought about these homes as outriders of the goals and mores of the *paese*. It is through the households and neighbourhoods that 'the high proportion of temporary migrants […] often associated with large numbers of apparently "broken" or "incomplete" families and of people living with friends and relatives rather than their nuclear family'[42] began the process of reasserting the social controls of the village and some of the original goals of migration. The Italian Mission (Methodist) in Toronto, 1908, complained that 'there are so many homeless men in this community it makes it necessary for every woman to accommodate as many boarders as she can crowd into her house.'[43]

Moving from camps and working-class hotels to live with families did not just reflect the emergence of job opportunities in the city. The price of home-cooked food and family chatter, clean clothes and a safe mailing address was that migrants themselves had to clean up, to overcome cafonism, [rude, boorish behaviour] and to make conversation without constant vulgarity. In the city, living with families or visiting families from the *paese* on Sundays marked either the settling-in for a long sojourn or the beginnings of thinking about true immigration. Married men had been unable to envisage their womenfolk living near most non-urban Canadian work sites.[44] Becoming *bordante* [a lodger or border] also meant that the decline into brutishness and the constant but idle chatter about sex ended. The family with whom one boarded, particularly *la padrona*, might know the boarder's family as well as his commitments at home and his dreams. Often the lady of the house had her own dream of playing matchmaker. If the *bordante* was not betrothed or married, there was invariably a niece of the household who could be sent for as a bride. In such simple human terms the needs of the old country family and of the *paese* itself were served. No one who boarded with a landlady from his own village had much chance of being either promiscuous or exogamous.

Often the lady of the house was as young as the youngest boarders, but if they were *paesani*, they most likely addressed her as *zia* (auntie). Respect, recognition of her connection with the Old World family structure, and a guarantee of propriety were all in the use of the word auntie.[45]

Probably that proximity to the occasion of sin which so exercized the critics of emigration came into play occasionally between *la padrona* and the *bordante*, although in the homes as in the village and camp, the problem of *where* remained complex. The chance arrival of husbands, children, neighbours, other boarders, visiting city nurses, water meter readers, settlement house workers, and Methodist missionaries could make a farce of the most passionate scenario. The central actors themselves also made passionate scenarios unlikely. Whether from morality and familial honour or a good sense of status and self-preservation, trysts were not likely. […]

The social and moral structures of the *villagio pettegolo* which had been weakened but never vanished in the all-male work camps recovered in the city's Little Italy. The Rev. Taglialatela, Methodist colporteur to the Italians of Toronto, saw social abnormality in transience itself: 'They are not under the eyes of their friends and relatives and do not feel obliged to look better and act well.' He, of course, thought that they had improved with time in the city; perhaps the sense of the *paese* and its controls simply reasserted itself through family and campanilist density.[46]

Vecoli's 'Contadini in Chicago,' a decade ago, noted the crucial place of the family in Little Italies: 'If the South Italian retained a sense of belongingness with his fellow townsmen the family continued to be the focus of most intense loyalties.'[47] The point, I think, could be pushed further. Just as the village or agrotown was a collectivity of families, so potentially were the *colonie* of the *paese* in North America. A migrant or sojourner was at all times within the system whether as a potential *ritornato* or as a colonist of the new *piccolo paese*. He was also at all times a member of a family, nuclear and extended. In fact, families—new ones, old ones, broken ones, potential ones in the form of young sojourners, girls awaiting dowries, husbands, fiancées, sons with insufficient inherited land, fathers toiling abroad so that family status kept pace with fecundity—were the impelling cause of migration.

Remittances made one economic world of the village and the many faraway lands where there were migrants sojourning. In the same way, families and neighbours in the New World reimposed the social coercion, jealousies, and affectionate familiarity of the *paese*:

> Most of the Cinisari in the 69th St. group intend to return to Sicily. The town of Cinisi is forever in their minds: 'I wonder if I can get back in time for the next crop? […] I hope I can get back in time for the *festa* […]' They receive mail keeping them informed as to the most minute details and about all gossip that goes on in Cinisi; in addition, they keep their hometown informed as to what is going on here. They write home of people here who have transgressed home custom: 'So and so had married an American girl. The American girls are libertines. The boy is very disobedient.' He has married a stranger […] that is, an Italian of another town. In this way they blacken a man's name in Cinisi so that a bad reputation awaits him on his return.[48]

We have long known about this pattern of contact between a specific *paese* and a specific part of some American city. The instances of it are very numerous.[49] Such networks of communication and transit existed between most towns of emigration and their *colonie*. [...] The abnormality of the migrant condition came, as we have seen, not from decline into boorishness or unbridled sexuality, but from the suspended animation in matters of marriage, sex, and inheritance which came with separation. The logical end of sojourning was either creation of a new nuclear family or reconstitution and completion of one. This could come about by 'going home,' sending for a wife or bethrothed, or marrying endogamously in the new land. [...][50]

The ethnic groups who provided the shock troops for turn-of-the-century industrialization—Italians, Hungarians, Greeks, South Slavs, Poles, Lithuanians, Finns, and Chinese—all had tremendous imbalances of male over female in the sex ratio of their migration statistics. And the boardinghouse stereotypes of rowdiness, insobriety, ignorance of English, and transience persist to one degree or another about all these groups, but perhaps less so about the Italians than the others. [...]

If immigration was a matter of intention and attitude rather than duration of sojourn, one is tempted to suggest that true immigration did not really commence until the questions of marriage and inheritance were settled. A migrant's search was ended when he had fulfilled his target, but his target was almost always to live a normal life, i.e., married life, among his own kind, somewhere in the psychical world of his *paesani* where he could make a living. [...]

The real history of the sojourners and of Canadian Little Italies will only be within our reach when all the possible archival and statistical sources are used along with the 'memory culture.' Church records, minutes of *mutuo soccorso* and other benevolent societies, stub books of payment, receipts and remittances from immigrant banks, and the sparse records of *paese* clubs are the internal ethnic sources we need to use. Photographs and city directory analysis also help to show the place of the migrants and *bordanti* in the birth of a *paese's* colony.[51]

Much of this essay should be read as a plea and perhaps an agenda for further study—study of the villages and towns of emigration and study of the migrant's mind set as a key to his North American experience. Until studies of such topics as changes in marriage and betrothal patterns, cuckolding, alcoholism, mental problems among *ritornati*, endogamy rates among sojourners, and a myriad of attitudinal and cultural subjects are done, plausible constructs

such as this essay provide our glimpse of the men who entered Canada in the 1900s [...]

Notes

1. Leonello De Nobili, 'L'Emigrazione in Calabria. Effetti dell'emigrazione in generale,' *Revista di Emigrazione* 1:5 (July, 1908).

2. R. Foerster, *Italian Emigration of Our Time* (Harvard, 1918). See F. Cerase, *L'Emigrazione di Ritorno* (Rome, 1971); Betty Boyd Caroli, *Italian Repatriation for the U.S., 1900–1941* (New York, 1973); T. Saloutos, *They Remember America* (Berkeley, 1956).

3. C. Cronin, *The Sting of Change: Sicilians in Sicily and Austria* (Chicago, 1970), pp. 85–89. C. Ware, *Greenwich Village, 1920–1930*, p. 197: 'A child would be expected to sacrifice his own ambition and advancement to the interest of the family group.' Pitkin shows the obverse of this: the parents' duty to *sistemare* their children's lot. See D. Pitkin, 'Marital Property Considerations Among Peasants: An Italian Example,' *Anthropological Quarterly* 33:1 (Jan., 1960): 37.

4. C. Cronin, The Sting of Change, pp. 58–59; John J. Baxevanis, *Economy and population movements in the Peloponnesos of Greece*, Athens: National Centre of Social Research 1972. See especially Chapter IV, 'The Decision to Migrate.'

5. This, of course, can be seen from the perspective of the 'stern family or from the person's own sense of family responsibility as a 'target migrant.' The clearest discussion of migrant intentions that I have found is in Joan M. Nelson's Temporary versus Permanent Cityward Migration: Causes and Consequences (Migration and Development Study Group, MIT, 1976).

6. The response of the mayor of Albano di Lucania to commissioners is in A. Rossi's Vantaggi e Danni dell'emigrazione, p. 1550.

7. See testimony about timing and length of sojourn throughout. A. Rossi's Vantaggi e Danni dell'emigrazione. An anthropological study of a Lebanese village shows that there was both a real and ideal pattern of migration deviation and income. See L. Sweet, 'The Women of Ain and Dayr,' Anthropological Quarterly Vol. 140:171.

8. Taped interview with Mr. Jones Yla, former Lithuanian-Canadian newspaper editor (Multicultural History Society of Ontario collection, 1976).

9. Typical would be the idyll in G. Fortunato's *In Mezzogiorno e lo stato itlaiano, Discorsi politici*, 1880–1910 (Bari, 1911):502: 'But the peasant, oh the peasant pick up the zappa and the vanga willingly again, happy enough to be free from the usurious slavery of rents, of being able to acquire for himself and for his a bit of his own and a piece of land.'

10. J. Nelson, *Temporary versus Permanent Cityward Migration*, p. 37.

11. De Nobili, 'L'Emigrazione in Calabria,' p. 7, and A. Milani, 'L'Emigrazione e una partita del suo bilancio morale passive,' *Rivista di Emigrazione* 1:7 (Sept., 1908): 17.

12. Again the contemporary Lebanese case study echoes the many cases recorded by Nitti, Fortunato, Del Nobili, etc., in the 1900s: 'Then some families have land but not labour, some have sheep and goats but no land, some have both, and many receive money from overseas which aids the exchange of food and work necessities among all.' Sweet, 'Women of Ain ad Dayr,' p. 173.

13. Some of the more damning *bollettini* about Canada were D. Viola's 'Le condizioni degli opera: italiani nel distretto minerario di Cobalt nella provincial di Ontario,' Anno 1910 no, 13; E. Rossi's 'Delle condizioni del Canada rispetto all'immigrazione italiana,' Anno 1903 no. 4; B. Attolico's 'L'agricoltura e l'emmigrazione nel Canada,' Anno 1912 no. 5. There were also complaints in the Italian parliament in 1901 which led to the *Corriere della Sera's* investigative reporter accompanying immigrants.

14. See D. Avery, 'Canada's Immigration Policy and the Foreign Navvy, 1874–1914,' *The Canadian Historical Association, Historical Papers* (1972), pp. 135–156.

15. The best account of this 'commerce of migration' through Chiasso to Canada is in B. Brandenberg's *Imported Americans* (New York, 1903). His is the only account of the notorious E. Ludwig who operated on the Swiss-Italian border as a labour agent for a number of Canadian companies.

16. The testimony of many labourers before the Royal Commission of 1904 confirms their transience and 'target' intention. See *Royal Commission appointed to inquire into the Immigration of Italian Labourers to Montreal and the Alleged Fraudulent Practices of Employment Agencies* (Ottawa, 1905).

17. *Corriere della Sera's* report, 'Emigration of Italian Peasants to Canada' (March 18, 1901), includes *Solimbergo's Report*, Public Archives of Canada, Immigration Branch, RG 76, Vol. 128, File 28885:1.

18. See *Royal Commission* (1904) for details.

19. See reports to the *Corriere della Sera* through 1901. Some 'target migrants' apparently even found themselves recruited to fight for Great Britain in the Boer War.

20. *Corriere della Sera*, 'In Canada the Landing of the Emigrants New Delusion,' Quebec May 3rd and the dispatch of May 5th in PAC, Immigration Branch, RG 76, Vol. 129, File 28885:1.

21. See W.D. Scott, 'Immigration and Population,' in *Canada and Its Provinces*, ed. A. Shortt and A. Doughty, VII:561 (Toronto, 1914) for the system of counting immigrants. Since so many Italian migrants to Canada came and went through U.S. ports, the figures are particularly unreliable. The sex ratio in Italian migration to Canada in the 1900s overpoweringly suggests seasonal and target migration. In 1906–1970 [sic; should be 1907], 5,114 Italians arrived in Canadian ports in steerage, 17 in other classes; 4,430 were men and 384 were women. Some reconstruction of such arrivals can be made from the annual immigration reports in Parliamentary sessional papers, but they cannot answer questions about Italian migration between U.S. Little Italies and Canada. Even in Toronto, where there should have been more balance between the sexes, there were three times as many Italian men as women according to the Census of 1911.

22. The 'memory culture' describes many South and East European bachelor migrants being caught in a cycle of inadequate summer work, winter indebtedness, and thus, no opportunity to end the sojourn. For some, the turn-of-the-century 'reconnoitring of North America elided with the Depression years.' The impact of harsh winters on the seasonal migrant continued a traditional problem of Canadian social history. See Judy Fingard, 'The Winter's Tale: Contours of Pre-Industrial Poverty in British America, 1815–1860,' *The Canadian Historical Association Historical Papers* (1974), especially p. 67.

23. See R. Berrier and T. Wolf, *Internal Migration*, a selected bibliography (Migration and Development Study Group, MIT, 1975).

24. The concern could range from the health of a parent to that of a fig tree, but it tended to involve jealousy about property and female virtue. Foerster, in *The*

139

Italian Emigration, quotes Coletti as claiming that in 'some parts of South Italy men who marry just before emigrating sometimes, by way of precaution, leave the wives immaculate,' p. 441.

25. For examples of a literature which put the migrant himself at the centre of study, see J. Berger and J. Mohr, *A Seventh Man* (London, 1975); Jane Kramer 'Invandrare,' *New Yorker Magazine* (22 March 1976). Ann Cornelisen's *Women of the Shadows* (Boston, 1976) provides a good picture of those left behind.

26. T. Cyriax, *Among Italian Peasants* (Glasgow, 1919), pp. 216–217.

27. Ibid., p. 10.

28. A brilliant, if a bit cruel, analysis of the relationship between South Italian male sexual fantasizing and banter on the one hand, and their feelings of poverty and powerlessness on the other can be found in A. Cornelisen, *Women of the Shadows*.

29. See the pattern described by V. Nee and his wife in San Francisco's Chinatown where men actually did go home only to beget sons or to bring them to America when they reached puberty: *Longtime Californ. A Documentary Study of an American Chinatown* (Boston, 1973), pp. 60–124.

30. See S. LaGurnina, *Wop: A Documentary History of Anti-Italian Discrimination in the United States* (San Francisco, 1973). See *Jack Canuck* 1:12 (25 Nov. 1911), City Archives of Toronto.

31. Foerster, *The Italian Emigration*, p. 441.

32. See P. Roberts, *The New Immigration* (New York, 1914), for U.S. work camps; E. Bradwin, *The Bunkhouse Man* (New York, 1928), for Canadians. Neither account details the degradation as well as the Italian *bollettini* and some of the oral 'memory cultures' do. See note 13.

33. Roberts, *The New Immigration*, p. 112.

34. Notiziario in *Rivista di Emigrazione* 1:3 (May, 1908). See John Davis, 'Town and Country,' *Anthropological Quarterly* 42:3 (July, 1969). This view was confirmed very forcefully by all the former migrants interviewed. Davis' local study is based on Pisticci which happened to be the hometown of many Italians who came to Toronto.

35. Roberts, *The New Immigration*, p. 115.

36. The limits of the 'memory culture' and of oral history sources generally are discovered when one asks about sex habits among the migrants. Even the oldest survivors will talk about the heterosexual prowess of their youth, but little else.

37. C. Arensberg, *The Irish Countryman, An Anthropological Study* (New York, 1968), p. 77. Interviews with Poles, Macedonians, Ukrainians, Italians, Lithuanians, and Croats confirm this view.

38. J. Baxevanis, in *Economy and Population Movements*, writes that 'Emigration is the historical solution to land fragmentation,' p. 67. The point is true but not subtle enough for the Italian situation. For some, 'target migration,' for others, seasonal migration, and for others, longtime sojourning were the alternatives, not simply emigrating. The Italian folk song, 'Quando Saro in America,' shows how complicated the matter was. See T. Cyriax, *Among Italian Peasants*, p. 196–197.

39. On the complicated question of whether the *padrone*, steamship agent, and boardinghouse keeper were one and the same, see testimony before *Royal Commission* (1904), p. 167.

40. In North America, the usual usage was *bordante* or *bordisti* although variations of the Italian *covivenze* were used as well.

41. J. MacDonald and L. MacDonald, 'Chain Migration, Ethnic Neighbourhood Formation and Social Networks,' in *An Urban World*, ed. C. Tilly (Boston, 1974), p. 230. The MacDonalds view the *bordanti* more as the product of serial migration than as migrants from the camps coming to the city.

42. Nelson, *Temporary versus Permanent Cityward Migration*, p. 62.

43. *Missionary Outlook* (June, 1908), XXVLLL:6:141. 'As these are not employed all the time in winter, but spend the idle hours around the house, it gives the housekeeper much extra work and makes it hard to leave and attend meetings.'

44. John Davis, 'Town and Country,' p. 174 'and the very strong associations of women with town make it difficult for men to accept that the women should work in the country.'

45. The use of terms of respect or affection for *la padrona* came out in many interviews. One of the most detailed accounts was that of Mrs. M. Caruso about her grandmother (taped interview, 7 Dec. 1976, MHSO collection). Mrs. Gina Petroff remembers that as a young wife, she always referred to her older boarders as uncle (taped interview, 27 Oct. 1976, MHSO collection).

46. A Taglialatela, 'Our Italian Citizens,' *Missionary Outlook* (April 10), XXX:4.

47. R. Vecoli, 'Contadini in Chicago,' in *Journal of American History* LI:3 (Dec., 1964): 409.

48. Cusumano account of Cinisi colony in New York. R. Park and Miller, *Old World Traits Transplanted* (New York, 1921), pp. 150–151.

49. See C. Bianco, *The Two Rosetos* (Indiana, 1974); L.W. Moss and S.C. Cappannari, 'Patterns of Kinship Comparaggio and Community in a South Italian Village,' *Anthropological Quarterly* 33:1 (Jan., 1960), and the bibliographical references in MacDonald and MacDonald, 'Chain Migration.'

50. Endogamous marriage, to have real meaning for this essay, would have to be between people from the hometown or surrounding villages. Marriage between people from the same province is really out-marriage in *paese* terms. [...]

51. The Multicultural History Society of Ontario has found many sources to be richer than assumed and others to be disappointing. [...]

Article 3: A Roumanian Pioneer

Anne B. Woywitka

Mrs. Veronia Kokotailo came with her parents to Canada in 1898 when she was four years old. Her father had decided to leave the village of Boian in Roumania because his native land could no longer offer sustenance to him and his growing family. He owned the house they lived in, plus a scrap of land no larger than a small city lot. Over the preceding generations, the original land holding had been divided and subdivided among members of his family so that there was hardly enough to grow a garden. How could he hope to raise a family on this meager bit of land? Much less, how could he hope to give anything to his own children when they were ready to go on their own? For these reasons, he decided to emigrate to Canada. Four other families decided to join him, including his father-in-law with a wife by a second marriage.

The sale of his property in Boian brought him enough to pay their passage, but little was left over to re-establish them in the new land. They arrived in Canada in the summer of 1898 to settle in a district northeast of Willingdon which was to form the nucleus of the first Roumanian settlement in Alberta. Though they left behind them the poverty of the Old Country, they also left behind all things dear and familiar to them—their homes, relatives, and friends, church and their way of village life. In exchange, they hoped to establish a better life on the 160 acres of land the Canadian Government was giving away

for $10—never dreaming how hard the transition from 'rags to riches' would be, nor how long it would take to make a decent life for themselves.

They brought with them such tools as spade, shovel, axe, hammer, saw, scythe and sickle. One family brought a quem for grinding wheat into flour, another a spinning wheel and loom. They brought with them their bedding and personal effects. The little extra money they still had went for hiring teamsters and wagons to take them from Edmonton to the area they had chosen to settle. In truth, to them the place was a dot on the map which they chose because there were other settlements nearby—Willingdon, Shandro and Whitford. They planned to call the new settlement Boian, after their native village.

When their teamster dropped them off, they could see little else than a forest of poplar trees and a glimmer of sky above. So this was to be their home in Canada!

'Well,' said Veronia's father, 'at least we will never run short of wood here. There is more than enough for our buildings and even more for fuel and fences than we ever dreamt of in the Old Country!'

For economic reasons, they decided that for the first little while, it would be better for the two families to live together.

They immediately set to clearing a space in the woods for their primitive shelter which they called a 'burdey.' It was a dugout large enough to accommodate the family with a pole-roof like a tepee over it. The poles were covered with sedge and sod. The burdey afforded them shelter from wind and sun and even kept out most of the rains that fell frequently that summer.

The two men had no sooner completed the burdey and dug a well when they left the women and children in search of work. They had to earn a few dollars for winter food supplies.

Source: *A Nation of Immigrants*, Iacovetta, et al. (originally from *Alberta Historical Review* 21 (4) (1973) 119–25.)

As the women enlarged the clearing for a garden, the pile of logs grew. Then Veronia's mother saw the possibility of a log house. She resented living like an animal in a lair and had cried bitterly over it. She longed for the clean white-washed home she'd left behind. From then on she worked with the vision of a log house uppermost in her mind. Before the men returned in the fall, the house had been built.

Veronia recalls how hard her mother worked as she cut, limbed and sawed the logs into equal lengths. With the mother-in-law's help, they dragged the logs into place and set them upright into the soil, side by side, to make a wall. Her mother was young and her body was yet to be hardened by hard work. Before she was finished building the house, both her shoulders were a mass of raw bleeding flesh. But she refused to give up and in time all four walls were standing. The only thing that baffled her was the roof, for which she was forced to call for help from a neighbour.

She left a space for the door and arranged for a window on the south wall. In place of glass she used a linen pillow case. As a final touch to the house, she made a porch over the door. Its walls and roof were made by weaving willows over a frame. She then plastered everything, inside and out, using a mixture of clay and chopped sedge.

Later, when she discovered a deposit of white clay, she carted it home by hand and used it to smooth and brighten the dark walls. The dirt floor bothered her, but there was no way to improve on that other than to surface it with clay and tramp it down. She kept the loose dirt down by sprinkling it with water and sweeping it off with a broom made of birch switches.

Now there remained the problems of a door, a chimney and an oven. Again, the willow came in handy. For the door she made a cross frame over which she wove thick batts of sedge. She wove a willow frame for the chimney and plastered it thickly, inside and out. She made a clay bake-oven, the top of which served as a warm bed for the children on cold winter nights. She laid rocks for a cook stove but had to wait until she could get a galvanized iron sheet for the stove-top. Thus, without spending a penny and improvising as she went, Veronia's mother built them a home in which they lived for many years. [...]

That summer and fall they lived mostly off the woods and meadows around them, picking berries, mushrooms and edible roots. They had some flour and a bag of potatoes which they had used sparingly. Their supplies had to last indefinitely.

The men returned in the fall with enough money to replenish food supplies and to buy the barest necessities. Because it was necessary to live on one's homestead part of the year in order to 'prove' it, they built a shelter on the father-in-law's quarter and he moved into it with his wife. About this time, Veronia's mother gave birth to another child.

That fall and winter, Veronia's parents chopped down trees, enlarging the clearing around the house. Come spring they would hire someone to break it. They did not spare themselves as they worked. When the snows grew deep, they sawed stacks of firewood for fuel and trimmed trees for posts and fence rails. Young as she was, Veronia took care of the baby and her brother and kept the fire going.

Before the spring thaw came, the father went working again. The food supply was running short and they needed money to pay for the breaking and the seed. Soon after he was gone it became necessary to ration their food. When the last handful of flour had been used and the last potato had gone into the soup pot, death by starvation became a very real possibility. The baby cried and the other children begged for something to eat. There was no one to whom the mother could turn for help, knowing other settlers were all in the same predicament.

Without too much hope, she went into the woods looking for mushrooms, though it was still early in the season. However, she did find little yellow button-sized mushrooms growing. These she picked not knowing whether they were edible or not. What difference if they died of mushroom poisoning or by starvation? Beggars could not be choosers. She added chopped green grass to the mushrooms in the pot and boiled it. They ate that day and did not die. Then for two weeks without a break, they ate the same unpalatable food. The mother cried each night and prayed that they not wake when morning came. But every morning they awoke, alive as ever and hungrier than the day before. The mother would go into the woods again and hunt for more mushrooms and pick more grass, and pray for the father to return.

At the end of the second week the father arrived home, carrying on his back 50 pounds of flour and a pig's head. He had walked a hundred miles over

142

rough trails bringing food for his family. Later, the mother earned her husband's displeasure when she cut off the ears from the pig's head and gave them to her parents for a pot of soup.

They broke a plot of land that spring and planted it to potatoes, a bit of garden, and the rest of wheat.

In the meantime, Veronia's mother and a neighbour woman, hearing that a Mr. Johnson at Whitford had raised a log barn and was looking for someone to plaster it, offered their services in hopes of earning a bit of money. They walked twice a day to work through five miles of bush. It was a back-breaking job and for lunch they were given raw carrots out of the garden. [...]

At the end of two weeks of hard labour, they each received a pail of potatoes in lieu of payment.

Because her father was away from home so much of the time and her mother worked outside the house, Veronia at the age of five had already learned responsibility. She took care of the younger children and ran errands for her mother.

In 1899, her mother harvested their first crop of wheat by sickle, tying it into sheaves and putting it in stooks [method of stacking wheat sheaves] to dry. The day she threshed, she took a panful of the precious grain, put it in a bag over Veronia's shoulder and sent her up the path to a neighbour's home where they had a quem. Veronia came back with the flour and by night-time they were eating buns and potato soup made from the produce of their own little bit of land.

It was a great day for rejoicing when Veronia's father bought a cow. Her grandfather had also bought one and when they purchased a plough, the two men teamed their animals. Now, not only did they have milk, but were able to break more land without hiring anybody.

The mother was heartbroken the day their cow died. They had come to depend on the milk, the bit of cream and cheese the cow had supplied them. It was hard to reconcile themselves to the loss. However, being a practical woman, she skinned the cow and tanned the hide. At least she had leather for making moccasins for her family.

Then, in time, her father bought another cow, and also an ox. This time he kept the cow for milking purposes only and used the ox for heavy work.

During those first years they were always only a step away from hunger and starvation. Mostly, they lived off the land. Meat was almost an unknown commodity. Though wild game was plentiful, her people were not hunters. Without a gun, they had no way to get the ducks and upland game-birds to their table.

One day when Veronia was on an errand to a neighbour's home, she sniffed the heavenly aroma of meat cooking on the stove. As she waited hopefully to be invited to eat, her attention was drawn by a cat yowling at the door.

The old woman turned to the door.

'Oh, here's my Machko back home. Be a good girl and let him in. 'He's been out all morning,' she said to Veronia.

Veronia opened the door and drew back with a gasp. She had never seen such a large cat before. He was twice the size of an average tom. His face and ears were nicked with battle scars, the end of his tail bitten off. On the doorstep lay a fat prairie chicken he had brought home. Padding softly into the house, he went straight to his mistress, rubbing himself affectionately against her legs and purring like a distant thunderstorm.

While the woman bent over to fondle the cat, speaking endearingly and praising him, the wheels in Veronia's head began to turn madly. She did not think the woman had seen the prairie chicken. Though she had never stolen anything before, hunger did not leave her much choice. Through the half-open door she could see the dead bird. It lay there, tempting her with visions of broth and succulent meat. Maybe if she snatched it and ran [...] ? Surely the woman could not miss something she had not seen? Besides, Veronia told herself convincingly, there was meat bubbling in her pot already. She did not know what it was to be hungry.

Putting her thoughts into action, the little girl slid out of the door, grabbed the prairie chicken under her arm and ran. But she had not gone far before she heard the woman shouting:

'What are you doing? Where are you going with that chicken? It's mine. Wait till I tell your mother what you did. Just wait.'

Caught in the act red-handed, Veronia dropped the bird and dived into a tall growth of green, too scared to look where she landed. Immediately, she felt the sharp sting of nettle on her legs and arms, but mostly on her bare buttocks. She scrambled out of the nettles even faster and ran home crying, shedding tears of shame and humiliation combined with a painful itch of nettle stings. She shriveled inside when she thought of her mother's wrath. Now even hunger seemed preferable.

The neighbour came to their door later in the day carrying the plucked bird in her hand. The little girl looked for a place to hide but saw none. Hanging her head in shame and resignation, she waited for the sky to fall on her. But as it turned out, the neighbour had a heart after all. While Veronia watched fearfully, the woman handed the bird to her mother.

'Perhaps you would like to make some soup. My cat is a hunter and brings me more than I can use.'

No word or mention of what had really happened.

Veronia's mother seized the old woman's hand and kissed it. Her eyes were bright with unshed tears. 'God will repay you for this! My husband is not home and my children are hungry. Thank you! Thank you so much!'

The neighbour nodded sadly. 'Forgive me! But like the saying goes, the well fed do not know the hungry.'

The lean years continued. What little income rolled in from the father's work was ploughed back into the homestead. The clearing in the woods grew ever larger. The family increased and so did the mother's responsibilities. Soon Veronia was to shoulder much of the work her mother had done before. She helped clear land, picked roots, and learned to work with the machinery her father had acquired. They grew a large garden and laid in a store of potatoes, dried peas, beans and broadbeans. They krauted cabbage, picked saskatoons and dried them for the winter. The whole family contributed to the welfare of the home for there was no room for a drone in their midst.

As more settlers came in, they brought with them various things like an oil press, mortar, and a grist mill. Her mother availed herself of their use, making oil from poppy seed, sunflower seeds and mostly from the oil rich seed of the cannabis, all of which she grew in her garden. She used the oil in all her baking and her cooking. She used the mortar to take the coarse hulls off the barley, wheat and millet and used the hulled grains to cook as cereal or as filling for cabbage rolls. They caught fish in the river using box-traps. These fish they pickled for later use or salted and dried them for winter eating. They picked mushrooms and dried them.

From the cannabis or hemp plant, they processed a coarse fibre which they wove into horse blankets. From these same fibres, they made strong rope. The mother made her own soap using waste fat and lye made from ashes. She scrubbed clothes on a wooden scrub board. She sewed and mended, first by candlelight, later by the light of a kerosene lamp.

In times of sickness, Veronia's mother reverted to the use of herbs and roots to make her own medicinal teas and salves. As a carryover from the Old Country she, like the rest of the settlers, believed in the power of witchcraft and the 'evil eye.' Usually in every district of Central European settlers, there was an old woman versed in the art of 'pouring wax' or 'throwing coals,' which was supposed to be able to relieve many aches and pains as well as take away illnesses of an emotional nature. These may have been primitive practices but the power of believing in them was strong and seemed to help in many instances.

By 1910 Veronia's father had horses for working on the land, a breaker for turning the sod, a plough, a disc, drill, harrows and a binder for harvesting.

The Boian Marea school was opened in 1909, and though fifteen-year-old Veronia wanted to go, her father felt that she was too old for that. Besides, he needed her help on the homestead. Three of the oldest children missed school because they were needed at home. The father felt that though he was illiterate, he had done well. Why waste time on school when there was still more land to be cleared, more work to be done? Perhaps that was why, when Veronia married and had children of her own, she made certain that no sacrifice on her part was too great in order to give them the education she had missed.

144

WHAT DID IT MEAN TO BE CANADIAN?

Conflicting Views on Nationalism and Identity (1880s–1920s)

Marcel Martel
York University

WHAT DID IT MEAN TO BE CANADIAN? CONFLICTING VIEWS ON NATIONALISM AND IDENTITY (1880s–1920s)

Introduction by Marcel Martel

147

●INTRODUCTION

Marcel Martel

The arrival of more than 3 million immigrants between 1896 and 1914, Canada's relations with Great Britain, and the place of Aboriginal peoples and French Canadians in the development of the country triggered a debate about the meaning of being Canadian. Nationalist sentiments were exacerbated and many citizens called for strong measures. Although nationalist sentiments are perceived as benign today, especially when a Canadian or a group of Canadians win an award or make an important discovery or achievement, these feelings have often been denounced as the cause of alienation, discrimination, and intolerance, as indicated in Phyllis Senene's analysis of the Canadian experience with nationalism. Her analysis offers a critical account of nationalism and the negative impact that nationalism has had on Canadians and ethnic relations. Although some prefer to condemn nationalism, we cannot deny the impact that nationalism has had on Canadians, as it was the case between 1880 and 1920.

At the end of the nineteenth century, English-speaking citizens strongly believed that they constitued the dominant group in the country and should remodel Canada according to their cultural preferences: a territory where the English language, Protestant churches, the affection for British institutions and, naturally, for the monarchy, would dominate. As stated in Carl Berger's study of nationalism, English Canadian nationalism was connected to the rise of imperialism. English-speaking nationalists envisioned a special destiny for Canada, one in which nationhood would be achieved within the British Empire—the imperial connection, after all, was seen as the best means to fulfill Canada's destiny.

Social Darwinism shaped the nationalist ideas of these people. Nationalists perceived themselves as part of a superior race, a view supported by recent events in world history. Most significantly, the United Kingdom had been able to build a powerful Empire. This vision underlay the transformation of Canada into a utopia where English, Protestantism, and British political and social institutions would thrive.

Canada's link to the Empire had brought economic and political advantages, according to English-speaking nationalists. Among them, Canada would be able to resist the dangerous charm of American continentalism. Moreover, due to its strategic geographic position, Canada had a special mission within the Empire. The utopian vision of the English Canadian nationalists was nourished by the possibility that Canada would one day take over the leadership of the Empire. Consequently, Canada had to be ready to defend the interests of the Empire anywhere.

These nationalists had a negative opinion of French Canadians as a group. According to them, French Canadians belonged to a non-progressive race that represented an obstacle for English-speaking people in their attempt to shape the country according to their utopian vision. The rights of French Canadians to preserve their culture, religion, and language were tolerated as long as they did not try to impose their nationalist project outside Quebec.

English-speaking nationalists used various organizations, such as Orange lodges, labour unions, and women's groups, to put pressure on provincial and federal governments to take measures aimed at containing this stream of newcomers, especially when they were not from the British Isles. They forced the federal government to implement policies, sometimes radical, in order to limit the arrival of immigrants defined as undesirable. A prime example is the restrictive immigration policy based on racial prejudices and the perceived incapacity of certain ethnic groups to assimilate. These groups met with partial success, notably with the implementation of a Head Tax for Chinese, starting in 1885, and a restrictive policy on Japanese following the 1907 anti-Asian riots in Vancouver.

However, these measures were not in themselves sufficient, because these English-speaking nationalists feared for the future of British culture. They pressed politicians to adopt a policy of assimilation intended to deny the multicultural character emerging in Canada, notably in the Canadian Prairies. So, first in Manitoba in 1890 and 1916, then in those areas that became Alberta and Saskatchewan in 1905, and finally in Ontario in 1912, they used the school system as an instrument of assimilation into the Protestant English-speaking culture, by making English the only language of instruction.

The English-speaking nationalist project collided with that of the French Canadians, especially when it threatened the realization of the English-speaking imperialist utopia, which was the conquest of western Canada.

The emigration of French Canadians and Acadians characterizes the development of these national groups in the second half of the nineteenth century. Certain members of the French-Canadian elite were quick to condemn this migratory movement. However, unable to stop it, they then tried to channel it. But a debate divided the elite. Where to go? Somewhere in Quebec? Yes, answered certain propagandists who praised the merits of Saguenay and the Eastern Townships in Quebec. For his part, the legendary Antoine Labelle, a priest in Saint-Jérôme north of Montreal, hoped to convince those who wanted to emigrate to go to the Laurentians instead of the United States of America. But was there somewhere else in Canada? Yes, answered those who worked in the Canadian Prairies. In the Prairies, colonization took place in an imperialist context because it meant dispossessing First Nations populations by signing treaties, thus facilitating the opening of the West to the colonists. In this process, French speakers tried to make their voice heard, but because French-speaking elites were divided on strategies for the settlement of the Prairies, they quickly found the limits of their influence.

149

The archbishop Alexandre-Antonin Taché and his successor, L.-Ph. Adélard Langevin, envisioned recreating a second Quebec in Manitoba in order to support French speakers who had already settled there. Their idea of populating the areas was based on French-speaking bloc settlements. In this vision, French speakers would live side by side with other French-speaking people, which would facilitate the constitution of an institutional network intended to ensure the development of the French fact.

The pleas of these people did not bend the will of their Quebec colleagues. Strategic considerations prevailed over the solidarity that should have animated French speakers. What would be the use of emptying Quebec to fill the Prairies? The West was perceived as a vast territory in which it would be difficult to ensure the dominance of French Canadians. A territory to be conquered, but at what price? Would this not create a danger to the political weight of Quebec in Confederation? In the geopolitical calculation that concerned the Quebec Catholic episcopate, Quebec triumphed. After all, what was the use of robbing Peter to pay Paul?

At the same time, Western Canada came to be associated with intolerance and hostility toward the French fact. Riel's trial in 1885, and then the Manitoba school crisis from 1890 to 1897, consolidated the belief of those who depicted the West as hostile toward the French Canadians. These conflicts changed the perception of Quebec toward the rest of the country and led Henri Bourassa, a French Canadian politician and intellectual who founded the daily newspaper *Le Devoir*, to articulate a vision that came to characterize the essence of French Canadian nationalism. Sylvie Lacombe's article offers a critical account of Henri Bourassa, the French Canadian leader who often received a hostile reaction among English Canadian nationalists.

French Canadians identified with Bourassa's views which led them to adopt a vision of society based on the notion of the coexistence between two nations treated equally. Within the context of *la survivance,* those whom we now call francophone minority communities in Canada played a defining role. This role was epitomized by the analogy of outposts and fortress. The minority francophone groups formed the former, whereas Quebec constituted the latter. Any loss of an outpost would inevitably affect the fortress, and the opposite was also true. Furthermore, the idea of outposts and fortress reflected a fear of English Canada with whom French Canadians shared the country. First Nations were ignored in this context or were integrated among English Canadians. School conflicts in New Brunswick, Manitoba, the North West Territories, and Ontario reinforced the perception of French-speaking communities as being under siege. Finally, disagreements over the relations between Canada and Great Britain, especially when Great Britain was at war such as in South Africa and during the First World War, led to clashes between French Canadian and English Canadian nationalists.

Despite profound disagreement over the meaning of being Canadian and the relations of Canada with Great Britain, there were attempts to reconcile differences. H. Viv Nelles's article analyzes the celebrations surrounding the tercentenary of Quebec City and exposes the competing visions of what Canada was in 1908.

QUESTIONS

1. What is nationalism? Should we make a distinction between a civic form of nationalism and an ethnic one?
2. Phyllis Senese offers a critical analysis of nationalism. Is racism intrinsically part of nationalism?
3. When Canadians gathered in Quebec City for the tercentenary of the city in 1908, was this a celebration of Canada's past, an occasion to celebrate French Canadian nationalism, or the British connection? What roles did French Canadians, Anglo-Saxons, First Nations, and ethnic communities perform?
4. Henri Bourassa proposed a vision of Canada based on equality. What was his definition of equality? Was his nationalist discourse inclusive?

FURTHER READINGS

Berger, Carl, *The Sense of Power: Studies in the Ideas of Canadian Imperialism, 1867–1914,* (Toronto: University of Toronto Press, 1970).

Lacombe, Sylvie, *La rencontre de deux peuples élus: Comparaison des ambitions nationale et impériale au Canada entre 1896 et 1920,* (Sainte-Foy, Québec: Presses de l'Université Laval, 2002).

Levitt, Joseph, *Henri Bourassa on Imperialism and Bi-culturalism,* (Toronto: Copp Clark, 1970).

Nelles, Henry Vivian, *The Art of Nation-Building: Pageantry and Spectacle at Quebec's Tercentenary,* (Toronto: University of Toronto Press, 1999).

Page, Robert, *Boer War and Canadian Imperialism,* (Historical Booklet: no. 44) (Ottawa: The Canadian Historical Association, 1987).

Silver, Arthur. *The French-Canadian Idea of Confederation, 1864–1900.* 2nd ed. Toronto: University of Toronto Press, 1997.

▲ Document 1: John A. Macdonald and Louis Riel

WHAT WILL HE DO WITH HIM?

● This cartoon published in 1885 depicts Prime Minister John A. Macdonald wondering what he should do with the Métis leader Louis Riel, found guilty of high treason. Should he spare Riel's life? English Canadians and French Canadians had opposite views on what should be done to Riel.

Source: Charles and Cynthia Hou, *Great Canadian Political Cartoons, 1820 to 1914*. Vancouver: Moody's Lookout Press, 1997, p. 61. Grip, May, 1885.

▲ Document 2: Depiction of the Perception that French Canadians Had of the War in South Africa (Boer War, 1899–1902)

JOHN BULL: Comme ces Canadiens se souviennent bien, comme ils sont reconnaissants de la tendresse que j'ai témoignée à leurs pères!

● This cartoon depicts the perception that French Canadians had of the war in South Africa (Boer War, 1899–1902). For French Canadians, the British involvement in the African colony reminded them of how Britain dealt with the rebellions of 1838 in Lower Canada. What do the various characters reveal about French Canadians, Great Britain and Imperialism?

Source: Charles and Cynthia Hou, *Great Canadian Political Cartoons, 1820 to 1914*. Vancouver: Moody's Lookout Press, 1997, p. 102.

▲ Document 3: Immigration Policy

HAND PICKED ONLY

JACK CANUCK: I want settlers, but will accept no culls.

THE SAME ACT WHICH EXCLUDES ORIENTALS SHOULD OPEN WIDE
THE PORTALS OF BRITISH COLUMBIA TO WHITE IMMIGRATION.

● These cartoons offer an explanation of immigration policy and its selection process. Not every immigrant was welcome. How is the selection process depicted in the cartoons?

Source: Charles and Cynthia Hou, *Great Canadian Political Cartoons, 1820 to 1914*. Vancouver: Moody's Lookout Press, 1997, p. 154. (a) *Daukt Herald*, Jan 1907; (b) *BC Saturday Sunset*, August 1907.

▲ Document 4: Answering the Call

ANSWERING THE CALL
" The whelps of the lion are joining their sire."

● This cartoon represents how the British colonies would behave in the advent of a war. They would "answer the call" issued by Great Britain. Compare and contrast Canada to the other colonies.

Source: Charles and Cynthia Hou, *Great Canadian Political Cartoons, 1820 to 1914*. Vancouver: Moody's Lookout Press, 1997, p. 220. *Vancouver Daily Province*, August 1914.

▲ Document 5: French Canadians and Canadian Nationalism

Henri Bourassa

Few in number, the French Canadian people are in a singularly difficult position.

We are the subjects of a power that was the age-old enemy of our country of origin. Our political allegiance belongs to a nation we value, with whom we have been able to have a marriage of convenience but whom it is impossible for us to love with the spontaneous love that makes living together and mutual sacrifice easy: the call of the blood and our own traditions are barriers.

We are surrounded by the more numerous descendants of a race which is foreign to us in its origin, its language, its religion, its laws and by its customs. This serious disadvantage is surely aggravated by the lack of intimate contact with them, the result of the scattering of the Canadian people over too large a territory; by the diversity and even the antagonism of economic concerns; and above all by the nefarious work of politicians and journalists who emphasize rather than mitigate the diversity of our aspirations.

This complex situation makes active patriotism very difficult. That love of the soil, of its institutions, of its nationality, which among other peoples is centred on a simple and strong patriotism in us is divided and presents us with three distinct duties: our duties towards England, towards our fellow countrymen of foreign origin; toward ourselves and our nationality....

DUTIES TOWARDS ENGLAND

155

In the present state of the world, it would be easy for me to reap applause by denouncing the British people, her government and her policies. I shall not do this for two reasons. I by no means believe in the efficacy of appeals to popular passion in order to enlighten the national conscience. It would seem to me cowardly to enflame an exclusively French audience when I come to preach mutual understanding between our two Canadian races. Moreover, it seems to me supremely unjust to hold the entire English people responsible for the foolish and criminal policy of those who govern them to-day.

I believe I have earned the right to judge England. I have denounced her deeds and her present tendencies at a time when there were many disadvantages to opposing the jingoist wave that was sweeping over our country. These tendencies I abhor and I shall always fight against them. It is our duty as French Canadians to tirelessly resist this policy of monopolization and military domination. But I repeat to-day what I have never ceased to proclaim at the height of the storm: this policy is contrary to the best traditions of the English nation. There exists still a truly liberal England: she hates this frenzy of brutal force, she has fought it constantly and soon, I hope, will overcome the misguided evil men who dominate the British Empire to-day. This England I love and admire; and as long as we are British subjects, it is to her that we must look. In organizing resistance to the attacks of the English Imperialists we must always take into account the existence and the feelings of a sane, liberal England.

Our obligations towards Great Britain have been and still are the theme of numerous and passionate disputes. To understand these responsibilities well and to fulfill them, it is

Source: Henri Bourassa. "French Canadians and Canadian Nationalism," in Joseph Levitt (ed.), *Henri Bourassa on Imperialism and Bi-Culturalism, 1900–1918.* Toronto: The Copp Clark Publishing Company, 1970, pp. 103–106.

sufficient enough to read our history carefully. Let us see the past clearly in order that we may ascertain our present duties and our future relations. This study helps us to see that England has done us much good and much harm. Men who love peace better than honor will find that the good triumphs over the bad and that in giving us political liberty, Great Britain has generously compensated for her wrongs towards us. These people forget that liberty has been the fruit of a long and arduous fight and that if England had refused us much longer, there would not be left an inch of British territory on the American continent.

In short, this historical study, if it is done without baseness or passion, leads us to the conclusion that we owe England neither bitterness nor gratitude. A detailed calculation of the good deeds and misdeeds of the Mother-Country would perhaps result in a slight imbalance to the detriment of British justice. Our English compatriots are apt to say willingly that we are not "business like". I would like us to give them new proofs of this by offering to close forever the accounts of the past. To this, however, I impose one essential condition: that is that no new accounts are opened, and that neither England nor our fellow citizens of English origin attempt to impose new obligations on us. Nothing in our past, nothing at the present time, nothing in the future obliges us to assume new burdens on England's account. And when I say "nothing", I mean moral obligations equally as much as material interests.

DUTIES TOWARDS CANADA AND ENGLISH CANADIANS

First, our duties in the political sphere.

Our line of conduct, it seems to me, is completely spelled out by the legal framework which the Act of Confederation has imposed on us. The benefits and the disadvantages of our constituency are numerous. It is not a part of this study to examine them in detail nor to decide if it would have been preferable for us to have rejected the federal idea.

Taking our situation such as I find it, I say that we should make the best of it. Let us avoid living or falling into an overnarrow provincialism; let us resist the encroachments of an absorbing federalism. Let us keep in the provincial domain all that is essential to the maintenance of our national character: education, civil laws, municipal organization. Equally let us work for the proper functioning of the federal system; in this area let us take the place which belongs to us and let us inspire the confidence of our neighbors by showing ourselves to be worthy of participating with them in common government.

Let us be generous without being weak, where we are the majority. Let us not yield the least of our rights where we are the minority. Let us not forget that we are not hired servants, even less are we parasites tolerated at the table of the rich: we are partners with equal rights. The strength and extent of our rights in the Canadian Confederation are measured by neither the number of our people nor by size of our fortunes: here is something perhaps we are often led to forget on a continent and in a century where the powers of numbers and even more brutal that fact of gold tend to become the supreme arbiters of justice. . . .

The two dangers that we must avoid are assimilation and isolation. We should look for all those common grounds where it is possible for us to co-operate with our fellow English citizens without losing our dignity or altering our national individuality.

On the question of language, I do not believe that it is possible or desirable for the mass of our people to learn and speak English. The common man can generally use only one language. The diffusion of the English language among the populace will take place at the expense of the national idiom and will soon harm the inner fibres of our ethnic temperament. This would be the surest road to the annihilation of our nationality. The case is not the same for our elite, those who by their wealth, intellectual culture and political and social position, ought to lead our people and maintain the union between ourselves and our neighbors. On them falls the duty of learning English, of drawing close to the elite of the English majority, of thoroughly studying the temperament, aspirations and the traits of English Canada. Moreover, the English elite have the same responsibility. If the most influential and most enlightened of the two races tried to have more to do with each other and got to know each other better, our national future would not be so precarious. We would see that there is among Anglo-Canadians, particularly in the great province of Ontario, much less fanaticism than we generally thought. Moreover, our neighbors would discover that we were not the inferior race that a great number of them scorned with such naive arrogance. They would realize that the acquisition of gold does not constitute the only talent and if they know the means of earning large dividends better than we, in other fields we have superior abilities.

To make this contact fruitful and this study useful, we should bring to them certain essential qualities: sincerity, uprightness, tolerance and a strong dose of altruism, in order to place ourselves within the point of view of the other before condemning what we call race prejudices. From our part, being less numerous and poorer, it is above all necessary to avoid obsequiousness when we speak in the presence of the English, and abuse when we are far from them.

DUTIES TOWARDS OURSELVES

These are the most important: for it is in the fidelity to our national duties that we will draw the necessary strength and enlightenment to accomplish all the others.

The first problem which comes to mind is this one: should we be more French than Canadian or more Canadian than French? In other words, should we be the French of Canada or Canadians of French origin? . . .

We should be French as the Americans are English. We should reserve and develop the instincts, the traditions and the intellectual powers which our origin has bequeathed to us; but we must centre our political allegiance and our national aspirations on Canadian soil.

Some of our compatriots happily envisage the day when we will recreate in America a free state where our race will prevail entirely. Assuredly, this is a legitimate and attractive dream; and the work of centuries may realize it more quickly than appearances indicate. But it is still a dream; and what must be carried out is the obligation of the present.

The best means of preserving our national traditions and preparing our future, whatever it may be, is not to live in yesterday's memories and to-morrow's aspiration but to perform faithfully the work of to-day.

We are the neighbors and partners of the English majority. We do not with our fellow citizens to tighten the ties which attach us to England nor to upset for their advantage the equilibrium between the two races in Canada. In return we should not hurt their nationalist feelings and their justified susceptibilities by desiring a political rapprochement with France or a rupture of Canadian Confederation. Let us remain solidly on the ground where the circumstances of history have placed us. Let us resist firmly the political absorption of Canada into the Empire and the extinction of our nationality in Canada. Let us respect the vow we have sworn to England and the Anglo-Canadian majority: this is the way to make them respect their own word.

It is important for our security to convince Anglo-Canadians of one undeniable fact: it is not as Frenchmen but as Canadians that we do not wish to draw closer to England and assume new obligations in the Empire....

■ Article 1: Weeds in the Garden of Civic Nationalism

Phyllis M. Senese

The ideology of nationalism has been an agent of social and political discord in Canada ever since its arrival in the early nineteenth century. Its effects are still evident in the strains that competing visions of nationalism create in Canadian life almost daily.[1]

In recent years, especially in English-speaking Canada, it has become common to identify two kinds of nationalism in this country, mirroring the asymmetrical 'two nations' model of Confederation: a civic nationalism of shared political institutions and progressive social values in English-speaking Canada, contrasted with an ethnic nationalism of a common language and culture and exaggerated homogeneity in Quebec. This is a false dichotomy.

Civic nationalism is, in my view, little more than a rhetorical device obscuring in a cloak of respectability and presumed moral superiority what is nothing more than nineteenth-century nationalism. Bluntly, it is a formula designed—in response to the renewed and reinvigorated movement for national self-determination that has been entrenching itself in Quebec for more than thirty years—to persuade the peoples of what is called English-speaking Canada that their nationalism is open, virtuous, fee from ethnic posturing, and altruistic (good), in contrast to the inward-looking, reactionary, ethnic, selfish (bad) nationalism of Quebec. Those who make this distinction—who think of Canada as being torn apart by ethnic nationalism and/or held together by civic nationalism—fail not only to recognize civic nationalism for the false front it is; they also fail to give full consideration to nationalism as an ideology. In essence, civic nationalism is simply the same old lament: if only 'they' would be more like 'us', all 'our' problems would disappear.[2] In trying to unravel a complex problem, let us begin at the beginning, with nationalism.

Source: Phyllis Senese. "Weeds in the Garden of Civic Nationalism," in Michael D. Behiels and Marcel Martel (eds.), *Nation, Ideas, Identities: Essays in Honour of Ramsay Cook.* Don Mills, Ontario: Oxford University Press, 2001. (c) Oxford University Press. Reprinted by permission of the publisher.

What keeps nationalism alive? Why, at the end of the twentieth century, when it was supposed to have disappeared as a relic of a troubled past, does nationalism flourish everywhere? Why does a preoccupation with 'blood and belonging'[3] still consume so much human energy and generate so much passion? Why have Canadians become 'addicted to ideologies'?[4]

Nationalism is an ideology. It claims to know when a nation exists, who belongs to it and who does not, and why. It advocates the creation of an independent state as a nation's natural right, a precondition for realization of its fullest potential. Nationalism invents a group of people who recognize in each other a shared community of culture, history, and future expectations.[5] Moreover, in Elie Kedourie's words, 'it pretends to supply a criterion for the determination of the unit of population proper to enjoy government exclusively on its own.'[6] With utter certainty, nationalists claim special knowledge of the nation and its people: their unique origins, glorious triumphs, singular sorrows; the threats that imperil the nation; how to mould the nation and its people to assume their rightful destiny. But things have never been that simple, because humans have not obligingly distributed themselves geographically so as to achieve the perfect correlation between territoriality and a specific people (ethnicity) that is increasingly taken to be the mark of a nationality. Nor have human populations remained ethnically pure. Over time, by choice, by chance, by force, populations have intermingled continuously to produce a multiplicity of groups of mixed origins who do not observe any rules of geographic precision. In short, there are no pure nations, no neat geographical boundaries. 'Nationalism requires too much belief in what is patently not so.'[7] Any nation that proposes to create an independent political state to fulfil itself will contain minority populations of numerous kinds. In the end, like other ideologies, nationalism has become a way for powerful elites, powerful classes, to restructure politics for their own ends. And the style of politics that nationalism invokes '[runs] to extremes. It represent[s] politics as a fight for principles, not the endless composition of claims in conflict.'[8]

Thus nationalism is a far more dangerous set of ideas than we generally acknowledge. Nationalists everywhere, always, insist that their nationalism is based on a set of self-affirming principles, and that it is not directed against any other nation. Yet somehow neither proposition turns out to be entirely true. This is so because nationalism rests, at base, on a foundation of opposition and exclusion. In Kedourie's formulation of nationalist rhetoric, 'humanity is divided into nations' and 'nations are known by certain characteristics which can be asceertained.'⁹ And Benedict Anderson has observed that a nation is 'an imagined community—and imagined as both inherently limited and sovereign.'¹⁰ Nationalism, notwithstanding its protestations of simple self-affirmation, always needs one essential ingredient to stimulate and sustain national solidarity: a threat. At some point every nationalism seeks out an Other—an enemy—on which to focus attention.

Belonging to a nation has no particular meaning unless it is exclusive: some people must be excluded, and that exclusion requires a reason. The prerequisites for belonging can be extremely precise or purposefully vague: all that matters is that belonging must be capable of being compared to not belonging. Nationalism A is compelled to insist that it is better than—superior to, more authentic than—nationalism B; otherwise there is no point in espousing nationalism. In its exclusivity, its anxiety about security, its belief that differences contaminate and destroy national cohesion, its rejection of the Other, nationalism is always about being afraid. Consider how nationalism appeals to the dark side of human nature; how it brings out the worst, not the best, human impulses; and, especially, the extent to which it provides ideological camouflage for racism.

Racism in a formal sense—defined as a series of theories about human origins that divided humanity into biological categories of distinct species and sub-species, and insisted that physical attributes and moral qualities were biologically linked, creating superior and inferior species—was an invention of the late eighteenth and early nineteenth centuries. By the time of Darwin's *On the Origin of Species* and Spencer's popularization of the 'survival of the fittest' notion, this set of theories was popularly accepted under the guise of 'scientific racism'. But such theories about 'races' of humans merely provided a new conceptual language for the age-old effort to manage the observable differences between and among groups of people. What preceded these biological theories of 'race' was a much longer and deeper cultural tradition of aggression and hostility

in accounting for human differentiation. Simply put, racism is the preoccupation over time with the observation, categorization, representation, valorization, and ranking of *perceived* human differences—differences consisting of largely false assumptions and assertions that can be manipulated to create stereotypes upon which—against which—action has to be taken. This pattern has been a basic feature of the intellectual landscape of Western culture at least since the time of the Greeks. Although it was not until the nineteenth century that biological, 'scientific' explanations for human diversity became available, the fear of indelible, dangerous group characteristics, embodied in some imagined Other, had existed for millennia. This fear is racism.

Among the many Greek contributions to Western civilization was a preoccupation with drawing boundaries to contain 'contending opposites'.¹¹ It has bequeathed to us a way of comprehending the world through polarized dualities: good/evil, white/black, young/old, male/female, civilized/barbarian, us/them. Greek thinkers grappled with the realization that while human beings in all their variety shared a common nature as humans, individuals could be seen as belonging to different groups. Undercutting any sense of common humanity sharing a common destiny was a 'fear of diversity—a fear that differences bring on chaos and thus demands that the world be put into an orderly pattern.'¹² Some 2,500 years later, Western society still thinks in dualistic terms, and has found few ways of successfully harmonizing unity and diversity. '[T]he one idea that has scarcely varied is that there is an "us" and a "them", each quite settled, clear, unassailably self-evident.'¹³

Western culture has shown a consistent pattern of hostile response to differences—every kind of difference. Initially, an attempt would be made, by a variety of means, to persuade those who differed in some vital aspect from a given dominant community to change, to conform, to convert, to recant—to abandon their differentness in order to belong. A significant element in the demand for change was the idea that differentness posed a danger of some kind to the dominant community. Moreover, those who refused to transform themselves demonstrated their inherent unfitness to belong by that very act of defiance. Of course, transformation was never really sufficient. The convert was always suspect, never quite legitimate. When persuasion failed, repression followed. And when repression did not obliterate differences, the next step was demonization—and, finally, extermination. The history of antisemitism, a species of racism, demonstrates the point. The road to Auschwitz has a long history in Western culture. The Jews were not, however, the only people to face this kind of onslaught.

Until relatively recent times, at least in most places in the West, the excluded, the Other, was demonized: linked—literally, not just metaphorically—to Satan. While the religious need to personify evil, so deeply embedded in the fabric of Christianity, may no longer be the norm in most of Western society, a secular version is still widespread. Deviance from a given norm was taken as evidence of satanic liaison; frequently, in medieval as well as modern times, the Other was also described as a disease, a plague to be eradicated. The notion that identifiable groups of people are not just different but an infection to be purged is easily recognizable in the contemporary practice of 'ethnic cleansing'. The insistence on seeing those who differed from the norm as members of a separate species, as a source of inherent, permanent infection, was a precursor of the biological determinism that took hold in the nineteenth century. In fifteenth-century Spain, for instance, proof of 'blood purity' was required, in order to preserve Catholicism from allegedly insincere and subversive Jewish converts: belonging was explicitly linked to blood lines, genealogy, lineage. Racism, then, existed long before it acquired a 'scientific' explanation. Nor has it limited itself to distinctions based on inherited characteristics (skin pigmentation, hair type, shape of eye): it has included religious affiliation, ethnicity, gender, sexuality, and illness. In fact, there are many kinds of racism, each shaped by specific historic contexts and continuities. Racism depends on images, stereotypes and assumptions about the Other that are fluid, that move and reshape across time; Europe's Other was always 'a simultaneous reaffirmation and reconstruction of earlier representations.'[14]

Racism constitutes an ideology which insists that natural and unchanging biological features are the paramount criteria for defining specific human groups, for assessing their worth in relation to one another, and for ascribing negative qualities to, and subsequent actions against, those deemed inferior. Racism is always about exclusion. This ideology appeals to an uncritical commonsense supposition that 'race' provides the explanation of observable human differences that is required to make sense of the world and to impose order on diversity. The Other is never confined to a specific time or place: it is constantly reimagined over time as circumstances dictate. As Robert Miles puts it:

> Different racisms are…not necessarily independent of each other, are not continually created anew in any absolute sense. Rather, any one instance of racism will be the product of both a reworking of at least some of the substance of earlier instances, and a creation of novel elements.[15]

The ideology of racism has been an all-purpose vehicle for expressing deep-seated fears about human differences.[16] Like nationalism, racism first invents groups of people who supposedly share distinctive commonalities and then devises criteria for inclusion and exclusion. Like nationalism, racism demands belief in imaginary creations. Like nationalism, racism claims to 'offer a semblance of order, an empowerment, or at minimum an affectation of power'.[17]

The racism woven into the fabric of Western experience was carefully packed in the cultural baggage that Europeans brought with them to the Western hemisphere. This way of looking at human differences as dangerous, to be transformed or eliminated, has deep roots in Canada. The ideology of racism mingled with, intensified, and inflamed the new ideology of nationalism as it emerged in Enlightenment Europe: first in the language of liberalism, then in the emotional absolutism of Romanticism, and finally in the false rationality of pseudo-science.

The most dangerous and least considered dimension of nationalism is its historic tendency to intersect with racism.[18] As David Theo Goldberg puts it: 'The popular Enlightenment concern with national characteristics often identified those characteristics racially. Similarly, the great nationalist drives of the late nineteenth century, as well as their imperialist counterparts, commonly invoked the banner of race as a rallying cry.'[19] What made this intersection possible was the fact that both 'nation' and 'race' are essentially empty terms—they can be continuously refilled with invented, and reinvented, notions "explaining" human difference. When nationalism insisted that each 'nation' possessed singular identifying attributes, those same attributes also served to demarcate and separate 'races'. Nationalism and racism alike strove to define and reinforce understanding of the self and the Other, of those included and excluded, and each resorted to natural law to validate its claims. 'Scientific racism' tightened the interdependence between the two: if ' "race" determined both cultural capacity and hierarchical development, . . . it therefore followed that each "nation" was the expression of a particular biological capacity'.[20] And it is this intersection of nationalism and racism that inspires my doubts about civic nationalism.

It is the attempt to disentangle nationalism from racism that has resulted in the supposed distinction between civic and ethnic nationalism, according to which racism skulks in the latter but not the former. One well-known and highly regarded proponent of this approach is Michael Ignatieff. He has written passionately about civic nationalism, which he argues 'envisages the nation as a community of equal, rights-bearing citizens, united in patriotic attachment to a shared set of political practices';[21] '. . . a nation based in citizenship rather than ethnicity'.[22] What Ignatieff writes about is the idea of nationalism refracted through liberation. 'This idea of the nation as a progressive, universalizing force was common both to Enlightenment discourse and that of nineteenth century liberals.'[23]

Liberalism stresses individualism, universal principles applicable to all humans, reform of society through reasoned action, progress of all sorts through education and institutional improvements, and commitment to human equality. Ignatieff is convinced that *civic nationalism* reflects these liberal ideals:

> [a]ccording to the civic nationalist creed, what holds a society together is not common roots but law. By subscribing to a set of democratic procedures and values, individuals can reconcile their right to shape their own lives with their need to belong to a community. This in turn assumes that national belonging can be a form of rational attachment.[24]

Yet consideration of 'law', 'rights', and 'belonging' suggests that in fact the liberal underpinnings of civic nationalism are precisely what make it substantively no different from ethnic nationalism. Early on, the egalitarian and universalist impulses of liberalism were subverted by the realization that neither principle conformed to social reality. European societies were riddled with inequalities that liberals had no intention of eliminating, and before long 'race theory provided legitimacy for inequality.'[25] Both individual liberty and its applicability to all peoples became contingent on 'rational capacity'—the standard used to define and put a 'limit upon the natural equality of all those beings ordinarily taken to be human.'[26] Until quite recently the notion of rights and equality under the law has been shaped by the view that it included only those deemed to possess—inherently and naturally—the capacity to reason, on the assumption that only rational individuals shared common 'interests' and thus qualified for the protection of law. Liberalism, then, especially as it developed in Britain, championed liberty and property rights for some over equality of all: social realities such as class and gender were reduced to irrelevancies. In practice those who lacked property or 'interest', by virtue of their rational incapacity, were excluded from political participation, equal protection under the law, and personal liberty. In effect, in its formation and application, liberalism became tainted with racism. As Goldberg has noted: 'By working itself into the threads of liberalism's cloth just as that cloth was being woven, race and the various exclusions it licensed became naturalized in the Eurocentered vision of itself and its self-defined others, in its sense of Reason and rational direction' to become 'the racializing paradox at liberalism's heart'[27] 'They' are not 'us'; 'they' should assimilate to become 'us'; if 'they' disappear, how would 'we' know 'we' are 'us'? As Yael Tamir has observed, 'there is a long-standing though much denied alliance between liberal and national ideas that might explain the inconsistencies pervading modern liberal theory.'[28] Contrary to the theory of liberalism, in its practice 'all men' were not equal: 'the rational, hence autonomous and equal subjects of the Enlightenment project turn out, perhaps unsurprisingly, to be exclusively white, male, European, and bourgeois.'[29]

In the Canadian experience, civic nationalism has simply been ethnic nationalism in disguise: the nationalism of nineteenth-century British liberalism, one in which, by the early nineteenth century, the ideologies of nationalism and racism had developed

161

'an interdependence such that the parameters of each ideology overlapped to determine the criteria for membership of the emergent state'.[30] After 1800, the steady migration from Britain to British North America of administrators, bureaucrats, businessmen, clergy, educators, farmers, half-pay officers, labourers, and tradesmen—all those displaced by deep, rapid social and economic dislocation in Britain—guaranteed the transfer of that ideological convergence to Canada. As Frantz Fanon was to observe: 'the settler makes history and is conscious of making it. And because he constantly refers to the history of his mother country, he clearly indicates that he himself is the extension of that mother country.'[31] From the early nineteenth century until very recently, Canada, outside Quebec, has been shaped by the conviction that, in Miles's words,

> the people of the Anglo-Saxon [English] 'race' had a special capacity for self-government by constitutional means, from which it was concluded that those not so biologically endowed should be excluded. Thus the idea of the Anglo-Saxon 'race' sustained a belief in a sense of superiority of both 'race' and 'nation.'[32]

Today, the appeal of civic nationalism for some Canadians lies in the mistaken belief that this form of nationalism is *only* about the political institutions, principles, and values that would best serve the interests of the citizens of an independent state containing many nationalities, many ethnicities. But *which* political institutions, principles, and values would prevail? And *who* would apply them to governance? From the days of British colonialism until long after the Second World War the answer was clear: British men would govern on the basis of British institutions, principles, and values[33]—institutions, principles, and values that had been contoured by cultural racism.

The search for an appropriate framework for civic nationalism has been driven by a narrow and selective reading of Canadian political history. In tracing the country's political evolution, many point to the winning of responsible government by Robert Baldwin and Louis-Hippolyte LaFontaine, and the crafting of Confederation under the leadership of John A. Macdonald and George-Étienne Cartier, as evidence of a unique non-ethnic nationalism at

work. George Brown, whose willingness to join Macdonald and Cartier in a coalition government for the express purpose of creating a federation made it all possible, is given much less prominence. In fact, he is usually left unmentioned—as are his bigotry and the powerful economic forces he represented that played a major role in securing a new political arrangement. As a result of those omissions, the standard version of Canadian history centres on the ability of French and English politicians (no other groups need be included) to work together in nation-building, that elusive pursuit that seems to hold such promise today. It is true that Baldwin and LaFontaine found ways for Reformers on either side of the ethnic divide to join forces, but each had a different reason for pursuing responsible government. What tends to get overlooked is the extent to which their collaboration was rooted in a British *colonial* setting. Baldwin's commitment to responsible government was always tempered by a refusal to accept any reform beyond elementary local control, lest more sweeping reform threaten the monarchy; hence his displacement by radical Reformers in the 1850s. LaFontaine, for his part, saw responsible government chiefly as a means to secure *la survivance* for the Canadiens as a distinct people. All their gestures of respect and solidarity between French and English in Canada were limited by the two men's social conservatism and their profound attachment to Britain. It was the *colonial context*, together with their personalities, that made their collaboration possible, a collaboration that illustrates how colonialism manipulates nationalism to maintain the status quo.[34] They would retire from public life to watch a younger generation, representing new economic and political interests, use the themes of nationalism to create newer, nastier relations between French and English in Canada.

Macdonald and Cartier are similarly hailed for creatively linking their political fortunes in such a way as to carry on the work of Baldwin and LaFontaine. Yet they too were prisoners of their own ethnic nationalisms. Cartier continued LaFontaine's strategy of using political arrangements to protect the language, culture, and religion of the Canadiens within a British colonial framework. At every turn he praised the British connection and the importance of being a British subject. In 1865 he defended the Quebec Resolutions by connecting the survival of British power in North America to the survival of the Canadiens; it was their loyalty and steadfastness, especially against the Americans, that had made the British connection possible.

> These historical facts teach us that French Canadians and English-speaking Canadians should have for each other a mutual sympathy, having both reason to congratulate themselves that Canada is still a British Colony. . . . If we unite we can form a political nationality independent of the national origin and religion of individuals.[35]

What Cartier failed to appreciate was that the British connection and the British institutions developing in Canada were wrapped in a British ethnic nationalism. The point would be obvious when the final form of Confederation left minority rights, those of Canadian Catholics, weakly protected and vulnerable to assault outside Quebec; rights for other minorities were not even considered. Moreover, the federal system itself encouraged the continued cultivation of British and Canadien nationalisms. The splitting of jurisdictions between Ottawa and the provinces ensured that nothing like a new nationality developed; the provinces became the repositories and advocates of all the old nationalisms. Cartier's hope for a new political nationality was rarely echoed by Macdonald; more commonly he imagined post-Confederation Canada as a British, even 'Arian',[36] nation. As colonials, Macdonald and Cartier never escaped a colonial mentality. They wanted greater powers for Canada, but only within the empire; and, unhappily, they were not immune to the confluence of nationalism and racism that the empire represented.

Both the political reform and the compromise that these men achieved were certainly of consequence, but the long-term effects were limited because of the dominance of British liberal nationalism. In English-speaking Canada that nationalism blinded citizens to their colonial condition (after all, Canada was part of Britain; it just happened to be across a larger than usual body of water). In turn, colonialism created a garrison mentality in English-speaking Canada in which 'the official culture [became] more and more willed, more and more threatened by hostile forces without and by subversive forces within.'[37] It was to escape those colonial confines that Stephen Leacock would later embrace imperialism: 'I . . . am an Imperialist because I will not be a Colonial.'[38] But only a muddled notion of nationalism, infused with the racism concealed in liberalism, could claim that imperialism was an improvement on colonialism. Meanwhile, the Canadien identity was growing stronger as a result of the protections that Cartier had secured in Confederation. And it grew stronger still with the realization that outside Quebec an ethnic nationalism had come to dominate and control Canada's political, economic, and social institutions: British liberal nationalism, a nationalism that had a *particular* cultural hegemony at is core.[39] For many in English-speaking Canada, Confederation was predicated on the assumption that the new Dominion, however it might expand territorially, was and would remain British. A French component in Canada might be tolerated (never entirely accepted) on the Quebec 'reserve' but nowhere else—as the experience of Louis Riel and the Franco-Manitobans would attest.

That British-Canadian nationalism merits closer scrutiny. In fact, it was an *English*-Canadian nationalism based not just on the primacy of the English language but on an English God, history, culture, and society. The term 'British' included the Scots, Irish, and Welsh in a united front against other nationalities, but within the category 'British' existed a hierarchy in which all things English were privileged. And despite the eventual chipping away of English primacy in religion and education, the English element has remained dominant in Canadian culture (until the post-1945 onslaught of the US version), political institutions, and historical outlook until very recently. Late-nineteenth-century imperialism only underscored the ethnicity of nationalism in English-speaking Canada. This English-Canadian nationalism was the nationalism of the élites, its strength tied not to numbers but to power. What made this nationalism especially successful and long-lived was its capacity to incorporate into itself members of other ethnic communities. Through seduction and intimidation it urged them to transform themselves; it persuaded them that to become English was to become truly Canadian and hence eligible (at least theoretically) to share in the power of the state—a prospect that by the late nineteenth century included the possibility of participation in imperial grandeur on a global scale. This sort of persuasion became increasingly evident after 1885, as non-British immigration to Canada began to soar.

163

Immigrants were rated, officially and in popular culture, on a scale of desirability, suitability, and assimilability that, not surprisingly, reflected the racism of the late nineteenth century. In reality, the chances of admission depended on how easily and quickly an immigrant could become English.[40] After all, as the young Sandor Hunyadi put it in John Marlyn's novel *Under the Ribs of Death:*

> 'Pa, the only people who count are the English. Their fathers got all the best jobs. They're the only ones nobody ever calls foreigners. Nobody ever makes fun of their names or calls them "balogny-eaters," or laughs at the way they dress or talk. Nobody,' he concluded bitterly, ''cause when you're English it's the same as bein' Canadian.'[41]

Like every other nationalism, the English-Canadian variety needed an enemy to promote solidarity. From the late eighteenth century it has been 'blessed' with two; the neighbouring American republic and the French-speaking Canadians concentrated largely in Quebec.[42] Baldwin, La Fontaine, Macdonald, and Cartier had all worked to ensure that an international boundary kept the Americans at bay, while the Canadiens (later Québécois), by virtue of Confederation, were no ordinary neighbours. Confederation may have been intended by the more fanatical among the English migrants to Canada to contain, if not smother, Quebec nationalism, but it failed to accomplish either objective. The result has been an unending dance of the two nationalisms.

The way English and Canadien nationalisms contended to define Canada after 1867 created a nationalist quagmire for non-British immigrants to the new Dominion.[43] Immigration served not just to populate the Prairies and make the National Policy work; it had the additional purpose of swamping the Canadiens through numbers. Numbers equal votes; votes equal power in Ottawa. Up to Confederation, immigration patterns suggested that the primary, if not exclusive, source of immigrants for the foreseeable future would continue to be Britain. It would have come as no surprise if Canadien nationalists were not enthusiastic about such immigrants. If that immigration pattern were sustained, there was every expectation that the rest of Canada would become a demographic replica of Ontario (perhaps a pale

reflection of the Atlantic region). But—as usual—circumstances changed, and with them immigration patterns. Immigrants from eastern, central, and southern Europe, from Asia, the Caribbean, the Middle East, all learned quickly and painfully that neither 'nation' in Canada really wanted them. For the majority of non-British immigrants who established themselves outside Quebec, three conditions of settlement became obvious.

First, immigrants had to accept the all but total loss of their own ethnic identity to have any hope of being considered desirable. In order to become Canadian, they had to find a way to become English, abandoning dress, foods, music, and names that shrieked 'foreigner'—though for increasing numbers it would be impossible ever to appear English enough. Second, immigrants had to adopt the English-Canadian nationalist definition of the nation's enemies. Finally, however, the true test of belonging was the cultivation of hostility to things French and Québécois. To become an insider required attacking the outsider, and if in some way Quebec francophones could be seen as presenting a direct threat to an immigrant community, the chances for success of an English assimilationist drive were enhanced. One need only think of Irish Catholics in Ontario or Ukrainian Catholic immigrants on the Prairies, at odds with French clergy and bishops from Quebec. Even today, recent (and not so recent) immigrants are encouraged to see recognition of a 'distinct society' in Quebec as an affront to the 'nation's heritage'. What nation? What heritage? Although the Englishness of Canada is fading now, it has not completely disappeared,[44] and nothing obvious looms on the horizon to take its place; thus immigrants still understand that, at least for now, their acceptance as Canadians is tied to adopting the residue of English attitudes, including English-Canadian nationalism. Until demography alters the balance (as it will), inclusion will continue to depend to a high degree on appearing to be English. As many Canadians with African, Asian, Middle Eastern, or Caribbean roots find, nationalism in English-speaking Canada frequently insists that 'home' for them must be somewhere else, no matter how long they and their families have been here. For them, assimilation never means truly belonging here, at least not yet.

I once heard Pierre Berton wonder aloud how differently Canada might have turned out if non-British immigrants and the Canadiens had ever made common cause against the English. English-Canadian nationalism ensured that the price for non-British immigrants would be too high to contemplate. Assimilation into the dominant English culture demanded imitation of its anti-Quebec, anti-French attitudes and behaviour as the price of belonging. And nationalism always insists that belonging matters more than anything else.

Canadien nationalism, like its English counterpart, saw (and sometimes still sees) immigrants as unwelcome, threatening Others. Neither was ever able to choose the immigrants it wanted; each had to find ways of making do with those who came its way. As a minority in Canada, the Canadiens were insufficiently secure about their own collective future to develop subtle techniques for incorporating the Other. Heavy-handed strategies (all in the name of the national good) offered immigrants little positive inducement to side with the Canadiens in what would appear to be a losing cause. There was, too, a wall of incomprehension dividing immigrants and Canadiens, a barrier greater even than differences of language, religion, and culture. Part of the mystique about the past that every nationalism cultivates is its own litany of past sorrows, sufferings, humiliations, conquests, and bloodshed. While it was not uncommon for early Canadien nationalists to correspond with Irish or Polish nationalists, the conditions of life for French Canadians were not comparable to the real suffering experienced elsewhere. In the late nineteenth century and into the twentieth, Jews fleeing pogroms, Ukrainians escaping tsarist and later Soviet repression, Mennonites seeking sanctuary, African Americans evading lynch laws, Chinese labourers exchanging famine for hard work and a hate-filled reception, First Nations peoples surviving the exterminationist provisions of the various Indian Acts—not one of these groups recognized anything familiar in the experiences of the Canadiens.[45] This gulf separating divergent memories of experience helps to explain why, to this day, it is easy to whip up anti-Quebec, anti-French sentiments, especially in western Canada. For those whose personal and ethnic histories (not least their histories in Canada) have been brutal, Quebec and its predominantly French-speaking population look like the pampered darlings of Confederation. Nationalism always demands comparison. More than anything, though,

Canadien nationalism lacked sufficient power within Canada to make a difference. True power terrifies, intimidates, subdues, manipulates, and controls; it does not merely irritate.

English-Canadian nationalism kept reinventing, reimagining, itself so that successive waves of immigrants (at least those from some parts of Europe) could be invited to play 'let's pretend'. Let's pretend that English-speaking Canada is white, Anglo-Saxon (English), Protestant—pretend even if it is not. Let's pretend that everyone, from anywhere, can join this 'nation', even when in reality they will be excluded in some fashion. Let's pretend that Ontario and Nova Scotia never legislated segregated schools to spare white children from the 'contamination' of their Black neighbours. Let's pretend that Asian immigrants, their children, and even their grandchildren were never denied full citizenship rights until 1947. Let's pretend that Jews fleeing Nazi Germany were never barred entry into Canada, or that for decades Jews were not kept out of professions, universities, social and recreational facilities. Let's pretend that the Indian Acts, land grabs, residential schools, and bureaucratically induced poverty never tore Aboriginal communities apart. Let's pretend that the Supreme Court of Canada never sanctioned racial discrimination. And there is so much more we could pretend never happened. The 'let's pretend' strategy succeeded because the game was so easy and—at least at first glance—so painless to play. Its greatest 'success' can be detected in the numbers of those of non-British ancestry who snap to an anti-Quebec stance at the drop of a 'distinct society'. They have forgotten that persecution and exclusion—the lost names, the lost languages, the lost cultures—were the price their parents, grandparents, even great-grandparents paid as the price of admission. The 'let's pretend' strategy appeared to express the power of the English, though in fact it was shaped by anxiety, by fear of rivals and of eventual decline.[46] 'Let's pretend' is the way a liberal state that 'prefer(s) birthright over choice as a criterion of membership'[47] always operates. 'Let's pretend', most dangerously for all who live in Canada, has induced historical amnesia about the undercurrents of hatred in Canada inspired by the racism that riddles every nationalism, including civic nationalism.

But times change. As the English contours and flavours of Canada continue to diminish, national identity for Canadians outside Quebec is less and less clear. Canada is officially bilingual and multi-cultural, but there is no consensus on what those concepts mean in practice, beyond the anger and resentment they provoke all around. In the midst of all this the idea of civic nationalism has gained a certain currency in English-speaking Canada. With no single ethnic group yet able to dominate as the English once did, civic nationalism appeals to a non-ethnic, multicultural view of society in which no ethnicity dominates, all are equal, Native people are entitled to nothing special, Quebec must be a province like all the rest, no one is entitled to a distinct society, the rights of unpopular or inconvenient claimants are limited, then . . . what?[48] Neither civic nor ethnic nationalism offers a way out of our Canadian dilemmas. Nationalism in any guise creates confusion, not clarity; anxiety, not tranquillity. Isaiah Berlin once reminded us that nationalism

> started in alliance with other forces: democracy, liberalism, socialism. But whenever they fell out among themselves, nationalism invariably won, and enslaved its rivals, and reduced them to relative impotence. German romanticism, French socialism, English liberalism, European democracy were compromised and distorted by it. They proved powerless against the torrent of nationalist pride and greed which culminated in the conflict of 1914.[49]

And nationalism's record since 1914 inspires little confidence.

Civic nationalism, finally, implies endorsement of multiculturalism and tolerance. Multiculturalism is the latest liberal attempt to deal with differences. Yet in its celebration of diversity and differences racism is not eradicated—merely shifted from the public to the private sphere. It becomes simply one more 'attempt to impute rational meaning to inequality.'[50] In fact, minorities remain at the margins. According to Goldberg: 'The more ideologically hegemonic liberal values seem and the more open to difference liberal modernity declares itself, the more dismissive of difference it becomes and the more closed it seeks to make the circle of *acceptability*.'[51] And this is the central issue: *acceptance,* not tolerance. Tolerance, often trumpeted as the highest Canadian virtue, denies the relevance of the Other; to tolerate is to endure, grudgingly, the objectionable Other as he really is—someone who needs to be made over. What the Other wants, needs, demands is to be embraced in all the dimensions of otherness, not merely tolerated.

Northrop Frye once made an observation about Canada that, for me, captures why English-speaking Canadians should be wary of civic nationalism.[52] Recounting his train journeys, as a student, from Fredericton to Toronto, he described the eagerness with which he waited for the view of Quebec City from Lévis: Here was one of the imaginative and emotional centres of my own country and my own people, yet a people with whom I found it difficult to identify; what was difficult being not so much language as cultural memory. But the effort of making identification was crucial: it helped me to see that a sense of unity is the opposite of uniformity. *Uniformity, where everyone 'belongs', uses the same clichés, thinks alike and behaves alike, produces a society which seems comfortable at first but is totally lacking in human dignity. Real unity tolerates dissent and rejoices in variety of outlook and tradition,* recognizes that it is man's destiny to unite and not divide, understands that creating proletariats and scapegoats and second-class citizens is a mean and contemptible activity. Unity, so understood, is the extra dimension that raises the sense of belonging into genuine human life.[53]

Civic nationalism is still nationalism after all. To achieve the kind of Canada that would meet the aims of its proponents, nationalism needs to be edited out. The focus must be on creating political and legal institutions that could secure an ethical society entrenched not in any nationalism, or in a perpetual 'let's pretend', but in social justice. As Canada continues to change rapidly in every respect, democracy, freedom, civility, and human dignity must remain the collective goal of all who live in this country. Canada needs and deserves more debate about how to build a society that includes everyone and excludes no one on the basis of ethnicity, skin colour, beliefs, sexuality, health. If civic nationalism does not offer a solution, perhaps (and only perhaps) liberalism's original optimism about human potential might suggest directions for the future, but only after liberalism divests itself all links to nationalism.

In the 1998 Massey Lectures Jean Vanier offered a non-nationalist perspective on how to achieve both individual freedom and a sense of belonging.[54] And recently, in the wake of the NATO entry into Kosovo, Michael Ignatieff has argued that no lasting progress towards peace can be made in that region until Serbs are willing to acknowledge and come to terms with their recent history, especially the actions of their government and military forces in Kosovo.[55] Ignatieff is right in insisting that meaningful reconciliation can begin only with an honest evaluation of what has occurred there. If Serbs and Albanians are to find any measure of reconciliation, both will need to abandon the ideology of nationalism.

Nationalism has been imagined, created, learned. Imagine what Canada might have become without it! Are we ready to risk unlearning nationalism?

Notes

This essay is dedicated to the memory of two people: Stephanie Gilbert, who died as I was first writing it; and Pierre Savard, whose unexpected death came as I struggled with revisions. It is also my thanks to Ramsay Cook, who always encouraged me, as his student, to discover my own conclusions, even when he disagreed with them. This essay has benefited from the insightful criticisms of Xavier Gélinas, Michael Behiels, Marcel Martel, and anonymous readers, all very generous with their time.

1. Consider the furor in May 1998 when David Levine was appointed CEO of the about-to-be merged hospitals of Ottawa; see, for example, Graham Fraser, 'The David Levine Affair: Fear and Loathing in Ottawa', *Globe and Mail* (23 May 1998), D3.
2. Michael Ignatieff, *Blood and Belonging: Journeys into the New Nationalism* (Toronto, 1993), 134, slides towards this formula: ' . . . and wish, suddenly, that we actually did love the same nation and not merely cohabit the same state'.
3. Ibid.
4. John Ralston Saul, *The Unconscious Civilization* (Toronto, 1995), 2.
5. See Ernest Geller, *Nations and Nationalism* (Ithaca, NY, 1983), 7, 53–8.

6. Elie Kedourie, *Nationalism* (New York, 1960), 9.
7. E.J. Hobsbawm, *Nations and Nationalism Since 1870: Programme, Myth, Reality*, 2nd (Cambridge, 1990), 12.
8. Kedourie, *Nationalism*, 18.
9. Ibid., 9.
10. Benedict Anderson, *Imagined Communities: Reflections on the Origin and Spread of Nationalism*, rev. edn (London, 1991), 6.
11. Arlene W. Saxonhouse, *Fear of Diversity: The Birth of Political Science in Ancient Greek Thought* (Chicago, 1992), 2.
12. Ibid., x.
13. Edward W. Said, *Culture and Imperialism* (New York, 1993), xxv.
14. Robert Miles, *Racism* (London, 1989), 25.
15. Ibid., 84.
16. Two excellent examples of work in this vein are Jeffrey Richards, *Sex, Dissidence and Damnation: Minority Groups in the Middle Ages* (London, 1994) and R.I. Moore, *The Formation of a Persecuting Society: Power and Deviance in Western Europe 950–1250* (Oxford, 1990).
17. David Theo Goldberg, *Racist Culture: Philosophy and the Politics of Meaning* (Oxford, 1993), 210.
18. Miles, *Racism*, 87–98.
19. Goldberg, *Racist Culture*, 78–9.
20. Miles, *Racism*, 89.
21. Ignatieff, *Blood and Belonging*, 3–4.
22. Ibid., 5.
23. Kenan Malik, *The Meaning of Race: Race, History and Culture in Western Society* (New York, 1996), 135.
24. Ignatieff, 4. John Ralston Saul has addressed these issues similarly in *Reflections of a Siamese Twin: Canada at the End of the Twentieth Century* (Toronto, 1997).
25. Malik, *Meaning of Race*, 100.
26. Goldberg, *Racist Culture*, 27; see also Malik, *Meaning of Race*, 55–70.
27. Goldberg, *Racist Culture*, 10.
28. Yael Tamir, *Liberal Nationalism* (Princeton, 1993), 117.
29. Malik, *Meaning of Race*, 28.
30. Miles, *Racism*, 90.
31. *The Wretched of the Earth*, cited in Said, *Culture and Imperialism*, 270.
32. Miles, *Racism*, 91.
33. See Goldberg, *Racist Culture*, 69–83.

34. For example, see David Spurr, *The Rhetoric of Empire: Colonial Discourse in Journalism, Travel Writing, and Imperial Administration* (Durham, NC, 1993).

35. J.-C. Bonenfant, 'Sir George-Étienne Cartier', *Dictionary of Canadian Biography X*, 147.

36. House of Commons, *Debates*, 30 April 1883, 905; see also Carl C. Berger, 'Race and Liberty: The Historical Ideas of Sir John George Bourinot', *Historical Papers* (1965), 87–104.

37. D.G. Jones, *Butterfly on Rock: Images in Canadian Literature* (Toronto, 1970), 36. Northrop Frye first described the 'garrison mentality' in the 'Conclusion' to *Literary History of Canada*, ed. Carl Klinck (Toronto, 1967), 830. Although Frye was referring specifically to English-Canadian literature, one could make the same argument about the Québécois literary imagination and its relationship to nationalism; but that is another paper.

38. Stephen Leacock, 'Greater Canada: An Appeal', *University Magazine* (April 1907), 133.

39. See Tamir, *Liberal Nationalism*, 140–50, for a discussion of the cultural imperative of liberalism.

40. 'For a type of middle-class English gentry, the French and the Irish, the Italians, the Poles and various others could be lumped together among *the children of the devil, to be ignored or refashioned in the image of their betters*'; Jones, *Butterfly on Rock*, 36; italics added.

41. John Marlyn, *Under the Ribs of Death* (Toronto, 1964), 24. Sandor's father's retort—that 'we are all foreigners here. . . nationality is of no consequence' (24)—reflects the dream that most immigrants had, but few realized. See also Terrence Craig, *Racial Attitudes in English-Canadian Fiction, 1905–1980* (Waterloo, 1987).

42. There were, of course, minor players in the category of 'enemy', but they were never accorded the same status as the Canadiens or Americans. The First Nations and Blacks were the two most notable. That they were both usually marginalized in nationalist squabbles accounts in no small way for their absence from the writing of Canadian history (in either official language) until relatively recently.

43. It also served as a device to derail and deny Aboriginal claims; see Goldberg, *Racist Culture*, 212.

44. Examples of this crop up from time to time: see the reaction ('We are not amused', *Globe and Mail*, 23 May 1998, D7) to the earlier suggestion by Donald B. Smith ('From Here to Heritage Day', 18 May 1998) to remove the English vestiges of the May holiday and make it more truly Canadian. For some time now, at my own university's Convocations, many First Nations students have worn their own traditional ceremonial clothing instead of replicas from British institutions, enriching and transforming the ceremonies; the sky has not yet fallen.

45. Consider the visit of Catalonia's Jordi Pujol to Quebec in July 1996, when his observations about Quebec's relative lack of real suffering generated a furor in nationalist circles.

46. For example, see Arthur Herman, *The Idea of Decline in Western History* (New York, 1997), 13–46; see also Carl Berger, *The Sense of Power: Studies in the Ideas of Canadian Imperialism 1867–1914* (Toronto, 1970), 4–11.

47. Tamir, *Liberal Nationalism*, 125; 128.

48. Positions taken by the Reform Party of Canada—attacks on the Supreme Court of Canada for extending Charter protection to homosexuals and lesbians, and calls for Parliament to legislate limits to Aboriginal land claims in the wake of the Delgamuukw decision—underscore the grim prospects that civic nationalism really offers: see "Reform seeks curbs on judicial activism'; 'Restrict native land claims, Reform says', *Globe and Mail* (9 June 1998), A4.

49. Isaiah Berlin, *The Sense of Reality: Studies in Ideas and Their History*, ed. Henry Hardy (London, 1996), 251. Many proponents of civic nationalism look to Berlin's formulation of British liberalism to support their claims. Ian Buruma notes that for Berlin (and many other anglophiles) England was a '*fabled* land of common sense, fairness and good manners'; *Anglomania: A European Love Affair*, (New York, 1998), 275; italics added.

50. Malik, *Meaning of Race*, 170; 169–77.

51. Goldberg, *Racist Culture*, 6–7, italics added.

52. I would insist that this applies equally to nationalisms in Quebec.

53. Northrop Frye, *The Bush Garden: Essays on the Canadian Imagination* (Toronto, 1971), vi; italics added.

54. Jean Vanier, *Becoming Human* (Toronto, 1998).

55. Michael Ignatieff interviewed on *The Magazine*, CBC-TV, 16 June 1999.

■ Article 2: Historical Pageantry and the "Fusion of the Races" at the Tercentenary of Quebec, 1908

H. V. Nelles

The idea of celebrating the 300th anniversary of Champlain's founding of Quebec in 1608 originated amongst the irrepressible members of the Société Saint-Jean-Baptiste of Quebec as yet another festival of survival and *nationaliste* emergence.[1] Ambitious city councillors and civic boosters saw the tourist, commercial, and political potential of broadening the event beyond these municipal and provincial origins into a national (pan Canadian) celebration of the founding of Canada.[2] A meddlesome and intriguing Governor General, Earl Grey, seized the opportunity as an occasion for an elaborately staged festival to give fractious Canadians a nobler image of themselves as a new nation, fused from two races, united within a grand empire.[3]

Local politicians led by Quebec City's Mayor Garneau thought mainly of using tourism as one way of arresting the economic decline of Quebec that had been going on for a generation. Earl Grey had another agenda. If he were to have his way the 300th anniversary of Champlain's arrival would be celebrated with a national and imperial festival uniting governments, voluntary organizations, and a mass movement of citizens in a campaign to consecrate the Plains of Abraham. This would be accomplished by the removal of the monstrous jail and munitions factory that in his mind disfigured the sites of heroic battles, and the creation of a suitably landscaped historic park adorned by a massive Statue to Peace larger than the Statue of Liberty to symbolize the subsequent harmonious union of two peoples in one country under the Imperial Crown.[4] He inherited the Quebec "embellishments" project from his predecessors, Dufferin and Minto. The fixation with the Plains of Abraham was his contribution. In his mind the consecration of the historic battlefields as a national park would contribute mightily to the project of

Source: H. V. Nelles. "Historical Pageantry and the 'Fusion of the Races' at the Tercentenary of Quebec, 1908," in *Histoire sociale/Social History*, vol. 29, no. 58 (1996), pp. 391–415. Reprinted with permission.

"race fusion", bringing French and English Canadians together in terms of mutual respect, that he believed to be the guiding principle of Wilfrid Laurier's public life. Grey convinced himself of this but found Laurier at first curiously unmoved.

The wily and reticent Prime Minister, all too familiar with the explosive potential of French-Canadian nationalism and British imperialism, and justifiably wary of the Governor General's not entirely innocent enthusiasms, dragged his feet. Alert to the snares of history, Laurier suggested combining Champlain's anniversary with a more neutral celebration of progress and technology—the opening of the Quebec Bridge scheduled for 1909. Amidst such forward-looking festivities Quebecers might transcend their all-too-troublesome past. According to the frustrated and impatient Governor General, Laurier was haunted by the "mischievous movements" of "ambitious Ultramontanes," whose intrigues he believed would "eventually lead to another abortive Papineau trouble"...[5] Laurier hoped to avoid playing their game as well as the Governor General's.

However, when the bridge collapsed ignominiously in the fall of 1907, so too did the Prime Minister's resolve. With pressure mounting for a major celebration of Champlain's 300th anniversary within his own Liberal organization in Quebec City and the Governor General building a grassroots Canadian Club organization with his enthusiasm, the Prime Minister gave in—though he waited until virtually the eleventh hour to do so. Quebec needed something to take its mind off the twisted wreckage in the St. Lawrence, and, if the rest of the country was forcing him to spend hundreds of thousands of dollars in Quebec on the eve of the election, well, so be it.

A modest municipal celebration of the 300th anniversary of Champlain's founding of his habitation at Quebec became transformed, then, by these complex and sometimes contradictory forces into the Tercentenary of the Founding of Canada with its object the consecration of the Plains of Abraham as an Historic Park—something quite different from the originators' intentions. In March 1908 the Canadian government established the National Battlefields Commission, endowed it with $300,000, empowered it to receive additional sums raised through voluntary efforts, and authorized it to expend those funds initially on a festival celebrating the Tercentenary of the founding of Canada/Quebec and subsequently

169

on the purchase of lands and construction of works necessary to create a permanent memorial park marking the sites of the Battle of the Plains of Abraham in 1759 and the Battle of Ste. Foy in 1760. [6]

Publicly funded and infused with the zeal of voluntarism, an ambitious programme unfolded in late July 1908 that gathered warships from three navies to the river below Quebec and featured processions, illuminations, fireworks, parades, reconstructions, a massed military tattoo, regatta, sail-pasts, Canada's first set of commemorative historical stamps, concerts, a gathering of learned societies, performances of the symphonic ode "Christophe Colombe", a solemn open-air mass, church services, state dinners, balls, garden parties, and, crowning the occasion, the presence of them heir to the throne, His Royal Highness the Prince of Wales. The centrepiece of this extravaganza would be a magnificent Historical Pageant in which the citizens of Quebec would recreate before their soon-to-be sovereign and thousands of spectators scenes from their past.

The Tercentenary of Quebec in 1908 was thus the Canadian counterpart of those elaborately staged festivals of national invention that have been the subject of much recent scholarly investigation,[7] but its lineage extends back to the spectacles of Renaissance princes and medieval royal entries, tournaments, and fêtes.[8] The state-sponsored Historical Pageant at the centre of the Tercentenary provides a fascinating glimpse into the contested world of public memory in a divided community. Through careful selection and deft balancing and by either avoiding or wilfully misrepresenting the unmentionable, history could be made to serve various present purposes.

It was a strange logic that deemed it appropriate to honour the founding of Quebec with a memorial park to its fall, but seen from a certain perspective it did make sense. Scholars have become accustomed to the "contested" character of ceremonial events. One now expects to find divided objectives and multiple interpretations embedded in such socially constricted rituals. Antagonists could, on occasion, co-operate for different purposes. Earl Grey learned that to celebrate imperial triumph he must also commemorate a British defeat. Laurier cleverly used the fact that "Champlain has not been without honour in the city he founded"—he already had a magnificent statue—to justify doing something novel: celebrating the history of Quebec with a festival and a national historic

park.[9] As well, it must be remembered that the ultranationalist Armand Lavergne, though he objected to the imperialist packaging, in the end found enough substance in the proposal to vote in the House of Commons in favour of the National Battlefields Commission. Hegemony and resistance can be acted out in the same public space, and there is room for quite a lot of dissonant activity in between. Celebrating the past is never completely straightforward, particularly in a divided polity. In this instance the issue of contention extended to what in fact was being celebrated: the founding of Quebec or its conquest? If the object was "race fusion", who were the races?

On another occasion the contending political divisions could be examined in all their baroque splendour. There are many other aspects of this event, having to do with the issues of representation, "ocularity", participation, and opposition, that also warrant attention. Here, however, the focus will be upon theatre, more particularly upon the ideology of historical pageantry, the nature of the "imagined past" put on display, the social structure of performance, and the unanticipated way in which the agenda of "race fusion" was both represented and subverted in spectacle.

The Grand Design

The Historical Pageant presented during the Tercentenary of Quebec held in July 1908 was designed to establish and to broaden the middle ground of understanding between English and French Canadians and, in the minds of some of the more enthusiastic celebrants, inspire a new consciousness of shared nationhood. The pageants displayed, in the most powerful dramatic form available, a view of Canadian history designed to serve explicit political goals. In the spectacle of the Historical Pageants power summoned art to help consolidate the state. Directed by one of the leaders of the contemporary British historical pageant movement and lavishly funded, Quebec's Tercentenary was in a real sense the "Ur" pageant in North America and was recognized as such by contemporaries. Its importance lies not only in its theatrical but also in its recognition as one of the mot ambitious attempts at the theatre of social transformation, whereby "history could be made into a dramatic public ritual through which the residents of the town, by acting out the right version of their past, could bring about some kind of future social and political transformation."[10]

Louis Napoleon Parker, a musician, actor, playwrite, and ardent Wagnerian, invented modern English historical pageantry in 1905. In his hands the twelfth centenary of the founding of Sherbourne, where he had formerly been music master at the school, grew into an open air "folk play" acted out by students, teachers, and townspeople on the lawns in front of the village's ruined abbey. The Sherbourne Pageant—the use of the word to cover this new form was also his invention—was an immediate if unlikely success, drawing overflow audiences. For a time Parker built a career as pageant master as did numerous imitators, whom he naturally scorned. Although he seems to have made up the rules as he went along, with a sense of proprietorial *amour propre* he later codified his art in 12 imperious commandments.

After insisting first upon what a pageant was not (a street procession, gala, wayzgoose, fête, beanfest, pageant wagon, or *tableau vivant*), he pronounced upon what a proper pageant should be: a "festival of brotherhood" in which social divisions are dissolved in a common effort to recreate scenes from a glorious past.[11] In essence Parker insisted upon the local, democratic, and participatory nature of these events. He took great delight in the social mixing and status inversions his "folk plays" produced onstage. The pageant should be presented not for tourists or for money but to brighten and enoble the lives of the citizens of the community, "to reawaken civic pride" and "increase self respect". There were to be no sets; the antiquity (preferably ruined) of the community itself was the stage. Self-reliance, local initiative, and learning together were to take the place of store-bought goods. The pageant was intended to serve as a mass school of arts and crafts; participants had to make their own costumes and properties, research their past, write the script, compose the music, organize the event, and serve as both actors and audience. Here Parker's pageantry joined with the contemporary arts and crafts movement to reawaken pre-industrial skills, revive the "moral principles associated with the past", and thereby rekindle a sense of historical organic community.

Above all, a proper historical pageant in Parker's formulation had explicit anti-modern impulses. The aim, apart from community education and entertainment, was to combat the spirit of the age: "This modernising spirit, which destroys all loveliness and has no loveliness of its own to put in its place, is the negation of poetry, the negation of romance... This is just precisely the kind of spirit which a properly organized and properly conducted pageant is designed to kill."[12] Reason had literally disenchanted society; historical pageantry aimed at nothing less than the re-enchantment of daily life.

In 1906 the London *Times* index contained no references to pageants of any kind. By 1908 it required a full column to itemize articles dealing with a score or more English pageants, and more than two columns to index the Quebec Tercentenary including its pageant.[13] There is no evidence, however, that in the planning stages the promoters of the Champlain Tercentenary knew much if anything of the development of historical pageantry in England before January 1908. Influenced by recent examples in the United States and their own experience, they tended to think in terms of formal ceremonies, buildings, reconstructions, and costumed processions. The World's Columbian Exposition at Chicago in 1893 seems to have been the inspiration for some of the early thinking about reconstruction of Champlain's habitation and his ship the *Don de Dieu*, as well as a parade of people dressed up as historical figures. By stages, as various committees worked over the idea and as the possibilities of federal money provided more scope for the imagination, the notion of "un grand cortège historique" [a great historic procession] evolved towards a theatrical spectacle representing, in the words of the municipal Comité d'Histoire et d'Archéologie, "des grandes scènes dramatiques prises dans les plus belles pages de notre histoire" [major dramatic scenes taken in the most beautiful pages of our history]. According to this group of historians, charged by the city council with the task of determining what might be celebrated and how, those scenes ought to include Jacques Cartier claiming possession of Canada for France, Champlain's return to Quebec in 1633, Dollard's exploits at the Long Sault, Mademoiselle de Verchères with the Iroquois, and Guy Carleton repelling the American invaders in 1775.[14]

As politicians, businessmen, and men of letters had been working themselves towards a more theatrical and spectacular means of representing the past before a mass audience during 1907, those more familiar with the contemporary British cultural milieu

171

had become aware of the current metropolitan fashion, historical pageantry. The good offices of the Governor General, who may well have planted some of the articles about pageantry in the Canadian press, brought these two currents together at Quebec. Louis Napoleon Parker was unavailable because of other commitments; however, late in February the local organizing committee announced that Frank Lascelles, producer of the Oxford Pageant, had accepted an invitation to direct a pageant at Quebec.[15]

When Lascelles arrived in the city in March, after having spent a weekend in Ottawa being briefed by the Governor General, he entered a community divided, though by far the dominant consensus of the city favoured the full-blown Tercentenary. The Société Saint-Jean-Baptiste had withdrawn to the sidelines. Having seen "its" festival inflated into this gargantuan and in some respects grotesque caricature, the SSJB refused to accommodate the Tercentenary by moving its own unveiling of the Laval Statue from the national day of June 24 to late July, when it would be swallowed up in the larger event. In this the Society was fully supported by the hierarchy of the Church. In St. Roch, the working class and commercial district north of the old city, public meetings denounced the celebration. Jules-Paul Tardivel the younger and Omer Heroux directed the *nationaliste* attack against the transformation of the tercentennial into an imperial festival in *La Vérité*, a newspaper whose 3,000 copies circulated weekly primarily amongst the clergy, religious orders, and devout lay Catholics of the province. Tardivel and Heroux put aside their fevered campaigns against conspiracies of Jews, Freemasons, Orangists, Odd Fellows, immigrants, trade unions, anarchists, liberals, and socialists of all stripes to expose the imperialist plot to take over the celebration and the hidden agenda of "race fusion".[16] For them the concept meant race suicide for French Canadians.

Lascelles began an intensive round of discussions with Mayor Garneau, H.J.J.B. Chouinard, the city clerk, who had proposed the celebration in the first place and served as the behind-the-scenes organizer and go-between with the Société Saint-Jean-Baptiste, and the Comité d'Histoire et d'Archéologie, guardians of a past of which Lascelles knew virtually nothing. In effect, the local committee had by this stage produced a "book" from which he could design a pageant.[17] With the full backing of the National Battlefields Commission, the pageants went into

production under Lascelles's guiding hand and with a budget of $155,000. The Dominion Archivist, Arthur Doughty, was commissioned to compose a brief history of Canada to provide context for the pageants and authoritative historical continuity for each of the scenes. Ernest Myrand, a member of the Comité d'Histoire et d'Archéologie, a historian and musicologist, set about writing dialogue for each of the scenes and producing appropriate and authentic music. The locally famous artist Charles Huot was engaged to design the costumes for the historical procession and the pageants. Charles Vézina and the Symphonic Society were recruited to perform the music. Lascelles went shopping for an exotic list of properties not readily fabricated locally (wigs, hats, muskets, swords, halberds, bows and arrows, cannon, drums, bugles). Architects and contractors threw together plans for a temporary stadium seating 15,000 spectators to be built on the site of the race track.

The new celebrity, Frank Lascelles, offered a preview of his art as the guest speaker for the first meeting of the newly formed Quebec City Canadian Club at a luncheon in the Empire Room of the Château Frontenac on Saturday, April 11. A strikingly handsome man with the dramatic flair of a trained actor, Lascelles held the 110-member audience in a thrall with his flowing, mellifluous cadences describing the wonders that would unfold in the midsummer eve. He assured his audience he had not come all of this way to put on "a mere theatrical or spectacular show". Rather he came to help the city, the country, and the world learn about Quebec's glorious history but in a new way through a new art form. "Things seen were mightier than things heard," he reminded his hearers, as he invited them to:

> Imagine that you dream a dream on a summer's day and see passing before you in quick succession visions of the great heroes who have gone, the peasants, the great founders, the soldiers, the martyrs, and the saints. And you wake up to find that it is really true, there in the flesh and blood before you are their prototypes, living, moving, walking, talking as they used to do and you can hardly believe that you are not dreaming still.

The process of bringing the past to life would in turn transform people's lives, draw rich and poor into a closer, working relationship, promote mutual understanding, and inspire "greater sympathy and a greater pride in your common heritage". History linked Quebec as no other place on the continent to "all that is noblest and best in the days of old France, the days of romance and chivalry, when that fair country was in the zenith of her religious and artistic life". Lascelles offered a lyrical hint in the form of a plot synopsis of the splendour that would unfold on the grass of the Plains of Abraham, with the sky overhead, the sweep of the historic countryside in full view, and the river flowing majestically in the background. Then with all of the eloquence he could command he summoned the city to action with the biblical injunction "let us now praise famous men and the fathers who begat us."[18]

The Pageant Unfolds

The story of the recruitment of the cast and the way in which opposition to the Tercentenary and its pageants was overcome must be told another time. Suffice it to say here that the women's movement in Quebec City, the organized business elites, and finally the Church hierarchy, all for quite different reasons and with varying degrees of enthusiasm, eventually threw their support behind the festival. For some the Tercentenary had positive attractions. For others the all-too-likely consequences of failure were too great to contemplate. These interventions by the social hierarchy and the bishops changed the atmosphere dramatically. The *nationalistes* became comparatively subdued. *Le Soleil* reported with some relief: "We are pleased to note that for the particular organization of historical pageants shows apathy, manifested in the early days especially by French Canadians gradually disappears."[19]

Gradually the massive grandstand began to rise from a pile of lumber at the race course, a wonder (and a fire hazard) to be viewed on a spring evening. Decorations festooned the streets. The reconstructed Habitation took shape in Lower Town. When the costumes were distributed families rushed out to have their pictures taken by Quebec's portrait photographers. The militia had begun to assemble in their camps; hotels and boarding houses filled up; a tented city received the overflow. Naval squadrons were reported cruising up the river, and of course HRH the Prince of Wales was aboard one of those ships.

Nothing quickened excitement more than the arrival of the Indians. Native people had figured in the planning for the festival from an early date, inspired by memories, or more likely photographic images, of the Chicago World's Fair. Chouinard originally hoped to include a settlement of Native people as welcoming parties for Champlain. Mayor Garneau's 1907 proposal to Laurier also allowed for an Indian encampment of several tribes along with their Catholic and Protestant missionairies.[20]

Indians with their costumes added necessary "colour" to the programme. Obviously there was a certain carnivalesque dimension to all of this, the mingled excitement and fear of having the exotic "other" represented across the reassuring separation of the stage. Identities in the process of formation were better recognized in the presence of the people with visibly different identities. Of course the representation of Native identity, too, would be largely constructed by the observers.[21] Here the Quebecers were attempting to replicate the dramatic effect of the ethnographic villages of the World's Columbian Exposition in which the status hierarchy of the human race was on display on the Midway Plaisance.[22] Quebec culture at this point was in what might be called the twilight of the "fearsome savage" interpretive period. Indians brought to the celebration a sense of implicit but contained danger.[23] Native people, represented in villages, tents, costumes, and ritual performances at the Tercentenary, would reinforce progressive symbolism, showing explicitly the measure of civilization's advance. The addition of missionaries and the domesticated encampment of families framed the scene as both past and pastorale.

The Native people themselves, recruited by agents of the Canadian Pacific Railway, L.O. Armstrong and J.R. Blaney, consisted of Iroquois from Caughnawaga near Montreal, Ojibway from Sault Ste. Marie, and local Native people from nearby Ancienne Lorette. The Native people's camp of upwards of 100 families, located on the Plains close to the pageant ground, attracted a steady stream of curious townsfolk. Geneva in the women's page of *Le Soleil* devoted a column to the local Native people: "among the last Hurons".[24] The presence of the Natives energized the rehearsals, especially the Dollard scene. American Horse, a veteran of several Wild West Shows, directed the Native people in theatrical technique. Decked out at public expense in gaudy Plains Indian headresses

173

and leather-fringed clothing, brandishing tomahawks and shouting war whoops, American Horse and his colleagues determined to act the part expected of them.

By the end of the dress rehearsals the city and its visitors could not only sense the mounting excitement, but also see with their own eyes the evanescent enchantment of historical pageantry:

> Emperors and princes, court ladies and lords of high degree, explorers and adventures, pages, soldiers and Indians, the flower of chivalry and the pride of court and castle, the heroes of fort and log cabin, and the hardy campaigners of a bye-gone age, all clad in striking costumes of three hundred years ago, mingled yesterday with the soberly clad citizens of the present day, and rode democratically on street cars, or wagons, or walked to the Plains of Abraham.

On the same day *Le Soleil* commented: "The Quebec city public began to relive this fascinating period of three centuries ago of the golden age of chivalry where the cream of French society was in full bloom, full of grace, full of charm, full of dignity."[25]

The Tercentenary celebrations opened on July 21 with the ceremonial arrival of Champlain, his tiny *Don de Dieu* in full sail overwhelmed by the monstrous fuming warships anchored in midstream. For our purposes we need not be distracted by the events of the Tercentenary save the grand historical procession, the *cortège historique*, in which the characters from the pageants marched through the streets of Quebec up to Champlain's monument by the Château where they paid their simultaneous respects to the founder of Canada and their future King. The history of Canada and much of that of France were thus drawn under the British imperial yoke. Two small matters about this parade warrant comment before we move to the pageants proper. First of all, the procession was not complete. The ecclesiastical characters did not march; thus it was an entirely secular affair. Secondly, when the procession passed the Ursuline Convent, Montcalm's army halted and gave a moving salute to the remains of its deceased commander interred within.[26]

For six evenings from 5:00 to 8:00 p.m.—to provide cool, dramatic gloaming and more practically

to allow actors to assemble after their day's work—the magic of the pageants unfolded. The sky stayed blue, the temperatures moderate; the sunsets were glorious, and the rain on one day held off until the end of the last scene. The pageants overcame sceptics with a narcotic combination of music, a mass cast, colour, staging, a dramatic setting, and a stirring finale. As a measure of his theatrical success, it might be noted that Lascelles went considerably over budget and the sale of tickets provided much less revenue than expected, yet there were no complaints from the notably tightfisted Commissioners. To the contrary, Lascelles was hailed as a genius and voted a special silver sculpture of the *Don de Dieu* as an honorarium. It is quite likely, then, that the pageants as spectacle exceeded even Lascelles's extravagant expectations.

How did the history of Canada unfold under his direction? The show begins with an empty field. A solitary Indian spots a French ship in the distance. The village gathers to welcome the strangers with songs and greetings. Cartier and his crew offer bread and wine and lay hands on the halt and lame; a great cross of wood is planted, prayers given, speeches made, and gifts exchanged. Amidst cries of jubilation from the Native people, the newcomers withdraw to their ship taking Donnacona with them.

Cartier and Donnacona reappear in the gardens at Fontainebleau to be presented to Francis I. Courtiers emerge from the forest on horseback. The King rides under a canopy on a horse draped in gold. Fauns and satyrs dance through the gardens. Cartier kneels; Donnacona falls prostrate before the King, then rises to tell his wondrous tale of the New World.

The second pageant takes place at the court of Henry IV in the throne room of the Louvre. Champlain is presented to the King and the glittering court by Sieur de Monts and receives his commission, following which members of the court form up for a stately pavane or peacock dance. In the next scene Champlain leads his young bride to her simple home in "rock bound" Quebec. They are greeted by the entire population of 80 people; the young bride charms the assembly. Native people gather, smoke the calumet, present her with gifts of clubs and war trophies, then dance their welcome as a cask of wine is broken open.

Rustic sociability gives way to the civilizing power of women and faith in the third pageant.

Mother Marie de l'Incarnation, the Ursulines, and the Jesuits are welcomed to New France by the Governor, Sieur de Montmagny. The nuns and priests kneel and kiss the soil, rise, and form a procession to a little church to thank God for their safe arrival. En route, Madame de la Peltrie kisses Indian children while Marie de l'Incarnation gathers a crowd of settlers' children about her for instruction.

Civilization hangs on the brink in the exciting fourth pageant in which the stalwart Dollard and his 16 colleagues hold out bravely against the murderous onslaught of the Iroquois. Then, after a stirring war dance, a massed attack of Indians overruns the paltry fort. "To the beat of drums the train moves off uttering plaintive and mournful sounds and bearing the bodies of the dead in procession, with their trophies elevated on poles."

Order is restored and civilization secured by the Church, reinforced by the secular power of the state. In the fifth pageant Mgr Laval, under a glittering canopy, surrounded by a splendid entourage, "ceremonially receives" the representative of the King, Marquis de Tracy, as New France becomes a Royal Colony in 1665. Cannon roar their welcome to the new Governor and his regiment, the Carignans-Salières. Twelve Indian Chieftains lay bows and arrows at the Governor's feet to symbolize peace. The church bells peel out their welcome, and a *Te Deum* is sung.

Taking possession of *le pays d'en haut* is the subject of the sixth pageant. Saint Lusson sets out for the west accompanied by *voyageurs*. The party is greeted by a succession of Indian tribes to mark progression along the way. Jesuits bless a cross and pray. Saint Lusson, sword raised and with a volley of muskets, claims the territory for France. A eulogy to the King is pronounced and the assembly concludes with a *Te Deum* "to thank God on behalf of these rude savages that they are now the subjects of so great and powerful a Monarch".

It is an hour before dawn on Monday, October 16, 1690, as the seventh pageant begins. Phips's English fleet of 34 vessels is reported to be three leagues from the city. A messenger from Phips arrives imperiously demanding the capitulation of Quebec. Governor Frontenac jauntily rejects this arrogant request with his memorable retort: "Je vais répondre à votre maître par la bouche de mes canons!" [I will answer your master from the mouth of my cannons!] Thus thwarted, Phips's squadron retreats in disarray.

Then comes the climax. In the French-language programme, written by Ernest Myrand, the eighth pageant is simply described as a "Grande parade d'honneur", in which

> Montcalm and Wolfe, Lévis and Murray, Carleton and Salaberry, at the head of their respective regiments, marched to the sound of cannon and trumpets. General salute to the troops which was answered by the firing warships anchored in the harbor.

> Grouping of all the characters in the Historic Procession and Pageants. Singing of both national anthems: O Canada! and God Save the King! Salute to the Flag.[27]

By contrast the official programme, written by the Dominion Archivist, Arthur Doughty, devotes four tightly printed pages of text to describing in detail the military engagements of 1759–1760.

The drama does not end in a mock battle, although the guns of the ships give the effect of the bombardment of the city. Instead, the armies of Wolfe and Montcalm form up and manoeuvre side by side The two generals exchange honours, and jointly, at the head of a unified army, they march across the field to the strains of "O Canada" and "God Save the King". Who would notice that Carleton's loyal French-Canadian militia of 1775 and de Salaberry's Voltigeurs of 1812 had joined the throng? As a climax, all the pageant participants gather as the children release a flock of white doves of peace.[28]

According to *Le Soleil* the crowd watched the simple opening scene "en religieux silence" [in religious silence]. Excitement mounted during the frenzy of the Dollard scene (which occupied a disproportionate amount of space in all the newspaper accounts). For Laval "les cloches chantent gaiement" [bells sing cheerfully]. Following Frontenac's boldness: "Un frisson d'admiration secoue les rangs des milliers de spectateurs." [A thrill of admiration shakes the ranks of thousands of spectators] Then, in a moment of heightened apprehension, the glorious finale unfolded:

> And after an interlude of a few moments, came the British and French armies marching side by side and fraternizing in peace.

The flags are flying, the breeze weaves their pleats and the English grenadier was walking along the French grenadier. The battalions marched, greeted by the cheers of the crowd and they leave the ground leaving all still imbued with different emotions, ten thousand people ... who reluctantly leave the scene or come in to relive all their authenticity and local color three centuries of the existence of the Canadian people.[29]

Reading the Pageants

Like most mysteries this one dissolves on close examination. The pageants at the Quebec Tercentenary fulfilled some of Louis Napoleon Parker's conditions. They brought back to life a distant, romantic, chivalrous age. They recovered mystical elements—fauns and satyrs—and thereby brought a natural spirituality to the surface of bourgeois regimentation. Dance, music, and drama were united. The costumes were sumptuous; the staging breathtaking. Roles brought forth new or hitherto distinguished talents in doctors, lawyers, wives, and merchants. Past and present mingled in the streets. Above all the physical setting was sensational, drawing attention to the dictum that the site itself be the subject celebrated. A visiting pageant enthusiast, Ellis Oberholzer, believed the pageant field at Quebec the most beautiful he had ever witnessed.[30]

On the other hand the pageants were put on by a national commission as a festival of national identity with a view to entertaining and instructing royalty, visiting dignitaries, tourists, and locals. Admission was charged and it was not cheap, leading to some grousing that more performances ought to have been arranged to allow orphans and others without means access. Lascelles unashamedly aimed for and attained spectacular effects. Properties were purchased and the costuming aspect of the affair generated an enormous business amongst the civil and military tailors, seamstresses, milliners, dry goods dealers, and merchants of the city. The aim of mixing the classes succeeded in part but was confounded somewhat by recruitment processes that depended upon existing social networks, clubs, organizations, and business or religious associations. Rather than subvert social distinctions, to a certain extent Lascelles's pageant put them on display.

What did the audience make of what it saw? It would be relatively easy to pile up self-congratulatory effusions from anglophones who thought it a wonderful coming together of two peoples into one. Earl Grey was specially commended by the Colonial Office for "the faculty you have of bringing into harmony elements which might be discordant". The Prince of Wales loved the pageants—so he said in a Marconigram from the *Indomitable* received at Quebec. He enthused about them later to his wife as well.[31] The English press, of course, was ecstatic.

But what of French Canada? Amidst its fulsome denunciations of the imperialist fête, the grudging one-sentence evaluation of the pageants by Tardivel's *La Vérité* speaks volumes: "The historical representations were generally appreciated." The weekly Catholic publication, *La Semaine Religieuse de Québec*, went considerably further:

> The "pageants"—English word that we did not take long, in all circles, to pronounce à la française-were among so many other items of the program, the centerpiece of the celebration. We frankly confess that we are absolutely unable to express the strong and powerful emotions that we experienced in these performances of the incomparable French period in our history.[32]

The pageants were particularly important, seen from this author's perspective, in precisely the terms Lascelles described: things seen are more powerful than things heard.

> We see in these "pageants" the main part of the festivities, because the popular masses, instead of vague notions that they had previously had taken there by the intuitive method, the exact knowledge of the great facts of our history; because our fellow English-speaking countrymen of all provinces, and foreign visitors, especially from the United States, saw the nobility and the heroism of the founders of our French-Canadian race. All these English people and Americans have seen and applauded our French and Catholic glories! Who says that there is not a great event, and that there will not have considerable effects?[33]

Genevra, the women's columnist for *Le Soleil*, agreed with this assessment. She insisted that the pageants had recruited participants from all social ranks; women had neglected their duties and homes, businessmen had neglected their affairs to bring a distant and noble past to life. English and French had worked together in a theatrical enterprise certain to have lasting effects:

> In each of these scenes, exclusively French and Catholic, the English people were the first ones to accept roles, leaving us with the greatest historical characters who belonged to us by right, but whom we neglected to take. They never had a smile of disdain for our religious costumes and the emblem of our culture, they have proven that they respected our sincere convictions. We could learn a great advantage in ordinary life, a more accurate understanding of the mentality of our fellow English-speaking citizens without ever sacrificing the interests of our language or those of our faith; without ever making concessions that we diminish in the spirit of those who we do and rob an antagonism as old as the conquest and who has more reason to be.[34]

From this perspective pageants taught French Canadians about themselves and delivered a message to English Canada that it would otherwise not hear.

Lascelles and the social organization that formed around the pageants influenced the way in which these scenes would be presented. Dramatic necessity as well as social imperatives drove production values. The view of history depicted in the pageant was constructed in a particular social and political matrix. The English were still numerous and powerful in the city. The French-Canadian intelligentsia was still attached to empire. The Liberal party provided the power structure at the local, provincial, and federal levels. The route to status, position, and honour ran through collaboration. Within that context several aspects of the pageants deserve comment: time, language, the cast, the role of women, the Native contribution, and the version of history put on display.

The pageants presented scenes from the "heroic" period of New France. But for the fleeting sighting of de Salaberry the nineteenth century was essentially invisible. So too, for that matter, was most of the eighteenth century. The pageants dramatized a few selected vignettes from the seventeenth century. Time leapt forward from scene to scene without any intervening continuity. The marchpast at the end encompassed three separate events covering more than a half a century. So as to diffuse the impression that the conquest was the object of celebration or the end of Canadian history, two costumed groups also marched in the procession and joined the armies of Wolfe and Montcalm in the eigth pageant: Guy Carleton and the defenders of Quebec in 1775, and de Salaberry and a contingent of Voltigeurs, French-Canadian heroes of another defence against the Americans in 1812. The historical committee chose the time frame, included and excluded as it saw fit, and did its utmost to ensure that the closing bracket of time did not correspond to 1759–1760, but for all practical purposes that is where Lascelles, for dramatic effect, brought things to a close.

Theatre had a way of spilling out into the streets, however. Costumed soldiers from Montcalm's army marched in the *nationaliste* Catholic Youth parade.[35] At one of the last pageants the two armies marched out of the stadium to the nearby Monument to General Wolfe, where they paid their respects. Usually the soldiers from the last scene maintained ranks and marched back through the crowds of the Grande Allée to their dispersal points. On at least one occasion Montcalm's army marched triumphally through the gaily decorated *nationaliste* district of St. Roch, prompting requests from anglophone quarters that Wolfe's army do the same thing there. In the streets it was possible to invert meaning. In this sense the pageants did not end at the conquest.

As befits the subject, the language of the pageant was entirely French. However logical a decision this might have been, it was nevertheless a bold move in view of the number of anglophone tourists anticipated. The organizers concluded that the inconvenience to unilingual English speakers was vastly outweighed by the offence that might be given if the past were rendered to French-speaking Quebecers in another language. The English members of the community and the tourists—duly provided with programmes and translations of the text if they were interested — registered no complaint. The only exception to the all-French dialogue came in the seventh pageant in which Phips's delegate delivers his

● **TABLE 1.1**

Anglophone and Francophone Participation

Scene	Total	LEADING ROLES		OTHER PARTS	
		Ang	Fr	Ang	Fr
Cartier	285	25%	75%	13%	87%
Francis I	456	0%	100%	33%	67%
Henry IV	624	29%	71%	43%	57%
Champlain	259	5%	95%	19%	81%
Ursulines	241	0%	100%	7%	93%
Dollard	100	6%	94%		
Laval	683	7%	93%	14%	86%
Lusson	185	0%	100%	18%	82%
Frontenac	767	0%	100%	19%	81%
Armies					
Wolfe	632	100%	0%	86%	14%
Montcalm	539	0%	100%	3%	97%
Totals	4,771	14%	86%	31%	69%
Quebec population	73,475	14%	85%	14%	85%

Sources: See note 37.

written ultimatum in English. Frontenac responds: "I've never been familiar with English, so, Mr. de Bienville, you would be very kind and translate this document for me." Later in the scene, when the agitated English delegate bursts out into French, Frontenac interjects: "Mister speaks good French, pleasant surprise! I am delighted. You know our history better than our language. Bravo. Your gesture is nice." Language was a serious business, but it could also be a laughing matter.[36]

The director did indeed seek out a cast for his script, but by the same token the volunteers made a script for themselves; they determined to a certain extent the balance of representation through the casting. It is also the case that the process of social conscription by which the recruiting for this labour-intensive production was done worked somewhat in opposition to the objective of social mixing.

The accompanying tables offer a dim and none too reliable reflection of a social phenomenon. Names are not a very good indicator of cultural origins. In an extensively exogamous, bilingual, and bicultural setting cultures change even though names stay the same. Classification of the personnel by type of name, gender, and scene does offer some insight, however, into the social processes that underlay the pageant.[37] In round numbers anglophone Quebecers provided 15 per cent of the starring roles and 33 per cent of the extras; francophones occupied 85 percent of the principal roles and made up 67 per cent of the extras in the roughly 3,000-member cast, almost a mirror reflection of the general population of the

● **TABLE 1.2**
Men and Women in the Cast

Scene	Total	LEADING ROLES		OTHER PARTS	
		Women	Men	Women	Men
Cartier	120	0%	100%	0%	100%
Francis I	291	25%	75%	66%	45%
Henry IV	459	25%	75%	49%	51%
Champlain	94	5%	95%	19%	81%
Ursulines	76	89%	11%	57%	43%
Dollard	17	0%	100%		
Laval	518	57%	43%	22%	78%
Lusson	20	0%	100%	0%	100%
Frontenac	602	0%	100%	18%	82%
Armies	841	0%	100%	0%	100%
Totals	3,038	31%	69%	23%	77%
Civilian parts only	2,197	33%	67%	42%	68%

Sources: See note 37.

179

● **TABLE 1.3**
Anglophone and Francophone Casting

Segment	Total	Anglophone	Francophone
Francis 1 court	134	48%	52%
Henry IV noblemen	111	39%	61%
Henry IV noblewomen	200	62%	39%
Laval: merchants' wives	33	58%	42%
Laval: peasants	66	52%	48%
Laval: regiment	99	1%	99%
Frontenac: court ladies	75	99%	1%
Frontenac: court men	101	17%	83%
Wolfe's army	463	86%	14%
Montcalm's army	369	3%	97%

Source: See note 37.

city of approximately 85 per cent francophones and 14 per cent anglophones. Although the two cultural groups were mixed in most scenes, some exceptions warrant notice: the principal parts in the Laval and the Ursuline scenes were played exclusively by francophones. It also would seem to be the case that francophones made up the ranks of Montcalm's army, anglophones that of Wolfe—though there was more intermixing in the latter. The casting of certain segments provides a better indication of greater anglophone enthusiasm for pageantry. Compared to the general population, anglophone women were significantly overrepresented in the court scenes.

Several forces seem to have been at work in the selection process: fantasy, identification, inversion, and, in all likelihood, coercion. English women in particular fulfilled an overwhelming desire to play at being French royalty, princesses, courtiers, and women of quality. Many of them appeared on horseback in the Francis I scene. On the other hand, some groups sought to identify themselves with their peers or their organizations in the past. Soldiers from the militia and the garrison made up large parts of the armies; sailors from the Yacht Club manned the *Don de Dieu*; businessmen and their wives, families, and children played at being merchants and bourgeois. Priests filled all of the ecclesiastical roles. The same was not the case, however, for nuns. The cloistered orders could not participate. The Ursulines did make the costumes for this scene, however; they took pains to ensure that the costumes were treated with due respect and were delighted when young women from good families, graduates of their convent school, were chosen to play the roles of Marie de l'Incarnation and Madame de la Peltrie. They kept in contact through friends and gathered a huge postcard collection of the pageant scenes.[38]

There seems to have been some inversion of roles, too: bourgeois English women took on the role of French-Canadian peasants. There was also a good deal of straightforward conscription into ranks—an orphanage provided the children of New France. Some participants sought to live out fantasies; others sought their own identities in the past.

The numbers available swelled the ranks of some scenes and left others thinly populated. The court scenes were much larger than might otherwise have been the case on account of the willingness of women in particular to volunteer. These scenes, though not the most dramatic, were the most colourful and popular. Thus women were not invisible in this history; 42 per cent of the civilian participants were female. Moreover women played starring roles in many of the scenes and left a lasting impression with the colourful mass of their costumes. This reflected the power of women as organizers and their greater interest in the theatrical aspects of the Tercentenary.

It may have been true that the actors were drawn from many ranks of society; however, the pageant made stars of lawyers, doctors, their wives and daughters, prelates, and politicians. Mr. Moise Raymond as Cartier received universal praise. The notary Boilly made a striking impression as Francis I; the advocate Antonio Couillard and his Queen, Mme L. A. Carrier, carried off their roles with panache. Sheriff Charles Langelier as Champlain and Mlle Yvonne de Lery as his young wife formed a heroic couple. Male members of the clergy were allowed to participate. L'abbé Vachon recreated the saintly and powerful Laval with grace and authority. The reviewer in the *Chronicle* singled out Frontenac as one of the most outstanding performances.

The professional bourgeoisie of the city seems to have supplied the leading actors of this pageant if the impression of casual empiricism bears up under closer scrutiny. Acting in the pageants fed their sense of self-importance between other powerful social hierarchies, and it drew upon their special communication skills. Business people stayed safely in the background. It has not been possible at this stage to determine the extent to which figures associated with the Société Saint-Jean-Baptiste became involved. The initial indications are that the two festivals for Laval and the Tercentenary involved substantially separate casts. As a working hypothesis it might be ventured that this was not the full range of Quebec's social structure on display, but rather the Liberal Party in costume.

Everyone had played a key part in the success of the pageants, it was affirmed on all sides in the flow of self-congratulation that followed. But all agreed, English and French, and *Le Soleil* in particular, that the Native people stood out. This is somewhat surprising since, as originally designed, Native people were to be supporting actors at most. As it turned out they starred in most of the scenes. The Native people had a great deal of artistic leeway; they largely directed their own scenes. Moreover, they showed themselves to be extremely pleased with the roles they had been given and could make for themselves. Afterwards, in an elaborate ceremony, American Horse and his colleagues invested Lascelles as an Indian Chief. Even though he was an actor among actors on this occasion, Lascelles was deeply moved by the event and took the whole thing very seriously. His obituary noted that he bore the name Tehonikonraka (man of Infinite Resources) as a chief of the Iroquois nation.[39]

From another perspective it is not at all surprising that the Natives made the deepest dramatic impression. They had the most energetic roles and great costumes. They fulfilled all expectations for nobility as well as savagery. Some of them were, after all, trained actors who knew how to work the crowd. The Native participants had reason to think well of Lascelles and the pageant. In this Wild West Show they got to win—in the Dollard scene. More to the point, they had key roles in most of the scenes. They did not just greet the European explorers and quietly disappear. They welcomed, guided, resisted, and showed different aspects of their characters. Their cultural differences were not only displayed to the extent that this was possible, but also used to indicate the passage up-country through different national territories. The Indians of the pageants greatly pleased the spectators. Similarly, the Native people who played these parts, with the approval of the director, made their own statement, and that obviously pleased them.

For Lascelles, working within the pageant tradition, Native peoples represented the natural, elemental spirits of the land. Native people were more effective assassins of modernism than wood sprites, sylphs, satyrs, and fairies. Moreover, they were multipurpose elements of the drama. They could be used in Christian symbolic terms as terrible foes bringing God's retribution. They could bring a genuine tremor of fear to the play; at the same time, they could be menials, functioning as the stage crew sweeping the huge carpet onto the field for the Henry IV court scene. Their wild dancing counter-balanced the measured civility of the pavane. Their presence, singing, dancing, smoking, looking after children, hunting, and guiding, served like a Greek chorus as a mordant commentary on the drama being enacted. Their continuing presence mediated cultural difference. Here was a third force interspersed between English and

French, and, within the theatrical conventions, they were able to present themselves as peoples with a history and a claim to the future deserving of consideration too. It is also clear that "race fusion" as seen by Earl Grey and "pan-Canadian nationalism" as seen by the moderate French-Canadian nationalists did not include Native people. The pageant, in its own way, said they should. In that respect the Indians stole the show.[40]

The past on display in the pageant was, of course, a highly selective, even idiosyncratic representation. One could go through each scene showing how issues were slanted or distorted. The selection of scenes itself emphasized heroism, nobility, grandeur, paternalism, community harmony, Christian sacrifice, mission, loyalty, survival, providential destiny, and transcendence. Royal involvement in the history of New France was greatly exaggerated by the selection and casting. The recently invented Dollard martyrdom was played to the hilt. The romantic aspects of the past were emphasized at the expense of the quotidian. The Church appeared not only a central force in history, but also was seen through an ultramontane lens; it rivaled the state in both majesty and power. The music (Mendelssohn's "War March of the Priests") and the gorgeous costumes and glittery canopy made this point.

But it must be said that the dramatic representation of the past in the pageants was not significantly unfaithful to the spirit of the contemporary historiography. Parkman laid out the grand sweep of this view of the past. Thomas Chapais (who was active on the Historical Committee) and Benjamin Sulte, writing in French, carried on the heroic tradition, clericalizing it and heightening the notion of the organic unity of the collectivity. George Wrong published *A Canadian Manor and its Seigneurs* that year. Arthur Doughty was hard at work turning the history of New France into the dramatic and stirring origins of a distinctly Canadian nation. His *Cradle of New France* was composed in 1907; he actually wrote the preface in Quebec during March 1908 while he was working on the pageants and the Battlefields plan. That the pageants bore this mark is not surprising given the direct hand both Chapais and Doughty took in the script. The notion of a romantic past, conceived as the biography of heroes, with New France as the beginning of Canadian civilization, in which priests and nuns shared honours with generals, governors,

181

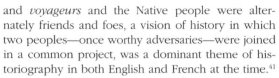
and *voyageurs* and the Native people were alternately friends and foes, a vision of history in which two peoples—once worthy adversaries—were joined in a common project, was a dominant theme of historiography in both English and French at the time.[41]

Most obviously history was altered in this representation to be made more palatable. There was an ongoing struggle between the local francophone script writers on the one side and Earl Grey's forces, including the English director, on the other, over when the pageants would end. The battle for Quebec in 1759 is, in the local committee's version, melded into a military action in which the French-Canadian population is loyal to the crown in 1775 and again in 1812. For imperialists like Earl Grey history ended and began in 1759; battlefield commemoration was what this was all about. For Lascelles too, though for theatrical reasons, the natural climax and conclusion unfolded on the Plains of Abraham in 1759. The imperialist forces, supported by the director, won out on the pageant ground. However, soldiers might dress up, but they could not fight; they could only express fraternity. The Battle of Ste. Foy was amplified in importance and made to represent an act of triumphant self-defence in which French Canadians preserved for all time enjoyment of their language, culture, and Church. Historians might demur (interestingly, on this occasion they did not), but what actually happened was beside the point. In 1908 both sides won and all the gunpowder, marching, and shouting on the Plains celebrated a century and a half of peaceful cohabitation in mutual respect. This, of course, was history as someone wanted it to be, not the way it was.

Performance reflects power. In this instance power was divided, and art offered some openings for the powerless. Overall, historical pageantry at the Tercentenary reflected the balance of power in Quebec City between the overlapping categories of social class, English and French, *nationaliste* and Liberal, Church and state, men and women, historians and dramatists. The conflicted origins of the festival, its multiple purposes, the ability of participants to make a show of their own, and a culturally divided audience all worked against hegemonic messages from one side or the other, or subverted them when they occurred. The past as "re-presented" had multiple meanings; even the disagreeable could be confronted

if appropriately costumed and choreographed. Some things were more acceptable as theatre than history, and more agreeable as theatre in the form of comedy rather than tragedy.

In the detumescent glow of the theatrical experience, we can see that the "race fusion" objectives momentarily succeeded at a sentimental level. Sentiment, as Laurier famously observed, bore a unique relation to politics in Quebec. It nevertheless had its limits. Excitement over the fleet did not have much bearing upon the subsequent Naval Debate although it was undoubtedly intended to do so. Another "race" crowded onto the stage at Quebec, but that did not necessarily put it in the picture. As for theatre and its influence over politics, a turbulent and violent history could be made to teach tolerance, but what actors and audiences chose to remember is another matter.

Notes

1. H. J. J. B. Chouinard, secretary of the Quebec City Société Saint-Jean-Baptiste, man of letters and clerk (*greffier*) of the City Council, contributed an article to the Christmas number of the *Daily Telegraph* (December 24, 1904) proposing a celebration honouring the tercentenary of Champlain's founding of Quebec. The society picked up his suggestion as one of several projects of national revitalization, the most notable other one being the funding of a statue of Laval to be unveiled on the 200th anniversary of his death, coincidentally in 1908. Early in 1906 the Société Saint-Jean-Baptiste (SSJB) successfully lobbied the city to take on this responsibility. See H. J. J. B. Chouinard, *Troisième Centenaire de la Fondation de Québec Berceau du Canada par Champlain, 1608–1908* (Quebec: Laflamme & Proulx, 1908), pp. 1–21, for documents and letters; see also Archives du Séminaire de Québec (hereafter ASQ), Fonds Chouinard.

2. Archives de la Ville de Québec (hereafter AVQ), Préliminaires de la célébration du 3e centenaire de la fondation de Québec (Comité Centenaire), *Procès-verbaux*, Comité exécutif, Comité d'action, 1906–1908, contain the minutes of the municipal body that took over planning the celebration. Many of these documents are reprinted in Chouinard, *Troisième Centenaire*. Right from the start this committee thought in terms of provincial and federal

funding to give "un cachet national de la Fête" (October 24, 1906). See also Archives Nationales du Québec (hereafter ANQ), Fonds Sir Georges Garneau, APG, 90/1–8, *boîte* 5, for additional material.

3. Mary Elizabeth Hallet, "The 4th Earl Grey as Governor General of Canada, 1904–1911" (Ph.D. dissertation, University of London, 1966), p. 134. Chapter 5 of this thesis provides an excellent account of Earl Grey's involvement in the Tercentenary. See also her research note, "The Quebec Tercentennial: Earl Grey's Imperial Birthday Party", *Canadian Historical Review,* vol. 54 (1973), pp. 341–352. Grey formulated his plan for a battlefields national park—based loosely on the model of Gettysburg—in a series of conversations and an exchange of memoranda beginning in 1906 with the recently appointed Dominion Archivist, Arthur Doughty. See National Archives of Canada (here-after NAC), National Battlefields Papers, vol. 1, Arthur Doughty to Earl Grey, June 15, 1906. See also NAC, Doughty Papers, M2244, for correspondence with Grey. Early in 1908 Doughty helped draft a plan for the Battlefields Park after consulting with Gettysburg authorities.

4. Earl Grey set forth his proposal in a series of speeches which he had printed and widely distributed, most notably to the Women's Canadian Club of Montreal on December 12, 1907, and the Canadian Club of Ottawa on January 15, 1908. He appealed to the women of Canada to help in the campaign to restore the site of battles "in which the contending races were alternately victorious, and in both of which the victor and the vanquished were entitled to equal honour, will be fittingly commemorated". The texts of both these addresses in pamphlet form are to be found with related material in NAC, National Battlefields Commission Records, RG90, vol 1. He expanded on his plans, in particular the Angel of Peace, in an extensive correspondence with Colonial Office officials, Canadian political figures, and friends. See Hallett, "The 4th Earl Grey", pp. 136–178; NAC, Grey of Howick Papers, MG27 II B2, vols. 1, 2, 8, 14, 28, 30, 31; NAC, Quebec Battlefields Association Papers, MG28 I 38, vol. 1, part 2 (portions of which were obviously transferred from Earl Grey's files), which contains correspondence between Grey, Garneau, and others. By 1907 Earl Grey and Mayor Garneau were working hand in glove on Laurier; see ANQ,

Fonds Garneau, *boîtes* 1 and 4, for Grey correspondence and *boîtes* 3 and 5 for Laurier letters.

5. NAC, Grey Papers, vol. 14, 4001, Grey to Lord Crewe, May 18, 1908. Understanding tensions between *nationalistes* and Liberals within the province of Quebec was a central preoccupation for at least two generations of Canadian historians. See, *inter alia*, Robert Rumilly, *Henri Bourassa* (Montreal: Chanteclerc, 1953); Pierre Savard, *Jules-Paul Tardivel* (Quebec: Laval, 1967); Mathieu Girard, "La pensée politique de Jules-Paul Tardivel", *Revue d'histoire de l'Amérique française*, vol. 21 (1967), p. 397; A. I. Silver, Introduction to J.-P. Tardivel, *For My Country* (Toronto: University of Toronto Press, 1975); Mason Wade, *The French Canadians* (Toronto: Macmillan, 1968), vol. 2; H. Blair Neatby, *Laurier and a Liberal Quebec* (Toronto: McClelland & Stewart, 1973); Joseph Schull, *Laurier* (Toronto: Macmillan, 1965); Ramsay Cook, *Canada and the French Canadian Question* (Toronto: Macmillan, 1966); Susan Mann Trofimenkoff, *The Dream of Nation* (Toronto: Gage, 1983). Denis Monière recast some of these sources in a cultural Marxist garb in *Le développement des idéologies au Québec* (Montreal: Éditions Québec/Amérique, 1977). Patrice Dutil's estimable *Devil's Advocate: Godfroy Langlois and the Politics of Liberal Progressivism in Laurier's Quebec* (Montreal and Toronto: Robert Davies, 1994) is the most recent contribution.

6. *Statutes of Canada*, 1907–1908, 7–8 Edw. VII, chaps. 57 and 58, Acts Respecting the National Battlefields at Quebec. For the debate on these bills, see *House of Commons Debates,* 1908, vol. 3, March 5 (4376–4401) and March 6 (4497–4536); vol. 7, July 18 (13496–13506). For a lavishly illustrated history of the National Battlefields, see Jacques Mathieu and Eugen Kedl, *The Plains of Abraham: The Search for the Ideal* (Quebec: Septentrion, 1993), in English; for a brief account of the relationship of the National Battlefields Commission to the broader historical landmarks movement, see C. J. Taylor, *Negotiating the Past: The Making of Canada's National Historic Parks and Sites* (Montreal and Kingston: McGill-Queen's University Press, 1990), pp. 3–25.

7. See, for example, Mona Ozouf, *Festivals and the French Revolution* (Cambridge: Harvard University Press, 1988), E. Hobsbawm and T. Ranger, eds., *The Invention of Tradition* (Cambridge:

183

Cambridge University Press, 1983); John Bodnar, *Remaking America: Public Memory, Commemoration and Patriotism in Twentieth Century America* (Princeton: Princeton University Press, 1992); John R. Gillis, ed., *Commemorations: The Politics of National Identity* (Princeton University Press, 1994).

8. Roy Strong, *Art and Power: Renaissance Festivals, 1450–1650* (Berkeley: University of California Press, 1984), and *Splendour at Court: Renaissance Spectacle and Illusion* (London: Weidenfeld and Nicolson, 1973); more recently see Barbara Hanawalt and Kathryn Reyerson, eds., *City and Spectacle in Medieval Europe* (Minneapolis: University of Minnesota Press, 1994).

9. Canada, *House of Commons Debates*, 1908, vol. 3, March 5, 1908, p. 4377.

10. David Glassberg, *American Historical Pageantry* (Chapel Hill: University of North Carolina, 1990). See also Michael Kammen, *Mystic Chords of Memory* (New York: Vintage, 1991), pp. 279–280. The standard work on the subject, Robert Withington's *English Pageantry: An Historical Outline* (Cambridge: Harvard, 1918, reprinted 1963), vol. 2, pp. 240–241 and 262–264, comments on the "historical importance" of the Quebec pageant in the chapter on the transfer of pageantry to the United States. See also the contemporary guide to pageant making, Ester Willard Bates, *Pageants and Pageantry* (New York: Ginn, 1912), pp. 5, 6, 14, 15, 19. The "grand effects" of the massed armies were thought to be especially striking. The local legacy is dealt with in Rémi Tourangeau, *Fêtes et spectacles du Québec* (Quebec: Nuit Blanche, 1992).

11. Louis Napoleon Parker, *Several of My Lives* (London: Chapman Hall, 1928), p. 278 and following. He also contributed an essay of the principles of historical pageantry to the *Journal of the Society of Arts*, vol. 54 (1905), which Glassberg and Withington quote.

12. See Withington, *English Pageantry*, vol. 2, p. 195 and following, for a full chapter on the Parkerian paeant; see also Glassberg, *American Historical Pageantry*, p. 44, for a perceptive commentary. Parker's aims are spelled out along with a bemused account of his harried life as pageant master in his autobiography, *Several of My Lives*.

13. *The Times Annual Index*, 1908, pp. 803–804, 915–916.

14. ANQ, Fonds Garneau. *boîte 5, Premier Rapport de la Commission d'Histoire et Archéologie nommée par son honeur le maire de Québec* (Quebec, 1907). It fell to the Commission d'Histoire et d'Archéologie, consisting of the Sheriff, Mr. Charles Langelier, a former mayor, scholar and professor of law, E.E. Taché, the provincial Minister of Lands and Forests and a noted architect and designer, and Col. W. Wood, author, specialist in the Seven Years' War, and chairman of the Literary and Historical Society of Quebec, to focus effort on a particular objective. The core of this report on the best means of celebrating Champlain's tercentennial is a detailed account of the Battle of the Plains of Abraham! A municipal subcommittee of historians identified particular scenes for reenactment in January 1908; see Chouinard, *Troisiéme Centenaire,* Rapport du sous comité d'histoire et d'archéologie, January 23, 1908, pp. 183–196.

15. AVQ, Comité Centenaire, *Procès-verbaux,* February 19 and 24, 1908. Although the word "pageant" is of French origin it was not understood by French Canadians. The term was always placed in question marks as an Anglicism. There would be irritation in some quarters that a more suitable French word could not be found to describe the form.

16. *La Vérité,* December 21, 1907; February 1, 8, 15 and 27, 1908.

17. AVQ, Comité Centenaire, *Procès-verbaux,* January 17, 1907, and January 23, 1908.

18. The Quebec *Chronicle* on April 13, 1908, printed a verbatim transcript. *Le Soleil* on the same date provided a front-page translation of the speech, which was given in English, with this comment: "Il était beau de voir cet étranger de distincion véritablement 'British to the core', prononcer avec un si bel accent les noms français de tous nos illustres ancêtres, les grands noms de Laval, Jacques Cartier, Champlain, Montcalm, Dollard et les Frontenac, les Veudreuil, les Lévis, sans omettre la mere 'Mary of the Incarnation' et tant d'autres de nos gloires nationales. M. Lascelles possède une belle eloquence et son programme si bien coordonné a soulevé à divers réprises des applaudissments prolongés." On Lascelles's visit to Toronto, *Saturday Night* offered a profile as well of his acting career (June 20, 1908).

19. Translation of "Il nous fait plaisir de constater que pour l'organisation en particulier des pageants des spectacles historiques l'apathie manifestée dans lespremiers temps surtout de la part des

Canadiens-français disparaît peu à peu". *Le Soleil*, June 10, 1908. At this point the papers had daily bulletins on Tercentenary progress.

20. AVO, *Rapport du Comité spécial du programme au Comité exécutif,* October 9 and 11, 1907.

21. Here I am following Robert Berkhofer, *The White Man's Indian* (New York: Knopf, 1978), and the more recent Canadian counterpart, Daniel Francis, *The Imaginary Indian* (Vancouver: Arsenal, 1992).

22. Robert Rydell, *All the World's a Fair* (Chicago: University of Chicago, 1984), pp. 48–71; Douglas Cole, *Captured Heritage* (Vancouver: Douglas and McIntyre, 1985), pp. 122–140; Julie K. Brown, *Contesting Images: Photography and the World's Columbian Exposition* (Tucson: University of Arizona Press, 1994), pp. 49–55, 107–113.

23. Don Smith, *Le Sauvage: The Native People in Quebec Historical Writing on the Heroic Period (1534–1663) of New France* (Ottawa: National Museums of Canada, 1974).

24. Translation of "Chez les derniers Hurons". Quebec *Chronicle*, June 29, July 13 and 14, 1908; *Le Soleil*, July 14 and 18, 1908. Some of the Native people were veterans of the Nile Voyageurs. Mr. Armstrong claimed to possess a peace pipe "wrought from the same red stone as Hiawatha obtained his".

25. Translation of "Le public de Québec a commencé à revivre cette époque séduisante d'il y a trois siècles à l'âge d'or de la chevalerie ou la fine fleur de la société française avait son complet épanouissement, plein de grâce, plein de charme, plein de dignité." *Le Soleil,* July 17, 1908; Quebec *Chronicle*, July 17, 1908.

26. The procession is fully covered in the various photograph and stereoscopic slide collections in AVO, ANO, and the York University Archives. The salute of the army is noted in the Ursulines' *Journal*. Archives Ursulines. *Journal*, 1908, pp. 84–85: "Par une bienveillante permission de l'autorité ecclésiastique il nous est donné de contempler du haunt de nos fenêtres garnies de rideaux de dentelle et d'oriflammes, cette merveilleuse procession de Pageants (mot anglais-français au pays qui veut dire triomphe ou pompe) qui fait halte devant notre chapelle pour y rendre hommage aux restes mortels de d'illustre Montcalm." The cloistered orders had been given a dispensation to attend the Laval unveiling, but not the Tercentenary.

27. Translation of "Montcalm et Wolfe, Lévis et Murray, Carleton et Salaberry, à la tête de leurs régiments respectifs, défilent au bruit du canon et des fanfares. Salut général des troupes auquel répondent les salves des vaisseaux de guerre ancrés en rade. Groupement de tous les personnages du Cortège Historique et des Pageants. Chant des deux hymnes nationaux: O Canada! et Dieu Sauve le Roi! Salut au Drapeau." Ernest Myrand, *Pageants du Tricentenaire de Québec* (Quebec: Laflamme & Proulx, 1908), p. 36.

28. The full text of the pageants is provided in the Quebec *Telegraph*'s commemorative volume: Frank Carrel, Louis Feiczewicz, E.T.D. Chambers, and Arthur Doughty, *The Quebec Tercentenary Commemorative History* (Quebec: Daily Telegraph Printing House, 1908), pp. 130–162; see also Myrand, *Pageants,* and the National Battlefields Commission's official *Historical Souvenir Book of the Pageants* (Montreal: Cambridge Corporation, 1908), the text of which appears to have been written by Doughty. The corrected proofs are in his papers in the National Archives of Canada. The newspapers contain lengthy accounts of the pageants as well, which have been used to double-check the printed text.

29. Translation of "Et après un intermède de quelques instants, arrivent les armées anglaises et françaises défilant côte-à-côte et fraternisant dans la paix. Les drapeaux flottent, la brise entremêle leurs plis et à côté du grenaider anglais marche le grenadier français. Les bataillons défilent, salués par les acclamations de la multitude et ils quittent le terrain laissant encore tous imprégnés des émotions diverses, les dix mille personnes ... qui quittent à regret cette scène ou viennent de revivre dans toute leur authenticité et leur couleur locale les trois siècles de l'existence du peuple canadien." *Le Soleil*, July 22, 1908; Quebec *Chronicle*, August 1, 1908.

30. "On the Plains of Abraham, with the St. Lawrence's silver surfaces beyond, and the green, fir-clad hills of Canada piled high above the stream, in the fading lights of the far Northern summer evening, the scene was incomparably beautiful." Quoted in Kammen, *Mystic Chords of Memory*, p. 279.

31. NAC, Grey Papers, vol. 14, p. 4092. Crewe to Grey, September 23, 1908. Vols. 38 and 31 contain his exchange of correspondence with the Prince of Wales and the King.

185

32. Translation of "Les 'pageants'—mot anglais que nous n'avons pas tardé, dans tous les milieux, à prononcer à la française—ont été parmi tant d'autres articles grandioses du programme de nos fêtes, la pièce de résistance de la célébration. Nous avouons sans détour que nous sommes absolument incapable d'exprimer les fortes et grandes émotions que nous avons éprouvées à ces représentations de l'incomparable période française de notre histoire".

33. Translation of "Nous voyons dans ces 'pageants' la partie principale des fêtes, parce que les masses populaires, au lieu des notions très vagues qu'elles avaient auparavant, ont pris là, par la méthode intuitive, la connaissance exacte des plus grands faits de notre histoire; parce que nos compatriores de race anglaise de toutes les Provinces, et la foule des visiteurs étrangers, surtout des États-Unis ont vu, de leurs yeux, la noblessse et l'héroisme des fondateurs de notre race canadienne-française. Tous ces Anglais et Américains ont contemplé et applaudi nos gloires françaises et catholiques! Qui dira qu'il n'y a pas là un grand événement, et qu'il n'en restera pas des effets considérables?" Archives de l'Archidiocèse de Québec, l'abbé V-A. Huard, directeur, *La Semaine Religieuse de Québec*, vol. 20 (1908), pp. 804–807.

34. Translation of 'Dans chacune de ces scènes, exclusivement françaises et catholiques, les Anglais ont été les premiers à accepter des rôles, en nous laissant cependant ceux des plus grands personnages, qui nous appartenaient de droit, mais que nous négligions de prendre. Ils n'ont jamais eu un sourire de dédain pour nos costumes religieux et l'emblème de notre culture, ils ont prouvé qu'ils respectent les convictions sincères. Nous pourrions tirer un très bon parti dans la vie ordinaire, d'une plus exacte connaissance de la mentalité de nos concitoyens de langue anglaise et sans jamais sacrifier les intérêts de la langue ou ceux de notre foi; sans jamais faire des concessions qui nous diminuent dans l'esprit même de ceux à qui nous les faisons et dépouiller un antagonisme aussi vieux que la conquête et qui n'a plus raison d'être." *Le Soleil*, August 8, 1908.

35. *L'Événement*, July 20, 1908.

36. Translation of "Je n'ai jamais été familier avec l'anglais, aussi, M. de Bienville, vous seriez fort aimable de me traduire ce document." "Monsieur parle le français et bon français, l'aimable surprise! J'en suis ravi. Vous savez encore mieux notre histoire que notre langue. Bravo. Votre geste est charmant.' Myrand, *Pageants*, p. 33; *Le Soleil*, July 9, 1908.

37. The names of the individual participants are listed in Carrel *et al., The Quebec Tercentenary*, pp. 130–162. The list is obviously not complete; whole groups of participants are missing from the roster. The most obvious omissions are the names of the Natives (with the exception of American Horse) and the orphans. Data for the city are the means of the 1901 and 1911 census counts. *Census of Canada*, 1901, vol. 1, pp. 380–381, and 1911, vol. 2, p. 372.

38. Archives Ursulines, *Journal*, 1908, pp. 85–86. See also pp. 90–91: "Tous ces dialogues et discours étaient l'oeuvre de M. Ernest Myrand, de Québec, qui a fait connaître et aimer d'avantage l'histoire de son pays[;] de concert avec M. Lascelles (protestant) il montre à tous la noblesse et l'héroïsme des fondateurs de notre race."

39. *Who Was Who*, vol. 3, 1929–1940 (London: Adam and Charles Black, 1941), p. 781.

40. At Quebec Lascelles found a theatrical device that would serve him well in other commissions. He would go on to produce similar pageants in England, at various World Expositions on behalf of Great Britain, in other divided politics such as South Africa, and at the great Imperial Durbar in India. He would direct another pageant in Calcutta before this same Prince, then King, and there, too, he would divide and unite Hindu and Islam by interspersing between the two a mythological people of warlike and pacific capacities. See *The Historical Record of the Imperial Visit to India, 1911* (London: John Murray, 1914), pp. 256–258 for details of the Calcutta Pageant. See also Hon. John Fortescue, *Narrative of the Visit to India of Their Majesties King George V and Queen Mary and of the Coronation Durbar held at Delhi, 12th December, 1911* (London: Macmillan, 1912), pp. 236–241.

41. On this subject see Serge Gagnon, *Le Québec et ses historiens de 1840–1920* (Quebec: Les Presses de l'Université Laval, 1978), pp. 123–208; Smith, *Le Sauvage*, pp. 43–54; Carl Berger, *The Writing of Canadian History* (Toronto: Oxford, 1976), pp. 1–21.

■ Article 3: Henri Bourassa: A Nationalist Leader Against British Imperialism

Sylvie Lacombe

We have a strong sentiment of love for Canada—not a Platonic love, nor a declamatory love of the pompous, heated spirit of election times. Our creed is that all the resources of Canada shall be developed for the people of Canada, that the representatives of the two great races[1] should devote themselves unitedly to the development of our intellectual, moral and material advantages in the best of real Canadian sentiment. (Henri Bourassa[2])

To those who worked on the project in 1867, the Confederation was supposed to lay down a brand-new type of nationality. These men were proud to say that the Dominion of Canada did not come out of a revolution, nor a war, neither a civil war or against a foreign country. Rather the Canadian nationality was the result of a pacific agreement and that was completely original, or so they felt.[3] On July 1 1867, the Dominion of Canada was granted a special statute indeed for it was born a "self-governing colony" of the British Empire. In a sense, it supposed a separation between domestic and foreign affairs. On one hand, all matters of strictly local concern were under jurisdiction of the federal government: Canada could exercise all the rights of self-government and therefore act like a sovereign nation. On the other hand, however, Canada had limited, if any, powers regarding foreign affairs: her diplomatic and economic relationship with other countries were negotiated and decided by London.[4] Such provisional statute gave rise to different interpretations among French and English Canadians as to what Canada exactly stood for and what her destiny was. In particular, two main visions opposed one another at the

Source: Sylvie Lacombe. "Henri Bourassa: A Nationalist Leader against British Imperialism," *Journal of Indo-Canadian Studies (A Special Issue on Quebec and French Canada)*, Vol. 2, No. 2 (July 2002): 83–92. Reprinted with permission from the author.

turn of the last century, and after a brief look at the Canadian context at the time, one of them may be partly examined. It can be seen that Henri Bourassa's definition of the Canadian constitution as a double compact was related to the ambiguous statute of self-governing colony.

At the turn of the century, thirty years or so after the Confederation, Canada witnessed great transformations. First of all, in the census of 1901, there were about 5,300,000 Canadians while the census of 1921 reports more than 8,800,000 inhabitants, an impressive increase of more than 60% mostly due to immigration. In the 1890s, the federal government organized a vast campaign depicting Canada as "the land of opportunity." The great majority of newcomers established themselves in the wide and wild Prairies. They were so numerous that in 1905, in order to give them social and political institutions, the provinces of Saskatchewan and Alberta were created. With the settlement of the West came also the wheat boom allowing Canada to enlarge exports in international markets. Besides, the opening up of the northern regions of Quebec, Ontario and British Columbia brought extended mining and forestry development. Consequently, the national and international scope of the Canadian economy was strengthened. The various lines of communication from coast to coast were highly improved, for example, the great Canadian railway systems were completed by the beginning of the century. But Canada was still a young country lacking the kind of money necessary to build huge development programs. Foreign investments were very high and the Canadian economy was developing essentially on borrowed money. Around 1900, it came mainly from the United Kingdom but after the First World War, American money became the main source of foreign investment. The development of business relied mostly on the establishment of large corporations, monopolies and trusts, based mainly in the provinces of Ontario and Quebec. Canada soon changed from a rural to an urbanized country. These rapid changes, only mentioned here to give an idea of the Canadian context at the time Bourassa entered politics,[5] have nonetheless transformed the country "in quality and in spirit."[6]

Furthermore, Canadian intellectuals were eager to forward their country on the path to nationhood inasmuch as they feared American annexation, for they distrusted even the slightest influence from their powerful neighbour. But their solutions were different whether they were advocated by French or English Canadians. To the latter, the majority, the connection with Great Britain was seen as an easy and comfortable counterpoise. In fact, they responded almost with zeal to the wind of imperialism blowing from the London Colonial Office, with more intensity since the appointment of Joseph Chamberlain as Colonial Secretary. Anglo-Canadians wished for close co-operation with their Motherland on every imperial matter, and particularly, they expected a strong commitment on the part of Canada regarding the defence question.[7] On the French Canadian part, the imperial mood was Henri Bourassa's mainspring to work out his nationalism which was quite widely espoused by his co-religionists.

Henri Bourassa, the Man

For people who met him, Bourassa was an honourable and stately politician with great skills and extensive knowledge in history, politics and law. He also had the power to electrify crowds.[8] Yet some commentators presented him as an uncompromising person lacking pragmatism, and for this reason, unable to raise constructive opposition.[9] Others have noted that he always appealed to reason but could also arouse moral passion.[10] During his lifetime he was mainly cheered by his fellow French Canadians and his ideas stirred enthusiasm particularly among them but his nationalism nevertheless appealed equally to English Canadians.[11] Even though Canada had not yet achieved complete sovereignty, she was in Bourassa's mind already a nation-state rather than a mere colony, but she was a British country with an Anglo-French nation.

Early in his life, Bourassa found the principles he believed in and stood for them during his whole career. Above all, his loyalty went to them and he constantly claimed his complete freedom of thought, refusing to follow blindly any party line, any party leader. What he called the nationalist doctrine was a combination of Catholic conservatism and liberal principles. Such paradoxical features partly explain why the character was so controversial a figure. But it must be said that in his thought, the Catholic element was not in contradiction with the Liberal one, rather both were integrated within a very consistent system.[12]

The Liberal tradition to which Bourassa claimed to belong was a British movement among the Whigs and initiated by men like Burke, Fox and Gladstone, later labelled as "Little Englanders." The image most often used to picture their vision of the Empire is that of a tree with its fruits representing the colonies. Just like a ripe fruit naturally falls off the tree, each colony in its own time will achieve independence. In this view thus, the Empire will eventually break apart, producing as many nations as there were colonies. Each one having been made on the pattern of the Motherland will then become a "little England." According to Bourassa, the Confederation was carved out of that Liberal tradition, and therefore liberty, decentralization, and respect of minorities were its founding premises. Pressures coming from both the Colonial Office and the English Canadian majority to tighten up the imperial bond were considered by him totally opposite to the natural evolution of Canada. Not only did they jeopardize her course, they could even lead to her being swallowed up by the United States. He thus opposed forcefully the pervading imperialism, whatever the shape it took.

But if Bourassa foresaw the Canadian independence from Britain, he did not wish to see it unfold too soon, and certainly not before the sound Liberal spirit would have been instilled into Canadian politics.[13] Independence in his mind would only result in the "largest measure of autonomy for Canada compatible with the maintenance of the British connection." Yet to many English Canadians he was no less than a traitor and some of them went as far as to claim his head. Bourassa acknowledged his own lack of loyalty to the Empire but he unflaggingly professed sincere and true loyalty to the British Crown. Since the former had come to betray the principles personified by the latter, it had to be opposed. There was no other solution but to denounce Great Britain in the very name of the ideas and values she once stood for:

> All that is good in British ideals, and there is much of it, would be better served by the free action of several independent British communities than by the common action of a monstrous Empire, built up by force and robbery, and kept together for no other purpose than allowing one race and one nation to dominate one-fifth of the

human race. British nations have to choose between British ideals and British domination. I stand for ideals against domination. I may be hanged for it, in the name of British liberty, but that does not matter.[14]

In order to save Canada from the influence of the false doctrine embraced by English Canadians, one needed only to be aware of the spirit of the British North American Act giving birth to the Confederation for soundness and rationality formed its basis and they supposed a fair balance between liberty and responsibility, between rights and duties, or so believed Bourassa. Although he is not the sole father of the notion according to which a double compact embodied the Canadian constitution, he certainly gave it its wider publicity. And though he himself never explicitly mentioned it, it may be argued that in Bourassa's mind the two compacts were logically derived from Canada's legal statute. In fact, they are better understood when related to the dependency towards Britain in foreign affairs for the first compact, and to the autonomy of the colony concerning local matters for the second one.

Two Compacts

The first compact is said to be an agreement between Canada and Great Britain concerning the Canadian responsibility in warfare matters. Bourassa argued that these responsibilities were strictly limited to the defence of the Canadian territory. When there were no territorial threats, Canada had absolutely no moral or legal obligation to contribute in manpower or money to Britain's wars. And the nationalist leader firmly stood by this interpretation on every occasion a Canadian contribution was in question. The first one came in 1899 when the South African war broke out. After only a few months of confusion and tortuous developments, Canada decided to send a contingent, and later a second, of volunteer forces to fight against the Boers who had defied the Empire.[15] One, and by no means the least, irregularity was that the decision had been taken without the consent of Parliament. Of course, Bourassa resigned his seat to protest against what he considered a dangerous precedent clearly violating the Constitution.[16] But the problem arose again in 1909 when the Liberal government proposed a naval policy, later partly resumed by the Conservatives, and once more in 1914 when the First World War broke out. Each time, the English Canadian majority saw a fortunate opportunity to push further the cause of imperial unity. But each time Bourassa restated his theory: the Constitution does not compel Canada to be at war each time Great Britain is at war. It was only logical and consistent with Canada's legal statute. Indeed having no proper national existence outside her own territory and without any official voice regarding her foreign affairs, Canada's imperial duty could not, in all fairness, include responsibility in warfare matters. Since she was treated as Britain's mere possession, it would be pure act of colonial servility for Canada to contribute to British imperial wars. The nation-to-be ought instead to force the respect of her constitution by which she was entitled to full British protection without any compensation. And if she really wanted a share in the burden of imperial defence, she must firmly claim to be duly consulted on international affairs within Imperial councils. The second constitutional compact can be related to the rights of self-government but only insofar as it concerned what distinguishes Canada on the American continent, that is, without any references to the Empire. This compact settled an agreement between "the two founding races" of Canada. Indeed in Bourassa's understanding, Canada was a marriage between the French and English Canadian communities and the Confederation stated them as equal partners. According to God's will, as he put it, the long time enemies were now at peace with one another, and in that lay the Canadian greatness:

> The free alliance of both races and nationalities, with absolute equality in every part of Canada, was the basic principle of the British North American Act…But above all, the principle acknowledged that, in each province, the rights of the minority, Catholic or Protestant, as the case may be, were to be respected, in matters of Church organisation and religious teaching, and in the preservation of the two national languages of the country. In other words, the inspiring thought and primary object of Confederation was not fusion, but union, of races.[17]

189

Consequently every French Canadian community in the English provinces, and not only in Quebec, had the right to its own separate and confessional schools. Moreover it was tremendously vital for the safeguard of the nation that it should be so. In Bourassa's nationalism, the main threat to Canadian nationhood was American annexation,[18] and for at least three reasons, French Canadians were thought to be better than English Canadians at avoiding such a calamity. First and foremost, because they had been established on Canadian soil for a longer period than their fellow countrymen, their patriotism was more naturally and spontaneously directed to Canada alone. In Bourassa's view, English Canadians inappropriately vowed to England and her Empire the kind of devotion they should instead feel for Canada. But French Canadian patriotism could also serve as a model for newcomers' nascent love for their country. Secondly, because of their "Frenchness," French Canadian communities would act as cultural and linguistic barriers preventing American thinking from filtering into the Canadian mind. For English Canadians shared numerous, perhaps too many, features with Americans, and for that reason could always be suspected of perverting the emerging national culture. Finally, French Canadians somehow were the best safeguard against American influence because they were Catholic. Indeed Catholic traditions and faith were seen as the most effective antidote against the appalling materialism typical of American culture. For all these reasons, Canadian dualism was not only a question of French Canadian rights but truly a matter of national scope, of national benefit.

In addition, Bourassa conceptualized the nation as similar to an individual, that is, as having a soul and a body. The two dimensions were fundamental but of course the soul was more important to foster than the body. Roughly speaking, the soul was given through the catholic traditions and faith, while the territory represented the body. The latter included exploitation of natural resources and more broadly speaking the whole economic sphere. Bourassa believed French Canadians to be the natural guardians of the Canadian soul because of their religion whereas Anglo-Canadians, known to be more skilled in businesslike activities, were to make the nation's body flourishing. In other words, he thought each group was superior to the other in taking care of one component of the nation, and because of that

saw them as totally equal in rights. In fact from his perspective, both communities needed each other in order to keep Canada a healthy nation.

Yet the so-called second compact was not accepted either by Anglo-Canadians who never saw themselves "engaged" in an equal partnership with the French Canadians. Consequently, when Alberta and Saskatchewan were created, the majority in Parliament refused to subsidize the French and Catholic schools in those provinces. Again in 1912, when the district of Keewatin was annexed to Manitoba a similar legislation deprived the French Canadians of the separate and confessional schools they hitherto enjoyed. Then later the same year, the government of Ontario decided to stop supporting with public funds its bilingual schools and strictly limited the teaching of French. On each occasion, Bourassa was prompt to protest against these decisions which he saw as blatant violations of the Constitution, though without much success.

Conclusion

The nationalist battles Bourassa fought during his political career were directly connected to his conception of the Canadian constitution as a double compact. He opposed Canadian contribution to imperial wars whenever the Canadian territory was not clearly an issue, and protested whenever the rights of French Canadians were not acknowledged, all the more infringed, by the English Canadian majority.

Bourassa's ideological legacy is blurred and complex as, perhaps, was the man. The majority of Anglo-Canadians were opposed to his nationalism during his most influential years, but afterwards they progressively turned away from the cause of imperial unity to espouse a similar kind of truly Canadian patriotism. Then decades later, and for a short while only in the 1950s, they supported an even softer version of his national dualism but it did not last and today, there is not much left of the recognition that French Canadians, as such, are one of Canada's founding people.[19] As for French Canadians, in the face of Bourassa's repeated failures to enforce their rights among Anglo-Canadians, they gradually reserved their support to other, more radical, nationalist leaders. They somehow concluded that they were better off within the province where they formed the majority, and eventually developed instead a Quebec nationalism.

Notes

1. It is worth noting that the term "race" was widely used at the turn of the century with a slightly different meaning than today. It underlined the social belonging of man, the fact that given members of a community share together the same social and political institutions, and to a certain extent common ideas and values. In brief, emphasis was laid on social inheritance rather than biological heredity. Bourassa, for example, believed common moral features typified both the French and French Canadian due to their shared forefathers and common law. But he also conceptualized the race similarly as we understand the notion of civilization or culture, for he added geographical and historical parameters: the Frenchmen living in what was then New France soon turned into Canadians as the way of living of new generations was better adapted to their environment. They later rounded off their "Canadianness" through adaptation to the British political institutions.

2. "The Nationalist movement in Quebec," January 22, 1907, in *Addresses Delivered before the Canadian Club of Toronto*, 1906–07 (Toronto: Warwick Bro's and Rutter, 1907) 56–64.

3. F. Underhill, "The Image of Confederation," *The Massey Lectures: Third Series* (Toronto: CBC, 1964) 1–12.

4. See R. MacGregor Dawson, *The Government of Canada* (Toronto: U of Toronto P, 1970) 20–39.

5. Born in 1868, Bourassa died in 1952. He was first elected in Parliament in 1896 under the banner of the Liberal party during Wilfrid Laurier's leadership. Except for a short episode in 1899 he sat in Parliament until 1907 and later came back from 1925 to 1935. Meanwhile from 1908 to 1912, he sat in the Quebec Legislature as an "Independent candidate," that is, with no party affiliation.

6. The expression is taken from R.C. Brown and R. Cook, *Canada 1896–1921, A Nation Tansformed* (Toronto: McClelland and Stewart, 1988) 1–6.

7. They did not campaign to extend British domination over new parts of the world but they upheld the cause of imperial unity. See C. Berger, *The Sense of Power, Studies in the Ideas of Canadian Imperialism, 1867–1914* (Toronto: U of Toronto P, 1970) 277.

8. See the short entries from J. P. Archambault, L. Groulx, O. Héoroux, R. Gauthier and A. Laurendeau in the brochure "Henri Bourassa" in *Mes fiches, Revue documentaire mensuelle* (Montréal: Fides, 1953) 32.

9. C. Murrow, "Henri Bourassa and the French Canadian Nationalism," *Opposition to Empire* (Montreal: Harvest House, 1968) 143.

10. J. Levitt, "Henri Bourassa and the Golden Calf," *The Social Program of the Nationalists of Quebec, 1900–1914* (Ottawa: U of Ottawa P, 1972) 178.

11. M.P. O'Connell, *Henri Bourassa and Canadian Nationalism*, Ph.D. thesis, Philosophy, University of Toronto, 1954, 304.

12. In this paper, emphasis will be on the Liberal elements only, without stressing the connections between the ideas and values included in it. To know more about the structural dimension of Bourassa's thought which perfectly qualifies what the French social anthropologist Louis Dumont called a hierarchy of values ("On Value," Radcliffe-Brown Lecture in Social Anthropology, The British Academy, 1980, 207–241), see S. Lacombe, *La recontre de deux peuples élus. Comparaison des ambitions nationale et impèriale au Canada entre 1896 et 1920* (Québec: Presses de l'Université Laval, 2002) 291.

13. For a short while around 1916 when the imperial mood reached its acme, Bourassa advocated complete independence from Britain. He was so fearful of American annexation that even a hasty independence appeared to him the lesser of the two evils.

14. Except from a letter from H. Bourassa, reproduced in *Canadian Nationalism and the War*, an interview from Bourassa to the Toronto Star representative, M. Arthur Hawkes, Montreal, (no editor), 1916, 14.

15. See the last three chapters of N. Penlington, *Canada and Imperialism, 1896–1899* (Toronto: U of Toronto P, 1965) 225–260.

16. He was re-elected by acclamation.

17. H. Bourassa, "Ireland and Canada," An address delivered in Hamilton, Ont., on Saint-Patrick's Day, 1914, under the auspices of the Ancient Order of Hibernians.

18. In his mind, certainly imperialism was hindering the Canadian nationhood but U.S. annexation would put a definitive end to it.

19. For an analysis of what will probably be the last or one of the last steps of Quebeckers' alienation to the Canadian nation, see K. McRoberts, "Misconceiving Canada," *The Struggle for National Unity* (Toronto, OUP, 1997) 395.

191

THE EARLY CANADIAN WOMEN'S MOVEMENT AND THE STRUGGLE FOR THE VOTE, 1870s–1918

Lynne Marks
University of Victoria

THE EARLY CANADIAN WOMEN'S MOVEMENT AND THE STRUGGLE FOR THE VOTE, 1870s–1918

Introduction by Lynne Marks

195

● INTRODUCTION

Lynne Marks

In mid-nineteenth century Canada, women lacked many of the rights that women today take for granted. Then it was assumed that a woman's primary role was to remain in the home as a wife and mother. This role was captured in the ideal image of "the Angel in the Home." Women were expected to create warm, moral, and nurturing havens for their children, as well as for their husbands who had to venture into the "rough and tumble" public sphere to earn money to support their families. This ideal contrasted sharply with reality for the many working-class women who had to venture beyond the home to contribute to the family income. For the middle-class women who could afford to remain in the home, this "domestic ideology", as it has been called, very much limited their options. Because a woman's role was to be a wife and mother, university education was closed to women, as such education was considered damaging to women's reproductive functions and inappropriate to their future roles. Access to professions such as medicine and law was also denied. Although single women had property rights, upon marriage women lost these rights, including any wages that they might earn. All of this came under their husband's control.[1] Women also lacked the right to vote or to hold public office, as this was considered far outside their "proper sphere" of the home.

In the United States, where similar restrictions applied, women started publicly debating and organizing around these issues in the 1830s and 1840s, but this did not begin to happen in Canada until the 1870s. Some of what we would consider the first feminist struggles took place over higher education, with women first gaining access to certain Canadian universities in the 1870s and early 1880s. However, even when it became possible, only a tiny minority of women were able to attend university.

Many more women were involved in activities beyond the home through local churches, since Christian faith and practice were particularly important to women in this period. By the 1870s and 1880s women became increasingly involved in Christian women's organizations not only at the level of their local church, but also through provincial and national organizations, particularly missionary societies, but also Christian women's organizations for social reform. The 1880s and 1890s saw increasing concern about social issues among middle-class men and women, as the effects of industrialization and urbanization made poverty more visible, and as increasing immigration from non-British countries led to growing concerns about the need to maintain the white, English-Canadian nature of the nation. One example of a woman's Christian social reform group was the Young Women's Christian Association (YWCA), an organization intended to safeguard young working-class women who were coming to the cities to work by providing them with respectable boarding houses and wholesome amusements. In Quebec, middle-class francophone women became involved in the Fédération Nationale St.-Jean-Baptiste. This organization developed programs to assist poorer women and children, for example, by providing pasteurized milk to children and babies, in cities where unpasteurized milk was a major cause of high infant mortality rates.

Women involved in social reform argued that white middle-class, Christian women needed to get involved in these efforts as their innate moral and nurturing qualities, so important to their roles in the home, were also crucial if they were to help improve and "mother" the larger society, particularly poorer and non-white women and children. In this way, they used the existing ideas about women's domestic roles to justify their activity within the broader society.

Another influential women's organization was the Women's Christian Temperance Union (WCTU). The WCTU had a number of social and moral reform objectives, but its central concern was over the use and abuse of alcohol. There were very few restrictions on the sale of alcohol in this period, and drinking was seen as the cause of a number of major social problems. Because it was considered socially unacceptable for women to drink at this time, most of the problems associated with drinking were linked to men. The WCTU thus campaigned against alcohol as a major cause of wife abuse and other violence. Members argued that the free availability of alcohol led many husbands and fathers to drink away their earnings, leaving many wives and children in deepest poverty. The WCTU supported temperance education, and developed programs to encourage both children and adults to promise to not drink alcohol, but their main tactic was to call for prohibition, government legislation against the sale of alcohol. Their largely fruitless efforts to convince governments to bring in prohibition legislation helped to convince the women of the WCTU that they needed to have the franchise, the right to vote, if they were going to have any impact on government alcohol policy. In the 1880s the WCTU thus increasingly called for women's right to vote not primarily because women were equal to men and thus entitled to the vote, but because they held unique moral qualities to improve society. While there were a few women's suffrage organizations in Canada in this decade, the WCTU was the largest women's organization calling for women's suffrage in Canada until the early twentieth century.

As the 1880 WCTU excerpt reveals, these women demanded the vote so that women would be able to vote to protect their homes and families from the ravages of alcohol. Historians have called this kind of justification for women's rights "maternal feminism," in that the justification for women's right to vote, and for other rights, was on the basis of what were considered to be women's particular maternal qualities. We can see these attitudes in some of the cartoons included in the module. Sometimes women's organizations also used what have been called "equal rights feminist" arguments (i.e., it was only just and fair that women should have the same political rights as men). In a social context where there was a great deal of hostility to women gaining political rights (see Stephen Leacock's piece), it may have seemed politically safer to argue for the vote on the basis of what were seen as women's more conventional qualities of morality, purity, and maternal nurturing abilities. However, Stephen Leacock's piece shows that arguments about how women would reform society if they got the vote did not always convince opponents. Leacock, who liked his scotch, was also opposed to women's suffrage because he feared if they got the vote, prohibition would soon follow. He was right.

As we see in WCTU excerpts from 1888 and 1911, a more racist argument was also used by the WCTU, as well as by other women fighting for the suffrage. These women were almost exclusively white, primarily middle class, and were very proud to see themselves as loyal subjects of the British empire, as we see in the description of the WCTU float in Victoria. Like most white Canadians of British background, they believed themselves superior to non-British immigrants, and they felt that it was very unfair that they be denied the right to vote, while immigrant men could vote.

How historians should deal with these racist elements of the women's suffrage movement has been a subject of intense debate, as we can see in the Valverde and Fiamengo pieces. These concerns came to the fore during World War I. In the years immediately before World War I, many more women and women's organizations came to support the right to vote, including farm women's organizations, and many working-class women, who felt that acquiring the vote was important not only for women's equality and to help "clean up" society, as earlier feminists had argued, but also to increase the political clout

197

of farmers and working people, and allow them to gain much needed reforms. The emergence of the suffrage movement is thus a complex mix of attitudes not only about gender, but also about race and class.

By 1914 when World War I began, the majority of those who supported women's right to vote, including leading advocates of suffrage such as Nellie McClung, supported women's war efforts as part of the way that Canadian women could do their part for Britain. Women's efforts in supporting the war, both in taking on non-traditional jobs so men could go and fight overseas, and in the range of volunteer work that women took on during the war, also helped to justify women's right to attain the suffrage.

In addition, maternal feminist arguments, in which women argued that granting women the right to vote would help to create a better and purer society, had increasing resonance during World War I, when there was a strong feeling that the deaths of so many soldiers in France had to lead to the creation of a better society after the war. Partly as a result of such arguments, women began to acquire the provincial franchise during the war, first in the prairie provinces of Alberta, Saskatchewan, and Manitoba in 1916, and in British Columbia in 1917.

At the federal level, some women received the vote in a way intended much more as a political ploy for Robert Borden, the prime minister, than for equality for women. By 1916 Borden came to believe that conscription (mandatory male enlistment in the armed forces) was necessary to help reinforce Canadian troops in Europe and to give Canada more credibility with British leaders. However, he had to call an election before bringing in conscription, so the election was fought primarily on the basis of this issue. To ensure his victory, Borden passed the *Wartime Elections Act* of 1917, which took the vote away from those he thought would oppose the government, including all voters who came from enemy countries and had become Canadian citizens since 1902. The Act gave the vote to women who were the mothers, wives, and sisters of Canadian soldiers fighting overseas, who he assumed would support conscription. This effort worked, and Borden's government won the election. The election divided the suffragists, many of whom opposed this measure as a blatant political ploy. But many also supported it, because they believed that conscription was necessary to help Canada win the war. Only a very few, such as Francis Marion Beynon, a Western feminist who opposed the war itself, also opposed the racism of taking the vote away from so many immigrant men.

In 1918, women were granted the federal franchise on the same basis as men. This still did not mean that all Canadian women were enfranchised. Women in Quebec did not gain the provincial franchise until 1940, because the Catholic Church hierarchy in Quebec, and some French-Canadian nationalist leaders, felt particularly strongly that if women voted in the public sphere, they would be abandoning their traditional God-given place in the home. Any threat to the home was seen as a threat to the survival of the French Canadian nation.

Other Canadian women did not receive the vote until after the Second World War. Like Chinese and East Indian men, Chinese and East Indian women did not receive the right to vote in Canada until 1947. Japanese women and men did not acquire the right to vote until 1949, and the franchise was not available to all Canadian First Nations women and men until 1960.

While 1918 did not see all Canadian women gain the franchise, the white women who had been fighting for the vote saw the granting of the franchise as a great victory. Historians looking back on these events have labelled this suffrage victory as the end of the "first wave" of the women's movement (with the second wave beginning with the women's liberation movement of the 1960s). More recently, scholars have recognized that feminist

198

activism remained strong in the years between 1918 and the 1960s, with women struggling for increased rights on a number of fronts, including the right to be legally defined as 'persons', as well as for greater equality within family and property law and the workplace, and improved resources for women's health, including legal access to birth control. In some of these struggles, the racist assumptions of the suffragists remained. For example, many feminists in the 1920s and 1930s advocated the sterilization of people they defined as mentally challenged, who they deemed "unfit" to have children, because they believed this would improve the health of the nation. In many other ways, however, the efforts of these early feminists had a major positive impact on the lives of many Canadian women.

NOTE

1. Over the course of the nineteenth century, married women's right to property did improve, although these improvements were uneven across the country. Document 1 notes that significant inequities remained in British Columbia regarding married women's property rights in the early twentieth century.

QUESTIONS

1. What kinds of arguments did women use in arguing for the vote? Why do you think they used these arguments?
2. What is Valverde arguing about the role of racism among early feminists? What is Fiamengo arguing? In what ways do they differ, and in what ways do they agree?
3. Do you prefer Valverde's article or Fiamengo's? Whose arguments did you find more convincing, and why?
4. What do you think about Nellie's McClung's arguments in *In Times Like These*? Do you think her work here more closely reflects Fiamengo's arguments about first-wave feminists, or Valverde's? Are any of McClung's concerns still relevant today?
5. Why did Stephen Leacock not support women's suffrage? What was his belief about women's role and women's nature?
6. Look closely at the description of the WCTU float in the excerpts from the WCTU; how many things can this float tell us about the WCTU's program, membership, values, and beliefs?

FURTHER READINGS

Bacchi, Carol Lee, *Liberation Deferred?: The Ideas of the English-Canadian Suffragists, 1877–1918* (Toronto: University of Toronto Press, 1983).

Cook, Sharon Anne, *"Through Sunshine and Shadow": the Woman's Christian Temperance Union, Evangelicalism, and Reform in Ontario, 1874–1930* (Montreal and Kingston: McGill-Queen's University Press, 1995).

Forestell, Nancy, "Mrs. Canada Goes Global" *Atlantis* Vol.30, No.1 (2005), pp. 7–20.

Kealey Linda, ed., *A Not Unreasonable Claim: Women and Reform in Canada, 1880s–1920s* (Toronto: Women's Educational Press, 1979).

McKay, Ian, "The Woman Question," *Reasoning Otherwise: Leftists and the People's Enlightenment in Canada, 1890–1920* (Toronto: Between the Lines, 2008).

Valverde, Mariana, *The Age of Light, Soap and Water: Moral and Social Reform in English Canada, 1885–1925* (Toronto: McClelland and Stewart, 1991).

▲ Document 1: Points in the Laws of British Columbia Regarding the Legal Status of Women

Note on front page of pamphlet: This pamphlet was written by Mrs. C.R. Townley in 1911 when she was president of Vancouver Branch, Political Equality League. She did not use her name as she felt it might be less effective if people knew it had been written by a woman.

The British Columbia Political Equality League is an organization of men and women who, convinced of the fairness and wisdom of allowing to men and women equally a voice in the government of their country are working with the object of obtaining for the women of this province a like municipal and parliamentary franchise as that now enjoyed by men. It was formed in the early months of this year (1911). It is a Provincial Society having local branches. [. . .]

There is nothing of the "suffragette" [the term for the more radical women in Britain who were campaigning for the franchise for women—some of these women went on hunger strikes, broke windows and chained themselves to fences to bring further attention to their cause] in the sane and quiet movement that is taking place in our midst. It is rather the gradual outcome of thought and education amongst an admittedly intelligent, observant and progressive people.

With regard to any change, there are always a few narrow and determinedly prejudiced persons of both sexes who refuse to look into a question on its merits—who apparently prefer not to inform themselves lest they should be convinced—but they grow fewer daily. It is the experience of the Political Equality League that the majority of men are not opposed to suffrage for women and that practically all our loyal women are united in the desire for a voice in the government of the country they love [...]

Points in the Laws of British Columbia Regarding Legal Status of Women

The British system of law is admittedly the best and fairest in the world. Yet times and circumstances of life change and even in law there is evolution. Constant amendments to existing laws go on. Sometimes a step backward is taken, more often a forward movement. The general principle in our laws is based on justice to all [...]

In our own province there are in existence certain laws that are not suited to the social progress of this day and generation and yet that remain unchanged.

Some of these are of vital interest as intimately touching family life and the solidity of the home. They bear upon the legal status of women, the protection and care of children, property rights and the distribution of estates [...] laws of property, status and civil rights are provincial matters. [. . .]

A wife is not entitled to dower in any land in the ownership of her husband. [Dower was a woman's right to a life interest in a third of the property held by her husband. Dower rights prevented a husband from selling property without her consent. The concept of dower existed in many other British jurisdictions.] He may sell or give it away without consulting

Source: Issued by the Vancouver Branch of the British Columbia Political Equality League, UBC Special Collections.

I would like to thank Melanie Ihmels for bringing this source to my attention—L. Marks.

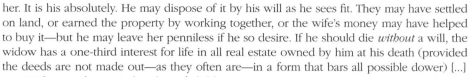

her. It is his absolutely. He may dispose of it by his will as he sees fit. They may have settled on land, or earned the property by working together, or the wife's money may have helped to buy it—but he may leave her penniless if he so desire. If he should die *without* a will, the widow has a one-third interest for life in all real estate owned by him at his death (provided the deeds are not made out—as they often are—in a form that bars all possible dower) [...]

With regard to guardianship of children:

The father has sole authority in the education and disposition of the child, although the mother is equally responsible with the father for the maintenance of the child.

The father has the right to arrange by will the guardianship and education of his child (even if unborn), till it shall be twenty-one years of age. No matter how unsuitable she may find this to be, the widow must abide by it. The mother may, however, petition the court for the care of the child until seven years of age if other guardian has been appointed by the father and after it is seven years old to have the right of access (go to see) to it.

These privileges are usually graciously granted her—but they are privileges, not rights. A mother has no right of possession in her legitimate child.

By going to law it is often possible to modify or rearrange matters. It is said "There is always a remedy in equity." But often this is no remedy, because of the expense entailed.

The consent of parents and guardians is necessary to the marriage of minors of either sex under twenty-one years of age—but the consent of the mothers is not needed if the father (or guardian appointed by will of the father) gives consent.

A girl of twelve years of age or a boy of fourteen years of age may be legally married in this province.

In the case of a deserted wife: The husband has the right to come and collect the earnings of their minor children. The wife may obtain an order of protection from the court to prevent this. But the very woman who needs this most, often is ignorant, or so situated by reason of distance or family cares that she cannot readily take the necessary steps.

The husband also may collect and use his wife's wages under certain circumstances.

These laws may well make men think. They are naturally of special interest to women—in whose lives "children" and "home" are the very watchwords of existence.

Though home is popularly regarded as woman's sphere in life, her children as her especial care and interest, it would seem that in reality the very roof may be sold over her head, the children she has borne be taken from her, and her little daughter of twelve years of age given in marriage without the mother's consent.

Cases influenced by these conditions come to the notice of every philanthropic society daily. Wives and families that might have been provided for are left destitute. Worthless husbands subdue their wives to their wishes by threatening to take their children away ...

The government has been approached at various times by women of the province with requests for amendments to these laws. It is not that men are against alterations, but that they have so many other political interests at heart—and these things do not restrict their personal liberty and legal status as they do that of women [...]

Ours is a progressive country. The men of British Columbia are in the main, broadminded as its wide flung area—sufficiently free from prejudice and old world trammels to consider with dispassionate common-sense and freedom from arrogant egotism, the possibility of advanced legislation along national lines. They know too well the worth, comradeship, and good judgement of the women who have stood by them in their efforts to build up homes in a new land—who have their interest and prosperity at heart—to deny them (if they want it) the voice in their country's welfare that is eagerly pressed upon fresh-coming ignorant foreigners as soon as possible by politicians. In Australia where women have the franchise, there is admittedly the best domestic legislation in the world [...]

201

▲ Document 2: Excerpt from *In Times Like These*

Nellie L. McClung

This seems to be a good time for us to jar ourselves lose [sic] from some of the prejudices and beliefs which we have outgrown. It is time for readjustment surely, a time for spiritual and mental housecleaning, when we are justified in looking things over very carefully and deciding whether or not we shall ever need them again.

Some of us have suspected for a long time that a good deal of the teaching of the world regarding women has come under the general heading of 'dope.' Now 'dope' is not a slang word, as you may be thinking, gentle reader. It is a good Anglo-Saxon word (or will be), for it fills a real need, and there is none other to take its place. 'Dope' means anything that is calculated to soothe, or hush, or put to sleep. 'Sedative' is a synonym, but it lacks the oily softness of 'dope.'

One of the commonest forms of dope given to women to keep them quiet is the one referred to in a previous chapter: 'The hand that rocks the cradle rules the world.' It is a great favorite with politicians and not being original with them it does contain a small element of truth. They use it in their pre-election speeches, which they begin with the honeyed words: 'We are glad to see we have with us this evening so many members of the fair sex; we are delighted to see that so many have come to grace our gathering on this occasion; we realize that a woman's intuition is ofttimes truer than a man's reasoning, and although women have no actual voice in politics, they have something far more strong and potent—they have the wonder power of indirect influence.' Just about here comes in 'the hand that rocks!'

Having thus administered the dope, in this pleasing mixture of molasses and soft soap, which is supposed to keep the 'fair sex' quiet and happy for the balance of the evening, the aspirant for public honors passes on to the serious business of the hour, and discusses the affairs of state with the electorate. Right here, let us sound a small note of warning. Keep your eye on the man who refers to women as the 'fair sex'—he is a dealer in dope!

One of the oldest and falsest of our beliefs regarding women is that they are protected—that some way in the battle of life they get the best of it. People talk of men's chivalry, that vague, indefinite quality which is supposed to transmute the common clay of life into gold.

Chivalry is a magic word. It seems to breathe of foreign strands and moonlight groves and silver sands and knights and earls and kings; it seems to tell of glorious deeds and waving plumes and prancing steeds and belted earls—and things!

People tell us of the good old days of chivalry when womanhood was really respected and reverenced—when brave knight rode gaily forth to die for his lady love. But in order to be really loved and respected there was one hard and fast condition laid down, to which all women must conform—they must be beautiful, no getting out of that. They simply had to have starry eyes and golden hair, or else black as a raven's wing; they had to have pale, white, and haughty brow, and a laugh like a ripple of magic. Then they were all right and armored knights would die for them quick as wink!

Source: *In Times Like These,* with an introduction by Veronica Strong-Boag (University of Toronto Press, 1972 [1915]), pp. 38–55, 57–58, 84–88, 90–91, 93–94.

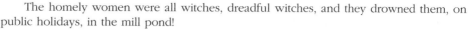

The homely women were all witches, dreadful witches, and they drowned them, on public holidays, in the mill pond!

People tell us now that chivalry is dead, and women have killed it, bold women who instead of staying at home, broidering pearls on a red velvet sleeve, have gone out to work—have gone to college side by side with men and have been so unwomanly sometimes as to take the prizes away from men. Chivalry cannot live in such an atmosphere. Certainly not!

Of course women can hardly be blamed for going out and working when one remembers that they must either work or starve. Broidering pearls will not boil the kettle worth a cent! There are now thirty per cent of the women of the U.S.A. and Canada, who are wage-earners, and we will readily grant that necessity has driven most of them out of their homes. Similarly, in England alone, there are a million and a half more women than men. It would seem that all women cannot have homes of their own—there does not seem to be enough men to go around. But still there are people who tell us these women should all have homes of their own—it is their own fault if they haven't; and once I heard of a woman saying the hardest thing about men I ever heard—and she was an ardent anti-suffragist too. She said that what was wrong with the women in England was that they were too particular—that's why they were not married, and, she went on, 'any person can tell, when they look around at men in general, that God never intended women to be very particular.' I am glad I never said anything as hard as that about men.

There are still with us some of the conventions of the old days of chivalry. The pretty woman still has the advantage over her plainer sister—and the opinion of the world is that women must be beautiful at all costs. When a newspaper wishes to disprove a woman's contention, or demolish her theories, it draws ugly pictures of her. If it can show that she has big feet or red hands, or wears unbecoming clothes, that certainly settles the case—and puts her where she belongs.

This cruel convention that women must be beautiful accounts for the popularity of face-washes, and beauty parlors, and the languor of university extension lectures. Women cannot be blamed for this. All our civilization has been to the end that women make themselves attractive to men. The attractive woman has hitherto been the successful woman. The pretty girl marries a millionaire, travels in Europe, and is presented at court; her plainer sister, equally intelligent, marries a boy from home, and does her own washing. I am not comparing the two destinies as to which offers the greater opportunities for happiness or usefulness, but rather to show how widely divergent two lives may be. What caused the difference was a wavy strand of hair, a rounder curve on a cheek. Is it any wonder that women capitalize their good looks, even at the expense of their intelligence? The economic dependence of women is perhaps the greatest injustice that has been done to us, and has worked the greatest injury to the race.

Men are not entirely blameless in respect to the frivolity of women. It is easy to blame women for dressing foolishly, extravagantly, but to what end do they do it? To be attractive to men; and the reason they continue to do it is that it is successful. Many a woman has found that it pays to be foolish. Men like frivolity—before marriage; but they demand all the sterner virtues afterwards. The little dainty, fuzzy-haired, simpering dolly who chatters and wears toe-slippers has a better chance in the matrimonial market than the clear-headed, plainer girl, who dresses sensibly. A little boy once gave his mother directions as to his birthday present—he said he wanted 'something foolish' and therein he expressed a purely masculine wish.

203

A man's ideal at seventeen
Must be a sprite—
A dainty, fairy, elfish queen
Of pure delight;
But later on he sort of feels
He'd like a girl who could cook meals.
Life is full of anomalies, and in the mating and pairing of men and women there
    are many.

Why is the careless, easy-going, irresponsible way of the young girl so attractive to men? It does not make for domestic happiness; and why, Oh why, do some of our best men marry such odd little sticks of pin-head women, with a brain similar in caliber to a second-rate butterfly, while the most intelligent, unselfish, and womanly women are left unmated? I am going to ask about this the first morning I am in heaven, if so be we are allowed to ask about the things which troubled us while on our mortal journey. I have never been able to find out about it here.

Now this old belief that women are protected is of sturdy growth and returns to life with great persistence. Theoretically women are protected—on paper—traditionally—just like Belgium was, and with just as disastrous results.

A member of the English Parliament declared with great emphasis that the women now have everything the heart could desire—they reign like queens and can have their smallest wish gratified. ('Smallest' is right.) And we very readily grant that there are many women living in idleness and luxury on the bounty of their male relatives, and we say it with sorrow and shame that these are estimated the successful women in the opinion of the world. But while some feast in idleness, many others slave in poverty. The great army of women workers are ill-paid, badly housed, and their work is not honored or respected or paid for. What share have they in man's chivalry? Chivalry is like a line of credit. You can get plenty of it when you do not need it. When you are prospering financially and your bank account is growing and you are rated Al, you can get plenty of credit—it is offered to you; but when the dark days of financial depression overtake you, and the people you are depending upon do not 'come through,' and you must have credit—must have it!—the very people who once urged it upon you will now tell you that 'money is tight!'

The young and pretty woman, well dressed and attractive, can get all the chivalry she wants. She will have seats offered her on street cars, men will hasten to carry her parcels, or open doors for her; but the poor old woman, beaten in the battle of life, sick of life's struggles, and grown gray and weather-beaten facing life's storms—what chivalry is shown her? She can go her weary way uncomforted and unattended. People who need it do not get it.

Anyway, chivalry is a poor substitute for justice, if one cannot have both. Chivalry is something like the icing on the cake, sweet but not nourishing. It is like the paper lace around the bonbon box—we could get along without it.

There are countless thousands of truly chivalrous men, who have the true chivalry whose foundation is justice—who would protect all women from injury of insult or injustice, but who know that they cannot do it—who know that in spite of all they can do, women are often outraged, insulted, ill-treated. The truly chivalrous man, who does reverence all womankind, realizing this, says: 'Let us give women every weapon whereby they can defend themselves; let us remove the stigma of political nonentity under which women have been placed. Let us give women a fair deal!' ...

This is the new chivalry—and on it we build our hope.

I hold it true—I will not change,
For changes are a dreadful bore —
That nothing must be done on earth
Unless it has been done before.

—Anti-Suffrage Creed

If prejudices belonged to the vegetable world they would be described under the general heading of: 'Hardy Perennials; will grow in any soil, and bloom without ceasing; requiring no cultivation; will do better when left alone.'

In regard to tenacity of life, no old yellow cat has anything on a prejudice. You may kill it with your own hands, bury it deep, and sit on the grave, and behold! the next day, it will walk in at the back door, purring.

Take some of the prejudices regarding women that have been exploded and blown to pieces many, many times and yet walk among us today in the fulness of life and vigor. There is a belief that housekeeping is the only occupation for women; that all women must be house-keepers, whether they like it or not. Men may do as they like, and indulge their individuality, but every true and womanly woman must take to the nutmeg grater and the O-Cedar Mop. It is also believed that in the good old days before woman suffrage was discussed, and when woman's clubs were unheard of, that all women adored housework, and simply pined for Monday morning to come to get at the weekly wash; that women cleaned house with rapture and cooked joyously. Yet there is a story told of one of the women of the old days, who arose at four o'clock in the morning, and aroused all her family at an indecently early hour for breakfast, her reason being that she wanted to get 'one of these horrid old meals over.' This woman had never been at a suffrage meeting—so where did she get the germ of discontent?

At the present time there is much discontent among women, and many people are seriously alarmed about it. They say women are no longer contented with woman's sphere and woman's work—that the washboard has lost its charm, and the days of the hair-wreath are ended. We may as well admit that there is discontent among women. We cannot drive them back to the spinning wheel and the mathook, for they will not go. But there is really no cause for alarm, for discontent is not necessarily wicked. There is such a thing as divine discontent just as there is criminal contentment. Discontent may mean the stirring of ambition, the desire to spread out, to improve and grow. Discontent is a sign of life, corresponding to growing pains in a healthy child. The poor woman who is making a brave struggle for existence is not saying much, though she is thinking all the time. In the old days when a woman's hours were from 5 A.M. to 5 A.M., we did not hear much of discontent among women, because they had not time to even talk, and certainly could not get together. The horse on the treadmill may be very discontented, but he is not disposed to tell his troubles, for he cannot stop to talk.

It is the women, who now have leisure, who are doing the talking. For generations women have been thinking and thought without expression is dynamic, and gathers volume by repression. Evolution when blocked and suppressed becomes revolution. The introduction of machinery and the factory-made articles has given women more leisure than they had formerly, and now the question arises, what are they going to do with it?

Custom and conventionality recommend many and varied occupations for women, social functions intermixed with kindly deeds of charity, embroidering altar cloths, making strong and durable garments for the poor, visiting the sick, comforting the sad, all of which

205

women have faithfully done, but while they have been doing these things, they have been wondering about the underlying causes of poverty, sadness and sin. They notice that when the unemployed are fed on Christmas day, they are just as hungry as ever on December the twenty-sixth, or at least on December the twenty-seventh; they have been led to inquire into the causes for little children being left in the care of the state, and they find that in over half of the cases, the liquor traffic has contributed to the poverty and unworthiness of the parents. The state which licenses the traffic steps in and takes care, or tries to, of the victims; the rich brewer whose business it is to encourage drinking, is usually the largest giver to the work of the Children's Aid Society, and is often extolled for his lavish generosity: and sometimes when women think about these things they are struck by the absurdity of a system which allows one man or a body of men to rob a child of his father's love and care all year, and then gives him a stuffed dog and a little red sleigh at Christmas and calls it charity!

Women have always done their share of the charity work of the world. The lady of the manor, in the old feudal days, made warm mittens and woolen mufflers with her own white hands and carried them to the cottages at Christmas, along with blankets and coals. And it was a splendid arrangement all through, for it furnished the lady with mild and pleasant occupation, and it helped to soothe the conscience of the lord, and if the cottagers (who were often 'low worthless fellows, much given up to riotous thinking and disputing') were disposed to wonder why they had to work all year and get nothing, while the lord of the manor did nothing all year and got everything, the gift of blanket and coals, the warm mufflers, and 'a shawl for granny' showed them what ungrateful souls they were.

Women have dispensed charity for many, many years, but gradually it has dawned upon them that the most of our charity is very ineffectual, and merely smoothes things over, without ever reaching the root. A great deal of our charity is like the kindly deed of the benevolent old gentleman, who found a sick dog by the wayside, lying in the full glare of a scorching sun. The tender-hearted old man climbed down from his carriage, and, lifting the dog tenderly in his arms, carried him around into the small patch of shade cast by his carriage.

'Lie there, my poor fellow!' he said. 'Lie there, in the cool shade, where the sun's rays may not smite you!'

Then he got into his carriage and drove away.

Women have been led, through their charitable institutions and philanthropic endeavors, to do some thinking about causes.

Mrs. B. set out to be a 'family friend' to the family of her washwoman. Mrs. B. was a thoroughly charitable, kindly disposed woman, who had never favored woman's suffrage and regarded the new movement among women with suspicion. Her washwoman's family consisted of four children, and a husband who blew in gaily once in a while when in need of funds, or when recovering from a protracted spree, which made a few days' nursing very welcome. His wife, a Polish woman, had the old-world reverence for men, and obeyed him implicitly; she still felt it was very sweet of him to come home at all. Mrs. B. had often declared that Polly's devotion to her husband was a beautiful thing to see. The two eldest boys had newspaper routes and turned in their earnings regularly, and, although the husband did not contribute anything but his occasional company, Polly was able to make the payments on their little four-roomed cottage. In another year, it would be all paid for.

But one day Polly's husband began to look into the law—as all men should—and he saw that he had been living far below his privileges. The cottage was his—not that he had ever paid a cent on it, of course, but his wife had, and she was his; and the cottage was in his name.

So he sold it; naturally he did not consult Polly, for he was a quiet, peaceful man, and not fond of scenes. So he sold it quietly, and with equal quietness he withdrew from the Province, and took the money with him. He did not even say good-by to Polly or the

206

children, which was rather ungrateful, for they had given him many a meal and night's lodging. When Polly came crying one Monday morning and told her story, Mrs. B. could not believe it, and assured Polly she must be mistaken, but Polly declared that a man had come and asked her did she wish to rent the house for he had bought it. Mrs. B. went at once to the lawyers who had completed the deal. They were a reputable firm and Mrs. B. knew one of the partners quite well. She was sure Polly's husband could not sell the cottage. But the lawyers assured her it was quite true. They were very gentle and patient with Mrs. B. and listened courteously to her explanation, and did not dispute her word at all when she explained that Polly and her two boys had paid every cent on the house. It seemed that a trifling little thing like that did not matter. It did not really matter who paid for the house; the husband was the owner, for was he not the head of the house? and the property was in his name.

Polly was graciously allowed to rent her own cottage for $12.50 a month, with an option of buying, and the two little boys are still on a morning route delivering one of the city dailies.

Mrs. B. has joined a suffrage society and makes speeches on the injustice of the laws; and yet she began innocently enough, by making strong and durable garments for her washwoman's children—and see what has come of it! If women would only be content to snip away at the symptoms of poverty and distress, feeding the hungry and clothing the naked, all would be well and they would be much commended for their kindness of heart; but when they begin to inquire into causes, they find themselves in the sacred realm of politics where prejudice says no women must enter.

A woman may take an interest in factory girls, and hold meetings for them, and encourage them to walk in virtue's ways all she likes, but if she begins to advocate more sanitary surroundings for them, with some respect for the common decencies of life, she will find herself again in that sacred realm of politics—confronted by a factory act, on which no profane female hand must be laid.

Now politics simply means public affairs—yours and mine, everybody's—and to say that politics are too corrupt for women is a weak and foolish statement for any man to make. Any man who is actively engaged in politics, and declares that politics are too corrupt for women, admits one of two things, either that he is a party to this corruption, or that he is unable to prevent it—and in either case something should be done. Politics are not inherently vicious. The office of lawmaker should be the highest in the land, equaled in honor only by that of the minister of the gospel. In the old days, the two were combined with very good effect; but they seem to have drifted apart in more recent years.

If politics are too corrupt for women, they are too corrupt for men; for men and women are one—indissolubly joined together for good or ill. Many men have tried to put all their religion and virtue in their wife's name, but it does not work very well. When social conditions are corrupt women cannot escape by shutting their eyes, and taking no interest. It would be far better to give them a chance to clean them up.

What would you think of a man who would say to his wife: 'This house to which I am bringing you to live is very dirty and unsanitary, but I will not allow you—the dear wife whom I have sworn to protect—to touch it. It is too dirty for your precious little white hands! You must stay upstairs, dear. Of course the odor from below may come up to you, but use your smelling salts and think no evil. I do not hope to ever be able to clean it up, but certainly you must never think of trying.'

Do you think any woman would stand for that? She would say: 'John, you are all right in your way, but there are some places where your brain skids. Perhaps you had better stay downtown today for lunch. But on your way down please call at the grocer's, and send me a scrubbing brush and a package of Dutch Cleanser, and some chloride of lime, and now hurry.' Women have cleaned up things since time began; and if women ever get into politics there will be a cleaning-out of pigeon-holes and forgotten corners, on which the dust of years has fallen, and the sound of the political carpet-beater will be heard in the land.

There is another hardy perennial that constantly lifts its head above the earth, persistently refusing to be ploughed under, and that is that if women were ever given a chance to participate in outside affairs, that family quarrels would result; that men and their wives who have traveled the way of life together, side by side for years, and come safely through religious discussions, and discussions relating to 'his' people and 'her' people, would angrily rend each other over politics, and great damage to the furniture would be the result. Father and son have been known to live under the same roof and vote differently, and yet live! Not only to live, but live peaceably! If a husband and wife are going to quarrel they will find a cause for dispute easily enough, and will not be compelled to wait for election day. And supposing that they have never, never had a single dispute, and not a ripple has ever marred the placid surface of their matrimonial sea, I believe that a small family jar—or at least a real lively argument— will do them good. It is in order to keep the white-winged angel of peace hovering over the home that married women are not allowed to vote in many places. Spinsters and widows are counted worthy of voice in the selection of school trustee, and alderman, and mayor, but not the woman who has taken to herself a husband and still has him.

What a strange commentary on marriage that it should disqualify a woman from voting. Why should marriage disqualify a woman? Men have been known to vote for years after they were dead! [reference to corrupt voting practices where men vote by impersonating men who have died, but whose names are still on the voters' rolls]

Quite different from the 'family jar' theory, another reason is advanced against married women voting—it is said that they would all vote with their husbands, and that the married man's vote would thereby be doubled. We believe it is eminently right and proper that husband and wife should vote the same way, and in that case no one would be able to tell whether the wife was voting with the husband or the husband voting with the wife. Neither would it matter. If giving the franchise to women did nothing more than double the married man's vote it would do a splendid thing for the country, for the married man is the best voter we have; generally speaking, he is a man of family and property—surely if we can depend on anyone we can depend upon him, and if by giving his wife a vote we can double his—we have done something to offset the irresponsible transient vote of the man who has no interest in the community.

There is another sturdy prejudice that blooms everywhere in all climates, and that is that women would not vote if they had the privilege; and this is many times used as a crushing argument against woman suffrage. But why worry? If women do not use it, then surely there is no harm done; but those who use the argument seem to imply that a vote unused is a very dangerous thing to leave lying around, and will probably spoil and blow up. In support of this statement instances are cited of women letting their vote lie idle and unimproved in elections for school trustee and alderman. Of course, the percentage of men voting in these contests was quite small, too, but no person finds fault with that.

Women may have been careless about their franchise in elections where no great issue is at stake, but when moral matters are being decided women have not shown any lack of interest. As a result of the first vote cast by the women of Illinois over one thousand saloons went out of business. Ask the liquor dealers if they think women will use the ballot. They do not object to woman suffrage on the ground that women will not vote, but because they will.

'Why, Uncle Henry!' exclaimed one man to another on election day. 'I never saw you out to vote before. What struck you?'

'Hadn't voted for fifteen years,' declared Uncle Henry, 'but you bet I came out today to vote against givin' these fool women a vote; what's the good of givin' them a vote? they wouldn't use it!'

Then, of course, on the other hand there are those who claim that women would vote too much—that they would vote not wisely but too well; that they would take up voting as a life work to the exclusion of husband, home and children. There seems to be considerable misapprehension on the subject of voting. It is really a simple and perfectly innocent performance, quickly over, and with no bad after-effects.

It is usually done in a vacant room in a school or the vestry of a church, or a town hall. No drunken men stare at you. You are not jostled or pushed—you wait your turn in an orderly line, much as you have waited to buy a ticket at a railway station. Two tame and quiet-looking men sit at a table, and when your turn comes, they ask you your name, which is perhaps slightly embarrassing, but it is not as bad as it might be, for they do not ask your age, or of what disease did your grandmother die. You go behind the screen with your ballot paper in your hand, and there you find a seal-brown pencil tied with a chaste white string. Even the temptation of annexing the pencil is removed from your frail humanity. You mark your ballot, and drop it in the box, and come out into the sunlight again. If you had never heard that you had done an unladylike thing you would not know it. It all felt solemn, and serious, and very respectable to you, something like a Sunday-school convention. Then, too, you are surprised at what a short time you have been away from home. You put the potatoes on when you left home, and now you are back in time to strain them.

In spite of the testimony of many reputable women that they have been able to vote and get the dinner on one and the same day, there still exists a strong belief that the whole household machinery goes out of order when a woman goes to vote. No person denies a woman the right to go to church, and yet the church service takes a great deal more time than voting. People even concede to women the right to go shopping, or visiting a friend, or an occasional concert. But the wife and mother, with her God-given, sacred trust of molding the young life of our land, must never dream of going round the corner to vote. 'Who will mind the baby?' cried one of our public men, in great agony of spirit, 'when the mother goes to vote?'

One woman replied that she thought she could get the person that minded it when she went to pay her taxes—which seemed to be a fairly reasonable proposition. Yet the hardy plant of prejudice flourishes, and the funny pictures still bring a laugh.

Father comes home, tired, weary, footsore, toe-nails ingrowing, caused by undarned stockings, and finds the fire out, house cold and empty, save for his half-dozen children, all crying.

'Where is your mother?' the poor man asks in broken tones. For a moment the sobs are hushed while little Ellie replies: 'Out voting!'

Father bursts into tears.

Of course, people tell us, it is not the mere act of voting which demoralizes women— if they would only vote and be done with it; but women are creatures of habit, and habits once formed are hard to break; and although the polls are only open every three or four years, if women once get into the way of going to them, they will hang around there all the rest of the time. It is in woman's impressionable nature that the real danger lies.

Another shoot of this hardy shrub of prejudice is that women are too good to mingle in everyday life—they are too sweet and too frail—that women are angels. If women are angels we should try to get them into public life as soon as possible, for there is a great shortage of angels there just at present, if all we hear is true.

Then there is the pedestal theory—that women are away up on a pedestal, and down below, looking up at them with deep adoration, are men, their willing slaves. Sitting up on a pedestal does not appeal very strongly to a healthy woman—and, besides, if a woman has been on a pedestal for any length of time, it must be very hard to have to come down and cut the wood.

These tender-hearted and chivalrous gentlemen who tell you of their adoration for women, cannot bear to think of women occupying public positions. Their tender hearts shrink from the idea of women lawyers or women policemen, or even women preachers; these positions would 'rub the bloom off the peach,' to use their own eloquent words. They cannot bear, they say, to see women leaving the sacred precincts of home—and yet their offices are scrubbed by women who do their work while other people sleep—poor women who leave the sacred precincts of home to earn enough to keep the breath of life in them, who carry their scrub-pails home, through the deserted streets, long after the cars have stopped running. They are exposed to cold, to hunger, to insult—poor souls—is there any pity felt for them? Not that we have heard of. The tender-hearted ones can bear this with equanimity. It is the thought of women getting into comfortable and well-paid positions which wrings their manly hearts.

Another aspect of the case is that women can do more with their indirect influence than by the ballot; though just why they cannot do better still with both does not appear to be very plain. The ballot is a straight-forward dignified way of making your desire or choice felt. There are some things which are not pleasant to talk about, but would be delightful to vote against. Instead of having to beg, and coax, and entreat, and beseech, and denounce as women have had to do all down the centuries, in regard to the evil things which threaten to destroy their homes and those whom they love, what a glorious thing it would be if women could go out and vote against these things. It seems like a straightforward and easy way of expressing one's opinion. [...]

Then there is the problem of the foreign woman's vote. Many people fear that the granting of woman suffrage would greatly increase the unintelligent vote, because the foreign women would then have the franchise, and in our blind egotism we class our foreign people as ignorant people, if they do not know our ways and our language. They may know many other languages, but if they have not yet mastered ours they are poor, ignorant foreigners. We Anglo-Saxon people have a decided sense of our own superiority, and we feel sure that our skin is exactly the right color, and we people from Huron and Bruce feel sure that we were born in the right place, too. So we naturally look down upon those who happen to be of a different race and tongue than our own.

It is a sad feature of humanity that we are disposed to hate what we do not understand; we naturally suspect and distrust where we do not know. Hens are like that, too! When a strange fowl comes into a farmyard all the hens take a pick at it—not that it has done anything wrong, but they just naturally do not like the look of its face because it is strange. Now that may be very good ethics for hens, but it is hardly good enough for human beings. Our attitude toward the foreign people was well exemplified in one of the missions, where a little Italian boy, who had been out two years, refused to sit beside a newly arrived Italian boy, who, of course, could not speak a word of English. The teacher asked him to sit with his lately arrived compatriot, so that he might interpret for him. The older boy flatly refused, and told the teacher he 'had no use for them young dagos.'

'You see,' said the teacher sadly, when telling the story, 'he had caught the Canadian spirit.'

People say hard things about the corruptible foreign vote, but they place the emphasis in the wrong place. Instead of using our harsh adjectives for the poor fellow who sells his vote, let us save them all for the corrupt politician who buys it, for he cannot plead ignorance—he knows what he is doing. The foreign people who come to Canada, come with burning enthusiasm for the new land, this land of liberty—land of freedom. Some have been seen kissing the ground in an ecstacy of gladness when they arrive. It is the land of their dreams, where they hope to find home and happiness. They come to us with ideals of citizenship that shame our narrow, mercenary standards. These men are of a race which has gladly shed its blood for freedom and is doing it today. But what happens? They go out to work on construction gangs for the summer, they earn money for several months, and when the work closes down they drift back into the cities. They have done the work we wanted them to do, and no further thought is given to them. They may get off the earth so far as we are concerned. One door stands invitingly open to them. There is one place they are welcome—so long as their money lasts—and around the bar they get their ideals of citizenship.

When an election is held, all at once this new land of their adoption begins to take an interest in them, and political heelers, well paid for the job, well armed with whiskey, cigars and money, go among them, and, in their own language, tell them which way they must vote—and they do. Many an election has been swung by this means. One new arrival, just learning our language, expressed his contempt for us by exclaiming: 'Bah! Canada is not a country—it's just a place to make money.' That was all he had seen. He spoke correctly from his point of view.

Then when the elections are over, and the Government is sustained, the men who have climbed back to power by these means speak eloquently of our 'foreign people who have come to our shores to find freedom under the sheltering folds of our grand old flag (cheers), on which the sun never sets, and under whose protection all men are free and equal—with an equal chance of molding the destiny of the great Empire of which we make a part.' (Cheers and prolonged applause.)

If we really understood how, with our low political ideals and iniquitous election methods, we have corrupted the souls of these men who have come to live among us, we would no longer cheer, when we hear this old drivel of the 'folds of the flag.' We would think with shame of how we have driven the patriotism out of these men and replaced it by the greed of gain, and instead of cheers and applause we would cry: 'Lord, have mercy upon us!'

The foreign women, whom politicians and others look upon as such a menace, are differently dealt with than the men. They do not go out to work, *en masse*, as the men do. They work one by one, and are brought in close contact with their employers. The women who go out washing and cleaning spend probably five days a week in the homes of other women. Surely one of her five employers will take an interest in her, and endeavor to instruct her in the duties of citizenship. Then, too, the mission work is nearly all done for women and girls. The foreign women generally speak English before the men, for the reason that they are brought in closer contact with English-speaking people. When I hear people speaking of the ignorant foreign women I think of 'Mary,' and 'Annie,' and others I have known. I see their broad foreheads and intelligent kindly faces, and think of the heroic struggle they are making to bring their families up in thrift and decency. Would Mary vote against liquor if she had the chance? She would. So would you if your eyes had been blackened as often by a drunken husband. There is no need to instruct these women on the evils of liquor drinking—they are able to give you a few aspects of the case which perhaps you had not thought of. We have no reason to be afraid of the foreign woman's vote. I wish we were as sure of the ladies who live on the Avenue. [. . .]

After one has listened to all these arguments and has contracted clergyman's sore throat talking back, it is real relief to meet the people who say flatly and without reason: 'You can't have it—no—I won't argue—but inasmuch as I can prevent it—you will never vote! So there!' The men who meet the question like this are so easy to classify.

I remember when I was a little girl back on the farm in the Souris Valley, I used to water the cattle on Saturday mornings, drawing the water in an icy bucket with a windlass from a fairly deep well. We had one old white ox, called Mike, a patriarchal-looking old sinner, who never had enough, and who always had to be watered first. Usually I gave him what I thought he should have and then took him back to the stable and watered the others. But one day I was feeling real strong, and I resolved to give Mike all he could drink, even if it took every drop of water in the well. I must admit that I cherished a secret hope that he would kill himself drinking. I will not set down here in cold figures how many pails of water Mike drank—but I remember. At last he could not drink another drop, and stood shivering beside the trough, blowing the last mouthful out of his mouth like a bad child. I waited to see if he would die, or at least turn away and give the others a chance. The thirsty cattle came crowding around him, but old Mike, so full I am sure he felt he would never drink another drop of water again as long as he lived, deliberately and with difficulty put his two front feet over the trough and kept all the other cattle away [...] Years afterwards I had the pleasure of being present when a delegation waited upon the Government of one of the provinces of Canada, and presented many reasons for extending the franchise to women. One member of the Government arose and spoke for all his colleagues. He said in substance: 'You can't have it—so long as I have anything to do with the affairs of this province—you shall not have it!' [...]

Did your brain ever give a queer little twist, and suddenly you were conscious that the present mental process had taken place before. If you have ever had it, you will know what I mean, and if you haven't I cannot make you understand. I had that feeling then ... I said to myself: 'Where have I seen that face before?' [...] Then, suddenly, I remembered, and in my heart I cried out: 'Mike!—old friend, Mike! Dead these many years! Your bones lie buried under the fertile soil of the Souris Valley, but your soul goes marching on! Mike, old friend, I see you again—both feet in the trough!' [...]

If any person doubts that the society of the present day has been made by men, and for men's advantage, let them look for a minute at the laws which govern society. Society allows a man all privilege all license, all liberty, where women are concerned. He may lie to women, deceive them—'all's fair in love and war'—he may break many a heart, and blast many a fair name; that merely throws a glamour around him. 'He's a devil with women,' they say, and it is no disadvantage in the business or political world—where man dominates. But if a man is dishonest in business or neglects to pay his gambling bills, he is down and out. These are crimes against men—and therefore serious. This is also a sore thought! [...]

Since women's sphere of manual labor has so narrowed by economic conditions and has not widened correspondingly in other directions, many women have become parasites on the earnings of their male relatives. Marriage has become a straight 'clothes and board' proposition to the detriment of marriage and the race. Her economic dependence has so influenced the attitude of some women toward men, that it is the old man with the money who can support her in idleness who appeals to her far more than the handsome, clean-limbed young man who is poor, and with whom she would have to work. The softening, paralyzing effects of ease and comfort are showing themselves on our women. [...]

The time will come, we hope, when women will be economically free, and mentally and spiritually independent enough to refuse to have their food paid for by men; when women will receive equal pay for equal work, and have all avenues of activity open to them; and will be free to choose their own mates, without shame, or indelicacy; when men will not be afraid of marriage because of the financial burden, but free men and free women will marry for love, and together work for the sustenance of their families. It is not too ideal a thought. It is coming, and the new movement among women who are crying out for a larger humanity, is going to bring it about.

But there are many good men who view this with alarm. They are afraid that if women were economically independent they would never marry. But they would. Deeply rooted in almost every woman's heart is the love of home and children; but independence is sweet and when marriage means the loss of independence, there are women brave enough and strong enough to turn away from it. 'I will not marry for a living,' many a brave woman has said.

The world has taunted women into marrying. So odious has the term 'old maid' been in the past that many a woman has married rather than have to bear it. That the term 'old maid' has lost its odium is due to the fact that unmarried women have made a place for themselves in the world of business. They have become real people apart from their sex. The 'old maid' of the past was a sad, anemic creature, without any means of support except the bounty of some relative. She had not married, so she had failed utterly, and the world did not fail to rub it in. The unmarried woman of today is the head saleslady in some big house, drawing as big a salary as most men, and the world kowtows to her. The world is beginning to see that a woman may achieve success in other departments of life as well as marriage. [...]

When women are free to marry or not as they will, and the financial burden of making a home is equally shared by husband and wife, the world will enter upon an era of happiness undreamed of now. As it is now the whole matter of marrying and homemaking is left to chance. Every department of life, every profession in which men and women engage, has certain qualifications which must be complied with, except the profession of homemaking. A young man and a young woman say: 'I believe we'll get married' and forthwith they do. The state sanctions it, and the church blesses it. They may be consumptive, epileptic, shiftless, immoral, or with a tendency to insanity. No matter. They may go on and reproduce their kind. They are perfectly free to bring children into the world, who are a burden and a menace to society. Society has to bear it—that is all! 'Be fruitful and multiply!' declares the church, as it deplores the evils of race suicide. Many male moralists have cried out for large families. 'Let us have better and healthier babies if we can,' cried out one of England's bishops, not long ago, 'but let us have more babies!' [...]

When the cry has been so persistently raised for more children, the women naturally wonder why more care is not exerted for the protection of the children who are already here. The reason is often given for not allowing women to have the free grants of land in Canada on the same conditions as men, that it would make them too independent of marriage, and, as one commissioner of emigration phrased it: 'It is not independent women we want; it is population.'

Granting that population is very desirable, would it not be well to save what we have? Six or seven thousand of our population in Canada drop out of the race every year as a direct result of the liquor traffic, and a higher percentage than this perish from the same cause in some other countries. Would it not be well to save them? Thousands of babies die every year from preventable causes. Free milk depositories and district nurses and free dispensaries would save many of them. In the Far West, on the border of civilization, where women are beyond the reach of nurses and doctors, many mothers and babies die every year. How would it be to try to save them? Delegations of public-spirited women have waited upon august bodies of men, and pleased the cause of these brave women who are paying the toll of colonization, and have asked that Government nurses be sent to them in their hour of need. But up to date not one dollar of Government money has been spent on them notwith-standing the fact that when a duke or a prince comes to visit our country, we can pour out money like water! [...]

If children die—what of it? 'The Lord gave and the Lord hath taken away.' Let us have more. This is the sore thought with women. It is not that the bringing of children into the world is attended with pain and worry and weariness—it is not that: it is that they are held of such small value in the eyes of this man-made world. This is the sorest thought of all! [...]

Women have carried many a sore thought in their hearts, feeling that they have been harshly dealt with by their men folk, and have laid the blame on the individual man, when in reality the individual has not been to blame. The whole race is suffering from masculinity; and men and women are alike to blame for tolerating it.

The baby girl in her cradle gets the first cold blast of it. 'A girl?' says the kind neighbor, 'Oh, too bad—I am sure it was quite a disappointment!'

Then there is the old-country reverence for men, of which many a mother has been guilty, which exalts the boys of the family far above the girls, and brings home to the latter, in many, many ways, the grave mistake of having been born a woman. Many little girls have carried the sore thought in their hearts from their earliest recollection.

They find out, later, that women's work is taken for granted. A farmer will allow his daughter to work many weary unpaid years, and when she gets married he will give her 'a feather bed and a cow,' and feel that her claim upon him has been handsomely met. The gift of a feather bed is rather interesting, too, when you consider that it is the daughter who has raised the geese, plucked them, and made the bed-tick. But 'father' gives it to her just the same. The son, for a corresponding term of service, gets a farm. [. . .]

There are some places, where a law can protect the weak, but there are many situations which require more than a law. Take the case of a man who habitually abuses and frightens his family, and makes their lives a periodic hell of fear. The law cannot touch him unless he actually kills some of them, and it seems a great pity that there cannot be some corrective measure. In the states of Kansas and Washington (where women vote) the people have enacted what is known as the 'Lazy Husband's Act,' which provides for such cases as this. If a man is abusive or disagreeable, or fails to provide for his family, he is taken away for a time, and put to work in a state institution, and his money is sent home to his family. He is treated kindly, and good influences thrown around him. When he shows signs of repentance—he is allowed to go home. Home, very often, looks better to him, and he behaves himself quite decently.

Women outlined this legislation and it is in the states where women vote that it is in operation. There will be more such legislation, too, when women are given a chance to speak out!

A New Zealander once wrote home to a friend in England advising him to fight hard against woman suffrage. 'Don't ever let the wimmin vote, Bill,' he wrote. 'They are good servants, but bad masters. Over there you can knock your wife about for five shillings, but here we does jail for it!'

The man who 'knocks his wife about' or feels that he might some day want to knock her about, is opposed to further liberties for women, of course.

But that is the class of man from whom we never expected anything. He has his prototype, too, in every walk of life. Don't make the mistake of thinking that only ignorant members of the great unwashed masses talk and feel this way. Silk-hatted 'noblemen' have answered women's appeals for common justice by hiring the Whitechapel toughs to 'bash their heads,' and this is another sore thought that women will carry with them for many a day after the suffrage has been granted. I wish we could forget the way our English sisters have been treated in that sweet land of liberty!

The problems of discovery have been solved; the problems of colonization are being solved, and when the war is over the problem of world government will be solved; and then the problem will be just the problem of living together. That problem cannot be solved without the help of women. The world has suffered long from too much masculinity and not enough humanity, but when the war is over, and the beautiful things have been destroyed, and the lands laid desolate, and all the blood has been shed, the poor old bruised and broken heart of the world will cry out for its mother and nurse, who will dry her own eyes, and bind up its wounds and nurse it back to life once more.

214

▲ Document 3: Nellie McClung

● Nellie McClung ca. 1910-1918. Nellie McClung was one of the most prominent leaders of the English Canadian women's suffrage movement. She lived most of her adult life in Manitoba and then Alberta, where she worked for women's rights and other social reform issues. She was also a noted author of both fiction and non-fiction.

Source: Glenbow Museum NA-273-2.

215

▲ Document 4: Canada Needs a Clean-up Week (1915)

CANADA NEEDS A "CLEAN-UP" WEEK

Most of the cities of Canada have an annual "Clean-up" Week each spring, when the winter's accumulation of rubbish and filth is raked together and destroyed. It has been found that the health as well as the appearance of the cities is improved and flies and other pests are greatly minimized by this process. Here we see our artist's conception of the "Clean-up" week which is needed in the public life of Canada.

● What are they burning? What message does this cartoon send about women's roles and abilities, in the home and the public world? What message does this cartoon send about men's role in social reform?

Source: Archives of Manitoba/ Archives du Manitoba, Arch Dale 22, N8929, 1915.

▲ Document 5: The Woman Question

Stephen Leacock

Stephen Leacock was a professor of political economy at McGill University in the first third of the twentieth century. He is best known as a popular writer of humourous fiction, the most well known of which is Sunshine Sketches of a Little Town *(1912)*

I was sitting the other day in what is called the Peacock Alley of one of our leading hotels, drinking tea with another thing like myself, a man. At the next table were a group of Superior Beings in silk, talking. I couldn't help overhearing what they said at least not when I held my head a little sideways.

They were speaking of the war.

'There wouldn't have been any war,' said one, 'if women were allowed to vote.'

'No, indeed,' chorused all the others.

The woman who had spoken looked about her defiantly. She wore spectacles and was of the type that we men used to call, in days when we still retained a little courage, an Awful Woman.

'When women have the vote,' she went on, 'there will be no more war. The women will forbid it.'

She gazed about her angrily. She evidently wanted to be heard. My friend and I hid ourselves behind a little fern and trembled.

But we listened. We were hoping that the Awful Woman would explain how war would be ended. She didn't. She went on to explain instead that when women have the vote there will be no more poverty, no disease, no germs, no cigarette smoking and nothing to drink but water.

It seemed a gloomy world.

'Come,' whispered my friend, 'this is no place for us. Let us go to the bar.'

'No,' I said, 'leave me. I am going to write an article on the Woman Question. The time has come when it has got to be taken up and solved.'

So I set myself to write it.

The woman problem may be stated somewhat after this fashion. The great majority of the woman of to-day find themselves without any means of support of their own. I refer of course to the civilised white women. The gay savage in her jungle, attired in a cocoanut leaf, armed with a club and adorned with the neck of a soda-water bottle, is all right. Trouble hasn't reached her yet. Like all savages, she has a far better time—more varied, more interesting, more worthy of a human being—than falls to the lot of the rank and file of civilized men and women. Very few of us recognise this great truth. We have a mean little vanity over our civilisation. We are touchy about it. We do not realise that so far we have done little but increase the burden of work and multiply the means of death. But for the hope of better things to come, our civilisation would not seem worth while.

But this is a digression. Let us go back. The great majority of women have no means of support of their own. This is true also of men. But the men can acquire means of

Source: 'The Woman Question' in *The Social Criticism of Stephen Leacock*, edited and introduced by Alan Bowker, University of Toronto Press, 1973.

support. They can hire themselves out and work. Better still, by the industrious process of intrigue rightly called 'busyness,' or business, they may presently get hold of enough of other people's things to live without working. Or again, men can, with a fair prospect of success, enter the criminal class, either in its lower ranks as a house breaker, or in its upper ranks, through politics. Take it all in all a man has a certain chance to get along in life.

A woman, on the other hand, has little or none. The world's work is open to her, but she cannot do it. She lacks the physical strength for laying bricks or digging coal. If put to work on a steel beam a hundred feet above the ground, she would fall off. For the pursuit of business her head is all wrong. Figures confuse her. She lacks sustained attention and in point of morals the average woman is, even for business, too crooked.

This last point is one that will merit a little emphasis. Men are queer creatures. They are able to set up a code of rules or a standard, often quite an artificial one, and stick to it. They have acquired the art of playing the game. Eleven men can put on white flannel trousers and call themselves a cricket team, on which an entirely new set of obligations, almost a new set of personalities, are wrapped about them. Women could never be a team of anything.

So it is in business. Men are able to maintain a sort of rough and ready code which prescribes the particular amount of cheating that a man may do under the rule. This is called business honesty, and many men adhere to it with a dog-like tenacity, growing old in it, till it is stamped on their grizzled faces, visibly. They can feel it inside them like a virtue. So much will they cheat and no more. Hence men are able to trust one another, knowing the exact degree of dishonesty they are entitled to expect.

With women it is entirely different. They bring to business an unimpaired vision. They see it as it is. It would be impossible to trust them. They refuse to play fair.

Thus it comes about that woman is excluded, to a great extent, from the world's work and the world's pay.

There is nothing really open to her except one thing—marriage. She must find a man who will be willing, in return for her society, to give her half of everything he has, allow her the sole use of his house during the daytime, pay her taxes, and provide her clothes.

This was, formerly and for many centuries, not such a bad solution of the question. The women did fairly well out of it. It was the habit to marry early and often. The 'house and home' was an important place. The great majority of people, high and low, lived on the land. The work of the wife and the work of the husband ran closely together. The two were complementary and fitted into one another. A woman who had to superintend the baking of bread and the brewing of beer, the spinning of yarn and the weaving of clothes, could not complain that her life was incomplete.

Then came the modern age, beginning let us say about a hundred and fifty years ago. The distinguishing marks of it have been machinery and the modern city. The age of invention swept the people off the land. It herded them into factories, creating out of each man a poor miserable atom divorced from hereditary ties, with no rights, no duties, and no place in the world except what his wages contract may confer on him. Every man for himself, and sink or swim, became the order of the day. It was nicknamed 'industrial freedom.' The world's production increased enormously. It is doubtful if the poor profited much. They obtained the modern city—full of light and noise and excitement, lively with crime and gay with politics—and the free school where they learned to read and write, by which means they might hold a mirror to their poverty and take a good look at it. They lost the quiet of the country side, the murmur of the brook and the inspiration of the open sky. These are unconscious things, but the peasant who has been reared among them, for all his unconsciousness, pines and dies without them. It is doubtful if the poor have gained.

The chaw-bacon rustic who trimmed a hedge in the reign of George the First, compares well with the pale slum-rat of the reign of George V.

But if the machine age has profoundly altered the position of the working man, it has done still more with woman. It has dispossessed her. Her work has been taken away. The machine does it. It makes the clothes and brews the beer. The roar of the vacuum cleaner has hushed the sound of the broom. The proud proportions of the old-time cook, are dwindled to the slim outline of the gas-stove expert operating on a beefsteak with the aid of a thermometer. And at the close of day the machine, wound with a little key, sings the modern infant to its sleep, with the faultless lullaby of the Victrola. The home has passed, or at least is passing out of existence. In place of it is the 'apartment'—an incomplete thing, a mere part of something, where children are an intrusion, where hospitality is done through a caterer, and where Christmas is only the twenty-fifth of December.

All this the machine age did for woman. For a time she suffered—the one thing she had learned, in the course of centuries, to do with admirable fitness. With each succeeding decade of the modern age things grew worse instead of better. The age for marriage shifted. A wife instead of being a help-mate had become a burden that must be carried. It was no longer true that two could live on less than one. The prudent youth waited till he could 'afford' a wife. Love itself grew timid. Little Cupid exchanged his bow and arrow for a book on arithmetic and studied money sums. The school girl who flew to Gretna Green in a green and yellow cabriolet beside a peach-faced youth—angrily pursued by an ancient father of thirty-eight—all this drifted into the pictures of the past, romantic but quite impossible.

Thus the unmarried woman, a quite distinct thing from the 'old maid' of ancient times, came into existence, and multiplied and increased till there were millions of her.

Then there rose up in our own time, or within call of it, a deliverer. It was the Awful Woman with the Spectacles, and the doctrine that she preached was Woman's Rights. She came as a new thing, a hatchet in her hand, breaking glass. But in reality she was no new thing at all, and had her lineal descent in history from age to age. The Romans knew her as a sybil and shuddered at her. The Middle Ages called her a witch and burnt her. The ancient law of England named her a scold and ducked her in a pond. But the men of the modern age, living indoors and losing something of their ruder fibre, grew afraid of her. The Awful Woman—meddlesome, vociferous, intrusive—came into her own.

Her softer sisters followed her. She became the leader of her sex. 'Things are all wrong,' she screamed, 'with the *status* of women.' Therein she was quite right. 'The remedy for it all,' she howled, 'is to make women "free," to give women the vote. When once women are "free" everything will be all right.' Therein the woman with the spectacles was, and is, utterly wrong.

The women's vote, when they get it, will leave women much as they were before.

Let it be admitted quite frankly that women are going to get the vote. Within a very short time all over the British Isles and North America in the States and the nine provinces of Canada woman suffrage will soon be an accomplished fact. It is a coming event which casts its shadow, or its illumination, in front of it. The woman's vote and total prohibition are two things that are moving across the map with gigantic strides. Whether they are good or bad things is another question. They are coming. As for the women's vote, it has largely come. And as for prohibition, it is going to be recorded as one of the results of the European War, foreseen by nobody. When the king of England decided that the way in which he could best help the country was by giving up drinking, the admission was fatal. It will stand as one of the landmarks of British history comparable only to such things as the signing of the Magna Carta by King John, or the serving out of rum and water instead of pure rum in the British Navy under George III.

So the women's vote and prohibition are coming. A few rare spots—such as Louisiana, and the City of New York—will remain and offer here and there a wet oasis in the desert of dry virtue. Even that cannot endure. Before many years are past, all over this continent women with a vote and men without a drink will stand looking at one another and wondering, what next?

For when the vote is reached the woman question will not be solved but only begun. In and of itself, a vote is nothing. It neither warms the skin nor fills the stomach. Very often the privilege of a vote confers nothing but the right to express one's opinion as to which of two crooks is the crookeder.

But after the women have obtained the vote the question is, what are they going to do with it? The answer is, nothing, or at any rate nothing that men would not do without them. Their only visible use of it will be to elect men into office. Fortunately for us all they will not elect women. Here and there perhaps at the outset, it will be done as the result of a sort of spite, a kind of sex antagonism bred by the controversy itself. But, speaking broadly, the women's vote will not be used to elect women to office. Women do not think enough of one another to do that. If they want a lawyer they consult a man, and those who can afford it have their clothes made by men, and their cooking done by a chef. As for their money, no woman would entrust that to another woman's keeping. They are far too wise for that.

So the woman's vote will not result in the setting up of female prime ministers and of parliaments in which the occupants of the treasury bench cast languishing eyes across at the flushed faces of the opposition. From the utter ruin involved in such an attempt at mixed government, the women themselves will save us. They will elect men. They may even pick some good ones. It is a nice question and will stand thinking about.

But what else, or what further can they do, by means of their vote and their representatives to 'emancipate' and 'liberate' their sex?

Many feminists would tell us at once that if women had the vote they would, first and foremost, throw everything open to women on the same terms as men. Whole speeches are made on this point, and a fine fury thrown into it, often very beautiful to behold.

The entire idea is a delusion. Practically all of the world's work is open to women now, wide open. *The only trouble is that they can't do it.* There is nothing to prevent a woman from managing a bank, or organising a company, or running a department store, or floating a merger, or building a railway—except the simple fact that she can't. Here and there an odd woman does such things, but she is only the exception that proves the rule. Such women are merely—and here I am speaking in the most decorous biological sense—'sports.' The ordinary woman cannot do the ordinary man's work. She never has and never will. The reasons why she can't are so many, that is, she '*can't*' in so many different ways, that it is not worth while to try to name them.

Here and there it is true there are things closed to woman, not by their own inability but by the law. This is a gross injustice. There is no defence for it. The province in which I live, for example, refuses to allow women to practice as lawyers. This is wrong. Women have just as good a right to fail at being lawyers as they have at anything else. But even if all these legal disabilities, where they exist, were removed (as they will be under a woman's vote) the difference to women at large will be infinitesimal. A few gifted 'sports' will earn a handsome livelihood, but the woman question in the larger sense will not move one inch nearer to solution.

The feminists, in fact, are haunted by the idea that it is possible for the average woman to have a life patterned after that of the ordinary man. They imagine her as having a career, a profession, a vocation something which will be her 'life work' just as selling coal is the life work of the coal merchant.

219

If this were so, the whole question would be solved. Women and men would become equal and independent. It is thus indeed that the feminist sees them, through the roseate mist created by imagination. Husband and wife appear as a couple of honourable partners who share a house together. Each is off to business in the morning. The husband is, let us say, a stock broker: the wife manufactures iron and steel. The wife is a Liberal, the husband a Conservative. At their dinner they have animated discussions over the tariff till it is time for them to go to their clubs.

These two impossible creatures haunt the brain of the feminist and disport them in the pages of the up-to-date novel.

The whole thing is mere fiction. It is quite impossible for women—the average and ordinary women—to go in for having a career. Nature has forbidden it. The average woman must necessarily have—I can only give the figures roughly—about three and a quarter children. She must replace in the population herself and her husband with something over to allow for the people who never marry and for the children that do not reach maturity. If she fails to do this the population comes to an end. Any scheme of social life must allow for those three and a quarter children and for the years of care that must be devoted to them. The vacuum cleaner can take the place of the housewife. It cannot replace the mother. No man ever said his prayers at the knees of a vacuum cleaner, or drew his first lessons in manliness and worth from the sweet old-fashioned stories that a vacuum cleaner told. Feminists of the enraged kind may talk as they will of the paid attendant and the expert baby-minder. Fiddlesticks! These things are a mere supplement, useful enough but as far away from the realities of motherhood as the vacuum cleaner itself. But the point is one that need not be laboured. Sensible people understand it as soon as said. With fools it is not worth while to argue.

But, it may be urged, there are, even as it is, a great many women who are working. The wages that they receive are extremely low. They are lower in most cases than the wages for the same, or similar work, done by men. Cannot the woman's vote at least remedy this?

Here is something that deserves thinking about and that is far more nearly within the realm of what is actual and possible than wild talk of equalizing and revolutionising the sexes.

It is quite true that women's work is underpaid. But this is only a part of a larger social injustice.

The case stands somewhat as follows: Women get low wages because low wages are all that they are worth. Taken by itself this is a brutal and misleading statement. What is meant is this. The rewards and punishments in the unequal and ill-adjusted world in which we live are most unfair. The price of anything—sugar, potatoes, labour, or anything else—varies according to the supply and demand: if many people want it and few can supply it the price goes up: if the contrary it goes down. If enough cabbages are brought to market they will not bring a cent a piece, no matter what it cost to raise them.

On these terms each of us sells his labour. The lucky ones, with some rare gift, or trained capacity, or some ability that by mere circumstance happens to be in a great demand, can sell high. If there were only one night plumber in a great city, and the water pipes in a dozen homes of a dozen millionaires should burst all at once, he might charge a fee like that of a consulting lawyer.

On the other hand the unlucky sellers whose numbers are greater than the demand—the mass of common labourers—get a mere pittance. To say that their wage represents all that they produce is to argue in a circle. It is the mere pious quietism with which the well-to-do man who is afraid to think boldly on social questions drugs his conscience to sleep.

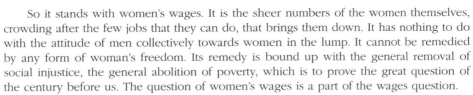

So it stands with women's wages. It is the sheer numbers of the women themselves, crowding after the few jobs that they can do, that brings them down. It has nothing to do with the attitude of men collectively towards women in the lump. It cannot be remedied by any form of woman's freedom. Its remedy is bound up with the general removal of social injustice, the general abolition of poverty, which is to prove the great question of the century before us. The question of women's wages is a part of the wages question.

To my thinking the whole idea of making women free and equal (politically) with men as a way of improving their *status*, starts from a wrong basis and proceeds in a wrong direction.

Women need not more freedom but less. Social policy should proceed from the fundamental truth that women are and must be dependent. It they cannot be looked after by an individual (a thing on which they took their chance in earlier days) they must be looked after by the State. To expect a woman, for example, if left by the death of her husband with young children without support to maintain herself by her own efforts, is the most absurd mockery of freedom ever devised. Earlier generations of mankind, for all that they lived in the jungle and wore cocoanut leaves, knew nothing of it. To turn a girl loose in the world to work for herself, when there is no work to be had, or none at a price that will support life, is a social crime.

I am not attempting to show in what way the principle of woman's dependence should be worked out in detail in legislation. Nothing short of a book could deal with it. All that the present essay attempts is the presentation of a point of view.

I have noticed that my clerical friends, on the rare occasions when they are privileged to preach to me, have a way of closing their sermons by 'leaving their congregations with a thought.' It is a good scheme. It keeps the congregation, let us hope, in a state of trembling eagerness for the next instalment.

With the readers of this essay I do the same. I leave them with the thought that perhaps in the modern age it is not the increased freedom of woman that is needed but the increased recognition of their dependence. Let the reader remain agonised over that till I write something else.

221

▲ Document 6: Women's Christian Temperance Union (WCTU) Excerpts

Excerpt 1

1880

[The WCTU's political effort to gain the vote] is not the clamor of ambition, ignorance, or frivolity trying to gain position, It is the prayer of earnest, thoughtful Christian women on behalf of their children and their children's children. It is in the interest of our homes, our divinely appointed place, to protect the home against the licensed evil (liquor) which is the enemy of the home, and also to aid in our efforts to advance God's Kingdom beyond the bounds of our homes.

It is only by legislation that the roots of great evils can be touched, and for want of the ballot we stand powerless in face of our most terrible foe, the legalized liquor traffic. The liquor sellers are not afraid of our conventions, but they are afraid of our ballots.

Source: Annual Report, WCTU Ontario, 1880, p. 10. Cited in Wendy Mitchinson, "The WCTU: 'For God, Home and Native Land': A Study in Nineteenth Century Feminism," in *A Not Unreasonable Claim: Women and Reform in Canada, 1880–1920s*, Linda Kealey, ed., (Toronto: The Women's Press, 1979).

Excerpt 2

1888

"[...] we are placed below all men, no matter how ignorant or wicked they may be, even the foreigner who perhaps can neither read or write, who by residing on Canadian soil one year and taking the oath of allegiance, though he may know nothing of our laws, nothing of the men who aspire to office, perhaps cannot speak one word of English, and yet he can say who shall be our legislators while we women are placed side by side with idiots, lunatics and children."

Source: From a 1888 speech by Maria Grant, Victoria WCTU, WCTU Yearbook, 1890, p. 52. Cited in Lyn Gough, *As Wise as Serpents: Five Women and an Organization that Changed British Columbia, 1883–1939* (Victoria: Swan Lake Publishing, 1988).

Excerpt 3

1900

Description of the WCTU float in the Victoria Day Parade, Victoria, B.C., 1900.

[The float was] [...] pure white, magnificently symbolizing the purity of aims actuating that great organization of Christian Women, who have become such a power in the world. In this triumphal "car" were fully forty children, representing the home upon which the labours of the parent organization exert their first and beneficent influence. In the hand of each child was a British flag, while on their dresses were pinned a maple leaf, a combination of which, although an incidental in the whole arrangement was of striking significance. A young lady was seated at each of the corners of the float, the first being engaged in tying a white ribbon around the world, the preserving commendable work of "Woman" for the past two decades. The second knelt before a golden cross representing the word "Christian", and "Temperance" was represented by a young lady grasping a goblet of pure water which she freely offered to all. There was a beautiful representation of the word "Union", in which the last young lady held in her hand a chain of 28 white links, representing the 28 departments of work under the control of the organization. The white ribbon tied into three links beautifully united the four representatives, making splendid allegory the words "Women's Christian Temperance Union". The Queen (the superintendent of the Band of Hope) sat in the centre of the float crowned by her pages who sat at her feet representing the loyal subjects. The monogram of the society was born on shields on each side and on the back of the float. Above all floated proudly the Union Jack [...] The children in the float sang appropriate hymns and the spectacle presented was beautiful indeed.

Source: *The Victoria Times,* May 25, 1900.

Excerpt 4

1911

[...] May they [young women members of the WCTU] be power in bringing about the day when the womanhood of our land shall be recognized to be citizens, and invested with the rights and privileges of citizens. To-day we stand aside and see the ignorant, debased, and even the lowest type of foreigner given the birthright denied to Ontario's pure and loyal womanhood, and we feel like crying out, "How long, O Lord, how long?" shall men of foreign birth and lowest intellect hold the balance of power in many of our elections, or votes on questions of temperance and moral reform? May every woman realize that this question of suffrage is one of intensest [sic] interest to her, and may every Union have a Franchise Department that will make itself felt in the community. Never say it is a question on which you are indifferent, it carries too momentous interests to be lightly set aside [...]

Source: Report of the corresponding secretary, Ontario Union, in report of the Annual Convention, Ontario WCTU, 1911. Ontario Archives F855.

223

▲ Document 7: The Door Steadily Opens (1910)

The Door Steadily Opens

● Who is in the room? What is the woman trying to do? What kind of feminist argument for woman's suffrage is expressed here?

Source: Grain Growers Guide, 21 September, 1910.

▲ Document 8: "A Nice Mess You Men Folks Make of Running a House" (date unknown)

● Aunt Suffragette to Bachelor Whitney: "A nice mess you men folks make of running a House. I've come to look after things a little." What does this cartoon suggest about women's abilities in the public sphere? What does it suggest about stereotypes about feminists in this period? Are these stereotypes similar to or different from today's stereotypes about feminists?

Source: Source and date unknown.

225

■ Article 1: 'When the Mother of the Race Is Free': Race, Reproduction, and Sexuality in First-Wave Feminism

Mariana Valverde

That the vast majority of English-speaking first-wave feminists were not only ethnocentric but often racist is by now widely acknowledged. It is also acknowledged that this led to the exclusion of native women, immigrant women, and women of colour from a movement which claimed to be based on gender, with negative political consequences reverberating into our own day.[1] Racist strategies were not confined to situations in which topics such as immigration were directly at issue: they were integral to the movement as a whole. An aspect of this pervasive racial politic that has seldom been examined is the way in which racist assumptions and strategies were implicated in the reproductive and sexual politics of the movement. Because women without children or husbands, as well as those in traditional family situations, justified their claims to political and social rights by reference to their quasi-maternal public and private roles, ideas about sexuality and reproduction had an impact on all women, regardless of individual situations. The purpose of this article is thus to undertake a critical analysis of the racial specificity of that key figure in our past, 'the mother of the race,' and of the discourses on sex and reproduction within which this symbolic figure was constructed.

While most first-wave feminists believed that women deserved political and social rights as a matter of equal justice, they also used utilitarian and organicist arguments that grounded women's cause in an affirmation of their role in biological and social reproduction. In this sense, the conceptualization of women's work in reproduction was key to feminism as a whole. While today feminists tend to analyse reproductive politics in terms of individual women's rights and collective gender oppression, at the turn of the [twentieth] century reproduction was generally seen, by feminists as well as anti-feminists,

as inextricable from racial and imperial politics.[2] Women did not merely have babies: they reproduced 'the race.' Women did not merely have just enough babies or too much sex: through their childbearing they either helped or hindered the forward march of (Anglo-Saxon) civilization.[3] Phrases such as 'race suicide,' or, in a feminist context, 'mothers of the race,' organize sexuality and reproduction under racial categories. Feminists challenged the sexist elements of the evolutionary theories of Darwin, Spencer, and other scientific and social Darwinists, but they did not, with one or two exceptions, question the fundamental racism of mainstream theories of social and biological evolution, and in many ways they reinforced racist theories of biological and social progress by adopting them for feminist purposes. [. . .]

Evolution and Race 'Degeneration'

> When the mother of the race is free, we shall have a better world, by the easy right of birth and by the calm, slow, friendly forces of social evolution.[4]
> —Charlotte Perkins Gilman

It was an article of faith among the Anglo-Saxon ruling classes in England, the United States, and English Canada that the ambiguous entity 'the race' was, at the turn of the [twentieth] century, in imminent peril of what was equally ambiguously known as 'degeneration.' Feminist intellectuals participated in the debate about who was responsible for degeneration and who was to take a leadership role in 'regeneration,' elaborating complex theories of women and evolution countering the misogynist assumptions of male-stream evolutionists. Feminist evolutionism, however, not only failed to question the racist presuppositions of evolutionary thought, but produced a profoundly racist form of feminism in which women of 'lower' races were excluded from the specifically Anglo-Saxon work of building a better world through the freeing of 'the mother of the race.'

Male evolutionary theorists used sexist assumptions about gender roles in their debates about the mechanisms of natural and sexual selection (mechanisms which, prior to the acceptance of Mendelian genetics in the second quarter of the twentieth century, occasioned much speculation). One of these assumptions was that women did not contribute to

Source: Abridged from *Gender Conflicts: New Essays in Women's History,* Franca Iacovetta and Marianne Valverde (eds.), (University of Toronto Press, 1992), pp. 34, 7–11, 13–26. © University of Toronto Press, 1992. Reprinted with permission of the publisher.

226

natural selection because conservatism was inscribed in their very eggs, while the male sperm was not only quick but 'progressive.' A popular book on heredity stated, in 1883, that 'the male element is the originating and the female the perpetuating factor; the ovum is conservative, the male cell progressive.'[5] The 'male element' was responsible for evolution, because, as it was generally believed, there was more genetic variability among men than among women. Women's bodies were mere storage bins, unable to generate new and potentially progressive mutations. Females were thus portrayed as in an analogous position to the so-called less evolved races—they were dragged along the evolutionary path rather than marching at the head. Darwin himself had drawn a parallel between women's role in evolution and that of 'lower' (that is, less evolved) races: 'It is generally admitted that with women the powers of intuition, of rapid perception, and perhaps of imitation, are more strongly marked than in man; but some, at least, of these faculties are characteristic of the lower races, and therefore of a past and lower state of civilization.'[6]

Women of all races, then, were the passive conservers of past biology. [. . .]

Feminist intellectuals challenged the misogynist consequences of evolutionary theories, but without questioning the overall shape of evolutionary argument or its reliance on racist categories. [. . .]

[Feminists argued that] European women were… more morally evolved than other women, and insofar as women's contribution to 'the race' was seen to lie in moral reform and education as well as in childbearing, then it was European women who led both their own race and the human race. [. . .]

White women's contribution to world progress was not limited to their private role in bringing up their children as good Christians and citizens. Some Protestant women participated in foreign missions with the idea that, as 'mothers of the race,' they had a particular role to play in evangelism, especially in Eastern societies, where sexual segregation, as Ruth Brouwer's study shows, was exaggerated by women missionaries in order to ensure a demand for their services.[7] Women missionaries envisioned Third World women as downtrodden victims of cultural practices more sexist than anything existing in Christian countries. A text written by a man but used by many women's missionary societies stated as a trite fact that 'we have been accustomed to speak of the disabilities of women in India,

her degraded position, seclusion and illiteracy. It is true that the women of India have been among the greatest obstacles to progress in that land.'[8] Third World women may have been mothers in their own right, and occasionally they were addressed as 'sisters': but the role assigned to them by the foreign female missionary was really that of devoted daughter, as a missionary poem entitled 'Work in the Zenana' vividly illustrates:

Do you see those dusky faces
Gazing dumbly to the West—
Those dark eyes, so long despairing,
Now aglow with hope's unrest?
They are looking, waiting, longing
For deliverance and light;
Shall we not make haste to help them,
Our poor sisters of the night?[9]

In this poem as well as in countless descriptions of widow-burning and other 'primitive' practices found in missionary and travel literature produced by women,[10] Third World women's own mothering is unacknowledged. Third World women are presented as either too victimized or too corrupt to qualify as real mothers. Rather, they need to be themselves mothered—by wiser Anglo-Saxon Protestant women.

While Canadian women saw their domestic and international mothering in primarily moral terms, some English and American feminists debated antifeminist male intellectuals on their own terrain. Claiming not just moral but even biological equality or superiority, they tried to turn the discourse of biological evolution to their own advantage. One of the most systematic attempts to build a feminist social theory by adapting evolutionism was made in the United States by Antoinette Brown Blackwell. She did not challenge the view that women's and men's bodies, and female and male social abilities, were totally different [...] She even admits that men have larger brains than women; but she argues that for every male superiority there is a corresponding inferiority. A chart in her 1875 book, *The Sexes throughout Nature*, shows that men are superior in size and strength, but inferior in 'endurance,' direct nurture,' and 'structure' (the latter meaning that women's physical structure is more complex than men's). As a whole, then, gender traits balance each other, so that although claiming equality for women would be biologically incorrect, the changes due to evolution

227

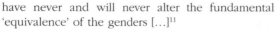
have never and will never alter the fundamental 'equivalence' of the genders [...][11]

The feminist critique of the gender bias of evolutionism was a fairly narrow one. The same antifeminist writers who deplored that college-educated women were not bearing children in large numbers usually also—and often more centrally—used the concept of racial degeneration to attack lawbreakers, the mentally ill, and people of colour. White feminists attacked only the gender bias of evolutionary and eugenic thought, leaving its basic framework intact. This was tantamount to creating a new hierarchy among women, with nefarious consequences for women who were stigmatized and oppressed not only through gender but also through their labelling as 'feeble-minded,' 'unfit,' or 'primitive.' Some women—of 'healthy' middle-class Protestant stock—claimed a spot higher up the evolutionary scale, but the majority of the world's women were in an ambiguous position between hapless victims of their own cultures and active agents of the dreaded process of 'degeneration.'

'Degeneration,' a term originally referring to the decay of nerve tissue, was in the 1880s and 1890s appropriated to refer to wider social processes of decadence and decay. As George Moss and Robert Nye have argued for Germany and for France, respectively, anxieties about urban crime and political upheavals were welded to fears about mad people, criminals, anarchists, and the racially 'other.'[12] There was in particular a fear about the reproductive excesses of 'degenerates,' whose numbers were perceived to be swelling at the expense of those of the more reproductively cautious middle classes.

Sometimes the term 'degeneration' was simply a synonym for 'biologically and morally inferior.' At other times, however, the term had a more specific meaning, and was used primarily to refer to Asian cultures. While Africans were regarded as 'primitive'—as not sufficiently evolved—Asians (most notably the Chinese, but also the vague category of 'Oriental') were seen as belonging to a civilization long past its prime, to a race that was overly evolved, decadent. When Roosevelt described the Chinese as 'an ancient and effete civilization,'[13] while Sir John A. Macdonald labelled them 'a mongrel race,'[14] they were saying that 'the Orient' (which since Marco Polo could hardly be regarded as primitive by Europeans) had had its glorious epoch in the long-ago past, but was now decayed and had lost its virility, just like Oscar Wilde.[15] The North American

panic about the role of Chinese men in so-called 'white slavery,' a panic in which feminists played a major role, was justified by reference to this general theory of racial evolution and degeneration. Black men were perceived as primitive, as unable to control their instincts; Chinese men, by contrast, were perceived as decadent perverts in need of opium and other drugs to fuel their flagging sexual energies. These mythological differences account for the varying modes of racist persecution: while black men were constantly suspected of impulsively raping or wanting to rape white women, Chinese men were suspected of hatching intelligent but devious plots, such as luring young white women into apparently harmless 'chop suey palaces' and opium dens, and from there into the 'white slave traffic.' The anti-Chinese and other racist agitations that took place in Canada in the 1920s were legitimized partly through sexual and reproductive myths.[16] Many of these myths were, unfortunately, not challenged but rather supported by Canadian maternal feminists.

Canadian Feminism and the Question of Racial Degeneration

A leading first-wave Canadian feminist, the magistrate and popular writer Emily Murphy, published an expose of the drug trade entitled *The Black Candle*, which raised the spectre of white women being lured to (perverted) sex through opium. This book, published in 1922, was part of a wider anti-Chinese campaign that was particularly virulent in western Canada. The book's sensationalist pictures of drugged individuals (mostly Chinese men) included a photo of a *black* man apparently in bed with a white woman. The connection between that photo and drug trafficking is not explained, but it is clear that white readers had their anti-black racism fuelled by the book, along with their anti-Chinese prejudices.[17] That Murphy's feminism was designed for white women only is equally clear, since, gender divisions aside, she believed that the 'Nordic' races were inherently superior: 'I think the proximity of the magnetic pole has something to do with the superiority of the Northmen. The best peoples of the world have come out of the north, and the longer they are away from the boreal regions in such proportion do they degenerate.'[18]

Murphy's sense of racial superiority was by no means unique. In the work and discourses of the largest grassroots feminist organization in turn-of-the century Canada, the Woman's Christian Temperance Union (WCTU), one can see that the white ribbon worn by female temperance activists was a symbol not only of the healthy pure milk they would substitute for alcohol but also of the kind of racial composition they favoured for Canada. The WCTU did not, at least in the 1880s and 1890s, exclude women of colour: in fact, there were a few local 'coloured unions' in southern Ontario (whose activities need to be researched by local historians). Nevertheless, the scant mentions of women of colour in the WCTU press are condescending and maternalistic, in keeping, with missionary societies' portrayal of 'natives' in Canada and 'heathens' abroad.

The WCTU was by no means impervious to the new, 'scientific' racism promoted in the later nineteenth century by anthropologists and writers on social evolution, and in the first few decades of the twentieth century by the eugenics movement. As early as 1889, the dominion WCTU had organized a separate department of 'Heredity and Hygiene' which evidenced some activity at least in Ontario and Quebec, where provincial department superintendents produced irregular reports. [. . .] While promoting addresses to local unions by physicians, the leaders of this department were obviously not interested in a strictly determinist view of genetics; such a view would have led to resignation and passivity, or possibly to joining the eugenic campaign for sterilization of the unfit. (The National Council of Women of Canada, a less evangelical and more state-oriented organization, put more work into investigating the 'problem' of 'feebleminded women.') The WCTU preferred to leave medical and scientific strategies to others; in its own work it promoted a cheerful validation of the ability of Christian mothers to overcome genetic obstacles.[19] In calling on women to 'uplift the race,' the WCTU was arguing that mothers (actual and symbolic) could do a great deal to shape both their children and the future of the nation—a contribution which would have been negated if a strict genetic determinist argument had been accepted. That women could shape the genetic pool was a necessary premise in the WCTU's argument for political rights: 'Governments rise and fall by votes, and until women have electoral value, their reforms, their labours, their dreams of an uplifted race, a purified country with 'protected' homes, will lack fulfillment.'[20]

The WCTU, however, did not directly challenge biological determinism. Some of their members, such as Mrs (Dr) Wickett, Wentworth County superintendent of heredity and hygiene, were firm believers in the reality of 'race suicide'. She warned that Canadian Anglo-Saxons were in peril of being overcome by the 'less moral' but more prolific French Canadians, 'and all because we women, for various reasons, shrink from the duty and the joy of motherhood.' As wealthy women pursued careers and other selfish goals, 'among the outcast, the feebleminded and the criminal, reproduction will still go on.'[21] It is clear that in Mrs Wickett's eyes not all actual mothers qualify as 'real' mothers. [. . .]

The strongest call for eugenic measures was heard at the Ontario WCTU 1911 convention, which passed a resolution asking the government to investigate the problem of 'the marriage of moral degenerates'; an editorial in the dominion journal followed this up with a call for compulsory pre-marital medical exams. Even this contribution to the panic about the prolific 'unfit' however, had a certain ambiguity absent from the work of Canada's scientific racists, in so far as the term 'moral degenerates' was not clearly race-based.[22]

WCTU leaders, then, were aware of developments in genetic and eugenic theory and occasionally endorsed these scientific discourses on race and heredity, but they seemed relatively lukewarm about them, in contrast with the enthusiasm for eugenics shown by Canada's physicians, especially public health doctors. This was not because of the quantity of racism present in eugenics: in 1906 the WCTU journal began to publish inflammatory articles on the vices of immigrant men and their relative worthlessness as voters compared with Anglo-Protestant women, and into the 1902s articles raising the spectre of Jewish control over the liquor trade used anti-Semitism to fuel the fire of prohibition.[23] If the WCTU did not prioritize its 'heredity and hygiene' departments, and even within those departments stressed hygiene over heredity, it was rather because of a conflict between scientific determinism and the WCTU's optimistic evangelism. A typical compromise is found in an editorial entitled 'The Law of Heredity.' [...] This editorial acknowledges that inherited *tendencies* are important, since it is clear that pipe-smoking fathers, for instance, often have sons who take up the cigarette habit. (Cigarettes were the second most important target of WCTU anger, after alcohol.) After painting a pessimistic picture of a father passing on his acquired tastes to his children, the writer quickly introduces a more prominent and brighter figure: a heroic mother who countered a hereditary taste for alcohol among her offspring through careful childrearing. The conclusion, that 'environ[m]ent in this instance prov[ed] itself stronger than heredity,' was in keeping with the WCTU's practical work in mothers' groups.[24] Shortly afterwards, an editorial on 'Patriotism' concluded that, despite Canada's mixed genetic inheritance, a pure and Christian nation could be produced through hard work, because 'heredity doesn't count for much in the presence of good environment.'[25]

This is not to say that the WCTU was necessarily less racist than the female and male advocates of science. The discourse of evangelism allowed ample opportunity to decry the wrongdoings of 'heathens' who insisted on selling ice-cream and candy on Sundays in defiance of Sunday observance laws, and of male 'aliens' who were allowed to vote although they did not own as much property as white Canadian women. In respect to Sunday observance, the WCTU thundered: 'Every decent Canadian citizen should make up his mind that foreign hosts that are sweeping down on this country shall obey its laws, or find it a decidedly uncomfortable abiding place';[26] and in respect to the vote, the spectre of hordes of 'Assyrians, Italians, and others' is invoked as the WCTU asks: 'Why should the ballot be given to these aliens, who own not a tithe of the property owned by Canadian women who are without the ballot?'[27]

The WCTU's form of racism, although influenced by the scientific discourse of eugenics, was primarily shaped by an older religious tradition labelling people of colour as 'heathens'—as culturally and morally inferior—and not necessarily as genetically inferior. The shopworn allegory equating Europe with light/morality and Africa with darkness/sin was the dominant trope utilized by WCTU women in their conceptualization of race and culture, as evidenced in the use of 'light' as a metaphor both of Christianity and of freedom in the missionary poem quoted above. The exercise suggested for young people by a British missionary textbook published in 1906 was one familiar to Canadian churchgoers of both sexes in this time period: 'Contrast the darkness of Africa with the light of civilization in England. Show how applicable the title "the Dark Continent" is to Africa, as inhabited by the Negro race, as the "Great Unknown Land" and as

the country that, more than any other, has been given over to the Works of Darkness.'[28]

The WCTU's approach to race, culture, and heredity was, in conclusion, somewhat contradictory, but it tended to rely on old missionary ideas about darkness and light more than on the new scientific racism. This evangelical perspective was less rigid and had the potential to view all people, whatever their race, as potentially useful members of society—as long as they followed Christian morality, identified by the WCTU with Canadian mores. Putting the missionary zeal at work, the WCTU proselytized among the black communities in Chatham and Windsor; in St Catharines there was a committee to recruit black women, and in Hamilton there was a 'coloured' local union.[29] The contradictory position in which black women found themselves in a movement characterized by metaphors of whiteness is clear in the following passage, in which a white WCTU member reports on a conversations she had with a black mother: 'With eyes flooded with tears, one [black] woman said, "Our children are precious and although their faces are black, yet we want their lives to be white. We do not know how to combat a terrible sin that is prevalent in our school."'[30] The black mother is not a 'real' mother, since she is quite unable to prevent her children from falling into sin. Again, here race marks the adult woman as a non-adult, as a tearful girl in need of guidance.

Although an evangelical perspective differs from a genetic-determinist one in not automatically precluding black women or children from being 'pure,' the fact that purity was equated with whiteness,[31] and hence indirectly with European culture, made it difficult if not impossible for Canada's women of colour to identify with the brand of feminism elaborated by the WCTU, and in general by the overwhelmingly Protestant women of first-wave Canadian feminism. First-wave feminism was envisaged as the freeing of 'the mothers of the race:' but not all adult women, even if they had children, qualified to mother either their own children or 'the race.'

The irony of the evangelical feminist theorization of race and culture may have been that, had they emphasized women's strictly biological role in reproduction, there might have arisen a potentially cross-racial sense of women's work in reproducing the human race. The heavy emphasis on women's role as moral teachers of children, however, privileged those women whose cultural and racial background marked them as more adult, more evolved, more moral, and better 'mothers of the race.' By proclaiming that 'the standard of morality is in the keeping of our women,'[52] the WCTU indirectly narrowed the scope of feminism to women from dominant cultures/races, since, as seen in the first section, women of colour were usually regarded as less moral and maternal and as more corrupted by their culture. Women of colour were largely invisible, making cameo appearances only as grateful recipients of the moral reform message, never as potential active agents of the feminist project.

Since the consequences of the racism and ethnocentrism of first-wave feminism are still being felt in the 1980s, it is important to understand not only that many suffragists were racist, but exactly how they were racist. As Canadians become aware of the shady past of the eugenics movement in Canada, it is important to note that racism was not the exclusive province of biological determinists. Different discourses (evangelism, science, tourism) produce specific varieties of racism performing distinct functions in the Canadian social imaginary. The WCTU employed both scientific and evangelical discourses on race in their conceptualization of 'the mother of the race,' but as a rule the latter predominated over the former. The feminist theorization of race, finally, was not only evident in their views on immigration but was also centrally implicated in their thoughts about what they saw as the core of women's gender identity and hence of the feminist project—biological and social reproduction.

Notes

Many thanks to my friends in the feminist history group, especially Lynne Marks, and also to Himani Bannerji.

1. Angela Davis, *Women, Race, and Class* (New York: Vintage 1983): Carol Bacchi, *Liberation Deferred? The Ideas of the English-Canadian Suffragists 1877–1918* (Toronto: University of Toronto Press 1983); Angus McLaren, *Our Own Master Race: The Eugenic Movement in English Canada* (Toronto: McClelland and Stewart 1990). My thanks to Angus McLaren for allowing me to read his book in manuscript.

2. Anna Davin, 'Imperialism and Motherhood,' *History Workshop no. 5* (1978):1–75; Lucy Bland, *Banishing the Beast: Feminism, Sex, and Morality 1885–1918*

(forthcoming 1992). My thanks to Lucy Bland for sharing her work with me.

3. See Hazel V. Carby, '"On the Threshold of Woman's Era": Lynching, Empire, and Sexuality in Black Feminist Theory,' in H.L. Gates, Jr, ed., *Race, Writing, and Difference* (Ithaca: Cornell, University Press 1986), 301–16; Jacquelyn Dowd Hall, 'The Mind That Burns Each Body: Women, Rape, and Racial Violence,' in A. Snitow et al., eds., *Powers of Desire* (New York: Monthly Review 1983). 328–49.

4. Charlotte Perkins Gilman, *Women and Economics 1898*; New York Harper & Row 1966), 340.

5. W.K. Brooks, The Law of Heredity, quoted in Cynthia E. Russett, *Sexual Science: The Victorian Construction of Womanhood* (Cambridge Mass.: Harvard University Press 1989), 94. See also Eveleen Richards, 'Darwin and the Descent of Woman,' in D. Olroy and I. Langham, eds., *The Wider Domain of Evolutionary Thought* (Dordrecht and London: Reidel 1983), 57–111.

6. Darwin, The Descent of Man, quoted in Flavia Alaya, 'Victorian Science and the "Genius" of Woman,' *Journal of the History of Ideas* 38:2 (1977): 261. This passage is also quoted by Richards, 'Darwin and the Descent of Woman'; Richards points out that Darwin explicitly rejected J. S. Mill's argument about the socialization of women in favour of biological determinism.

7. Ruth Compton Brouwer, *New Women for God: Canadian Presbyterian Women and India Missions, 1876–1914* (University of Toronto Press 1990), 97–101.

8. Canadian Council of the Missionary Education Movement, Canada's Share in World Tasks (np 1921), 90.

9. Quoted in 21 Ruth Compton Brouwer, *New Women for God: Canadian Presbyterian Women and India Missions, 1876–1914* (Toronto: University of Toronto Press 1990), New Women, 87.

10. A good example is Lucy Guinness, *Across India at the Dawn of the Twentieth Century* (London: Religious Tract Society 1902). The engravings in this book create a sharp contrast between the literally dark and frightening images of Indian 'superstitions' with the well-lit portraits of virtuous Anglo-Saxon women playing hymns at the piano.

11. Antoinette Brown Blackwell, *The Sexes throughout Nature* (New York: Putnam's Sons 1875), 58.

12. George Mosse, *Nationalism and Sexuality* (New York: Fertig 1985); Robert Nye, *Crime, Madness and Politics in Modern France* (Princeton: Princeton

University Press 1984); and Frank Mort, *Dangerous Sexualities: Medico-Moral Politics in England since 1800* (London: Routledge 1987).

13. Roosevelt quoted in Richard Hofstadter, *Social Darwinism in American Thought* (Philadelphia: University of Pennsylvania Press 1945), 155.

14. Macdonald quoted in Donald Avery, 'Canadian Immigration Policy and the 'Foreign Navvy' 1896–1914,' in M. Cross and G. Kealey, eds., *The Consolidation of Capitalism 1896–1929* (Toronto: McClelland and Stewart 1983), 52.

15. For an attack on Wilde, Nietzsche, impressionist painters, and other intellectual degenerates, see the influential work by Max Nordau, *Degeneration* (New York: Appleton 1895).

16. Mariana Valverde, *The Age of Light, Soap, and Water: Moral Reform in English Canada, 1885–1925* (Toronto: McClelland and Stewart 1991), chap. 4

17. Emily Murphy, *The Black Candle* (Toronto: Thomas Allen 1922). Murphy played a leading role in the passing of provincial laws allowing 'eugenic' sterilization. See Angus McLaren, 'The Creation of a Haven for 'Human Thoroughbreds': The Sterilization of the Feeble-Minded and the Mentally Ill in British Columbia,' *Canadian Historical Review* 67:2 (1986).

18. Emily Ferguson [Murphy], *Janey Canuck in the West* (Toronto: Cassel 1910), 38

19. See, for instance, the article 'Hygiene and Heredity' by the local superintendent of this department in Oxford County, Ontario, in *Canadian White Ribbon Tidings (CWRT)* 15 April 1907, 879–80; and the untitled article on hygiene by WCTU leader Dr Amelia Yeomans in ibid., 1 May 1907, 886.

20. 'Woman's Franchise,' *Woman's Journal*, Feb. 1892, 7

21. 'Race Suicide,' *CWRT*, 15 Aug. 1908, 1221

22. *CWRT*, 1 March 1911, 1861. See McLaren, *Our Own Master Race.*

23. An article reprinted from the Ford publication, *The Dearborn Independent*, entitled 'Aspects of Jewish Power,' claimed that governments were reluctant to implement prohibition because of the undue influence of Jews controlling the liquor traffic; *CWRT*, Dec. 1924, 256. My thanks to Lynne Marks for this reference.

24. Editorial, 'The Law of Heredity,' *CWRT*, 15 April 1907, 874–5.

25. *CWRT*, 15 June 1908, 1184.

26. Editorial, *CWRT*, 15 June 1907, 938.

27. *CWRT*, 15 March 1905, 228. Note the obviously literary reference to the ancient Assyrians, who are here typically mixed with the more plausible Italians. The WCTUwomen, like other reasonably educated Anglo-Saxons of their time, saw racial and ethnic groups through the filters of both learned and popular texts and images of 'the Orient.' The Thousand and One Nights imagery is seldom explicitly invoked, but it would have been employed by both writers and readers of such allegedly 'factual' pieces as the description of immigrant men's drunkenness in *CWRT*, 1 May 1905, 251–2.

28. Quoted in Lorimer, *Colour, Class and the Victorians*, 76. A similar racial hierarchy, expressed in somewhat more benevolent terms, is found in Canadian texts such as William T. Gunn, *His Dominion* (Canadian Council of the Missionary Education Movement 1917), and John R. Mott, *The Decisive Hour of Christian Missions* (New York: Student Volunteer Movement for Foreign Missions 1911). Mott's book was used as a textbook by Canadian Presbyterians.

29. A Miss Phelps, whose race is not indicated, was active among St. Catharines blacks in the early 1890s. See AO, WCTU Collection, minutes of Ontario WCTU for 1894 annual convention. The existence of a 'coloured union' in Hamilton has been pointed out to me by Lynne Marks, whose own work will shed further light on some of the issues raised in this paper. Lynne Marks, 'Religion and Leisure in Three Ontario Towns, 1880–1902 (PhD thesis in progress, Department of History, York University).

30. *CWRT*, 15 March 1904, 50. The 'terrible sin' is probably masturbation, vigorously denounced by Arthur W. Beall, the WCTU's paid sex hygiene educator for boys.

31. In its first issue, the *Woman's Journal* (July 1885, 1) declared: 'The distinctive badge of the WCTU Union is a white ribbon, denoting purity in the heart, in the home, in society.'

32. Ibid., Nov. 1885, 3.

■ Article 2: Rediscovering Our Foremothers Again: Racial Ideas of Canada's Early Feminists, 1885–1945

Janice Fiamengo

The full article includes a discussion of four early feminists: Sara Jeanette Duncan, Nellie McClung, Agnes Maule Machar, and Flora MacDonald Denison. This excerpt includes only Fiamengo's discussion of McClung.

The past decade witnessed a sea change in scholarship on the early Canadian women's movement as feminist scholars came to recognize (or were forced to see[1]) the racism of white feminist 'foremothers' and wrestled with its implications for critical practice. Whereas scholars in the 1970s and 1980s tended to celebrate the achievements of early suffrage and reform activists, often 'white-washing' (Smith, 1995: 93) their ideological impurities so that they might stand as icons of resistance, more recent scholarship by Carol Lee Bacchi, Angus McLaren, Mariana Valverde, and others has emphasized the imperialist and racist foundations of early Canadian 'feminism'.[2] Such work has been crucial in redressing the error and omissions of white feminist scholarship. Critical reassessment, however, has often shaded into outright dismissal, and in the process some of the complexities of early feminist discourse have been lost in the reductive conclusion that all first-wave feminist writing promoted a monolithic racism. Investigation of Canada's past is, as Veronica Strong-Boag has suggested, an ongoing and open-ended process of reexamination guided by current concerns and theoretical perspectives, and it is perhaps time to take another look at early feminist engagements with race. [. . .]

Recent developments in postcolonial and critical race theory, especially Homi Bhabha's emphasis on the ambivalence of colonial discourse, point the way to a nuanced reading of this complex archive.

Particularly important for my purpose is the recognition that ideological formations such as white supremacy are rarely stable or coherent (Hall, 2000: 15), John Comaroff (1977) has stressed that scholars studying colonialism's history do well to pay attention to its 'moments of incoherence and inchoateness, its internal contortions and complexities' (165), because they often provided the points where resistance came to be focused.[3] Race was always a contested subject in nineteenth- and early-twentieth-century Canada,[4] and competing understandings of race within Social Darwinism and evangelical Christianity made the term itself highly unstable.[5] Scientific debate raised unanswered questions about how profound racial differences were and whether they were primarily biological or cultural (Anderson, 1991: 40–4). Furthermore, early white feminism also contained competing claims. Although Darwinian beliefs about the superiority of the Anglo-Saxon race and evangelical emphasis on the civilizing mission often fit smoothly with white feminist self-positioning as 'mothers of the race' (Valverde, 1992: 1) and 'crusaders for Empire' (Carty, 1999:37), feminist rhetoric of equal justice for all complicated acceptance of racial hierarchy and made possible statements of empathy and solidarity with nonwhite people. [. . .]

Emphasizing the variety of white feminist conceptions of racial difference is useful because it demonstrates that white supremacy, undeniably the dominant ideology during this period,[6] was nonetheless not absolute in Canadian society before the Second World War. Recognizing the diverse positions that whites could occupy in those years is crucial in avoiding extremes of apology (everyone thought like that, so we can't judge them for it) or disavowal (they were all racist, so their work isn't worth reading carefully) in order to understand how well-intentioned individuals negotiated the racial and racist discourses of their day. In this discussion, I follow Kwame Anthony Appiah and David Theo Goldberg in distinguishing between racism and racialism, problematic as such a manoeuvre is. Because the writers considered in this paper used a racial discourse, it is necessary to attempt a distinction in order to notice where racialism does not lead to racism. Put simply, racialism is the belief that particular races share certain inherited traits (whether produced through culture or biology) that define 'a sort of racial essence' (Appiah, 1990: 5). Racism, in contrast, uses these traits

233

to create a physical, intellectual, and moral hierarchy. It is probably safe to say that, because racialism was a constituent part of the formation of Western subjects, few white persons could have escaped racialist thinking; as Kay Anderson (1991) has argued, by the end of the nineteenth century, most white Canadians believed 'that the mental, moral, and physical differences between "the races" were profound' (61). Just how they understood those differences in relation to their own whiteness is the question that I explore in the following pages. [. . .]

Prairie reformer Nellie McClung (1873–1951), was a tireless campaigner for temperance, women's suffrage, peace, democracy, and church reform, McClung was an effective leader who saw herself as a 'voice for the voiceless' (1935: 281).[7] Her vision of social reform developed at a time of expanding white settlement on the Prairies, racist fears about the immigration to Canada of 'foreigners', and developing international tensions between imperial powers. As previous references have indicated, Christianity and love for the British Empire (McClung once wrote 'My heart has been thrilled with what it is to be a citizen of the British empire'[8]) underpinned much of her thought: she was committed to Methodism (later the United Church) and to British justice even though a critic of their failings. Her commitment to justice was at least partly forged by the hard conditions of rural life, especially the poverty and government neglect that destroyed struggling white settler families on the Prairies. The two ideological strands of ethnocentrism and a commitment to democratic citizenship produce a complex racial ideology in which racism and antiracism are difficult to separate. Arun Mukherjee (1995) and, to a lesser extent, Mariana Valverde (1991) have highlighted the racist and imperialist assumptions in McClung's fiction and essays, showing how belief in Christian mission work led McClung to dismiss the civilizations of non-Christian peoples and to mobilize racist stereotypes, particularly her association of Chinese men and opium. Valverde notes that 'the very origins, as well as the form of McClung's feminism are shaped by ethnocentric ideas' (120). Mukherjee's discussion indicates the difficulty of defining McClung's beliefs about race as Mukherjee shows, nearly every 'politically incorrect' (20) statement can be countered with a more progressive one. Here I will concentrate on some of McClung's uncollected writings in order to consider lesser known aspects of her thought and

activism. These writings indicate that McClung struggled with the meaning of race throughout her life and showed herself capable of rethinking racist assumptions when the occasion demanded it; her sympathetic interest in racial Others highlights the progressiveness of her feminism even while she continued to rely on racial and racist discourses to frame her arguments.

The paradoxes of Christian commitment are everywhere in McClung's writing. Her belief in the ideals of Christian civilization limited her apprehension of the damage that settlement and government policies inflicted on Native peoples, yet that very commitment to Christian justice also galvanized some empathy for Native struggles. In *Clearing in the West* (1935), for example, McClung recounts how, as a child, she defended Métis and Indian rights to land and autonomy during the Riel Rebellion, arguing with her parents that the Métis had 'a grievance, a real one' (168). At the same time, her adult conception of Canada as a new country ('a great blank book' with 'no precedents to guide us' [1915:96]) dismissed the First Nations entirely. A scene from *The Stream Runs Fast* (1945) demonstrates McClung's willingness to extend membership in the British imperial family to a Native father whose son is fighting in the First World War; McClung recognizes that 'He was one of us— and one who had made a big contribution. We were all citizens of the British Empire; we were all of the great family of the Next-of-Kin' (158). Family membership in the empire is clearly negotiated on white terms in this scene. Equal citizenship meant assimilation to Britishness, an inclusive alternative to the early-twentieth-century assertion of Native biological inferiority. At the same time, McClung often characterized Native peoples using more or less benign racial stereotypes invoking inherent difference. For example, she records how she was prevented from being lost in London's streets while attending a Methodist conference by a young Native woman (also attending the conference) who had the 'blessed native instinct' for direction (1945: 224): in linking this young woman's ability to negotiate direction with a wild bird's homing instinct, she betrays a tendency to equate Native peoples with God's lesser creatures. The autobiography in which these passages occur was the last book that McClung published, making it difficult to argue, as one might be tempted, toward antiracism as she grew older. However, evidence from her papers reveals that she participated actively in antiracist causes toward the end of her life, most notably in defence of Japanese Canadians before and during the Second World War when she was nearing seventy years of age. McClung was more concerned about racial injustice than many of her white feminist contemporaries, and her belief in the God-given common humanity of all people anchored the liberating potential of her Social Gospel activism.

McClung was unusual in her stress on a multiracial vision of the country at a time when most whites took for granted that Canada would always be a white nation. At the London Methodist meeting cited above, she reacted with anger when southern American delegates refused to sit with the 'coloured people' of the African Methodist Church. 'We were seated near the malcontents, and quickly changed seats with them, wondering if they would carry their race prejudices to heaven,' she records sarcastically, reflecting that 'my soul was scorched with shame for my race' (1945: 221). From the early years of her career to the end of her life, McClung articulated a vision of Canada based on equal justice for all. 'One of my most glorious dreams,' she wrote famously for the Ottawa *Citizen* in 1915, 'is that Canada shall be known as the land of the fair deal.'[9] When she defined that phrase for In *Times like These* (1915), she listed racial justice as her first criterion of fairness: 'Canada should be a place where every race, colour and creed will be given exactly the same chance' (97). Living in a country that blended many peoples, Canadians, she believed, had an unprecedented opportunity for interracial understanding.[10] Too often, 'however, we are a pretty self-centred race, we Canadians', she lamented.[11] During the Second World War, McClung held on to the hope that a new world order might emerge from the fight against Hitler, dreaming of a regenerated society in which it would be recognized that 'all men are equal in God's sight, irrespective of race or colour. There are no superior races.'[12] The confusing elasticity of her use of the term *race* (which is sometimes synonymous with ethnicity, sometimes linked with colour, and at other times identified with nation) makes precise analysis of her meaning difficult but also seems to have enabled McClung to think flexibly about Canadian national identity. Her faith that all peoples could find a 'spiritual cement' to bind them together in communities of fellowship helped her to avoid the racist extremes of some fellow reformers.

As Mukherjee (1995) has stressed, such idealistic statements need to be considered in the context of McClung's racist and imperialist culture and weighed against her complicity with or opposition to the racism that McClung encountered in her daily life. For example, Mukherjee notes that McClung supported overseas Christian mission work, campaigned for women's suffrage with American racists, and wrote nothing about racial inequality when she travelled through the southern United States, 'Would it not seem interesting to know how McClung responded to the Jim Crow south and the racist feminism of the southern suffragists?' she asks (22). Indeed, while some of Mukherjee's queries about the extent to which McClung challenged friends and colleagues (e.g., Emily Murphy), on their racism may never be definitively answered, Mukherjee signals important future directions for work on McClung. Uncollected newspaper articles in McClung's personal papers give evidence of some of her more decisive and public antiracist stands and answer a few of Mukherjee's questions about McClung's antiracist practice.

Unlike some white suffragists, who voiced bitterness that they were denied the vote, while it was granted to ignorant men such as 'untutored Ruthenians and Galicians' [Ukrainians] (Bacchi, 1983: 53), McClung largely refused such postures of wounded racial superiority. In 1915, on the suffrage trail, she managed to avoid being drawn into racist arguments. The *Winnipeg Free Press* reported that McClung 'spoke passionately in defence of the foreign women' on the question of suffrage. 'Let it be remembered,' the newspaper quoted McClung, 'that there are far more foreign men that women in the county and there is no objection to their voting. It has even been urged that the vote should be taken from these foreign men because corrupt politicians have bought their votes. I wouldn't take away their vote, but I would remove their ignorance. There is no menace to be feared from the foreign women.'[13] In this instance, McClung does not refute the charge that 'foreign' men, mainly, it seems, Eastern and Southern Europeans, were particularly vulnerable to corrupt voting.[14] Her assumption that foreigners probably did need education betrays the paternalistic racialism of her thinking, but she does not call for exclusions, preferring a rhetoric of inclusivity and possibility. A number of newspaper articles from this period report McClung's '[s]tirring defence of foreign women'[15]

235

during her wartime suffrage campaigns. In 1917, McClung seemed to contradict her earlier position by calling for the vote to be given to Canadian and English-born women first, as a special war measure however, she withdrew this suggestion and publicly acknowledged her error when Francis Marion Beynon criticized the idea in the pages of the *Grain Growers' Guide*.[16] While McClung likely believes that not all people understood democracy as well as the British, she rarely allowed that thinking to limit her commitment to voting rights for all citizens.

Angus McLaren has noted that racist and anti-immigrant mobilizing reached a peak during the Depression years, when economic hardship and the threat to public order caused by hordes of unemployed people exacerbated the racism of many Canadian officials, politicians, and business leaders. McClung's public statements during the 1930s on behalf of the Doukhobors in British Columbia, European Jews, and Chinese and Japanese Canadians reveal resistance to the fear-mongering of public officials and community elders, who frequently warned of racial threats to Canadians by unassimilable aliens (Valverde, 1991: 104–28). In fact, McClung was one of the few commentators to argue that the danger lay not in racial contamination by these others but in Canada's failure to fulfill its Christian obligation to people seeking refuge. Commenting on Canada's humanitarian obligation to accept Jews fleeing Hitler, she charged that 'in spite of our broad territory Canada has not been generous with the 'stranger at our gates' and insisted that 'unless we adopt a new policy […] the verdict of history will be that the Canadian people were both short-sighted and hard of heart.'[17] She chided 'narrow racial groups of great political power', clearly naming and deploring the racism of whites.[18] 'Noted Author Bursts Bomb at City Rally' was the title of a Vancouver newspaper report for 10 October 1935, when McClung addressed a Liberal Party rally at the Empress Theatre in Vancouver to disagree explicitly with the Liberal MP's opposition to Oriental franchise. 'In my opinion every class and every creed of people should have equal rights,' McClung was reported to have said in explanation of her disagreement with Ian Mackenzie, Liberal MP for Vancouver Centre.[19] Two years later, when Japanese military aggression in China, combined with economic tensions at home, seemed to validate anti-Japanese discourse, McClung was urging Victoria

residents to maintain justice in their dealings with the local Japanese Canadian population. 'It was a time,' the *Colonist* reported McClung as saying on 9 October 1937, 'to show kindness and understanding and not blame those who are powerless to help what is being done by the militia party.'[20] These statements reveal that, although her conception of the nation was ethnocentric in its celebration of British heritage, faith in British justice led her to oppose racial exclusivity and persecution.

After the bombing of Pearl Harbor by the Japanese on 7 December 1941, McClung's insistence on fairness was even more unusual and difficult to maintain.[21] Although a few individuals and newspaper editors counselled calm and consideration for the difficult position of Japanese Canadians, 'those voices advocating either a "tolerant" or even a "moderate" attitude were quickly submerged in the wave of anti-Japanese protest' (Adachi, 1976: 201). At this time, McClung wrote some of her most notable newspaper columns on Canadian race relations, revealing a commitment to justice in troubled times.[22] Her providential view of history enabled her to understand the so-called problem of Japanese Canadians in British Columbia as an opportunity for Canadians to test their commitment to justice. 'We have in this province of British Columbia 23,000 Japanese people, many of them natives of Canada and some of the second generation.' she wrote on 3 January 1942[23]

> We have an opportunity now of showing them that we do respect human rights and that democracy has a wide enough framework to give peace and security to all people of goodwill irrespective of race or colour. I believe that all precautions must be taken at this time, but we must not sink into Hitler's ways of persecution. We must not punish innocent people. The Canadian Japanese are not to blame for the treacherous attack on Pearl Harbor, nor for the other misdeed of their misled people.

McClung went on to ask readers to remember that Canada's treatment of its citizens would be judged by history. 'A great opportunity is ours today to show a kindly spirit of watchful tolerance. Let us guard well, not only our bridges and our plants, but our good name for fair dealing. We must have precautions, but let us think of our Japanese, as human beings, not as enemy aliens.' 'Our Japanese' has a ring of paternalism but also stresses Japanese Canadian inclusion in the national family. The call to think outside racial categories and to see the full humanity of Japanese Canadians indicates the extent to which McClung could mobilize patriotic myth ('our good name for fair dealing') to oppose xenophobia. Given that, as a resident of Victoria, she believed herself to be in imminent danger of an air attack, this was no small achievement. Two weeks later, McClung returned to her theme of Canada's moral obligations. 'Last week I made a plea for the individual Japanese, that they should be treated fairly,' she reminded readers,

> [...] and I know these sentiments will be challenged, for this is a time of excitement, when prejudices run riot. But we must remember we are a Christian people. On New Year's Day we confessed our sins and asked God to guide us. If we are to merit that guidance we must not allow hate centers to develop here. [. . .] Let us, the free people, do all in our power to keep open the gates of mercy, no matter what comes. A great purpose and design for humanity is being worked out in the world now before our eyes and we must not blot our part of the pattern.[24]

McClung's insistence that God's hand was guiding history and that Canadians had a vital role to play in its unfolding show her use of a Christian narrative of good warring against evil that made the protection of racialized victims a cornerstone of Canada's wartime mandate.

Mary Hallett and Marilyn Davis, authors of McClung's biography, have suggested that outsight criticism of government policy would have been censored at this time. It certainly seems that McClung was under orders from her editor to avoid 'political' matters. In one article, she prefaced a few remarks on conscription with the injunction 'now don't be nervous, Mr Editor, I am not dealing with it in a political way.'[25] Whatever the reason, there is no record that McClung protested the internment of Japanese Canadians, which occurred shortly after these columns were published; the announcement of partial evacuation occurred on 14 January 1942; total evacuation of all persons of Japanese ancestry

was announced on 26 February 1942. Rather than focusing on the internment, McClung turned her sights to the future, imagining the better Canada that should be built after the war, hoping that the Oriental franchise would be implemented immediately once the war ended as evidence that Canada would finally be 'through with racial antipathies' and characterizing the war as 'a war against all racial superiorities'.[26] Even to McClung, such statements must have seemed optimistic. As the war dragged on, many of her columns were devoted to strengthening morale: she urged all-out support for the war effort, with boosterish articles on conserving sugar, sharing food, making sacrifices, and salvaging useful materials. She continued to devote a good deal of print space to intemperance, which she occasionally targeted as one of the causes of the war. Her attention to wartime racial injustice was, in the end, weakened by her belief that God was on the Allies' side and that Canadians' moral energies should be fully concentrated on the war effort. Nonetheless, her articles on fair treatment for Japanese Canadians reveal that, unlike the majority of white Canadians in Western Canada, McClung was not swayed by wartime propaganda. Ultimately, her emphasis on Canada as a nation of immigrants and her belief in Christian democracy meant that she did not appreciate the unique situation of Native peoples; she promoted assimilation to British civilization as the answer to racial conflict. Nevertheless, her sense of her role in an unfolding Christian narrative often prompted concern for racial justice and explicit antiracism work. [. . .]

Constance Backhouse ends her study of the legal history of racism in Canada by noting that cases of resistance demonstrate that 'Those who espoused philosophies of white supremacy were not speaking in a moral vacuum' (278). Although racism was the dominant ideology in the period under consideration, it was not simply the air that early Canadians breathed, as is often asserted. Feminist reformers, like others, made choices from among a range of discourses, some of which enabled antihegemonic thinking about race. [...] [In addition to the writings of Agnes Maule Machar and Flora MacDonald Denison] McClung's [concept of the] fair deal, [...] seems to have favoured the development of inclusive understandings of race that saw difference as at least potentially an opportunity rather than a threat. [. . .] Important work remains to be done to contextualize and analyse the ideologies that frequently limited, but occasionally furthered, a racially inclusive white feminist vision in the early years of the Canadian women's movement.

Notes

1. Women of colour and Native women in Canada have been primarily responsible for prodding white feminists into this realization. As Donna Haraway has noted, to say that white women 'discovered' or 'came to 'realize' their complicity in racism really means that they 'were forced kicking and screaming to notice it' (157)! For a good example of such prodding, see Mukherjee, 'Right', on white feminist silence about Charlotte Perkins Gilman's racism.

2. McLaren see Valverde (1991), Perry (2001), Newman (1999), Gerson (1997), and Devereux (2000).

3. For an overview of scholarly interest in the tensions and contradictions of empire, see Stoler and Cooper (1997).

4. For an overview of Canadian thinking about race and national identity, particularly the relationship between Aboriginal peoples and Euro-Canadians, see Strong-Boag and Gerson, 2000: 19–32.

5. The instability of race in the late nineteenth century was exacerbated because it could mean 'different things simultaneously' (Valverde, 1992: 5). As Louise Michele Newman has suggested in her analysis of early American feminism, race often 'functioned as an absent presence' in white women's suffrage arguments (57). I deliberately keep the waters muddy by following the usage of my writers, evoking 'race' when referring to any people defined as foreign, non-Anglo-Saxon, or nonwhite in situations where power and exclusion are at issue. I intend such conceptual muddiness to signal my disbelief in any immutable or absolute basis for racial distinction following recent theorists in understanding race not as a biological given but as a historically inflected ideal produced through representation and constantly being remade in particular discursive situations. For an overview of central issues in race thinking, see Cornell and Hartmann, 1998: 15–38; for a history of race thinking, see Anderson, 1991: 15–38; for a history of race thinking, see Cornell and Hartmann, 1998: 15–38; for a history of race thinking, see Anderson, 1991: 38–44, and Bernasconl and Lott, 2000: vii–xviii.

6. See Backhouse for a study of 'the central role of the Canadian legal system in the establishment and enforcement of racial inequality' (15). For a discussion of moves to prevent the immigration of 'inferior' races, including Slavs, Jews, Southern Europeans, Orientals, and Blacks, see McLaren, 1990: 46–67.

7. For a biography that discusses McClung's activism, see Hallett and Davis (1993); for a 'scrapbook' with extensive quotations, see Savage (1979). For an analysis of McClung's fiction from a feminist perspective, see Warne (1993).

8. Unidentified clipping, Nellie McClung Papers, PABC, vol. 17.

9. Untitled clipping, Nellie McClung Papers, PABC, vol. 17.

10. Untitled Clipping, *Regina Star*, 9 November 1937, Nellie McClung Papers, PABC Vol. 17.

11. 'How Should We Celebrate July 1?" *Western Home Monthly*, July 1927, Nellie McClung papers, PABC, vol. 15.

12. 'What Holds the British Empire Together'. Unidentified Clipping: Nellie McClung Papers, PABC, vol. 14.

13. Unidentified Clipping, Nellie McClung papers, PABC, vol. 17.

14. But McClung also recorded how 'in our blind egotism we class our foreign people as ignorant people, if they do not know our ways and our language. They may know many other languages, but it they have not yet mastered ours they are poor, ignorant *foreigners*, we Anglo-Saxon people have a decided sense of our own superiority, and we feel sure that our skin is exactly the right color' (1915: 53).

15. Undated clipping, Nellie McClung Papers, PABC, vol. 17.

16. Untitled clipping, *Grain Growers'* Guide, 24 January 1917, Nellie McClung Papers, PABC, vol. 17.

17. Unidentified clipping, Nellie McClung Papers, PABC; vol. 17.

18. For a discussion of Canada's protracted unwillingness to offer refuge to European Jews, see Abella and Trooper (1982).

19. Unidentified clipping, Nellie McClung Papers, PABC vol. 17. In the federal election campaign of 1935, the Liberals opposed the newly created CCF's stand on enfranchising Chinese and Japanese Canadians, vowing to defend the white electorate.

20. 'Urges Women to Consider Local Japanese People', *Victoria Colonist*, 9 October 1937, Nellie McClung Papers, PABC vol 17.

21. Within a week of the attack, demands were being made across British Colombia that all people of

238

Japanese heritage be interned, and soon newspaper editorials began to support the majority public opinion, See Adachl, 1976: 201–2.

22. Mary Hallett and Marilyn Davis (1993: 274–6) also discuss these columns.

23. 'What Did We Learn in 1941?' Unidentified clipping, 3 January 1942, Nellie McClung Papers, PABC, vol. 52.

24. Unidentified clipping, 17 January 1942, Nellie McClung Papers, PABC, vol. 52

25. Unidentified Clipping, 21 February 1942, Nellie McClung Papers, PABC, vol. 52.

26. 'That We May Not Forget,' *Winnipeg Free Press*, 14 November 1942, Nellie McClung Papers, PABC, vol. 53.

References

Abella, Irving, and Harold Trooper, 1982. *None is Too Many: Canada and the Jews of Europe, 1933–1948*. Toronto: Lester.

Adachi, Ken. 1976. *The Enemy That Never Was*. Toronto: McClelland.

Anderson, Kay J. 1991. *Vancouver's Chinatown: Racial Discourse in Canada, 1875–1980*. Montreal: McGill-Queen's University Press.

Appiah, Kwame Anthony. 1990. 'Racisms', pp. 3–17 in *Anatomy of Racism*, D. Goldberg, ed. Minneapolis: U of Minnesota Press.

Bacchi, Carol Lee. 1983. *Liberation Deferred? The Ideas of the English-Canadian Suffragists, 1877–1918*. Toronto: University of Toronto Press.

Backhouse, Constance. 1999. Colour-Coded: *A Legal History of Racism in Canada, 1990–1950*. Toronto: University of Toronto Press.

Bernasconl, Robert, and Tommy L. Lott, eds, 2000. *The Idea of Race*. Indianapolis: Hackett.

Bhabha, Homi. 1997. 'Of Mimicry and Man: The Ambivalence of Colonial Discourse', pp. 152–60, in *Tensions of Empire: Colonial Cultures in the Bourgeois World*, F. Cooper and A.L. Stoler, eds. Berkeley: University of California Press.

Carty, Linda. 1999. 'The Discourse of Empire and the Social Construction of, Gender', pp. 35–47 in *Scratching the Surface: Canadian Anti-Racist Feminist Thought*, Enakshi Dua and Angela Robertson, eds. Toronto: Women's Press.

Comaroff, John L. 1997. 'Images of Empire, Contests of Conscience: Models of Colonial Domination in South Africa', pp. 163–97 in *Tensions of Empire:*

Colonial Cultures in the Bourgeois World, F. Cooper and A.L. Stoler, eds. Berkeley: University of California Press.

Cook, Ramsay. 1985. *The Regenerators: Social Criticism in Late Victorian English Canada*. Toronto: University of Toronto Press.

Cooper, Frederick, and Ann Laura Stoler, eds. 1997. *Tensions of Empire: Colonial Cultures in the Bourgeois World*. Berkeley: University of California Press.

Cornell, Stephen, and Douglas Hartmann. 1998. *Ethnicity and Race: Making Identities in a Changing World*. Thousand Oaks, CA; Pine Forge.

Devereux, Cecily. 'Writing with a "Definite Purpose": L.M. Montgomery, Nellie L. McClung, and the Politics of Imperial Motherhood in Fiction for Children', *Canadian Children's Literature* 26:3 (2000): 6–22.

Gerson, Carole. 'Nobler Savages: Representations of Native Women in the Writings of Susanna Moodie and Catharine Parr Traill', *Journal of Canadian Studies* 32.2 (1997): 5–21.

Goldberg, David Theo, ed. 1990. *Anatomy of Racism*. Minneapolis: University of Minnesota press.

Hall, Catherine. 2000. 'Introduction: Thinking the Post-colonial, Thinking the Empire', pp. 1–33 in *Cultures of Empire: A Reader. Catherine Hall*, ed. New York: Routledge.

Hallet, Mary, and Marilyn Davis. 1993. *Firing the Heather: The Life and Times of Nellie McClung*, Saskatoon; Fifth House.

Haraway, Donna J. 1991. *Simians, Cyborgs, and Women: The Reinvention of Nature,* New York: Routledge.

McClung, Nellie. [1915] 1972. *In Times like These*. Toronto: University of Toronto Press.

——. 1935. *Clearing in the West*. Toronto: Allen.

——. 1945. *The Stream Runs Fast*. Toronto: Allen.

McLaren, Angus. 1990. *Our Own Master Race: Eugenics in Canada, 1885–1945*. Toronto: McClelland & Stewart.

Mukherjee, Arun P. 'In a Class of Her Own', *Literary Review of Canada* (July–August 1995); 20–3.

——. 1993. '"Right our [sic] of 'Herstory': Racism in Charlotte Perkins Gilman's Heriand and Feminist Literary Theory'. pp. 159–75 in *Returning the Gaze: Essays on Racism, Feminism, and Politics, Hlmani Bannerji,* ed. Toronto: Sister Vision.

Newman, Louise Michele. 1999. *White Women's Rights*: *The Racial Origins of Feminism in the United States*. New York: Oxford University Press.

Perry, Adele, 2001. *On the Edge of Empire: Gender, Race,*

239

and the Making of British Columbia, 1849–1871. Toronto: University of Toronto Press.

Savage, Candace. 1979. *Our Nell: A Scrapbook Biography of Nellie L. McClung*. Saskatoon: Western Producer Prairie.

Smith, Susan L. 'Whitewashing Womanhood: The Politics of Race in Writing Women's History', *Canadian Review of Comparative Literature* 22.1 (1995):93–103.

Staslulis, Daiva, and Nira Yuval-Davis. 1995. 'Introduction: Beyond Dichotomies—Gender, Race, Ethnicity and Class in Settler Societies', pp. 1–37 *Unsettling Settler Societies: Articulations of Gender, Race, Ethnicity, and Class*, Dalva Staslulis and Nira Yuval-Davis eds. London: Sage.

Stoler, Ann Lama, and Frederick Cooper. 1997. 'Between Metropole and Colony: Rethinking a Research Agenda', pp. 1–56 in *Tensions of Empire: Colonial Cultures in the Bourgeois World*, F. Cooper and A.L. Stoier, eds. Berkeley: University of California Press.

Strong-Boag, Veronica. 'Contested Space: The Politics of Canadian Memory', *Journal of the Canadian Historical Association* 5 (1994): 3–18.

Strong-Boag, Veronica, and Carole Gerson. 2000. *Paddling Her Own Canoe: The Times and Texts of Pauline Johnson (Tekahionwake)*. Toronto: University of Toronto Press.

Valverde, Mariana. 1991. *The Age of Light, Soap, and Water: Moral Reform in English Canada*, 1885–1925. Toronto: McClelland & Stewart.

——, 1992. '"When the Mother of the Race is Free": Race, Reproduction, and Sexuality in First-Wave Feminism', pp. 3–26 in *Gender Conflicts: New Essays in Women's History*, Franca Iacovetta and Mariana Valverde, eds. Toronto: University of Toronto Press.

Warne, Randl R. 1993, Literature as Pulpit: *The Christian Social Activism of Nellie McClung*. Waterloo: Wilfrid Laurier University Press.

240

THE GREAT WAR

Leaders, Followers, and Record-Keepers

P. E. Bryden
University of Victoria

THE GREAT WAR: LEADERS, FOLLOWERS, AND RECORD-KEEPERS

Introduction by P.E. Bryden

243

● INTRODUCTION

P. E. Bryden

The Canadian nation was not yet 50 years old when war broke out in Europe in 1914. The Great War, as it was known until an even greater war began 25 years later, affected Canadians of all walks of life. More than 60,000 lost their lives, and more than half a million served in the armed forces; those who remained in Canada argued over who should fight, but they also bought war bonds, rationed food, and contributed to an economy turned over almost entirely to the prosecution of the war effort. Like all wars, there were winners and losers; there were also, like in all wars, those who led and those who followed. In Canada, where reputations were still being forged in the early decades of the twentieth century, considerable thought has gone into determining when and where Canada led, and when and how Canada followed. Those people who remember the Great War, and those who kept a record of what happened so we could all remember, have played an important role in assessing the role of leaders, and the role of followers, and in determining which of those role Canadians played.

There is little question that Canada entered the war as a follower of sorts: hostilities began at the end of July 1914 with Austria-Hungary's declaration of war on Serbia, leading to Germany's declaration of war on Russia and France, and then Britain's entry into the field on 4 August. As a colony of Britain, Canada was automatically at war on 4 August as well, following the mother country into a battle over the division of Europe. But even if the war was far away, Canadians were enthusiastic about following Britain into the fray: the boom of the first decade of the twentieth century had given way to slumping markets, and a distant war seemed to be just the thing to jump-start the economy.

Robert Borden was Canada's wartime leader, a Conservative prime minister who had been in power since 1911 when he defeated Wilfrid Laurier by advocating a protectionist economic policy and making common cause with some of the nationalist politicians in Quebec. Borden was a great supporter of the British imperial connection, a quality he emphasized in 1911 in contrast to Laurier's advocacy of free trade and therefore more continentalist outlook. It comes as no surprise, then, that he enthusiastically joined the fight against Germany in the summer of 1914. His thoughts in the early months of war are apparent in the selection from his memoirs that is included in the documents. But there were limits to the extent to which Borden would blindly follow the British, and as war dragged on for the next four years, he had a number of opportunities to press for an increasing leadership role for Canada abroad, and a number of opportunities to test his own leadership at home. The two roles were intimately linked.

Although Canadians had entered war reasonably enthusiastically, they did so largely because it was assumed that hostilities would not last particularly long; with each passing year that war raged, fewer and fewer Canadians offered to serve in the armed forces. Rather than volunteering to enlist, many people argued that they were already making a contribution at home or that Canadians should stop shedding their blood over foreign territory. Farmers and their sons were choosing to contribute to the war effort by producing foodstuff; factories had made the transition to producing shells and other products necessary to the war effort, and therefore factory workers were finding both steady employment and a regular paycheque at home without needing to fight overseas; most importantly, French Canadians were beginning to question the utility of Canadians participating in a foreign war with foreign ideals, and therefore their enlistment figures were dropping precipitously. All in all, Canadians were becoming less willing to continue to follow Britain into the trenches of France with each passing year of war.

Borden, on the other hand, was struggling to secure a stronger leadership role for Canada in the decision-making centre of London, and to some extent he regarded that as contingent upon continued high levels of enlistment. The first group of Canadian soldiers had reached France in the spring of 1915, following rudimentary training in Valcartier, Quebec, and then more substantial training in England through the fall and winter of 1914–15; they were part of what would become a four-division corps within the British Expeditionary Force. But by the end of 1915, Borden was convinced that that was not enough, and announced that Canada's new recruitment target would be half a million men—a huge percentage of Canada's population of about 8 million people. Only by making a substantial manpower contribution would Canada earn the respect that Borden, and others, were certain was due.

Canadians fought as part of the British army, and thus looked to Britain for leadership and for decisions regarding strategy and the broad management of war. This would have been fine, and would have suited Canada's sense of the order of the Empire, had the Great War been a short one. It was not, however, and as casualties mounted and little or no progress appeared to be made, Borden began to question British leadership. Prime Minister H. H. Asquith had little time for military input from the colonies, but when he was replaced as prime minister by David Lloyd George at the end of 1916, there was a new approach to Empire at Whitehall. Borden was given some encouragement: Lloyd George established an Imperial War Cabinet, composed of leaders of the British colonies, to advise on military strategy and be privy to the basis for British decision making. Finally, Canadians were allowed a modicum of influence—or at least the appearance of influence—in the determination of wartime strategy. Borden began his attendance at the Imperial War Cabinet in 1917, and virtually simultaneously determined that to achieve his 500,000-man enlistment goal, which had proven impossible through voluntary means, his government would have to enact conscription.

The issue of conscription came close to tearing Canada apart, and certainly wreaked havoc with the Conservative Party. Canadians were divided on the issue of whether conscription was an appropriate response to the manpower shortage at the front. French Canadians were almost entirely opposed to the proposition, and Laurier, who was invited to join a coalition government with Borden in 1917, refused to continue to support the Conservative government, necessitating an election. Borden made certain that he continued to lead Canada's war effort by introducing a number of electoral changes designed to shore up the pro-conscriptionist forces in Canada. First, he created a Union government of all those who were in favour of conscription, which meant most of the English-speaking members of Parliament. The election of 1917 was thus waged between the English and the French, under the guise of the Unionists and what remained of the Liberal party. Second, the government passed the *Wartime Elections Act* disenfranchising immigrants who had come to Canada since 1900 from an enemy nation—a group that evoked little sympathy from most Canadians and who were generally Liberal in their voting inclinations. The Act also gave the vote to close female relatives of men serving overseas, implying that the Union government favoured giving women the right to vote, but in reality handing ballots to people who were most likely to vote in favour of conscription. Third, the passage of the *Military Voters Act* allowed the government to use the votes cast overseas in any constituency of its choosing—presumably using them in ridings where pro- and anti-conscription forces were most closely matched. Finally, in the final weeks of the 1917 campaign, Borden promised that conscription would not apply to farmers or their sons in a last ditch effort to win over a group that had been generally opposed to conscription. Borden and the Unionists won the election of 1917 handily, with 153 seats to 82, and while he remained leader it was with a far different following than he had been able to command at the start of the war.

In Britain, where the Canadians received the majority of their training, and in France, where most of the fighting occurred, there was far less interest in securing a position for Canada in the Imperial War Cabinet, or in Borden's ability to carry on as prime minister; leading and following occurred in the trenches, where a misstep might mean death and where both those who led and those who followed faced the grim reality of war. The Great War was different from those that had been waged before not only in its global reach, but also, ironically, in its stagnation. This was a war in which almost 10 million soldiers' lives—more than 60,000 of them Canadian—were lost in battles fought over a few feet of territory; such was the horrifying nature of trench warfare. Years later, when Canadians were asked to remember what military life was like, they had some interesting things to say about war, about what was worth remembering, and about the nature of leadership, as you will see from the interviews included here.

The Great War is remembered differently in different quarters: some people focus on the heroism, some on the tragedy, and others still on the camaraderie of wartime. But a great deal of what is remembered is helped by those who recorded the events—to the best of their abilities—when they happened. More than 60 war artists were hired by the Canadian War Records Office to keep a visual record of the activities on the home front and the slaughter in Europe. The result was about 800 finished paintings, sculptures, and sketches, a tiny collection of which are included here, that provide a striking commentary on what each artist thought should be remembered about the Great War.

The Canadian War Records Office also recorded, in breathtaking detail, the activities of the Canadian Corps in Europe. Like the war art, the written record not only provides an important archive of information about the Great War, but also sheds some light on the way people at the time wanted the events to be remembered. In the articles, author Terry Copp provides an overview of Canada's military experience in the war, and Tim Cook examines Max Aitken's efforts in the Canadian War Records Office, which forms a large part of the basis for our understanding of Canadian participation in the First World War. Ultimately, figuring out who was leading and who was following—and where—rests on how the record of the war was kept in the first place.

QUESTIONS

1. How did Borden represent his leadership at the outset of war?
2. In what ways did the men and women who participated in the Great War oral history project choose to remember the role of leaders and followers?
3. In Terry Copp's interpretation of the events of the Great War, where did Canadians lead and in what circumstances did they follow?
4. After examining the paintings that have been reproduced here, discuss what aspects of the Great War each was designed to record for posterity.
5. According to Tim Cook, what was the significance of Max Aitken's efforts with the Canadian War Records Office?
6. How are Borden, the war artists, and the people whose stories have been collected all engaged in the act of propaganda, as Cook discusses it in reference to the Canadian War Records Office?

FURTHER READINGS

Cook, Tim, *At the Sharp End: Canadians Fighting the Great War, 1914–1916*, (Toronto: Viking, 2007).

Cook, Tim, *Clio's Warriors: Canadian Historians and the Writing of the World Wars*, (Vancouver: University of British Columbia Press, 2006).

Cook, Tim, *Shock Troops: Canadians Fighting the Great War, 1917–1918*, (Toronto: Viking, 2008).

Granatstein, J. L., and J. M. Hitsman, *Broken Promises: A History of Conscription in Canada*, (Toronto: Oxford University Press, 1977).

Keshen, Jeffrey A., *Propaganda and Censorship During Canada's Great War*, (Edmonton: University of Alberta Press, 1996).

Tippett, Maria, *Art at the Service of War*, (Toronto: University of Toronto Press, 1984).

Vance, Jonathan F., *Death So Noble: Memory, Meaning, and the First World War*, (Vancouver: University of British Columbia Press, 1997).

247

▲ Document 1: House of Ypres

● Some of Canada's war artists, like A.Y. Jackson, were better known as painters of the Canadian wilderness. What sense does this painting try to convey of the countryside in war-torn Europe?

Source: A.Y. Jackson: House of Ypres. 19710261-0189, Beaverbrook Collection of War Art. © Canadian War Museum.

▲ Document 2: Canadian Artillery in Action

● How does the artist depict soldiers? How does he view technology?

Source: Capt. Kenneth Forbes: Canadian Artillery in Action. 19710261-0142, Beaverbrook Collection of War Art. © Canadian War Museum.

▲ Document 3: Canadian Gunners in the Mud, Passchendaele

● Mud was a constant companion and an ever-present enemy for everyone in the Great War, as this painting suggests.

Source: Alfred Theodore Bastien: Canadian Gunners in the Mud. 19710261-0093. Beaverbrook Collection of War Art. © Canadian War Museum.

▲ Document 4: The Battle of Vimy Ridge, 1917

● Here and in Document 5, in perhaps Canada's most famous battle, there are other enemies apparent. How do the two artists depict Vimy Ridge?

Source: Richard Jack: The Taking of Vimy Ridge. 19710261-0160, Beaverbrook Collection of War Art. © Canadian War Museum.

▲ Document 5: The Crest of Vimy Ridge

● *The Crest of Vimy Ridge,* **Gyrth Russell**

Source: Gyrth Russell: The Crest of Vimy Ridge. 19710261-0617, Beaverbrook Collection of War Art. © Canadian War Museum.

▲ Document 6: At the Front

More than fifty years after the end of the Great War, a group of historians inter-
viewed some of those who had participated in the war either in the trenches, or in
war industries or support services. The following are some of their recollections of
what happened. While you read through these oral interviews, think about what
each person chose to remember, and consider what each thought about the leaders
and the followers during the war.

Keith Fallis

There's one memory that stands out in my mind very clearly. I was in the group that were mostly young fellows in their twenties. We were in the Signals, it was engineers then. We were held in England until we were nineteen, because they had come to the conclusion that it wasn't good to send eighteen-year olds out to the trenches. Too many were breaking down nervously and so on. So we were given all kinds of special training. One day we were taken out to be taught bayonet-fighting. They had straw men there, you see. After you had done a certain amount of training about how to hold your rifle, then you had to prac- tise taking a run and a jab at this straw man. 'In, out, and on guard' is what the sergeant would shout. The two places that you tried to slam your bayonet in are his throat and his stomach. I think more than half of us just couldn't eat our supper that evening. From that time on, I always had this kind of ambivalence: 'I'm glad that I'm in the Signals, at least I'm only doing the telephoning,' but knowing that that was not a moral position. If the war is justified, then you have to accept all your responsibilities, you see. But I never went over to Siegfried Sassoon's position that, because of the nature of it, you have to repudiate it. But I think that because of that experience and also going over to the front and seeing men killed for the first time, and horses shot to pieces, I froze up. I just wouldn't think about it. I just hung on to this: the best we could hope was that this war would make the world safe for democracy; and it's a helluva business, and the sooner we get it over with, the better.

Basically I sort of froze up. I didn't want to discuss moral questions or religious ques- tions. I did sometimes feel after my experience in battle, how could anyone believe in God as having an influence in human life and have this sort of thing happen? But I never went on to discuss it. I just froze up intellectually.

Mark Tanner

We were sent out to the Isle of Shapiay, Eastchurch, where we had our training. I'm aston- ished, when I think of the way they train pilots today, at the quick training they gave us. They used to turn out pilots with as little as two and a half or three hours flying time with your instructor, not solo. After two or three hours, the instructor would step out and say, 'Well you go alone now.' Quite a feat! When each one of us would start off on our solo flight, spectators on the ground would all be watching, expecting the poor bloke to crash. Getting off is hard enough, but getting back on the ground again is the real difficult thing. Sometimes they wrecked the machine. They didn't break themselves—it wasn't that haz- ardous, but it was an experience. They used to talk in the squadron that the average life

Source: Oral History Interview from *The Great War and Canadian Society: An Oral History,* Toronto: New Hogtown Press, 1978. Reprinted with permission.

of a pilot on the front line in France was ten hours' flying time, and I think that's accurate. The casualties were quite severe.

Michael Sheehan

I'll never forget our first sight of the Germans. We had those beautiful Ross rifles. They were absolutely the slickest rifles you could find anywhere, but no good for war. The Germans were coming, we could see them coming across down there. So we opened up with these Ross rifles, and I bet we didn't fire more than a dozen shots before it seized. It got hot. (It was made so beautifully.) They had absolutely seized, everything just as tight as could be. We stood on the bolt to try to open the breech, nothing doing! The rifles were absolutely useless, and here the Germans were, coming down the road down below us, about a couple of hundred feet. We had barbed wire about as high as a table—it wouldn't stop anything. And we looked down at this great big column of men, about a thousand of them marching down there, just keeping step, the officer ahead and a couple of them behind. You wouldn't believe it! They could have walked up that hill, and we didn't have anything. We didn't even have a revolver. We couldn't have done a thing. They could have just walked up and then walked right through for the next fifty miles. We were the last line, you see. We don't know yet why, but they turned around, about turned, and marched right back.

Robert Swan

After a certain length of time we became fatalists, because there wasn't any rhyme or reason. You could ask why a man, So-and-So, was killed, and why you weren't killed, or why this was done, or why that was done. There wasn't any answer to it—*never*! Couldn't find an answer. So you just had to accept it and roll with the punches and say, 'Well, I'm here today and I'll make the best of it and get as much out of it as I can, and keep out of trouble.' But if you stopped to try and reason it out and make any sense out of it, it was just impossible. We'd no explanation for many of the things that happened.

There was another factor which I think had a bearing on the whole situation. Here you had a very large number of young men at the very height of their physical condition and under rigid training. So they were honed down and tuned down, as fit as they ever would be, and with all the natural instincts of a young man. Yet we were facing the fact that, 'Well, we're here today, but we might be gone tomorrow. So if we're going to have any life at all, we'll take it when we can get it.' And if they were inclined in that way, and there were very large numbers what where, without any doubt, they went to the women. I think that they had much more reason, there was much more excuse for them doing it than there is in the modern attitude toward sex as it is today. These boys just didn't know whether they were going to have any of that, or whether they weren't, or how long they were going to have it. And being, as I say, in the prime of physical condition, with all the human natural urges that result, you can't blame them if they took what they could get while the going was good. I don't say that every man did that, because there were many, many who didn't. But it was a very general experience, particularly after a long trip in the trenches or something like that. [...]

You know, the first baths we had, they didn't have any special bathing facilities, nor did they have any new replacement underwear or anything. But they had built these shacks out of any old boards they could get. There were cracks through the boards, and you could feel the wind coming through like nobody's business. You went into a dressing room section, and they had nails in the wall, big spikes, and you took off your stuff and hung it up on that. And then you went to a hole in the wall, and you threw in your underwear and your socks, and went into the bath house. The bath house had tubs made out of beer barrels cut in two—they were good and big, you see. There were ten tubs in this one that I'm thinking of. You worked in gangs of twenty men, two men to a tub. You were given a piece of yellow soap, like laundry soap, and you got two buckets of cold water and one bucket of hot water. The hot water was heated on an old boiler that they had out in the yard, which they fired with anything that would burn. The bath attendants filled the tubs, and the two men stood in a tub, washed each other with the soap, and sloshed themselves off. You were given three minutes, and then you had to get out. Then you went to another door where you got a towel to dry yourself. You went up to another wicket and you got a suit of underwear and a pair of socks. It was the old army game of one man, one shirt, and you never knew when you got them what size they were. You might be six feet tall and get a suit of underwear for a midget, and some other guy would get one where they had to roll the sleeves right up to his elbows. There was a lot of horse-trading in the dressing room, trying to get something that would halfway fit you. And this was all reconditioned underwear that somebody else had had, but it had been disinfected and smelled of creosote. But at least it was clean!

That's the kind of bath you got once in a dog's age when you came out. Otherwise, if the weather was halfway decent, and if you were out in the camp somewhere, all around that place there, there were shell holes that had been filled full of water. By that time, the mud would have settled, and the water would be clean—it would be rainwater. If you could get some sort of biscuit tin or something to scoop it out without disturbing the mud, you could get yourself enough fresh water to strip off and wash yourself right out there in the open. At least you could get some kind of relief in that way. But if it was raining cats and dogs, which it did most of the time, that wasn't pleasant or possible. But you took any kind of means you could to keep yourself clean.

Later on of course, they built real bath houses with shower heads in the roof, and then you'd go there. Then they got new clothing. The army began to bring in clothing frequently, so that when you turned in this dirty, filthy underwear that you were wearing, you never got that back at all. I don't know what they did with it.

Ben Wagner

The drinking was perhaps a sore point in the early days with the Canadian army. The army camps in Canada, in the days of our wonderful militia, had always been dry. I don't know why, but they had. But they went to England, and on Salisbury Plain, they found that all these little villages had pubs. And although there was no place they could drink in the camp, they went to these villages. And they got obnoxious, they got too much to drink, you see. The usual city bloke from down around Jarvis Street got too much to drink and became obnoxious. So the army commander, who was an Englishman, opened what they called 'wet' canteens. Now they could only get beer, they couldn't get hard liquor. But the wet canteens served two purposes. They kept a man at home where he could more or less be kept under cover (I've seen a man lugged off to the clink lots of times on a fella's shoulders) it kept them from annoying the English people who were very friendly to us Canadians. And ten percent went to a fund that was used to buy things for the soldiers. So although there was an outcry from the WCTU (Women's Christian Temperance Union) across Canada about this whole thing of the wet canteens, it was a very good thing.

In the camps we had what we called the 'wet' canteen and the 'dry' canteen. In the dry canteen you got 'coffee'—quotation marks around the coffee—biscuits and things which you had to pay for. Very rarely did you get anything free. Now *that* was one of our bitter points.

At the YMCA you got nothing free; at the Salvation Army, if you didn't have the money for the coffee, you got the coffee just the same. Its coffee was a little bit worse than the YMCA's, but not too much, because the English don't know how to make coffee anyway.

As for the diseases, there was regular inspection that kept them under control. It wasn't like in civilian life where a boy might become almost rotted with VD without ever going to a doctor. There you had regular inspection. Whenever you went sick, it was on your daily orders: 'So-and-so: diphtheria, So-and-So: VD.' It was always public. I might say that perhaps 5% of the battalion had had VD. But they were immediately put in hospital and under treatment, so that there wasn't the bad effects of it. It was checked.

Eric Rosen

Every unit had its padré. The RCs, of course, would always have an RC padré and their church service on a Sunday—that would be all it would amount to—and the same with the denominational churches. Mostly the padrés were Anglican, as far as I know. Unfortunately, in our unit we didn't have a very good padré because he too used to drink, and that was a very poor example to us. I had gone to the Baptist Church, and we were under pretty evangelical preaching, but when we got over there, there seemed to be just the formal Sunday morning church parade which you had to go to.

Myself, I always had a hatred of anyone who would ridicule the Bible. One of my best friends (I don't know why we chummed up like that) was bad like that, to my mind. One night we were all in bed on the floor, and he was opposite me, and he said something about Bible-thumpers, so I heaved my boot at him.

Another thing that used to annoy me: we had one man in particular, who was a very boisterous fellow. I seen him stand outside and shake his fist to the heavens when it was raining and say—he used to refer to God as 'Huey'—'Send it down, Huey!' and it used to make me cringe. He'd get out there and shake his fist. He was one of our runners and one night, he and another runner were out. We were in a rough spot, and they were being shelled. When they came in, the chap that was with him says, 'Boy, he didn't shake his fist tonight, he got down on his knees and prayed. We were really in a spot,' he said, 'He didn't shake his fist.' That shows you what it'll do to some people.

I often used to talk to my brothers about it. I can't understand myself. It used to annoy me no end, but I dodged church parade or anything if I could, and I wasn't any better than a lot of the fellas. But that used to really get me when anybody said anything like that.

Another thing: prostitution was very, very easy, particularly in France. When we were out on leave, it was on every hand. It was nothing to walk down the streets of a town, and the little boys would be out touting for their sisters. Little boys would take men to where there [*sic*] sisters were. Possibly as young fellas we didn't have too strong views on those things, even though we were instructed from the time we entered the army very, very strongly against this sort of thing—not so much from the angle of the moral aspect of it, as the danger of infection. Some of the lectures they gave us—I can see them now—were terrible, awful! We'd come away from them, and they would be saying they'd never look at a girl again, but that lasted for about five minutes. It was unfortunate that there was so many that did become infected. In France it was easy. It was licensed, I guess, so it was easy. And of course, in England, where we go on leave, there was always somebody, particularly if you went into the pubs. Myself, I found it rather difficult, because everything of that sort of thing was hush-hush in our family life. I'll say this: there were some—men who were old enough to be our fathers—who led us younger guys into things that they had no business doing. To me, as a father now, I see how wrong it was.

255

Robert Swan

His 'Love Poem'

Dear Maizy,

If I last another week, my leave comes up, and I will be on my way to London to see you again. If you enjoy the birds, the bees, and the flowers, take a good look at them before I get there. After that, you will not see anything but the ceiling for the next six days. Hold everything and hope for the best.

XXXX Arthur

Mrs Jane Walters

Patients had a habit of falling in love with you. They were so glad to get back home and have young girls around who weren't too hard to look at and who were kind, who helped them. I remember there was one Roumanian soldier, and he thought he was in love with me. I kinda thought I was in love with him too. He was very attractive. You know, a girl who has ideals—and we had ideals in those days, I hope you have now—to be thrown in with men like that, all kinds from all over the world, it took some doing to keep level, not have your head turned. But you had your heart hurt very often.

Mrs Anita Phillips

We had a doctor on our ward, Dr Robertson, I think it was. He'd been there for quite a long time, and I had been there for a long time too. And he came in one morning, and he said, 'Have we got Nursing Sister White here?' [She nurseed in hospitals in England and France] White was my name. We all looked so amazed at him. I said, 'Why, of course. What's the matter?' He says 'Well, you tell your boyfriends that are flying over this place to stop dropping bombs on my head.' (laughs) They had little things that they put weights on, and they put a note inside it, and they dropped them. He happened to be passing, and it dropped right on his head. (laughs) The notes told me where they had been, and when they'd be back, and hope you'd be at a little dance, or something like that. Just nice notes.

Quite often, yes. Not the dropping of the bombs! But friends coming to the hospital, you know.

▲ Document 7: Memoirs

Robert L. Borden

Here, Borden records for posterity his recollections of the early days of war. He obviously has clear views on the question of leadership.

The War

Never was a holiday dream followed by a more terrible awakening. During my visit to England in 1912, I had reached the conclusion that war was probably inevitable; but European conditions had seemed peaceful. The assassination of Archduke Franz Ferdinand at Sarajevo on June 28th, had been alarming but on both sides of the Atlantic none, I imagine, believed that the situation would develop, with such startling suddenness, into a war that in its effect upon both belligerent and neutral nations would almost shatter the very framework of modern civilization.

Telegrams from Ottawa began to acquaint me with the possibility that a general European war was impending. On July 28th, I learned that Great Britain was endeavouring unsuccessfully to keep peace but that she would almost certainly be involved if France should be attacked. It was reported that Germany and Russia were quietly mobilizing. On July 30th, a telegram arrived from my secretary, A.E. Blount, that the situation was serious but that the Ministers thought I need not come if I could be ready to leave on short notice. I decided to go immediately; and, after despatching telegrams, I left early on the thirty-first for Ottawa where I arrived the following morning. The Governor-General was absent in the West;[1] and very few Ministers were in Ottawa. Under my telegraphic instructions Blount had requested the Ministers to return immediately. The King's secretary had cabled to the Duke that, although the situation was most serious, there was a faint hope of peace.

With the approval of such colleagues as were available, I immediately despatched to the British Government on August 1st, the following telegram in the name of the Governor-General:

> "My advisers while expressing their most earnest hope that peaceful solution of existing international difficulties may be achieved and their strong desire to co-operate in every possible way for that purpose wish me to convey to His Majesty's Government the firm assurance that if unhappily war should ensue the Canadian people will be united in a common resolve to put forth every effort and to make every sacrifice necessary to ensure the integrity and maintain the honour of our Empire."

To this message which was made public immediately, the following reply was received:

> "With reference to your telegram of August first, His Majesty's Government gratefully welcome the assurance of your Government that in the present crisis they may rely on wholehearted co-operation of the people of Canada."

On the following day I despatched to the British Government in the name of the Governor-General a further telegram which was made public subsequently:

257

Source: *Robert Laird Borden: His Memoirs*. Toronto: Macmillan, 1938, pp. 451–471.

"In view of the impending danger of war involving the Empire, my advisers are anxiously considering the most effective means of rendering every possible aid and they will welcome any suggestion and advice which the Imperial naval and military authorities may deem it expedient to offer. They are confident that a considerable force would be available for service abroad. A question has been mooted respecting the status of any Canadian force serving abroad as, under section sixty-nine of Canadian Militia Act, active militia can only be placed on active service beyond Canada for the defence thereof. It has been suggested that regiments might enlist as Imperial troops for a stated period, Canadian Government undertaking to make all necessary provision for their equipment, pay and maintenance. This proposal has not yet been maturely considered here and my advisers would be glad to have views of Imperial Government thereon."

In reply to this message the following cable was received:

"With reference to your cypher telegram of August second, please inform your Ministers that their patriotic readiness to render every aid is deeply appreciated by His Majesty's Government but they would prefer postponing detailed observations on the suggestions put forward pending further developments. As soon as situation appears to call for further measures I will telegraph you again."

While in England in 1912 I had felt it my duty to become acquainted with the arrangements effected by the Imperial Defence Committee and its organization for immediate, effective action upon the outbreak of war. Details were procured from Lieutenant-Colonel Sir Maurice Hankey, Secretary of that Committee, and in January, 1914, proceedings were taken to consummate similar arrangements in Canada. A conference of deputy heads of various departments was constituted under the chairmanship of Sir Joseph Pope, then Under Secretary of State for External Affairs

As a result of this systematic organization the communications from the Imperial authorities were acted upon promptly and with an entire absence of confusion. Each detail was worked out with precision.

On Sunday and Monday (August 2nd and 3rd) we spent practically the whole day in Council. We established censorship, declared bank notes legal tender, authorized excess issue of Dominion notes, empowered the proper offices to detain enemy ships, prohibited the export of articles necessary or useful for war purposes and generally took upon ourselves responsibilities far exceeding our legal powers. All these measures, which were wholly without legal validity until they were afterwards ratified by Parliament, were accepted throughout the country as if Council had possessed the necessary authority.

The Canadian banks were extremely apprehensive of a devastating run upon their funds and it was learned that in several cities safety-deposit boxes had been secured for the purpose of hoarding gold. Any such attempt became absolutely futile as soon as we decreed that bank notes should be legal tender. The anticipated run on the banks did not take place; and the preparations for hoarding gold to be withdrawn from the banks became entirely useless.

We placed the Canadian naval vessels at the disposal of the King for co-operation with British naval forces; and we purchased at Seattle two submarines which got away just ahead of the United States' order to detain them, and succeeded in evading United States' cruisers which pursued them.

There were many rumours as to German attacks upon our coasts and guns were provided from Quebec for the defence of Vancouver, Glace Bay, Canso, Sydney and St.

John. The *Rainbow* went south, in the face of powerful German cruisers in the Pacific which easily could have sunk her, to bring back two small boats, the *Shearwater* and the *Algerine,* which were in southern waters at the outbreak of war. Some deck hamper thrown overboard in preparation for action drifted to the United States coast and gave rise to a rumour that she had been sunk.

We were in Council on August 4th at eleven and again at four. During the evening, while again in Council, at 8:55 p.m. the momentous telegram arrived announcing that war had been declared. Immediately, an Order-in Council was passed summoning Parliament to meet on August 18th.

Although the events of the past few days had quite prepared us for this result, it came at the last as a shock. None of us, at that time, anticipated the terrible duration of the war agony; but we did realize that the struggle would be intense. White graphically described it as "the suicide of civilization". It was difficult to retain one's balance in the unexpected and bewildering environment that had enveloped us in what seemed but a moment.

A question that arose at once was our attitude towards German and Austrian army reservists resident in Canada. There was pressure from the British Government to arrest or intern them. We had no reason to believe that they were animated by the militarist tendencies which influenced the German and Austrian Governments, or to doubt that they would be loyal to the country of their adoption. Therefore, by Order-in-Council and proclamation, we declared that these persons, as adopted citizens of our country, were entitled to the protection of the law and would receive it; that they should not be molested or interfered with unless they should attempt to aid or abet the enemy or to leave Canada for the purpose of fighting against Great Britain and her Allies, in which case we should be obliged to follow the laws and usages of war but with all possible humanity.

259

When I formed my Government in 1911 I was extremely doubtful as to including [Sam] Hughes; while he was a man of marked ability and sound judgment in many respects, his temperament was so peculiar, and his actions and language so unusual on many important occasions that one was inclined to doubt his usefulness as a Minister. There was much pressure on his behalf from various sources; and my cousin, Sir Frederick Borden, who sought an interview with me on behalf of Hughes, expressed the firm, and I believe the sincere opinion that Hughes, under proper control, would be of great service to the country. I discussed with Hughes when I appointed him his extraordinary eccentricities. On one occasion when I impressed strongly upon him the mischievous and perverse character of his speech and conduct, he broke down, admitted that he often acted impetuously, and assured me that if he were appointed I could rely on his judgment and good sense. This promise was undoubtedly sincere but his temperament was too strong for him. He was under constant illusions that enemies were working against him. I told him on one occasion that I thoroughly agreed that he was beset by two unceasing enemies. Expecting a revelation he was intensely disappointed when I told him that they were his tongue and his pen. In my experience his moods might be divided in three categories; during about half of the time he was an able, reasonable, and useful colleague, working with excellent judgment and indefatigable energy; for a certain other portion of the time he was extremely excitable, impatient of control and almost impossible to work with; and during the remainder his conduct and speech were so eccentric as to justify the conclusion that his mind was unbalanced.

Throughout the training of the First Division at Valcartier Camp, Hughes could not resist his absurd inclination to fill not only the role of Minister of Militia but that of Military Commander. His intense vanity and a rather vindictive temper which developed during this period, contributed to the difficulty of the situation. However, notwithstanding all this, his inexhaustible energy and resourcefulness were a great asset to Canada at that time. No other man could have accomplished during a similar period what he did achieve in the training and organization of the First Canadian Expeditionary Force.

All through September there was much outcry from officers and prominent citizens with regard to his language and conduct. His usual dictatorial attitude towards subordinates (except those for whom he had an especial liking) had been accentuated by the strain and anxiety of his work. Quarrels developed between him and officers of the Expeditionary Force but in some cases these were due not entirely to his excitable temperament but to unfortunate provocation.

Considerable pressure was brought to bear to permit Hughes' promotion to the rank of Major-General. Although not particularly impressed with the advisability of such a step, I eventually consented.

It was at first proposed that the Canadian Expeditionary Force should consist of about 20,000 men. More than 30,000 arrived in camp; and there arose the difficult problem of selecting those who should go overseas and those who should remain. The intense disappointment of the latter can be imagined; they had sacrificed every material consideration and surmounted every difficulty in order to reach camp and have an opportunity of enlisting. The duration of the War was, of course, uncertain. Financial experts had loudly proclaimed that it could not last long, as the financial burden would become intolerable. Wagers were laid in August, 1914, that, with the beginning of the coming year, we would see the end of the struggle.

What were we to do with the additional 10,000 or 12,000 men? I had but the faintest appreciation of the inevitable wastage when our men reached the Front, but I felt certain that reinforcements and reserves would be required at no distant date. Accordingly, I proposed to my colleagues that we should send the entire force assembled at Valcartier; and I gave them my reasons for that conclusion in which they instantly concurred. Thereupon I proceeded to Valcartier and at a conference with General Hughes, I announced without preliminary discussion, that I had decided to send abroad the entire contingent. He was silent for a moment and then he suddenly broke down and sobbed audibly. He presently explained his emotions as joy and relief; he had been, he told me, agonized by the thought of a selection for which he would be responsible and which he must determine. In reviewing his character and actions, allowance must always be made for his extremely emotional temperament.

When the Expeditionary Force finally sailed from Gaspé on October 3rd, its safe passage was assured by strong naval forces protecting the convoy. As to the adequacy of that force, we had had much correspondence with the Admiralty. On October 14th I received the welcome tidings that it had reached Plymouth.

Hughes delivered (and later published) a flamboyant and magniloquent address to the troops, based apparently on Napoleon's famous address to the Army of Italy. It did not enhance his prestige; and indeed excited no little mirth in various quarters. After the departure of the forces, he became obsessed with a desire to visit England. This proposal did not arouse our enthusiasm. Finally we consented but not before I had given him grave warning that he must control his temperament and have no friction with the authorities on the other side.

In Hughes' absence Hazen was acting as Minister of Militia, and we immediately began consideration of preparation for further contingents, as the news from the Front indicated that the War would not be of short duration. On October 17th, I held conference with

Hazen, Gwatkin, Chief of Staff, and Denison, Adjutant-General. They urged a programme of training for 30,000 men. We went over the whole question of defence; and on the following day I sent for the Acting Minister and told him to instruct Gwatkin to get up such a programme—30,000 men continuously in training to go forward by detachments of 10,000.

Throughout the period—August 1st to December 31st, I was working at very high pressure, sometimes under the care of a physician; but occasionally I obtained relief from a short holiday. It would be tiresome to enumerate the thousand and one incidents, some of them of a highly disturbing and exciting character, which pressed upon me during that period and which are mentioned in my diary. There was constant correspondence with the British Government and with the Acting High Commissioner respecting our co-operation in the War and touching upon our capacity to supply food, arms, munitions, and indeed every description of material necessary for war purposes. Further, there was disturbing unemployment in some of our cities; and, unfortunately, British officials seemed disposed in some instances, to obtain supplies from the United States which could have been procured in Canada and the provision of which would have given employment to some of our people. I made sharp protests against this practice; and on one occasion I learned that a British official had sent a considerable order to a city in the United States under the impression that he had placed it in Canada.

Note

1. The Governor-General did not return until the morning of August 4th.

■ Article 1: The Military Effort, 1914–1918

Terry Copp

Most of the world remembers the First World War as a time when 'innocent young men, their heads full of high abstractions like Honour, Glory and England […] were slaughtered in stupid battles planned by stupid Generals.'[1] English-speaking Canadians, while generally accepting this view, have supplemented it with an imaginative version of a war in which their soldiers won great victories and forged a new national identity. Both of these approaches have served to promote literary, political, and cultural agendas of such power that empirical studies of what actually happened during the war have had little impact upon the historiography. Recently, a new generation of

Source: Terry Copp, "The Military Effort, 1914–1918," in *Canada and the First World War: Essays in Honour of Robert Craig Brown*, David Mackenzie, ed., Toronto: University of Toronto Press, 2005: pp. 111-130. (c) University of Toronto Press, Inc., 2005. Reprinted with permission of the publisher.

scholars has challenged this approach, insisting that 'the reality of the war and the society which produced it' are also worthy of study.[2] If historians are to continue to study the past to further understanding of what happened and why it happened that way, they need to remember that the men and women who participated in events like the First World War were not concerned with the views of later generations. The meaning of their war was constantly changing, and since no one know the outcome or the consequences of decisions which needed to be made, they relied upon the best information available at the time and tried to act in ways that did not violate their shared values. This essay is therefore intended to introduce readers to the events of the war as well as the way historians interpret them.

It is clear, for example, that while Canadians were surprised that the assassination of an Austrian archduke should lead to war, those citizens interested in world affairs had long been aware of the possibility of such a conflict. The enmity between Germany and France, the alliance system, and the increasingly bitter rivalry of the German and British empires were topics of informed discussion throughout most of the decade that preceded the war.[3] The 'naval question,' which along with reciprocity of free trade with the United States, dominated pre-war political debate, sensitized many of those normally indifferent to such topics. Canadians were divided on issues of war and peace and especially divided on military and naval expenditure precisely because they thought they understood what was at stake.

French-Canadian opinion, at least within Quebec, was almost universally opposed to any form of military expenditure which might underwrite Canadian participation in foreign wars. Within English-speaking Canada there were sharp divisions between pro-empire activists, Canadian nationalists, anti-militarists and declared pacifists. While newspapers such as the *Montreal Star* and the Toronto *Mail and Empire* offered strong support for military preparedness, the Toronto *Globe*, the Methodist *Guardian*, and the voice of the western farmer, the *Grain Growers' Guide*, were equally adamant about the dangers of militarism.[4]

Canada's leaders played no part in the decision for war in 1914, and it is literally true that Canada went to war because Britain was at war. This statement, while accurate, does little to help us make sense of the events of August 1914 in Europe or in Canada. To achieve understanding we must answer three different questions: (1) Who was believed to be responsible for the outbreak of war? (2) Why was Britain involved? (3) What kind of war was it going to be? The answers to these questions seemed obvious to informed Canadians. Germany was threatening the peace of Europe and violating Belgian neutrality as part of an attack on France. Britain was defending France against German aggression and coming to the assistance of Belgium. The war was likely to be over by Christmas, after decisive battles between standing armies, but it might last until 1915.

The response of most English-speaking Canadians was predictable. Canada was part of the empire and must actively support the mother country in a just war which Britain had tried to prevent. This view of the origins of the war was dismissed as simplistic in the 1920s, when historians developed a revisionist interpretation which ignored evidence of German intentions. Today, the scholarly consensus presents a picture not very different from the one accepted by Canadians in 1914.[5]

The country's commitment to the war effort was not in doubt, but Canada could not provide any immediate assistance. Wilfrid Laurier's attempt to create a Canadian navy, able to defend Canada's coasts and assist in the protection of imperial sea lanes, ended with his defeat in 1911. The Liberal-controlled Senate then blocked Prime Minister Robert Borden's Naval Aid Bill, which offered direct financial assistance to the Royal Navy. As a result, in 1914 the Royal Canadian Navy possessed one seaworthy, if obsolescent light cruiser, HMCS *Rainbow* and two submarines hastily purchased from the neutral United States by the government of British Columbia.[6]

Canada's regular army of 3,000 all ranks, plus some 70,000 volunteers serving in the militia, constituted a far more considerable force than the navy. Under the energetic if eccentric leadership of Sam Hughes, minister of militia since 1911, fifty-six new armouries and drill halls were built and training camps created or expanded. Hughes is usually remembered for his misguided commitment to the Ross rifle, a Canadian-designed and manufactured weapon, which proved deficient under combat conditions. But if Hughes is to be condemned for his errors of judgment, he must also be remembered for encouraging more realistic training, marksmanship, the acquisition of modern guns for the artillery, and the expansion of the militia.[7]

Whatever view one takes of Hughes, it is evident that no Canadian field force could possibly have gone into action on a European battlefield in 1914. This reality did not deter the minister. On 6 August he sent 226 night telegrams directly to unit commanders of the militia ordering them to interview prospective recruits and wire lists of volunteers for overseas service to Ottawa. Hughes bypassed existing mobilization plans requiring the Canadian Expeditionary Force to assemble at a new, yet to be built, embarkation camp at Valcartier, near Quebec City.

Would the original plan have worked more smoothly? Would a conventionally recruited force of 30,000 men have been ready to leave for England in October? We will never know, but it is impossible not to be impressed with what Hughes and William Price, who created camp Valcartier and organized the embarkation of troops, accomplished in just seven weeks.

Who were the men who volunteered to go to war in 1914? Desmond Morton suggests that, 'for the most part, the crowds of men who jammed into the armouries were neither militia nor Canadian-born.'[8] Most, he argues, were recent British immigrants

262

anxious to return to their homeland in a time of crisis, especially when Canada was deep in a recession which had created large-scale unemployment. The best available statistics suggest that close to 70 per cent of the first contingent 'were British born and bred' though the officer corps was almost exclusively Canadian. Command of the First Division went to a British officer, Lieutenant General Sir Edwin Alderson, but Hughes appointed Canadians to command the brigades, battalions, and artillery regiments. Much the same pattern held for the second contingent: 60 per cent were British born, but their officers were Canadian.[9]

When news of the war reached the colony, Newfoundlanders were still mourning the loss of more than 300 fishermen in a spring blizzard. The response nevertheless was enthusiastic, and in the absence of a recent British immigrant population, recruits were drawn from a cross-section of town and outport communities. Less than 250,000 people lived in Newfoundland in 1914, but thousands volunteered to serve in the Newfoundland Regiment and the Royal Navy.[10] Imperial ties were no doubt basic to this response, but many were drawn to serve by the promise of decent pay and a meaningful role in a war which could not be much more dangerous than the sea.

The men who gathered at Valcartier were supposed to be at least five feet, three inches, tall with a chest measurement of thirty-three and a half inches, between eighteen and forty-five years of age, and ready to serve for one year 'or until the war ended if longer than that.' Officers received from $6.50 a day for a lieutenant colonel to $3.60 for a lieutenant. Non-commissioned officers could earn as much as $2.30 a day, while the basic rate for a soldier was $1.10. The Canadian Patriotic Fund […] provided additional support for families from private donations. The fund, with chapters across Canada, offered support only after a humiliating investigation of the recipients and then provided assistance on a sliding scale which paralleled the army's rates of pay. A dollar a day was not far below the income of a junior clerk or unskilled labourer and was far above the cash paid to a farm worker. The army was thus an attractive proposition to many single men seeking escape from the dull routines of work or the harsh experience of unemployment. A large number of married men

also volunteered, but Sam Hughes, who insisted participation had to be voluntary in every sense of the word, decided that 'no recruit would be accepted against the written protest of his wife or mother.' According to the newspapers 'long lists of men were struck off the rolls' because of this regulation.[11]

As the Canadian Expeditionary Force and the Newfoundland Regiment departed for England, a second contingent, which would become the 2nd Canadian Division, was authorized. This decision (7 October) was made in the context of the German advance on Paris, the dramatic retreat of the British Expeditionary Force from Mons, and the miracle of the Battle of the Marne, which saved France from immediate defeat. If the war was seen as a romantic adventure in early August, by October the harsh reality of high casualties and the prospect of a German victory created a more realistic view.

By October Canadian opinion was also deeply affected by the plight of the Belgian people. Voluntary organizations including farm groups, churches, and ad hoc committees responded with offers of money, food, clothing, and plans to aid Belgian orphans and refugees. This spontaneous outpouring of sympathy preceded the first atrocity stories, which served to further intensify anti-German sentiments and public support for participation in a just war.[12]

The 1st Division arrived in Britain on 14 October and reached its tented camp on Salisbury Plain near Stonehenge just in time for the worst, wettest winter in recent memory. Over the next four months the contingent trained and equipped itself to join the British army in Flanders as a standard infantry division. Major General Alderson, an experienced British officer, was given command. The establishment of 18,000 men included three brigades, each consisting of 130 officers, 4,000 men, and 272 horses. Each brigade contained four infantry battalions of approximately 900 men commanded by a lieutenant colonel. A battalion was made up of four rifle companies, each divided into four platoons. Additional firepower was provided by two sections of two Colt machine guns per battalion. The three divisional artillery brigades, equipped with modern fifteen-pounder field guns, provided the firepower that was supposed to permit troops to assault enemy positions neutralized by shelling.[13]

There is no consensus among historians as to how well prepared the Canadians were when they entered the line in March 1915. Desmond Morton describes the Canadians as 'woefully unready.'[14]

A recent study of the 4th Infantry Battalion offers a detailed analysis which suggests that the 'mad Fourth' worked hard at a comprehensive training program in both England and Europe. Paired with the Royal Welsh Fusiliers in Belgium, platoons were rotated through the trenches and prepared by repeated exercises in rapid fire, fire control, and close combat drill. When first ordered into action in April 1915, the companies leapfrogged forward in perfect order using fire and movement. They were stopped some 600 yards short of their objective and suffered heavy losses, but their counter-attack towards Mauser Ridge played a significant part in stemming the enemy's initial advance.[15] Further studies at the battalion level are necessary before firm conclusions can be drawn, but it is important to recognize that the events of the war may not lend themselves to simple notions of the transformation of raw recruits into experienced professional soldiers. The reality may well be that no Canadian formation fought a more important or more successful battle than 2nd Ypres.[16]

The German army's experiment with chlorine gas, as a method of breaking the stalemate on the Western Front, has been re-examined by Tim Cook in his book *No Place to Run*.[17] The Canadians were, he reminds us, sent into a salient which 'protruded into the German lines like a rounded tumour, eight miles wide and six miles deep.' The positions they took over from the French covered 4,500 yards north of Gravenstafel Ridge and were overlooked by German observers on Passchendaele Ridge to the east. 'Shells came from everywhere except straight behind us,' one gunner noted in his diary. The Canadians were shocked by the state of the trenches, which resembled muddy holes rather than those created in training.

Eight days after their tour of duty began a period of quiet which had settled over the salient was broken by an intense artillery barrage beginning in the late afternoon. 'Along with the shells came an ominous grey-green cloud four miles long and half a mile deep' which crept upon the 45th Algerian and 87th French divisions. 'One by one the French guns fell silent only to be replaced by screaming choking Algerians running into and past the Canadian lines

[...] The victims of the gas attack writhed on the ground. Their bodies turned a strange gas-green as they struggled to suck oxygen into their corrupted lungs. The chlorine attacked the bronchial tubes, which caused the membranes to swell into a spongy mass and ever-increasing amounts of fluid to enter from the bloodstream. The swiftly congested lungs failed to take in oxygen, and the victims suffocated as they drowned in their own fluids.'[18] The Canadians were spared all but the edges of the cloud, and it was evident that they would need to launch a counter-attack to check the expected German advance. There was much confusion as well as indecision and moments of panic, but the counter-attacks mounted by the 1st and 3rd brigades that night were carried out with skill and resolution.

Early on the morning of 24 April, as the Canadians and the first British reinforcements struggled to build new defensive positions, a second gas attack began. The 15th and 8th battalions of Canada's 2nd Brigade, holding the original lines in what was now the apex of the salient, saw the gas drifting towards them and urged each other to 'Piss on your handkerchiefs and tie them over your faces.' Urine, the chemistry students in the army recalled, contained ammonia, which might neutralize the chlorine.

Courage and determination were no proof against the full force of the gas, however, and as the Canadians slowly retreated, wounded and severely gassed soldiers were abandoned to become prisoners or to face execution. A new defensive line some 1,000 metres further back was established with the assistance of British troops, and the next day the Germans launched a series of conventional attacks near the village of St Julien, where the famous 'brooding soldier' Canadian war memorial now stands. After the German advance south of the village was halted, General Alderson was ordered to recapture St Julien and 're-establish our trench line as far north as possible.' This absurd order compounded the growing chaos and led to further heavy losses. Stopping the German advance was one thing; retaking ground in a salient valued solely for reasons of Belgian pride and British prestige was quite another. On 26 April yet another attack into the German positions was launched. The Lahore Division of the British Indian Army advanced until gas, used for the first time defensively, broke the impetus of the attack.[19]

The Canadians emerged from the battle with horrendous casualties: over 6,000 men, including 1,410 who became prisoners of war. This casualty rate, 37 per cent of the troops engaged, would never be exceeded, not even at the Somme.[20] The British and Canadian press lauded the Canadian achievement and the enemy acknowledged their 'tenacious determination,' but behind the scenes there were serious conflicts over the conduct of the battle, including sharp criticism of Brigadiers Arthur Currie and R.E.W. Turner. Many Canadian officers were equally unhappy with the performance of senior British commanders.[21] After April 1915 this tension between British and Canadian officers helped to ensure that the 1st Division became the core of Canada's national army rather than an 'imperial' formation drawn from a dominion.

News of the gas attack and the valour of the country's soldiers reached Canada on 24 April before the battle was over. The newspapers reported that Canadian 'gallantry and determination' had saved the situation, but they hinted at heavy losses. The Toronto *News* described the mood: 'Sunday was one of the most anxious days ever experienced in Toronto, and the arrival of the officers' casualty list only served to increase the feeling that a long list including all ranks was inevitable. Crowds scanned the newspaper bulletin boards from the time of arrival of the first lists shortly before noon, until midnight, while hundreds sought information by telephone. Historian Ian Miller, writing of Toronto, describes the dawning awareness that whole battalions had been devastated. At first it was impossible to believe that battalions such as the 15th, made up of men from the city's 48th Highlanders, had been wiped out, and the press assumed that many were prisoners of war. When the full lists were available in early May, the truth was apparent. The 15th Battalion had virtually ceased to exist, and 'half the infantry at the front have been put out of action.'[22] The events of the spring of 1915 transformed the war from a great adventure to a great crusade. A week after the enemy introduced the horrors of gas warfare, the *Lusitania* was torpedoed off the coast of Ireland with a loss of 1,369 civilians, including 150 children. Newspapers across Canada published heart-rending stories about the victims and survivors of the sinking alongside further accounts of the fighting in the Ypres salient. The war was now recognized as a struggle against a brutal, barbaric enemy.

In revisionist accounts of the Great War some writers have sought to minimize German war crimes in 1914–15, but at the time Canadians recognized policies designed to inspire terror for what they were. Recently, historian Jeffrey Keshen has added to the revisionist approach, arguing that Canadians were 'manipulated' by elites and a 'jingoistic press,' which presented 'unrealistically blithe images about trench warfare.'[23] In his study, *Propaganda and Censorship during Canada's Great War*, based on government censorship files, he suggests that Canadians at home were denied the opportunity to learn the realities of war and were force-fed a romantic version of heroic sacrifice.

This view of the home front is contradicted by Ian Miller's detailed study of Toronto in which he cites examples of private letters routinely published in the press describing the war in gruesome detail. This was particularly true after the first gas attack when, to cite just one example, a letter from the front printed in the Toronto *World* informed readers that 'the dead are piled in heaps and the groans of the wounded and dying never leave me. Every night we have to clear the roads of dead in order to get our wagons through. On our way back to base we pick up loads of wounded soldiers and bring them back to the dressing stations.'[24]

The censors could do little to prevent the printing of such letters, and they proved equally unable to control the content of articles on the war. One attempt to stop the publication[25] of Robert W. Service's gritty descriptions of his experiences as an ambulance driver was ignored by editors determined to print front-line reports from the popular author and poet. Service's description of the 'Red Harvest' of the trenches, with its images of 'poor hopeless cripples' and a man who seemed to be 'just one big wound,' left no room for doubt about the ugliness of war.[26] The effect of such accounts was to inspire young Canadians to enlist in a great crusade against an evil enemy.[27] Historians who are uncomfortable with this reality should avoid imposing their own sensitivities on a generation which had few doubts about the importance of the cause they were fighting for.

The Canadians returned to the battlefields of Flanders on 17 May, capturing 'one small orchard and two muddy ditches' at a cost of 2,468 casualties. The capture of the 'Canadian Orchard' was a small part of a major Franco-British offensive which included a futile attempt to seize Vimy Ridge.[28] Overall Allied losses in May and June totalled more than 200,000 men, a clear demonstration that battles could not be won with the weapons available in 1915. The British and French field commanders were convinced that with more and better shells for the artillery, including ones filled with gas, they would break the German defences. Lord Kitchener, who was striving to create a 'New Army' which would place seventy divisions in the field, was less sure. He was preparing for a long war but admitted he had no idea of how it might be won.[29] It is evident that the British generals, like their French and German counterparts, were totally surprised by the harsh realities of trench warfare. They simply had no idea of how to get men across the zones of machine-gun, mortar, and artillery fire to close with the enemy. They were equally unprepared to exploit any breach in their opponent's defensive position if it should occur.

Senior British officers, with a few outstanding exceptions, demonstrated a profound lack of imagination and initiative in the early years of the war. The first suggestions for a tracked armoured vehicle which could overcome barbed wire and cross trenches were made in Britain during the fall of 1914, but the army was uninterested. Instead, experiments were carried out by a 'landships committee' formed by Winston Churchill through his control of naval expenditures. The first such vehicles, known for security reasons as 'tanks,' were ready for use in July 1916 and employed for the first time on 15 September, though another year passed before large numbers were available.[30] Steel helmets, which saved many lives, were issued by the French in early 1915, but British and Canadian troops waited another year before helmets became standard issue. The Germans made extensive use of trench mortars, but it was not until August 1915 that the British War Office authorized the mass production of the British-invented Stokes mortar.[31] The shortage of artillery shells was not resolved until 1916. The public were not aware of these problems, but they were well informed about machine guns, which were said to account for German success in trench warfare.

The arrival of the 2nd Canadian Division in England in June 1915 raised an important question about the future of Canadian formations in the British Army. Sam Hughes was determined that they should serve together and proposed the formation of the Canadian Corps. Normally, the composition of a British corps, made up of two or more divisions, varied according to the exigencies of war, but Kitchener agreed that an exception could be made for the Canadians. Alderson was appointed to command the Corps and two Canadian militia officers, Arthur Currie and R. W. Turner, were promoted to command the 1st Division and the 2nd Division, respectively.[32]

Despite the evident stalemate and heavy casualties, Allied generals and their political masters agreed that the war must continue. At the Chantilly conference of July 1915 a decision was reached on a massive Anglo-French offensive to be carried out in the spring of 1916. Preparations, especially the production of enough guns and shells to destroy the enemy's barbed wire and crush his defences, were to be the foundation of an attack they hoped would rupture the enemy front, leading to a mobile war and victory on the field of battle. The same optimism was evident within the German army, where plans for an offensive designed to win the war in 1916 culminated in the attack on the French fortress city of Verdun. The intent was not to capture ground but to bleed the French army and destroy its will to fight.[33]

The Canadians spent a relatively quiet winter, and it was not until spring 1916 that 2nd Division was committed to a major action. Georges Vanier, the future governor general, who was serving with the 22nd Battalion, wrote to his mother describing the emotions he felt when marching through France, 'the country I love so much in order to fight in its defence.'[34] Then, as the French and German armies tried to destroy each other at Verdun, his battalion and the rest of 2nd Division were ordered to take over positions near St Eloi, which a British division had fought to capture and hold. The British had sunk mine shafts under the German lines and set off explosions that wiped out the landmarks and created seven craters, the largest of which was 50 feet deep and 180 feet across. The attempt to relieve that British division in the midst of the battle compounded a bad initial plan, and the Canadians were soon caught up in a disaster which cost the division 1,173 casualties.[35]

The battle of St Eloi led to another crisis in command relationships when the Corps commander sought to dismiss General Turner and one of his brigadiers for alleged incompetence. The new British commander-in-chief, General Sir Douglas Haig, refused to confirm the decision because of 'the danger of a serious feud between the Canadians and the British [...] and because in the circumstances of the battle for the craters mistakes are to be expected.'[36] Canadian historians have tended to side with Alderson and condemn Turner, noting that political interference from Hughes and his representative Sir Max Aitken (later Lord Beaverbrook) saved Turner and cost Alderson his job as Corps commander.[37] But the case against Turner is made on Clausewitzian grounds, suggesting that a competent commander is by definition one who reacts properly and masters the situation. If this standard is applied, uniformly few generals on either side make the grade, and we are left with fallible, stubborn, imperfect humans, unable to foresee the future and almost always overwhelmed by the chaos of battle.

The Canadians, now including the 3rd Division, spent the summer of 1916 in familiar positions north of Ypres. The enemy was still able to shell the salient from several directions, making life in the forward lines both miserable and very dangerous. Many Canadian (and British) officers expressed their bitter opposition to orders to hold and attempt to expand the Ypres salient. Sam Hughes, always suspicious of decisions made by British professional soldiers, created a major controversy when he publicly denounced the policy. By the spring of 1916 Hughes had little credibility left, and Borden moved to dismiss his troublesome minister.[38]

[...]

While the Canadians endured life in the Ypres salient, the British began their major 1916 offensive: the Battle of the Somme. The Somme is now remembered chiefly for the first day, when 21,000 men were killed and 35,000 wounded,[69] the worst single-day disaster in British military history. Canadians did not take part, but the Newfoundland Regiment, part of the British 29th Division, lost 272 men killed and 438 wounded from a strength of 790 men; that is why 1 July is Memorial Day in Newfoundland.[40]

The failure to achieve the hoped-for breakthrough did not mean the battle was over, and the Somme fighting continued throughout the summer. One of the few bright spots was the success of the Royal Flying Corps in winning air superiority over the battlefield. S.F. Wise, who wrote *Canadian Airmen and the First World War*, notes that with new tactics and the concentration of 400 aircraft the RFC was able to dominate the sky, forcing the enemy to find the resources to meet this new threat. Fully 10 per cent of the pilots engaged at the Somme were Canadians who had transferred from the army.[41]

The RFC also played a major role in the new offensive which began on 15 September 1916. The Canadian Corps, three divisions strong, was part of an attack which involved two British armies. The battle of Flers-Courcelette began with the first ever attempt to employ tanks on the battlefield. Haig's decision to use the small number of tanks then available to assist in a set-piece attack was and continues to be criticized, because it sacrificed the element of surprise.[42] It is evident that Haig believed a breakthrough was still possible in 1916, and he insisted on using whatever was available. The Canadians, attacking astride the Albert-Baupaume road, were supported by two detachments of three tanks each. According to Nicholson, the 'presence of the tanks encouraged many Germans to surrender,' but most were put out of action in the first hours of the battle.[43] The RFC, which attacked the enemy's trenches with machine-gun fire, may well have played a larger role in securing the initial modest gains. Despite improvements in artillery doctrine and a vast increase in the supply of shells, Flers-Courcelette quickly degenerated into an attritional battle which was to cost the Canadians 24,029 casualties. These losses included 1,250 men of the 4th Canadian Division, which fought its first battle in November 1916.

Haig's policy of continuing the Somme battle after it was evident that there was little hope of defeating the enemy in 1916 was bitterly opposed by many British political leaders, including David Lloyd George, who became prime minister in December 1916. Lloyd George's criticisms of Haig and the war of attrition on the Western Front would continue until the armistice, but in the absence of a convincing alternative strategy the British and French armies continued to plan to renew the offensive in 1917.[44]

Lloyd George was anxious to limit the slaughter in the trenches, but he was not prepared to endorse the various peace proposals put forward by American president Woodrow Wilson, the papacy, and the German government.[45] The proposals were widely discussed in Canada, but since it was evident that negotiations were bound to produce a settlement faavourable to Germany because of its occupation of important parts of France, most of Belgium, and large areas of the Russian Empire, few Canadians endorsed the idea of an armistice in 1917. As there was no hope of peace on German terms, the Kaiser and his chief advisers decided to employ 'unrestricted submarine warfare' as a means of ending Britain's capacity to continue the war. This policy, implemented in February 1917, led to the sinking of American ships and a declaration of war against Germany by the United States on 6 April 1917.[46]

Allied military commanders remained committed to victory on the Western Front. The British preferred a plan to win control of the Belgian coast but agreed to cooperate with a French proposal for a coordinated Anglo-French attack designed to encircle and destroy large elements of the German army. Before the 'Nivelle offensive,' named for the new French commander Robert Nivelle, began, however, the enemy withdrew its forward defences to a new position known as the Hindenburg Line, some twenty miles to the east. This manoeuvre shortened and strengthened the German lines, destroying what little prospect of success the offensive had promised, but the operation was not cancelled.

The British part in the April offensive, known as the Battle of Arras, included plans for the capture of Vimy Ridge, a feature which dominated the Lens-Douai plain to the east. The Germans did not abandon the ridge when they withdrew to the Hindenburg Line, since the ridge was considered of vital importance and the defences were thought to be impenetrable. The Battle of Arras, like the rest of the Nivelle offensive, yielded little except death and destruction except at Vimy, where the Canadian Corps won an important local victory announced to the world as 'Canada's Easter gift to France.' The success of the Canadian Corps has given rise to a peculiar myth, which relates the capture of Vimy Ridge to the emergence of Canada as a nation. This is a theme requiring analysis of the construction of post-war memory rather than reflecting the actual events of April 1917.[47]

Canadian historians have also been drawn to the battle for Vimy Ridge when seeking to examine the idea that the Corps was a particularly effective component of the Allied armies. The most systematic study of these issues is Bill Rawling's *Surviving Trench Warfare*, in which he examines the changes in weapons and tactics between 1914 and 1918. Rawling argues that 'each soldier' became 'a specialist with a specific role to play in battle.' The Canadian Corps, he writes, 'moved away from the concept of the citizen-soldier who could ride and shoot to an army of technicians which, even in infantry battalions, specialized in particular aspects of fighting battles.'[48] Rawling believes that the growing sophistication of the Canadian Corps helps to explain the dramatic success at Vimy and in the battles of 1918.

There is much to be learned from this and other explorations of the evolution of tactics, but Vimy was primarily a set-piece battle dominated by artillery. The troops were carefully rehearsed to move quickly to their assigned objectives, relying on 'one heavy gun for every twenty yards of front and a field gun for every ten yards, twice the density available in the Somme battles.'[49] This enormous firepower, most of it British, together with the elaborate counter-battery work of British and Canadian gunners permitted the Corps to move steadily across the sloping, featureless terrain. By early afternoon on 9 April three of the four divisions had reached the crest of the ridge. When Hill 145, the objective of 4th Division, fell three days later, the entire ridge was in Canadian hands. The victory was costly, 3,598 dead and 6,664 wounded,[50] but the attack, Rawling argues, 'ended with a different balance between cost and results.'[51]

After Vimy the Corps commander, Sir Julian Byng, was promoted, and Arthur Currie took over the task of directing what had become Canada's national army. As Jack Hyatt has demonstrated in his biography of Currie, the transition to Corps commander was fraught with personal and political difficulties. To Currie's everlasting credit these issues did not interfere with his leadership of the Corps in action.[52] In August 1917 Currie orchestrated the capture of Hill 70 on the outskirts of Lens and forced the enemy to try to retake it at enormous cost.[53] Many historians regard this action as the outstanding achievement of the Corps.

Currie did his best to prevent the Canadians from being drawn into the Third Battle of Ypres, known to history as Passchendaele. Even Haig's most ardent defenders are unable to persuade themselves that the continuation of offensive operations in Flanders made sense in the fall of 1917.[54] The original plan, with its promise of an advance to the Belgian coast, may have had some merit, but by October, when the Canadians were sent into action, the battle could be justified only as an effort to pin down and wear out the German army. Attritional warfare is a two-edged sword, however, and British losses at Passchendaele were at least as great as those suffered by the enemy.[55]

Currie protested vigorously against participation in the battle and tried to enlist Prime Minister Borden in the cause. Hyatt suggests that his opposition was overcome only when Haig intervened to personally persuade Currie that Passchendaele must be captured. Because he had great respect for Haig, Currie obeyed, and the Canadians were committed to a battle which has come to symbolize the horrors of the Western Front.

Currie's opposition to Canadian participation at Passchendaele did not mean that he was opposed to Haig's overall strategy of wearing down the enemy by attacking on the Western Front. What Currie and a number of other generals questioned was Haig's stubborn persistence in continuing operations which had little chance of success. At Passchendaele the Canadians did succeed in capturing the ruins of what had once been the village, but the cost of the month's fighting, more than 15,000 casualties, was a price no Canadian thought worth paying.[56] As Third Ypres ended, the first large-scale tank battle in history was fought at nearby Cambrai, and for a brief moment it appeared that the long-sought breakthrough had been achieved. Then the Germans counter-attacked, regaining most of the lost ground. The war would continue into 1918.

At home Canadians reacted to the war news and the endless casualty lists in varying ways. In French-speaking areas of Quebec the war had never seemed of much importance and few young men had volunteered. The exploits of the one French-Canadian battalion, the 22nd, were featured in the daily newspapers, but public opinion remained generally indifferent or hostile to pleas for new recruits. Henri Bourassa and other nationalist leaders demanded redress from the 'Boche' of Ontario, where French-language schools had been abolished, but there is no evidence that reversal of this policy would have altered French-Canadian attitudes towards the war. The Canadian victory at Vimy Ridge had no discernable nation-building impact in Quebec.

The situation was very different in most English-speaking communities.[57] Hundreds of thousands of young men had joined and tens of thousands had been killed or wounded. Winning the war, thereby justifying these sacrifices, was a shared goal which few challenged. When the pool of able-bodied volunteers dried up in late 1916, public opinion favoured conscription long before Prime Minister Borden announced its introduction. The near unanimity of opinion in English-speaking Canada was evident in the 1917 federal election, when most opposition candidates, ostensibly loyal to Wilfrid Laurier and the Liberal Party, campaigned on a win-the-war, pro-conscription platform.[58]

Arthur Currie tried to keep the Canadian Corps out of politics, but the Unionist political managers were determined to use the military vote to influence the outcome in marginal ridings. The manipulations of the soldiers' vote for partisan political purposes should not be allowed to obscure the overwhelming endorsement the men serving overseas gave to the Unionist cause.

The prospect of an Allied victory appeared remote in January 1918. The collapse of czarist Russia and the seizure of power by the Bolsheviks led to negotiations to end the war in the east. Inevitably the peace treaty, signed at Brest-Litovsk, was dictated by Germany and included vast transfers of territory. The German army could now bring large numbers of troops to the Western Front and seek victory on the battlefield before the American Expeditionary Force was ready for combat.[59] The French government and military believed that the best they could hope for was to withstand the expected German attack and prepare to renew the offensive in 1919, relying on the full force of the American army. The British government shared this view, though General Haig insisted that, after defeating a German attack, the Allies could win the war in 1918 by vigorous action.[60]

In 1918 the Canadian Corps played a major role, out of all proportion to its relative size. One reason was the decision to maintain all four Canadian divisions at full strength rather than follow the British example and reduce the number of infantry battalions from twelve to nine. The Canadian Corps found the men it needed not through conscription but as a result of the decision to break up the 5th Division forming in England and use its battalions to reinforce the four divisions in the field. This move allowed the Corps to solve its manpower problems for the spring of 1918, though it was evident that if the war continued, tens of thousands of conscripts would be required. Currie was also responsible for improvements in the training and organization of the Corps, including a reorganization of Bruitnel's machine gunners into a mobile reserve 'mounted in armoured cars and directly under the control of the corps commander.'[61]

Between March and June 1918 the Germans unleashed four major operations, recovering all the ground gained by the Allies since 1914, capturing 250,000 prisoners, and inflicting more than 1 million casualties on the Allied armies.[62] It was all in vain. The German commanders gambled everything on a collapse of Allied morale, but when the offensive ended in July, their armies, overextended and exhausted, faced a powerful and resolute Allied coalition under the command of Marshal Ferdinand Foch.

The Canadian Corps, holding ground well to the north of the main point of the German attack, was initially required to place divisions under British command, but after Currie protested, the Corps was reunited under his control. Although this policy was bitterly resented by the British senior officers, who were fighting a life-and-death struggle with the German army, Currie and Borden were adamant: the Canadians would fight together.[63]

On 8 August 1918 the Corps, deployed alongside Australian, British, and French formations, launched an attack at Amiens which was so successful that it became known as the 'black day' of the German army. S.F. Wise, who is preparing a book-length study of the Amiens battle, emphasizes the effect the Allied advance had on the German high command. 'They had struck,' he writes, 'a crippling blow at the will of the enemy, surely the chief object of strategy.'[64] The offensive soon lost momentum, but this time Haig agreed to break off the action and mount a new attack at Arras to be spearheaded by the Canadians. The period from 8 August to 11 November 1918 became known as the 'Hundred Days,' a period in which the Allied armies made spectacular gains, defeating the German armies in a series of battles which many historians believed determined the outcome of the war.[65] Throughout the Hundred Days the Canadians were in action at Amiens, Drocourt-Quéant, Canal du Nord, Cambrai, Valenciennes, and Mons.[66] The cost of these victories, more than 40,000 casualties,[67] was high, but they were seen as the necessary price of ending the war in 1918. Recently, British military historians have concentrated their research on this period, arguing that too much attention has been paid to the attritional battles of 1916 and 1917. Developing the themes first argued by John Terraine,[68] historians associated with the Imperial War Museum in Great Britain have begun an assessment of every division which fought in the armies of the British Empire. Their preliminary work suggests that many British as well as the Canadian, Australian, and New Zealand divisions were highly effective military organizations before and during the Hundred Days.[69]

Canadians were not involved in the negotiations which led to the armistice of 11 November 1918, but it is evident that both Currie and Borden shared the views of British, French, and American diplomats who were determined, in President Wilson's words, 'to make a renewal of hostilities on the part of Germany impossible.' This meant that Germany would have to surrender more or less unconditionally, and so proved. Canada's military effort in the First World War allowed the prime minister to insist upon the right to sign the Treaty of Versailles and to secure separate membership in the League of Nations.[70] Canada's new international status was only one sign of the growing sense of nationhood felt by English-speaking Canadians.

The Canadian Corps and the Canadian people had accomplished great things together in what they believed to be a necessary and noble cause. Most Canadians held to this view of their war experience despite the rise of revisionist accounts of the causes of the conflict and efforts by poets, novelists, and historians to portray the Great War as an exercise in futility. When the decision to build a great memorial at Vimy Ridge was made, the purpose was 'to commemorate the heroism [...] and the victories of the Canadian soldier.' The memorial was to be dedicated to 'Canada's ideals, to Canada's courage and to Canada's devotion to what the people of the land decreed to be right.'[71] It was this view of the war that sent enthusiastic crowds into the streets when General Haig visited Canada in 1925.[72] It was this memory of the war that sustained the regular army and militia volunteers throughout the years of retrenchment and depression.

270

NOTES

1. Samuel Hynes, *A War Imagined: The First World War and English Culture* (London, 1990), ix.

2. Martin Stephan, *The Price of Pity: Poetry, History and the Myth of the Great War* (London, 1996), xv.

3. Ian Miller, 'Our Glory and Our Grief: Toronto and the Great War,' PhD thesis, Wilfrid Laurier University, 1999, 28–53.

4. Newspaper opinion on these and other issues can be found in J. Castell Hopkins, ed., *The Canadian Annual Review of Public Affairs* (Toronto, 1914–18), (hereafter CAR), as well as in the newspapers themselves, available on microfilm.

5. A good introduction to the current research may be found in Keith Wilson, ed., *Decisions for War, 1914* (London, 1995).

6. Marc Milner, *Canada's Navy* (Toronto, 1994).

7. The story of Hughes's deeds and misdeeds may be followed in *CAR* and the *Debates* of the House of Commons. See Ronald Haycock, *Sam Hughes: The Public Career of a Controversial Canadian, 1885–1916* (Waterloo, 1986).

8. Desmond Morton, *When Your Number's Up: The Canadian Soldier in the First World War* (Toronto, 1993), 9.

9. *CAR, 1914,* 180.

10. Ibid., 197.

11. *CAR, 1914,* 182, 227, 190.

12. Evidence for the public commitment to Belgium and its refugees may be found in every Canadian newspaper. See *CAR, 1914,* 228, for a summary.

13. A.J.M. Hyatt, *General Sir Arthur Currie: A Military Biography* (Toronto, 1987), 16.

14. Morton, *When Your Number's Up,* 31.

15. Andrew Iarocci, 'The Mad Fourth,' MA thesis, Wilfrid Laurier University, 2001.

16. For the most detailed account of 2nd Ypres see A.F. Duguid, *Official History of the Canadian Forces in the Great War, 1914–1919,* Vol. 1 (Ottawa, 1938). No further volumes were published. See also Daniel G. Dancocks, *Welcome to Flanders Fields, the First Canadian Battle of the Great War: Ypres, 1915* (Toronto: McClelland and Stewart, 1988).

17. Tim Cook, *No Place to Run: The Canadian Corps and Gas Warfare in the First World War* (Vancouver, 1999), 13.

18. Ibid., 21

19. Nicholson, *Canadian Expeditionary Force,* 78, 83–4.

20. Rawling, *Surviving Trench Warfare,* 221.

21. Timothy Travers, 'Currie and 1st Division at Second Ypres, April 1915,' *Canadian Military History* (hereafter CMH), 5, 2 (1996), 7–15.

22. Quoted in Miller, 'Our Glory and Our Grief,' 115, 117–18.

23. Jeffrey A. Keshen, *Propaganda and Censorship during Canada's Great War* (Edmonton, 1996) xi–xii.

24. Miller, 'Our Glory and Our Grief,' 131.

25. Keshen, *Propaganda and Censorship,* 29.

26. Toronto *Star,* 14 December 1915.

27. A total of 42,000 men had been accepted for enlistment in the 2nd and 3rd contingents before Second Ypres. A further 35,000 men enlisted immediately after the battle and by the end of 1915 212,000 men were under arms. The Canadian-born proportion of this total was 30 per cent. *CAR 1915,* 208–9.

28. Nicholson, *Canadian Expeditionary Force,* 103.

29. Llewellyn Woodward, *Great Britain and the War of 1914–18* (London, 1967) chap. 4.

30. B.H. Liddel Hart, *The Tanks* (London, 1959), Vol. 1, chap. 2.

31. Woodward, *Great Britain,* 43–4.

32. Nicholson, *Canadian Expeditionary Force,* 114.

33. Ibid., 160–100.

34. Deborah Cowley, ed, *Georges Vanier: Soldier* (Toronto, 2000), 79.

35. Nicholson, *Canadian Expeditionary Force,* 137–45.

36. Quoted in Hyatt, *General Sir Arthur Currie,* 55.

37. See the recent articles, Tim Cook, 'The Blind Leading the Blind: The Battle of the St. Eloi Craters,' *CMH,* 5, 2 (1996), 24–36; and Thomas P. Leppard, 'The Dashing Subaltern: Sir Richard Turner in Retrospect,' *CMH,* 6, 2 (Autumn 1997), 21–8.

38. The events are outlined in *CAR, 1916,* 260–1.

39. Ian McCulloch, 'Batty Mac: Portrait of a Brigade Commander of the Great War, 1915–1917,' *CMH,* 7, 4 (1998), 22.

40. Woodward, *Great Britain,* 148.

41. Nicholson, *Canadian Expeditionary Force,* 507–9. See also David Facey-Crowther, ed., *Better Than the Best: The Story of the Royal Newfoundland Regiment, 1795–1995* (St John's, 1995).

42. S.F. Wise, *Canadian Airmen and the First World War* (Toronto, 1980). See also Guy Hartcup, *The War of Invention: Scientific Developments, 1914–1918* (London, 1988).

43. Trevor Pidgeon, *The Tanks at Flers* (Cobham, U.K., 1995), 21–30.

44. Nicholson, *Canadian Expeditionary Force,* 169.

45. Ibid., 198.

46. Woodward, *Great Britain,* 227–42.

47. Holger H. Herwig, 'Total Rhetoric, Limited War: Germany's U-boat Campaign, 1917–1918,' in Roger Chickering and Stig Forester, eds, *Great War, Total War* (Cambridge, 2000), 189–206.

48. Jonathan Vance, *Death So Noble: Memory, Meaning and the First World War* (Vancouver, 1997).

49. Rawling, *Surviving Trench Warfare,* 217. For a parallel discussion of British tactical innovation see Paddy Griffith, ed., *British Fighting Methods in the Great War* (London, 1996).

50. Rawling, *Surviving Trench Warfare,* 219.

51. Nicholson, *Canadian Expeditionary Force,* 265.

52. Rawling, *Surviving Trench Warfare,* 219.

53. Hyatt, *General Sir Arthur Currie,* 74–5.

54. Nicholson, *Canadian Expeditionary Force,* 272–97.

55. Robin Prior and Trevor Wilson, *Passchendaele: The Untold Story* (New Haven, Conn., 1996).

56. Hyatt, *General Sir Arthur Currie,* 84–5.

57. Nicholson, *Canadian Expeditionary Force,* 327.

58. See, for example, Leslie Frost, *Fighting Men* (Toronto, 1967).

59. Patrick Ferraro, 'English Canada and the Election of 1917,' MA thesis, McGill University, 1971.

60. Holger H. Herwig, *The First World War: Germany and Austria-Hungary* (New York: 1997), 392–5.

61. Woodward, *Great Britain,* 324.

62. Hyatt, *General Sir Arthur Currie,* 102–3, 102.

63. Ibid., 105–6.

64. Nicholson, *Canadian Expeditionary Force,* 460.

65. S.F. Wise, 'The Black Day of the German Army: Australians and Canadians at Amiens, August 1918,' in Peter Dennis and Jeffrey Grey, eds, 1918: *Defining Victory* (Canberra, 1999), 32.

66. G.D. Sheffield, 'The Indispensable Factor: The Performance of British Troops in 1918,' in Dennis and Grey, *1918,* 72–94. For a more critical approach, see Timothy Travers, *How the War Was Won: Command and Technology in the British Army on the Western Front, 1917–1918* (London, 1992).

67. Shane B. Schreiber, *Shock Army of the British Empire: The Canadian Corps in the Last 100 Days of the Great War* (Westport, Conn., 1997).

68. Nicholson, *Canadian Expeditionary Force,* 485–506.

69. John Terraine, *To Win a War: 1918, the Year of Victory* (London, 1998).

70. John Lee, 'The SHLM Project—Assessing the Battle Performance of British Divisions,' in Paddy Griffith, ed., *British Fighting Methods in the Great War* (London, 1996), 175–181.

71. Robert Craig Brown, *Robert Laird Borden: A Biography. Vol. II, 1914–1937* (Toronto, 1980), 155–8.

72. Canada, *House of Commons Debates,* 1922.

73. John Scott, 'Three Cheers for Earl Haig,' *CMH,* 5, 1 (1996), 35–40.

Article 2: Documenting War and Forging Reputations, 1914–18

Tim Cook

The Canadian Corps was one of the finest fighting formations in the Great War, regarded by both allies and enemies as shock troops that were thrown into the bloodiest campaigns to deliver victory. With an almost non-existent professional army before the war, Canada raised 600,000 men, of whom 424,000 served overseas from 1914 to 1919. As with other national armies fighting on the Western Front, the casualties were appalling; by the armistice, more than 60,000 Canadians were dead, and another 138,000 had been wounded in combat. Despite this bloodletting, or perhaps as a result of it, the Canadians earned a reputation as determined and efficient soldiers. [...]

Despite frequent allusions to the country being populated by a race of sportsmen and hunters, the Canadians were not immediately viewed as an elite force. Drawn from the harsh dominion of the North, Canadians were seen as undisciplined, unruly troops who had proved their unconventional but adept fighting skills during the South African War; however they were deemed more brawlers than soldiers.[1] Moreover the difficult learning curve on the Western Front was cruel to all inexperienced troops and the Canadians were no exception. They went through several difficult and costly battles in the first two years of the wear that left them viewed as suspect by their British commanders. This changed by the end of the Battle of the Somme in 1916. Like their Australian counterparts, who were also seen as an elite force by the end of the war, as the Canadian gained fighting confidence and skills, they began to develop an independent identity. In the process, the Dominion armies demanded recognition from the British who fought next to them. This sense of distinction helped to foster sprite to corps within Canadian units, but the creation of an identity did not happen by chance. The Canadian Corps had an active propaganda campaign that publicized Canadian uniqueness throughout the war.

The organization behind this promotion was the Canadian War Records Office, headed by Sir Max Aitken, later Lord Beaverbrook, an expatriate Canadian millionaire with close ties to Military and Political leaders in both Canada and the United Kingdom. With characteristic passion, Aitken employed his considerable skills as a press baron, member of parliament, and influential peer to advance a relentless campaign extolling the heroic deeds of Canadians in battle. Journalistic features accentuating Canadian exploits, the commissioning of artists, photographers, and cinematographers to craft Canadian-content works, the creation of commemorative journals, and even the publication of the first popular ward histories, all helped to shape a distinctive Canadian identity. Largely at his own discretion, but also supported by Prime Minister Sir Robert Borden, Minister of Militia and Defence Sir Sam Hughes, and the Ministers of Overseas Military Forces, Sir George Perley and Sir A.E. Kemp, Aitken's active campaign, when combined with the very real accomplishments of the Canadian Corps on the battlefield, enshrined the Canadians' reputation within the British Expeditionary Force (BEF). With an eye on the future, Aitken would provide a steady barrage of media products to manufacture a sense of distinctiveness and identity for the Canadian soldier, while at the same time gathering, writing, and preserving a legacy of war records that would be employed by future historians to understand the Great War.

Many Canadians followed the deteriorating situation in the summer of 1914, and the government turned to a number of experts for advice. One of the most prominent, Sir Max Aitken advised his acquaintances Robert Borden and Sam Hughes that it was unlikely that Britain would ever go to war over an issue in the Balkans. Yet as brinkmanship spiralled into war ultimata, Aitken changed his appreciation, supplying the now scrambling Canadian government with inside information gleaned from British social circles, which included friends such as Winston Churchill, Andrew Bonar Law and Rudyard Kipling. And when Great Britain declared war on 4 August, Canada too, as a dominion in the British Empire, was at war. The Cabinet needed someone to keep it abreast of the ever-changing situation on the Western Font and in the backrooms of London. Notwithstanding a somewhat darkened reputation, Aitken was well suited for the job.

273

Max Aitken was born in 1879 and raised in New Brunswick. While excelling neither at studies nor sports, he exhibited a command of business, running several profitable schemes at an early age. He began to acquire small companies in his twenties, sell shares in them, and purchase new companies with his profits. An exuberant and energetic figure, short in stature and with an enormous grin, Aitken revelled in deal-making. He earned grand profits while others floundered in his wake. After making millions from buying up, amalgamating, and creating monopolistic conglomerates, and then selling out at the right time, Aitken left Canada for England in 1910 under a cloud of suspicion.[2] Viewed by some as a market exploiter, perhaps he had simply made too much money too quickly. He had certainly not spread enough of it around to the powerful men who effectively controlled the burgeoning Canadian economy.

Aitken wasted little time in establishing himself in British society. He won a parliamentary seat in 1911, was knighted for his support of the Tory party, and began to buy up newspapers shortly thereafter. Nonetheless, Aitken was mistrusted for his dealings in Canada and possibly for his "new money" wealth. Socially active in some of the best London clubs—certainly more so than he was in the House of Commons—he also contributed journalistic pieces to Canadian newspapers. He kept in touch in other ways too, providing support and money to the Canadian Conservative Party, especially Borden and Hughes, to whom he gave campaign money for the 1911 election. When war was declared, Aitken was thus not only seen as the Canadian expert in Britain, but also as a political ally. Yet Sir Max was expected to be asked to assist the Herbert Asquith government in prosecuting the war effort, and he was bitterly disappointed when the appointment failed to materialize. After some soul searching, he appealed to his Canadian friends for a fitting position to serve his country of birth.

But Aitken was not without his faults. Borden was unsure if Aitken, who still had powerful enemies among the Canadian business élite, was more of a handicap than an advantage. Undeterred by Borden's lukewarm responses to his initial offer of assistance, Aitken appealed to his Sam Hughes at the end of 1914, claiming that the 'most important section of London Press agrees to give me opportunity to describe Canadian mobilization in series of illustrated articles.' His fervent desire to assist was evident, being sure that he could be 'a service in the whole Canadian situation'.[3] However, this service did extend to enlisting in the Canadian Expeditionary Force (CEF); he was far too rich and plagued by asthma to serve in the front lines.

On Hughes's urging, the Canadian Cabinet appointed Aitken to the position of Eye Witness, in which he would supply Canadians with wartime information.[4] [...]

To document the war work of the Canadian Division, Aitken traveled behind the front in his Rolls-Royce and interviewed scores of Canadian soldiers and officers in the field. He became a recognized figure and was adept at drawing stories out of tired men, even when the staff officers at the rear disliked his involvement.[5] Aitken's role was nearly unique as there were few war correspondents at the front.[6] Moreover, when he encountered problems with British staff officers bent on enforcing rules to quash all unauthorized information, Aitken utilized his status as special envoy for the Canadian government, as well as his influential position in the Conservative Party, to ensure that he was not impeded. An opponent of censorship throughout the war, Aitken was able to force the military's hand and to relax its strict rules regarding the dissemination of information to the public. "The trouble about the Eye Witness business is that the Eye Witness is ipso facto more or less official," wrote one army censor. "I could not undertake to vet the writings of the correspondent with regard to the truth."[7] His information-gathering skills, money, and official status placed him in a better position to comprehend the events of war than any other person in the CEF. And while General Alderson neither trusted nor liked him, the more junior Canadian brigadier generals and battalion commanders were generally enthusiastic in supporting Aitken, the man who was to chronicle and publicize their actions.[8] In addition to sending back weekly communiqués to Borden and the Canadian government, Aitken's journalistic accounts were published widely in Canadian newspapers. His very readable narratives must have been reassuring for many Canadian families. That was all to change in less than a month, however, as the Canadian Division would be shattered at the Battle of Second Ypres. [...]

Canada's Eye Witness made his name—as well as that of the Canadian Division—significantly more prominent with his vivid account of the heroic

Canadian stand at Ypres. Aitken's piece was published on 1 May 1915, and through his friendships with other press barons, his own newspapers, and his position as Eye Witness, his account of the brave Dominion soldiers was read widely throughout the Empire.

It appeared that the untried Canadian Division had stopped the Germans alone. The idea that Canadian troops were holding out against impossible odds and the nefarious release of chlorine gas resulted in a stirring narrative for readers in the super-charged patriotic atmosphere in England and in Canada. "The battle ... was bloody, even as men appraise battles in this callous and life-engulfing war." The Canadians were, according to Aitken, "enormously outnumbered" and their performance was "amazing" as the division consisted of "men who ... at the outbreak of the war were neither disciplined nor trained."[9] Further accounts stressed that the division was formed by the "Canadian people," who had joined partly for the "glory of adventure but more of the spirit of self-sacrifice."[10] Aitken turned the battle into an epic story, in line with the rousing accounts of the British Army's last stands against legions of natives in one of their many nineteenth-century colonial battles. This time, though, it was the Canadian boys who held off overwhelming odds, falling in droves, but keeping chins up, and eventually stopping the hordes of Huns advancing behind their death clouds. Aitken's success in carving out a distinguished record for the Canadians as an almost separate fighting force, rather than as Dominion troops fighting within a much larger British Expeditionary Force (BEF) structure, left some British politicians and officers complaining that it appeared to be only the Canadians fighting the Germans, with a little support from the British.[11] They were not, of course, but Aitken's publicity machine was far more effective than that supporting British troops. With the focused nature of his writing, Aitken's account of the Canadians, along with their obvious bravery in battle, began to forge their reputation.

With this journalistic success, Aitken realized that the Canadians needed more than one man to disseminate information about their deeds. He began to build a small office to both protect the Canadian war records and to fashion propaganda on Canadian military exploits. As early as January 1915, Aitken had reported to Hughes that the Canadian records kept by the British at the War Office were "in a state of

chaos."[12] This did not sit well with the minister who was already smarting from being denied the opportunity to command and who felt that the British were consistently displaying a haughty attitude towards him and his soldiers. With the full support of Hughes and Borden, and in the wake of his celebrated Ypres account, Aitken acquired a new role for himself as the official Canadian Records Officer in May 1915.[13]

With this title, he began to negotiate with the British Historical Section of the Committee of Imperial Defence to gain possession of the original Canadian War Diaries and operational war records. In one of the most prescient moves related to documenting the war, Aitken—once again at his own behest—pushed for and succeeded in controlling the records and thus the future history of the CEF. The nation that oversees its own archives is able to shape and manufacture its own history and eventually guard its own memory while creating its own identity. Aitken realized this from the start and believed in leaving a legacy of war records that would "lay down the bedrock of history."[14]

[...]

AFTER CHRONICLING the Canadians in action, Aitken did not have the time nor seemingly the inclination to visit the front again after witnessing the grim fighting of Second Ypres. Instead, he gathered a small team of wounded veterans and experienced writers to assist him in carrying out his twin mandates of collecting war records and publicizing the Canadian Corps. The Canadian War Records Office (CWRO) was established in January 1916.

Realizing that his vision of leaving a legacy of records would not have been possible if he waited for financial support from the budget-conscious Canadian government, Aitken paid for the CWRO, including the hiring of staff and the purchase of all supplies, out of his own pocket for six months before the government allocated $25,000 to cover some of the costs. In rooms donated by the Public Record Office, the CWRO staff registered, arranged, and examined the Canadian War Diaries sent to them from the field. Other historical material was also collected to better document the CEF, both units training in England and those serving in France and Belgium. General and routine orders, honours, and awards conferred on officers and men, photographs, soldier-published trench newspapers, and an assortment of other historical ephemera were gathered and catalogued. Later in

275

the war, the CWRO would actively create records to capture the Canadian war experience. Photographers, war artists, cinematographers, and historical officers would go into the field to capture their countrymen's actions for all history. "My office," wrote Aitken, "has a voracious appetite for historical documents."[15]

The CWRO became much more than a simple archives, however. Aitken was one of the principal figures administering the Canadian forces in England. Henry Beckles Wilson, who worked briefly in the CWRO, gave a description of the organization: it was almost "a corps headquarters in the field ... It was as if Aitken had clandestinely built up a simulacrum of Sir Sam Hughes's office in Ottawa, where place-hunters, contractors, officials, politicians and pressmen came and went all day ... It was, in effect, the real and immediate source of authority of the Canadian Corps in Europe."[16] Willson's exaggerated prose should not detract from Aitken's importance in England. He was recognized by his friends as a man of importance and feared by his enemies as a force to be reckoned with.

From the start, Aitken began to build his historical empire by making sure that senior officers in both England and France knew that he was now responsible for documenting the war and ensuring a legacy for the Canadian soldier. There were stumbling blocks, however. Alderson was particularly concerned that Aitken, whom he rightly associated with Sam Hughes, the minister who constantly interfered in the command of his Canadian Corps, would uncover and publish secret documents.[17] With his honorary military status, Aitken appeared to be just another political crony. To be clear, this was exactly what Aitken was—yet, at the same time, he took his role, as CEF archivist and historian seriously. If the responsibility of guarding documents for future generations did not sway the corps commander, the Eye Witness could reposition himself by promising not to reveal battle secrets irresponsibly but, instead, to "make the deeds of Canada shine brightly in this War. No effort will be spared to attain this end."[18] Aitken needed the war records not only to create a proper historical legacy but also to add legitimacy to his publicity projects. Even though Aitken was willing to present the Canadians in the best possible light in his publications, there is no evidence that the CWRO's staff censored or destroyed damning war records.

As Aitken moved from Eye Witness to official record keeper and unofficial publicist, he was assisted by several gifted individuals in his goals: Lieutenant Colonel (later Brigadier General) R.F. Manly Sims, a former British regular officer and businessman, was his chief liaison officer in France; Captain Theodore G. Roberts, the younger brother of the New Brunswick poet and writer Charles G.D. Roberts, took up much of the day-to-day writing; Henry Beckles Willson, historian and man-of-letters, was in charge of War Diaries until his stormy relationship with Aitken forced his resignation; and later, Talbot Papineau, a well-known French-Canadian nationalist, collected war records and wrote dispatches before returning to the front where he was killed. The CWRO's self-proclaimed guiding principle was to be the "spokesman for the Canadian Army; it was the official reporter of what was good to report; it was the eyes and the pen of the great inarticulate mass of men who were too busy fighting to tell just how they were fighting."[19] The CWRO officers may have been the spokesmen for the army, but they certainly were not neutral or objective in their approach—they judged what to report, and they defined what was to be emphasized and what would be forgotten.

Alderson remained wary of Aitken, but with his removal from command in May 1916, the CWRO had a better relationship with the new corps commander, Lieutenant General Sir Julian Byng. Attesting his power, Aitken had orchestrated the dirty business of undermining Alderson's position, ensuring that General Sir Douglas Haig, commander of the BEF, kept the questionably competent Canadian-born Major General Richard Turner, VC, in command of the 2nd Division while at the same time sacrificing Alderson for the sake of good relations between the Canadians and the British.[20] As Hughes's right-hand man in England, Aitken was more than an archivist gathering records for some future official historian: this was the man whom had manipulated the command of brigades and battalions, had the Canadian Corps commander removed, and would, in due course, have a hand in bringing down the Asquith government.[21] "Sir Max Aitken is a power in the land—at present—has immense influence in both Canadian and English governments and consequently upon the Army," wrote one observer.[22] Although Byng despised civilian interference from Canada and Britain, he was astute enough to curry favour with the powerful Sir Max whenever he had a chance. And if they went against his professional and personal instincts, then so be it.[23]

[...]

WITH BYNG'S CONTINUED SUPPORT, R.F. Manly Sims and Theodore Roberts, who were collecting war records at the front, supplied Aitken with information for the CWRO's newspaper communiqués and for the preparation of a second volume of *Canada in Flanders*.[24] However, this was never easy, and Manly Sims confided to Aitken, who was anxious to receive records of the Canadian fighting at Mount Sorrel in June 1916, that he would need a "seer" to understand the true picture of the battle.[25] The confusion and chaos of attack and counterattack did not lend itself to an easy retelling, primarily since most of the witnesses were dead, maimed, or had seen little and understood less outside of their couple of hundred metres of battlefield. Noting that War Diaries and appendices varied in quality, Aitken appealed to Byng to reiterate to his subordinates the importance of keeping accurate and detailed war records.[26] The corps commander did this through a series of orders—one going so far as to warn that, "units which have not kept full and accurate reports may find that injustice has been done to them in [future] historical works.'[27] Despite such threats, it was found that many units still produced weak War Diaries and operational reports that failed to provide adequate information or coverage. The 18th Battalion's War Diary on the Somme was so useless that someone within the regiment added a note: "Not much help to a historian."[28] Understanding the need to gather war records and ensure their creation at the front prompted a small team of CWRO officers to be stationed in France.

There had been no CWRO representative on the Somme battlefield from September to November 1916, and the War Diaries and reports created there were considerably weaker than earlier historical records. With horrific casualties, it was not uncommon to lose most forward officers in an engagement, thereby leaving no one qualified to write up the reports of operations. At other times the strain of battle ensured that "some of the diaries are so illegible that they can scarcely be read."[29] The CWRO field historians, therefore, played an important role in assisting in the creation of records. This active intervention and actual authoring of war records in some cases was essential for providing documentary evidence of the ebb and flow of the war; as one CWRO report noted, "these records were snatched from the firing line and from men still red hot from the fiery ordeal of action." In the war records lay the "rigid testimony of truth," which must not "be allowed to perish with" the men who created them.[30] Without the CWRO's intercession, the records available to subsequent generations of Canadians and historians would have been far less comprehensive.[31]

In addition to the collection of war records, the CWRO historical officers assisted the regimental war diarists and officers tasked with writing up operations. Besides being overworked, exhausted, and sometimes without the necessary literary skills, the battalion war diarists often did not have a full picture of the battle. How were they to describe an engagement raging across a broad front when they were stationed at rear headquarters? As a result, they often turned to the historical officers to supply them with information or add overlooked details. Captain Talbot Papineau described his role as an historical officer in the field, emphasizing in a letter home that, "You must understand that I am not a mere newspaper correspondent. Nothing makes me angrier. I write many official staff documents as well. For instance yesterday I made a complete tour of our whole battle front—interviewed almost all the Battalion commanders—personally examined the enemy lines and finally wrote a long report which the General favourably commented upon today."[32]

[...]

All of this active work in creating and safeguarding records had been the result of the energetic interventions by Sir Max Aitken. However, he would not stop there. As part of his desire to promote Canadian soldiers, Aitken hoped to commemorate their deeds by producing a collection of their own writings. With that in mind and basing the project on the very successful Australian *Anzac Book*, he instructed Manly Sims in July 1916 to write to commanding officers that the CWRO wished to publish stories, poems, cartoons, and personal accounts of battle from frontline soldiers in a commemorative "war book for the masses."[33] Unfortunately, the response by most Canadian soldiers was lukewarm. Even then, Aitken complained that the submissions he did receive were "of very low order."[34] As such, he chose only those works that conformed to his own image of the Canadian soldier.[35] Accounts that emphasized fear and bitterness were excluded in favour of stories emphasizing abilities to stick it out and remain cool under fire. One submission read: "A C.O. detailed two Highlanders to escort four German Prisoners back to the prisoners' pen, about one and one half miles in the rear. In less than ten minutes they returned, and being questioned by the C.O., about the four German prisoners, replied;—"They all dropped dead Sir, and we didna [sic] want to miss this fight, so we returned."[36] Titled "Fact," the passage was both a mixture of trench humour and the grim nature of fighting on the Western Front—both considerations that were largely unknown to those on the home front. However, a record of the deliberate execution of German prisoners did not fit into Aitken's vision of a book that would glorify Canadian deeds. "Fact" was never published, and instead readers were treated to a collection of anecdotes of the "stiff-upper lip" variety that spoke to bravery, sacrifice, and nationalistic aspirations.

Although touted as a work by Canadian soldiers for Canadian soldiers, volume 1 of this commemorative work, published in January 1917 and entitled *Canada in Khaki*, consisted of a large number of journalistic and CWRO accounts, not to mention articles by Sir George Perley and other noteworthy Canadians. Nonetheless, there were poems and cartoons from soldiers that gave the journal a sense of authenticity. It was immensely successful, selling 40,000 copies in the first week.[37] Two more volumes followed, each selling tens of thousands of copies, and *Canada in Khaki* helped to create an image of the Canadian soldier that was thoroughly different from that of the British Tommy.

Yet what defined the Canadian soldier? Looking at the First Contingent, it was clear that the Canadian soldier was more likely to be British born than anything else. But with Aitken's products, the line between Canadian and Briton became blurred. *Canada in Khaki* is a useful example for analyzing Aitken's approach to myth making. Perley wrote that the Canadian forces were "native-born, British-born, and young men from all the varied races that in recent years have been carried by the tide of immigration into the Golden West." T.G. Roberts, Aitken's most trusted writer at the CWRO, went one step further, musing that although some of the Canadians may have been born outside of Canada, "He is no less a Canadian, either in his own heart or in the hearts of his friends [...] Whatever a man used to be, he is now what his cap badge proclaims him." These Canadian soldiers were, according to A.M. De Beck, editor of *Canadian News*, and another contributor to the journal, "Men from the prairies, from the wheat fields and the lumber-yards of the West; men accustomed to the saddle and to sport of all kinds; men who can wield an axe more deftly than I can hold a pen; men accustomed to face death twenty times a year or more, and who have waged war with Nature or with wild beasts all their lives—what wonder that they sprang to the call of war as surely never men sprang before. The clash of battle was as music to their ears." This "hardy breed of men, the stalwart children of nature" seemed, according to *Canada in Khaki*, bred for war. One final example must suffice: a cartoon by H.M. Bateman, entitled "The Canadian in Peace and War, as Imagined by an English Artist," goes to the heart of the image that Aitken was trying to construct. The drawing showed a young man stalking a bear, lumberjacks sitting on a great log, voyageurs exploring the land, gold prospectors striking it rich, and cowboys shooting bottles off a barrel. This "peacetime" iconography led directly to an image of a Canadian infantryman with bayonet herding three German prisoners through the line. Depicting a devil-may-care grin and stone-hewn features on the Canadian soldier, it was clear that our English artist clearly equated the rugged Canadian land with a rough and determined soldier. From cartoons, photographs, and editorials, a unique image of the Canadian soldier was being constructed in the pages of the CWRO-sponsored works.[38]

Along with these publications, Aitken felt that the public should have a chance to experience the deeds of the Canadian Corps by visualizing their exploits: "We must see our men climbing out of the trenches to the assault before we can realise the patience, the exhaustion, and the courage which are assets and the trials of modern fighting men."[39] Aitken would ensure that not only did the people of Canada know exactly what their sons, brothers, husbands, and fathers were doing in France and Belgium, but also that the rest of the world was told—over and over again—that it was Canadian soldiers fighting as a distinct unit, rather than as colonial cannon-fodder within the larger BEF, who were contributing to winning this war. Although it is beyond the scope of this work, Aitken also organized a media blitz involving photographs, film, and art. It is most remarkable that once again it was Aitken who, in order to meet his self-declared dual mandate of publicizing and documenting the war, forged ahead and established official photographers, cinematographers, and artists to document the war for future generations.[40] "There is no event of any importance that ever happens up and down that long line in France," boasted the CWRO, "which is not chronicled, photographed or painted for the benefit of the people who sit at home."[41]

[...]

The writing of contemporary history is always difficult, especially when one's subjects are alive or recently martyred, and it is all the more trying during the uncertainty of an ongoing war. Despite their overwhelming success among he public, all three volumes of *Canada in Flanders* were subject to criticisms by Canadian soldiers.[42] The innate suspicion of soldiers at the front of all tings in the rear (basically anything farther back than company headquarters) was keenly directed towards Beaverbrook's work. For those who already knew about his close ties to Hughes, there was the added misgiving that Beaverbrook was producing political propaganda to prop up his friends. Certainly Generals Sir Richard Turner, Garnet Hughes, and David Watson received aid, with the Eye Witness even going so far as to manipulate the appointment of commanding officers to ensure that his friends received their proper due—for example, saving Turner's job after St. Eloi; ensuring that Hughes (the minister's son) received command of the 1st Brigade and later the 5th Division; and removing competitors to Watson so that he was given the 4th Division.[43] That is not to say that without Beaverbrook's support others did not thrive—as generals such as Louis Lipsett, Archibald Macdonell, and Arthur Currie obviously did—but it was clear to many in the highly political and partisan Canadian military structure that Aitken looked out for his friends. Would he also do so in his histories? Some certainly thought so, and when volume 3 of *Canada in Flanders* was published in early 1918, the Canadian Corps commander, Lieutenant General Sir Arthur Currie, responded with vehement criticism.

With his appointment as corps commander in June 1917, Currie was the first Canadian-born officer to take the position. He had been a Militia officer before the war and what he lacked in military appearance—with his pear-shaped body seemingly ready to topple from his horse—he made up for with a planned, methodical approach to warfare. Although Currie had little charisma with which to inspire his men, he was one of the finest generals in the war, leading the Canadian Corps to a series of victories.

While Currie was fully engaged in perfecting the fighting capabilities of his corps, he was also highly cognizant of how he and his men would be remembered in history. When the general read the most recent volumes of *Canada in Flanders* and found that his former division, the 1st, had been nearly left out, he was furious that this self-styled "official history" had slandered the memory of his men and their accomplishments on the Somme. Currie fumed in letters to both Prime Minister Borden and Overseas Minister Kemp that "it is my opinion that no one should have the privilege of publishing to the world a work described as the official story of the Canadian Expeditionary Force which is not a true narrative of the facts.' One of the most vicious battles of the campaign, the 26 September attack on Regina Trench received only five lines, and according to Currie, his men had been denigrated by a history that proclaimed at no time "did the attacking troops get within striking distance of this last objective." That was untrue, as the 2nd and 3rd Brigades had reached the enemy trenches, suffering 2,800 casualties and receiving over 100 honours and decorations. But the loss of nearly 3,000 1st Division soldiers for no appreciable gain was not the image that Beaverbrook and the CWRO wished to portray to the public. The work of Currie's division had indeed been overlooked; moreover, what was written was inaccurate. Currie insisted that this slight was intentional and raged that the author, Roberts, never even came to see him while he was researching the narrative, this despite being at his headquarters.[44] Seething that the history had "no value whatever as an historical document," Currie was largely accurate in his criticisms.

Roberts had indeed written an uneven history of the Canadians on the Somme. Despite his reputation as a celebrated writer and poet, no major wished to feel the full wrath of his corps commander, and so Roberts pleaded in a personal letter for "allowances" when one has a "huge mass of undigested material, often conflicting, to deal with in a very limited time." But the focus of volume 3 was on the 2nd Division's attack at Courcelette on 15 September 1916, rather than the less successful and costly battles that followed (by the 1st, 3rd, and 4th Canadian Divisions), because he was writing in a style that mimicked Beaverbrook's own work. The CWRO histories emphasized Canadian success, which was very evident at Courcelette, and downplayed the failures.

279

Although Currie demanded more recognition for his men, and a balanced history would have reflected it, he probably would not have wanted Roberts to reveal the futility of the attack, the uncut barbed wire that funnelled the infantry into killing grounds, and the uneven artillery barrage that left his troops vulnerable while crossing No Man's Land. The objectivity of history had been sacrificed at the altar of shaping public opinion and encouraging support for the war. Despite Currie's demands for more historical accuracy—or, more likely, for greater coverage that emphasized the bravery and sacrifice of the 1st Division—Beaverbrook was unmoved. Having been appointed to Lloyd George's War Cabinet as minister of Information in March 1918, Beaverbrook did not readily accept Currie's criticisms, writing that with the "fortunes of war … a history cannot be divided off into spaces equally allotted to each unit." That was true, but units, and especially their powerful commanders, could and did insist on proper recognition.

Aware of the partisan hierarchy of command in the CEF and back in England, Currie worried constantly that Turner or another Canadian general waiting in the wings would supplant him.[45] Beaverbrook had done his best to ensure that his friends would be given the most important command positions, and when Currie had bucked at this influencing peddling, most prominently by blocking the appointment of Garnet Hughes to command of the 1st Division, he had suffered a campaign of lies and slander intended to ruin his name.[46] Currie could never pin down his enemies, but he believed that Beaverbrook and the Hughes (father and son) were involved. Furthermore, Currie knew that his operational victories from 1917 onward, although garnering the Canadian Corps a reputation as shock troops, had been won at a heavy cost. The casualty lists continued unabated, and Currie needed the historians and publicists to show the full extent of the victories, which would help justify the terrible losses.

The first histories to come out, therefore, had an enormous impact not only on the public but also on the soldiers. As Currie's correspondence made clear, he was aware that his position was insecure, and he therefore could not accept semi-official histories that ignored his men or their acts. There was more, thought Currie and the rest of the Canadian generals, to Beaverbrook's history than the simple scribblings of a political manipulator: he and the CWRO had the

power to shape contemporary perceptions and to lay the foundation for future interpretations of the war.[47] If a man as powerful as Currie took notice, then it is clear that others did too.

Although Currie and the CWRO were able to put aside their differences for the rest of the war, it is perhaps not surprising that Beaverbrook cancelled work on the fourth volume of *Canada in Flanders*. Currie had also learned something from the acrimonious exchange: in late 1918 he established his own historical group, the Canadian War Narrative Section, to write his official account of the fighting rather than turning to the accomplished CWRO chroniclers. Despite having his grievances largely ignored, Currie still remained convinced of the essential work of the CWRO and passed several additional orders to all units in the corps, noting the importance of creating proper war records to document their actions and of sending them later to the CWRO for safe archiving.[48] In the end, despite the general's dislike for Beaverbrook, the two agreed to work together because they were both consumed with seeing the Canadian Corps receive its due credit. Currie prepared for both the war of No Man's Land and the war of reputations that would follow.

In this wartime struggle for recognition, the CWRO continued in its role of writing supportive Canadian accounts. The Eye Witness reports of 1915 had been replaced, by 1917, with a concentrated barrage of journalistic dispatches emanating from the CWRO that emphasized the unique nature of the Canadian soldier and were aimed at the British and Canadian public on the home front. The result was an effective propaganda program that disseminated short sketches of Canadian courage throughout the Empire[49] For example, the CWRO ran a series of special articles at the end of 1917 "for the benefit of the British Public" in order to emphasize "what a democratic Army Canada possesses."[50] This was not a far leap from the enduring militia myth forced after the War of 1812, which provided a convenient set of Canadian heroes and did not require the government to invest in a professional military. The CWRO continued its publicity campaign with the British press in 1918 by sending out pre-written stories to all British newspapers. A similar article by Major T.G. Roberts, which was published in a series of British newspapers, underscored how Canadian boys had been fashioned into a great fighting army: "The prize-fighter may make a good soldier, but the mild young man in the corner book-shop makes a better soldier … The junior clerk who yesterday trembled before the displeasure if his paunchy employer today dies gloriously for England on the field of battle." Although Roberts did not detail how or why the civilian made this transition to soldier, the notion of a democratic army was stressed repeatedly in CWRO-disseminated accounts. The idea of the inherently superior civilian soldier who put down pen and plough for rifle to defeat the professional German soldier was in direct contrast with what most British generals, especially Haig and Currie, saw as the key factors in the Canadian operational success from 1917 onward. Instead, it was continuous training and the maintenance of strong discipline in the ranks that had forged the corps' effectiveness.[51] With their long-standing and multi-faceted publicity campaign, the CWRO could rightly claim that its work "has done more than a little to increase Canadian prestige and correct still prevalent misconceptions as to Canadian affairs."[52] Yet some of the ideas emanating from the CWRO conflicted with reality, while others avoided the real structural and tactical reasons for success in favour of highlighting racial or national characteristics that supposedly animated all Canadian soldiers.

From April 1917 onward, the Canadians won an unbroken series of victories: Vimy Ridge in April, Fresnoy in May, Hill 70 in August, Passchendaele in October-November, and the many battles that made up the last Hundred Days offensives. The Canadians had honed their attack doctrine of close infantry and artillery support and evolved into an elite force within the BEF, and Currie was not shy about claiming that his corps was the "hardest-hitting force" in the "British Empire."[53] Nonetheless, due to censorship restrictions, the imperial war journalists were not always able to distinguish between the initiatives of British troops and those of the Canadians and Australians. Many of the successful Dominion operations (the capture of trenches, villages, or what was left of them) had therefore been attributed to British units or the BEF in general. With the Dominion forces now viewing themselves as national armies, Currie was furious at the thought of being cheated out of recognition, and as a result he wrote, "the people in Canada would like to receive the fullest accounts of the doings of the Corps." That was a diplomatic way of demanding proper recognition for hard-won deeds. To codify the sacrifice, Canadian Corps intelligence tabulated

that during the battles of Amiens and the crashing of the Hindenburg Line in the Hundred Days campaign, a two-month period of fierce fighting, the Corps had captured 21,000 prisoners and 300 guns, and defeated 34 German divisions. During this time the Canadian Corps, with its four over-strength divisions, accounted for more than 25 percent of the prisoners and 40 percent of the guns for the entire BEF. It was necessary for Currie that those at home understood the extent of their corps' contribution in battle. Such figures had to be disseminated in order to strengthen his position against the political intriguers calling for his sacking due to the high casualties suffered in these successful but costly campaigns.[54]

Despite both political and military urging by the Canadians, many of the British journalists and press censors continued to believe that there was no need to distinguish between Dominion and British troops.[55] Against this perceived discrimination, the Canadian Corps was forced to rely heavily on its established publicity machine to propagate its deeds. The CWRO remained the focal point for disseminating information from Canadian war correspondents such as F.A. Mackenzie, J.F.B. Livesay, Rowland Hill, Fred James and its own CWRO staff, whose job it was to "stiffen the war-weary backbone of Canada."[56] A conscious effort was made to have Canadian press stories sent to all British newspapers in the hope of combating what staff officers at Canadian General Headquarters (GHQ) viewed as a bias against them.

At the same time, these perceived slights to the Dominion armies were viewed differently within the rest of the BEF, with many imperial divisional commandeers complaining that their units were largely ignored in favour of the more easily identifiable Dominion troops.[57] Despite conflicting and chauvinistic views of the coverage, it is clear that armies fighting in the field were also keenly aware of the battle over shaping and sharpening their own reputations. Without the CWRO, it is likely that the Canadians would not have garnered the same recognition. The notion of the colonial storm trooper, which has since been codified in much of the historical writing over the twentieth century and was based primarily on the success of the Australians and Canadians in the last two years of the war, might very well have been more muted. It was not, with one *Manchester Guardian* reporter noting sarcastically shortly after the Armistice that it was "long open

281

to doubt whether there was anybody but Canadians fighting in France."[58] Such an observation reflected Canadian operational victories no doubt, but it also reflected Beaverbrook's work in record creation and archiving and the effective exploitation of such documentary resources in producing pro-Canadian publicity in many forums and media.

[…]

BORDEN AND CURRIE met shortly after the war, and the prime minister informed the general that "certain sections of the American press have adopted the attitude of belittling the importance of operations of the Canadians." Although Currie supplied Borden with a short narrative on recent operations, it was clear that a full history was needed to defend the reputation of the Canadian Corps.[59] With Currie still smarting from the belief that both the British press and GHQ had downplayed the success of his corps, an official account based on authentic documents would offer, he believed, just rewards. Equally important, an official report might help to defend against the rumours that were beginning to spread relating to Currie's command in the last year of the war, which had been enormously successful but equally costly to his men.

One of the CWRO reports noted that it was necessary to "secure for Canada those facts of War, which in the dim future may come to be regarded simply as legend or folk-lore unless they are carefully recovered in black and white at the present time and are carefully preserved for all time."[60] Although Currie agreed with the sentiment, he did not want to leave the task of writing the official report of operations to the CWRO. Having lost more than a few battles to Beaverbrook over the nature of the first semi-official CEF history, Currie set up his own historical section to ensure that he had control over how the Hundred Days would be codified in print and presented to the public.

Although there is no indication that Currie interfered with the writing of the history, the corps commander did order one of his gifted and respected senior officers, Brigadier General Raymond Brutinel, who had been an innovator of machine-gun tactics during the war, to oversee the historical work. "I am very anxious that this report should be very complete and very accurate," wrote Currie, and under Brutinel the Canadian War Narrative Section (CWNS) was established on 20 December 1918.[61]

Currie ordered all divisional commanders to give full support to the narrators. The cooperation was nearly total, as Currie was clearly anxious to see the work published, but also because any failure to comply might result in units being ignored in the final report.[62] Currie also ordered that documents be loaned to the CWNS, which must have been worrisome to the members of the CWRO, as this maws obviously an overlap of responsibilities. However, with Currie's backing the CWNS had priority in the collection, arrangement, and use of operational records to craft this history.

Brutinel set guidelines, in particular that the CWNS historians should strive for "clearness and accuracy … [but that] no adverse comment need be made respecting the leadership or conduct of formations or Troops acting in conjunction with the Canadian Corps."[63] As we have seen, however, Currie wished to see the Canadian Corps receive its full credit. With a mass of documents at its disposal and even more arriving every day, within three months the CWNS compiled a competent, if dry, history of the Corps in the Hundred Days. The pounding nature of the fighting was highlighted and that helped to explain why almost 20 percent of all Canadian battlefield casualties occurred during these ninety-six days of battle. Having spearheaded the BEF, the four over-strength Canadian divisions met and defeated parts of forty-seven German divisions. While Canadian intelligence officers counted every enemy soldier confronted min battle to reach this astounding figure, Currie still crowed to one friend that "We took care of 25%" of the total German armies on the Western Front, "leaving it to the American Army, the French Army, the Belgian Army and the rest of the British Army to look after the balance."[64]

The final history was an important document for Currie as Sir Sam Hughes had publicly voiced the long-standing undercurrent of rumours against Currie in the House of Commons in early March 1919. Protected by parliamentary immunity, Hughes accused Currie of "needlessly sacrificing the lives of Canadian soldiers" in order to elevate his own status among the British. Currie should be "tried summarily by court martial and punished so far as the law would allow … You cannot find one Canadian soldier returning from France who will not curse the name of the officer who ordered that attack on Mons," lectured Hughes to his fellow members of parliament.[65] Currie

282

was deeply hurt by the attack, even more so since there were few politicians who were willing to stand up for him and against the fiery ex-minister. Without accurate reports, however, many of Currie's friends in parliament had been hamstrung in their ability to rebut Hughes's wild claims. Although the corps commander was eventually defended by Cy Peck, a newly elected MP, former battalion commander, and Victoria Cross winner, no minister rose in defence.[66] Borden, to whom Currie had offered key advice during the war on how to deal with his British political counterparts, refused to engage Hughes until months later, and even then he never effectively refuted the claim that Currie had needlessly killed Canadian soldiers. The CWNS report, then, was an important first step for Currie in reclaiming his damaged reputation from Hughes, his cabal, and the Canadian soldiers, many of whom both believed and added to the rumours.[67]

The CWNS history was also a concern to Currie's divisional commanders. Major General David Watson of the 4th Division wrote to Currie in early February that he wished to read a draft before it was published tom ensure that his division received a fair accounting. "I have no objection whatever to your seeing this narrative," wrote Currie, "in fact I would like you to see it, because I am very anxious that it should not only be complete but accurate; but to intimate that, under the arrangements now pertaining, justice would not be done to your Division, is to insinuate something which I don't like." Currie finished somewhat menacingly by indicating that Watson should have "confidence in my ability to do justice to the operations of the Fourth Division."[68] It appeared that Currie, while demanding full glory for the Canadian Corps, would be the final arbiter for ensuring the accuracy and fullness of those first accounts, which laid the groundwork for conceptualizing the conflict.

Currie also paid attention to what other historians were writing about his corps. When *The Final Blow of the First Army in 1918* was published that same month, Currie had the unenviable task of complaining to his old Army commander, General Sir Henry Horne, that the accomplishments of the Canadian Corps had been largely ignored in this history. Just a during the war, when the British press downplayed or referred mistakenly to Canadian battles as British ones, "it seems as if the author was reluctant to refer to the Canadians at any time," wrote Currie. No mention was made of the hard fighting on 30-31

August against the Fresnes-Rouvroy line, and no credit was given to the 1st and 4th Divisions' monumental crashing of the Canal du Nord on 27 September. Currie once again showed his desire to have his corps recognized.[69] Horne wrote back to Currie a week later, downplaying the problems of the monograph by noting that it was not an "official history," but indicating that he regretted the Canadians had been ignored.[70] In an often-quoted and decontextualized remark that was originally made in private, however, Horne complained that, "the Canadian Corps is perhaps rather apt to take all the credit it can for everything, and to consider that the BEF consists of the Canadian Corps and some other troops."[71] To the British, the Canadians again appeared bent on self-promotion; to the Canadians, it confirmed that they would have to be vigilant in securing proper recognition for their deeds.

[…]

ONE EARLY REVIEWER of *Canada in Flanders* observed that them book "lifts the veil of war and tells us not only what our heroes did, but who they were."[72] Beaverbrook and the CWRO may have revealed an aspect of the war that was previously unavailable to the public, but their unveiling was not a disinterested act: while pulling away the curtain, they had their own agenda to present. Not everyone liked Beaverbrook or his work: one Canadian staff officer categorized his writing as "products of hearsay and collaboration, these spurious masterpieces of an incompetent absentee."[73] Currie was not much kinder, describing the historical series as bearing "no more resemblance to the true story of the period it depicts than a mutton stew does to the sheep itself."[74] Beaverbrook was well aware of the pitfalls of writing contemporary history, warning that his history was based on records "snatched from the firing line, and what they gained in vividness, they may have lost in accuracy. It is for the historian of the future to decide."[75] Future historians would indeed clear up mistakes that were made because of a lack of time to consider or even locate evidence. Until then, though, several generations would rely heavily on the first histories produced or supported by the CWRO, and all historians are in debt to Beaverbrook and his staff for their work in collecting and shaping the war archives of the CEF.

Beaverbrook had his enemies, as all powerful men do, but it was his important role in the initial chaotic Canadian administrative hierarchy and his close friendship with Sir Sam Hughes that allowed him to exert considerable power, as no historian or archivist would have been able to in the same situation. Beaverbrook was also one of the propagandists of the war. "This strange attractive gnome with an odour of genius about him," was little liked and much feared; more than ma few called him "Beenacrook," but they did so behind his back.[76] And although he was distrusted by all three Canadian Corps commanders in the field, both Byng and Currie came to recognize the important work of the CWRO in not only preserving their legacy through the archiving of war records, but also in publicizing the deeds of the Canadian soldier at the sharp end.

Our understanding of the past is always changing, ever nuanced, and always reinterpreted by subsequent generations. Despite Beaverbrook's impressive work, he was practical enough to realize that his histories were but the first of many to follow. Nevertheless, with the actual sources at his fingertips, Beaverbrook and the CWRO were able to "steal a march" on other chroniclers and present their version of the war and the role of the Canadians in it. Beaverbrook wrote with a purpose in mind—to glorify the deeds of the Canadians. And he did so with a flare and style that made his histories bestsellers. Along with his CWRO officers and their vast output during the war, Beaverbrook constructed an image of the Canadian soldier reflecting his own ideals. Canadians were depicted as a northern race of rugged civilian-soldiers who were separate from their British cousins. This image was embraced because it was consistent with British prewar views of the Canadian frontier and the men who tamed it. Yet there was more to it than that. Beaverbrook's writing built on these myths and the CWRO's primary goal, despite the medium used, was a steady barrage of propaganda to distinguish the Canadians within the wider context of the BEF. Beaverbrook laid the groundwork for collecting the war records, and then he used those same records to fashion the first depictions of the war, to present the Canadian soldier in a superior light, buttressed with seemingly authentic official records.

The archival records, then, remained an essential component in supporting the publicity function of the CWRO, and later underpinned all subsequent interpretations of the Great War. It is also clear, however, that archives are not just the bare bones of history for future generations; they are part of the history-making process. Archives are not neutral, nor are their creation impartial.[77] There is always a mandate to collect something to privilege some voices while silencing others. Such was the case with the CWRO intent on documenting Canadian actions that glorified the heroics of battle over the futility of trench warfare, and emphasized the success of the democratic citizen in defeating the professional German military machine. These records eventually helped to form the official archives that subsequent generations of historians have used to formulate their views of the Canadian Corps. The notion of an objective archival record, collected in a disinterested fashion, is problematic. It is nearly impossible to gauge the influence of the CWRO officers on the war diarists and other creators of war records, but it is clear from the CWRO officers' reports back to London that their prime mandate was to ensure that records were created to document actions. That alone suggests that it was not simply the soldiers at the front who wrote up their daily accounts. They were influenced by regulations, orders, time constraints, and the inability to know what was happening along the front, not to mention the constant prodding by CWRO staff who visited the battalions to inquire into and influence the recordkeeping process. There is no evidence to suggest that Canadian records were fabricated to cover up disasters in the war—as disasters, along with the victories, are plainly evident in the war archives. However, one should be cautioned by the anecdote offered by Sir Basil Liddell Hart, who recounted the story of a French general. During the desperate March Offensive, French reinforcements were ordered to counterattack. It was found, however, that the line had already been lost the day before. Upon being informed of the loss, the general refused to destroy the order, and "with a knowing smile, thereupon remarked: '*C'est pour l'histoire.*'" Much time was spent during the war, warned Liddell Hart, in "preparing the ground for its historians."[78] With the CWRO's involvement and the various factors affecting the creation of Canadian war records, these primary documents are products more of process and influence than accurate and disinterested mirrors of acts and facts.

Whatever the operational successes of the Canadian Corps on the Western Front from 1917 onward—and there was an unbroken run—one must at least acknowledge that a portion of the Canadian reputation as shock troops came from the CWRO's publicity campaign. Beaverbrook's desire to nurture a Canadian image separate from that of his British counterparts, when coupled with the Canadian Corps' operational successes, helped to forge a distinct Canadian identity as elite troops. As the sole agency of publicity in the CEF, the CWRO developed a steady deluge of stories, photos, exhibitions, films, commemorative works, and histories to ensure that Canada received its full credit. It is always difficult to estimate the impact of publicity campaigns, but anecdotal evidence suggests the CWRO made an impression. British war correspondent Philip Gibbs commended Beaverbrook in his 1920 memoirs, writing that the Canadians "organized their publicity" in a "masterful way, and were determined that what Canada did the world should know—and damn all censorship."[79] Attesting to that same publicity campaign, John Buchan, the director of Britain's Department of Information, famous novelist, and future Canadian governor general, certainly saw the results of this "human dynamo's" work. He observed somewhat incredulously that the wide circulation of CWRO books and pamphlets, as well as photographs and film, might lead one to believe "that Canada is running the war."[80]

Beaverbrook wisely noted in the preface to the second volume of the *Canada in Flanders* series that the gathering of the war records allowed for the "framework [to be] erected for an official narrative. This is a prudent measure which will be endorsed by Canadian students of history, since there is a growing tendency to demand a full and intelligent documentary record of our progress." Soldiers were often forced to create records in "the face of grave danger and complete exhaustion when they might well have been excused from troubling about such trivialities as to what posterity would think of them."[81] But posterity would be very interested in these Great War heroes, and countless historians would study them over the next century. These same historians would rely heavily on the war records. The conscious moulding of memory and laying of an historical foundation by Lord Beaverbrook has had an enduring legacy in Canadian historiography since the guns fell silent on 11 November 1918.

NOTES

1. Carman Miller, "The Crucible of War: Canadian and British Troops during the Boer War," in *the Boer War: Army, Nation and Empire*, ed. Peter Dennis and Jeffrey Grey (Canberra: Army History Unit, 2000).

2. For the best account of Aitken during this period, see Gregory P. Marchildon, *Profits & Politics: Beaverbrook and the Gilded Age of Canadian Finance* (Toronto: University of Toronto Press, 1996).

3. Library and Archives Canada (hereafter LAC), Lord Beaverbrook papers (BP), MG 27 II G 1, Series E, reel A-1764, Aitken to Hughes, 28 December 1914. These are microfilmed copies of the Beaverbrook papers held in the Beaverbrook library.

4. LAC, Records of the Department of External Affairs (RG 25), v. 259, file P-3-19, Order-in-council 3117, 6 January 1915.

5. Lord Beaverbrook, *Politicians and the War, 1914-1916,* vol. 1 (London: Thornton Butterworth, 1928), 189.

6. On the problems of war journalists, see Keith Grieves, "War Correspondents and Conducting Officers on the Western Front from 1915," in *Facing Armageddon: The First World War Experienced,* ed. Peter Liddle and Hugh Cecil (London: Leo Cooper, 1996), 719-35; Martin Farrar, *News from the Front: War Correspondents on the Western Front 1914-1918* (Thrupp, UK: Sutton Publishing, 1998).

7. BP, reel A-1764, Aitken to Hughes, 13 October 1916. For Aitken's violations of censorship rules, see Peter Buitenhuis, *The Great War of Words: Literature as Propaganda, 1914 and 1918 and After* (London: B.T. Batsford, 1989), 80.

8. For problems with Alderson, see RG 9, v. 4676, 4/3, Aitken to Alderson, 14 February 1916.

9. Tom Driberg, *Beaverbrook: A Study in Power and Frustration* (London: Weidenfeld and Nicolson, 1956), 84.

10. Sir Max Aitken, *The Official Story of the Canadian Expeditionary Force* (London: Hodder and Stoughton, 1916), 4.

11. A.J.P. Taylor, *Beaverbrook* (New York: Simon and Schuster, 1972), 88; Lord Beaverbrook, *Men and Power, 1917-1918* (London: Hutchinson, 1956), 268.

12. BP, reel A-1765, Aitken to Borden, 1 January 1915. A similar letter had been sent to Hughes to garner his support.

285

13. BP, reel A-1765, Borden to Aitken, 14 September 1915; Aitken to Borden, 25 August 1916; Borden to Aitken, 11 July 1917. Borden was also very supportive of Aitken, and he was particularly pleased with the historical legacy that Aitken was gathering for future generations of Canadians.

14. RG 9, v. 4746, 175/1, CWRO, Report, 11 January 1917. Denis Winter has gone so far as to say that the Dominions' control over their records allowed them to keep more documents than the British, who culled many of the war records. Although Winter's arguments are sometimes based on conjecture or negative evidence, and are coloured by his palpable dislike for British senior commanders, his point on the Canadian control of their own records is important. Denis Winter, *Haig's Command: A Reassessment* (London: Penguin Books, 1991), chs. 14 and 15.

15. RG 9, v. 4270, 114/18, Aitken to Major General J.W. Carson, 27 December 1916.

16. Henry Beckles Willson, *From Quebec to Piccadilly* (London: Jonathan Cape, 1929), 201.

17. At this point in the war, the Canadian Corps consisted of the 1st and 2nd Divisions. The 3rd and 4th Divisions had been added by the end of 1916.

18. RG 9, III-D-3, v. 4676, 4/3, Aitken to Manly Sims, 9 February 1916.

19. RG 9, v. 4770, 143/7, CWRO in France, n.d. [ca. 1918].

20. For Aitken's role in the removal of Alderson, see BP, reel A-1764, Aitken to Hughes, 24 April 1916; Morton, *A Peculiar Kind of Politics,* 72-5.

21. For examples of Aitken's power in Canadian war politics until Hughes was asked to resign, see BP, reel A-1764, Aitken to Hughes, 19 September 1915; Aitken to Hughes, 26 September 1915; Hughes to Aitken, 28 September 1915; Aitken to Hughes, 6 October 1915; Hughes to Aitken, 2 November 1915. For Aitken's role in bringing down the Asquith government, see Driberg, *Beaverbrook: A Study, 86-109;* and the more recent book by Anne Chisholm and Michael Davie, *Beaverbrook: A Life* (London: Hutchinson, 1992).

22. 'LAC, MG 30 E52, Talbot Papineau papers, v. 4, Papineau to Dear B., 26 October 1916.

23. See Jeffrey Williams, *Byng of Vimy: General and Governor General* (Toronto: University of Toronto Press, 1983, 1992), XIV:

24. LAC, MG 30 E 300, Victor Odlum papers, v. 3, T.G. Roberts, "I remember Currie," pt. 2, *The Ottawa Journal,* 9 April 1940.

25. BP, A-1765, Manly Sims to Aitken, 5 June 1916.

26. RG 9, v. 4458, 19/4, Aitken to Byng, 25 July 1916; RG 9, v. 4746, 176/2, Report on War Diaries, 8 February 1917.

27. RG 9, v. 4458, 19/3, G.40, 30 March 1917.

28. LAC, T-10721, War Diary, 18th Battalion, p. 2, September 1916.

29. LAC, T-10750, War Diary 73rd Battalion, Aitken to Byng, 25 July 1916

30. RG 9, v. 4746, 175/1, CWRO, Report submitted to … Sir Robert L. Borden, 11 January 1917. The CWRO representatives at the front often "stimulated" battalion officers to craft better testimonials of their unit's actions; see RG 9, v. 4740, 159/1, CWRO memorandum, 19 February 1918; and RG 9, v. 4741, 161/2, Roberts to Watkins, 24 May 1917.

31. Official historian A. F. Duguid wrote in 1938, after having used the CWRO-shaped records to craft his history, that the Canadian War Diaries were at least twice as detailed as that of the British and Australians; "this excellence … must in fairness be laid to Beaverbrook and his emissaries at the front 'urging upon units in the field the historical importance of making their own war diaries complete.'" LAC, Records of the Department of National Defence (RG 24), v. 1755, DHS 10-10, pt. 2. Duguid to Sir Andrew Macphail, 8 February 1938.

32. LAC, MG 30 E52, Talbot Papineau papers, Papineau to Dear B., 9 October 1916.

33. For basing the Canadian book on the Anzad book, see RG 9, v. 4746, 175/3, Minutes of Meeting, 22 September 1916, which referred to how the CWRO was looking for a publisher for the Canadian "Anzac" Book. Quotation from RG 9, v. 4746, 175/1, CWRO Report, 11 January 1917. It is interesting to note, however, that Charles Bean, the Australian reporter, archivist, and official historian, modeled his Australian War Records Section after Beaverbrook's CWRO. See Ann Millar, "Gallipoli to Melbourne: The Australian War Memorial, 1915-19," *Journal of the Australian War Memorial* 10 (April 1987): 34.

34. RG 9, v. 4732, 140/9, Aitken to Roberts, 30 August 1916.

35. Charles Bean conducted a similar selection of material to conform to his image of the Digger. See D.A. Kent, "The Anzac Book and the Anzac Legend: C.E.W. Bean as Editor and Image-maker," *Historical Studies* 84, 21 (1985); Denis Winter, "The Anzac Book: A Reappraisal," *Journal of the*

Australian War Memorial 16 (April 1990); Alistair Thomson, "Steadfast until Death'? C.E.W. Bean and the Representation of Australian Manhood," *Australian Historical Studies* 23, 93 (1989): 462-79.

36. RG 9, v. 4733 140/10, "Fact."

37. LAC, KP, v. 52, file 9, Beaverbrook to Kemp, 21 April 1917.

38. The quotations are taken from *Canada in Khaki: A Tribute to the Officers and Men Now Serving in the Canadian Expeditionary Force, No. 1* (London: CWRO, 1917).

39. RG 9, v. 4746, 175/1, CWRO, Report submitted to … Sir Robert L. Borden, 11 January 1917.

40. For photography, see RG 9, v. 4746, 175/1, CWRO, Report submitted to … Sir Robert L. Borden, 11 January 1917; Peter Robertson, "Canadian Photojournalism during the First World War," *History of Photography* 2, 1 (1978): 371; W. Rider, "With a Camera at the Front," in *Canada in Khaki: A Tribute to the Officers and Men Now Serving in the Canadian Expeditionary Force, No. 3* (London: CWRO, 1917). For films, see KP, v. 133, file C-27, Second Report of the War Office Cinematography Committee, September 1918; Nicholas Reeves, *Official British Film Propaganda Film during the First World War* [London: Croom Helm, 1986); Peter Morris, *Embattled Shadows: A History of Canadian Cinema, 1895-1939* (Montreal and Kingston: McGill-Queen's University Press, 1978): 58-61. For the CWMF and the war artist program, see Tippett, *Art at the Service of War*; and Laura Brandon, "Shattered Landscape: The Great War and the Art of the Group of Seven," *Canadian Military History* 10, 1 (2001): 58-66.

41. RG 9, v. 4770, 143/7, draft article, CWRO in France, n.d. [ca. 1918].

42. See for example, RG 9, v. 4732, 140/7, correspondence; ibid., J.B. Murphy to Beaverbrook, 25 June 1917; RG 9, v. 4732, 140/8, CWRO to Gascoigne, 29 May 1918; BP, A-1766, Sanders to HQ, 2nd Division, 3 April 1917; Aitken to Manly Sims, 19 April 1917.

43. The Beaverbrook papers contain ample evidence of Aitken's interference in the appointments of senior officers to make way for his friends and ensure that they received plum positions during 1915 and 1916.

44. RG 9, v. 4678, 10/1, Currie to Beaverbrook, 22 May 1917; and RG 9, v. 4732, 140/6, Davy to Aitken, 15 December 1916.

45. LAC, MG 30 E100, Sir Arthur Currie papers (LAC, CP), v. , file "M-R," Currie to Perley, 10 December 1917; Smart to Currie, 6 January 1918; A.M.J. Hyatt, "Sir Arthur Currie and Politicians: A Case Study of Civil-Military Relations in the First World War," in *Swords and Covenants,* ed. Richard Preston and Peter Dennis (London: Croom Helm, 1976), 148; Daniel Dancocks, *Sir Arthur Currie: A Biography* (Toronto: Methuen, 1985), 126-7.

46. Hugh M. Urqhart, *Arthur Currie: The Biography of a Great Canadian* (Toronto: J.M. Dent and Sons, 1950), 205-6.

47. For the controversy, see KP, v. 135, file C-48: Currie to Beaverbrook, 3 July 1918; Roberts to Currie, 11 July 1918; Beaverbrook to Currie, 12 July 1918; Currie to Kemp, 4 July 1918.

48. RG 9, v. 4746, 176/1, Extract of Routine Orders by Sir Arthur Currie, 6 September 1918.

49. The CWRO also published a newspaper for the Canadian soldier: the *Canadian Daily Record.* The paper contained general news on Canada and the war, with sporting and social news forming the majority of the content. From mid-1917 onward, the circulation of the paper was more than 15,000 copies a day. The 787th and final issue was published on 31 July 1919. RG 9, v. 4746, 176/7, CWRO—*The Canadian Daily Record*, 31 May 1918. For a few examples, see RG 9, v. 4770, 143[7; and Willson, *From Quebec to Piccadilly,* 204.

50. RG 9, v. 4770, 143/7, CWRO to Roberts, 16 October 1917.

51. LAC, CP, v. 1, Currie to Brewster, 32 May 1917; Dancocks, *Sir Arthur Currie,* 131.

52. BP, A-1765, Report by Sir Max Aitken to Rt. Hon. Sir Robert Borden on … Canadian Representative at the Front, n.d. [ca. 19 May 1916].

53. See Shane B. Schreiber, *Shock Army of the British Empire: The Canadian Corps in the Last 100 Days of the Great War* (Westport, CT: Praeger, 1997); Tim Cook, *No Place to Run: The Canadian Corps and Gas Warfare in the First World War* (Vancouver: UBC Press, 1999). Canadian War Museum, Sir Arthur Currie papers (hereafter CWM, CP), file 58A 1 61.4, Currie to Dobie, 9 February 1919.

54. RG 9 III-A-2, v. 353, file 106, Major E. Bristol to Embury, 23 October 1918. Also see LAC, CP, v. 1, file 1, Currie to Borden, 26 November 1918; ibid., v. 1, file 2, Currie to Kemp, 1 November 1918.

55. RG 9 III-A-2, v. 353, file 106, Memo: Re Press Censorship, 31 October 1918; Embury to C.P., GHQ, 1

November 1918; Embury to Bristol, 10 November 1918.

56. Quote from BP, A-1766, William Dennis to Beaverbrook, 28 September 1918.

57. For Dominion anger regarding coverage, see John F. Williams, *ANZACs, the Media and the Great War* (Sydney: University of New South Wales, 1999), 179, 199-201, 245-6.

58. *Manchester Guardian*, 23 December 1919, as cited in Tippett, *Art at the Service of War,* 21,

59. Robert Scott Demill, "The 1928 Cobourg Trial of Sir Arthur Currie and the Port Hope Evening Guide: The Rehabilitation of the Reputation of a Corps Commandeer," (MA thesis, University of Ottawa, 1989), 65-6.

60. RG 9, v. 4746, 175/4, Supply of Reports and Narratives on Recent Fighting, n.d. [ca. late 1916 early 19170.

61. CWM, CP, file 58A 1 61.4, Currie to Sir Arthur Conan Doyle, 1 February 1919.

62. RG 0. 111-B-1, v. 1033, file W-4-3, G.8/6-19, 30 December 1918; also see the correspondence in RG 24, v. 1733, file DHS-1-13.

63. `RG 9, v. 4809, file 196, General directions for guidance in the compilation of detailed narrative of operations of the CANADIAN CORPS, 5 September 1919.

64. LAC, CP, v. 1, file 2, Currie to Lt. Col. W. Ridgway Wilson, 10 December 1918.

65. House of Common Debates, 1919, v. 1, 3 March 1919, 207.

66. CWM, CP, file 58A 1 61.7, Peck to Currie, 8 April 1919; House of Commons Debates, 1919 v. 1, 14 March 1919, 468.

67. See Tim Cook, "The Butcher and the Madman: Sir Arthur Currie, Sir Sam Hughes and the War of Reputations," *Canadian Historical Review* 85, 4 (2004): 693-719

68. *CWM, CP, file 58A 1, 62.7, Peck to Currie, 8 April 1919; House of Commons Debates, 1919 v. 1, 14 March 1919, 468.*

69. *CWM, CP, file 58A 1 62.4, M.H. Dobie to Currie, 4 January 1919; Currie to Dobie, 9 February 1919.*

70. CWM, CP, file 58A 1 61.5, Currie to First Army, 20 March 1919; Horne to Currie, 27 March 1919. Burstall was also angry because he thought that several "published reports" had ignored his division. He pleased for Currie to rectify the matter,

especially in any official publications, LAC, CP, v. 3, file 1, Burstall to Currie, 8 April 1919.

71. Desmond Morton, *Canada and the War: A Military and Political History* (Toronto: Butterworths, 1981), 133.

72. RG 9, v. 4732, 140/7, Extracts from Press Opinion of *Canada in Flanders,* n.d. [ca. March 1916].

73. RG 9, v. 4676, 3/5, untitled [memoirs by Colonel J.J. Carrick], n.d. [ca. late 1915].

74. LAC, CP, v. 1, file 1, Currie to Harold Daly, 26 October 1918; v. 1, file 2, Currie to Sir William Hearst, 14 November 1917.

75. RG 9, v. 4746, 175/5, CWRO, [draft history, 21 February 1918]; Aitken, *Canada In Flanders,* vol. 2, vii-viii.

76. See Peter Buitenhuis, *The Great War of Words: British, American and Canadian Propaganda and Fiction, 1914-1933* (Vancouver: UBC Press, 1987), 80, 98-101; and Williams, *ANZACS, the Media and the Great War,* 171, 265 for assertions that Beaverbrook was the war's premier propagandist. For the quotation, see Chisholm and Davie, *Beaverbrook: A Life,* 163.

77. The traditional concept of archives and self-image of archivists concerns notions of neutrality, objectivity, and impartiality. In other words, the archivist is constructed as a kind of invisible, honest broker between original creators and users of records. Such views have been challenged in recent debates in archival theory. For the most significant discussion on the topic, see Terry Cook, "What Is Past Is Prologue: A History of Archival Ideas since 1898, and Future Paradigm Shift," *Archivaria* 43 (Spring 1997): 17-63; Brien Brothman, "The Limits of Limit: Derridean Deconstruction and the Archival Institution," *Archivaria* 36 (Autumn 1993): 205-20; and Richard Brown, "Death of a Renaissance Record-Keeper: The Murder of Tomasso da Tortona in Ferrara, 1385," *Archivaria* 44 (Fall 1997): 1-43.

78. Basil Liddell Hart, *Why Don't We Learn from History?* (London: George Allen and Unwin, 1944), 9.

79. Philip Gibbs, *Realities of War* (London: Heinemann, 1920), 191.

80. Quotation from Arthur R.M. Lower, *My First Seventy-Five Years* (Toronto: Macmillan, 1967), 106; Buchan cited in Tippett, 21.

81. Lord Beaverbrook, *Canada in Flanders,* vol. 2, 4th ed. (London: Hodder and Stoughton, 1917), viii-ix.

CANADA IN THE 1930s

Surviving Canada's Great Depression

P.E. Bryden
University of Victoria

CANADA IN THE 1930s: SURVIVING CANADA'S GREAT DEPRESSION

Introduction by P.E. Bryden

● INTRODUCTION

P.E. Bryden

In Canada, perhaps the worst year of the Great Depression was 1933. More than one-quarter of Canadians were out of work, and in some sectors the figures were considerably higher. Agriculture was severely compromised by drought conditions in the prairies, the closing of international markets, and plummeting prices for commodities; manufacturing had slowed and in some cases virtually stopped thanks to a decreasing demand for products. The infra-structure for dealing with this sort of long-term economic crisis was fragile, and politicians of all stripes struggled to identify solutions to a problem they did not understand. But while these were difficult times for many, it is important to remember that almost three-quarters of the population remained employed, and for them the dropping prices meant that they could often afford luxuries in the 1930s that ten years earlier would have been well beyond their means. The Depression thus affected people in Canada differently depending on where they lived and where they worked. But despite these differences, the experience of the Depres-sion had a profound impact on the way Canadians viewed their world, and particularly on how they viewed the role of government in society. Much of the design of the postwar Can-adian state can find its origin in the experience of the Depression in the 1930s.

It is difficult to pinpoint the beginning of the Depression. Certainly the collapse of the New York stock exchange in October 1929 provided people with a moment from which to begin their assessment of the economic collapse of the following decade, but the real origins of depression can be found much earlier. Almost a decade of war and economic recession, extending from about 1914 until the early 1920s, left most North Americans eager for prosperity. Manufacturing industries expanded to meet the demand, farmers increased their acreage to feed a hungry public, and the remainder of the 1920s seemed to "roar." But prosperity was achieved at a price: both employers and employees borrowed money to take advantage of the opportunities for expansion, and when the economy had reached its limit, many Canadians were unable to afford their debt. The expansion of the 1920s had thus been somewhat artificial, and the height of the good times was partially responsible for the depths of the bad times.

Individual perceptions of Depression differed widely. Included here are two different ways of understanding what people experienced in the 1930s. The first are oral recollections of people who lived through the Depression, collected in the 1970s; the second is a quantita-tive glimpse of the contours of the Depression across Canada as graphically illustrated. Both offer only a tiny indication of the way different people across the country lived through the 1930s, but they do give some idea of the broad range of experiences that people had. Clearly, living through a long period of economic collapse had an effect on people regardless of whether they were better or worse off in the 1930s. The interviews in particular remind us that people *remembered* the Depression, and in many cases, sought to take lessons from it.

In retrospect, those in power seemed blinkered in their response to the Depression. William Lyon Mackenzie King, the Liberal prime minister for most of the 1920s, suggested during the 1930 election campaign that only those provinces with Liberal governments would receive assistance from Ottawa. That partisanship, combined with his clear inability to either recognize the extent of the economic collapse or offer any solutions, meant the end of King's tenure in office—at least for the time being. R.B. Bennett, the millionaire leader of the Conservatives, took his place. He also, unfortunately, echoed King's approach to the Depression. Unable to embrace new solutions to the economic crisis—like those that were being considered south of the border with American President Franklin Roosevelt's interventionist collection of legislation known as the New Deal—Bennett followed the same old approach to an economic downturn that had been used by generations of politicians before him. He raised the tariff in order to protect Canadian manufacturers from competition, he introduced a modest relief scheme starting in 1932, and he preached the doctrine of self-help. These were orthodox solutions. The tariff barrier simply isolated a Canadian economy that could thrive only by exporting its excess product—particularly in the agricultural and primary resource sectors—and essentially closed any doors for Canadian trade that might have existed. The relief scheme, introduced as an emergency measure in 1932 and continued thereafter, was designed to give single, unemployed men room and board in return for physical labour. It was limited in its availability, and was designed simply to keep people alive rather than to jump-start the economy in any meaningful way. And the constant reminders to scrimp and save and help each other were cold comfort when the last avenues of assistance had already been explored. So desperate were Canadians that many of them wrote to Bennett himself and, not being a heartless man, he often replied. But that sort of personal appeal did nothing to alter the direction of the Depression.

Outside Ottawa, there seemed to be a much clearer sense that this economic collapse needed to be handled differently than earlier recessions. Across the country, provincial politicians explored alternative economic models than those that had been tried before. In British Columbia and Ontario, for example, populist Liberals Duff Pattullo and Mitch Hepburn charted courses that veered quite dramatically from the path followed by the Mackenzie King Liberals in Ottawa. In British Columbia, health insurance was investigated and massive public works projects were initiated, while in Ontario the premier began his administration by attacking big business, proceeded to attack the big labour unions that were controlled by their American parent unions, and ended by attacking the federal Liberals. There was nothing of the "wait-and-see" attitude in these provinces that seemed to characterize the federal government.

Other provinces were even more innovative. In Alberta, William Aberhart swept to victory in 1935 promising a "social credit" for everyone as a means of putting money into the hands of people who would spend it, thereby priming the economy. The economic idea didn't work, but the Social Credit party would have a lasting influence on politics in first Alberta, then BC, and then Quebec. Quebec followed more well-worn political territory in the 1930s, but even there, people were keen to elect a politician and a party that would tackle the growing crisis head on. Maurice Duplessis of the newly formed Union Nationale seemed to want to wrest control from business and ensure that government provided for people's social well-being; once he was elected in 1936 his innovative program failed to materialize and he offered more of the same, but his election underlined the desire for change in Quebec. In the Maritimes, there was no flirtation with new parties, but the old Liberals and Conservatives were quick to try to pressure the federal government into providing more aid for an increasingly destitute population.

Politicians tried—usually without success—to design and pass legislation that would ease the effects of the Depression. One way that people tried to influence politicians was to lobby government. During the Depression, this occurred in both bold public expressions of discontent with the political response to the economic situation, and in more private terms that were nevertheless equally insistent that governments needed to change their approach. One of the most public displays of disapproval came in the summer of 1935. Unemployed men who had been the recipients of meager federal assistance through relief camps and make-work projects were finally fed up with the futility of their situation and sought an audience with Prime Minister Bennett. Congregating in Vancouver in

June, a group of at least 1,000, and very quickly double that, began a journey across the country to confront the prime minister about his plans for dealing with the high levels of unemployment. Riding the freight rails and picking up supporters, the On-to-Ottawa trek, as it became known, soon attracted federal attention as well. Bennett called in the RCMP to stop the trekkers in Regina; he would meet with a small delegation of representatives, but certainly not with a mob of thousands. The meeting with Bennett achieved nothing, and the trekkers in Regina bristled at being forced to disband under federal terms rather than of their own volition. The resulting violence of the Regina Riot is remembered here in three different versions of events.

Surviving the Depression was ultimately a personal challenge, and the articles and documents included here examine the various ways people managed. Some Canadians, for example, tried to lobby politicians privately, a topic that Lara Campbell examines in her article about Ontarians during the Depression. Some of the survivors of the Depression remembered the ways that their family coped with the Depression, and a sampling of these oral reminiscences have been included here. And in her article on women in Montreal, Denyse Baillargeon also examines some of the private strategies that were used to make ends meet and weather the economic downturn as a family, and shows the important role that was played by the women of the household.

This collection thus shows that individuals were able to develop new strategies for dealing with the new circumstances caused by the Depression in Canada, but it is important to remember that governments also ended up designing new policies as a result of the experiences of the 1930s. As usual, it took governments quite a bit longer than individuals to learn from the Depression, but the results have had important consequences. Much of the postwar social safety net, including the implementation of national programs of pensions, hospital and health insurance and, most explicitly, the unemployment insurance program, owe their existence to the memories of the experience of the Depression.

QUESTIONS

1. Are there differences between the concerns as people expressed them to the premiers in their letters, and the way they remembered the Depression later? If so, what might explain this?
2. What sorts of things can we learn about the Depression from the graphical information included here? What other sorts of materials might you use to present a more complete picture of Canada in the 1930s?
3. How did the experience of women in the Depression differ from that of men?
4. How did the experience of people living in cities differ from that of people living in rural areas?

FURTHER READINGS

Campbell, Lara A., *Respectable Citizens: Gender, Family and Unemployment in Ontario's Great Depression* (Toronto: University of Toronto Press, 2009).

Glassford, Larry A., *Reaction and Reform: The Politics of the Conservative Party under R.B. Bennett, 1927–1938* Toronto: University of Toronto Press, 1992.

Grayson, L.M. and Michael Bliss, eds. *The Wretched of Canada* (Toronto: University of Toronto Press, 1971).

Neatby, H. Blair, *The Politics of Chaos: Canada in the Thirties* (Toronto: Macmillan of Canada, 1972).

Thompson, John Herd with Allen Seager, *Canada, 1922–1939: Decades of Discord* (Toronto: McClelland and Stewart, 1985).

▲ Document 1: Memories of Canadians Who Survived the Depression

Barry Broadfoot

In 1971 journalist Barry Broadfoot crossed the country several times, interviewing people wherever he came upon them about their recollections of the Depression. Almost all of the people he talked to were strangers, willing to offer a few words about the 1930s to an interested traveller. He talked to people in their homes, on the street, wherever a conversation could be struck up. Some of the interviews he taped, some he simply remembered and wrote down later. The result was an extremely popular collection called Ten Lost Years, *Broadfoot's attempt to keep the memory of the Depression alive for a later generation of Canadians. The following are a few of the oral recollections that people offered Broadfoot. They are highly personal, opinionated, and potentially insulting. Are they any different from the recollections that people might offer today if asked to remember a hardship?*

Ten Lost Years

"Some people just want to forget it ever happened, that God-fearing, third-generation Canadians starved to death in city alleyways and on their lousy farms out on the prairie. But it happened. The drought, of course, nobody could survive that, and that was just extra misery piled on top. At the time, the Canadian governments, the economists, the experts, did they know what was happening? No. They still don't.

President Roosevelt when he came in in 1933 took over an unholy mess in the U.S. and his New Deal started things going. He knew he had to spend money, even if he didn't have it. Why, print more. But get people working, so they could spend money, so other people could spend money so there would be money percolating through the economy. Roosevelt wasn't all that successful, but there was one thing so important that people have forgotten it. He had the appearance of success. I'll repeat that. He had the appearance of success. Other way of saying it, he gave people confidence. That fear was going away. Remember he said, 'We have nothing to fear but fear itself.' In a way, that was witch doctor stuff, but it worked. People wanted to be told, to be assured that things would go okay. And in about three or four years he started to get the country turned around and of course, Canada benefited too. Sure we did. There's no denying it.

But Bennett (*the Canadian prime minister*) did precious little for us and a lot of the things he did was bad, the relief camps for one thing, and William Lyon Mackenzie King? Hah! There was a winner. A tiny cautious man hyped on spiritualism who thought any problem could be solved by setting up royal commissions which would report back years later and by that time, by that time they hoped, the problem would have gone away. Or calling top level provincial conferences and all you got was the wealthy or the big provinces, Quebec, Ontario, British Columbia, their premiers ready and quite happy to sacrifice the weaker and poorer provinces so they could get a bigger share of federal funds. Oh, they were a bunch of dandies. Any man who was a Liberal or a Tory in those days cannot say he served his nation.

Source: *Ten Lost Years 1929–1939: Memories of Canadians Who Survived the Depression* by Barry Broadfoot. Copyright (c) 1973, 1997 by Barry Broadfoot. Published by McClelland & Stewart Ltd. in trade paperback in 1997. Used with permission of the publishers.

Of course, it all came out not too bad. The war, of course. People even talk about the Good Old Days now. Yes, and they still don't realize that Canada came out of the Thirties and Forties in good shape but not really through too much of our own doing. The Second World War, that gave us our leg-up, and then that crazy post-war prosperity when everyone had money to spend which they hadn't been able to spend during the war, and everyone wanted our goods.

But don't tell me we actually survived the Depression as such. No, it destroyed us for those ten years. Nineteen-twenty-nine to nineteen thirty-nine. The country stopped. Hardly a thing moved. Plans and all that, but not many were put into effect. Those that were put into effect, how many worked? Yes, ten lost years."

A Conspiracy to Hide Those Years

"One thing that has always astonished me is the way the Depression has been handled by school text books, histories, that kind of book. Even at the university level, the Depression is not handled in any depth. There are textbooks of Canadian history where the Depression gets three or four paragraphs, and I actually saw one book where it got *one* sentence, and went something like this: 'Between 1929 and 1939 the Canadian nation suffered a Great Depression, and the western wheat farmer was the most seriously hit.' Period. That was all. Then they went on to the war, as if the war, in a twist of meaning, healed all wounds.

It is almost a conspiracy to hide these ten years, although I hate to use the word 'conspiracy' because it often has a criminal connotation. Of course I don't think that. But [...] There seems to have been an attitude right up till now of 'Let's shove it under the carpet, let's not talk about it, let's not even admit that we walked around with holes in our soles and souls and let's never admit the fact we had to work for a dollar a day or we had to take relief and do things which our pride and our upbringing and our heritage would never allow us to do before.' I don't know why this attitude should prevail.

I can't come up with any true explanation, but it is a fact that in the U.S. and other countries this same attitude prevails. It is almost as if to say, if we don't talk about the Great Depression, then there will never be another one. Of course, it's true, too, that people were ashamed, collectively, that there was such a thing as a Depression, that the whole system just broke down and nothing could be done to make it work. But why have ten years of our contemporary history, ten years of the greatest trauma this continent has faced, and that includes all the wars, been virtually blotted out?

Remember, in some ways it was a tremendously exciting time. People found strengths they did not know they had. They learned they could endure, and endure and endure some more. It was almost a trial by battle. Yes, it was a battle in that sense and the Canadian nation came out of it stronger than before. Think about it. There was solid stuff there in the beginning, integrity, willingness to work and work very hard, faith, a defined goal and a good base of English, Scotch, Irish, French, German, Scandinavian, Polish, Russian, Ukrainian, Italian, all these providing a diverse but strong base to build upon.

But in the schools and universities today, what is known? A few paragraphs. At most, one or two pages. But more often, nothing! I meet people under thirty and I ask them what the Depression means to them. Or, to put it in more simple terms, what was the Depression? They will say, 'Oh, that was when times were hard,' or 'Dad said that was when he didn't have any money,' or 'That was when my parents couldn't go to the cottage at the lake each summer.' And of course, anybody in high school or university, likely as not, they will just giggle.

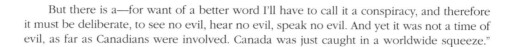

But there is a—for want of a better word I'll have to call it a conspiracy, and therefore it must be deliberate, to see no evil, hear no evil, speak no evil. And yet it was not a time of evil, as far as Canadians were involved. Canada was just caught in a worldwide squeeze."

A Crime to Be Poor

I never so much as stole a dime, a loaf of bread, a gallon of gas, but in those days I was treated like a criminal. By the twist in some men's minds, men in high places, it became a criminal act just to be poor, and this percolated down through the whole structure until it reached the town cop or the railway bull and if you were without a job, on the roads, wandering, you automatically became a criminal. It was the temper of the times.

I was not a hobo. A hobo, by definition, is a regular bum, a professional bum; and there probably were hoboes in the time of the Crusades and there are hoboes now. There always have been that kind of people, whether they are on the highways or in the slums, in the Skid Roads or sitting beside a fire sipping Scotch whiskey in Rosedale (*a fashionable part of Toronto*) and living off their wife's inherited wealth. Hoboism is a state of mind.

I was, you could say, a wanderer. One of the unfortunates: A victim of the economic system? Perhaps: Certainly, most certainly a casualty in the battle between ignorant men who were running this country. There are two places in Ontario, in the fair city of Toronto and down at the even fairer city of London, where ancient records will show that I am a criminal. A criminal in that I violated the Criminal Code of Canada and thereby gained a criminal record for begging. Jail.

And I once got 30 days for riding a freight car long ago into a God-forsaken little Saskatchewan city which, thank God, the economic ebbs and flows of the past two decades, have served to reduce to a position of impotence. I refer, sir, to the metropolis of Moose Jaw. I am too old to check and not interested enough to care if the police court records have long since gone into the incinerator. But I do have a criminal record, and to me, as one who survived what we call The Great Canadian Depression, that is a badge of honor.

You will notice this train we are on? Perhaps it is indicative of how far our civilization has come, or gone, that I consider the passenger service between Toronto and Montreal of 40 years ago to be far superior to what it is today. If it were not for this drink in my hand, in this luxurious car, I would say there could not even be any comparison. Why, I ask you, can they not run the trains on time?

But enough, back to the criminal poor. I was born on a small farm across the Red River from a town called Morris, Manitoba, and when I was 14, in 1932; my father drowned in that river. The stupid son of a bitch tumbled into the river and that was the end of him. We didn't own the farm anyway. The bank did, and they were quick to assert the sovereignty of the Almighty Dollar. Four days after the funeral, we were out. Oh, no, not evicted, no possessions by the roadside. No, the foreclosure papers had been flashed through the courts: Judges seemed just as cooperative to those whom they deemed The Powers then as they do now. The judiciary and the bankers' association walked hand in hand, stopping occasionally to smile into each other's faces like lovers walking through a green park. We were not evicted. In fact, we were asked to stay. 'Mrs. Desjardins, the man from the bank said, you and your family can stay here as long as you want.

And why not? Why not, my friend? It made perfect sense. Who would rent 160 acres of grazing land, a house and its outbuildings in those years? No one, my friend. But if the widow Desjardins, who was a clean and industrious and honest woman, was induced to stay and if her six children stayed and continued to farm in the desultory manner of the past, a few cows and pigs and eggs sold in the nearby town, why, the house and buildings and fences and land would not deteriorate too much. It was a perfect arrangement, for the widow and her brood and for the bank: But it didn't work. My mother was a wise old hen and she clucked that man out of the house with some of the choicest language I have heard a woman utter. To this day. I have no idea where she picked up those words. It was years until I considered myself fluent enough in them to use them in public.

So we left. (*Snaps his fingers.*) To Winnipeg. Our few possessions, a hundred dollars or so, and into the ghetto of North Winnipeg, by the Canadian Pacific tracks where the trains shook the house day and night and the little Jew boys got behind the counters of their father's stores on Selkirk. vnue when they could barely see over the counter, and they learned the arts of commerce, which have made that race paramount since long before Christianity inflicted itself upon us.

But I ramble. You obviously do not believe that the Depression should be kept out of sight, like the pregnant and unmarried daughter at the Christmas feast or the retarded son when the priest comes to call: Why have we run from those ten years, which, if I may set the record straights, could have continued on and oh, yea, verily on and on until the last syllable of recorded time, if there had not been a war? A Hitler. For him, cousin, many thanks. Because Canadians, English-Canadians like you, French-Canadians like me, Ukrainian-Canadian, Chinese-Canadian, we were ashamed of it. Why? Because of what we call the Protestant Ethic, of course, which in essence says 'work your ass off all your life and do what the boss tells you and the big guy in the sky, when your time comes, he'll see you get your reward. The streets of Heaven are paved with gold, and hell is a fiery inferno.' We believe all this, you know. Even today, I believe it. You believe it. That gentleman and his wife over there, they believe it. I know.

So when I found out I could not survive in Winnipeg, I left, I left that crummy house the relief had put us in, and before I left I hammered out pork and bean cans, hammered them flat, and then I nailed them over the holes where the rats came in and I told my mother not to tell the relief examiner that I was gone but to keep claiming my allowance, my share, and I said goodbye to her and Jean and Marie and all the rest and I took to the road with my two blankets wrapped around my Bible and my poor clothes and tied together with two leather thongs, and that is what they called a turkey. I roamed back and forth. I got in fights, and I was in one which concerned maybe 10 or 12 men and one man died later from his wounds, but by that time we had scattered to the far winds and he was just another casualty of that undeclared war. Potter's field for him. Tough, fellow, tough.

I worked in harvest fields for the cheapest farmers in Canada and I worked for some damn fine fellows too. I picked apples and I picked tobacco and I picked peaches in the Okanagan, and in those days, the Okanagan Valley was Paradise. I must go back to Paradise someday, and I wonder if a very fine family outside of Penticton named Williams … Williamson? … will remember me? I worked for them for several months and they treated me like a son. I was a skinny little 16 year old. But, even so, when I would go into Penticton, because of the way I was dressed, because I had a French accent, maybe because of just the way I looked, the police would sometimes question me. I was a transient, but not a hobo.

If they wanted you to pick fruit in a hurry and get them out of a jam, you were an economic savior, but the rest of the time you were shit.

If you were poor but had a house and sent your kids to Sunday school, if you had no money and nothing for food, then you were unfortunate and people looked after you. If you left home, like I did, so my brothers and sisters would have more food and more room to sleep, then you became a criminal. You did not have to commit a criminal act. Mr. (*R.B.*) Bennett saw to that. You just had to be you, without money. Throw the guy in jail. Get him out of town. Lay the stick to his backside. Hustle him along. There's no more soup and bread and there won't be tomorrow so you guys get the hell out of here, see! How many times have I heard these things.

I was not bitter then. No, I can honestly say that, but I didn't know any better. The Communists used to come into the jungles or ride the freights with us, but what they were saying just wasn't making sense to me, or anybody else. If they had talked about a little farm with good pastures and a nice stream with fish in it and big trees around the house, and some cows and pigs in it and maybe a car in the garage, then I would have understood. If they had talked about that, that I could have this and that, I would have understood.

But I didn't understand and I didn't care when they talked about Lenin and what was happening in Russia and that we should go into Vancouver and smash the telegraph station and break store windows and make the police so mad at us that they'd crack a few hundred heads. That kind of talk was just so much baloney. Bullshit.

I went to war like the rest and I saw a lot and I came back and I went to university and got in with this company, the one I'm with now. They've been good to me and I've worked hard and I make a lot of money. You could call me a success. My brothers and sisters did okay too. One's a doctor. One girl's a nun, but getting kind of restless, she writes me. It was only when I started thinking it all over, after it had digested for so many years, that I realized just how terrible things were in the Thirties and how it was criminal to be alone and poor and on the roads when, for most of us, that was the only place we could be.

You've heard my story and I guess you're asking yourself, how could a guy that thinks the way this guy thinks be riding in this car and drinking Scotch and not doing anything about it. It is simple, and you should know it. The war smoothed out a lot of us, took away the memories of the Thirties, levelled off the bumps, like that, see. Most of us never had it so good, looking back on it. The great experience, eh? Then university. Money in the pocket, pretty girls. A big company. A good job. District sales manager. Fine, eh?

Now I'll tell you something, my friend; if there hadn't been a war there would have been a revolution. Two, three more years, and then poof! Some leaders would have come along. But the war came along and it killed a lot of good guys but it did a lot for a lot of other guys too. Maybe I'm not saying exactly how I feel it, but it is all over and done with. Nobody thinks about it, because it is still a shameful thing to be poor in Canada. Things haven't changed that much. It was shameful to be poor then, and it is shameful now, except some people just don't seem to care about it all that much. That's my story, and for that, you owe me a drink. Ballantine's."

... I Was Up and They Were Down

"If you had money the Dirty Thirties were a good time to live in. I was senior apprentice to a master miller in a big flour mill and I got $100 a month and you bet ya, I was in clover. Yes, I can remember everything about those times.

As I said I got $100 a month and that was a good wage. For a single man that was $25 a week and there was no taxes, the income tax didn't start until you made $2,000 a year, and I had a fine little apartment and a garage for $17.50 a month, kitchen, living room, two bedrooms and bathroom and big storage space in the basement. Not bad, eh?

I belonged to the canoe club over on the Red River and I curled, and in summer two other fellows and myself had a cottage all summer at Winnipeg Beach and we went to all the junior hockey games, following the Winnipeg Monarchs in those days, and I had a big Victor Northern Electric radio. They weren't called radios in those days. They were called radio receivers, which makes sense, doesn't it? The set received radio signals. There was Moore's Restaurant, and Child's down at the corner of Portage and Main, and the Royal Alex had a fine restaurant and so did the Fort Garry but it was always too stuffy for me. Life was good on $100 a month, and I saved money too. About $15 each month.

Oh, yes, I had a snazzy little 1929 Auburn roadster, painted sort of a silvery grey and as I remember I bought it cheap. I offered them $100 down and paid it off at $15 a month and they were glad to take it. I think it was Webb Motors. A lot of those firms went belly up later—just not enough $100 a month bachelors around. It was a great little car, travelled over mud roads like a skater on ice, and it was sure good to get the girls. Later I bought a big Nash from Leonard and McLaughlin Motors.

Food was cheap. Meat was shockingly cheap. You could buy a pound of fresh filetted pickerel straight from Lake Winnipeg that morning for something like 15 cents a pound. Lamb, 10 cents a pound. Stew lamb, why they practically gave it away. Sirloin, 20 cents, even less. Everything was rock bottom, and I heard the cost of living dropped more than 35 per cent from 1927 to 1933.

No, we never thought of the poor people. The reliefers. We'd see them on these make-work jobs, cleaning up back lanes, digging dandelions, hauling coal. I never thought to pity them, or help them. Far as I knew, nobody did. They were just there. If I went up to the public library on William Avenue and I saw how the people lived around there, sometimes I'd wonder. But only how people could live in such poverty, such conditions. I can't remember ever asking myself what made such poverty, such conditions. I was up and they were down and I expected to see my name in the sport pages as part of the team that won such and such a race at the canoe club, and if those people, if their name showed up in the 'Free Press' as having been sent to jail for stealing from Eaton's or the Bay, then so be it. What I mean is, I equated poverty with the sort of low life that criminals led and, I guess, if you were a criminal or that way inclined, then you lived in poverty and poor conditions.

No, I can't really say that I had a social conscience. Of course, you must realize that such a phrase had not even been invented then. There were always people in Market Square in the evenings ranting about hard times and corruption and R. B. Bennett and why weren't more jobs being made. We would just say they were 'Commies' although I believe the usual word was 'Bolshevists.' The newspapers ignored them, usually.

I remember I was stopped for speeding by a motorcycle cop one afternoon, on West Portage, and it turned out to be a chap I'd gone to school with and we got to jabbering and he said he was making $19 a week and he was tickled pink with it. I said I was making $25 a week and he said, 'In that case, Ernie, you get a ticket. This way it sort of spreads things a bit more evenly.' I remembered that, not to blab about how much you were making. There were too many thems and not that many of us and it was best to just let sleeping dogs lie.

Good times: When I married my wife in 1939 I was making $120 and it looked like I was going to get a good shot at that miller's job. It didn't work out that way because I went into the army two years later and there was no job for a captain working as 2-i.c. in a 40-year-old flour mill for me after. I was a big shot and wanted a big shot job. I moved to Saskatchewan and started a feed store, bulk oil dealership and had a small mill on the side. Just to keep my hand in. I did well.

Does all that sound phoney?"

Bridge Parties Kept Us Going

"It was the bridge parties which kept us alive. Literally alive. I mean it.

My husband was on the Faculty at Saskatoon, the university, and contrary to what most people though, academics in those days were graded pretty low, very low in the salary schedule. You talk about a janitor, pardon me, a structural custodian, these days making almost as much as a teacher in an elementary school, well let me tell you it wasn't all that much different in the Thirties. Tenure was a fine thing, you couldn't get fired, but don't you believe me, they knew how to cut in those days.

I had three children to bring up and I followed all the advice in the papers, like buying day-old bread because it was better and steaming it, and saving the water that greens had been boiled in and using it—but it still tasted awful—and using cheese and dried beans as a meat substitute.

There was one that was a dandy. Don't drink tea because it has no food value. Well, let me tell you this, I like my tea. It may not have food value but it has philosophical value and heart-warming value.

But to bridge. October through to the end of April, and once a week, every Thursday, we started at 1:30, quite early, and played for about nearly two hours and then had a lovely lunch and talk and went home to another week of the Depression. One year it was two tables, eight ladies, but the rest, it was four ladies, just four good friends. We all lived near the campus and we did have nice homes but it was those days and nobody really did any entertaining. Couldn't afford to, that was the real reason. But we did have our lovely living rooms and our furniture and our best china, and we could still cook. So important. We were starved for talk. 'Socializing' as a farm woman might call it.

My turn came around every four weeks and the week before was the anticipation, the planning what to have. Let's see, Monday I'd do a bit of cooking and the floors, and Tuesday I'd scrub and polish the hall and bathroom and living room and kitchen, and Wednesday I'd prepare. God, how I'd prepare a luncheon. Scrumptious, I can tell you, just scrumptious. Somebody used that word, scrumptious, in one of the radio shows. We didn't compete to see who could put up the best lunch but we all did our best, and there was no jealousy. We were such good friends.

Poor bridge players, I might add. Contract bridge was really quite new in those days so we'd often play auction, which was simple.

It was the anticipation, that's what counted. Having them come to your house, your home, and going to their homes even though they just lived around the neighborhood. When Mrs. Hensley died, it was like we had lost our best friend and it took a lot of deciding who would take her place. Oh, lots of ladies wanted to join. In that way it was a kind of exclusive club. Not snobby, but in a way, yes, you could say it was, if you understand.

Those were such hard time. As I remember there were times when you heard of somebody leaving, a fine letter of recommendation and all that, but the thing remained, he and his family would be around Saskatoon when the fall classes began. Saskatoon was such a nice town, such a pretty place with all its trees and the river, and it also was a place where everybody knew everybody else's business and there was an awful lot of talking at those bridge parties. Of course I should have said that it was very inexpensive, these little parties. You must remember that prices were quite low, you know, good brown bread for four cents a loaf and sugar at practically nothing a pound and a little money would go a long way and besides, the papers were full of economy recipes, oh they had fancy names for them, but they were still Depression recipes. I still remember those weekly tea parties so well. They were such good times." ...

The Regina Riot: One View

"I wouldn't say it was a riot, not at first. We were behaving peaceably enough there in Regina, and then the police on one side and the Mounties on the other started to pull the guys, our speakers, off the platform. There was whistles blowing and horses charging and you could say it was the police doing the rioting, clubbing and charging. We took it for a few minutes and then we let go, against them.

There might have been about 1,500 of us, all pretty pissed off, and those newspaper reports that there was about 4,000 of us was crazy. There never was more than 2,000 trek boys at any time. What the others were, they were Regina people down to Market Square to hear the speakers. Then when trouble started they were gone, just like that. Citizens of Regina, and not wanting any trouble.

It began for me after I'd been in a relief camp at Deroche which was about 50 miles up the Fraser Valley from Vancouver. We got bed and blankets, meals, tobacco and twenty cents a day. Not even two bits. Twenty cents a day to buy luxuries. The camp was lousy and the food was lousy. Oh, it was good enough food, I guess, but it was cooked so bad, in the same pots, not cleaned, day after day. There was fights over the smallest things, like a game of checkers and whose move it was, and the Reds, the Communists were everywhere. Whenever there was trouble beginning, they had been there before to start it or had their hats off fanning the flames. They were easy to spot, in fact, as I recall, they never made much of a try at saying they weren't. Most of them came from the Old Country.

I just can't remember why I walked out of the camp and headed for Vancouver but it had something to do with chickenshit regulations. Most of the administrators were First World War veterans, friends of politicians. The whole relief camp business, you must understand, was a political thing. They wanted all the young guys off the streets and stuck hellandgone up in the woods where they wouldn't start no revolution. That was a laugh. We did a lot of bitching but not much about revolution. That was just talk. I think the main thing was that we felt we were just dumped into the bush to rot, and the food was awful. That ass; Mayor Taylor of Vancouver, said the food we got was better than the food on his own table. If that is so, then his wife must have been married for her looks and sure as hell not her cooking.

About 100 of us got to Vancouver, hitching, in boxcars but a lot just plain walked. As I recall, we bunked down at the Ukrainian Hall and then a labor temple. People brought food, and I think the city helped out, and we had enough to eat.

I just can't remember too many of the details and I never believed anything I read in the newspapers. There was a few newspaper reporters along and they gave us a few laughs. They tried to be unemployed trekkers but they didn't dress right and they didn't act right and they sure as hell didn't know the lingo. How could they? We let them come along, though. The Communists were behind the whole thing, you know, from the beginning and I guess to the end, although a lot of them would fade out at the final curtain. They didn't believe in going to jail.

There was Arthur Evans, Art Evans, and he was a real hard nut but his trouble was he couldn't get along with anybody. Even with this, Evans could organize, but we all thought he was more of a front man. I was 19 at the time, or 20, and even I could see it took a lot more than one man to get a thing like this going. But he was doing something and that was more than anybody else was doing. His idea, his speeches said that the only way to get things was to go down to Ottawa and see R.B. Bennett—now there was a man who was easy to hate—and get something going for us. Decent relief, or jobs: Evans insisted that we behave ourselves. No violence, none at all. No stealing, and that was going to crimp an awful lot of guys' style. Be polite. Thank people when they gave us food or allowed us to sleep beneath their apple orchards. Evans was right, of course, and while I think very few of the boys were Communists they could see he made sense. It was a case, more than anything, of follow the leader.

Vancouver had a mayor then, Gerry McGeer, and Gerry was a smart boy. He was a Liberal politician and if he could stick it up the ass of the Conservatives and R.B., those initials to us meant Rotten Bastard, then he could get some votes, and also he'd like to see a lot of us single fellows to hell and gone out of town. Let us be Ottawa's headache, if we got there. So Old Gerry tapped a lot of his rich friends and he set up a tag day in down-town Vancouver and they came through with about $5,000, which, was an awful lot of do-re-mi in those days, an awful lot. In a way, it was bribe money for us to get out of town, and there we were, led by Arthur Evans, jumping a C.P. freight and heading to Ottawa.

I read that about 1,000 left Vancouver, and to a lot of Vancouver people it must have been good-riddance-to-bad-garbage. Along the way about another 1,000 or so joined us and we worked our way across to Calgary: We bunked down in Kamloops one day and got a soup kitchen set up by the town and tobacco passed out, and it went okay. It seems we spent another day in Golden, a divisional point, and the people were nice and Calgary was okay too, as I recall.

In fact things were just going along like free beer out of a spigot until the C.P.R. said they weren't going to let us ride their freights any more. That was a laugh. A million guys were riding freights in Canada, and suddenly no more riding. Evans and his boys told us it was a dirty plot to stop us, but we all knew that. What we didn't know was whether the C.P.R. or the Bennett government was behind it. It didn't really matter. The railways and the government were so close in cahoots together you couldn't tell them apart, anyway. I read something later that the interest paid by the government every year on the Canadian National debt was more during the Depression than was ever paid to men, women and children in Canada during those years to keep from starving, to be able to go out with decent clothes and to keep a decent roof over their heads, and, god damn it all, to keep from going mad. So we weren't going to be allowed to ride the freights, and Regina was the last stop.

Okay, so Evans and some of his boys went down to Ottawa to see old Rotten Bastard Bennett and that didn't work out too well. In fact, it didn't work out at all. Evans was hot-headed and couldn't work with people who didn't do just what he said, and you've heard of R.B. Bennett. I remember Evans calling the prime minister a liar, and if I know Evans, he probably swore when he did it. So you see how it would go. It was after this that Bennett must have decided that that was it.

As I recall we were going to have a mass meeting in the Market Square in Regina. We'd been sleeping on the ground and getting handouts and hanging around town for more than ten days, two weeks and some of the boys had gotten into a little trouble, some stealing, theft by night, that sort of thing, and the locals weren't all that kindly disposed towards us.

Bennett ordered that Evans and his boys were to be arrested at the meeting. That was on Dominion Day It was a stupid thing, but just about everything you care to name which the government did in those days was stupid. Well, as soon as the meeting got going they jumped us. I don't think our boys had any guns but the police sure as hell did, and they were using them. Shooting at legs. We didn't even have rocks, nothing but our bare hands, but if we could pull a cop off his horse then we had boots and he got it. One cop was dead and some people were wounded, shot. A lot of guys were arrested, and I can't remember what happened, to them. Probably three months, taking part in a riot.

I can't remember even what happened to Arthur Evans. He'd get jail, of course. He'd never be able to talk his way out of that one. But it wasn't all that much of a riot. The papers played it big but it wasn't all that much. A lot of guys just thought it was a lark, a chance to yell at cops and snap a lighted cigarette in their faces and then run like hell.

303

The C.P.R. assembled a train and got us sorted out and we got on it and went back to the coast, although there were guys dropping off along the way. It was a free ride for some, both ways. A lot of fun a chance to break the monotony for others. I let off a little steam and so did a lot of others and we were fed pretty well.

That's about all I remember of it, except Old Gerry McGeer did a pretty good job of sticking it to the Tories. They got a lot of bad publicity. If my dates are a little off and I'm out on some things, well, it was a long time ago and I haven't thought of it for years."

The Regina Riot: Second View

"I always thought the Regina Riot was what you would today call a snow job. A police riot, and against us, the trekkers, and believe you me when I say an awful lot of those smashed windows and stolen goods were the work of good Regina citizens. I know. I saw them. Men in good clothes who weren't with our bunch who came out from Vancouver and so I can say, those guys that did the looting were a lot of Regina people. Well mostly.

Look, look at it this way. We were disciplined. Art Evans told us it had to be this way, that being polite and organized and neat even in our old duds was the way to gain public support, and we'd got it all along the line. Suppose a trekker was found with a pen and pencil set or a wrist watch or something in his pocket. Well, they would have thrown the key away. Five, eight, ten years. Looting was the worst crime against property and you know what property was in those days. Like the Trinity, God, the Son and the Holy Ghost.

There were a lot of store windows bashed in. I read that the square looked like a battleground. Holy Hell, those reporters then never saw a battleground, and I have. For three years, '15 to '18. There was a lot of damage but two days later, after Dominion Day, you couldn't tell the difference.

I'm sorry the policeman was killed and some of our boys got arrested and it made a lot of noise across the country but as I said, it was a snow job. Old R.B. Bennett wanted a showdown and he got it, piling all those cops into vans and banging them into the square. Guns were firing. Guess who had the guns? He wanted to discredit the trek and he did. Oh, yes, he succeeded. We were, in the eyes of a lot of people, just a bunch of Reds. Carrying the card. It wasn't like that at all. We were just a bunch of ordinary guys, but Bennett stuck the label on us and it stuck. He did a lot of harm that day, that guy."

On the Road to Regina

"The boys were getting a bit restless. Nothing was happening, and they would wander around town and back to the grounds for meals and back and forth. Of course, the Communist agitators were working on them and there was one good slugging match with police and RCMP in a vacant lot across from the city hall and a shouting match another time, but nothing really happened.

Of course we knew the Communists, and while they hung around the soup lines, I don't think I ever saw one of them in the line. They ate up at a cafe and ate pretty well, I'd say. Then the gang came in from Vancouver, mostly boys out of the relief camps and this was the start of the March On Ottawa. You know, it only got as far as Regina, where they had the riot.

To this day, I don't think that riot had to happen, and Miller (*the policeman who was killed*) didn't have to die. They just didn't handle it right. I mean, the boys down at Victoria Park, they weren't ready to start any revolution but Art Evans was determined to push it through. You know, I never thought Evans was really a bad actor, and who is to say 35 years later that he was all that wrong. Anyway, about 250 of the boys at Victoria Park got sick and tired of sitting around so we joined the march, pretty much all together, and away we went for Ottawa. We were on a freight and if the CPR arranged it this way, I don't know, but only the last six cars were empty and everybody piled in these and away we went.

It was late at night when we got into Medicine Hat and there was a lot of shunting and pushing around and nobody thought much of anything of it. There always was that kind of activity in the yards, but in an hour or so, the cops came along and said we all had to get off. What had happened was this. They had just unhooked the last six cars and pushed them onto a siding. The boys were all herded into a warehouse and told they would be charged with violating the Railway Act, trespassing on CPR property.

The boys took it as a joke, saying they'd go on the next march, things like that. I had to stay with them, of course, and nothing happened. No charges were laid and they were put on other trains going back west or told to hit the road and as far as I know, none of that bunch got to Regina.

If someone had used his head they could have done the same thing at every divisional point between Vancouver and Regina, quietly, no fuss or muss, and nothing would have happened. You would have had a lot of screaming agitators but nothing else. As it was, there was a lot of trouble, and Evans and his merry little band, about 10 in all, I think, did cause a lot more trouble than they should have. They made it a lot tougher on the unemployed man, believe you me."

▲ Document 2: A Maritimer Speaks His Mind

● **A Maritimer Speeaks His Mind,** *Maclean's,* **1 February 1933. Resentment over the uneven effects of the Depression was a theme in this political cartoon of the era.**

Source: A Maritimer Speeaks His Mind, *Maclean's,* February 1, 1933. Charles and Cynthia Hou, *Great Canadian Political Cartoons, 1915 to 1945* (Vancouver: Moody's Lookout Press, 2002).

▲ Document 3: Annual Wage-Earners by Province and Sex, 1921 and 1931

PROVINCE AND CENSUS YEAR	AVERAGE EARNINGS		PROVINCE AND CENSUS YEAR	AVERAGE EARNINGS	
	Male	Female		Male	Female
P.E. Island			Manitoba		
1921	657	334	1921	1,162	693
1931	679	364	1931	929	559
Nova Scotia			Saskatchewan		
1921	890	423	1921	1,030	663
1931	762	431	1931	761	524
New Brunswick			Alberta		
1921	873	455	1921	1,143	701
1931	755	437	1931	890	599
Quebec			British Columbia		
1921	1,030	480	1921	1,048	676
1931	925	478	1931	897	623
Ontario			Canada		
1921	1,102	613	1921	1,057	573
1931	1,005	636	1931	927	559

Source: Adapted from Statistics Canada, Canada Year Book 1937.
http://www66.statcan.gc.ca/cdm4/document.php?CISOROOT=/eng&CISOPTR=5461&REC=

307

▲ Document 4: On-To-Ottawa Trek

● The On-to-Ottawa trek was a very public display of opposition to the system of relief camps. What does this picture suggest about the people who were involved in the trek and about the image that was being presented of them?

▲ Document 5: The Impact of the Great Depression on People

Relief Budget
One Week for a family of five, Montreal, 1932

Food	Amount	Approximate Cost	Subtotal	
Milk	13 quarts	$1.30	Dairy	1.45
Cheese	1 pound	.15		
Brown Bread	10 loaves, 240 oz	.60		
Rolled Oats	3 pounds	.15	Grains, Cereals	1.00
Flour	2 pounds	.10		
Rice, Barley	2 pounds	.15		
Tomatoes	3 tins, 6 pounds	.18		
Potatoes	25 pounds	.25		
Carrots, Turnips	4 pounds	.16		
Cabbage	2 pounds	.05		
Onions	2 pounds	.08	Vegetables, Fruits	.94
Dried beans	1 pound	.04		
Dried peas	1 pound	.06		
Prunes, figs	1 pound	.12		
Chuck roast	3 ½ pounds	.46	Meat	.54
Beef or Pork Liver	½ pounds	.08		
Butter	1 pound	.25		
Peanut butter	½ pound	.08		
Shortening	½ pound	.08	Other	.65
Molasses	1 pound	.13		
Sugar	2 pounds	.10		
			One-week total	$4.58

Source: The Impact of the Great Depression on People, *Historical Atlas of Canada*, (Volume III, Plate 41, Concise Plate 41) Donald Kerr, Deryck W. Holdsworth, and Geoffrey J. Matthews. (Toronto, ON: University of Toronto Press, 1990).

■ Article 1: "'A Barren Cupboard at Home': Ontario Families Confront the Premiers During the Great Depression"

Lara Campbell

On 9 October 1933, Mr. T. Frith of Pembroke, Ontario, wrote his fourth of six letters to Premier George Henry. Unemployed and supporting a family, he unsuccessfully petitioned Henry for a job: 'I am getting fed up with everything. It looks strange to me men that never did anything for the Government can be holding down permanent jobs and the likes of me face poverty [...] I would just like too [*sic*] know how you would like it yourself if you fought 3 1/2 years for your government [...] do you think you would be getting a fair deal if they didn't give you a little work to keep your wife and family.'[1]

Unemployed citizens of Ontario wrote thousands of similar letters to Premiers George Henry and Mitchell Hepburn during the Great Depression. In 1931, 18 per cent of wage earners in the province were officially out of work, and by 1935 in some cities, such as Niagara Falls, Windsor, and the Toronto suburbs, 33–45 per cent of the population relied on relief.[2] At the beginning of the Depression, state-run social welfare programs were limited in scope, consisting of Mothers' Allowance, Workmen's Compensation, and a means-tested Old Age Pension. Unemployment relief, funded by the federal government and administered by the municipalities, was inadequate and stigmatizing, and was viewed by the federal and provincial governments as a temporary emergency measure. To qualify for relief, the unemployed had to be completely destitute, and were forced to forfeit cars, radios, phones, and liquor permits. Relief payments were often made in kind or by a voucher system, and were different in each community across Canada.[3]

Source: Laura Campbell, "'A Barren Cupboard at Home': Ontario Families Confront the Premiers During the Great Depression," in *Ontario Since Confederaton: A Reader,* Edgar-André Montigny and Lori Chambers, eds., (University of Toronto Press, 2000), pp. 284–306. Reprinted with permission.

In response to high unemployment and inadequate and stigmatizing relief policies, many Ontario citizens wrote directly to the premier of Ontario. Some of these letters consist of criticisms of government policy, complaints against those on relief, or proposed economic solutions to the Depression, but most are requests from unemployed, white, working-class men and women for jobs or financial aid. The only Canadian study looking at similar sources is *The Wretched of Canada,* a collection of letters to Prime Minister R.B. Bennett. The editors, Michael Bliss and L.M. Grayson, argue that these letters were written by the poorest of the population, those whose lives were 'a single-minded struggle for survival, monotonous and dreary.' They claim that 'the Canadian people had too much discipline, too much individualism [...] too little political sophistication to fight back in a radical protest against a whole economic and social system.'[4] While some of the letters to the prime minister and the premiers were indeed desperate pleas for help, many were clearly articulated demands based on notions of rights and entitlement. As citizens, letter writers believed that, in return for service and duty to the state, they and their families were entitled to economic security. Letters written by breadwinners, wives and mothers, homeowners, veterans, and Canadians of British background used the idea of a reciprocal relationship between citizen and state, and the language of respectability, service, and duty, to claim entitlement to jobs and financial aid. Rather than interpreting these letters as expressions of helplessness, this essay examines them as a fundamental part of the shift to the postwar welfare state.

The history of the welfare state has been well documented in Canada, but most historians have used a top-down approach to debate the development of policies, institutions, and the origins and objectives of welfare state programs. Historians have discussed the influence of government, business, religion, and party politics, the role of intellectuals and the social sciences, and the desire of the state to preserve the capitalist economic order and to avoid social disorder. Written mainly from an institutional approach, this history leaves little room in which to locate the agency of welfare recipients or to understand their role in the development of the postwar welfare state.[5] Most people in the 1930s did not belong to an organized political party or protest group, but they voiced concerns and criticisms to friends and neighbours,

310

and in letters written to politicians. Letters to the premiers demonstrate that popular pressure must not be overlooked as a major source of political influence. In Canada, the thousands of letters received by federal and provincial governments demanding that the state take moral responsibility to protect and nurture its citizens, along with relief protests, strikes, and other forms of unrest, helped to push the government towards a more interventionist rights-based welfare state.[6] A broad consensus of public opinion began to develop around the belief that the stigma of charity-based relief was no longer acceptable for Canadian citizens.

The concept of 'rights' articulated by the letter writers was not one of universal entitlement to economic security. Although letter writers thought that every citizen was entitled to a set of rights, they also believed that citizenship itself had to be earned. One way that people attempted to influence the government and assert their fundamental sense of belonging and status as citizens was by making claims, on the state,[7] through which they defined the meaning and limits of citizenship. A proper citizen was understood as someone who had a strong work ethic, fulfilled proper gender roles, was married and raising a family, and was white and of British background. Meeting most or all of these requirements meant that one was a citizen and had a right to enter into a moral relationship with the state. In return, the state had a duty and a responsibility to protect its citizens from poverty and unemployment, both of which interfered with the ability to practise good citizenship. Letter writers explicitly used the language of citizenship, a powerful word connoting 'respect, rights, and dignity,'[8] to argue that the government should take the problems of unemployment and poverty seriously. Writers understood themselves to be fully participating members of a larger community; as such, they were entitled to formulate demands and claim a central place in the social and economic order.[9]

Linda Gordon and Nancy Fraser argue that social welfare policy is based on the dichotomous principles of contract or charity. They define charity as a stigmatizing handout symbolizing dependence, 'a gift on which the recipient had no claim, and for which the donor had no obligation.'[10] Contract, however, is associated with rights and dignity; it is based on the free-market economy and the historic rights of free male citizens to own their property and their

labour power.[11] This opposition between charity and contract has formed the basis of the twentieth-century welfare state, and runs throughout most social welfare programs and policies in Canada.[12] Whether social welfare should be temporary, minimal, and stigmatizing, or a 'guarantee of a decent standard of living, economic security and honorable entitlement,'[13] is still a topic of debate in late twentieth-century politics.

Feminist historians have argued that this contrast between contract and charity is gendered, creating a two-tiered welfare state intended to uphold the traditional family model of the male breadwinner and the dependent female homemaker. Programs that serve a mainly female constituency, such as Mothers' Allowances or Family Benefits, are, they argue, charity, based programs that are low-paying, stigmatizing, intrusive, and based on the applicant meeting a particular moral standard of female propriety,[14] Programs that develop in the tradition of contract and are based on male patterns of participation in the paid labour force, such as Workmen's Compensation and Unemployment Insurance, are less stigmatizing and more generous. However, it is important to remember that there is no neat division between charity and contract-based social welfare programs. Even in the contract-based model, concerns over upholding the work ethic and preserving the difference between the deserving and the undeserving are often incorporated into the programs.[15]

A comparison of the principles of contract and charity is helpful in interpreting how specific welfare state programs were implemented and how claimants articulated their demands. By examining the grassroots level in the development of social welfare, such as letters written to the premiers, it is possible to develop a more complex and nuanced appreciation of the relationship between the citizen and the state. It is useful to think of charity and contract not as dichotomous categories, but as a continuum with a variety of positions in between. Where particular claimants fit themselves, or are situated by the state, is mediated by such characteristics as class, race, gender, and marital status. In the Depression years, both men and women attempted to incorporate the dignity and sense of entitlement associated with the language of citizenship and a rights-based discourse in order to negotiate a space of greater equality and security for themselves and their families. The

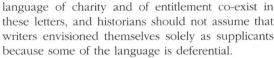

language of charity and of entitlement co-exist in these letters, and historians should not assume that writers envisioned themselves solely as supplicants because some of the language is deferential.

The letters, read carefully and as a whole, clearly demonstrate that the Depression years were a meeting point between traditional values of character, duty, and charity and developing ideas of entitlement and state-sponsored welfare in opposition to government bureaucracy and charity. What emerged was both a desire to reform rather than completely eradicate the capitalist economic structure, and a discourse that never completely challenged deeply held inequities and hierarchies of gender, ethnicity and race, and marital status.[16] While recognizing that the welfare state was limited in scope, and was never intended to create full social and economic equality, the postwar welfare state was still an important shift in policy that recognized a right to a certain minimum level of income. Programs such as unemployment insurance or family allowances, and, later, universal old age security and health insurance, were non-means-tested social programs that, at a minimum, 'have been crucial breakthroughs in the fight against poverty and insecurity, and have helped to create a sense of social rights linked to national citizenship.'[17] The language and values of service, duty, and respectability framed writers' demands for economic security and helped to shape the extent of government responsibility for social welfare.

To most letter writers, having a job was crucial to feeling fully human. Unemployed men in particular claimed that working and earning a wage was central to maintaining responsible citizenship, pride, and self-worth. This 'right' to a job, however, was not unconditional. Unemployed people, either those on relief or those refusing to take it were careful to point out their strong work ethic and willingness to perform any type of labour for good pay. Because the stereotype of the lazy, unemployed worker persisted into the 1930s, the jobless were careful to distance themselves from such images.[18] There was little agreement on who, exactly, deserved employment or had the right to it. In the fight for limited jobs, forceful divisions based on gender and marital status existed among those who were unemployed. It is clear, however, that most men believed they had a right to work before women, and that both men and women thought that married men were the most entitled to jobs. Ideally, men were the breadwinners

who would support their dependent wives and children.[19]

Men articulated their demands for jobs or financial aid through a discourse of independent breadwinner status, claiming they had never needed help and insisting they wanted work, not relief. Although it was usually considered humiliating to ask for relief, men did not feel it was shameful to remind the government of its responsibility to help them find work. They consistently reminded the government that they were 'entitled, deserving and in dire need of work.'[20] This demand for work was based on a powerful sense of masculine entitlement, one that enabled a man to claim respectable status and avoid the shame of charity. The state, men declared, had an obligation to help them fulfil their manly duties, as it would 'lift a man up to be given work instead off [*sic*] charity.'[21]

Not surprisingly, letters clearly indicate that men's status and self-esteem was intricately bound up with the ability to work.[22] As one man pointed out, 'I love to work [...] But, if I work or run the race, I want to win some sort of prize.'[23] The ideal prize, for many, was a family wage and the opportunity to marry and raise new citizens. For married men, masculinity and self-respect were linked to the right to work and the ability to support a family. Even though the family wage was a reality for only a small minority of the population, the idea of the man as the main monetary contributor to the family economy was dominant in the 1930s. As one unemployed man stated: 'I respectfully request that the Government will give me the opportunity to work [...] and provide fully all that is needed for the support of my wife and child [...] for whose welfare, both the Government and myself are legally and morally responsible.'[24]

Indeed, while men argued for entitlement from the contract and rights-based position of employment, it is crucial to remember that they spoke of these rights within a familial context. Their rights as wage-earners drew additional strength from their role as providers and were inseparable from their position as husband and father within the family. Men continually referred to their obligations and duties as family providers, and to the emotional and psychological trauma of failing in these roles. By the interwar period, the representation of fatherhood had shifted slightly to accommodate the more involved roles expected of men in the ideal companionate family. The father's main contribution to the family was still breadwinning, but he was also expected to take on a more active and involved role with his children.[25] Cynthia Comacchio argues that breadwinning came to symbolize the emotional ideals of 'fatherly devotion' and 'paternal protection' as well as material provision.[26] For fathers, seeing their children going hungry was a visible and painful reminder of their failure as providers, a challenge to the duties surrounding the societal definitions of respectable manhood.[27]

Unemployment could lead not only to the loss of 'manhood and self-respect' but to a serious threat to the social order, once men could no longer be rewarded for fulfilling the expected roles of husband, father, and provider. 'You can readily understand [that] a hungry man,' claimed Sam Harris, president of the Navy League, 'especially if he has children, is dangerous. Holdups, robberies, purse-snatchings, porch-climbings, and other things, might easily happen'[28] Men could use their role as father to remind the government that the stability of the state and the security of the family were intricately bound together. 'It will be a strong man patriotically who this winter will drown out the cries of his children for bread with the strains of The Maple Leaf Forever,' claimed one unemployed veteran.[29] Another unemployed man told Hepburn: 'We hear our little ones crying for many things that they cannot have under this wave of charity, they do not get enough to eat and they have to starve and suffer these evictions … and see Bailiffs throwing their home on the street their toys and Belongings can you wonder why men are clamering [*sic*] for a Revolution.'[30]

The argument that the state's fundamental responsibility was to protect families from instability created a powerful demand for increased state support of welfare programs. As Annalee Golz argues, by the postwar reconstruction period the state accepted a moral obligation to protect and ensure the stability and welfare of the Canadian family.[31] This concern over the stability of the family did not exist only in social welfare or state discourse, however. Part of the powerful rhetoric of postwar welfare programs, such as the Family Allowance Act, was rooted in the demands of Depression-era families for their right to protection by the state.

Women wrote to the premiers as frequently as men, but the basis of their arguments for entitlement differed. While men consistently referred to their status as breadwinners, women were viewed as wives and mothers who had no rightful claim to a position in the paid labour force, especially when male unemployment was so high. But women used the language of rights and entitlement even though these rights were not based on their position within the market economy. As wives and mothers, women demanded help on behalf of their husbands' and families' well-being and independence. Like men, women viewed the family as an independent and self-supporting unit that was, ideally, free from dependence on charity. They were careful to point out the respectable status of their families and their husbands' strong work ethic. 'We want work, not charity' was the refrain from women on behalf of their families just as much as it was from unemployed men.[32]

Married women in particular were labelled as dependants of men and were located in the private sphere where domestic reproduction and caregiving work was unpaid and. privatized.[33] Women tended, therefore, to make indirect claims on the state, rooted in their position as wife, mother, and dependant.[34] They asked for jobs for husbands and aid for children, so as to maintain the pride and security of the family. 'My husband feels terrible[;] he loves his family, is willing to work hard,' wrote a mother of seven whose university-educated husband lost his job as a salesman. Her husband, and many other men, she claimed, were 'people who have always paid their way [and are] people unaccustomed to hardship [and] are losing everything they ever worked for through no fault of theirs.'[35] Although the claims women made for their families' right to economic security were not as strong as men's, their requests for help should not be interpreted as a form of begging or charity. Certainly, male breadwinners claimed a more direct form of entitlement predicated on independent wage-earning status and a broad public consensus around their right to paid employment. But women still found room to argue for their right to economic security, even within a position of subordination and the framework of a familial status that defined them primarily as dependants.[36]

Even though the idea of the family wage excluded women from the public sphere, women could draw on the rights associated with it to criticize government unemployment policy and the lack of adequate relief, and to argue for their families' right to economic security. As one woman wrote 'It is almost

313

winter and our men have had no work for ages and we have no winter clothes and no prospects of any my own children have no clothes [...] Its work we want not relief. We don't our living [*sic*] for nothing we want work and lots of it.'[37] Women repeatedly insisted on their children's need for adequate food and clothing as well as school books and medicine, reminding the premiers that their husbands required jobs to meet these necessities. Protesting on behalf of husbands and children by using the rhetoric of 'militant mothering' was one way that women could subvert assumptions of female domesticity to make claims on the state.[38]

The Great Depression drove home the disparity between idealized prescriptions for womanhood and the reality of taking care of a family on a limited budget. As women's ability to manage households and raise children grew increasingly constrained due to high male unemployment, women challenged the traditional roles in which they held a sense of pride and accomplishment.[39] In doing so, they politicized the rhetoric associated with the family wage and with family duties and obligations. A letter signed by the 'mothers of Sturgeon Falls' illustrates women's ability as wives and mothers to make collective demands on the state:

> There are many fathers without work, some with only three days a week. Fathers have these young, unemployed men to care for. As a father, Hon. Sir, you will understand the situation, we mothers are up against, who have our young sons on our hands, who cannot get employment [...] the people will need relief money, or some means given by the Government that the people may have a way of living to keep body and soul together.[40]

Wives and mothers expected men to protest against the unemployment that robbed them of their ability to provide and made it difficult to manage the household. One woman from Welland observed: 'There are millions of men driven to being red. A man can stand a good deal but when his wife and children suffer if *he is a man* he becomes desperate.'[41] When men protested against low wages or inadequate relief, their wives clearly framed those actions within the proper duties and responsibilities of manhood. After the arrest of Stratford relief strikers

in 1936, one of many wives wrote to Hepburn in protest: 'Surely it is no crime to ask for more food that our children may not suffer from malnutrition.'[42] Another wife asked the premier, 'Why should our children and I be denied having a good husband and father in our home just because he protested against the low standard of relief?'[43]

The arguments made by women on behalf of their families may not have challenged traditional gender roles, but their actions demonstrate that they did not see themselves as passive victims. These letters were a form of political resistance, where women actively voiced opposition to the way the government handled unemployment, threatened to withhold their vote in the next election, and demanded political accountability.[44] As one woman admonished Henry, after writing him three times in vain to request a farm loan and school books for her daughter, there was 'one vote here the last time and will be three this time if i get no help i give none.'[45] Although women were generally excluded from higher-paying administrative positions and policy making, and were labelled as dependants or excluded from the better-paying and less-stigmatizing welfare programs, they were still pivotal in 'shaping the broad outlines of the welfare state.'[46] As Linda Gordon points out, when women made demands for relief, they were rejecting charity, 'inventing rights,' and claiming the status of rightful citizen.[47] Married women were not accorded the same respect and status as men, but their demands for respectability and security should be recognized as a crucial factor in transforming state obligations for social welfare.

Women with husbands could make claims on the government based on the family wage, but women who were deserted or widowed also used the language of entitlement to claim the right to Mothers' Allowance. Mothers' Allowance may have been a form of moral regulation, yet these letters indicate that women understood it as a form of entitlement,[48] not charity. They adopted the language of contract to clothe their claims in a discourse of rights that validated their needs as legitimate entitlements tied to marriage and motherhood. 'To raise a future Canadian in the way he should be raised,' claimed one widow, 'is an important and full time job, enough responsibility for any woman however strong, without the added burden of trying to find a job.'[49] Women drew on the gendered expectations of womanhood to legitimate their requests and to demand recognition,[50] arguing that the state owed them support in return for fulfilling their proper roles as wives and mothers. A deserted wife whose remarriage disqualified her from a veteran's pension drew on her status as a mother as well as the language of service and sacrifice used by veterans, claiming, 'at the same time after I have struggled to raise my boys up to manhood the Government would expect my boys to step out and do their share to protect the country should a war break out; that go [sic] to show how much respect the Government has for the citizens of the country.'[51] Women protested when allowances were cut off or denied, contacted local Mothers' Allowances, Boards, and wrote to politicians. 'Why do innocent children have to suffer the loss of a good home,' asked one woman,'[…] when we are Canadians, and our parents before us.'[52] While not always successful, their determination indicates that women were serious in attempting to force the state to recognize their maternal concerns and duties.

Historians have argued that Mothers' Allowance acted as a form of state moral regulation by making women's eligibility dependent on their moral propriety and respectability, such as proper housekeeping standards and the cleanliness and behaviour of their children.[53] Sexual standards were of particular concern to administrators, and many women were cut off from the allowance after being accused of immorality.[54] But even those recipients who were accused of impropriety could draw on the rhetoric of some reformers who had originally envisioned the allowance as a form of entitlement that recognized that 'the reproductive work of women merited some degree of entitlement.'[55] A woman accused of moral impropriety for keeping a male boarder in her home unsuccessfully protested the removal of her allowance by claiming, 'I am a member of the Church of England and a conservative and I am trying to bring my children up right.'[56] In some cases, however, being a good mother was enough to maintain the allowance, even in the face of sexual scandal. A woman from Toronto, whose application for a mother's allowance was rejected because she had two children by a man who turned out to be a bigamist, appealed successfully, saying: 'I am a Canadian girl born and raised in Toronto and I am a Mother. I think I am deserving of that allowance.'[57] Claiming entitlement based on fulfilling the gendered duties of wife

and mother could be a source of power for women, who could use those accomplishments to demand financial aid from the state. Like most women who wrote to the premiers, single mothers believed they and their children were entitled to economic and family security.

Letter writers used the language of respectability to claim that the proper relationship between the citizen and the state was reciprocal, and they emphasized certain moral qualities as necessary preconditions of citizenship. One argument closely associated with respectability and the demand for work was the declaration by many letter writers that homes were in danger.[58] To both men and women, owning their own home was a clear sign of moral worth within the community. In her study of male workers in Hanover, Joy Parr shows how home ownership gave families economic security and a sense of pride rooted in community respectability.[59] Men and women took great satisfaction in the presentation of their homes, since a home was where a family could 'live in a sanitary condition,' and where a man could fulfil his obligation to his family and 'bring my wife, and children up right.'[60] Suzanne Morton argues that workers in Halifax achieved respectability by establishing privacy and meeting common standards of good taste, reflected in consumer purchases and the decoration of the family home.[61] While most of the people in her study were tenants rather than owners, homeownership would have further increased the pride and self-worth of men and women within the community. Letter writers were determined to maintain their homes at great cost, and were worried about the possibility of foreclosure and eviction.

Homeowners placed themselves within the circle of respectability by emphasizing such values as thrift and economic responsibility. City councils and homeowners' associations worried that men were 'becoming ill in mind and body for want of their regular employment, and the happiness and peace of our homelife is almost destroyed through the enforced idleness of the breadwinners.'[62] Councils passed resolutions that explicitly linked homeownership to respectability, pride, and self-respect, and demanded that unemployed homeowners be given special opportunities to work off tax arrears and mortgage payments. Homeowners were praised for thriftiness and savings 'at a considerable sacrifice,' for paying taxes and taking 'a pride in the Municipality,'

315

and for their 'praiseworthy efforts [at] maintaining themselves without recourse to relief.'[63] Homes were important because they were a powerful symbol of a person's position in the social order and the most visible evidence of hard work and thrift, the very moral qualities needed to be a good citizen. To be evicted from one's home, citizens claimed, destroyed the 'family's self-respect and morale.'[64] Women could also appeal to the government as homeowners, since they were an essential part of the family economy when buying and maintaining a home. One woman told Henry: 'I worked like a man on our place to help my husband and saved every cent I could to help get along […] it is no fault of ours that we cannot meet our way.'[65] For a married woman, the home was the centre of domestic production and the heart of her responsibilities as a wife and mother. 'Making do' was a skill many women perfected in order to stretch a man's low wage and to manage the household on limited resources.[66] Preventing foreclosure was a crucial job for women in the Depression years, and letters indicate that women saved and spent money carefully, took in sewing and boarders, sold their own produce and baking, and performed domestic service to help save their homes.[67]

While men and their wives made claims on the state based on fulfilling proper gender roles, respectability, and home ownership, First World War veterans and their families were also able to draw on the language of sacrifice and service to the country. To veterans, service in the Great War set their demands apart from all other claims on the state. The letters of unemployed veterans carefully pointed out their years of service and duty, claiming that patriotic loyalty was the duty of the soldier, but that the government had a moral obligation to protect and support them in return. Many unemployed veterans felt abandoned and ignored by a government that was reluctant to offer them special status in recognition of their sacrifices. 'It certainly does not make me feel very nice,' explained one unemployed man, 'to think I helped to defend a country that will not help me in times when I and my family need it badly.'[68] Veterans' associations complained to the government that veterans' dismissals from jobs were contrary to 'British justice,' and that returned men should be given preference for employment.[69] One veterans' group protested the arrests of Etobicoke relief strikers because some of the men were vets 'who at the country's call willingly

went through hell, believing they were fighting for Justice, Peace and Freedom and now when they dare Fight for even a miseryable [*sic*] existence for themselves and their wives and Families you have them thrown into prison cells.'[70] Jobs and economic security, veterans claimed, were basic rights that they had earned overseas while proving themselves as worthy Canadian men and citizens.

Veterans' criticisms of the government in the 1930s were rooted in their collective protest against inadequate government compensation after First World War, when they began to mobilize against poor training programs, inadequate pensions for disabled soldiers, and unfair differentials in pensions based on rank.[71] They made their claims for compensation, Desmond Morton argues, on the basis of 'moral entitlement,' not charity.[72] By 1919 the Great War Veterans' Association advocated state policies such as public housing, minimum wage, nationalization of primary resources, profit controls, and age, sickness, and unemployment insurance.[73] Veterans insisted that their wartime sacrifices of lost wages and family separations had yet to be properly rewarded,[74] and linked their status as soldiers to the respectability associated with manly breadwinning and family duty. Their fulfilment of the masculine call to sacrifice deserved special recognition, they believed, particularly when high unemployment made it increasingly difficult to support their families. 'When MEN were needed to save our nation,' claimed the Canadian Legion, 'the boys responded to the call unselfishly, upholding the best traditions of our Empire. They gave their all. Promises of Freedom and Security have been broken or forgotten.'[75] The discourse of sacrifice and duty, combined with the privilege associated with the role of breadwinner, was, for many veterans, a powerful argument for their right to employment. One veteran with an ill wife and four children told Henry to give the men who 'wallowed in the mud of Flanders a chance to make a few dollars and keep the Respectability of ourselves and our families.'[76]

Veterans' families also used the concepts of duty and sacrifice to make claims on the government, often linking war service to the powerful image of protecting the home. Some families were literally on the verge of foreclosure, but, for others, the word *home* represented economic security. One mother reminded Henry: 'If this country ever has to fight again it can call on my eight boys to protect it well you cannot expect them to protect homes they haven't got.'[77] Future soldiers were the same young men who were unemployed and unable to fulfil the basic duties of citizenship. Their families reminded the government that its success in future international conflicts depended on the willingness of young men to serve, and, therefore, they expected protection on the home front in times of economic crisis. As one father reminded Henry, 'We thought that when two of our boys went overseas, that they went to protect our home.'[78]

Closely tied to values of duty and respectability were particular notions of ethnicity. It is not surprising that in a time of social and economic upheaval, an affirmation of Canadian national identity should appear in popular discourse. Although historians have discussed the rise of an independent Canadian cultural nationalism beginning in the 1920s, few have looked at how national identity was formed outside the intellectual elite.[79] Yet, if a nation is an 'imagined community,' it is crucial to understand how conceptions of nationality were shaped and understood at the popular level.[80] Letter writers used the discourse of national identity to place themselves, along with the politicians they were addressing, within a collective, although narrowly defined, Canadian identity. Anyone who was white and of British heritage was a true Canadian, and therefore worthy of financial aid and economic justice. Letter writers clearly indicated who was and was not included in a hierarchy of entitlement. Those who were 'Canadian by Birth'[81] or of British heritage were seen as the only truly deserving citizens of Canada. For many, true Canadian identity was established through generations of Canadian ancestry. To letter writers, the United Empire Loyalists and the early pioneers symbolized the belief in an organic community where generations of Canadians were linked together in the creation of the Canadian nation. An unemployed man on the verge of foreclosure wrote to Henry to ask for help in saving his family's home, saying: 'My wife is a Canadian of three generations back and myself I am forty-five years in Canada a British subject at that.'[82] United Empire Loyalist 'stock' was a vital signifier of status to both men and women, and to Conservative and Liberal supporters. One woman explicitly linked the Hepburn government with 'pioneer British stock' from 'the Stirring days of Alexander McKenzie.'[83]

By drawing on the status of ethnicity, women could be true Canadians on an equal basis with men and could claim a crucial place for themselves within the national narrative.[84] A woman's status as a member of the Anglo-Canadian community could be used to argue for greater recognition and entitlement, and a stronger position on the continuum of charity and contract. The native-born, according to female letter writers, played a crucial role in building the nation, and should therefore receive recognition from the state. Genealogy became a calling card and signifier of special status. 'I am no foreigner,' wrote a widow who was facing foreclosure. 'I was born in Ontario from parents that [were] also born in Ontario. My grandfather was a U.E.L. my grandparents on my mothers side were Irish. My husband was also a good Canadian born in Canada from English blood.'[85] Another woman wrote: 'Are we not true, loyal Canadians from the same descent as your wife Mrs. Henry. Her ancestry [sic] Laura Secord was mine also as well as Sir Allen McNab and the other faithful early settlers.'[86] Single mothers could also call on Canadian ethnicity to more forcefully argue their status of respectability. A woman who was turned down for Mothers' Allowance wrote to say: 'We are respectable citizens of Canada and have been for generations back. I am bringing up my family deasent and respectabel [sic] and educating them the best I can [...] I feel I have been dealt out of my rights by some-one who thinks it there [sic] duty to save government money.'[87]

This tendency to use ethnicity as a claim for entitlement can be seen as both a radical and a conservative impulse. Canadian identity became a way for the unemployed and poor to claim respectability and to make demands for economic and political justice. But the narrow definition of a true Canadian excluded the non-Canadian born and those 'foreigners' who were not of British background, and were therefore unable to demand the entitlements claimed by those considered full members of the Canadian state.[88] 'Is there a chance,' asked one unemployed man, 'for a good honest Canadian Citizen to make an honest living for himself and Family [...] Why do our Governments [...] permit our own Canadians to be shut out and all classes of foreigners placed in their positions.'[89] Writers complained with bitterness and hostility that 'foreigners' were taking away Canadians' rightful place in the labour force and stealing away potential opportunities. As one unemployed woman stated: 'It is impossible for a single man, during the last five years, to have any

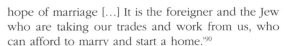
hope of marriage [...] It is the foreigner and the Jew who are taking our trades and work from us, who can afford to marry and start a home.'[90]

In the public imagination, the fear of immigrants was also associated with the fear of communist protest against the capitalist system. The rhetoric of 'British justice' was commonly used to set criticism of the government and claims for entitlement apart from more radical critiques of the economic and political system, although the distinction between radical and 'British justice' could be ambiguous. 'I don't want any Czar of Russia methods in what I have always been taught was a free Canada for Canadians,' claimed an unemployed miner from Cobalt. 'But in my case it is far from being a free country [...] I do not want you to think I am a Red or an agitator, but I do feel that I have been very unfairly dealt with.'[91] Many individuals wrote to say they were not communist agitators or radicals, just ordinary people who desired 'British justice,' which they defined variously as 'the Right to work in a man's own country,'[92] to receive a living wage and provide for a wife and family, to criticize government relief and policy measures freely, and to receive priority for jobs if a veteran or Canadian born. Using the threat of communism or 'turning red' within their letters was one way that writers expressed the depth of their concerns about the economic condition. An unemployed veteran told Henry in 1931, 'I am no extremist or radical,' but 'starvation breeds revolution,' particularly when 'my children are receiving less nourishment than I received while in a Soviet prison in Moscow.'[93] A woman with an unemployed husband and a sick child, and who proudly claimed Loyalist descent, asked Henry, 'Do you wonder in the face of such suffering that people become radicals?'[94]

As men and women wrote formal requests to the government, they were attempting to establish their needs as legitimate political concerns and participating in a debate to define how those needs should be properly met.[95] Using the language of rights and entitlement, letter writers attempted to link their demands to the dignity associated with the principle of contract, claiming that economic security and stability should be provided in return for service to the state. This language of contract, rights, and entitlement was at once progressive and limiting. While it argued for greater government responsibility for the welfare of its citizens, expanded government obligation for social welfare was never intended to eradicate economic inequality completely, and many people were excluded from the status of a fully entitled and deserving citizen. The dignity associated with a rights-based discourse in this era still presumed the existence of the oppositional categories of charity and dependence.[96] The assertions by letter writers that they were entitled citizens who had fulfilled certain duties implied that others had failed to meet the obligations required of citizenship, and were therefore not entitled to aid. The way that claimants understood state responsibility and individual obligation left little room for a conception of state welfare beyond contractual obligations based on individual duties.[97]

Yet individuals did have some room to act and to manoeuvre. While some letters received a formulaic response, others obtained some form of help. After a direct appeal to the premier, some men were given temporary work on government public works projects in the early 1930s. Many others received answers to their questions on government policy and legislation, or promises of investigation into denial of, for example, relief payments or Old Age Pensions or Mothers' Allowance Benefits. With a few notable exceptions, however, most people who wrote to the premiers did not offer a radical critique of the capitalist economic order or demand sweeping changes to the political system. Still, their actions should be seen as no less important than those of organized political parties or labour unions. They made their demands and criticisms on a basis of duties, obligations, and moral values, including a willingness to work, proper gender roles, and a moral character emphasizing thrift, sobriety, and honesty. Recommendations to Henry and Hepburn from reeves, ministers, and prominent members of the community, remarking on workers' responsibility and honesty, demonstrated that good character was considered an essential component of good citizenship. Letter writers used traditional notions of hard work, good character, and duty to make claims on the state and to argue for increased state responsibility for its citizens. Within a limited discourse and range of possibilities, writers were attempting to create a positive vision of a society where citizens within an industrial capitalist order could expect protection from the economic insecurity and instability produced by unemployment. Ultimately, viewing these letters as

318

political actions means re-evaluating the way historians have defined the meaning of the word *political*. Taken seriously, these letters suggest an active and politically aware population determined to write to politicians and government officials to keep them accountable, and to ensure that their claims were seriously acknowledged. In Depression-era Canada, the letters and appeals of unemployed men and women for a reciprocal relationship between citizen and state should be viewed as an important force in the transition to the postwar welfare state.

Notes

1. Archives of Ontario (AO), RG 3-8, GS. Henry Papers, MS 1759, file Department of Public Works, Mr T.F. to Henry, 9 October 1933.

2. John T. Saywell, *'Just Call Me Mitch': The Life of Mitchell F. Hepburn* (Toronto: University of Toronto Press, 1991), 84; James Struthers, *The Limits of Affluence: Welfare in Ontario, 1920–1970* (Toronto: University of Toronto Press, 1994), 92.

3. See James Struthers, *No Fault of Their Own: Unemployment and the Canadian Welfare State, 1914–1941* (Toronto: University of Toronto Press, 1983); and Dennis Guest, *The Emergence of Social Security in Canada* (Vancouver: UBC Press, 1985), 84–5.

4. Michael Bliss and L.M. Grayson, eds. *The Wretched of Canada: Letters to R.B. Bennett, 1930–1935* (Toronto: University of Toronto Press, 1971), xxv.

5. See, for example, Alvin Finkel, *Business and Social Reform in the Thirties* (Toronto: James Lorimer, 1979); Allan Moscovitch and J. Albert, *The Benevolent State: The Growth of Welfare in Canada* (Toronto: Garamond Press, 1987); Struthers, *No Fault of Their Own* and *The Limits of Affluence;* Doug Owram, *The Government Generation: Canadian Intellectuals and the State* (Toronto: University of Toronto Press, 1986); Michiel Horn, *The League for Social Reconstruction* (Toronto: University of Toronto Press, 1980); Larry Glassford, *Reaction and Reform: The Politics of the Conservative Party under R.B. Bennett, 1927–1938* (Toronto: University of Toronto Press, 1992); Walter Young, *Anatomy of a Party: The National CCF, 1932–61* (Toronto: University of Toronto Press, 1969); and Nancy Christie and Michael Gauvreau, *A Full-Orbed Christianity: The Protestant Churches and Social Welfare in Canada, 1900–1940* (Toronto: McGill-Queen's University Press; 1996). For an examination of grassroots activism, see Frances Fox Piven and Richard A. Cloward, *Regulating the Poor: The Functions of Public Welfare* (New York: Random House, 1971). In Canada, see Victor Howard, *'We Were the Salt of the Earth': The On-to-Ottawa Trek and the Regina Riot* (Regina: Canadian Plains Research Center, 1985); Ronald Liversedge, *Recollections of the On-to-Ottawa Trek* (Toronto: McClelland & Stewart, 1973); Dominique Marshall, 'The Language of Children's Rights, the Formation of the Welfare State, and the Democratic Experience of Poor Families in Quebec, 1940–55,' *Canadian Historical Review* 78, 3 (1997): 409–39; and Shirley Tillotson, 'Citizen Participation in the Welfare State: An Experiment, 1945–57,' *Canadian Historical Review* 75, 4 (1994), 511–42.

6. See Craig Jenkins and Barbara G. Brents, 'Social Protest, Hegemonic Competition, and Social Reform: A Political Struggle Interpretation of the Origins of the American Welfare State,' *American Sociological Review* 54 (1989): 891–909; Saywell, *Just Call Me Mitch,* 265–6; and Linda Gordon, *Pitied but Not Entitled: Single Mothers and the History of Welfare, 1890–1935* (Cambridge: Harvard University Press, 1994), 243–51.

7. Gordon, *Pitied but Not Entitled,* 274.

8. Nancy Fraser and Linda Gordon, 'Contract versus Charity: Why Is There No Social Citizenship in the United States?' *Socialist Review* 22, 3 (1992): 45.

9. T.H. Marshall argues that social citizenship ranges from the 'right to a modicum of economic welfare and security to the right to share in the social heritage and to live the life of a civilized being according to the standards prevailing in the society.' T.H. Marshall, *Citizenship and Social Class* (London: Pluto Press, 1992), 6. For a critique of Marshall, see Gordon and Fraser, 'Contract versus Charity,' 48–56, and Carol Pateman, *The Disorder of Women: Democracy, Feminism and Political Theory* (Stanford: Stanford University Press, 1989), 184–5.

10. Gordon and Fraser, 'Contract versus Charity,' 59.

11. Ibid., 55, and Pateman, *Disorder of Women,* 185.

12. See Guest, *The Emergence of Social Security,* and Michael Katz, *In the Shadow of the Poorhouse: A Social History of Welfare in America* (New York: Basic Books, 1986), ix–xiv.

13. Fraser and Gordon, 'Contract versus Charity,' 48.

14. See Veronica Strong-Boag, 'Wages for Housework: Mothers' Allowance and the Beginning of

319

Social Security in Canada,' *Journal of Canadian Studies* 14 (1979–80): 24–34; Struthers, *Limits of Affluence*, 19-49; Margaret Little, 'The Blurring of Boundaries: Private and Public Welfare for Single Mothers in Ontario,' *Studies in Political Economy* 47 (summer 1995): 89–109; Jane Ursel, *Private Lives, Public Policy: 100 Years of State Intervention in the Family* (Toronto: Women's Press, 1992); Ruth Roach Pierson, 'Gender and the Unemployment Insurance Debates in Canada,' *Labour/Le Travail* 25 (spring 1990): 77–103; Dominique Jean, 'Family Allowances and Family Autonomy: Quebec Families Encounter the Welfare State, 1945–1955,' in Bettina Bradbury, ed., *Canadian Family History: Selected Readings* (Toronto: Copp Clark Pitman, 1992), 401–37; Annalee Golz, 'Family Matters: The Canadian Family and the State in Postwar Canada,' *left history* 1, 2 (1993): 9–50. For the United States, see the essays in Linda Gordon, ed., *Women, the State and Welfare* (Madison: University of Wisconsin Press, 1990); Ann Shorla Orloff, 'Gender and the Social Rights of Citizenship: The Comparative Analysis of Gender Relations and Welfare States,' *American Sociological Review* 58 (1993): 303–28: Mimi Abramovitz, *Regulating the Lives of Women: Social Welfare Policy from Colonial Times to the Present* (Boston: South End Press, 1988).

15. James Struthers argues that the principle of less eligibility was written into unemployment insurance by making benefits lower than market-based wage rates and by favouring those who had steady, full-time employment. See Struthers, *No Fault of Their Own,* 211–12; Pierson, 'Gender and the Unemployment Insurance Debates'; Guest, *Emergence of Social Security,* 146–7.

16. See Tillotson, 'Citizen Participation in the Welfare State,' where she argues that a form of citizen participation can be found in the early years of Brantford's recreation movement.

17. Struthers, *Limits of Affluence,* 4. Family Allowance benefits were never adequate, argues Dominique Jean, but they still 'led parents to incorporate the idea of an adequate allowance into their concept of their rights as Canadians … [and] to enlarge their concepts of their rights as citizens.' Jean, 'Family Allowances and Family Autonomy,' 430.

18. Struthers/Limits *of Affluence,* 94–5.

19. Margaret Hobbs, 'Gendering Work and Welfare: Women's Relationship to Wage-Work and Social Policy in Canada during the Great Depression' (PhD thesis, University of Toronto, 1995), and 'Rethinking Antifeminism in the 1930s: Gender Crisis or Workplace Justice? A Response to Alice Kessler-Harris,' *Gender and History* 5, 1 (1993): 4–15; Lois Scharf, *To Work and to Wed: Female Employment, Feminism, and the Great Depression* (Westport: Greenwood Press, 1980).

20. AO, RG 3-8, Henry Papers, MS 1759, file Department of Public Works, Mr G.D. to Henry, 20 July 1933.

21. Ibid., MS 1752, file Department of Public Works, Mr S.J. to Henry, 11 May 1932.

22. For a discussion of the importance of the male breadwinner ideal, see Cynthia Comacchio, 'A Postscript for Father: Defining a New Fatherhood in Interwar Canada,' *Canadian Historical Review* 78, 3 (1997): 305–408; Robert Griswold, *Fatherhood in America: A History* (New York: Basic Books, 1993); and Joy Parr, *The Gender of Breadwinners: Women, Men, and Change in Two Industrial Towns, 1880–1950* (Toronto: University of Toronto Press, 1990); and Suzanne Morton, *Ideal Surroundings: Domestic Life in a Working-Class Suburb in the 1920s* (Toronto: University of Toronto Press, 1995).

23. AO, RG 3-8, Henry Papers, MS 1755, file Legislation, mortgage, Mr R.H. to Henry, 7 January, 1932.

24. Ibid., MS 1759, file Department of Public Works, T.H.G. to Henry, 3 October 1933.

25. Morton, *Ideal Surroundings,* 72; Comacchio, 'Postscript for Father'; Parr, *Gender of Breadwinners,* 82.

26. Comacchio, 'Postscript for Father,' 395.

27. Michael Roper and John Tosh argue that male power is continually 'contested and transformed,' partly because the ideal of financial self-sufficiency has always been hard to achieve. Michael Roper and John Tosh, *Manful Assertions: Masculinities in Britain since 1800* (London: Routledge, 1991), 18. See also the essays in Mark Carnes and Clyde Griffen, *Meanings for Manhood: Constructions of Masculinity in Victorian America* (Chicago: University of Chicago Press, 1990); and Morton, *Ideal Surroundings,* 82.

28. AO, RG 3-8, Henry Papers, MS 1757, file Navy League, Sam Harris, president, Navy League of Canada, to Henry, 27 March 1933.

29. Ibid., MS 1747, file Unemployment Relief no. 3, Lt. W.J.O. to Henry, 8 October 1931.

30. AO, RG 3, Series 9, M.F. Hepburn Papers, no. 180, file Unemployment Relief, no. 2, L.W. to Hepburn, 24 June 1934.

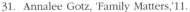
31. Annalee Gotz, 'Family Matters,' 11.

32. AO, RG 3, Series 9, Hepburn Papers, no. 180, file Unemployment Relief no. 2, Mrs M.G. to Hepburn, 27 July 1934.

33. Pierson, 'Gender and the Unemployment Insurance Debates'; Pateman, *Disorder of Women,* 182–5, 192–5.

34. Evans, 'Divided Citizenship,' 91, 95.

35. AO, RG 3-8, Henry Papers, MS 1745, file Relief, asked for, Mrs W.A. Rowland to Henry, 1 October 1931.

36. See Linda Gordon, *Heroes of Their Own Lives: The Politics and History of Family Violence,* 1880–1960 (New York: Penguin, 1988).

37. AO, RG 3, Series 9, Hepburn Papers, no. 180, file: Unemployment Relief, Mrs W.H. to Hepburn, 1934.

38. See Joan Sangster, *Dreams of Equality: Women on the Canadian Left,* 1920–50 (Toronto: McClelland & Stewart, 1989); Irene Howard, 'The Mothers' Council of Vancouver: Holding the Fort for the Unemployed, 1935–38,' *BC Studies* 69–70 (1988): 249–87; Annelise Orleck, '"We Are That Mythical Thing Called the Public": Militant Housewives during the Great Depression,' *Feminist Studies* 1 (1993): 147–72.

39. See Lois Rita Helmbold, 'Beyond the Family Economy: Black and White Working-Class Women during the Great Depression,' *Feminist Studies* 13, 3 (1987): 629–49.

40. AO, RG 3-8, MS 1747, Henry Papers, file Unemployment relief no. 3, Mrs W.G. on behalf of the mothers of Sturgeon Falls, 29 September 1931.

41. AO, RG 3-10, Hepburn Papers, no. 250, file Comments on unemployment relief, 29 July 1935.

42. Ibid., no. 203, file Provincial Secretary's Department, Mrs J.J. to Hepburn, 14 May 1936.

43. Ibid., Mrs L.M. to Hepburn, 10 May 1936.

44. Ann Snitow, 'A Gender Diary,' in Marianne Hirsch and Evelyn Fox Keller, eds., *Conflicts in Feminism* (New York: Routledge, 1990), 9–43.

45. AO, RG 3-8, Henry Papers, MS 1736, file Agricultural Development Board, Mrs A.S. to Henry, 26 August 1931.

46. Frances Fox Piven and Richard A. Cloward, 'Welfare Doesn't Shore Up Traditional Family Roles: A Reply to Linda Gordon,' *Social Research* 55, 4 (1988): 633.

47. Gordon, *Pitied but Not Entitled,* 627.

48. Margaret Little notes that lobbyists and recipients in British Columbia saw Mothers' Pensions as payment for a service performed. Margaret Little, 'Claiming a Unique Place: The Introduction of Mothers' Pensions in British Columbia,' in Veronica Strong-Boag and Anita Clair Fellman, eds., *Rethinking Canada: The Promise of Women's History* (Don Mills: Oxford University Press, 1993), 285–303. In *No Car, No Radio, No Liquor Permit: The Moral Regulation of Single Mothers in Ontario, 1920–1997* (Toronto: Oxford University Press, 1998), Little notes that women receiving Mothers' Allowances tended to direct complaints to the premier or local politicians rather than risk a direct protest to the investigator (105).

49. AO, RG 3-10, Hepburn Papers, no. 190, file Public Welfare Department, Mothers' Allowance, Mrs R.H. to Hepburn, 21 February 1935. Quoted in Struthers, *Limits of Affluence,* 99.

50. Recent literature has argued that the welfare state can provide a potential escape route for women from dependence on individual men by providing a direct relationship to the state. See Pateman, *Disorder of Women,* 196; Evans, 'Divided Citizenship,' 95; Gordon, 'What Does Welfare Regulate?' *Social Research* 55, 4 (1988): 609–30; Orloff, 'Gender and the Social Rights of Citizenship,' 305.

51. AO, RG 3, Series 9, Hepburn Papers, no. 180, file Unemployment Relief no. 2, Mrs J.W. to Hepburn, 6 September 1934.

52. AO, RG 3-8, Henry Papers, MS 1745, file Relief: asked for, Mrs C.G. to Henry, 9 June 1931. See also Mothers' Allowances files, ibid., MS 1742, 1931, and MS 1757, 1933.

53. Margaret Little, 'The Blurring of Boundaries,' and Little, 'Manhunts and Bingo Blabs: The Moral Regulation of Ontario Single Mothers,' in Mariana Valverde, ed., *Studies in Moral Regulation* (Toronto: Centre of (Criminology, 1994).

54. Little, 'Blurring of Boundaries'; Struthers, *Limits of Affluence,* 43.

55. Struthers, Limits *of Affluence,* 48.

56. AO, RG 3-8, Henry Papers, MS 1742, 30 October 1931, file Mothers' Allowances Commission, Mrs C.C. to Henry, 30 October 1931.

57. Ibid, MS 1757, file Mothers' Allowances Commission, Mrs R.C. to Henry, 5 March 1933.

58. In a clipping from a 1934 Perth newspaper, the homes of seventeen people were listed for sale owing to tax arrears; seven of these homes belonged to women. AO, RG 3, Series 9, Hepburn Papers, no. 180, file Unemployment no. 2, Mrs A.F. to Hepburn, 2 August 1934 (enclosure).

59. Parr, *The Gender of Breadwinners.*

321

60. AO, RG 3-10, Hepburn Papers, no. 225, file M.F. Hepburn, private no. 3, Mrs G.A. to Hepburn, July 1934; AO, RG 3-8, Henry Papers, MS 1759, file Department of Public Works, Mr V.G. to Hepburn, 19 September 1933.

61. Morton, *Ideal Surroundings,* 32–8.

62. AO, RG 3-8, Henry Papers, MS 1760, file Resolutions, Toronto Ward Two Property Owners Joint Executive to Henry, 24 April 1933.

63. Ibid., file Resolutions, Peterborough City Council to Henry, 7 February 1933; file Resolutions, Kitchener City Council, 14 June 1933; and file Resolutions, Hamilton City Council, 13 June 1933.

64. Ibid., MS 1755, file Legislation, mortgage, Mr W.F.P. to Henry, 9 January, 1933.

65. Ibid., MS 1760, file Relief, asked for, Mrs T.P. to Henry, 18 March 1933.

66. Morton, *Ideal Surroundings,* 38. On 'making do,' see Denyse Baillargeon, '"If You Had No Money, You Had No Trouble, Did You?": Montreal Working-Class Housewives in the Great Depression,' *Women's History Review* 1, 2 (1992): 217–37; Laura Hollingsworth and Vappu Tyyska, 'Hidden Producers: Women's Household Production in the Great Depression,' *Critical Sociology* 15, 3 (1988); Jeane Westin, *Making Do: How Women Survived the Thirties* (Chicago: Follet Publishing, 1976).

67. See, for example, AO, RG 3-8, Henry Papers, MS 1760, file Relief, asked for, Mrs T.P. to Henry, 18 March 1933; MS 1759, file Department of Public Works, Mr R.M. to Henry, 24 June 1933; RG 3-10, Hepburn Papers, no. 225, file Hepburn, private no. 3, Mrs G.W.A. to Hepburn, July 1934. For the role of women in the family economy, see Meg Luxton, *More Than a Labour of Love: Three Generations of Women's Work in the Home* (Toronto: Women's Press, 1980); and Bettina Bradbury, *Working Families: Age, Gender and Daily Survival in Industrializing Montreal* (Toronto: McClelland & Stewart, 1993).

68. AO, RG 3, Series 9, Hepburn Papers, no. 180, file Unemployment Relief no. 1, Mr W.K. to Hepburn, 17 December 1934.

69. See letters in AO, RG 3-10, Hepburn Papers, no. 171, file B.E.S.L., 1934.

70. Ibid., no. 205, file Resolutions, Progressive Veterans in Canada to Hepburn, 27 July 1936.

71. Desmond Morton, The Canadian Veterans' Heritage from the Great War,' in Peter Neary and J.L. Granatstein, eds., *The Veterans Charter and Post-World War II Canada* (Montreal and Kingston: McGill-Queen's University Press, 1998), 22–3, and Morton, '"Noblest and Best": Retraining Canada's War Disabled 1915–23,' *Journal of Canadian Studies* 16, 3 and 4 (1991): 75–85.

72. Morton, 'Canadian Veterans,' 22.

73. Jeffrey A. Keshen, *Propaganda and Censorship during Canada's Great War* (Edmonton: University of Alberta Press, 1996), 204.

74. Morton, 'Canadian Veterans,' 23.

75. AO, RG 3, Series 9, Hepburn Papers, no. 180, file Unemployment Relief, Canadian Legion Unemployment Committee, B.E.S.L Hamilton Branch to Hepburn, December 1934.

76. AO, RG 3-8, Henry Papers, MS 1759, file Department of Public Works, East Block, Mr F.K to Henry, 24 May 1933.

77. Ibid., MS1744, file Positions, general, Mrs A.B. to Henry, 27 June 1931.

78. Ibid., MS 1762, file Unemployment Relief, homeowners, Mr H.V.W. to Henry, 8 September 1933.

79. See Carl Berger, *The Writing of Canadian History: Aspects of English Canadian Historical Writing since 1900* (Toronto: University of Toronto Press, 1986); Mary Vipond, 'Nationalism and Nativism: The Native Sons of Canada in the 1930s,' *Canadian Review of Studies in Nationalism* 9, 1 (1982), 81–95; Vipond, 'The Nationalist Network: English Canada's Intellectuals and Artists in the 1920s,' *Canadian Review of Studies in Nationalism* 7, 1 (1980): 32–52.

80. Benedict Anderson, *Imagined Communities: Reflections on the Origins and Spread of Nationalism* (London: Verso, 1983).

81. AO, RG 3-8, Henry Papers, MS 1761, file Soldiers' Aid Commission, Mr E.L. to Henry, 14 January 1933.

82. Ibid., MS 1762, file Unemployment Relief no. 1, Mr T.H. to Henry, 7 August 1933.

83. AO, RG 3-10, Hepburn Papers, no. 225, file M.F. Hepburn, private no. 3, Miss M.E.M. to Hepburn, 3 July 1934.

84. See Antoinette Burton, *Burdens of History: British Feminists, Indian Women, and Imperial Culture, 1865–1915* (Chapel Hill: University of North Carolina Press); and Ann Curthoys, 'Identity Crisis: Colonialism, Nation, and Gender in Australian History,' *Gender and History 5, 2* (1993): 165–76.

85. AO, RG 3-8, Henry Papers, MS 1750, file Mothers' Allowances Commission, Mrs S.B.S. to Henry, 24 February 1932.

86. Ibid., MS 1760, file Relief, asked for, Mrs C.R.C. to Henry, 2 August 1933.

87. Ibid., MS 1745, file Relief, asked for, Mrs A.H.M., 29 December, 1931.

88. Although it is difficult to assess the exact ethnic background of letter writers, a careful study of the letters reveals few non-British names.

89. AO, RG 3-8, Henry Papers, MS 1744, file Positions, general, Mr B.C. to Henry, 19 November 1931.

90. Ibid., MS 1750, file Mothers' Allowances Commission, Miss A.M. to Henry, 26 August 1932.

91. Ibid., MS 1760, file Relief, asked for, Mr H.L.S. to Henry, 26 July 1933.

92. Ibid.

93. Ibid., MS 1747, file Unemployment Relief no. 7, Lt. W.J.O. to Henry, 8 October 1931.

94. Ibid., MS 1762, file Unemployment Relief: home-owners, Mrs K.H. to Henry, 21 July 1933.

95. Nancy Fraser, 'Struggle Over Needs: Outline of a Socialist-Feminist Critical Theory of Late Capitalist Political Culture,' in Gordon, ed., *Women, the State, and Welfare,* 202.

96. Fraser and Gordon, 'Contract versus Charity,' 59.

97. Ibid., 64, 47.

■ Article 2: Working for Pay and Managing the Household Finances

Denyse Baillargeon (trans. Yvonne Klein)

Author Denyse Baillargeon conducted interviews in 1986 and 1987 with 30 women who were married at the beginning of the 1930s and were willing to discuss their experience of the Depression as young wives in Montreal. Most of the women were working class, but their specific identities have been protected by code. In the following excerpt, Baillargeon discusses the various ways they made ends meet.

My mother-in-law used to laugh at me—she'd say, if I gave you a nickel, you'd turn it into a dollar." (E11)

Studies dealing with the period just before the Depression years of the 1930s show that, without exception, workers' wages were insufficient to ensure a decent standard of living for an average family.[1] In the absence of a family wage, children and women as well had to do what they could through various kinds of work to increase the family income. Even in a period of relative prosperity, additional pay was as necessary a part of balancing the household budget as were the wages of the principal earner, but so was extremely strict management and very careful housekeeping.

Because of unemployment, however, the Great Depression came to exercise additional pressure on family finances. In these conditions, how did families ensure their survival?

... In this chapter, we will first of all consider the question of income. It is important to examine this subject at the outset because income determines the family's standard of life, the quantity of housework as well as what equipment the women had at their disposal to do it with, and the degree to which households had to turn to other means of support. We will concern ourselves not only with income deriving from the husband's principal activity, but also with the contributions deriving from the wife's labour, with budget management, and with the impact of unemployment on the household economy and on the sexual division of labour.

A LIVING WAGE

It was generally understood that, after marriage, women would quit their jobs in order to take care of the house and children. In addition to these tasks, the majority would also take over the management of the family finances, which initially comprised the husbands' wages as principal breadwinner. The funds they had to spend would depend on his occupation. In most cases, this factor would also determine whether or not the wives would have to undertake some sort of paid activity in order to make up for a lack of income.

Source: *Making Do: Women, Family, and Home in Montreal during the Great Depression* (translated by Yvonne Klein WLU Press, 1999). Reprinted with permission from Wilfrid Laurier University Press.

323

The following table indicates the husbands' occupations just before the beginning of the Depression or at marriage if this occurred after 1929:

● TABLE 1
Husbands' Occupations in 1929 or at Marriage

Status	Number
Self-Employed Shopkeepers, tradesmen	3
Waged Non-manual Workers	6
Manual workers	20
Out of Work	1
Total	**30**

As we may observe, only one of the husbands, who had been in fact unemployed since the couple was married in 1927, did not have a permanent job at the beginning of the thirties, while three had small businesses (a barber shop, a corner restaurant, two taxicabs). Among the manual workers, eleven were factory workers, while the rest were working in construction (a bricklayer, two labourers), in small businesses (barbershop employee, butcher shop employee, delivery man), and in services (two maintenance workers, one auto mechanic). The nonmanual workers included a laboratory technician, a junior manager, two shop assistants, and two office clerks.

According to the unemployment statistics, a number of these occupations were especially vulnerable as the Depression set in. This was particularly true for industrial and construction workers,[2] but in fact almost every one of the couples in the sample was affected one way or the other by the economic crisis. Of the three small businessmen, for example, only the barber was able to retain his business, although he suffered from a decline in revenue as he had to lower his prices by 30 percent, while his clientele also shrank. In 1934, he had to get rid of the second-hand car he had purchased the year before. The other two had to sell up their businesses to avoid bankruptcy. According to their wives' recollections, their failure was the result of their clients' overwhelming demand for credit and the general decline in business:

When the Depression came, we were obliged to extend too much credit, even though we had to buy for cash. We could have wound up on the street. We had already lost $900 in bad debts. Before we lost everything, we sold up. As for myself, I didn't want to buy on credit—I wouldn't have been able to sleep. ... There are always people who don't pay. But during the Depression, they always had an excuse. Or they would pay us, but not the whole thing. We lost control over our lives. (E7)

When I first met [my husband], he owned two taxicabs. And when I got married, in 1929, that's when the crash happened. Then a year later he sold his two cars. He had one man working for him but ... he had to sell, he wasn't making enough. Marriages in those days—he got paid five dollars for a wedding party. I was happy [when he sold his cabs] I was happier when he had a job and a salary we could count on. He had lots of money in his pockets, but you couldn't count on it ... he had to make the payments every month. We did not live well. We were doing very well if we managed to have enough to eat all the time. (E29)

Both of them experienced unemployment, and in one case, home relief, before finding a paying job, which one of them kept for the rest of his life, the other until the Depression was over. The fate of these small businessmen was not very far removed from that of elements of the working class on whose members they depended to make a living and from which they had often themselves originated. Without sufficient assets to pay their obligations and wait for better times, fearful of falling into too much debt and losing everything or refusing outright to go into debt at all, large numbers of them would be vulnerable to a major economic crisis like that of the 1930s.

Of the twenty-six who worked for wages, only four escaped any loss of employment or cut in salary. Four others had their workweek cut to one or a couple of days and three, while working the same number of hours, had their wages cut by 20 percent. Seven were without a steady job for more than three years, six others for a period of between one and two years, and the last, and most fortunate, for several months only. Two others—including one whose husband was out of work at the time they were married—had to turn to the Saint Vincent de Paul Society or to relief, but according to their accounts, their husbands' laziness and refusal to provide for the family were to blame rather than lack of jobs during the Depression. All in all, fifteen couples needed governmental aid to survive and two chose to go back to the land as a solution.

With the exception of two informants who were never told, the women remembered very clearly what their husbands were earning when they got married. As they recalled, the level was very low—if two of them were earning as much as thirty-five dollars a week, others made as little as ten and more than half less than twenty dollars a week. According to the data of the federal minister of labour, however, it required $20.18 a week in Quebec in December 1929 and $14.29 a week in December 1933 simply to cover the costs of food, heating, light, and rent for an average family of five.[3] In 1931, the living wage for Canadians was figured at $1050 a year, or about twenty dollars a week, while it would take at least $1500 a year ($28.84 a week) to provide a comfortable standard of living.[4] In this sample, only five men made more than twenty-five dollars a week at the end of the 1920s or at the beginning of the 1930s.[5] The unemployment and short weeks from which more than two-thirds of the respondents' husbands suffered obviously involved a reduction in income and accentuated the financial difficulties they were already experiencing. So, in addition to paying $8.50 in rent directly to the landlord, the Unemployment Relief Commission of Montreal established the sums of $7.15 a week in winter and $6.55 in summer as the amount of aid to be paid to a family of five. These amounts were supposed to cover all other necessities of life (food, heating, clothing) and represented a total of $39.48 and $36.88 a month, depending on the season.[6] Even if we take into account the decline in prices of around 29 percent, according to the data cited previously, these sums represent barely more than half of the $14.49 required in 1933 to cover the basic living expenses of a family of five each week.

It seems clear that the families of the unemployed could not survive merely on the grants they received.

Income to Balance the Budget

The inadequacy of workers' wages is already well known. What remains to be documented is the range of other forms of work undertaken by men and women to manage to balance the family budget.[7] Participating in informal economic enterprise was more often left to women because their family and household responsibilities, which, although preventing them from entering the job market, still did allow them a greater flexibility with which to organize their time, so that they were able to engage in different activities in the home.[8] Nevertheless, a considerable number of men were looking for additional income, as the recollections of our informants indicate.[9]

Odd Jobs

Given the inadequacy of their wages, it comes as no surprise to learn that even when they had steady jobs, several of the husbands did other work or made some sort of exchange in order to supplement their incomes, either during or after the Depression. During the Depression years themselves, seven of the husbands looked for ways to increase their incomes.

Thus, a mechanic made money fixing cars after work, while an office worker did different kinds of maintenance at night and on the weekend for the recreation club he worked for. Together with his wife, a woodworker made checkerboards which he disposed of in a draw after his grocer had sold ten dollars worth of ten-cent tickets in his shop, where they were on display. In a flagrant violation of the law forbidding lotteries, one of the husbands sold "hockey cards" at the factory where he worked. Another kept the books for a small grocery on top of his work as a civil servant. The man who owned a corner store retained his sales job while his wife kept the shop during the day and he took over in the evenings. It was, moreover, exactly for this reason that he decided to get married right away: "That's why we got married, so we wouldn't have to pay a store clerk" (E7). Another, who was working for a Montreal department store as a receiving clerk, got permission to run a little snack bar for the use of store employees. He had one woman helping him

325

at lunchtime and he called upon his wife to make certain purchases:

> When he was working, he had the restaurant and at noontime he hired a woman. [...]. It brought in enough. He sold soft drinks, chocolate, gum. There were people who came downstairs to grab a chocolate bar. When he could get hold of some fruit, he bought it. I didn't mind, sometimes he'd call me up and tell me, "Come bring me this or that." I would go and walk down there with the baby in the carriage." (E21)

Clearly the Depression only made it more pressing to turn to all sorts of expedients to make up for shortages in the family income. Before going to the Saint Vincent de Paul Society or the Montreal Unemployment Relief Commission for help, or even while they were receiving benefits,[10] six of the husbands had sought to support their families by undertaking all kinds of activities. Some of the notable stopgaps which the men, newly unemployed, turned to in order to find new sources of income included digging out a cellar with a shovel, washing walls and ceilings, shovelling snow in the affluent districts of the city, reselling breads and cakes bought directly from a commercial bakery at the end of the day when the unsold merchandise was returned, peddling the remainders of blocks of ice or bootlegging alcohol which the man made in his shed (and hid in the baby carriage for delivery), and opening a little "restaurant" at home. The informants also report other activities or deals carried out by different members of their acquaintance, suggesting that this phenomenon was very common. For example, a brother-in-law went hunting and sold the game he had killed and butchered, a neighbour cultivated eight garden plots on land furnished free by the city and sold the vegetables, and so on.

To this list should be added the different jobs that the men accepted on a temporary and often part-time basis before they found permanent employment. In the majority of cases, indeed, their years of unemployment were interspersed with periods when they had jobs (not counting the public works that some of them were required to do), which brought, along with a supplementary income, just enough hope to support the next period of joblessness. These odd jobs and other forms of paid activity did not always mean that their wives could avoid having to find ways to earn money.

Working in Your "Spare Time"

We generally tend to think of women in this period as homemakers and this is largely how they appear in the census figures. In the sample collected here, however, only six did not engage in any paid activity after they were married. Among those who did contribute to the family income, six began work after 1939, when it was easier for them to free themselves of family responsibilities and at a time when paid work for married women, if not altogether acceptable, was in any event more tolerated. One of the others decided to go to work in a munitions factory at the beginning of the war in order to recoup the family finances that had been sapped by the six years that her husband, a bricklayer, had been almost constantly out of work.

Among the women who worked for pay during the decade of the 1930s, five had jobs outside the house, while the thirteen others worked at home in one or several paid capacities. Needlework of various sorts—dressmaking, embroidery, beading, smocking, knitting—represented the most common kind of work, with eight of the informants engaging in it either for companies or independently. Another worked for two years for her mother-in-law, who was keeping a rooming house, in exchange for room and board for herself and her husband, while six let rooms or took in boarders.[11] In four cases, the lodgers were parents or friends of the family, who would sometimes put up with living conditions that a stranger might have had more difficulty accepting, like sharing a sofa bed in the living room with one of the sons of the family or sleeping on a folding cot set up for the night in the hall leading to the kitchen. Taking in roomers or boarders in fact involved a small investment that not all were able to make. A flat with an extra room was required and it was necessary to get hold of an extra bed, a set of sheets and some blankets, none of which could be managed by the poorest and largest families. A study conducted by the federal government into the Canadian family concluded:

> It is clear that the families who take in lodgers are not those who are living in uncomfortable living quarters or with limited facilities. ... It would appear that taking

in lodgers is more a source of revenue for the more prosperous class of wage earners than for the poorest class and that this practice cannot be turned to as a way of relieving poverty.[12]

Two informants took in washing and hired themselves out as cleaning women,[13] while three others ran a little business. One of these first managed her husband's business until he was forced to sell. After being out of work for several months, she sought work as a private dressmaker from the owner of the concern where she had worked before her marriage. He, however, preferred to employ her husband as a private chauffeur on a permanent basis, while hiring her as a maid when he needed extra help, for parties and so on. Another woman invested an insurance payment that she received following an accident in a little "restaurant" which she ran with her husband for a short period while he was out of work:

I think we started with about fifty dollars worth of stock. Nothing much—a little candy, a few cigarettes, a little of this, a little of that. Nothing much. We lasted about a year. Yes indeed! Five cents for a Coke! There were a lot who didn't have the five cents to buy it. (E26)

An informant, widowed in 1930, also decided to open a little restaurant. She rented out a room as well to different relatives and also did dressmaking for her neighbours. Despite all her efforts, the income she derived from these three occupations was not enough to support her children. After exhausting the life insurance payment from which she paid her rent, she had to contemplate, with some reluctance, the solution of remarrying:

When you see you have no more money. ... The Depression was starting. When you were selling only five or ten cents worth a day, you're not making much. ... You start thinking about a lot of things. You say, my children what are they going to do? Soon I'll have no more money. That'll be it. You say, OK, I'll get married. ... If I'd had a pension ... I would have kept my restaurant. I wouldn't have remarried. For a while, I wanted to

go to Ontario. If I'd known anyone there I would've gone because they paid widows a pension there. (E3)

This extract highlights the economic importance of marriage for women. As fate would have it, the second husband lost his job a month before they were married and the couple finally decided to go back to the country to live.

Finally, the third woman sold her baking while she was living in the country for a time in hopes of improving the health of her paralyzed daughter:

I said to my husband, "Do you know, I'd like to make pies and cakes. I think I can sell them on Sundays." Yes, indeed, that's what I started to do, madame. ... I never had enough of them! I sold out. My husband said, "You'd do better with a store." Well, I said, "If only I could." We had a kind of little shed, it was about as big as my hand and we used to put the wood in there. It was not exactly a good store. But he made me a counter and I put it in there. On Saturdays, I would have to spend my whole day making pies and cakes! I would make them on Saturday, I would make my pastry, my cakes. (E17)

This informant was not the only one to make money from her culinary talents. Another of the women, who also cleaned houses and did dressmaking, made baked beans and maple butter (out of black-market brown sugar) during the war that her husband sold for twenty-five cents a container at the grocery where he was working. "I made them in my spare time, all by myself," she said. Sewing and cooking, traditional feminine accomplishments and two important elements in the domestic labour of women, could be easily transformed into paid work. These strategies are a tribute to the resourcefulness of these women who sought to take advantage of the skills they had mastered so well and demonstrate as well that the line between the marketplace and the unpaid economy was, for them, a slender one indeed.

The work that married women did for pay was thus indeed far from being inessential, even if it was, for the most part, accomplished at home, unseen and unrecorded.[14] When we look at the list, the first thing that strikes us is precisely the variety of things that

327

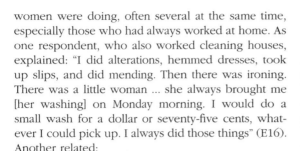

women were doing, often several at the same time, especially those who had always worked at home. As one respondent, who also worked cleaning houses, explained: "I did alterations, hemmed dresses, took up slips, and did mending. Then there was ironing. There was a little woman … she always brought me [her washing] on Monday morning. I would do a small wash for a dollar or seventy-five cents, whatever I could pick up. I always did those things" (E16). Another related:

> We didn't have enough money. I used to smock baby clothes. Then I had my boarder who gave me six bucks a week. That helped a little, my husband was making ten dollars a week. … I was always doing some kind of sewing to make money. I was sewing for practically thirty years. (E13)

Clearly, it was economic necessity that motivated the women who decided to earn a little money. Some did not look for ways to improve their level of income, however, despite their husbands' inadequate wages, while others, whose husbands were doing better or who had smaller families, nevertheless did work, often for specific purposes, like paying off a debt or educating their children. In other words, the notion of what was necessary to assure the well-being of a family varied from woman to woman according to individual standards. The amount of the husbands' income was therefore not the sole factor that came into play when a woman decided to work, although in a majority of cases, it was the determining one.[15] As we shall see later on, their husbands' opposition meant that certain women did not go to work, regardless of their financial difficulties.

In general, the majority of the women who contributed to the family income during the 1930s had begun working even before their husbands were laid off or had their wages cut:

> He was making ten dollars a week. We couldn't manage on that. I started to work. I sewed for everybody, I knitted, and I did everything to make ends meet. … I did dressmaking, knitted for everybody, made little dresses—I knitted socks and mittens, I braided rugs—fifteen cents for mittens, thirty-five cents for socks, a dollar and a

quarter for a braided rug. It wasn't a fortune. Although for me, it helped me a lot. (E22)

According to their recollections, only three informants began to work specifically because their husbands were out of work. On the other hand, nine of the husbands lost their jobs for periods ranging from several months to several years without there being any question of their wives going to work. A number of reasons were brought forward to explain what might appear as a paradox:

> I thought, but who would I leave the kids with? There wasn't any daycare. You were taking a chance leaving kids with a neighbour. … There wasn't any point in trying to get work to do at home, because there wasn't any. Or if there was, then it paid practically nothing. … You couldn't have stayed on relief. … I felt it was better if my husband did odd jobs here and there. (E25)

The number of dependent children as well as the husbands' opposition comes up constantly in the oral histories, revealing a considerable ambivalence: "I would have liked to go to work," one of them maintained, "but he didn't want me to. Anyway, the children were too little, I couldn't leave them. In those days, you didn't leave your babies with someone else" (E20). Another was sure that she would not have been able to find work:

> There wasn't any more work for girls than there was for men in those days. … And I'd never had a job,[16] let me tell you I'd have had a lot of trouble finding work too. Later on, when I was older, I figured things out. Then I was too timid. Maybe if I had more guts I could have found myself some kind of job. But my mother-in-law had never worked outside the house. Myself, I felt I had to be like her. (E19)

Underneath these arguments, one detects a certain reluctance, as much on the women's part as on their husbands', to bring about a reversal in roles that would be incompatible with defined and accepted social norms. The presence of young children especially represented a major obstacle to women's working for pay, even if the out-of-work father would have been available to take care of them. The majority of the women also were positive that there was no work for women without actually having looked for any. In fact, in the nine cases where the wife had never made any financial contribution to the family, the sexual division of labour was so rigidly ingrained that it prevailed over the need to find additional income.

Otherwise, when we look more closely at the five women who did work outside the home before 1939, we realize that two of them worked for less than a year, while another was employed only part time. Only two became the principal family bread-winner—one for a period of four years—and only one of the two husbands had totally stopped working at the time. Moreover, neither had more than two children and these were cared for by someone other than their husbands even when he was free to do it.

The women who were already doing paid work at home before their husbands became unemployed continued their work and even increased their efforts whenever possible; as a result of the Depression, however, many of the private dressmakers lost a part of their clientele. But no one of this group ever entertained the notion of replacing their work at home with work outside it: "I sewed for other people for housekeeping money during the Depression. I was a big help to my husband—he was doing what he could and so was I," one respondent said. But when she was asked if she ever thought about getting a paying job, she answered, "My husband wouldn't have allowed it, no. He said that a wife ... we could only go out by the day,[17] there wasn't any other work" (E5). Just like the men whose wives made no financial contribution to the household before they were unemployed, those who accepted their wives working at home for pay would never have stood for her finding a job outside the home. This reversal of roles would have been a direct threat to their superior position as head of the household and would have represented too sharp a blow to their pride which had already been fairly well shaken by failure to fulfil this role adequately. It would seem that the family model of breadwinner/homemaker was so entrenched that even extreme poverty was insufficient to dislodge it.[18]

In general, and in an altogether astonishing way, the women had more trouble recalling their own incomes than their husbands' wages. Two factors may explain this phenomenon. On the one hand, the relative lack of importance that they accorded to the money they made, which they regarded as a secondary income, hardly aided recollection. On the other, the amounts they got varied enormously, depending on their clientele (if they were self-employed, for example), or the amount of work they could do when they were paid by the piece. "It was an extra. It didn't give me a steady income" (E22), as one of them said. The proportion of women's earnings in the total household income is therefore almost impossible to establish. From the information we have, we observe, however, that these earnings varied from three to ten dollars a week and that, in certain cases, they might represent up to 50 percent of the husband's wages. One thing is certain—the money they earned went toward the needs of the household and not those of the women, as they paid the rent and bought groceries and clothes for the children. The following is a representative statement from the histories: "It didn't pay a helluva lot, but it was only that it gave me a little something at the end of the week. ... When [my husband] didn't have enough, then I was the one who paid, I would put it toward the rent or to buying clothes for the kids" (E17).

Less commonly, as we have already pointed out, the sums were accumulated with an eye to paying for the children's schooling. "With that money, I was able to send two to high school," one informant proudly declared. But this form of savings was only possible in smaller or better off families, where the husband's paycheque was enough to cover basic expenses. In most cases, the wife's earnings were used to pay for part of the rent or the groceries. This contribution could, moreover, make the difference between living below or just a little above the poverty line.

Managing the Budget and Women's Economic Power

Regardless of any additional revenues, the income of these households remained generally very low. Making ends meet was a real feat and one which confronted most of the women in this sample. According to a tradition that was deeply rooted in the working class in Quebec as well as elsewhere, it was most often the wife who was had the responsibility of administering the family budget.[19] How money was handled between husband and wife could, however, take on different forms, revealing power relations within the family.

In half of the families in the sample, the husband turned over his entire pay to his wife, who gave him an allowance for his personal expenses. The practice was prevalent throughout the working class, especially among those who earned the least, thus tending to confirm the hypothesis that holds that it represented, for men, a way of avoiding the challenge of managing on wages insufficient to support a family.[20] Quite frequently, these men did not even know what the household financial situation was, as they had no interest in the subject:

> I was always the one who handled the budget because my husband was not good at it. He would always say, "You take care of it." Like with the insurance and so on. He would never know how the insurance got paid and all. It wasn't his problem." (E19)

Even if they only rarely interfered once the money was given to their wives and did not demand a precise accounting of expenses, this way of handling money did not necessarily mean that they had given up all their economic power. Some of them, for example, expected that there would always be something left over to supply their need for extra cash. "That's why he gave me the wallet, he knew I would take care of it and when he asked me for five dollars, he knew I would have it. I always had it. If I'd said, 'I don't have it,' he wouldn't have liked that. You learn these things once you get married" (E2). Others threatened to take over the family finances where they were badly managed. "My husband told me, I am going to give you my pay. But if I see you're wasting it, then I'll keep it and take care of things myself" (E5). Whether they were completely detached from household matters or managed to retain a certain degree of control by insisting on their own demands or floating the possibility of interfering in the management of the money, these men did not have as their first concern balancing the budget.

In nine families, the husbands exercised a greater degree of power over how the money was used. Some of them kept the amount they wanted for their expenses (tobacco, transportation, etc.) and gave the rest to their wives, while others gave over only the amounts required to pay part or all of the running expenses. The two following recollections illustrate these different modes of operation. "When Friday night came around, he kept his expenses and the rest I had. I was the one who took care of everything. I was the one who paid the rent, the lights, I was the one who saw to everything" (E8). "He gave me the money to meet our expenses. But it was my husband who handled the purse strings and he knew how to manage. He didn't drink" (E29). This way of handling money appears most often among the families where the husband was earning a higher wage, but also where the husband had his own business or where part of his income came from tips or commissions. As these situations resulted in variable incomes, the wives we interviewed did not know precisely how much their husbands earned. Such was the case for another informant, married to a barber:

> I never knew exactly how much he made, never. Because they made tips. Anyway, he had to keep them to pay for everything— cleaning his outfits, his tools, he was the one paid for those things. He had to be sure to have enough. But I always had enough for the household expenses. (E24)

This practice of keeping the extras also occurred in connection with other kinds of activities, not always entirely legal, that brought in money, as we see here:

> He would come home and give me all of his pay. There wasn't any lottery in those days, but he sold hockey cards and he sold a lot of them. The guy who ran the whole thing would bring him the complete series and he would sell them at the plant. So he made money that way. It wasn't an enormous amount, but for his expenses. ... Because a man, he needs money in his pocket. ... That money was his. I was lucky that he made that money because I didn't have to give him a cent. (E11)

Wiser because of the experience of her mother, who had had to solve by herself the problems arising from an inadequate family income, one informant insisted that this task be shared: "When I got married, I said that the money had to be dealt with by both of us. That way, it's not always the same one who has to worry. ... I said that we both had to handle it. We had the best system. We talked about it before we got married" (E6). This way of managing was, however, only adopted by three of the couples in the sample.

At the opposite extreme, three participants, married to workers, never had any money at all in their possession, their husbands taking over paying all the bills, including the groceries. Philosophically, one of them said, "I said to myself, if anything happens, I won't get the blame" (E30). She insisted, however, on the fact that her husband had "always fed her" very well, suggesting that he had therefore fulfilled his obligations toward her. In this regard she was, nevertheless, better off than another woman, whose husband drank and played cards:

> I didn't have anything to manage, he wouldn't give me money. You know, there were men in those days. ... I didn't know he was playing cards. He was drinking, too, when he played. I knew, I found out all about it a little while later. He would pay some of the rent and the food. At first, he was the one who bought the food. He didn't want me to buy just anything. He only bought what was strictly necessary. ... I used to cry a lot. I asked my mother, "Is this what marriage is?" (E18)

This last example, although it might seem unrepresentative, is nevertheless not unique and allows us a glimpse of how far the economic dependence of women could go. This situation has, moreover, much in common with that of two other of the women whose husbands, who also had drinking problems, only worked now and then, both during the Depression and after it. One of them, pathologically jealous, refused even to allow his wife to work to support the family. All in all, seven of the husbands were in the habit of drinking regularly, often to excess. In at least four cases, the money they spent on their addiction deprived their families of the minimum they need [sic] to live and forced their wives to rely on their own paid work or on charitable organizations, the government, or their relatives to get by. In three other cases, the informants stated that their husbands had prevented the family from improving its economic condition. Excessive drinking, apparently quite common as it affected more than 20 percent of the husbands in

the sample, had grave consequences for the standard of living of these families. Their behaviour also shows with total clarity that the pay envelope belonged by right to the husband and that he could dispose of it virtually as he chose. It was, furthermore, because so many men were given to drink that the Dorion Commission had agreed to recommend changes to the Civil Code in this connection.[21]

Refusal to support was clearly against the law, but it was difficult for wives to launch proceedings and these often proved ineffective. One of the informants brought her husband to court on three occasions. As she herself said, the spouses who were found guilty were liable to a month in jail, which would not have given their wives any greater means of supporting the family decently, in fact, quite the contrary: "when the judge saw him the third time, he told him, 'if you come before me one more time ... there won't be any more talking. ... I won't listen to your wife and you'll go inside.' Inside! What good would that have done me?" (E27).

When we raised the question of their management, the majority of the women, especially those who held the purse strings, were quick to say that they were not wasteful, that they always tried to get all they could out of everything they had, and that they managed on the money they had at their disposal. "We always got by on what he made," one of them said. "We never went into debt" (E4). In fact, making ends meet without complaining about having too little money seemed to be a mark of a good homemaker and a good wife. On the one hand, it was a way of showing that their housekeeping and managerial skills were advanced enough to compensate for a lack of income; on the other, by being undemanding, the women also avoided placing their husbands' breadwinning capabilities into question, thus preserving their dignity. For both these reasons, they were generally very proud of having successfully coped on their own with balancing the budget. In the end, however, some of them realized the drawbacks of a system which rested the entire weight of this responsibility on their shoulders while opening the door to their husbands' complaints:

> In the beginning, I didn't mind because I was a good manager. But what happened was that he didn't actually do the shopping anymore and he didn't know what things cost.

He'd fuss about the prices. It was all right at the beginning. But afterwards when our expenses got bigger, he didn't know what things cost and he'd say, "That cost an awful lot! Where is the money going?" Then you feel guilty, you say, "My God! Am I wasting your money? Am I a bad housekeeper?" You feel guilty and it's not your fault. (E16)

This guilt is linked to the fact that the women felt that the money was not theirs but belonged to their husbands, even when the men did not go out of their way to make them feel that way. The sense that they were spending someone else's money also explains why they so seldom complained of being short of money and why they generally did not feel they had the right to intervene on the subject of their husbands' work, even when the possibility of better-paying jobs existed.[22] One informant, whose husband worked as a machinist in a textile factory, said of his pay:

We had to be careful—he didn't make a lot of money. He could have made more, as other factories were paying better. But he was so used to working there, he'd been there for years ... he loved where he worked. I never told my husband what to do because it's important to have a man who's working and who loves his job." E11)

Some of them even had qualms about asking for money, relying on their husbands' goodwill: "I had a cup—he'd leave me money in it. Every day he'd leave me some. It embarrassed me to ask him for money. I didn't like it—he was the one who left it for me" (E4). The status of breadwinner also conferred certain privileges which, as we have seen, were demonstrated not only in the habit of some of the husbands of keeping back part of their earnings for drink, but also in the custom of some of the wives of reserving the best of the food for their husbands: "I was always careful that he got served first," one of them said, "and always the best piece of meat. Sometimes, I thought it was unfair" (E2). If the purchase of furniture was generally decided by both of them, the husband generally got what he wanted when it came time to think about more important expenditures. Thus, one respondent had to accept her husband's decision to buy a house, which they lost during the Depression:

"I was never fussy about buying houses in the city. I didn't like the idea. But it was my husband's money and that's what he wanted. It was his money and no one could say anything about it" (E17). Another woman, in contrast, would have preferred to invest in a house rather than borrowing to buy an automobile: "My husband wanted to have a car. I wanted a car too but it would have been better to buy a house, but my husband didn't think of that" (E2).

Giving over the pay envelope to the wife, whether in whole or in part, was far from representing a form of power for the women, something of which they were, for the most part, perfectly aware.[23] On the contrary, these oral histories tend rather to refute the thesis that holds that the domestic sphere represents an area of power or of counterpower for women because it is there that they exercise control.[24] At first sight, it would seem logical that women who were in charge of making purchases should be left with the money to do so. Too often, however, this practice allowed the husband to get away cheaply from a permanent headache, all the while maintaining the illusion that he was adequately fulfilling his role as breadwinner. If disaster overtook the family finances, he could always place the blame on his wife's bad management. She herself would tend to take the blame and to say as little as possible about the difficulties she was facing because she felt that her homemaking skills were at stake.

Making Ends Meet

As we have just seen, most often it was the wives who took on the responsibility for managing the household budget and who had to plan for what it was spent on. Without question, the most critical aspect of women's domestic labour was their making ends meet on an income that was generally insufficient, as the welfare of the whole family depended on their ability to make do on the money they had available. Checking prices, buying only what was strictly necessary, wasting nothing, not going into debt were constant bywords in their oral histories: "I never wasted anything"(E1); "Every cent counted" (E2); "You had to count the pennies all the time" (E5). One respondent explained just how she managed to get along despite her large family and a desperately low income: "Only I never had my hair done, never bought lipstick, never bought a stick of gum. Never make an unnecessary expense, eh? Never, ever, ever. I never went to the movies—I didn't know anything about it" (E22).

Looking back, all of these women were surprised themselves to observe that they had managed to get by on so little. When asked what she had done to manage, one of them answered, "I can't tell you. All I can say is that God was with me. I never went into debt. When I wanted to have a little something, I had the money saved up. ... How did I do it? I don't know" (E22). "For a while," said another, "I had to work miracles" (E2). A third maintained, "Don't ask me how I did it. I don't know" (E28).

In fact, as they described in detail how they managed, it became evident that these women had a very strict set of priorities that they tried to observe, even when the intervals between paydays sometimes made their task complicated. This was particularly true of those whose husbands were paid twice a month, which sometimes required them to get through three weekends on one pay.

First of all, they had to pay the irreducible expenses like electricity and rent, the last of which the landlord generally collected at the door, encouraging promptness. "Rent and electricity, those are the first things to put on the budget" (E5). "The rent money was the first thing of all. I would rather skip eating" (E14). Thus, the rent and the electricity were seen as "debts" that they made a point of honour of paying regularly. Once these obligations were met, the remainder of the money went to pay for food, for wood or coal for the stove, and, in last place, the expenses connected to clothing, transportation, insurance, and if there were a few pennies left, to recreation.

If we look in detail at each line of these budgets, we note that the women tried first of all to find a place to live with a rent that was no more than their husbands' weekly salary. Given the smallness of their wages, this meant that the living quarters open to them were often of very poor quality or too cramped for the size of their families.

Once the family was housed, it was next necessary to think about feeding it. According to data furnished by the Labour Gazette, feeding a family of five cost on average $11.02 in December 1929 and $6.72 in December 1933; these figures indicate that for these two years, food represented 54 percent and 46 percent respectively of basic expenses.[25] Despite this reduction, food represented an important item in the budget. In order to meet their families' needs without putting too great a strain on the household finances, these housewives performed feats of ingenuity both in buying and preparing food for the table. They chose the cheaper cuts of meat and avoided purchasing prepared foods that were too expensive. "We never bought anything already made" (E2), as one of them said. Tinned products were largely confined to tomatoes, corn, salmon, peas, and beans for the majority of the women. Fresh fruit, with the exception of apples and bananas, appeared only rarely on the menu, and in general, they contented themselves with a rather narrow range of vegetables: potatoes, carrots, turnips, and onions making the most frequent appearance on the table.[26] The tiny sums paid by home relief would further reduce the quality and variety of food consumed. As one informant noted, "We bought potatoes. In those days, potatoes didn't take too much out of your pocket. ... They cost less than anything else, so you could eat more of them. It was a way of filling yourself up without it costing too much" (E19).

The importance of food, as a basic need that had to be satisfied, and the difficulties that might accompany the task of feeding the family appeared spontaneously in the comments that were collected on this subject. Quite frequently, indeed, the informants insisted on saying that despite all their financial difficulties, and despite the Depression, their families, the children in particular, never lacked for food, which implies that nourishing the family was a constant worry. "To want for food, that was the worst possible thing. I would rather not have had clothes on my back. Eating was enough" (E2). "We always ate our three meals a day" (E14). Not missing a meal did not, however, necessarily mean that the food was the best quality or that the menus were well balanced, as some of the women were well aware. "We always ate, maybe not as well as we might—but we always ate" (E23). "I used to put all kinds of things together to make one big dish. We couldn't eat steak, but we never, ever suffered because of a meal" (E28). For others, "not having food" meant literally not having something to eat, without regard to the quality of the meal: "We often had mustard spread on bread. But we always had something to eat" (E19). Another informant said, "We were never really destitute during the Depression. We always had something to eat" (E8); her comments express

333

the idea that it is the total absence of all food that was often associated with genuine poverty. That is to say, their desires, even at the level of satisfying their basic needs, remained very modest.

Among these needs, spending on clothing came in last place and was often reduced to the minimum. The husband and the older sons almost always wore store-bought clothes while the clothing of the other children was made at home, either from new material or, more frequently, remade out of old garments donated by relatives. In order to cut costs, the youngest children wore hand-me-down clothes and even shoes when their father was handy at replacing soles. Those who were less talented at sewing would buy their clothes from Saint Vincent de Paul and the Salvation Army or from pedlars who would charge interest for spreading out the payments.

What with the husband, who had to go out every day to work and the children, who had to be decently dressed for school, the women, who spent more of their time at home, found their needs being met well after those of everyone else. Their wardrobe was limited to a couple of cheap cotton housedresses and one or two better dresses that were suitable for the rare occasions that they went out: "At home, with the kids, we wore cotton housedresses. We never put pretty dresses on our backs. We had cheap cotton housedresses with an apron over them. On Sundays, we wore a good dress. When we went out, we dressed up" (E11). One of them, who for fifteen years wore the same winter coat she had bought the year she got married, explained, "After I took care of my children and my husband, there wasn't anything left for me. So I wore other people's stuff that I fixed up for myself. I wore other people's clothes for a long time" (E16). Another recounted, "I remember when we had the restaurant, I had just two dresses—wash the dress, iron the dress. Day after day—wash the dress, iron the dress. ... Me, who hates to iron!" (E26).

In the majority of families in the sample, virtually the entire budget was devoted to basic necessities, and that was even before the effects of the Depression made themselves felt. Because of job losses and wage cuts the crisis often required them to make cuts in their essential outlays—housing, food, clothing, and heating—despite the reduction in prices that the Depression brought about. The women did not, by the way, comment on this price reduction, probably because it coincided with the growth in

the size of their families. In order to maintain at least a minimum quality of life, the women would utilize even more energetically those various strategies with which they were familiar or which they were forced to adopt—increasing their work in the home to supplement their income, but also packing the family into a smaller flat, keeping a closer watch over the budget, buying less and buying cheaper, inventing yet more economical recipes, calling more on relatives when possible. [...]

Examining the incomes of the families in the sample, the sources of this money, and how it was managed has allowed us to observe that the breadwinner/housewife model did not correspond to the reality experienced by the majority of the families under consideration, as eighteen of them were dependent for their survival on the combined incomes of the two partners, in the 1930s alone. The Depression is not, however, altogether responsible for husbands' working two jobs or wives' working for pay, as the majority of these households (fifteen out of eighteen) depended on various sources of income even before unemployment deprived them of the wages of their principal breadwinner. Rather than changing the nature of the remunerative activities that women engaged in, since they, for the most part, continued to turn to work in the home, the Depression caused housewives to intensify their efforts. In fact, the sexual division of labour was rooted so deeply that just one woman was in the position of chief family breadwinner during the period of her husband's joblessness.

The overwhelming majority of these women was responsible for making the purchases and paying the running expenses of the household. Because they were required to translate their husbands' wages into goods for their family's consumption and because where they lived was often the place where they also worked for pay, there was no clear distinction for these women between the public and the private sphere.[27] The interconnection between different forms of work which were carried out in the two spheres was especially visible during the Depression while the importance of their role as housewife and administrator only grew in proportion to the degree that unemployment deprived them of their normal sources of income.[28]

To guarantee the well-being of their family while buying the least they could at the best possible price sums up the challenge faced daily by the majority of these housewives. Regardless of the additional income they could raise from their paid activities, there is no doubt that they would not have met it without extremely careful household management. As one informant explained, "I never went without food or clothes. But if I hadn't sewed and bought cheap, I would have gone without" (E3). [...]

Notes

1. The average family, used as a point of reference to establish the minimum budget necessary to support a working-class family, generally comprises five persons: two adults and three children, a composition that does not correspond to the reality of every family. For a discussion of wages before the Great Depression see Terry Copp, *The Anatomy of Poverty: The Conditions of the Working Class in Montreal, 1897–1929* (Toronto: McClelland and Stewart, 1974) 149–63 and the publication of the Federal Ministry of Labour: *La Gazette du Travail et Salaires et Heures de travail au Canada.*

2. Leonard Marsh, *Canadians in and out of Work: A Survey of Economic Classes and Their Relation to the Labour Market* McGill Social Research Series 9. Toronto: Oxford University Press, 1938) 345–46.

3. Quebec, *Annuaire statistique du Québec*, 1930, 1934: 400, 426; *La Gazette du Travail*, Canada, ministère du Travail, Feb. 1933, 249.

4. Andrée Lévesque, *Virage à gauche interdit. Les communistes, les socialistes, et leur ennemis au Québec 1929–1939* (Montréal: Boréal Express, 1984) 22.

5. According to a study carried out in 1935, eighty-five percent of the population of Montreal was dependent on an income of less than $1250 a year (around twenty-four dollars a week) and fifty percent on an income of less than $850 (about sixteen dollars a week) (Montreal Board of Trade, *Housing and Slum Clearance for Montreal*, cited in Lévesque, *Virage* 22).

6. Montreal Unemployment Relief Commission, *Renseignements à l'usage des chômeurs nécessiteux et des propriétaires*, n.d.10–11. In other directives issued in 1937, the amounts went to $8.51 a week in summer and $9.11 in winter, always for a family of five.

7. Investigations into workers' wages carried out by government agencies and charities obviously did not take into account the money that derived from these activities as well as the savings produced by the domestic labour of housewives. See Martha

May, "The 'Good Manager': Married Working-Class Women and Family Budget Studies, 1885–1915," *Labour History* 25 (1984): 351–72.

8. Bettina Bradbury, "Women's History and Working-Class History," *Labour/Le Travail* 19 (1987): 38.

9. We have virtually no data on the incidence of men working two jobs before the Second World War. In the 1950s, Fortin and Tremblay state that 18.4 percent of the heads of households in their sample had a second job (72).

10. It should be noted that it was not prohibited to earn a little money while receiving aid from Saint Vincent de Paul, since the society provided only food or food vouchers but did not pay for rent or other expenses. According to the rules laid down by the Unemployment Relief commission of Montreal, the head of the family and his wife could earn up to three dollars a week each without losing their benefits. Still, the commission deducted 50 percent of the income derived from renting rooms from the relief payment, even if this income did not exceed three dollars a week (Montreal Unemployment Commission, *Renseignements à l'usage des chomeurs nécessiteux et des propriétaires* (Montréal, n.d.) 6).

11. Unlike boarders, roomers only got a place to stay; they had to take their meals elsewhere and do their own washing, though not all the boarders automatically had their laundry done for them.

12. A.J. Pelletier, F.D. Thompson and A. Rochon, *La Famille canadienne, Recensement du Canada 1931* (Ottawa: King's Printer, 1942) 69. Bettina Bradbury likewise notes that in nineteenth-century Montreal, the poorest families were more likely to live with other families than to take in boarders, whereas the property-owning and professional families, perhaps influenced by the ideology of the home, were less and less involved in this activity. (Bradbury, "Pigs, Cows, and Boarders: Non-Wage Forms of Survival among Montreal Families" *Labour/Le travail* 14 (1984): 33–35). For a discussion of the decline in this practice among the middle class in the United States in the nineteenth century, see John Modell and Tamara Hareven, "Urbanization and the Malleable Household: An Examination of Boarding and Lodging in American Families," *Journal of Marriage and the Family* (1973): 467–79. This article notes that the Depression temporarily reversed the tendency, observed in all social classes, to cease taking in boarders, in the United States at least.

335

13. We must emphasize that the Depression involved an increase in the proportion of women working in the personal service sector where domestics are classified. In Montreal, for example, 20.2 percent of female labour was listed in this sector in 1921, compared to 29.3 percent in 1931 and 26.9 percent in 1941 (Lavigne and Stoddart, "Ouvrières et travailleuses montréalaises 1900–1940" in Marie Lavigne and Yonlands Pinard, eds. *Travailleuses et feminists: les femmes dans la societé québécoise* (Montréal: Boréal Express, 1983, 101). These census figures do not always permit us to establish what proportion of them were married.

14. The observations only confirm the theories about the invisibility of married women's work that several scholars with an interest in paid female labour have advanced. See for example, Bettina Bradbury, "L'economie familiale et le travail dans une ville en voie d'industrialisation: Montréal dans les années 1870" in Nadia Fahmy-Eid and Micheline Dumont, eds. *Maîtresses de maison, maîtresses d'écoles: femmes, familles et éducation dans l'histoire du Québec* (Montréal : Boréal Express, 1983); Suzanne D. Cross, "La majorité oubliée: le rôle des femmes de Montréal au 19 e siècle"; Lavigne and Pinard 99–114; Lavigne and Stoddart, "Ouvrières et travailleuses"; Veronica Strong-Boag, *The New Day Recalled : Lives of Girls and Women in English Canada, 1919–1939* (Toronto: Copp Clark Pitman, 1988) 41–71.

15. In this regard, see Elizabeth Roberts, *A Woman's Place: An Oral History of Working-Class Women, 1850–1940* (Oxford: Blackwell, 1984) 229.

16. In fact, this informant had taught for a year before getting married, but she did not seem to consider this a real job.

17. That is, as a daily cleaning woman.

18. Concerning the impossibility of reversing these roles during the Depression, see Mirra Komorovsky, *The Unemployed Man and His Family* (New York: Arno, 1971); Ruth Milkmann, "Women's Work and Economic Crisis: Some Lessons of the Great Depression," *Review of Radical Political Economics* 8 (1976): 85.

19. Meg Luxton, *More than a Labor of Love: Three Generations of Women's Work in the Home* (Toronto: Women's Press, 1980) 161–99; Strong-Boag, *New Day* 133–44; Roberts 125–68; Pat Ayers and Jan Lambertz, "Marriage Relations, Money, and Domestic Violence in Working-Class Liverpool, 1919–39," in Jane Lewis, ed. *Labour and Love: Women's Experience of Home and Family, 1840–1940* (Oxford: Blackwell, 1986) 195–219.

20. Ayers and Lambert 197.

21. Jennifer Stoddart, "Quand des gens de robe se penchent sur les droits des femmes: le cas de la commission Dorion 1929–1931," in Lavigne and Pinard 321.

22. This statement must, however, be qualified as three informants intervened to find work for their husbands while another called her husband's boss to get him a raise.

23. Philippe Garigue also observed that women did not feel that they had more authority, even when they controlled the purse strings (*La Vie familiale des canadiens francais* (Montreal: University of Montreal Press) 38).

24. Andrée Fortin, for example, states, "It may well be said that this administrative power is not large, managing poverty not being a secure job; one notes that "queen of the home" is not merely a symbolic title—she is the regent and the steward" ["La famille ouvrière d'autrefois," *Recherches sociographiques, La Famille de la Nouvelle-France à aujourd'hui* 28. 2–3 (1987): 283].

25. Quebec, *Annuaire statistique du Québec*, 1930 and 1934, 400 and 426. According to a federal study in 1938, francophone families in Montreal devoted on average 34 percent of their budget to this expenditure [*Canada, BFS, Family income and Expenditure in Canada: A Study of Urban Wage-Earner Families, Including Data on Physical Attributes* (Ottawa: King's Printer, 1941) 26].

26. The study undertaken in 1938 also looked into consumption habits regarding foodstuffs [and] noted that, compared to the sample as a whole, among French-Canadian families in Quebec, "Purchases per person ... were noticeably above the average for meat, white bread, potatoes, canned fruit, and bananas. They were below the average for brown bread, cheese, milk, and oranges" (Canada BFS 54). We should note that it was rare that wages would permit buying in bulk; in any event, cramped quarters hardly encouraged the storage of provisions.

27. Elizabeth Roberts, "Women's Strategies, 1890–1940," *Labour and Love: Women's Experience of Home and Family 1840–1940*, ed. Jane Lewis (Oxford: Blackwell, 1986), 223.

28. Strong-Boag, *New Day* 137.

A NATIONAL CRIME

Residential Schools in Canada, 1880s to 1960s

Maureen Lux
Brock University

A NATIONAL CRIME: RESIDENTIAL SCHOOLS IN CANADA, 1880s TO 1960s

Introduction by Maureen Lux

339

● INTRODUCTION

Maureen Lux

In June 2008 Prime Minister Stephen Harper stood in the House of Commons to deliver a most unusual speech:

> Mr. Speaker, I stand before you today to offer an apology to former students of Indian residential schools. The treatment of children in Indian residential schools is a sad chapter in our history. [...]
>
> The government of Canada built an educational system in which very young children were often forcibly removed from their homes, often taken far from their communities. Many were inadequately fed, clothed and housed. All were deprived of the care and nurturing of their parents, grandparents and communities. First Nations, Inuit and Métis languages and cultural practices were prohibited in these schools. Tragically, some of these children died while attending residential schools and others never returned home. The government now recognizes that the consequences of the Indian residential schools policy were profoundly negative and that this policy has had a lasting and damaging impact on aboriginal culture, heritage and language. [...]
>
> The government of Canada sincerely apologizes and asks the forgiveness of the aboriginal peoples of this country for failing them so profoundly. We are sorry. [...][1]

The apology and the limited financial compensation for survivors went some way to acknowledge the damage done to many generations of Aboriginal people and their communities. But the formal apology, coming 128 years after the residential school system began, and more than a decade after the worst abuses were widely known, made many wonder whether government efforts were not too little, too late. The Christian churches that managed the schools on the government's behalf had already apologized a few years before, although the Catholic Church issued a Papal apology only in 2009.

The residential schools' tragic legacies—the loss of language and history, damaged lives, and corroded communities—were not unforeseen or unintended consequences, but rather were the *raison d'être* of the schools. Indeed, the foundation of the residential school system rested on what was called in the late nineteenth century "aggressive civilization," or the forced assimilation of Aboriginal people into Christian, capitalist Canadian society by actively repressing their languages, cultures, religion, and medicine. To that end, residential schools, which removed children from their parents' influence, forced them to speak English (or French in Quebec), and indoctrinated them in the Christian faith that denigrated Aboriginal spirituality, became the centrepiece of government policy. For nearly a century, from the 1880s to the closure of most of the schools in the 1960s, the moral authority of the Christian churches joined forces with the legislative and financial power of the state to create and perpetuate the school system. It is important to note that some students had a positive experience at residential schools, and not all Aboriginal children attended the schools. As for the numbers of children enrolled, the *Report of the Royal Commission on Aboriginal Peoples* notes that the records do not allow a precise accounting, but "the impact of the system was felt not only by the children who attended schools but by the families and communities that were deprived of their children and had to deal subsequently with children who returned damaged from the schools. In that sense, communities, parents and, indeed, children later born to former students of the residential schools were all 'enrolled'.[2] At its height in 1931 there were 80 schools in the Northwest Territories and every province except Prince Edward Island, New Brunswick, and Newfoundland. The question must be, why? How did Christian stewardship and state responsibility become so perverted as to create such a tragic end?

In 1879 Canadian Prime Minister John A. Macdonald sent Nicholas Flood Davin, failed Conservative candidate and journalist, to investigate the American Indian Industrial schools and to report on the advisability of establishing such schools in Canada. Davin's confidential 1879 *Report on Industrial Schools for Indians and Half-Breeds* (excerpted here) recommended the establishment of Industrial schools. Davin's consistent and objectionable (to our twenty-first-century ears) references to "race" sheds some light on Victorian perceptions of Aboriginal peoples and the notions of racial superiority that influenced the establishment of the residential school system. As Davin noted, "[...] if anything is to be done with the Indian, we must catch him very young. The children must be kept constantly with the circle of civilized conditions."

As historian John Milloy explains in "The Tuition of Thomas Moore," the state policy of assimilation that attempted to make Aboriginal peoples strangers in their own lands found a most accommodating partner in the Christian churches. But the school system, always underfunded, increasingly forced the churches to economize on food and clothing, while the children spent less time in the classroom and more time working in the fields, barns, kitchens, and laundries to maintain the schools. Despite ample evidence that the "circle of civilized conditions" was creating appalling conditions, those responsible, the churches and government, each blamed the other.

In "The Charge of Manslaughter: Disease and Death, 1879–1946," Milloy examines the dreadful conditions in some of the schools. Rising concerns over costs and the alarming state of the children's health led government and the churches to lower their expectations. The original distinction between Industrial schools (intended to teach trades to older students) and the less expensive boarding schools (for younger students) had become negligible, and after 1923 all were simply known as residential schools.

One of those intimate with the dangerous condition of the schools and the subsequent deterioration in the children's health was the department of Indian Affairs medical officer, Dr Peter Bryce. In the excerpt of his 1922 pamphlet *The Story of a National Crime: Being an Appeal for Justice to the Indians of Canada,* Bryce recounts how the department, especially Departmental Accountant and later Deputy Minister Duncan Campbell Scott, actively suppressed his 1907 report on the conditions of the schools, and ignored his recommendations to ameliorate the children's misery. It is important to note, however, that Bryce's condemnation of the government was motivated not only by the deplorable state of health, but also by his own resentment at being passed over in 1919 for a position in the new federal Department of Health.

School children, their parents, and communities were not passive victims of the assimilationist policies pursued by state and church in the residential schools. Granted, the power relations were hardly equal and the Indian department had considerable resources to force children into school and keep them there. Amendments to the *Indian Act* in 1894 and again in 1920 legislated compulsory attendance at school; police charged parents who refused to comply, and rounded up and returned children who made a run for home. Besides sheer compulsion, there were also the concerted efforts of school principals, Indian Agents, and missionaries to coerce parents and communities to surrender their children. Nevertheless, children and their parents accepted what they could not change, but resisted when and where they could. As historian J.R. Miller explains in "You Ain't My Boss," children and their communities resisted their maltreatment, but their voices were rarely heard beyond the local school. But perhaps ironically, when concerted Aboriginal political action emerged as a national force in the 1960s it was often residential school graduates who were the most effective leaders. The schools themselves created those who mounted the most effective forms of resistance.

Even after the end of the church–state educational relationship in 1969 and the closure of most schools, the story of neglect and abuse was still not widely known beyond the Aboriginal communities that continued to struggle with its legacy. As John Milloy explains, what finally broke the silence was "[...] ironically, the deepest secret of all—the pervasive sexual abuse of the children."[3] In the 1980s, harrowing reports of sexual abuse of non-Aboriginal children at orphanages in Newfoundland and Ontario prompted a public dialogue that eventually listened to Aboriginal revelations of similar abuse. In British Columbia, police uncovered widespread sexual abuse by priests at Williams Lake school; in 1990, Phil Fontaine, chief of the Assembly of Manitoba Chiefs, spoke out about his mistreatment at the hands of priests at Fort Alexander school in Manitoba: "I think what happened to me happened to a lot of people. It wasn't just sexual abuse, it was physical and psychological abuse. It was a violation."[4] Revelations of abuse continued and lawsuits mounted, but it was the aftermath of the failed Meech Lake Accord and the clash between police and Mohawks at Kanestake (Oka) that prompted the establishment of the Royal Commission on Aboriginal Peoples in 1992. With a mandate to explore the relationship among Aboriginal peoples, the government, and Canadian society, and to propose solutions to the problems that plagued the relationship, the Royal Commission reported in 1996. One of its priorities was to investigate the history of the residential schools, and the Commission recommended a public inquiry to allow survivors to tell their stories and begin the healing process. Further, the Commission recommended a compensation package for victims and a government apology. After much prompting and pressure by Aboriginal and non-Aboriginal groups, the apology came 12 years later, while the public inquiry, the Truth and Reconciliation Commission, has yet to begin its work. For very many former students all of this comes far too late, but the opportunity for public debate of this sad history may go some way to honour their memory.

NOTES

1. Prime Minister Stephen Harper's statement of apology, 11 June 2008.
2. Royal Commission on Aboriginal Peoples, *Looking Forward, Looking Back,* Vol. 1, Part 2, Chapter 10, "Residential Schools," n. 15.
3. John Milloy, *A National Crime: The Canadian Government and the Residential School System,* 1879–1986 (Winnipeg: University of Manitoba Press, 1999), 298.
4. *The Globe and Mail,* 31 October 1990, quoted in J.R. Miller, Shingwauk's *Vision: A History of Native Residential Schools* (Toronto: University of Toronto Press, 1996), 328.

QUESTIONS

1. Why was the nineteenth-century policy of "aggressive civilization" actively pursued into the late twentieth century?
2. How was it that the worst abuses of the residential schools did not become the subject of public debate for more than a century? Has there been a public debate?
3. Prime Minister Harper's apology to Aboriginal people is similar to the government's 1988 apology to Japanese Canadians for their internment during World War II. Why

did it take another two decades for an apology to Aboriginal Canadians? Do government apologies create the impression that past wrongs have somehow been corrected or forgiven?

4. What does Davin's 1879 Report tell us about late nineteenth century views of Aboriginal people? What does it say about their views on education? Why were there no plans to train Aboriginal teachers for the schools?

5. Peter Bryce, a physician and powerful public health expert, was eventually drummed out of government service for his public criticisms of the residential school system. What impact would criticisms by the children and their parents have had on the schools?

FURTHER READINGS

Barman, J., Y. Hebert, and D. McCaskill, eds., *Indian Education in Canada, Volume One: The Legacy,* (Vancouver: University of British Columbia Press, 1986).

Dyck, Noel, *Differing Visions: Administering Indian Residential Schooling in Prince Albert, 1867–1967,* (Halifax: Fernwood Publishing, 1997).

Haig-Brown, Celia, *Resistance and Renewal: Surviving the Indian Residential School,* (Vancouver: Tillacum Library, 1988).

Miller, J.R., *Shingwauk's Vision: A History of Native Residential Schools,* (Toronto: University of Toronto Press, 1996).

Milloy, John, *A National Crime: The Canadian Government and the Residential School System, 1879–1986,* (Winnipeg: University of Manitoba Press, 1999).

Royal Commission on Aboriginal Peoples, *Looking Forward, Looking Back,* Volume 1, Part 2, Chapter 10, "Residential Schools," accessed from http://www.collectionscanada.gc.ca.

The following are memoirs by former students or based on interviews with students. See, for example, Celia Haig-Brown, *Resistance and Renewal: Surviving the Indian Residential School* (Vancouver: Tillacum Library, 1988); Isabelle Knockwood with Gillian Thomas, *Out of the Depths, The Experiences of Mi'kmaq Children at the Indian Residential School at Shubenacadie, Nova Scotia* (Lokeport, Nova Scotia: Roseway Publishing, 1992); Basil H. Johnston, *Indian School Days* (Toronto: Key Porter Books Limited, 1988); G. Manuel and M. Posluns, *The Fourth World* (Don Mills: Collier-Macmillan Canada Ltd., 1974); Linda Jaine, ed., *Residential Schools: The Stolen Years* (Saskatoon: University [of Saskatchewan] Extension Press, 1993); Geoffrey York, *The Dispossessed: Life and Death in Native Canada* (Toronto: Lester & Orpen Dennys, 1989); Assembly of First Nations, *Breaking the Silence, An Interpretive Study of Residential School Impact and Healing as Illustrated by the Stories of First Nations Individuals* (Ottawa: First Nations Health Commission, 1994).

▲ Document 1: Report on Industrial Schools for Indians and Half-Breeds

Nicholas Flood Davin

Ottawa, 14th March, 1879

To the Right Honourable

The Minister of the Interior

SIR,—I have the honour to submit the following report on the working of Industrial Schools for the education of Indians and mixed-bloods in the United States, and on the advisability of establishing similar institutions in the North-West Territories of the Dominion.

In accordance with your directions of the twenty-eighth of January, I went to Washington. His Excellency Sir Edward Thornton, the Honourable Carl Schurtz, Secretary of the Interior, and the Honourable E. A. Hayt, the Commissioner of Indian Affairs, secured for me every facility for becoming acquainted with the establishment, cost and practical value of industrial schools among the Indian populations of the United States.

The industrial school is the principal feature of the policy known as that of "aggressive civilization." This policy was inaugurated by President Grant in 1869. But, as will be seen, the utility of industrial schools had long ere that time been amply tested. [...] After eight years' experience of the partial carrying out of these recommendations, the Board pressed for a still more thorough policy; they urged, among other things, that titles to land should be inalienable from the family of the holder for at least three generations. From 1869 vigorous efforts in an educational direction were put forward. But it was found that the day school did not work, because the influence of the wigwam was stronger than the influence of the school. Industrial Boarding Schools were therefore established, and these are now numerous and will soon be universal. [...]

The Indian character, about which some persons find such a mystery, is not difficult to understand. The Indian is sometimes spoken of as a child, but he is very far from being a child. The race is in its childhood. As far as the childhood analogy is applicable, what it suggests is a policy that shall look patiently for fruit, not after five or ten years, but after a generation or two. [...]

[...]

The Indian is a man with conditions of his own, which make civilization a puzzle of despair. He has the suspicion, distrust, fault-finding tendency, the insincerity and flattery, produced in all subject races. He is crafty, but conscious how weak his craft is when opposed to the superior cunning of the white man. [...]

The first and greatest stone in the foundation of the quasi-civilization of the Indians, wherever seen, was laid by missionaries, men who had a supreme object and who did not count their lives dear unto them. Schools are scattered over the whole continent, wherever Indians exist, monuments of religious zeal and heroic self-sacrifice. These schools should be utilized as much as possible, both on grounds of efficiency and economy. The missionaries' experience is only surpassed by their patient heroism, and their testimony, like that of the school teachers, like that of the authorities at Washington is, that if anything is to be done with the Indian, we must catch him very young. The children must be kept constantly within the circle of civilized conditions. [...] The plan now is to take young children, give

---

Source: Nicholas Flood Davin, *Report on Industrial Schools for Indians and Half-Breeds* (14 March 1879), Library and Archives Canada, MG26A, Sir John A. Macdonald Papers, Vol. 91, 35428-45.

them the care of a mother, and have them constantly in hand. Such care must be *pari passu* with religious training.

[…]

The recommendations I venture to submit are as follows:—

(1.) Wherever the missionaries have schools, those schools should be utilized by the Government, if possible; that is to say, a contract should be made with the religious body controlling the school to board and educate and train industrially a certain number of pupils. […]

(2.) Not more than four industrial boarding schools ought to be established at first. […]

(3.) An industrial boarding school should be established somewhere in the fork of the North and South Saskatchewan, near Prince Albert, in connection with the Episcopalian Church. The land is wonderfully fertile. There are a good many Indians in the neighbourhood. There are Bands of Indians near Carlton and near Dutch Lake. There is plenty of fish and timber.

(4.) In no place could an industrial boarding school in connection with the Methodist body be more properly placed than near Old Bow Fort. The Blackfeet and Stoneys, wild but noble types of Indians, would thus be reached. […]

(5.) At Qu'Appelle it might well be thought we should find an appropriate site for an industrial boarding school to be conducted by Roman Catholics.[…]

(6.) An industrial boarding school, in connection with the Presbyterian Church, should be established on Riding Mountain. […]

The importance of denominational schools at the outset for the Indians must be obvious. One of the earliest things an attempt to civilize them does, is to take away their simple Indian mythology, the central idea of which, to wit, a perfect spirit, can hardly be improved on. The Indians have their own ideas of right and wrong, of "good" Indians and "bad" Indians, and to disturb this faith, without supplying a better, would be a curious process to enlist the sanction of civilized races whose whole civilization, like all the civilizations with which we are acquainted, is based on religion. […]

(7.) Some distinction should be made between the treatment of parents who send their children regularly to the day-school, and of those who are either careless whether their children go to school or not, or who are wholly opposed to their children attending school, as some are. To the first, an additional ration of tea and sugar might be given.

(8.) Where practicable, some inducement of a special nature should be held out to the child.

(9.) As Bands become more amenable to the restraints of civilization education should be made compulsory.

(10.) The character of the teacher, morally and intellectually, is a matter of vital importance. If he is morally weak, whatever his intellectual qualifications may be, he is worse than no teacher at all. If he is poorly instructed or feeble in brain, he only enacts every day an elaborate farce. […]

(11.) In order to secure that the education given would be efficient, there ought to be competent inspection. […]

(12.) Where boys or girls, whether Indians or half-breed, show special aptitudes or exceptional general quickness, special advantages should be offered them, and they should be trained to become teachers and clerks in connection

345

with the Department, as well as fitted to launch out on commercial and professional careers.

(13.) The salary of a teacher must be such as will induce good men to offer
themselves. The teacher should be paid according to his qualifications. [...]

I have the honour to be,
Sir,
Your obedient servant,
Nicholas Flood Davin.

▲ Document 2: Anglican Indian School, Siksika (Blackfoot) Reserve

ALL ONE IN CHRIST JESUS

● Anglican Indian School, Siksika (Blackfoot) Reserve, Alberta, ca. 1901–1910. Who might have taken this photograph? Why?

Source: Glenbow Museum, NC-5-1.

▲ Document 3: Students Filling Mattresses with Straw, Kanai (Blood) Anglican School

● Students filling mattresses with straw, Kanai (Blood) Anglican school, ca. 1916. What does this tell you about the kinds of work schoolchildren did? What does it tell you about the living conditions at the school?

Source: Glenbow Museum, NA-1400-31.

▲ Document 4: The Story of a National Crime: Being an Appeal for Justice to the Indians of Canada

Dr. Peter Henderson Bryce, M.A., M.D.

The Story of a National Crime Being a Record of the Health Conditions of the Indians of Canada from 1904 to 1921

I. By Order in Council dated Jan. 22nd, 1904, the writer was appointed Medical Inspector to the Department of the Interior and of Indian Affairs, and was entrusted with the health interests of the Indians of Canada. [...]

For the first months after the writer's appointment he was much engaged in organizing the medical inspection of immigrants at the sea ports; but he early began the systematic collection of health statistics of the several hundred Indian Bands scattered over Canada. For each year up to 1914 he wrote an annual report on the health of the Indians, published in the Departmental report, and on instructions from the minister made in 1907 a special inspection of thirty-five Indian schools in the three prairie provinces. This report was published separately; but the recommendations contained in the report were never published and the public knows nothing of them. It contained a brief history of the origin of the Indian Schools, of the sanitary condition of the schools and statistics of the health of the pupils, during the 15 years of their existence. Regarding the health of the pupils, the report states that 24 per cent of all the pupils which had been in the schools were known to be dead, while of one school on the File Hills reserve, which gave a complete return to date, 75 per cent. were dead at the end of the 16 years since the school opened.

Recommendations of school report 1907

Briefly the recommendations urged, (1) Greater school facilities, since only 30 per cent. of the children of school age were in attendance; (2) That boarding schools with farms attached be established near the home reserves of the pupils; (3) That the government undertake the complete maintenance and control of the schools, since it had promised by treaty to insure such; and further it was recommended that as the Indians grow in wealth and intelligence they should pay at least part of the cost from their own funds; (4) That the school studies be those of the curricula of the several Provinces in which the schools are situated, since it was assumed that as the bands would soon become enfranchised and become citizens of the Province they would enter into the common life and duties of a Canadian community; (5) That in view of the historical and sentimental relations between the Indian schools and the Christian churches the report recommended that the Department provide for the management of the schools, through a Board of Trustees, one appointed from each church and approved by the minister of the Department. Such a board would have its secretary in the Department but would hold regular meetings, establish qualifications for teachers, and oversee the appointments as well as the control of the schools; (6) That Continuation schools be arranged for on the school farms and that instruction methods similar to those on the File Hills farm colony be developed; (7) That the health interests of the pupils be guarded by a proper medical inspection and that the local physicians be encouraged through the provision at each school of fresh air methods in the care and treatment of cases of tuberculosis.

Source: Dr. Peter Henderson Bryce, M.A., M.D., *The Story of a National Crime: Being an Appeal for Justice to the Indians of Canada.* Ottawa: James Hope and Sons, 1922.

349

II. The annual medical reports from year to year made reference to the unsatisfactory health of the pupils, while different local medical officers urged greater action in view of the results of their experience from year to year. As the result of one such report the Minister instructed the writer in 1909 to investigate the health of the children in the schools of the Calgary district in a letter containing the following:—

"As it is necessary that these residential schools should be filled with a healthy class of pupils in order that the expenditure on Indian education may not be rendered entirely nugatory, it seems desirable that you should go over the same ground as Dr. Lafferty and check his inspection."

Recommendations based upon examination of 243 school children

These instructions were encouraging and the writer gladly undertook the work of examining with Dr. J.D. Lafferty the 243 children of 8 schools in Alberta, with the following results:—

(a) Tuberculosis was present equally in children at every age; (b) In no instance was a child awaiting admission to school found free from tuberculosis; hence it was plain that infection was got in the home primarily; (c) The disease showed an excessive mortality in the pupils between five and ten years of age; (d) The 10,000 children of school age demanded the same attention as the thousand children coming up each year and entering the schools annually.

Recommendations, made in this report, on much the same lines as those made in the report of 1907, followed the examination of the 243 children; but owing to the active opposition of Mr. D. C. Scott, and his advice to the then Deputy Minister, no action was taken by the Department to give effect to the recommendations made. [...]

The writer had done no regular inspection work since Mr. D. C. Scott was made Deputy minister in 1913, but had in each year up to 1914 prepared his medical report, printed in the annual report of the Department. [...]

Thus we find a sum of only $10,000 has been annually placed in the estimates to control tuberculosis amongst 105,000 Indians scattered over Canada in over 300 bands, while the City of Ottawa, with about the same population and having three general hospitals spent thereon $342,860.54 in 1919 of which $33,364.70 is devoted to tuberculosis patients alone. The many difficulties of our problem amongst the Indians have been frequently pointed out, but the means to cope with these have also been made plain. [...]

The degree and extent of this criminal disregard for the treaty pledges to guard the welfare of the Indian wards of the nation may be gauged from the facts once more brought out at the meeting of the National Tuberculosis Association at its annual meeting held in Ottawa on March 17th, 1922. The superintendent of the Qu'Appelle Sanatorium, Sask., gave there the results of a special study of 1575 children of school age in which advantage was taken of the most modern scientific methods. Of these 175 were Indian children, and it is very remarkable that the fact given that some 93 per cent. of these showed evidence of tuberculous infection coincides completely with the work done by Dr. Lafferty and the writer in the Alberta Indian schools in 1909.

It is indeed pitiable that during the thirteen years since then this trail of disease and death has gone on almost unchecked by any serious efforts on the part of the Department of Indian Affairs, placed by the B. N. A. Act especially in charge of our Indian population, and that a Provincial Tuberculosis Commission now considers it to be its duty to publish the facts regarding these children living within its own Province.

▲ Document 5: School Boys from Tsuu T'ina (Sarcee) Reserve, 1920

● School Boys from Tsuu T'ina (Sarcee) Reserve, 1920; note the bandages on the boys' heads, likely covering 'scrofula' sores or tuberculosis of lymph nodes of the neck. One-quarter of the boys have their heads bandaged. If these are the 'healthy' boys, what might this say about the other children in the school?

Source: Glenbow Museum, NA-192-13.

▲ Document 6: Schoolchildren at the United Church School on the Stoney Reserve, Morley, Alberta, ca. 1950

● Class in session at the Residential School on the Stoney Reserve, Morley, Alberta. Note the pictures of the Royal Family on the wall. Why would all the children be dressed in their coats?

352

Source: Glenbow Museum, NA-5719-4.

▲ Document 7: Bed-time Prayers at Girls' Dormitory, Old Sun School, Siksika (Blackfoot) Reserve

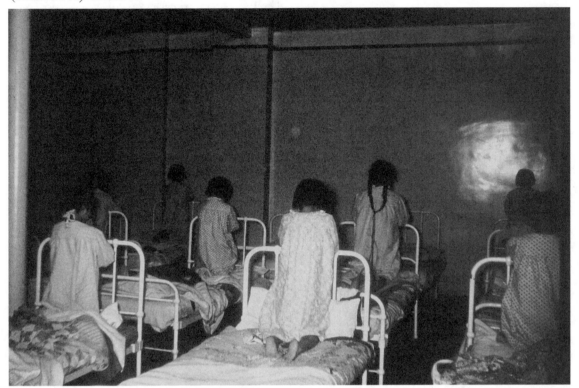

● Bed-time prayers at the girls' dormitory, Old Sun School, Siksika (Blackfoot) Reserve, ca. 1955. Note the ordered beds in the crowded dormitory. Who might have taken this photo? Why?

Source: Glenbow Museum, NA-4817-22.

■ Article 1: The Tuition of Thomas Moore

John Milloy

In its *Annual Report* of 1904, the Department of Indian Affairs published the photographs of the young Thomas Moore of the Regina Industrial School, "before and after tuition." The images are a cogent expression of what federal policy had been since Confederation and what it would remain for many decades. It was a policy of assimilation, a policy designed to move Aboriginal communities from their "savage" state to that of "civilization" and thus to make in Canada but one community—a non-Aboriginal one.[1]

At the core of the policy was education. It was, according to Deputy Superintendent Duncan Campbell Scott, who steered the administration of Indian Affairs from 1913 to 1932, "by far the most important of the many subdivisions of the most complicated Indian problem."[2] In the education of the young lay the most potent power to effect cultural change—a power to be channelled through schools and, in particular, through residential schools. Education would, Frank Oliver, the Minister of Indian Affairs, declared in 1908, "elevate the Indian from his condition of savagery" and make "him a self-supporting member of the State, and eventually a citizen in good standing."[3]

The pictures are, then, both images of what became in this period the primary object of that policy: the Aboriginal child, and an analogy of the relationship between the two cultures—Aboriginal and White—as it had been in the past and as it was to be in the future. There, in the photograph on the left, is the young Thomas posed against a fur robe, in his beaded dress, his hair in long braids, clutching a gun. Displayed for the viewer are the symbols of the past—of Aboriginal costume and culture, of hunting, of the disorder and violence of warfare and of the cross-cultural partnerships of the fur trade and of the military alliances that had dominated life in Canada since the late sixteenth century.

Source: John S. Milloy, *A National Crime: The Canadian Government and the Residential School System, 1879–1986*. Winnipeg: University of Manitoba Press, 1999, pp. 3–9. Reprinted with permission.

Those partnerships, anchored in Aboriginal knowledge and skills, had enabled the newcomers to find their way, to survive, and to prosper. But they were now merely historic; they were not to be any part of the future as Canadians pictured it at the founding of their new nation in 1867. That future was one of settlement, agriculture, manufacturing, lawfulness, and Christianity. In the view of politicians and civil servants in Ottawa whose gaze was fixed upon the horizon of national development, Aboriginal knowledge and skills were neither necessary nor desirable in a land that was to be dominated by European industry and, therefore, by Europeans and their culture.

That future was inscribed in the photograph on the right. Thomas, with his hair carefully barbered, in his plain, humble suit, stands confidently, hand on hip, in a new context. Here he is framed by the horizontal and vertical lines of wall and pedestal—the geometry of social and economic order; of place and class, and of private property the foundation of industriousness, the cardinal virtue of late-Victorian culture. But most telling of all, perhaps, is the potted plant. Elevated above him, it is the symbol of civilized life, of agriculture. Like Thomas, the plant is cultivated nature no longer wild. Like it, Thomas has been, the Department suggests, reduced to civility in the time he has lived within the confines of the Regina Industrial School.

The assumptions that underlay the pictures also informed the designs of social reformers in Canada and abroad, inside the Indian Department and out. Thomas and his classmates were to be assimilated; they were to become functioning members of Canadian society. Marching out from schools, they would be the vanguard of a magnificent metamorphosis: the savages were to be made civilized. For Victorians, it was an empire-wide task of heroic proportions and divine ordination encompassing the Maori, the Aborigine, the Hottentot, and many other indigenous peoples. For Canadians, it was, at the level of rhetoric at least, a national duty—a "sacred trust with which Providence has invested the country in the charge of and care for the aborigines committed to it."[4] In 1880, Alexander Morris, one of the primary government negotiators of the recently concluded western treaties, looked back upon those agreements and then forward, praying: "Let us have Christianity and civilization among the Indian tribes; let us have a

• Thomas Moore, as he appeared when admitted to the Regina Indian Industrial School (Saskatchewan Archives Board, R-82239 [1]). [Source: Saskatchewan Archives Board R-A8223-1]

• Thomas Moore, after tuition at the Regina Indian Industrial School (Saskatchewan Archives Board, R-82239 [2]). [Source: Saskatchewan Archives Board R-A8223-1]

wise and paternal Government…doing its utmost to help and elevate the Indian population,…and Canada will be enabled to feel, that in a truly patriotic spirit our country has done its duty by the red men."[5]

In Canada's first century, that "truly patriotic spirit" would be evident in the many individuals who devoted their "human capabilities to the good of the Indians of this country." In the case of Father Lacombe, Oblate missionary to the Blackfoot, for example, the "poor redman's redemption physically and morally" was "the dream of my days and nights."[6] According to Canada's first Prime Minister, Sir John A. Macdonald, the nation, too, dreamed of discharging its benevolent duty. A national goal, he informed Parliament, was "to do away with the tribal system and assimilate the Indian people in all respects with the inhabitants of the Dominion, as speedily as they are fit to change."[7] With the assistance of church and state, wandering hunters would take up a settled life, agriculture, useful trades and, of course, the Christian religion.

Assimilation became, during Macdonald's first term, official policy. It was Canada's response to its "sacred trust" made even more alluring by the fact that supposedly selfless duty was to have its reward. The Deputy Superintendent General of Indian Affairs, L. Vankoughnet, assured Macdonald in 1887 that Indian expenditures "would be a good investment" for, in due course, Aboriginal people, "instead of being supported from the revenue of the country,…would contribute largely to the same."

Education, as Scott indicated, was the most critical element of this assimilative strategy. Vankoughnet, in his memo of 1887 to the prime minister, was doing no more than reflecting the common wisdom of the day when he wrote:

Give me the children and you may have the parents, or words to that effect, were uttered by a zealous divine in his anxiety to add to the number of whom his Church called her children. And the principle laid down by that astute reasoner is an excellent one on which to act in working out that most difficult problem—the intellectual emancipation of the Indian, and its natural sequel, his elevation to a status equal to that of his white brother. This can only be done through education….Only by a persistent continuance in a thoroughly systematic course of educating (using the word in its fullest and most practical sense) the children, will the final hoped and long striven for result be attained.[8]

"That most difficult problem" was to be solved not only through "persistent" tuition but also, more specifically, by residential school education, which, initially, took two forms: "boarding" schools, which were situated on or near a reserve, which were of moderate size and which taught reading, writing and arithmetic, agriculture, and the simple manual skills required by farmers and their wives; and "industrial" schools, such as Thomas's Regina Industrial School, which were large, centrally located, urban-associated trade schools and which also provided a plain English education. "It would be highly desirable, if it were practicable," the Department wrote in its *Annual Report* of 1890 "to obtain entire possession of all Indian children after they attain to the age of seven or eight years, and keep them at schools…until they have had a thorough course of instruction." The Department was confident that if such a course were adopted "the solution of the problem designated 'the Indian question' would probably be effected sooner than it is under the present system" of day schools.

By 1890, the government had been committed for just over a decade to the development of a system of residential schools of "the industrial type."[9] That commitment had sprung from the recommendations of the now-famous *Davin Report* of 1879. Nicholas Flood Davin, a journalist and a defeated Tory candidate, had been rewarded for his electoral effort by Macdonald with a commission to "report on the working of Industrial Schools…in the United States and on the advisability of establishing similar institutions in the North-West Territories of the Dominion." Senior American officials who Davin visited, Carl Schurtz, the Secretary of the Interior, and E.A. Hayt, the Commissioner of Indian Affairs, evinced the greatest confidence in the efficacy of the industrial school, which was, Davin was informed, "the principal feature of the policy known as that of 'aggressive civilization,'" their policy of assimilation. Day schools had proven a failure "because the influence of the wigwam was stronger than the influence of the school." Indeed, support for this thesis came, he claimed, from Cherokee leaders he met in Washington. They described the "happy results of Industrial Schools" and convinced him "that the chief thing to attend to in dealing with the less civilized or wholly barbarous tribes, was to separate the children from the parents."

Next on Davin's agenda was a trip to the school at the White Earth Agency in Minnesota. He was obviously impressed. The school was 'well attended and the answering of the children creditable….The dormitory was plainly but comfortably furnished, and the children…were evidently well fed." The whole reserve had an air of progressive development, traceable, in the opinion of the agent, to the school. Subsequent meetings in Winnipeg with "the leading men, clerical and lay, who could speak with authority on the subject" must have confirmed his American observations, for Davin's report gave unqualified support to the "application of the principle of industrial boarding schools." He submitted, as well, a detailed plan for beginning such a school system in the west that he probably worked out with those authorities—Bishop Taché, Father Lacombe, the Honourable James McKay and others.[10]

While the *Davin Report* may properly be credited with moving the Macdonald government to inaugurate industrial schools in the 1880s, it is far from being, as it is often characterized,[11] the genesis of the residential school system in Canada. Indeed, when Davin submitted his report, there were already in existence in Ontario four residential schools, then called manual labour schools—the Mohawk Institute, and the Wikwemikong, Mount Elgin, and Shingwauk schools; and a number of boarding schools were being planned by missionaries in the west.

Furthermore, the report does not answer the most important questions about the beginning and intended character of the residential school system.

Why did the federal government adopt a policy of assimilation? What was the relationship between that policy, its ideology and structures, and education, particularly residential schools? Not only are the answers to such central questions not in the *Davin Report*, but neither are they found in any single report in the early years after Confederation. Indeed, to discover the roots of the Canadian residential school system, we must make recourse to the history of the pre-Confederation period of Imperial control of Indian affairs. It was in that earlier era that the assimilative policy took shape with the design of programs for the "civilization" of the Indian population of Upper Canada. The policy was then given a final legislative form, in the first decade after Confederation, with the determination of the constitutional position of Indian First Nations expressed in two early Indian acts: 1869 and 1876.

The Imperial policy heritage of the 1830s, 1840s, and 1850s, supplemented by federal legislation and programming in the first decade of Confederation, was both the context and the rationale for the development of residential schools, which in turn constituted part of the most extensive and persistent colonial system—one that marginalized Aboriginal communities within its constitutional, legislative, and regulatory structure, stripped them of the power of self-government, and denied them any degree of self-determination. As a consequence, Aboriginal people became, in the course of Canada's first century, wards of the Department of Indian Affairs and increasingly the objects of social welfare, police, and justice agencies.

The result of the federal government's colonization of First Nations was sorrowful, indeed. When, in 1946, a joint committee of the House of Commons and Senate met "to examine and consider the Indian Act"[12] and the record of federal administration of Indian affairs, the members found not only a policy that had remained largely unchanged since the Confederation era—"an unwritten heritage of the past"[13]—but also one that had clearly fallen far short of its goal and showed no sign of imminent success. By every indicator—health, employment, income, education, housing—Aboriginal people, far from being assimilated, were still separate and second-class citizens. What unfolded before those parliamentarians was a complex social, economic, and political tapestry with a single unifying thread—growing Aboriginal poverty.

One of the darkest hues in that tapestry came from the fact that the main thrust of the colonial system's assimilative strategy had concentrated on the young, on the thousands of Thomas Moores, boys and girls, Indian, Métis, and Inuit, across the land. They were the vulnerable future of communities and of Aboriginal culture, and they had been removed from their homes and placed in the care of strangers, many of whom were hostile to their culture, beliefs, and language. For the sake of civilization, in the discharge of a national duty, they were placed in the residential schools. For those children and their communities and, indeed, for all Canadians, the consequence of those schools, of Thomas Moore's tuition, has been truly tragic.

Notes

1. For a review of Canadian policy see: J.L. Tobias, "Protection, Civilization, Assimilation: An Outline History of Canada's Indian Policy," in *As Long as the Sun Shines and Water Flows*, edited by I. Getty and A.S. Lussier (Vancouver: University of British Columbia Press, 1983); J.R. Miller, *Skyscrapers Hide the Heavens: A History of Indian/White Relations in Canada* (Toronto: University of Toronto Press, 1989); and O. Dickason, *Canada's First Nations: A History of Founding Peoples from Earliest Times* (Toronto: McClelland and Stewart, 1992).

2. *Annual Report of the Department of Indian Affairs* [hereinafter referred to as the Annual Report] 1911, 273.

3. N.A.C. RG 10, Vol. 6039, File 160-1, MR C 8152, F. Oliver to Joint Church Delegation.

4. *Annual Report* 1891, x.

5. A. Morris, *The Treaties of Canada with the Indians of Manitoba and the North-West Territories* (Toronto: Belfords, Clarke and Col. 1880), 278.

6. N.A.C. MG 27, I C4, E. Dewdney Papers, A. Lacombe to E. Dewdney, 25 November 1889, 2, 189–192.

7. As quoted in M. Montgomery, "The Six Nations and the Macdonald Franchise," *Ontario History* 57 (March 1965): 13.

8. INAC File 1/25-1. Vol. 15, L. Vankoughnet to Sir John A. Macdonald, 26 August 1887.

9. *Annual Report* 1890, xii.

10. *The Davin Report,* 1–17.

11. See for example: J. Barman, Y. Hébert, and D. McCaskill, "The Legacy of the Past: An Overview," in *Indian Education in Canada*, edited by J.

Barman, Y. Hébert, and D. McCaskill, vol. 1: *The Legacy* (Vancouver: University of British Columbia Press, 1986), 6.

12. J. Leslie and R. Macguire, eds., *The Historical Development of the Indian Act* (Ottawa: Depart-

ment of Indian and Northern Affairs Canada, 1979), 133.

13. J. Taylor, *Canadian Indian Policy during the Inter-War Years, 1919–1939* (Ottawa: Indian and Northern Affairs Canada, 1983), 4.

■ Article 2: The Charge of Manslaughter: Disease and Death, 1879–1946

John Milloy

The provisions of the 1911 contract and the discussions during the negotiating sessions make it clear that there was a crisis in conditions, sanitation, and health in the schools. Neither the Department nor the churches could have pretended otherwise. Dr. P. Bryce's first report was published in 1907 just as the discussions were about to get under way, and another report, by F.H. Paget, a Departmental accountant, which was highly critical of the condition of school buildings, came to hand in 1908. The Honourable S.H. Blake, a lawyer conducting a review of Anglican mission work, who was an influential force in the negotiations, characterized the situation in the schools for the Minister, Frank Oliver, in the most blunt fashion: "The appalling number of deaths among the younger children appeals loudly to the guardians of our Indians. In doing nothing to obviate the preventable causes of death, brings the Department within unpleasant nearness to the charge of manslaughter."[1]

The residential school system began its drift to that "unpleasant nearness" right from its inception. The "appalling number of deaths among the younger children" was the result of removing children, as Blake explained to the minister, from a healthy "out of door life" to the confines of badly constructed schools made worse over time by neglectful and inadequately funded maintenance programs. Perhaps even more pertinent, careless administration of health regulations, a lack of adequate medical services and

the effect on children of the harsh and alien routines of education added their deadly weight.

In those hundreds or thousands of deaths (extant records do not allow an accurate count)[2] the churches, Department and government shared complicity.[3] The disease and deaths and the cause of them were known to all. Indian Agent MacArthur commented, in 1910, in view of the situation at Duck Lake, where he estimated that, in the past, nearly fifty percent of the children sent to the school died: "[No one] responsible can get beyond the fact that those children catch the disease while at school" confined for months on end "in a building whose every seam and crevice is, doubtless, burdened with Tuberculosis Baccilli."[4] To those entering the circle of civilization for the first time, the all-too-common conditions could be a shock. For the new Principal of Red Deer school, Dr. J.P. Rice, arriving in 1903 from his comfortable Toronto parish, "the sight of the ragged ill-kempt and sickly looking children was sufficient to make me sick at heart." Enrollment was down due to deaths, the removal of children by their parents, and because the "sanitary conditions of the buildings are exceedingly bad."[5]

It all began with the buildings. Those many schools that were opened by the churches in advance of government grants were routinely "erected on very primitive plans"[6] by amateurs without the guidance of professional architects.[7] They often received grants sight unseen, without any Departmental inspection, and despite the fact that senior officials, like Scott, admitted that they were "intensely apprehensive" about the quality and safety of church-built structures.[8] This was such a common concern that Hayter Reed, when drafting the 1894 regulations, included a proposal that the Department, before any grant was authorized, should have the right to inspect the plans or, if already built, the school premises.[9] Such a regulation, had it been adopted and enforced, may well have been useful for when schools were finally visited; the Department discovered, in some instances, that their decision to proceed had not been wise.[10]

Source: John S. Milloy, *A National Crime: The Canadian Government and the Residential School System, 1879–1986*. Winnipeg: University of Manitoba Press, 1999, pp. 77–107. Reprinted with permission.

The Department's own record was not a great deal better, however. Benson, in a general assessment of the school system in 1897, pulled no punches: "The buildings have been put up without due consideration for the purpose for which they would be required, hurriedly constructed of poor materials, badly laid out without due provision for lighting, heating or ventilating."[11]

From the outset, schools had been built with an eye to economy. E. Dewdney, who supervised the construction of the first three industrial schools in the west, insisted that they be of the "simplest and cheapest construction." Putting them near railway lines would facilitate the acquisition of construction materials and supplies. In the course of time, he reasoned, with the growth of settlement, construction costs would drop and the schools could be upgraded.[12] That was, it turned out, a foolish assumption. The trains, when they came, brought settlers, but certainly no federal funds for reconstructing schools.

[…]

It is important (and it illustrates the range of problems, rooted in construction deficiencies, siting, and short budgets) to give some indication of the degree of crisis that existed in the fabric of the residential school system as a whole. Moreover, it is important to give an indication of how conscious officials in the Department were, or could have been, of the situation.

A single report, submitted in 1908 by F.H. Paget, an accountant with the Department, gives some sense both of the scope of the problem and of senior Departmental staff's awareness of it. The report was commissioned by the Department during the negotiations for the contracts when information on the condition of the system was vital. It amounted to a review of a cross-section of nearly one-third of the system including both industrial and boarding schools.

[…]

Paget's report revealed that the schools ran the gamut from good to deplorable. The majority—fifteen out of the twenty-one—were in the latter category. He was impressed with the Qu'Appelle School, which was rebuilt after its fire "with all the modern conveniences." Lacombe's High River School "was splendidly conducted,…neat and clean." He was impressed most with the Duck Lake Boarding School, despite what Indian Agent MacArthur said only two years later

about its historic fifty-percent death rate: "Excellent order, neat and clean throughout, [and] very much a self-contained institution, all clothing being made, and meats, roots, grains and vegetable raised."

All of this was overshadowed by Paget's descriptions of schools that did not pass muster. Not surprisingly, Regina and Red Deer topped the industrial school list. Red Deer was "not modern in any respect." Regina was a sorrowful school: "Driving up it looked more like a deserted place than a Government Institution," The "building is old and the floors are worn, the plaster broken and marked in places and the paint worn off." The children "did not have that clean and neat appearance that was in evidence at other schools."

[…]

Finally, the report indicated what was by 1908 a commonplace, the connection between the condition of the schools and the ill health of children, particularly through tubercular infection. Though Paget covered much of the same ground as Bryce's report of the year before had, he had not been directed to check the doctor's findings. He was, however, certainly familiar with Bryce's report and even referred to it obliquely in his description of Old Sun's Boarding School, which he "found to be all that had been said of it by others in regard to being unsanitary and the building unsuitable in every way for such an institution." In addition, he brought forward similar observations of other schools.[13]

The Department, of course, was fully aware, before either the *Bryce Report* or the *Paget Report*, of the plague of tuberculosis affecting the Aboriginal population and the fact that it had insinuated itself into the schools. The tubercular epidemic, which had moved across the country with the tide of settlement, was the result of white presence coupled with the Aboriginal community's lack of immunity to infectious diseases. It was also, however, a consequence of the process of colonization, of the forces that marginalized communities, divorcing them from their traditional life ways. Confinement to reserves and overcrowded European-style lodgings of the lowest quality provided the fertile ground with malnutrition, lack of sanitation, despair, alcoholism, and government parsimony, from which the infection ran its mortal course through communities.

The impact of tuberculosis, statistically expressed, was out of all proportion to the size of the Aboriginal

359

population. A study by Bryce revealed that the rate of tubercular infection for Indians was one in seven "and the death rates in several large bands 81.8, 81.2, and in a third 86.1 per thousand." The "ordinary death rate for 115,000 in the city of Hamilton was 10.6 in 1921."[14]

The tubercular bacilli infested the body in a multitude of manifestations. "Contracted in infancy [it] creates diseases of the brain [tubercular meningitis], joints, bones and to a less degree the lungs [pulmonary tuberculosis or consumption] and ...if not fatal till adolescence it then usually progresses rapidly to a fatal termination in consumption of the lungs."[15] It was signalled by a wide range of symptoms: head and joint aches, pain in breathing, and glandular swelling and eruption (scrofula) being some of the more common ones. In its most contagious phase, that is, consumption, coughing and spitting blood or sputum spread the infection to others; and fever, weakness, and wasting led to death.

One mode of transmission that particularly affected the children in the schools was drinking milk infected with bovine tuberculosis. Industrial and boarding schools kept cows, and the children routinely drank unpasteurized milk. As with the school buildings, the outbuildings for livestock were often a problem. The principal of St. George's School in Lytton, for example, was told by the Department of Agriculture that he would have to pull down his barn because it was a log structure and could not be disinfected. The school had lost eighteen head of cattle in the previous three years.[16]

Not only was it impossible to isolate the schools from the epidemic, but, as well, the schools themselves were expeditors; they aggravated the problem by simulating in an exaggerated fashion many of those problematic conditions that affected reserve communities.[17]

[...]

The root of overcrowded dorms and classrooms, as with the deteriorating condition of school buildings, could be traced back to funding arrangements and particularly to the per-capita system. The critical need that principals had to maintain high enrollments to qualify for the full grant that had been assigned to their school led to practices that contributed directly to the health problem. Pushing enrollments to and past the point of overcrowding was one of these. The Crowfoot School in 1909 provided a striking example

of this. In that year, Duncan Campbell Scott, then the Department's Chief Accountant, had before him a request from the principal for more students and information supplied by Benson that the dormitories were overcrowded and the ventilation was poor. Scott told the deputy superintendent, rather angrily, that of the fifty-two pupils that had been in the school since it had been in receipt of grants eight years earlier, eight had died, seven of those in the school and the other within a month of leaving. Of the thirty-nine children in the school who had been examined in the previous few months by Dr. J.D. Lafferty, twenty-two were infected with tuberculosis in the lungs:

This is what we have to show for an expenditure of $15,611. The outlook for the remaining pupils in attendance is not very bright and there is very little hope that the graduates of the School will attain maturity and be able to exercise any civilizing influence....The accommodation at the School is inadequate for the number of pupils in residence, and the unhealthy pupils should be discharged.[18]

Principals, of course, were contending with problems flowing directly from just the sort of funding that Scott referred to. As the per-capita ceiling remained stubbornly unchanged at $72 until 1911, they could increase their grant only by having their authorized student number raised. Annually, the Department was besieged with such requests. Additionally, principals had to strive to recruit up to the maximum number authorized, which might already have been a figure that permitted the overcrowding of the living spaces of the school, as was evident in the case of Crowfoot and many other schools.

The pressure that principals worked under to secure adequate funds meant that there was a tendency to be less than careful about the condition of the children they brought into the school. In 1907, the Anglican bishop of Caledonia wanted to turn over Metlakatla to government control because of the anxiety, and perhaps the moral disquiet, that he felt over recruitment. He admitted candidly: "The per capita grant system encourages the taking in of those physically and intellectually unfit simply to keep up numbers."[19]

[...]

Of course, neither the principals nor the churches were solely responsible for the schools. If school administrators were driven into excess by funding needs and led there by missionary zeal, they were not restrained in any effective way by the Department. The 1892 and 1894 Orders-in-Council and the 1911 contracts established the government's responsibility for providing medical services to the schools and the Department's right to inspect the schools was made a condition of the grant. Regulations were issued in 1894 and retained, throughout the period, stipulating that children had to have a medical certificate signed by a doctor before admission.[20]

Unfortunately, the implementation of those regulations left much to be desired. There was no regular inspection of the schools nor any guarantee that forms were being filled in or doctors consulted. In 1909, the Departmental secretary sent out new admission and certificate-of-health forms, which he thought were "sufficiently stringent to guard against tubercular children being taken into the school." They were not enough, however, to keep Louise Plaited Hair out of St. Mary's Boarding School on the Blood Reserve. Her form was signed by Dr. O. Edwards and accepted without question by the Department, in 1911, despite the fact that there was evidence that she had contracted tuberculosis. To a question that asked if there were signs of scrofula or other forms of tubercular disease, Edwards had written, "Glands on right neck slightly enlarged."[21]

According to Scott, when he reviewed the situation with other senior officials in 1925, Louise represented hundreds who had been admitted despite the regulations. The "indiscriminate admission of children without first passing a medical examination" continued. It was not only the principals, he realized, but "our own officers who are picking up orphans, delinquents and others, that are causing the difficulty, as occasionally no application forms are forwarded." There had to be, as well, "more careful checking of the medical officers' remarks in the case of all applicants."[22]

The administrative difficulties identified in Scott's review encompassed more, however, than lax implementation of regulations by officials or attempts to evade those regulations by principals desperate to keep up enrollments. The system simply did not have the medical support that the Department was pledged to provide and that was required to properly protect the children and attend to their health needs.[23] That tragic omission had to be laid on the Department's doorstep.

The scope of this tragedy was measured in 1907 by Dr. P.H. Bryce, then the "Medical Inspector to the Department of the Interior and Indian Affairs." He had been appointed to that position in 1904 after a career in public health with the Ontario government. In February 1907, the Deputy Superintendent, F. Pedley, directed him to inspect the schools in the west, reporting particularly on "the sanitary conditions at each of these schools."[24] After visiting thirty-five schools, he submitted his report in November. It was printed and distributed to members of Parliament and to the churches.

[…]

The impact of the report lay not in his narrative of the disease nor in its scientific tone. It was the statistical profile of the extent of the white plague among the children that projected the stunning gravity of his findings.[25] It was the stuff of headlines. The *Ottawa Citizen* on 16 November ran its story of the report under the banner: "Schools Aid White Plague—Startling Death Rolls Revealed among Indians—Absolute Inattention to Bare Necessities of Health."

The article published by *Saturday Night* on the twenty-third of that same month screamed just as loudly. The report should "startle the country" and "compel the attention of Parliament….Indian boys and girls are dying like flies in these situations or shortly after leaving them….Even war seldom shows as large a percentage of fatalities as does the education system we have imposed on our Indian wards." It revealed "a situation disgraceful to the country."[26]

Bryce's statistics were based upon questionnaires that he distributed to all thirty-five schools eliciting the health history of the children who were then, or had been, in the schools. He received only fifteen replies, all from boarding schools founded between 1888 and 1905. Nevertheless, he was convinced that he had "valuable information and food for thought." The information related to the history of 1,537 children. Of these, twenty-four percent had died. Invariably, the cause of death is given as "consumption or tuberculosis," and just as regularly, whenever an answer was given to the question "Condition of the child on entry?," it is "given as good."

The situation was even worse, however, than his initial calculations suggested. The death rate inevitably moved beyond the twenty-four percent mark. Close analysis by Bryce of some of the returns revealed "an intimate relationship between the health of the pupils while in the school and their early death subsequent to discharge." For example, of the thirty-one pupils who had been discharged from the File Hills Boarding School, fifteen left in coffins. An additional seven died from within a few months to three years after returning home. In total, seventy-five percent of those on the discharge roll were actually dead. When the File Hills ratios are applied to Bryce's sample of 1,537 children, it results in an increase from twenty-four percent to forty-two percent as the percentage of those children who died from their school experience. Assuming that these ratios were constant, and projecting them throughout the system in 1907, when there were 3,755 students in the schools, would mean that some 1,614 of those children would die prematurely. And every year more children came into the schools and more became infected.[27]

[...]

With the *Bryce Report* in hand and corroborative comments from local agents, it is not surprising that the Church and Department negotiations turned to the question of the tuberculosis epidemic in the negotiations that took place between 1908 and 1910. In fact, the *Report* had carried recommendations for the reform of the school system. These urged the government to press on with residential education with the stress on reserve-based boarding schools, to place the management of the schools wholly in Departmental hands, relegating the churches to an advisory capacity, and to insure that "the health interests of the pupils be guarded by a proper medical inspection and that the local physicians be encouraged through the provision at each school of fresh air methods in the care and treatment of cases of tuberculosis."[28] Bryce's recommendation of "fresh air methods" was shorthand for sanatoria. This would have been a very expensive approach to the problem necessitating considerable remodelling of buildings and high levels of medical staffing.[29]

Not surprisingly, perhaps, the contract took a different approach,[30] with regulations aimed at improving the medical screening of children entering the schools, ending overcrowding and suggested revisions to the funding system to facilitate better maintenance and improvements in the vital areas of ventilation, health and sanitation. That focus was laid out in a memorandum of agreement sent by the Departmental Secretary, J.D. McLean, to the church representatives who had met with Oliver in November 1910. The contract embodied the conditions upon which the increased grant was to be paid.

"Those conditions require that the school buildings shall be sanitary and that the school management shall be such as to conduce to the physical, moral and mental well-being of the children." The revised per-capita rates were designed to assist in that.

[...]

Unfortunately, the concern for the children reflected in the contract did not give any priority to the improvement of the condition of the schools. By the end of the First World War, it was "business as usual," business as it had been since the 1880s. In 1918, Duncan Campbell Scott briefed the Superintendent General, Arthur Meighen, on the state of Indian education. He reviewed the contract system, pointing out that one of its central purposes had been to deal with the "inadequate" buildings, which "were unsanitary and … were undoubtedly chargeable with a very high death rate among the pupils." For a few years after 1911, "until the outbreak of the war," the Department, he continued, "had been able to do its share" toward improving conditions. Then, "as the war continued[,] all new projects were abandoned."[31]

While the Department was able to hold the line on per-capita rates, and even managed a $10 advance in 1917, it lost ground in its attempt to fund improvements in the physical condition of the schools. Increasingly, the "circle of civilized conditions" was a crumbling edifice. If it had been Blake who briefed Meighen in 1918, he may well have added to Scott's commentary a sobering reflection; because the Department was still, a decade later, "doing nothing to obviate the preventable causes of death," it continued to be "within the unpleasant nearness to the charge of manslaughter."[32]

[...]

The Department, too, had it within its power to make a greater effort, if not through improved funding, at least through its authority. It could have insisted that its officials carry out inspections and that the churches follow regulations directed to the care of the children. It did not do so. The Departmental watch dog was far from vigilant; it rarely barked and, despite the conditions over which Bryce, Paget, Corbett, local doctors, and even senior Departmental officials had shaken their heads,[33] it certainly did not bite. Grants were not withdrawn, schools were not forced to close or principals to resign. The Orders-in-Council of 1892 and 1894 and the contracts of

1911 were in fact administrative fictions. They constituted powers, authorities, and agreements that did not facilitate effective, efficient, or even what seemed the most constant, goal—economical management.

The reality was that, from the moment the school system was launched in the 1880s and 1890s, it drifted without a firm hand, without concerted intervention. And this was despite the knowledge that many children were held in dangerous circumstances and that the death rate was not only of tragic proportions but was, in addition, undercutting the whole purpose and strategy of the system. Many, many children—perhaps as high as fifty percent according to Scott's estimate—would not "attain maturity and be able to exercise any civilizing influence" in their communities.[34]

A significant cause of this lay with personnel in the Department and in the churches involved directly in the management of the system. These many men and women failed to act decisively in the face of the suffering and death of so many children. They were not alone, however. They were joined in complicity and insensitivity by non-Aboriginal society as a whole. The devastation that the white plague brought to the children in the schools and through their deaths to their parents and communities drew out the fundamental contradiction between the persistent cruelty of the system and the discourse of duty, of the "sacred trust with which Providence has invested the country in the charge of and care for the aborigines committed to it."[35]

It was a contradiction that the country was not prepared to face, and did not in fact face, throughout the rest of this period to 1946. The editor of *Saturday Night* seemed to sense this contradiction from the very moment of the publication of the 1907 *Bryce Report*:

> His report is printed, many people will scan the title on the cover, some will open it, a few will read it and so the thing will drift along another year. And so with the next year and the year after. So will be the course of events...unless public opinion takes the question up and forces it to the front. Then Parliament will show a quick interest, pigeon holes will give up their dusty contents, medical officers will have a wealth of suggestions and the scandalous procession

of Indian children to school and on to the cemetery may possibly be stopped.[36]

Of course, none of those conditions was fulfilled. There was no "public opinion," Parliament showed no interest, quick or otherwise, and the children continued to go to the schools and to the schools' cemeteries, as Bryce's pamphlet in 1922 revealed.

In 1922, the issue of Aboriginal people had long since been swept into the darker reaches of national consciousness. The deaths, and the condition of the schools pricked no collective conscience, wrought no revolution in policy, or even any significant reformulation. Sir George Murray's comment in 1830 about the old Imperial policy was just as true nearly one century later. This federal policy "was persisted in...as a matter of routine, [rather] than upon any considered grounds of preference."[37] There was no reconsideration, no second thoughts, no questioning of the assumptions of assimilation or of residential schools as an appropriate method of achieving that end. There appeared to be no thought or reaction at all.

The "routine" of residential education after the industrial school era, in the years after 1923 through to 1946, simply persisted. Unlike so many children, the school system survived the tubercular infection. It even grew, if more slowly than in the initial decades in the life of the system. In 1923, there were seventy-two residential schools. That number grew to a high of eighty in 1931.[38] The number then gradually fell through closures, many because of fires, to seventy-five in 1943.

The much slower rate of growth after the First World War did not indicate any waning in the enthusiasm for expansion. Churches continued to push to open schools in the few remaining untapped educational areas.[39] There were simply not that many areas left. Departmental cooperation continued. Scott, himself, led the way in moving the system into one of those areas—the east, Quebec, and Nova Scotia. The first school commissioned in Quebec was the Anglican Fort George School followed by Fort George Roman Catholic School, and in Nova Scotia the first and only school was the Roman Catholic Shubenacadie School. Scott was particularly dedicated to this latter project: "When we have this school established," he wrote to the Catholic church in 1926, sounding more like Vankoughnet than himself, "one of the desires of my official life will have been accomplished."[40]

363

As well as there being but limited horizons by the 1920s, finance continued to be a restraint and a detrimental factor in the condition of existing schools. Wartime reductions, which had blighted the program of improvements of 1911, ushered in yet another era of underfunding. Initially after the war, there were advances in the level of per capitas. A $10 increase was authorized in 1919.[41] Other increases followed in 1921, 1924, 1926, and 1931, moving the average per capita to $172.[42] These increases were never enough, however, to satisfy the churches' appetites for government funds nor to prevent them from again "encountering huge deficits."[43]

With the Depression, the situation got worse because, as the minister responsible for Indian Affairs, T.G. Murphy, phrased it, the "financial condition of the country [was] such that economies" were then "imposed on" the government.[44] In 1932, it was "found necessary … to make a flat decrease in per capita grants." Other cuts followed.[45] In 1938, the Committee of Churches Cooperating with the Department of Indian Affairs calculated that between 1932 and 1938 the reductions amounted to a $840,000 loss to the churches.[46]

The Department put the best public face on the situation.[47] Privately, senior staff knew that the per-capita average, claimed to be still about $180 in 1938, was "exceptionally low" and inadequate particularly in relation to the funding available to other residential child-care facilities. R. Hoey, the Department's Superintendent of Welfare and Training, supplied H. McGill, the Director of Indian Affairs, with revealing comparative figures. The government of Manitoba provided per-capita grants of $642 and $550 respectively to the Manitoba School for the Deaf and the School for Boys. Private institutions in that Province were also more generously funded. The Knowles School for Boys in North Kildonan was sponsored by the Community Chest at $362 per boy. The Catholic Church provided St. Norbert's Orphanage with $294 and St. Joseph's Orphanage with a $320 per-capita grant. Finally, an international comparison was not in the Department's favour either. The child Welfare League of America estimated that the average per-capita grant in the United States of large child-care institutions was $541, with the smaller ones running only as low as $313.[48]

The Second World War pulled the country out of the deep economic trough of the Depression, but it brought no benefits to the school system. Wartime military expenditures meant reductions "to almost every appropriation"[49] for the Department and a building freeze. In the face of this, Hoey realized that it would be "exceedingly difficult to secure the funds necessary …at any time during the years that [lay] immediately ahead."[50]

The persistence of underfunding undercut the maintenance and repair of buildings. Under the terms of the 1911 contracts, the Department had been charged with that expense, and, even after the contracts lapsed, it agreed to continue.[51] Indeed, in the relatively optimistic days following the First World War, the policy of the Department was to buy up the church schools and then to be responsible for all capital costs including repairs and new construction.[52] Scott went so far as to propose that the cost of purchasing all the church-owned schools be placed in the supplementary estimates in order that the whole matter "may receive the careful consideration of the government."[53] This would have meant acquiring forty-three of the seventy-five schools then operating in 1922.

The Department's promise and Scott's proposal remained good intentions only. In the early years of the Depression, expenditures (combining the per-capita grants and capital funds) fell from an average of $28,000 per school to $16,000.

By the Second World War, the Department was so far behind that Hoey and P. Phelan, Chief of the Training Division, estimated that they had less than half the funds necessary to meet repair commitments.[54] McGill admitted, in fact, that they had "been experiencing for the [previous] 10 or 12 years the utmost difficulty in securing the funds necessary to keep [the] schools in a state of repair."[55] They were not, he concluded, being maintained "in a reasonable state."[56]

As in the industrial school era, the net result of underfunding could be seen both in the condition of the schools and in the care given to the children. The building stock was in poor shape at the outset. A Departmental survey in 1922 concluded that of the seventy-five schools the great majority were not "modern up to date buildings in good condition," nor were they "adequate for the purpose of Indian education." A smaller number were condemned as "dilapidated and inadequate."[57]

Needless to say, the condition of the system was not improved by the reductions in funding in the 1930s and the wartime freeze. In 1931, one of the system's flagship schools, Shingwauk, was condemned.[58] Long lists of repairs from every corner of the system were submitted and ignored, as were pleas for urgent assistance.[59]

Bad and badly maintained buildings continued to translate into bad health.[60] However, the extent of the tuberculosis problem in the schools in the 1930s and 1940s is hard to assess. There were no reports of the scope or calibre of the Bryce or Corbett reports. Routine agents' reports, which are the most common documentation, are of limited value because agents were not trained medical observers. In many cases, however, the condition of the children was sorrowfully obvious even to such amateurs.[61]

It was obvious, too, from those reports that the Department's administrative system regarding health certificates was still far from watertight. Dr. C. Pitts, who attended the children at Lejac School in British Columbia, certainly held that position. He had special knowledge of the school system because his father was a long-serving principal, and he had friends who were school doctors. He went so far, in 1935, as to suggest that the regulations were a farce and their enforcement a practical impossibility: "As for the general medical examination…this is not done in any other school that I have any knowledge of….Where is the point of this [examination], when I know that were I to apply the standards of health to them that is applied to children of the white schools that I should have to discharge 90% of them and there would be no school left."[62]

An equally serious impediment to any attempt to care for the health of the children was the inability of the Department to acquire funds to underwrite attacks on tuberculosis in the schools. Only at the end of the 1930s did funding for sanatoria treatment appear, and that was largely owing to pressure from the Canadian Tuberculosis Association. No special funds were set aside especially for the schools, however.[63]

The 1920s, 1930s, and 1940s had more in common with the previous Industrial era than underfunding, the woeful condition of the buildings, and the infection and death of children from tuberculosis. Connected to each of these issues, nested in reports on them, is another persistence: abundant evidence of the failure of the churches and the Department to adequately parent these children, to operate institutions that were above reproach as homes and as

schools. In part, this was again due to the issue of finance. Whenever correspondence turned to the per capitas or maintenance funds, someone was bound to point out that this affected the children, that it would "render almost superhuman the task of feeding, clothing and treating the children in the manner required by the Department."[64] And there were numerous reports from schools confirming this. Principals were forced to meet budget shortfalls, as the Principal of Christie School in British Columbia, Victor Rassier, O.S.B., had had to do, "by economizing to the bone in every department."[65] And Agent J. Smith at Kamloops School stated: "If the children are to be kept they ought to be reasonably clothed and fed, and it is utterly impossible to do from the present per capita grant."[66]

But the failure to care properly for the children was rooted in more than the issue of funding, and in more than just the difficulties of building and managing the system. The "manner required by the Department [for] feeding clothing and treating the children,"[67] a standard of care, was both an ill-defined and a rarely achieved goal. Bryce, Paget, and Corbett stand as witnesses to the inherent structural flaws in the system. The Reverend Thompson Ferrier comes forward to add to their witness the human failings and the resultant suffering of the children who were neglected by Departmental-church "parents," cruel or incompetent, who presumed that they should and could supplant the childrens' natural Aboriginal parents but who did not consistently carry out their parenting responsibilities.

In July 1925, just three years after Bryce's *Story of a National Crime* was published, Ferrier, who had then been in charge of Methodist industrial and boarding schools and hospitals for twenty-five years, set down on paper his memory of a cross-country tour of those schools when he first took up his position. Only Coqualeetza School in British Columbia was, in his opinion, in good order. The others were not circles of civilized conditions:

> Mount Elgin Institute at Muncey looms up in memory with its untidy yard and a lot of old sheds, outbuildings and dilapidated barns that had passed their day all unconscious of their need of repairs and paint. The main building had accommodation for about one hundred pupils who were receiving such

365

harsh treatment as to call forth numerous complaints from the Indian people and the Indian department. Several attempts were made on the part of the pupils to burn up the whole business all because it was under the management of a man who had the idea that physical strength was to take the place of what ought to be done by the heart and head in educating and training young life, who believed that it was safer to deal with the hide than the honour of the pupil and a man who took more interest in hydraulics than hygiene.

When Ferrier got to Brandon, he found ninety children who seemed to have the upper hand. They were "destructive, untrained young men and women from thirteen to twenty-three years of age. They were having their own way, smashing everything they could not eat or wear and running roughshod over a discouraged staff. It looked as though the institution had fallen into a pit and was waiting for someone to come and give it a decent burial."

At Norway House, they had a poor barn shaped building with broken doors, worn out floors, no modern conveniences of plumbing, heating or lighting, a cold shell of a place with partial accommodation for about thirty-five pupils who were obliged to live without a balanced ration as there was no garden, poultry or stock. An incompetent staff were trying to penetrate the stronghold of heathenism with the belief that the problem would never be solved. Red Deer was no better. The school comprised a miserable lot of buildings, the boys home being very dark and unsanitary. There was a stable for horses but none for stock. The management was unconscious of the great possibilities of the rich fertile land of the farm and the opportunity presented as a training school for farmers and stockmen. For many reasons the whole institution was very unpopular with the Indian people of Alberta. The office appeared to be used more for a real estate business than to make a contribution toward civilizing and educating the people.

Finally, Ferrier went to the west coast and to Port Simpson, where they "had twenty boys housed in a building and under a management that was a disgrace to the Methodist church."[68]

As had been the case with all the previous reports (Bryce's, Paget's, and Corbett's), none of the conditions described by Ferrier was news to the Department or the churches. They already had a flood of evidence, a spate that continued through to and beyond 1946, that indicated that in too many cases the children were not being adequately fed, clothed, or taught and that discipline often crossed the line into abuse. The vision of life and learning in the "circle of civilized conditions" had not become a reality. The promise that children would receive the "care of a mother"[69] and an education that would elevate the child "to a status equal to that of his white brother" remained unfulfilled.[70]

Notes

1. Anglican Archives, MSCC, Series 2-14, Special Indian Committee, 1905–1910, S.H. Blake to the Hon. Frank Oliver, Minister of the Interior, Sunday Morning, 27 January 1907, printed in *To the Members of the Board of Management of the Missionary Society of the Church of England in Canada*, by The Hon. S.H. Blake, K.C., 21.

2. Given the incomplete state of student records in the school files, it is impossible to arrive at the number of deaths from disease in the schools in any year or decade. Later in the chapter, a sense of how "appalling" the number was is given through percentages supplied in large part by Dr. Bryce. In light of the anecdotal evidence, Bryce's figures seem to have been supported generally by Departmental staff and to have applied nation-wide.

3. There is no statistical base for determining the number of children who died from disease in the schools. The Bryce Report of 1907 gives some indication of death rates when tuberculosis was most rampant (N.A.C. RG10, Vol. 4037, File 317021, MR C 10177, P. Bryce. Report on the Indian Schools of Manitoba and the Northwest Territories, Ottawa, Government Printing Bureau, 1907).

4. N.A.C. RG 10, Vol. 6305, File 652-1, MR C 8682, Agent MacArthur to Secretary, 27 December 1910. To be fair, some children came to school already infected, having contracted the disease in

over-crowded and squalid living conditions in their reserve homes.

5. N.A.C. RG 10. Vol. 3920, File 116818, MR C 10161, Dr. J.P. Rice to C. Sifton, 3 August 1903: M. Benson to Deputy Superintendent General of Indian Affairs, 9 September 1903.

6. N.A.C. RG 10, Vol. 7185, File 1/25-1-7-1, D.C. Scott to Hon. Charles Stewart, 31 October 1927.

7. N.A.C. RG 10, Vol. 4037, File 317021, MR C 10177, D. Laird to Secretary of Indian Affairs, 7 December 1907.

8. N.A.C. RG 10, Vol. 7185, File 1/25-1-7-1, D.C. Scott to Hon. Charles Stewart, 31 October 1927.

9. N.A.C. RG 10, Vol. 3836, File 68557, MR C 10146, H. Reed, Suggestions for the Government of Indian Schools, 27 January 1890.

10. N.A.C. RG 10, Vol. 6467, File 889-1 (1-2), MR C 8785, C. Perry to Dr. H. McGill, 25 May 1900. The Squamish school was a case in point. It was built by the Catholic missionary and funded in 1900 after a direct appeal to Clifford Sifton by the local member of Parliament and the Catholic bishop. It was, when inspected by the Assistant Indian Commissioner of British Columbia, C. Perry, shortly after its opening, in such ramshackle condition that Perry thought it should be closed immediately.

11. N.A.C. RG 10, Vol. 6039, File 160-1, MR C 8152, M. Benson to J.D. McLean, 15 July 1897.

12. N.A.C. RG 10, Vol. 3674, File 11422, MR C 10118, E. Dewdney to Father Lacombe, 22 July 1883; and E. Dewdney to Superintendent General of Indian Affairs, 16 April 1883.

13. N.A.C. RG 10, Vol. 4041, File 334503, MR C 10178, E.H. Paget to F. Pedley, 25 November 1908.

14. Bryce, *The Story of a National Crime*, 11. The Canadian Tuberculosis Association circulated figures that detailed the percentage of Aboriginal tuberculosis deaths by province compared to their percentage of the population. In Manitoba, of the total deaths, forty-one percent were Aboriginal, though Aboriginal people made up only 2.2 percent of the population; in Saskatchewan it was twenty-seven percent of the deaths and 1.6 percent of the population; in Alberta it was thirty-four percent of the deaths and 2.1 percent of the population; and in British Columbia it was thirty-five percent of the deaths and 3.7 percent of the population (Wherrit, *The Miracle of Empty Beds*, 110).

15. Bryce, *The Story of a National Crime*, 11.

16. Wherrit, *The Miracle of Empty Beds*, 16–17; and N.A.C. RG 10, Vol. 6462, File 888-1 (2-3, 6-7), MR C8781, Rev. A. Lett to D.C. Scott, 6 March 1922.

17. Wherrit, *The Miracle of Empty Beds*, 16-17 and 100-103.

18. N.A.C. RG 10, Vol. 6348, File 752-1, MR C 8705, D.C. Scott to Deputy Superintendent General of Indian Affairs, 23 April 1909.

19. N.A.C. RG 10, Vol. 3937, File 120048-1, MR C 10164, Bishop of Caledonia, to A. Vowell, 11 November 1907.

20. See, for example, N.A.C. RG 10, Vol. 6210, File 469-1 (1-3), MR C 7941, Deputy Superintendent General of Indian Affairs to J. Lawlor, 8 November 1894.

21. N.A.C. RG 10, Vol. 1543 [no file number], MR C 14839, J.D. McLean to R. Wilson, 2 October 1909; and D. Laird to R. Wilson, 7 March 1911 (Application for Admission attached).

22. N.A.C. RG 10, Vol. 6015, File 1-1-13. MR C 8141, D.C. Scott to W. Graham, 16 February 1925.

23. See, for example, the explanation from a field official citing the lack of doctors in remote areas as the reason for non-compliance with the medical regulations: N.A.C. RG 10, Vol. 6015, File 1-1-13, MR C 8141, Acting Agent to R. Ferrier, 9 March 1925.

24. N.A.C. RG 10, Vol. 4037, File 317021, MR C 10177, Deputy Superintendent General of Indian Affairs to J.D. McLean, 14 February 1907.

25. N.A.C. RG 10, Vol. 4037, File 317021, MR C 10177, P. Bryce, *Report on the Indian Schools,* 1907, 17–19.

26. N.A.C. RG 10, Vol. 4037, File 317021, MR C 10177. Copies of stories in the *Citizen,* 16 November 1907, and *Saturday Night,* 23 November 1907, as well as the *Montreal Star,* 15 November 1907, are in this file.

27. N.A.C. RG 10, Vol. 4037, File 317021, MR C 10177, P. Bryce, *Report on the Indian Schools*, 1907, 17–20.

28. Bryce, *The Story of a National Crime,* 4.

29. N.A.C. RG 10, Vol. 6039, File 160-1, MR C 8152, Bishop of St. Boniface et al. to R. Rogers, 24 November 1911 and 15 November 1912. Bryce's recommendations may also have been sidelined in the negotiations by political considerations. The Catholic church was opposed to many of the reforms—Bryce's and even some of those eventually included in the contracts. The schools, the church charged, were being "submitted to vexatious requirements by physicians, whose interests therein appear to have been in large measure confined to making unnecessary demands."

367

30. For further details on the government's approach, see N.A.C. RG 10, Vol. 6039, File 160-1, MR C 8152, F. Oliver to Reverend and Dear Sirs, 21 March 1908. See particularly Oliver's discussion of Winnipeg Resolution No. 7.

31. N.A.C. RG 10, Vol. 6001, File 1-1-1 (1), MR C 8134, D.C. Scott to A. Meighen, n.d. January 1918. The effect of the war on expenditures was dramatic. In 1914, the Department spent on average $8,684 on each boarding school and $16,146 on each of the remaining industrial schools. In 1918, those figures had fallen to $5,738 and $12,338 respectively. Total expenditures for the system fell by thirty-three percent from $811,764 to $542,568.

32. Anglican Archives, MSCC, Series 2-14, Special Indian Committee, 1905–1910, S.H. Blake to the Honourable Frank Oliver, Minister of the Interior, Sunday Morning, 27 January 1907, printed in To the Members of the Board of Management of the Missionary Society of the Church of England in Canada, by The Hon. S.H. Blake, K.C., 21.

33. See, for example, correspondence on the Chapleau School: N.A.C. RG 10, Vol. 6191, File 462-1, MR C 7926, J.D. McLean to Rev. J. Anderson, 29 December 1914; Extract of Inspection Report by W. Hamilton, 3 May 1915; and J. Sheahan, M.D., to J.D. McLean, 2 July 1917. See also the correspondence relating to St. Cyprians: N.A.C. RG 10, Vol. 6368, File 763-1, MR C 8720, Assistant Deputy and Secretary to E. Yoemans, n.d. 1911; S. Stewart to Archdeacon J. Tims, n.d. 1911; J.D. McLean to Archdeacon J. Tims, 22 January 1913; J.D. McLean to Archdeacon J. Tims, 15 February 1913; J.D. McLean to A. Gunn, 15 February 1914; and W. Graham to Secretary, 21 July 1925.

34. N.A.C. RG 10, Vol. 6348, File 752-1, MR C 8705, D.C. Scott to Deputy Superintendent General of Indian Affairs, 23 April 1909.

35. *Annual Report* 1891, x.

36. N.A.C. RG 10, Vol. 4037, File 317021, *Saturday Night*, 23 November 1907.

37. N.A.C. C.O. 42/27, G. Murray to J. Kempt (No. 95), 25 January 1830.

38. There was then one school in Nova Scotia, thirteen in Ontario, ten in Manitoba, fourteen in Saskatchewan, twenty in Alberta, sixteen in British Columbia, four in the Northwest Territories, two in the Yukon, and plans for two schools in Quebec.

39. See, for example, N.A.C. RG 10, Vol. 6040, File 160-3A, Part 1, MR C 8153, Rev. T. Ferrier to D.C. Scott, 8 July 1920.

40. N.A.C. RG 10, Vol. 6041, File 160-5, Part 1, D.C. Scott to J. Guy, 11 July 1926. See Appendix, p. 307 herein, for school list, 1931.

41. N.A.C. RG 10, Vol. 6039, File 160-1, MR C 8152, J.D. McLean to Sir James Lougheed, 24 August 1920.

42. N.A.C. RG 10, Vol. 6040, File 160-3, Part 1, MR C 8153, Rev. T. Ferrier to D.C. Scott, 6 December 1921; and Vol. 7185, File 1/25-1-7-1, R.T. Ferrier, Superintendent of Eduacation, Memorandum to File, 5 April 1932.

43. N.A.C. RG 10, Vol. 6040, File 160-3A, Part 1, MR C 8153, Joint Church Delegation to Minister of the Interior, 7 January 1921; Canon S. Gould to D.C. Scott, 23 September 1924; D.C. Scott to C. Stewart, 7 March 1927; and Memorandum to File, 8 February 1926.

44. N.A.C. RG 10, Vol. 6730, File 160-2 (1-3), MR C 8092, T.G. Murphy to Canon S. Gould, 26 April 1931.

45. N.A.C. RG 10, Vol. 7185, File 1/25-7-1, R.T. Ferrier, Memorandum to File, 5 April 1932; and N.A.C. RG 10, Vol. 6041, File 160-5 Part 1, MR C 8153, H. McGill to Rev. J. Scannell, O.M.I., 17 February 1936; and Vol. 7185, File 1/25-1-7-1, Deputy Superintendent General of Indian Affairs, Circular, 26 March 1936.

46. United Church Archives, WMS Fonds, Accession 83.058C, File 3, Memorandum of the Committee of Churches Cooperating with the Department of Indian Affairs in Indian Education, 8 February 1938.

47. N.A.C. RG 10, Vol. 7185, File 1/25-1-7-1. R. Hoey to H. McGill, 4 November 1938.

48. N.A.C. RG 10, Vol. 7185, File 1/25-1-7-1, R. Hoey to H. McGill, 4 November 1938. Hoey provided additional figures that were equally depressing. The Children's Aid Society of Alberta estimated that the minimum per-day maintenance cost for a neglected child was $1. The Ontario figure was slightly lower at seventy-five cents, Manitoba was between sixty-three and seventy-two cents, B.C. was at fifty-seven cents and Saskatchewan was at fifty cents. This worked out to an average of seventy cents. The Department's national average, using its $180 figure, was forty-nine cents, and it was supposed to cover more than just food and clothes.

49. N.A.C. RG 10, Vol. 6041, File 160-5, Part 1, MR C 8153, R. Hoey to Rev. J. Plourde, 15 October 1940.

50. N.A.C. RG 10, Vol. 6730, File 160-2 (1-3), MR C 8092, Director of Indian Affairs to Rev. T. Westgate, n.d. 1940.

51. N.A.C. RG 10, Vol. 6041, File 160-5, Part 1, MR C 8153, D.C. Scott to Charles Stewart, 7 March 1922.

52. N.A.C. RG 10, Vol. 6039, File 160-1, MR C 8152, R.F. Ferrier, Memornadum—Impression of the Interview between Church Representatives and the Superintendent General, 13 April 1922.

53. N.A.C. RG 10, Vol. 6041, File 160-5, Part 1, MR C 8153, D.C. Scott to Charles Stewart, 7 March 1922.

54. N.A.C. RG 10, Vol. 6479, File 940-1 (1-2), MR C 8794, R. Hoey to H. McGill, 16 November 1942.

55. N.A.C. RG 10, Vol. 6479, File 940-1 (1-2), H. McGill to Rev. W. Geddes, 21 November 1942.

56. N.A.C. RG 10, Vol. 6482, File 941-2, MR C 8796, H. McGill to Rev. J. Plourde, 15 February 1940.

57. N.A.C. RG 10, Vol. 6039, File 160-1, MR C 8152, R.F. Ferrier to Charles Stewart 12 May 1922.

58. N.A.C. RG 10, Vol. 6730, File 160-2 (1-3), MR C 8092, Rev. T. Westgate to Secretary, 29 October 1931. It did not, however, close.

59. See, for example, the plight of the Catholic Sturgeon Lake School in: N.A.C. RG 10, Vol. 6041, File 160-5, Part 1, MR C 8153, Bishop J. Guy to Secretary of Indian Affairs, 10 October 1936; and R. Hoey to Father Plourde, 16 October 1940.

60. See, for example, the reports in 1927 from Dr. P. Wilson and C. Perry on St. George's, Lytton, in which overcrowding and defective plumbing, ventilation, and sanitation are charged with the death of thirteen children from mumps and influenza (N.A.C. RG 10, Vol. 6462, File 888-1 (2-3, 6-7), MR C 8781, Dr. P. Wilson to H. Graham, 23 February 1927; and C. Perry to Secretary, 6 May 1927).

61. N.A.C. RG 10, Vol. 6452, File 884-1 (1-3), MR C 8773-8774, Extracts of a Report by C. Perry attached to W. Ditchburn, 16 June 1930.

62. N.A.C. RG 10, Vol. 6443, File 881-1 (1-3), MR C 8767, C. Pitts, M.D., to R.H. Moore, 22 October 1935.

63. See: Wherrit, *The Miracle of Empty Beds*, 107 and 111–14, for a discussion of these events; and INAC File 961/23-5, Vol. 1, G.H. Berry to Major D.M. Mackay. This Inspection Report notes the opinion of Dr. R.N. Dick, who claimed that the children's health, at Kuper Island School, was threatened by budget restrictions.

64. N.A.C. RG 10, Vol. 6041, File 160-5, Part 1, MR C 8153, Rev. U. Langlois, O.M.I., to H. McGill, 28 April 1936.

65. INAC File 951/23-5, Vol. 1, V. Rassier, O.S.B., to The Secretary, 15 April 1934.

66. N.A.C. RG 10, Vol. 3918, File 116659-1, MR C 10161, J. Smith to Assistant Deputy and Secretary, 8 February 1918. For additional examples see: N.A.C. RG 10, Vol. 6327, File 660-1 (1-3), MR C 9807, M. Benson to Deputy Superintendent General of Indian Affairs, 23 December 1903; and N.A.C. RG 10, Vol. 6205, File 468-1 (1-3), MR C 7937, M. Benson to Deputy Superintendent General of Indian Affairs, 26 November 1902.

67. N.A.C. RG 10, Vol. 6041, File 160-5 Part 1, MR C 8153, Rev. U. Langlois, O.M.I., to H. McGill, 28 April 1936.

68. N.A.C. RG 10, Vol. 6040, File 160-3A, Part 1, MR C 8153, Rev. T. Ferrier to C.E. Manning, 1 July 1925.

69. *The Davin Report*, 12.

70. INAC File 1/25-1, Vol. 15, L. Vankoughnet to Sir John A. Macdonald, 26 August 1887.

369

Article 3: You Ain't My Boss:[1] Resistance

J.R. Miller

My grandmother was very, very upset. I distinctly recall the third time—my final year at the Baptist Mission school—when these missionaries came again to take me away, I was at that time living with my grandmother and my aunt ... who was a blind person. They in a sense were my immediate family ... When these missionaries came to the door and they said, 'Well, we have permission to take [named deleted] to this Whitehorse Baptist Mission school,' and they came to physically take me out of my home, I hung on to my grandmother's legs. I was crying, of course, and my grandmother was very angry. She was quite old—in her sixties, probably. I remember her taking her tut as we called it, walking cane—and beating this missionary, this white missionary over the backside, and saying, 'You leave my grandson alone. You are not taking him anywhere.' And my aunt Pat came out— and she was blind then, too—and saying the same thing, supporting her mother. And saying that you cannot take this child from this home no matter what permission you have. They didn't produce any written document at the time ...

My grandmother stood by me, and she was able to drive these white missionaries out of our home. And they finally left in defeat. And this is one Indian child who didn't get to go to the Whitehorse Baptist Mission school forever after.[2]

It is hardly surprising that the excesses that occurred in many residential schools provoked protest and resistance, from both parents and students. In due course, the same grievances would lead to collective recriminations and pressure for change that were transmitted through Indian political organizations. During the first six decades of the modern residential school system, however, opportunities to combine voices of protest were usually limited to the family or the band in the case of adults, and to the level of a dormitory among the student body. Though limited in scope for a long time, the forms that Native resistance took were surprisingly numerous. Among parents and family friends the reactions ranged from complaints, to withholding of cooperation, to violent retribution, to defiance of the underlying assimilative thrust of Indian Affairs policy. Within the ranks of the students themselves, there was a similarly large number of ways in which children and young adults could make their objections known. They could and did complain loudly to their families; they could disturb the schools' routine with behaviour that ranged from a lack of cooperation to outright disruption. When pushed too far to be satisfied by these modest responses, they had available more serious sanctions, such as desertion and destruction. Residential school children and parents protested and resisted in many ways.

The effectiveness of both students' and parents' protests depended on a series of particular, often local, circumstances. Headquarters staff of both government and the missionary organizations were usually inclined to discount complaints from Natives themselves. A Presbyterian group that visited a number of schools in Manitoba and Saskatchewan in 1913 reported dismissively that the complaints about the troubled Crowstand school on the Cote reserve near Kamsack were 'of a stereotype character' and tiresomely familiar.[3] Bureaucrats in the secular realm were usually even less inclined to pay attention to Natives' complaints than were those in the ecclesiastical. However, there were a series of circumstances that could force either or both to be more responsive. A principal who was already under a cloud with his superiors sometimes found it desirable to counteract, if not always to accede to, Indians' complaints. The Indian Affairs department was more inclined to seek a solution to protests if its officials were convinced that ignoring the objections would lead to political complications for which their elected masters might hold them responsible. Missionary bureaucrats were often anxious to conciliate parental opinion in situations where their schools were in competition with institutions of another denomination. Denominational rivalry was an especially sharp goad to action where the competition was between a Roman Catholic and a non-Catholic school. There were few threats more effective than removal of one's children from their school.

Source: J.R. Miller, *Shingwauk's Vision: A History of Native Residential Schools.* Toronto: University of Toronto Press, 1996, pp. 343–374. © University of Toronto Press Inc., 1996. Reprinted with permission from the publisher.

These factors sometimes created circumstances in which protests from parents could have limited effect. Such situations at times allowed Native communities and families to influence, if not control, the way in which individual schools treated their children. What emerges from a survey of the interaction of both schoolchildren and their adult communities is a picture not simply of authority and submission, but of a subtle and shifting interplay of forces. Influence and power could in some instances flow in favour of the Aboriginal constituency, in spite of the apparent dominance of government and church. Although too much should not be made of this phenomenon—it would be misleading to suggest, for example, that Native groups were able to force schools to operate as they wished—it is important to understand that protests and resistance could and did have some effect.

The simplest form of parental protest was a complaint lodged with either a missionary or an official of the Indian Affairs department. The Anglican bishop of Caledonia, for example, reported to Ottawa as follows: '"My child might as well be dead" said one mother bitterly when she found she could not get her child back for eight years.' That was one argument the cleric used to support the government's proposal to place more emphasis on day schools at the expense of industrial schools during the first decade of the century.[4] Complaints about the Anglican T.E. Clarke, principal at Battleford, led the Indian commissioner to dispatch the Department of Indian Affairs inspector to investigate, although dismissal of the principal in this instance did not come for another two years.[5] The Ojibwa whose children attended Wikwemikong in the 1890s proved unable to get the government official to force the missionaries to do anything about their complaints concerning excessive instruction in catechism, though the inspector was prepared to act on a father's fear that it was 'dangerous and indecent for his girl to get on the swing.'[6] And when Mr and Mrs Badger took their objections about mistreatment of their children at the Anglican school at Onion Lake to the DIA, they did get the satisfaction of having the agent report to the Indian commissioner, who quickly issued orders that the overwork and 'the ear-twisting for punishment should be dropped, the latter absolutely.'[7]

Sometimes principals responded to parental criticism themselves, although not always with an eye to correcting the conditions that had given rise to the complaints. Missionary supervisors of schools were often more interested in counteracting public criticism than in resolving the difficulty. The beleaguered Principal Clarke of Battleford, anticipating criticism of his regime at the next diocesan synod and cognizant of the likelihood that Ahtahkakoop (Star Blanket) would attend as a delegate, went to considerable trouble to ensure that friends of his school and of the DIA would be in attendance to counter the critics.[8] Missionaries sometimes found that efforts to involve Native leaders in the deliberations of their organizations provided occasions for criticism, such as the time Chief Rattlesnake told the annual convention of Presbyterian workers in Manitoba and Saskatchewan that he 'wanted [the] children to be taught so that they could help the older Indians. Children [were] not learning fast enough.'[9] On the other hand, the principal of Lestock school interpreted 'a large and representative delegation' that objected to an anticipated cancellation of 'the monthly holiday' as proof that the sisters had blabbed to their charges, and complained to his superior in Ottawa.[10] Other forms of complaint that could have some effect were to the church superiors of those in charge of a school to which parents objected. Two Presbyterian worthies from head office in Toronto collected quite a number of objections to overwork, discipline, and inadequate care at several mission locations, including two boarding schools, on the west side of Vancouver Island.[11] Indians at Sandy Bay reserve in Manitoba forwarded their complaints about the Anglican Elkhorn school through the rural dean and the field secretary of the church's principal missionary organization.[12] And, finally, the disgruntled Ojibwa of Couchiching reserve near Fort Frances, Ontario, demanded a meeting with the Oblate provincial to pursue objections to the way the school in their region was being run.[13]

The aggrieved Couchiching band was engaging in another common form of protest against residential school conditions—the formal petition directed either to Indian Affairs or to church officials. Not all such petitions were critical; there were rare petitions *in favour of* missionaries. For example, the chief and head men of a band whose children attended the Crowstand school, where the principal had resigned because he could not secure adequate housing for his ailing wife, sent a message to the Presbyterian committee in Winnipeg asking 'that your resignation be not accepted and that a house be built for your accommodation.'[14] By far the majority of formal protests, however, criticized school leadership.

In this case, too, there was a familiar pattern of denial on the part of those who were accused of contravening the wishes of parents. A request that the principal of the Alberni school be removed in 1905 because he did not provide adequate supervision of the senior girls met a rejoinder that the letter came from 'the father of the only illegitimate child born of a girl in this Mission in recent years.'[15] Ojibwa in the Shoal Lake area of northwestern Ontario became quite expert in petitioning the Presbyterian officials about aspects of boarding-school administration to which they objected. In 1902 the leading men objected to the administration of the matron, who was perceived to be too strict, with the result that the woman tendered her resignation. She particularly objected to the fact that a contract between the Indians and her church limited what the missionaries could do and required that the children be 'well-treated.'[16] A few years later, the local Indian leadership had to protest again, this time against removal of the missionary who had tried to enforce their wishes in the operation of the school. Chief Red Sky threatened that if the Presbyterians removed this man, 'I will ask the Indian Agent to send the children to another school for we won't have them here at all.'[17] This threat proved unavailing, and the Indian parents found themselves petitioning against excessive corporal punishment the next year.[18]

[…]

A particular source of grievance to parents that might cause them to withhold their children was sickness and mortality at the schools. In northern Manitoba, Native people were 'dumb to entreaties' to send their children to the Methodists' Brandon or Norway House schools. 'Some years ago children were sent to Red Deer. Two have returned, two are at Brandon and will return this summer. The rest, the majority died. Seven were sent to Norway House this past summer. Two are already dead. These things completely knock the attempts re Brandon or Norway House in the head. They just sit right down on a fellow. And one must shut up because there is at least a degree of justice on their side.'[19] The most striking example of withholding children because of a school's bad reputation, particularly for health, was the Presbyterians' Regina school. Parents had

always had problems with the institution, and with its aggressive efforts to fill it with students. One mother even wrote another warning: 'You better bring here your children at once or they will be taken to Regina. They are taking children of[f] the Reserve to Regina. 19 children have been taken from the Reserves to the Regina School.'[20] Problems at the Regina school worsened steadily thanks to incompetent leadership and serious health problems that alienated parents from the institution. The trouble, noticeable early in the century, neared a crisis point towards the end of the decade.[21]

Regina's unhappy experience pointed up several aspects of residential school operations that gave parents at least a narrow area in which to protest effectively. First, when a school was located in a region with numerous institutions, parents had a certain amount of choice. A defective school could be taught a lesson by withholding students. In the southern prairies there were at least a dozen schools serving four denominations in the early decades of the twentieth century, and there were even instances where the same denomination had an industrial and a boarding school within a fairly short distance. The Presbyterians, unfortunately for Regina, operated boarding schools at File Hills in Saskatchewan and at Birtle, Manitoba, in addition to the unpopular industrial school at Regina. A veteran missionary contended 'that the feeling against sending children to the far away Industrial Schools is becoming stronger with the Indians themselves. Many of the old people say, that the worst element on the reserve is to be found among returned graduates who in a year or two, drift down sadly.'[22]

Regina was in bad odour with parents for many reasons. It was distant, run by an unpopular principal, had a reputation for overworking children, and experienced a lot of sickness and death among the students. A missionary on a reserve near the Birtle school reported to Presbyterian head office that 'some of the parents intimate that they will send their children to Birtle when they are bigger. The Regina is looked upon with disfavour. It is a long way off and of the seven who were sent there only one is alive to-day, all the rest dying of tuberculosis. The parents are really afraid to let the children go.'[23] A meeting with a group of parents in the chief's house on Muscowpetung reserve resulted in a list of reasons that explained why, although all wanted education for their children, 'some graduates absolutely refuse to send their children from home any more':

(a) The secrecy observed by most schools as to sickness among the pupils.
(b) The use of the pupils for work about the farm and the school when they should be in the classroom.
(c) The breaking up of their home circle.[24]

As long as there were other schools in the region, parents enjoyed some latitude in seeing that their children were educated without sending them to a distant and threatening institution. Even where dissatisfaction did not reign, 'parents prefer to keep their children in the schools nearest their homes.'[25]

[...]

In some cases, avoidance of schooling appeared to be part of a strategy chosen by the leaders of a particular community. Chief White Bear adhered to Treaty 4 in 1875, but he and his followers clearly were not interested in sedentary agriculture as an alternative to the buffalo economy. Instead, the band selected a reserve with rolling land, lakes, and numerous trees, and it proceeded to develop a mixed economy of hunting, fishing, selling products such as tanned hides and charcoal to townspeople, and limited gardening. As the farmer in charge of the reserve observed in 1897, the White Bear band 'try to live as they did before treaty was made with the North-west Indians.' Their strategy, which was in marked contrast to the Pheasant Rump and Ocean Man bands in the same agency, worked. White Bear lost fewer people to disease compared with these other two bands, and his people maintained themselves well on the varied sources of income.

What was instructive was that White Bear, his sons, and their followers among the leadership rigorously eschewed both missionaries and residential schools. The farmer who commented adversely on their economic activity in 1897 continued his plaint by adding, 'and they will hardly allow any one talk on the subject of education to them, and simply say that their "God" did not intend them to be educated like white people; they will not allow that there would be any benefit to be derived from having their children taught.' Tom White Bear, for example, reportedly would 'not farm or keep cattle himself, and uses all his influence to prevent other Indians from doing

so.' White Bear's son would 'not allow his children to be sent to school, says he would sooner see them dead, and on every chance he gets speaks against education and the Industrial schools provided by the Government.' In an effort to induce White Bear to cooperate on farming and schooling, Indian Affairs deposed him as chief, provoking a kind of boycott by the old chief's followers. When Ottawa noticed in 1897 that there was no chief or councillors on the White Bear reserve, the agent proposed the appointment of a 'good hardworking man, [who] has the best farm and buildings in the Agency, has had five of his children sent to school (three have died there) and does all in his power to help on the work on the reserve, and has a large following.' Eventually, Indian Affairs had to capitulate to the stubborn White Bear traditionalists. Ottawa restored the old chief not long before his death, and the reserve received the day school the leaders sought a couple of years later.[26]

[...]

The ability of parents to resist schools was not confined to the prairie region or to the period before the Great War, when problems of disease and student deaths were at their most intense. In the 1920s the Chooutla school in Yukon experienced severe financial problems because of a persistent inability to get and maintain enrolment at the authorized pupilage. In 1925, when enrolment was ten below the authorized forty, the Anglicans' head office chastised the principal, noting that a loss of 'confidence of the parents' was usually part of the explanation of such problems, along with the competition provided by day schools.[27] The venerable bishop, Isaac Stringer, conceded four years later that the continuing problem of under-enrolment owed much to illness and death at the school, not to mention the fact that 'for some time the idea has gone abroad that the children have not been well fed.'[28] Much later Clara Tizya recalled of the same era that when a girl from Rampart Landing died at Chooutla and 'they sent the body back there were many rumours about the children receiving bad treatment and this scared the parents or gave them an excuse for not sending their children to school.'[29]

[...]

The final way in which the adult community could resist the schools was to persist with the traditional practices that residential schooling was designed to eradicate through assimilation. The Ojibwa at Shoal

Lake in northwestern Ontario had inserted in the 'contract' that they signed with Presbyterian missionaries a provision 'that parents shall be allowed to take their children to their religious festivals, but only one child at a time and the child shall not remain over night.'[30] On the File Hills Colony, which was home to selected graduates from the Lebret and File Hills schools, 'fiddle dances, pow-wows and tribal ceremonies were forbidden.' Nonetheless, Eleanor Brass can 'remember as a child accompanying my parents to some secret fiddle dances held in private homes. There were numerous violin players and the dances were quite lively.'[31]

Charles Nowell used to participate in children's potlatch ceremonies when he was a boy at Fort Rupert, before going to Alert Bay school. When he was twelve, his ailing father sent for him in order to instruct him on the necessity of carrying on the potlatch tradition and to have him use his newly acquired learning—writing—to record essential traditional lore. '"I think the only way for you to remember the main positions and all the ancestors is for you to write them down, because it seems to me that everybody is forgetting all their ancestors and names," said his father. "The first thing, you will write down our ancestors till now." So I did—all our ancestors right down to him.' Soon after having his son record their ancestors, names, position in the clan, the dances and their names—all information vital to the preservation of potlatch practice—Nowell's father 'lay down to sleep' and 'he died.'[32] Nowell as an adult not only observed potlatch practices, but he also helped anthropologists to record for prosperity considerable Kwagiulth heritage.

Other adults, such as the men on a reserve in Manitoba, took action immediately to defend their practices. When the agent and DIA inspector came to the reserve and 'cut down or tore down the booth that had been erected for their dance,' the people were so angry that they boycotted the missionary's services for months afterwards.[33] The centrality of traditional Aboriginal ceremonies to both parents and students from Plains cultures was also demonstrated in the early decades of the modern residential school system by the way in which the onset of dancing provoked a rash of runaways, as at the Regina school in 1891.[34] In some cases, as with the Assiniboine Dan Kennedy, the reaction against church-government efforts to suppress traditional practices came after graduation. Kennedy, a graduate of Lebret, turned out to be one of the most energetic and persistent champions of traditional dancing.[35]

Unlike Dan Kennedy, many residential school children did not wait until after graduation to resist the oppressive program to which they were subjected. Like their parents, the pupils themselves had a variety of means to register their protest and try to change the conditions to which they objected. Even more so than the older generation, they were in a vulnerable position as inmates of institutions staffed by the object of their complaints, facilities that were sometimes far removed from countervailing home influences. However, vulnerability did not mean total incapacity or impotence. Residential school children had a range of sanctions from which to select, although their position usually led them to indirect forms of protest and complaint. They might, for example, seek outside help against the school officials, rather than tackling the situation themselves. Or they might register their objections by lack of cooperation and various forms of 'acting up.' In extreme cases they resorted to avoidance techniques that ranged from getting away from the source of the problem to a direct attack on the school. As was often the case in all sorts of institutional settings, the inmates showed an astonishing inventiveness and energy in combating and trying to reshape the forms and forces that held them.

What gave student opinion at least limited influence was the pupilage system and parents' ability in some situations to withhold their children. These background factors ensured that school authorities, if only sporadically, would make an effort to secure good opinions from the children for home consumption. Censorship could stifle negative reports, but it could not generate positive ones. To get endorsement required effort by the staff. An Oblate wrote enthusiastically from Moose Factory to the principal of the order's Fort George school that parents there 'qui ont des enfants chez vous en recoivent que d'excellentes nouvelles,' and predicted that the 'recrus seront probablement trop nombreuses dans un avenir prochain.' On the other hand, he gently chided the principal for failing to ensure that the children from Moosonee wrote home. 'Les parents des enfants à votre école ont restés surpris de ne pas reçevoir de lettres par les derniers courriers.'[36] In 1936 the official publication of the Chooutla school near Carcross, Yukon,

374

indirectly acknowledged the influence of Native opinion when it congratulated itself on being 'full to over-flowing,' with more 'awaiting admittance.' Chooutla, 'under the popular and efficient leadership of Rev. H.C.M. Grant, its Principal, seems to be more than ever highly regarded by the Indians [sic] parents.'[37] And school officials were quick to celebrate when student opinion seemed favourable, as when Chief Starblanket's son was unexpectedly enrolled in the File Hills school, or a student of the Chapleau institution wrote a positive composition on 'Indian Education' that was published in the Toronto *Globe*.[38] These instances were merely the favourable side of the coin of student opinion. Most of the examples of parental protest and pressure noted above were the result of student complaints, sometimes transmitted surreptitiously by the pupils outside censored channels.

Within the walls of the schools themselves, disgruntled students were most likely to indicate their unhappiness with ridicule and a lack of cooperation. One practice that residential school students shared with pupils everywhere was the use of derisory nicknames for teachers and childcare workers. Among themselves, children at Shubenacadie tagged Sister Mary Leonard, the heavyset supervisor they feared, with the name 'Wikew,' which was Micmac for 'fatty.'[39] At St Philip's school a nun who was particularly hated by the students was known as 'Little Weasel' in Saulteaux.[40] At Shubenacadie during Isabelle Knockwood's time as a student, some 'boys developed nicknames for various nuns based on elaborate and obscene wordplays in Mi'kmaw.' One sister who the boys believed 'was sexually "loose" was named *Bujig'm*—a nonsense word which sounds similar to *Bijag'n*—which translates literally as "throw it in."' One of the girls would alter Latin words in hymns into ribald Micmac. For example, *Resurrecsit sicut dixit* became *Resurrecsit kisiku iktit*, changing the meaning from 'He said he would rise again' to 'When the old man got up, he farted.' What made the episode all the more delicious was that the sister presiding would stop the singing and 'patiently teach Clara the proper pronunciation. Clara would just stand there and grin. Even the holy ones had to laugh.'[41]

Non-cooperation was more overt than name calling. A former student of the Anglicans' Pelican Lake school vividly remembered an 'older boy' in one of her early classes who never participated in the work of the classroom. He simply sat stolidly at his desk ignoring everything around him.[42] At Moose Factory, Billy Diamond defied a supervisor by refusing to finish his vegetables. The future chief 'sat without eating for eight hours, the plate in front of him and the supervisor pacing behind until finally, at two o'clock in the morning, with the vegetables cold and still untouched, the supervisor caved in and sent the boy up to the darkened dormitory, where dozens of boys still lay with their eyes closed, feigning sleep while they awaited the outcome of the vegetable standoff.'[43] The Methodists' Coqualeetza school in British Columbia recorded in its register of admissions and discharges several students who were 'Discharged because of indisposition for work or study,' or 'Sent away as incorrigible,' or discharged because of an 'indisposition or inaptitude for study.'[44] The Oblate principal at Fort George also expelled a young fellow whom he described as 'unusually stubborn and would not cooperate with school authorities.'[45] Offences might range from refusal to do school work to misbehaviour in chapel; an almost unlimited number of possibilities was available. Isabelle Knockwood delighted in defying Wikew's 'Don't dare move a muscle' at bedtime by 'wiggling my toes under the blankets thinking, "You ain't my boss and I'll wiggle all I want." At the same time, I was looking straight at her wearing the Indian mask which I had discovered over the years she couldn't read.'[46] More overt were the boys at Lytton who threatened the principal to his face that they would steal food if he didn't provide them with better rations. They were pleasantly surprised when their challenge succeeded.[47]

Indeed, the favourite form of misbehaviour among students was stealing food. The young women at Kamloops school organized elaborate schemes to pilfer apples and other food that they shared in the dormitory.[48] Similar stunts were carried out at most schools at one time or another. The boys at Elkhorn in the 1940s killed one of the school's pigs by spraying it with water and leaving it to freeze to death. When the school authorities could not figure out what had killed the pig, they ordered it incinerated. The boys who leapt to dispose of the carcass in fact roasted and hid it, treating the contraband pork as snack for many days.[49] Food pranks that involved staff were fondly remembered. One woman took advantage of the assignment of clearing the staff dining room to sample delicacies with a spoon she had brought. When she found the large jar of horseradish not to her liking, she spat the condiment back in the jar and screwed the lid on.[50] A male former student of Shubenacadie told Isabelle Knockwood that boys working in the barn sometimes urinated in the milk destined for the sisters and priest.[51] A particularly wicked thrill could be obtained by directing misbehaviour at the religious practices of the missionaries. Some students conscripted into assisting with services indulged in mockery, and a former altar boy recalled how they used to mock the Mass that all were compelled to attend every morning.[52]

More daring—and more rewarding—was theft of communion wine, either by suborning a person who looked after the sacristy or through a nighttime raid.[53] Getting drunk on the stolen wine, however, gave the game away with dire consequences.[54] A man who had attended several residential schools in Ontario recalled that at Shingwauk he and another boy had made homebrew in the attic of the carpenter's workshop. They had a fright one day when the carpenter smelled something strange and noticed a leak in his shop ceiling. The artisan said that they would have to reroof the building because it was obviously leaking. The boys, who knew better, moved their illegal brew to the barn, where they later got roaring drunk on it.[55]

Another guilty pleasure for multitudes of residential school students was getting around the strict rules on segregation of the sexes. Justa Monk 'had my first sexual experience with another student, a girl I really liked, within the walls of Lejac, just a few feet from one of the brothers who was peeling potatoes at the time.'[56] In some schools, like Shingwauk, where the girls' and boys' dormitories were wings at opposite ends of the same building, contact could be made by going over the rooftop at night—a dangerous resort even if one was not apprehended.[57] Boys at Blue Quills who thought access to the latest technology was the solution to their isolation discovered that science could be their undoing, too. 'I remember one time we used walkies talkies to socialize with the girls,' recalled one, 'but we were found out because of the wiring system or the pipes. Somehow it got connected with the television and we got caught because our voices came on the television.'[58]

Where the living quarters of the sexes were completely separate, as at Spanish where the girls' school was across the road from the boys', more elaborate arrangements were necessary. There a complicated communications system was worked out, one that, ironically, relied on the daily visit of one of the Jesuits to the girls' chapel to say Mass. A boy who wanted to communicate surreptitiously with a girl would arrange for a message to be slipped into the priest's hatband. When the celebrant reached the vestibule at the girls' school, his hat would be placed on a stand, whence it would be quietly picked up and the slip of paper with the illicit message extracted. A return note could be sent back to the boy with the priest on his return after Mass. Another means used at Spanish capitalized on the fact that shoe repairs were carried out in the cobbler shop in the boys' building. A girl would sew a message into the lining of a pair of boots that was being sent across for repair. This system worked reasonably well, too, although the girls sometimes damaged the newly refurbished boots extracting the return message.[59] Some students simply arranged for regular meeting places and times with either siblings or members of the opposite sex in whom they had a romantic interest.[60] Charlie Nowell in British Columbia eventually got expelled from Alert Bay school when one of his notes to a girl whom he met regularly in the evenings was intercepted by her stepfather.[61] Peter Webster got out of Ahousaht at the age of fourteen when 'I took the blame for the pregnancy of one of my classmates.'[62]

In situations where extensive flouting of the rules about segregation of mature males and females occurred, complications generally ensued. In the early days, a small boarding school such as Alberni on Vancouver Island had considerable difficulty dealing with such a problem. Lax supervision by a trusting matron led to her dismissal, only to be replaced by new officers who upset children and parents by locking the girls in their dormitory every night.[63] At the Anglicans' Sarcee school, similar concerns led to protracted discussions over the design of dormitory windows. The local missionary wanted windows with sashes that could be opened, necessitating, in his opinion, the installation of bars on the outside of the window openings. But the Indian agent ruled that no bars were necessary, leaving the cleric with grave concerns about security.[64] As the new regime at Alberni learned a couple of years after the window debate at Sarcee, open windows led to nocturnal visits, which in the Alberni case led to nailing the windows closed.[65] In extenuation, the Alberni principal contended that 'in other schools similar difficulties have arisen and in Regina we had a share and a great deal more serious than ours.'[66] Indeed, both the Cecilia Jeffrey and the Regina schools had had encounters with the problem. Things so degenerated at the Presbyterian schools that one missionary charged 'the conduct has become almost like that of a brothel instead of a Church home,' while the principal of the File Hills boarding school stated flatly that 'I for one will never consent to send my children that I am treasuring with a mother's love where they would be exposed to such dangers.'[67]

At the Methodists' Brandon school, some of the boys obtained duplicate keys and used them to visit the girls' dormitory before they were caught.[68] When principals at Regina and Alberni responded to renewed scandal by locking the dorms from the outside or by barring the windows, they encountered objections from the Indian Affairs department, which 'objects to the bars lest the building should be a fire trap in case of accident.'[69] Concerns over the students' persistent success in violating the rules against fraternization contributed to the problems that caused closure of both Crowstand and Regina.[70] Others, such as Alberni, carried on for many decades in spite of recurrent problems. At Alberni, the staff put 'a wax stamp and a chain' across the window of the most accessible boys' dormitory, but this merely forced the amorous to take a more dangerous route 'through the window on the west side of the building, and along a ledge of the roof. There was a drop of thirty feet to the ground.'[71] Whether it was a Presbyterian school on Vancouver Island or an Anglican institution near Sault Ste Marie, adolescents found similar ways to flout the rules and get in touch with members of the opposite sex.

Sometimes there was a connection between illicit relations and what was probably the most commonly reported manifestation of student resistance—running away from school. A former administrator of the Pelican Lake school recalled an incident in which an Indian boy who lived with a family in the town of Sioux Lookout paddled across the lake to rendezvous with his girlfriend, a classmate. The following morning they were discovered in a tent not too far off from the school.[72] Although there could be many reasons for students' deserting, the reaction that flight evoked

among staff was uniformly negative. For one thing, runaways caused considerable difficulties and anxieties. Early in the century, the missionary principal of Norway House in northern Manitoba had to make a January trip 320 kilometres northeast accompanied by a Mountie to retrieve pupils who had not returned after the summer vacation.[73] At a crasser level, unauthorized absences, if detected by Indian Affairs officials, would lead to a decrease in revenue. For example, when six girls ran away from a Manitoba school 'to attend a dance on the Reserve,' it cost the Anglican Missionary Society a thirteen dollar fee to the police.[74]

[...]

Even more dramatic a form of rebellion than truancy was arson. For students who were unable to escape, often an emotionally satisfying substitute was to attack the school with fire. Once again, as with the problem of runaways, there tended to be a suspiciously high correlation between troubles at a school and a mysterious outbreak of fire. For example, at Wikwemikong in the 1880s, during a period of some tension between missionaries and parents, there were two unexplained fires early in 1885, and another fire at the girls' school in the autumn of 1888 that had definitely been set by two students.[75] At the Presbyterian school at Birtle, Manitoba, a young boy calmly went into the pantry, took matches, and proceeded to set fire to the barn on a September day in 1903.[76] Alberni home burned down in suspicious circumstances in 1917.[77] The Anglicans in the 1920s experienced arson at Alert Bay, which was full to overflowing—sometimes a sign of parental confidence in a school—and at Onion Lake, which was always in some difficulty.[78] The Onion Lake fire in 1928 appeared to be 'copycat' incendiarism: two boys at the Anglican school seem to have been influenced by a recent fire at the neighbouring Catholic school that had completely destroyed the institution. The razing of the Cross Lake school in Manitoba, also in 1928, probably was a coincidence.[79] The Oblates had a suspicious fire at Duck Lake in 1926, and two boys attempted arson at the Sioux Lookout school in 1931. The principal of the Elkhorn residential school was not very pleased when the two would-be arsonists were transferred to his school.[80] The Oblates at Pine Creek, Manitoba, in 1930 had the distinction of double arson, one boy 'having set the church on fire and another boy … tried to do the same to the School.'[81] In less than a decade after 1936, nine residential schools were destroyed by fires of various origins.[82]

[…]

Arsonists and runaways were merely the extreme of a continuum of unhappy and angry students who, like their parents, often resisted and protested as best they could against the iniquities of residential school life. From complaints, to acts of non-cooperation and defiance, to antisocial actions—these students often expressed by their words and actions what many others felt, others who often were too timid or intimidated to follow suit. What is less clear about resistance by both parents and schoolchildren is how effective their deeds and arguments were. Certainly, when a leading Blood man came to Canon Middleton and objected to his children being taught Blackfoot syllabics, the missionary was more than happy to oblige his desire for solely English instruction.[83] Often missionaries evinced concern to maintain good relations with children and parents, and they trumpeted any small victories they experienced. Kate Gillespie of File Hills was delighted when Chief Starblanket let his son attend the Presbyterian school rather than Catholic Lebret.[84]

[…]

Probably the best symbol of Native resistance to the intrusive and oppressive nature of residential schools was found in the persistence of traditional cultural practices, such as dancing among Plains peoples and the potlatch on the Pacific. That former residential school students, as noted earlier, were among the most energetic in defending the practices that assimilative education was supposed to consign to oblivion is among the most pointed ironies of the history of residential schooling. Also ironic was the fact that, by the time Native resistance led to removal of such coercive elements as the potlatch and prairie dancing bans in the 1951 amendment of the Indian Act, a dramatically new chapter in the residential school story was opening. This instalment—the conclusion, as it turned out—was the increasingly assertive and influential campaign of Native political organizations to eliminate residential schooling in Canada. The irony in this process, which stretched from the first major outpouring of Native political process in the later 1940s to the elimination of government-controlled residential schools in the late 1960s and 1970s, was that it was often former residential school students who provided the most vociferous criticism of education and the most effective political leadership. In helping to shape the generations of political leaders who emerged after the Second World War, residential schools contributed to the most effective of the many forms of Native resistance that had been spawned by these institutions.

So, anyway, after I finished sweeping—she kept following me around like this, cutting me [up], cutting my people up. All of a sudden I just swung my broom like this. 'F you!' Oh, I swore. 'Don't swear.' I said, 'F you.' I kept on. I just went wild. I just snapped. 'You f-ing, fucking…' Oh, did I ever use that F word! Did I ever swear! 'Keep quiet! Everybody's listening.' 'I don't give a damn. I don't give a fuck!' I just went completely wild. And I stood up to her like this.

She said, 'You come upstairs. I'm going to fix you.' 'You're f-ing right I will,' I said. In the meantime, even the boys came running towards the girls' side. And they're all prompting me, 'Don't be scared of her. Keep it up. Keep it up.' They took me upstairs. Those other two—that nun that made trouble for me and another nun—came running. Three of them, they grabbed brooms on the third floor. They beat me up with brooms. Brooms all over. And I grabbed ahold of her … I grabbed her veil like this. And she was hanging on, and she had me by the hair. And another nun was hitting me all over. I just didn't care. One of them nuns, I grabbed ahold of her like this and swung like this. She landed far [away]. Oh, she landed like at the end of that wall. That's how far [away] she landed. I really went wild that time. And the other one, I grabbed her and flung her like this. And I hung on to this one. And then she told them in French to go. They went crying 'cause I made them cry.

There was me and her now. I said, 'Kill me first; I'm not giving up.' I just hung on to her. Every time she'd hit me, I'd hit her right back. Oh, I had her good. 'Let me go,' she said. I'd jerk her like this. And she'd hang on to it [her veil]. Finally, she said, 'In the name of God, please let me go, Pauline.'[85]

Notes

1. Isabelle Knockwood, *Out of the Depths: The Experience of Mi'kmaw Children at the Indian Residential School of Shubenacadie, Nova Scotia* (Lockeport, NS: Roseway Publishing 1992), 125

2. Interview, 21 June 1990, Whitehorse, with a Han male who attended Whitehorse Baptist Mission school 1951–3 (interview by Lu Johns Penikett)

3. United Church of Canada Archives [UCA], Records of the Presbyterian Church [PC], Foreign Mission Committee [FMC], Western Section [WS], Indian Work in Manitoba and the North West [IWMNW], box 7, file 155, Report of Visit to Indian Missions, 15 Aug. 1913. Other examples concern Mount Elgin in Ontario, both before the Great War (ibid., A. Sutherland Papers, box 8, file 154, T.T. George to A. Sutherland, 27 May 1908, and Sutherland to George, 3 June 1908) and during the 1940s (ibid., E.E. Joblin Papers, box 1, file 3, Notes on the Survey of the Education of Indian Children in Western Ontario, 15 Sept. 1943). In commenting on complaints made in the 1890s about the Wikwemikong schools on Manitoulin Island, the Jesuit historian noted, after conceding that Indian Affairs investigated parental complaints, that the outcome 'shows that the Indians were still capable of thinking and speaking nonsense.' Regis College Archives, Father Julien Paquin, 'Modern Jesuit Indian Missions in Ontario' (unpaginated manuscript)

4. General Synod Archives [GSA], GS 75-103, Papers of the Missionary Society of the Church in Canada [GS 75-103], Series 2-14, Special Indian Committee [Series 2-14], box 19, S.H. Blake correspondence, file Mar/08–June/09, F.H. DuVernet to S.H. Blake, 23 Mrch 1909, enclosing copy DuVernet to Secretary, Department of Indian Affairs, 23 March 1909.

5. National Archives of Canada [NA], MG 29, E. 106, Hayter Reed Papers, box 20, 1255, H. Reed to Inspector J.A. Macrae, 30 June 1892.

6. Paquin, 'Modern Jesuit Indian Missions'

7. NA, Records of the Department of Indian Affairs [RG 10], School Files, vol. 6320, file 658-1, part 1, 305595, (copy) David Laird to Indian Agent Sibbald, 28 Nov. 1906,' enclosed with Laird to Secretary, DIA, 4 March 1907. Laird continued to the Agent: 'When the children have sore necks or are tender about the throat, this sort of punishment is cruel. 'I think it would be well to call the meeting of Indians you propose, speak to them in a persuasive manner, assure them the overwork and ear-twisting will be discontinued, and tell them the Indian Commissioner [Laird] and the Department are most anxious that they should send their children to school.'

8. Reed Papers, vol. 12, file 'Rev. T. Clarke 1891-92,' 132, T. Clarke to Hayter Reed, 14 July 1891

9. Archives of the Manitoba and Northwestern Ontario Conference of the United Church of Canada, University of Winnipeg [UCA-Wpg], Minute Book of Presbyterian Workers among the Indians, Synods of Manitoba and Saskatchewan, 1909–1915, 68, Fifth Convention, Crowstand school, 23–24 July 1912

10. Archives Deschâtelets [AD], L 535 .M27L 349, William Moss, OMI, to J. Magnan, OMI, 18 April 1932. Father Moss was replaced as principal shortly after this incident. Ibid., 351, J. Magnan to A.S. Williams, 21 May 1932

11. PC, FMC, WS, Indian Work in BC [IWBC], box 1, file 16, Hamilton Cassels and Andrew Jeffrey to R.P. MacKay, 4 Aug. 1897

12. GS 75-103, Series 2-15, Papers of the MSCC [Series 2-15], Records of the Indian and Eskimo Residential School Commission [IESRC], box 21, 9, Minute of 28 Aug. 1928. In this case, since the principal at Elkhorn had already rejected similar complaints, 'No further action was considered necessary' by the central body.

13. AD, L 912 .M27C 195, Maurice Bruyere and Joe Mainville to Rev. Fr. Magnan, Provincial OMI, nd [1933]. The following year a new principal was appointed and, apparently, conditions improved for a number of years. However, by the end of 1940, the president of the Columbus Indian Mission Club on the reserve was objecting to another deterioration in conditions at the school.

14. UCA-Wpg. A.B. Baird Papers, box G, G 1393-4, A.B. Baird to Rev. C.W. Whyte. The principal's resignation (Whyte to Baird, 12 March 1897) is ibid., G 1214-18.

15. PC, FMC, WS, IWBC, box 3, file 174, A.W. Vowell to Dr John Campbell, 13 May 1905 (enclosing letter from Dan Watts, Big George, Tatoosh Jimmie George, Tyee Bob of 6 May); ibid., James R. Motion to R.P. MacKay, 27 May 1905. Swewish, who claimed to be 'chief of the Shesaht people,' later wrote to denounce the petitioners and to endorse the work of the principal. Ibid., file 75, Shewish to R.P. MacKay, 5 July 1905 (translated and typed by James R. Motion)

16. PC, FMC, WS, IWMNW, box 2, file 41, petition from Shoal Lake Reserve, 22 Sept. 1902 (enclosed with A.G. McKitrick to MacKay, 23 Sept. 1902); ibid., Maggie A. Nicoll to R.P. MacKay, 23 Sept. 1902;

ibid., file 42, same to same, 13 Oct. 1902; ibid., file 40, same to same, 25 Aug. 1902. See also ibid., box 3, file 55, J.O. McGregor and Sarah McGregor to R.P. MacKay, 27 Nov. 1903, in which a new principal and matron complained that the missionary, A.G. McKitrick, interfered with their work by insisting that the original promise 'that the children would not be taught religion' be honoured.

17. Ibid., box 5, file 95, Petition dated Shoal Lake, 4 March 1907, to Foreign Mission Society, Toronto (interpreted by Miss Mary Begg and transcribed by Miss E. Robertson, teacher)

18. Ibid., file 111, Report of the Subcommittee of Synodical Indian Mission Committee, Manitoba and Saskatchewan, July 1908. See also ibid., box 6, file 117, Agnes Sibbald to Rev. Dr J. Farquharson, 30 Jan. 1909.

19. Ibid., W.W. Shoup (Nelson House) to A. Sutherland, 17 March 1907

20. Reed Papers, vol. 19, file 'May 1891,' 619, Knatakasi-wisine (Piapot Reserve) to D[ea]r Sister in law (Mrs Mistassini], 21 May 1891

21. PC, FMC, WS, IWMNW, box 1, file 24, J.A. Sinclair to R.P. MacKay, 19 April 1901; ibid., box 5, file 115, (copy) R.P. MacKay to J. Farquharson, 30 Nov. 1908; ibid., file 116, J. Farquharson to R.P. MacKay, 3 Dec. 1908

22. Ibid., box 4, file 70, Neil Gilmour (Norway House) to R.P. MacKay, 11 Feb. 1905. Gilmour was referring specifically to 'the reserves that form the Regina School constituency.'

23. Ibid., file 72, F.O. Gilbart to R.P. MacKay. 28 April 1905

24. Ibid., box 7, file 145, W.W. McLaren, report on tour of reserves and schools in southern Manitoba and southern Saskatchewan, 22 April 1912

25. Report of Deputy Superintendent General James A. Smart, in Annual Report of DIA for 1900, Canada, *Sessional Papers [CSP] (No. 27) 1901,* xxxiii. The deputy minister went on: 'equally natural is it for the teachers of boarding schools to desire to retain their pupils instead of drafting them to the higher institutions.'

26. The materials for the White Bear story, which were assembled by Mary Miller for my benefit, are found in RG 10, Black Series, vol. 3940, file 121,698-13, part 0; and Annual Reports of the Department of Indian Affairs, 1880–1906. The materials quoted are from letters written in 1897, and from the report for 1897. Concerning the resistance to residential schooling, the 1897 department report (*CSP[No. 14] 1898,* 161) was clear and revealing: 'There are twenty-five children of school age in the band, and seven of them are attending the industrial schools at Regina, Qu'Appelle and Elkhorn. It is very difficult to get the parents to allow the children to be sent away to school, more especially those Indians who are in any way connected with the deposed chief White Bear and his sons, who will have nothing to do with anything in the shape of education, and who try to live as they did before treaty was made with the North-west Indians.'

27. Archives of Yukon [AY], Anglican Diocese of Yukon Records, box 7, file 9, T.B.R. Westgate to W. Barlow, 7 July 1925

28. Ibid., I.O. Stringer to T.B.R. Westgate, 21 Oct. 1929. Westgate, the Anglican's head man in missionary work in Canada, in turn lamented to DIA that an enrolment of twenty-six in a school with a pupilage of forty meant serious financial problems for the school and the church. Ibid., T.B.R. Westgate to Secretary, DIA, 16 Dec. 1929

29. L.G.P. Waller, ed., *The Education of Indian Children in Canada* (Toronto: Ryerson Press 1965), 103–4. Mrs Tizya also recalled: 'And so, for the next 25 years, no children were sent out to the Carcross Indian Residential School and it was for this reason that we decided to bring our children out to where they could become educated. We realized that we could not do anything for our children in an atmosphere where no one else cared about his children' (104).

30. PC, FMB, IWMNW, box 1, file 33, 'Agreement' of 14 Jan. 1902 enclosed with J.C. Gandier to R.P. MacKay, same date. The first clause of the agreement provided: 'That while children are young and at school they shall not be baptized without the consent of their parents …'

31. Brass, *I Walk in Two Worlds,* 13

32. Clelland S. Ford, *Smoke from Their Fires: The Life of a Kwakiutl Chief* (New Haven, Conn.: Yale University Press 1941), 85–6 and 107

33. PC, FMC, WS, IWMNW, box 3, file 46, D. Spear to R.P. MacKay, 26 Feb. 1903. The agent's visit had occurred a little before Christmas.

34. Baird Papers, box 3, E1156-9, A.S. McLeod to A.B. Baird, 4 June 1891

35. See PC, FMC, WS, IWMNW, box 4, file 59, E. MacKenzie to R.P. MacKay, 7 March 1904; James R.

Stevens, ed., *Recollections of an Assiniboine Chief* [Dan Kennedy, Ochankuhage] (Toronto: McClelland & Stewart 1972), 103–4. See also RG 10, Black Series, vol. 3825, file 60, 511-1, J.D. McLean to Indian Commissioner, 5 Jan. 1903: 'Chief Wanduta, of the Oak River Sioux Band, has called at the Department with his son, who is a graduate of the Brandon Industrial School.'

36. AD, LCB 3445 .G46M 65, J. Cyr, OMI, to Father Labrèche, 13 Feb. 1944 [families that have children at your school have received only excellent reports, (and) recruits probably will be too numerous in the near future]; ibid., 66, same to same, 28 March 1944 [families of children at your school remain surprised at not receiving letters by the last mail].

37. AY, Anglican Yukon Records, *Northern Lights* 25, 4 (Nov. 1936): 3

38. PC, FMC, WS, IWMNW, box 3, file 55, K. Gillespie to R.P. MacKay, 20 Nov. 1903; *Globe,* 9 Oct. 1926, 'Certified by G.T. Snowden, Acting Principal,' The published letter was noted by the Anglicans' missionary body: GS 75-103, Series 2-15, box 21, 812

39. Knockwood, *Out of the Depths*, 32. The students had other, somewhat less derogatory names in their own language for other sisters.

40. Joe Severight interview, Cote Reserve, 19 Feb. 1992. Mr Severight also recalled that some boys— 'peeping Toms,' he called them—spied on two of the sisters, whose bedroom adjoined the boys' dormitory.

41. Knockwood, *Out of the Depths,* 124

42. Interview with an Ojibwa woman who in the 1940s attended Pelican Lake from age seven until about age eleven, 2 Feb. 1991, Sioux Lookout, Ont. She recalled that this boy ran away several times and was strapped for it once.

43. Roy MacGregor, *Chief: The Fearless Vision of Billy Diamond* (Toronto: Penguin 1989), 25–6. The episode clinched young Billy's role as leader of the students.

44. Vancouver, United Church of Canada Conference of BC Archives, Coqualeetza Register of Admissions and Discharges, numbers 38, 049, 89, and 90

45. AD, LCB 3346 .G46M 112, (copy) W.S. Gran to Regional Supervisor, 14 Feb. 1961

46. Knockwood, *Out of the Depths*, 125

47. 100 Verna J. Kirkness, ed., *Khot-La-Cha: The Autobiography of Chief Simon Baker* (Vancouver/Toronto: Douglas & McIntyre 1994), 36–7

48. Haig-Brown, *Resistance and Renewal,* 89–90

49. Telephone interview with Ernest Hall, 3 Aug. 1993. I am indebted to Regina writer Jim Anderson, who first told me of this incident.

50. This anecdote was told by an unidentified woman, who said that it had been experienced by another woman, during a public session of the 'Journey to Healing' Conference, 26 Sept. 1991, Saskatoon.

51. Knockwood, *Out of the Depths*, 55. The workers knew which milk was headed for the staff dining room because it always came from the cows that gave milk of higher quality than the rest.

52. Interview, 21 Jan. 1992, Saskatoon, with male Saulteaux student who attended St Philip's, 1955–62, and Marieval 1962–5

53. Haig-Brown, *Resistance and Renewal,* 91, recounts an organized system at Kamloops for the theft and sale of eucharistic wine.

54. Joe Severight interview. Mr Severight, who attended St Philip's school in the 1930s, recalled that he and his companions were punished—after they had sobered up.

55. A male (surname Kakeegesic) who attended Chapleau, Moose Factory, and Shingwauk schools, speaking at the public session of Shingwauk reunion, 4 July 1991

56. Bridget Moran, *Justa: A First Nations Leader* (Vancouver: Arsenal Pulp Press 1994). 54. On another occasion, 'Sister Alphonse saw me kissing a girl in the priests' dining room' and 'started slapping me. I grabbed her wrists and squeezed them hard and I said to her, "You're not my teacher now,"' Ibid., 55

57. Recollection in public session at Shingwauk reunion, 4 July 1991

58. Diane Persson, 'The Changing Experience of Indian Residential Schooling: Blue Quills, 1931–1970,' in Jean Barmen, Yvonne Hébert, and Don McCaskill, *Indian Education in Canada*, vol. 1: *The Legacy* (Vancouver: University of British Columbia Press and Nakoda Institute 1986), 164

59. Interview with Miss Ann Berrigan, SFM (La Société des Filles du Coeur de Marie), Montreal, 16 Oct. 1990. Students at St Philip's school in the 1950s used a wood box as a 'drop' for messages between boys and girls. On one occasion, a staff member found a note, assembled the students, and read the message aloud to embarrass those involved. Interview, 21 Jan. 1992, Saskatoon, with male Saulteaux student of St Philip's, 1955–62, and Marieval, 1962–5

60. Interview, 15 Dec. 1987, Regina, with Joy Mann

61. Ford, *Smoke from Their Fires*, 104–5

62. Peter Webster, *As Far as I Know: Reminiscences of an Ahousat Elder* (Campbell River, BC: Campbell River Museum and Archives 1983), 42

63. PC, FMC, WS, IWBC, box 1, file 22, M. Swartout to R.P. MacKay, 22 Feb. 1899; ibid., file 23, K. Cameron to R.P. MacKay, 30 May 1899; ibid., B.I. Johnston to R.P. MacKay, 17 June 1899

64. Calgary Indian Missions Papers, box 3, vol. 1, 124–7, J.W. Tims to Mr Scott, 11 Aug. 1903

65. PC, FMC, WS, IWBC, box 3, file 72, K. Cameron to R.P. MacKay, 1 and 25 March 1905: ibid., Mrs J.R. Motion to R.P. MacKay, 29 March 1905

66. Ibid., file 75, J.R. Motion to R.P. MaKay, 17 June 1905

67. Ibid., IWMNW, box 3, file 55, A.G. McKitrick to R.P. MacKay, 14 Nov. 1903; ibid., box 5, file 74, Kate Gillespie to R.P. MacKay, 22 June 1905

68. Ibid., box 6, file 123, W.W. McLaren to R.P. MacKay, 5 July 1909. McLaren also noted of Brandon, 'The older boys too whenever they got a chance when on leave down town often frequent the redlight district of the city.'

69. Ibid., box 5, file 1095, (copy) D.M. Laird to Rev. Sir, 14 Jan. 1908; ibid., BFM, Correspondence with WFMS, box 1, file 24, (copy) R.P. MacKay to Mrs C. Clark, 5 May 1910

70. For a sample of the material on the Crowstand dormitory problems, see PC, FMC, WS, IWMNW, box 5, file 99, (copy) E. McWhinney to J. Farquharson, 8 July 1907.

71. PC, BFM, Correspondence with WMS, box 5, file 84. Helen W. Horne, assistant secretary for Indian Work, WMS to J.H. Edmison, 6 Jan. 1923; Chief Earl Maquinna George's Life Story (typescript), 25

72. Derek and Hazel Mills interview, 2 Feb. 1991, Sioux Lookout, Ont.

73. UCA-Wpg. J.A. Lousley Autobiography (manuscript), chapter 11, 2–3

74. GS 75-103, Series 2-15, box 20, minutes of 23 Oct. 1924. See also Archives of Yukon, YRG 1, Series 1., vol. 11, file 2335, part 6, (copy) John Hawksley (DIA) to Rev. Principal, Chooutla Indian School, 20 July 1932.

75. Paquin, 'Modern Jesuit Indian Missions': and 'Synopsis of the History of Wikwemikong'

76. PC, FMC, WS, IWNMW, box 3, file 53, E.H. Crawford to R.P. MacKay, 30 Sept. 1903

77. PC, BFM, Correspondence with WMS, box 4, file 61, Jessie Wilson to R.P. MacKay, 31 May 1917

78. GSA, M 75-1, Bishop Lucas Papers, box 2, Minutes of Commission, 23 Oct. 1924 re Alert Bay; GS 75-103. Series 2-15, box 21, Minutes of 6 March 1928

79. AD, LC 6201 .K26R 1, clipping from *Le Patriote*, 21 Oct. 1931

80. AD, HR 6671, .C73R 47, (copy) J. LeChevalier, OMI, to W.M. Graham, 4 May 1926, concerning Duck Lake; GS 75-103, Series 2-15, box 22, Minutes of 7 April and 30 April 1931

81. RG 10, School Files, vol. 6041, file 160-5, part 1, J. Magnan, OMI, to Duncan C. Scott, 2 Dec. 1930

82. Joblin Papers, box 1, file 3, (copy) R.A. Hoey to G. Dorey, 29 May 1944. With all these fires, missionaries might be forgiven the odd bit of paranoia. The Oblates, for example, thought that a fire at Fort Frances school had been set by an American socialist in revenge for the principal's discouraging organizing on the nearby reserve. *Missions*, no. 214, (Sept–Dec. 1921): 307–8

83. Middleton Papers, box 2, file 7, (copy) S.H. Middleton to Roberta Forsberg, 7 Nov. 1960

84. PC, FMC, WS, IWMNW, box 3, file 55, K. Gillespie to R.P. MacKay, 20 Nov. 1903

85. Interview with Pauline Pelly, former St Philip's student, 6 Sept. 1991, Saskatoon. The altercation between Pauline and the sister lasted some time, and eventually the confrontation shifted to the student's home on the reserve, because the principal followed her there. Pauline's father sternly admonished the Oblates for the behaviour of the sister and the principal.

WORLD WAR II AND THE INTERNMENT OF ENEMY ALIENS

Circumscribing Personal Freedoms

Marcel Martel
York University

WORLD WAR II AND THE INTERNMENT OF ENEMY ALIENS: CIRCUMSCRIBING PERSONAL FREEDOMS

Introduction by Marcel Martel

385

● INTRODUCTION

Marcel Martel

When Canada declared war on Germany on September 10, 1939, Canadians were resigned to the fact that this new era of war would cause them to make sacrifices and bring limits to personal freedoms and domestic consumption. But they also had fears, especially when Canadians enlisted and many went abroad to fight the enemy. These reactions stemmed from First World War experiences. Yet some hope persisted, in particular that the sacrifices and other restrictions imposed by the state would end and peace would return.

More than one million Canadians answered the call to enlist and fight the enemy. Canada's role in military operations was crucial. Besides training air pilots and escorting convoys across the Atlantic (and preventing German U-boats from sinking them), the Canadian military effort involved preparing troops for the war. Most of the Canadian troops were sent to Europe and took part in important military operations. After the ill-conceived Allied attack on the French coast at Dieppe in 1942, Canadian troops took part in the liberation of Italy and played a significant role in Normandy on June 6, 1944, and in the liberation of the European continent, especially the Netherlands.

While Canadian troops experienced successes in Europe, those who were sent to defend the British colony of Hong Kong on December 7, 1941, met a different fate. Although they fought hard and many soldiers paid with their lives, most were captured and became prisoners of war. For four years, these Canadians PoWs faced harsh treatment: They were underfed, suffered from malaria and other illnesses, and worked in slave labour camps. More than 550 died during the Japanese attack or in the slave labour camps.

During that period of the war, the role of the federal government was to mobilize material and human resources, put in place strategies to win the war, and reassure Canadians that their sacrifices were worth it. At the same time, the federal government adopted policies that restricted personal freedoms and imposed censorship. As people learned from wars in the twentieth century, the first casualty of war is truth. Newspapers and letters sent by soldiers to their loved ones and relatives were censored in order to remove any information considered sensitive or likely to undermine morale. The federal government collected information on those who might constitute a security threat because of their beliefs, their opposition to the war, or the suspicion that they were helping Canada's enemies.

It was not the first time the federal government had adopted policies aimed at controlling the flow of information in the country and conducting surveillance activities. The government had done so during the First World War, but in this case it made its policies known before declaring war. First issued on September 3, 1939, the Defence of Canada Regulations remained in force until August 1945. The regulations gave the government the power to censor letters and newspapers and control radio broadcasts. Furthermore, Section 21 gave government the power to detain and intern anyone who threatened public order and enlistment efforts. Enemy aliens—that is, individuals who were not British subjects and possessed the nationality of a state at war with Canada—were required to register. If they did not comply or were suspected of helping the enemy, they could be detained and interned.

Contrary to what happened during the First World War, the internment process was more selective. Being in charge of implementing the policy, the RCMP was well informed and knew precisely who to arrest and intern, according to Reg Whitaker and Gregory S. Kealey. Several hundred enemy aliens who were naturalized after 1922, including Germans,

Italians, and communists, were interned. Conscientious objectors, among them Mennonites, were sent to camps where they performed tasks such as fighting forest fires or planting trees. Membership in the Jehovah's Witness religion became illegal under the Defence of Canada's Regulations and Jehovah's Witnesses could be arrested for proselytizing.

Japanese Canadians were the ethnic group that faced the greatest injustice during the Second World War. In 1941, there were 23,149 Japanese in Canada (0.2 percent of the population), and 22,000 of them lived in British Columbia. As Japan conquered territories in the Far East, Canadians started looking on Japanese Canadians with suspicion and expressed racist sentiments toward them. The Japanese attack on the naval base at Pearl Harbor on December 7, 1941, led the United States to declare war against Japan and to relocate and intern Japanese citizens. The Japanese attack also convinced many Canadians that Japan was planning to invade North America and had the military capacity to do so. Various organizations, provincial politicians, newspapers, and Ian Mackenzie, a friend of Prime Minister Mackenzie King and the voice of British Columbia in the federal cabinet, demanded the relocation of Japanese Canadians. Racism and fear led to the request for this repressive measure despite the fact that the RCMP had found no evidence of subversion among Japanese Canadians.

Prime Minister Mackenzie King took action, hoping the measures would appease Canadians. Canada declared war on Japan, and the federal government arrested 38 Japanese and seized the entire Japanese fishing fleet. On January 14, 1942, the federal government announced the partial evacuation of all male enemy aliens—that is, Germans, Italians, and Japanese. On February 24, 1942, the evacuation order was applied to all Japanese Canadians living in British Columbia.

The relocation experience has shaped the lives of many Canadians, as illustrated in Pamela Sugiman's article. For his part, well-known environmentalist David Suzuki wrote a few pages about his experience as a young child. In the excerpt from his autobiography included in this module, Suzuki recalls his experience and his move to Ontario once the war was over. Although some Japanese families agreed to move to Japan, the Suzuki family chose Ontario. This excerpt demonstrates how Suzuki became aware of his ethnicity and how events external to him played a role in how other Canadians interacted with him.

The federal government pursued a process of displacement by interning Japanese Canadians and seizing and selling their properties. It also planned to deport them to Japan, because as an ethnic group they were perceived by senior government officials as a source of tensions among white Canadians; by deporting them, the government hoped to put an end to these tensions. In 1946, about 4,000 Japanese Canadians were deported to Japan. However, the federal government was unable to carry out its plan in full because of the costs and the logistics involved. Although many moved to other parts of Canada, Japanese Canadians were prohibited from returning to British Columbia until 1949. In 1941, 95 percent of Japanese Canadians lived in British Columbia; 10 years later, that number had dropped to 33 percent, while 39 percent now lived in Ontario and 22 percent in the Prairies.

Although internment and relocation as a state policy have remained controversial, the victims sought an apology. In 1988, the federal government apologized to Japanese Canadians and offered them financial compensation. In the case of Italian Canadians interned during the war, the Canadian government did not offer an official apology or financial compensation. Instead, in November 2005, the government agreed to create a fund. These different responses raise the issue of apology as a means of reparation. Is this a course of action worth pursuing?

QUESTIONS

1. Who was interned in Canada during the Second World War and why?
2. Compare and contrast Suzuki's testimony with the testimonies contained in the letters analyzed by Pamela Sugiman.
3. According to Whitaker and Kealey, the RCMP was well informed when it arrested and interned individuals who constituted a threat during the Second World War. What evidence did they use to reach their conclusion?
4. What do we learn about the role of the state and the internment of Canadians? Was this an unjustified repressive policy?

FURTHER READINGS

Durflinger, Serge Marc, *Fighting from Home: The Second World War in Verdun, Quebec*, (Vancouver: University of British Columbia Press, 2006).

Iacovetta, Franca, Roberto Perin, and Principe Angelo, *Enemies Within: Italian and Other Internees in Canada and Abroad*, (Toronto: University of Toronto Press, 2000).

Keshen, Jeffrey, *Saints, Sinners, and Soldiers: Canada's Second World War*, (Vancouver: University of British Columbia Press, 2004).

Nishiguchi, Gabrielle, "The Trip with a Trap: The 1946 Deportations of Japanese Canadians," *ACS Bulletin AEC*, Vol. 20, No. 1, (Spring 1998): pp. 1, 5–6.

Roy, Patricia, Jack L. Granatstein, Masako Lino, and Hiroko Takamura, *Mutual Hostages: Canadians and Japanese during the Second World War*, (Toronto: University of Toronto Press, 1990).

Roy, Patricia, *The Oriental Question: Consolidating a White Man's Province, 1914–1941*, (Vancouver: University of British Columbia Press, 2003).

Ward, Peter W., *White Canada Forever: Popular Attitudes and Public Policy toward Orientals in British Columbia*, 3rd ed. (Montreal: McGill-Queen's University Press, 2002).

▲ Document 1: My Happy Childhood in Racist British Columbia

David Suzuki

Buffered from the world by my parents, I didn't know Japan had attacked Pearl Harbor in Hawaii on December 7, 1941, and I didn't sense any fear or consternation in Mom or Dad. Many years later, my father told me that when he heard the announcement of the attack, he immediately went to a barber and had his hair restyled into a crew cut, which he retained for the rest of his life. "I knew we were going to be treated like 'Japs,' so I figured I might as well look like one" was the way he put it. Cutting his hair was an act of both defiance and submission to what he knew was inevitable. The treachery implicit in Japan's "sneak attack" against the United States Navy and the terrible war that followed threw my family and some twenty thousand other Japanese Canadians and Japanese nationals into a turbulent sequence of events, beginning with Canada's invocation of the iniquitous War Measures Act, which deprived us of all rights of citizenship.

In 1941, Canada was still a racist society. In Prince Rupert in northern British Columbia, First Nations people existed under conditions akin to apartheid in South Africa: they were not allowed to stay in most hotels, they were refused service in restaurants, and they were forced to sit in certain designated sections of theaters. There were also prohibitions against any First Nations person in pubs. (My uncle Mar, who was quite swarthy, was once asked in a bar what tribe he was from. He replied, "The Jap tribe.")

One of the terrible dilemmas of democracy is that only under conditions of duress or crisis do those cherished rights even matter, but that's when they are often rescinded in the name of national security. What good are high ideals of we guarantee them only when times are good? We now know there was not a single recorded case of treachery among Japanese Canadians during the war, despite the conditions to which they were subjected.

But to the white community we looked different; we looked just like the enemy and thus deserved to be treated like the enemy. Most Japanese Canadians were totally loyal to Canada, and many young Japanese Canadian men signed up and willingly fought and died for Canada. Sadly, the evacuation of Japanese nationals and Canadians from the coast of British Columbia and their incarceration in internment camps generated enormous resentment within the community, and many Japanese Canadians gave up citizenship and abandoned Canada for Japan after the war. Under the War Measures Act, property was confiscated and sold at bargain-basement prices, possessions were looted, bank accounts were frozen, and people were warned they would be removed from coastal British Columbia, where they were thought to pose a threat. Within months we were sent to other provinces or relocated to hastily constructed camps deep in the interior of B.C.

As a child, I was not aware of any of these events apart from our relocation, and I can only marvel at how my parents shielded us from the turmoil they must have undergone. Much later, as a teenager, I realized that we—Japanese Canadians—had not been deemed worthy of full membership in the nation. It was an alienation not so much from my country, Canada, as it was from Canadian white society. In my teen years, my identity was based on the consciousness that in the eyes of white Canadians, I was Japanese first, Canadian second. All my life as an adult, my drive to do well has been motivated by the desire to demonstrate to my fellow Canadians that my family and I had not deserved to

389

Source: David Suzuki, "My Happy Childhood in Racist British Columbia," in *The Autobiography*. Vancouver: GreyStone Books (an imprint of D&M Publishers), 2006, pp. 14–25. Reprinted with permission from the publisher.

be treated as we were. And if that was the psychic burden I carried as a result of our experiences during the war, just think of the consequences for First Nations people from the terrible treatment they have been subjected to since first contact.

Of course, Japanese Canadians still held strong ties to Japan. Like those of English heritage who had lived in Argentina for generations yet felt enormous turmoil when Britain attacked the Falkland Islands, the Japanese who came to Canada (called Issei, or first generation) still had family and friends back in the "old country." Like all immigrant people, the first generation of Japanese-heritage kids born in Canada (called Nisei, or second generation) had to grow up without grandparents or an extended family here. This was a sharp break from traditional values surrounding family and elders, and Issei were especially concerned about the loss of those values. As a Sansei (third generation) born of Canadian-born parents, I did have grandparents living in Vancouver and saw them regularly, but, being unilingual, I was almost as cut off from them as I would have been had they lived on the other side of the Pacific. Most of those among the first wave of Issei were like my grandparents: desperately poor, lacking formal education, and in search not of freedom or democracy but of opportunity. They accepted the bigotry they encountered and the restrictions on their entry into society. The War Measures Act consolidated their belief that in Canada, equality and democracy didn't apply to everyone, only to certain privileged racial groups.

Ironically, it was in the internment camps that I became aware of the pain and irrationality of discrimination, and from the Japanese Canadian community at that. It was my first experience of alienation and isolation, and it gave me a lifelong sense of being an outsider. Soon after Pearl Harbor, my father had volunteered to go to that road camp where Japanese Canadians were helping to build the Trans-Canada Highway. He had hoped that by volunteering, he would demonstrate his good intentions, trustworthiness, and willingness to leave his family as hostages to ensure his continued good behavior, therefore ensuring we would be allowed to remain in Vancouver. But it wasn't to be. I am amazed that somehow my parents, still in their early thirties, were able to shield my sisters and me from the pain, anger, and fear that must have threatened to overwhelm them, as the only country they had ever known branded them enemy aliens who could not be trusted.

One day in early 1942, my father was gone. Yet I don't remember feeling any anguish leading up to his sudden departure, nor during the prolonged absence of the one male in my life, who also was my best buddy, hero, and role model. Left with three young children, my mother had to sort through our possessions, winnowing the necessities from everything else, which then had to be sold, given away, or discarded before we made the long train ride to our eventual destination in the Rocky Mountains. I didn't wonder why everyone on the train was Japanese. I just played games with Martha Sasaki, whose family was seated next to ours, and we had a delicious time.

Our destination was Slocan City, a ghost town. Built during the silver rush of the 1890s, when thousands of people mad with silver fever flooded into the beautiful, isolated Slocan Valley, the town was abandoned when mining declined. Now another wave of people poured into the mountains. I found myself surrounded by hundreds of other Japanese Canadians housed in rotting buildings with glassless windows. We lived in a decaying hotel that must have been quite impressive when Slocan City was booming but had become so derelict that I had to learn to avoid the hazardous floorboards on the porch that encircled the building. My mother, my two sisters, and I were placed in one of the tiny rooms, which were still reeking from past generations of occupants, and we would wake each morning covered in bedbug bites. Cleanliness for Japanese is like a religion, and I can imagine the revulsion my mother must have felt in those first weeks.

The massive upheaval, movement, and incarceration of twenty-two thousand Japanese Canadians who were supposed to be a threat to the country posed an immense logistical challenge. Camps made up of hastily thrown together tents and shacks were soon filled. Food had to be supplied by a nation already preoccupied with war across the oceans. There were shortages, especially of trained personnel like nurses, doctors, and teachers. There was no school for the first year, and for a kid suddenly plunked down in a valley where the rivers and lakes were filled with fish and the forests with wolves, bears, and deer, this was paradise.

I had lots of time to play. One of my playmates was a girl named Daisy, who was about my age and who had ended up in Slocan along with her Japanese Canadian mother. Her father was a Caucasian who was serving in the army, defending the democratic guarantees denied his family. Daisy was one of the few kids I felt comfortable playing with, but she was set upon cruelly by the other children, who would reduce her to tears by taunting her as an *ainoko*, which can be roughly translated as "half-breed." She was my friend, and I would never participate in harassing her, but I have felt shame that I didn't have the courage to stand up to the others and defend her. Years later, when we were teenagers, I met Daisy in southern Ontario. She was breathtakingly beautiful but filled with rage toward Japanese Canadians for the torment she had experienced in the camp. I understood the terrible psychic repercussions of discrimination, because I too was on the receiving end of that prejudice.

Although Dad had been taken to Japan for a month when he was about five, Mom had never visited that country. They were Canadians. Both my Nisei parents were bilingual, but they spoke English at home unless they didn't want us to know what they were saying. Almost all the other children in the camps were Nisei, so they were fluently bilingual and could switch into Japanese at will. I as a Sansei didn't speak Japanese and often could not understand what they were saying. Because of my linguistic deficiency, I was picked on by and isolated from the other children.

About a year after we arrived in Slocan, a school was built in a settlement called Bayfarm, perhaps a mile away. I had to knuckle down and start in grade 1. I loved school and was a good student. Dad and Mom would grill me on what I had learned each day, patiently listening to me prattle on. I thought what I had to say was riveting, but now I know their quizzing was a very effective way of going over lessons and helping to correct or guide me along.

I was seven when I enrolled in grade 1, but I was soon skipped through three grades and passed into grade 4 in a year. My father said that at one point I seemed to lose interest in studies and began to complain about having to go to school. He and Mom were very worried, because our education was one of their highest priorities, so one day Dad decided to go to the school to find out what was going on. As he walked along the railroad track that connected Slocan to Bayfarm, he saw a group of kids in the distance chasing a boy. It was winter, and there was a thick blanket of snow on the ground. The victim would slip and fall and the kids would catch up, kicking and hitting him as he struggled to his feet to flee again. The boy was me. Mercifully, I have no recollection of that particular mode of harassment, although I do remember much taunting in the school yard. It took a long time for me to overcome my mistrust and resentment of Japanese Canadians as a result of the way I was treated in those camp days.

White kids we saw rarely, and those we did encounter were Doukhobors accompanying their parents, who visited the camps to sell fresh fruit, meat, and vegetables. I am ashamed of one incident in which I took part as a result of ignorance and childhood stupidity. I have always felt grateful to the Doukhobor farmers, who perhaps were motivated in part by their own memories of repression and injustice in Russia, but to me at that time they seemed alien and mysterious as they rode into Slocan on their laden, horse-drawn carts. One day, a chum told me a "bad word" in Russian, giggling as he made me repeat it until I had it memorized. We didn't know what it meant, and I have no idea how he knew the word or even whether it was a curse or a sexual term. We leaned out of a second-floor window when a farmer's cart came trundling down the alley and stopped below us. My friend and I shouted out the word. When the farmer ignored us, we kept chanting until he picked up the knife he used to cut the tops off vegetables, shouted something at us, and climbed off the wagon.

I guess the shot of adrenaline from fear is why little boys do such things, but I did not enjoy being terrified for my life. We bolted out of that room and into my place and under the bed, trembling and trying to stifle our heavy panting. I doubt the farmer even came into the building, but I was absolutely convinced he was going to kill us. A long while later, we finally crept out of the room, and you can bet we never repeated that stunt. Years later, I apologized for the prank to an audience in the Doukhobor Centre in Castlegar and thanked the Doukhobor community for its support of Japanese Canadians during those trying years.

As the war was drawing to a close, those who renounced their Canadian citizenship and were to receive a one-way ticket to Japan were separated from those who chose to stay in Canada. There was strong coercion among camp members to demonstrate their anger at Canada by signing up to "repatriate" to Japan, and more than 95 percent did. Those who did not sign up were castigated as *inu*, or "dogs." My mother met regularly with a group of women to socialize and gossip, but after word got out that we had chosen to remain in Canada, someone in the group insulted her, nobody spoke up for her, and she never went back. To her death, she would not tell my father who had made the remark or what had been said. I have never forgotten that. My mother, one of the gentlest, kindest people I have known, a person who had had to work hard all her life, who would never have knowingly hurt another person, had been deeply wounded by people she considered friends. One of my worst characteristics is that I find it hard to forgive and forget insults and hurts, and this expulsion of my mother further estranged me from the Japanese "community."

Once the first boatloads of people (including my mother's parents and her older sister's family) arrived in Japan, word quickly came back to Canada that conditions were terrible. Japan had been flattened by bombing, and the people were further demoralized by the atomic bombs dropped on Hiroshima and Nagasaki in 1945 to finally prompt unconditional surrender. Food, clothing, and shelter were extremely hard to find, and people struggled to survive.

At that point, those who had renounced their citizenship began to change their minds and clamored to stay in Canada. They remained in the B.C. camps for so long as they fought deportation to Japan that the government finally allowed them to stay in Canada and resettle wherever they wanted. Many chose to return to the B.C. coast, and Dad was very bitter about that. He hadn't wanted to leave B.C., yet he had been evicted from the province, whereas those who had said they wanted to leave B.C. and Canada ended up staying. My father contemptuously referred to them as "repats" and said they were gutless. First they did not have the strength to decide to stay in Canada and fight for their rights, and then they chickened out of moving to Japan.

After we said we would remain in Canada, we were moved from Slocan to Kaslo, still in the Kootenay region but a much larger urban area on Kootenay Lake. For the first time,

I attended a school with lots of white kids. But now they seemed alien, and I shied away from them, content to explore this new area of lakes and mountains by myself. The valley in the Kootenay region was rich in pine mushrooms, and that fall I learned where they were likely to be found and how to recognize the bulges on the ground, beneath trees, that indicated where the *matsutake* were. We filled potato sacks with them and my mother bottled the fragrant mushrooms. Today *matsutake* pickers do a thriving business exporting them to Japan. Kootenay Lake had a population of kokanee, which are landlocked miniature sockeye salmon. We took the *Moyie*, a passenger stern-wheeler steamboat, to Lardo, a landing at the head of the lake, where we witnessed a spectacular kokanee run. Like their oceangoing relatives, kokanee turn bright red at spawning time, and the river bottom was carpeted with undulating scarlet ribbons.

One summer day in Kaslo in 1945, I was in the communal bath with an old Japanese man when bells began to peal. "Damme! Maketa!" he exclaimed, meaning "That's bad! We've been beaten!" I didn't know what he meant by "we," because as far as I was concerned, my side must have won. I dressed and rushed out to the street, where people were celebrating and setting off firecrackers. I edged closer to the crowd, hoping someone might hand me a firecracker. Instead, a big boy kicked my behind and shouted, "Get lost, Jap. We beat you!" That's why the old man was rooting for the other side. The evacuation and the boy had shown me I was not a Canadian to the government or to him; I was still a "Jap."

We finally left Kaslo on a long train ride across the prairies, all the way to a suburb of Toronto where Japanese Canadians were kept in a hotel until we found places to go. Dad eventually located a job working as a laborer on a hundred-acre peach farm in Essex County, the southernmost part of Canada. We were supplied with a house, and my sisters and I attended a one-room schoolhouse in Olinda. There were probably thirty students, many of German background, but they were white and had not suffered the kind of discrimination we had felt during the war. My sisters and I were the only non-white kids in the area.

On the first day of school in Olinda, I was so shy that I couldn't look any other students in the eye. When recess came, I was stunned when the other children came up to us and dragged us into games and kept us at the center of all the fun. I later learned that our teacher, Miss Donovan, had told all the other students that my sisters and I were coming and that we were to be welcomed into their midst. What a wonderful gift she gave us.

I loved that year in Olinda, but we moved to the town of Leamington the next year when Dad found a job in a dry-cleaning plant. It was 1946, and when we arrived there, some Leamingtonians boasted to me that "no colored person has ever stayed here beyond sunset." We were the first "colored" family to move into the town, and we were nervous.

In postwar Ontario, Japanese Canadians were sprinkled across the province. In southern Ontario, a handful of families worked on farms, and they kept in touch and became the social circle for my parents. The adults would get together periodically to share stories, offer help, and feast on some of the treasured Japanese food prepared for the occasion. Dad became active in the Japanese Canadian Citizens Association, a group that sprang up to help people settle in their new province and to begin the long struggle for redress and apology. Meeting other Japanese Canadians filled me with mixed emotions because I still remembered the way I had been treated in the camps, but the hormones surging through my body spurred me to check out the only possible dating opportunities—Japanese Canadian girls.

Children are wonderful. They are blind to color or race until they learn from their parents or peers what to notice and how to respond. I was playing with one of my chums when my father came along on a bicycle. I called out to him, and he waved and cycled on past. My friend was dumbfounded and asked, "How do you know him?" When I replied, "Because he's my dad, stupid," he gasped, "But he's a Chink!"

In grade 6 at Mill Street School in Leamington, my teacher was a woman after whom the school is now named. I was an obedient, well-behaved student, so it was a shock one day when, as I was sitting quietly in class, she ordered me to get out. I stumbled into the corridor, stunned and humiliated, and trembled with apprehension as I sat on a seat. After an interminable wait, the teacher came out. "But what did I do?" I stammered. She retorted, "You were smirking at me. I know what you people are thinking. Now get back in there, and don't ever let me catch you looking at me like that again!" I was completely confused but seething with an anger I had to hide.

From that experience, I understood that my physical appearance must be threatening to people like her. Ignorance and the relentless propaganda during the war, portraying buck-toothed, slant-eyed "Japs" in the cockpit of a plane on a kamikaze mission, must have caused mystery and fear just as today's image of a Muslim extremist strapped with explosives. Every time I looked in a mirror, I saw that stereotype. To this day, I don't like the way I look on television and don't like watching myself on my own TV programs.

▲ Document 2: Right on the Job

RIGHT ON THE JOB

● *The Toronto Daily Star* published a cartoon (June 13, 1940) supportive of the RCMP arrests of individuals who constituted a security threat. How did the cartoonist depict these individuals as a security threat?

Source: Charles and Cynthia Hou, *Great Canadian Political Cartoons, 1915–1945*. Vancouver: Moody's Lookout Press, 2002. Reprinted with permission, Torstar Syndication Services.

▲ Document 3: Strategic Withdrawal to Prepared Positions

● *The Toronto Daily Star* published a cartoon supportive of the federal government's decision to intern Japanese Canadians (January 21, 1942). In the depiction of Japanese Canadians, compare and contrast the way Japanese Canadians and RCMP officer were depicted.

Source: Charles and Cynthia Hou, *Great Canadian Political Cartoons, 1915–1945*. Vancouver: Moody's Lookout Press, 2002. Reprinted with permission, Torstar Syndication Services.

▲ Document 4: Let Canada Answer *This*

● In March 1942, a cartoon in *The Halifax Herald* asked readers if it was acceptable to treat Canadian prisoners of war the way the Japanese army did. Compare and contrast the way the Japanese soldier and the Canadian prisoner of war are depicted.

Source: Charles and Cynthia Hou, *Great Canadian Political Cartoons, 1915–1945*. Vancouver: Moody's Lookout Press, 2002. Reprinted with permission from Anita Chambers.

▲ Document 5: Japanese Canadians Signing a Petition to Stay in Canada

● This cartoon deals with the policy of deporting Japanese Canadians after the war and the request by some to stay. How are the characters depicted in the cartoon? (*The Daily Colonist, Victoria,* 20 December 1945.)

Source: Charles and Cynthia Hou, *Great Canadian Political Cartoons, 1915–1945*. Vancouver: Moody's Lookout Press, 2002. *Daily Colonist*, December 30th, 1945.

■ Article 1: Passing Time, Moving Memories: Interpreting Wartime Narratives of Japanese Canadian Women

Pamela Sugiman

The story of internment of Japanese Canadians during World War II has become part of the collective memory of most Canadians of Japanese descent. Promoted as part of the community's efforts to seek redress for wartime losses, the collective narrative has centred around loss of property, the indignities of detainment in Vancouver, expulsion to ghost towns, and violation of human rights and principles of democracy. The Redress Settlement with the Canadian government in 1988 has prompted a further unearthing of personal memoirs, in a conscious effort of Japanese Canadians to recover their history. The individual experiences examined here, through the author's personal memories, from private letters written during the war by Japanese Canadian women and intercepted by the Canadian government, and from recent interviews with second-generation Japanese Canadian women, reveal diverse experiences within the collective story. In particular, these accounts challenge the image of the silent, unresisting, and uncritical Japanese Canadian woman.

The wind is so sickly warm. Perhaps the same wind has blown over the bloody battle fields of the Pacific. I have so much to write to you about tonight, I mustn't waste my time by letting my imagination get the better of me—my mind wanders so easily these days—could it be what they call the "ghost town rot"? Even with the certain amount of freedom that's allowed us in the ghost towns, we're getting so sick of the place. We're getting so dull and dry, and uninteresting. I can't help but wonder what boredom and monotony you must have to endure behind those nasty barbed wires! It's more than three years now, *Niesan*, three long years. [...] [from sister in Bay

Farm to her brother in Angler, Ontario, June 1945, written in English][1]

Acts of Political Violence[2]

The pain caused to all persons of Japanese descent by the Canadian government's actions during the years of the Second World War is etched in my memory. It has become an integral part of my existence, as well as the defining moment in my own family's history. Throughout the better part of my adult life, I have reflected on the wartime internment of my mother, father, grandparents, aunts, and uncles. As a sociologist, I have been researching these injustices for years. I do not know how familiar most Canadians are with these events in history. By now, many must know the rough contours of the story, at least the one that has entered the public discourse and been legitimated by the written word and the published record.[3]

In the years prior to the Second World War, over 95 per cent of Japanese Canadians lived in British Columbia, the first immigrant from Japan settling in this western province in 1877. Discriminatory legislation, in addition to ostracism from the Anglo-Celtic population, forced a concentration of Japanese settlements in the southwest corner of B.C. People of Japanese origin owned fishing boats along the coast, as well as berry farms and gardens throughout the Fraser Valley, and in Vancouver a Japanese business and residential community (known as Japan Town) flourished on and around Powell Street. Yet, in spite of their economic and cultural presence, Japanese Canadians had extremely circumscribed rights. By law, they were prohibited from holding public office, from voting in an election, and from entering most institutions of higher learning and hence the professions.

Anti-Asian sentiment was strong and unabashed in B.C. in the decades leading up to the war.[4] However, racism took on new dimensions and its impact on the community intensified dramatically when Japan bombed Pearl Harbor in December 1941. Days after the bombing, with claims that "all people of Japanese racial origin" posed a threat to national security, the Canadian government closed down Japanese-language newspapers, impounded fishing boats, and began plans to remove forcibly 21,000 persons of Japanese ancestry from their homes (75 per cent of this group were naturalized or Canadian-born citizens).[5]

Source: Pamela Sugiman, "Passing Time, Moving Memories: Interpreting Wartime Narratives of Japanese Canadian Women," *Social History, 37,* 73 (May 2004), pp. 51–79. ISSN: 0018-2257. Reprinted with permission.

399

Along with the uprooting, Japanese Canadians were subject to a dusk-to-dawn curfew and had their homes searched by officers of the Royal Canadian Mounted Police. Over time, thousands were herded into the stench-filled livestock buildings of Hastings Park in Vancouver, a "clearing site" for those who would later be dispersed to isolated parts of the province. The majority of Japanese Canadians (approximately 12,000) were eventually sent to "internment camps", where they were forced to live in hastily prepared shacks or run-down hotels.[6] These "settlements" were situated in various parts of the B.C. interior: Greenwood, Sandon, Kaslo, New Denver, Rosebery, Slocan City, Bay Farm, Popoff, and Lemon Creek. Tashme, another site, was set up on vacant land just outside the 100-mile "protected area" close to Hope. A smaller number of families (approximately 1,150) were relocated to so-called "self-supporting" camps in Lillooet, Bridge River, Minto City, McGillivray Falls, and Christina Lake. These families supposedly possessed the financial resources necessary to assume full responsibility for their own relocation and maintenance. Another small group (about 4,000) were sent to perform gruelling labour in family units on the beet farms of Alberta and Manitoba.

In the first phase of the internment, many sons, brothers, and husbands were separated from their families and sent to labour in work camps in B.C. and Ontario. Approximately 1,000 men were sent to road camps. Japanese nationals were placed in camps around the B.C./Alberta border, while the Canadian-born *Nisei* were sent to the Hope/Princeton highway or to Schreiber, Ontario. Men who showed even the most mild form of resistance were interned as prisoners of war in Petawawa and Angler, Ontario. About 700 men were incarcerated in these sites, many of whom remained there for the duration of the war.[7]

With the defeat of Japan in 1945, all cleared Japanese Americans were permitted to return to the coast.[8] However, Japanese Canadians, by then interned for three years, faced a "second uprooting". At this time, the Department of Labour announced two policies: dispersal and "repatriation". People of Japanese ancestry were forced to leave B.C. by either dispersing east of the Rockies (Ontario or Québec) or "repatriating" to Japan. As noted by Roy Miki and Cassandra Kobayashi, the term "repatriation" was a euphemism for what was in fact "a forced exile". After all, "[T]he 'patria' or country of birth for the majority of these citizens was Canada, so they could not in this sense, be 'repatriated' to Japan."[9] Fearful, angry, and confused, approximately 10,000 Japanese Canadians signed up for expulsion. Many signed simply because they were reluctant to face the unfamiliar and racially hostile terrain of Eastern Canada, and thus a large number later changed their minds. Yet in 1946 roughly 4,000 individuals had already been deported (2,000 of these were Canadian born; one-third of the 2,000 were dependent children under the age of 16).[10] The government did not allow Japanese Canadians to return to the "protected zone" until 1949, roughly four years after the war's end. They were not granted the right to the federal vote until June 1948 (effective April 1949), and could not vote in the province of British Columbia until March 1949.[11]

These were acts of political violence. The government's actions resulted in dispossession, property loss (farms, fishing boats, vehicles, homes, and personal belongings of less monetary worth but great personal value), a violation of human rights, disruption of education, diminished aspirations, coerced employment (often highly exploitative in nature and typically for low pay and little recognition), the break-up of families, loss of culture (language, customs, art forms), and continued exposure to racism in its many guises. The more hidden and unquantifiable costs of these wartime injustices enter the realm of emotion and subjectivity, the most dramatic and tragic of these being suicide.[12] In short, the Second World War internment resulted in the destruction of a community and trauma to the individuals within it.

Situating the Narratives

If this story is not known to a general audience of *Hakujin* Canadians, it has no doubt been heard many times by most Canadians of Japanese descent.[13] Indeed, promoted over the last few decades as part of the community's efforts to seek redress for wartime losses, it has become part of our collective memory. The collective narrative has centred around loss of property, the indignities of Hastings Park, expulsion to ghost towns, and violation of human rights and principles of democracy. Since the Redress Settlement with the Canadian government in 1988, we have witnessed a further unearthing of personal memoirs, in a concerted effort on the part of Japanese Canadians to recover their history, consciously to remember, and to preserve memory through the literacization of experience.[14] This expanding cultural reservoir is of enormous value in enriching and extending our sense of ourselves.

Notwithstanding the political utility and empirical value of the official public history, I would caution, however, against the colonization of our thinking about Japanese Canadians and their communities by one (perhaps dominant) story. It is important to search for and listen to many different narratives, drawn from a wide array of sources. As Kirsten McAllister writes, we are somehow compelled by *the* story and therefore must ensure that *all* stories are not reduced to the same one.[15] One narrative alone may conceal the diverse experiences of people—experiences shaped by age, generation, and one's location within hierarchies based on gender and social class. A uniform story, moreover, obscures the ways in which complex systems of domination come together in shaping people's lives. The dominant narrative, though always changing, remains one in which the theme of resistance (in its varied forms) is not always strongly conveyed. Indeed, one might even suggest that much of the publicized literature on the internment has promoted the idea that Japanese Canadians generally, and Japanese Canadian women especially, have been a passive and acquiescent lot.[16] These traits, assumed to be cultural, are embraced by the popular phrase *shikata ga nai*—"what can be done" or an expression of resignation to the situation.[17] The concept of *shikata ga nai* and the silent, passive Japanese woman is part of a race and gender essentialism that must be challenged. While the Redress Movement has clearly disrupted the cultural amnesia that has for so long marked Canadian history, I am not convinced that the imagery of the silent and uncritical Japanese Canadian woman has been fully contested.

Multiple stories of internment from *Nisei* (second-generation) women and, to a lesser extent, their *Issei* (first-generation) mothers indeed challenge this image. I explore the ways in which these women asserted themselves in the face of the nightmares they endured during the war. I take up this theme by describing a range of narratives of Japanese-Canadian experience, each derived from a different source. The first is highly personal, embedded in my own memories. The second set of stories emerges from a selection of private letters written by and to

Nisei and *Issei* women in the mid-1940s. Finally, some images are drawn from the oral testimonies of 35 *Nisei* women currently living in Ontario and B.C.

Just as each of these narratives emerges from a distinct source, each is also communicated in a different way. My personal memories were indirectly experienced, born in childhood, travelled across generations, and strongly informed by a present-day collective remembrance. The private correspondence was crafted in the context of war, intercepted and edited by government officials, and most likely not intended for a public audience. In comparison, the oral testimonies were spoken to a researcher, rooted in personal memory, directly experienced. Rather than offer a direct point-by-point comparison of the narratives, I am interested in the ways in which they inform one another, bringing out the many and complex dimensions or layers of a story. At a general level, the narratives tell us something about the importance of interpretation for the construction of history and about the imposition of time and memory in the process of research and story-telling.

401

Personal Memory

Let me begin with a few words about my own memories of the internment.[18] For many decades, feminist academics have argued against the idea of scientific objectivity and academic distance.[19] In this project especially, I must immediately dispel any pretense of academic distance—and I make no claims of detachment. As Annette Kuhn writes about the process of exploring memory in her book *Family Secrets,* it has been a "story so far of a voyage that turned into an odyssey of the heart as much as of the intellect".[20] Like Kuhn, while working with the materials of my research, I found that "the distanced standpoint of the critic began to feel less and less adequate to my material, incapable of addressing such powerful responses to my critical objects". I too am "captivated" and "intrigued" by the stories that I have read and heard. Writes Kuhn, "Getting to grips with this response demanded that I should not stifle it by insisting upon a critical distance, but rather acknowledge it and bring it into play by embracing my own past and its representation through memory."[21]

My personal memories and the emotional essence of these memories have undeniably shaped my interpretation and construction of the two other narratives.[22] The letters and testimonies upon which I draw were never simply "sources of data", pieces in a project of historical reconstruction. Clearly, they informed my understanding of Japanese Canadian lives, but they have also been personally experienced and are very much a part of my own "journey through remembrance".

My early memories of the internment were gathered largely from my parents, my aunt, and, to a lesser degree, my grandparents. Given that I could not speak Japanese and they said that they could not speak English, communication with my grandparents was largely by way of an implicit understanding based on eye and body contact, as well as their tales as told by their *Nisei* children. The grandparents whom I knew seemed stoic, displaced, and highly dependent on one another. They seemed to be passing time in Ontario, very much rooted both emotionally and materially in their past lives. My mother taught me about the internment through her caution, in addition to her fragmented stories about life in Haney, then Hastings Park, Rosebery, and ultimately the long, lonely train trip to work as a domestic for a wealthy family in Toronto. My father conveyed anger and ambivalence, and offered snapshots of a carefree pre-war existence in Vancouver, followed by incarceration in a prisoner of war camp. The most vivid of these snapshots is the white shirt with red circle that he was forced to wear in Petawawa.

My knowledge of the internment was drawn from an extremely small and homogeneous group. Sheltered in my Anglo-Saxon/Eastern European neighbourhood of Toronto, my only contact with other Japanese Canadians was with people in my own family. Once in a while, I visited distant relatives, and on Sundays I saw familiar strangers at the Toronto Buddhist Church. During these years, I had curiously embraced the idea that we should not talk about the internment, that to ask too many questions would hurt my parents. This is odd because, in retrospect, my parents have no obvious indication that they did not want to share their memories with me. I furthermore believed, albeit with an increasingly critical eye, that Japanese Canadians may be best described by the phrase *shikata ga nai*. I asked my parents if they had not felt anger. I assumed that they had no critical feelings toward the Canadian government. I believed that Japanese Canadians then did not protest, and later just wanted to forget.

Memory, of course, is fluid. As I undertook this project, my memories have changed. In encountering new information, new sources of data, voiced by people beyond my own family, I have begun to remember in different ways. My memory has been transformed. I now turn to some of the sources of its transformation.

Private Letters

In the initial stages of my research, I came across a number of letters, written by and to Japanese Canadians, that had been intercepted and censored by government officials during the war. The extracted contents are now housed in the National Archives.[23] Among the first to catch my eye was a letter that had been written to my aunt by her brother. I later found correspondence by other members of my extended family. Many months passed before I gathered and read all of the 900 letters that I had collected, but, as I did so, another narrative began to unfold, one that contested my simple childhood memories.

The narrative that emerges from the private correspondence was produced in the context of war. Little time elapsed between the thought and the writing of that thought, the documenting and preservation of sentiments. In this sense, the letters have an immediacy and rawness. For Japanese Canadians, the time of writing was one of separation, uncertainty, and disruption. During these years, many women were living lives away from their fathers, brothers, husbands, sons, and boyfriends. Many *Issei* women were advancing to middle age, while the majority of *Nisei* were teens or relatively young. Some were children. The experiences about which they wrote were not mediated by decades of living. The letters and their authors are, in a sense, "fixed in time".[24]

This private correspondence seems to have served two main purposes. People used the letters to communicate information to one another about living and working conditions, finances, government policy, family decision-making. The letters also served as a vehicle of self-expression, a means by which to convey feeling and articulate personal opinion. One theme that is clear, perhaps more directly and consistently communicated than in the oral testimonies, is that of the violence imposed upon the community and the harsh impact of this violence on individuals. Most of the letters are highly personal, thus allowing for a sense of the intimate experience of the government's wartime actions. The outright disclosure of injustice, the open airing of misery and grief, is enlightening and profound.

The Emotional Experience of Political Violence

While both *Issei* and *Nisei* women conveyed anger in their correspondence, the *Issei* were more likely at the same time to declare their outright loyalty to Japan, and their criticism of the Canadian government specifically, and white people generally, was unqualified. While equally critical of government and politicians, letters written by *Nisei* women reveal more contradictory emotions. Their anger toward the government was tempered with disappointment and despair. Born and raised in Canada, good citizens, they were in disbelief about their treatment in this country. Because their unfair treatment was based on phenotypical racial qualities, they felt that much was beyond their control. Despite this, there are repeated assertions of national loyalty and national identity. In May 1945, for example, a *Nisei* woman wrote to her brother in Ontario:

> Through no fault of our own we happened to be born of Japanese parents, however, as you know, all were educated in Canadian system of governing Democracy. Right of free speech, etc. etc., no matter what race colour, or creed. Well, these ignorant "so-and'so's" think they're the only ones in this country thats entitled to live. [...] With all the raw deals and racial hatred towards us I'm still proud to say that I'm a Canadian of Japanese ancestry. I was created to be one and will live up to one. [From sister to brother?, May 1945, written in English]

A *Nisei* woman in Lemon Creek expressed similar feelings to a male friend in Angler, Ontario:

> No use going out East, when, wherever you go, the narrow minded whites call you "JAPS". Might as well stay here where there are practically no white people. The nisei are sure in a tight spot. We don't know whether we're a CANADIAN or a JAPANESE. Because we were JAPANESE they forced us from the coast and now as CANADIAN

they want us to evacuate EAST. Phooey and double phooey to the damn selective service guys. [From woman in Lemon Creek to male friend in Angler, Ontario, March 1944, written in English]

And in a letter to a male friend in Brantford, Ontario, a *Nisei* woman from Slocan wrote:

> It surely makes me sick—and angry ... they may take us for enemies just cuz our parents were born in Japan but they certainly don't give us much chance to let us prove ourselves worthy of this country. [...] Oh, it made my blood boil—"once a Jap, always a Jap". [...] The more I think of our standing the worse it is for my poor heart so I'll stop. [From woman in Slocan to male friend in Ontario, March 1944, written in English]

My present-day political outlook and sensibilities made it difficult for me to read, over and over again in these letters, the word "Jap". It was one thing to see this word used in official government documents or in *The Vancouver Province* newspaper, but quite another to read it in private correspondence written by and to Japanese Canadians themselves. Given its author, the language took on an even more violent and obscene quality. A *Nisei* woman in Bay Farm wrote to a female friend in Alberta:

> [I]f we are loyal we have to go east, or on the other hand back to Japan. There's work outside of this place I guess but what is the difference, wherever you go a Jap is a Jap. [Between woman friends, Bay Farm to Alberta, April 1945, written in English]

Many *Nisei* repeatedly expressed feelings of entrapment. They were marked by their own faces—trapped by physical features that identified them as Japanese. Writing about Japanese American women, Jeanne Houston notes that slanted eyes and high cheekbones became not simply Japanese physical traits, but "floating signifiers of difference" linked to "negative behavioural characteristics". The inner self may have been Canadian, but the outer self was Japanese. This separation of self is part of the violence done to Japanese Canadians.[25]

403

Dichotomization of the inner and outer self is evident in the following letter written by a *Nisei* woman in Toronto to her girlfriend in Alberta:

> They call us "Japs" and think of us in the same light that they think of the native Japanese. I think there are very few people that really consider us as "fellow Canadians" …even among our occidental friends. I suppose it all boils down to the fact that we have black hair and oriental features and we look so different from the other races that we can never become quite as Canadianized as the rest. […] [Between woman friends, Toronto to Alberta, August 1944, written in English]

Imparting similar views, a *Nisei* woman in Tashme wrote her brother in British Columbia:

> I think a *Nisei* has a better a chance as we know English and customs, but pretty hard for *Isseis*. Bad enough that we have black hair and slant eyes. [From sister in Tashme to brother in Sicamous, B.C., May 1945, written in English]

Interned in Tashme, a woman wrote to a girlfriend in Rosebery:

> Imagine we the *Niseis* have to do, what the Selective Service tells us to do, when we don't even get the rights of *Canadian citizen*. Really we are treated like skunks anywhere we go—we are not wanted because of black hair and brown eyes. […] [Between woman friends, Tashme to Rosebery, October 1943, written in English]

Reference to what had become conspicuous aspects of the physical self is made repeatedly in many of the letters. The *Nisei* were painfully aware of the ways in which hair colour and the shape of one's eyes were used to homogenize a group and to deny the social factors of citizenship and cultural identity.

Daily Survival and Hardship

Much of the correspondence furthermore concerns the women's feelings about day-to-day survival, getting by. In their letters, gendered divisions and experiences are prominent. They braved the internment as women whose oppression had been strongly shaped by both sexual and racial subordination. Some revealed a strong consciousness of this. While husbands, sons, and boyfriends wrote about exploitative working conditions in the road camps, in lumber mills, and in factories and about the inhuman treatment they endured as POWs, women wrote of their own gendered hardships: the burden of supporting a family in the absence of a male provider. This was particularly true of *Issei* women who were mothers and therefore shouldered heavy financial and familial responsibilities. To her husband in Angler, an *Issei* woman in Lemon Creek wrote:

> My worries are greater than yours. Every day with the temperature at hundred and twenty degrees I have to go to negotiate and every time I go to the Welfare I have to fight. Not receiving sufficient for our daily necessities I have had to use what I had but had saved…. And who has made us suffer in this way taking away my husband who is guiltless and interning him. And is it not a wilful thing to do by taking away the subsistence and then telling me to go out to work. [From wife in Lemon Creek to her husband in Angler, July 1944, written in Japanese]

Similarly, a woman in Greenwood explained to her husband in Angler:

> I took all the notes of what I had earned by working in the fields, of what I spent and bills of things I had bought … I had twenty-seven dollars and eighty-one cents left…. With that [money received from the B.C. Security Commission] and the twenty-seven dollars and eighty-one cents I was told to maintain myself for three months. This was really too exasperating. I think one cannot be blamed for grumbling after being told a ridiculous thing like that and also after working so hard in the fields. They seem to think we can produce work for ourselves…. It really makes me miserable to think that we are getting no where except in years. [From wife in Greenwood to her husband in Angler, July 11, 1944, original language not specified]

Also telling are the letters that some *Nisei* women wrote about their treatment as domestic workers in private households. Many *Nisei* had been sent to work for *Hakujin* families in Ontario and Quebec, as well as in B.C. itself. In fact, some even cared for the children of their RCMP guards. Within these homes, they sometimes faced severe racist and sexist treatment. Though women (who continued to perform paid domestic work long after the war's end) today speak warmly, uncritically, of their *Hakujin* bosses and are particularly reluctant to broach an issue such as harassment, the latter problem is raised in some of the written letters. One young woman, for example, wrote her fiancé in Ontario about her experiences in Nakusp. Apparently, her male boss had sexually harassed her when the woman of the house was away. Not only does the tone of her correspondence convey disgust, but she openly declares her intention to fight against such treatment. She wrote:

> [T]he old lady went for her holidays so I was alone with this fat old [—] … he just walked right toward me and grab hold of me and he didn't let me go so I just hit me and scream and everything I could but he's a fat old pig so I was squashed I just told me I'll tell everything to your wife well I think that hurt him he sure was mad but its his fault eh…. I knew this will happen someday I didn't like her to go for holiday leaving 3 kids. [From woman in Nakusp to her fiancé in Ontario, January 1945, written in English]

The writer planned to leave the position immediately. However, because their employment had been arranged by the B.C. Security Commission, many did not have the option of leaving such situations.

Nevertheless many Japanese Canadian women did express a defiant spirit, in spite of forced inaction. The discourse on which they drew promoted cultural constructs of womanhood, sometimes embracing a distinct racial component. A number of *Issei* women, for example, asserted their resilience, their strength to persevere, as would be expected of a true Japanese woman. A wife in Lemon Creek wrote to her husband in Angler:

> Please do not worry about me … I'll like to do my best for the two children. I have

the same intention as I had at first and even if my hair turns grey in years of waiting I will be a true Japanese woman. [From wife in Lemon Creek to her husband in Angler, November 1944, original language not specified]

Another *Issei* woman writing from New Denver expressed these sentiments to her male friend in Angler:

> It is difficult for woman alone to move but [...] I fought and fought for it and won. I worried over it so much and what with the heat I was sick in bed for 7 days. [...] If they treat me like that just because I am a woman I won't give in even one step. [From woman in New Denver to male friend in Angler, July 1944, written in Japanese]

Some women additionally drew on maternal imagery in resisting racial oppression. An *Issei* mother in Manitoba wrote to friends in B.C.:

> We will keep our health until the day when we again tread the earth of our motherland. As a woman I may be looked upon as of the weaker sex, but as a mother I am strong. I have been able to work through the severe cold without one day of illness. I overcome all hardships as for my country and my children. [From woman in Manitoba to friends in B.C., March 1945, written in Japanese]

The Forced "Repatriation" Decision

As indicated by some of the letters that I have thus far cited, a prominent subject in the private correspondence was the issue of "repatriation" or dispersion.[26] Eager to eliminate the "Japanese race" from the province of B.C., and more generally to ensure that a concentration of such people not resurface elsewhere in Canada, in 1945 the federal government forced Japanese Canadians to "choose" either to "repatriate" to Japan or to move east of the Rockies. The pros and cons of moving to Ontario or Quebec or relocating to Japan began to saturate Japanese Canadian communities.[27] As noted, the government presented its policy as one of "choice". However, the *Issei* and *Nisei* alike

405

knew that this "choice" was illusory. Indeed, it was coercive. Repatriation decision tore apart many families, both physically and emotionally. Faced with this so-called choice, wives, mothers, and daughters not only asserted their will against government authorities; they also had to negotiate relations of power within their own families. Contrary to the popular image of the obedient *Issei* woman, many first-generation wives firmly opposed their husbands in decisions about repatriation. An *Issei* man incarcerated in Angler warned his wife about the consequences of her resolution to remain in Canada:

> If you carry out your desire to go East you will not be able to return to (our) country [Japan]. After the war there will be great hardship and, as at present, hell on earth [...] There is no object to be attained by going East on your own accord. [...] It is the Government's aim to separate and scatter. It is frightening. [...] Canada is a large country. Its ostracism is terrifying. [From husband in Angler to his wife in Lemon Creek, May 1944, written in Japanese]

In many cases, a wife's opposition to her husband's repatriation decision was met with the threat of desertion. For instance, an *Issei* man declared to his wife in Rosebery:

> If you disagree to go back to JAPAN with me I am afraid that I will have no more to do with you because I cannot see any other way. What is more, I will leave you behind and go back myself. [From husband in Angler to his wife in Rosebery, April 12, 1944, original language not specified]

A woman in Popoff wrote to her husband in Angler:

> No Sir, I won't go out of here even if you divorced me or they kill me. [...] No one in the families will move out of here so don't forget that. You think I am selfish and man but what can I do. [...] All this time I thought my husband was a man but not anymore. If you don't do or listen what I say well then, do anything you like but don't forget

I'll never forgive you, never. [From wife in Popoff to her husband in Angler, May 1945, written in English]

The repatriation question resulted in even more frequent conflicts between *Nisei* children and their *Issei* parents. On the whole, the Canadian-born *Nisei* had serious reservations about moving to Japan, a country that was foreign to them. One may surmise that the majority of young *Nisei* girls and women ultimately respected their parents' decisions, contrary to their own desires. Some of these women later returned to Canada on their own. Yet a number of *Nisei* daughters did resist their parents' will. A woman in Vernon disclosed her intentions to her girlfriend in Popoff:

> [M]y parents are keen on returning to Japan after the war [...] I guess they think me unpatriotic but I do not see things their way and I firmly believe my future is in this country. I know there are families in ghost towns and elsewhere where the children and parents take the different viewpoint on this survey. The parents think they control our body, mind and soul and believe they could make us do anything they want us to. They utterly believe we would never disobey them in any way, but I think they're mistaken there. Surely our life is not theirs, surely we aren't going to suffer because we had followed them to their homeland and can't adopt ourselves to their customs. [...] I haven't as yet said anything about my decision to my parents but when they start to survey here in Vernon they'll sure be surprised when they hear what I have to say about the whole darn nasty affair. If after all my objections I do go to Japan you'll know very well I never went because I desired to do so [...] I'll fight to my last energy to remain in Canada. [Between woman friends, Vernon, B.C., to Popoff, April 1945, written in English]

These letters dispel notions of a silent and accepting Japanese Canadian woman. Crafted in the immediacy of war, they impart strong emotion, notably anger, at times outrage. While historians have documented the resistance efforts of organizations such as the Nisei Mass Evacuation Group and the Japanese Canadian committee for Democracy, we have few narratives of informal, individual protest against racial and gender oppression, often articulated by women who possessed limited structural resources.[28] These letters are especially remarkable given that the women I interviewed claimed to have then known that their correspondence might be read by government authorities. In this light, their letter writing may be viewed as a symbolic gesture of defiance.[29]

Oral Testimony

My intent in bringing these letters together with narratives generated through oral testimony does not rest on the belief that the more data sources we consult, the more valid our history. Furthermore, I do not suggest that written documents (housed in archives) may serve as a measure of the accuracy or veracity of spoken reminiscences. In particular, there is no place in this analysis for accusations of faulty or distorted memory.[30] Rather, I wish to explore the process of remembering and the ways in which the derivation of our knowledge of history (sources of data and methods of gathering) may generate very different types of narratives that may be used to build upon one another and to disclose the role of subjectivity, of interpretation, and of the researcher herself in constructing the past.

Researcher and Narrator

My engagement with the oral testimonies forced me to confront a distinct set of concerns. Admittedly, in interpreting the written letters, I intervened, carefully selecting passages upon which to draw and comment in a formal analysis.[31] Indeed, when relying on written documents, it has been especially tempting to separate analysis on one hand from data on the other.[32] This is problematic, for, in dichotomizing data and analysis, in neatly separating the collection of data from their interpretation, we run the risk of overlooking the ways in which the data themselves are already the products of editing, reflection, and decision and are therefore not simply concrete indicators of historical objectivity. Yet, in gathering oral testimony, my role as researcher seemed even more intrusive. I was responsible for the generation

of the testimony itself. Without my intervention, the testimonies would simply not exist.[33] I entered the women's lives, asked them my questions, tape-recorded and transcribed their words. In comparison, the letters rest in the archives, whether or not I examine them. Moreover, without my shaping, the spoken narratives would assume a different form. As I have noted in other writings, in gathering *Nisei* women's stories, I imposed my own agenda and sensibilities. Initially at least, I enforced a reliance on a linear historical chronology and yet, at the same time, imposed a feminist logic, highlighting the significance of the personal and its links to a wider political existence. Furthermore, my questions were guided by the collective internment narrative with which I was most familiar.[34]

As well, over the course of the interviews, my relationship with the women evolved and itself informed the research inquiry.[35] Just as the women's narratives are the product of this unfolding relationship, so too was my own understanding of them and their stories. At the outset, I believed that the differences between myself and the narrators might pose a barrier, in spite of our apparent bonds. But, with each interview, I discovered that the differences between us in age and generation were important in helping the women to establish a sense of their value as "informants". My (comparatively young) age and different status (*Sansei* or third-generation) rendered me ignorant in some ways and marginal to "their" history. Furthermore, inequalities based on class and education proved to be far less important than I had anticipated. Though most of the women themselves lived working-class lives, their *Sansei* children have achieved remarkably high levels of education. Research projects, book manuscripts, and doctoral degrees were therefore not foreign to many of the women. More meaningful than my educational credentials was my family background. The most significant bond between us proved to be one based on "racial" identity and family relations and thereby an implicit understanding of the impact of internment by virtue of my place in a cross-generational "community of memory".[36] Before we started to talk about her life, Sue (whom I had never met before) told me that we were distant relatives.[37] She conveyed stories about my grandmother: her penchant for sweets, her sense of humour, her characteristic toothy smile. At the beginning of another interview, I discovered that Yoshiye had grown up in the same small community as my mother.[38] (I never before knew that my mother had played baseball, not to mention that she was good at it.) And no one had ever told me that Yoshiye, who became a nurse after the war, was working in a Toronto hospital and happened to be on duty at my father's side when he died over 30 years after the war's end.

In the evolving relationship between researcher and narrator, secrets were exchanged. Few of the women hesitated to ask me about my own family, about my current situation and emotional sentiments. In turn, some of them shared their secrets with me. It is paradoxical that some of these shared stories, which now dot my own narrative, are ones I cannot tell. The women's secrets, "small and fragile", are now most vivid in my own memory of the internment.[39] Of course, some memories will never be shared with anyone. These are purely autobiographical. Others will be kept within a particular community, shared with some but not others.[40] In a hushed voice, Rose, for instance, asked me to promise never to disclose some of her sentiments to a *Hakujin* audience.[41]

Time and Memory: In Retrospect

Compared with written documents, the women's testimonies have a different relationship to time. The time at which the interview takes place, the time that passes over the course of an interview, the passage of time from the events discussed to memories conveyed are all significant in shaping the narrative. In the words of Alessandro Portelli, "Tales go with time, grow with time, decay with time…. Life histories, personal tales, depend upon time, if for nothing else, than because there are additions and subtractions made to them with each day of the narrator's life." As Portelli states, there is only so much material that can be preserved in individual and collective memory.[42] In interpreting the spoken narratives, it is important to keep in mind that, in a way not possible with the letters, the women's thoughts have been filtered through the passage of roughly 60 years—and all that has unfolded during these years. What we are hearing, then, are the women's memories of internment.

Many of the women who participated in this project had trouble remembering events that are now prominent in the public narrative. There are silences in their narratives. Some women do not remember dates that have taken on an official importance. "What

year did the war end? When did we have to head East?" Some do not remember the sequencing of events in their lives and in the larger history. "How could I have come to Toronto in 1947, if the war ended in 1945? That must be a mistake. Well, let's see, I got married in '45. I must have left B.C. before then."

Some women comment on these omissions as deliberate and wilful.[43] As noted by Eviatar Zerubavel, people make choices about what to "put behind them."[44] As she showed me her collection of photos from the war years, Amy talked about having to leave business school because of the internment. I inquired about this.

> *Pam:* How long were you in business school?
> *Amy:* Well, from September until oh, March, I think. I don't remember. That part I can't remember. And I don't remember—if it's because I don't like to think of unpleasant things. I don't remember that.

Further in her testimony, she noted another gap in her memory.

> *Pam:* Did you have any communication with your father who was in the road camp?
> *Amy:* Well, I guess my mother did. But I don't remember that. It's very shattering not to remember.
> *Pam:* I think it's because of age, probably. […]
> *Amy:* But I know that when he was moving to New Denver […] when we arrived in New Denver, we were all sick. […] We all vomited.[45]

Similarly, Rose stated,

> It's funny. I was twenty-two, twenty-three. Isn't it funny that I don't have too… maybe it's […] like you try to block what you know. But I remember that we didn't get out 'til October of that year. […] We moved from our home […] on Powell Street […] across the street there was a Japanese department store.

The most distinct and graphic memories of some women seem unrelated to official facts of the

408

internment. Yet they are very much a part of the women's personal memory of the wartime suffering. In her testimony, Ruby explained that, when she was growing up in British Columbia, there was one boy who was "really nasty" [racist].[46] To this she quickly added that there had been "an English couple who were always being nice to us". She maintained that, once the war was over, racial discrimination was not a problem. In her words, "I'm sure there's always a few even up to now, you know. [...] Certain people don't like certain nationality or whatever. But on the whole, I would say it's not too bad." However, later in her testimony, Ruby reintroduced the racist boy. She remarked, "I don't know what he's like now. I think he still lives in Winfield. [...] 'Cause I mean, he was a real jerk." She continued, "But I often think, I wonder what that guy is doing. I wonder what kind of life he has or whether he's still that way. I don't know." She remembered him again at the end of her testimony: "Oh, he was a real mean kid [...] I don't think he was much older than we were but he's just a mean bully. Yes, real bully. Oh, he used to be a real nasty kid. I don't think there's anybody as nasty as him."

Since the war's end, *Nisei* women have lived in neighbourhoods and entered workplaces in which there have been few Japanese. Importantly, as their sons and daughters have married, most have acquired *Hakujin* daughters- and sons-in-law and grandchildren that are part *Hakujin*, part *Nihonjin*, and thoroughly integrated into the dominant (*Hakujin*) society.[47] Betty explained,

> I don't talk about it much to my children. We remember a few things but try not to dwell on it. We're hoping our children won't have to go through the same things we did. In those days it was all Japanese or all *Hakujin*. There was no intermarriage. Now it's different.[48]

Some no longer speak openly about "race" and racism. Ruby concluded her commentary on the racist bully by asserting, "But I don't think there's that mean of a kid around any more." Neatly demarcating the war years from all those that followed, some women maintained that the experience of racism was specific to the pre-war period and the duration of the Second World War. While some women did offer powerful and damning stories of racist assault in post-war

B.C., Ontario, and Quebec, others claimed that they seldom, if ever, heard racist remarks or encountered discrimination within employment, education, or housing. When these women spoke of racism in particular, it was almost as though the decades immediately following their internment had disappeared from memory, or at least faded in significance. Indeed, some women promoted the liberal equation of cultural/ethnic assimilation and the denial of difference with equality and the eradication of racial intolerance. Long regarded as the "orientalist" other, they are relieved to have become culturally and economically integrated into the nation. While most no longer speak with passion about their inhuman treatment as the racialized "other", the women did offer clear descriptions of the long, horrible train trip from one internment site to the next and from B.C. to Ontario, the nothingness, the loss of opportunity, the ways things could have been.

Nostalgia and Critical Memory

Testimony reveals many layers of feeling. In hearing the women's memories, I was also struck by the positive sentiments, indeed the happiness, in the recollections of some. Happy moments existed alongside thoughts about forced exile, the violation of rights, and losses incurred. Some women described their years in the sites of internment as "fun" and "the best times" of their lives. Hideko, for instance, explained,

> Those were very interesting years for me. That's where I met all my friends. [...] Nobody's rich or poor or educated. We were all the same. And we all helped each other. [...] In fact, the whole Tashme was [...] we were happy. Nobody sad. We all encouraged each other, you know. And helped each other so.[49]

Similarly, Sugar remarked, "We had a lot of fun as kids, you know."[50]

On the surface, these remarks stand in stark contrast to the narratives drawn from the letters. Yet it is not surprising that these women uphold a time in their lives, experienced in youth, free of heavy domestic burdens, in a situation of shared oppression. Though families were often separated, groups of *Nisei* women lived together in forced communities that were characterized by age, sex, and racial and

409

ethnic homogeneity. Isolated in desolate parts of the B.C. interior, communities of internees established close bonds. Over time, these bonds have no doubt taken on heightened meaning. By the war's end, the government shattered these communities, severing the ties.

Moreover, thinking about years past, the women remembered not only what they themselves had directly experienced. They also placed their memories in the context of families, friendships, and other social relationships. Hideko commented, "What we had to do to keep the family together … it must have been horrible for my mother." Similarly, Masako remarked, "I myself, I guess, I've been fortunate to be born right in the middle. I didn't suffer. But it's my oldest brother and my mom and dad. They really suffered. And it's the person who really suffered, they didn't even get their Redress."[51]

The same woman who recalled good times, in which she learned to sew, danced to Benny Goodman, and went ice skating with the girls, has also embraced in memory the whippings that her husband endured as a prisoner of war and the hours spent by her mother scavenging for discarded pieces of coal to heat the family's leaky shack in the cold of winter. As noted by Zerubavel, notwithstanding diverse experience and particular memories, we may speak of a common, shared memory. The common nature of memories suggests that they are not purely personal and individual.[52] Memory reveals a strong social dimension. Like the researcher herself, *Nisei* women delve into "communities of memory".[53]

In reading the women's stories, furthermore, it is important to consider the broader process of transmission, the ways in which people convey meaning beyond words, and the disjuncture at times between the written (transcribed) word and vocalized utterances. Much is lost or concealed in the transcribing of voices and words and in the writing of oral testimony. We do not see the tears, the visible inability to talk, the emotion welling up in a woman's eyes as her words continue to flow with calm. The women's narratives are punctuated with emotion, with throw-away phrases such as "I don't know" and "That's what I think, anyway." Their recollections of both "good" and "bad" times were interspersed with defensive laughter that attempted to mask hurt and consequence.

Also telling is that the very women who spoke of the internment as the "good old days" voiced

strong objections to the actions taken against them, their words more subdued but nevertheless echoing sentiments articulated in the old letters. Yoshiye commented, "It was a foolish, expensive adventure that the federal government took. […] At least [with the Redress Settlement] it came out in public that it was a horrible thing." Similarly, after providing decades of faithful domestic service to the same *Hakujin* woman, Ritsuko recollected with exasperation her former employer's remarks about the internment.

> Like [Mrs. Whitton] said, "Well, that was a great mistake." She used to say that Mackenzie King, he made a big mistake. Well, I don't think that was a mistake! […] How can she ever say that was a mistake! […] To evacuate is different. But the thing what the Japanese went through, leaving their things behind, leaving their business […] behind. Just like that in twenty-four hours? You lose everything? And [Mrs. Whitton] calls that a mistake of Prime Minister? It was so crazy for her to tell me that! I think there was a better way […] I know. I guess they were so afraid of Japanese after the war. […] That's why it happened you know. I guess they weren't afraid of the Germans.[54]

In many women, nostalgia co-exists with a critical eye toward the injustices that they and their families endured. Leo Spitzer's concept of "critical nostalgia" is useful in understanding this juxtaposition of happiness and suffering.[55] While critics of nostalgia have regarded it as "inauthentic, reactionary, and offering a falsification of the past", Spitzer argues that, although nostalgic memory may be viewed as "the selective emphasis on what was positive in the past", it is not by any means antithetical to a critical awareness of the negative aspects of one's past.[56]

Roughly six decades after the war's end, the women also offered explanations as to why, back then, they did not and could not collectively (effectively) resist the government's actions. Having witnessed the emergence of a human rights framework, a discourse of liberalism, and most immediately the successful campaign of the Redress activists, they were prompted to explain. Indeed, an explanation of their apparent lack of resistance has become part of the narrative. However, these explanations do not rest on ideas about essential cultural traits. Rather, the women highlighted their past position of structural powerlessness. During the war, they were young, propertyless, uneducated—and female. Pauli remarked,

> There was some young men that resisted, naturally, back at the Coast. But then men at the RCMP got word of it. They were pilfered out and taken right away. They were the ones that were sent to the internment camps [POW camp]. And of course, all the younger men, able men, were all sent out to the road camp. So only the older, and the women and children. So there couldn't have been much resistance. There just was no way.[57]

She continued, "[M]any people just sort of gave up, you know, if we were here so what else can we do. [...] There's no way you could write a letter or anything and have somebody come out and help you and say, well, we'll send you here or there, you know. There was nothing like that." Sachi likewise commented,

> But there was nothing we could do. We're too young to fight. [...] "Why didn't you fight? Why didn't you stand up against the Government? They were taking your legal rights." Well, heck, we're only teenagers. We weren't old enough to think. Well, some did but the fighting only meant they were incarcerated and sent to a prison camp. So, there was no way we could stop that racial prejudice that was so great in Vancouver days. And I know, you might think we were dumb not to fight but we couldn't. We could do anything.[58]

The passing of time is important in shaping these responses. Though we can never accurately predict the pieces that will appear in unfolding narratives, one wonders whether, 20 years earlier, these women would have freely volunteered an analysis of their powerlessness.

Just as the women told a story of the past, they also presented an image of themselves in the present.[59] In doing so, they remained keenly aware of the audience to whom they were speaking. The women in this study presented their past suffering partially, selectively. While they wanted their pain to be acknowledged, they also did not wish to reduce themselves to the status of victims.[60] They told their stories in such a way that highlighted their endurance, as well as their agency. Judy Giles's concept of "composing subjectivities of dignity and self-respect" aptly describes this manner of presentation. Giles notes that women sometimes create stories as expressions of their attempts to compose subjectivities that offer dignity and self-respect in a world characterized by their own powerlessness.[61]

In asserting dignity, the women gave me many happy endings. The conviction of a happy ending indeed was resonant at the conclusion of most of the testimonies. In their narratives, one could detect an ideology of positive thinking and the theme of "triumphant social mobility".[62] Echoing the words of many others, Hannah said,

> Well, if this hadn't happened and we were still living at the coast, we'd probably be discriminated. And people have been able to further their education and they wouldn't be what they are today, a lot of people. So in a way, maybe it was, it was terrible to go through that, but I guess in the end, you look at it now. People are scattered all over. [...] And maybe it was a good thing [*softly spoken*].[63]

According to Michiko, "Everybody has done well because of the suffering. They achieved."[64]

There is a corrective sense to these reminiscences. *Nisei* women frequently voiced the view that the suffering of the past has been "a blessing in disguise", but this statement contains many layers of meaning and therefore should not necessarily be taken at face value. It is not a statement of forgiveness. It is not redemptive. Nor is it spoken by women who have neatly put the past behind them. Rather, it is part of an attempt at healing, though, in hearing their memories, we see that this process of healing will never be complete. Nonetheless, the women attest: we have not only survived; we have succeeded. The past is remembered but will not be relived. Though they experienced violation at the hands of the state, their children did not endure

411

such suffering, and they are resolved in the belief that their grandchildren never will. They have not been defeated.

Conclusion: A Multiplicity of Stories

Writing about her edited collection on memory and working-class consciousness, Janet Zandy notes that the essays "do not dissolve into one blended working-class essence".[65] Like the collection that Zandy describes, the narratives that I present here do not simply merge into one single story. Rather, they suggest a multiplicity of stories. When we consider them together, when we think about the ways in which the different narratives weave in and out of one another, we begin to see the complexity of the internment experience. The conditions of their creation—the different sources from which they stem and the social process of their communication—lead us to reflect on the significance of time and memory in the construction of these narratives.

If we turn to documents written in the midst of war, we read one set of stories. When we ask women to remember the past in the present time, we hear different tales. To all of this, the researcher brings her own past as well as her current concerns, sensibilities, and political agenda. These narratives inform one another. They present history itself as a social and political construct, and the process of historical/sociological research as one that must be self-conscious and multi-layered. According to Walter Benjamin, "it is the task of those who deal not only with chronicles, but with history, to study not just the mechanics of the material event, but the events of the remembering and of the telling—the patterns of the remembering, the forms of the telling"—the conditions under which our "historical materials" have been created. In this sense, though the event may be over, the telling of that event is "boundless".[66]

In what ways has this study contributed to a reconfiguring of the historical narrative and the telling of history? Much of the early literature points to a silent and uncritical Japanese Canadian woman. This portrayal, one so familiar as to be at times compelling, is much too narrow. Growing up with fragments of memory, imparted by the close members of my small family, I long viewed the internment of Japanese Canadians as a shameful episode in our nation's past, a blatant act of injustice but one far removed from our present existence. My own

exposure to racism as a child growing up in an Anglo/European neighbourhood of Toronto, along with my parents' unspoken warnings about the safety of staying at the social margins of my world, suggested however that the wartime violations still touched our lives. As a teenager, I was burdened with many questions about my family's history in this country. Why didn't my parents and their generation fight back? Why hadn't they stood up for their rights and resisted? Over the years, why had they chosen to remain silent about such an blatantly unfair and tragic experience?

Prompted by the Redress campaign in the 1980s, I took these questions beyond my family and began to read the early published accounts of the internment.[67] I participated in a growing "community of memory". As this community broadened, encompassing both those who had lived through the war and those born afterward, it seemed to offer new space and thereby legitimated my presence. My active intervention as a researcher revealed many dimensions to the story that I had heard years ago. The multiple stories, voiced and written, uncovered detail where before there seemed only to be silence. The contents of old letters housed in archives revealed intense emotion, notably anger and despair. Upon reading them, I learned that many *Nisei* women had indeed displayed a strong spirit of resistance, contained by a structural powerlessness. In the narratives, I detected a range of emotions and forms of defiance—inside the individual, if not presented to an external, public audience. These feelings may or may not have been seen or noticed.

Alongside the emotion, the different narrative sources unfolded layers of injustice. Beyond property loss and the stench of Hastings Park, I heard and read about diminished aspirations, lost opportunities, troubled relationships, generational conflict, a yearning for privacy, boredom to tears, deportation, work-related injuries, attempted rape, suicide, and death due to inadequate medical care. All of this produced in me a heightened sense of loss. In their oral accounts, women carefully selected memories for sharing with an unfamiliar audience. They conveyed some thoughts as secrets, experiences that had no clear fit with the collective history. These secrets told of episodes that had caused their holders memorable grief. When I asked them to sum up their stories as a way of concluding their narratives, most women

412

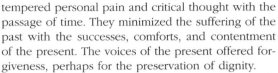

tempered personal pain and critical thought with the passage of time. They minimized the suffering of the past with the successes, comforts, and contentment of the present. The voices of the present offered forgiveness, perhaps for the preservation of dignity.

In *The Battle of Valle Giulia*, Alessandro Portelli writes about presenting a paper to an academic audience and afterward receiving comments such as "Yes, nice, very interesting—but what difference does it make?" Portelli writes in reply, "[F]ieldwork is always a form of political intervention because it encourages an effort at self-awareness, growth, and change in all those involved."[68] Hearing the women's testimonies, reading their letters, has inspired me to nuance my own narrative and to reconsider the ways in which I study women's lives. More importantly, I regard the women themselves as active participants in the creation or production of the narratives, and thereby of images of themselves. In short, I see both the act of putting pen to paper and articulating thought, as well as sharing memories in the oral tradition, telling personal stories and disclosing thoughts to a researcher and her community of listeners, to be a deliberate and interpretive act—an act of agency. The women's narratives are "a mixture of the telling of their lives" and a statement of their minds.[69]

Notes

* Pamela Sugiman is associate professor in the Department of Sociology at McMaster University. An earlier version of this paper was presented at the "Diaspora, Memory and Silence" Conference, Centre for Feminist Research, York University, Toronto, Ontario, October 24–25, 2003. Parts of this paper were also presented at the *BC Studies* Conference, University of British Columbia, Vancouver, May 1–3, 2003. This project was funded by the Social Sciences and Humanities Research Council of Canada and the National Association of Japanese Canadians. For their assistance with this research, carried out with skill and sensitivity, the author wishes to thank Tomiko Robson, Gillian Anderson, and Candace Kemp. Rose Aihoshi generously helped introduce the author to many of the narrators. The author also acknowledges the insights and support of Kathryn McPherson, three anonymous reviewers for *Histoire sociale/Social History*, and especially Robert Storey and Tamura Sugiman-Storey.

1. This and all subsequent censored letters are located in the National Archives of Canada [hereafter NAC], Record Group [hereafter RG] 27, Department of Labour, Japanese Division, "Intercepted Letters", vols. 655, 661, 662, 1527, 1528. To respect the privacy of the individuals named in these letters, I specify relationships only and do not disclose names.

2. I employ the term political violence to describe the uprooting, dispossession, and incarceration of various groups of Japanese Canadians by the federal government, in an effort to convey the devastating and long-term impact of these acts on individuals and the community as a whole, I do not "compare" this form of violence to historical acts of genocide, massacre, lynching, bodily rape. I see the need to consider, however, the government's treatment of Japanese Canadians as part of a continuum of political violence that takes into account emotional and physical pain and suffering, as well as material losses.

3. See Kirsten Emiko McAllister, "Captivating Debris: Unearthing a World War Two Internment Camp", *Cultural Values*, vol. 5, no. 1 (2001), p. 98.

4. In a thoughtful analysis, Mona Oikawa argues that the violations committed against Japanese Canadians should be more generally viewed as "reflective of the war for white bourgeois supremacy being waged against people of Japanese origin (and against Aboriginal people and other marginalized communities) living *in* Canada". Pointing to exclusionary laws against Asians in British Columbia from the time of their immigration to Canada, Oikawa is critical of the representation of the internment as a "wartime event". See Mona Oikawa, "Cartographics of Violence: Women, Memory, and the Subject(s) of the 'Internment'" (PhD dissertation, OISE/University of Toronto, 1999, p. 13). For a discussion of anti-Asian sentiment, see, for example, Gillian Creese, "Class, Ethnicity and Conflict: The Case of the Chinese and Japanese Immigrants, 1880–1923" in Rennie Warburton and David Coburn, eds., *Workers, Capital, and the State in British Columbia* (Vancouver: University of British Columbia Press, 1988); Patricia E. Roy, *The Oriental Question: Consolidating a White Man's Province, 1914–41* (Vancouver, University of British Columbia Press, 2003). "Visible Minorities and Political Participation", in Jorgen Dahlie and Tissa Fernando, eds., *Ethnicity,*

413

Power, and Politics in Canada (Toronto: Methuen Publishing, 1981), pp. 151–171, and "British Columbia's Fear of Asians, 1900–1950", *Histoire sociale/Social History*, vol. 13, no. 25 (May 1980), pp. 161–172; Timothy J. Stanley, "White Supremacy, Chinese Schooling and School Segregation in Victoria: The Case of the 1922–1923 Chinese Students' Strike", *Historical Studies in Education/Revue d'histoire de l'éducation*, vol. 2, no. 2 (Fall 1990), pp. 287–305; W. Peter Ward, *White Canada Forever: Popular Attitudes and Public Policy Toward Orientals in British Columbia* (Montreal and Kingston: McGill-Queen's University Press, 1978).

5. On January 16, 1942, the federal government passed Order-in-Council PC 365, calling for the removal of male Japanese nationals, 18 to 45 years of age, from a designated "Protected Area" 100 miles from the B.C. coast. Three weeks later, the government passed Order-in-Council PC 1486, expanding the power of the Minister of Justice to remove all persons of Japanese origin from the "protected zone". As military officers responsible for defence of the Pacific coast did not regard the Japanese in Canada as a security threat, the government established the B.C. Security Commission. This civilian body carried out the expulsion of Japanese from the area. For a comprehensive discussion of these events, see Ken Adachi, *The Enemy That Never Was: A History of the Japanese Canadians* (Toronto: McClelland & Stewart, 1991); Ann Gomer Sunahara, *The Politics of Racism: The Uprooting of Japanese Canadians During the Second World War* (Toronto: James Lorimer, 1980).

6. Here I use the term internment to describe a wide range of experiences, including forced relocation to ghost towns, "self-supporting camps", and sugar-beet farms; incarceration in prisoner of war camps; movement to labour camps; compulsory resettlement from B.C. to Ontario or Quebec; and deportation to Japan. In some government documents, in comparison, the term refers only and specifically to the incarceration of Japanese and Japanese Canadian men in prisoner of war camps. Ann Sunahara notes that, legally, the *Nisei* could not be interned, as they were Canadian citizens. Under the Geneva Convention, internment is a legal act that applies only to "aliens". As a result, the federal government referred to the "detainment" of Japanese Canadians. Sunahara, *The Politics of Racism*, p. 66.

7. Roy Miki and Cassandra Kobayashi, *Justice in Our Time: The Canadian Redress Settlement* (Vancouver and Winnipeg: Talonbooks and National Association of Japanese Canadians, 1991), p. 4. For more information about the conditions in these internment sites, see Robert K. Okazaki, *The Nisei Mass Evacuation Group and P.O.W. Camp "101" Angler, Ontario* (Scarborough, Ont.: n.p., 1996); Yon Shimizu, *The Exiles: An Archival History of the World War II Japanese Road Camps in British Columbia and Ontario* (Wallaceburg, Ont: Shimizu Consulting and Publishing, 1993).

8. For a comparison of American and Canadian wartime policies toward persons of Japanese origin, see Daniel J. O'Neil, "American vs. Canadian Policies Toward their Japanese Minorities During the Second World War", *Comparative Social Research*, vol. 4 (1981), pp. 111–134. For a more comprehensive discussion of the wartime internment of Japanese Americans, see Lawson Fusao Inada, ed., *Only What We Could Carry: The Japanese American Internment Experience* (Berkeley and San Francisco: Hey-day Books and California Historical Society, 2000); Report of the Commission on Wartime Relocation and Internment of Civilians, *Personal Justice Denied* (Seattle and London: The Civil Liberties Public Education Fund and University of Washington Press, 1997).

9. Miki and Kobayashi, *Justice in Our Time*, p. 49. Writing about the Japanese American experience, Raymond Okamura presents an important critique of the language used by the United States government during the years of internment. Okamura demonstrates how the U.S. government relied on euphemisms such "evacuation" and "relocation", which concealed the harsh impact of its treatment of persons of Japanese origin during the war. See Raymond Y. Okamura, "The American Concentration Camps: A Cover-up Through Euphemistic Terminology", *Journal of Ethnic Studies*, vol. 10, no. 3 (Fall 1982), pp. 95–109.

10. Deportation took place between May and December 1946.

11. Adachi, *The Enemy That Never Was;* Miki and Kobayashi, *Justice in Our Time;* Sunahara, *The Politics of Racism.*

12. Mentions of cases of suicide within the Japanese Canadian community were found in NAC, RG 27, "Intercepted Letters". In at least one of these cases,

the suicide was directly linked to the experience of extreme racism in Canada. Out of respect for surviving family members, I do not discuss these cases in detail.

13. *Hakujin* is a Japanese term translated as "white person" or Caucasian.

14. The Redress Agreement was signed by the National Association of Japanese Canadians and the Canadian government on September 22, 1988. For a discussion of the Redress Movement and Agreement, see Audrey Kobayashi, "The Japanese Canadian Redress Settlement and its Implications for Race Relations", *Canadian Ethnic Studies*, vol. 24 (1992). pp. 1–19; George Kurian, "Bittersweet Passage: Redress and the Japanese Canadian Experience", *Journal of Comparative Family Studies*, vol. 26 (1995), pp. 286–287; National Association of Japanese Canadians, *Democracy Betrayed: The Case for Redress* (National Association of Japanese Canadians, 1985, 2nd printing); Maryka Omatsu, *Bittersweet Passage* (Toronto: Between the Lines, 1993).

15. As Kirsten McAllister (citing Lifton, 1979) states, there is often a "compulsion to repeat *the* history of Japanese Canadians". This compulsion "has the power to impose stasis, halting the impulse to extend outwards towards the fleeing, tumbling motion of the ongoing world and thus to incorporate new experiences. Within its grasp, all stories are reduced to the same story." See McAllister, "Captivating Debris". p. 98.

16. It is interesting that some of the earlier wartime literature on Japanese Canadians highlights the protests of Japanese Canadians against the Canadian government. For example, after interviewing Japanese Canadians interned in B.C. during the war, sociologist Forrest E. La Violette wrote at length about their complaints and demands to the B.C. Security Commission, federal government representatives, and the Spanish Consulate. Forrest E. La Violette, *The Canadian Japanese and World War II* (Toronto: University of Toronto Press, 1948). Mona Oikawa notes that La Violette's analysis stands in contrast to that presented by Ken Adachi. Adachi's post-war account presents an image of Japanese Canadians as "relatively docile" and "co-operative". Writes Oikawa, "What is stunning to me in the literature is the shift from the depiction of protesting Japanese Canadians to a prevailing image of docile

people co-operating with the government." See Oikawa. "Cartographies of Violence", p. 32; Adachi, *The Enemy That Never Was*.

17. In conducting interviews with aging *Issei* in Canada in the contemporary period, sociologist Atsuko Matsuoka has observed that the Western interpretation of *shikata ga nai* may differ from the meaning given by the *Issei*. In the context of her interviews, Matsuoka discerned *shikata ga nai* to mean "we do/did the best we can/could" rather than resignation or "giving up". She further found that the *Issei* revealed a remarkable resiliency. Atsuko Matsuoka, personal correspondence, November 2003.

18. Though a more detailed story of my own family's experience of internment would add richness to this discussion, I provide here only a cursory account. I believe that to convey the wider, sociological meaning of a personal story, one must present it in the context of a comprehensive analysis that links biography to a broader theoretical and empirical literature. Such a project is beyond the scope of this article. I consider more fully the relationship among biography, personal memory, and history in Pamela Sugiman, "These Feelings that Fill My Heart: Exploring Japanese Canadian Women's Lives Through Oral Testimony" (paper presented to the "Feminism and the Making of Canada" Conference, McGill University, May 7–9, 2004). For an interesting and thoughtful discussion of research and self-reflexivity, see Franca Iacovetta, "Post-Modern Ethnography, Historical Materialism, and Decentring the (Male) Authorial Voice: A Feminist Conversation", *Histoire sociale/Social History,* vol. 32, no. 64 (November 1999), pp. 275–293.

19. Many of the issues that inform this discussion have been taken up by feminist historians in a critique of positivism and the assumption of objective historical research. See, for example, Susan Geiger, "What's so Feminist About Women's Oral History?", *Journal of Women's History*, vol. 2, no. 1 (Spring 1990), pp. 169–182: Sherna Berger Gluck and Daphne Patai, eds., *Women's Words: The Feminist Practice of Oral History* (New York: Routledge, 1991); Joan Sangster, "Telling Our Stories: Feminist Debates and the Use of Oral History", in Robert Perks and Alistair Thomson, eds., *The Oral History Reader* (London: Routledge, 1998), pp. 87–100.

20. I refer here to an article in which Kuhn reflects on her experiences in writing *Family Secrets: Acts of Memory*

and Imagination (London: Verso, 2002). These ideas are expressed in Annette Kuhn, "A Journey Through Memory", in Susannah Radstone, ed., *Memory and Methodology* (Oxford: Berg, 2000), p. 179.

21. Kuhn, "A Journey Through Memory", p. 185.

22. For a discussion of the researcher's emotional engagement with the research, see Ruth Behar, *The Vulnerable Observer: Anthropology that Breaks Your Heart* (Boston, Mass.: Beacon Press, 1996); Antoinette Errante, "But Sometimes You're Not Part of the Story: Oral Histories and Ways of Remembering and Telling", in Sharlene Nagy Hese-Biber and Michelle L. Yaiser, eds., *Feminist Perspectives on Social Research* (Oxford: Oxford University Press, 2004), pp. 411–434; Suzanne Fleishman, "Gender, the Personal, and the Voice of Scholarship: A Viewpoint", *Signs: Journal of Women in Culture and Society*, vol. 23, no. 4 (Summer 1998); Iacovetta, "Post-Modern Ethnography", Personal Narratives Group, eds., *Interpreting Women's Lives: Feminist Theory and Personal Narratives* (Bloomington and Indianapolis: Indiana University Press, 1989); Valerie Yow, "'Do I Like Them Too Much?' Effects of the Oral History Interview on the Interviewer and Vice-Versa", *Oral History Review*, vol. 24, no. 1 (Summer 1997), pp. 55–79.

23. In correspondence with the office of Arthur MacNamara, Deputy Minister, Department of Labour, T. B. Pickersgill, Commission of Japanese Placement for the Department of Labour, stated that most of the private letters intercepted by the federal government were written by individuals who had family members either interned in prisoner of war camps or relocated outside British Columbia (NAC, RG 27, Department of Labour, vol. 1528, Japanese Division, Intercepted Letters, Pickersgill to MacNamara, March 2, 1946). Most of the letters cited here were originally written in English. Those letters that had been composed in Japanese had been translated during the war by employees of the federal government. I have read only the translated versions of these letters, retyped by the Directorate of Censorship, Department of National War Services. The majority of the intercepted letters that can be found in the collections at the National Archives appear in translated form only. As a result, some of the nuance and meaning in the original letters may be lost. Most likely to facilitate censorship and review by politicians and bureaucrats who were not fluent in Japanese, the Canadian Postal Censor in Vancouver instructed that all letters be written in English. Correspondence in Japanese was to be restricted to "essential news and information" and free of "inconsequential gossip". The Censor furthermore warned that use of unusual Japanese symbols would delay their reading (Adachi, *The Enemy That Never Was*, p. 267). The Censor also indicated whether or not correspondence was to be "held", "released", or "condemned". Most of the letters cited here were released, some with passages deleted.

24. See Alessandro Portelli, "The Peculiarities of Oral History", *History Workshop Journal*, vol. 12 (1981), pp. 96–107.

25. Jeanne Houston (1973) cited in Traise Yamamoto, "'The Other, Private Self'" Masking in Nisei Women's Autobiography", in Traise Yamamoto, ed., *Masking Selves, Making Subjects: Japanese American Women, Identity, and the Body* (Berkeley: University of California Press, 1999), p. 116.

26. The "repatriation survey" as well as the general dispersal of Japanese Canadians were administered by T.B. Pickersgill, Commissioner of Japanese Placement. Beginning on April 13, 1945, in Tashme, an RCMP detachment under Pickersgill's authority canvassed all Japanese and Japanese Canadians over the age of 16. Before asking people to sign the repatriation forms, RCMP officers posted two notices in each internment site. The first notice stated that anyone who sought repatriation would receive free passage to Japan. In addition, the notice explained that, upon signing, Canadian citizens were expected to declare a desire to relinquish their "British nationality and to assume the status of a national of Japan". The second notice offered (limited) financial support to people who agreed to move east of the Rockies. This support, however, was contingent on one's willingness to accept whatever employment the government deemed appropriate. Failure to do so would be regarded as evidence of disloyalty to the nation. Adachi, *The Enemy That Never Was*, p. 298. For a full discussion of family, gender relations, and repatriation policy, see Pamela Sugiman, "Home and Family: Acts of Intimacy in the Transnational Politics of Wartime Canada", in Lloyd Wong and Victor Satzewich, eds., *Transnational Communities in Canada: Emergent Identities, Practices, and Issues* (Vancouver: University of British Columbia Press, forthcoming).

27. Miki and Kobayashi, *Justice in Our Time*, pp. 46–55.

28. The Japanese Canadian Committee for Democracy was established by a small group of *Nisei* in 1943. Its initial goal was to achieve full citizenship rights and to assess the financial losses incurred during the war. The Nisei Mass Evacuation Group was formed in protest of the government's decision to split apart Japanese Canadian families. Initially, the group requested that people be relocated as family units. Later, the Mass Evacuation Group advocated resisting the government's orders until families could stay together. Miki and Kobayashi, *Justice in Our Time*, pp. 36, 56.

29. After reading the letters in the archives, I began to ask the women narrators in this study whether or not they had known that their personal correspondence was being censored during the war years. Thinking back, all of them said assuredly that everyone in the ghost towns knew that letters were being read by government authorities. Whether or not they believed that their own correspondence had been intercepted, however, is not clear. It is significant, though, that the authors of a small number of the letters in the Department of Labour collection did make direct reference to the Censors, claiming that they did not care what the Censor thought of their feelings of anger and violation.

30. See Iwona Irwin-Zarecka, *Frames of Remembrance: The Dynamics of Collective Memory* (New Brunswick, N.J.: Transaction Publishers, 1994); Portelli, "The Peculiarities of Oral History".

31. In part, these letters have also been authored by government censors. Surely, there were hundreds, perhaps thousands, of other letters that moved directly from sender to receiver read in full by friends and family. Just as the women's testimonies are products of our culture, the letters too have been constructed in time.

32. See Alessandro Portelli, *The Battle of Valle Giulia: Oral History and the Art of Dialogue* (Madison: University of Wisconsin Press, 1997).

33. Among many others, this issue has been discussed by Michael Frisch and Dorothy L. Watts, "Oral History and the Presentation of Class Consciousness: The *New York Times* versus the Buffalo Unemployed", *International Journal of Oral History*, vol. 1, no. 2 (June 1980), pp. 88–110; Ronald J. Grele, *Envelopes of Sound* (Chicago: Precedent Publishing, 1985); Judith Modell, "Stories and Strategies: The Use of Personal Statements", *International Journal of Oral History*, vol. 4, no. 1 (February 1983), pp. 4–11; Portelli, "The Peculiarities of Oral History", p. 103.

34. In the words of Alessandro Portelli, "Let our history be as chronological, factual, logical, reliable, and documented as a history book is supposed to be. But let it also be, like a literary text, a book about itself. Let it contain the history of its making, the history of its maker. Let it show how he grows, changes, and stumbles through the research and the meeting with other subjects. Speaking about the Other as a subject is far from enough, until we see ourselves as subjects among others, until we place time in ourselves, and ourselves in time" ("The Peculiarities of Oral History", p. 179).

35. The oral testimonies on which this discussion draws were gathered by myself, in addition to two research assistants, both young women. One research assistant was a *Yonsei* (fourth-generation) Japanese Canadian. Some of the early interviews were conducted by a *Hakujin* graduate student. I decided to employ this student because of her strong interview skills, maturity, and intelligence. As well, she was given the task of interviewing only those women (a minority) who have been active (leaders) in the Japanese Canadian community. I recently communicated with some of these women about the interview experience. They said that they felt more obliged to provide details about the internment because the researcher was a *Hakujin*. Recognizing the importance of race and subjectivity in shaping the researcher/narrator relationship, I have arranged to conduct a second and, in cases, a third interview myself with some of these women. In doing so, I hope to understand more fully the interaction between researcher and narrator, as well as the role of time in shaping narratives.

36. The concept of "community of memory" is introduced by Iwona Irwin-Zarecka. A community of memory, she writes, in its most direct meaning, "is one created by that very memory". Irwin-Zarecka notes that, as increasing numbers of second-generation writers and artists "work through the meanings of living with the memory of the Holocaust, the community bonded by that memory grows to include all the empathetic witnesses as well". Rather than severing the direct link between experience and remembrance, the connection "is redrawn to

capture the complexity of effects of that experience beyond individual memories". A shifting of the boundaries of the community is ongoing. It extends as, over time, the trauma functions as a "key orienting force" in the lives and public actions of others who did not themselves live through that trauma. Irwin-Zarecka further writes, "what underlies that bonding ... or what defines the community through its many transitions, is a shared, if not always explicated, meaning given to the experience itself.... Personal relevance of the traumatic memory, and not personal witness to the trauma, here defines the community" (*Frames of Remembrance*. pp. 47–49).

37. Sumi (Sue) Kai, Toronto, Ontario, February 7, 2003.
38. Yoshiye Kosaka, Toronto, Ontario, July 10, 2001.
39. Irwin-Zarecka, *Frames of Remembrance*, p. 55.
40. Eviator Zerubavel, "Social Memories: Steps to a Sociology of the Past", *Qualitative Sociology*, vol. 19, no. 3 (1996), p. 284.
41. Rose Kutsukake, Toronto, Ontario, April 7, 2003.
42. Portelli, "The Peculiarities of Oral History", p. 163. For a more complete reading of Portelli's thinking about oral history, time, and memory, see the collection of essays in Alessandro Portelli, *The Death of Luigi Trastulli and Other Stories: Form and Meaning in Oral History* (Albany: State University of New York Press, 1991).
43. In addition, though we have witnessed a recent proliferation of writing on the internment, the women in this study were still reticent about some topics and spoke with greater ease and energy about others. It was extremely difficult, if not impossible, to broach with most women issues pertaining to sexuality. This matter seemed to be off-limits. To put it on the agenda would be to risk violating the shared understanding that existed between researcher and participant. In the rare case that a woman did raise the issue on her own initiative, it seemed to generate such discomfort, embarrassment, and unease that I decided not to communicate this part of her testimony to other listeners, perhaps less known and trusted. In making this decision, I myself have participated in a selective remembrance.
44. Zerubavel, "Social Memories", p. 286.
45. Amy Miyamoto, Montreal, Quebec, March 1, 2003.
46. Ruby Hanako Ohashi, Vernon, B.C., July 29, 2002.
47. As noted by Audrey Kobayashi, marriages between Japanese Canadians and individuals of other ethnic backgrounds currently make up over 90 per cent of all marriages. Audrey Kobayashi, *A Demographic Profile of Japanese Canadians and Social Implications for the Future* (Ottawa: Department of the Secretary of State, 1989), p. 40. For a discussion of inter-marriage among Asian Americans, see Harry Kitano, Wai-Tsang Yeung, Lynn Chai, and Herbert Hatanaka, "Asian-American Interracial Marriage", *Journal of Marriage and the Family,* vol. 46, no. 1 (February 1984), pp. 179–190.
48. Berry (a pseudonym), Steveston, B.C., August 24, 2002.
49. Hideko (a pseudonym), Kamloops, B.C., July 20, 2002.
50. Sugar Sato, Toronto, Ontario, March 26, 2003.
51. Masako Yakura, Vernon, B.C., July 17, 2002.
52. Zerubavel, "Social Memories", p. 284.
53. Irwin-Zarecka, *Frames of Remembrance,* pp. 47–65.
54. Mrs. Whitton is a pseudonym. Ritsuko Sugiman, Toronto, Ontario, July 16, 2003.
55. Leo Spitzer, "'Back Through the Future': Nostalgic Memory and Critical Memory in a Refuge from Nazism", in Meike Bal, Jonathan Crewe, and Leo Spitzer, eds., *Acts of Memory: Cultural Recall in the Present* (Hanover, N.H.: University Press of New England, 1999), pp. 87–104.
56. See, for example, Herbert J. Gans, "Symbolic Ethnicity", in Herbert Gans *et al.*, eds., *On the Making of Americans: Essays in Honor of David Reisman* (Philadelphia: University of Philadelphia Press, 1979), pp. 193–220; Christopher Lasch, "The Politics of Nostalgia", *Harper's*, November 1984, pp. 65–70; Raymond Williams, *The Country and the City* (New York: Oxford University Press, 1974); Suzanne Vromen, "The Ambiguity of Nostalgia", *YIVO Annual*, vol. 21 (1994), p. 71.
57. Pauline (Pauli) Inose, New Denver, B.C., July 28, 2002.
58. Sachi Oue, Toronto, Ontario, May 24, 2001.
59. This point is elaborated upon by Portelli. He notes that, while "[t]he historian is mainly interested in reconstructing the past; the speaker seeks to project an image..." ("The Peculiarities of Oral History", p. 166).
60. See Mary M. Childers, "'The Parrot or the Pit Bull': Trying to Explain Working Class Life", *Signs: Journal of Women in Culture and Society*, vol. 28, no. 1 (special issue on "Gender and Cultural Memory", Autumn 2002), p. 214.

61. Judy Giles, "Narratives of Gender, Class, and Modernity in Women's Memories of Mid Twentieth Century Britain", *Signs*, vol. 28, no. 1 (Autumn 2002), p. 36. I present a more comprehensive discussion of these points in Sugiman, "Memories of Internment: Narrating Japanese Canadian Women's Life Stories", *Canadian Journal of Sociology* (forthcoming).

62. Childers. "'The Parrot or the Pit Bull'", p. 204.

63. Hannah Tabata, Kamloops, B.C., July 21, 2002.

64. Michiko [a pseudonym], Vernon, B.C., August 14, 2002.

65. Janet Zandy, *Liberating Memory: Our Work and Our Working-Class Consciousness* (New Brunswick, N.J.: Rutgers University Press, 1995), p. xi.

66. Walter Benjamin cited in Portelli, "The Peculiarities of Oral History", p. 175.

67. Most importantly, Adachi, *The Enemy That Never Wars;* Sunahara, *The Politics of Racism*.

68. Portelli, *The Battle of Valle Giulia*, pp. 51–52.

69. *Ibid.*, p. 80.

■ Article 2: A War on Ethnicity? The RCMP and Internment

Reg Whitaker and Gregory S. Kealey

The story of internments during the Second World War can be told from various points of view. One of these is from the perspective of the security service of the Royal Canadian Mounted Police (RCMP), the agency charged with developing the intelligence base for identifying those considered, according to government criteria (to which the RCMP itself contributed), sufficiently dangerous threats to national security and the war effort to require internment. How did the 'Mounties' view the internment process? What did their performance reflect of their strengths and weaknesses as a security intelligence force? What lessons did they draw from the experience? This essay attempts to address these questions by looking at what the RCMP did for internments, at ethnicity and ideology, at ethnicity on trial, at homegrown fascism, and at what internments did for the RCMP.

What the RCMP Did for Internments

Nothing in the wartime experience has led to more notoriety for the RCMP's security service than the internment of various people under the Defence of Canada Regulations (DOCR). Depriving people of their liberty without the normal safeguards of charges under the Criminal Code, legal counsel, habeas corpus, and a 'day in court'—all possible to some degree under the draconian provisions of the DOCR that put the safety of the state first—was bound to rouse resentments on the part of those on the receiving end. Internment of unpopular minorities was widely applauded at the time by the majority. This only deepened the anxieties of affected minorities, especially in retrospect, when a new era of postwar multiculturalism spurred feelings of ethnic victimization that could not have been openly articulated during the war itself. The Japanese-Canadian community has been offered an official apology by the Canadian government for the forcible relocation and confinement of the entire Japanese population of the Pacific coast and the confiscation of its property. Italian Canadians too have received an official apology from Ottawa for the internment of 600 Canadians of Italian origin, while at the same time criticism of how that apology was obtained has surfaced from within the Italian-Canadian community.[1] Scholarly arguments have also been made about the efficacy of the internments of 847 German Canadians.[2] In other cases where ethnicity was replaced by ideology as grounds for internment, complaints of serious injustice have also been sounded.[3]

The RCMP was the agent of the state in this activity, as in other intelligence and national security matters. The commissioner of the RCMP was appointed Registrar General of Enemy Aliens under the authority of the DOCR. By March 1940, 16,000 'enemy aliens' (Canadian residents of German birth

Source: Reg Whitaker and Gregory S. Kealey, "A War on Ethnicity? The RCMP and Internment," in Franca Iacovetta, Roberto Perin, and Angelo Principe, eds. *Enemies Within: Italian and Other Internees in Canada and Abroad*. Toronto: University of Toronto Press, 2000, pp. 128–147. (c) University of Toronto Press, Inc. (2000). Rerpinted with permission of the publisher.

not British subjects by 1922) had been registered through a special branch of the RCMP set up for this purpose.[4] The Mounties were expected to gather intelligence on subversive activities carried out by groups banned under the DOCR by the cabinet, to prepare lists of persons associated with such groups designated for internment, and to take such persons into detention when their names were approved by an advisory internment committee of senior government officials. Under an order-in-council of 4 June 1940, RCMP officers were made justices of the peace for the purpose of issuing search warrants regarding illegal organizations. As William Kaplan explains, 'The effect of the new regulation was that any time an RCMP officer wished to search any premises all he had to do was prepare in his own hand an order giving him the authority to enter and search for any reason, or no reason.'[5]

Police forces are rarely heard to complain about being given too many powers: the Mounties were no exception. The DOCR and the atmosphere of wartime emergency allowed the force to exercise a degree of intrusive surveillance and control over groups that it considered suspicious, without the usual set of peacetime constraints. Policies such as national registration of aliens offered the force the opportunity to expand its surveillance database, as did security screening of government employees and the application of fingerprinting.[6] These developments accelerated the acceptance of modern techniques of political policing and as such were welcomed by a force eager to build up its overall capabilities.

Ethnicity and Ideology

The actual conduct and conditions of internment were not an RCMP responsibility. The instance of apparent ethnic victimization that has gained most attention—that of the Japanese relocations—actually fell outside the internment program as such; ironically, the RCMP was taken off this case precisely because its advice was *not* alarmist about the supposed threat of a Japanese 'fifth column.' Nor was the RCMP particularly hawkish about the threat posed by German and Italian Canadians, despite well-founded concerns about Nazi and fascist activists among their ranks.[7] Another group that drew unwelcome attention because of its pacifism and unconventional social customs—the Mennonites (of largely German

extraction)—was viewed with some sensitivity by the Mounties.[8]

When ethnicity was mixed with left-wing ideology, it was a different story. The RCMP, in keeping with the always dominant anti-communism of the security service, was implacable in pursuit of pro-communist Ukrainians, Red Finns, and other ethnic associations of leftist bent. While able to conceive of the notion that most Canadians of German, Italian, and Japanese origin were probably loyal and law-abiding, especially if treated fairly, to be firmly distinguished from the potentially disloyal minority of activist trouble-makers, the RCMP showed few signs of any sympathy for members of leftist ethnic associations—even when these associations were enthusiastic supporters of the war effort, as they were following the Nazi invasion of the USSR in 1941. One of the groups that did suffer from internments and from property seizures was the Ukrainian Labour-Farmer Temple Association (ULFTA), which had its string of cultural centres across the country closed and their assets disposed of. The RCMP not only kept close scrutiny on the ULFTA but invariably interpreted the words and behaviour of its officers in the worst possible light.[9]

Close to a hundred Communists or those associated with communism according to the dossiers of the security service were interned, eventually all together in the Hull Jail just across the Ottawa River from Parliament Hill.[10] Even after the USSR entered the war on the allied side, many of the communist internees were kept behind prison bars for close to another year. In this and in the maintenance of the ban on the Communist party throughout the war, the RCMP was not simply a silent agent but an active lobbyist within government against any legitimation of the Communists.

Yet when it came to drawing up the 'particulars,' as the official charges against the internees were called, the security service, which would have contributed the bulk of the evidence, was not always very precise, or even credible. Ludicrous particulars in the case of individual Communists (that X had attended a civil liberties meeting or that Y 'associated' with Z, who associated with Y, thus demonstrating a conspiracy) eventually drew unfavourable press attention. One communist internee was even charged with contesting the constitutionality of Quebec's notorious Padlock Law![11] Despite detailed knowledge

420

of who was who in the party, amassed from under-cover sources, evidence of actual treasonous or even illegal behaviour by individual Communists seemed hard to come by. Perhaps there was no such evidence, despite revolutionary rhetoric that the RCMP no doubt found seditious. Or perhaps what evidence there was would have pointed to secret sources the RCMP had no wish to disclose, nor any need, given the expansively draconian scope of the DOCR.

Ethnicity on Trial?

The Italian Community

A major criticism made of the RCMP in relation to the German and Italian groups is that the force lacked intelligence resources of sufficient quality to identify properly and then isolate the small minority of actively disloyal agents of the Axis powers from the wider ethnic communities in which they were hiding. Some critics have gone so far as to deny the very existence of enemy agents. The result is that in the eyes of these critics, innocent persons were rounded up and interned, on the basis of their ethnicity alone: thus, critics argue, the RCMP and the Canadian state in effect abused minorities in the name of WASP hegemony, making the internments a case of 'ethnicity on trial.' The security service was certainly aware of its own deficiencies with regard to the Japanese community. In its internal report for 1941–2, the Intelligence Branch conceded that surveillance of the community was 'maintained only with difficulty, as due to racial and physical dissimilarities, our sources of contact are limited.'[12] Yet similar arguments regarding the German and Italian communities do not stand up to close scrutiny.

For one thing, the security service did generally possess adequate language facilities to watch political developments in these communities. For another, its surveillance of pro-Nazi and pro-fascist activities had long antedated the war. In fact it had been acting closely with Norman Robertson, a senior official in the Department of External Affairs soon to become under-secretary of state, and other senior civil servants through the latter half of the 1930s to monitor such activities. J.L. Granatstein describes this as a 'desultory process of planning' and a 'belated effort' and implies that Robertson had to do some of the RCMP's intelligence work. No doubt Robertson, who semi-humorously described his role to his parents as

a 'one man Cheka or Gestapo […] civilian commissar with the RCMP' did marshal some useful intelligence (including information on fascists quietly acquired from Communist and later convicted Soviet spy Fred Rose),[13] but its misleading to suggest that the RCMP had no interest of its own in Nazi and fascist activities in Canada.

Intelligence on fascism in the Italian community began prior to Robertson's initiative. Interest was spurred, several scholars suggest, by the Ethiopian invasion of 1935–6, which revealed to the Canadian government the potential dangers of Fascist oaths taken by Italian Canadians when Canadian and Italian foreign policies came into conflict.[14] Constant reports flowed from Commissioner Wood to Robertson.[15] Translations and analysis of the Italian-language press in North America (including the United States) were supplied, but, much more important, sources were developed within the various Italian communities around the country, which yielded increasingly detailed reports in the late 1930s.[16] The RCMP found especially useful a network of informants from the communities. Willing collaboration was fairly widespread, perhaps reflecting anti-fascist sentiments and resentment against some of the community leaders enlisted by the Italian diplomats, in other cases involving more mixed motives.[17] Undercover RCMP operatives, such as John Leopold and Frank Zaneth, who had been employed to penetrate the Communist party and labour unions, proved less useful than voluntary informants from the community: there were few RCMP officers with the requisite language skills to be credible undercover 'Italians.'

When Italy and Canada formally went to war in June 1940, the RCMP was very well prepared. According to an internal RCMP memorandum, 95 per cent of the Italian Fascists were 'known to us': 'We have complete files and enough evidence to warrant their immediate arrest.'[18] As McBride puts it, 'Essentially […] the Canadian government interned those whom the Italian community told it to arrest.'[19] A crucial distinction was made between leaders and rank-and-file followers. The registration of enemy aliens was also a key surveillance tool. Fingerprinted, the dangerous could be detained while the 'sheep,' the words of a Justice Department official, could be 'kept track of.'[20] Once Canada was at war with Italy, the DOCR permitted the seizure of documents that led police to make further arrests. In Quebec, the RCMP

421

asked the Quebec provincial police to assist them, using Maurice Duplessis's Padlock Law.

It is hard to square this account with the image of a force too ill-informed to finger those likely to cause trouble or potentially vulnerable to Mussolini's agents. Indeed, despite retroactive protestations of innocence, it does seem that the activities of most of those rounded up in 1940 constituted prima facie threats to national security in a war in which Italy was an enemy state.

The German Community

Similar points could be made with regard to pro-Nazi organization among Canadians of German background, although the latter community was more dispersed than the Italians, especially in the west, where pro-Nazi activity was most successful, and thus a somewhat more difficult target for surveillance. According to Jonathan F. Wagner, the Germans, predominantly farmers, who settled the prairies were more recent arrivals than the more urban workers and artisans in the east, were less assimilated than their eastern counterparts, and were more likely to have been exposed to strong German nationalist ideas prior to emigration. Moreover, during the Depression years they tended to be more economically insecure, thus easier targets for pro-Nazi agitation.

Not surprisingly, much of the pro-Nazi activity was in fact directed at the west, but the small, rural, rather self-contained German communities on the prairies were perhaps somewhat harder targets for the RCMP to penetrate than the urban Italian communities.[21] The RCMP had been keeping tabs on German-Canadian political activities (of both left and right) as early as 1931,[22] but after Hitler's ascension to power in 1933, the politics of anti-communism sometimes played against building an effective dossier on pro-Nazi organizations. For instance, when the Deutscher Bund, one of the most important tools for Nazi influence in Canada, applied for a beer licence in 1936, the RCMP determined that the Bundists were 'anti-communist' and thus less dangerous than their left-wing rivals.[23]

By mid-1938, however, public opinion in Canada had turned sharply against Nazi Germany, increasingly seen as a potential adversary. The RCMP began directing closer attention to the influence sought by the Nazis over the Auslandeutsche (ethnic Germans living outside the Reich) and to the specific mechanisms of influence through various German-Canadian organizations with connections to the homeland. Obviously, the racial ideology of Nazism lent itself to potential extensions of the Nazi state through 'Aryan' brethren abroad. Yet if notions of the 'master race' and of German cultural and racial superiority were breeding grounds for Canadian Nazism, they also limited the potential reach of these ideas. German Nazis had little or nothing to do with homegrown Canadian pro-Nazi activists, whom they tended to look down on as racially inferior. There was thus little likelihood of any pro-Hitler infection spreading into the wider population from the seeds planted by the German government in the German-Canadian community—unlike the potential of a common conservative Catholicism to lead to links between the Montreal Italian pro-fascists and the extreme right wing in Quebec, as noted in RCMP reports.

The Canadian government made a serious error, as senior officials later admitted among themselves, in not making some official statement indicating the potential disloyalty implicit in membership in suspect pro-Nazi organizations. Consequently, some German Canadians may have joined such groups without realizing that it put them in jeopardy when war broke out with Germany.[24] Scholars argue that Canada had failed its ethnic communities in the 1930s by not stopping the actions of the German and Italian consuls earlier and then had little choice with the war 'but to attempt to protect the rest of the country from the potential problems of allowing a portion of its population to embrace fascism.'[25]

Whatever the limitations of past practices, when war did break out, it would seem that the RCMP did have relatively good intelligence on potential German troublemakers—not perhaps as detailed or as rich as the information on the Italian pro-fascists—but good enough to yield a list of virtually all the leaders. Wagner declares that by 1939 'little escaped the force at this point, as informers and agents reported on any activity which might be construed as pro-Nazi.' He adds that within the space of a few days at war's outset, 'the country's leading Nazis were rounded up and detained.'[26] The first and biggest sweep was accomplished in lightning police raids before dawn on 4 September 1939 (before Canada was officially at war, thus pre-empting some, though not all evasive action). Some of those initially detained were later

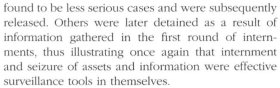

found to be less serious cases and were subsequently released. Others were later detained as a result of information gathered in the first round of internments, thus illustrating once again that internment and seizure of assets and information were effective surveillance tools in themselves.

That some Germans rounded up may not have been real Nazi activists would not be surprising; mistakes can be made in such wide sweeps. Some 'mistakes,' however, may have been deliberate. For instance, the German-Canadian League, an anti-Nazi organization, reported that a detainee in the initial sweep was one of its 'undercover' members. The League did not wish to see him released, however, as he might prove a useful informant to the police from within the internment camp. While the RCMP had been reluctant earlier in the 1930s to cooperate with anti-Nazi elements in the German-Canadian population because of its anxieties about communist influence, it was actively cooperating with the German-Canadian League as well as other anti-Nazi forces in 1939. A handwritten note to the commissioner in October 1939 gloats that it is 'interesting to note how dog eats dog, thus simplifying our campaign.'[27]

Keyserlingk condemns the RCMP for interning farmers and workers, whom he assumes were unlikely to be effective agents of Nazi sabotage or subversion. Yet he admits that almost all those included in the initial sweep were members of pro-Nazi organizations. Keyserlingk derides the arguments of the RCMP that such action broke the back of potential Nazi activity against the war effort.[28] The RCMP's claims were indeed stated somewhat extravagantly. Clifford Harvison of the Intelligence Branch, later an RCMP commissioner, wrote that within forty-eight hours 'more than 200 leaders and sub-leaders of Nazi groups were arrested' in Quebec, mostly in Montreal. 'Due to the surveillance work that had continued up to the last moment, all but two or three of the leaders were among those apprehended and they were arrested within the next few hours [...] Years of painstaking investigation that had at times brought severe criticism proved its value.'

Harvison claimed that captured enemy agents later told the RCMP that the 'speedy arrests had completely wrecked the carefully built German espionage apparatus in Canada.' As additional proof of the 'effectiveness of the anti-subversive work [...]

not one case of enemy sabotage occurred during the war.' Harvison went further to state that the German High Command confirmed all this after the war. There appears to be no evidence to support this latter assertion. Another official in the security service, Charles Rivett-Carnac, was only slightly less restrained in his praise of the branch that he supervised in the late 1930s, asserting that 'we were able to take effective measures against those aliens in Canada who could otherwise have proved hostile to the Allied cause.'[29] Keyserlingk assumes, along with other critics, that because little or no pro-Nazi activity against the war effort was later uncovered, no threat existed in the first place. It is surely equally reasonable to conclude that prompt action had pre-empted such activity by removing those whose previous links with pro-Nazi or pro-fascist organizations would make them the nucleus of any potential enemy-directed plots. After all, Nazism and fascism were racial ideologies that claimed the loyalties of 'blood brothers' across the seas.

The fifth-column scare in the spring of 1940 serves to highlight a marked gap between popular anti-German hysteria and the relative coolness and professionalism of the RCMP. As Harvison recalled years later, 'Each setback in Europe was followed by a flood of calls, letters and visitors volunteering information' on alleged fifth columnists. After the fall of France, 'the flood became so heavy as to require the setting up of a large, special staff to receive visitors and to handle mail and telephone calls [...] Almost always, the information was the result of over-wrought imaginations, but every scrap of information required checking. There was always the long chance that the information might contain a grain of truth. More important was the need for reassuring the public as to the interest and alertness of the security service.'[30] While it was important that the RCMP be seen to be responding to public anxieties, it is evident in retrospect that they remained steady in the face of the anti-German prejudices that were animating many people.

The internments were more remarkable for their relative selectivity than for putting 'ethnicity on trial,' striking not at the ethnic communities in general but at the ideologically suspect minority—in striking contrast to the experience of the 1914–18 war. At most, 847 pro-Germans were interned (out of a potential population base of more than a half-million), with most released by late 1944 or early 1945—in striking contrast to the 9,000 or so persons of German and Austro-Hungarian origin interned during the first war. The total numbers of Italian internees peaked at 632, with most released by the end of 1943. If we add in Communists and Canadian Nazis, the total number of internees appears to have reached just over 1,200 in 1940. This total excludes the 'relocated' Japanese population of British Columbia, and also the refugees from Hitler's Germany, many of them Jewish, sent from Britain to Canada and kept behind bars for much of the war [...]. The Japanese experience is of course a notorious exception to this observation, as this community was indeed severely penalized on the basis of ethnicity, but again the RCMP played no active role in this sorry tale. Where it was directly involved, the RCMP might actually be given some credit for the relative selectivity that the state did demonstrate.

Homegrown Fascism

The RCMP's intelligence on the homegrown varieties of Nazis and Fascists[31] was not as good at the outbreak of war as its knowledge of the German and Italian communities. The leading force on the extreme right in Canada was Adrien Arcand, the firebrand *'führer'* whose activities were centred in Quebec. Although investigation of Canadian fascism was launched seriously in 1935, detailed information on Arcand and his followers (whose public activities were systematically scrutinized from 1938 on) came with internment, rather than preceding it. When Arcand was interned in 1940, an impressive array of documents was seized relating to correspondence with German Nazis since 1933, and membership lists from the Arcand group and others across Canada came into possession of the police.[32] By that time, war with the fascist powers put paid to any future for homegrown Canadian Fascists in the postwar era.

Perhaps the RCMP had not taken these groups as seriously as it might have before the war, but it was clear that they hardly posed a continuing security threat. This may explain the absence of much mention of Nazi activities in the RCMP's internally circulated Intelligence Bulletins,[33] a point noted by critics of the RCMP within the civil service.[34] While this has led some to conclude that the RCMP was blind to right-wing extremism allied to Canada's foreign enemies while hypersensitive to left-wing groups allied to the USSR (which take up most of the attention in the Intelligence Bulletins), McBride makes the entirely sensible point that Fascists were considered by the RCMP important enough to be candidates for internment, but not to be as significant long-term security threats as the Communists.[35] The notion that there was some active sympathy in the RCMP with Fascists, apart from a shared anti-communism, is not very convincing. It is true that on the eve of the Nazi-Soviet pact, Charles Rivett-Carnac, then head of the Intelligence Branch, attempted to assure Norman Robertson that communists were a worse menace than Nazis, since fascism did not involve 'the overthrow of the present economic order—and its administrative machinery [...] Fascism is the reaction of the middle classes to the Communist danger and, as perhaps you are aware, the Communists describe it as "the last refuge of capitalism."'[36]

Yet despite this predisposition to view fascist activity less seriously *as a security threat* than communism, and despite an official Canadian attitude towards Hitler's Germany in the late 1930s that combined isolationism with occasional naïveté (at least on the part of Prime Minister Mackenzie King), evidence of positive pro-Nazi sentiment, or even a willful blind eye, on the part of the RCMP is simply not there. Certainly the doctrine of German racial supremacy was hardly calculated to appeal to a force thoroughly impregnated with the ideals of a Canada loyal to the British imperial mission. Nor were the clandestine, 'subversive' aspects of extreme right-wing organizations, with their overtones of foreign interference, likely to commend themselves to a force fully committed to the conservative political policing of Canadian society. Once war with the Axis powers had begun, the RCMP knew very well who Canada's enemies were and who their potential Canadian allies were—although this did not diminish its certainty that the Communists remained once and future threats, despite the wartime alliance with the USSR.

What Internments Did for the RCMP

If the RCMP and its small Intelligence Branch were key instruments of the state in the implementation of the internment policy, internment also represented concrete advantages for the RCMP's security intelligence role. Emergency wartime powers, especially of detention, search and seizure, and censorship, provided unparalleled opportunities to extend and consolidate political policing. Internment particularly contributed to the delegitimation of political extremism in ways especially helpful to the RCMP. The idea that certain kinds of political activity were subversive had always been a powerful tool, but the Intelligence Branch had always been constrained to a degree by the need to fit its political policing into a framework of criminal law enforcement. Policing of the communists had reached a peak in the early 1930s with the use of section 98 of the Criminal Code, deportations of foreign-born communist union organizers, and the jailing of a number of communist leaders following the *Rex v. Buck et al.* treason trials of party officials in 1931, but this had proved controversial and allowed communists such as Tim Buck to pose as martyrs.

In 1938, the RCMP prepared a nation-wide assault on the Communist Party of Canada (CPC) with detailed plans for the arrest of the leadership for violations of neutrality and passport regulations relating to recruitment for the Spanish Civil War. Cooler heads prevailed, however, and the memories of CPC successes in the aftermath of the Buck trial played a major role in the decision not to arrest and prosecute people. The DOCR, with their banning of political associations and arbitrary powers of internment, provided a far more flexible and politically effective instrument in the context of wartime patriotism and national discipline. Above all, the linkage between extreme ideologically motivated political movements and Canada's foreign enemies served to discredit these movements and to place them in a kind of special quasi-legal status as legitimate targets for permanent surveillance.

For the RCMP, the quiet go-ahead given the Intelligence Branch to penetrate and monitor Italian and German pro-fascist groups in the late 1930s was a very useful precedent. These groups were not illegal entities under the current law of the land, and the government of Canada had given no official warning that membership or participation in such groups should pose any concern to individuals. Yet under the shadow of war the government had, in its secret councils—in which the RCMP was a key participant—made certain definitive judgments about the potential disloyalties attached to membership in specific groups and had then charged the RCMP with responsibility to identify and locate the leaders and potential troublemakers from within the groups, for internment the instant the previously prepared orders were enacted. The relative effectiveness of the force in carrying out these responsibilities, along with the apparent nullification of the espionage, sabotage, or subversion threats believed to have been posed by these groups, ensured that the RCMP would carry out of the war an enhanced prestige within the Canadian state and some surety of a continued pre-eminent role in security intelligence in the postwar era.

In retrospect, it is apparent that the wartime internment experience helped lay the groundwork for the Cold War anti-communist security measures that followed. Once again, as it had been since the labour revolt of the First World War, the RCMP's security service was given the task of developing intrusive surveillance of a legal political entity—the CPC—and its various arms and fronts.[37] Once again, such extraordinary peacetime political policing was set up by a government decision that communists, in the context of a possible future war with the Soviet Union, would constitute a serious security risk that would require internment. Once again, lists were to be drawn up for action when warranted. The maintenance of such lists was part of the justification for a vast postwar surveillance operation against Communists, Communist allies, and people with any associations with Communists. Such was the scale of this operation that a royal commission in the late 1970s discovered that the RCMP held security files on some 800,000 individuals and organizations.[38] Potential internment was not the only basis for such a vast operation—the security clearance system in the public service and immigration lent powerful impetus to the accumulation of secret dossiers as well—but especially in the 1950s, when war sometimes seemed a very real possibility, preparation and maintenance of the lists of internees (code-named operation PROFUNC) ate up some of the security service's time and resources.

There was one other lesson that the RCMP may have drawn, to its profit, from the wartime internment experience. Indiscriminate internment of 'enemy aliens,' as in the First World War, or the direct targeting of an entire ethnic community for relocation and detention, as with the Japanese in the Second World War, were inherently divisive in a country with large immigrant communities. The

425

RCMP record for 1939 to 1945 on this issue is not at all as questionable as some critics have claimed. On the whole, and given the obvious limitations imposed on it, the RCMP proved fairly adept at distinguishing ideology from ethnicity. There is a complex wartime history of the relationship between the Ukrainian-Canadian community and the Canadian state and the relationship between pro-communists and nationalists within that community that illustrates the difficult passage that had to be negotiated by the force. Pro-communist Ukrainian groups were of course fundamentally suspect, and in 1940 the Canadian government had taken an active hand in creating the Ukrainian-Canadian Committee as an umbrella group of respectable anti-communist nationalists.

After the Nazi invasion of the USSR the following year, however, a delicate problem presented itself: pro-communist Ukrainians were now vociferously supporting the war, while the loyalties of some of the anti-Soviet nationalist Ukrainians might be considered suspect. The RCMP kept a close watch on all factions and employed well-placed informants to pass on detailed information.

For a time in 1941, a key figure in the wartime effort by Ottawa to develop a policy towards ethnic communities was employed by the RCMP as a temporary director of the 'European section.' Tracey Philipps, an Englishman with interwar experience in British intelligence, was cautiously anti-communist but above all interested in building unity behind the war effort. Following his stint with the RCMP, he continued as an advisor on nationalities but ran into fierce (and unfair) criticism from the pro-communist Ukrainian-language press—criticism that in the prevailing atmosphere of the Grand Alliance was picked up by some sections of the mainstream press as well. External Affairs, pressured by its new Soviet allies, was doubtful about allowing public assertions of Ukrainian independence, and Phillips was eventually squeezed out of official Ottawa. So was a close ally on minorities policy, Professor Watson Kirkconnell, who, though never directly employed by the RCMP, was to be an ally of sorts in the coming Cold War as an inveterate anti-communist public crusader.

While official policy on minorities never formally gelled around firm support of anti-communist ethnic organizations during the war, the RCMP, in its careful handling of the prickly Ukrainian-Canadian problem, showed the way towards the future of state–ethnic relations. Keeping a watchful eye on all factions, the RCMP nevertheless steered towards legitimizing and thus domesticating the more conservative ideological tendencies, while identifying and isolating the pro-communist Ukrainians as potential security threats.[39] The contrast with the much blunter sweep of the First War against 'enemy aliens' was sharp and instructive. This lesson was to stand the RCMP in good stead in the Cold War days ahead, when it was careful to target only the pro-communist ethnic associations and to establish working relationships with anti-communist organizations from the same communities.

It cannot be said that in the wartime internments the RCMP showed any great respect for civil liberties.[40] Of course, it did not have to, given the extraordinary wartime state of emergency and the powerful forces, both populist and governmental, demanding stern and swift action in the name of national security. Nor was there in the Canada of the 1940s any Charter of Rights or the same consciousness of the rights of minorities as exists in the 1990s. In any event, the RCMP's Intelligence Branch was a security force and a political police; concern for civil liberties was neither part of its job description nor on the list of tasks presented it by the government. That said, it is noteworthy that it acted within the parameters set for it with reasonable restraint, especially in the face of the temptations to exploit ethnic prejudices – temptations to which other agencies of the Canadian government succumbed in the case of the Japanese Canadians, to Canada's lasting shame.

Notes

1. Bruno Ramirez, 'Ethnicity on Trial: The Italians of Montreal and the Second World War,' in Norman Hillmer, Bohdan Kordan, and Lubomyr Luciuk, eds., *On Guard For Thee: War, Ethnicity, and the Canadian State, 1939–1945* (Ottawa: Canadian Committee for the History of the Second World War, 1988), 71–84; papers presented at the 'Internment of Italian Canadians during World War II' conference at York University, Toronto, Oct. 1995; and the Introduction and the essay in this volume by Iacovetta and Ventresca.

2. Robert H. Keyserlingk, '"Agents within the Gates": The Search for Nazi subversives in Canada during World War II,' *Canadian Historical Review*, 66, no. 2 (1985), 212–39, and 'Breaking the Nazi Plot:

Canadian government Attitudes toward German Canadians, 1939–1945,' in Hillmer, Kordan, and Luciuk, eds., *On Guard for Thee,* 53–70.

3. William Repka and Kathleen M. Repka, *Dangerous Patriots: Canada's Unknown Prisoners of War* (Vancouver: New Star Books, 1982). Reg Whitaker, 'Official Repression of Communism during World War II,' *Labour/Le Travail* 17 (spring 1986) 135–66.

4. Carl Betke and Stan Horrall, *Canada's Security Service: An Historical Outline,* 1864–1966 (Ottawa: RCMP Historical Section, 1978), 484.

5. PC 2363, 4 June 1940. William Kaplan, *State and Salvation: The Jehovah's Witnesses and Their Fight for Civil Rights* (Toronto: University of Toronto Press, 1989), 49–50.

6. On screening and fingerprinting, see Larry Hannant, *The Infernal Machine: Investigating the Loyalty of Canada's Citizens* (Toronto: University of Toronto Press, 1995).

7. Caution and moderation with regard to the 'enemy alien' minorities are quite evident from the annual wartime reports of the security service. During the height of the fifth column scare in 1940, RCMP headquarters was flooded with denunciations by Canadians of German-origin neighbours, including a list of 'traitors' submitted by the Canadian Chamber of Commerce. The RCMP handled these complaints with what can best be described as weary forbearance: those checked out invariably proved unfounded. See the papers of the House of Commons Committee for the Defence of Canada Regulations, Office of the Clerk of the House of Commons, Ottawa, and the essays by Principe and Bruti-Liberati in this volume.

8. Gregory S. Kealey and Reg Whitaker, eds., *RCMP Security Bulletins: The War Series, Part II,* 1942–1945 (St John's: Canadian Committee on Labour History, 1993), 1 March 1943, 64–6, and Introduction, 22.

9. On the ULFTA, see Whitaker, 'Official Repression of Communism.' The ULFTA's complaint that its property and halls had in come cases been sold by the Custodian of Alien Enemy Property to its 'bitter political enemies,' the Ukrainian National Organization (a complaint echoed by a number of respectable civil libertarians in mainstream Canadian society), was dismissed by the RCMP in its internal Intelligence Bulletin in the following extraordinary fashion: 'The psychological effect upon the … membership through loss of their halls to its [*sic*] opposition helps to keep alive the enthusiasm in their organization and produces a state of exuberance [!] so necessary to back their demands to the Government.' Kealey and Whitaker, *War Series Part II,* 1 March 1943, 56.

10. See the essay by Radforth in this volume.

11. The 'Padlock Law' allowed the Quebec government to close premises deemed to be used for the dissemination of 'Communist propaganda,' the latter term being defined not in the law but arbitrarily by the attorney general. The law was passed by Maurice Duplessis's Union Nationale government in 1937 and ruled unconstitutional by the Supreme Court of Canada in 1957.

12. Report dated 14 April 1942.

13. J.L. Granatstein, *A Man of Influence: Norman A. Robertson and Canadian Statecraft, 1929–1968* (Ottawa: Deneau, 1981), 81–90. A. Grenke, 'From Dreams of the Worker State to Fighting Hitler: The German-Canadian Left from the Depression to the End of World War II,' *Labour/Le Travail* 35 (spring 1995), 65–105, points out (94) that Robertson's advice overrode the RCMP's intention to intern left-wing German Canadians on the basis of information that they were anti-Nazi and pro-war, despite the Hitler-Stalin pact.

14. See, for example, Michelle McBride, 'From Internment to Indifference: An Examination of RCMP Response to Fascism and Nazism in Canada from 1934 to 1941,' MA thesis, Memorial University, 1997, 33, and the essays on Italian Canadians in part I of this volume. An account of 'consular fascism' can be found in Martin Robin, *Shades of Right: Nativist and Fascist Politics in Canada, 1920–1940* (Toronto: University of Toronto Press, 1992), 207–32.

15. Wood to Robertson, 1 Feb. 1938, with reference to initial letter from Robertson dated 27 April 1936.

16. See the essay by Bruti Liberati in this volume.

17. Michelle McBride, 'Fascism, Secret Agents, and the RCMP Security Service, 1939–41: Preliminary Remarks on Three Secret Agents in the Italian-Canadian Community of Montreal,' paper presented to joint session of the Canadian Historical Association and the Canadian Association for Security and Intelligence Studies, University of Ottawa, 31 May 1998.

18. CSIS 87-A-130, V.A.M. Kemp, Superintendent O Division, to the Commissioner, 15 May 1940.

19. McBride, 'From Internment to Indifference,' 170, and the essays in part I of this volume. Some

427

informants, she writes, and as others have shown, were secret agents, others vindictive neighbours, while others were simply trying to be good Canadian citizens.

20. Quoted in McBride, 'From Internment to Indifference,' 169.

21. Jonathan F. Wagner, *Brothers beyond the Sea: National Socialism in Canada* (Waterloo, Ont.: Wilfrid Laurier Press, 1981), 18–21. On German-Canadian Nazism, see also Robin, *Shades of Right*, 233–64.

22. CSIS 117-89-94.

23. McBride, 'From Internment to Indifference,' 39–40.

24. CSIS 87-A-130, Norman Robertson, memorandum to O.D. Skelton, 17 April 1940, and Robertson to Bavin, 17 April 1940.

25. McBride, 'From Internment to Indifference,' 200–1, and the essays by Pennacchio and Principe in this volume.

26. Wagner, *Brothers*, 131–2.

27. CSIS 117-89-94, 7 Sept. 1939.

28. Keyserlingk, '"Agents within the Gates."'

29. C.W. Harvison, *The Horsemen* (Toronto: McClelland and Stewart, 1967), 101. Rivett-Carnac, *Pursuit in the Wilderness* (Boston: Little, Brown, 1965), 295.

30. Harvison, *Horsemen*, 144.

31. On homegrown fascists, see Lita-Rose Betcherman, *The Swastika and the Maple Leaf: Fascist Movements in Canada in the Thirties* (Toronto: Fitzhenry and Whiteside, 1975); Robin, *Shades of Right*, 125–206.

32. CSIS 87-A-130. After his release from internment, Arcand sued unsuccessfully to regain possession of his papers.

33. Gregory S. Kealey and Reg Whitaker, eds., *RCMP Security Bulletins, The War Series, 1939–1941* (St John's: Canadian Committee on Labour History, 1989); *War Series, Part II, 1942–1945.*

34. H.S. Ferns, *Reading from Left to Right: One Man's Political History* (Toronto: University of Toronto Press, 1983), 182.

35. McBride, 'From Internment to Indifference.'

36. NA, Norman Robertson Papers, vol. 12, f. 137, Rivett-Carnac to Robertson, 24 Jan. 1939

37. For the early history of these files, see Gregory S. Kealey, 'The Early Years of State Surveillance of Labour and the Left in Canada: The Institutional Framework of the RCMP Security and Intelligence Apparatus, 1918–26,' *Intelligence and National Security* 8, no. 3 (1993), 129–48.

38. Commission of Inquiry Concerning Certain Activities of the RCMP, second report, vol. 1, *Freedom and Security under the Law* (Ottawa: Minister of Supply and Services, 1981), 518.

39. On the Ukrainian Canadians and the Canadian wartime state, see Bohdan Kordan, 'Disunity and Duality: Ukrainian Canadians and the Second World War,' MA thesis, Carleton University, 1981; Thomas M. Prymak, *Maple Leaf and Trident: The Ukrainian Canadians during the Second World War* (Toronto: Multicultural History Society of Ontario, 1988); N.F. Dreisziger, 'The Rise of a Bureaucracy for Multiculturalism: The Origins of the Nationalities Branch,' 1–30, William R. Young, 'Chauvinism and Canadianism: Canadian Ethnic Groups and the Failure of Wartime Information,' 31–52, and Bohdan Kordan and Lubomyr Luciuk, 'A Prescription for Nationbuilding: Ukrainian Canadians and the Canadian State, 1939–1945,' 85–100, all in Hillmer, Kordan, and Luciuk, eds., *On Guard for Thee;* and Frances Swyripa's essay in this volume.

40. For a critical account of RCMP failures in this regard, see John Stanton, 'Government Internment Policy, 1939–1945,' *Labour/Le Travail* 31 (spring 1993), 203–41, and his *My Past Is Now: Further Memoirs of a Labour Lawyer* (St John's: Canadian Committee on Labour History, 1994).

CONSTRUCTING A CANADIAN ICON

The Medicare Debate to the 1960s

Maureen Lux
Brock University

CONSTRUCTING A CANADIAN ICON: THE MEDICARE DEBATE TO THE 1960s

- **Introduction by Maureen Lux**

431

● INTRODUCTION

Maureen Lux

Canadians take great pride in their national health insurance program, or Medicare. As an icon of Canadian identity, it is one of the few issues on which we can agree, and although we love to complain about it, voters consistently tell politicians to keep their hands off Medicare. In 2002, in response to another "crisis" over healthcare costs and increasing wait times for treatment, Roy Romanow led a Royal Commission on the future of health care. He found that Canadians strongly support Medicare's core values of "equity, fairness and solidarity. These values are tied to their understanding of citizenship."[1] In November 2004 the CBC asked its audience to name the "greatest Canadian of all time." Canadians overwhelmingly chose a politician—T.C. (Tommy) Douglas—for his role as the "Father of Medicare."

The notion that Medicare was born of a single parent is a simplification, of course. Moreover, only about 70 percent of services (doctor visits and hospital treatment) are financed by taxation; private payments cover the other 30 percent, which includes such services as dental care and prescription drugs.[2] But there can be no question that Medicare has come to define what it means to be Canadian, even though the national program, not established until 1968, is fairly recent. It might seem strange that an insurance program should carry such importance, but Medicare distinguishes Canadians from Americans and allows Canadians to feel not a little superior.

It was not always so. The national health insurance program, like much public policy, emerged out of struggle between a vision of a much more comprehensive program and the demands of Medicare's opponents.

In June 1944 Saskatchewan elected the Co-operative Commonwealth Federation (CCF, later NDP), the first social democratic government in North America, led by Tommy Douglas. The CCF ended the decade-long Liberal party rule and captured 47 of 52 seats in the provincial legislature. Douglas' CCF emerged out of the social, political, and economic circumstances of the province, especially the searing experience of the Depression.

The international economic decline began in the late 1920s, and the Canadian economy reacted quickly since Canada exported so much of its resources. In the prairie West the "Dirty Thirties" began in 1931 with the weather: hot, dry winds blew month after month, year after year, drying fields, destroying crops, covering everything with dust. Some years were worse, some better, but by 1938 the drought led to a plague of grasshoppers that ate anything that managed to stay green.[3] Worse yet, the international market for prairie grain collapsed, leaving farmers with accumulated debt and little income. Unemployment rose to dangerous levels in central Canada when prairie farmers could no longer afford the cars, tractors, radios, and refrigerators that the factories produced. Understandably more than a quarter-million people gave up on the place and left the prairies in the 1930s, but what is surprising is how many remained. Municipalities, responsible for assistance, made the experience of collecting "relief" in the form of vouchers for food and clothing sufficiently humiliating in order to deter all but the most destitute. It seemed to many during the Depression that capitalism itself could not, or should not, survive.

The CCF's political and ideological program, a practical blend of socialism and Christian values, was spelled out in the Regina Manifesto at its founding meeting in 1933. The CCF, declared the Manifesto, would not rest until cooperation replaced competition, until socialism replaced capitalism.

> We aim to replace the present capitalist system, with its inherent injustice and inhumanity, by a social order from which the domination and exploitation of one

432

class by another will be eliminated, in which economic planning will supersede unregulated private enterprise and competition....[4]

This Depression-inspired document called for wide-ranging social and economic change, including socialized health services and "insurance covering illness, accident, old age and unemployment."[5] During the Depression doctors' bills were often the last to be paid, if they were paid at all. A survey of rural physicians in the early 1940s found that most worried that private practice was no longer possible. One physician despaired: "Any system is to be preferred to the present. Collections appear hopeless."[6] By 1943 the Canadian Medical Association (CMA) endorsed a scheme of compulsory medical insurance, acknowledging the Depression's impact on the health of Canadians, as well as its impact on doctors' incomes.[7] As Bothwell and English argue in "Pragmatic Physicians" included here (Article 1), organized medicine's stance on health insurance waxed and waned depending on the economic climate. By the 1930s its solid support for 'socialized medicine', led by government, reflected doctors' plummeting economic and social position. But this was the last time organized medicine would agree on the need for a comprehensive program of health insurance; in the postwar period organized medicine was the most strenuous opponent of Medicare.

The CCF's first electoral victory came not during the Depression but in 1944 during wartime's full employment. Certainly the memory of the Depression was still vivid for voters, but the CCF also appealed to voters by tempering some of the Manifesto's more radical proposals. Just as important to the victory was Douglas himself. A Baptist preacher in Weyburn, Saskatchewan, he was a fiery campaigner and a gifted speaker. One of his more famous speeches, "Mouseland," is reproduced here. He used humour, sarcasm, and allegory to criticize the economic and political status quo, which appealed to hardworking Canadians. Another of his famous speeches, "The Cream Separator," likened economic society to the cream separator where milk (produced by farmers) was churned by workers, to separate the skim milk from the cream, which was consumed by the "corporate elite" that owned the machine. The farmer and worker were made to fight over the thin skim milk, and each blamed the other. And when there was too much cream and the corporate elite couldn't consume it all, the worker was laid off and markets for farmer's milk disappeared. The moral of the story, and the promise of the CCF, was that one day the farmers and workers would take control of the machine "so that it begins to produce homogenized milk in which everybody'll get a little cream."[8]

Douglas as premier and minister of health committed his government to health insurance. A rough chronology of events leads to the impression that Saskatchewan led the way: in 1947 Saskatchewan established hospital insurance; a national hospital insurance program followed in 1958; in 1962 Saskatchewan enacted universal health insurance after a bitter doctor's strike; in 1968 the federal government developed a national health insurance program. But such a chronology dismisses the struggles and compromises that lay behind the policies; it creates the notion that the development of Medicare was a story of inevitable progress. History rarely happens that way.

In July 1962 Saskatchewan doctors withdrew their services, hoping to force changes to the government's medical insurance plan. "Keep Our Doctors" committees formed in reaction to a well-funded propaganda campaign that threatened the province's doctors would leave rather than work under the government plan. The images of protest and conflict reproduced here suggest that many Saskatchewan residents supported the physicians and loudly opposed health insurance. The bitter three-week doctors' strike ended with a compromise agreement that allowed physicians to work on a fee-for-service basis rather than as salaried employees; they could continue to see patients in their private offices rather than as part of a healthcare team in clinics. Medicare emerged out of this sort of protest and compromise.

Gerard Boychuk's article is part of a larger work that examines the history of health insurance in a comparative North American political framework that asks why Canada established a national insurance program while the Americans did not. His perspective is thoroughly political, and he concludes that the debate over health insurance in each country was fundamentally influenced by the larger political temper of the 1960s. American public policy, influenced by the politics of civil rights and "race," fragmented into a system of private health insurance, while Canada, threatened by Quebec nationalism, worked to integrate citizens into a national program. Boychuk's approach suggests that Medicare and its "core values" emerged by political negotiation from above rather than social pressure from below. But Boychuk does suggest an intriguing notion of how Medicare grew to iconic status in Canada.

Alvin Finkel's chapter highlights the material basis of public policy and the struggle between Medicare's proponents and its detractors. Finkel does not ignore politics, but he emphasizes the contingency of history. Nothing about Medicare was inevitable, and the program that emerged was less than its founders desired, but more than its opponents wanted.

NOTES

1. Roy Romanow, *Building on Values: The Future of Health Care in Canada* (Ottawa: Final Report of the Royal Commission on the Future of Health Care in Canada, 2002), xvi; Romanow was Saskatchewan's premier from 1991 to 2001.
2. Gregory P. Marchildon, *Health Systems in Transition: Canada* (Toronto: University of Toronto Press, 2005), 39.
3. Gerald Friesen, *The Canadian Prairies: A History* (Toronto: University of Toronto Press, 1987), 386.
4. Quoted in A. W. Johnson, *Dream No Little Dreams: A Biography of the Douglas Government of Saskatchewan, 1944–1961* (Toronto: University of Toronto Press, 2004), 21.
5. Johnson, 22.
6. Quoted in Gerard W. Boychuk, *National Health Insurance in the United States and Canada* (Washington: Georgetown University Press, 2008), 103.
7. Bernard Blishen, *Doctors and Doctrines: The Ideology of Medical Care in Canada* (Toronto: University of Toronto Press, 1969), 147.
8. Quoted in Dennis Gruending, ed., *Great Canadian Speeches* (Markham, ON: Fitzhenry and Whiteside, 2004), 152–3.

QUESTIONS

1. If Medicare was so important to Canadian identity, how can you explain the opposition to its implementation?
2. How did Medicare move from a contentious issue to an icon of identity so quickly?
3. As the Americans currently debate a public health insurance scheme, can you see parallels with the Canadian debate?
4. How does Finkel's approach differ from Boychuk's? Why?
5. In Douglas' "Mouseland" speech, who are the cats? Who are the mice?

FURTHER READINGS

Badgley, Robin F., and Samuel Wolfe, *Doctor's Strike: Medical Care and Conflict in Saskatchewan,* (Toronto: Macmillan, 1967).

Blishen, Bernard, *Doctors and Doctrines: The Ideology of Medical Care in Canada,* (Toronto: University of Toronto Press, 1969).

Boychuk, Gerard W., *National Health Insurance in the United States and Canada,* (Washington: Georgetown University Press, 2008).

Johnson, A. W., *Dream No Little Dreams: A Biography of the Douglas Government of Saskatchewan, 1944–1961,* (Toronto: University of Toronto Press, 2004).

Marchildon, Gregory P., *Health Systems in Transition: Canada,* (Toronto: University of Toronto Press, 2005).

"Medicare: A People's Issue," accessed February 1, 2010, from http://scaa.sk.ca/gallery/medicare/index.php.

Romanow, Roy, *Building on Values: The Future of Health Care in Canada*, (Ottawa: Final Report Royal Commission on the Future of Health Care in Canada, 2002).

435

▲ Document 1: Mouseland

Tommy Douglas

Mouseland was a place where all the little mice lived and played, were born and died. And they lived much the same as you and I do.

They even had a Parliament. And every four years they had an election. Used to walk to the polls and cast their ballots.

Some of them even got a ride to the polls. And got a ride for the next four years afterwards too. Just like you and me. And every time on election day all the little mice used to go to the ballot box and they used to elect a government. A government made up of big, fat, black cats.

Now if you think it strange that mice should elect a government made up of cats, you just look at the history of Canada for the last ninety years and maybe you'll see that they weren't any stupider than we are.

Now I'm not saying anything against the cats. They were nice fellows. They conducted their government with dignity. They passed good laws—that is, laws that were good for cats. But the laws that were good for cats weren't very good for mice. One of the laws said that mouse holes had to be big enough so a cat could get his paw in. Another law said that mice could only travel at certain speeds—so that a cat could get his breakfast without too much effort.

All the laws were good laws, for cats. But, oh, they were hard on the mice. And life was getting harder and harder. And when the mice couldn't put up with it any more, they decided that something had to be done about it. So they went en masse to the polls. They voted the black cats out. They put in the white cats.

Now the white cats had put up a terrific campaign. They said: "All that Mouseland needs is more vision." They said: "The trouble with Mouseland is those round mouse holes we got. If you put us in we'll establish square mouse holes." And they did. And the square mouse holes were twice as big as the round mouse holes, and now the cat could get both paws in. And life was tougher than ever.

And when they couldn't take that anymore, they voted the white cats out and put the black ones in again. Then they went back to the white cats. Then to the black cats. They even tried half black and half white cats. And they called that coalition. They even got one government made up of cats with spots on them: they were cats that tried to make a noise like a mouse but ate like a cat.

You see, my friends, the trouble wasn't with the colour of the cat. The trouble was that they were cats. And because they were cats, they naturally looked after cats instead of mice.

Presently there came along one little mouse who had an idea. My friends, watch out for the little fellow with an idea. And he said to the other mice, "Look, fellows, why do we keep electing a government made up of cats? Why don't we elect a government made up of mice?" "Oh," they said, "he's a Bolshevik. Lock him up!" So they put him in jail.

But I want to remind you: That you can lock up a mouse or a man but you can't lock up an idea.

Source: T. C. Douglas, "Mouseland" (c. 1944). Originally broadcast on CBC Radio News Special, January 1, 1961. Reprinted with permission from the Canadian Broadcasting Corporation. To hear Tommy Douglas' speech, go to http://archives.cbc.ca/politics/parties_leaders/topics/851/

▲ Document 2: Doctors' Strike

TO OUR PATIENTS

THIS OFFICE WILL BE CLOSED AFTER
JULY 1st, 1962

WE DO NOT INTEND TO CARRY ON PRACTICE
UNDER
THE SASKATCHEWAN MEDICAL CARE
INSURANCE ACT

437

Source: Saskatchewan Archives Board S-A998.

▲ Document 3: All Doctors Are Out

Source: Courtesy of the *Leader Post*.

▲ Document 4: The Doctors' Position

June 16, 1962
The Doctors' Position on Medical Insurance

Doctors do not object to the Saskatchewan Government-controlled medicare plan because of money. Even Government leaders admit that doctors would get more money under the Act. **So it is not a matter of fees or of money.**

Genuine medical insurance is something every doctor wants to see. But this plan proposed by the Government, no matter what the Government says, is much more than just medical insurance. It places the control of medicine in the hands of the Government and a political Commission.

In an effort to solve the impasse with Government, your doctors proposed that the Cabinet accept an insurance plan similar to the one which has been so successful in Australia. This would have provided you with all the benefits of the Government Plan **but it would have prevented Government control of medical practice.**

The Government, by its actions, has indicated that it will accept no plan other than its own Act because it wants absolute control over doctors and patients. These controls are long-term rather than immediate. Many of them will not appear in the first draft of Commission regulations. However, these regulations can be changed any time at the whim of the politicians and the politically appointed Commission. **Subsequent versions will contain more and more controls.**

Both Government and the Commission have given doctors their "assurance" they do not want to control doctors. **They have "promised" this and "promised" that** in recent weeks in an attempt to manoeuvre the doctors into accepting their Act.

WHY
can't the doctors accept this act?

POLITICAL MEDICINE
Your doctors are concerned about the future quality of medical care. We believe that you, too, are concerned that the medical care you will receive in the future will be of the same quality that you have received in the past. We don't believe that you want to have your doctor directly responsible to politicians or a Commission which is politically controlled.

CONTROL
This Act provides for control of patients as well as doctors. The Commission takes away your rights whether you would want them to or not. It controls doctors in a very special way—as we understand Section 49(1)(g), the Commission has the right, for example, to tell doctors where to practice, whom they may care for and how they may provide care. **We believe that you would react as the doctors have done because you would not tolerate such control by Government for one minute.**

POLITICAL ASSURANCES
Government spokesmen have admitted that these controls exist in the Act but they say that they will never use them. Your doctors wonder why they were written into the Act, if the politicians don't intend to use them. We consider that the health of our patients and the future of the practice of medicine are too important to depend on the promises of politicians. Promises are too

easily broken and in the experience of the doctors of Saskatchewan in dealing with this government, promises have been broken too many times in the past.

BROKEN PROMISES
Doctors were promised by "duly elected representatives" that they would have an opportunity to study this Act before it was presented to the Legislature.

THIS PROMISE WAS NEVER KEPT
Our then "duly elected" Premier T. C. Douglas promised us that any plan must be acceptable to those giving the services as well as those receiving them.

THIS PROMISE WAS NEVER KEPT
"Duly elected representatives" promised that the Thompson Committee would have ample time to study and report on all the health needs of the people before legislation was introduced.

THIS PROMISE WAS NEVER KEPT
These are just three examples of broken promises. There are many more. Would you, under these circumstances, place any trust in the promises of "duly elected" politicians?

We ask all thoughtful citizens to consider this question—Could you bring yourself to accept such an Act and such a Commission?

Your doctors face a dilemma. They have decided that they cannot continue in practice under this Act after July 1st. They hope that you, as free men, will appreciate their position. What is at stake is the future quality of medical care and the right of doctors to practice medicine without political direction.

WE ASK THAT YOU SUPPORT THE IMMEDIATE WITHDRAWAL OF THE GOVERNMENT PLAN AND RESUMPTION OF NEGOTIATIONS ON A BASIS ACCEPTABLE TO THE PROFESSION

(Authorized by the Saskatchewan Division of the Canadian Medical Association)

439

Source: Courtesy of the Saskatchewan Division of the Canadian Medical Association.

▲ Document 5: Hanging T. C. Douglas in Effigy, July 1962

440

● **Hanging Douglas in Effigy During Rally in Support of Striking Doctors, July 1962. Why are these women so angry? What role did the media have in the Doctors' strike?**

Source: Saskatchewan Archives Board RB-39801.

▲ Document 6: Rally in Support of Doctors, July 1962

● What do these images of the July 1962 rally indicate about the doctors' supporters? By their professionally produced protest signs, and their clothes, can you make some assumptions about their social and economic position in society? What groups did not attend the rally?

Source: Morris Predinchuck, Saskatchewan Archives Board, Morris Studio Fonds.

▲ Document 7: Rally in Support of Doctors, July 1962

Source: Morris Predinchuck, Saskatchewan Archives Board, Morris Studio Fonds.

■ Article 1: Pragmatic Physicians: Canadian Medicine and Health Care Insurance, 1910–1945

Robert S. Bothwell and John R. English

It has become a ritual in Canada to view the medical profession as unalterably opposed to state-sponsored health insurance. It is usually assumed that this is so, was so, and has always been so.

In fact, the history of the medical profession's attitude to health insurance belies this common stereotype. The first mention of health insurance in the *Canadian Medical Association Journal* was in 1912. Lloyd George had just introduced his famous Insurance Act in Great Britain, and Canadian doctors took note of this new phenomenon. In the words of the editor of the *Journal,* the conservative Sir Andrew Macphail, "a spirit of charity will be replaced by a cold official atmosphere. When physicians become civil servants, those who peculiarly adapted for healing the sick will be automatically forced out of the service and into private practice." Prophetic words perhaps, and similar reservations were expressed in 1914 by Dr. A. R. Munroe of Edmonton, who claimed that Lloyd George was "exploiting the medical profession either in the name of charity or religion." Nevertheless, Munroe believed that commercial methods of insurance should be studied and that the medical profession could agree on four points: universal access to medical care; no "charity" treatment; increases in doctors' incomes; the need to have insurance schemes calculated on the basis of "the medical schedule of fees." Munroe added that it was "worth every man's while studying."[1] Who could disagree?

Macphail and Munroe assumed that health insurance would be a long time coming to Canada. The First World War, however, created an atmosphere of mutual sacrifice and an acceptance of state

Source: Robert S. Bothwell and John R. English, "Pragmatic Physicians: Canadian Medicine and Health Care Insurance, 1910–1945" in SED Shortt, ed., *Medicine in Canadian Society: Historical Perspectives* (Montreal: McGill-Queen's University Press, 1981), pp. 479–493. Reprinted with permission.

involvement in a broader range of social services than hitherto contemplated. In 1917 the president of the CMA, Dr. A. D. Blackader, reflecting the anti-materialist sentiments so prevalent during the war, warned the CMA that it must avoid the imputation of "mercenary reasons" in its opposition to health insurance. Moreover, all doctors should now begin to prepare for the consideration of health insurance in Canada, and in this process the CMA should seize the initiative "to safeguard the true interests of our own profession."[2]

Still, by the war's end in 1918 no prominent Canadian doctor had explicitly stated a preference for state-directed medicine. But in 1919 Professor D. F. Harris told the Association of Medical Health Officers of Nova Scotia that since preventive medicine was already and properly the concern of the state, curative medicine should be a state concern as well. This was a fairly common attitude among public health doctors, who, being already civil servants, could see few terrors and no degradation in the prospect of universal state medicine. In the same year the first Royal Commission was appointed to study health insurance, in British Columbia, and its Report recommended a state-supported system of health insurance.[3]

The British Columbia government, however, took no action on the Royal Commission Report, because, as Premier Oliver informed the legislature, there was much doubt that health insurance was a provincial responsibility. The Royal Commission recommendation was therefore ignored, and medical insurance, like so many wartime social schemes, was all but forgotten during the 1920s. When the general secretary of the CMA, Dr. T. C. Routley, told Saskatchewan doctors in 1923 that health insurance was a serious proposition which deserved study, the secretary of the Saskatchewan Medical Society replied that he was "sure that this is just a flight of imagination in Dr. Routley's mind, and if he keeps quiet about it the country will never hear of it again."[4]

In fact, the country did begin to hear about health insurance again in 1928 and 1929 when a parliamentary committee held hearings in Ottawa to determine Canada's social security needs. Health insurance, the committee decided, was one of the needs, but the committee bowed to an advisory legal opinion which stated that social security was really

443

the responsibility of the provinces. This did not prevent the House of Commons from debating health insurance, which it did annually, but it did insure that health insurance would be talked out every time.

The CMA itself discussed health insurance once again in 1929. In a debate at the annual meeting that year speakers indicated uncertainty, opposition and, in a few cases, support for health insurance. Dr. T. B. Green of British Columbia claimed that in his association meetings he had "never heard, with one exception, any voice favouring health insurance." On the other hand, Dr. George Wilson of Toronto stated his belief "that state medicine is coming and we need not fight against it. It behoves {sic} this Association to get behind it and direct it." Speakers from eastern Canada tended to be less specific than those from the West. One doctor from Saint John hoped that the idea of health insurance "will die before it reaches us," but was willing to support an investigation, providing that it was done "as quietly as possible, let those {of us} in the East may hear of it."[5]

In the same year the British Columbia government abandoned its position that health insurance was a federal matter and appointed yet another Royal Commission to consider the possibilities of a provincial scheme. Before the commission submitted its report in 1932, a general economic depression had settled over the country, a depression which fundamentally altered both the state's and the medical profession's perspective on health insurance.

Quite suddenly the CMA began to perceive health insurance not as a threat but rather as an antidote for the economic ills of the profession. The CMA's Committee on Medical Economics pointed out how severely doctors were affected by the depression. In a survey of doctors in Hamilton, which the committee carried out in 1933, it was found that doctors' practices had declined in volume by 36.5 percent between 1929 and 1933. Even worse, in 1929 77.5 percent of doctors' work was remunerative; in 1932, the proportion had fallen to 50 percent. Almost half of the doctors surveyed claimed that their professional income was insufficient to pay their expenses and provide the necessities of life. The respondents estimated that only 30 percent of the population was willing to pay for medical care, and that many patients failed to secure medical attention early enough in cases of serious illness solely because they could not afford it.[6]

In rural areas the situation was reportedly even more desperate. Dr. Ward Woolner of Ayr, Ontario, described his own experience in an article in the *CMA Journal*:

> Since 1929, rural areas have many families who cannot pay anything to their doctor. Even farmers, who a few years ago were considered well to do—had electricity installed, had motor cars and telephones—cannot pay for medical care today. We are asked to accept all kinds of produce on our accounts. The writer received over twenty chickens, several ducks, geese, a turkey, potatoes and wood on account during last winter. Many country doctors have trouble collecting sufficient to purchase the bare necessities of life.[7]

Dr. Woolner concluded that only a province-wide scheme of medical care could alleviate the situation. Many others had come to the same conclusion.

In 1932 the Province of Quebec Medical Association recommended a system of compulsory health insurance to cover complete service, cash benefits, and the right to free choice of physician by the patient.[8] The B.C. Royal Commission set up before the depression reported in favour of a health insurance plan covering employed persons making less than $2,100 per annum. The unemployed, however, were still left to charity. This meant, inevitably, that indigents would continue to receive a considerable amount of free service from doctors, or continue to add to the municipal relief burden. Doctors generally found this to be intolerable, and, in response to the British Columbia proposals, the CMA instructed its economics committee to prepare its own health insurance plan.[9]

Medical care for the unemployed and payment for such care was the CMA's greatest concern. Accordingly in 1933, Dr. Routley, the CMA's general secretary, went to see Prime Minister Bennett about the problem. He pointed out to Bennett that the doctors were in effect providing their own subsidy to the unemployed by giving free service, but Bennett offered little hope of federal aid. With no solution in sight, the editor of the *Bulletin of the Vancouver Medical Association* called for the "socialization" of medicine. He urged doctors to accept a situation that was not only unavoidable, but actually desirable. A generous response from the medical profession would restore doctors' self-esteem and return "the medical profession to the pinnacle on which it once stood, and from which to a great extent … it has fallen.[10]

The CMA Committee on Economics finally presented its "Plan for Health Insurance in Canada" to the CMA's Council in 1934. The committee pointed out that provincial and municipal governments had shirked their responsibility for the provision of medical care for the indigent. The only solution to the problem was "State Health Insurance." State health insurance would be organized as a division of provincial departments of health and a central health insurance board, "representative of all interested parties," would furnish advice. The supervision of the plan would, of course, be handled by doctors, who would ensure that "the systematic practice of preventive medicine" would be properly carried out. The plan covered indigents, whose premiums would be paid for by the state, as well as single persons with incomes below $1,200 and families with incomes below $2,400. Above those income levels, participation in the plan would remain voluntary. The committee did not specify how doctors should be paid, although they noted that in sparsely populated rural areas doctors would have to rely on a contractual salary.[11]

In the same year, the president of the Toronto Academy of Medicine, Dr. E.A. McDonald, argued in his presidential address for state medicine. Doctors, he claimed, were "being driven into the indigent class" because they were forced to treat penniless patients free of charge. He advocated that Canada follow the British model for health insurance, but he recommended rather more generous salaries than the British paid. The general practitioner, McDonald suggested, "shall be paid a salary sufficient to enable him to live in comfort and continue his post-graduate studies to enable him to keep abreast of the progress of medicine, say, $6,000.00 per year." Specialists would be paid proportionately more, "say $8000 to $10,000 yearly." In 1930–31 the average male wage-earner in Canada was estimated to have earned only $927 per annum, and the salary of a member of Parliament was $4,000. It is therefore unlikely that McDonald's salary proposals met with much favour outside the medical profession.[12]"

When British Columbia introduced a draft health insurance scheme in 1935, the medical profession began to realize that health insurance presented many difficulties which had not been anticipated. By the time the draft pill became law in 1936, the B.C. medical profession was thoroughly alarmed. The Health Insurance Act proposed a restricted coverage—wage-earners making less than $150 a month, leaving out domestic servants, casual labourers, the indigent, part-time workers, and recipients of old age pensions and mothers' allowances. In short, those least likely to pay their accounts remained uninsured. The act was, the *Bulletin of the Vancouver Medical Association* declaimed, "a pale shadow of its former self, anaemic and paralyzed in its lower limbs, or its lower income levels, if you prefer." Equally disturbing was the act's failure to make specific provision for the rates and manner of payment and to give doctors a large role in the act's administration. Subsequent negotiations with the doctors failed to produce agreement, and the government postponed implementation of the scheme—indefinitely, as it turned out.[13]"

The British Columbia experience, however, did not cause Canadian doctors to reject the concept of health insurance. Indeed, the problem was that governments were not prepared to go far enough. In some provinces, therefore, the medical associations took the lead in developing voluntary health care schemes. In 1937, Manitoba began the study of voluntary hospital insurance (Blue Cross) and by 1939 the plan was in operation. Other Canadian provinces soon followed. In Ontario, Associated Medical Services and the Windsor Medical Services were established in 1937; both were sponsored by the OMA. A similar scheme was put into operation in Regina in 1939.[14]

These plans were local in coverage and voluntary in nature, and it seems that the CMA regarded them as a stop-gap. In 1939, the CMA's Committee on Economics reported that it had completed a comprehensive study of the working of health insurance in other countries, but recommended that the task of completing a health insurance plan had to be left to the government: "the Government must be the lead horse and … the Canadian Medical Association should be an essential and recognized running mate." The lead horse soon came round the corner, in the person of Dr. J.J. Heagerty, the director of public health for the federal Department of Pensions and National Health.

Before 1939, Pensions and National Health had failed to win, show, or place in the health insurance sweepstakes. It was regarded in Ottawa as a mediocre

445

department filled with second-raters. Its functions were confined to house-keeping on the health side, and it had never developed a comprehensive approach to health insurance, which it believed was a provincial responsibility. But in September 1939, Pensions and National Health acquired a new minister, Ian Mackenzie, who had been hastily transferred from the sensitive Department of National Defence on the outbreak of war. Mackenzie was naturally anxious to re-establish his reputation, and within months he had adopted social welfare as his instrument.

In January 1941, the King government summoned a Dominion-Provincial Conference to discuss the recommendations of the Rowell-Sirois Royal Commission. One of the special studies prepared for the commissioners by A. E. Grauer dealt with public health, which Grauer reported was in dismal shape. As Ottawa prepared for the conference, Mackenzie approached the deputy minister of finance, Clifford Clark, to ask that "consideration {be] given to the possible inclusion of public health as one of the subjects for discussion." "Someone," Clark rudely noted, "has called his attention to Professor Grauer's report."[16] While Mackenzie did not succeed in having health insurance placed on the agenda, he did create the impetus within his own department for a re-examination of the possibilities of health insurance.

A small committee, chaired by Dr. Heagerty, reported in January 1941 that "The principle of health insurance is approved." Its recommendations were to form the nucleus of the future federal health insurance scheme. The committee urged that public health (Heagerty was a public health doctor) be "an integral part" of any health insurance plan, that coverage be universal below a certain income level, and that provincial departments of health administer the plan in consultation with medical practitioners.

In October 1941, the CMA's executive visited Ottawa, where they were informed by Mackenzie of the work in progress. Mackenzie emphasized that nothing had been decided as yet, and that he wished to keep in touch with the doctors. A subcommittee of seven, including Routley, was appointed for this purpose. More important, the CMA itself in the same year approved the principle of health insurance, expressing reservations mainly about direct employment of doctors by the state.

The stumbling block was not the medical profession but rather the federal Department of Finance.

Pensions and National Health's early proposals envisaged a federal enabling act which would authorize federal contributions to provincially legislated plans. These plans would have to exclude indigents, but would allow fairly comprehensive medical treatment. In a letter to the minister of finance, Mackenzie estimated the cost of the program at $20 million, but alas, the Finance Department did not believe Mackenzie, and the minister's project was returned to him with a recommendation for more study.[17]"

An exchange of letters in the *CMA Journal* of April 1942, between Heagerty and Routley, was intended to show that a health insurance bill was very near—something that was far from the truth. Dr. Routley sounded the alarm: the doctors must consider their position before it was too late. A great change was coming, and the CMA must be in the vanguard. Routley urged all doctors to join the CMA so that the CMA's answer to the anticipated question "Whom do you represent?" would be too embarrassing. To the current wartime slogans of "Remember Hong Kong! Remember Pearl Harbor!" Routley suggested adding, "Remember Great Britain, and remember New Zealand when you think of Health Insurance!"[18]

At the annual meeting of the CMA in June 1942, the results of a questionnaire on health insurance were tabled. The 2,500 doctors who replied strongly supported the 1934 principles. They wanted: "an independent Health Insurance Commission" in each province, "the majority of whom shall be representatives of organized medicine"; medical care for indigents paid for by the government; freedom of choice for physician and patient; remuneration "according to the method or methods of payment which [doctors] select." With this mandate the committee of seven could take the initiative in defining more precisely the association's attitude towards the prospective health bill.[19]

The next draft of Heagerty's bill reflected the CMA's concerns. There was to be both a dominion Council on Health Insurance and separate provincial councils, with a majority of the membership being practising doctors. There was to be fee for service payment, and all indigents were to be included. In effect, Heagerty's bill gave the doctors everything they wanted. As far as Pensions and National Health were concerned, the bill was complete by December 1942, "except as to matters relating to costs." But costs, as it turned out, were close to the heart of the matter.

On 18–19 January 1943, a special meeting of the CMA Council was convened in Ottawa. (Heagerty and his deputy minister, Dr. Wodehouse, were members of the council.) The meeting adopted two resolutions:

1. The Canadian Medical Association approves the adoption of the principle of health insurance.
2. The Canadian Medical Association favours a plan of health insurance which will secure the development and provision of the highest standard of health services, if such plan be fair both to the insured and to all those rendering the services.

The *CMA Journal* approvingly noted that Heagerty and Wodehouse's attitude throughout was one of satisfying frankness. While the council was pleased with the progress made to date, it nevertheless refrained from approving the specific plan put forward by Pensions and National Health.[20]

Heagerty and Wodehouse had achieved a qualified success on the medical front, but Mackenzie, their minister, had lost the political battle for immediate implementation of the plan. The day after the CMA Council approved the principle of health insurance, Mackenzie learned that the cabinet would not support the enactment of health insurance in 1943. Instead, Heagerty's draft bill would be sent to a House of Commons committee, the Committee on Social Security, for study.

The Special Committee on Social Security convened in March 1943. It held four months of frequently wild and woolly sessions as lawyer-MPs and medical MPs had at one another. Routley and Dr. A. E. Archer, the CMA president, appeared on behalf of the association. Routley repeated the conclusions of the special council meeting of the previous January: the doctors anticipated "great and in some respects unwelcome changes," but they had accepted the principle of health insurance. Reflecting a common fear among doctors that politicians would meddle in their daily work, Routley warned the committee that health insurance must be run by a "non-political independent commission."

Other medical opinions were given at the hearings. The Catholic Hospitals Council's representative told the committee that they feared a loss of autonomy and confessional identity in a national hospital scheme; the majority of Canadians, after all, were Protestants. The osteopaths, the chiropractors, the Christian Scientists, and even the "Anti-Vaccination and Medical Liberty League of Canada" came forward. The gist of their testimony was objection to the predominant role of" doctors in the administration of health insurance, and the restriction of benefits to strictly medical forms of treament. Heagerty firmly rejected their arguments, insisting on the control of all medical treatment by the medical profession.

Finally, in July, the committee reported to the House of Commons that it thought that the principle of health insurance was a good one, and that the government should scout out the provinces' reactions. In the meantime the committee should be reconstituted next session. Heagerty's project had survived, chloroformed.[21"]

The CMA, which may have been disturbed by the attitude of some who had appeared before the Social Security Committee, seemed to welcome this pause. An August 1943 editorial in the *CMA Journal* saw the delay in Ottawa as providing an opportunity to think things over. Archer echoed this sentiment in his presidential address, and while not repudiating the CMA's support for the principle of health insurance, he suggested that health insurance should be delayed until after the war.[22] The doctors' hesitations gained force in December 1943 when a financial committee on health insurance reported that health insurance would cost the federal government approximately $100,000,000, four times as much as Mackenzie's original estimate. This report undermined much of Heagerty's testimony to the Special Committee. This committee's conclusions did not become public for a few months and in the meantime, the *CMA Journal* described Heagerty's testimony on finance as "not always consistent." Heagerty, who must have known by this point that his financial estimates were unsound, tried to reply that the criticisms were "erroneous" and unjust. As the chairman of the B.C. Division of the CMA's Committee on Economics observed, "Dr. Heagerty's subsequent reaction has seemed to rather prove that we have hit a tender point."[23]

The tone of the discussion had changed, a fact noted by Dr. M. G. Burris in a letter to the *CMA Journal* in March 1944:

> The profession of Canada as a whole is only now realizing the true nature of the

447

proposed Bill. In my opinion the section of the profession included within the Canadian Medical Association has been altogether too complacent and too compliant in the matter hitherto. We have proceeded apparently in the belief that State control was inevitable and as if the legislation had already been enacted. We have neglected to examine adequately the theories underlying and the theorists responsible for the present situation. The philosophy of the proposal is as plain an example of National Socialism and State Control as one could imagine or desire.

The *Journal* also took note of the American Medical Association's hostile attitude on health insurance, an attitude quite unlike the CMA's "too complacent and too compliant" attitude. The *Journal* also began to publish unfavourable comments on the proposed measures for British health insurance, in one case repeating a warning issued to Canadian doctors by Lord Dawson of Penn, "Chief Physician to His Majesty the King."[24]

It was, however, the Health Insurance Act passed by the Saskatchewan legislature in the early spring of 1944 which crystallized doctors' fears about politicians and their use of health care schemes. The Saskatchewan medical profession strongly protested "the fact that no opportunity was given to make representations on this bill and the hasty manner in which it was rushed through in the last hours of the legislature." They were understandably alarmed that no provision had been made for the representation of doctors on the Health Insurance Commission. The responsible minister replied that the bill was merely an enabling act and that no health insurance could be set up immediately under its provisions. Nevertheless, the doctors treated this Saskatchewan experience as an evil omen. The profession, Saskatchewan doctors argued, had been subjected to slanders and abuse. Rather plaintively, they summed-up their position: "We all know that individually, the doctor is everyone's friend but as a group we are regarded as anything but that."[25]

The fears of the Saskatchewan doctors were premature: there was no possibility that a poor province like Saskatchewan could finance a health insurance scheme without federal aid. Just as the Patterson government in Saskatchewan was passing its "innocuous enabling act," the federal scheme was collapsing in Ottawa, the victim of miscalculations and political exigencies. When the Mackenzie King government decided to proceed with family allowances, health insurance was abandoned and not revived as a separate measure. Far from being imminent and inevitable as CMA President Archer had claimed in 1943, a comprehensive health insurance scheme was a generation away. By the mid-1960s when the Pearson government introduced medicare, the Heagerty plan was all but forgotten; so too was the CMA's previous support for health insurance for Canadians.

The CMA's support for health insurance in the 1930s and early 1940s contrasted strongly with organized medicine's opposition to health insurance in the United States and Britain. Indeed, in the 1930s and even in the early 1940s, the most vocal supporters of health insurance were prominent members of the Canadian medical profession. It was always a qualified support and enthusiasm varied inversely with the economic condition of the profession. It also seems that the greater the degree of familiarity with the politician and his schemes, the greater were the doctors' doubts. Nevertheless, to the "indigent" medical profession of the 1930s, health insurance promised paid accounts and security. In the 1940s and 1950s there appeared to be better ways, and the medical profession then chose to confront the perils of prosperity alone, without the politician's help.

Notes

1. *Canadian Medical Association Journal* (hereafter *CMAJ*) 3 (1912): 228; ibid. 4 (1914): 1112.
2. Ibid. 7 (1917): 582.
3. H. E. MacDermot, *History of the Canadian Medical Association*, 2 (Toronto, 1958): 60–61.
4. Cited in ibid., p. 61.
5. A transcript of this discussion may be found in ibid., pp. 61–64.
6. *CMAJ* 31 (September 1934), Supplement: 51.
7. Ward Woolner, "Medical Economics in the Rural Districts of Ontario," *CMAJ* 30 (1934): 307.
8. *CMAJ* 31 (September 1934), Supplement: 51.
9. H. E. MacDermot, "A Short History of Health Insurance in Canada," *CMAJ* 50 (1944): 448–49.
10. Cited in ibid.

11. Report of the Committee on Economics, "A Plan for Health Insurance in Canada," *CMAJ* 31 (September 1934), Special Supplement: 25–62.

12. E. A. McDonald, "State Medicine," *CMAJ* 31 (1934): 666–67.

13. Reproduced in *CMAJ* 34 (1936): 685.

14. *Royal Commission on Healthy Services* 1964 1: 387-88.

15. Cited in MacDermot, *History of the CMA,* p. 73.

16. Clark to Alex Skelton, 23 December 1940, RG 19 E2C, v. 108, Public Archives of Canada. See, generally, R. S. Bothwell, "The Health of the People," Paper presented to Canadian Historical Association Annual Meeting, June 1975. Reprinted in John English and J. Stubbs, eds., *Mackenzie King: Widening the Debate* (Toronto: Macmillan, 1978), pp. 191–220.

17. See Bothwell. "Health of the People," pp. 11–13.

18. *CMAJ* 46 (1942): 390–91.

19. Ibid. 47 (1942), Special Supplement: 3-5

20. Ibid. 48 (1943): 93.

21. Canada, House of Commons, Special Committee on Social Security, *Minutes; Journals of the House of Commons*, 23 July 1943.

22. *CMAJ* 49 (1943): 123–27.

23. Ibid. 50 (1944): 72, 174–75, 276.

24. Ibid., pp. 164–65, 276.

25. Ibid., pp. 273–74.

■ Article 2: Excerpts from National Health Insurance in the United States and Canada

Gerard W. Boychuk

Federal Failure, Provincial Success—Reform in Canada, 1945–49

The Failure of Comprehensive Health Insurance at the Federal Level

The initial push for public health insurance reform in the World War II period took place at the federal level in Canada. Federal proposals in the early 1940s initially contemplated a federally administered system of comprehensive health insurance coverage. Others proposed federal matching grants for provincial provision of public insurance for a similarly comprehensive range of health services. Finally, others recommended leaving health insurance completely to the provinces. The system that emerged roughly fifteen years later was a federal–provincial system limited to hospital insurance that, while setting broad national principles, left administration to the provinces—a system that none of the early proponents of reform had envisioned. In large part, this outcome reflected the degree to which public health insurance reform was intertwined with territorial politics and was the result of a reform process in which successful outcomes were highly tenuous. In contrast with early proposals for reform illustrating the different visions—one federalist and one provincialist—informing proposals for public health insurance reform, more moderate proposals (tilting toward the latter vision) came to dominate but even these initially floundered on the shoals of the territorial politics inscribed in Canadian federal–provincial relations.

...

After securing reelection, the Liberal government included public health insurance reform as part of the broader package of "Green Book Proposals" for postwar reconstruction in 1945. The federal government, at the Dominion–Provincial Conference on Post-War Reconstruction of 1945, offered grants-in-aid for medical, hospital, dental, pharmaceutical, and nursing benefits. The terms of the proposals were very open-ended, and "the original plan for national legislation in the interests of promoting national uniformity and adequacy had been dropped" (Guest 1997, 132).

The government of Québec rejected the social insurance proposals. Other elements of the overall package also met with serious provincial resistance.[1] Despite the softening of federal proposals as outlined above, the Québec premier opposed federal proposals on the basis that they were "incompatible with the autonomy of the province" and "would inevitably lead to interference in all these fields which ought to be free of Dominion authority."[2] Of course, the provincial government had no plans of its own to enter the public health insurance field; rather, it was protecting existing arrangements in which the Catholic Church had largely assumed the responsibility for providing the province's health services. The provincial government was not willing to be subjected to the political pressure that would have undoubtedly been generated by a federal cost-sharing program. Nor was it willing, on principle, to cede the initiative to federal social policy in an area of provincial jurisdictional competence. As a result of the inability to achieve federal–provincial consensus on this and other issues, the "entire package was jettisoned and the first significant plan for a comprehensive medical care system in Canada was stillborn" (Guest 1997, 132).

...

Hospital Insurance in Saskatchewan

The story of the emergence of public hospital insurance in Saskatchewan in this period is more complex and nuanced than is often portrayed. Public health insurance did not emerge simply as the natural result of a government with a socialist public philosophy holding power in a parliamentary system. The outcome was far more contingent than such an interpretation suggests and dependent on the perception—mistaken though it was—that a federal program for cost-sharing health insurance was imminent.

Necessity as the Mother of Reform

Various government programs in the hospital and medical-care sectors had developed incrementally over a long time in Saskatchewan—less as a matter of ideological predisposition than as a response to necessity. First allowed under provincial legislation in 1916, Saskatchewan had, in various localities, municipal doctor arrangements by which physicians in rural municipalities were paid a stipend by the municipality to supplement their fee-for-service income (Houston 2002, 23).[3] This was seen as a pragmatic response to an immediate problem—the difficulty of retaining physicians in sparsely populated agricultural areas especially during economic downturns that, in a one-crop agricultural economy subject to drought and other natural hazards and based on world commodity prices, were not infrequent.[4]

The Depression and its aftermath provided a strong impetus for some government intervention to provide health services in Saskatchewan. In a survey of ninety rural physicians in the early 1940s, the response was "almost unanimous in declaring that private practice was no longer feasible" (Houston 2002, 36). One particular reply captures the urgency of the mood of rural physicians: "Any system is to be preferred to the present. Collections appear hopeless. I do not know how medical men can hope to carry on out here under present and future conditions" (Houston 2002, 36).[5]

In keeping with the existing pattern of local development, universal hospital and medical insurance first came into being on a regional rather than provincial basis. The Swift Current area in southwestern Saskatchewan was drought stricken and facing serious doctor shortages (Houston 2002, 82). As the private health care system faltered, some sort of public plan appeared to be a necessity. By special legislation, the Swift Current Health Region was created, and universal medical and hospital care was implemented in the region in mid-1946—half a year before universal hospital insurance would be offered across the province. Physician support for such an initiative was split between rural doctors, some of whom believed that they could not continue to practice under existing conditions, and urban doctors, who did not share the plight of their rural colleagues. Physicians in the province's two urban areas, Regina and Saskatoon, "looked askance at this experiment in 'socialized medicine'" (Houston, 2002, 84).

These early programs of government intervention in the provision of health services had resulted in public opinion that was favorably predisposed toward public health insurance and led the Saskatchewan College of Physicians and Surgeons as well as the Saskatchewan Association of Rural Municipalities to endorse public hospital insurance (Taylor 1978, 79).

The Role of the Cooperative Commonwealth Federation

It is tempting to assume that since a provincial hospitalization program was implemented after the election of the Cooperative Commonwealth Federation (CCF) in 1994 that it was implemented as a result of that election.[6] The reality is again more complex. As argued above, necessity placed health care on the political agenda. The proposals for health insurance reform at the federal level provided a template for reform as well as the likelihood of future federal cost-sharing. The Liberal government in Saskatchewan in 1944 had already adopted enabling legislation to allow for Saskatchewan's participation in a federal health insurance program before the CCF's election (Naylor 1986, 129).

Hospital insurance proposals that emerged under the Liberals prior to the CCF's election placed public provision on a social insurance basis (e.g., requiring contributory premiums) and limited its provision to hospitals. These design decisions came from an abiding belief on the part of Saskatchewan policymakers that a federal cost-sharing program was imminent. The Select Special Committee on Social Security, which had been appointed by the governing Saskatchewan Liberals, had considered both direct state provision of medical services as well as public health insurance but concluded that "since federal assistance was a prerequisite to the adoption of a scheme of health services in Saskatchewan, and inasmuch as the Dominion government would probably determine which of the two systems it could support, the choice for Saskatchewan was not theirs to make" (Taylor 1978, 76). The Liberal government came to the same conclusion—a plan in Saskatchewan required prior action by the federal government. The Liberals passed enabling legislation for public health insurance that allowed the province to implement a health insurance plan as soon as a federal program was announced (Taylor 1978, 77).

451

In contrast to these tentative proposals for hospital insurance, the CCF was firmly committed to socialized health services and had been since the Great Depression. In its Regina Manifesto of 1933, the CCF called for "socialized" health services. Health, hospital, and medical services would be "publicly organized"—moving health services from the existing system based on private enterprise to making such services freely available on the same basis as education—the same principle underpinning proposals in the state of New York in 1939 (CCF 1933).[7] The 1944 CCF campaign under T. C. "Tommy" Douglas focused on the issue of health service but argued that health insurance akin to that proposed by the Heagerty committee would be inadequate (Naylor 1986, 137).

Immediately after being elected in 1944 the Douglas government appointed a health commission under Henry Sigerist, a professor of medical history at Johns Hopkins University (Houston 2002, 69). Following the recommendations of the Sigerist report, the province first moved to provide comprehensive health care for social assistance recipients, pensioners, and widows on the fee-for-service basis (Houston 2002, 72). The plan was in operation by January 1, 1945, and provided medical, hospital, and dental care and pharmaceuticals on a means-tested basis for recipients of Old Age Assistance and social assistance (Taylor 1954, 751–52).

At the same time, the government began making plans for universal hospital insurance. As had been the case under the Liberals, the CCF considered it essential that the hospital insurance plan be designed to meet federal requirements (Taylor 1987, 98).[8] It jettisoned its commitment to socialized health services and, instead, adopted the approach that had been initiated under the former Liberal government—universal premium-based insurance limited to hospital services.

Strategic Miscalculation

The Dominion–Provincial Conference on Reconstruction had been launched but not concluded when the Saskatchewan government decided to move ahead with hospital insurance (Taylor 1978, 69). Believing that having a public health insurance program up and running successfully before the next election would be crucial to their reelection, the Saskatchewan officials proceeded with the hospital insurance initiative and took "the gamble to introduce the program

before the federal policy had been decide upon" (Taylor 1990, 72–73). The Saskatchewan government, of course, could not know that the federal–provincial negotiations would break down and that federal cost-sharing would, as a result, not be available for another dozen years.[9] As it stood, the provincial government was now publicly committed to instituting a hospital insurance program, and province-wide universal hospitalization insurance became available on January 1, 1947. Given the belief that federal support was essential, the Saskatchewan government would certainly not have proceeded with the hospital insurance plan had it realized that no federal cost-sharing would be forthcoming for more than a decade. The expectation of federal cost-sharing temporarily suspended the constraining dynamics typically faced by provinces attempting to implement major social programs on their own.

The crucial contribution of the CCF government in Saskatchewan in this period was not to be the first provincial government to seriously pursue reform (which the government of British Columbia had done a decade earlier) or to be the only provincial government to undertake reforms (as discussed below, British Columbia adopted a program of social assistance medical care at the same time as Saskatchewan and would implement universal hospital insurance two years after Saskatchewan) or even to be the originator of the idea of public health insurance (in this period forceful impetuses for reform existed in Ottawa including, for example, the Heagerty committee, which had a great influence on debates in Saskatchewan).

Rather, the major contribution of the CCF government was to follow through with the implementation of its hospital insurance program even after its strategic miscalculation in regard to federal cost-sharing became clear. Despite the serious setback represented by the failure of the Conference on Reconstruction to produce cost-sharing, the Saskatchewan government implemented hospital insurance in an administratively effective and politically adroit manner—providing an impressive example that every single other provincial government sent a delegation to Saskatchewan to study. Had the Saskatchewan government wavered or, alternatively, been less successful in its implementation of hospital insurance (as would later be the case in British Columbia), the historical development of public health insurance in Canada would undoubtedly have taken a significantly different path.

National Public Hospital Insurance and Medical Care Insurance in Saskatchewan, 1950–62

The advent of hospital insurance at the provincial level did not automatically translate into the successful implementation of a hospital insurance program at the federal level. Instead, the failure of the federal–provincial negotiations in 1945 pushed subsequent reforms at the federal level into a period where they would have to be undertaken without the support of the medical profession and, as outlined in the following section, under political leadership considerably less predisposed toward direct public intervention in the health insurance field. Neither the federal government nor the Ontario government—whose agreement was key to the adoption of a federal plan—was enthusiastic about the prospect of public intervention in the health insurance field. Despite provincial precedents, the outcome remained far from assured and subject to the vagaries of the politics of Canadian federalism.

Nevertheless, as a result of federal–provincial dynamics, the federal government and Ontario provincial government became caught up in a game of one-upmanship driven by electoral pressures—the result of which was the hospital insurance program, which still constitutes one of two major planks of Canadian medicare today. A number of characteristics of the emergent system now seen as representative of the philosophical underpinnings of health care in Canada (such as universality and first-dollar coverage) came about as pragmatic responses to the immediate administrative problems of implementing a federal–provincial program.

One major consequence of federal cost-sharing for hospital insurance was to set the stage for the inception, four years later, of public insurance for physician care in Saskatchewan. Medical care insurance faced vociferous opposition in Saskatchewan from the medical profession, business, the media, and significant segments of the public—echoing earlier debates over public health insurance in the United States. However, in this case, reform would ultimately be successful.

National Hospital Care Insurance in Canada

In comparison with 1945, none of the key protagonists by the early 1950s—including the prime minister and federal government, the Ontario government, and the CMA—was keen on the idea of public health insurance. St. Laurent as leader of the Liberal Party was clearly not predisposed toward public health insurance although the Liberal cabinet was deeply split philosophically. On the other side of this debate, Paul Martin Sr., as minister of health, was a strong proponent of national health insurance and, over the period that hospital insurance was debated in the federal government, his support and influence in the cabinet grew (Taylor 1987, 128). At the provincial level, the governing Conservatives in Ontario were committed to the principles of free enterprise and limited government, and many individual members of the government were ardent opponents of government health insurance (Taylor 1987, 110, 118–19).

...

Certain characteristics of the hospital insurance plan as adopted later contributed to the rise of public health insurance to iconic status in Canada. They also helped foster public health insurance's role as a powerful tool of territorial integration. However, it is critical to note that, for the most part, these characteristics were incidental elements of the federal plan.

Certainly the federal program recognized and reinforced a central role for the provinces in shaping their own hospital insurance programs. The program was relatively conditional and certainly more highly conditional than future programs, such as federal cost-sharing for medical care insurance, would be. However, at the same time, it was not nearly as specific in its conditions as the initial federal proposal (based on the Heagerty recommendations) had been in 1943. The sequencing of events was crucial in this outcome. The failure of federal reforms in 1945 had opened up political space for the provinces to proceed on their own, and some of them did. In the wake of provincial experimentation, the federal government simply could not enforce a specific model of hospital insurance on the provinces once four provinces already had programs fully operating (Taylor 1987, 202).

At the same time, the federal conditions on cost-sharing for hospital insurance introduced elements that helped make public health insurance a symbol

453

of national unity and identity—including universality and public insurance as an entitlement unrestricted by payment of premiums or coinsurance fees. Policy-makers, however, did not deliberately intend either of these outcomes. Despite later revisionist histories that elevated universality to iconic status as a philo-sophic principle underpinning the health care system in Canada, the requirement that insurance be uni-versally available on uniform terms and conditions simply meant that federal cost-sharing funds could not be used to subsidize insurance provision through private plans—thus banning the transfer of public funds to private control. This provision reflected a desire to keep direct public control over public funds more than a commitment to egalitarian ideals (Naylor 1986, 166).

...

Medical Care Insurance in Saskatchewan

The advent of federal cost-sharing for hospital insur-ance allowed the provincial government in Sas-katchewan the financial latitude to move ahead with medical care insurance. In stark contrast with the ear-lier development of hospital insurance in Saskatch-ewan, the decision to embark on public medical care insurance was made with no expectation that federal cost-sharing would be forthcoming and was truly a decision to "go it alone." There were, of course, strong precedents on which to base the expansion of health insurance to the coverage of physician services in Saskatchewan, including the hospital insurance scheme that had in been in operation for roughly fifteen years as well as the more geographically lim-ited experiment in comprehensive coverage in the Swift Current Region. Nevertheless, from the outset the success of this venture was far from assured. Despite contemporary claims that Saskatchewan had a political culture strongly predisposed toward public medical insurance, the endeavor encountered serious resistance from the medical profession, broad segments of the public, and the media. Despite this opposition, universal medical care insurance became a reality—but only after a bitter twenty-three-day physician strike that made news around the world.

...

The doctors had already experienced some suc-cess in forestalling earlier attempts at expansion of

public insurance coverage for physician services at the regional level. In 1955 proposals for two addi-tional comprehensive regional medical care plans (following the model of the Swift Current plan) were subject to referendums in their respective areas. The college and its voluntary prepayment plans launched a massive publicity campaign contributing to the resounding defeat of medical care in both regions (Taylor 1990, 98; Naylor 1986, 179). These earlier battles had contributed to reinforcing the solidarity of the profession as well as steeling their resolve to resist further expansions of public medical care insurance (Taylor 1990, 98).

The doctors had also aggressively adopted a strategy of expanding physician-controlled voluntary prepayment plans (Taylor 1990, 98). Roughly 40 per-cent of the population was already covered under enrollment in the two profession-sponsored plans (Naylor 1986, 179; Taylor 1987, 266n71). Further-more, the province also had a categorical system of comprehensive coverage for recipients of old-age pensions and social assistance for more than six-teen years at the time when universal medical care insurance became a reality. Thus roughly one-quarter of the Saskatchewan population has "more or less" comprehensive coverage for medical services under various public programs including the Swift Current plan for comprehensive health service coverage in that region, the social assistance medical care pro-gram, and the municipal doctor contract system (Naylor 1986, 177). Only the remaining one-third of the population was without medical care coverage.

In addition to its own considerable political power, the College of Physicians and Surgeons received the support of extraprovincial interests including the CMA and the insurance industry, which were both committed to defeating public physician service insurance in Saskatchewan. This support sig-nificantly increased the pressure the college could bring to bear on the provincial government (Taylor 1990, 105). The Saskatchewan government was con-fronted not only by its own physicians but also by the national profession.

...

Finally, the coalition of interest opposed to the Saskatchewan plan was as broad as the coalition resisting public insurance in the United States. In the 1960 provincial election the college was joined in its opposition to public medical care insurance by the Saskatchewan Liberal Party, the dental and pharmaceutical associations, and the Chambers of Commerce (Taylor 1990, 104). During the actual doctors' strike in 1962, the press was universally critical (Taylor 1990, 118–19). Popular resistance to medical care insurance was organized through the development of a series of Keep Our Doctors Committees, which were vocally and vociferously opposed to the plan. These committees staged a series of impressive public rallies against the medical insurance plan.

The anti-insurance coalition also used rhetoric as drastic and misleading as the AMA campaigns in the United States. As noted by Lord Taylor, a leading figure in resolving the Saskatchewan doctors' strike, "'The American Medical Association was at this time, hysterically opposed to Medicare; and it endeavored, not without some success, to communicate its hysteria to the doctors and the public in Saskatchewan" (quoted in Taylor 1990, 121). Organized medicine in Saskatchewan portrayed public health insurance as communistic and a threat to freedom. Typical press coverage in Saskatchewan referred to the medical insurance program as "ferocious" and the government as "dedicated to the destruction of our economic system" (Taylor 1990, 118–19).

The 1962 Doctors' Strike and Its Resolution

In response to the announcement of Premier Douglas during a provincial by-election campaign in early 1959 that the provincial government intended "to embark upon a comprehensive medical care program that would cover all our people," the college emphasized its support for voluntary prepayment plans that, in this case, it controlled.[10] To the degree the college was willing to countenance a role for government in health insurance, it argued in favor of the CMA policy of subsidizing coverage for low-income people provided through voluntary agencies (Taylor 1990, 106). As outlined above, the college waged a massive publicity campaign in the 1960 election.

Initially the CCF government was far from certain as to how the public would react to the plan (Taylor 1987, 269). In the 1960 election the government received only 40 percent of the vote. In reaction to these results, "the college contended that the election, which had been virtually converted into a referendum on medical care insurance, had indicated

majority opposition to the government's policy" (Taylor 1990, 104). In the 1962 federal election the CCF was badly beaten in Saskatchewan (including the defeat of former CCF premier Tommy Douglas who had left provincial politics to run federally), and this defeat was widely perceived to be a reaction against public medical care insurance (Taylor 1987, 300). Nevertheless, an internal assessment presented by the head of the college to the CMA in July 1962 noted: "Over the past two and a half years, the public in that province seems to have accepted and approved of the fact that they will be provided with some form of plan for comprehensive, all-inclusive medical care insurance" (Taylor 1990, 114). Rather than responding to public opinion demanding public insurance, the CCF was shaping public opinion.

Despite the strident opposition of the profession, legislation was introduced and passed in the fall of 1961 making provision for a compulsory, premium-based system of public medical insurance. In response, the primary objective of the college was to preserve a role for the prepayment plans in the expectation that the CCF government would be replaced after the next election. If the move to public insurance was to later be reversed, the college believed it was critical that the prepayment plans survive so they might provide a voluntary alternative to the public program (Taylor 1990, 116). In response to the college's refusal to even negotiate in regards to a public plan, the government offered a major concession: The doctors could directly bill their patients who would then be reimbursed by the public plan according to the negotiated fee schedule. The college rejected the concession and called again for a system of subsidization of voluntary plans (Taylor 1990, 109). The gulf between the two sides could not be bridged, and on July 1, 1962, the doctors withdrew their services.

The strike presented huge political risks for both sides—no one knew where the public would lay blame if deaths were attributed to the strike (Taylor 1987, 314). Under mounting pressure, after twenty-three days an agreement was reached as a result of a major concession on both sides. The medical profession agreed to accept that the plan would be universal and compulsory with the government collecting premiums and disbursing payments. For its part, the government agreed that the existing organizational structure of the voluntary plans remain in place to act as billing and payment agents for physicians who did not wish to deal directly with the government health commission (Taylor 1990, 125).[11]

With the strike ended, universal compulsory public health insurance for physician services was fully in operation in the province of Saskatchewan although the physician-controlled prepayment plan organizations remained in place. The medical profession viewed the end of the strike as a cease-fire rather than a cessation of hostilities (Taylor 1987, 325–27). As the profession's leadership had hoped, twenty-one months later, in early 1964, the CCF government fell and the Liberals, who had opposed the public medical insurance plan and supported the doctors, were elected. But "to the surprise of the public and the dismay of the profession, the Liberal government did not change the format of the program, and the profession-controlled plans were never returned to their prior status" (Taylor 1990, 129). Comprehensive universal compulsory health insurance in Saskatchewan had become a reality.

Medical Care Insurance in Canada, 1962–84

I suppose we'll be proposing grocery-care next.
—Ernest Manning, Premier of Alberta

The principles of the Canada Health Act began as simple conditions attached to federal funding for medicare. Over time, they became much more than that. Today, they represent . . . the values underlying the health care system. . . . The principles have stood the test of time and continue to reflect the values of Canadians.
—Roy J. Romanow, *Health Canada Act Overview*

It is difficult to overstate the seriousness of the crisis facing Canadian unity during the period in which medical care insurance was debated and introduced. As *independentiste* sentiment in Québec flared, bombings first took place in Québec's largest city, Montréal, in 1963. The tension reached crisis proportions seven years later when, in the wake of the

kidnapping of the British Trade Commissioner James Cross and kidnapping and murder of Québec cabinet minister Pierre Laporte, the federal government temporarily suspended civil liberties across Canada on the basis of "apprehended insurrection" in Québec. Over this period, the rise of the militant separatist movement, the Front de Liberation du Québec (FLQ), as well as the creation of nonviolent parties dedicated to the establishment of an independent Québec by constitutional means—such as the Rassemblement pour l'Indépendence Nationale in 1960 and Ralliement National in 1966, which were both superseded by the Parti Québécois (PQ) in 1968—signaled the force of this challenge to Canada's territorial integrity.[12] It was from within this context that a national system of medical care insurance emerged in Canada.

. . .

The development of national public medical care insurance in Canada is often viewed as the result of a relatively natural evolution flowing out of earlier federal and provincial policy innovations such as universal hospital care insurance at the federal level and medical care insurance in Saskatchewan. The development and consolidation of national universal medical care insurance, however, in the period from the mid-1960s to the mid-1980s was highly tenuous. In this contingent process of development, the conjuncture at key points between the politics of health care and politics of territorial integration played an important role. Powerful political currents—especially those developing in Québec—provided a central dynamic driving the development of a national system of medical care insurance designed to touch the lives of all Canadians regardless of where they lived.

. . .

Political Resistance to Federal Medical Care Insurance

While it is often argued that the development of public medical care insurance in Saskatchewan set in motion positive feedback dynamics that created pressure for federal reforms, the political context for federal medical care insurance proposals in the wake of the developments in Saskatchewan was not particularly propitious. Although universal public medical care insurance had been implemented in Saskatchewan, this development, in itself, triggered negative feedback dynamics auguring against the

456

adoption of a similar program at the federal level. First, it generated even more serious resistance by the CMA to public physician-care insurance at the national level than had existed prior to the Saskatchewan experiment. Second, it contributed to the adoption of alternative health insurance plans in other provinces. Finally, it created serious concern at the federal level about the degree of resistance that a federal program might encounter.

One of the crucial effects of Saskatchewan adopting medical services insurance was to steel the CMA's resolve against compulsory public insurance for physician services. Organized medicine in Canada viewed the development of public medical care insurance in Saskatchewan as a "serious breach" (Taylor 1990, 129). In response to the developments in Saskatchewan, the president of the CMA made a "ringing call to the profession to reinforce the private governmental structure it had created to prevent any further breach in the system. And it made very clear its fear of, and determination to exclude, any other influence in the arrangements the profession controlled" (Taylor 1990, 130). As the CMA campaigned vigorously against national medical insurance, it issued constant warnings that "the introduction of medical care insurance, which they pejoratively referred to as socialized medicine, would lead to an exodus of doctors from the country" (Taylor 1990, 26).

...

Finally, the Saskatchewan experience generated considerable concern among federal policymakers. The difficulty of implementing medical care insurance in Saskatchewan demonstrated just how politically risky the venture would be for a minority Liberal government at the federal level. Certainly, the Saskatchewan doctors' strike removed any perception at the federal level that medical care insurance would be a natural evolution from hospital care insurance.[13] Federal policymakers were acutely aware that there was "a hell of a lot of opposition" to the plan in Saskatchewan. In light of the developments in Saskatchewan, the federal decision to proceed would have to be made on the assumption that an expansion of public health insurance would be campaigned against vigorously—which it was, especially by the insurance industry, which argued that the federal proposals would "ruin the nation."[14]

The omens for the successful achievement of a national plan "now were increasingly dark" (Taylor 1990, 144). In the view of the CMA, "The odds in favor of the market-economy approach . . . were shifting most favorably" (Taylor 1990, 140). Encouraged by these outcomes, the CMA was stepping up its publicity campaign against universal compulsory public health insurance as well as directly lobbying at the highest political levels.[15] Furthermore, public support of compulsory public physician-care insurance was weak. In a public opinion poll conducted in the fall of 1965 as the government was preparing to introduce legislation, support for a voluntary plan (52 percent) outstripped support for a compulsory plan (41 percent) by a significant margin.[16]

The provinces, on the whole, were recalcitrant. At the annual Provincial Premiers Conference, "so strident were the tones, so angry the voices, and so vehement the opposition that one journalist summed it up, 'The federal government's proposed legislation lies torn, tattered, and politically rejected'" (Taylor 1990, 149). When the federal government announced its medical care insurance proposals in 1965, Premier of Alberta Ernest Manning commented acerbically, "I suppose we'll be proposing grocery-care next."[17]

Nevertheless, the Liberal minority government elected in 1963 and reelected as a minority again in 1965 persevered in pursuing a national plan, and the federal government eventually pushed through a conditional cost-sharing program for public medical care insurance. Of course various compromises were made. For example, the medicare program would have "principles" rather than "conditions," a semantic measure intended to make the plan more palatable to the provinces. These principles, later to become enshrined in the CHA, were portability, public administration, comprehensiveness, universality, and accessibility.[18]

From the outset the Québec government flatly refused to participate in any federal scheme in an arena of primarily provincial jurisdiction. Premier of Québec Jean Lésage argued that Québec would bring in its own plan of medical care insurance but that "when our plan is introduced, it will be operated outside any joint Federal–Provincial program in line with our general policy of opting out of all areas within our competence" (quoted in Taylor 1990, 147).[19] The Québec position had been and remained clear: its overriding objectives were complete provincial autonomy in all areas of provincial jurisdiction and securing the financial capacity to fund programs in these areas independently of conditional federal transfers.

This provincial recalcitrance was overcome, however, by a brilliant federal maneuver of dubious constitutional legitimacy—certainly breaking the spirit, if not the letter, of the Canadian constitution. In the fall of 1968 the federal finance minister announced an increase of 2 percent in federal income tax. Although it was formally called the social development tax (as it would have been unconstitutional for the federal government to levy a health care tax), the tax was clearly intended to finance federal contributions to health insurance. Taxpayers in all provinces would be, in essence, paying for medical care insurance regardless of whether or not their province had a program eligible for federal cost-sharing. This action created significant political pressure on provincial governments to acquiesce to the program (Taylor 1987, 392). As a result, all provinces, even those that were less than enthusiastic about the federal plan, such as Québec, quickly developed programs eligible for federal cost-sharing (see table 8.1).

In a context in which provinces could opt out of established programs, a new cost-sharing program offered unique opportunities for renewing a strong federal role. Constitutional questions aside, the relevant political question was whether public opinion in favor of universal medical care insurance was sufficiently strong in Québec that the federal government could put pressure on the provincial government that it could not resist. Federal policymakers were well aware that universal public medical care insurance has as much popular appeal within Québec as anywhere else.[20]

. . .

The political prospects for a straight federal program of either a universal or categorical (e.g., limited to children) variety were radically transformed by a number of factors. The first was the report of the Royal Commission on Health Services (Hall Commission) in 1964. The Hall Commission provided, in large part, the philosophical rationale for the expansion of universal public insurance to medical care.[21] The Hall Commission, reflecting its own concern with issues of territorial integration, recommended a "Health Charter," the essence of which was as follows: "The achievement of the highest possible health standards for all our people must become a primary objective of national policy and a cohesive factor contributing to national unity. . . . The objective can best be achieved

through a comprehensive, universal Health Services Program for the Canadian people" (Taylor 1990, 135).[22]

. . .

As Kent outlines, the role of Québec was "absolutely crucial" to the endorsement of medical care insurance by the federal government: "There would have been no Canadian welfare state if pre-1960 Québec politics had continued."[23] Changes in Québec were "absolutely essential to moving ahead." The new Lésage government was as keen on social policy as was the federal Liberal government. Federal officials perceived the Pearson government and Lésage government of Québec as having the same broad objectives in health care, and federal officials believed that a federal cost-sharing program could be made politically acceptable even in light of Québec nationalism. In so doing, the federal cost-sharing proposal for medical care was significantly different from cost-sharing for hospital care, with the former being based on broad principles rather than federal monitoring of a detailed program. Federal policymakers fashioned a proposal that proved impossible for the Liberal government in Québec to resist.

As soon as the federal government announced its intentions to initiate a federal cost-sharing program for medical care insurance, the Québec government declared that it intended to bring in its own program outside the rubric of any federal shared-cost plan (Taylor 1987, 356). To this point, there had been very little government action in Québec to support this claim. It was after the conference that the Québec premier "set events in motion," announcing that health insurance would be introduced the following year and establishing a committee to study the issue (Taylor 1987, 386, 392). The two governments now were jockeying to be the first to occupy the political space created by the issue of medical care insurance—engaging in competitive state-building, to use Banting's apt phrase.

Although the Liberal government in Québec was replaced by the Union Nationale government in mid-1966, the Québec government continued to insist that it had full jurisdictional competence over health care and demanded that the federal government cede further tax room and return to Québec the tax capacity that it required to exercise this competence (Taylor 1987, 386). Despite the fact that the influential Castonguay committee (which had been appointed by the Québec Liberals) recommended the establishment of a comprehensive, universal provincial health insurance program, the Union Nationale publicly committed itself to a policy of subsidizing health insurance provided to those with low income through existing agencies (Taylor 1987, 389–90).

Two factors combined to make this policy position futile. First, the structure of the federal "health insurance tax" meant that even if the Québec government were to refuse to go along with the federal plan, Québec citizens would still be taxed and the proceeds transferred to other provinces. Of course the Québec government (and some Québec members of parliament) vociferously protested against the federal position; however, the federal government, from the outset, refused to budge. As the national program was implemented and Québec stayed out, federal intransigence was reinforced by the election results of 1968: "The federal government with its recently acquired large majority in the Commons, and especially its success in Québec, was in no mood to compromise" (Taylor 1987, 392). Second, the position of the Québec government ran against strong public support for medicare inside the province of Québec—a factor that the federal government was counting on. Support for the federal medicare program in Québec proved to be higher than in any other region in Canada by a considerable margin (see table 8.2).

Given the immense pressure on the Québec provincial government generated by federal maneuvering, it seemed largely a foregone conclusion that Québec would eventually join the program despite its efforts to resist (Taylor 1990, 150).[24] Regardless of aspirations

to exercise full provincial autonomy, the Québec government could not resist the federal offer even in the face of federally stipulated "national principles."

The Iconic Status of Health Care in Canada, 1984–2008

National Unity and National Distinctiveness

Support for public health insurance became increasingly strongly linked to issues of national unity as well as Canadian distinctiveness. In a 1978 poll, 72 percent of respondents agreed that medical care "should be guaranteed by the government" (Mendelsohn 2001, 28). By 1985, 95 percent of Canadian respondents agreed. In 1965, 52 percent of people responding to a poll favored a voluntary plan while only 41 percent favored a universal plan, and in 1968, only 55 percent of respondents (and less than half in Ontario) felt that the federal government should bring in Medicare as it had promised (Taylor 1987, 391). In contrast, by 2000, 88 percent of respondents said that it was "very important" to them to have a "strong national system of publicly funded health care"—only 3 percent felt it was "not important" (Mendelsohn 2001, 25). As Marmor and coauthors noted: "None of the major studies of the origins of Medicare [in Canada] . . . have concluded that the overwhelming support for the egalitarian values of the Medicare program preceded the passage of

459

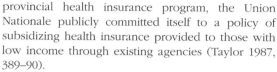

TABLE 8.2

Support for Medicare, Canada, by Region, 1968 (Percentage)

	NATIONAL	QUÉBEC	ONTARIO	WEST
Federal government should bring in:				
Medicare as promised	55	64	49	55
Medicare should be postponed	19	20	19	19
Medicare should be dropped	19	12	23	19
Can't say	7	4	9	7

Source: Taylor 1987, 391.

national health insurance legislation." Rather, "the values expressed by the . . . operating principles of Medicare . . . have in large measure arisen from Medicare's performance, not its origins" (Marmor, Okma, and Latham 2002, 16). Public support for the program is not explained solely by its performance, however. These shifts were also related to public perceptions of the role of health insurance in fostering national unity and defining a national identity precisely as intended, though to a degree not anticipated by, federal policymakers.

Public Health Insurance, Citizenship, and National Unity

Public health insurance has come to be seen in Canada as a right of citizenship. In a 1998 poll 69 percent of respondents agreed (48 percent agreed "completely") and only 11 percent of respondents disagreed that "Medicare is a right of citizenship" (Mendelsohn 2001, 28) Perceived in this way, health care fosters national unity by defining the national community as the community through which this right is granted. The central principles of the CHA, especially universal coverage, equal access, and cross-provincial portability of benefits, "have come to define the citizenship dimensions of health provision in Canada" (Maioni 2002). When asked in a 1994 poll to identify what "most ties us together as a nation," the two responses garnering substantial agreement were health care and hockey (Stanbury 1996).

The corollary of perceiving health care as a right is the demand for a high degree of national uniformity in the provision of public health services. The degree of provincial variability that is politically acceptable in delivering a service that is a right of national citizenship is necessarily limited. In a 1996 poll 63 percent of respondents felt that it was "very essential" to have national standards for health care across the country while another 25 percent felt it was somewhat essential (Mendelsohn 2001, 80).[25] The federal role in health care through its link with citizenship is imbued with considerable symbolic significance. As Maioni puts it:

> The federal government can claim to have "nationalized" health care and promoted "equal citizenship" among Canadians and guaranteed health benefits to all. In debates about provincial autonomy, national unity,

or constitutional renewal, this is of enormous significance: the federal government has no constitutional role in health care but can claim to defend the "integrity" of the popular features of the "Canadian" health care model. The federal government achieves clout without the headache of administering and budgeting for health care services. (2001, 100)

All relevant political actors "recognize the extent to which disputes about health care involve struggles over economic and political space in the federation" (2001), 88).

. . .

Footnotes

Federal Failure, Provincial Success—Reform in Canada, 1945–49

1. Another unresolved issue was tax rental—an arrangement by which the provinces during wartime had ceded certain issues of provincial taxation to the federal government in return for unconditional federal grants. The agreement proposed an extension of these arrangements. Both Ontario and Québec opposed the proposals. The former disagreed with the structure and level of proposed federal compensation for ceded tax room (Naylor 1986, 133–4). However, the Premier of Québec, Maurice Duplessis, objective on the basis of constitutional principle—arguing that the proposals undermined the federal–provincial division of powers enshrined in the British North America Act, Canada's central constitutional document at the time.

2. Premier Maurice Duplessis quoted in Taylor and friends 1987, 62–63).

3. According to C. Rufus Rorem, a researcher for the U.S. Committee on the Costs of Medical Care (CCMC) who studied the Saskatchewan municipal doctor system in the period, "Each of the municipalities which has adopted the municipal doctor system had already had unsatisfactory experiences with the conventional methods of private practice.... In several instances a local physician placed before the municipality the alternative of employing him on an annual salary or having him move to another

community." The CCMC in the United States recommended that a similar program be implemented in particular areas in the United States.

4. An important innovation in 1941 was a municipal system of tax prepaid hospital and physician care that allowed residents to choose from any doctor or hospital anywhere in the province (as opposed to limiting choice to salaried doctors in that particular municipality) (Houston 2002, 78).

5. Full results of the survey are reported in the Saskatchewan Medical Quarterly.

6. The CCF philosophy, although it clearly could be considered a democratic socialist party, was at root an extension of the "social gospel" vision. This vision originated in the United States: it was influential after the Civil War and peaked during the Progressive Era (from the turn of the century to the end of World War II). For an overview of the social gospel doctrine in the United States, see Morone (2004).

7. Under the heading "Socialized Health Services—Publicly Organized Health, Hospital and Medical Services," the Regina Manifesto states: "Health services should be made at least as freely available as are educational services today. But under a system which is still mainly one of private enterprise the costs of proper medical care, such as the wealthier members of society can easily afford, are at present prohibitive for great masses of the people. A properly [i.e., publicly] organized system of public health services including medical and dental care . . . should be extended to all our people in both rural and urban areas" (CCF 1933).

8. Thus, for example, the decision to make the plan a contributory social insurance program based on premiums was in direct response to the Green Book proposals, which emphasized premiums (Taylor 1990, 70).

9. The provincial legislation was passed in February 1946, and the federal–provincial negotiations ended in failure in early May 1946 (Taylor 1990, 58).

National Public Hospital Insurance and Medical Care Insurance in Saskatchewan, 1950–62

10. At the first opportunity following Douglas's speech, the College of Physicians and Surgeons unanimously passed a resolution avowing that "medical care has always been readily available to the public regardless of ability to pay, and that no one has ever been denied medical attention because of his financial position"; "we firmly believe that the standards of medical services to the people will deteriorate under such a system"; and "we oppose the introduction of a compulsory government-controlled, province-wide medical care plan and declare our support of, and the extension of health and sickness benefits through indemnity and service plans" (Taylor 1990, 100–101).

11. As a result of this compromise, doctors had a number of choices of ways to practice (a) receiving direct payments from the commission as payment in full (either salary or fee for service); (b) billing through a voluntary agency (and accepting billing as payment in full); (c) billing payments at doctors' sole discretion (providing an itemized list so that the patient could apply to the commission for reimbursement from the minimum fee schedule); (d) practice entirely for private fees (no itemized statement required) (Taylor 1990, 125–26). Initially it appeared as if the voluntary agencies (option B) would become a key component of the new system. Direct billing of the government, however, came to supercede billing through voluntary agencies: "In 1963, the proportion of physicians billing the commission directly was minimal, amounting to only 21.5 percent. By 1970 this proportion had increased to 51.5 percent, with the proportion billed through the prepayment plans declining from 68.0 percent to 40.5. With the proportion continuing to decline, in 1988 all physicians' claims were sent directly to the commission" (Taylor 1990, 129).

461

Medical Care Insurance in Canada, 1962–84

12. The territorial challenges facing the federal state were not limited to those emanating from Québec. As contemporary observers noted at the time, even had Québec remained quiescent, "the pressures for decentralization have been so fired up by resurgent provincialism that many have questioned the very survival of the federal government as a decisive body" (Black and Cairns 1966, 34).

13. Tom Kent, principal assistant to Prime Minister Lester B. Pearson, interview with author, April 2005.

14. Ibid.

15. The CMA executive met with the minister of health and prime minister in June 1965 (Taylor 1990, 141).

16. When asked about the apparent support in public opinion polling for a voluntary plan rather than a compulsory plan, Tom Kent emphasized that senior policymakers did not put much stock in public opinion polls—believing that the answers were largely shaped by the way the questions were asked. They believed that, in the last analysis, a straight public plan was "what people would vote for." As Kent points out, the real evidence of public support for the proposal was that it was voted for unanimously in the House of Commons. Kent, interview.

17. Ibid.

18. For an overview of these principles, see chapter 9. The federal contribution would match total spending by all provinces with this total amount being divided among provinces on a per capita basis.

19. Rather than calling for federal financial aid for health care (or any other specific program area), the Québec government called for the federal government to "make it easier for provinces to exercise their constitutional powers, for example, by rectifying the present system of sharing revenue sources in Canada" (Lésage quoted in Taylor 1990, 147). This continues to be the position of the Québec government in 2008.

20. Kent, interview.

21. The Hall Commission was appointed in mid-1961 and issued its report three years later, in mid-1964.

22. The report recommended public insurance coverage of a comprehensive range of services including medical services; dental services for children, expectant mothers, and public assistance recipients; prescription drug services; optical services for children and public assistance recipients; prosthetic services; and home care services.

23. According to Kent, far more than people appreciated, there was a real alliance between the Lésage and Pearson governments (Kent, interview). According to Peter C. Newman, "Pearson's main policy preoccupation was his attempt to sponsor some kind of accommodation between Québec and the rest of the country" (Newman 1968, 45).

24. Québec Premier Bertrand was resigned: "Ottawa has placed us in a position where we might be one of the last provinces to sign. . . . Either Quebec joins the programme, and thus flies squarely in the face of the Canadian constitution, or else we do not join up and thus deprive our people of a lot of money to which they have the right. What does one do in a case like this? Don't we have to be realistic and make the best of the situation, that is, sign the agreement with Ottawa, counting on its being the last time?" (Taylor 1987, 392).

The Iconic Status of Health Care in Canada, 1984–2008

25. In a 2000 poll, just under 60 percent of respondents felt that the federal government "should ensure that all Canadians, no matter where they live, have access to similar levels of health care services" (Mendelsohn 2001, 77).

■ Article 3: The Medicare Debate, 1945–80

Alvin Finkel

"The government sponsors the TB testing of cattle, pays for loss and has blood testing every year free of charge. What about humans? Let's take our hats off to Russia as far as health is concerned."[1] This was the conclusion of a group of farmers in Seaforth, Ontario, meeting in late 1943 to discuss the idea of a national universal medical care program. Sponsored by *Farm Radio Forum*, a CBC radio series, groups of farmers across the country responded to the proposals that were being mooted for state medical insurance. But the proposals being discussed were more radical than Canada's current medicare system. Medical care was to be removed from the private marketplace completely, and the costs of hospital care, doctors' visits, pharmaceutical costs, dental care, and eye care were to be covered by a state-funded regime.

The farmers' groups revealed that conditions of health care in Canada, particularly in rural areas, were often grim. For example, a farmer in Elderbank, Nova Scotia, stated "Our doctor has 275 miles of highway to travel. Many do not consult him because of cost of services. Immediate federal action is needed." In Leader, Saskatchewan, another reported: "Our school is never visited by either doctor or nurse. This fall one family had a child with contagious disease…finally the school was closed up, as teacher and all pupils were sick. Mothers here, who never have a doctor at the birth of a child, least of all pre-natal care, most of them are wrecks and old long before their time."[2] Polls suggested that a national medicare scheme was the most popular reform discussed during the Second World War and its aftermath. In both 1944 and 1948, 80 per cent of Canadians expressed support, with the Québécois sharing this sentiment despite the claims of their provincial government and the Catholic Church that national medicare posed a threat to Quebec's traditions of individualism and Church control of social services.[3]

The dismal state of health services across the country fuelled the demand for state action. Canadians had reason to believe that they did not enjoy the full benefits of the medical knowledge of their time. While Sweden and New Zealand, both with universal state medical programs, had the world's lowest infant death rates in 1942—29 per 1,000 live births—Canada's rate was 54: In all provinces, the infant mortality rate in rural areas was higher than the urban rate, usually quite significantly, for example 79 to 51 in Nova Scotia, 76 to 43 in Manitoba, and 63 to 30 in British Columbia. Significantly, Saskatchewan, where pressure from women's groups in the interwar period had led to the hiring of municipal doctors and the creation of "union" hospitals (hospitals operated by several municipalities uniting to pay for their construction and operation), had the country's lowest rural death rate for infants. In that province, 52 children per 1,000 died in their first year of life compared with 43 in the province's cities.[4]

Still, the State Hospital and Medical League of Saskatchewan estimated that 34 per cent of all deaths were premature and that half of all provincial residents suffering disabling illnesses could have been free of disease if preventive care had been applied. As Tommy Douglas, soon-to-be-premier of that province and generally regarded as the "father of Canadian medicare,"[5] noted in a broadcast in 1943, "If the average person were checked over by a clinic at stated intervals, and treatment were available before the illness had reached a critical stage, not only would we live longer but the cost of health services in the aggregate would be less than it is now."[6] The National Committee for Mental Hygiene reported in 1939 that only 10 per cent of Canadians could comfortably pay for their medical services in a free-market system while 25 per cent were completely dependent on charity; the remaining 65 per cent could pay for normal services but were forced into debt or rejection of treatment if an operation or long-term care was required.[7]

Yet, despite popular support for medicare, it was not implemented in the early postwar period and, over the next two decades, pro- and anti-medicare forces were locked in constant battle. Advocates of medicare seemingly won, but the program that emerged disappointed them both in the limitations of its coverage and the structure of medical care that it embraced. This chapter explores the structures of

463

Source: Alvin Finkel, "The Medicare Debate, 1945–80," *Social Policy and Practice in Canada: A History* (Waterloo, ON: Wilfrid Laurier University Press, 2006), chap. 8. Reprinted with permission from Wilfrid Laurier University Press.

political decision making, formal and informal, that resulted in the creation of a particular type of medicare in 1968.

From the Green Book to Hospital Insurance

Though the federal government balked at the potential costs of national health insurance in 1945, it recognized that Canadians expected governments at all levels to invest in health care.[8] In 1948, it announced a program of conditional health grants to provinces to build and operate hospitals, train medical personnel, and carry out health research. The wealthier provinces, in turn, also provided funding to expand their network of hospitals and to increase the number of graduates from medical schools. From 1948 to 1953 alone, forty-six thousand hospital beds were added across Canada.[9]

Saskatchewan had elected a CCF government led by T. C. Douglas in 1944, and it had pledged to take steps towards the creation of a universal medicare scheme. Despite the unavailability of matching federal funds after the collapse of the Green Book process, Saskatchewan forged ahead with plans to create universal hospital insurance in the province and end the distinction in hospitals between paying clients and charity cases. It immediately undertook a hospital construction project to ensure that most residents lived close enough to a hospital to receive care close to home. Then it legislated tax-funded hospitalization insurance in 1947, becoming the first jurisdiction in North America to implement such a program. The province's general revenues as well as a prepaid monthly premium levied on families and singles would pay the costs of insuring that need, and not financial means, determined who used 'Saskatchewan hospitals. Saskatchewan physicians largely supported this measure, while hospital administrators who opposed the legislation kept quiet after the premier threatened that the province could take control of the hospitals if the existing administrators no longer wished to run them.[10]

British Columbia's Coalition government of Liberals and Conservatives faced serious competition from that province's CCF and also decided to implement a universal hospital insurance program, financed by premiums and a 3 per cent sales tax. Claiming that it wanted to blend the concepts of private and public responsibility, it included "co-insurance" (user fees) within its hospital insurance program, despite protests from the CCF and the labour movement. Alberta presented yet a third model for paying hospital and other medical bills. Decrying both compulsory participation and centralization, the government established a series of health districts in 1946. District boards, which included both physician and consumer representatives, negotiated a health insurance scheme with municipalities, including the services to be covered for a maximum payment of $10 per adult. While most costs were borne by the voluntary subscriber to the insurance scheme, hospital fees were set at $1 per day, with the municipality and the province splitting the remaining operating costs. Manitoba and Newfoundland also had voluntary programs, which had been established before Newfoundland joined Canada, enrolling about half the province's population.[11]

Louis St. Laurent, like Mackenzie King, was less than enthusiastic about the federal government creating a national health insurance scheme. But he was under tremendous pressure from the five provinces that were heavily subsidizing patients' costs to implement a national program and lift at least half the burden of costs from the provines.[12] Ontario weighed in on the provinces' side in 1955. About 70 per cent of Ontario residents enjoyed some form of hospital insurance coverage, but Premier Leslie Frost faced public pressure for the government to fund hospital insurance. This included pressure from hospital authorities. The community elites that ran the hospitals had been dealt a body blow by the Depression, as the number of paying customers dwindled while charity cases climbed. In the postwar period, they came to believe that their institutions needed the economic stability that public insurance alone could provide.[13]

Frost responded by insisting that federal involvement was required, a viewpoint he stressed at federal-provincial discussions on hospital insurance. These discussions led to the Hospital Insurance and Diagnostic Services Act of April 1957, which established a formula for federal grants to provinces that implemented a provincial hospital insurance scheme. About half of all hospital costs would be borne by the federal government. The provinces chose the method of financing for their plans, but there were penalties for provinces that levied user fees. Passage of the legislation was eased by the lack of opposition from the Canadian Medical Association (CMA), which, since 1949, had supported user-pay hospitals.[14] Their change of heart was dictated by the need to assuage public anger regarding high costs for hospital stays and to avoid more radical medicare programs that included costs of doctors' visits. The private insurance companies were the big losers in the debate, but were determined to fight to maintain the rest of their health insurance business by denouncing further state intervention in medical care.

Towards Medicare

The CMA's rejection of public hospitals insurance in 1949 was part of a broader rejection of health insurance by Canadian doctors after the war. With average incomes rising quickly, physician groups expanded or launched health insurance plans that proved successful beyond the doctors' expectations. The plans tabulated total annual medical bills for given populations and set insurance rates that would yield the income expected by physicians plus administrative costs needed to run the plan. For physicians, it meant that they collectively set the rates for various types of treatment. Private insurance companies, which covered over 1.5 million Canadians in 1962,[15] were required to accept the physician-dictated rates as the price for having a place in the health insurance industry.

By contrast, if governments were to get involved in medical insurance, it was likely that they would require physicians to accept lower rates for various procedures as a means of reducing overall medical costs. In the United States, the growth of the private health insurance industry, also dominated by physicians, gave the American Medical Association (AMA) an incentive to spend lavishly to lobby politicians and propagandize Americans regarding the evils of a public health insurance program. Their efforts forestalled President Harry Truman's plans in the late 1940s to introduce a national universal medical insurance scheme despite widespread popular support for such a policy. In the context of the Cold War, the AMA painted state medicine as an exemplar of the programs that unfree Communist states imposed upon their hapless citizens, an image that was ironic in light of the introduction of state medicine in Britain and other European democracies. Supported by big business organizations, the AMA developed an impregnable opposition to state

medicine in Congress that united northern Republicans with southern Democrats, the latter often wealthy conservatives elected from pro-medicare constituencies but able to avoid the issue by making the preservation of racial segregation the key to their election strategies.[16]

At the federal-provincial conference in 1955, St. Laurent indicated that the federal government would only consider a national health insurance program when a majority of provinces representing a majority of citizens were prepared to institute provincial programs. The three Atlantic premiers responded that they could only consider a program if the federal government promised in advance to provide most of the funding. The premiers of Alberta and Manitoba wanted more unconditional grant money from the federal government in preference to universal medicare, and wanted any universal scheme to incorporate the private insurance schemes already in operation rather than replace them with a public plan. Ontario was only willing to commit to a national study of the possible scope and costs of a federal health scheme while Premier Duplessis of Quebec a federal program.[17]

As with hospital insurance, it was the provinces that stepped up to the plate first to offer universal programs and then put the federal government on the hot seat for failure to make such provision a national responsibility. Once again, it was Saskatchewan CCF government that led the way. Tommy Douglas, running for re-election in 1960, announced that with the federal government now paying half of Saskatchewan's hospital bills, his government could afford to implement universal medicare. Both the urban and rural poor, including most farmers, were unable to buy medical coverage, and the Saskatchewan government, like other provincial governments, was picking up the tab for medical bills for a growing section of the poor. It argued that this was unfair, first because it stigmatized those required to rely on state aid and discouraged them from seeing doctors, and second because it placed heavy financial burdens on the state that a universal plan would offset with the tax or premium contributions of the better-off, which the private insurers claimed for themselves. But Saskatchewan faced a huge fight in implementing its program.

Saskatchewan had played a pioneering role in the provision of medical services in Canada. Its municipal doctor schemes and union hospitals of the interwar period, the result of the work of the

465

farm women's movement, and particularly Violet McNaughton, challenged the notion of health as a commodity to be purchased by those with the wherewithal to do so. Nonetheless, such programs relied on voluntary participation by doctors rather than state coercion. The CCF's experiments with full-state operation of medical services before the 1960s were limited to a few areas of the province in which the government was able to enlist the support of progressive-minded physicians. However, after the government announced its intentions to have a province-wide medical insurance scheme, a community clinic movement sprang up, a natural outgrowth of the populism that had produced both the major farm movements in Saskatchewan and the CCF itself. Health clinics with a holistic model of health, in which nurses, social workers, nutritionists, and dentists worked alongside doctors, enrolled about fifty thousand people in thirty-five regional associations in a province of less than 1 million people.[18]

Most physicians had no intention of becoming salaried professionals working in state-run clinics whose policies were determined by elected boards of non-physicians. In line with the CMA, which aided them in carrying out an extensive propaganda campaign against the government's plan, Saskatchewan doctors insisted that individuals and families should pay their medical bills via private insurance. If the province insisted that all citizens should be insured, it should direct them to buy insurance from a private plan. Only the poor should have their bills paid by the state, with the state paying physician-dictated rates for services that private plans paid. In July 1962, when the government proved adamant that it would proceed with its plans, the Saskatchewan branch of the CMA organized a withdrawal of physician services.[19]

Upper- and middle-class supporters of the physicians formed "Keep Our Doctors" committees that accused the government of imposing an unworkable policy for socialist ideological reasons. The corporate-owned daily papers, always hostile to the CCF government, terrified people by suggesting that the province might lose most of its doctors. With both the CMA and national business organizations spending extravagantly to reinforce this message through television and radio advertising, as well as by using the appearances of "expert" witnesses on news shows, Saskatchewan residents were subjected to non-stop propaganda against state medicare. This

was offset by the support for medicare from the Saskatchewan Federation of Labour and the major farm organizations, though these groups had limited access to the media.

The doctors' strike ended after twenty-two days as a result of government negotiations with the Saskatchewan branch of the CMA, in which the doctors conceded a universal state program and the government conceded many of the demands of the doctors. There would be no salaries for doctors or payments by the number of patients that they served. Instead, fee for service, the principle that governed private insurance plans, would remain sacrosanct. Doctors would continue to operate from their own private offices, and not only would doctors not be forced to participate in a community clinic, but those who chose to practise in a clinic would receive direct funding from the state rather than have to deal with the community clinic board. Finally, doctors would have the choice of participating directly in the state plan either by requiring patients to pay bills and then bill the plan or by staying out of the plan altogether and billing patients with whatever fees they deemed appropriate. This was simply a face-saving measure since both sides understood that most patients would choose to patronize doctors who were in the prepaid medicare scheme.

The Hall Commission

Saskatchewan's decision to launch a compulsory, state-run medicare scheme placed pressure on the national political parties to respond to demands from Canadians in all provinces for universal medical insurance. The NDP made implementation of a national medicare scheme a central plank in its platform. Out of office, the Liberals as well recommitted themselves to the national medicare program that they had promised in the 1945 election but had never delivered. Business stalwarts among former ministers, including C. D. Howe, Charles Dunning, and Brooke Claxton, opposed medicare. But the reformers who had taken over the party machinery in the late 1950s convinced delegates at the 1961 national convention to recommit the party to a national medicare program.[20]

While John Diefenbaker faced fewer demands within his party for state medicare, and considered business pressures against such a measure, he was leery of simply dismissing any solution that might appease public demands for guaranteed access to medical care.

He turned in 1961 to Justice Emmett Hall, a fellow Saskatchewan Conservative, to head a commission to study options for improving the health care available to Canadians. Commentators assumed that the commission, largely composed of hand-picked Tory supporters, would opt for a non-compulsory scheme.

While the commission deliberated, the Social Credit governments of Alberta and British Columbia attempted to counter the "socialist" Saskatchewan scheme with state programs that avoided "coercion" of doctors or "conscription" of citizens into a state plan. First, Alberta in 1963, and then British Columbia in 1964, announced voluntary plans that directed most residents into existing doctor-controlled and insurance-company plans, but provided state subsidies for the poor so that they could also receive coverage. The Alberta plan was endorsed by the provincial College of Physicians and Surgeons, which the government consulted as it set the premium and determined what services were covered. Such plans left many families who were just above the low-income cut-offs in the position of having to decide whether they could afford the high costs of private insurance or should risk going without coverage. Even in wealthy Alberta, the province calculated that only 60 per cent of provincial residents were covered by the voluntary medical-care scheme.[21]

The commission heard ample testimony from organized groups as well as individuals who favoured the Alberta and British Columbia approach over the Saskatchewan plan. While 40 per cent of Canadians had no medical insurance and many more had coverage only for catastrophes, elite groups that opposed a universal state program, led by the CMA and the Canadian Chamber of Commerce, insisted that only 15 per cent of Canadians were unable to afford medical coverage.[22] This figure seemed suspicious in light of a Statistics Canada study in 1961 that placed 27 per cent of Canadians below the poverty line and another 14 per cent on or just over that line.[23] However, to admit that private medical insurance was a hardship for almost half of the population would weaken the argument against state medicine.

Medicare's Opponents

Supporters of continued privatization and voluntary participation in medical insurance included the Canadian Medical Association, the Canadian Dental Association, the Canadian Chamber of Commerce, the entire private insurance industry, the pharmaceutical industry, and representatives of most other industries. The premiers of British Columbia, Alberta, Manitoba, and Ontario opposed medicare while Quebec's Premier Lesage was opposed to federal legislation in a sphere of provincial competence. The Atlantic premiers generally supported medicare but wanted the federal government to pay the lion's share of the costs and to give them time to phase in any universal program because they faced shortages of medical personnel. Only Woodrow Lloyd in Saskatchewan was an unequivocal supporter of a fully state-operated scheme.[24]

The advocates of private insurance used a variety of arguments before the commission. For example, the British Columbia Medical Association, following the lead of the CMA,[25] argued that the monies that medicare would absorb could be better spent on "scholarships for medical students, to add rehabilitative and chronic care kids to our hospitals, to extend our mental health programme, and for many other important services." Directing taxes instead towards paying medical insurance was "foolhardy" because it meant "providing a service to those who are already providing it for themselves, as most British Columbians are doing through our system of voluntary health insurance."[26]

The CMA's brief added that the hospital insurance program, which the physicians regarded favourably, had expanded demand for hospital beds. The federal and provincial governments, it suggested, having created this demand by making hospitalization a free good, now had to cough up the money for more beds. Implicit, however, in this argument was that prior to the existence of a public program, the real health needs of the population, in the area of hospitalization, had been underserved despite the availability of private hospitalization insurance.[27] Nor did the physicians try to claim that private health insurance was meeting everyone's needs. They conceded that to achieve universal medical insurance coverage, about 3 million Canadians would have to have their bills paid by taxes collected from the rest of Canadians, who, in turn, would also have to pay for their own private insurance.

The CMA, while avoiding the Cold War rhetoric of its American counterpart in its opposition to state

467

medicine, emphasized that doctors as a group would be hostile to state medical insurance and even more hostile to any efforts by the government to move them away from individual practice into group settings that might also include other types of medical practitioners. "Physicians by nature and by training are strongly individualistic and it is not given to all doctors to function happily and efficiently as a member of a group." It could lead, in any case, to "assembly-line medicine."[28]

The Canadian Dental Association (CDA) also claimed that state monies could be better directed at other goals than a national insurance program. Admitting that most Canadians had little or no access to dentists, they pointed out that there was a dismal ratio of dentists to population—1 to 3,000, compared with 1 to 1,900 in the United States, with regional gaps that were best demonstrated by Newfoundland and Labrador's ratio of 1 dentist per 11,000 residents. If all Canadians suddenly had access to dental services, there would simply be too few dentists to accommodate them. Steps to increase the number of dentists would have to precede the implementation of any government plan, and, in any case, any such plan had to be placed under the control of dentists. The dentists called for greater state funding for dental programs and lower fees for dental students.

The dentists admitted that "education and income separately and together are strongly associated with going to the dentist." Yet the dentists largely ignored their own insight that money kept many Canadians from properly caring for their teeth, focusing instead on "people's lack of interest in preventative measures" as the way to improve dental health. They recommended that provinces make fluoridation of water supplies mandatory for municipalities, that Canadians consume less sugar, and that more government funds go to dental research. While cool to state involvement in dentistry, outside of dental education and research, the CDA did recognize some need for governments to fund potential consumers of dentists' services. Like the physicians, they supported state funding of necessary services for destitute Canadians. If governments were going to provide state dental service programs, they should restrict their programs to children.[29]

Not one recognized organization of health professionals in Canada placed itself on record as supporting medicare, with the exception of the nurses' association in Saskatchewan where medicare already was an established program.[30] The rest of the nursing profession in Canada, which later would become a militant supporter of public medicine, restricted itself to calling for greater public support for nursing education and better salaries for nurses.[31]

Both pharmacists and the pharmaceutical industry strongly opposed inclusion of prescription drugs in a state medical insurance plan, since it carried the implicit threat of state regulation of drug prices. The Canadian Pharmaceutical Manufacturers' Association (CPMA) reported soothingly that competition was lively at the manufacturing and retail levels of the industry: "The competitive aspect of research and development, combined with behaviour of prices and promotional activities, indicates that a satisfactory level of competition exists in the industry. Furthermore, this competition is directed in a manner which is socially desirable. Growth, product development and the general level of prices have been favourable rather than unfavourable to the consumer."[32] The pharmaceutical manufacturers assured the commissioners that after-tax profits of the industry were modest and the industry's expenditures on promotion were fairly restrained and served the purpose of informing physicians and others about useful pharmaceuticals.

In fact, the industry's profits, measured as a percentage of invested capital, were double the average for Canadian industries as a whole from 1953 to 1958. A study prepared in 1961 for the federal Department of Justice by the director of Investigation and Research, Combines Investigation Act, noted that apart from making large profits, the industry was absolutely profligate in its promotion expenditures, as it worked tirelessly to press physicians to use various new drugs. Patent laws protected drug companies that developed a new pharmaceutical product, and it was the knowledge that they had a monopoly for many years over a particular drug that caused pharmaceutical companies to spend millions trying to convince physicians to prescribe their product.

But, while monopolistic practices affected only "certain drugs" at the manufacturing level, the retail level was a dead loss to market forces despite being wholly private. Wrote the justice investigator: "The practices of retail druggists … have resulted in the virtual elimination of price competition at the retail level."[33] Such monopolistic practices did not lead to calls for either a public takeover of the manufacture and distribution of pharmaceuticals in Canada or for new public regulations over the industry from any segment of the health care industry. Health care providers, such as doctors, dentists, and pharmacy owners, had a common interest in establishing a high price for their services, and happily confounded private provision with competition and efficient pricing.

Ultimately, the two arguments that were heard most frequently to discredit a compulsory public medical system were that it would deprive health practitioners of the freedoms that all business people ought legitimately to have in a democratic society, and that it would be so costly as to provoke crushing levels of taxation that would destroy Canada's industrial competitiveness. The CMA stated starkly: "We consider government intervention into the field of prepaid medical care to the point of becoming a monopolistic purchaser of medical services, to be a measure of civil conscription. We would urge this Royal Commission to support our view that, exclusive of states of emergency, civil conscription of any segment of the Canadian population is contrary to our democratic philosophy."[34] Premier Leslie Frost of Ontario was prominent among anti-medicare politicians to invoke the industrial competitiveness argument. The country, he averred, "has already become a high cost economy. And that is affecting our trading and developmental position."[35]

Medicare's Supporters

Medicare's supporters suggested that Canadians had collective rights to the best medical treatments that were available regardless of income, and that the right of individuals to receive affordable medical service outweighed the alleged rights of medical practitioners to price their services as they deemed best. Despite the crushing majority support for medicare evident in opinion polls, few Canadians were willing to come forward as individuals and suggest that they had received second-rate medical treatment because they were poor. A careful scouring of the thousands of briefs before the Hall Commission reveals only one case where an individual Canadian denounced her doctors for providing her family mediocre care because of their inability to pay. Her physician's scathing personal attack upon her in response demonstrated why few

Canadians had the temerity to reveal personal cases of receiving poor treatment or being driven to bankruptcy to obtain necessary medical attention.[36] Instead, the horror stories that the commission heard as well as the main arguments countering the claims of private medicine came from organizations. Trade unions, social worker and welfare organizations, farmers' federations, and the United Church of Canada convinced the commissioners that they should adopt an ambitious national program.

The Canadian Association of Social Workers placed the case before the Hall Commission that programs that limited free state care to the destitute, which were in operation in many Canadian provinces, did not work. Many were deterred from seeking medical assistance at clinics because several hours might be required for them to fill out forms at the accounting department. Meanwhile, many people of middle means who did not qualify for the state care available to the indigent avoided seeking medical care because "it is going to come out of the food budget, or come out of the youngsters' clothing budget or something like this." The social workers observed that the stigma of receiving a charitable service discouraged usage of the service. It also created problems regarding the proper cut-off income for recipients. Better to have medicare available to all Canadians so that no one had to see it as either a special right or a special shame.

The social workers unsurprisingly made a strong pitch for closely co-ordinating health and welfare services so as to improve the physical and mental health of the population. Many of their clients suffered poor health because of poor housing and the stresses that resulted from limited incomes. They also called for the definition of medical services under medicare to include convalescent hospitals, home care and replacement homemakers for convalescing mothers, and the provision of prosthetic appliances.[37]

The Canadian Federation of Agriculture (CFA) and several other major farm groups appeared before the commission and indicated that the majority of farmers could not afford private health insurance.[38] The United Church of Canada, whose General Council had called for a contributory national health plan since 1952, confirmed the CFA's impressions. The United Church brief added that urban immigrants, particularly unskilled workers from southern Italy, were perhaps even more vulnerable. These people were underpaid, ill-housed, insecure about their income, and prone as a result to both physical and mental illness. Yet they were too impoverished to be able to set aside the money for private health insurance.[39]

But the trade union movement probably proved the most effective in demolishing the arguments of industry and physicians that Canadians were gradually meeting their medical needs privately. In the postwar period, the trade union movement, which enrolled about a third of Canadian workers thanks to wartime and early postwar organizing successes, had succeeded in winning a variety of "fringe benefits" for their members in addition to wage increases and improvements in working conditions. A medical benefits package had become a common gain for trade unionists, and such prepaid medical insurance swelled the numbers of families whom the private insurance companies could claim as they pooh-poohed the need for a public program.

Unions' characterizations of the limitations of private coverage undermined such insurance industry boasting. National, provincial, and labour federations complained to the Hall Commission that the profit-driven insurance schemes that enrolled their members tended to severely restrict or deny coverage altogether in such areas as preventive health services, rehabilitation, mental health, dental services, and social services. Prescription drugs, nursing aid, appliances, eyeglasses, and hearing aids were rarely covered. Yet most of these plans had "costly deductible and co-insurance charges." As the Canadian Labour Congress (CLC) concluded, "It is too much to expect that a complete range of services can be made available on a universal basis to the Canadian people within the near future through the mere extension of the private pre-payment schemes. It is not physically financially nor administratively possible."[40]

The CLC led the way in labour's deliberations before the commission, answering point-by-point the claims made to the commission by the CMA. It noted that, even using the CMA's definition of poverty, 4.5 million Canadians would require that their medical bills be paid for by the state. Apart from the layouts for these people, the state would have to spend millions in carrying out the means tests necessary for determining who was eligible, in the process of stigmatizing them.[41]

Trade union federations in poorer provinces emphasized the disparities in medical services

among Canada's regions that resulted from a market-driven allocation of resources. In Newfoundland, for example, the number of doctors per capita was less than half the Canadian average, while many rural areas had no physicians at all. The imbalance in the availability of nurses with the rest of Canada was similar. There were few dentists outside the two major cities, and St. John's institution for the aged and infirm was "a blot on the decency of the Canadian nation." Not only was a national medicare plan needed, according to the Newfoundland Federation of Labour, but such a plan had to provide for regional hospitals and clinics to be built and staffed in deprived provinces.[42]

The Hall Report and the Implementation of Medicare

Emmett Hall and the majority of his fellow commissioners were won over, in large part, by the values and arguments of the supporters of a universal medicare program. Their 1964 report made some obeisance in the direction of business and physicians by recognizing that no doctor should be forced to join a national medicare program, and that doctors should remain in private practice even if they joined medicare rather than becoming civil servants working in government offices. Even more of a victory for the physicians was the commission's rejection of the National Health Service model of salaried physicians, which the labour movement had endorsed. Instead, the commissioners supported continuation of the fee-for-service model which was a hallmark of private insurance.[43]

However, the overall direction of the report reflected the persuasiveness of the opponents of the argument made by businesses and physicians. Wrote the commissioners: "The achievement of the highest possible health standards for all our people must become a primary objective of national policy and a cohesive factor contributing to national unity, involving individual and community responsibilities and actions. This objective can best be achieved through a comprehensive, universal Health Services Programme for the Canadian people." "Comprehensive," in Hall's view, included "all health services, preventive, diagnostic, curative and rehabilitative, that modern medical and other services can provide."[44] This meant that governments should not only

470

provide universal coverage for physicians' services and for hospitalization but should also cover prescription drug payments for all Canadians, home care and prosthetic services as required, dental services for children, expectant mothers, and public assistance recipients, and eyecare for children and the poor. Most of these programs would exclude user fees, though each prescription would bear a dollar user fee and adults would be expected to pay one-third the cost of eyeglasses, which would however be free for children.[45] Taxation would pay for all Canadians to be covered by the national health program. In short, Hall had rejected the voluntary medical insurance schemes that Ontario, Alberta, and British Columbia had proposed as alternatives to the potential of full coverage to all Canadians for all necessary medical services.

Hall recommended that the federal government pay half the costs for any provincial medicare scheme that provided universal coverage. The provinces could determine their priorities in terms of the various components of the medicare scheme and the timing of their introduction. Federal government grants would help to establish the training programs required to produce the additional personnel needed once medical services were universally available, as well as he facilities required to build the medical and dental clinics to house these services. The federal government would, for example, share with the provinces the costs of building mental health wings in regular hospitals so that most inmates of mental health institutions could receive care in their community. It would also aid the provinces in providing funds that allowed parents to raise mildly intellectually disabled children at home.[46]

The Hall Report put pressure on Lester Pearson's Liberal government, which had been elected in 1963, albeit without a parliamentary majority, to live up to its medicare promises. The Liberals had promised a national medicare program that would provide comprehensive services free of charge to children till they left school and to Canadians over sixty-five years of age. Everyone else would have services by general practitioners, specialists, and surgeons, along with diagnostic services, covered, except for the first $25. Even the left-wingers in the government were taken aback by the scope of services that Hall wanted a national program to cover. For a year the government waffled, and even in the throne speech

of 1965, the government committed itself to medicare in only the vaguest terms. The NDP, which had endorsed the Hall Report *in toto*, demanded that the government implement its full set of recommendations immediately.[47]

An exhaustive review of the Hall recommendations by the Department of National Health and Welfare demonstrated the substantial bureaucratic support for the tenor of the reforms proposed by the commissioners. Department officials endorsed Hall's views that "deterrent fees," that is user fees, could not be allowed for basic services because they contradicted the principle of universal availability of medical services. Federal funding of medical services along the lines of the existing federal formula for hospitals was "fundamental in making the most effective use of the nation's health resources to achieve the highest possible health standards for residents of Canada." The bureaucrats also endorsed the children's dental program and subsidizing of prescription costs, but with Finance and Privy Council officials serving as observers to the committee's deliberations, they couched such support with indications that both of these sets of services should be phased in over an unspecified period. Potential costs also caused the officials to reluctantly oppose Hall's embrace of government financing of home care.[48]

The eventual compromise reached within the government called for medicare to be introduced in phases. The first phase would add physician and diagnostic services to the existing hospitalization coverage, while other components of the Hall vision would be introduced as fiscal means became available. In practise, though few Canadians could know it at the time, there would be no second phase for medicare at least during the twentieth century.

The government had a built-in excuse for delay because of the need to convince the provinces to implement medicare programs. There were meetings in April and May of 1965 in which federal officials representing the cabinet and the Department of National Health and Public Welfare along with the Department of Finance heard the views of ministers of health and their officials from the provinces. Two federal–provincial conferences that year also provided the provinces with a forum for their disparate views, but provided little detail from Pearson regarding the federal government's plans. Pearson did, however, insist that the federal

471

government, following Hall, would insist that federal funds would only to go provincial programs that met four criteria: comprehensive coverage of physicians' services, universality of coverage, public administration, and portability of services so that citizens were covered when they lived outside of their home province.[49]

In Quebec, an exhaustive provincial review of social programs, headed by Claude Castonguay, had recently begun and tentatively looked favourably upon a program of universal medicare. Federal dollars to help fund such a program were desirable, but federal input into the design of the program was unacceptable. Alberta's Premier Manning continued to fulminate against any program that was universal and that did not involve co-insurance. His government was furious that Ottawa had penalized the province financially for its insistence on user fees in the hospitalization plan. Ontario, Manitoba, and British Columbia also insisted that provinces have more scope for the design of medicare than Pearson's four principles might allow. Other provinces accepted the principles of the Hall Report but wanted sufficient federal funding to make it affordable for them to establish a program. Only Newfoundland was anxious for a federal plan to be legislated immediately, though New Brunswick was committed to establishing a plan and Saskatchewan wanted a federal contribution to its program.[50]

The Liberals called a federal election in late 1965 but narrowly failed again to form a majority government. Their commitment to a modified version of the Hall recommendations during the election left them little alternative afterwards but to legislate a medicare bill. In 1966, the government introduced legislation to provide an average of 50 per cent of the costs of provincial schemes that met the four medicare principles (a formula was used that would provide a larger portion of federal funds per capita in poorer provinces),[51] but the legislation lacked a date for implementation. Initially, Pearson aimed for 1 July 1967, the one hundredth birthday of the country. However, continued provincial reluctance to accept the federal principles argued against such speed, as did the change in the balance of forces in the Liberal cabinet after the election.

Walter Gordon, the progressive finance minister, took responsibility for having advised Pearson to hold an early election, and resigned from cabinet.

His replacement, Mitchell Sharp, held views similar to those of organized business and appeared in no hurry to implement medicare, which he claimed could have an undue impact on the federal treasury. Robert Stanfield, the new leader of the Conservative party, denounced "a vast new spending program."[52] But Sharp and his supporters were only able to delay medicare's implementation by one year.[53] On 1 July 1968, funds would be available to provinces with a medicare scheme that met the four principles of medicare. Still, the division within the Pearson cabinet encouraged provinces that opposed universality and public administration to move slowly. Only Saskatchewan and British Columbia presented plans in the month after the medicare deadline and began to receive federal funding in July.

By then, the dithering Pearson had been replaced as head of the government by the more decisive Pierre Elliott Trudeau. Trudeau scotched any further attempts from within the cabinet or the provinces to allow for either delays or modifications of the medicare legislation. Within a year all provinces but Quebec had announced plans that met the criteria of the Medical Services Act of 1968. Quebec entered the plan in 1972.[54]

Medicare, Health, and Hierarchy

The Hall Report was less about health overall than about how to ensure that access to physicians was generally available and that physicians were adequately paid.

Hall did not challenge the medical profession's monopoly over medical care. The commissioners heard a variety of briefs from non-allopathic healers, but they largely accepted the equation of physicians with healing. Even the officials of the Department of National Health and Welfare who reviewed the report's recommendations observed the narrowness of Hall's focus: "Attention in the Recommendations was actually focused on personal health services provided mainly by physicians and others in private practice to the exclusion of public health services."[55]

In addition, the commissioners paid little attention to environmental pollution, which a few trade briefs suggested was a factor in the health of individuals.[56] They had little to say about the roles of fitness, stress, nutrition, and poverty, outside of its impact on ability to pay medical bills. Industrial accidents were not addressed. The commissioners gave no consideration to the community-care model, which had already been piloted in Saskatchewan, accepting unquestioningly a hierarchical model of medical care in which physicians dictated the roles of other medical practitioners and patients had no input into either the character or payment structures of services.[57]

Native Peoples and Medical Care

Nothing illustrated better the argument that physician care alone could not guarantee a healthy population that the continued oppression and suffering of indigenous Canadians. In 1977, when the average age of death for Canadians was 66, the comparative figure for natives was 42.4 years. They were four times as likely to die violent deaths in their twenties or thirties as other Canadians. Babies on reserves died in large numbers of gastroenteritis and pneumonia, diseases of poverty. Waters upon which Natives depended for their fish were often poisoned with waste mercury from chemical plants. On poor, isolated reserves with shabby housing and few facilities, Native children sniffed gas while their parents abused alcohol. Though the residential schooling system, which snatched children from their parents and placed them in environments where physical and sexual abuse were often rife, was being phased out, its scars on the Native psyche were reflected in substance abuse and poor parenting skills.

These woes were compounded by a lack of health workers, including doctors and nurses, on many reserves. There were only ten physicians and 221 nurses of Native descent in Canada in the mid-1970s and there was no national program to change this situation.[58] The federal government had over time taken a degree of responsibility for Native health care, always claiming, however, that constitutionally it was not compelled to do so. Until 1945, Indian Affairs had authority over Native health. After 1945, the Department of National Health and Welfare (DNHW) was given charge of this responsibility, and in 1962, a branch of DNHW called Medical Services was formed with a variety of programs under its control, including the former Indian Health Services.[59]

Community control initiatives at the grassroots attempted to compensate for government indifference and to pressure the federal government to provide Native communities with the wherewithal to deal with both their social and health needs. Reserves began to organize their own community medical schemes to hire doctors and nurses, to make up for the lethargy of Medical Services and to establish the right of Native communities to govern themselves in all areas, including health services. Native nurses formed an organization to promote nursing as an occupation for Native girls. Shamanistic healing practices, long suppressed by the colonial authorities on reserves, but never completely eradicated, made a comeback. The colonialism experienced by Native peoples and the health of the Aboriginal population seemed inextricably linked, and campaigns for community control over health services formed part of the struggle to shed the legacy of paternalistic, remote control by Ottawa over Native lives.[60]

The creation of a national network of provincial medicare programs, all subscribing to the principles of comprehensiveness, universality, portability, and public administration, represented a major victory for progressive forces in Canada, backed by overwhelming public opinion. The combination of public campaigning by important social movements, including labour, farmers, and social workers, with support from key elements of the Liberal Party and the civil service, resulted in a Tory-appointed royal commission failing to suggest some sort of public–private mix that largely subordinated health service provision to profit-seeking health insurance companies and physicians. In turn, this led the Liberal government, divided for two decades on whether to implement its promises originally made in 1919 for a national public program, to finally deliver.

The success of reformist forces in Canada in the area of medicare was a contrast with the United States where the politics of race, the lack of a social-democratic party, the bias of public expenditures towards military spending, and the immense power of organized medicine continued to prevent the introduction of a universal medicare program. As Canada legislated universal medicare, American President Lyndon Johnson, spending billions of dollars on an unpopular war in Indochina, felt only able to support medicare for the elderly and a Medicaid program for the destitute that held down costs for medical services for the poor by sending them to special medical clinics, which were generally understaffed and involved long waits for service.[61]

473

By contrast, Canada's "first phase" of medicare provided far less comprehensive coverage for illness prevention and treatment than the National Health Service in Britain and similar programs in Scandinavia and Holland. The Soviet Union and its Cold War satellites in eastern Europe all provided sweeping free comprehensive medical care programs. The Hall Commission had looked to western European models rather than the United States in framing its recommendations, and the government rhetorically accepted the commission's conclusions. In practice, the desire to keep costs down resulted in a watering down of Hall's proposals that saw medicare's "first phase" limited to coverage of visits to hospitals and physicians, and diagnostic services. Further phases were not legislated. The late 1960s represented the high point of social reform rather than a first installment on social reforms that would fundamentally redistribute wealth in Canada. The next three chapters examine areas in which the postwar welfare state largely failed to meet the needs of Canadians—daycare, housing, and poverty.

Notes

1. Health Study Bureau, *Review of Canada's Health Needs and Insurance Proposals* (Toronto, ON: Health Study Bureau, 1946), 41.

2. Ibid., 40–3.

3. Malcolm G. Taylor, *Health Insurance and Canadian Public Policy: The Seven Decisions That Created the Canadian Health Insurance System* (Montreal, QC: McGill-Queen's University Press, 1978), 166.

4. Health Study Bureau, *Review of Canada's Health Needs*, 3–4.

5. Historian Georgina Taylor nuances the notion of medicare having been single-parented by a male, recalling that farm women, led by Violet McNaughton, had created the prototypes of medicare at a municipal level in the province. See Georgina M. Taylor, "'Ground for Common Action': Violet McNaughton's Agrarian Feminism and the Origins of the Farm Women's Movement in Canada" (PhD thesis, Carleton University, 1997). See also Georgina M. Taylor, "'Let Us Co-operate': Violet McNaughton and the Co-operative Ideal," in *Co-operatives in the Year 2000: Memory, Mutual Aid, and the Millennium*, ed. Brett Fairbairn and Ian Macpherson (Saskatoon, SK: Centre for the Study of Co-operatives, University of Saskatchewan, 2000), 57–78.

6. "CCF Broadcast by T. C. Douglas, MP," William Lyon Mackenzie King Papers, MG 26, J1, Vol. 346, p. 297811, *Library and Archives of Canada* (LAC).

7. Ibid., p. 297809.

8. Many organizations expressed disappointment that the promised national health insurance program did not materialize. For example, the National Council of Women of Canada voted at their 1947 convention to "commend the Dominion Government on the Health Insurance Plan already prepared and urge its implementation as soon as possible." "Resolutions, Annual Meeting, held in Regina June 6–11, 1947," National Council of Women of Canada (NCWC) Papers, MG 28 I 25, Vol. 90, File 1, LAC.

9. Malcolm G. Taylor, "The Canadian Health-Care System: After Medicare," in *Health and Canadian Society: Sociological Perspectives*, 2nd ed., ed. David Coburn, Carl D'Arcy, George M. Torrance, and Peter New (Toronto, ON: Fitzhenry and Whiteside, 1987), 74.

10. Duane Mombourquette, "'An Inalienable Right': The CCF and Rapid Health Care Reform, 1944–1948," in *Social Welfare Policy in Canada: Historical Readings*, ed. Raymond B. Blake and Jeff Keshen (Toronto, ON: Copp Clark, 1995), 298–302.

11. Taylor, "The Canadian Health-Care System," 74, 84; Margaret A. Ormsby, *British Columbia: A History* (Vancouver, BC: Macmillan, 1958), 487; Alvin Finkel, *The Social Credit Phenomenon in Alberta* (Toronto, ON: University of Toronto Press, 1989), 123.

12. Eugene Vayda and Raisa B. Deber, "The Canadian Health-Care System: A Developmental Overview," in *Social Welfare Policy*, ed. Blake and Keshen, 315.

13. David Gagan and Rosemary Gagan, *For Patients of Moderate Means: A Social History of the Voluntary Public General Hospital in Canada, 1890–1950* (Montreal, QC: McGill-Queen's University Press, 2002).

14. Brief of Canadian Medical Association, April 1962, Canada, Royal Commission on Health Services, RG 33, Series 78, Vol. 19, File 278, LAC.

15. "Brief from Great West Life and Metropolitan Life Insurance Company," n.d., Royal Commission on Health Services, Vol. 15, Exhibit 200.

16. Monte M. Poen, *Harry S. Truman Versus the Medical Lobby: The Genesis of Medicare* (Columbia, MS: University of Missouri Press, 1979); Lawrence R. Jacobs, *The Health of Nations: Public Opinion and*

474

the *Making of American and British Health Policy* (Ithaca, NY: Cornell University Press, 1993).

17. "Reports of 1955 Federal-Provincial Conference," Department of National Health and Welfare Papers, RG 29, Vol. 918, LAC.

18. Joan Feather, "From Concept to Reality: Formation of the Swift Current Health Region," *Prairie Forum* 16, 1 (Spring 1991): 59–80; Joan Feather, "Impact of the Swift Current Health Region: Experiment or Model," *Prairie Forum* 16, 2 (Fall 1991): 225–48; Stan Rands, "Recollections: The CCF in Saskatchewan," in *Western Canadian Politics: The Radical Tradition*, ed. Donald C. Kerr (Edmonton, AB: NeWest, 1981), 58–64.

19. On the doctors' strike, see Robin E. Badgley and Samuel Wolfe, *Doctors' Strike: Medical Care and Conflict in Saskatchewan* (Toronto, ON: Macmillan, 1967).

20. P. E. Bryden, *Planners and Politicians: Liberal Politics and Social Policy, 1957–1968* (Montreal, QC: McGill-Queens University Press, 1997), chap. 2 and 3.

21. Finkel, *The Social Credit Phenomenon*, 144; "Discussions with Provinces on Health Services Matters," Meeting with Alberta Officials, 22 April 1965, Department of National Health and Welfare Papers, RG 33, Vol. 45.

22. Evidence of Canadian Medical Association, April 1962, Canada, Royal Commission on Health Services, Vol. 19, File 278; Evidence of Canadian Chamber of Commerce, March 1962, Vol. 14, File 188.

23. Canada, Economic Council of Canada, *The Challenge of Growth and Change*, Fifth Annual Review (Ottawa, ON: Queen's Printer, 1968), 104–105.

24. "Discussions with Provinces on Health Services Matters," Department of National health and Welfare Papers, Vol. 45.

25. Evidence of Canadian Medical Association, April 1962, Royal Commission on Health Services.

26. Evidence of British Columbia Medical Association, February 1962, Royal Commission on Health Services, Vol. 12, File 150.

27. Evidence of Canadian Medical Association, April 1962, Royal Commission on Health Services.

28. Ibid.

29. Evidence of Canadian Dental Association, March 1962, Royal Commission on Health, Vol. 14, Exhibit 192, 1962.

30. Evidence of Saskatchewan Registered Nurses Association, January 1962, Royal Commission on Health Services, Vol. 9, File 84.

31. See, for example, Evidence of New Brunswick Association of Registered Nurses, 9 November 1961, Vol. 8, File 44; Evidence of Manitoba Association of Registered Nurses, January 1962, Vol. 9, File 65; and Evidence of Association des Infirmières de la Province de Québec, April 1962, Vol. 15, File 219, Royal Commission on Health Services.

32. Evidence of Canadian Pharmaceutical Manufacturers Association, May 1962, Royal Commission on Health Services, Vol. 20, File 291.

33. Canada, Director of Investigation and Research, Combines Investigation Act, *Material Collected for Submission to the Restrictive Trade Practices Commission in the Course of an Inquiry Under Section 421 of the Combines Investigation Act Relating to the Manufacture, Distribution and Sale of Drugs* (Ottawa, ON: Department of Justice, 1961) 258.

34. Evidence of Canadian Medical Association, 16 October 1962, Royal Commission on Health Services, Vol. 6, File 67.

35. Canadian Press Report of Leslie Frost Interview, 29 March 1961, Royal Commission on Health Services, Vol. 8.

36. Evidence of Mrs. Marguerite Miles, Toronto, n.d., File 355; Evidence of Dr. C. Collins-William, Toronto, n.d., File 375, Vol. 22, Royal Commission on Health Services.

37. Evidence of Canadian Association of Social Workers, 28 May 1962, Royal Commission on Health Services, Vol. 6, File 61.

38. Evidence of Canadian Federation of Agriculture, 27 March, 1962, Royal Commission on Health Services, Vol. 14, File 190.

39. Evidence of United Church of Canada, April 1962, Royal Commission on Health Services, Vol. 22, File 352.

40. Evidence of Canadian Labour Congress, 17 October, 1962, Royal Commission on Health Services, Vol. 6, File 68.

41. Ibid.

42. Evidence of Newfoundland Federation of Labour, October 1961, Royal Commission on Health Services, Vol. 7, File 25.

43. Royal Commission on Health Services, *Report*, vol. 1 (Ottawa, ON: Queen's Printer, 1964), 29.

44. Ibid., 11.

45. Ibid., 19.

46. Ibid., 19, 24–25, 36, 41.

47. "Election 1963 Pamphlets," National Liberal Federation Papers, MG 28, IV–3, Vol. 1024, LAC; Bryden, *Planners and Politicians*, 136.

48. "Departmental Review of the Report of the Royal Commission on Health Services: Departmental Appraisal and Proposals and Recommendations," March 1965, 23, 25, 28, 59, 62, 77, 87–92. Quote is from 28. Department of National Health and Welfare Papers, Vol. 45.

49. Ibid., 142.

50. Bryden, *Planners and Politicians*, 159; "Discussions with Provinces on Health Services Matters," Meeting with Quebec Delegation, 12 and 13 April 1965, Department of National Health and Welfare Papers, Vol. 45; Finkel, *The Social Credit Phenomenon in Alberta*, 150–51.

51. Eugene Vayda and Raisa B. Deber, "The Canadian Health Care System: A Developmental Overview," in *Social Welfare Policy*, ed. Blake and Keshen, 316. In 1973–74, the federal grant to Newfoundland covered 81.5 per cent of the province's medical bills and 57.6 per cent of its hospital costs while the grant to Ontario paid 44.8 per cent of medical care and 49.4 per cent of hospital costs. "For medical insurance, each province received 50 per cent of the average national per capita medical care expenditure multiplied by its population."

52. The continued opposition of the premiers was clear in File 618.4, "Correspondence with Premiers," Lester B. Pearson Papers, MG 26, N-4, Vol. 199, LAC. Other than Saskatchewan and British Columbia, no provinces were clearly prepared to join the medicare program in February 1968. Nova Scotia and Newfoundland were believed by the federal government to be only prepared to join if Ontario did. But Ontario, New Brunswick, and Alberta were unprepared to join the program. Manitoba planned to defer participation for at least a year beyond July 1 in the hopes of convincing the federal government to concede support for a plan more in tune with Manitoba's free-enterprise views.

53. Ibid., 152–63.

54. Ibid., 164–67.

55. Department of National Health and Welfare, "Departmental Review," 2.

56. Evidence of United Electrical, Radio and Machine Workers of America, May 1962, Royal Commission on Health Services, Vol. 21.

57. Donald Swartz, "The Politics of Reform: Conflict and Accommodation in Canadian Health Policy," in *The Canadian State: Political Economy and Political Power*, ed. Leo Panitch (Toronto, ON: University of Toronto Press, 1977), 311–43; and Vivienne Walters, "State, Capital and Labour: The Introduction of Federal-Provincial Insurance for Physician Care in Canada," *Canadian Journal of Sociology and Anthropology* 19, 2 (1982): 157–72.

58. Paul Grescoe, "A Nation's Disgrace," in *Health and Canadian Society*, ed. Coburn, D'Arcy, Torrance, and New, 127–40.

59. James S. Frideres and René R. Gadacz, *Aboriginal Peoples in Canada: Contemporary Conflicts*, 6th ed. (Toronto, ON: Prentice Hall, 2001), 68–69.

60. Maureen K. Lux, *Medicine That Walks: Disease, Medicine, and Canadian Plains Native People, 1880–1940* (Toronto, ON: University of Toronto Press, 2001); T. Kue Young, *Health Care and Culture Change: The Indian Experience in the Central Subarctic* (Toronto, ON: University of Toronto Press, 1988).

61. Poen, *Harry S. Truman Versus the Medical Lobby*; Paul Starr, *The Social Transformation of American Medicine* (New York, NY: Basic Books, 1982).

476

THE SIXTIES

A Youth Revolution or A Few Angry Baby Boomers?

Marcel Martel
York University

THE SIXTIES: A YOUTH REVOLUTION OR A FEW ANGRY BABY BOOMERS?

Introduction by Marcel Martel

● INTRODUCTION

Marcel Martel

The 1960s was a period rich in ideological turmoil, political events, and social and cultural changes. This period of turmoil and change is often attributed to the arrival of a generation known as baby boomers—referring to those born between 1945 and the beginning of the 1960s, although there is no consensus on precisely when the baby boom ended. The word *revolution* is used to characterize the radical nature of change that society underwent because of new attitudes toward sexuality, gender roles, and social values. At the time, members of the media, politicians, and even university professors credited young people with being at the centre of social unrest and ideological challenges. The fact that, in 1966, youth constituted 50 percent of the population of Canada under age 21 gave credit to those who believed that this age cohort had the power, energy, and abilities to provoke change. Even the well-known American magazine *Time* designated the baby boom generation as the Man of the Year in 1967. This designation helped fix in our imagination how this generation would be remembered and celebrated; the magazine associated baby boomers with terms such as *rebellious, liberty, disobedience, challenge to the status quo,* and *anti-conformism.* The document "Turn On, Tune In, Take Over!!!" included in the module is an ironic view of the famous motto popularized by Timothy Leary. First published in the Vancouver underground newspaper *Georgia Straight,* the author of this piece provided advice aimed at changing the school system. Instead of dropping out, people should organize peaceful activities and be critical of their education.

Some baby boomers rejected social conservatism, promoted liberal attitudes toward sexuality, and did not hesitate to experiment despite the fact that their behaviours tended to disturb conservative elements in society. They argued in favour of being different in terms of behaviour, clothing, and societal expectations. Many of those who went to college and, in particular, to university did not hesitate to get involved in social, cultural, and political issues. In 1969, 18 percent of Canadians aged 18 to 24 were enrolled in colleges and universities. The university system went through a period of expansion to accommodate the arrival of baby boomers. Existing universities expanded their facilities and new universities were created, such as Brock, Simon Fraser, Trent, York, and the Université du Québec network. However, these institutions either were unprepared to welcome these inquisitive students or were overwhelmed by the task of hiring new faculty members, developing curriculum, and delivering quality education.

At the time, university students were concerned with international issues such as preventing a nuclear war, promoting disarmament, stopping the Vietnam war, and denouncing universities as imperialist institutions. But they were also concerned with issues such as university governance, paternalistic attitudes dictating how universities dealt with students, greater student input in university curriculum, teaching evaluation, better delivery of educational programs and courses, and changes to how students were disciplined—which led some students to publish manifestos, stage protests, send petitions, and organize sit-ins and even strikes. In other cases, protests were organized over the issue of access to university where it was being severely affected by increased tuition fees. Occasionally, police put an end to student protests.

If student activism on campus captured the attention of many, others were not convinced that students as a group were an agent of social change. In the excerpts of the manifesto entitled "The Student as Nigger" and included in this module, university professor

Jerry Farber depicts students as consenting victims of the educational system. Writing in 1967, the author tried to awaken students to their state of slavery and encouraged them to become critical. Farber was at that time actively involved in the civil rights movement and was jailed seven times for participating in protests against racial discrimination in housing, employment, and education. His eyewitness account of the Watts Riots of 1965 has been reprinted in *Reporting Civil Rights*, published by the Library of America. Just as some people today may find the use of the term *nigger* disturbing or totally inappropriate, others at the time tried to prevent its dissemination on campuses, fearing that it would trigger student unrest.

Many of the protests did not gather a lot of support among students, but those who took part in them believed that their collective action was part of an international movement. Their protests comforted them in their belief that their battles, which in many cases were prompted by local circumstances, were nevertheless part of a wide geographical movement that had no boundaries. Student activism, especially in 1968, was spreading in the western hemisphere (France, Italy, Mexico, Spain, and the United States), as well as in Asia and communist countries such as Poland and Czechoslovakia.

If students got media attention because of their demands and actions, so did others such as hippies. These people, who were characterized as having long hair and colourful clothes, gathered in towns and cities, especially Vancouver (Gastown), Toronto (Yorkville), and Montreal (Carré Saint-Louis), to live according to their non-materialistic values. Their presence triggered strong reactions, often very critical, as demonstrated by the cartoons. However, Vancouver alderman Harry Rankin offered an alternate view of hippies. In his piece, first published in the *Georgia Straight* and included in this module, he argued that society should understand the meaning of hippies' quest for a better world.

481

Some politicians, media, and parents opposed the value system promoted by hippies. In their scholarly articles, Stuart Henderson and Bruce Douville offer contrasting portrait of hippies. Henderson's article analyzes the factors that led to the destruction of Yorkville as one of the centres of the counterculture movement in Canada. The hepatitis scare became a useful expedient to chase hippies out of this Toronto neighbourhood. For his part, Bruce Douville's article gives new meaning to the terms *counterculture, religion,* and *hippies*. Although attendance at institutional churches declined in the 1960s, some youth saw in the hippie lifestyle a way to live according to original Christian principles.

Popular mythology transformed baby boomers into the prime movers of change in the 1960s without paying too much attention to the fact that in terms of gender, class, and ethnic differences this generation was not a uniform and unanimous age cohort. Not all baby boomers had it easy in the 1960s. Young black people who were forced to move out of Africville in Nova Scotia or First Nations people living in abject housing conditions on reserves force us to revisit the representation of this generation.

Looking back at this time period, can it be said that these young people triggered a revolution that changed society forever? Or was society confronted by a few angry individuals who were successful in speaking on behalf of their generation? Specialists are still debating the causes, meaning, and legacy of the 1960s, and the selection of documents and articles that are part of this module illustrate the various meanings associated with that period.

QUESTIONS

1. According to the manifesto and the article entitled "Turn on, Tune In, Take Over!!!", what was wrong with the educational system? Is the content of these documents still relevant today?

2. In his definition of hippies, what did Vancouver alderman Harry Rankin try to achieve? Did he display a real sympathy for hippies?
3. Why was the gathering of youth and hippies in Yorkville defined as a threat? Were hippies a threat in Douville's article?
4. What contributed to the end of Yorkville as a meeting place for youth and hippies?
5. According to Douville, were young people who embraced religious beliefs revolutionary in their beliefs and behaviours?

FURTHER READINGS

CBC Archives, *Yorkville: A Hippie Haven,* and *Yorkville: From Hippies to Highrises.* http://archives.cbc.ca/IDD-1-69-580/life_society/hippies

Martel, Marcel, *Not This Time: Canadians, Public Policy and the Marijuana Question, 1961–1975.* (Toronto: University of Toronto Press, 2006).

National Film Board of Canada, *Flowers on a One-Way Street,* Montreal, 1967.

Owram, Douglas, *Born at the Right Time: A History of the Baby Boom Generation.* (Toronto: University of Toronto Press, 1996).

Palmer, Bryan D., *Canada's 1960s. The Ironies of Identity in a Rebellious Era.* (Toronto: University of Toronto Press, 2009).

Ricard, François, *The Lyric Generation: The Life and Times of the Baby Boomers.* (Toronto: Lorimer, 1994).

482

▲ Document 1: "The Student As Nigger"

Jerry Farber

Students are niggers. When you get that straight, our schools begin to make sense. It's more important, though, to understand why they're niggers. If we follow that question serioulsy, it will lead us past the zone of academic bullshit, where dedicated teachers pass their knowledge on to a new generation, and into the nitty-gritty of human needs and hangups. From there we can go on to consider whether it might ever be possible for studnets to come up from slavery.

First, look at the role students play in what we like to call education. At Cal State where I teach, the students have separate and unequal dining facilities. If I bring a student into the faculty dining room, my colleagues get uncomfortable, as though there were a bad smell. If I eat in the student cafeteria, I become known as the educational equivalent of a "nigger-lover". In at least one building there are even rest rooms which students may not use. Also there is an unwritten law barring student-faculty lovemaking. Fortunately, this anti-miscegenation law, like its Southern counterpart, is not 100 per cent effective.

CHOOSE HOMECOMING QUEEN

Students at Cal State are politically disenfranchised. They are in an academic Lowndes County. Most of them can vote in national elections—their average age is about 26—but they have no voice in the decisions which affect their academic lives. The students are, it is true, allowed to have a toy government of their own. It is a government run, for the most part, by Uncle Toms, concerned principally with trivia. The faculty and administrators decide what courses will be offered; the students get to choose their own Homecoming Queen. Occasionally, when student leaders get uppity and rebellious, they're either ignored, put off with trivial concessions, or maneuvered expertly out of position.

A student at Cal State is expected to know his place. He calls a faculty member "Sir" or "Doctor" or "Professor" and he smiles and shuffles some as he stands outside the professor's office waiting for permission to enter. The faculty tell him what courses to take (in my department, English, even electives have to be approved by a faculty member); they tell him what to read, what to write, and, frequently, where to set the margins on his typewriter. They tell him what's true and what isn't. Some teachers insist that they encourage dissent but they're almost always lieing and every student knows it. Tell The Man what he wants to hear or he'll fail you.

When a teacher says "jump" students jump. I know of one professor who refused to take up class time for exams and required students to show up for tests at 6:30 in the morning. And they did, by God! Another, at exam time, provides answer cards to be filled out—each one enclosed in a paper bag with a hole cut in the top to see through. Students stick their writing hands in the bags while taking the test. The teacher isn't a provo; I wish he were. He does it to prevent cheating. Another colleague once caught a student reading during one of his lectures and threw her book against the wall. Still another lectures his students into a stupor and then screams at them in rage when they fall asleep.

Source: Jerry Farber, "The Student as Nigger," *Senate Debates*, September 19, 1968, pp. 80–84. Reprinted with permission from Jerry Farber.

483

CLASS IS NOT DISMISSED!

During the first meeting of a class, one girl got up to leave after about ten minutes had gone by. The teacher rushed over, grabbed her by the arm, saying "This class is not dismissed!" and led her back to her seat. On the same day another teacher began by informing his class that he does not like beards, mustaches, long hair on boys, or capri pants on girls, and will not tolerate any of that in his class. The class, incidentally, consisted mostly of high-school teachers.

Even more discouraging than this Auschwitz approach to education is the fact that the students take it. They haven't gone through twelve years of public school for nothing. They've learned one thing and perhaps only one thing during those twelve years. They've forgotten their algebra. They're hopelessly vague about chemistry and physics. They've grown to fear and resent literature. They write like they've been lobotomized. But, Jesus, can they follow orders! Freshmen come up to me with an essay and ask if I want it folded and whether their name should be in the upper right hand corner. And I want to cry and kiss them and caress their poor, tortured heads.

Students don't ask that orders make sense. They give up expecting things to make sense long before they leave elementary school. Things are true because the teacher says they're true. At a very early age we all learn to accept "two truths," as did certain medieval churchmen. Outside of class, things are true to your tongue, your finger, your stomach, your heart. Inside class, things are true by reason of authority. And that's just fine because you don't care anyway. Miss Wiedemeyer tells you a noun is a person, place or thing. So let it be. You don't give a rat's ass; she doesn't give a rat's ass.

SIRENS AND A RATTLE OF BULLETS

The important thing is to please her. Back in kindergarten, you found out that teachers only love children who stand in nice straight lines. And that's where it's been at ever since. Nothing changes except to get worse. School becomes more and more obviously a prison. Last year I spoke to a student assembly at Manual Arts High School and then couldn't get out of the goddam school. I mean there was no way out. Locked doors. High fences. One of the inmates was trying to make it over a fence when he saw me coming and froze in panic. For a moment, I expected sirens, a rattle of bullets, and him clawing the fence.

Then there's the infamous "code of dress". In some high schools, if your skirt looks too short, you have to kneel before the principal, in a brief allegory of fellatio. If the hem doesn't reach the floor, you go home to change while he, presumably, jacks off. Boys in high school can't be too sloppy and they can't be too sharp. You'd think the school board would be delighted to see all the spades trooping to school in pointy shoes, suits, ties and stingy brims. Uh-uh. They're too visible.

What school amounts to, then, for white and black kids alike, in a 12 year course in how to be slaves. What else could explain what I see in a freshman class? They've got that slave mentality: obliging and ingratiating on the surface but hostile and resistent underneath. Like black slaves, students vary in their awareness of what's going on. Some recognize their own put-on for what it is and even let their rebellion break through to the surface now and then. Others—including most of the "good students" have been more deeply brainwashed. They swallow the bullshit with greedy mouths. They honest-to-God believe in grades, in busy work, in general education requirements. They're like those old grey-headed houseniggers you can still find in the South who don't see what all the fuss is about because Mr. Charlie "treats us real good". [...]

RESPECT FOR AUTHORITY

The general timidity which causes teachers to make niggers of their students usually includes a more specific fear—fear of the students themselves. After all, students are different, just like black people. You stand exposed in front of them, knowing that their interests, their values and their language are different from yours. To make matters worse you may suspect that you yourself are not the most engaging person. What then can protect you from their ridicule and scorn? Respect for authority. That's what—it's the policeman's gun again. The white bwana's pith helmet. So you flaunt that authority. You wither whisperers with a murderous glance. You crush objectors with erudition and heavy irony. And, worst of all, you make your own attainments seem not accessible but awesomely remote. You conceal your massive ignorance—and parade a slender learning.

Finally, there's the darkest reason of all for the master-slave approach to education. The less trained and the less socialized a person is, the more he constitutes a sexual threat and the more he will be subjected by institutions, such as penitentiaries and schools. Many of us are aware by now of the sexual neurosis which makes white man so fearful of integrated schools and neighborhoods, and which makes castration of Negroes a deeply entrenched Southern folkway. We should recognize a similar pattern in education. There is a kind of castration that goes on in schools. It begins, before school years, with parents' first encroachments on their children's free unashamed sexuality and continues right up to the day when they hand you your doctoral diploma with a bleeding, shriveled pair of testicles stapled to the parchment. It's not that sexuality has no place in the classroom. You'll find it there but only in certain perverted, and vitiated forms.

PERVERSION IS INTELLECTUAL

How does sex show up in school? First of all, there's the sadomasochistic relationship between teachers and students. That's plenty sexual although the price of enjoying it is to be unaware of what's happening. In walks the student in his Ivy League equivalent of a motorcycle jacket. In walks the teacher—a kind of intellectual rough trade—and flogs his students with grades, tests, sarcasm and snotty superiority until their very brains are bleeding. In Swinburne's England, the whipped school boy frequently grew up to be a flagellant. With us their perversion is intellectual but it's no less perverse.

Sex also shows up in the classroom as academic subject matter—sanitized and abstracted, thoroughly divorced from feeling. You get "sex education" now in both high school and college classes: every one determined not be embarrassed to be very up-to-date. These are the classes for which sex, as Feiffer puts it "can be a beautiful thing if properly administered". And then of course, there's still another depressing manifestation of sex in the classroom: the "off-color" teacher, who keeps his class awake with sniggering sexual allusions, obscene titters and academic innuendo. The sexuality he purveys, it must be admitted, is at least better than none at all.

UNDERNEATH THE PETTI-PANTS

What's missing from kindergarten to graduate school is honest recognition of what's happening turned-on awareness of what's underneath the pettipants, the chinos and the flannels. It's not that sex needs to be pushed in school; sex is pushed enough. But we should let it be, where it is and like it is. I don't insist that ladies in junior high school lovingly caress their students' cocks (someday, maybe); however, it is reasonable to ask that the

485

ladies don't by example and structures teach their students to pretend that they aren't there. As things stand now, students are psychically castrated or spayed—and for the very same reason that black men are castrated in Georgia: because they're a threat.

So you can add sexual repression to the list of causes, along with vanity, fear and will to power, that turn the teacher into Mr. Charlie. You might also want to keep in mind that he was a nigger once himself and has never really gotten over it. And there are more causes, some of which are better described in sociological than in psychological terms. Work them out, it's not hard. But in the mean time what we've got on our hands is a whole lot of niggers. And what makes this particularly grim is that the student has less chance than the black man of getting out of his bag. Because the student doesn't even know he's in it. That, more or less, is what's happening in higher education. And the results are staggering.

For one thing damn little education takes place in the schools. How could it? You can't educate slaves; you can only train them. Or, to use an uglier and more timely word, you can only program them. [...]

MAKE THEM WILLING SLAVES

Another result of student slavery is just as dangerous—students don't get emancipated when they graduate. As a matter of fact, we don't let them graduate until they've demonstrated their willingness—for 16 years—to remain slaves. And for important jobs, like teaching, we make them go through more years just to make sure.

What I'm getting at is that we're all more or less niggers and slaves, teachers and students alike. This is the fact you have to start with in trying to understand wider social phenomena, say, politics, in our country and in other countries.

Educational oppression is trickier to fight than racial expression. If you're a black rebel they can't exile you; they either have to intimidate you or kill you. But in high school or college, they can just bounce you out of the fold. And they do.

Rebel students and renegade faculty members get smothered or shot down with devastating accuracy. In high school, it's not usually the student who gets it; it's more often the teacher. Others get tired of fighting and voluntarily leave the system. But dropping out of college for a rebel, is a little like going North, for a Negro. You can't really get away from it so you might as well stay and raise hell.

ORGANIZE FOR FREEDOM NOW

How do you raise hell? That's another article. But for a start, why not stay with the analogy? What have black people done? They have, first of all, faced the fact of their slavery. They've stopped kidding themselves about an eventual reward in the Great Watermelon Patch in the sky. They've organized. They've decided to get freedom now, and they've started taking it.

Students like black people, have immense unused power. They could theoretically, insist on participating in their own education. They could make academic freedom bilateral. They could teach their teachers to thrive on love and admiration rather than on fear and respect, and to lay down their weapons. Students could discover community. And they could learn to dance by dancing on the IBM cards. They could make coloring books out of the catalogs and they could put the grading system in a museum.

They could raze one set of walls and let life come blowing into the classroom. They could turn the classroom into a "field of action" as Peter Marin describes it. And they could study for the best of all possible reasons—their own resources.

They could. They have the power. But only in a very few places, like Berkeley, have they even begun to think about using it. For students as for black people, the hardest battle isn't with Mr. Charlie. It's with what Mr. Charlie has done to your mind.

▲ Document 2: Turn On, Tune In, Take Over!!!

If you drop out of school, you'll probably have to get a job. You'll hate *that*, too. The pay will be low, and it'll be even more boring than school was.

If you don't get a job, your parents will do all they can to make life rough for you.

You could leave home, but what happens then? It's getting too cold for sleeping outside or hitchhiking around the country. Staying with friends can be fun—for a little while. But you'll find it impossible to *do* anything. You'll soon grow tired of "making the scene" and living on somebody else's terms.

ACTION is the answer. When you close yourself up in your own little world, you're just avoiding questions that will have to be answered, sooner or later. If school is a drag, it's up to you to make it better. If you're thinking of leaving school anyway, what's wrong with getting KICKED OUT?

Nobody had the right to tell you how to run your life. You know more than the "elders" do about the things that are really important today. *Make* school interesting, by taking it over. How can you begin? Here are some ideas:

- Organize a union, to put pressure on the teachers and principals, so they'll give you what you want.
- Petitions can be circulated, to get rid of bad teachers and principals.
- A delegation can be sent to every PTA meeting, to present student demands. Don't ask for permission; tell them what you intend to do.
- Fight against all age restrictions. If you want to do something, go ahead. If you get caught, call the *Georgia Straight* Defence Fund. The "laws" are so bad that, nowadays, it is dishonourable not to have a criminal record. Just forget about building a future in *their* society. *You* can do better.
- Organize love-ins in schoolyards, perhaps for every noon hour.
- During fire drills, act as if there were a real fire. Once you get outside, keep going.
- If you don't like a textbook, lose it.

TAKE OVER!

- Stamp out corporal punishment. If any teacher or principal hits you, charge him with assault. One student actually hit back when a teacher attacked him. This is not recommended, however, except in extreme emergencies.
- Insist that schools be left open at night, so you can have a place to sleep in case home conditions become unbearable.
- Plan out your own courses, and teach them yourselves. Ask sympathetic teachers to help you.
- Start up school newspapers. *Georgia Straight* will help in any way possible. If you are interested, come and watch us in action (?). Also, send us anything you think we can use.
- Let your imagination run wild. Each day should bring new ideas. Once you get started, nothing can stop you.

All ideas and questions will be gladly received and personally dealt with. Write to: Project X, *Georgia Straight*.

Source: "Turn On, Tune In, Take Over!!!," in *The Georgia Straight*, September 8, 1967. From *The Georgia Straight: What the Hell Happened?* Vancouver: Douglas & McIntyre, 1997, pp. 47–48. Reprinted with permission from *The Georgia Straight*.

▲ Document 3: What Makes a Hippie?

Harry Rankin

City Council has set up a committee to investigate the "hippies" of Vancouver. I opposed the motion in council. Investigating people just because they are different smacks of a political inquisition.

When City Council decided to go ahead and investigate the "hippies," I agreed to go on the committee, mainly to make sure they received a fair hearing.

What makes a "hippie"? What are they after?

"Hippies" are rebels, even if rather unconventional ones. They're rebelling against the widespread violence and wars of our society. They're disillusioned with false middle-class values and standards, with status seekers, with people living beyond their means, with the vulgar materialism and the bitter competition so prevalent today. They're suspicious that automation will make man into a workhorse, a cog in an immense machine.

"Hippies" want a more rational world, with the emphasis on the freedom of each individual to develop his own personality. Their disillusionment with unhealthy aspects of our social order and their opposition to the hypocrisy of the Establishment is understandable. I don't like these things myself.

What is more difficult to understand, of course, is their form of protest.

The outlandish appearance of many "hippies" is not only a source of despair to barbers and shoe salesmen, it's a source of wonder to many of us.

Apparently they don't believe in action to abolish the evils against which they protest. Their philosophy is to withdraw from society, to turn their backs on the world, to do no more work than is necessary, to follow their own interests, and to help each other.

This "opting-out" doesn't make sense to me. I believe we can only make society better by chipping in and doing our share.

However, you can't wish "hippies" away just because you may disagree with some of the things they do or don't do. They're here; they're one of the facts of life. Personally I don't think they can stay forever in this in-between make-believe world of turning their backs on a society that they must live in whether they like it or not.

What we should avoid at this stage is being stampeded into taking police or legal action against them. Ideas can't be suppressed by force, but we can act to correct the conditions that give rise to those ideas.

489

Source: Harry Rankin, "What Makes a Hippie?," in *The Georgia Straight*, September 8, 1967. From *The Georgia Straight: What the Hell Happened?* Vancouver: Douglas & McIntyre, 1997, pp. 47. Reprinted with permission from Connie Fogal.

▲ Document 4: RCMP and Hippies

TRIBULATIONS OF THE GENERATION GAP

New recruit : Peace, man... like which of you cats do I rap with?

Drill Corporal : There there, Sergeant Major, take it easy. It must be a prairie heat mirage. Let's keep our cool and it'll go away.

● This cartoon of a hippy officer joining the RCMP force was published in *The RCMP Quarterly*, a magazine published by the RCMP. Looking at the hippy officer, what makes this character different from the others? Did the officer that looked like a hippy constitute a threat to the RCMP?

Source: *The RCMP Quarterly*, Vol. 37, No. 1 (January 1972), p. 2. Reprinted with permission from the RCMP Veterans Association.

▲ Document 5: The Most Forgettable Generation

● This cartoon about hippies was published in a mainstream magazine. Pay attention to the depiction of hippies. Do they all wear long hair? Could you identify female and male hippies? Were hippies depicted in a threatening way?

Source: R. Jones, *Saturday Night*, Vol. 84, No. 9 (September 1969), p. 35.

▲ Document 6: Youth

● The author of this cartoon depicts the youth movement as international in scope. Is this the case when you look at the list of countries mentioned? Is the young person included in the cartoon a hippy? If so, why? What is the political meaning of this cartoon?

Source: John Collins, about 1968, McCord Museum M965.199.6633.

Article 1: Toronto's Hippie Disease: End Days in the Yorkville Scene, August 1968

Stuart Henderson

In theory, any visitor to Yorkville who ate in a café, bought any object or contacted *any person*, may have been exposed to the disease [...] which can eventually lead to death. (emphasis added)
—*Toronto Star,* 7 August 1968

All sorts of guys are swearing at you if you come near them [...] One lady screamed at me, 'Don't *breathe* near me, you ——!' (emphasis added)
—"Luke the Drifter," *Toronto Star,* 13 August 1968

It's a bellybutton, a natural point of intersection. Yorkville, a tiny district consisting of two main arteries sandwiched between Avenue Road to the west, Yonge Street to the east, Bloor Street to the south and Davenport Road to the north, sits in the geographic centre of Metropolitan Toronto.[1]

And, during the 1960s this one-half square kilometre of boutiques, cafés, and art galleries also found itself at the centre of Toronto's youthful counter-culture—its students, hippies, artists, greasers, bikers, and others who congregated in and around the district, enjoyed the live music and theatre in its many coffee houses, its low-rent housing in overcrowded Victorian walk-ups, and its perceived saturation with anti-establishment energy.[2] For a period of roughly 10 years, and to the distress and consternation of local merchants and their well-heeled patrons, Yorkville served as a crossroads for Toronto's youth culture, as a venue for experimentation with hip lifestyles and beliefs, and as an apparent refuge from hegemonic ideology and the stifling common-sense it constructs.[3]

Source: Stuart Henderson, "Toronto's Hippie Disease: End Days in the Yorkville Scene, August 1968," *Journal of the Canadian Historical Association 2006*, Vol. 17, No. 1, New Series, pp. 205–234. Reprinted with permission from the Canadian Historical Association.

The early Yorkville scene is often remembered (by both its observers and its participants) as a largely happy, even idyllic neighborhood peopled by bohemian artists, poets, and musicians, whose calm was eventually shattered by relentless police incursions, "weekend hippies," under-age girls (derisively termed "teenyboppers"), injectable amphetamines, and unabated coercive municipal pressure.[4] Indeed, as the early 1960s became the late Sixties—a paradigm shift frequently characterized (both then and now) as a swing from innocence to cynicism, idealism to nihilism—Yorkville moved beyond its role as a mere popular nuisance in the public imagination.

When Syl Apps, Chair of Parliament's Select Committee on Youth (and former captain of the Toronto Maple Leafs), famously decried Yorkville as "a festering sore in the middle of the city" in the spring of 1967, a new era was beginning in earnest.[5] By the end of that year, Yorkville was increasingly linked to violence, drug abuse, addiction, homelessness, and disease; for many of the Villagers who had been a part of the scene prior to the summer of 1967, the Village no longer offered what they were looking for. One year later most of the earlier waves of hip youth had turned away from their former haunts—all of "the true hippies"[6] had left, according to Yorkville activist and media darling David DePoe.[7]

What remained in their stead as Yorkville entered the summer of '68 was a sizeable, diffusive assortment of young people. While many of them were committed in the same ways as their predecessors to what they took to be the hippie ideals of authenticity and peacefulness, continuing to get high on LSD, marijuana, and the psychedelic music scene, a small but crucial minority of them were experimenting with newly available, and highly addictive, injectable amphetamines. Moreover, many of these new Villagers, having traveled across great distances to make the scene, were homeless, and were perpetually suffering from the effects of privation. To make matters worse, the availability of casual sex had increased the spread of various venereal diseases, while overcrowding in Village crashpads was promoting poor sanitation and hygiene practices. Many of the issues so loudly harped upon by Apps and his ilk the previous year were now indisputably apparent.

Finally, in mid-summer 1968, the notion that Yorkville's hippie ghetto represented a pox on the face of Toronto became a kind of reality. Throughout

July, Women's College Hospital (which supervised a Yorkville-based "hippie clinic" under the charmingly literal name "Trailer") admitted an unusual number of patients suffering from hepatitis.[8] Aware of rumours that this social disease was an issue in the *über*-hip Haight-Ashbury district of San Francisco, the clinic became concerned about the prospect of a similar outbreak.[9] Although Trailer and Women's College tried to keep their findings quiet while awaiting the results of further tests, local media were surreptitiously alerted to the possibility of a "hippie disease" at work right in the heart of English Canada's biggest city. Rather predictably for media that had become collectively obsessed with covering the tiny enclave of Toronto youth culture, they over-reacted.[10]

The next morning, front page headlines warning of the spread of a contagious, mutable form of a fatal disease likely terrified local readers. Dire admonitions to keep out of Yorkville came from all directions. Within days, "hippies," and anyone who might be associated with them, were denied service at restaurants and shops outside of the Village. Throughout the month of August 1968, Yorkville's hip youth became the lepers of Toronto. Even after all available evidence showed that the hepatitis rate in Yorkville was in no way indicative of an epidemic—all but two of the Villagers turned out to be intravenous drug users, suggesting that the disease was being spread through dirty needles, not food or water—the damage was done.[11] As fears over the degenerating character of Yorkville reached their apotheosis, the scene was delivered a killing stroke by this specious, media-exaggerated hepatitis "epidemic."

This article outlines the process whereby Yorkville became the expected stage for the performance of "counterculture," a process which saw the "Village" re-cast as a foreign territory and, eventually, a "cancer." Its main purpose is to demonstrate that with the exaggerated hepatitis "epidemic" came a long-awaited opportunity for conservative authorities (and others unhappy with the development of a hip youth centre in the heart of Toronto) to officially declare Yorkville to be a "sick community," and to initiate its "break-up." As conservative discourse over Yorkville moved from the figurative (speculation about hip irrationality, madness, and foreignness) to the literal (Yorkville as the manifestation of the infectious potential of hip hedonism), the Village faced its final confrontation with a Toronto establishment bent on its destruction.

"Making the Scene" in Yorkville, 1960–1968

By the end of the 1950s, Toronto's diminutive bohemian community began to descend upon Yorkville after having been driven out of the area around Gerrard Street, a few blocks south, when it was torn down to make room for an expanding Toronto General Hospital. At the time, Yorkville played host to a very few clothing stores and restaurants, and the flats above these establishments were often occupied by their proprietors, many of whom were recent immigrants from war-scarred Eastern Europe. Following years of post-war suburbanization projects, which had drawn many Torontonians from the core of the city further North, East, and West, Toronto's newly empty inner-city Victorian and Edwardian houses had become home to European transplants.[12] As such, 1950s Torontonians knew of Yorkville (and generally lamented its status) as an ethnic ghetto.[13]

Throughout the 1950s, Yorkville's new immigrant population established distinctly European enterprises. Among these, the coffee house was among the freshest innovations, and certainly the most significant for the future of Yorkville. For many bored students and artists, perhaps equally enamored of Baudelaire, Sartre, and Kerouac, the coffee house suggested a hip hangout unlike any previously known to the city. According to Clifford Collier, part of the first wave of Village hipsters, such tastes of Euro-flavour were a revelation: "I mean there were *never* coffee houses in Toronto," he explained. "The closest thing we had to anything fancy was Diana Sweets [a tea room]! [And] because of the Europeans coming into Toronto after the war, here were coffee houses."[14]

Toronto's City Council was generally supportive of such developments, at least at first. Yorkville, as part of a much-lauded gentrification project at work in the Bay-Bloor area, was, at least by day, becoming known as a centre for Euro-chic fashion and design, and for what was still being referred to as the "carriage trade"[15] But, after dark, European residents, shopowners, and some of their clientele took to mixing with curious youth from around the city in local coffee houses. It was through this fruitful intermingling of European émigrés, middle-class Torontonians, and Beat youth (a short-lived and vague movement comprised of aspiring poets, musicians,

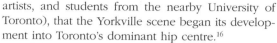

artists, and students from the nearby University of Toronto), that the Yorkville scene began its development into Toronto's dominant hip centre.[16]

If *hip* is forged through the alchemy of intermingled Others, a position suggested by journalist John Leland in his entertaining study of the vicissitudes of hipness in American culture, then Yorkville offered Toronto a veritable crucible.[17] Within the ranks of artists, poets, and musicians flocking to the Village by 1963 were middle-class WASPS, Jews, homosexuals, Southern Italians and Eastern Europeans, all breathing the same smoke-dry coffee house air.[18] Opening their eyes to the others around them, sharing misgivings and frustrations with liberal capitalist hegemony, and aiming to devise new and perhaps less formalized social conventions, Yorkville's coffee house scenesters promoted open-eyed awareness and escape from the *mauvaise foi* they believed to have enslaved their contemporaries in the suburbs.[19]

Into the 1960s, Yorkville would emerge as Canada's expected stage for the twinned performances of youth and hip. Set apart, circumscribed by boundaries both arbitrary and ultimately significant, Yorkville became known to all as "the Village"; it was a zone of difference, a kind of unhinged space in which participants could play at alternative identity performance. Outside of the confines of the district, such apparently countercultural activities as drug use or liberated sexuality, or such countercultural aesthetics as long hair and thrift shop fashions, were read by Torontonians as performances of *Yorkville*.[20] As such, Yorkville played out for many Canadians (as thousands of young people crossed the country to take part in the scene) and for most Torontonian baby boomers curious enough to check it out, as a means to approach social rebellion merely be *being* someplace.

People, in the idiom of 1960s hip culture, used the expression "making the scene" to refer to this *being someplace*, as though it was the people, not the structures, which constituted the scenery in any given location. (*We made the scene last night around 10 o'clock; Sally made the scene a few hours later*, and so on.) There is a connotation here, perhaps hidden after decades of disuse, which suggests that these hip folks recognized the power of *presence* in creating meaning in any particular locus. The same way that an actor on a sparse, even empty stage can

make the scene around her seem to respond to *her*, and not the other way around; the phrase "making the scene" can refer to the way that we, as human actors, do something of the same thing to our own surroundings.

"Making the scene" in Yorkville, then, was what everyone was up to, and all the time, as the place was up for grabs, as it became a battleground over identity, meaning, and truth. In effect, the politicians, hippies, bikers, speed freaks, shop owners, and teenyboppers alike were all active participants, all performers, in the continuous making and re-making of *Yorkville* throughout the 1960s, as each tried to imbue the stage with his own meaning.[21] The competing heuristics variously endorsed and propagated by each interest and identity group all shared the same central point of reference: Yorkville was a cultural theatre, the central stage on which this pageant would play out.[22]

Into the mid-1960s, the coffee house scene exploded in Yorkville. Offering outdoor patios and cramped stages for the suddenly cool folk musicians and poets who claimed the neighborhood, the coffee houses were, very early on, a kind of hip theatre.[23] As local artists hung their neo-Dadaist work on the walls, as poets stood spontaneously upon their benches and shouted impulsively concocted verse, as folksingers sat scribbling their thoughts at tables littered with crumpled papers and cigarette ash, any visitor to the scene could see that at least part of the allure of the coffee house was its spectacle of difference.[24] Indeed, many commentators on the scene emphasized this very point—Yorkville was a symbiosis of Beat artistry and foreign energy, an exciting, theatrical, and ultimately participatory experience for the tourist.

As a geographic location, Yorkville was figuratively cut off, re-cast as a strange land, an unstable and subversive zone of decadent self-absorption and vice. As a business district it was teetering on the precipice, apparently about to fall, its impending economic doom always blamed on the young, rowdy Villagers. As a metaphor for a Canadian failure to control an increasingly inscrutable and volatile youth culture, it was potent, vivid, and fearsome. In an era when so many of Canada's institutions were forced to grapple with the huge influx of young people brought on by the Baby Boom—no fewer than seven major Canadian universities were established in this period[25] here was another, more impromptu

495

institution: a pseudo-college for the disenchanted, the thrill-seeking, the alienated, the stoned.[26]

To the horror of many Depression-raised parents, no one group took to the scene more readily than middle-class, suburban youth—at least at first. As a consequence, hip Yorkville, after a few years of rather quiet, below-the-radar expansion, grew into a *bona fide* cultural concern by 1964. As Beatlemania swept across North America, media were paying more attention to middle-class youth culture than ever before; the public was curious, and the City was getting nervous. By the following spring, as huge street parties began to characterize weekend nights on Yorkville Avenue, Toronto's City Council turned activist in an effort to curb the development of the scene.[27]

In perhaps the most telling example, the Council tried to curtail Yorkville's popularity by instituting a moratorium on licenses for coffee houses in the spring of 1965, an act which served as a rather effective bit of accidental propaganda for young people, who found it to be incontrovertible evidence that Yorkville was, indeed, cool. Meanwhile, after yet another street party had been characterized by local media as a "riot," undercover and beat cops were dispatched to fill the streets in impressive numbers, charged with rooting out the "rowdys" and the "toughs," along with the drug-takers, the drug dealers, and the prostitutes whom many feared had set up shop in the area.[28] City Council even tried to institute a by-law prohibiting motorcycles—a move which demonstrated its fundamental misunderstanding of the hip scene—hoping that this would help return Yorkville to its predestined path toward boutiques, upscale galleries, sophistication, and affluence.[29]

Such attempts to coerce hipsters to forego Yorkville for fields less fair met with virtually no success—every summer fresh hordes of young people flocked to this supposed hippie wonderland, the centre of all things counterculture in Eastern Canada. The local media played a key role in all of this, shining their often blinding light on the tiny area, illuminating all aspects from the tawdry to the fascinating, from the raucous to the sublime. Indeed, their role was crucial, and did not go unnoticed by local merchants: one boutique owner complained to the *Globe and Mail* in the spring of 1965 that "every newspaper that re-counts trouble on Yorkville 'is like an ad for every punk in town to come down here.'"[30]

In Yorkville, political identity (including performances of racial, sexual, and class identity) and what I shall refer to as the phenomenon of *local-foreignness* operated in interwoven, indivisible ways.[31] Widespread sexual promiscuity (including whispers of prostitution and homosexuality) and pervasive drug use were generally cited as the two worst results of allowing Yorkville's "character" to be shaped by the hands of an unchecked and morally bankrupt culture.[32] While there was no "Jack the Ripper" to terrorize the Yorkville denizens, no outright personification of the danger of social transgression, the ever-present threats of hippie sex fiends, speed-peddling greasers, and hulking bikers preying on poor, out-of-pocket girls emphasized an atmosphere of pervasive, or at least potential, sexual violence and moral depravity which was readily exploited by both local media and City Councilors.[33] In the view of Deputy Chief of Police Bernard Simmonds, Yorkville was little more than a roiling cauldron of class and sexual devastation. "They come to the Village as good kids," he lamented, "mixed up perhaps, many from fine homes, and these beatniks grab them and within two days they are *ruined*."[34] (emphasis added)

It was the very foreignness of Yorkville's culture that truly set it apart and established the district as a zone of difference. From the moment a place is set apart as separate, as somehow distinct, it becomes a *de facto* foreign territory.[35] At the most basic level, the casting of Yorkville as a *Village*, while tied to a historical reality (Yorkville *was* a Village until it was annexed by the city in 1883), served to establish the district as a zone of local-foreignness, at once present and removed from the local and the foreign contexts.

As semiologists have argued for decades, once a thing is named, is bounded through language and common-sense, it is only then rendered comprehensible.[36] This thing can now be characterized (as 'thing'), its meaning(s) debated, evaluated, (mis)understood.[37] In terms of geography, such a process is doubly important, because often we are speaking in the abstract when we discuss place—we may never have been there, and are never going to go; but because it is named, we are able to develop a sense that it *is*. And so we develop mental maps, onto which we can project our understandings of these places. Geographer Peter Jackson has argued that such maps of meaning "are ideological instruments in the sense that they project a preferred reading of the material world, with prevailing social relations mirrored in the depiction of physical space."[38]

Because Yorkville was understood as a place in which flourished both subversion and dissent, the map of meaning through which the area was read by most observers was reflective of this common sense. In other words, hegemonic distrust and fear of cultural and social dissent fostered a treatment of Yorkville as a distinct, local-foreign land—a common-sense view which served both as a warning to some to stay away, and, importantly, as an invitation to the curious to come and partake.[39] This process, in turn, helped to inculcate the characterization of the Yorkville youth culture as somehow unfathomable, alien, and dangerous.

Sex, drugs, and rock'n'roll (the hip holy trinity in the 1960s) characterized the (foreign) activity that was "Yorkville" in newspaper editorials, magazine articles, and television exposés.[40] In most media treatments of the scene after 1965, "free love" (or, in the crudest sense, free *sex*) was an expected Yorkville pastime, drug use defined participation and conferred status in the Village scene, and rock'n'roll (having recently supplanted folk music) was the soundtrack to experiences both psychedelic and sexual. In fear, frustration, and palpable fury, City Council (and untold numbers of Torontonians) watched as their every attempt to legislate the young people out of the district seemed not only to backfire, but to actually incite *more interest* in the Yorkville scene. And, through it all, the numbers of shaggy-haired and peasant-skirted Villagers grew while their activities became ever more outlandish. To the more conservative Council members, Yorkville was being lost: lost to a swelling youth culture increasingly obsessed with the weird, the subversive, the irrational.

These were young men who refused to work, and young women who refused to be ladies; refusals of class privilege, cultural imperatives and norms, and even the most central tenets of the "civilized" society fairly defined the scene.[41] To many onlookers, having so recently lived through the calamity of a world at war, Yorkville and its Villagers were maddeningly incomprehensible. In 1965, Horace Brown, a prominent Toronto Alderman, actually referred to the neighborhood as "a foreign country," after touring it with media in tow, sparking wide media-driven debate over Yorkville exceptionalism and the apparent Generation Gap.[42] But, the

Yorkville-as-a-foreign-land-taken-over-by-teenagers frame was not malevolent enough to dissuade the curious from stopping in. And so, City Council, their conservative wing represented by former Mayor and all-around hippie-hater Allan Lamport, turned away from the associations with foreignness in 1967, and began to emphasize the unclean, unshaven, and generally unkempt aesthetic of hip youth in their efforts to dispose of all of this hip magnetism.[43] Soon enough, in the bloated rhetoric of at least a handful of City Councilors, this inflamed population of hip youth was said to constitute a kind of social disease, "a cancer that is spreading through Metro as more teenagers crowd in from around the nation."[44] Yorkville, they began to argue, wasn't just a foreign, morally toxic zone of difference: it was an *infection*.

Many young people, invited to engage with what they had been taught was *their* place, *their* community, couldn't help but be swayed by the politicization of youth caught up in this discourse. If young people are localized, their activities characterized and categorized, their identity is then *politicized* as different, foreign, and deviant. As a result, a central ideological shift—part of a process which had begun with the Juvenile Delinquency preoccupations of the 1950s and which approached its apotheosis with the counterculture in the 1960s—saw youth culture re-cast as a political project.[45]

As cultural historian Peter Braunstein has underlined, by the late 1960s, youth was widely appreciated to be an ethic, even a *performance*, not so much about age as it was about spirit.[46] And youth, like Yorkville, was accessible to all—that is, if you were up to the performance. Considered in this way, the battle for Yorkville was both a battle for the physical space *Yorkville* and the meaning of that space. Could Yorkville be liberated from its overlords? As the popular Hollywood film *Wild in the Streets* cleverly exploited, by the mid-1960s the political dimensions of youth were—following black writers such as Eldridge Cleaver and Frantz Fanon—being expressed in terms of a Third World-ism, as if youth were an identity (even a race) in need of liberation from the repressive colonizing establishment.[47]

In the new conservative discourse, hip, foreign Yorkville was a community at risk, overwhelmed by a symbolically sick population. This apparent sickness was manifest in what appeared to be the Villagers' insane pride: a pride taken in their lack of interest in work, their austere lifestyles, their general disdain for social conventions, their propensity toward beards and other conspicuous body hair, and their embrace of psychedelic drug use as a radical avoidance of reality (that is, their refusals of hegemonic performances of gender, race, class, and religion).

In 1967's so-called Summer of Love—a season re-packaged as an advertising slogan—unprecedented numbers of young people flocked to the Village from all over the country, bumming rides in overcrowded vans from Shediac, Thompson, or Hay River, and arriving to find the greatest sustained party of their young lives. A Canadian parallel to the American obsession with San (be-sure-to-wear-some-flowers-in-your-hair) Francisco, the Yorkville scene had become a cultural firestorm, dividing many Torontonians (and Canadians) over the value of this urban youth centre.[48] August 1967 led to some very loud and public events, which seemed unlikely to stem the flow of interest in the Village, or the hip youth who claimed it as their own. First, charges of police brutality dogged the local force (after a non-violent protest over Yorkville's traffic problem turned into a paddy wagon free-for-all), prompting the public to face the issue of repressive anti-hippie coercion. Second, Allan Lamport's campaign of vitriol and insult culminated in a series of farcical face-offs between the Diggers (a group of political hippies led by a media-savvy Villager named David DePoe) and members of the City Council at which etiquette and hygiene were the hot button topics of discussion, suggesting to many liberal-minded Torontonians that the Council was badly out of touch on these issues.[49] Third, in a hotly reported national story, it was suggested in the House of Commons that while two National Film Board camera crews were at work documenting the whole wooly experience of hippiedom in mid-town Toronto, they (backed by government funding) had been complicit in illegal activities in the district.[50]

Amid this surge in public interest, Villagers began to perceive a change in the air—by the end of the year, it was not uncommon to hear Villagers declaring that Torontonians had witnessed the end of their scene. Citing media over-exposure, overcrowding, poverty, and the pernicious (and recent) influx of amphetamines and drug-addicted teenagers, many frustrated Villagers tolled the death knell amid the fallen autumn leaves.[51] In San Francisco's Haight-Ashbury, the hip old guard had already symbolically killed the Hippie, holding a mock funeral in early autumn as a statement on the co-optation and commercialization of the scene, and the saturation of the district by media, municipal, and other wanted attention.[52] But what of Yorkville? Since winter was never a particularly hopping season in the Village—cold, rain and snow tended to frustrate the ascetic and frugal lifestyle of many indigent hippies accustomed to sleeping where they lay during the balmy summer months—all eyes were turned toward the following summer. Hepatitis Attacks!: Yorkville, the Hippie Quarantine

In mid-summer 1968, Yorkville became the very "cancer area" that Allan Lamport and other conservative City Councilors had claimed it to be.[53] Throughout July, Dr. Anne Keyl of Women's College Hospital (through her role as supervisor of Trailer, the "hippie clinic" in Yorkville) admitted an "unusual number" of patients suffering from hepatitis, most of whom, "both in-patient and out-patient, were associated with the Yorkville district."[54] June Callwood, persistent hip ally and landlady at hippie shelter Digger House, explained Keyl's role in fostering the appearance of an epidemic:

> Dr. Anne Keyl [...] she was sympathetic [...] And she wanted to know what was going on in Yorkville. She was worried about their health and [for me, it was:] *finally, here was the establishment starting to worry about them.* She was in her fifties, a short stout woman, plain spoken. And when I told her about the conditions, the health condition of these kids, she was appalled. Then somebody came in [and was] diagnosed with Hep B. And she took off on it, huge. Everybody had to get immunized.[55]

Keyl (and her staff) met with the Medical Officer of Health for the City of Toronto and the Provincial Epidemiologist on 30 July, and then again on 2 August, where it was concluded that, although "the number of cases of infectious Hepatitis reported in Toronto in July 1968 [...] was still less than half the number reported in July 1966," the right move would be to undertake a survey to try to determine the extent of hepatitis in Yorkville.[56]

According to the final Report of the hastily assembled Hepatitis Co-ordinating Committee, published in September 1969, "Subsequently, two unforeseen events took place, either of which would have been sufficient to transform the 'quiet' survey into a Front Page news story".[57]

On the afternoon of the first survey clinic (August 2), at least two newspapers telephone messages advising that the clinic would begin work that day and suggesting that this would be a good opportutnity for a news story. The second incident was the wide distribution in Yorkville, on August 5, of a typewritten single-sheet flier headed, 'Danger! Danger! Hepatitis". The source is unidentified but the news media wer in possession of copies in time for the daily papers of August 6.[58]

This well-timed invitation was actually the brainchild of Wilfred (Bill) Clement, chief pharmacologist at Queen Street Mental Health Centre, and popular Yorkville character. Following a particularly unproductive meeting with local health officials, Clement took matters into his own hands:

I recall being in a meeting [on Yorkville and hepatitis] with the people from Toronto General and Women's College Hospital [...] the nice ladies from Women's College Hospital were asking the Province to put up the money for needles to score the blood. The Province doesn't want to pay for it. This goes on for half an hour—they're arguing about the fucking spikes![59]

Clement, infuriated by this apparent lack of interest in helping the Villagers—Toronto's hospitals were notorious for their indignant response to hip youth and their health issues—was also dumbfounded that the Province wouldn't pay for the needles necessary to measure the spread of the illness.[60] "We're talking about maybe 1000 dollars," he explained recently. "We were also talking about an epidemic that we were trying to nip in the bud. That's the whole purpose—we're going to nip this fucking thing in the bud. [Hepatitis] is a drag!"[61] In the end, Women's College Hospital found the money to buy the needles, but not before Clement, enraged

by the apathy he had witnessed in the meeting, had alerted the local press to the situation.[62]

Trailer played a central role in the effort to contain the hepatitis outbreak, being (with The Grab Bag, a popular convenience store catering to local hippies) among the first spots in the district to offer free testing for the disease.[63] The incendiary leaflet, it must be assumed, was designed to coax certain otherwise indolent Villagers into action on this potentially devastating issue. Yet, in constructing the possibility of a hepatitis epidemic as a kind of foregone conclusion, the flyer acted as the first successful *anti*-advertisement to the district. And, Clement's alerting of the media both to the flyer and to the hepatitis testing stations helped to re-establish boundaries around Yorkville, and to re-enforce the perception that it was a community in crisis. With this abrupt hepatitis epidemic came the opportunity to establish Yorkville as a new variety of sick community: Yorkville was no longer figuratively ill, it was now quite literally *infected*.

Almost immediately following the initial newspaper articles of 3 August, the Villagers began to evacuate. Although the first report in the *Toronto Star* made it plain that the suspected cause of the outbreak was needle-sharing, it also explicitly claimed (incorrectly) that intravenous drug use was a typical hippie behavior: "Ten doctors from two Toronto hospitals spent last night in Yorkville looking for cases of a form of Hepatitis *often found among hippies*. The disease is believed to be transmitted by hippies using contaminated hypodermic needles."[64] (emphasis added) The *Globe and Mail* went a step further, referring to an apparent epidemic of "a little known variety [of the disease] that has come to be known as *hippie Hepatitis*."[65] (emphasis added)

Meanwhile, many members of the Toronto Police, hugely overrepresented in the Yorkville district in their efforts to curb illegal drug activity, vandalism, and underage vagrancy, became concerned that their beat was hazardous to their health. When the Yorkville detail lined up to get their prophylaxes against infection, photographers from local newspapers caught the images that would define the episode: a throng of uniformed police (read: the establishment) queuing up to get the shots needed to protect them from infection (read: the counterculture).[66] To the casual observer, there was no question: Yorkville was indeed infected with a hazardous and unpredictable social disease.

The only way to safely visit the Village was by getting immunized against its pernicious effects.

As the Trailer and the Grab Bag established their testing stations, reporters and observers from various media took up their vantage points in the Village.[67] And, because frenzied reports of a probable epidemic were floated by doctors and police even before the results of blood testing came back, reporters were left with a very easy front page headline for the following Tuesday morning: "Hepatitis among Villagers now an Epidemic, Doctors Fear."[68]

Toronto was about to get a crash course in epidemiology. A combination of Serum Hepatitis (today known as Hepatitis B) and the more communicable Infectious Hepatitis (Hepatitis A) was apparently found in up to 20 Villagers on that first weekend.[69] While the Serum form of the liver disease had been expected (as it was well-known to be communicated through needle-sharing and sexual contact), the second form was not. The evident presence of Infectious Hepatitis, which could be spread through contaminated food, water, human contact, and a variety of other media, threatened to move the epidemic beyond the boundaries of hippiedom.[70]

A.R.J. Boyd, the Medical Officer of Health for the City of Toronto, was quick to make it clear in press statements that Infectious Hepatitis had yet to be conclusively found in Yorkville, and he emphasized that until it was found, the word *epidemic* was being misused. "And," he cautioned, "the word epidemic is itself sometimes misleading. All the word means is that a great many more cases of a certain disease are showing up than is usual. So far, that is not the case with Hepatitis. After all, there have been some years we've had 500 reported cases of the disease."[71]

Rather than heeding his words, reportage of the apparent epidemic continued unabated—and Dr. Boyd, along with those City Councilors who took up his line, was castigated for dragging his feet.[72] Even on 8 August, when Boyd was forced to admit that two cases of Infectious Hepatitis had been conclusively found among the Villagers, he still refused to bend to pressure from the press (and, increasingly, the community at large) to dub the situation an epidemic. He also attempted to clarify the muddied results of the initial rounds of testing in Yorkville, which had come back variously reporting up to 500 possible cases of the disease: "[These] blood tests

are inconclusive," he stressed. "The same test could be positive if someone were beaten up and badly bruised. It just shows tissue damage. I want more than that. The picture is still not at all clear."[73]

Suzanne DePoe (sister of David DePoe) had a unique perspective on the "epidemic." As one of a very few full-time volunteers at Trailer, DePoe was alerted to the prospect of a hepatitis predicament very early on. She recalls:

> What happened is that they were getting some sick kids in [Keyl's] clinic with liver functions off, and they figured out it was Hepatitis, and they knew that because of the way [hippies] lived in communal houses and probably the hygiene wasn't that great and Hep A spread so easily that they had to get them [tested]. So, that was my next job: pinching sick kids off the street and getting them into the clinic for blood tests.[74]

But, her proximity to the disease—she had, for weeks prior to August 1968, been working with the Villagers who came to Trailer seeking help and advice—proved to be a problem when, very early on in the development of the outbreak in August, she was counted among the two initial cases of Infectious Hepatitis:

> And then I got Hepatitis. I got taken out just as it got big. You see, I was getting a blood test once a week because I was dealing with them [sick Villagers]. And the minute my liver function went off the tiniest bit they whacked me into isolation in Women's College [Hospital]. And there was a picture of me in the Globe and Mail in bed in the hospital.[75]

And so, the young woman became a cause célèbre for a media and public who were, by now, very familiar with the name DePoe, and its close association with the Yorkville scene. Clement is quick to remind us, "needless to say [their father, CBC newsman] Norman DePoe was decidedly pissed off!"[76]

Meanwhile, the nefarious tourist activity that was *Yorkville* was being explicitly re-constructed in media reports, and likely in the minds of many frightened

Torontonians, as potentially lethal. Just *going* to Yorkville could kill you. The *Toronto Star*, on 7 August, underlined this characterization with a dire front page pronouncement: "In theory, any visitor to Yorkville who ate in a café, bought any object or contacted *any person*, may have been exposed to the disease, a liver infection which can eventually lead to death."[77] (emphasis added)

The three local newspapers (the *Toronto Star*, the *Toronto Telegram*, and the *Globe and Mail*), not often in agreement on the Village scene, now united in painting a grim portrait of a community in peril. As the apparent numbers of victims escalated—almost 150 people, including as many as 6 policemen, were reportedly felled by the disease by 9 August—editorials appeared, critical of the City for its slow response to such an obvious catastrophe.[78] Before the end of the week, the Province had taken over the investigation "because people in Yorkville may have spread the disease outside the city of Toronto."[79] While Dr. Boyd attempted to quell the fears of a frightened public by blaming the press for overzealous and inflammatory reportage,[80] downtown hospitals were overrun by spooked kids, "desperate" for a test.[81] Fear, knowing no boundaries, was hardly confined to Toronto: it was reported that three days after the initial accounts of the Yorkville outbreak, a public swimming pool in London, Ontario (some 200 kilometres away), was being drained as a "precautionary measure."[82]

By the following Monday, the Province of Ontario was formally asking the public to "stay out of Yorkville," and appealing to them to "satisfy their curiosity at a later date."[83] Businesses began to suffer. Coffee houses and rock'n'roll clubs sat empty. There were reports that, even in 30-degree heat, cars passing through Yorkville were rolling up their windows.[84] One Villager, who provided the pseudonym Luke the Drifter, explained to the *Star* that hippies were being treated as pariahs, more then ever before, on the streets surrounding the Yorkville district: "All sorts of guys are swearing at you if you come near them. They all think you're going to give them Hepatitis. One lady screamed at me, 'Don't breathe near me, you ——!'"[85] On 12 August, York Council voted five to four to ask the Province to close off Yorkville to the general public—establishing a makeshift quarantine—and to order all of the restaurants and coffee houses in the district to close down.[86]

Fears of diseased hippies spreading their infection throughout Metropolitan Toronto, along with an apparent desire to keep countercultural youth in one place, culminated in the scuppering of a project to build a badly-needed youth shelter at the corner of Queen and Bathurst Streets, about four kilometres from Yorkville. Originally *for* the project, if only grudgingly and apprehensively, the Queen-Bathurst Merchant Association had now turned vehement in its attempts to quash the venture. Armed with the profoundly effective (apparent) evidence that hippies carried an infectious and lethal disease, the Association petitioned Mayor Dennison and Controller Margaret Campbell to shut down the plan. "We said we would go along with the shelter," explained George Starr, president of the Merchant Association, "but that was before the sickness."[87]

Even local celebrities found themselves subject to a new kind of prejudice. Three members of the psychedelic rock band Kensington Market, among the biggest draws on the Toronto scene, were asked to leave a coffee shop on Bloor St. (at Lothian Mews, just adjacent to Yorkville) because they looked like Villagers. "I don't care too much about who we serve," explained Stephen Kefkoto, manager of the Coffee Mill, "[b]ut, you know—the Hepatitis scare. They were obviously Village residents. Usually they don't come in here."[88]

For businesses in the Village, it was not so much a question of turning people away as *attracting* them. On the first Friday after the outbreak was reported, it was estimated that the crowds on Yorkville Ave. were but one-tenth their usual size. Coffee houses and other hangouts were sparsely populated, and dining spots were reporting a dip (by up to 80 percent) in reservations. As Marilyn McHugh (of the Penny Farthing coffee house) put it, "The whole street is down."[89]

By 15 August, blame for the outbreak was ascribed to the lax laws, which had allowed Yorkville to become a hotbed for infection. As a result, City Controllers concluded that "stronger laws [were] needed to put down hippies." Now afforded the opportunity that many on the Board of Control had been looking for—a viable reason (and workable mandate) to rid Yorkville of its hippie population—the move to clean up the district was underway. "As strange as it may seem," speculated Controller Fred Beavis, "this [hepatitis outbreak] may have done a lot of good for Yorkville."[90]

501

In a sense, Beavis' assumption was correct: hip Yorkville was beginning its long goodbye, fading into the murky twilight of the late 1960s. The hepatitis outbreak was just another signpost along the way, but it was the one which clearly marked the beginning of the end. Following almost a month of constant media and municipal announcements that it was the epicentre of an incurable infection, hip Yorkville would never recover.

Yet the truth is that the famous Yorkville hepatitis "epidemic" never really took place. When, more than a year late, the Report by the Co-ordinating Committee for the Ontario Department of Health was published, it admitted that the vast majority of the (very few) cases of the illness were easily traced back to the unsanitary practices of intravenous drug users, never more than a small minority in the Yorkville scene, the basic point that Dr. Boyd made all along. In fact, the Final Report concluded that, of the total 32 patients hospitalized for probable hepatitis during the outbreak, "the 27 who were classified as *probable* [Serum] Hepatitis and the three as *possible* Hepatitis used drugs intravenously. The remaining two, who did not use drugs intravenously, [were] classified as probable infectious Hepatitis."[91] According to one clinical account which was included in the Final Report, only 25 patients with a diagnosis of hepatitis were admitted to Women's College Hospital during the period 3 July to 30 September—a period three times the length of the "epidemic" episode. Of these 25 patients, 20 were male, and the age range spanned 16–27, with a mean age of 19. Only *one* of these patients did not use any drugs, but the remaining 24 *all* used amphetamines intravenously.[92]

All of the turmoil and confusion, the fear and anxiety, it would seem, was massively embellished.[93] There was no epidemic—rather, there was, as the Medical Officer of Health had maintained throughout the three-week panic, a minor outbreak that was virtually confined to intravenous drug users, and had nothing to do with the water, food, or sanitary practices of the vast majority of Villagers.[94]

The Aftermath

In late summer 1968, amid the din of the hepatitis "epidemic," *Canadian Welfare* magazine published the substance of a speech given to the Women's Canadian Club by hippiedom's most famous middle-class ally, June Callwood. Discouraged, and nearly

hopeless, Callwood's speech unleashed upon her audience of upper middle-class, mostly white and Christian women, a hail of horrific and damning revelations. Opening with a reminder that she had spent the past months playing landlady to Digger House, a shelter designed to house the kind of young people who "disgust" her audience. Callwood's agenda appears to have been to attack her addressees for holding to the erroneous belief that all hip youth were responsible for their lot as street kids. Not so, she explained, before going on to describe these "children" as "society-damaged." The fault for their predicament was, according to her assessment, anyone's but their own.

"Let me tell you who they are," Callwood began:

> They are the loneliest, most frightened people in this land [...] They are the children of alcoholics and prostitutes and child-beaters; they are the children no one wanted in the first place; they are the children who went to eleven schools and lived in 14 foster homes and can call any woman mother; they are the children of middle class parents whose own despair and ambition and anxiety occupied all their attention, with nothing left over for a child; and of the parents who truly thought that love is something that can be given in the form of toys and television sets.[95]

According to Callwood, this "damaged" youth culture, comprised of unfortunates from all social classes, all walks of life, was "the visible mark of our disgrace [as Canadians]."

But Callwood's pronouncements, vividly realized and rhetorically insistent, were based on a contentious view that "the original hippie movement" (which she brazenly romanticizes) had come and gone, leaving behind a "*new wave* of badly mangled and desolate kids who now form the core of the movement." (emphasis added) Her argument (which she maintains today) was that these "original hippies"—like the "true hippies" mentioned by David DePoe, above—were concerned with "trying to find room somewhere on this crowded earth and practice simple generosity, from the heart and to strangers [sic]," while these new hip kids were merely troubled pretenders to that fine pursuit. "They have the aspiration to be beautiful, loving people," she explained, "but their mental and emotional faculties are almost destroyed. They could imitate, but they could never understand" those "original hippies" and their lofty goals.[96]

Callwood's case, that whatever the hippies had represented had evaporated sometime after the summer of 1967, although surely refused by many Villagers who were offended by this generalization, gained credence in the context of a post-hepatitis Yorkville. By mid-summer 1969, the conservative daily *The Toronto Telegram* even went so far as to declare that Yorkville's "hippies are gone." The article, entitled "Yorkville Re-visited," took a retrospective view of a by-gone era, an era which was said to have reached its zenith during the highly publicized "Siege of Yorkville" in August 1967, that two-week period characterized by sit-ins, confrontation, and police overzealousness. But, at the *Telegram,* this zenith had come into focus only with a little perspective: "[L]ooking back now from the distance of two years, the famous hippie sit-down in the middle of Yorkville Ave takes on another coloration. It seems, if anything at all, rather quaint."[97] Written on the occasion of the end of the last of the criminal trials of participants in the protest—David DePoe had been recently acquitted of two counts of causing a disturbance—the article reads like a sinister eulogy. Casually reducing the phenomenon of Yorkville youth culture to a quadrumvirate of interrelated (perhaps identical) shorthand, the article related, but certainly did not lament, that since "David DePoe is gone, the hippies are gone, the Yorkville of 1967 is over, [and] the trials have ended," Yorkville can now move on.[98]

If, in 1966, one could be said to be performing "Yorkville" by donning hippie garb and smoking drugs in suburban Lawrence Park, by 1969 to do so would simply be to perform as "hippie." The idea of a specific hip space was losing relevance, ceasing to carry any deeper meaning. Performances of hipness—from the outlandish clothing to the heretofore underground psychedelic music, from the spread of dope through public schools and universities to the liberalization of sexual relations amongst young people—were no longer specifically tied to Yorkville in the public imagination.

And so, the notion of a "Yorkville youth" took on new connotations in these years, as people like Callwood emphasized the essential differences between the new Villagers and the so-called original

wave of hip youth who had colonized the Village. No longer was "Yorkville youth" shorthand for "hippie"; by the end of the summer of 1968, it had become synonymous with a certain needy, distressed and alienated portion of the counterculture: its homeless, its disturbed, its junk-sick, its infected. And the truth is that from 1968 to 1970, as developers tightened their hold on the district, as police managed to arrest ever more Villagers on dope offences, as disease and addiction were spread thick as oil on water over the dwindling numbers of young people who haunted Yorkville's all-night restaurants and cafés, the Village community fell into a complicated, and often bleak downward spiral into depression.

Moreover, Yorkville was so closely associated with hip behaviour and identity, an association especially evident in the local press' emphasis on "Villagers" and "Yorkville Youth" as specific identity categories, the death of the Yorkville hippie scene, after the events of August 1968, was read by many observers as the death of the hippie phenomenon itself. It didn't help that most of the Villagers who would otherwise have been spending their days and nights very visibly on Yorkville Avenue and Cumberland Street had found a new, invisible home at nearby Rochdale College. The highly experimental College—an 18-storey apartment complex and "free school" completed in 1968 at the corner of Bloor and Huron Streets, not half a kilometre from Yorkville—began to gobble up Villagers immediately upon its inception in September 1968 (just as the hepatitis scare wound down).

Off the streets, effectively erased from the visage of the city, Rochdale's hip scene operated as a (mostly) self-contained, even self-reflective unit. Throughout the 1960s the Village scene may have been *metaphorically* cut off from Toronto, tied to a map of meaning that treated it as a circumscribed island of difference within the wider cityscape; but Rochdale actually *was* cut off. Its inhabitants cloistered (some rarely ever left the building!), under a kind of self-imposed exile from the wider community, Rochdale in some ways represents the failure of integrationist politics in the hip world. But, in a very real sense, it *was* the end of the Yorkville scene.[99] Yorkville increasingly appeared as a hip ghost town, its hippies suddenly less conspicuous, less obtrusive, no longer milling about on the sidewalks of Toronto's tiny boutique sector in all their numbers.

503

The hepatitis epidemic (that never was) offered depth and authority to the view that Yorkville and the hippies were played out. The "true hippies" were gone, and the new ones were sick, infected, "damaged." The petals thus off the flower, the Yorkville activity was associated more and more with the new Villagers, people like "Beatle Bill" and "Murray the Speed Freak," well-known to many in the scene toward the end as exemplars of the scourge of speed (methedrine) and indigence in the Village. According to Suzanne DePoe:

> Beatle Bill was the most famous speed freak in Yorkville. Oh, and Murray the Speed Freak. There was Murray and Beatle Bill. They're probably dead. They were characters around the Village, so people knew them. They were social. Well, Beatle Bill wasn't social. He was just famous because he did so much fucking meth that nobody could figure out how he was walking around, you know? And his teeth were rotten. It's what meth does. His general health was terrible. These guys were young, too!

In post-hepatitis Yorkville, with Villagers such as these now carrying the "counterculture" mantle, allies of the scene slipped into the shadows, eventually disappearing from sight altogether.

The end days of hip Yorkville saw the hurried development of hotels and other commercial enterprises, further distancing the Village from its quaint early 1960s atmosphere. Rents went up, forcing more artists, students, and otherwise under-funded young people further away from the little district. Police crackdowns on drug use (especially speed) were stepped up; biker violence was more common, and gang rapes at their hands were being reported with alarming frequency.[100] When the *Health of Yorkville* report (begun as an offshoot of the hepatitis study of 1968–1969) came out in 1970, it left little doubt as to the sorry state of the majority of the locals it surveyed. But, it also maintained that whatever Yorkville had been prior to the hepatitis outbreak of August, 1968, and whoever its Villagers had been, *it* was no longer anything of the sort, and *they* were all gone.[101] Into the 1970s, Yorkville was quickly developed into the very district the City Fathers had always wanted

it to become: a bastion of consumerism and conspicuous affluence.

Ultimately, the hepatitis "epidemic" serves as a lesson in civil responsibility. How often must we fall prey to such "epidemics," such media-driven panics over impending calamity designed to buoy conservative policy initiatives? In this final major episode in hip Yorkville's brief narrative, we see the destructive power of a media-driven system (merely in its adolescence in the late-1960s) which, however unconsciously, uses fear to product political results. For fear, like liquid, runs downhill; from a trickle to a torrent, its momentum grows steadily.

Be mindful of what you drink.

Notes

The author wishes to express his thanks to Karen Dubinsky and Ian McKay for their commitment to this project. This article was prepared with support from the Social Sciences and Humanities Research Council of Canada.

1. Portions of this article appeared, in another form, in the *Toronto Star*, 28 May, 2006.

2. For a problematic, but comprehensive anthropological study of such identity categories, see Reginald G. Smart, et al., *The Yorkville Subculture: A Study of the Life Styles and Interactions of Hippies and Non-Hippies*, prepared from the field notes of Gopala Alampur, (Toronto: Addiction Research Foundation, 1969). For our purposes below, I shall employ such identity categories with care, recognizing their mutability while appreciating their centrality and relevance to the scene at the time. Virtually every one of my interview subjects painted Villagers inside of these four frames; only when pressed did they admit the instability of the categories.

3. Hip and hipness are difficult, ephemeral categories. However, they are used below with a deliberate hand, and should be defined before we continue. The word 'hip' is, like the word 'cool', ancient black American argot which was, through a complicated process of cultural appropriation, brought into urban white North America in the early twentieth century. Hip, from the Wolof *hepi* (to see, to have one's eyes open), is a rare surviving slave term, and clearly retained significance among slaves living through the persistent physical threat that was the 'peculiar institution'. Thus 'hipness' refers,

in its original and purest definition, to an ability to understand, to be aware, to be enlightened. Hip youth, then, in the Yorkville context, were those who sought out new ways of understanding, awareness, and enlightenment (often through drug use, alternative sexual relations and experience, and a rejection of material wealth and culture). See Clarence Major, *Juba to Jive: a Dictionary of African American Slang* (Harmondsworth: Penguin, 1994). See also John Leland, *Hip: The History* (New York: Echo, 2004) for a fun, wide-ranging and informative account of the complicated process of hipness and American culture. It should be noted that Leland's book rather unapologetically glosses over the 1960s youth movement for no apparent reason.

4. This frame can be observed in at least three retrospective treatments of the district. See, for example, Doug Owram, *Born at the Right Time: A History of the Baby-Boom Generation* (Toronto: University of Toronto Press, 1996), 210–15; Myrna Kostash, *Long Way From Home* (Toronto: James Lorimer and Co., 1980), 107–44; Pierre Berton, *1967: Canada's Turning Point* (Toronto: Seal Books, 1997), 163–92. This article is part of a continuing project, a Ph.D. dissertation entitled "Making the Scene: Yorkville and the Toronto Counterculture, 1960–1970." Through my research, I have uncovered a variety of episodes and other evidence that counterbalances this romantic memory of pre-1967 Yorkville.

5. *Globe and Mail* (April 7, 1967), 1. While a player, Apps was famously pure and chaste in his lifestyle and manner. "Maple Leafs owner Conn Smythe would often introduce him at banquets as 'Syl Apps, my captain, who doesn't drink, smoke, or swear.'" Salvatore Ianni, *Syl Apps: A Maple Leafs Legend,* <www.penaltybox.com/legends/syl_apps.html. 3/15/2001>, (viewed 22 April 2006).

6. This category is problematic, and prone to the vicissitudes of opinion. However, David DePoe's own romantic definition of what comprised the "true hippie" (altruism, individualism, and activism) harmonizes with most others from the period: "A true hippy [*sic*] is somebody who has dropped out of normal society because he doesn't like the dehumanization and de-personalization that goes on. Having dropped out of all that jazz he is actively engaged in trying to create a new society with more meaning. You never find a true hippy [*sic*] just sitting around. He's talking or organizing or working.

He's got something going for himself ...," *Voice of the Annex* (Autumn 1967): 1. In many ways, this paper (and my dissertation) aims to unpack this notion of "authentic" Village identity.

7. DePoe was profiled on the cover of the *Toronto Star*-produced *Star Weekly Magazine* in September 1967. He was given the moniker "Super Hippie" in a move he now refers to as a betrayal. David DePoe, interview by author, 20 December 2004.

8. Trailer was housed in a *trailer*, parked in an empty lot on Avenue Road, at the corner of Yorkville Ave. Run under the auspices of the Jewish Family and Child Service. Trailer was among the first street clinics in Toronto. According to Suzanne DePoe, who ran Trailer in 1968 (until she was felled by hepatitis): "My job was to basically be a referral point. So, it just required some basic organizational skills and smarts. Like, what we were there to do was to get underage kids off the streets, get bad trips treated, get them down to Queen Street [Mental Hospital] to get treated. Get people with medical problems into the hospital, and into the clinic at Women's College [Hospital]. There was a lot of V-D in the Village. Like that. So, that's what I was doing. People would, you know, stagger into the Trailer and I would deal with them." Suzanne DePoe, interview by author, 14 March 2006.

9. For a good, tight overview and history of the relationship between a counterculture ghetto and health crises, see David E. Smith, et al., "The Health of Haight-Ashbury" in Howard S. Becker, ed., *Culture and Civility in San Francisco* (San Francisco: Transaction Inc. 1971), 77–100.

10. The three Toronto newspapers (the *Star*, the *Telegram*, and the *Globe and Mail*) had their own particular takes on the Village scene throughout the 1960s, and it is dangerous to lump them together. If, in general, the *Star* was cautiously liberal, the *Globe* centrist, and the *Telegram* conservative, each of them offered at least one staff writer or editorialist who frustrated these general expectations. For instance, the *Star* had Ron Haggart, unrelenting champion of the scene throughout the 1960s; the *Globe* had Michael Valpy, himself a Villager and friend to the Diggers; and the *Telegram* had Sheila Gormley, who would openly criticize her paper's anti-hip stance in a 1970 book on youth and drug use. See Marcel Martel, *Not This Time: Canadians, Public Policy and the Marijuana Question,*

505

1961–1975 (Toronto: University of Toronto Press, 2006), 15–16. However, in the case of the hepatitis epidemic, all three outlets reacted with a similarly exaggerated response.

11. E.W.R. Best, "Introduction," *Hepatitis in Yorkville, 1968: Report of the Co-ordinating Committee* (Ontario Department of Health, 15 September 1969), 4.

12. The related processes of suburbanization and immigration verily defined Toronto's demographic shifts in the post-war period. For a detailed discussion of the distribution of immigrants in Toronto following World War II (and of the variety of challenges they were made to meet), see Franca Iacovetta, *Such Hardworking People: Italian Immigrants in Postwar Toronto* (Montreal and Kingston: McGill-Queen's University Press, 1993). On suburbanization, see Richard Harris' excellent *Creeping Conformity: How Canada Became Suburban, 1900–1960* (Toronto: University of Toronto Press, 2004) for an account of the development of "corporate" suburbs in the post-war period. For a synthetic examination of these key processes, see Veronica Strong-Boag, "Home Dreams: Women and the Suburban Experiment in Canada, 1945–1960," *Canadian Historical Review* 72, 4 (1991): 471–504.

13. Mary Millichamp, daughter of a prominent Toronto family, opened a pioneering restaurant in Yorkville in the late 1940s, only to be admonished by her high society friends. As she told a journalist in the early 1960s, her friends swore up and down that they would "never patronize anything 'on that street!'" Quoted in Barbara Elizabeth Key, "The Growth of Yorkville" (B.A. thesis, York University, 1967), 32.

14. Clifford Collier, interview by author, 15 June 2006.

15. The "carriage trade" was really a euphemism for upper-class female shopping and consumption. The predominance of expensive gown shops and artisans' boutiques in the Village throughout the 1960s suggests that many of the people frequenting the district would have been counted among the wealthier women in the city and beyond. For example, Yorkville, by 1967, was home to Helmar of London (a dress designing salon boasting a selection of imported fabrics and nine in-house seamstresses, offering gowns for between $100 and $1000); Pot Pourri (a similar, but somewhat less dear, dress designing salon); the Recamier Boutique (the owner of which traveled to Europe twice each year to buy new gowns); along with a number of "sportswear, hats, furs, and wig boutiques as well as several *haute couture* salons for styling hair, [all of which] cater[ed] to the female customer." Moreover, bath boutiques, candle shops, and stores devoted to imported merchandise and curios from India, Persia, and Japan helped fill out the short blocks. Key, "Growth of Yorkville," 41.

16. Beat identity, knotty and defiant of simple definition, must be understood as the dominant influence on what would come to be known as the Hippie identity. However, any over-emphasis on the sway Beat Toronto had in their immediate time period (say, 1957–1962) would be foolish. At their height, the Toronto Beats were but a tiny manifestation of youth identity; they were among the most fascinating to the established order, perhaps, but were by no means the vanguard of some immediate groundswell. Their greatest contemporary contribution, and the contribution with which this study is most concerned, was the Beat propensity for new, exciting, and otherwise under-appreciated innovations in the world of art, film, music, and literature. Their experimentalism contributed to an atmosphere, in those few establishments that catered to their ilk, of spontaneity and cacophonous energy. For an investigative report on Toronto's Beat scene, see *Toronto Star* (3 March 1959). For a detailed and important study of the Beats (in America), see Leerom Medovoi, *Rebels: Youth and the Cold War Origins of Identity* (Durham: Duke University Press, 2005), especially Chapter Six.

17. See Leland, *Hip*.

18. For example, a gay coffee house (The Mousehole), run by Clifford Collier, was a popular Yorkville haunt, and Collier recalls there being generally positive gay-straight relations in the early 1960s. Clifford Collier, interview by author, 5 June 2006. The "Greasers" (working-class youth, usually of southern or eastern European extraction), for example, had begun to drift through the scene at the same time as had their Beat counterparts. Throughout the 1960s, in fact, Greasers comprised a key identity group in the Yorkville scene, despite persistent reports emphasizing the exclusively hippie identity of the Village. For a subjective, but instructive insider's history of the Greaser scene, see James E. Smith, "I Wish I Was A Fish: A Search For

Live Options in Yorkville" (unpublished memoir, 1972). Throughout the 1960s, Smith ran a Drop-In Centre at St-Paul's-Avenue Road United Church, on the periphery of the Village.

19. Dave DePoe recalls the early, Beat-influenced scene: "When I first started to go there in '63 it was very Beat, basically. Sort of like: you go there and you listen to poetry, music, and y'know. That year I had a friend who was a poet in residence at U of T and together we started going to Yorkville, to this coffee house where a poet could just get up and read something and then somebody would sing a couple of songs." David DePoe, interview by author, 29 December 2004.

20. Throughout the 1960s, and especially after 1966, the words "hippie" and "Yorkville" were used interchangeably in the local media: "Yorkville youth" was shorthand for hippie.

21. In making this claim, I am following gender theorist Judith Butler, and in particular her assertion that "there is no gender identity behind the expressions of gender ..., identity is performatively constituted by the very 'expressions' that are said to be its results." In her view, gender is not a stable, foundational feature of one's identity, but rather the expected manner in which one might act. Gender (like other apparently immutable aspects of identity) is a role to be performed. The common-sense performances of gender, race, and class correspond to hegemonic ideology which suggests (or, in some cases, decrees) the manner in which to act within the boundaries of normalcy. See Judith Butler, *Gender Trouble: Feminism and the Subversion of Identity* (London: Routledge, 1990), 25. See also Butler's elaboration on these themes in *Bodies That Matter* (New York: Routledge, 1993).

22. As Joel Lobenthal has suggested (echoing arguments made by Judith Butler, among other identity theorists), in contrast to the more staid fashions of the 1950s, in the 1960s "the individual remade himself daily, trying out new stances of dress and behavior, internalizing some, [while] keeping others at arm's length as theatrical alter egos." Joel Lobenthal, *Radical Rags* (New York: Abbeville Books, 2003), 217.

23. For a lively history of the Yorkville coffee house and music scene, see Nicholas Jennings, *Before the Goldrush: Flashbacks to the Dawn of the Canadian Sound* (Toronto: Penguin Books, 1997).

24. A cousin to Beat experiments in uniting disparate forms of art into messy harmony, neo-theatre events called "Happenings" were increasingly popular in the Yorkville of the early 1960s. Often held in local galleries such as the Isaacs' or the Sobot, but just as habitually held at apartments, lofts, and coffee houses such as the Gaslight or the 71 Club in the budding scene, "Happenings" were designed around neo-Dadaist preoccupations with juxtaposition, surrealism, and disorder. A transparent attempt to refigure the expected manner (grave and conventional as it is) of viewing art in silent, empty, cold galleries and museums, "Happenings" were designed to err on the side of chaos. Denise Leclerc and Pierre Dessurealt, *The Sixties in Canada* (Ottawa: National Gallery of Canada, 2005), 167.

25. Doug Owram establishes this point at every turn in his study of the effect of the Baby Boom on Canadian society. Owram, *Born at the Right Time*.

26. A similar phenomenon occurred in late nineteenth-century London. See Judith R. Walkowitz, *City of Dreadful Delight* (Chicago: University of Chicago Press, 1992), 20.

27. In May 1964, a Village of Yorkville Association sponsored Festival was brought to an embarrassing conclusion as police and young people sparred in the streets when the milling crowds refused to disperse; see *Toronto Star* (16 May 1964). Six months later, a massive sing-along in the street became another bloated fracas as police tried to clear Yorkville of revellers; see *Toronto Star* (19 October 1964), and *Globe and Mail* (19 October 1964).

28. Even City Councillors took to patrolling the streets, both to prove that the police presence was maintaining order, and as part of a fact-finding project designed to "curb rowdyism," the misleading term widely used by local media to describe hip youth in 1964 and 1965; see *Globe and Mail* (31 May 1965).

29. See *Globe and Mail* (10 April 1965). Motorcycles were a weird choice. Although some biker gangs (especially the Satan's Choice and the Vagabonds) were beginning to hang around the area in the spring of 1965, they hardly constituted a major thrust in the burgeoning hip scene.

30. *Globe and Mail* (28 May 1965).

31. Walkowitz refers to similar phenomenon as "urban spectatorship." I have chosen to redefine this category in order to emphasize the significance of

507

foreignness in the case of Yorkville. See Walkowitz, *City of Dreadful Delights,* 15–24.

32. The role of young women in Yorkville as victims of hip sexual depravity was assumed, expected, and underlined in most every study of the district after 1965. The truth behind this position is debatable, largely because it relies on a simplistic view of sexual power, and the conservative assumption that a young woman's sexual innocence was to be protected at all costs. As Alice Echols, Beth Bailey, and a growing number of other astute commentators on the hip 1960s have underlined, sex and gender in the context of the "sexual revolution" must be viewed through the prism of an expanding moral panic over female sexual agency. See Alice Echols, *Scars of Sweet Paradise: The Life and Times of Janis Joplin* (New York: Henry Holt, 200), especially Chapters Four and Five. See also Beth Bailey, "Sex as a Weapon," in Peter Braunstein, ed. *Imagine Nation* (New York: Routledge, 2002), 305–24.

33. By the mid-1960s, white slavery narratives began to colour the discourse surrounding young women in the Yorkville scene. As ever more young women turned to Yorkville for fun and community, the assumption that they were being held powerless, under the sway of their hippie (male) oppressors, forced to take drugs and have "free" sex, cropped up with increasing frequency. This frame was particularly apparent in the autumn of 1967—for a concise example of the association between Yorkville and sexual violence/depravity, see *Globe and Mail* (2 November 1967). For more on the white slavery narratives, and a historical example of their use to frame illicit drug use in Canada, see Catherine Carstairs, *Jailed for Possession* (Toronto: University of Toronto Press, 2006).

34. *Globe and Mail* (2 November 1967).

35. George Chauncey, in his landmark work on gay culture in New York City, demonstrates the multiplicity (and the overlapping) of such *de facto* foreign zones inside the modern cityscape, a characteristic which enables Others to float in and out of local and foreign contexts, and which underlines the mutability of spacial meaning. George Chauncey, *Gay New York: Gender, Urban Culture, and the Making of the Gay Male World, 1890–1940* (New York: Basic Books, 1994).

36. See especially, Jacques Derrida, *The Ear of the Other*, Peggy Kamuf, et al., trans. (Lincoln: University of Nebraska Press, 1998).

37. Crucially, as Judith Butler has elaborated, "[The] name, as a convention, has a generality and a historicity that is in no sense radically singular, even though it is understood to exercise the power of conferring singularity." Judith Butler, *Excitable Speech* (New York: Routledge, 1997), 29. In this way, appelation is a profoundly powerful act—it is both to endow a thing with a recognizable individuality and to establish its social and political (not to mention historical) context/meaning. It must be understood to have one and many meanings simultaneously, each politically and socially constructed, each bound to interpretations of common-sense in a particular context.

38. Peter Jackson, *Maps of Meaning* (New York: Routledge, 1993), 186.

39. For many, what they saw in Yorkville was precisely what they wanted to see: a hip wonderland, a subversive slum, fresh ground for business. The notion of tourism and of "the tourist's gaze" is, of course, appropriate here. As Karen Dubinsky has shown with regard to the tourist *über*-destination of Niagara Falls, the meaning of a particular destination is, at any given moment, as mutable and as shifting as sand or smoke. Karen Dubinsky, *The Second Greatest Disappointment: Honeymooning and Tourism at Niagara Falls* (New Brunswick, NJ: Rutgers University Press, 1999). See also John Urry, *The Tourist Gaze: Leisure and Travel in Contemporary Societies* (London: Sage, 1990).

40. Marcel Martel, in his recent study of marijuana legislation in the 1960s, focuses a great deal of his attention on Yorkville, as did most observers in the period. Yorkville acted as a crucible, a test tube for the study of marijuana and other drugs as young people devoured them. Martel's fascinating *Not This Time* offers an in-depth discussion of the meteoric rise of drug consumption among teens and young adults.

41. One recalls Michel Foucault's argument that madness has traditionally been understood as (or, at least associated with) the inability (or lack of desire) to be productive. Michel Foucault, "The Birth of the Asylum," in *The Foucault Reader*, Paul Rabinow, ed. (New York: Pantheon, 1984), 141–67. Indeed, the refusal of work was a central concern for conservative responses to (and disdain for) the Village scene. In the most extreme example, City Controller Herbert Orliffe famously suggested in the Spring of 1967 that Yorkville's "undesirables"

508

should be put into Work Camps: "If Work Camps were established ... it would instill in them a sense of discipline." *Globe and Mail* (12 May 1967).

42. This saga played out in the local newspapers between 27 May and 10 June 1965.

43. Allan Lamport made no bones about his disgust with the hippie scene. Indeed, his very role as a member of Toronto Council in 1967 and into 1968 can be reduced to his efforts to eradicate the hippies from Toronto. See *Christopher's Movie Matinee* (Mort Ransen, National Film Board of Canada, 1968). See also its sister film, *Flowers on a One-Way Street* (Robin Spry, National Film Board of Canada, 1968).

44. *Toronto Telegram* (17 April 1967).

45. English professor Leerom Medovoi has recently published an important book on this topic, a survey of the juvenile delinquent in the immediate postwar era and his centrality to the development of the youth as political project. This fascinating study carefully lays out the inexorable trajectory between the Beat rebel of the early 1950s to long-haired hippie of the late 1960s. Leerom Medovoi, *Rebels*.

46. "No longer simply an age category, youth became a metaphor, an attitude toward life, a state of mind that even adults could access." Peter Braunstein, "Forever Young: Insurgent Youth and the Sixties Culture of Rejuvenation," in Peter Braunstein, ed., *Imagine Nation* (New York: Routledge, 2002), 243.

47. Black Panther guru and astute cultural commentator Eldridge Cleaver voiced this particular trend very early on, while still in prison: "The characteristics of the white rebels which most alarm their elders—the long hair, the new dances, their love for Negro music, their use of marijuana, their mystical attitude toward sex—are all tools of their rebellion. They have turned these tools against the totalitarian fabric of American society—and they mean to change it." Eldridge Cleaver, *Soul on Ice* (New York: Delta, 1968), 75.

48. San Francisco's Summer of Love is best explored in Alice Echols' essay, "Hope and Hype in Sixties Haight-Ashbury," in her book *Shaky Ground: The Sixties and its Aftershocks* (New York: Columbia University Press, 2002), 17–50. See also Scott McKenzie's anticipatory anthem *San Francisco (Be Sure to Wear Some Flowers in Your Hair)* (Raven Records, 2004).

49. The transcript of the meeting reveals the centrality of this issue to Lamport: "But you refer to the word *dignity*. Now that's a very good word. A number of them there [as he points to the thirty-or-so hip onlookers] haven't been washed for weeks. Now, they aren't seeking dignity, are they?" See *Christopher's Movie Matinee*. One representative article explained the meeting very deliberately as a clashing of two distinct worldviews, effectively ridiculing them both, reducing the respective arguments to "Love and opting out vs. the need to wash." *Globe and Mail* (18 August 1967). See Owram, *Born at the Right Time*, and Berton, *1967* for overviews of this fractious two-month period.

50. In 1967, the National Film Board of Canada sent a film crew to Yorkville to study the district, its counterculture, and its nightlife. The plan was simple: observation of the Yorkville scene in an effort to explore the curious forms of social rebellion taking place in mid-town Toronto. However, while the crew was at work (filming what would become *Christopher's Movie Matinee*) it became clear to everyone that more was at stake here than just a collection of weird young people vying for freedom. As political tensions began to rise leading up to the protests of late August, another film crew was sent in (under the direction of the late Robin Spry) to chronicle the deepening conflict. When the late-August protests turned violent, there were allegations that the film crews had helped to incite the mêlée to enhance the entertainment value of their respective documentaries.

51. See, for example, *Globe and Mail* (4 November 1967); also see *Globe and Mail* (23 November 1967)

52. See Echols, *Shaky Ground*, 46.

53. In late August 1967, Lamport made this important comparison: "I took it upon myself to talk to these people called hippies. Now, they're not all bad, nor all the kids are bad. But, sometimes you get a cancer area ... and we're trying to ferret that out." *Christopher's Movie Matinee*.

54. Best, "Introduction," *Hepatitis in Yorkville*, 1.

55. June Callwood, interview by author, 11 March 2005.

56. Best, "Introduction," *Hepatitis in Yorkville*, 1.

57. Ibid.

58. Ibid., 2.

59. W.R. Clement, interview by author, 5 March 2006.

60. A full-blown study of the "Health of Yorkville," while allowing that some doctors and nurses (and hospitals in general) had begun to grapple with effective ways to approach the "complex task" of treating Yorkville youth, lamented that "others

509

appear to have no motivation to adapt to the problems created by widespread drug use and have virtually atrophied to the point of consistent irrelevance." This project was born of the confusion and interest surrounding the 1968 Hepatitis fracas. Merrijoy Kelner, et al., "The Health of Yorkville" (unpublished report for the Department of Behavioural Science, University of Toronto, 1970), 72.

61. W.R. Clement, interview by author, 5 March 2006.

62. Ibid. Clement, it should be stressed, still maintains that the exaggerated approach taken up by the medical authorities in their effort to contain the possible spread of Hepatitis was the right move.

63. For more on the role of Trailer in the daily lives of Villagers, see: John Kileeg, *Village Service Unit for Alienated Youth: The 'Trailer' in Yorkville* (Report to the Social Planning Council of Metropolitan Toronto, 1968).

64. *Toronto Star* (3 August 1968).

65. *Globe and Mail* (3 August 1968).

66. See, *Toronto Telegram* (8 August 1968); and *Toronto Star* (8 August 1968).

67. The shopkeepers at the Grab Bag had taken to wearing surgical masks, a point that the *Toronto Star* was quick to document. *Toronto Star* (8 August 1968).

68. *Toronto Star* (6 August 1968).

69. *Globe and Mail* (5 August 1968).

70. According to June Callwood, "Everybody had to get immunized. And, it was a nasty shot—my son Casey who was 6 or 7 years old at the time had to be immunized because he was with me all the time at Digger House." June Callwood, interview by author, 11 March 2005.

71. Best, "Introduction," *Hepatitis in Yorkville*, 1

72. *Globe and Mail* (7 August 1968).

73. Ibid. (8 August 1968). This story appeared on the front page.

74. Suzanne DePoe, interview by author, 14 March 2006.

75. Ibid.

76. W.R. Clement, interview by author, 5 March 2006. The DePoes are the children of Norman DePoe, then among the best-known journalists in the country, having been chief parliamentary correspondent since 1952, among other highly visible assignments. At this time, both children were estranged from their father. Still, his shadow was cast over them at every turn, hugely influencing the press' interest in following any story related to their name. See Allan Levine, Scrum Wars: The Prime Ministers and the Media (Toronto: Dundurn Books, 1993).

77. *Toronto Star* (7 August 1968).

78. Ibid. (10 August 1968).

79. Ibid.

80. Ibid. (8 August 1968).

81. Ibid. (9 August 1968).

82. Ibid.

83. Ibid. (12 August 1968).

84. Ibid. (13 August 1968)

85. Ibid.

86. *Globe and Mail* (13 August 1968).

87. *Toronto Star* (14 August 1968). Elsewhere in this edition, a headline ran, "Nail her death certificate all over Yorkville": a man whose wife had been felled by Hepatitis four years previously was anxious to do anything he could to alert people to the dangers of the disease. Neither he nor his unfortunate wife, it should be noted, had ever even been to Yorkville.

88. Ibid. (13 August 1968).

89. *Globe and Mail* (10 August 1968).

90. Ibid. (15 August 1968).

91. J.C. Sinclair, "Clinical Aspects, Section II: Review," *Hepatitis in Yorkville, 1968: Report of the Co-ordinating Committee* (Ontario Department of Health, 15 September 1969), 10.

92. Caroline Hetenyi and F.M. Hill, "Clinical Aspects. Section I: Clinical Report," *Hepatitis in Yorkville*, 1968, 7–8.

93. Callwood maintains that Anne Keyl did the right thing by raising the spectre of epidemic, because we will never know if she stopped it in its tracks by acting so deliberately. "But she got all the shots, she did it in the Trailer, set up a little clinic there, and everyone thought she was overreacting. But there *wasn't* an epidemic. So, did she nail it, or was she overreacting? We'll never know, but there wasn't an epidemic." June Callwood, interview by author, 11 March 2005.

94. The immediate fallout from the "epidemic" on Yorkville businesses and hangouts was, as was pointed out above, dire; but it was its combination with the more organic result of the end of summer vacation which served to devastate Yorkville merchants in the following months. According to Bill Clement, "It was the end of August; it was a natural event. Go home, have baths, get haircuts, go to school. I mean: these are *middle class* kids!" Bill Clement, interview by author, 5 March 2006.

95. June Callwood, "Hippies," *Canadian Welfare* 44 (September-October 1968): 17.

96. A year later, Callwood's writing on the scene had darkened to the point that her feelings of horror, frustration and helplessness were left exposed, stark, and naked at the fore. "The regulars now," she wrote late in 1969, "are those too tired to move. Plugged into drugs that are killing them slowly, they languish. They came to find love, but it's gone, and what can you do? As they decay, the police pick them over; so do the dealers who cut the product with poisons and the thugs who take the girls and sell them." June Callwood, "Digger House," in W.E. Mann, ed., *The Underside of Toronto* (Toronto: McClelland and Stewart, 1970), 123–30.

97. "Yorkville Re-Visited," *Toronto Telegram* (22 July 1969).

98. Ibid.

99. Rochdale became Toronto's new epicentre of hip—improving on Yorkville in a variety of ways (no cops, no parents, no politicians, no snow, no money, fewer hassles) and re-creating, apart from live music, the best of what the Village had to offer (plentiful drugs, abundant sex, like-minded young people, a sense of community). Rochdale was the pushbroom that swept through the Village in the late Sixties, carrying most everyone away. See the documentary *Dream Tower* (Ron Mann, National Film Board of Canada, 1994), for a limited but useful overview of the relationship between the end of the Yorkville scene and the rise of Rochdale. See also: David Sharpe, *Rochdale: The Runaway College* (Toronto: Anansi, 1987); Henry Mietkiewicz and Bob Mackowycz, *Dream Tower: The Life and Legacy of Rochdale College* (Toronto: McGraw-Hill Ryerson, 1988); Ralph Osborne, *From Someplace Else: A Memoir,* (Toronto: ECW Press, 2003).

100. David DePoe, in recalling the role of bikers in the scene after 1968 emphasized their taste for sexual violence. "The Vagabonds [motorcycle club], I mean, they did things that we didn't like. Like gang rape. You know? They would call girls a *splasher.* And they'd take her to their clubhouse and they'd, ten guys would, y'know, basically *fuck* her, and that's what they did." David DePoe, interview by author, 20 December 2004.

101. Kelner, et al., *The Health of Yorkville.*

■ Article 2: "And We've Got to Get Ourselves Back to the Garden": The Jesus People Movement in Toronto

Bruce Douville

I came upon a child of God;
He was walking along the road,
And I asked him, 'Where are you going?'
And this he told me:
"I'm going on down to Yasgur's farm;
I'm going to join in a rock 'n' roll band,
I'm going to camp out on the land,
And try and get my soul free."
We are stardust,
We are golden.
And we've got to get ourselves
Back to the garden.[1]

At its core, the counter-culture of the late 1960s and early 1970s was a movement for emotional and spiritual liberation. The young people of the generation immortalized in Joni Mitchell's "Woodstock" sought to free their souls, and articulate for themselves what it meant to be children of God. In William McLoughlin's words, the "young were far from irreligious, but they sang and marched to a different beat and saw the world in a different light."[2] They proclaimed a message of peace and love, and they denounced warmongering, consumerism, and an "establishment" system that they found de-humanizing. With spiritual values such as these, it is little wonder that many of them responded readily to Christianity.

The Jesus People movement[3] took place when many hippies turned from eastern mysticism to Pentecostal Christianity, from "free love" to the love of God, and from street pharmaceuticals to being "filled with the Spirit." In many ways, the movement was an extension of the counter-culture. The "Jesus freaks" retained the "hip" vocabulary, long hair, unorthodox clothing, psychedelic artwork and rock music. They also adopted the social institutions of the counter-culture: communes, coffeehouses, teach-ins, and rock festivals. These, however, are only surface similarities. The Jesus people shared much more fundamental characteristics with the hippies and student activists: their reaction against "technocracy" and materialism, their experiential focus, and their vitality. Equally as important were crucial differences between the two movements: the Jesus people were largely apolitical, unlike the counter-cultural left, and they explicitly rejected drug use, permissive sexuality, and the occult.

Both the Jesus movement and the secular counter-culture emerged in their prototypical forms in California in the late 1960s, and spread throughout the United States and Canada. In Toronto, the counter-culture manifested itself in the Yorkville hippie scene, Rochdale College, and activist organizations such as the Student Union for Peace Action.[4] The Jesus movement manifested itself in communal experiments such as the Jesus Forever Family at Rochdale College and the House of Emmaus on Draper Street, and the large weekly worship services of "the Catacombs" at St. Paul's Anglican Church, Bloor Street.[5] While there were notable differences between the Canadian and American counter-cultures, the Jesus movement in Toronto was remarkably similar in nature to its prototype in southern California. There was little to distinguish the practise, theology, sociology, or eventual fate of the two groups. In this essay, I will explore the nature of the Jesus People movement—particularly its similarities to and differences from the broader counter-culture—using Toronto as my chief example. My primary sources are contemporary assessments of the Jesus People in mainstream Canadian publications, particularly the "Religion" section of the *Toronto Star.*

In the late 1960s, hippies, student activists, and sympathetic observers perceived the counter-culture to be a reaction against "technocracy." Both terms—"counter-culture" and "technocracy"—gained wide currency through sociologist Theodore Roszak's *The Making of a Counter Culture: Reflections on the Technocratic Society and Its Youthful Opposition*. Roszak defines technocracy as "that society in which those

Source: Bruce Douville, "'And We've Got to Get Ourselves Back to the Garden': The Jesus People Movement in Toronto," in *Historical Papers 2006: Canadian Society of Church History*, pp. 5–24. Reprinted with permission from the author. Bruce Douville is a PhD student in Canadian history at York University (Toronto). His dissertation focuses on the relationship between Christianity and youth revolt in the sixties.

who govern justify themselves by appeal to technical experts who, in turn, justify themselves by appeal to scientific forms of knowledge. Any beyond the authority of science, there is no appeal."[6] In the dominant technocratic culture, Roszak explains, experts manage all aspects of life, and "the prime goal of the society is to keep the productive apparatus turning over efficiently."[7] In such a society, humans become technical beings, impersonal and unemotional. (As the persona in Joni Mitchell's "Woodstock" describes it, "I feel to be a cog in something turning.") It is a perfect form of totalitarianism, he argues, precisely because it is subliminal: "even those in the state and/or corporate structure who dominate our lives must find it impossible to conceive of themselves as the agents of a totalitarian control."[8] The counter-culture, then, was the conscious rejection of all institutions of technocratic social control.

As this essay will show, repudiating technocracy meant rejecting many traditional values. Two of these were economic: the sanctity of work, and of private property. Both were seen as aspects of de-humanizing materialism. The disdainful attitude of Toronto's counter-culture towards private property is evident in the history of Rochdale College. On a grand scale, the college was an experiment in collective ownership, and it was also the site of many smaller experiments in communal living. For three years after Clarkson, Gordon and Company took ownership of the building, Rochdale residents resisted eviction.[9] The counter-culture's disdain for the Protestant work ethic is evident in Toronto hippie David DePoe's observation, "Work isn't everything, work isn't holy."[10]

Likewise, the Jesus People were not devoted to the Protestant work ethic. They did not oppose wage labour, but since Christ's return was imminent, materialistic goals were unimportant, and long-term financial planning was foolish.[11] Susan Mousley, a sixteen-year-old resident of Rochdale's Jesus Forever commune, believed that God led her to quit her job and, as she explained to a sceptical reporter, she awaited further direction from the Lord.[12] Philip Marchand wrote about Roy, a resident of the House of Emmaus, parents "wouldn't mind it if Roy got a job. But he tells them only, 'I'll be patient, and the Lord will provide.'"[13]

From its inception, the Jesus People movement also embraced communal living. They wished to pattern themselves after the first-century followers of Christ, and many of them were impressed to discover that communal living was normative in the early church.[14] Christian communes also served practical purposes. First, they provided accommodation, which was important since Jesus People ministered to a largely transient population. Second, they provided relatively stable environments where new converts could avoid their old acquaintances and habits, and replace them with new ones. In Toronto, the two most well-known Jesus People communes were the House of Emmaus on Draper Street, and Jesus Forever Family on the third floor of Rochdale College.

Robert Vellick established the House of Emmaus as a result of a seminar he started at Rochdale College. Out of that seminar "came an awareness of the need for a body or community to grow together with." In a 1971 *Toronto Star* article, Vellick explained the importance of community:

> "You have to live Christianity," Vellick points out. "It's not out there somewhere—it's right here between people. What's missing in the churches is a deep personal relationship among the members. They don't really know each other: how can they love in any depth?"[15]

Besides Vellick, whom the article describes as "a lean, bearded figure with the intense eyes of an Old Testament prophet," and presumably his wife, an adult education teacher, the House of Emmaus also included about fifteen members.[16] According to Vellick, many of them came from difficult backgrounds (i.e., drug use and home problems), though at least one associate of the House of Emmaus was a University of Toronto student.[17] The residents engaged in street evangelism in Yorkville, and provided practical assistance to transients.[18]

According to one Rochdale College resident, the Jesus Forever group on the third floor was "one of the most stable communes in the building":

> They were the only cultural entity that ever came to Rochdale, squared off, and came out ahead. [Students who were not Jesus Freaks] would move in and would be crewcut, hard-working, do-their-home-work-every-day students in September. By

513

November they had dropped out and had gotten into politics and drugs and sex and all that s**t. The Hare Krishna moved in and moved out almost immediately because they kept losing members. But the Jesus Freaks had a cultural identity.[19]

The commune's leader was a former drug dealer "who had a mouth full of rotten teeth, played guitar badly and sang much worse. But he was the actual charisma that held it all together."[20] The Jesus Forever group appears to have operated in a manner similar to the House of Emmaus, but its primary mission field was Rochdale itself. For example, Susan Mousley, mentioned above, was a Rochdale resident prior to converting and joining the third-floor Christian commune.[21] In 1974, one of the group members told Tom Harpur that "the group had been looking at a house in case they were evicted along with other residents. 'But we'd like to stay here because the need is greater."[22]

The history of the movement in Toronto shows that the Jesus People shared the counter-cultural disdain for materialism. Without question, they had unique motives. Their apathetic attitude towards the Protestant work ethic probably reflected eschatological concerns rather than political ones. Likewise, their communalism was not an end in itself, but a means to achieving more effective evangelistic outreach and discipleship, and to strengthen the bonds of Christian community. Nevertheless, the Jesus People clearly distanced themselves from the economic values of the dominant technocratic society, because these values were not consistent with the gospel of Christ as they understood it.

Like their secular counterparts, the Jesus People also rejected other aspects of the technocratic culture: the primacy of intellectual expertise, logic and tradition. In its place, both the counter-culture and the Jesus movement embraced experience, emotion, and immediacy. Furthermore, because the dominant social institutions cherished these values that the counter-culture rejected—such as knowledge, training and historical continuity—the counter-culture was anti-institutional. One of these institutions was organized religion, which the Jesus People saw as being part of the problem, not the solution. Many churches, in turn, were uncomfortable with the Jesus People.

According to Doug Owram, the counter-culture was "a romantic revolution, resisting the pre-eminence of the rational and scientific world." For the youth of the 1960s, the rationality of the dominant culture "seemed to shut out the very possibilities of passion and experience":

> So few people find real love, argued one writer, because "severely dehumanized societies like North America in the grip of a liberal or materialistic philosophy destroy the ability to feel. We are a generation of romantics—unable to really touch one another—only to dream about it."

Emotion had to be restored through experience. Without emotion both the individual and the society became a mechanism rather than a living organism.[23]

To restore their ability to feel, most hippies turned to drugs. Marijuana and LSD provided the kinds of experience that they craved to fill the emotional void. Indeed, many took LSD "as a semi-religious experience."[24] Like the romantics of the previous century, the counterculture glorified intense feelings and emotional experiences.

The Jesus People rejected drug use, but like their secular counterparts, they placed great emphasis on emotional experiences. Conversion was necessary for salvation, and for many Jesus People, it was a profoundly emotional experience. As Susan Mousley described it, "I never got around to speed that day. I didn't need it. I was too high on the Lord [...] . It was like somebody pouring something into me. He cleaned out the darkness. I was forgiven all my sins. It's as if a door behind me had closed."[25] Even more intense, for many of them, was the experience of being "filled with the Holy Spirit." Like Pentecostals, most Jesus People believed that subsequent to salvation, all Christians must receive the baptism in the Holy Spirit, with the evidence of speaking in tongues.[26] When Roy, a House of Emmaus resident mentioned above, "felt the presence of the Holy Spirit in him for the first time, [it was] a presence like a spiritual high so powerful he couldn't stand on his feet for five hours afterwards."[27]

It is no coincidence that Jesus People, many of them former drug users, used terms such as "spiritual high" and "trip" to describe these events. The Jesus "freaks" replaced narcotics with Christ and

514

Holy Spirit. These experiences, however, were not merely ends in themselves. Rather, they were seen as proof that God was at work in their lives. When the doubting reporter questioned the validity of Susan Mousley's religious experience, Mousley responded, "I got the gift of tongues eight hours after I became a Christian and I now have the gift of discernment."[28] Powerful emotions and the "gifts of the spirit" (e.g., speaking in tongues, physical healing, miracles) were evidence of God's reality, and His presence. In contrast, a lack of emotion was perceived as evidence of God's absence. "If you can't get emotional," Merla Watson of the Catacombs is quoted as saying, "I feel sorry for you."[29]

Critics of the Jesus People were most disturbed by their heavy reliance on emotion and experience. As Tom Harpur observed, the "emotionalism and the tendency to give simple answers to complex issues could result in just another 'trip' destined to end in a rude shock once the initial 'high' is over."[30] In their analysis of the movement in California, Ronald Enroth and his colleagues noted that Jesus People used experience as the criterion to determine the validity of Christianity, (i.e., "But I've had this experience, and I know it's true. I know I'm right."): "The Bible, however, exhorts its readers to test the spirits. Other persons have had other experiences, and for them these experiences have been most profound and earthshaking. According to what criterion can these competing experiences be judged? The criterion must lie outside the realm of experience itself." Emotion and experience alone are not sufficient, Enroth argues. One must also use one's intellect, and according to Enroth, this was something that many Jesus People were not prepared to do.[31]

The Jesus People movement inherited its anti-intellectualism and anti-traditionalism from the broader counter-culture. Owram writes that "the emotionalism of the counter-culture made it impatient with intellectual canon," and that the hippies and student activists "felt exempt from history."[32] Indeed, like other twentieth-century revolutionaries, they sought to liberate themselves from the burden of history. Centuries of accumulated scholarship in the sciences and humanities had failed to produce a just, peaceful society; therefore, cultivating one's intellect was irrelevant at best, and harmful at worst. For Jesus People, all the truth that they needed could be found in the Bible, and in the leading of the Holy Spirit. The truth

was out there, and the truth was simple. This attitude provoked the journalist who interviewed Susan Mousley to remark that the Jesus People were "victim[s] of a voluntary frontal lobotomy. [...] Susan and the rest of her family don't question life anymore. They're not exercising the intelligence that distinguishes them from dogs and cats. Tame animals accept direction from their master, and the Jesus Forever family accepts direction from its master."[33] While her criticism was extreme, even more sympathetic observers warned of the dangers of privileging experience over intellect. In a *Toronto Star* article about the Jesus People, W. Stafford Reid, a professor of Reformation history at the University of Guelph, remarked:

> One other danger indicated by the Reformation is that of anti-intellectualism, with an over-emphasis upon emotion and personal experience. Groups with such tendencies arose in the sixteenth century but usually they were soon fragmented by divisions over experience, since all experiences were not the same. It was the groups that had a well-articulated structure of thought that survived and ultimately exercised a wide influence.[34]

Hand in hand with their distrust of intellectual cultivation and tradition, the Jesus People also distrusted the established churches—even evangelical churches. House of Emmaus leader Robert Vellick told Tom Harpur that churches "are trying to play patsy with God on the one hand and the world on the other; that's why they're just lukewarm." One of his colleagues explained that they were not anti-church, and that many of them belonged to established congregations, but they felt "that too often the traditional churches are bound up in materialism and conformity to the world." Their attitude reflected the primitivist drive of the movement. In Harpur's words, they wanted "to be known simply as followers of Jesus—Jesus People—trying to embody apostolic Christianity in twentieth-century garb." Their attitude also reflected the counter-cultural distrust of their parents' generation and its institutions. In Vellick's words, "this is a new generation, and we're not in anybody's camp."[35]

Unfortunately, the distrust between Jesus People and older Christians was mutual. When Roy of the

515

House of Emmaus converted to Christianity, there remained a great deal of conflict between him and his Christian parents. "He had become a Jesus freak," Marchand writes, "but the freak part was still almost as important as the Jesus part in the eyes of his parents. Now, in fact, his parents want him to show how Christian he is by getting a haircut and wearing decent clothes."[36] Wilber Sutherland, a former worker with Inter-Varsity Christian Fellowship, relates the episode of a Toronto church that had supported an effective Christian coffeehouse in Yorkville: "When some of the converts wanted to attend communion still in their 'hippie' garb, bare feet and all, there was strong opposition unless they 'cleaned up.' They chose to establish their own Sunday service instead." When the issue was debated at a gathering of Toronto's clergy, an evangelical minister "was very distressed at the thought of administering communion to these uncouth 'kids' who probably had never been baptized."[37]

Some established churches were able to bridge the distrust. Ronald Enroth and his colleagues provided several examples of "straight churches" that welcomed the Jesus People, perhaps the most successful being Pastor Chuck Smith's Calvary Chapel in Santa Ana, California.[38] In London, Ontario, Rev. David Mack of King Street United Church allowed a group of Jesus People to host a regular Christian coffeehouse, known as Jesus Rap, in the church basement. The experience rejuvenated the church, which had been on the verge of closing.[39] Furthermore, as the Jesus People matured, they concluded that the established church had much to offer. In 1974, Robert Vellick informed the *Toronto Star* that he had become a Roman Catholic, and the House of Emmaus was "an evangelical, Roman Catholic lay community." Vellick made this move, he said, because he needed roots, and "you can't completely cut yourself off from the history and tradition of the church."[40] In the same article, David Mack noted that a significant number of the original Jesus People had eventually joined established churches. "Where the churches have been willing to bend in regard to worship and other structures," Mack said, "the young people have come in and found a depth of tradition and knowledge they knew they themselves were lacking."[41]

In the early days of the movement in Toronto, the Jesus People, like their secular counterparts, celebrated warm emotion and living experience. They rejected cold intellect and dead tradition, and they criticized the church, because they believed that it embodied these characteristics. Eventually, they came to believe that a living, experiential faith could not be divorced from the life and experience of the historic church, and that emotion could not be divorced from intellect. Undoubtedly, they would have agreed with Tom Harpur's opinion that the optimum "would be a new religious synthesis where reason and emotion find again their proper balance. The Bible words about marriage are appropriate here as well. They say: 'Those whom (which) God hath joined together let no man put asunder.'"[42]

Another trait that the Jesus movement shared with the counter-culture was its vitality. The hippie, the student activist, and the Jesus "freak" each made the same claim: that he belonged to a dynamic international grassroots movement, one that held the unique potential to transform society. Each movement grew rapidly, and was evangelistic and idealistic in nature. Moreover, the optimism and vigour of the counterculture was rooted in the Baby Boomers' sense that they belonged to a special generation. The Jesus People shared this sense, but took it a step further: they believed that they belonged to the last generation before Christ's return. Their intense interest in eschatology contributed to the dynamism of the movement.

Toronto's best example of the Jesus movement's rapid growth and vitality was the weekly gathering known as the Catacombs. In 1968, two students at Birchmount Park Collegiate approached Merv Watson, a music teacher, about forming a Christian club at the school. They decided to call it The Catacombs Club, because they considered themselves "an underground presence on the high school scene." By the following year, the Catacombs had developed into a charismatic prayer group that met in individual homes.[43] The group grew rapidly, and kept moving its prayer meetings to larger venues: from private living rooms to the basement of Bathurst Street United Church, to Cody Hall at St. Paul's Anglican Church, Bloor Street, and ultimately to the sanctuary of St. Paul's.[44] In 1972, Tom Harpur observed that there were about four hundred to five hundred, largely teenagers, in attendance at the weekly Thursday night meetings, and in 1974, he reported attendance of up to one thousand.[45] According to Merv Watson, about thirty to forty per cent of those attending were Jesus People, while the remainder were "straight kids from every church and from every part of town." They were drawn by the exuberant, Pentecostal-style worship (i.e., raising one's hand in prayer, praying out loud and "speaking in tongues"). They were also drawn by the music ministry of Merv and Merla Watson, who often performed their own compositions. Tom Harpur described the Catacombs gatherings as "a mixture of the old-time revival meeting, a modern hootenanny and a classical concert."[46] Clearly, the group members were convinced that something exciting and unique was happening at the Catacombs. Many church pastors throughout southern Ontario were also convinced, and they chartered buses so that their youth groups could take part in the experience.[47]

This sense of uniqueness had its roots in the Baby Boomers' sense of being special, both personally as individuals, and collectively as an emerging generation. Doug Owram attributes this trait to several factors. Parents, who had lived through times of deprivation and disruption, aspired to prove a materially and emotionally secure environment for their children. The affluence generated by a booming postwar economy led young people to believe that they occupied a world without limits. Finally, the Baby Boomers were conscious of their demographic importance. "For a period of twenty to twenty-five years," Owram writes, "not only was there demographic imbalance, but that imbalance tilted the values and politics of the Canadian nation towards the values and politics of Canadian youth." From the vantage point of hippies and student activists, they belonged to a generation with substantial power and unlimited opportunities.[48]

For Jesus People, their generation was indeed special, not simply because of its demographic importance, but because they believed it to be the final generation before the second coming of Jesus Christ. Their expectation of Christ's imminent return rested on two principal lines of argument, both involving biblical prophecy. First of all, they were convinced that the Jesus movement itself was a fulfilment of the Old Testament prophet Joel's prediction that in the last days, God would pour out His Spirit, and that miracles would occur. Enroth explains:

In his sermon on the day of Penecost, Peter quoted that prophecy [...] But since the Jesus People collapse all history between the Book of Acts and the present moment, they see themselves as the continuing

fulfilment of Joel's words. As the church in the Book of Acts represented "the former rain" that brought the first fruits, the Jesus People adhere to the standard Pentecostalist view that they are "the latter rain" referred to by the prophets and that will immediately precede the second coming.[49]

Their other line of argument was to point to the turbulent world of the late 1960s and early 1970s as fulfilments of biblical prophecy, and harbingers of Christ's return. Many Jesus People read Hal Lindsey's *The Late Great Planet Earth*, which argued that world events indicated that Christ's second advent may be imminent.[50] Jesus People in Toronto eagerly awaited that final event. Toronto's Jesus People publication was entitled *Maranatha*, the Aramaic term for "Come, Lord."[51] Roy told journalist Philip Marchand "that the Second Coming might be indicated as well by the fact that the ranks of Christians are swelling: 'Down at the House of Emmaus there's been, in the past two weeks, somebody saved every night.'"[52]

Furthermore, many Jesus People were preoccupied by the eschatological importance of the state of Israel. They believed that the 1948 re-establishment of the state of Israel and the 1967 reclamation of the holy sites of Old Jerusalem paved the way for the eventual building of the third Temple.[53] They also believed that many Jews would convert to Christ in the last days. For this reason, Jesus People were keenly interested in efforts to spread the gospel in Israel, and in the development of Messianic Judaism (i.e., Jews who believe that Jesus is the Messiah). In 1972, Merve and Merla Watson informed a gathering of the Catacombs "how they believe God is calling them to a special ministry in the Holy Land," and by May 1974, the two had left the Catacombs and formed a new group, whose "members aim at 'ministering to Jews' through music and praise."[54] Though many would dismiss such missionary efforts as, at best, quixotic, they are an example of the vitality and optimism of a movement eager to save as many souls as it could before Christ's imminent return.

Without question, the Jesus People owed much of their excitement and evangelistic energy to their confidence that these were the last days, and that their movement was a special end-times dispensation from God. However, while this confidence offered short-term benefits (i.e., motivation, rapid growth), it

517

posted long-term dangers for the movement. Enroth and his colleagues concluded that after talking to California's Jesus People, "we felt that Christ had better come soon, because they could not long sustain the emotional high and the intensity of life that they were presently enjoying."[55] Disillusionment and waning enthusiasm, they feared, could cause the movement to decline rapidly. Despite such concerns, the Jesus People retained their vitality. As with any religious revival, many conversions proved to be ephemeral; many, however, proved to be lasting. The Catacombs, for example, maintained its momentum well into the 1970s, and continued to exist until the late 1980s—long after the demise of the Yorkville hippie scene, SUPA, and Rochdale College. Clearly, the Jesus movement was both energetic and relatively durable.

So far, this essay has examined the similarities between the Jesus movement and the counter-culture. However, one must not minimize the differences between the two groups. Unlike their secular counterparts, the Jesus People were essentially apolitical. They did not engage in social or political activism, because Christ's second advent was the only solution for social injustice. Moreover, the Jesus movement was an explicit reaction to and repudiation of significant parts of the counter-culture: chaos, drug use, permissive sexuality, and non-Christian spirituality.

Social and political protest was the most visible aspect of the counter-culture. In Toronto, New Left activists demonstrated against the Vietnam War, occupied the University of Toronto senate chamber to "stop the power structure," and formed a variety of protest groups.[56] However, there is no evidence that Toronto's Jesus People took part in any events to protest systemic poverty, the Vietnam War, nuclear proliferation, or any of the other causes of the New Left social activists. The Jesus People's lifestyle may have been an implicit rebuke to materialism, but they did not work to create a society in which material wealth was redistributed to meet human needs. Indeed, to the extent that they had anything to say about politics, it was to support the power structure. At Rochdale, for example, some students were upset when it appeared that the Jesus Forever Family was too closely aligned to Clarkson, Gordon and Company:

> When Clarkson gave the Jesus People a rent-free room, suspicions immediately

came to a boil. Alex MacDonald expresses some of them: "Jesus freaks do as they're told. When the Clarkson Company told them to get out, they were one of the very, very few groups in the building who said okay and left. They didn't go to court, they didn't fight it. 'Authority is good.' Certain of their members were on staff—they got down that low."[57]

In the contemporary news sources reviewed for this essay, Jesus People mentioned social and political evils only to explain why so many young people were turning to Christianity, or to hold them up as signs that Christ was coming soon.[58] Undoubtedly, their firm belief in an imminent apocalypse was an important reason for their indifference to social and political activism. The kingdoms of this world, they believed, were dominated by Satan, and no amount of amelioration could bring about a just society. Conversion was an individual affair, not a social one.[59]

Consequently, the Jesus People were activists, but their activism was aimed at saving individuals rather than saving society. And in the mission fields of the counter-culture, they found many that desperately needed saving. The Jesus People were unequivocal in their denunciations of many aspects of the counter-cultural lifestyle. Most of the individuals featured in contemporary news articles on the Jesus movement were refugees from that lifestyle. Robert Vellick had been a drug user and a student of the occult.[60] Likewise, Roy of the House of Emmaus, and Susan Mousley of the Jesus Forever Family had been heavy drug users.[61] Finally, the leader of the Jesus Forever commune had been a drug dealer, who reportedly became a Christian following a prolonged LSD trip.[62] These young people believed that by turning to Christ, they were set free from substance abuse and other self-destructive behaviours. Without question, the Jesus People could have done more to respond to the relevant social and political issues of the early 1970s. Nevertheless, while they did not restructure society, they managed to restructure their own lives.

On a theological level, there was little to distinguish the Jesus People from Pentecostals in the "straight" churches. Jesus People believed in biblical inerrancy, justification by faith, baptism in the Holy Spirit, the pre-millennial return of Jesus Christ, and adult baptism by immersion. In spite of these similarities, however, they knew that there were substantial differences between their movement and "old-time religion." In fact, theologian Erling Jorstad calls the Jesus movement a "new-time religion." He contends that previous revivals in late-nineteenth and twentieth-century America affirmed traditional values. In contrast, he argues, the Jesus movement repudiated nationalism, materialism, and the institutional church.[63] The Jesus People combined evangelical faith with the counter-cultural rejection of technocracy. It is for this reason that some within the movement called it the "Jesus Revolution."

The Jesus movement may not have been a revolution, but what was it? There are three other possibilities to consider: reaction, revitalization or revival. The first two terms come from William McLoughlin's *Revivals, Awakenings and Reform*. Citing the work of Anthony F.C. Wallace, McLoughlin argues that as a society develops, it reaches a crisis point at which its traditional values are no longer practicable. When this "period of cultural distortion" occurs, there are two possible responses. The first is reaction: a traditionalist movement emerges, led "by those with rigid personalities or with much at stake in the older order." Their solution is to "call for a return to the 'old-time religion,'" and "find scapegoats in their midst [...] upon whom they can project their fear." Ultimately, Wallace explains, this response is unsuccessful, and the only viable response is revitalization. He defines this as the process in which charismatic individuals lead the society to accept new "mazeways"—new values and mores to replace the old, unworkable ones.[64]

In one sense, the Jesus movement was a reaction—to the trauma, excesses and instability of the late 1960s and early 1970s. The values and beliefs that its adherents embraced were, in many respects, very traditional indeed. However, these were not the values of the dominant, technocratic society of the twentieth century. The Jesus People responded to gospel's promise that Christ would "make all things new," and their lives wee changed. To dismiss the Jesus people as mere "reactionaries" fails to capture the nuances and complexities of this movement.

In another sense, the Jesus movement was a revitalization. However, it did not revitalize North American society, but rather one segment of that society; namely, the sub-culture of evangelical Christianity.[65] As the Jesus People matured, many of them made peace with the institutional church, and became members. Others joined the new denominations that emerged from the movement, notably Calvary Chapel and the Vineyard fellowships.[66] In addition, many current leaders in the North American evangelical community were influenced by the movement in its early days.[67] The Jesus movement was clearly "private" religion, in the sense that José Casanova uses the term to distinguish it from "public" religion. Ironically, however, the energy that the Jesus People infused into the North American church undoubtedly contributed to the "Year of the Evangelical" in 1976, and may have contributed to the "deprivatization" of evangelical Christianity in the late 1970s and early 1980s.[68]

Some evangelical Christian scholars of the movement propose a third possibility, that it was a revival—a divine intervention in human history. Both Di Sabatino and Jorstad endorse this interpretation of the Jesus People movement.[69] Clearly, few academics would find this a satisfactory explanation. Nevertheless, one must acknowledge that this is how the Jesus People themselves understood it. Yet even if one sees the movement—quite literally—as the work of a *deus ex machina*, it was still a drama that involved human players, with human motives and fallibilities. In other words, one can believe that the movement had transcendent dimensions *and* still analyze its sociological or psychological dimensions.

More research needs to be done on the Canadian Jesus People movement. This essay only focused on Toronto, and did not examine issues of race, class, or gender. Furthermore, this study had little to say about evangelical Christian student groups at Toronto's post-secondary institutions, particularly the University of Toronto. Did these groups attempt to reach out to student radicals (i.e., as the Christian World Liberation Front did at University of California at Berkeley)?[70] If so, how successful were they? Also, if history is to be understood as a dialogue, then it is important to find out how the hippies and New Left activists responded to the Jesus People. Furthermore, what role did evangelical churches in downtown Toronto play in reaching out to hippies, or to Jesus People? Finally, what can the movement tell us about the nature of secularization (in all three senses of the word as José Casanova defines it) in urban Canada during the 1960s and 1970s?[71]

519

This essay began with the "Woodstock" generation, and its search for emotional and spiritual freedom. In Joni Mitchell's song, the child of God looked for this freedom at Yasgur's farm. In Toronto in the early 1970s, other children of God looked for this freedom at a communal house on Draper Street, or at a Thursday night prayer meeting at St. Paul's Church. Both the counter-culture and the Jesus movement were attempts to get "back to the garden," to an idyllic world that transcended technocracy and materialism. While the Jesus People could not recreate Eden, they did create Christian communities that celebrated mutual support, emotional warmth, and spiritual freedom, as they understood it.

Notes

1. Joni Mitchell, "Woodstock," from *Ladies of the Canyon*, Reprise Records, 1970.
2. William G. McLoughlin, *Revivals, Awakenings and Reform: An Essay on Religion and Social Change in America, 1607–1977* (Chicago: University of Chicago Press, 1978), 210.
3. Throughout this essay, I will use the terms "Jesus People movement" and "Jesus movement" interchangeably. At least one scholar prefers the former term, since the latter is often used to denote first-century Christianity. See David Di Sabatino, "The Spiritual Sixties and the Jesus People Movement," introduction to *The Jesus People Movement: An Annotated Bibliography and General Resource* (Westport, CT: Greenwood Press, 1999), 4n.
4. Doug Owram, *Born at the Right Time: A History of the Baby Boom Generation* (Toronto: University of Toronto Press, 1996), 185–307.
5. Di Sabatino, "The Spiritual Sixties," 13.
6. Theodore Roszak, *The Making of a Counter Culture: Reflections on the Technocratic Society and Its Youthful Opposition* (Garden City, NY: Doubleday and Company, Inc., 1968), 8.
7. Roszak, *The Making of a Counter Culture*, 7.
8. Roszak, *The Making of a Counter Culture*, 9.
9. Roszak, *The Making of a Counter Culture*, 185–86. See also David Sharpe, *Rochdale, the Runaway College* (Toronto: Anansi, 1987); and Henry Mietkiewicz and Bob Mackowycz, *Dream Tower: The Life and Legacy of Rochdale College* (Toronto: McGraw-Hill Ryerson, 1988).
10. Owram, *Born at the Right Time*, 205.
11. Pre-millennial eschatology, especially the belief that the *parousia* would occur in their lifetime, was

a central part of the theology of the Jesus People. It did not merely influence their actions; it determined them. The importance of eschatology in the Jesus movement will be discussed at greater length later in this essay (see Ronald M. Enroth, Edward E. Ericson, Jr., and C. Breckinridge Peters, *The Jesus People: Old-Time Religion in the Age of Aquarius* [Grand Rapids: William B. Eerdmans Publishing Company, 1972], 179–93).

12. Heather Chisvin, "The Conversion of Susan Mousley," *Miss Chatelaine* 8, no. 6 (18 November 1971): 75, 97. By the end of the article, Chisvin informs readers that Susan felt led to return to complete her high school education.
13. Philip Marchand, "Moments of Grace in Sinful Toronto," *Saturday Night* 86 (November 1971): 35.
14. David Di Sabatino, "The Jesus People Movement: Counterculture Revival and Evangelical Renewal" (MTS thesis, McMaster Divinity College, 1994), 36. Also, see Enroth, et al., *The Jesus People*, 207–20.
15. Tom Harpur, "'Turning on with Jesus': Fad or True Revival?" *Toronto Star*, 28 August 1971, 81.
16. Marchand, "Moments of Grace," 35.
17. Robert Douglas, "Jesus Movement comes to Toronto," *Toronto Star*, 8 May 1971, 61.
18. Harpur, "Turning on with Jesus"; and Marchand, "Moments of Grace," 35.
19. Sharpe, *Rochdale*, 137.
20. Mietkiewicz and Mackowycz, *Dream Tower,* 48–9.
21. Chisvin, "Conversion of Susan Mousley," 97–8.
22. Tom Harpur, "Jesus People blend into the 'straight' churches," *Toronto Star*, 11 May 1974, 4(E).
23. Owram, *Born at the Right Time*, 205–6.
24. Owram, *Born at the Right Time*, 209.
25. Chisvin, "Conversion of Susan Mousley," 98.
26. Enroth, et al., *The Jesus People*, 194–220.
27. Marchand, "Moments of Grace," 35.
28. Chisvin, "Conversion of Susan Mousley," 99.
29. Tom Harpur, "Fervent teenagers say: Isn't Jesus wonderful!" *Toronto Star*, 19 February 1972, 85.
30. Harpur, "Fervent teenagers say: Isn't Jesus wonderful!" 85.
31. Enroth, et al., *The Jesus People*, 164–68.
32. Owram, *Born at the Right Time*, 208.
33. Chisvin, "Conversion of Susan Mousley," 99–100.
34. Reid mentioned Calvin's *Institutes of the Christian Religion* as one example of such a "well-articulated structure of thought." Since Reid is also a Presbyterian minister, his example is not surprising (W.

Stafford Reid, "Jesus People may bring about a new Reformation," *Toronto Star,* 18 September 1971, 85).

35. Harpur, "'Turning on with Jesus.'"

36. Marchand, "Moments of Grace," 35.

37. Wilber Sutherland, "Some reached out, some rejected Jesus People," *Christian Week,* 14 February 1995, 11.

38. Enroth, et al., *The Jesus People,* 84–101.

39. Jim Sheppard, "High on Jesus," *United Church Observer* (November 1972), 24–6.

40. Harpur, "Jesus People blend into the 'straight' churches."

41. Harpur, "Jesus People blend into the 'straight' churches."

42. Tom Harpur, "Revivalism is sweeping North America," *Toronto Star,* 15 June 1974, 5 (H).

43. Di Sabatino, "The Jesus People Movement: Counterculture Revival and Evangelical Renewal," 65–68.

44. Al Reimers, *God's Country: Charismatic Renewal* (Toronto: G.R. Welch, 1979), 23.

45. Harpur, "Fervent teenagers say: Isn't Jesus wonderful!"; and Harpur, "Jesus People blend into the 'straight' churches." Di Sabatino claims that attendance "steadily ranged between 2,000 and 2,500 during a three year peak period," though he doesn't specify when that was—possibly in the late 1970s ("The Jesus People Movement: Counterculture Revival and Evangelical Renewal," 67).

46. Harpur, "Fervent teenagers say: Isn't Jesus wonderful!"

47. Di Sabatino, "The Jesus People Movement: Counterculture Revival and Evangelical Renewal," 67.

48. Owram, *Born at the Right Time,* 308–11. One potential weakness in Owram's thesis is that many Canadians did not share in this postwar affluence. Indeed, the bulk of his book deals with middle-class and upper-middle-class baby boomers. Several chapters deal particularly with university students in the 1960s. While the post-secondary system expanded enormously in these years, university students still represented an affluent minority of baby boomers. Furthermore the student radicals Owram writes about were a minority within that middle-class minority. In spite of these reservations, I still find his analysis useful.

49. Enroth, et al., *The Jesus People,* 184.

50. Enroth, et al., *The Jesus People,* 187–90.

51. Douglas, "Jesus Movement comes to Toronto."

52. Marchand, "Moments of Grace," 36.

53. Enroth, et al., *The Jesus People,* 187–88.

54. Harpur, "Fervent teenagers say: Isn't Jesus wonderful!"; and Harpur, "Jesus People blend into the 'straight' churches." Eventually, Merva and Merla Watson moved to Israel.

55. Enroth, et al., *The Jesus People,* 241.

56. Owram, *Born at the Right Time,* 224, 233, 293–96.

57. Sharpe, *Rochdale,* 264.

58. Douglas, "Jesus Movement comes to Toronto"; and Marchand, "Moments of Grace," 36.

59. Enroth, et al., *The Jesus People,* 172–74.

60. Harpur, "'Turning on with Jesus.'"

61. Marchand, "Moments of Grace," 34–35; and Chisvin, "Conversion of Susan Mousley," 97–98.

62. "He'd been a dope dealer. And at one point, the cops nabbed him but forgot to search him. So he did all this acid—eighteen hits—in the back of a police car. When the cops realized what had happened, they got pissed off and threw him out of the car in the middle of the night in High Park. He told me that he just walked around High Park for two days and two nights because he couldn't find his way out. He just kept walking in circles. And since he was on acid the whole time, Jesus kept popping out from behind the trees and pointing to him. So he took that as a sign and he became born again" (Mietkiewicz and Mackowycz, *Dream Tower,* 48–49).

63. Erling Jorstad, *That New-Time Religion: The Jesus Revival in America* (Minneapolis, MN: Augsburg Publishing House, 1972), 120–22.

64. McLoughlin, *Revivals, Awakenings and Reform,* 12–16.

65. Di Sabatino, "The Spiritual Sixties," 18–19.

66. Incidentally, the "Toronto Blessing" of the 1990s, which had a powerful impact on charismatic and Pentecostal churches throughout the world, began in a Toronto Vineyard fellowship.

67. The American televangelist, Benny Hinn, was involved in the Catacombs when he lived in Toronto. Di Sabatino, "The Jesus People Movement: Counterculture Revival and Evangelical Renewal," 68n.

68. José Casanova, *Public Religions in the Modern World* (Chicago: University of Chicago Press, 1994), 11–74, 135–66.

69. Di Sabatino, "The Jesus People Movement: Counterculture Revival and Evangelical Renewal," 14–15; and Jorstad, *That New-Time Religion,* 120. It should

521

be noted that Enroth and his colleagues are also evangelicals, but they are critical of several traits of the Jesus People: "their simplistic mentality, the excessive emphasis on experience and feeling, and their bias against intellectual pursuits, social involvement, and human culture in general." They avoid passing judgment on the movement as a whole, for to do so "would be to fall into their own error of oversimplification" (17).

70. Enroth, et al., *The Jesus People*, 102–14.

71. Casanova, *Public Religions in the Modern World*, 211–34. Casanova distinguishes between three meanings of secularization: differentiation, decline and de-politicization.

PEACEKEEPING MISSIONS, 1956-1990s

Canada's Real Contribution to World Affairs?

Marcel Martel
York University

525

● INTRODUCTION

Marcel Martel

In their attempt to define Canada's role in the world, Canadians often refer to their country's record of peacekeeping. Although over the last decade Canadian contributions to United Nations (UN) peacekeeping missions have declined both in terms of human resources involved and the number of missions that Canada has taken part in, Canadians are still proud of their country's role. The song written by well-known folk singer Tom C. Connors, about peacekeeping missions and their role in shaping Canadian identity, encompasses many representations—some would say myths—associated with peacekeeping that reinforce the idea that Canada is in essence a peacekeeping nation.

It was in 1956 that Lester B. Pearson, then Canada's secretary of state for external affairs, suggested the idea of peacekeeping forces. That year, Egypt's nationalization of the Suez Canal triggered an international crisis that involved France, Great Britain, and Israel. Looking for a peaceful way of resolving this crisis, Pearson proposed the resolution to the UN General Assembly which created a United Nations Emergency Force. The international community embraced this initiative and Pearson received the Nobel Peace Prize for this great diplomatic achievement in 1957. Cartoons included in the module refer to the Suez Canal crisis and Pearson's role. Since then, Canada has taken part in several UN Peacekeeping missions, notably in Cyprus, Lebanon, and more recently in Bosnia and Herzegovina, and Rwanda.

Despite the fact that Canadians are usually proud of the country's peacekeeping role, those taking part in UN peacekeeping missions have had a different understanding of their significance and usefulness. The selected excerpts of Lieutenant-General Romeo Dallaire's moving testimony on the UN mission that witnessed genocide in Rwanda in 1994 offer a grim depiction of how the role of the international community, and in particular of Western powers such as the United States and France, led to the inability of the UN mission to stop the Rwanda genocide. Although critical of his role and admitting his own failures as well as those of the UN and the international community, Lieutenant-General Dallaire does not throw in the towel: He still believes in the necessity of the UN missions. In contrast to Dallaire, Major-General Lewis MacKenzie did not deal with genocide but was confronted with a civil war and ethnic cleansing in former Yugoslavia when he was in Sarajevo from March to August 1992. Although critical of the UN and how the international organization handled the situation, MacKenzie still believes in the usefulness of peacekeeping missions.

Peacekeeping missions have led Canadians and scholars to debate Canada's role in the world. In their attempt to characterize Canada's role, some have argued that it is a slow evolution from colonial status to sovereignty. For others, such as Harold Innis, it is an evolution from colony to nationhood and then back to colony again. Innis's statement describes how Canada lost its colonial status, briefly enjoyed the feeling of being a nation (in the 1930s), and then became a colony of the United States after the Second World War. Others argue that in terms of constitutional and political evolution, Canada slowly gained its sovereignty. In 1931, Canada became independent through the Statute of Westminster, which provided the right to self-government in all matters, external as well as internal. In 1982, the patriation of the Canadian constitution gave Canada the power to amend the *British North America Act*, which until then had remained under British authority. However, the characteristics of the Canadian economic structure that rely on export, the emergence of the United States as a world leader after the Second World War, and international

526

commitments have had an impact on the degree of autonomy Canada has been able to exercise. Since the Second World War, Canada has had to acknowledge the military, economic, and political consequences of sharing a continent with its powerful neighbour, the United States. The period after the Second World War is being called the "golden age" of Canadian foreign policy history. Costas Melakopides depicts strategies that allowed Canada to make its voice heard in the international community, at the same time taking into consideration the fact that the world was divided into two important camps, one led by the United States and the other by the Soviet Union.

If Canadian participation in peacekeeping missions has constituted a crucial contribution to world's politics, scholars still disagree on its meaning for Canada and Canadians and its impact on international relations. Historian Jack Granatstein launches a frontal attack against the perception that Canada is by nature a peacekeeping nation. Joseph T. Jockel picks up where Granatstein left off and explores why Canadians are proud of being defined as a peacekeeping nation.

Peacekeeping missions are one element of Canadian foreign policy. Yet they should not obscure the fundamental question that has obsessed Canadian politicians, diplomats, bureaucrats, intellectuals, international relations specialists, and Canadians in general since the end of the Second World War: Which definition best describes Canada's foreign policy? Is Canada a satellite of its powerful neighbour, the United States of America? Is Canada a sovereign nation capable of developing a foreign policy that reflects its economic, political, and military interests? Or is Canada a state that is sovereign in name only because the military, economic, and other international treaties and conventions it has signed over the years have circumscribed its ability to develop its own foreign relations and policy?

527

QUESTIONS

1. How did Dallaire and MacKenzie perceive their role? How did they deal with murders, crimes, and casualties?
2. Both Dallaire and MacKenzie were critical of the United Nations. Did they formulate similar criticisms?
3. How does Tom C. Connors describe the work done by peacekeeping forces? Do these tasks have similarities with Canadians' perceptions of their country's role in the world?
4. How does Costas Melakopides define functionalism? Which evidence does he provide to support his thesis? Are you convinced by the evidence?
5. How do Jack Granatstein and Joseph T. Jockel justify Canada's role as peacekeepers? Do they use similar arguments and evidence?

FURTHER READINGS

Bothwell, Robert, *Alliance and Illusion: Canada and the World, 1945–1984*, (Vancouver: University of British Columbia Press, 2007).

English, John, and Norman Hillmer, eds., *Making a Difference? Canada's Foreign Policy in a Changing World Order*, (Toronto: Lester Publishing Ltd., 1992).

Granatstein, Jack L., and David Bercuson, *War and Peacekeeping from South Africa to the Gulf —Canada's Limited Wars*, (Toronto: Key Porter Books Limited, 1991).

Hillmer, Norman, and J. L. Granatstein, *Empire to Umpire: Canada and the World into the 21st Century*, (Toronto: Thomson Nelson, 2008).

Legault, Albert, and Manon Tessier, *Canada and Peacekeeping: Three Major Debates,* trans. George Tombs, (Clementsport, Nova Scotia: Canadian Peacekeeping Press, 1999).

Melakopides, Costas. *Pragmatic Idealism: Canadian Foreign Policy 1945–1995*. (Kingston: McGill-Queen's Press, 1998).

NOTE

*I would like to thank Colin McCullough for the selection of the primary documents.

▲ Document 1: Check Out Rwanda and You're in Charge

Lieutenant-General Roméo Dallaire

I confess that when General Roy called, I didn't know where Rwanda was or exactly what kind of trouble the country was in. The next day, he told me more about the tiny, heavily populated African nation. Rwanda was in the midst of negotiating a peace agreement to end a vicious two-and-a-half-year civil war between a rebel force, the Rwandese Patriotic Front (RPF), and the government. The rebel movement had grown out of a refugee population of Rwandans who had fled north to Uganda in the early sixties, after independence had changed the political balance in their homeland. In the early nineties, the rebel army had twice pushed into the northern region of Rwanda and was now hunkered down behind a demilitarized zone monitored by a group of neutral military observers under the auspices of the Organization of African Unity (OAU). While the parties negotiated the terms of a peace agreement in Arusha, Tanzania, the UN had been asked by the president of Uganda, Yoweri Museveni, to send in a small force to monitor the border to ensure that weapons and soldiers were not crossing from Uganda into Rwanda to reinforce the RPF.

This was to be my mission, dubbed the United Nations Observer Mission in Uganda and Rwanda (UNOMUR). General Roy described it as a classic peacekeeping operation, a confidence-building exercise designed to encourage the belligerents to get down to the serious business of peace. It was extremely modest in scope and size: I would have under my command a total of eighty-one unarmed military observers, who would operate on the Ugandan side of the border.

Why pick me to lead this tiny mission in a place I'd barely heard of? I was about to begin an unprecedented third year as commander of the 5ième Brigade Group; in four days we were going to celebrate the twenty-fifth anniversary of its founding with more than a thousand troops on parade. The 5th still faced plenty of challenges, many of them in the area of peacekeeping. We were still too ad hoc in our preparation of troops for deployment on ever more challenging missions. Much of our training was still focused on classic war-fighting, even though the conflicts we were sending troops into usually were not unfolding like classic wars. As far as I was concerned, it wasn't yet time for me to leave, but I was being asked—ordered—to deploy. Whether it was a big force, a small force or just me alone, I was going over. Knowing that Major General Maurice Baril was heading up the military component of the UN Department of Peace-keeping Operations (DPKO), I surmised that there must be more to this mission than met the eye. In the end I decided that this was my chance to learn first-hand what would work in the changing nature of conflict in the post–Cold War world.

However, I was stunned to find out that Canada was only willing to supply me, and not a single soldier more, to the mission. I protested to the defence department, which remained adamant about the decision until I noticed a tiny loophole in the arrangement. I was being hired by the UN under a civilian contract—in essence being seconded by the government of Canada to UN service—and so the defence department was still on the hook to supply the one Canadian officer it had approved for UNOMUR. The director of Canadian peacekeeping operations at National Defence Headquarters gave me a list of ten names from which to choose the officer who would become my military assistant. Since

529

Source: Excerpted from *Shake Hands with the Devil: The Failure of Humanity in Rwanda* by LGen Roméo Dallaire. Toronto: Vintage Canada, 2004, pp. 43–45, 48–53, 289, 295–96, 512–15. Copyright © 2003 Roméo Dallaire, LGen (ret.) Inc. Reprinted with permission of Random House Canada.

the mission was so tiny, picking the right MA was crucial: he would take care of a large portion of the paperwork and the administrative burden so that I could concentrate on operations, training and political matters.

I didn't recognize any of the names on the list of ten, and truth be told I was miffed that none of the officers from my brigade was on it. The people of Rwanda spoke French as well as Kinyarwanda; the RPF spoke English. I wanted my MA to be bilingual, but none of the officers on the list met that requirement—short notice and a lack of volunteers was the department's lame excuse. I finally stopped at one name: Major Brent Beardsley of the Royal Canadian Regiment, the senior infantry regiment in the army. At thirty-nine, he was older than most of the others on the list and he was currently involved in drafting the Canadian Forces peacekeeping manual. On paper he seemed to have the background to balance off my limited experience with UN headquarters and with peacekeeping.[...]

[...] I was carried away by the idea of adventure that Africa represented to me. Growing up Catholic in Quebec in the fifties, I had been captivated by missionary tales from "the dark continent." [...]

Downtown Manhattan in mid-July was hot, and the streets were littered with tourists. It was not the best time of the year to be in New York, but the shimmering glass tower of the United Nations headquarters beckoned, and sometimes I had to pinch myself to realize I wasn't dreaming.

Like many first-timers at the UN, I was impressed by the grandeur of the chambers of the General Assembly and the Security Council. But I soon learned that the real work went on in a rabbit warren of offices that lay just out of sight of the general public. The drabbest and most cramped offices seemed to belong to the DPKO. Staff were working in dreadful conditions: desks squeezed together, phones jangling constantly, outdated computers crashing (in some cases, employees were still using typewriters), people often short of the most basic office supplies. Not to put too fine a point on it, the DPKO was essentially a thirty-sixth-floor sweatshop. Its sorely under-equipped state was possibly part of the image game that the UN plays in order to avoid the wrath of irresponsible media and the international political vultures who use any excuse to accuse it of "wasting" money. But I soon noticed that other UN agencies, such as the United Nations Childrens Fund (UNICEF) and the United Nations High Commissioner for Refugees (UNHCR), were not only better quartered but enjoyed a better quality of life all around.

Maurice Baril was a member of a triumvirate that led the DPKO. The other members were Kofi Annan, the under-secretary-general of peacekeeping, and Iqbal Riza, who was Annan's number two and essentially the chief of staff for the department. The appointment of Baril in June 1992 had been celebrated as a coup for Canada. But the task he had set himself—building the office into an effective military-strategic, as well as operational, headquarters—was a huge challenge. Critics charged that the DPKO was staffed by a bunch of incompetent boobs who kept bankers' hours and disappeared when situations in the field came to a head. Canada's Major General Lewis MacKenzie, who had led the UN peacekeeping contingent in Sarajevo, had heaped scorn on the DPKO for its generally negative attitude toward those in the field, its lack of response to immediate needs, and the way its staff and leadership seemed to be consistently unavailable when urgent decisions had to be made. His criticisms had made headlines in Canada and most of the capitals in the world and had sunk morale in the DPKO.

[...] April 11, the fifth day of slaughter. The Security Council and the office of the secretary-general were obviously at a loss as to what to do. I continued to receive demands to supply them with more information before they would take any concrete action. What more could I possibly tell them that I hadn't already described in horrific detail? The odour of death in the hot sun; the flies, maggots, rats and dogs that swarmed to feast on the dead. At times it seemed the smell had entered the pores of my skin. My Christian beliefs had been the moral framework that had guided me throughout my adult life. Where was God in all this horror? Where was God in the world's response?

[…] Too many parties have focused on pointing the finger at others, beyond the perpetrators, as the scapegoats for our common failure in Rwanda. Some say that the example of Rwanda proves that the UN is an irrelevant, corrupt, decadent institution that has outlived its usefulness or even its ability to conduct conflict resolution. Others have blamed the Permanent Five of the Security Council, especially the United States and France, for failing to see beyond their own national self-interest to lead or even support international intervention to stop the genocide. Some have blamed the media for not telling the story, the NGOs for not reacting quickly and effectively enough, the peacekeepers for not showing more resolve, and myself for failing in my mission. When I began this book, I was tempted to make it an anatomy of my personal failures, which I was finally persuaded would be missing the point.

I have witnessed and also suffered my share of recriminations and accusations, politically motivated "investigations" and courts martial, Monday-morning quarterbacking, revisionism and outright lies since I got back to Canada in September 1994—none of that will bring back the dead or point the way forward to a peaceful future. Instead, we need to study how the genocide happened not from the perspective of assigning blame—there is too much to go around—but from the perspective of how we are going to take concrete steps to prevent such a thing from ever happening again. To properly mourn the dead and respect the potential of the living, we need accountability, not blame. We need to eliminate from this earth the impunity with which the génocidaires were able to act, and re-emphasize the principle of justice for all, so that no one for even a moment will make the ethical and moral mistake of ranking some humans as more human than others, a mistake that the international community endorsed by its indifference in 1994.

There is no doubt that the toxic ethnic extremism that infected Rwanda was a deep-rooted and formidable foe, built from colonial discrimination and exclusion, personal vendettas, refugee life, envy, racism, power plays, *coups d'état* and the deep rifts of civil war. In Rwanda both sides of the civil war fostered extremism. The fanatical far right of the Hutu ethnicity was concentrated in the MRND and its vicious wing in the CDR party, and was nurtured by an inner circle around the president, Juvénal Habyarimana, and his wife. The Tutsis also had their hard-liners, in the persons of some of the embittered refugees of the 1959 revolution, and sons and daughters raised in the poverty and double standards of Uganda, permanently gazing across the border to a homeland denied to them until they took it by force; among them also were vengeful Hutus who had been abused by the Habyarimana regime.

Together these extremists created the climate in which a slaughter of an entire ethnicity could be dreamed up—an attempt to annihilate every Tutsi who had a claim on Rwanda, carried out by Rwandans on Rwandans. The violent extremism was nurtured over decades of an armed peace, but it could have been controlled or even eradicated before Hutu Power enacted its "final solution." Through our indifference, squabbling, distraction and delays, we lost a great many opportunities to destabilize the génocidaires and derail the genocide. I can easily delineate the factors that might have guaranteed our success, beginning with having the political and cultural savvy from the start to ensure an effective military and civilian police presence on the ground in Rwanda as soon as the Arusha Peace

531

Agreement was signed; providing UNAMIR with hard intelligence on the ex-belligerents' intentions, ambitions and goals so that we didn't have to fumble in the dark; providing the mission with the political and diplomatic muscle to outmanoeuvre the hard-liners and also to push the RPF into a few timely concessions; reasonable administrative and logistical support of the mission; a few more well-trained and properly equipped battalions on the ground; a more liberal and forceful application of the mandate; and to bring it all off, a budget increase of only about US$100 million.

Could we have prevented the resumption of the civil war and the genocide? The short answer is yes. If UNAMIR had received the modest increase of troops and capabilities we requested in the first week, could we have stopped the killings? Yes, absolutely. Would we have risked more UN casualties? Yes, but surely soldiers and peacekeeping nations should be prepared to pay the price of safeguarding human life and human rights. If UNAMIR 2 had been deployed on time and as requested, would we have reduced the prolonged period of killing? Yes, we would have stopped it much sooner.

If we had chosen to enhance the capabilities of UNAMIR in these ways, we could have wrested the initiative from the ex-belligerents in reasonably short order and stymied the aggression for enough time to expose and weaken the "third force." I truly believe the missing piece in the puzzle was the political will from France and the United States to make the Arusha accords work and ultimately move this imploding nation toward democracy and a lasting peace. There is no doubt that those two countries possessed the solution to the Rwandan crisis.

Let there be no doubt: the Rwandan genocide was the ultimate responsibility of those Rwandans who planned, ordered, supervised and eventually conducted it. Their extremism was the seemingly indestructible and ugly harvest of years of power struggles and insecurity that had been deftly played upon by their former colonial rulers. But the deaths of Rwandans can also be laid at the door of the military genius Paul Kagame, who did not speed up his campaign when the scale of the genocide became clear and even talked candidly with me at several points about the price his fellow Tutsis might have to pay for the cause. Next in line when it comes to responsibility are France, which moved in too late and ended up protecting the génocidaires and permanently destabilizing the region, and the U.S. government, which actively worked against an effective UNAMIR and only got involved to aid the same Hutu refugee population and the génocidaires, leaving the genocide survivors to flounder and suffer. The failings of the UN and Belgium were not in the same league.

My own *mea culpa* is this: as the person charged with the military leadership of UNAMIR, I was unable to persuade the international community that this tiny, poor, over-populated country and its people were worth saving from the horror of genocide—even when the measures needed for success were relatively small. How much of that inability was linked to my inexperience? Why was I chosen to lead UNAMIR? My experience was in training Canadian peacekeepers to go into classic Cold War–style conflicts; I had never been in the field as a peacekeeper myself. I had no political expertise, and no background or training in African affairs or manoeuvring in the weeds of ethnic conflicts in which hate trumps reason. I had no way to gauge the duplicity of the ex-belligerents. The professional development of senior officers in matters of classic peacekeeping, let alone in the thickets of the post-modern version (which I prefer to call conflict resolution), has often been reduced to throwing officers into situations and seeing whether they can cope. While the numbers of UN troop-contributing nations has increased well beyond the more traditional contributors (among which Canada was a major player), there are still no essential prerequisites of formal education and training for the job.

▲ Document 2: Peacekeeper

Major-General Lewis MacKenzie

In UNPROFOR [United Nations Protection Force in the former Yugoslavia], our problem was equally pressing. We had no mandate from the UN Security Council to get involved in the affairs of Bosnia, yet the situation was deteriorating all around us. The European Community was supposed to be taking the lead in peacemaking; the EC's Lord Carrington had a special representative in Bosnia, Colm Doyle, an Irish army major, who was doing his best, like the rest of us, to find out what was actually happening. Until we knew that, there was little we could do, except to offer to provide our "good offices" if a neutral setting were required for intercommunal discussions.

[...] APRIL 22

Keeping UN New York up-to-date on developments was taking most of our time. Officials there were concerned that we were getting involved in the conflict. Frankly, we had no choice: to sit in our headquarters while the city fell apart all around us would have destroyed what little credibility we had. The people of Sarajevo did not understand that we had no mandate in Bosnia and, quite understandably, expected us to help them with their humanitarian needs. Regrettably, every time we tried, we were accused of collaborating with the side we assisted.

[...] JULY 12

It took a while to realize it, but I think to this day that our main problem was our title, UNPROFOR. The term "United Nations Protection Force" was appropriate for the initial deployment of our peacekeepers in Croatia. The 14,000 UN soldiers were sent there to protect the people living in the UNPAS, primarily Serbs, from outside attack. The UN had assumed the responsibility for relieving the JNA [Yugoslav People's Army] of its protection role, thereby permitting it to return to Serbia, and reducing the risk of confrontation between Croatia and Serbia. Things turned out differently, of course; the threat to people living in the UNPAS came from within, particularly from the Serbs, who started to evict non-Serbs from the UNPAS. In addition, many JNA [Yugoslav People's Army] soldiers merely took off their uniforms and stayed put. Nevertheless, the title of UNPROFOR was applicable to the task that the UN had been given in Croatia.

But not in Bosnia. Along came our 1,400-strong force to Sarajevo riding white vehicles and wearing blue helmets and calling ourselves UNPROFOR, because that was the name of the organization we belonged to. The city was frequently the target of heavy shelling, and civilian casualties were high. Most of the damage was done by the Bosnian-Serb guns located in the hills around Sarajevo; but the local citizenry was not aware that the government's TDF forces initiated a good many of the incidents, to which the Serbs usually overreacted with their heavy weapons.

With a name like United Nations Protection Force, it was not unreasonable for the citizens of Sarajevo to expect that our job was to protect *them*. Certainly, the Presidency was perpetuating the idea that we had a responsibility to take their side in the conflict. Their reasoning followed the logical but impractical assumption that as a member of the UN, Bosnians should be able to rely on any UN peacekeeping force to be on their side. As

533

Source: Excerpt from *Peacekeeper: The Road to Sarajevo* by Major-General Lewis MacKenzie, pp. 137, 158-59, 291-93, 330-32, published 1993 by Douglas & McIntyre, an imprint of D&M Publisher Inc. Reprinted with permission from the publisher.

citizens of a new country that started fighting for its existence the day it was born, Bosnians didn't understand, or refused to accept, that an international peacekeeping force had to deal with both sides on a regular basis, and to pass objective judgment on events as they transpired. Any suggestion that anyone but the Serbs or Bosnian Serbs were 100 per cent responsible for each and every incident was unacceptable to the Presidency.

As far as the Presidency was concerned, I represented the impotence of the United Nations. The UN traditionally tries to avoid civil wars like the plague; there is seldom an effective way to bring international pressure to bear on any of the sides in a civil conflict. In the case of Bosnia, the UN was trying to pressure the Bosnian Serbs by imposing economic sanctions on Serbia; however, there was a lack of conclusive evidence that President Milosevic in Belgrade was actually controlling Dr. Karadzic in Pale, or providing him with significant military support. On the other hand, the official government of Bosnia-Herzegovina led by President Izetbegovic, a full-fledged member of the UN, was asking the international body for help, and the best that the UN could offer was to open the Sarajevo airport. Consensus could not be found within the Security Council for a more ambitious intervention. Izetbegovic was understandably disappointed by the lack of military action by the UN, and by the world body's reluctance to lift its embargo on arms shipments to the region. And thanks to efforts by members of his Presidency and the TDF, it appeared that I had become the lightning rod for the dissatisfaction of his people.

Rumours were being circulated that my wife was a Serb, and that she had been introduced to me by the "Serbian terrorist, Mila Mulroney", the wife of Canadian Prime Minister Brian Mulroney. Mrs. Mulroney was indeed born a Serb but left Sarajevo permanently for Canada when she was five years old, and so must have started her "terrorist" career at a very young age. Before I was to leave, various members of the Presidency asked me to pass on their regards to Mila, as they had liked her very much when they had attended university with her in Sarajevo. A terrorist *and* a university student by five years of age—I was impressed.

After some twelve hours of consideration, I kept returning to the same conclusion: UNPROFOR might be unpopular, but it was at least doing some good for the people; I, on the other hand, was an obstacle to the peace process, and the disinformation campaign against me was endangering the lives of everyone who worked with me. Having witnessed the reasonable level of co-operation that had quickly developed between the new UN officers in town, such as Michel Jones, and the Presidency, I reluctantly decided that a new sector commander would probably have a much better chance to advance the peace process than I did. Even more importantly, in my eyes, the hatred being directed towards UN personnel in my name would, I hoped, subside on my departure.

I met with General de Chastelain; he listened to my logic, which culminated in my telling him I intended to ask General Nambiar to replace me. To my pleasant surprise, the CDS said he understood; he'd considered pulling me out earlier. In fact, he thought I should leave as soon as possible.

[…] Since returning from Sarajevo, I have been publicly critical of the UN's ability to command, control and support logistically its burgeoning peacekeeping forces in the field. Numerous UN commanders have expressed similar criticisms in the past; however, due to the extensive media coverage given to my command, my views received a considerable amount of attention and, regrettably, resulted in some hard feelings at the UN.

I say "regrettably" because I am a staunch supporter of the UN. I feel it is the only international organization that has the potential to cope with an increasingly complex and unstable world. Unfortunately, it was not possible to encourage the debate needed to bring about a review of the UN's shortcomings without resorting to the strident sound bites that capture the media's, and the public's, imagination.

The vast majority of the people I worked with in UN New York were hard-working, dedicated individuals. They gave me every bit of support within their capacity to do so. Unfortunately, they were handcuffed by systemic inefficiencies within the overall UN bureaucracy.

"If you are a commander of a UN mission, don't get in trouble after five P.M. or on the weekend. There is no one in the UN to answer the phone!" Yes, I said that. My friends and former bosses in the UN were hurt and replied that, indeed, they had talked to me many times after five P.M. They were absolutely right, but they missed my point: they talked to me from home, a reception or, in some cases, from bed, but that isn't the same as being able to report to a command headquarters on a twenty-four-hour basis.

To give the UN credit, communicating with its commanders in the field during office hours was good enough from the first observer mission in 1947 until 1992. Peacekeeping forces were doing just that, keeping the peace; most of the time, except for some violent exceptions in the Congo and Lebanon, there was ample time to react to a crisis during office hours. A UN commander was given a mandate, resources and a budget, and told to get on with it. He didn't need or desire a lot of contact with UN headquarters in New York. I felt exactly the same way when I commanded the UN mission in Central America in 1991.

All of that changed when the UN decided to place the headquarters of its Croatian UNPROFOR operation in Sarajevo in 1992 and was inexorably drawn into the Bosnian conflict. The numerous crises in that city required urgent input by the UN, but the diplomatic technique of exchanging coded cables was not up to the challenge. Soldiers are used to talking to other soldiers at their headquarters—superiors who speak their military language and, more importantly, who understand what's going on, day to day, in the operational theatre.

Over the past few years, the number of UN peacekeepers deployed around the world has grown from fewer than 5,000 to well over 60,000, and yet, at the time of writing, there is still no military-style command centre in UN New York: no one on duty twenty-four hours a day, seven days a week; no communications room with maps of the various operational areas on the wall, and mission-knowledgeable duty officers manning the radios and keeping a log of all the information and requests coming in from the field. No army in the world would deploy its troops with so little direct control over what they were doing. The UN shouldn't either.

The solution is simple, and various nations are ready to take on responsibility for helping to provide it: a full-time UN peacekeeping operations centre should be established as a matter of priority. It should be manned by experienced officers with previous UN peacekeeping service, and it should have planning capability.

Another problem is that the UN is currently incapable of providing adequate logistics support to its various missions around the world. In theory, national military units are supposed to arrive in the theatre self-contained for a period of sixty to ninety days, after which a system of internationally-let contracts is supposed to kick in and provide the necessary logistics support. But unfortunately, many countries are not capable of or willing to send their units self-contained. Within UNPROFOR, as an example, the battalion from Nepal arrived without vehicles. Germany ultimately gave them what they needed, but the requisite spare parts and personnel to maintain the German fleet were not included.

Within UNPROFOR, there were six different headquarters, comprised of individuals from a cross-section of nations. No concerted, overall plan was drawn up to meet the

535

logistics needs of these groups, and obviously they were incapable of being "self-contained". Months after our arrival, they were still missing the basic items to permit them to carry out their responsibilities.

Recent UN missions have experienced dramatic changes to their mandates and responsibilities on a month-to-month basis. The UN is willing to take on expanded roles for its missions, but cannot generate the expanded logistics support in anything approaching a timely manner. In UNPROFOR, the role of the officer observers grew tremendously in importance; however, the vehicles and radios critical to their effectiveness never did show up in adequate numbers. Lives were put at risk as the observers' vehicles were forced to go on patrol singly, when pairs of vehicles were absolutely necessary for safety.

A solution to the logistics problem is not easy, but has to be addressed. A chain of logistics bases is required around the world to support UN peacekeeping operations. They must have the necessary equipment on hand, or at least the ability and the budget to purchase it. Such bases exist today; they are American military bases.

The U.S. is delinquent in payment of its UN dues for peacekeeping purposes. Since the Americans are the largest contributor to the UN budget, their debt has a tremendously detrimental effect on UN operations in the field. The U.S. is not keeping up with its payments because it knows peacekeeping money is being wasted on overly generous allowances and benefits, and a bloated peacekeeping bureaucracy. If I were in the Americans' position, I wouldn't pay all of my UN bills either. Fortunately, their predicament has the makings of a solution.

▲ Document 3: Support in the Nick of Time

SUPPORT IN THE NICK OF TIME

Source: "Support in the Nick of Time." *The Toronto Daily Star,* 8 November 1956. Reprinted with permission by Torstar Syndication Services.

▲ Document 4: End of the Debate

END OF THE DEBATE

● **Documents 3 and 4 are cartoons published in a Toronto newspaper following the announcement of the creation of peacekeeping forces in 1956. These cartoons reflect not only the new meaning for the military of participating in peacekeeping operations, but also the debate over Lester B. Pearson's proposal and its impact on Canadian foreign policy. How is Canada portrayed in the cartoons? What do we learn about peacekeeping missions?**

Source: "End of the Debate." *The Toronto Daily Star*, 16 October 1957. Reprinted with permission by Torstar Syndication Services.

538

▲ Document 5: The Blue Berets

T. C. Connors

Yes we are the Blue Berets
We're up and on our way
With another UN flag to be unfurled
Till the factions are at bay and peace is on its way
We'll display our Blue Berets around the world

Yes we are the Blue Berets
We're always proud to say
We'll stand between the mighty and the frail
And where children cannot play because war is in their way
We shall send in our blue berets without fail

For we are the Blue Berets
And we know we're far away
Tell our family and our friends that come to call
If you count the lonely days
You'll see you blue berets marching home again to say We Love You All

Yes we are the Blue Berets
We're marching on our way
Where bullets fly and rockets madly hurl
And where hungers never cease
And mothers cry for peace
We try to bring some hope to an ugly world

We are the Blue Berets
We're marching on our way
With another UN flag to be unfurled
Till the factions are at bay and peace is on its way
We'll display our Blue Berets around the world

For we are the Blue Berets
And we know we're far away
Tell our family and our friends that come to call
If you count the lonely days
You'll see you blue berets marching home again to say "We Love You All"

If you count the lonely days
You'll see you blue berets marching home again to say "We Love You All"

539

▲ Document 6: Serbs and the U.N.

● Documents 6 and 7 depict the relations between Serbs and the United Nations. How do the cartoonists convey a sense of domination on the part of the Serbs? Compare and contrast how the United Nations Organization and peacekeeping forces are depicted in both cartoons.

Source: Aislin (alias Terry Mosher), 1994, McCord Museum M997.53.153.

▲ Document 7: Serbs Take On the UN

Source: Serge Chapleau, 1995, McCord Museum M997.52.101.

▲ Document 8: Canada's United Nations Peacekeeping Missions, 1947 to 1990s

The legend of the map lists:

1. Guatemala
2. Honduras
3. El Salvador
4. Costa Rica
5. Haiti
6. Dominican Rep.
7. Nicaragua
8. Croatia
9. Western Sahara
10. Iran
11. Iraq
12. Syria
13. Cyprus
14. Lebanon
15. Israel
16. Nigeria
17. Zaire
18. Angola
19. Namibia
20. Afghanistan
21. Kuwait
22. Jordan
23. Egypt
24. Pakistan
25. Yemen
26. Somalia
27. Laos
28. Cambodia
29. India
30. Korea
31. Vietnam
32. Indonesia

Past peacekeeping missions
Current peacekeeping missions

● Canada's United Nations peacekeeping missions, from 1947 to the 1990s.

Source: Adapted from *The Integrated Atlas: History and Geography of Canada and the World* (Toronto: Harcourt Brace, 1996), p. 120; and from *Destinies: Canadian History Since Confederation*, Sixth Edition, Francis, R. Douglas; Jones, Richard; Smith, Donald B. © 2008 Nelson Education Ltd. Reproduced by permission. www.cengage.com/permissions.

■ Article 1: The Golden Age, 1945–1957

Costas Melakopides

Canada's control over its foreign policy could not, by definition, begin before the recognition of the country's sovereignty. This recognition was legally conferred by the Statute of Westminster (1931), which followed the 1926 Balfour Declaration whereby Canada, along with the United Kingdom and the other dominions, became "autonomous communities within the British Empire, equal in status, in no way subordinate to one another in any aspect of their domestic or external affairs, though united by a common allegiance to the Crown."

The Department of External Affairs was established by Ottawa in 1909. Until 1945, however, Canada's external relations were conducted in a semi-autonomous fashion.[1] Thus, the declaration of war against Germany by London in 1914 entailed Canada's automatic involvement in the First World War. When Canada participated in the 1919 Paris peace conference, the country's representatives were part of the imperial delegation. During the interwar period, Canada opted for an isolationist policy both in an effort to avoid overseas entanglements and in view of the conscription crisis, caused by the First World War, which had divided anglophone and francophone Canadians. At the same time, and until the outbreak of the Second World War, Canada relied on London for the conduct of its external relations, having only five diplomatic legations abroad in addition to the High Commission in London. And in the spirit of isolationism, still favoured by Prime Minister Mackenzie King, Ottawa gave support to British Prime Minister Chamberlain's policy of appeasement towards the Nazis.

When war broke out, however, Mackenzie King submitted to Parliament the government's declaration of war on Nazi Germany, which did not receive approval until a whole week later. The delay was intended to signal that Canada's decision to join the allied effort was taken independently.[2] During the

war, Canada's performance was more than honourable. Its contribution involved placing over a million men under arms. Canadians suffered 85,000 casualties: 53,000 wounded and 32,000 dead. In addition, the country trained allied airmen; it supplied war material to the Allies, being a serious source of help to the Soviet armed forces; and its 1941 Defence Production Agreement with the United States allowed Canada to channel American support to Britain at a crucial juncture of the war effort.[3]

Having thus made an important contribution to the victory, and having been called by Winston Churchill in September 1941, "the linchpin of the English-speaking world," Canada emerged in 1945 as one of the world's economic powers, being the second-largest trading nation, while also possessing remarkable military strength.

Canada's former isolationist inclinations were now receding, and the country was poised to play an activist new role in the world. Indeed, already in July 1943, with hostilities still flaring, Prime Minister Mackenzie King expressed Canada's emerging internationalism. In a House of Commons speech, he enunciated the "functional principle." As King put it,

> on the one hand, authority in international affairs must not be concentrated exclusively in the largest powers. On the other, authority cannot be divided equally among all the thirty or more sovereign states that comprise the United Nations, or all effective authority will disappear [...] Representation should be determined on a functional basis which will admit to full membership these countries, large or small, which have the greatest contribution to make to the particular object in question.[4]

This principle has been captured memorably by Blair Fraser as amounting to the aphorism, "Let those who can, do." Functionalism was energetically and creatively employed by Canada's delegates to the United Nations San Francisco Conference in 1945. After the Bretton Woods Conference of December 1944, which founded the postwar international politico-economic order, this was the country's next major opportunity to help shape the postwar world. The San Francisco Conference ushered in the golden age of Canadian diplomacy.

Source: Costas Melakopides, *Pragmatic Idealism: Canadian Foreign Policy 1945–1999.* "The Golden Age, 1945-1597," pp. 37-51, 206-07. McGill-Queen's University Press, 1998. Reprinted with permission.

543

The 1945–57 period, also known as the St. Laurent–Pearson era, crystallized the principles of Canadian foreign policy for subsequent years. It established the major patterns of Canada's international behaviour and its conception of its role in the world. Telling manifestations of these principles and patterns relate to Canada's relations with the United Nations, the North Atlantic Treaty Organization (NATO), Britain and the Commonwealth, and the two superpowers, the United States and the Soviet Union.

Canada and the United Nations

At San Francisco, Canada emerged as a committed advocate of the United Nations' role as humankind's best hope to attain and maintain international security, cooperation, and peace. Canada also assumed a leading position among a group of countries that came to be known as middle powers. At the conference Canada aimed to achieve a number of objectives: to contain the great powers' overwhelming weight at the new global organization; to increase the voice and role of the middle powers, on the basis of the functional principle; to limit the veto power of the Security Council's five permanent members; to create a United Nations police force; and finally, to emphasize the importance of economic and social cooperation and development as the best means to consolidate international security and peace.[5]

Canada's energetic pursuit of middle-power functionalism bore impressive fruits. The entire United Nations Charter is marked by the Canadian delegation's influence. For instance, because of Canadian proposals, article 23(1) includes the declaration that, in the election of non-permanent members of the Security Council, "due regard [will also be] specially paid" to the contribution made by members of the United Nations "to the maintenance of international peace and security and to the other purposes of the Organization." Other examples of articles affected, and at times determined, by Canada's views and proposals include: articles 10 and 12 on some functions of the General Assembly; article 23 on the composition of the Security Council; article 24(3) about the Security Council's submitting reports to the General Assembly; article 44 regarding the participation of a member in Security Council deliberations, if that member's armed forces were invited to send contingents under the chapter VII "Action with Respect to Threats to the Peace, Breaches of the Peace, and Acts of Aggression"; and articles 100, 101, and 105 concerning the Secretariat. Finally, many of the proposals submitted by Canada regarding the Economic and Social Council (ECOSOC) were adopted and written into chapter 10 of the charter.[6]

Louis St. Laurent, as minister of external affairs, articulated explicitly the interests and principles of Canada's internationalist commitment in the Gray Lecture of January 1947[…]. That is why, as St. Laurent concluded, "We are preparing ourselves to fulfil the growing responsibilities in world affairs which we have accepted as a modern state"; and we have "a useful part to play in world affairs, useful to ourselves through being useful to others."[7]

The United Nations was the primary vehicle chosen by Canada for the fulfilment of these internationalist "responsibilities." In the same spirit, when Canada was elected to the Security Council, St. Laurent observed in September 1947: "We in this country continue to believe that the best hope for mankind lies in the establishment of a world organization for the maintenance of peace [...] [and] if we wish to enjoy the benefits of such a development we must also accept its responsibilities."[8] We must, of course, recall that by September 1947 the Cold War was in full swing. East and West, under the leadership of Stalin in Moscow and Harry Truman in Washington, were poised for confrontation. Mutual suspicions and mistrust had elevated the antagonism to the point where military conflict between the former Second World War allies could not be precluded. To recall this dramatic context (six months after the enunciation of the March 1947 Truman Doctrine) helps one appreciate the significance of St. Laurent's view of the United Nations as "the best hope for mankind."

Peacekeeping under United Nations' auspices was a major avenue that Canada employed to fulfil its internationalist vocation. It began participating in all UN peacekeeping activities although, strictly speaking, the term came into use only with the 1956 Suez mission. Thus, Canada's first observer missions began in 1948 in Palestine, with the setting up of the United Nations Truce Supervision Organization (UNTSO), and in 1949, with the UN Military Observer Group in India and Pakistan (UNMOGIP).

Quite clearly, the Suez crisis of October 1956 is properly regarded as having provided the opportunity for Canada's, and Lester Pearson's, most successful diplomatic intervention. Pearson's immediate goals seem to have been, first, to defuse the Suez crisis which was threatening regional and global security, given Nikita Khrushchev's vociferous threats that he would "shower" the West with nuclear rockets. Second, Pearson aimed to help Britain and France save face once their governments had been widely condemned as aggressors and abandoned at the Security Council even by the administration of President Eisenhower. The third goal was to save the Commonwealth from the nearly fatal blow to its integrity caused by the widespread perception that London's Suez action was an "imperialist adventure." And fourth, Lester Pearson wished to demonstrate the United Nations' capability to handle regional or global crises by diplomatic means.[9] Pearson's masterful 1956 initiative at the United Nations was rewarded, a year later, by the Nobel Peace Prize.

Meanwhile, however, the Korean War of 1950–3 had seriously threatened world peace. Here, too, Canada's skills of communication, moderation, and mediation were instrumental in ending the conflict. By the summer of 1952, it looked as though the Soviet Union might enter the war, thus widening the conflict and causing a new global conflagration. Canada, with Lester Pearson holding the presidency of the UN General Assembly, initiated a series of diplomatic contacts and behind-the-scenes negotiations which produced a resolution agreed to by the conflicting sides.

As former Canadian high commissioner to India, Chester Ronning, wrote in 1966, Pearson's historic success was due to a number of factors: to his cooperation with India and other member states which shared Canada's views; to persistent consultations with all UN members which secured support for the armistice resolution; and to "friendly behind-the-scene negotiations" with the United States and other participants in the UN-sponsored action in Korea. As a consequence, Canada's achievement, according to Chester Ronning, was "fully as important as the Suez success to which greater importance was attached because Korea was away off in Asia."[10]

Beyond these peacekeeping and peacemaking triumphs, Canada's role in the United Nations—which has been called "the cornerstone of the country's external relations" during this period[11]—included sustained contributions that spanned the entire spectrum of the UN's agenda and mandate. Thus, Canada's own representatives, and Canadians as international civil servants, dealt energetically and creatively with social, economic, educational, and technical issues, including those of disarmament and arms control. The success of Canada in the various committees, commissions, and councils of the UN's specialized agencies can be illustrated through the list of Canadians who held crucial posts. Dr. Brock Chisholm was elected as the first director of the World Health Organization (WHO). He had already helped prepare the International Health Conference of June 1946 and the draft constitution of WHO. Before accepting the post of WHO's director general in June 1948, he had been executive secretary of its Interim Commission for two years. When he retired from his WHO post in 1953 he had been offered a three-year extension. He declined arguing that "a permanent organization should not have the same head for too long, particularly at the beginning of its history."[12] Dr. George Davidson served as high commissioner for refugees, while Major-General Howard Kennedy was first director general of the United Nations Relief and Works Agency for Palestine Refugees in the Near East (UNRWA), an agency created in 1949. Dr. Hugh Keenleyside was the first director general of the UN Technical Assistance Administration. Escott Reid, among other activities, occupied an important position at the World Bank, while numerous Canadians served with the other international economic organizations created under the auspices of the Bretton Woods system. Finally, this list must recall that General E.L.M. Burns served both as chief of staff of UNTSO in Palestine (from 1954 to 1956) and as commander of the United Nations Expeditionary Force.[13]

A major ground for Canada's success story at the United Nations is associated with the superb diplomatic skills, the engaging personality, and the internationalist credentials of Lester B. Pearson. The great Canadian diplomat and statesman had attracted the respect of the international community even before receiving the Nobel Prize. Having already served as president of the General Assembly, he had played important roles in establishing the United Nations Relief and Rehabilitation Administration (UNRRA) and the Food and Agriculture Organization of the United Nations (FAO). Lester Pearson was also nominated twice for the post of secretary general—a nomination vetoed by Moscow. In a review of his book, *Diplomacy in the Nuclear Age*, John F. Kennedy wrote, in 1959, that "already 'Mike' Pearson has been the chief architect of the Canadian foreign service, probably unequalled by any nation; he has been a brilliant ambassador and foreign secretary; he has been a central figure in the growth of the Atlantic Community and NATO, even while taking a leading role in the shaping of the United Nations."[14]

"Clearly," wrote Peyton Lyon, "there is substance in the conventional judgment that Pearson's personal commitment and talent contributed greatly to Canada's internationalist image." Yet Pearson was not alone, neither was he "the most profound thinker within the Ottawa mandarinate." The period of the golden decade (as Peyton Lyon more modestly calls it) also witnessed the outstanding contributions of many more inspired Canadian internationalists than we have already mentioned. Thus, Peyton Lyon could hardly contain his enthusiasm about them. Hume Wrong "earned an awesome reputation for being right about global trends," being also "exceptionally influential in Washington." Norman Robertson "displayed comparable knowledge and a strikingly fertile imagination." Wynne Plumptre and Louis Rasminsky "made outstanding contributions" in the founding of the International Monetary Fund and the International Bank for Reconstruction and Development (World Bank). And Escott Reid, distinguished by "his faith in grand designs" (as recorded in his autobiography, *Radical Mandarin*) "proved extraordinarily effective as a drafter of international constitutions."[15]

The list of the internationals reserves a special place for two other contributors to the shaping of the postwar world through the UN and Canada's role therein. The first is Paul Martin, who successfully negotiated with Moscow—over strong opposition from Washington—the expansion of UN membership in 1955. The other is John Holmes, the distinguished diplomat, scholar, and teacher about whom Margaret Doxey has written:

> A firm believer in multilateralism, and in the United Nations as an important framework for diplomatic and peacekeeping initiatives, John [...] never tilted at windmills, but looked for practical ways to achieve progress towards a more peaceful and equitable world. And he was, of course, particularly concerned that Canada as a "middle power" should play its full part in this process.[16]

Behind-the-scenes bridge-building and informal but effective mediation became hallmarks of Ottawa's golden age middlepowermanship. The Canadians' talent for such mediation, as Peyton Lyon has stressed, is "a fact widely appreciated by foreign diplomats." In particular, Pearson's success in achieving the Korean armistice under United Nations auspices "did much to intensify the Canadian elite's conviction that as moderators of US behaviour, they were performing a service vital to mankind."[17]

It has already transpired, therefore, why the familiar appellations "honest broker" and "helpful fixer" became entrenched during the golden age of Canadian diplomacy. But these terms also derived from Canada's consistent pursuit of functionalist principles and internationalist values in a variety of other forums, including the North Atlantic Treaty Organization.

Canada and NATO

Idealist optimism fuelled the creation of the United Nations and sustained Canada's committed support for its mandate. This optimism, however, was dramatically undermined by the eruption of the Cold War between 1946 and 1947. Whatever one views as the precise locus of responsibility for the antagonism of the two camps or blocs, Ottawa was profoundly concerned with the ominous changes in the international climate. These changes followed Stalin's threatening conduct in the Middle East and Eastern Europe; Winston Churchill's March 1946 "Iron Curtain" speech at Fulton, Missouri; and President Harry Truman's March 1947 speech to the joint session of the US Congress which enunciated his historic doctrine.[18] From Ottawa, St. Laurent was among the first to call for the creation of an instrument of collective Atlantic defence, to parallel the UN's role as an institution of collective security.[19]

During the negotiations for the creation of NATO, from 22 March 1948 to 15 March 1949, Canada distinguished itself in at least two ways: by being an ardent supporter of the emerging Atlantic alliance, which would involve the United States in the defence of Europe and thus help "contain" Stalin's perceived expansionist designs; and by insisting that NATO would have to be more than a mere military bloc.

As Escott Reid has shown, Canada's principal objectives during the multilateral negotiations for NATO were: to produce a treaty, and not just a relevant declaration by the American president; to attain an article guaranteeing the collectiveness of the common defence; to include a strong article on non-military cooperation among the members; and to oppose Italy's membership and the treaty's extension to cover Algeria (then a French territory).[20]

Canadian negotiators succeeded fully in their first goal, but were not successful in keeping Italy out. And while Washington opposed a stress on non-military cooperation, Canada succeeded in inserting article 2 in the NATO Charter. This article has been known ever since as "the Canadian Article."[21]

Canada's contribution to the formation of NATO demonstrated the country's penchant for moderation, exemplified by less bellicose stands and less threatening options than other allied capitals would favour. Ottawa consistently advocated moderation in the handling of Moscow, attempting to dissuade the allies from rhetoric or tactics that might be perceived by the Soviet Union as provocative and thus fuelling the vicious circle of East-West mistrust and insecurity. In addition, Canadian statesmen (St. Laurent and Pearson in particular) tended to believe that the manifest superiority of Western political principles and values would suffice, ultimately, to win the Cold War:

> Perhaps naïvely—certainly naïvely in the opinion of some American leaders at the time—men like St. Laurent and Pearson never lost hope of piercing the Iron Curtain, of re-building confidence among the leaders of the two blocs, and of hammering out at the Conference table the conditions for peaceful coexistence. Even at the height of the Cold War, the view prevailed in Ottawa that as the West demonstrated its superior ability to meet human needs and aspirations, Communist Society would become more liberal.[22]

Be that as it may, from 1950 to 1957 Canada's defence expenditures averaged 6.3 per cent of the country's GNP. More than half of this was Canada's contribution to NATO. During this period, Canada deployed ground forces to Germany and air forces to France, thereby demonstrating its pragmatic endorsement of the concept that security for the Atlantic allies began at the central front in Europe. Canada's motives regarding NATO, however, also involved the persistent effort to attain an effective "counterweight."

Now that Britain's power as Canada's traditional protector had clearly receded, NATO Europe could be expected to counterbalance the overwhelming power and influence of the United States. In other words, while Canada's Western interests and credentials were being cultivated and enhanced through membership in NATO, Canada's consuming need for distinctness was also ever-present. The Atlantic alliance, therefore, being an organization for collective defence, could, among other things, meet Canada's need to contain the influence and raw power of the Western superpower.

Britain and the Commonwealth

During its golden age, Canadian diplomacy used the Commonwealth as another vehicle or forum for special contacts and relations with a large part of the Third World and the advanced industrial democracies of the United Kingdom, Australia, and New Zealand. Indeed, just as Canada was instrumental in the adoption of the Balfour Declaration by the 1926 Imperial Conference (which recognized the autonomy of the dominions), Canadians helped decisively in the expansion of the Commonwealth to cover the millions of people of the Indian subcontinent in the 1940s. Thus, the assurances of Mackenzie King to Prime Minister Jawaharlal Nehru convinced India to remain a member. Nehru's fears that the Commonwealth was just another name for the British Empire and membership would contradict India's status as a republic were assuaged. Nehru decided on Indian membership when Canada proposed, and had it adopted, that by also calling the British sovereign "Head of the Commonwealth" some states would not have to accept him/her as their monarch. In this connection, Thomson and Swanson have observed: "Nehru was touched by the Canadian attitude, and decided [...] that if a country like Canada could be a member without sacrificing its principles, then India, too, could perhaps do so."[23] When Nehru convinced his country's political elite to remain in the Commonwealth, Pakistan and Ceylon followed the Indian lead.

At the Commonwealth meeting in Colombo, Ceylon, in January 1950, Lester Pearson was the main protagonist in negotiations which resulted in the Colombo Plan for Cooperative Economic Development in South and Southeastern Asia. As Indian Ambassador Rajeshwar Dayal has written, "Lester Pearson's participation in the opening meeting [...]

547

helped to endow the plan with body and substance [...] Pearson was instrumental in assuring the Canadian government's generous financial contribution towards the plan's objectives."[24]

The Colombo Plan was the first multinational aid program of the postwar era. Lester Pearson's pledge of $25 million a year as Canada's contribution established the honourable, and later distinguished, Canadian record in the field of development assistance to the Third World. If India was the top recipient of Canada's aid among the Commonwealth nations, this was both because of that country's genuine development needs and the emergence of the "Indo-Canadian love affair." Fruits of this relationship included a number of common initiatives and diplomatic projects, such as collaboration during the crises of Korea and Suez as well as in peacekeeping.

At the same time, Britain remained a focal point of Canadian foreign policy, given the deep roots of historical, linguistic, cultural, and political commonality of interests and values. In addition to the sentimental ties developed by these interests and by Canada's support of Britain during and after the Second World War, there was also the sharing of many politico-strategic perceptions surrounding the Cold War and the need to ensure the continued American presence in Europe. Finally, if the Suez crisis caused a certain schism within Canada (the Conservative party argued that Ottawa had "betrayed" London), it is certainly the case that Pearson's performance in the United Nations served the best interests of both the Commonwealth and Britain itself.

Thus, the Commonwealth emerged as a major forum for the exercise of Canadian middlepowermanship. Canada's longer-term goals here included the strengthening of political, commercial, and cultural links with a host of Third World members. In addition, the Commonwealth offered Canada numerous opportunities for North-South mediation and for enhanced credibility and prestige. Finally, of course, the multi-ethnic and multi-racial organization could provide Canada with another counterweight to the indisputable power of its southern neighbour.

Canada and the Superpowers

If the facts of geography had resulted in Canada's being "sandwiched between two superpowers," the presence of the United States at Canada's southern border and the manifest asymmetry of their power resulted in the Canada–United States connection becoming one of the most convoluted, variegated, intimate, and at times intense postwar bilateral relationships. One inescapable by-product was Canada's perennial sensitivity to the retention of its normative autonomy and its treasured distinct identity.

That this special relationship also contained the potential for friction did not follow only from the two countries' differences in political culture, size, power and capabilities, security perceptions, and strategic interests. Their interdependence inevitably involved Canada's profound fear of economic dependence on the United States. Whereas British capital had supported Canadian growth until the First World War, American capital began flowing massively to Canada after 1946. While this capital sustained Canadian growth, it also produced a disconcerting indebtedness. Canada's total indebtedness during 1945–70 reached $40 billion, and of this sum, 80 per cent was owed to the United States. The spectre of American economic domination thus developed, reaching peaks by the late 1950s and the late 1960s. Canadians became concerned that American capital was being attracted by crucial sectors of the country's economy. These sectors included mining, and the manufacturing of transport equipment, machinery, petroleum and coal products, and rubber and chemical products. Walter Gordon, a former Liberal finance minister, put the issue dramatically in his 1966 book, *A Choice for Canada: Imperialism or Colonial Status*. He wondered whether "Canada had become free of Britain's colonial influence only to fall under the spell of the United States' economic imperialism."

As it developed, therefore, Canada's policy towards the superpowers amounted to a sensitive synthesis. Ottawa policymakers on the one hand aimed at close collaboration with the United States and the Western alliance. On the other hand, they were committed to moderation in both Cold War rhetoric and in corresponding actions. The former dimension stemmed from Canada's anti-communist attitudes and the need to establish unambiguous Western credentials. The latter dimension, deriving from Canada's political-cultural distinctness, permitted Canada to perform a mediating and moderating role, even at the height of the Cold War.

More specifically, a certain independence in Ottawa's relations with Moscow began as early as

548

the immediate postwar years. This relative Canadian autonomy … seemed anchored on the following principles: reduction of international tensions through East-West bridge-building; increased communication through diplomatic contacts, moderate pronouncements, and exchange of official visits; persistent stress on detente; emphasis on a broader conception of security; de-ideologization of Canadian trade; and finally, cultivation of Canada's sense of independence and distinctness. In sum, Ottawa's post-1945 policy towards Moscow was an eloquent and tangible reflection of Canadian internationalism in action.

In Ottawa, St. Laurent and Pearson were convinced that the West was bound, ultimately, to win the Cold War, given its moral and material superiority. In Moscow, Ottawa's ambassador, Dana Wilgress, was producing explanatory and predictive accounts of Soviet foreign policy designs which endorsed Washington's perceptions that led to the policy of containment. It was, however, an endorsement with a clear Canadian difference. As shown in his cable to Ottawa of 27 September 1945, Wilgress was also aware of the Kremlin's own alarmism vis-à-vis the West: "The Western World is living in dread that the Soviet Union is out to spread Communism throughout the world. Do they ever stop to think that the Soviet Union is also living in dread that the Western World is out to restore capitalism to the Soviet Union?" Wilgress's prescription was entailed in his reply to his own question: "If we would succeed in removing these two obsessions, cooperation between the Soviet Union and the Western World would become operative without the friction now so obvious."[25]

Similarly, Escott Reid channelled the policy analysis of the Department of External Affairs along the lines of what we now call "post-revisionism." In other words, both superpowers were expanding powers; the Americans were not bereft of all the blame; but, for the next decade, the possibility of war appeared to be "remote," since the balance favoured the United States and the Kremlin policymakers abhorred "adventurism."[26] Given, therefore, Canada's interests in seeing Cold War tensions reduced, two policy prescriptions followed. First, Canada should moderate the extremist proclivities of some Washington circles: "If Canada can follow a policy which is consistent in purpose, though variegated and resourceful in application, it can exert a very considerable influence upon United States policy."

And second, presaging Ottawa's philosophy that led to the insistence on article 2 of the NATO Charter, Escott Reid noted that the West's "firmness need not be accompanied by rudeness." He added: "We should endeavour to follow a course which is neither that of excessive flattery nor of excessive ostracism."[27]

Thus, Ottawa's Cold War premises amounted to what Larry Collins labelled "containment without ostracism" and "containment with a 'human face'." Canada's concomitant attitudes were manifested during the negotiations for the formation of NATO. And, along with the principle of Canadian distinctness, these attitudes help explain the Liberal cabinet's repeated refusals to join Washington and London in confronting the Soviets' Berlin blockade of 1948–9.

Prudential internationalism continued to distinguish Ottawa's decisions at the beginning of the 1950s. While the Korean War was under way, the Department of External Affairs produced another document that kept endorsing a policy of caution and non-provocation. Entitled *General Limitations on Canadian Foreign Policy*, the November 1951 study advised: "Canadian foreign policy has to aim at promoting conditions most favourable for the achievement of an understanding with the Soviet Union which will provide reasonable relief from fear of imminent war or subversion."

Canada's Cold War role, then, was identified as follows: "Canada must ensure the Atlantic alliance does not infringe on vital Soviet interests which would provoke the very Russian response the alliance was set up to discourage. In sum, Canada must work in the alliance to protect the West's security without threatening the Soviets."[28]

Then, in September 1955, another External Affairs study capitalized on "the spirit of Geneva" and on the rising hopes for an easing of East-West tensions in a post-Stalinist world. The study, *Canadian Policy in the Light of Soviet Tactical Changes Since Geneva*, noted the risks to Canadian sovereignty from any escalation of the Cold War, since Washington could then pressure Canada to accept US bases and troops. It concluded that Canada's twin aims of security and national independence converged on one policy: namely, to attempt "to exploit the present Soviet willingness to establish more peaceful and normal relations between the two power blocs."[29]

Solidly in the internationalist forefront of pragmatic optimism, such thinking was soon translated

549

into diplomatic action. Lester Pearson became the first NATO foreign minister to visit the Soviet Union in October 1955. His visit to Moscow, Leningrad, and the Crimea implied Ottawa's determination to employ palpable communication and a preparedness to negotiate as the vehicles for the normalization of Canadian-Soviet relations. Pearson's trip was certainly successful. Besides repeatedly assuring Nikita Khrushchev and his entourage of NATO's "peaceful intentions," the visit marked the start of Canadian-Soviet cooperation in the economic, technical, and cultural fields.[30] The January 1956 trade agreement between the two "northern neighbours" established a new pattern of lucrative Canadian exports of wheat to the Soviet Union and extended each other most favoured nation (MFN) status. Moscow agreed to buy annually between $60 and $75 million worth of wheat. Notable also was the shift in Soviet attitudes towards Canada, which seems to have began with *Pravda's* October 1955 piece, "For Good Neighbourly Relations Between the USSR and Canada."[31]

During the next year, however, when Moscow-led Warsaw Pact troops invaded Hungary, Canada joined in condemnation of the bloody aggression. Nevertheless, St. Laurent's telegram to Moscow exhibited traditional Canadian moderation: it employed the vocabulary and tone that were to become the hallmarks of a distinct style of Canadian internationalism. Assuring Moscow that Canada did not intend to influence the type of government chosen by the Eastern Europeans, St. Laurent appealed "in the name of humanity" for the minimization of suffering. After all, the Suez crisis, perpetrated by Canada's own allies, was taking place simultaneously.

It thus transpires that Ottawa's attitudes and policies towards Moscow were a faithful reflection of its entrenched decision to exercise middlepowermanship at the height of the Cold War. Similarly, Ottawa's attitudes towards Washington sprung from Canada's decision to strike a sensitive balance between the genuine commitment to its Western obligations and values and the parallel need to protect its distinctness. Ottawa's relevant attitudes towards American foreign and security policies were a function of two clear decisions: to cultivate as harmonious and cooperative relations as possible with Canada's NATO allies and with Washington itself; and to assert Canada's special perceptions, interests, and values whenever the situation warranted. As we have seen, the latter implied that Ottawa would express subtly its disagreements with Washington. The most notable such cases arose during the negotiations for the formation of NATO; during the Berlin blockade of 1948–9; during the Korean War; and during the 1956 Soviet invasion of Hungary. As for Ottawa's manner of expressing its occasional disagreements, it was only natural that quiet diplomacy would emerge as Canada's favourite policy option.

Conclusions

This overview of the golden age may suffice to establish the set of clearly defined Canadian foreign policy goals. Central among them were the following: to contain the role of great powers and the explosive potential of the superpowers; to increase the rightful room for action by the middle powers; to expand the role and the significance of multilateral institutions; to be ready and willing to defuse major crises and to enhance simultaneously the long-term prospects for stability and peace; to forge manifold links with individual states and groups of states; to establish solid credentials as a moderating influence and mediating force in the world; and to contribute to the advancement of world prosperity by assisting in economic, technical, and educational programs under bilateral and multilateral auspices.

The interests and values on which these goals were premised constitute the essence of Canadian internationalism. Arguably, Ottawa's actual international performance during the golden age transcended the expectations of the optimists. Certainly, Canada's diplomatic energy, imagination, and at times brilliance established its superb internationalist prestige. Simultaneously, of course, Canadian foreign policy served a broad set of domestic interests and needs.

We can now appreciate far better both Lester Pearson's own role in implementing the pragmatic idealism of Canada's foreign policy and the predictive wisdom of his 1948 speech in Vancouver: "We instinctively know that Canada cannot easily secure and maintain prosperity except on the broadest basis of multilateralism—which is another name for internationalism [...] We also know, or should know, that there can be no political security except on the widest possible basis of co-operation."[32]

Notes

1. For the early years of the Department of External Affairs, see Eayrs, "The Origins of Canada's Department of External Affairs."

2. On Canada's declaration of war, see Eayrs, *In Defence of Canada*, Vol. II: *Appeasement and Rearmament*. Vol. III, *Peacemaking and Deterrence* (1972) is invaluable for the period 1943–49.

3. Middlemiss and Sokolsky, *Canadian Defence: Decisions and Determinants*, wrote:

   During World War II Canada once again contributed out of all proportion to its size. More than in the previous war, Canada was able to exploit its contributions to play an active role in Allied diplomacy and also to reinforce the image of the country as a truly distinct and indeed major international player. With the fall of the Axis powers and the weakening of Britain and France, Canada, physically untouched by the war, had been strengthened relative to other nations by the boost it gave to the development of its industry and resources (p. 16).

4. Canada, House of Commons, *Debates*, 9 July 1943, 4558. On the meaning of "functionalism," see Tucker, *Canadian Foreign Policy*, and Blair Fraser, *The Search for Identity: Canada, 1945–67*.

5. Lester Pearson provided illuminating background information and authoritative judgments on the Canadian delegation's goals, and its life and times in *Words and Occasions*.

6. See Canada, Department of External Affairs, *Canada and the United Nations, 1945–1975, passim*.

7. Department of External Affairs, *Statements and Speeches*, no. 47/2, 13 January 1947, 3–11.

8. Quoted in Thomson and Swanson, *Canadian Foreign Policy: Options and Perspectives*, 26.

9. For details on the Suez crisis and Pearson's role, see Fraser, *The Search for Identity*.

10. Ronning, in *Canada's Role as a Middle Power*, ed. J. King Gordon, 42.

11. Thomson and Swanson, *Canadian Foreign Policy*, 26.

12. Sanger, ed., *Canadians and the United Nations*, 14.

13. Thomson and Swanson, *Canadian Foreign Policy*, 90. Writing in 1971, these authors added: "Canada has demonstrated an active interest in the activities of UNESCO and UNICEF, in the FAO, which was founded in Quebec City, and in ICAO, which had its headquarters in Montreal."

14. John F. Kennedy's book review of Pearson's *Diplomacy in the Nuclear Age* first appeared in *Saturday Review* and is reprinted in *International Journal*, 66–70.

15. Lyon, "The Evolution of Canadian Diplomacy since 1945." In Painchaud, ed., *From Mackenzie King to Pierre Trudeau: Forty Years of Canadian Diplomacy, 1945–1985*, 16.

16. Doxcy in "John Holmes: An Appreciation," *Behind the Headlines*, 6.

17. Lyon, "The Evolution of Canadian Diplomacy," 18.

18. See Gaddis, "Towards a Post-Revisionist Synthesis"; also LaFeber, *America, Russia, and the Cold War, 1945–1984*, 1–73.

19. See Thomson and Swanson, *Canadian Foreign Policy*, ch. 5.

20. Reid, "The Creation of the North Atlantic Alliance, 1948–1949," in Granatstein, ed., *Canadian Foreign Policy*, 158–82.

21. Article 2 reads as follows:

    The Parties will contribute toward the further development of peaceful and friendly international relations by strengthening their free institutions, by bringing about a better understanding of the principles upon which these institutions are founded, and by promoting conditions of stability and well-being. They will seek to eliminate conflict in their international economic policies and will encourage economic collaboration between any or all of them. *Nato Facts and Figures*, Brussels: NATO Information Service (1971), 270.

22. Thomson and Swanson, *Canadian Foreign Policy*, 63.

23. Ibid, 80.

24. Dayal, "The Power of Wisdom," 112.

25. Quoted in Donald Page, "Détente: High Hopes and Disappointing Realities," in Balawyder, ed., *Canadian-Soviet Relations*, 25–6.

26. Quoted in Collins, "Canadian-Soviet Relations during the Cold War" in ibid., 44–5

27. Ibid., 44.

28. Ibid., 51.

29. Ibid., 53.

30. Lester Pearson gave his own colourful account of the trip in *Mike: The Memoirs of the Right Honourable Lester B. Pearson,* vol. 2, ed. Munro and Inglis, 191–211.

31. Black and Hillman, "Canada and the Soviet Union as Neighbours," in *Nearly Neighbours: Canada and the Soviet Union*, 6.

32. Pearson, *Words and Occasions*, 69.

Article 2: Peacekeeping: Did Canada Make A Difference? And What Difference Did Peacekeeping Make to Canada?

J. L. Granatstein

If there is any one area of foreign and defence policy in which Canada did unquestionably make a difference, it is surely in the area of peacekeeping. Lester Pearson's role during the Suez Crisis of 1956 and his subsequent Nobel Peace Prize fixed Canadian—and global—attention on the idea of interposing troops from many nations between warring armies. Before 1956, U.N. and other peacekeeping operations were modest efforts, of limited success, and carried out by relatively modest groups of observers; after 1956, peacekeeping was often a large-scale operation, regrettably also of limited success, and carried out by infantry, armoured reconnaissance, and service troops, as well as air force personnel, sometimes in combat roles. The difference was marked, and much of the change had occurred because of Pearson's initiative, diplomatic skill, and assessment of the need at Suez. Later crises in the Congo, Cyprus, the Middle East, Vietnam, the Iran–Iraq borderlands, Latin America, and the Sahara built on the experience of 1956, and in every case Canadian service personnel and peacekeeping expertise played an important part. More to the point, Canada tried hard to ready its armed forces for peacekeeping and to spread its hard-won knowledge to other nations. The designation of a stand-by infantry battalion and of army and air force peacekeeping specialists was one sign of Canada's initiative. A military peacekeeping conference for like-minded nations held in Ottawa in the mid-1960s was another. Repeated efforts to improve the U.N.'s creaky organizational machinery and stabilize its financing of peacekeeping operations were still others. We have done our part and paid our dues in this area, and the world is likely a better place for our efforts.

Source: From *Making a Difference? Canada's Foreign Policy in a Changing World Order* by John English and Norman Hillmer (Lester Publishing, 1992), pp. 222–36. Copyright © 1992 J.L. Granatstein. With permission of the author.

Has Canada made a difference? There can be no doubt that, in peacekeeping, we have. But to ask only that question is to overlook other, more important ones. Why were Canadians so attracted to the idea of peacekeeping? What was the attitude of the bureaucracy and the armed forces to the concept? Has that attitude changed? And, if so, why and how? And, finally, has the idea of peacekeeping now come to play too large a role, taking precedence in the Canadian mind? Has the support for peacekeeping begun to affect policies in other areas? This brief essay examines these questions.

"Ours is not a divine mission to mediate," military historian John Holmes wrote in 1984. "Our hand is strengthened by acknowledged success," he went on shrewdly, "but it is weakened if planting the maple leaf becomes the priority."[1] Too often Canada's participation in peacekeeping operations (PKOs) has had some of this "planting the flag" idea about it, a sense that we must maintain our record as the country that has served on more PKOs than any other—whether or not those operations made sense, had much chance of success, or exposed our servicemen and servicewomen to unnecessary risks in an unstable area of the world.

Where did the idea of Canada as peacekeeper *par excellence* originate? Certainly it is not inherent in Canada's origins, which were as violent as those of any nation. The litany of our aboriginal wars, rebellions, bloody strikes, and participation in wars, large and small, is too well known to need reiteration here, and we should accept that violence has been, and might be in the future, as Canadian as apple pie. Probably the idea emerged out of the missionary strain in Canadian Protestantism and Roman Catholicism that saw Canadian men and women go abroad in substantial numbers in the nineteenth and twentieth centuries to bring the word of God to India, Africa, and China. Virtually every church in English and French Canada had a missionary family or religious order in its prayers and as the recipient of its contributions, and letters from the mission fields were staples of Sunday services and church bulletins. Missionaries nowadays do not command good press, the Christian preachers of those simple days before the Second World War more often being painted as despoilers of cultures than as saviours of souls and healers of the sick. But the "do-good" impulse that they represented

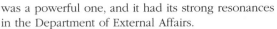
was a powerful one, and it had its strong resonances in the Department of External Affairs.

So many of External's diplomats were sons of missionaries or of the manse. Some were born in China or in other mission fields; others followed clergyman fathers from parish to parish, imbibing the idealism of the social gospel along with their Bible studies. J.S. Woodsworth exhibited this kind of idealism in political life, and it was not insignificant that one of his sons joined External. Lester Pearson, of course, was another whose Methodist upbringing undoubtedly shaped him profoundly.

But so, too, did Pearson's experiences—and those of his entire generation—in the Great War. The shattering cataclysm of the slaughter on the Western Front cannot be underestimated, especially as it was followed within twenty years by another and even more horrific war. The Great War had sprung from obscure troubles in the Balkans; the 1939 war arose from Hitler's expansionist aims, focused in the summer of 1939 on the Polish Corridor. Small patches of land of relative insignificance, in other words, could lead to global catastrophe. Surely there had to be a better way, and the United Nations was summoned forth in 1945 as an attempt to create a collective security organization with enough teeth to keep aggressor states in check.

Canada had played its part in resisting the aggressors during the world wars, and it had learned something from those two experiences. The most important lesson was that isolation was no guarantee of safety in the modern world and that isolationism as a doctrine was equivalent to fool's gold. Another lesson was that it was sometimes very difficult to get along with your friends. Canadian prime ministers from Macdonald on had realized that about the British, who were certain always that they knew best and that the colonial's duty was to contribute to England's defences and coffers.[2] In the Second World War, however, Canada for the first time cast its lot with that of the United States, and while Ottawa's men got on better with the Americans on a personal basis than they ever had with the British, there were perils, nonetheless. The new superpower was as arrogant in its conviction of rectitude as Britain had ever been, as convinced that God was on Washington's side, and that Ottawa's role was to follow dutifully in its wake. Canadian policy in the postwar world would try to maintain a careful balance between cooperation with

the United States and independent action. This was especially true at the United Nations.[3] And peacekeeping, while it often served U.S. interests, to be sure, nonetheless had about it a powerful aura of independence and the implicit sense that it served higher interests than simply those of the United States, or even the West.

The coming of the Cold War paralyzed most of the functions of the U.N., but peacekeeping, initially by observer forces in areas of the world that were either of little importance to the Great Powers or else too dangerous to be allowed to fester, somehow survived.[4] We have now forgotten that Canada initially was not enthusiastic about the idea of participation in U.N. peacekeeping operations. At the 1945 San Francisco United Nations Conference on International Organization, at a time when the focus was on large U.N. military forces to crush aggression, Mackenzie King's Canada inevitably worried about being forced to join in wars without a say in the decisions that led up to them. The United Nations could not become a larger and more powerful replacement for Downing Street and Whitehall, against which Sir Wilfrid Laurier and Mackenzie King had fought for a half-century. The plans of the U.N.'s Military Staff Committee went a-glimmering with the Cold War, but our continuing caution was evident when the U.N. set up observer missions around the borders of the new states of Israel and in the flashpoint state of Kashmir, strategically located between India and Pakistan. Requests for officer-observers in 1948 were treated very coldly by the Department of National Defence in Ottawa. The army was understrength and not very well trained; no one could be spared; and there might be difficulties with Jewish Canadians or with Commonwealth partners. "Ask someone else, please," was the message.

But, in fact, likely because Pearson had just become secretary of state for External Affairs and because Canada was on the Security Council at the time of the creation of the U.N. Military Observer Group in India–Pakistan, Canada did reluctantly agree to send four observers from the reserve army early in 1949. That number was increased to eight later that year, and, in 1950, the regular force took over the commitment. Canadian participation in the U.N. Truce Supervisory Organization (UNTSO) in the Middle East did not begin until 1954, when four officers were seconded for duty there. Before the end of the year, Major-General E.L.M. Burns, a corps commander during the Italian campaign and a senior bureaucrat as the deputy minister of Veterans' Affairs, became UNTSO's commander.[5] Burns's appointment was to have important consequences in shaping Canada's first major peacekeeping contribution.

The same year, Canada found itself unexpectedly asked to participate in a peacekeeping venture outside the ambit of the United Nations. The Geneva Conference, called to wind up the Korean War and provide a cover for France's extrication from the swamp it had made for itself in Indo-China, asked Canada, Poland, and India to create an International Control Commission (ICC) in each of the three successor states of French Indo-China. Canada was a Western democracy and the least objectionable of them to China; Poland was a Soviet satellite, but was deemed acceptable to the West; and India was anti-colonialist, neutral, and a Commonwealth member. Surprised by the request, Ottawa again was genuinely reluctant to participate, not least because the legal basis of the Geneva agreements was hazy and because the Americans were dissociating themselves from them before the ink had dried. Would participating involve us in continuing trouble with Washington? Another reason for Ottawa's reluctance was that the commitment was relatively large; officers, almost all of whom had to be bilingual, were needed, and the armed forces, as usual, were short of such individuals. But Canada found that it could not say no—"If [...] by participating [...] Canada can assist in establishing [...] security and stability in Southeast Asia," the government's press release put it, "we will be serving our own country as well as the cause of peace"—and accepted the commitment. Approximately 150 military personnel and External Affairs diplomats proceeded to Laos, Cambodia, and Vietnam, a group that included three major-generals, eighty army officers, a sprinkling of naval and RCAF officers, and a handful of enlisted men. That was a serious drain on limited resources, one that was resented by National Defence Headquarters at a time when the country's commitments to NATO were large and taken very seriously indeed.

The Indo-China commitment was wearing and wearying. The Indians maintained an air of biased impartiality; the Poles were openly partisan; and the Canadians, after trying to be judicious, soon found that fairness was unfair to the anti-communist elements in all three of the new countries. For the next nineteen years, the ICCs limped along in the midst of war; their presence in Indo-China "radicalized" a generation of military officers and diplomats, in the sense that their experience strengthened their conviction that the communists, Vietnamese and Polish, were totally unscrupulous.[6] On the other hand, Canada's ICC commitment turned out to be a blessing in disguise when the United States became militarily involved in a major way in Vietnam. U.S. allies around the world were pressured to contribute troops to the war, but Canada, sheltering behind its ICC role, was able to deflect Washington's demands. Still, Canadian servicemen and diplomats gathered information for the Americans in North Vietnam and delivered messages from Washington to the leadership in Hanoi. It was obviously sometimes hard to separate the peacekeeper's duty from that of the anti-communist ally.

Canada's military commitment to peacekeeping would soon increase substantially, in 1956, when the Suez Crisis erupted with the Anglo-French-Israeli collusion and attack on Egypt. Prime ministers Louis St. Laurent and Anthony Eden exchanged heated telegrams as the Canadian fumed over the lies despatched from Downing Street.[7] The "supermen of Europe," St. Laurent said in Parliament, had had their day. So it seemed, and especially so when the militarily weak British and French had to cut their attacks short, brought to heel by U.S. pressure on the pound sterling and the franc, and by outrage at the U.N.

Meanwhile, because General Burns was already on the scene at UNTSO, he was tapped to be the commander of the new United Nations Emergency Force (UNEF), created at New York by Pearson and Secretary General Dag Hammarskjöld. And because Burns was there, he was able to step into the problem caused by President Nasser's objection to having Canadian infantry as part of the UNEF. They marched under the same flag as the British invaders, they wore the same uniforms, and the name of the regiment selected for UNEF duty, the Queen's Own Rifles of Canada, was almost literally a red flag to the Egyptian leader, who feared that incidents between his people and the Canadians might cause serious difficulties. The simple truth is that Nasser was right. Burns found the way out of an increasingly embarrassing situation for the Liberals in Ottawa by suggesting that almost any country could provide infantry, and that what UNEF really needed were logistics personnel, which scarcely any of the potential eligible contributors, other than Canada, could provide.[8] In fact, that was precisely correct. Other than the Great Powers and a few of the Dominions (some of whom, like Australia, had taken too much of a pro-British position in the crisis to be even remotely acceptable to the Egyptians), very few nations had skilled military specialists or an air-transport capability. Canada did, because its military had always been prepared for overseas service and, in the 1950s, was relatively well equipped for its NATO role on the Central European front. The irony is clear: Canada's role as a Cold Warrior had given us the types of military forces that were most useful for peacekeeping. In the end, some one thousand Canadians in the various essential services (and including an armoured reconnaissance squadron to assuage Canada's military ardour) duly went to UNEF duty, where they remained until Nasser ordered them out of Egypt in the run-up to the 1967 Arab–Israeli War. That expulsion caused a traumatic shock to Canadian public opinion, dealing peacekeeping one of its very few blows here in the third of a century after 1956.

The impression persists that Nasser's objections to Canada in 1956 and 1967 came as a great surprise to Pearson and the country. Canadians (or English-speaking ones, at least), while still British in their outlook when the UNEF was established, were not used to having their bona fides questioned, and Pearson's initial idea in the heart of the crisis was that the British and French invaders might lay down the Union Jack and the *tricolore* for the blue flag of the United Nations. The invaders, in other words, could become the peacekeepers. It took almost no time for the Canadian to realize that this was simply not on in the atmosphere of the General Assembly at the end of October 1956, but it was nonetheless revealing that the anglocentric Pearson thought, however briefly, that it might be.[9] The Suez Crisis had made it clear, as it had not been before, that our British connections might not always be an asset in the world.[10]

What made all this even more difficult for the government was that the Progressive Conservative Opposition had had a field-day charging that Canada had sold out Britain and France, its mother countries and historic allies, and had slavishly followed a course laid down by Washington. Peacekeeping, in other words, was not going to be a bed of roses, and if Pearson soon won his well-deserved Nobel Peace

Prize and the Liberal leadership, John Diefenbaker and the Conservatives won the general election of 1957. Most accounts agree that Canada's UNEF role cut little ice with the electors, more of them seeming to turn against the Liberals for their "betrayal" of Britain than voting for them for Pearson's U.N. role.[11] In 1967, Canada's expulsion from Egypt apparently had little political weight, probably because Pearson, then prime minister, seemed to know what he was about and because the war that engulfed the region (and that caused death and injury to other nations' peacekeeping troops still in the Sinai) followed so quickly on the departure of Canadian troops. The prevailing mood here was simply relief.

In 1958, however, once the Liberals had been driven from office, virtually everyone in Canada had basked in the glow of Pearson's Nobel Prize. This was widely interpreted a sign of Canada's new maturity in the world, and in a curious way that is extraordinarily difficult to trace, peacekeeping became Canada's *métier*. So much so, in fact, that when John Diefenbaker and his Department of National Defence showed little desire to participate in the U.N. operation in the Congo in 1960 (ONUC), public opinion literally forced the government's hand. It was not that Diefenbaker was against peacekeeping or the U.N. While he had been unhappy with Pearson's role at the U.N. during the Suez affair, he was not backward in claiming that he was the first to advance the very idea of peacekeeping forces;[12] moreover, his government was the first to put an infantry battalion on stand-by for U.N. service in 1958, and he sent peacekeepers to Lebanon in the same year. But in 1960, the army, as always hampered by the demands of its NATO commitments, by tight budgets, and by a genuine shortage of signals personnel, now had to provide a squadron of the Royal Canadian Corps of Signals and other units, including RCAF transport aircraft and crews, for the new U.N. force. Once again, there were few other acceptable contributors to ONUC who could possibly provide such technicians. Soon after their arrival in the chaos of a suddenly liberated colonial state, Canadians were attacked and beaten by mobs of soldiery, apparently in the mistaken belief that they were Belgian paratroopers. Later still, Canadian units came under fire on a number of occasions as the U.N. force became involved in open war with separatist Congolese elements. While they did their tasks well in these difficult situations, it might well

555

be questioned whether Diefenbaker's initial response was not the correct one.

At least the Congo operation ended within a measurable time frame. The next major peacekeeping operation, that in Cyprus, did not. The Mediterranean island, divided between Greek- and Turkish-speaking Cypriots, was in turmoil in 1964. The Greek majority wanted *enosis*, political union with Greece; the Turks (and Turkey) adamantly resisted any such thing, and there was fighting in the streets and in the hills.

What made this crisis unusual was that Cyprus was a Commonwealth state (the British continued to maintain bases on the island), and that Greece and Turkey were both NATO allies. The other NATO partners, not least the United States, looked with dismay on the prospect of fighting between the Greeks and Turks, and contemplated the imminent collapse of NATO's southern flank with horror. It was inevitable that efforts to install a peacekeeping force should proceed with urgency, but neither NATO nor the Commonwealth was able to get President Makarios of Cyprus to agree to receive forces raised by them. It had to be a U.N. force, Makarios maintained.

Canada had been tapped to provide troops for Cyprus by both the Commonwealth and NATO, and it was asked once more by the U.N. For a time, indeed, despite their government's concerns about the way the force was being organized, financed, and administered, the Canadian infantry battalion was the only force the U.N. had on the island, other than the British, who were exceedingly uncomfortable in their role. Then secretary of state for External Affairs, Paul Martin, began to work the telephones, creating a force out of nothing. The Americans were duly impressed at the way Canada had rescued the situation, President Lyndon Johnson asking Prime Minister Pearson what he could do for him in return. "Nothing at the moment, Mr. President," Pearson replied, noting carefully that he had some credit in the bank of American goodwill.[13]

Canada's concerns about the Cyprus force were more than justified. The commitment begun in 1964, supposedly for a term of six months, has continued to the present, and promises to go on for the foreseeable future. The U.N. force has survived Turkish invasion, rioting, ennui, and the appalling inefficiencies of the U.N.'s administration,[14] and some Canadian servicemen of long service have put in six, seven, or eight six-month tours of duty on the island. Cyprus

was and is an object lesson that peacekeeping is not sufficient and that peacemaking has to be part of every U.N. mandate. The irony of the situation is that the Canadian military, once unhappy about the Cyprus commitment that took a battalion away from training to fight the Soviets in Germany, now look at the role very differently. With the end of the Cold War, the liberation of Eastern Europe, the dissolution of the Soviet Union, and the coming drastic reduction in Canada's NATO commitment, Cyprus is the only continuing locale for small-unit training in a near-combat situation. The once-dreary duty has become the army's main active role, hailed for its training value; with Canada's other commitments to PKOs, it is now the best argument the Department of National Defence can muster for continuing to maintain any credible forces at all in a world of *détente*.

My account thus far has lightly traced several of the early peacekeeping operations. There is little point in continuing to chronicle the operations and the Canadian role in them. But it is important to remember that Canadians were not asked to participate in any of the PKOs for their inherent neutralism or because our soldiers and airmen were the equivalent of a gendarmerie. Far from it. We were wanted in Cyprus primarily because we were a NATO power; we were needed in the Suez because, as a NATO ally with a tradition of overseas service in two world wars, we had sophisticated technical capabilities; and we were a natural choice for the ICCs because we were a *Western* democracy. Neutralism or military weakness, in other words, had nothing at all to do with our acceptability as a peacekeeper.

And yet, somehow, Canadians came to believe that they did. Partly, this belief came about because peacekeeping was a role that made us noticeably different from the Americans. The Yanks fought wars, Canadians said, pointing at Vietnam, Grenada, and Panama, while Johnny Canuck kept the peace. In an era in which the military called the shots around the world and defence spending ate up superpower budgets, Canada's main claim to fame was its peacekeeping, its *anti-military* military role. In an era of increasing continentalism, at a time when Canada's independence was seemingly under assault from foreign investors and the all-pervasive force of American culture, such simple myth-making was probably understandable, and perhaps even necessary. All the better, then, that peacekeeping was one of the few roles for our armed forces that could unite all Canadians. New Democrats who disliked NATO, NORAD, and Washington could burst with pride over Canada's U.N. efforts; Quebeckers, historically averse to overseas commitments, beamed at the exploits of the Vandoos in Cyprus or the gallant efforts of French-speaking officers in the Congo. Liberals and Tories vied with each other in urging more and more peacekeeping on the government. After all, were we not maintaining order among the fractious nations and peoples of the world? What could be more Canadian than that?

And so we sent a force to Vietnam once more in 1973, our decision aided by strong pressure from Washington, though sensibly, this time, the Trudeau government slapped some tough conditions in place and followed what it called an "open mouth" policy of telling the truth about violations of the truce. More to the point, when the new ICC could not carry out its role with any chance of success, Canada pulled out its forces. There was little criticism of that, however, probably because all Canadians recognized the intractability of the Vietnamese problem. "Canada would act for peace," two historians suggested, "but not in a charade."[15] It remains only to say that the United States was most unhappy at Canada's withdrawal; likely Washington's unhappiness helped mute any criticism that might have fallen on Ottawa from peacekeeping's Canadian supporters.

And those supporters were legion. Let me, in my anecdotage, give one personal example of the support peacekeeping had come to muster. In August 1988 the United Nations authorized the establishment of UNIIMOG, the U.N. Iran–Iraq Military Observer Group, set up to oversee the cease-fire that brought the eight-year-long war between Iran and Iraq to its end. Canada was asked to participate, once again with a signals unit. I was called by the *Globe and Mail* and asked my opinion of the nation's participation in UNIIMOG, and I suggested that it was a mistake to put Canadian troops into a situation in which they would be at the mercy of what I called "two lunatic governments." That quote, which the next day ended up on page one as the lead story—and which literally made me fall out of bed as I read the newspaper with my coffee—produced some fifteen telephone calls from radio and TV stations and newspapers within

three hours, almost all of them vehemently critical of me for daring to suggest that Canada ought not to participate. Both the Iranian and Iraqi governments *were* lunatic, of course, though happily we suffered no casualties in filling our role, probably because exhaustion had temporarily made peace seem to be in the combatants' best interests.

The point I made to the *Globe and Mail*, obviously, was that Canada had to pick its spots and ought not to feel obliged to participate automatically in every peacekeeping operation. We should insist on conditions, there should be a clear mandate, and the financing ought to be levied on all U.N. member states and not, as has all too often been the case, only on those who feel like contributing. Moreover, since the Canadian government is responsible to the public for the lives of its men and women in uniform, we ought not to put them in a position where their safety is at risk—as it undoubtedly was in UNIIMOG.

None of this mattered, however, to those who had made participation the *sine qua non* of Canadian nationalism. Peacekeeping was so popular, I had to conclude, because it was useful, to be sure, but primarily because it was something we could do and the Americans could not.[16] In other words, peacekeeping made us different from our friends and neighbours. And while that was a good thing, it also had about it something of the anti-Americanism that is part and parcel of our identity.

This became all the more obvious to me when Iraq invaded Kuwait in as clear an act of undoubted aggression as the world has witnessed since 1945. The United States mobilized a vast military coalition; Canada took part, though rather more hesitantly than I would have wished; and, in what I have no hesitation in characterizing as a just war under every canonical and legal definition, Iraq was driven from Kuwait at terrible cost to its military and people. This was not a peacekeeping operation, though it was authorized by the United Nations and was, indeed, a throwback to the kind of collective security envisaged by the drafters of the U.N. Charter in 1945 and practised only once before, in Korea.[17]

Canadian public opinion was sorely divided over the war, but in the end healthy majorities supported Canada's role in it. The Liberals and the New Democrats in Parliament went through conniptions trying to oppose the war while simultaneously supporting our servicemen and -women in the Gulf. The government,

557

one eye fixed on public opinion, gave the troops different and progressively more aggressive mandates several times during the struggle. One of the predominant trends in the public discourse, acerbically characterized by Charlotte Gray in the Canadian Institute for International Peace and Security's magazine as a mixture of "idealism, legalism, internationalism and knee-jerk anti-Americanism," was that by participating in the Americans' war Canada was destroying its hard-won credibility as a peacekeeper.[18] There was unquestionably an element of anti-Americanism about all this, not least in the Opposition's stances in Parliament, in much of the media coverage, and in the positions taken by peace groups. And peacekeeping, because it was Canada's particular skill, became one of the main vehicles for expressing it.

The critics who charged that the government had sacrificed Canada's peacekeeping role on the altar of Washington's war over Kuwait and oil were proven wrong almost at once. Within weeks of the end of the Gulf war, Canada was asked to participate—with seven hundred soldiers and the force commander—in a peacekeeping operation (MINURSO) being set up in the Sahara to supervise a referendum designed to end the long war between Polisario guerrillas and Morocco.[19] The country was also expected to participate in a U.N. force in Cambodia. Our role in Kuwait, in other words, proved to have no immediate effect at all on our ability to operate as peacekeepers. Nor should it have been expected to. We were, as I have suggested repeatedly herein, wanted as peacekeepers because of our military capabilities as much as or more than for our national attributes. Participation in a war in no way altered that, except perhaps to demonstrate that our pilots and ships' crews were as genuinely efficient in combat as in patrolling the Green Line in Nicosia. It must also be said that, if Canada cuts its armed forces down to nothing, as many of the supporters of a virtually disarmed Canada urge, and if it takes away the military's versatility, our future capacity to act in peacekeeping roles will be severely constrained, if not ended.[20]

The point of all this is that for too many Canadians peacekeeping has become a substitute for policy and thought.[21] Some countries (but no longer our budget-strapped nation) try to deal with problems by throwing money at them; our people and, to some substantial extent, our governments try to deal with the world's problems by sending peacekeepers.

This is not an ignoble impulse, but it is one that has to be checked with realism. Canada was right to participate with its allies in the war against Saddam Hussein, and those who objected to our role, whether out of misguided anti-Americanism or concern for our future as a peacekeeper, were wrong. We have also been right to participate in most of the peacekeeping operations in which we have served. But let us, at the very least, retain and enhance our right to consider which PKOs we shall participate in, just as we have the right to consider which wars we shall fight. Governments, like individuals, are supposed to be capable of rational decision making. And automatic responses—whether "My country right or wrong" or "Send in the Canadian peacekeepers"—are no substitutes for thought.

Notes

1. J. W. Holmes, "Most Safely in the Middle," *International Journal* 39 (Spring 1984): 384.
2. See J.L. Granatstein, *How Britain's Weakness Forced Canada into the Arms of the United States* (Toronto, 1989), chap. 2.
3. See, e.g., J.L. Granatstein and Norman Hillmer, *For Better or For Worse: Canada and the United States to the 1990s* (Toronto, 1992), chaps. 5–6.
4. See J.L. Granatstein, "Canada and Peacekeeping: Image and Reality," *Canadian Forum* 54 (August 1974).
5. See J.L. Granatstein, "Canada: Peacekeeper," in Alastair Taylor et al., *Peacekeeping: International Challenge and Canadian Response* (Toronto, 1968), pp. 100ff., 116–17.
6. The best study of Canada's experience is Douglas Ross, *In the Interests of Peace: Canada and Vietnam, 1954–73* (Toronto, 1984). See also Ramesh Thakur, *Peacekeeping in Vietnam: Canada, India, Poland and the International Commission* (Edmonton, 1984).
7. See the account in L.B. Pearson's memoirs, *Mike: The Memoirs of the Rt. Hon. Lester B. Pearson*, Vol. II: *1948–1957* (Toronto, 1973), chap. 10.
8. Burns's account is in his *Between Arab and Israeli* (Toronto, 1962), pp. 208ff.
9. Cited in J.L. Granatstein, "The Anglocentrism of Canadian Diplomacy," in Andrew Cooper, ed., *Canadian Culture: International Dimensions* (Waterloo, 1985), p. 37.

10. Pearson later suggested that his decision to give Canada a flag of its own had its genesis in the Suez Crisis and the troubles over the Canadian contingent. Interview, October 21, 1971.

11. John Meisel, *The Canadian General Election of 1957* (Toronto, 1962), pp. 254–55.

12. See John Diefenbaker, *One Canada: Memoirs of the Rt. Hon. John G. Diefenbaker*, Vol. I: *The Crusading Years, 1895–1956* (Toronto, 1975), p. 280.

13. L.B. Pearson, *Mike: The Memoirs of the Rt. Hon. L.B. Pearson*, Vol. III: *1957–1968* (Toronto, 1975), pp. 134–35.

14. On U.N. administration of peacekeeping, see E.H. Bowman and J.F. Fanning, "The Logistics Problems of a UN Military Force," *International Organization* 17 (1963).

15. See J.L. Granatstein and Robert Bothwell, *Pirouette: Pierre Trudeau and Canadian Foreign Policy* (Toronto, 1990), pp. 55ff.

16. Of course, even this was not true, though not one Canadian in a thousand realized it. The United States participated in the U.N. Truce Supervision Organization from its organization in 1948 and in the Multilateral Force of Observers (MFO) set up in the Sinai as one condition of the peace brokered by President Carter between Egypt and Israel. Eventually Canada would serve on the MFO as well. One might add that there is an irony in the way Japan is struggling with the problems posed for its constitution by the possibility of participating in peacekeeping. There, engaging in peacekeeping is largely seen by public and politicians as being obliged to accede to the Americans' wishes; here, the exact opposite is true.

17. See Kim Nossal, "Coalition-Building's Darker Side: Australia and Canada in the Gulf Conflict," a paper presented at the Australasian Political Studies Assn., 1991.

18. Charlotte Gray, "Home Grown Skirmishes. Canada and the War," *Peace & Security*, Autumn 1991, p. 8. See also Don Munton, "From Paardeberg to the Gulf: Canadians' Opinions About Canada's Wars," ibid., Spring 1991, p. 16.

19. See Richard Brûlé, "Western Sahara: A Settlement in Sight," *Peace & Security*, Autumn 1991, p. 15.

20. When the armed forces were unified in 1968, critics charged that Defence minister Paul Hellyer aimed to create a military that could only do peacekeeping, not fulfil a range of mandates. Ironically, a quarter-century later, defence cuts and the virtual end of Canada's NATO role may lead precisely to that result. The point, however, is that without many capabilities even peacekeeping will not be able to be performed well. On unification, see J.L. Granatstein, *Canada, 1957–1967* (Toronto, 1986), chap. 9.

21. See Desmond Morton's comment: "Peacekeeping is the great [Canadian] morale builder. It is the only thing the public think the military are any good for. It is a distraction from the military role, but it is unfortunately the one that everybody out there will put as priority one, and one has to respect that political reality": "What Is to Be Done? Canada's Military Security in the 1990s," *Peace & Security*, Summer 1990, p. 5.

559

Article 3: The "Committed Peacekeeper"

Joseph T. Jockel

The Canadian Senate's Standing Committee on Foreign Affairs reported in early 1993 that international peacekeeping "is the sole military activity which Canadians fully support."[1] It was not always so. And it will not necessarily remain so in the future.

The Once-Reluctant Peacekeeper

The distinguished Canadian historian J. L. Granatstein of York University has recently pointed out that "we have now forgotten that Canada initially was not enthusiastic about the idea of participation in UN peacekeeping operations."[2] In the first few years after the Second World War, the Canadian government saw peacekeeping as a drain on very scarce Canadian defense resources, a thankless task, a potentially divisive mission at home, and a way in which Canada might be dragged by other countries into distant conflicts in which it had little interest.

Only a handful of Canadian military personnel, and at first only reservists, were deployed on the earliest UN peace observation missions. Canadian participation in the frustrating International Commission of Supervision and Control (ICSC) in Indochina, which Ottawa reluctantly agreed to in 1954, only served to confirm Canadian skepticism, although a decade later Ottawa was pleased to be able to stave off the U.S. interest in having Canadian forces sent to fight alongside Americans in Vietnam by pointing to Canada's prior commitments there to peacekeeping.

In 1964, the Canadian secretary of state for external affairs, Paul Martin, could also still feel justified in telling an American audience that peacekeeping "is politically difficult at home because of the risks; and we get small thanks abroad for our work. We do it not for the glory but as a duty, since there are not many of us willing and able to move in quickly with an effective force."[3] In fact, though, Canadians had already begun to be captivated by Canadian peacekeeping.

An important catalyst for the change in attitude was the award of the 1957 Nobel Peace Prize to Lester B. Pearson, the first, and to this day the only, Canadian to receive that award.[4] As Canada's secretary of state for external affairs, Pearson had been the principal diplomatic engineer behind the creation of the first United Nations Emergency Force (UNEF I), which was deployed to the Sinai in the wake of the 1956 Suez crisis. Another Canadian, Major General E. L. M. Burns, was the first commander of UNEF I, serving for three years. Burns shaped UNEF I into the prototype of most successor international peacekeeping operations: a substantial multinational force under UN command, based on infantry, lightly armed for immediate self-defense, and consisting of several national contingents of both officers and enlisted personnel.

The Canadian public became so enthusiastic about peacekeeping that it, and editorial opinion, all but compelled a reluctant government in 1961 to contribute to the tumultuous UN operation in the Congo. Thereafter, international peacekeeping would formally be identified as a task of the Canadian Armed Forces, especially in a 1964 white paper on defense. But officials often remained skeptical. Ottawa was especially disillusioned when UNEF I, which Canadians had played such an important role in creating, was expelled from Egypt on the eve of the 1967 Six-Day War. Canadians were disheartened as well by their experiences in Vietnam, where the truces they were to monitor broke down, and by the apparently interminable operation in Cyprus. A 1971 defense white paper downgraded peacekeeping as a military priority. In 1973, with the Vietnam experience in mind, the government devised a set of criteria that, in principle, could be applied to determine whether it should accept invitations to participate in new peacekeeping operations.

But regardless of the formal criteria or the disillusionments and disappointments of the past, Canada's record of participation slowly grew longer in the cold war, operation by operation, and expanded very rapidly at the cold war's end. Ottawa lost much of its earlier skepticism about the value of peacekeeping to the world and to Canada. As the Mulroney government put it in 1992, "Canadians are justifiably proud

Source: Joseph Jockel, "The Committed Peacekeeper", *Canada and International Peacekeeping*, pp. 11-26, 79-81, Canadian Institute for Strategice Studies, 1994. Reprinted with permission from the author.

of the contributions the Canadian Forces have made to international peacekeeping. [. . .] Our experience and competence in this field are second to none, and the international community will continue to call upon Canada to assist in the design and conduct of such missions."[5]

If, during the past few years and until very recently, Ottawa ever had wanted to turn down an invitation from the UN to participate in a new peacekeeping operation, it would have had to brave substantial criticism at home. For as a result of its peacekeeping experiences, Canada seemed to have become, as the House of Commons Standing Committee on National Defence and Veterans Affairs put it in a 1993 report, a "committed peacekeepeer."

The Committed Peacekeeper

Why did peacekeeping become so important to Canada? It is not at all starry-eyed to conclude that Canadians and their government have been motivated in substantial part by altruism or simple international voluntarism. In other words, they often are self-prompted to go out and do good in the world. To the extent that peacekeeping has helped alleviate suffering and has contributed to regional and international stability, it has afforded Canadians the opportunity to do just that.

But there have been other important, self-interested motivations that have reinforced altruism. It was frequently argued during the cold war that peacekeeping in faraway regions ultimately contributed to Canada's physical security. This was a result of both Canada's proximity to the United States and the leading role of the United States in containing the Soviet Union and confronting it across the globe. The two superpowers could have been drawn into an escalating conflict in a region such as the Middle East, leading to the possibility of a nuclear war. In the event of a strategic nuclear exchange, Canada would have suffered almost as grievously as the United States itself. In a classic formulation of the problem, members of the Canadian Senate and House of Commons reported in 1986 that "we see practically no point in thinking of national security as distinct from international security. We start from the assumption that the threat to Canada is one and the same with the threat to international stability and peace."[6] Thus viewed, helping to dampen regional conflicts far from

home through participation in peacekeeping operations was an element of Canadian national defense.

Of course, the disappearance of Soviet global power severs this link between Canadian national defense and regional conflicts far away. As a result, Canada is today in a remarkably attractive position with respect to its physical security. One motivation for peacekeeping has thereby disappeared. Nonetheless, recent Canadian foreign policy formulations have replaced the notion that threats to international peace and security also physically threaten Canada with the much broader assertion that Canada's interests are generally served by a peaceful, stable world order and, ergo, peacekeeping remains in the Canadian national interest. This seems undeniable. But while it may renew the motivation for an active Canadian role, this affirmation hardly provides a standard for assessing where scarce Canadian military resources should be deployed in the regionally unstable post–cold war world.

From time to time during the cold war, Canadian contributions to peacekeeping have met specific Canadian foreign policy interests. For example, the deployment of UNEF I served to help put an end to a dangerous and deepening rift between, on the one hand, the United States, and, on the other, Britain and France, the three of which were Canada's principal allies. The long-standing peacekeeping operation in Cyprus (UNFICYP), which began in 1964, helped dampen conflict between Turkey and Greece, two other Canadian allies, both located on NATO's southern flank. Canada was skeptical as to the workability of the 1973 second peacekeeping operation in Vietnam, the International Commission of Control and Supervision (ICCS); pressured by Washington to participate in it, it got out quickly. But the Canadians served long enough on their second national tour of duty in Vietnam to help provide a fig leaf to cover the U.S. retreat from the quagmire. This certainly was in the Canadian interest, as the seemingly interminable war had been debilitating the United States, Canada's most important trading partner, friend, and ally.

Canadian governments have often sought to use small military contributions as demonstrations of solidarity to leverage Canadian influence in international forums and with allies. This was especially the case in NATO, where the small Canadian air and land force contingent in Germany, roughly 5,000 personnel during the 1970s and 1980s, was thought

561

necessary to guarantee Canada's "seat at the table" and to strengthen ties, including economic relations, with western Europe, especially Germany. The same approach was applied to North America: After the Soviet bomber threat to this continent was supplanted by the missile threat, vestigial Canadian air defense efforts at home, coordinated through the Canada-U.S. North American Aerospace Defense Command (NORAD), helped guarantee Canadian access to U.S. technology, defense procurement orders, and strategic planning. Similarly, the small but effective Canadian contribution to the allied coalition during the Gulf War, consisting of 24 CF-18 fighter aircraft, three ships, and a field hospital, not only was welcomed by the United States and others as a moral stand against Iraqi aggression but again helped to secure a Canadian say, especially in Washington, this time in the conduct of the war.

Today, the Canadian Armed Forces often serve the same, traditional function of buttressing Canadian diplomacy, but do so now through their international peacekeeping efforts. The UN, it should be added, is particularly important to Canada as a middle power, partially because in New York Canada can not only have its say but also seek to make common cause with other like-minded states. As a prime contributor to UN peacekeeping, Canada is entitled to a major voice in the international debates that have been under way over the future of the UN. Not only has the standing of the Canadian delegation probably been enhanced in addressing matters of international peace and security directly related to peacekeeping, but a Canadian major general has recently been named military adviser for peacekeeping to the UN secretary general.

More broadly, Canada's reputation as a good international "citizen," a reputation acquired partially through extensive peacekeeping, may have strengthened its position in the UN across a wide range of issues on the world agenda. It would be hard to measure effectively the exact relationship between peacekeeping activism and overall Canadian influence. An evaluation team assembled by the Canadian Department of National Defence found, on the basis of interviews it conducted, "disagreement between foreign and Canadian sources on this point." On the one hand, "almost all foreign interviewees, and a few Canadians indicated that peacekeeping was not a strong factor in national influence." But "most Canadians disagreed, saying it was of importance."[7]

Peacekeeping has sometimes also helped afford Canada the right to be heard in the management of regional conflicts in which it would otherwise not be involved. This was most dramatically demonstrated in early 1993, when the Mulroney government publicly joined the debate over the Clinton administration's tentative proposal to use air power in the former Yugoslavia to retard "ethnic cleansing" in Bosnia and preserve Muslim enclaves. The fact that there were Canadian peacekeepers in the UN operation there (who the Canadian government feared might come under retaliatory attack) lent legitimacy and power to the prime minister's opposition. Several European countries agreed with the Canadian position.

Still, as Peter Jones has pointed out, participation in peacekeeping sometimes has had the opposite effect, that of dampening the Canadian voice in the settlement of regional conflicts

> inasmuch as it is very difficult for a government to both field peacekeeping forces, which must be seen as absolutely impartial in order to be effective, and then turn around and issue Delphic pronouncements about the wisdom of a given state's actions. Rather than guaranteeing influence over a situation, then, having one's forces as peacekeepers often requires that a country practice a tremendous amount of diplomatic restraint about the issue, lest one's impartiality be compromised.[8]

Yet, undoubtedly, peacekeeping has become so very popular in Canada because it fulfills a longing for national distinctiveness, especially vis-à-vis the United States. In North America, the United States clearly dominates. Canada, although the world's second largest country (after Russia), has a population and an economy about one-tenth the size of the United States's. A trading nation, about 75 percent of its exports go to the United States, while the United States is Canada's most important source of foreign capital. Eighty percent of the Canadian population lives in a long, thin band, about 100 miles wide, running along the U.S. border, which means that Canadians, especially English-speaking Canadians, who form the majority of the population, have ample access to American culture, access Canadians make full use of. In the bilateral arrangements for

North American defense, Canada is a junior partner to the U.S. nuclear giant. Partially because of this pervasive American presence in Canada, the sense of overarching Canadian national identity is underdeveloped. Moreover, it is subject to further strain by domestic linguistic and regional divisions. Under all these circumstances, "perhaps the most striking thing about Canada is that it is not part of the United States."[9] With economic ties between Canada and the United States growing, especially under the 1988 Canada-U.S. Free Trade Agreement and the recently ratified North American Free Trade Agreement (NAFTA), many Canadians worry that their country's autonomy and distinctiveness (not to mention its prosperity) are being further eroded.

In world affairs, the United States also dominates. Although Canadians share many foreign policy interests with the United States, it is often frustrating to live in the global shadow of what was one of two superpowers and now is the only one. Debates over Canadian foreign policy often turn on how Canada can best influence the United States in the conduct of U.S. foreign and defense policies, which ironically can only intensify Canada's feeling of living in the American shadow.

Canadians are often irritated by the lack of a clear Canadian image outside their country. Especially galling to many is the perception, sometimes held in the United States and overseas, that Canada and the United States, as well as (English-speaking) Canadians and Americans, are scarcely distinguishable. So Canadians long for distinctive roles in international affairs, which will both differentiate them in the world's eyes and at the same time bolster their own sense of national identity in the face of both the benign, but very real, American challenge and the divisions at home.

There is a strong Canadian tradition of turning to external relations as a way to "balance" the United States, or form "counterweights" to "continentalism" (that is, increasing ties with the United States). Canada's attempts at economic diversification to reduce dependence on the United States, undertaken especially in the 1970s during the prime ministership of Pierre Trudeau, who sought to increase ties with the European Community and Japan, failed. But the quest for ways to "balance" the United States, and for a distinctiveness in Canadian foreign policy in which Canadians can take pride, remains.

Up until now, at least, participation in international peacekeeping, especially operations conducted under the aegis of the UN, has been seen as being especially suited to meeting these often strongly felt needs. As one Canadian analyst has put it, "to all intents and purposes, peacekeeping is the only major area of Canadian military activity that is not continental [. . .] peacekeeping is what we do that is not with the United States."[10] Or, another scholar has observed, "peacekeeping is seen as an independent, distinctively Canadian activity and our internationalism as an antidote to too much continentalism."[11]

It would be hard to deny much of the apparent success, thus far, of this reliance on peacekeeping. Canadians are not only intensely aware and enormously proud of their unparalleled record in peacekeeping, but have come to see it as an important element contributing to their national identity. These feelings have only intensified during the past few years as the number of peacekeeping operations rapidly increased, and Canadians have become accustomed to watching televised images of their soldiers wearing blue berets in distant lands. Symbols of Canada's peacekeeping record have been embraced by politicians and citizenry alike: Major General MacKenzie rapidly became a national hero and was courted by both major political parties to run for parliament. With great ceremony, a new national peacekeeping monument, apparently the first such monument in the world, was unveiled in Ottawa in 1992.

It is especially striking how powerfully this enthusiasm for peacekeeping has extended right across the country, especially transcending the often troubled linguistic line: peacekeeping is championed by English Canadians and Québécois alike. During Canada's most recent constitutional travails, which coincidentally peaked with the celebrations of the country's 125th birthday in 1992, federalists (including the federal government) repeatedly invoked images of Canadian peacekeepers to bolster national pride and unity. (Quebec sovereignists have emphasized, for their part, that a prime task of the armed forces of a sovereign Quebec would also be to contribute to UN peacekeeping operations.)

The impact has been gratifyingly felt abroad, as well. Vague images of snow, mounties, and hockey have been joined by those of Canadian peacekeepers. General MacKenzie became one of the most well-known Canadians outside his country, especially in

563

the United States. Americans who know little about the extent of Canada's role in world affairs will often know about Canadian peacekeepers. This has especially been the case as the murderous catastrophe continues in the former Yugoslavia and Americans also catch glimpses of Canadians there on their televisions.

Not surprisingly, recent Canadian enthusiasm for the country's role in international peacekeeping has sometimes crossed the line into mythmaking. In fact, there have been several such myths, which emphasize the distinctiveness, if not the uniqueness, of Canadian peacekeeping. In other words, they portray Canada as having a vocation, a special calling for international peacekeeping. Some of these myths are more well-founded than others.

The image of Canada as peacekeeper meshes well with the reality of life in Canada, especially when compared to life in the United States. It is not just foreigners who equate the symbolism of peacekeepers with policemen. Canadians have long known that their society, while less exhilarating, is also more orderly and much less violent than that of the United States. It can be added that they have always wanted to keep it that way. Peacekeeping abroad seems a natural extension of peacefulness at home.

Canada consists, in essence, of two societies or national communities, one English-speaking, the other French-speaking, a reality reflected in the federal government's two official languages. Especially in recent years, there has been substantial immigration to Canada from countries other than Britain and France. Both the federal and provincial governments pursue policies purported to foster multiculturalism. Many Canadians have liked to believe that national bilingualism and state-subsidized multiculturalism have especially suited them to international peacekeeping.

And, in fact, Canada alone can provide military contingents easily capable of functioning in the two major languages of the UN, which are also Canada's two official languages. The notion that the country's domestic affairs create an aptitude for peacekeeping often goes further, though. It extends to the idea that Canada's national character is shaped by such values as tolerance, compromise, and acceptance of ambiguity and by such political skills as cross-cultural communication, negotiation, and brokerage that can come from living in a country with two languages,

regional differences, and several ethnic groups. These values and skills, it has also been believed, make Canada and its soldiers especially well equipped for peacekeeping assignments.

It is still too early to tell whether these Canadian self-perceptions have been damaged by the bruising constitutional debates of the past few years, which often strained domestic tolerance and culminated in the Canadian electorate's rejection in an October 1992 referendum of a compromise constitutional package negotiated by the federal government, the provincial and territorial governments, and the aboriginal leadership, and endorsed by all major federal parties of the day. Ironically, another domestic clash, which occurred while the constitutional crisis was under way, has only served to strengthen Canadian perceptions that their armed forces are especially suited for peacekeeping.

During the summer of 1990 a skirmish between Mohawks and townspeople in Oka, Quebec, over the extension of a local golf course onto lands held sacred by the Mohawks turned ugly. Some well-armed Mohawks barricaded the local reserve as well as a major bridge leading into Montreal. A Quebec provincial policeman was killed. Thereupon the Canadian army was called in to seal off the barricaded areas and to preserve some distance between the Mohawks and the increasingly exasperated local citizenry, some of whom resorted to rock throwing. Although the Quebec provincial police were later criticized, by all accounts the army performed brilliantly and effectively. Many Canadians were especially taken by the image of one particularly young soldier remaining utterly calm in the face of provocation by a Mohawk. It was lost on almost no one in Canada that the army had been engaged in "domestic peacekeeping," relying on many of the professional skills and tactics that it would more normally employ in peacekeeping overseas.

One of the most widely held explanations for Canada's high profile in peacekeeping, sometimes held by those outside Canada as well as by Canadians, has been that the country has been called on so often by the international community to serve during the cold war because of Canadian "neutralism" in spirit or temperament, if not in formal alliance standing, making Canada a sort of honorary North American Sweden. It is easy to see why this idea has held sway. Again, it served to distinguish

Canada from the United States, which not only was the Western alliance's leader but, as one of the two superpowers, was kept from playing a highly visible role in peacekeeping during the cold war.

U.S. criticism of the UN during the Reagan years and the persistent delinquency of the United States in paying its UN bills further contrasted it with Canada, which paid its bills on time and whose ambassador to the UN very publicly took on American critics of the world organization. The distinction in international roles was further drawn for many Canadians when, while Canadian soldiers were wearing blue berets in several locales, the U.S. military was forcefully intervening in Grenada and later Panama. All of this brought back powerful memories of the war in Vietnam, where Americans were belligerents and Canadians peacekeepers. Operating in the background was the recognition that the United States was heavily armed, including with nuclear weapons, while Canada had no nuclear weapons and maintained only a small military establishment.

This notion of Canada as a sort of "neutral" peacekeeper, to be distinguished from the aligned and "belligerent" United States, is inaccurate in two respects, though. First, it tends to overlook entirely the roles that the United States has in fact played in peacekeeping. Although it certainly remains true that the Canadian experience is more extensive than that of the United States, Canadians are usually surprised to learn that the U.S. record of participation in UN peacekeeping operations is just slightly older than Canada's. The first such operation, the United Nations Truce Supervision Organization (UNTSO), established in 1948, consisted at first of only U.S., French, and Belgian officers, a composition retained until 1953. Canada's first peacekeeping assignment was to the 1949 United Nations Military Observer Group in India and Pakistan (UNMOGIP). Canadians later joined UNTSO in 1954.

U.S. legislation, namely the UN Participation Act of 1945, as amended, has long provided the president with the standing authority to detail up to 1,000 members of the armed forces to the UN in a noncombatant capacity, which has facilitated the participation of U.S. personnel in several other peacekeeping operations. As will be discussed below, U.S. involvement in UN peacekeeping operations has been growing.

The United States has also provided the support, above all transport capability, for peacekeeping operations in which it was not a formal participant. In fact, U.S. airlift and sealift has sometimes supported Canadian peacekeepers, including during the Suez operations that so heavily shaped Canadian thinking about peacekeeping. So, as Jones has pointed out,

> peacekeeping was not, in fact, an independent policy role for Canada, as peacekeeping forces were largely dependent upon at least one superpower for their logistical existence and upon both superpowers for their political existence. A prime result of the Suez experience for Canadians, then, was that many failed to see peacekeeping for what it really is.[12]

No doubt it has been easier for many Canadians to embrace the notion of Canada as a virtually "neutral" peacekeeper because it has roots in other, sometimes fondly held and generally dubious perceptions of their country's place in the world: Canada as "honest broker between the superpowers" and Canada as "peacemaker." Perhaps the most widely held, and among the most inaccurate, especially given Canada's record in the First and Second World Wars and efforts during the cold war, is that Canada has been an "unmilitary country." In this regard, it is striking that no new national monument has yet been erected to the Canadian contributions to collective defense through NATO and NORAD, even though these have exacted far greater Canadian contributions in money, military personnel and equipment, diplomatic exertions, and sheer decades-long allied steadfastness than international peacekeeping has.

In reality, though, Canada was asked to send peacekeepers on so many operations because of the high quality of its professional military and because in fact it was not "neutral." Granatstein underlines both these points, emphasizing that

[...] Canadians were not asked to participate in any of the peacekeeping operations for their inherent neutralism or because our soldiers and airmen were the equivalent of a gendarmerie. Far from it. We were wanted in Cyprus because we were a NATO power; we were needed in the Suez because, as a NATO ally with a tradition of overseas service in two world wars we had sophisticated technical capabilities, and we were a natural choice [in Indochina] because we were a Western democracy. Neutralism or military weakness, in other words, had nothing at all to do with our acceptability as a peacekeeper.

And yet Canadians came to believe that they did. [...][13]

The Still-Committed Peacekeeper?

In a sense, recently Canada has been too committed to peacekeeping. As will be explored in the next chapter, the Canadian Armed Forces recently were stretched far too thin by Ottawa's acceptance of peacekeeping commitments in the post–cold war world and could easily be so stretched again. Yet it may well be that this national commitment to peacekeeping will remain in place over the next decade, especially if it becomes the centerpiece of the Liberal government's new defense policy.

This is far from certain, however. For the first time Canada faces enormous "competition" from other countries that inevitably will challenge the idea of Canada's having a special international vocation as peacekeeper. Just like the Canadian Armed Forces, other national militaries have been freed from the exigencies of East-West competition. They have begun to find or be assigned new roles in the recent explosion in the number of peacekeeping operations.

At the same time, the old formulas for composing such operations with national contingents, which once took into account that East-West strife, are no longer being applied. Thus one of the major "comparative advantages" that Canada possessed in international peacekeeping, not "neutral" status but status as the West's prime peacekeeper during the cold war, is disappearing very rapidly.

Nowhere has this been more evident than in the new and until recently quite rapidly intensifying interest in peacekeeping shown by the United States, a country with unequalled global military resources to contribute to peacekeeping and, of course, the very country from which Canada has sought to distinguish itself through its own peacekeeping efforts. President George Bush first directly signaled that interest in an important September 1992 speech to the UN General Assembly in which he announced that he had directed the secretary of defense to "place a new emphasis on peacekeeping." He went on to outline a host of ways this was to be accomplished.

Not only would the U.S. armed forces "emphasize training of combat, engineering, and logistical units for the full range of peacekeeping and humanitarian activities," but they would seek to work more closely with the UN, allowing it to draw more effectively for peacekeeping upon the "considerable" U.S. military capabilities, especially in lift, communications, intelligence, and training. Apparently to emphasize the point that the old formulas for participating in peacekeeping could be abandoned, the president added that "there is room for all countries, large and small, and I hope all will play a part."[14]

Initially, the new Clinton administration strongly echoed its predecessor's sentiments. Secretary of State Warren Christopher told the U.S. Senate's Foreign Relations Committee in April 1993 that the government was placing a "new emphasis on promoting multinational peacekeeping and peacemaking" and that "we in the U.S. are ready to do our part."[15] During the spring and summer of 1993 administration officials began work on a policy directive on peacekeeping for President Clinton's approval, which would provide for further U.S. involvement not only in operations themselves but in training, planning, and management.

These steps were welcomed at the UN secretariat. "There is a definite change of mood and [a] willingness from the United States to be partners, the UN under secretary general for peacekeeping operations, Kofi Annan, said in mid-1993. "As UN operations become ever more complex and cumbersome to manage, U.S. participation becomes ever more important.[16]

The United States has already begun to do more in the field. The United Nations Protection Force (UNPROFOR) operations in Yugoslavia include a U.S. mobile surgical hospital unit of 229—the first time an entire U.S. unit has been provided to the UN. As of May 1993, 3,300 U.S. military personnel were assigned to six UN peacekeeping operations, the vast majority (2,976) in Somalia, under the authority of the UN commander, a Turkish general. (Earlier, 30,000 U.S. personnel had been assigned to Somalia as part of the U.S.-led Unified Task Force.) In June 1993, a reinforced company team of 300 U.S. soldiers was deployed to Macedonia. The U.S. Congressional Research Service described their responsibility there in terms that could only shake Canadian conceptions of the role of the U.S. armed forces: "The U.S. unit will wear blue helmets and conduct missions as directed by the UN commander."[17]

But the Clinton administration's initial enthusiasm for peacekeeping cooled over the course of 1993 after the October death of 18 U.S. servicemen in Somalia and policy debacles in both Somalia and Haiti. At the same time, congressional concerns about the emerging peacekeeping role of the United States rose, as did reluctance among the Pentagon leadership to undertake peacekeeping. The outcome of the interagency debate on peacekeeping was Presidential Decision Directive 13 (PDD-13), which was to be signed in early 1994. This classified document apparently sets three tough conditions for the U.S. armed forces to participate in peacekeeping: that U.S. interests will be served, that the U.S. contribution is of sufficient size to ensure success, and that sufficient political support exists in the United States for participation.

If, despite recent hesitations, the U.S. government remains committed to a cautiously expanded peacekeeping role for the U.S. military, peacekeeping for Canadians will become less and less "what we do that is not with the U.S." PDD-13 was under consideration just when the Clinton administration began planning to double the size of the U.S. peacekeeping contingent in Madedonia [sic]. Relying on the UN to "balance" the United States will become all the more difficult for Canada if the United States continues to take a greater interest in the planning and management of peacekeeping operations.

The other "competition" comes from a range of countries. By early 1993, no fewer than 69 countries were contributing to UN operations. Among them, Germany and Japan both took steps to alter their basic laws to permit participation in peacekeeping; as of March 1993, 200 Germans and almost 700 Japanese were participating in the UN's Cambodian operation. Germans also served in Somalia. The Soviet Union first entered active peacekeeping in 1973 and later notably provided airlift for Canadian military personnel who served in the early phases of the United Nations Iran-Iraq Military Observer Group (UNIIMOG). Recently, 1,000 Russians have been on peacekeeping duty in six operations, the vast majority in the former Yugoslavia, where almost 400 Ukrainians are also on duty.

With other countries prepared to play a greater role, and with Canada's traditional distinctiveness in peacekeeping thereby eroding, the possibility simply cannot be ignored that Canadians will want to reduce their share. Moreover, ... peacekeeping has become much harder: more dangerous more expensive, and involving more politically and morally difficult issues. As the House of Commons committee noted in The Dilemmas of a Committed Peacekeeer, Canadians have had their ideas "radically altered," coming to realize that peacekeeping is not just a matter of sending over troops equipped with "white jeeps and good intentions."[18] Especially in the wake of their long and often frustrating experience in Yugoslavia, there is no guarantee that they and their government will want to continue to bear these burdens.

NOTES

1. Canada, Senate, Standing Committee on Foreign Affairs, Meeting New Challenges: Canada's Response to a New Generation of Peacekeeping, Ottawa, February 1993, p. 83.

2. J. L. Granatstein, "Peacekeeping: Did Canada Make a Difference? And What Difference Did Peacekeeping Make to Canada?" in John English and Norman Hillmer, eds., Making a Difference: Canada's Foreign Policy in a Changing World Order (Toronto: Lester Publishing Limited, 1992), 225. See also Granatstein's "Canada: Peacekeeper—A Survey of Canada's Participation in Peacekeeping Operations," p. 93, in Alastair Taylor et al., Peacekeeping: International Challenge and Canadian Response (Toronto: Canadian Institute of International Affairs, 1968); this chapter remains the best history of the early period of Canadian peacekeeping.

3. Paul Martin, address at Wayne State University, June 18, 1964, quoted in Granatstein, "Canada: Peacekeeper," 181.

4. Although Canadians shared in the 1988 Nobel Peace Prize, which was awarded to all UN peacekeepers.

5. Canada, Minister of National Defence, Canadian Defence Policy 1992, Ottawa, April 1992, pp. 32, 11.

6. Canada, Parliament, Special Joint Committee of the Senate and of the House of Commons on Canada's International Relations, Independence and Internationalism, Ottawa, June 1986, p. 34.

7. Canada, Department of National Defence, Chief Review Services, Program Evaluation Division, Final Report on NDHQ Program Evaluation E2/90: Peacekeeping, 1258-77 (DGPE), June 30, 1992, pp. 127–128.

8. Peter Jones, "Canada's Peacekeeping Criteria," Peacekeeping: An Annotated Bibliography (Kingston,

Ontario: Ronald P. Frye & Company, 1989), xxv–xxvi. This book is now available from the Canadian Institute of Strategic Studies, which has acquired the rights to it.

9. J. Bartlett Brebner, Canada: A Modern History (Ann Arbor: University of Michigan Press, 1960), i.

10. Harold Klepak, in Canada, Senate, Standing Committee on Foreign Affairs, Proceedings of the Subcommittee on Security and National Defence, May 12, 1992, p. 3:11.

11. Norman Hillmer, in Canada, House of Commons, Standing Committee on National Defence and Veterans Affairs, Minutes of Proceedings and Evidence, Ottawa, April 1, 1993, p. 30:9.

12. Jones, Peacekeeping, xvi.

13. Granatstein, "Peacekeeping: Did Canada Make a Difference," 231.

14. "Address by the President of the United States of America, George Bush, to the 47th Session of the UN General Assembly," September 21, 1992, New York, U.S. Mission to the United Nations (USUN) Press Release 84-(92).

15. Quoted in Marjorie Ann Browne, "United Nations Peacekeeping: Issues for Congress," Washington, D.C., Congressional Research Service issue brief IB90103, updated June 16, 1993, p. 5.

16. Quoted in R. Jeffrey Smith and Julia Preston, "U.S. Plans Wider Role in U.N. Peacekeeping," Washington Post, June 18, 1993, p. A33.

17. Browne, "United Nations Peacekeeping," 5.

18. Canada, House of Commons, Standing Committee on National Defence and Veterans Affairs, The Dilemmas of a Committed Peacekeeper: Canada and the Renewal of Peacekeeping, Ottawa, June 1993, p. 27.